Short Story Criticism

Guide to Gale Literary Criticism Series

For criticism on	Consult these Gale series
Authors now living or who died after December 31, 1959	*CONTEMPORARY LITERARY CRITICISM (CLC)*
Authors who died between 1900 and 1959	*TWENTIETH-CENTURY LITERARY CRITICISM (TCLC)*
Authors who died between 1800 and 1899	*NINETEENTH-CENTURY LITERATURE CRITICISM (NCLC)*
Authors who died between 1400 and 1799	*LITERATURE CRITICISM FROM 1400 TO 1800 (LC)* *SHAKESPEAREAN CRITICISM (SC)*
Authors who died before 1400	*CLASSICAL AND MEDIEVAL LITERATURE CRITICISM (CMLC)*
Authors of books for children and young adults	*CHILDREN'S LITERATURE REVIEW (CLR)*
Dramatists	*DRAMA CRITICISM (DC)*
Poets	*POETRY CRITICISM (PC)*
Short story writers	*SHORT STORY CRITICISM (SSC)*
Black writers of the past two hundred years	*BLACK LITERATURE CRITICISM (BLC)*
Hispanic writers of the late nineteenth and twentieth centuries	*HISPANIC LITERATURE CRITICISM (HLC)*
Native North American writers and orators of the eighteenth, nineteenth, and twentieth centuries	*NATIVE NORTH AMERICAN LITERATURE (NNAL)*
Major authors from the Renaissance to the present	*WORLD LITERATURE CRITICISM, 1500 TO THE PRESENT (WLC)*

ISSN 0895-9439

Volume 30

Short Story Criticism

Excerpts from Criticism of the
Works of Short Fiction Writers

Anna J. Sheets
Editor

GALE

DETROIT · LONDON

STAFF

Anna Sheets, *Editor*

Laura Wisner-Broyles, *Associate Editor*

Lynn Koch, Debra A. Wells, *Assistant Editors*

Susan M. Trosky, *Permissions Manager*
Kimberly F. Smilay, *Permissions Specialist*
Stephen Cusack, Kelly Quin, *Permissions Associates*
Sandy Gore, *Permissions Assistant*

Victoria B. Cariappa, *Research Manager*
Tracie A. Richardson, Norma Sawaya, Cheryl L. Warnock, *Research Associates*

Mary Beth Trimper, *Production Director*
Deborah Milliken, *Production Assistant*

C. J. Jonik, *Desktop Publisher*
Randy Bassett, *Image Database Supervisor*
Michael Ansari, Robert Duncan, *Scanner Operators*
Pamela Reed, *Photography Coordinator*

Library of Congress Catalog Card Number 88-641014
ISBN 0-7876-2053-X
ISSN 0895-9439

Printed in the United States of America

10 9 8 7 6 5 4 3 2 1

Contents

Preface   vii

Acknowledgments   xi

Preface

A Comprehensive Information Source
on World Short Fiction

S *hort Story Criticism (SSC)* presents significant passages from criticism of the world's greatest short story writers and provides supplementary biographical and bibliographical materials to guide the interested reader to a greater understanding of the authors of short fiction. This series was developed in response to suggestions from librarians serving high school, college, and public library patrons, who had noted a considerable number of requests for critical material on short story writers. Although major short story writers are covered in such Gale series as *Contemporary Literary Criticism (CLC), Twentieth-Century Literary Criticism (TCLC), Nineteenth-Century Literature Criticism (NCLC),* and *Literature Criticism from 1400 to 1800 (LC),* librarians perceived the need for a series devoted solely to writers of the short story genre.

Coverage

SSC is designed to serve as an introduction to major short story writers of all eras and nationalities. Since these authors have inspired a great deal of relevant critical material, *SSC* is necessarily selective, and the editors have chosen the most important published criticism to aid readers and students in their research.

Approximately eight to ten authors are included in each volume, and each entry presents a historical survey of the critical response to that author's work. The length of an entry is intended to reflect the amount of critical attention the author has received from critics writing in English and from foreign critics in translation. Every attempt has been made to identify and include excerpts from the most significant essays on each author's work. In order to provide these important critical pieces, the editors sometimes reprint essays that have appeared elsewhere in Gale's Literary Criticism Series. Such duplication, however, never exceeds twenty percent of an *SSC* volume.

Organization

An *SSC* author entry consists of the following elements:

- The **Author Heading** cites the name under which the author most commonly wrote, followed by birth and death dates. If the author wrote consistently under a pseudonym, the pseudonym will be listed in the author heading and the author's actual name given in parentheses on the first line of the biographical and critical introduction.

- The **Biographical and Critical Introduction** contains background information designed to introduce a reader to the author and the critical debates surrounding his or her work.

- A **Portrait of the Author** is included when available. Many entries also contain illustrations of materials pertinent to an author's career, including holographs of manuscript pages, title pages, dust jackets, letters, or representations of important people, places, and events in the author's life.

- The list of **Principal Works** is chronological by date of first publication and lists the most importantworks by the author. The first section comprises short story collections, novellas, and novella collections. The second section gives information on other major works by the author. For foreign authors, the editors have provided original foreign-language publication information and have selected what are considered the best and most complete English-language editions of their works.

- **Criticism** is arranged chronologically in each author entry to provide a useful perspective on changes in critical evaluation over the years. All short story, novella, and collection titles by the author featured in the entry are printed in boldface type to enable a reader to ascertain without difficulty the works discussed. Also for purposes of easier identification, the critic's name and the publication date of the essay are given at the beginning of each piece of criticism. Unsigned criticism is preceded by the title of the journal in which it appeared.

- Critical essays are prefaced with **Explanatory Notes** as an additional aid to students and readers using SSC. An explanatory note may provide useful information of several types, including: the reputation of the critic, the intent or scope of the critical essay, and the orientation of the criticism (biographical, psychoanalytic, structuralist, etc.).

- A complete **Bibliographical Citation,** designed to help the interested reader locate the original essay or book, precedes each piece of criticism.

- The **Further Reading List** appearing at the end of each author entry suggests additional materials on the author. In some cases it includes essays for which the editors could not obtain reprint rights. Boxed material following the further reading list provides references to other biographical and critical sources on the author in series published by Gale.

Beginning with volume six, SSC contains two additional features designed to enhance the reader's understanding of short fiction writers and their works:

- Each SSC entry now includes, when available, **Comments by the Author** that illuminate his or her own works or the short story genre in general. These statements are set within boxes or bold rules to distinguish them from the criticism.

- A **Select Bibliography of General Sources on Short Fiction** is included as an appendix. This listing of materials for further research provides readers with a selection of the best available general studies of the short story genre.

Other Features

A **Cumulative Author Index** lists all the authors who have appeared in SSC, CLC, TCLC, NCLC, LC, and Classical and Medieval Literature Criticism (CMLC), as well as cross-references to other Gale series. Users will welcome this cumulated index as a useful tool for locating an author within the Literary Criticism Series.

A **Cumulative Nationality Index** lists all authors featured in SSC by nationality, followed by the number of the SSC volume in which their entry appears.

A **Cumulative Title Index** lists in alphabetical order all short story, novella, and collection titles contained in the SSC series. Titles of short story collections, separately published novellas, and novella collections are printed in italics, while titles of individual short stories are printed in roman type with quotation marks. Each title is followed by the author's name and corresponding volume and page numbers where commentary on the work is located. English-language translations of original foreign-language titles are cross-referenced to the foreign titles so that all references to discussion of a work are combined in one listing.

Citing Short Story Criticism

When writing papers, students who quote directly from any volume in the Literary Criticism Series may use the following general forms to footnote reprinted criticism. The first example pertains to material drawn from periodicals, the second to material reprinted from books:

[1]Henry James, Jr., "Honoré de Balzac," The Galaxy 20 (December 1875), 814-36; excerpted and reprinted in Short Story Criticism, Vol. 5, ed. Thomas Votteler (Detroit: Gale Research, 1990), pp. 8-11.

[2]F. R. Leavis, D. H. Lawrence: Novelist (Alfred A. Knopf, 1956); excerpted and reprinted in Short Story Criticism, Vol. 4, ed. Thomas Votteler (Detroit: Gale Research, 1990), pp. 202-06.

Comments

Readers who wish to suggest authors to appear in future volumes, or who have other suggestions, are invited to contact the editors by writing to Gale Research, Literary Criticism Division, 835 Penobscot Building, Detroit, MI 48226-4094.

Acknowledgments

The editors wish to thank the copyright holders of the excerpted criticism included in this volume and the permissions managers of many book and magazine publishing companies for assisting us in securing reproduction rights. We are also grateful to the staffs of the Detroit Public Library, the Library of Congress, the University of Detroit Mercy Library, Wayne State University Purdy/Kresge Library Complex, and the University of Michigan Libraries for making their resources available to us. Following is a list of the copyright holders who have granted us permission to reproduce material in this volume of *SSC*. Every effort has been made to trace copyright, but if omissions have been made, please let us know.

COPYRIGHTED EXCERPTS IN *SSC*, VOLUME 30, WERE REPRODUCED FROM THE FOLLOWING PERIODICALS:

American Literature, v. XLI, November, 1969. Copyright 8 1969 Duke University Press, Durham, NC. Reproduced with permission.—*American Mercury,* v. 19, February, 1930. Reproduced by permission of the Enoch Pratt Free Library in accordance with the terms of the will of H. L. Mencken.—*Book World - Washington Post*, v. XV, September 15, 1985. Copyright 8 1985, Washington Post Book World Service/Washington Post Writers Group. Reproduced by permission.—*The Canadian Forum*, v. 46, June, 1966 for "Clean Cuts" by Belle (Bella) Pomer. Reproduced by permission of the author.—*The Dreiser Newsletter*, v. 16, Fall, 1985. Reproduced by permission.— *German Life and Letters*, v. 21, 1967-68; v. 32, July, 1979. Copyright 8 1968, 1979 . Both reproduced by permission of Blackwell Publishers Limited.—*The German Quarterly*, v. XLIII, March, 1970. Copyright 8 1970 by the American Association of Teachers of German.—*Hebrew Annual Review*, v. 10, 1986 for "S. Y. Agnon's Art of Composition: The Befuddling Turn of the Compositional Screw" by Yair Mazor; v. 10, 1986 for "Sexual Symbols in `Another Face' by S. Y. Agnon" by Lev Hakak. Both reproduced by permission of the respective authors.—*Hebrew Studies*, v. 30, 1989. Reproduced by permission.—*Hispanic Journal*, v. 1, 1980; v. 3, Fall, 1981. Both reproduced by permission.— *Hispanofila*, v. 64, 1978; v. 113, 1995. Both reproduced by permission.—*The Hudson Review*, v. XI, Summer, 1958. Copyright 8 1958 by The Hudson Review, Inc. Reproduced by permission.— *Indian Journal of American Studies*, v. 13, July, 1983. Copyright 8 1983 by American Studies Research Centre. Reproduced by permission.— *Judaism: A Quarterly Journal*, v. 42. Fall, 1993. Copyright 8 1993 by the American Jewish Congress. Reproduced by permission from Judaism.—*Letras Femeninas*, v. 18, 1992. Reproduced by permission.—*Letras Peninsulares*, v. 2, Spring, 1989. Reproduced by permission.—*Melbourne Skavonic Studies*, v. 1, 1967. Reproduced by permission.— *Michigan Germanic Studies*, v. XI, Fall, 1985; v. 16, Spring, 1990. Both reproduced by permission.—*Modern Language Notes*, v. 86, October, 1971; v. 101, March, 1986. 8 copyright 1986, 1971 by The Johns Hopkins University Press. All rights reserved. Both reproduced by permission of The Johns Hopkins University Press.—*Modern Language Studies*, v. 13, Winter, 1983 for "'Edo and Enam' --The Ironic Perspective" by Esther Fuchs; v. 15, Fall, 1985 for "Wherefrom Did Gediton Enter Gumlidata?--Realism and Comic Subversiveness in `Forevermore'" by Esther Fuchs. Copyright 8 Northeast Modern Language Association 1983, 1985. Both reproduced by permission of the publisher and author.—*New Orleans Review*, v. 17, Winter, 1990. Copyright 8 1990 by Loyola University. Reproduced by permission.—*North American Review*, v. 265, Spring, 1980. Reproduced by permission.—*Ploughshares*, v. 4, 1978 for "The Short Fiction of George Garrett" by William Peden. Reproduced by permission of Margaret Sayers Peden for the author.—*Publications of the Modern Language Association of America*, v. 81, October, 1966. Reproduced by permission.—*The Nation*, New York, v. L, January-June, 1980; v. 262, June 24, 1996. Copyright 8 1980, 1996 The Nation magazine/ The Nation Company, Inc. Both reproduced by permission.—*The New York Herald Tribune*, v. 6, May, 1930. Copyright 1930, 8 renewed 1985, by The New York Times Company. All rights reserved. Reproduced by permission.—*The New York Times*, September 11, 1965. Copyright 8 1965 by The New York Times Company. Reproduced by permission.—*The New York Times Book Review*, March 2, 1958; September 19, 1965; January 9, 1983;October 6, 1985; May 5, 1996. Copyright 8 1958, 1965, 1983, 1985, 1996 by The New York Times Company. All reproduced by permission.—*Publishers Weekly*, v. 239, May 11, 1992; v. 243, February 5, 1996. Copyright 8 1992, 1996 by Reed Publishing USA. Both reproduced from Publishers Weekly, published by the Bowker Magazine Group of Cahners Publishing Co., a division of Reed Publishing USA.—*Revista de Estudios Hispanicos*, v. 11, 1977. Reproduced by permission.—*Romance Languages Annual*, v. 4, 1992. Reproduced by permission.— *Romance Notes*, v. 11, 1969. Reproduced by permission.—*Romance Quarterly*, v. 39, May, 1992. Copyright 8 1992 Helen Dwight Reid Educational Foundation. Reproduced with permission of the Helen Dwight Reid Educational Foundation, published by Heldref Publications, 1319 18th Street, NW, Washington, DC 20036-1802.—*Saturday Review*, v. XLVIII, November 13, 1965. Copyright 8 1965 Saturday Review Magazine. Reproduced by permission of Saturday Review Publications, Ltd.—*Saturday Review/World*, v. 1, January 12, 1974. Copyright 8 1974 Saturday Review Magazine. Reproduced by permission of Saturday Review Publications, Ltd.—*Seminar*, v. XV, February,

Novella, and the Short Stories" in *Shmuel Yosef Agnon: A Revolutionary Traditionalist*. Translated by Jeffrey M. Green. New York University Press, 1989. Copyright 8 1989 by New York University. All rights reserved. Reproduced by permission.—Sokoloff, Naomi B. From "Expressing and Repressing the Female Voice in S. Y. Agnon's `In the Prime of Her Life'" in *Women of the Word: Jewish Women and Jewish Writing*. Edited by Judith R. Baskin. Wayne State University Press, 1994. Copyright 8 1994 by Wayne State University Press. All rights reserved. Reproduced by permission.—Sokoloff, Naomi. From "Passion Spins the Plot: Agnon's `Forevermore'" in *Tradition and Trauma: Studies in the Fiction of S. J. Agnon*. Edited by David Patterson and Glenda Abramson. Westview Press, 1994. Copyright 8 1994 by Westview Press, Inc. All rights reserved. Reproduced by permission.—Stuart, Henry Longan. From *Theodore Dreiser: The Critical Reception*. Edited by Jack Salzman. David Lewis, 1972. Copyright 8 1972 by David Lewis, Inc. Reproduced by permission of the author.—Voss, Arthur. From *The American Short Story: A Critical Survey*. University of Oklahoma Press, 1973. Copyright 8 1973 by the University of Oklahoma Press. All rights reserved. Reproduced by permission.—Yudkin, Leon I. From *Escape Into Seige: A Survey of Israeli Literature Today*. Routledge and Kegan Paul, 1974. 8 Leon I. Yudkin 1974. Reproduced by permission

PHOTOGRAPHS AND ILLUSTRATIONS APPEARING IN *SSC*, VOLUME 30, WERE RECEIVED FROM THE FOLLOWING SOURCES:

Berriault, Gina (May 17, 1997), photograph by Ken Cedeno. AP/Wide World Photos. Reproduced by permission.—Dreiser, Theodore, photograph by Pirie MacDonald. The Library of Congress.—Tolstoy, Leo (seated on park bench, forked white beard), 1897, photograph. The Library of Congress.—Garrett, George, photograph. AP/Wide World Photos. Reproduced by permission.—Shoneui, Agnon, photograph. The Library of Congress.

S. Y. Agnon
1888-1970

(Born Shmuel Yosef Czaczkes; also transliterated as Josef; wrote under the pseudonym Shmuel Yosef Agnon) Israeli novelist, short story writer, novella writer, editor, and essayist.

INTRODUCTION

A major twentieth-century author, Agnon was one of two writers to receive the Nobel Prize for literature in 1966. Nevertheless, his international fame has been limited by the fact that he wrote primarily in Hebrew and devoted most of his fiction to the consideration of Judaic history, culture, and language. Yet Agnon's underlying commentary on the plight of the individual in the modern world has universal application, highlighting the growing disintegration of community and spiritual faith and the accompanying spread of secular and materialistic values and cultural rootlessness. Furthermore, his skill as a writer is unquestioned: Agnon is highly regarded for his adroit use of modernist literary techniques and exceptional control of language.

Biographical Information

Agnon was born Shmuel Yosef Czaczkes on July 17, 1888 in the city of Buczacz in Galicia, an historical region of southeastern Poland and western Ukraine. His father, an ordained rabbi and a fur trader by profession, was an Hasidic Jew who exposed his son to rabbinic texts, the Bible, and Talmud and maintained a family library in which his son spent much time. Agnon attended a small local school, studied privately with a teacher, and also received tutelage in German, which enabled him to read European literature in German translation. In 1906 Agnon became an assistant to the publisher of a small Jewish weekly journal; during the next year or so, a number of his poems appeared in that publication. In 1907, at the age of nineteen, he traveled to Palestine, where he stayed for six years, mainly in the city of Jaffa. There he became first secretary of the Jewish court and secretary of the National Jewish Council. Agnon also published several stories in the newspaper *Hapo'el Hatzair*. The title of one of these, "Agunot" (1908), was adopted—with slight modification—as his pseudonym.

Agnon departed for Berlin in 1913. At this time Germany was a melting pot of sorts. Agnon observed various Jewish groups coming into contact there, and the culture of persecuted Jews who had immigrated from rural villages in eastern Europe stood in stark contrast to that of the comparatively cosmopolitan German Jews and of Zionists (those Jews who called for the establishment of a Jewish homeland in Palestine). Agnon was struck by the

difference between the Judaism of tradition and that of modern Jews subsumed by secular society. While in Germany, Agnon became friends with the eminent Jewish scholar Gershom Scholem and the businessman Salman Schocken, with whom he shared an interest in old Hebrew books. Schocken served as Agnon's patron, enabling the young author to focus on his writing. Other noted figures with whom Agnon associated while in Germany include the philosopher Martin Buber, the poet Hayyim Bialik, and Ahad Ha'am, a vocal proponent of Zionism. Agnon returned to Palestine in 1924, settling permanently just outside Jerusalem. In 1931 the initial volumes of *The Collected Works of S. Y. Agnon* were published in Hebrew by Schocken. Agnon continued to live and write in Palestine (officially Israel as of 1948), and eventually became a celebrated figure in his country. In 1966 he received the Nobel Prize along with the German poet and dramatist Nelly Sachs. Agnon died in 1970.

Major Works of Short Fiction

Agnon's stories display striking diversity. His narratives include coming-of-age tales such as "The Kerchief";

magical fables such as "Pisces" and "Buczacz"; unusual love stories such as "Metamorphosis" and "First Kiss"; and accounts of modern alienation such as "A Whole Loaf" and "At the Outset of the Day." Other works, like "The Tale of the Menorah" and "Fernheim," explore the relationship of Judaism to political turmoil and exile. Agnon's stories often have the quality of folk literature and legend but incorporate modern literary techniques and devices such as shifting points of view, wordplay, symbolism, historical allusions, nonlinear narratives, and intermingling of fantasy and reality. Agnon's literary inspiration and allusions are rooted largely in Jewish culture, language, and history. Nitza Ben-Dov has observed that, "Most of Agnon's fictional works are composed of all the many linguistic strata of Hebrew, from the Bible and on through the Mishnah, the Talmud, the midrash, the prayerbook, the medieval Hebrew poets, the rabbinic commentaries, and the Hasidic tales of Eastern Europe." Nonetheless, Agnon was also familiar with the writings of German authors and those of Scandinavian, Russian, and French authors in German translation.

Like Austrian writer Franz Kafka, with whom he is often compared, Agnon occasionally depicted characters rendered ineffectual by vacillation, passivity, or psychological inertia. Employing a version of these themes, "The Face and the Image" tells of a man who is summoned to visit his sick mother but is prevented from doing so by a series of absurd obstacles. Similarly, "To the Doctor" revolves around the device of numerous delays, which in this tale contribute to the death of a sick man. Kafka and Agnon also shared the ability to create surrealistic, dreamlike stories in which the world seems menacing or inhospitable. Agnon's "The Lady and the Pedlar," which contains more atmosphere than plot, is of this mold. As well, many of Agnon's characters, like those of Kafka, suffer from alienation. Nahum N. Glatzer has observed that in Agnon's Kafkaesque stories, "Man is lonely, homeless, in exile; meaning disintegrates, lines of communication break down; there is no exit."

As already suggested, Agnon often focuses on the difficulty of establishing and sustaining relationships. The protagonist of "The Doctor's Divorce" is a doctor (and therefore a man of science trained to rely on reason and objectivity) who cannot dispel the unsubstantiated suspicion that his wife had an affair prior to their marriage. Eventually his inner turmoil brings the marriage to an end, in spite of the doctor's unabating love for his wife. In "The Tale of the Scribe" the main character's holy calling as a scribe of religious texts proves to be incompatible with normal human relationships, or with earthly existence for that matter. The novella *Betrothed*, which treats the subject of unfulfilled love, tells of a scientist lured away from his betrothed and from Judaism by the temptations of worldliness and modern life.

Critical Reception

Agnon is the most accomplished author of fiction to have written in Hebrew. Commentators have attributed part of

the subtlety and complexity of his writing to the capacity of that language. According to David Patterson, "The ancient vocabulary of Hebrew is pregnant with associations of all kinds, and the skillful juxtaposition of words and phrases can be made to yield a variety of nuances. Linguistically, as well as thematically, Agnon's writings can be read at different levels." With regard to many foreign-language authors, scholars have debated whether the art of their writing can be sufficiently conveyed in translation. In the case of Agnon, that question has often taken center stage. Noted author Cynthia Ozick observed that, "For decades, Agnon scholars (and Agnon is a literary industry) have insisted that it is no use trying to get at Agnon in any language other than the original. The idea of Agnon in translation has been repeatedly disparaged; he has been declared inaccessible to the uninitiated even beyond the usual truisms concerning the practical difficulties of translation. His scriptural and talmudic resonances and nuances, his historical and textual layerings, his allusive and elusive echoings and patternings, are so marvelously multiform, dense, and imbricated that he is daunting even to the most sophisticated Hebrew readers." Setting aside issues of translation, critics generally agree that Agnon was concerned foremost with the enduring relevance and meaning of Judaism through history. According to Lippman Bodoff, "The struggle to provide and maintain a Jewish identity as the core of Israeli culture, in the face of the chasm in Jewish life opened up by modernity between the self and reason at war with community and faith, is an underlying theme in much of Agnon's work." Agnon saw growing secularity and loss of tradition as threats to Judaism, community, and spiritual piety that would eventually lead to isolation and alienation. Conflicts and oppositions similar to these run throughout the author's works. Bodoff, though speaking specifically about *Betrothed,* identified a pervading theme in Agnon's fiction, "a battle between Past and Future, Religion and Nature, Spirituality and Science, Hebraism and Paganism, Jewish tradition and Greek and Roman culture, God and Nature . . . ." Agnon's subtlety as an artist is evidenced by the fact that the victor in those battles is not always apparent.

PRINCIPAL WORKS

Short Fiction

'Al Kapot ha-Man'ul 1922
Bidmi yameha (novella) 1923
**Sefer Hama'asim* 1932
Bi-levav Yamim [*In the Heart of the Seas: A Story of a Journey to the Land of Israel*] (novella) 1935
Elu va-Elu [*A Dwelling Place of My People: Sixteen Stories of the Chassidim*] 1941
***Shevu'ath Emunim* (novella) 1943
***Edo ve-Enam* (novella) 1950
Ad 'olam [*Forevermore*] (novella) 1954
Selected Stories of S. Y. Agnon 1970
Twenty-One Stories 1970

Ir Umeloah 1973
A Book That Was Lost, and Other Stories 1995

Other Major Works

Hakhnasath Kallah [*The Bridal Canopy*] (novel) 1931
Sipur Pashut [*A Simple Story*] (novel) 1935
Ore'ah Nta Lalun [*A Guest for the Night*] (novel) 1937
Yamim Nora'im [*Days of Awe: A Treasury of Jewish Wisdom for Reflection, Repentance, and Renewal on the High Holy Days*] (nonfiction) 1938
Tmol Shilshom (novel) 1945
Kol Sipurav Shel Agnon (collected works) 1947; standard edition 1953-62
Shirah [*Shira*] (novel) 1971
Bahanuto shel Mar Lublin [*In Mr. Lublin's Store*] (novel) 1974
Shai Agnon—Sh. Z. Schocken: Hilufe Igarot 1916-1959 (letters) 1991

*The title is commonly translated as "The Book of Deeds" or "Book of Fables." Expanded editions of this collection appeared in 1939, 1941, and 1951.

**Translated and collected in *Two Tales: "Betrothed" and "Edo and Enam,"* 1966.

CRITICISM

Curt Leviant (essay date 1970)

SOURCE: "Seeing into the Hidden Interior of Things," in *Saturday Review,* May 16, 1970, pp. 27-30, 46-8.

[*In the following excerpt, Leviant observes that Agnon incorporated some of his favorite themes into the narratives of* Twenty-One Stories, *a collection that the critic perceives as steeped in Hebrew history, culture, and language.*]

In *Twenty-one Stories* we see the themes that had become almost obsessive with Agnon throughout his long career: loss of home, exile from family, Diaspora, alienation, despair, loss of faith. Half of the stories come from Agnon's *Sefer ha-Maasim* (variously translated as *Book of Tales, Deeds,* or *Happenings*), one of the heights of Agnon's achievements. In these surreal works action takes place in a world devoid of laws of time and place, cause and effect, and, occasionally, life and death. Here Agnon accents modes of perceptions and experience normally blocked in realistic fiction. And in subverting the rational, normal order, Agnon instills in us a metaphysical fear as we see into the hidden interior of things.

Although some of the stories have no particularly Jewish slant, it should be remembered that Agnon is primarily a Jewish artist, fashioning the raw materials within the framework of the Hebrew word, Jewish imagery and allusions, and a Jewish world view. His method of shaping, converting and balancing the material, however, is West-

ern, inspired by his acknowledged reading of the French, Russian, and Scandinavian writers and the German Neo-Romantic masters. Agnon's esthetics should also be seen in the light of the Central European mode of writing which accents the meditative approach, and in which inner dynamics outweigh dramatic action, as in the Swiss Gottfried Keller, the Austrians Robert Musil and Adalbert Stifter, and the Czech Kafka.

Despite the nightmarish qualities of unresolved and occasionally paralyzed will, some stories end with hope or signs of positive resolution, an indication that even in a shattered world optimism is possible.

—Curt Leviant

Whereas extensive exegesis is not usually necessary for Agnon's other works, these stories, rich in allusion and Kafkaesque in complexity, nearly always need explication. Like all good fiction, they may be said to have an outer and an inner life; the latter is often evident only to the reader in Hebrew who can react to various motifs and crucial words and terms with multi-meanings, or phrases from the Bible and Talmud woven into the text.

Among the more memorable tales in *Twenty-one Stories* are the antipodal **"Metamorphosis,"** which begins with divorce and seems to end in love, and **"The Doctor's Divorce,"** where the reverse occurs. In **"Metamorphosis"** a divorced couple, Hartmann and Toni, achieve new degrees of communication and understanding after the bonds of their marriage are formally severed. Following a long walk in the country, they stop to eat supper at an inn and spend the night in separate rooms. Hartmann thinks of his two daughters and of Toni, whose image he embraces. Although not definite, the lyrical ending seems to indicate that a reconciliation is possible:

> Once again she appeared before him. . . . his eyes closed . . . his soul fell asleep, and his spirit began to hover in the world of dreams, where no partition separated them.

"The Doctor's Divorce," on the other hand, deals with the gradual erosion of love. A doctor who marries a nurse, Dinah, cannot rid himself of the suspicion that his wife has had an affair before their marriage. Despite the strong love that the nurse has for her husband, the irrational doubt by a man of science and rational sensibility destroys the marriage, just as monomaniac probing of a supposed flaw ultimately leads to destruction in Hawthorne's **"The Birthmark."**

The theme of absence from home and estrangement is pursued in **"Fernheim,"** in which a man returns from a prisoner-of-war camp and finds his wife gone, won over by another who he thought had been killed in a landslide. Stories with similar motifs thrust the reader into the world of homelessness from the very first sentence:

> The train was lost among the mountains and could not find its way. (**"On the Road"**)

> After the enemy destroyed my home I took my little daughter in my arms and fled with her to the city. (**"At the Outset of the Day"**)

> Close to the Passover holiday it happened. I was far away from my father's house and my home town. (**"To Father's House"**)

Yet, despite the nightmarish qualities of unresolved and occasionally paralyzed will, some stories end with hope or signs of positive resolution, an indication that even in a shattered world optimism is possible.

These stories contain various gradations of Jewish material. The simplest, and the common denominator, is Agnon's richly nuanced and stylized Hebrew, apparent in stories like **"Fernheim"** and **"Metamorphosis,"** which contain no Jewish milieu, imagery, or theme. The symbolic tales, though tangentially Jewish in background and general in plot (desire for a whole loaf in a restaurant, attendance at a concert) are weighted with meanings involving crucial Jewish issues such as faith, alienation, and wholeness of spirit. Another category, minimally represented in *Twenty-one Stories,* is that where the European Jewish milieu is fully recreated and where traditional Jewish referents, characters, plot, and language combine to make a completely Jewish tale.

Such a story is the nostalgic **"The Kerchief."** The young narrator longs for his father's return from the fair. The central object in the tale is a holiday kerchief which the father brings his wife. The narrator relates the joy of the father's return, and the tranquility and delight of the Sabbath when the family is reunited. The boy had previously dreamt of the Messiah who would lead everyone to the Land of Israel, and recalls the Jewish legend that the Messiah sits among beggars of Rome binding his wounds. The dream becomes vivified later in the story when a poor beggar (aligned with the Messiah) comes to town. The boy binds the beggar's sores with the most precious object he possesses: his mother's kerchief, given him for his Bar Mitzvah. In parting with the beloved possession to do a *mitzvah,* a good deed, he is accorded both supernatural approval ("the sun came and stroked my neck") and the approval of his mother ("Ere I had ended asking her to forgive me she was gazing at me with love and affection.").

One reason perhaps why so little of Agnon has appeared in English is the difficulty of translation. In translating fiction the problem of culture rather than language is uppermost. With Hebrew, whose literature is rooted in a religio-cultural tradition, this problem is compounded. One can readily translate words, but not cultural intimacy. To truly understand everything in a classically He-

brew work, a reader would have to be familiar with a good deal of the Jewish culture's usable past.

In sum, [Agnon] probes man's spiritual journey through a problem-laden twentieth century.

—Curt Leviant

This holds true especially for the writings of Agnon, whose Hebrew is inseparable from the mainstream of the classical Hebrew tradition. Although Agnon is difficult to translate, paradoxically he is not so difficult to read. The average Jew with a traditional Jewish education consisting of Hebrew, Bible, and some Talmud would have no difficulty in reading and understanding Agnon; yet this same person would find himself lost with contemporary Israeli writers who use mid-twentieth-century, post-State of Israel idiom, colloquialisms, and slang.

The vocabulary of S.Y. Agnon is classic and simple. The difficulty in translating him is not in rendering a recondite idiom, but in conveying the essence of his allusions and prismatic meanings. Like Dante, much of Agnon can be read on various levels. Beyond the story—the framework upon which all other levels of meaning depend—there can also be the allegorical, religious and mystical level, corresponding to the four categories of Hebrew Biblical interpretation.

A translator of Agnon must also be aware of the endless array of quotes and phrases from the entirety of Hebrew literature, the past of Jewish existence. At times Agnon warns the reader with the introductory words "As it is written" or "As it is said." The reader and translator are then on guard for the classical phrase that follows. But more often Agnon's allusions and phrases blend smoothly into the fabric of his prose. It is the reader's obligation to be prepared for these verbal enrichments and properly estimate their value, flavor, and tone.

Two examples from *Twenty-one Stories* should suffice. In the concluding line of a little folk tale, **"Fable of the Goat,"** which reads (in my translation): "May he flourish in old age, sprouting in verdure, in the land of the living, tranquil and secure," Agnon alludes to three different Biblical verses, and at the same time parodies the *maqama* technique. One phrase is from the Psalm of the Sabbath, Psalm 92; another is from Psalm 116, and the concluding phrase is from Jeremiah 30:10. The entire line is composed of two clauses, and the final word of each clause rhymes. . . .

In **"A Whole Loaf"** Agnon mentions a man who invented a better mouse-trap. No doubt, says the narrator, this "can greatly correct the evil"—the translator's rendering of the Hebrew *"tikkun gadol."* Now *tikkun* in Hebrew can mean a repair or an improvement, but it is also a technical religious term which means correction of worldly imperfections. In other words, there is both a physical and a metaphysical weight to the word, and its glance extends in many directions. The word *tikkun* can be applied to fixing a chair or to moral reformation. The expression may serve as a paradigm for countless other words and phrases which, through centuries of the Hebrew linguistic and literary tradition, have taken on multiple meanings.

Agnon's many allusions to the mainstream of Hebrew writings, however, do not give a conglomerate effect to his prose. To offer a parallel, his writing does not sound like a hodgepodge of Anglo-Saxon, Chaucerian, Elizabethan, and modern English. Since Hebrew was a written language for the nearly 2,000 years since the destruction of the Temple, and was not spoken continuously in the homeland, it did not undergo the radical changes in grammar, vocabulary, pronunciation, and syntax that have taken place in English. And, since Jews have made the study of their classical literature a religious duty, familiarity is something to be expected rather than wished for. It is this shared emotional and intellectual experience that Agnon uses and converts into art.

Agnon's style has over the years remained constant, although his forms and storytelling modes have changed. His word choice and prose rhythms are basically those of the Mishna and Midrash, stemming from the second to the fifth centuries of the Common Era. He also makes use of the Hebrew of the Hasidic and pietistic texts of the eighteenth-to-nineteenth centuries and some modern Hebrew. Although his allusions, direct quotations, and vocabulary extend to all layers of Hebrew, the basic style is his own version of rabbinic Hebrew, which Agnon has developed into a virtually inimitable linguistic instrument that is both poetic and precise.

There is a musical quality in Agnon's prose that offers the translator another problem: how to convey the sense of classic prose without sounding archaic (a trap which some of his translators fall into), and how to preserve the rhythm and occasional assonance, alliteration, word-play, and even rhyme. But, despite all this, Agnon has been translated into more than a dozen languages, including the major Indo-European tongues, as well as Hungarian, Arabic, and even Japanese. For it is his narrative mastery, his fully realized characters, and his universal themes of man spiritually lost and wrenched from his environment that have made his writing understandable in various cultures. . . .

Although Agnon's fame is secure abroad, his reputation among the younger writers in Israel is somewhat problematic. When he began to write, Hebrew literature was still relatively young; when he died, many sabras were already so secure in their native roots that they were scorning their own literary tradition and looking for others. This can in part be ascribed to ignorance of traditional Hebrew materials, and also to the more comprehensive rejection of many values and attitudes of the older generation. But Agnon stands at the forefront of Hebrew literature precisely because he made use of the interplay between Western and Jewish themes, modes, and stories. Hence his writings have a polychromatic luster that is lacking in much of the fiction of the younger generation. Some, however, have recognized Agnon's modernity, and in these writers the public pose of rejection has mellowed into private adoration and receptivity of influence.

What is modern, then, about Agnon if he writes a mannered Hebrew that is easy enough to read but has a faint patina of yesteryear to it, and if the tradition he describes is now only a nostalgic memory for some Jews, and foreign or exotic to non-Jews? His modernity lies in his ambiguity and irony: he questions the traditional social, moral, and spiritual conceptions; he dwells on despairing isolation; his protagonists grapple with existential problems. In sum, he probes man's spiritual journey through a problem-laden twentieth century.

Long thought to be a naïve folk artist, Agnon was shown midway in his career to be a complex, sentient artist. For those who have not read most of his works, the best comparison in English might be Nabokov or Faulkner— the former for his complexity, authorial control, linguistic brilliance, and humor, the latter for the entirety of his world. The little jokes, puns, and private myths (such as beginning all the characters names in *Edo and Enam* with the letter "G," prompting critics to build castles in the sand when all along Agnon is having a joke at their expense) merely show the playful mastery of his authorial world. Like Nabokov, too, he uses various recurring symbols and characters that are mentioned or reappear in several works. (The hero of the Zionist novel *In Days Gone By* is the great-grandson of Reb Yudel; Rechnitz, hero of *Betrothed,* is mentioned in *Edo and Enam*; the narrator of *A Guest for the Night* mentions several characters from Agnon's fiction.)

When Agnon received word in October 1966 that he had been awarded the Nobel Prize (for which he had been mentioned as early as 1935), he stated: "If God will grant me long life, they [the Nobel Committee] will yet see that they did not err in choosing me." That remark was perhaps the least modest of his public utterances. Despite his fame, he lived unostentatiously; despite his complexity, he had personal contact with people all over the world, from all walks of life. An indication of the character of the man might be the note found in his desk after his death, requesting that he be buried on the Mount of Olives next to a humble schoolteacher. Like Sholom Aleichem, who asked to be buried among the poor, Agnon did not wish to lie in a section reserved for the élite. This attitude is perhaps a fitting fusion of Sholom Aleichem and S. Y. Agnon, both culture heroes in Jewry, the two towering figures in twentieth-century Jewish literature.

Baruch Hochman (essay date 1970)

SOURCE: "The Whole Loaf: Agnon's Tales of the Ancestral World," in *The Fiction of S. Y. Agnon,* Cornell University Press, 1970, pp. 29-52.

[*In the following excerpt, Hochman surveys Agnon's short fiction treating the culture of the* shtetl, *the Hebrew village prior to the nineteenth century.*]

About a third of Agnon's work directly reflects the culture of the *shtetl* before its final decline. Entirely devoted to a limited range of experience in the century preceding Agnon's birth, such work takes the form of folk tales in the idiom of the faithful who enjoyed the "whole loaf" of experience within the ancestral tradition. The civilization of the *shtetl* had defined itself for centuries almost entirely in terms of that tradition. Agnon attempts to render the quality of experience within it.

If one seeks a spiritual center of gravity within the Agnonic *shtetl,* one finds it in the pervasive feeling that, ultimately, mortality holds no terrors for its folk. The denizens of Agnon's traditionalistic tales live in a world where pain and loss are pervasive. There are pogroms and persecutions; there is poverty; there is the final fact of death. But pain and loss can be placed in a larger conception of moral order in the cosmos, of an implicit logic in events. One craves the good things of the life of this world, but one is perpetually aware of their transience. The real life—the true, the intelligible world—is elsewhere. Though one does not negate the immediate conditions of one's existence—the tradition, after all, is essentially not otherworldly—one knows its limits and strives within the established order of faith to transcend it.

The culture of the *shtetl* had its upheavals. The life of East European Jewry between 1770 and 1880 was stormy, even in relatively peaceful Galicia. But Agnon is not occupied with its upheavals. His tales of the ancestral world are meticulous in historical detail, touching again and again upon the tensions and disruptions of the times. The emphasis, however, is not on the conflict in and for itself, but on its effect on the individual caught up in it. What really interests Agnon is the way individuals accommodate themselves to the stresses of life within village culture.

Those who celebrate Agnon as an epic writer do so because of the lucidity with which he conjures the actualities of the lost village past. And, indeed, his technique is highly objective. He writes folk tales full of people, things, events, evoking a world where the daily round of actions and responses unfolds at a leisurely pace. The emphasis, however, is not on the objective order, but rather on the strain of feeling that informs the lives of its people. The prevailing tone of the tales—even the broadly comic ones—is lyric in the extreme. Agnon tunes in on a delicate, tremulous strain of feeling that, he implies, suffused the culture at large and came to fruition in individuals. And the consciousness of these individuals is ordered by the governing patterns of consciousness in their civilization.

What characterizes the denizens of Agnon's *shtetl* is a radical limitation of individual consciousness and a peculiar passivity in confronting the conditions of their lives.

There is conflict, but it is always defined in conventional terms. There is struggle, but the struggle is rarely ultimate. Agnon's village folk never strike out boldly against the things that undo them, and they rarely reflect on themselves or the immediate causes of their anguish. When they do reflect on their circumstances, everything is referred back to the governing order of things—to God, to galut (exile, Diaspora), to schemes of sin and punishment that imply divine governance. The world is seen wholly in terms of the system of ideas and images that order their lives. Both nature and history are grasped in such terms.

The effect, aesthetically, is that of certain folk drawings, where stars modulate into Sabbath candles, and the world of nature arranges itself around a *sukkah* (tabernacle) or the Ark of the Covenant. The inner life is treated in a similar fashion. The life of the feelings is mediated through sets of prototypical patterns and analogues. To long for one's lost love is to be an *agunah,* that is, a grass widow, who is bereaved in this life; to sit among the ruins of one's shop is to be like the city that sat desolate.

The people of Agnon's tales of *shtetl* life have little individuality in our sense of the word. They are discrete beings, possessed of particular qualities and sharply distinguished from each other. They lack self-consciousness, however, and rarely turn in upon themselves. They never hurl themselves against the existing order of things, and they therefore have little inwardness in the way people in modern fiction ordinarily do. What they do have is an intensified experience of a clearly delimited range of feeling, which Agnon echoes and amplifies to the fullest. They are given to a deeply felt sense of ineffable longing, ineffable loss, ineffable pleasure in longing and loss—which Agnon devotes his formidable gifts to evoking. The most striking thing about his shorter tales is the lapidary elegance with which they dramatize the experience of relatively passive individuals, reaching beyond the flesh and the world. Even the comic tales, with their emphasis on incongruity and happy endings, are infused with a muted melancholy quaver and a constant sense of the something beyond.

Agnon's early tales are remarkably consistent in their evocation of these qualities. Though they vary in theme, in nuance of background, and—subtly—in technique, they share the peculiar beauty and harmony he casts on *shtetl* types in describing their response to the pain of existence. The tales this chapter discusses represent, in a way, variations on a unifying theme: the theme of loss, in a field of experience where loss can be undergone in a larger context, where harmonization of discord is possible, as well as an extraordinary aesthetization of pain. Such aesthetization of experience, but also of the spirit of the *shtetl* as Agnon sees it, is perhaps the most striking quality of these tales. It is also their most drastic limit.

"Agunot" (1908), Agnon's first major tale, sets the tone for the later tales; it is a kind of prelude to his life's work. Attuned to the moods of the *shtetl* as he apprehended them, though not specifically concerned with its milieu, it established the thematic and sentimental patterns that have dominated his work.

> What characterizes the denizens of
> Agnon's *shtetl* is a radical limitation of
> individual consciousness and a peculiar
> passivity in confronting the conditions
> of their lives.
>
> —*Baruch Hochman*

"**Agunot**" is a tale of thwarted love. Its heroine, Dinah, is a girl of fairy-tale loveliness, reared tenderly by a father who wishes to marry her to a renowned scholar. She falls in love, however, with an artist who has been commissioned to build an ark for the Torah scrolls in the house of study over which her husband is to preside. Ben Uri, the artist, is too deeply absorbed in his task to take notice of her, and she marries Ezekiel, a prodigious scholar her father has imported for her from abroad. Ezekiel in turn loves Freidele, a simple *shtetl* girl, the daughter of his father's housekeeper, who returns his love. After the marriage, Dinah dreams of Ben Uri, Ezekiel of Freidele.

The marriage does not work. Ahiezer, Dinah's father, who had gone to Jerusalem "to rebuild and refound her, from her ruins," acknowledges that his intentions have not prospered. He takes Dinah to the Rabbi, who had known of Dinah's predilections, and the Rabbi undoes the marriage knot. Ahiezer leaves Jerusalem, and Dinah goes with him. One night, the Rabbi dreams a disquieting dream, and after dreaming it once again, takes up a pilgrim's staff and wallet and goes out into exile with a view to "repairing" the bereaved souls, like Ben Uri's and Dinah's, that wander in droves through limbo.

The tale is suffused with thwarted yearning. Its basic motifs are sounded at the very outset:

> It is said: A thread of grace is spun and drawn from the deeds of Israel, and the Holy One, blessed be He, Himself, in His glory, sits and weaves a prayer shawl all grace and all mercy for the Congregation of Israel to enfold herself in. Radiant in the light of her beauty she glows, even in these the lands of her exile, as she did in her youth, in her Father's house, in the temple of her Sovereign and the city of sovereignty, Jerusalem. When He, of Ineffable Name, sees her, that she has been neither sullied nor stained even here, in the lands of her oppressors, He—as it were—leans toward her and says, "Behold, thou art fair, my love, behold thou art fair." And this is the secret of the power and the glory and the exaltation and the tenderness in love which fill the heart of every man in Israel.

> But there are times—alas!—when some temptation creeps up and snaps a thread in the loom. Then the prayer shawl is damaged. Evil spirits hover about it, . . . and tear it to shreds. At once a sense of shame assails all Israel, and they know they are naked. Their days of rest are wrested from them, their feasts are fasts, and their lot is dust instead of luster. At that hour the Congregation of Israel strays abroad in her anguish, crying, "Strike me, scourge me, strip away my veils from me!" Her beloved has slipped away, and she, seeking Him, cries, "If ye find my beloved, what shall ye say unto Him? That I am afflicted with love." And this affliction leads to direst melancholy which persists—Mercy shield us!—until from the heavens above He breathes down upon us strength of spirit to repent, and to muster deeds that are a pride to their doer, and again to draw forth the thread of grace before the Lord.

By setting the star-crossed lovers in a field of rich traditional associations, Agnon achieves a fine lyric resonance. It is no mere accident that sends bereaved souls into the world seeking their mates, but rather a near-cosmic fatality. Ben Uri and Dinah, Ezekiel and Freidele, and also Ahiezer and Jerusalem itself, figure within a prototypical pattern of loss, associated as they are with both the Shulamite of the Song of Songs and the Congregation of Israel in its distress. The Rabbi who takes up his pilgrim's staff to wander in the world is the prototype of the saint who wanders in the darkness of life, seeking to right its incomprehensible wrongs. Jerusalem is not merely a city, but *the* city, land of the pious heart's desire, whence men wander in gloom, coerced by the mysterious workings of chance or of fate—of the sin that, in the formulation of the tale's opening, "catches a thread in the loom." The rest of the world is outer darkness, Diaspora, exile—banishment, ultimately, from both terrestrial delight and the joy of existence in the light of the divine presence.

The title of the tale clinches the sense of universal bereavement. The *agunah* was the grass widow of the Jewish Law, which had no statute of limitations in family matters, so that a woman whose husband had disappeared could not remarry till he had been proved dead—or sent her a divorce. As it happens, every soul in this tale is in a state of *aginut*—including the mourning figure of the Holy Spirit (*shekhinah*) who appears to the old Rabbi in his dream, cooing mournfully like a dove. Everyone in the tale is an *agunah,* fatally bound to an inaccessible love object and unable to break out of the "web." And though there clearly is a cause, no one need struggle to know it. Whether the cause is an accident of human history or of an inevitability of the transcendent Law does not matter. It merely is. And the sadness of it is unspeakably lovely, its loveliness unspeakably sad.

"**The Crooked Made Straight**" (1912), Agnon's next major tale, is less penumbral than "**Agunot.**" Its action is more directly recounted; its characters are sharper and more vivid. It is a moral tale that projects an analogous mood far more obliquely. Its moral is stated at the outset: "The sage hath said, 'Wealth is less substantial than vanity,' . . . to make it known how frail and insubstantial money is, since it has no intrinsic value. . . . By its very nature . . . [it] evanesces . . . [and] for the least of reasons . . . it is lost." The story itself recounts a series of events involving a certain man, Menashe Haim by name, . . . who fell from prosperity . . . and was driven . . . into transgression. How he was oppressed . . . but did not oppress others, and [therefore] came into his own in his death and enjoyed a name and a memorial among the living, as is set forth at length . . . within the tale. It is of him and the likes of him that it is written, "And then they shall atone for their sins"; to which our rabbis added . . . , "They shall atone for their sins through suffering."

The tale tells of the progressive impoverishment of a decent but childless shopkeeping couple to the point where the husband must take to the road as a certified beggar. We watch the husband's deterioration from a householder's dignity to rank mendicancy. Menashe Haim sinks so low that, at the very moment he has enough alms in hand to justify his heading homeward, he sells his credentials to a professional beggar and then eats and drinks himself insensate. When he awakes, he finds that all his money has been stolen and takes to the road again, now as a common pariah.

Time passes. Finally, the other beggar drinks himself to death, and Menashe Haim, whose documents he carries, comes to be thought of as dead. By the time Menashe Haim has worked his way home again, Kraindel Charney, his long-suffering wife—who has languished patiently, first as an *agunah* and then as a widow—has finally remarried and is celebrating the birth of a son. Stunned, Menashe Haim takes to the road again. Finally, after much wandering, he stumbles into the cemetery where his wife has erected a monument to "him"—that is, to the beggar who has been mistaken for him. Menashe Haim, exhausted, dies there, and is buried by a kindly gravedigger alongside the monument that bears his name. In the end, he benefits from the prayers and offerings his still loving wife tenders in his name.

The imaginative emphasis of the tale is on the grotesquerie of Menashe Haim's life and death and the final, graveyard peace he achieves. At the center of the story is the selling of the begging certificate at a nightmarish fair, with its monstrous distractions and its deafening din. A beggar in shrouds sings mournfully of how he returned from the other world to find his door shut against him. A woman sitting on a pile of rags keens her misery as an *agunah*.

The fair seems to externalize something in Menashe Haim himself. What Menashe Haim sees at the fair anticipates what will happen to him in life. It suggests, moreover, that the "real" world is a nightmare of vanity, mortality, disincarnation. When Menashe Haim gorges and gluttonizes at the inn, we recoil from the sour taste in his mouth and his sodden flesh. The death of Menashe Haim's double is still more revolting.

Altogether, there is a sense of the hideousness of the flesh—and of its deathliness. The flesh is equated with selfhood, with a kind of death of the spirit. At the end, Menashe Haim is in a sense reborn in the spirit, having

purged himself through suffering and remorse. Thus, the tale bears out its "argument." We perceive the mutability of a happiness rooted in the world and the flesh. Menashe Haim is happy only when, insensate with suffering, he finds repose among the tombstones and comes to rest underground. Like **"Agunot," "The Crooked Made Straight"** suggests that the common condition of mankind is indeed a condition of disenfleshment without disenchantment, of pariahdom without final degradation, of *aginut* without desperation—only of incessant, muted desire.

Nor is the disenfleshment unpleasant. Menashe Haim, all passion spent, seems happier underground than anywhere else. But even underground and passionless, he has not stopped yearning. He still wants the tenderness of Kraindel Charney's love. From our point of view as readers of the tale, he gets them. Kraindel Charney lays offerings on his grave.

"The Legend of the Scribe" (1919), has a more positive emphasis, though it too moves toward dissolution and death. **"The Crooked Made Straight"** is a moral fable with Gothic touches, **"The Legend of the Scribe"** an idyl of love within the Law, with a moment of hallucination at the end. It suggests how fantasy and feeling can indeed be embodied in a marriage of tender beauty and essential innocence, even as they can be released in a moment of peculiar delight that neutralizes the horror of death. The opening sets the tone for what follows:

> These are the events of Raphael the scribe. Raphael the scribe was a wholly pious man, who used to prepare Torah scrolls and phylacteries and *mezuzot* in perfect sanctity. It was the way of householders who were afflicted with childlessness, God help us, and whose wives had been taken from them, to come to Raphael and say to him, "You know, good Raphael, what we are and what we will be. I had hoped to see my sons and the sons of my sons come to you and ask you to indite for them their phylacteries in their time. But now, alas, I am desolate and forlorn. My wife, whom I had hoped to await through the days and the years in the heavens above—my wife has suddenly passed on before me, and left me to nothing but tears. Perhaps you could bring yourself, good Raphael, to prepare a Torah scroll for me, in accordance, with my means, such as they are, as the hand of the Lord is kindly upon you. . . ." And Raphael the scribe would sit himself down and prepare him a scroll, that he might leave behind him some memory, some monument in Israel.

The action of the tale is radically simple. We learn how Raphael lived and worked, of the quality of his relationship to his wife, of their childlessness, and of the irony of his preparing Torah scrolls for the childless. And we learn of Miriam's tender yearning, how she prayed that the Lord might bless her womb, even as she tenderly ministered to the children of others. Then we see how their life is disrupted by Miriam's sudden death and learn how Raphael decides to prepare a Torah scroll in her memory. We watch Raphael immerse himself in the ritual of scroll-writing. And we watch him, when he has completed his labor of love, as he dances with the scroll, which he has decked out in a cover made of Miriam's wedding dress, and is carried back to that Simhat Torah (Festival of Rejoicing in the Law) long ago, when he was a boy and first joined the men in the dance. He recalls how Miriam, hardly more than a child, came to kiss his Torah scroll and, having burned his jacket with her candle, was engaged to him. He sings as he dances, signing the song and dancing the dance he had danced then, confounding the now and the then in the song. Though Miriam is dead and her wedding dress adorns the Torah scroll he has written in memory of her, he reaches into the closet to find the dress. Having looked and having found only a bag of earth from the Holy Land—the very earth he had placed in Miriam's grave—he dies, and is found with the wedding dress over his face.

The tale is remarkable in its capturing of the tenderness that informs Raphael and Miriam's life together, and in its modulating into the quiet ecstasy of Raphael's final dance. We have the sense that for Raphael, within the containing forms of the tradition, the life of love and the life of the Law are continuous, not dichotomous; for once, Eros and civilization do not collide. The one feeds the other, and is fed by it. To be a scribe, monastically dedicated to the transcription of the Law, and to be a man and a husband are not disjunctive; the kissing, the touching, the singing, the dancing—and also the fasting, the praying, the self-containment—that signify one aspect of life inform the other as well. Agnon captures the process whereby such congruence is made possible in his account of the Sabbath encounter between man and wife.

> While Miriam stands in the ritual bath, Raphael tarries in the house of prayer. When she comes home from the bath, she puts on garments as lovely as those of a bride on the day of her nuptials and stands in front of the mirror. At that moment it seems to her that the days of her girlhood have returned; she sees the inn that had stood at the crossroads, where lords and ladies used to come and cattle merchants used to lodge—where she had lived with her mother and her father and with Raphael, the lord of her youth, and she remembers for a moment the veil her mother had made for her marriage. For a moment, she thinks of adorning herself for her husband. But then she sees, glancing at her out of the mirror, the sampler she had made as a girl, which now hangs on the wall opposite—the pair of lions standing within it, their mouths open [to utter the glories of the Lord]. She recoils from her thought. "The earth is the Lord's and the fullness thereof!"

> So that when Raphael returns from his devotions and beholds his wife in her loveliness, . . . he draws near to whisper endearments in her ear. But when he reaches her, he sees the Lord's name reflected in the glass . . . and reads with reverence, "I shall hold Him always before me." Then he shuts his eyes and turns from her, to honor the Lord in his holiness. They part in silence. He sits in one corner of the room, reading the Zohar and its commentaries, and she sits in another, saying her prayers, until sleep comes to dim their eyes. They rise and take the copper bucket with the copper fish engraved on its bottom, and they wash their hands for their evening prayers.

There is nothing puritanical in Miriam's failure to adorn herself as a bride. She is intrinsically a bride. Consciousness of her place in God's world makes her one. Her memory of girlhood becomes part of her consciousness of a larger pattern to which she belongs. To see the sampler on the wall, with its evocation of the greater context of her existence, is to realize her essential form. Raphael and Miriam go to bed, like other couples. But their doing so seems an aspect of a larger reality of which they are a part.

What Agnon suggests is a kind of ladder of love, on which the movement from one plane of love to another is achieved without negation of the "lower" planes. It is this that makes possible the peculiar equanimity with which Raphael experiences the final hallucination, which is potentially so dissonant and yet so filled with a sense of the tenuousness of life.

In fact, the underlying life of the tale seems to stem from a paradox. What Raphael and Miriam are—and love—intimates a pattern of transcendence and is contained in a way of life that is the earthly vehicle for that pattern. But the delicate balance of feeling, its perfect poise, arises within life, and consists of the shifting, time-bound mortal realities: the human feelings which, however they are caught up in the governing pattern of transcendence, are subject to mortality and can themselves be disintegrated, under the pressure of experience, into the time-bound realities which have constituted them.

But even such disintegration need not finally disrupt. At the end of his life, Raphael is still dancing the dance of the Law with which his meaningful life as man and husband began. And, though *we* may perceive it differently, Raphael's experience remains integral. His dance of death is his dance of life. As he dances, his consciousness, which carries him back to the past, before the beginning of his love, is moving backward and forward at once, to what has become a timeless past and to what will be a timeless future, in death. But in both directions he moves toward the unifying goal of his life. And that goal is both in life and beyond life.

"The Outcast," published in the same year as **"The Legend of the Scribe,"** renders a similar theme more elaborately. It is concerned, not with the quiet felicity of a traditional marriage, but with the torment and upheaval in the life of a boy torn between two traditions. Set at the time of the first appearance of Hasidism in eastern Galicia, it is more concrete in social and historical detail than any of the tales discussed so far. It is also more directly concerned with open conflict. Yet its chief emphasis is on the inner turmoil of the boy in question—and in the resolution of that turmoil in a death of exquisite longing.

"The Outcast" tells how Uriel, a Hasidic rabbi, comes to a village one snowy Friday and is banished from the town by Avigdor, its rigidly sectarian *parnas* (burgomaster). The rabbi, as he leaves, curses his antagonist, saying that an outcast will arise from his seed. At just that time

Reb (Mr.) Avigdor's daughter dies, leaving a brood of children. Gershom, the eldest, is a gifted Talmudic scholar and the apple of his grandfather's eye. And indeed, when Gershom comes home for the first Passover after his mother's death, he is overwhelmed by melancholy and goes by chance into a little Hasidic prayer house, where he finds both pleasure and release in the Hasidic service. He immediately rejects the experience, however, and reverts to his grandfather's Way, splitting hairs in his Talmudic studies, afflicting his body with ascetic exercises, and "encasing himself in sadness like a worm." His soul suffers, however, and craving the union he senses can come only through the medium of Hasidic exaltation, he sets out to find Reb Uriel.

A Hasid finds him fainting in the snow and brings him home. He recovers but languishes, until a mysterious stranger initiates him into the vision of ecstatic union with the deity that informs the Hasidic cult.

> And since Gershom's heart was opened and came to glimpse the divine mystery within simple things, the stranger began to lead him from rung to rung on the ladder of wisdom. . . . At that moment the husk of that soul fell away, and all of Szibucz fell away from it. And such longings began to spring up in his heart as had never been known to the people of Szibucz, and they revealed themselves in his eyes, which labored in the Law and then sought to rise higher and higher, beyond. But his fingers were blind, and they groped in the world of truth as a blind man gropes in the darkness.

As a result, "melancholy suffused him, and the anguish of the world veiled his pleasant face." Suffering, he moves further and further from the ordinary plane of rabbinic learning and human contact, "pouring out his soul, as a child into its mother's bosom," climbing and soaring into the "intelligible world" and striving to sit "in the shadow of the Holy One, blessed be He" and to "suckle from holy thought." But when the inspiration leaves him,

> Gershom sits on the ground and puts his head between his knees like one who had been forced to alight from the chariot at the moment that the Holy Spirit went forth to greet its Father in Heaven. "My God, my God," Gershom cries, "you created Paradise and placed a sword at its gate. May it be your will that my bones burn in hell, if only a sixtieth part of them reach you in the end.". . . And a voice murmurs like a dove, "Alas, for the sons who were exiled from their Father's table." Exiled from Father's table, and when will they return? Has their time not yet come? The lowly world thou hast created—what remains for us within it?

His final sense of release comes only when his master reveals the mysteries of the Song of Songs.

> He had not yet finished when Gershom began to cry with all his might, "I will fly and wander far, and sing the Song of Songs. To the house of the Lord we will go, we will go; we will tell the house of Jacob how my soul has thirsted, has yearned for the Lord." So he cried and cried, like a bird that has scented the fluttering of its wings, and flies, and murmurs as it flies.

The scene then shifts:

> The eastern sky reddens, and the dome of the sky nearest the earth grows dark. The daughters of Israel light their candles and stand in the gateway of their houses, murmuring to each other, "A good and a blessed Sabbath." As they wait, their chaste daughters come, with their hair dressed, in their lovely garments, and stand with them, facing the synagogues and the houses of study in order to be able to respond with "Amen, may His hallowed name be blessed." The householders, with their sons, walk to the houses of study and chant the Song of Songs, and the good Lord sinks the wheel of the sun in the west in order to receive his beloved, the Sabbath Queen, in chaste darkness.

> At that moment Gershom entered the house of study and leaped onto the altar and lay his head between his hands for a moment. Then he lifted his head and began to read the Song of Songs with terrible ardor and awesome strength until he reached the verse, "Draw me after Thee, and we will run." And when he reached the verse, "Draw me after Thee, and we will run," his soul departed from his body, in its purity. His lips were still murmuring, "The King, he brought me into his chambers," when his soul expired with the words.

Formally, **"The Outcast"** is concerned with the working out of a curse in the context of a conflict between Hasidim (ecstatic pietists) and Mitnagdim (legalistic literalists) at the time (the 1770's) Hasidism reached Galicia. The issues are crystallized in the representation of Avigdor, the rich, worldly, repressive pillar of the old dispensation with its emphasis on Law, and Uriel, with his melting, ecstatic cult of love.

Gershom's tragedy stems from the conflict in him between the way of the world, which is Avigdor's, and the way of transcendence, which is Uriel's. The story's main emphasis is on Gershom's anguish and the horror—mixed with ecstasy—of his doom. It is terrible that he should have to suffer; it is terrible that he must die, reaching into the world beyond for tenderness and love. It is also marvelous: a total transcendence, in feeling, of the limits of life in the vale of tears. In taking the mystic way, which he does not altogether choose, Gershom reaches out to his dead, beloved mother, as well as to God. The imagery of suckling at the breasts of thought, and of pouring out his soul "like a child into its mother's bosom," straddles the conventional metaphoric language of mystic communion and the concrete psychological realities of the boy's life. The tale evokes essentially the same ambiguity that informs Raphael's relation to the Torah scroll and the same reconcretization of metaphor that is achieved in **"Agunot."** So integral is Gershom's melting out of life at the end that it induces neither pity nor terror in the ordinary sense. Gershom wants it so badly and needs it so much, that the pity lies only in the fact that it took so long for it to happen, the terror in the fact that it is not really pitiable at all. And yet it is all very sad.

The balance of the feeling evoked in **"The Outcast"** is characteristic of all the tales I have discussed here—and of many of Agnon's other tales of *shtetl* life. They exploit the imagery of faith and transcendence, of union and communion as a way of conveying a sense of experience that at once laments mortality and celebrates the pain that it brings. One might say that **"The Outcast"** renders a characteristic moment and a characteristic mode of experience in the *shtetl* culture. But the emphasis is not on the substance of that culture or on the ancestral values that inform it. Rather, it is on the emotional values that arise within it, without reference to the validity of the problems or attitudes that give rise to them.

The most striking thing about the stories is the apparent objectivity of their form. One might say that Agnon does a triple take in rendering actions set in the ancestral world. First, he enters, though in a limited way, into the experience of particular characters who act and react within it. Second, he renders their actions and reactions much as *they* would have rendered them. And third, he casts the tale itself in a literary mode that would be congenial to the participants in its action. Reading such a tale, we apprehend the people, scenes, and events that fill the tale, but also participate in the attitudes and perspectives of those who act in them. Thus it is not only an action that we see imitated, but—implicitly—an entire mode of consciousness and a total vision of experience.

Agnon never attempts a discursive presentation of the grounds for and qualities of this vision. In fact, he never talks about the vision as such. Quite the contrary. The tales—again—are composed in the manner of folk tales. They employ a narrative voice that assumes we are tuned in upon its assumptions and can therefore focus directly on the things that concern it. The vision that animates the entire world of the tales is, in a manner of speaking, completely dissolved in their narrative mode.

Yet the depersonalization that the form of these tales involves should not conceal the extent to which Agnon uses them to project his most personal, his most intimate predilections. And these predilections are both complex and devious. The "modern" tales, written since the early thirties, suggest that Agnon turns to the ancestral world for the "wholeness" of experience it engendered. In tales both traditional and modern, moreover, Agnon suggests that the ancestral world is possessed of a power and a vitality which stun the imagination. One story—**"The Fathers and the Sons"**—presents us with a series of fathers, each older than the one preceding him, and each more fresh, more vigorous, and more vital. The suggestion is that the narrator of that tale experiences a sense of impotence and insignificance in the face of the patriarchal world and the "fact" that the world is felt to deteriorate in power and glory with the passing of the generations. One presumes that Agnon resurrects the ancestral world to present us with images of that power and that glory.

Yet the power in question is a very peculiar one. It is, to be sure, the power to affirm life, but it is also the power to reconcile oneself utterly to life's negativity. The people and scenes depicted in these tales are always seen as diminutive—quaint, folksy, lovable. His people are, almost uniformly, little people with a quiet dignity. They are pious and prudent, deeply involved with the things that constitute their lives and remarkably gifted at letting go of them without crying havoc. Again and again we see them, in one of two perspectives. We see them experiencing pain and loss, not only stoically, but also with a kind of yearning pleasure. Or we see them comically abstracted from consciousness of the exigencies of ordinary life. In either case, there is beauty or amusement in their lives, but certainly not power or vitality in the ordinary meaning of the terms.

> **Agnon's finest noncomic work in the traditionalist mode has a kind of luminous loveliness and musicality, reminiscent of the medieval tale at its best.**
>
> **—*Baruch Hochman***

As a result, one has the sense that Agnon is performing a peculiar operation on the past which haunts him so persistently. If its grandeur lives in his imagination, that grandeur is cut down to size in the adulatory diminutives of his stories. It is as though he must shrink it to livable scale, not by directly challenging its existence or values, but by bringing it under aesthetic control. I often wonder whether Agnon's most pious evocations are not in fact voodoo exorcisms of a past that will not die.

If Agnon is indeed resurrecting the past in order at once to celebrate it and to diminish (if not to denigrate) it, if he is in this way indeed circumventing a very real confrontation with decisive elements in his own experience, then a further quality of the tales takes on a striking significance. The tales of the traditional world rarely involve confrontation of the tensions to which their characters are subject or an exploration of the inner grounds of their conflicts. Just as **"The Legend of the Scribe"** renders the way fantasy and feeling are integrated within a prescribed pattern of relationships, so it renders the disintegration of that life—and feeling—pattern within rather formalized conventions of feeling and belief. It is surely no accident that Raphael, like Gershom, breathes out his soul in song. In these tales, song is the vehicle for the unquiet, the longing, the fear that the characters experience: it is Ben Uri's song that haunts Dinah, for example. But song is also the medium of reconciliation and a final harmonization of discord, both for the characters in the stories and for their readers. That reconciliation comes in death. To expire is to breathe out the dying breath, and that breath is song, which both expresses the individual's craving for union and carries him toward the union he has craved.

The effect is peculiar. Agnon's finest noncomic work in the traditionalist mode has a kind of luminous loveliness and musicality, reminiscent of the medieval tale at its best. In it there is a fine orchestration of feelings that spring from pain and loss, but never a direct representation of the rawness and anguish they involve. Everything is harmonized within the dominant pattern of submission, and every discord is resolved within that pattern. The songs characters sing are one medium for expressing the feeling that there is a resolution. Another is the elaborate pattern of tropes from the repertory of traditional image and legend. But the final effect is somehow one of evasion. It is as though Agnon turns to the ancestral past partly because he finds within it a set of attitudes that permit a deeply desiderated transcendence of the harshness of inner conflict and a deeply felt need to circumvent the horror of death itself.

And that evasiveness leaves one uneasy. The stories have a quiet beauty. In sheer virtuosity there is little to match them in modern Hebrew letters. And they do, one feels, draw on something that was really present in the *shtetl* culture. Indeed, they do so with an authority and a compassion (despite the diminutives) that are moving. But the extraordinary aestheticizing of experience is suspect, as is the deep passivity they reflect. They are still more troubling when read in the light of Agnon's later work. There Agnon invokes dissonance. He renders characters who, like those in the earlier tales, yearn "beyond"— often back to the world of the earlier tales, that is, to the ancestral scene. And he projects, sometimes on a grand scale, the horror that informs such yearning in the modern world. Yet in the modern stories as well, however clearly the psychological and historical grounds of the dissonance are projected, one feels he is stepping away from the heart of the darkness—and illuminating it with an inadequate, aestheticizing light.

I am suggesting, in effect, that there is a much stronger affinity between Agnon's early, pathetic tales of *shtetl* life and his later, "modernist" work than at first meets the eye. There are stylistic affinities, of course, and there is the ever felt hand of the master craftsman at work. And there are the constant echoes of the classic Judaic idiom of faith. But beyond these formal and external elements there are the pervasive passivity, the recurrent "yearning beyond," and the constant craving for a wholeness unattainable in the present life.

One might see these qualities as the expression of a deep theological and existential intuition, of the awareness of man's deeply experienced sense of his vulnerability and violability, and of the only partial existence which is—at best—his in the flesh. One might hold that the melting sweetness and even ecstasy of the tales of the ancestral world evoke the way that the sense world is overcome by a tradition of faith, in which the felt presence of the deity creates the possibility of dealing with it satisfactorily. One might insist that the sense of loss and fragmentation of being that fills the modernist tales is the consequence of the characters' having been cut off both from the an-

cestral world and the deity who could be reached through the forms of life he prescribed.

But it seems to me that Agnon is writing about (or working with) something else: a deeply felt personal, one might even say infantile, sense of a wholeness that has nothing to do with the deity or his ways (unless one wishes simply to consider the religious feeling a direct projective of infantile needs). There is no question that he projects the sense of completeness with delicacy, mastery, and grace. But the struggle, the horror even, that ordinarily accompanies this craving for wholeness is never really there. There is no subversive resistance within the self to the felicities to which his characters consistently aspire.

Hence one comes away from the tales with a sense that something is lacking. It is impossible not to wonder whether the loveliness and musicality so worshipfully evoked are not, in the end, an evasion and a self-indulgence of Agnon's own wish to transcend the final terrors of mortality itself. Agnon, one notes, depicts pain, but never the pain of wayward inner resistance to striving toward objects of valid desire. And we rarely glimpse the larger, more dangerous impulses, which his people are generally and beneficently spared. When we do perceive them, as in Agnon's lyric evocation of a dreadful necrophiliac love, we perceive them in the glow of an aestheticizing so complete that it robs them of their life. Yet their luminous simplicity continues to beguile us.

Robert Alter (essay date 1972)

SOURCE: "Agnon's Mediterranean Fable," in *Defenses of the Imagination: Jewish Writers and Modern Historical Crisis,* The Jewish Publication Society of America, 1977, pp. 187-98.

[*In the following excerpt, Alter calls attention to Agnon's intermingling of ancient Hebrew and Greek worlds in* Betrothed, *a strategy that enhances the story's fabulous quality, according to the critic.*]

S. Y. Agnon was a writer often fascinated with fabulous antiquity, but what is peculiar about **Betrothed,** one of his most intricately devised and original tales, is its seemingly promiscuous intermingling of different ancient worlds. The story is set in the early Zionist community at Jaffa, all its chief characters are Jewish, and the language of narration is of course the richly traditional Hebrew, with predominantly medieval-rabbinic tonalities, that is Agnon's stylistic hallmark. Yet the protagonist, in his student days an impassioned reader of Homer, freely invokes "the good gods" in his speech (though when the whim moves him he also calls on a monotheistic "God"); has Zeus and Esculapius on his lips; tells the local girls in Jaffa stories about Sappho and Medea. He is pledged to a woman whom he remembers rising out of the waters of a pond, half-mermaid, half-Aphrodite; and, finally, in the climax of the story he becomes the prize in a weirdly reversed reenactment of an ancient Greek race for athletic laurels. Beyond this circle of allusions to ancient Greece drawn around the protagonist, we get momentary but significant glimpses of other ancient or exotic cultures. There are weighted references to the Egyptian art of mummification; a symbolically important invocation of Semiramis, mythological queen of Assyria and supposed founder of the garden-city of Babylon; a bizarre tale about a black African queen who rides the back of one of her ministers; and strategic reminders of the presence of Islam in the city of Jaffa.

Betrothed is a muted psychological study of one Jacob Rechnitz, who is the powerless captive of a profound Oedipal impulse, and, simultaneously, it is an "Oedipal" story in a rather different sense, of a geographical and imaginative return to the womb of Western cultures. It is this latter aspect of the story that I shall try to describe, though the symbolic argument is so intricately articulated that I can only sketch the general outline of a development that must be followed through minute attention to a whole series of interlocking passages in the actual experience of reading. The opening lines of the story set it in a broad perspective as a tale of the encounter of cultures: "Jaffa is the darling of the waters: the waves of the Great Sea kiss her shores, a blue sky is her daily cover, she brims with every kind of people, Jews and Ishmaelites and Christians. . . ." The use of the biblical term Great Sea for the Mediterranean in itself has the effect of shifting the viewpoint backward toward the ancient Mediterranean world, where this was the great sea of all the earth (for Odysseus as for Jonah), and of course these three peoples are all groups whose faiths first flourished at the eastern end of the Mediterranean basin. In the Hebrew, the first two words of the story are a pointed pun: *Yafo yefat yamim,* literally, "Jaffa, beautiful one of the seas," calling our attention to the supposed etymological derivation of *Yafo* (Jaffa) from *yafeh,* the word for beautiful, and reminding us that Japheth *(Yafet),* the biblical progenitor of the Greeks—a people associated with the ideal of beauty—is also according to one tradition the founder of the city of Jaffa. Later in the story, when Rechnitz is taking his fiancée Susan Ehrlich around town, he points out to her "the 'Nine Palm Trees,' planted by Japheth, the son of Noah, when he founded Jaffa: one for himself, one for his wife, and seven for his seven sons." It is clear that one of several central polarities with which the story elusively plays is that of Hebraism and Hellenism, or, to put it in more indigenously Hebrew terms, Shem and Japheth, the two cultural archetypes of Israel and Greece. The "Seven Maidens" who run the race for Jacob stand in strangely suggestive correspondence to the seven sons of Japheth, as do past and present, Hebrew and Greek, to each other in the tale.

Betrothed records the subtle but profound assimilation of the world of Shem by the world of Japheth through the character of Jacob Rechnitz. According to Noah's blessing to his two more fortunate sons in Genesis, "the Lord will deal bountifully with Japheth"—in another traditional interpretation of the enigmatic verb-form *yaft,* "will grant beauty to Japheth"—"and he will dwell in the tents of Shem." Rabbinic tradition understood the tents of Shem

as an epithet for the talmudic academies or study-houses of the Law, and imagined the offspring of Greek aesthetic culture coming to learn the moral law of the Jews, thus realizing a cultural ideal by combining "the loveliness of Japheth" *(yefeifiuto shel Yephet)* with "the Torah of Shem." Jacob Rechnitz—his first name, of course, is a biblical synonym for Israel—represents a reversal of this ideal: he is a Shem in the tents of Japheth, an amateur of ancient Greek culture, a sedulous student of the natural sciences that derive from Greece, pursuing his own specialty of marine biology in an eerily erotic fashion. "Another young man would ask for no more than such a life [walking by starlight with beautiful girls]; but as for Rechnitz, another world lay in his heart: love of the sea and research into her plants." And as his eyes feast on the magical marine world of colors and shapes and textures, his response is amorous rapture: "'My orchard, my vineyard,' he would say lovingly." It is not surprising that, when he comes to Palestine during the pre-World War I period in which the tale is set, he should settle in Jaffa, the city that has a mythological "Greek" founder. Japheth planted seven palm trees for his seven sons; Rechnitz at the end of the story will be trapped by a shimmering vision of seven girls on that same Jaffa shore. The switch from masculine to feminine is thoroughly appropriate for the passive, woman-ridden Rechnitz (is it any wonder he tells stories about Medea and man-bestriding queens?); and one even suspects that, despite the masculinity of Japheth and his sons, the story ultimately associates the Greek world into which Rechnitz moves with a female principle that stands opposed to the masculine world of the Semites. Jaffa is a city founded after the flood, yet Rechnitz chooses it for his residence not because it is the entrance to the Promised Land but, on the contrary, because it faces out on the verge of the ever-returning, never-receding flood of ancient waters.

The world of *Betrothed* is a remaking of the old biblical creation according to the ambiguous design of gods other than the Lord of Genesis. One of the two, seemingly disparate, ultimately complementary reasons given in the story for Rechnitz's interest in the sea is a kind of vision he has one night while reading Homer:

> He heard a voice like the voice of the waves, though he had never yet set eyes on the sea. He shut his book and raised his ears to listen. And the voice exploded, leaping like the sound of many waters. He stood up and looked outside. The moon hung in the middle air, between the clouds and stars; the earth was still. He went back to his book and read. Again he heard the same voice. He put down the book and lay on his bed. The voices died away, but that sea whose call he had heard spread itself out before him, endlessly, while the moon hovered over the face of the waters, cool and sweet and terrible.

The vision of the sea transmitted to Rechnitz by Homer is of a sphere of tremendous primal power, echoing in the power and vitality of Homer's own poetic creation. Rechnitz thus associates the sea simultaneously with the vital source-culture of early Greece and with the evolutionary source of life itself: "off he would sail to where, as he told himself, the earliest ancestors of man had their dwelling." But, in Rechnitz's Homeric vision, as the pounding of the waves dies down, he becomes aware of the moon (an actual moon outside his window) hovering over the face of the waters (waters conjured up by the lines of poetry before him)—not, as in Genesis, the spirit of the Lord, but the *moon*, "cool and sweet and terrible," like the call of sirens, like the allure of eros itself to this threatened male. The evocation of Genesis I by way of the Greek Homer becomes a new, stirring but ambiguous creation presided over not by the forthright biblical God but by an erotic lunar demiurge, associated with the female principle, with imagination and beauty, with a world of shadows and wavering reflections. The reverberations of this moment are heard again in an exchange between Rechnitz and the pious Yemenite caretaker of his school which he reports to the Consul:

> "Once he asked me, 'Why is it that King David says: *Thou hast set a boundary, they shall not cross it, they shall not return to cover the earth; thou hast set a boundary to the waters of the sea, that they shall not go up on the dry land?* And yet we see that the waters of the sea do go up on the dry land.'"

> "And how did you answer the Yemenite?"

> "What could I reply?" said Rechnitz. "I didn't give him any answer, but I sighed deeply, as one does when regretting that things are not as they should be."

The Psalms, here quoted by the Yemenite, are full of allusions to a primordial conquest of the intransigent sea by the Lord of Creation (in its ultimate derivation in Canaanite religion, it is the conquest of the sea god by the land god). The reality, however, inhabited by both the pious caretaker and the freethinking teacher, seems to contradict the authority of the Psalms. For, in the story, it is the sea that repeatedly asserts its dominion over the land, and that whole solid biblical world of divinely-set demarcations and boundaries dissolves into a marine flux where opposites merge. Shem and Japheth are fused—to borrow Joyce's phrase—into Jewgreek and Greekjew, life looks like death, or love becomes death (the climactic race that begins at the Hotel Semiramis ends by the old Muslim cemetery; the solemn pledge of betrothal between Jacob and Susan is itself renewed in the cemetery), and even the dividing line between personalities blurs, with Susan fading into her mother and her mother into Jacob's mother, in the sea-and-moonstruck mind of the protagonist.

For Rechnitz, the confusion of realms and identities is doubly appropriate. Whether life-spawning sea or womb, the primal source to which he is drawn implies a denial of the principle of individuation. And because that to which he would return is an ultimate taboo, it is fitting that he can make the approach only through a series of surrogates. Thus, the narrator suggests early in the story that Susan's mother becomes an uncanny substitute for Rechnitz's in his own mind: "Jacob's mother, too, had loved him as a mother should love her son, and he had returned her love in a son's normal way; but his affection for Frau

Ehrlich was something apart. It was a love that could be accounted for by no natural cause, though there was reason for it, no doubt, as there is reason for all things; yet the reason was forgotten, the cause was lost and only the effect remained." Rechnitz, impelled as he is by longings for this mother-figure, is the very type of a man caught in a web of motives that remain obscure to him, but hardly to the narrator and his audience. Agnon's technique for suggesting this condition is to set up a kind of verbal smoke screen, a merely seeming obfuscation, through which, however, the lineaments of Jacob's predicament are visible to the discerning eye. Characteristically, just a moment later in the narrative, Agnon conveys the transference of Jacob's affection from Susan's mother to Susan after the mother's death with a gesture of mystification that only partly hides the explicitness of his statement: "It was rather like a new motion of the soul, when the soul attached itself at once to one who is absent and another who is present, and is taken up into both as one." Years later, in a garden in Jaffa, Jacob will gaze at Susan's lovely hands and think, most unsettlingly, of "her mother's hands when she would place them on the table and his lips would long to touch them."

It is significant that the awareness of this chain of surrogates, always powerfully subliminal in Rechnitz and always ultimately associated with the sea, should reach the verge of consciousness in the penultimate moment of the story, when he closes his eyes to the limitless expanse of sea and listens to the pounding of the waves as the girls run down the beach:

> He saw his mother kneeling down before him. He was a small boy; she was threading a new tie round his collar, for it was the day Susan was born and he was invited to the Consul's house. But surely, thought Jacob to himself, she can't be my mother, and it goes without saying that she isn't Susan's mother either, because one is far from here and the other is dead; if I open my eyes I shall see that this is nothing but an optical illusion. The illusion went so far as to present him at once with his own mother and with Susan's; and since one object could not be two, it followed of necessity that here was neither his own mother nor Susan's. But if so, who was she? Susan herself, perhaps?

The threading of the tie around the collar looks forward to the moment when Jacob will crown Susan with a circlet of seaweed at the end, and catches up a series of images of circles and encirclement linked with women and water—the circular pond in the garden, the wreaths of flowers on Frau Ehrlich's bier, the entourage of girls on the beach, the golden ring of Susan's eyelashes that captivates Jacob, from which her voice seems to emanate at the end.

It is no wonder that Rechnitz, for all his love of the sea, is moved to pensive regret by the idea that its waters go up on the dry land. The sea is a never-forgotten presence in the story, effectively dominating all the action and all the personages. In various evocations of Susan Ehrlich, her mother, the moon, and Rechnitz's algae, water is associated with erotic experience, and both water and eros are linked with the imagistic motif of "the blue distances" intimating death. At the beginning of the story, Jacob observes in the Consul's office portraits of mother and daughter, before which is set "a moist rose in a glass of water"—the Hebrew for "Susan" means "rose"—and both female figures in the pictures seem about to disappear into blue mists. Later, when Susan herself identifies the blue distances with a nirvanalike death, she "seemed to hover over those blue distances she had spoken of," and she invites Jacob to kiss her closed, tear-moist eyes, his lips at once touching her flesh and salt water in a dream of love and death.

Elsewhere, less passively, the sea, glimpsed through the hotel windows or heard in the dark of a summer evening, is "like some being that lacked peace in its depths," the sound of its waves "like the distant roaring of beasts of prey," ominous, alien, ready to pounce. These are not the "mighty breakers of the sea" in Psalms whose might is as nothing before "God Who is mighty on high," but rather the savage man-breaking waves of Poseidon, if not the dark waters of still older Greek gods, Chaos and Old Night.

Why should the ancient Greek Mediterranean culture exert the seductive, perhaps fatal attraction that it does within the world of the story? The answer has to be sought, I think, not so much in the intrinsic nature of Greek culture as in the peculiar condition of the twentieth-century world to which Rechnitz, the Consul, Frau Ehrlich, and Susan belong. Perhaps the best way to see that condition is through the strange relationship of the principal characters to both personal and historical time. Though only Susan is afflicted with sleeping sickness, father, daughter, and lover are all weighed down in varying degrees and manners with an enormous sense of weariness and ennui. "There is nothing new," sighs the Consul, echoing Ecclesiastes, "the world goes on as usual," and he is by no means the only character who perceives time in the manner of Ecclesiastes as endless cyclicality with no meaningful progression or innovation.

If experience merely repeats itself endlessly, it is endlessly fatiguing, and so the two lovers of the story, Susan and Jacob, are seen in repeated flight from the time of adult experience into the timelessness of sleep or longed-for death, or into the radiant atemporality of remembered moments from early childhood or the mythic past. It is significant that the narrative is marked by a number of trancelike moments of vision when a fragment of the past seems to erupt into the present as though untouched by the flow of time. On the personal level, this occurs in Rechnitz's visions of the garden of his childhood, fixed forever with its pond, its flowers, its iron gate. On the cultural level, the same pattern is observable, for example, in the still presence of the Nine Palm Trees, which tremble slightly in the brilliant sunlight before Rechnitz's eyes as they must have done at the beginning of history before the eyes of Japheth and his seven sons.

Jacob Rechnitz, the most representative figure of the modern age in the story, is bloodless, will-less, direc-

tionless (except for his attraction to the vegetation of the watery depths)—in sum, the very image of an enervated humanity that has lived beyond its historical prime. The Consul's absurdly inappropriate remark to Rechnitz, "You look as fresh and blooming as a young god," accompanied by the old man's own wistful longings for a renewal of youth, point up the essential irony of Jacob's relation to Greek antiquity, for it is precisely his anemic character that explains both why he is drawn to the Homeric sea and why that magnetism is finally so dangerous to him. Like Dr. Ginath, the scientific seeker in Agnon's later story, *Edo and Enam,* Rechnitz tries to penetrate the mysteries of a primeval realm of vitality as the representative of an age sapped of vitality, an age out of touch with the inherent mystery of man, the gods, and the natural world. But any attempt to seek "renewal" in this way—as, for example, in the notable modern cults of archeology and anthropology, in the various modern spiritual flirtations with the carnal gods of the ancient Near East or of ancient Greece—is futile and may also be fatal, for man is no longer capable of belonging to the archaic world, however powerful his nostalgia for it. Too many centuries of accumulated cultural experience intervene, experience which, for better or for worse, has gradually modified man's nature and estranged him from his own beginnings. The fate of anyone who essays this route of no-return is likely to resemble that of the venerable sage Gevariah in *Edo and Enam,* who climbs to the top of a mountain to learn from the eagles the secret of the renewal of youth and instead receives from them his mortal wound. Agnon himself makes a point of comparing the magical appearance of the charmed leaves brought down from the mountain in *Edo and Enam* with the algae Rechnitz hauls up from the depths in *Betrothed,* and with "the silver strands we observe on the moon," as if to say: what is sought up above in the later tale is sought down below in the earlier one, and the fate of the seekers may be the same.

In *Edo and Enam* the quest for cultural origins leads clearly to death. In *Betrothed,* the story ends in poised ambiguity, with death lurking as a teasing spectral possibility—or is it a presence? The lovely lyric spookiness of the closing moments of the tale is a function not only of Agnon's peculiar sensibility but of the perilously seductive meaning that the pagan past and the primal sea must have for Rechnitz:

> Sea and sky, heaven and earth, and all the space between were grown into a single living being; a luminous calm enveloped by azure, or an azure transparent as air. Up above, and under the surface of the sea, the moon raced like a frenzied girl. Even the sands were moonstruck and seemed to move perpetually. Like the sands, like all the surrounding air, the girls, and with them Rechnitz, were taken up into the dream. If they looked overhead, there was the moon running her race, and if they looked out to sea, there she was again hovering upon the face of the waters.

This is beautiful, but it is the precarious beauty of a dream that can dissolve momentarily. Precarious, too, is the paradox of delicate balance between luminous calm and frantic, driven motion. The hovering upon the face of the waters from Genesis is once more invoked, for this is a grand final recapitulation of that pagan lunar cosmos where boundaries vanish and opposites fuse—sky and sea, heaven and earth, dry land and water. We can hardly forget that the double moon racing above and below here was first described as cool and sweet and terrible. Rechnitz is ready, then, for the eery race along the seashore in which he will at the end be claimed by a moonstruck girl—the Hebrew for sleepwalker also means moonstruck—who would call him on an impossible road back to another image of watery origins, the pond in the long-locked garden. Are Susan's night clothes her shroud? Has she arisen from a sickbed or the grave to fulfill her pact with Jacob? Agnon is careful to draw a veil of ambiguity over the conclusion by the suggestion of a possible continuation in the studied anticlimax of his final paragraph. Whatever the literal answer to these questions, such life as Susan can offer Jacob must be a kind of death, for what invites him to her is a return to the womb, as what draws him to the sea is a longing for the womb of human culture, and to man born of woman, the return to the womb can only mean in the end a turning to death. One understands, then, why an ambiguous hint of a dybbuk-motif—the spirit of the plighted bride returning to claim her own—is appropriate for the ending, and why the whole tale should be a reversal of the Sleeping Beauty legend, the kiss of the entranced maiden conferring on her redeeming prince a breath of eternal sleep.

The anticlimax of the last paragraph deserves reflection, because it suggests Agnon's conception of the nature of his fiction and perhaps something also of the larger use such fiction might serve:

> Here, for the time being, we have brought to an end our account of the affairs of Jacob Rechnitz and Susan Ehrlich. These are the same Susan and Jacob who were betrothed to one another through a solemn vow. Because of it, we have called this whole account "Betrothed," though at first we had thought to call it "The Seven Maidens."

At the very end, the artificer asserts what is in two senses his authority over his artifice, calling it a "composition" (*hibur*, rendered freely above as "account"), reminding us that the conventional matter of title is entirely the author's decision. The two titles are linked by an etymological pun, *SHEV'UAT Emunim* (literally, "The Solemn Vow") and *SHEV'A HaNe'arot* ("The Seven Maidens"), pointing to the connection in Hebrew between the taking of vows and the magical number seven. But this thematically central play on words also makes us aware that the absorbing reality of the tale is itself a construct of words—words, in the shimmering perspectives of Agnon's double vision, being both the stuff of their own reality and the means through which our historical reality is made accessible. It is hard to think of another extended piece of fiction by Agnon where the artistic control is so unflaggingly sure, its exercise so intricately consistent. That quality of control, surfacing in the placid authorial "we" of the final paragraph, constitutes an im-

plicit affirmation of a confident life-making impulse even in a tale that lingers so hauntingly over the watery depths. It is through the controlling intelligence of the writer's imagination that the story makes real for us the ultimate abyss at the brink of which our culture stands, and any truth the tale conveys could hardly be a consoling one. Yet the self-delighting, reader-delighting control of the artist, asserting itself openly at the end, cunningly shaping a narrative structure where no simple conclusion, whether apocalyptic or naively optimistic, can be drawn, is an intimation of possibilities beyond the sea of nothingness that beckons to the protagonist, and is a demonstration of the imagination's ability to cope with the world by being both in it and outside it. The switch in mood at the end to the prosaic reality of the writer's workroom is in its peculiar way tonic as well as anticlimactic. The ontological duality of all imaginative works is felt with especial sharpness here: inventing fictions, we conclude, is an arbitrary act but it may somehow also be, in the quandary of our whole culture, a necessary act as well.

Leon I. Yudkin (essay date 1974)

SOURCE: "Symbolic Analogue in Agnon's 'Metamorphosis'," in *Escape into Siege: A Survey of Israeli Literature Today*, Routledge & Kegan Paul, 1974, pp. 57-70.

[*In the following excerpt, Yudkin examines Agnon's narrative technique as it is demonstrated in "Metamorphosis" ("Panim aherot"), focusing on the author's ability to suggest character histories extending beyond the events explicitly described in the story. Note: The title of the story, here translated as "Metamorphosis," is also known as "Another Face" (see Lev Hakak, 1986).*]

The purpose of this [essay] is to examine a single story by S. Y. Agnon and thus investigate certain aspects of his narrative technique, used in much of his work. Clearly, a short story is more accessible to this sort of close examination than is a full-length novel. Each stage of the story can be seen in its immediate context, and each ingredient, each image, each event, each piece of dialogue, as well as its part in the total structure of the story may be seen in its relevant setting. The story that I have chosen is **'Metamorphosis'** (Hebrew **'Panim aherot'**). **'Metamorphosis,'** as the name suggests, treats of a relationship that reaches its crisis point at the time that the narrative takes place, and undergoes a vital change. In a very short space, the author has to put over to us the background of the relationship against which this metamorphosis happened. A complicated psychological process has to be realistically drawn within the limited confines imposed by the technique of the short story. As Leah Goldberg says:

> The problem is how to convey change within a short story and to throw light on the past of the active participants. . . . Sometimes, we have to feel within the

dramatic segment of life presented to us by the author that this grown man about whom the story is told had a childhood, had lived before this point, and has undergone other experiences.

[*Omanut ha-sippur*, 1963]

Concentration of suggestive narrative technique in a highly sophisticated form is achieved by Agnon, who was already an experienced master of the short story. An analysis of **'Metamorphosis'** would not only be helpful in learning how Agnon achieves his effects, but should also cast light on his narrative technique in general, and we may discover, in disguised form, some of the underlying themes in Agnon's work, and the means by which he implements some of his purposes.

In discussing this short piece, it is possible to examine the story stage by stage in the order of its presentation by the author. The situation is established immediately. The setting is outside the courthouse, where the divorce proceedings have taken place. The first to appear on the scene is Toni, the woman who has just been divorced: '. . . she came out of the Rabbi's house with the bill of divorcement in her hand.' The story opens with the words, 'She was wearing a brown dress, and her warm, brown eyes were moist.' Two things are conveyed here: the objective fact of Toni's emergence from the courthouse and her grief. Her moist eyes elicit sympathy from the reader. Agnon's language also establishes the subdued tone of the description. The word for brown (*hum*) is repeated and paired with the word for warm (*ham*), the stress being laid on the labials.

As Toni emerges from the courthouse, two other characters appear—Svirsh and Tenzer—'two bachelors who had become friendly with her since the first year of her marriage.' But, again, the description is not neutral—'Through the tears on her lashes she could see how overjoyed they were.' First, we had sympathy established for Toni. Now, this is clearly related from Toni's point of view—'through the tears on her lashes.' Svirsh and Tenzer are established through her eyes as vultures waiting to feed on the prey of an unfortunate victim. Tenzer (the gay dancer) is described as taking her hands 'in his large clammy hands.' Then he 'gazed at her with the cold furtive look of a sensualist who is uncertain of his pleasures.' Though this is apparently retailed by an omniscient narrator, the viewpoint is clearly Toni's and carries with it a bias against the encroaching Tenzer and guarantees the reader's hostility towards him. Toni is hostile to them and retreats from them both. The reader sympathizes with her, and is also made suspicious of the two people who are concerned only to exploit the situation.

But Tenzer and Svirsh remain with her until the emergence of Hartmann, her former husband, from the court. 'His face was lined and his forehead furrowed. For a moment he stood there looking about him like someone who has just come out of the dark and is wondering which way to go.' Thus Hartmann is seen (by Toni?) as a worried and uncertain man. At this critical moment, he approaches his former wife and asks whether she is going

with 'them,' Tenzer and Svirsh. Toni replies to this with another question, 'Don't you want me to?' The couple have just gone through the formal legal process of divorce, but we see here that their actual relationship is not determined merely by their formal relationship in law. Toni is apparently conditioned to acceptance of Hartmann's guidance and instruction and instinctively continues to follow his judgment. It is at this point that the narrative could have taken a different turn, with each of them going their separate ways in accordance with the implications of the divorce proceedings. But they stay together, bound by their own history and actual relationship to each other. We continue to see Toni as the helpless victim of circumstances, who instinctively attracts sympathy. Her 'sadness' is stressed: 'Her entire appearance seemed to say, "Do I look as if I could go alone?" '

So Toni is incapable of faring for herself and needs the protection of another. It could have been Tenzer or Svirsh. But they are swept out of the picture as suddenly as they were brought in. Although their names and characters have been established, they are entirely subsidiary. The fact that there are two of them is a guarantee of their insignificance in relation to Toni and Hartmann. And indeed they are concerned only for their own pride, as Tenzer says, after she is taken by Hartmann, 'After all it wasn't from me that he took her,' and then retreats into facetiousness. The presence of Tenzer and Svirsh melts away, angrily and humorously, in the face of a stronger tie.

Now Toni is alone with Hartmann, and we can observe their reactions to each other, and their behaviour towards each other. We are aware of Hartmann's clumsiness—his intention to perform actions that are then checked—'Hartmann made as if to take her arm, but desisted, so that she should not feel his agitation.' At this point the actual divorce ceremony can be recalled, and becomes very vivid in Hartmann's mind. Toni's eyes are still full of tears, evoking pity. And now we are brought into Hartmann's consciousness. 'Why are we standing here? he asked himself.' We begin to see the events from his angle. Reviewing the proceedings, he seems to detect a mistake in the scribe's words: '. . . and he thought there was a mistake in it. Why was the wretched man in such a hurry? Because Toni and I . . . the whole thing was so strange.' Two things occur to Hartmann: first, that there has been a mistake in connection with divorce proceedings, and second, that the whole thing is strange. It should also be noted that he does not articulate the fact of the divorce. Just at the point where it is to be mentioned, three dots intervene. Of course, he has a psychological block against its articulation. The mistake presumably applies to the divorce itself, although he does not say so. And the 'whole thing' that is so strange, no doubt is the divorce. None of this is stated. His regret, indeed his view of the event as unnatural and peculiar, is pushed to the back of his mind. But we clearly observe the workings of his unconscious through the consciously articulated, namely what is stated from his point of view in the Agnon story. Since he has come to an impasse here, because he will not allow himself to take the necessary remedial action, he has to do something else—'He felt he must do something. He

crumpled his hat and waved it about.' His action is ineffective and irrelevant. He then notices that he has not
shaved, and is annoyed with himself for appearing dishev-
elled before Toni on such a day—'today of all days.' So,
through lack of an effective course of action, he returns
to his supposed previous preoccupation with himself, and
his own pride. As in others of Agnon's stories, the beset-
ting fault of the central figure is his self-centredness that
prepares the way for his eventual tragedy.

Hartmann now feels himself free to express himself
through talk. But it goes wrong. We have already noted
the psychological block from which he is suffering which
prevents him from articulating his genuine concerns. He
still cannot say what he wants to say:

> Hartmann fixed his gaze on a window being opened
> across the way, trying to remember what it was he had
> wanted to say. He saw a woman peeping out. That's
> not what I meant, he thought, and he began talking not
> about what he'd been thinking, but about something quite
> different.

The appearance of the woman at the window causes him
to say that his preoccupation had not been erotic—in
other words, this must have preoccupied him. And what
he says is again irrelevant to his thoughts. Toni notices
this, too, and tries to understand him—'if only he would
speak coherently and calmly, she would understand everything.' And she comments on his sadness, thus trying
to enter his world and extend the necessary sympathy.
What Agnon is using here is the technique of substitute
action or substitute speech. When something cannot be
done or said, something else takes its place and illuminates by its irrelevance. This is the sense of the 'analogue'—the species that is representative of something
else, and is a device frequently used by the author when
his characters, through intellectual or psychological deficiencies, cannot express their deepest purposes. Thus
we have the story proceeding at two levels—the surface
level and the deeper level, only hinted at by the events of
the surface, by the ripples of the pool.

Toni tries to enter his mind, expressing a sympathy for
him while he is preoccupied with himself—'she felt as if
she were responsible for all his troubles.' She also begins to talk off the point, but this surface irrelevance may
be translated into deeper relevance: 'If she were aware of
what she was saying she would have noticed that she, too,
was talking to no particular purpose. But Hartmann accepted her replies as if they were to the point.'

Both Hartmann and Toni had thought of their children—
innocent witnesses of an adult estrangement. This thought
is concretized in the appearance on the scene of a little
girl with a bunch of asters. Hartmann gives the girl money and cannot understand why she is not satisfied. But
Toni takes the flowers, smells them, and thanks her. This
is what the little girl wanted. Hartmann is willing to offer
money, but Toni can allow others sympathy. Clearly, Toni
is more aware of other people's needs than is her former
husband. Hartmann regards things as 'transactions.' Re-

ferring to this incident of the little girl with the flowers,
he says, 'Well, this is one transaction I've emerged from
safely.' Toni takes up the hint. In keeping with the technique established by the author, things said hint at things
unsaid. If he says that he has emerged safely from this
transaction, it can only mean that there was another transaction in which he was not successful. At this point,
Hartmann begins to talk of his business affairs, a thing
that he has been unaccustomed to do. Toni does not understand, but now he gives full vent to his selfish preoccupations. Apparently this is the first time that he has
been prepared to explain his affairs to Toni; and 'she
began to get the drift of his story, and what she did not
grasp with her mind her heart understood.' A sympathy is
developed between them for the first time. The metamorphosis is beginning to take place—the 'new face' is beginning to emerge. 'Suddenly he realized that he was
seeing his affairs in a new light.' It is even said that the
problem became after all not so insoluble. Now Toni
begins to see that the whole affair of the divorce and his
anger is caused by his business frustration. She lends him
her full support: 'Michael, I'm sure you'll find a suitable
way out of it.' She assumes the role of the stronger partner, and the metamorphosis continues. 'He looked at her
as he had not looked at her for a long time past, and he
beheld her as he had not beheld her for a long time past.'
And he feels genuinely attracted to her: 'with difficulty
he kept himself from caressing her.' She has now become an erotic object, and the way is clear for a new
relationship to be established.

What had gone wrong between the two? At this point in
the story we are given the history of the present situation. As said above, the difficulty to be overcome in the
short story is that of presenting a three-dimensional character with a background and history within the confines
of a small space. Agnon solves this by his review of the
two central characters' relationship as seen by themselves
in their present relationship. We are not quite sure who
is telling the story at this point. The subject has been mainly Hartmann, and the point of view seems to be midway
between Hartmann, Toni and an external observer—the
narrator. Haim Hazaz, faced with a similar problem of
presenting a genuine confrontation between two rounded
characters within the limited confines of a short story,
adopts a similar technique. In the story **'Rahamim,'**
Menashke's potted history is presented in the form of a
brief oblique comment on the root of his bitterness and
frustration, and his counterpart, the name character of
the story—Rahamim—is presented through Menashke's
eyes in his idyllic contentment—of course, a theoretical
conjecture. Thus we get a picture of a confrontation between two people who have a past as well as a present
existence, and a life beyond the immediate circumstances. In **'Metamorphosis'** a crisis point has been passed
and the two protagonists are beginning to move towards
each other. But a fuller understanding is needed of the
rift that took place. One cause has already been hinted
at—Hartmann's selfishness and egocentricity. We now
hear of another—the fact that their life was not being
shared. Hartmann would not tell his wife of his business,
a large part of his life. 'From the day he had built his

house he had tried to keep home and office completely separate.' But he had not succeeded in creating this distinction to perfection because 'a man cannot control his thoughts, and they would come crowding in on him, turning his home into a branch of his shop.' Gradually, business came to assume more importance at the expense of other things, and he became further estranged from his wife. For lack of anything to do at home he took up smoking, which in this story is an image of Hartmann's discontent. He came to take no interest in his wife, and thus became jealous of her and all her activities. But 'eventually he reconciled himself to the situation, not because he condoned her activities but because she had come to assume less importance in his eyes.' Hence the root of the estrangement, the separation, the rift, and the background to this new encounter. Reconciliation can come about only on a basis of reversing the divisive process. In other words, if the rift occurred through one partner's selfishness and refusal to share his concerns, the reconciliation must develop through a willingness to open out his life and concern himself with others.

So Hartmann has to move in another direction towards Toni. This section describes his gropings, physical and mental. They are indeed summed up by the ineffectiveness of his actions, which leaves no doubt of their intention. 'Hartmann stretched his hand into the vacant air and caressed Toni's shadow.' His intention is not in doubt, but the action is pointless. Then he caresses the air. The general scene is described, but only to illuminate the situation of Hartmann and Toni. And then it is said, 'A boy and girl sat with their arms twined about each other, talking; then their voices broke off abruptly, and the scent of hidden desire hung in the air.' Presumably this is a description of an external fact. But if it is so, then it is brought in as a referent to the two central characters. And the statement, 'the scent of hidden desire hung in the air,' is presented neutrally, one degree away from the 'boy and girl.' It does of course apply to Hartmann and Toni; the metamorphosis involves growing erotic awareness. Thus again one thing is said by means of another. [In *Pesher Agnon*, 1968] M. Tochner calls this the 'technique of the other face,' which he describes as 'this artistic device . . . including the use of semantic, linguistic means or an open chain of associations or transparent, symbolic events, each one of which, or all together, form an aspect additional to the surface—a sort of dimension within the overt.' This story is particularly rich in this device, although it is used by Agnon in others of his stories.

Still in this section, ambiguities, associations and apparently mistaken impressions abound. Also everything said is not important in itself, but for what it indicates. Hartmann begins to denigrate Svirsh and Tenzer with Toni's approval. A distant light is taken by Toni for a firefly that reminds her of a childhood incident, and this reminds her of her child, which in turn brings her back to the present situation. A man with a ladder is seen as a very tall man. There is confusion over whether Toni had intended saying something or not:

Toni blinked her eyes and drew in her breath. 'Was there something you wanted to say?' Michael asked her. She looked down and said: 'I didn't say anything.' Hartmann smiled. 'That's strange, I fancied you wanted to say something.' Toni blushed. 'Did I want to say something?' She looked at her shadow in silence. Hartmann smiled again: 'So you didn't say anything. But I thought you did.'

This comical uncertainty points to the dialogues between themselves within their own divided minds and within their pasts. Toni is looking at her shadow. The shadow is the *alter ego,* and at the end of the section two shadows appear—'the head of one of them was close to Toni's while the other was close to Hartmann's.' The image of the boy and girl is repeated and the air is charged with 'unfulfilled desires.' Toni looks at her wedding ring. She is still wearing the wedding ring, and she is once again entering the situation of embarking upon marriage. Ironically, after the divorce, her marriage is becoming a reality.

Hartmann and Toni agree to go together to a restaurant. Toni now seems to have the capacity of entering Hartmann's mind and to know his unexpressed thoughts. They order food which has been freshly cooked; there are new dishes on the menu. They also have wine. Again, the external events point to the internal ones. There is fresh food available to replace the old dishes, an aspect of the 'other face,' but it has not yet been entered in the menu, in other words has not been officially recognized. Wine is drunk—wine that is suitable for a wedding celebration rather than for the aftermath of divorce proceedings. Although 'Toni was ashamed to eat too heartily, her bashfulness failed to blunt her appetite.' They seem to be enjoying a coming together, rather than mourning a separation. Toni is happier now, and Hartmann thinks, without the intervention or censorship of the narrator: 'Since the day I married her I never behaved so decently towards her as when I gave her the divorce.' And he proceeds to reflect on marriage, which he believes should only exist with love. Hartmann's growing love for Toni is hinted at in an expression of erotic desire—'Her shoulders seemed to him to be hidden and two white specks peeped at him, through the openings in her dress where her blouse had slipped down, exposing one shoulder. Now, Hartmann thought, we shall see the other one.' Everything seems to be going well. The meal was good. The wine was good, it was less expensive than was to be expected. They both smoke and we read: 'They sat opposite one another, the smoke from the cigar and cigarette mingling.' The mingling of their cigarette smoke is, of course, an analogue for their own drawing together. Then Hartmann tells of a dream that he had about one Suessenstein, a friend of his of whom he normally was fond. But his appearance in the dream was unwelcome. This Suessenstein is apparently tired of living in hotels and wants a flat, like Hartmann's own. They go to see such a flat. The landlady has a blemish, 'one leg shorter than the other, though this did not seem like a blemish in her.' Then Suessenstein begins to talk as though it is Hartmann who is looking for a flat, and he advises him against it. It would be too cold: there is a stove in the bedroom, but the study is all of glass.

Here Agnon is using the dream to comment on waking experience. Living in a hotel is contrasted to living in a permanent flat. The flat is the symbol of permanent stable existence, the home that includes house and family. Suddenly he is told that he himself is the one seeking to change his flat for another—here an unconscious motive for the divorce. There may be warmth in the bedroom, in other words there may be sexual satisfaction to be had, but a large part of life has to be devoted to work in the study, which is freezing. Finally, the comment on the landlady is a comment on the possibility of changing the appearance of something, its 'face,' by viewing it in a different light. Thus although she had a blemish, one leg being shorter than the other, this seemed more of a virtue: 'On the contrary, she seemed to dance along rather than walk.' Perhaps, now, he can begin to see Toni afresh in the manner of the dream.

Hitherto all has gone well, but when Toni and Hartmann leave the restaurant, it is said: 'The garden and the surroundings became dark. A frog jumped in the grass. Toni dropped her flowers in alarm,' and then—'something had obviously gone wrong with them,' referring to the electric wires. Again, the scenery is a referent to the psychological narrative, as is the stream lying in its 'bed,' with the clear, clear sexual overtones of the Hebrew in what is translated as 'bed'—*bet mirba'at*. Now Hartmann is feeling alert, but Toni is tired. Desire is being aroused in him, but for her there is discord: 'She was exhausted, and her legs were incapable of supporting her body.' Hartmann begins to feel sorry for her and wants to help her. He is responding to someone other than himself and thus drawing closer to her. He decides to take her back to the restaurant for the night—to the scene of their first growing reconciliation. Hartmann is appreciative now of Toni: 'It was good, he felt, that Toni existed for him in this world and at that hour.'

In the last stage of the story, Hartmann and Toni return to the restaurant in search of accommodation. The old man looking after the place is disturbed by this intrusion and assumes them to be a pair of lovers. His view of them does confirm this aspect of the couple that has been developing since the divorce. But they are split up. Toni is given a room, where the bed has a 'bridal wreath' hanging above. She is returning to the original condition of her marriage, but without the husband. Hartmann is left alone to sleep on the billiard table, where he notices the cigar that he had put down when he had begun to tell his dream to Toni. That was the last cigar that he had needed. It will be remembered that for Hartmann, smoking was the product of his domestic dissatisfaction, but with the recounting of the dream he has purged himself of this need. Thus the coincidence of the cigar, remaining from that time, is stressed. Then, he thinks again of smoking: ' "Now we'll have a smoke", he said. But before he could take out a cigar he had forgotten what it was he had meant to do.' Smoking is no longer a necessary substitute activity.

He does not smoke. But at the point when he is going to smoke he sees a mound in front of him, and feels the need to ascend it—'He had not really intended to do so,

but once he had told himself, he went and did it.' The symbolic device of the hill is also interposed by Agnon at the critical moment in the story called **'Gib'ath ha-hol' ('The Sand Hill')**. There, the central figure, Hemdat, finds himself at the moment of decision—a decision that he is unable to take. He wants to decide whether the love between him and Yael is permanent or not, and he seeks a sign to help him decide on his course of action. The sign is negative, an 'evil sign,' for it is Yael herself. But Hemdat does not see it, and he descends from the hill. The hill is a symbol of isolation, and in **'Metamorphosis,'** it reminds Hartmann of his youth, when he fell from such a mound. The fear that that incident would repeat itself attacks Hartmann, quite irrationally, for the mound is very small. But now he can come down safely and leave his isolation. He can be joined to others: 'Strange, he thought, all the while I stood on the mound, I was thinking only about myself, as if I were alone in the world, as if I did not have two daughters.' Further—'The incident of the mound had opened his heart.' He can now see the incident of the mound in a different light. What if he had fallen? He would simply have picked himself up and forgotten about it. And now he can reflect on the childhood incident anew as well, and recollect it with pleasure, not terror: 'his limbs felt relaxed, like those of a man who stretches himself after throwing off a heavy burden.' This childhood experience was, in actuality, uniquely pleasurable, and his recollection of it acts as a cathartic agent removing his fear of 'descending the mound,' and opening the way for his entry into life.

After this incident, he retires to sleep and thinks of Toni. He visualizes her body and 'the two white spots where her skin showed through the brown dress. . . . There's no doubt about it, she isn't young.' Then he reflects that perhaps she has a tooth missing. Toni's defects here begin to take on the character of the landlady's defects in Suessenstein's dream. There her defects became virtues. Here, too, now, 'he still thought of Toni critically, as he always had, but now he felt that all those shortcomings in no way detracted from her.' He feels now genuinely united with her, and imagines that she is in trouble, and needs him. Perhaps he could help her (the word Agnon uses is *l'hoshia*' 'to save', which generally has theological overtones. He wants to extend salvation to her). The effect of his new-felt closeness with her is to obscure the mound—'gradually the parasol vanished, the smoke dispersed. And the asters grew more numerous until they covered the whole mound.' But at this point—'his eyes closed, his head dropped on the pillow, his soul fell asleep and his spirit began to hover in the world of dreams where there was nothing to keep them apart.' This is how the story ends—ambiguously. Not on a point of genuine live contact between the two protagonists, but on a point of theoretical complete union in the only place where that union is possible—in the world of dreams. Hartmann has come a long journey—marrying Toni, becoming estranged from her, divorcing her, and once more, moving back towards her. But perhaps a completely successful return, the aspiration of so many of Agnon's heroes in various situations, is doomed to failure.

In this analysis we can see what means Agnon has employed to create the story. The narrative situation is of
two people who had been estranged; who, from the crisis
point, begin to move together—paradoxically, at the moment of official separation. In order to do this and to credit
the story with significance, Agnon has to invest his characters with a third dimension—with a past and a history
that lives in the present. The limitations of the short story do not allow lengthy discussions, so several levels have
to be presented within one surface. To this end Tochner's
'technique of the other faces' is used. Symbol, the image
standing for more than itself, dream (the surrealistic technique) and cutback (familiar to us throughout fiction and
as the flashback in films) cast light on the interdevelop-
ment of the two characters at this crucial moment, the
narration of which covers an evening spent between these
two people, but also the whole background of their lives
together. Their estrangement had a cause and this cause has
to be eradicated, the fatal flaw to be removed for the estrangement to be overcome. But whether a complete reversal is possible is doubtful. Perhaps this can take place
only in the world of dreams, where there is no divide.

For such a story, as indeed in all fiction, whether values
are consciously adopted or not, the point of view from
which the story is told is, of course, vital. [In *The Rhetoric of Fiction,* 1961] W. C. Booth has said, 'though the
author can to some extent choose his disguises, he can
never choose to disappear.' In this story Agnon has chosen a number of disguises and speaks with a number of
voices. We have most of the tale from Hartmann's point
of view, even though Hartmann himself is viewed critically. Most of the development takes place within Hartmann. His was the flaw, and he has to make the adjustment. He has to grow, to cease being selfish, to share his
life and to consider others. The options open to him and
the possibilities within such a pregnant situation are presented forcibly, subtly, and with the great narrative concentration of which Agnon is such a master.

Bernard Knieger   **(essay date 1975)**

SOURCE: "Shmuel Yosef Agnon's 'The Face and the
Image'," in *Studies in Short Fiction,* Vol. 12, Spring,
1975, pp. 184-85.

*[In the following essay, Knieger attempts to define the
central theme of the story "The Face and the Image"
("Ha-panim la-panim").]*

One of the Agnon stories in *Twenty-One Stories* is **"The
Face and the Image."** But this title is a metaphorical
translation of the Hebrew **"Ha-panim la-panim,"** which
literally translates into "The Face to the Face." The editor Nahum N. Glatzer in his "Editorial Postscript" writes
(on page 283) that the "Hebrew title of the story is taken
from Proverbs 27:19, which the standard translations
render as, 'As in the water face answereth to face, so the
heart of man to man.'" But what is the relevance of this
proverb to the story? Presumably the reference exists to

establish an ironic contrast: the proverb asserts than man
comforts man, but the narrator of the Agnon story is an
isolated individual.

As is characteristic of many titles, the title **"Ha-panim
la-panim"** provides crucial guidance to the central meaning of the story. But we do not realize the full nature of
this guidance unless we recognize that this phrase not
only appears in Proverbs; more crucially, it appears in a
variant form—*panim el panim,* "face to face"—in Genesis and in Exodus. In Genesis 32:30, after his famous
wrestling match where he has been renamed Israel, Jacob
says, "I have seen God face to face, and my life is preserved." And in Exodus 33:11 it is written, "And Jehovah
spoke unto Moses face to face, as a man speaketh unto
his friend." These are well-known passages: *panim el
panim* is as famous a phrase to a Hebrew speaker with a
minimum knowledge of Jewish culture as, say, "Home of
the Brave" would be to the average American. Therefore,
part of the content of the Agnon title is in its echo of
panim el-panim: that is, in the contrast between the face
confronted by its mirror-image and with "God."

The central plot situation in the story is the narrator's
failure to be able to visit his ill—dying or perhaps already dead—mother as a result of a series of awkward
mishaps set up by the narrator himself. **"The Face and
the Image"** is from the collection *The Book of Deeds,*
and the characteristic story there is non-realistic, as the
English reader can judge for himself, for Glatzer has
included nine other stories from this source in the *Twenty-
one Stories.* In any event, the mixture of realism and sur-
realism in **"The Face and the Image"** encourages a symbolic interpretation of this story in which the mother
emerges as, say, the "old faith," certainly as its representative. As Glatzer writes in a general comment on *The
Book of Deeds:* "Deep faith is a matter of the past. . . ."
Thus the narrator at the end of the story is not sitting
face to face with his mother, the representative of the
old faith, but rather in strange surroundings. He is surprised by a mirror-image of himself "reflecting back every
movement of the hand and quiver of the lips, like all
polished mirrors, which show you whatever you show
them, without partiality or deceit." Significantly, the "image rose" when he is trying to avoid recognizing the
consequences of his not being by his mother's side. In
the final line of the story, the "I" says that "it, namely, the
revelation of the thing, surprised me more than the thing
itself, perhaps more than it had surprised me in my childhood, perhaps more than it had ever surprised me before." Presumably what is revealed to him is his isolation, his folly, his impotence.

Instead of wrestling with God or speaking to Him face to
face, the narrator at the end is speaking with himself and
wrestling with his own self-image: man in his folly, his
self-confusion and isolation, in his impotence, and perhaps in his vanity as well, cannot return to the old faith—
some such statement emerges as the central theme of
this story, a meaning that is anticipated by the title **"Ha-
panim la-panim,"** and by its echo of the more famous
panim el panim.

Harold Fisch (essay date 1975)

SOURCE: "The Book of Fables," in *S. Y. Agnon,* Frederick Ungar Publishing Co., New York, 1975, pp. 68-83.

[*In the following excerpt, Fisch examines dreamlike aspects of the stories in* Book of Fables, *which is also known as* Books of Deeds.]

[There is a] combination in Agnon's fiction of the dreaming and waking consciousness, but [it remains to be] determined what kind of dreams these are. They are surely not typically Freudian or Jungian dreams, though it would be easy to find features to support a Freudian or Jungian analysis. What we seem to have is a specific Agnonian type of dream with a syntax all its own; with anxieties, hopes and terrors which can best be understood against the background of Jewish history both ancient and modern. For this is the fundamental context of all Agnon's thinking and experience.

A work which gives us a special insight into the contours of Agnon's dreamworld, and enables us also to judge its relationship with the world of everyday is a collection named simply *Sefer HaMa'asim* (*Book of Fables*). This is a group of twenty short stories, or rather antistories, written over a period from 1930 to 1951. Here, in these strange writings, the normal bonds of continuity fall away; effects fail to follow causes; the setting of Jerusalem changes without warning to that of Vienna or Buczacz; generations and periods are telescoped. The narrator, for instance, suddenly finds himself conversing with his dead grandfather. Forced to leave his work for a few hours whilst the painters are whitewashing his room, he lurches into the past, into the home of his childhood. The symbolic and everyday worlds are yoked together by violence in a way only found elsewhere in Kafka, though Agnon differs from Kafka in his greater degree of faithfulness both to the dream and to everyday observation. He also reminds us of Edgar Allan Poe with his strange world of mystery and imagination. But, in general, Agnon is not so romantically abstracted from his environment nor so totally immersed as Poe in his own psychic depths. His *Book of Fables* are not tales involving radical alienation of that kind.

The last of the *Book of Fables* in the 1951 edition, **"The Letter,"** may be read as a detailed, almost journalistic account of Jerusalem society in the thirties: there are the mandatory police, the bureaucracy, the German refugees with their unhappy complaints about everything they find in the new country. It is all there, even a brilliantly satirical account of a memorial meeting held in honor of some civic leader who has recently passed on. But there is also the faithfulness to the dream. When the narrator gets back home after the meeting, the dead gentleman himself, Mr. Gedalya Klein, is waiting for him; they talk about this and that. [About the name Gedalya Klein, the critic states in a footnote: "There is satire here on the naming of names. We could render this Mr. Bigger Little."] There is nothing frightening or unexpected about the meeting: it has all the thoroughly predictable and "normal" quality of a dream encounter. Mr. Klein and the narrator try to find their way to a certain prayer-house they once visited together (in an earlier dream). Finally, Mr. Klein makes some marks with his stick, and there is the prayerhouse suddenly in front of them! "The old man picked up his stick, knocked twice on the wall, a door opened, and in I went."

A typical dream situation which recurs throughout the *Book of Fables* is sudden amnesia. The narrator finds he cannot remember his address, or that he is tongue-struck, or that his feet are dragging and he cannot move, or that he is improperly clad. In the last case, he is in the synagogue without a head-covering or without a prayer shawl. Above all (as in so many dreams of those of us who have to give lectures or attend meetings), there is an obsession with time. The clock is mentioned in practically every fable: one is inevitably late; the post office is closed before he gets there; he misses the last bus; he has to board a ship by a certain time but the children are lost, and he and his wife chase around the town (which town?) to try and find them, but eventually they get back on board at the last moment as the ship casts off, and find the children waiting there for them.

The three fables I shall describe are **"The Last Bus," "The House,"** and **"The Whole Loaf." "The Last Bus"** begins with the narrator fumbling with a primus stove needed for boiling water to launder a shirt. Finding there is no kerosene in it, he leaves it and goes off to visit a Mr. Sarit who engages him in conversation regarding various people. The house seems to be a kind of furniture store; it is full of cupboards and chairs, and there is a strong smell of turpentine around. We get a fleeting glance of Mr. Sarit's daughter (by his first wife) "whose green eyes and well-developed limbs put [the narrator] in some confusion." Then Mrs. Sarit (the second) provides him with a kind of launderer's ladle to help him in dealing with the primus problem. Place-names and references to his childhood locate this scene in Buczacz in Galicia. Coming out into the street on a narrow black bridge he finds himself in Jerusalem waiting for the last bus home. A few girls who have been to the theater are waiting at the bus stop, but although they know him they ignore him. One of them has long hair and is wearing slacks. He starts talking to his grandfather but doesn't tell him about his visit to Mr. Sarit, because he remembers that his grandfather wasn't too friendly with Sarit. When the bus comes, he misses it, of course. The girls get in first and he drops the ladle that he is carrying. He is especially exasperated at the thought that the girls have left him behind without even bothering to stop the driver and make him wait for him. His grandfather refuses to let him hire a cab, but takes him to the office of the bus company, where they make inquiries about another "carriage."

> I was sorry that my grandfather had lowered his dignity to trouble himself to come from the other world, especially as when he left this one they didn't use buses. I was sorry that I had caused him humiliation.

The superintendent says there is another old carriage but he has no idea when it will start out. The narrator knows very well that it is hopeless to wait for this, but his grandfather urges him on, confident that they will soon move off. The narrator finds his tongue has "thickened" and he can say nothing. The official is obviously having a joke at the expense of them both. On the way to the old carriage (it is really not a bus but, judging by the quaint terminology, it is a disused railway coach from the Galician period) the old man slips and falls, but the narrator doesn't worry because "dead people can't hurt themselves." The problem is what to do now—the narrator starts walking home. It is a pleasant mild evening: he runs into five acquaintances, one of whom he knows by name and who has cause to dislike him. Another passerby of dignified appearance who might have befriended him leaves him with a barely muttered greeting and the faintest hint of a smile. He is left feeling lost and troubled, alone at night "walking behind those men of whom one was my enemy and the other four were not my friends."

Part of the vocabulary of this dream is evidently erotic. There is the ladle, the primus, the girls to whom he is attracted but who seem not to respond to his presence. The sense of emptiness and inadequacy (the empty primus) has evident sexual implications. But this is secondary to the main theme of the various episodes: the young girls just coming from the theater are, as we would say, "moving with the times"—they catch the bus; so is the superintendent who has his laugh at the pair of latecomers who cannot get home; so in a way is Mr. Sarit with his two wives, his successful business, and his careful timekeeping (he goes to bed early and has regular habits). The underlying symbolism of the dream enforces the contrast between the onward pressure of time, and the brooding presence of the past—the grandfather who is "behind the times" and to whom the narrator is still spiritually bound. hence his inability to respond as he would like to Sarit's daughter and to a girl wearing slacks. His involvement in the "new" world and the anxieties and discomfitures to which it gives rise are a source of "humiliation" to his grandfather. But on the other hand, his involvement in the old world gives him little comfort; his grandfather's foolish solicitude keeps him from "getting home" to his rest, and the patriarchal gentleman whom he meets at the end passes him by with barely a nod leaving him to the company of the somewhat hostile group of jerusalem residents.

The pervading theme of homelessness is here picked out with clear erotic and historical references. The pressure of onward time, and the remembrance of times past leave the narrator in "great distress." He is an alien in Shebush and an alien in Jerusalem. How will the man carrying the burden of the past and of his own inadequacies and unfulfilled desires finally reach home? The old coach will not enable him to make it, and the new indifferent generation cares little whether he makes it or not.

The historical theme is even more clearly underlined in the symbolism of **"The House."** We find ourselves in a well-ordered, comfortable and freshly cleaned Jerusalem house on the day before the Passover. Everything radiates a feeling of domestic sanctity and warmth. But there is also a sense of much activity and tension—the tension arising from the many preparations for the festival. They have not slept the whole week, says the narrator; the house has had to be thoroughly cleaned, the pots changed over, and the last traces of leavened bread have had to be scrupulously removed. There has been haircutting, washing, and baking. The following day, i.e., the eve of the festival itself, will also be a day of intense activity and preparation. And so, worn out with his exertions and in expectation of further exertions still to come, the narrator falls asleep almost before he has a chance to eat his evening meal. His sleep is pleasant and refreshing as befits a man whose home is what it should be on the eve of the Passover, but he is aroused at four o'clock (he hears the clock striking) and, going to the door, is annoyed to find that his nocturnal visitor is "a little Arab boy, somewhat ruddy and stout, of a strain bequeathed to the country by the crusaders." He feels a desire "to strike the little bastard on his jaw" for waking him so rudely in the middle of the night. But he overcomes the impulse and after asking what he wants gives him a drink of water. The child seems to be either impudent or incredibly simple, and remains stupidly where he is. Finally the narrator gives him some of the bread that had been left over before the final clearing out prior to the Passover. This is what the child was after, and he runs away with the bread. Going back to bed he finds he can no longer sleep; he now begins to worry about his landlord who has just got back to town and is threatening him with a notice of eviction. He feels he must go and see him, and try and get the matter smoothed over. In passing, the narrator mentions two customary dreams, one of a pleasant and heart-warming house of prayer in the old country, with its white walls, its candles and its fresh Sabbath smell; the other of a big cold house (evidently in central Europe) of forbidding aspect with many windows and a hostile landlady.

> This will help you to understand the feelings of a man like myself, and the fear he has of having to wander, especially of having to leave a place in which I felt at home immediately I entered it.

Looking around for his landlord, Mr. So-and-So, he pursues him from his home to the post office, and then to the bank, but time is short for he has left some leavened cakes at home which have to be finished during the forenoon prior to the festival. He finally meets up with Mr. So-and-So meaning to make some pleasant conversation. However, he finds himself unable to speak. After foolishly following him around for a while, he invites him to his house: to this his landlord brusquely replies that he will visit the house whenever he feels so inclined—indicating clearly that he looks upon the house as his own property and sees the narrator as an unwanted tenant. Finding himself now without money, the narrator has to walk home where, of course, he arrives at a late hour after the festival has already begun. To his profound dismay, he finds the leavened bread left from the night before still unburnt. The table is laid for the festive meal, but all is come to naught—the house is ritually disqualified, and they have to leave it. But the ritual disqualification is but the symbol for a deeper cause of homelessness:

A wife understands her husband. Looking at me she realized that all my efforts with the landlord had been in vain. She knew that we were condemned to leave our home. So she wrapped herself round; she took the boy and I took the girl, and we left.

Going down the street they hear from someone's home the sound of the recital of the Passover Story or *Haggada,* "This day we are here; next year in the Land of Israel. This year we are bondmen; next year we shall be free." Agnon draws the moral:

> It is not enough for a man to dwell in the Land of Israel, he must also pray to be free. . . . A home from which you can be ejected at any time is no true home.

This fable cannot be understood without bearing in mind the character of the Passover-archetype, which for the Jew is probably as powerful as any of the Jungian psychic structures. The sense of urgency and haste which the narrator and his family feel is right there in the biblical source:

> And the Egyptians were urgent upon the people, that they might send them out of the land in haste; for they said, We be all dead men. And the people took their dough before it was leavened, their kneading troughs being bound up in their clothes upon their shoulders.

(*Exodus* XII, 33-4)

The pressure upon the narrator and his family in the preparations for the Passover is the pressure of the ongoing challenge of Jewish history itself, the Exodus from Egypt being the classical prototype, the concrete symbolization of its terrors and its joys. For the Exodus spells both liberation and exile, and between these two poles Jewish history is lived in all its existential paradox. The narrator has come home: here in Jerusalem was a place where he had felt at home immediately on arrival. At the dream center of the fable it blends with the intimate warmth of the prayerhouse in his father's village in eastern Europe. The first sentences underline the calm and joy which the house radiates from its freshly whitewashed walls, and its sparkling floor. His sleep is the sleep of the man who has come home and presides over the festive board. But it is a troubled sleep. The little Arab boy who disturbs him is descended from some philandering crusader who eight hundred years before had mingled his strain with the local Saracens. He represents that alien series of occupations starting with the Romans—the word "ruddy" (*admoni*) to describe his color immediately suggesting *Edom* the traditional, hated name of Rome—and ending with the British, which has made the Jewish Homeland into a problematical home indeed. Romans, Byzantines, Nabateans, Arabs, Turks, and British have at one time or another taken possession of it, so that although he has come home at last, the Jew has not yet lost the sense of homelessness. He must still fight for his right of possession. The narrator's family ejected from their home and walking out into the street are reenacting the archetypal Passover ritual in terms of modern history.

It will be seen that symbol and allegory combine to form a narrative pattern which gains logical coherence only when the underlying mythic structure is understood. This structure might be termed the Jewish theme of linear history, which though seeming to consist of an endless cycle of exiles and returns, redemptions and catastrophes, is felt nevertheless to be moving on to some desired and all-justifying consummation. Hence the forward pressure, the feeling of having to reach a destination.

The clock is no peripheral symbol in Agnon's dreamworld. In a large number of these tales (as, for instance, at the beginning of *A Guest for the Night*) he projects the experience of the Day of Atonement—another fundamental Jewish archetype—and the constant underlying sensation is that the Day is moving on, it is drawing to a close, there is a further duty still to be performed. Will the narrator successfully discharge the burden of prayer and observance "in the time" remaining? And, always, there is the brooding presence of Days of Atonement gone by in eastern Europe, in central Europe; ancestral echoes and urgent present responsibilities, making together a microcosm of Jewish history.

Joyce in his dream novel, *Finnegans Wake,* celebrates a cyclical theory of history which he had derived from the Italian historiographer, Giambattista Vico. Finnegan blends with Adam, with Tristram, with Sinbad the Sailor and the ancient heroes of Ireland. All the heroes of the past become one hero. There is no change, no progress: it is, in short, an historical pattern which rests upon a nature myth, upon birth, copulation, and death—the pattern of the seasons. Agnon's fiction likewise rests on an underlying concept of history, but instead of the dreamy changelessness of *Finnegan* with its ever-recurring motifs, we have the onward pressure of things to be done invading the inner province of the psyche. Here is the special existential background of Agnon's fiction. The Arab boy has a definite historical existence: he belongs to the present as well as to the past, to the outer world of consciousness as well as to the inner world of the psyche. And the narrator is challenged to react. He will either strike him on the jaw or give him bread. But act he must; he cannot slip away from him into a dreamy indifference. Even in sleep, history throws out to us its challenges and choose we must.

"A Whole Loaf" with the same tendency to the grotesque, and the same obsessive concern with the passage of time as the other two stories just described, is a very much more "contrived" fable. The narrator having been kept indoors during the whole Sabbath day by the intense midsummer heat of Jerusalem, goes out in the evening to look for a restaurant to eat a meal—his first meal of the day. His wife and children are abroad, and he has to manage for himself. Here is a hint of the theme of homelessness . . . encountered in *Edo and Enam.* An elderly acquaintance, the scholarly Dr. Yekutiel Ne'eman, beckons him in passing and engages him in conversation about his family. They go on to discuss Ne'eman's book, a book about which there is some difference of opinion among scholars. Some say he made it up himself, and some say he drew his opinions from an earlier authority. At all events,

> from the day it was published, the world has changed a little for the better, and a number of people have even made a point of living according to what is written in it.

Before they part, Dr. Ne'eman gives him a bundle of letters which have to be sent off by registered mail, and asks him to be kind enough to take them to the post office.

The narrator, instead of going straight to the post office, turns aside to other concerns. First, he spends some time in a synagogue, then he is tempted to satisfy his hunger first instead of worrying too much about the letters. He walks along daydreaming about all sorts of succulent dishes but makes little progress either in the direction of a restaurant or the post office, until finally he runs into Mr. Gressler who diverts him from both objects. Mr. Gressler is a successful and materialistic hail-fellow-well-met individual, a Mr. Worldly-Wiseman, whom, says the narrator, he had known "as long as I can remember." Mr. Gressler's company had often given him great pleasure, and yet it is also owing to Mr. Gressler that the narrator's house had been burnt down, for it was Gressler who had persuaded a neighbor to set fire to his property in order to claim the insurance, and the fire had spread to the narrator's dwelling. To give a touch of fantasy to the incident it is related that the firemen, who had been at a party when called to deal with the blaze, poured brandy on the fire to keep it going instead of putting it out!

After a brief ride in Gressler's carriage, the narrator jerks at the reins in order to avoid meeting an undesired acquaintance—an inventor of mousetraps—and as a consequence both he and Gressler topple in the dirt, the narrator being badly shaken and bruised. Picking himself up out of the dirt he immediately makes his way to the nearest restaurant, a somewhat classy affair, where he places his order for dinner, adding that he wanted a whole or uncut loaf with it. This would make it a rather special kind of meal. Everyone else is served before him: time and time again the waiter comes along, but it turns out that the loaded tray is always intended for another diner. At one moment he spies a little boy munching a roll of bread,

> just like that which my mother of blessed memory used to bake us for *Purim.* I can still taste it in my mouth. There is nothing in the world I would not have given for just a taste of that roll.

Hour after hour passes until he hears the clock striking ten-thirty. At that he jumps up, suddenly remembering that this is the time the post office closes, and he must rush to mail Dr. Ne'eman's registered letters. Naturally, as he jumps up, he knocks over the tray containing his meal which the waiter is at last bringing to him. The proprietor begs him to wait until a fresh meal can be prepared, and so he waits, full of remorse at having failed in

his errand, until at last the restaurant is closed and he is locked in without his having eaten anything. Sitting looking at the soiled tablecloth and the remains of all the meals that have been eaten, he observes a cat and a mouse emerge, both intent on gnawing the leavings. Dr. Gressler passes by the window but fails to respond to his call. At last he falls asleep. In the morning when the staff arrives to clean up, he leaves the restaurant, weary, hungry and alone. The letters are preying on his mind, but it is Sunday, and in the Jerusalem of Mandate times the post office is closed on Sunday.

The symbolism is patent. As Israeli critics have pointed out, Dr. Ne'eman (Faithful) is a *persona* of Moses the Lawgiver, the man who had written a book which some might think his own but which others believe was copied from a greater authority than himself. The world has become a little better since it was written. He lays a charge on the narrator which the narrator must carry out. But the narrator has another friend, the egregious Mr. Gressler. He is the antitype of Ne'eman: coarse, living it up, and caring little who gets hurt in the process. The narrator, though drawn to his company, has in fact little to thank him for. For it is Gressler who, in the past, had brought it about that "his house was burnt down." Here the Jewish historical theme (the burning of the Temple) merges with an event in Agnon's own life, namely, the burning of his home in Germany in 1924, an event to which he often reverts. It is Gressler who diverts him from the task with which Dr. Ne'eman has charged him, and after being diverted, he forgets about the "letters" altogether and concentrates only on satisfying his hunger. This he fails to achieve, partly because in a dream such desires are usually frustrated, and partly because he sets himself a high aim—he wants "a whole loaf," something both satisfying and dignified, something like the Sabbath meal he has missed, a meal which will remind him of the delicious whole rolls which his mother used to bake for the feast of *Purim.* But he is left both hungry and alone. Gressler takes no notice of him at the end of the tale, and amid the garbage and the vermin of the locked restaurant he reaches his nadir. He has satisfied the demands neither of the "id" nor of the "superego." The charge laid on him by Ne'eman remains unfulfilled. But the letters are still in his pocket . . . and some day, maybe, he will get around to mailing them.

Here again we have the Jewish history-consciousness imposing itself on the pattern of the dream-symbols. The clock is moving on, tasks have to be performed, decisions have to be taken. It is not merely that the narrator makes the wrong decisions, but that at the crisis of the story he is unable to decide at all—should he eat or should he go to the post office? This is a natural enough dream-situation. But what gives it its special covenant dimension is the sense of responsibility (the word for "registered" in Agnon's Hebrew also means "responsibility") symbolized by the letters which, though covered with filth, spilt wine, and gravy by the overturned tray, still have to be delivered, together with the sense of a past world not "wholly" recoverable, symbolized by the special meal with its "whole loaf" to adorn and dignify it.

This is clearly an allegorical tale like so many of Kafka's tales, and like *Pilgrim's Progress*; but its force is not entirely owing to allegorical contrivance. We recognize the main features intuitively. We have known Mr. Gressler from infancy, and as for Ne'eman, he has existed from ancient times and he is still around. He reminds us of ancestral responsibilities still waiting to be discharged. Such a tale is thus an image of contemporary existence in the historical present. And here is where Agnon differs from Kafka. **"A Whole Loaf"** is, among other things, a naturalistic account of a Saturday night in Jerusalem in the twenties. We see the Arabs in their fezzes, the orthodox Jews in their fur hats (*streimels*); there is traffic, there are cafes and hotels; you see the different types coming out to take the air after a burning day of hot desert wind (*hamsin*). You meet the scholar at his lighted window, the successful man of property in his coach; you visit a little synagogue with its candles and benches, and a fine restaurant with its magnificent appointments and its babel of tongues.

If Yekutiel Ne'eman is the Moses of the Bible, he is no less the embodiment of that Moses who still exists as an active part of Agnon's religious consciousness and of the community of Jerusalem which he here describes. Just, as the Arab boy who disturbs the narrator's sleep in **"The House"** is both a symbol of the red-haired Edom-Esau whom Jacob-Israel had alternately fed and fought in the book of *Genesis,* and a living part of the human landscape of Palestine with which the new Jewish settlers have somehow to reckon. What binds together the world of symbol and the world of everyday is a biblical dimension of ongoing time which communicates with us simultaneously through dream and through our waking consciousness: it is both without and within, both near and far-off, both past and present.

Esther Fuchs   (essay date 1983)

SOURCE: "'Edo and Enam'—The Ironic Perspective," in *Modern Language Studies,* Vol. 13, No. 1, Winter, 1983, pp. 85-100.

[*In the following essay, Fuchs maintains that an understanding of* Edo and Enam *as an ironic story enables the reader to make sense of the story's "strangeness," namely its "digressions, internal contradictions, sudden transitions from realism to phantasy [sic], neologisms and anachronisms."*]

1. INTRODUCTION

It would seem that a story as widely explained and thoroughly interpreted as *Edo and Enam* requires no further explanations. The numerous allegorical interpretations of this enigmatic story left hardly any detail in its originally confusing state. What the momentous critical quest for clarity failed to acknowledge, however, is the literary significance of the presumably meaningless elements in the story. Based on the proposition that in literature meaningless elements are just as significant as meaningful ones, we shall focus precisely on the enigmatic and most disturbing thematic and structural properties of *Edo and Enam,* unexplaining, wherever possible, the allegorical explanations which layed the potential problems to rest.

The allegorical quest for meaning in *Edo and Enam* started with Baruch Kurzweil's partially allegorical interpretation of the story [*Masot al sipurav shel shai agnon,* 1975]. Substituting the Greifenbachs' house for the house of Judaism and their key for the futile attempts of modern Jewry to open it, Kurzweil maintains that *Edo and Enam* is a parable on the dilemma of Modern Judaism. Kurzweil does not explain his selective focus on the house and the key, to the exclusion of other objects represented in the story. This is the gap which Meshulam Tochner's comprehensive allegorical interpretation [*Pesher Agnon,* 1968] sought to fill. Carrying on the Judaic orientation of Kurzweil's interpretation, Tochner accords a historical or metaphysical status to almost all the objects, places and characters mentioned in *Edo and Enam*. Equating Amadia with Mount Sinai, Gamzu's magic leaves with the Torah, Gamzu himself—with the people of Israel; Gevaryahu, his father-in-law, with Rabbi Akiba, and the twenty two exotic dancers with the letters of the Hebrew alphabet, Tochner asserts that the "apparent" aspect of the story is secondary, almost peripheral to the "invisible" subtext. The text of the "visible story" is demoted to the status of mere literary "make-up", intended to camouflage the real meaning of the story. Tochner ignores the fact that what he considers to be the "primary text" constitutes his own interpretation of the story, and that by establishing a hierarchy of primary and secondary texts, he gives in fact, priority to his own interpretation over the original text. Most importantly, however, both Kurzweil and Tochner fail to defend their Judaic interpretation of *Edo and Enam* on the basis of the thematic field of the original text. With the exception of Gamzu's keen interest in ancient Jewish hymns, none of the other characters seems to be particularly concerned about Judaism. Jewish related motifs appear as tangential rather than primary elements in *Edo and Enam*; consequently, there is no inherent justification for this particular interpretative orientation. But this did not deter other critics from speculating on Agnon's Zionist ideology based on Tochner's moot allegorizations. Edi Zemach, for example, maintains [in an essay in Hebrew in *Hasifrut,* Summer, 1968] that *Edo and Enam* reflects Agnon's rejection of secular Zionism. Shlomo Zucker, on the other hand, affirms that Agnon decries the aestheticist and scientific approaches to Jewish traditional sources, rather than secular Judaism as a whole. This debate dramatizes the inherently arbitrary nature of the story's allegorical interpretation. Its substitutive nature paves the way for exegeses, which are mutually exclusive. By its very nature, the allegorical method precludes a multiplicity of approaches to the multifaceted literary work. The categorical nature of the allegorical method eclipses the multidimensionality of *Edo and Enam,* a drawback which was applauded by Hillel Barzel [in *Sipurei 'ahavah shel shai agnon,* 1975]. According to Barzel, the "excellent exegetical work" undertaken by Agnon's critics redeems the story from its oppressive "strangeness", and makes it more accessible to the average reader.

The underlying premise of the allegorical approach is that a "normal" story ought to be clear and accessible while a "strange" story must be clarified to be fully appreciated. The strangeness of **Edo and Enam** consists among other things in its digressions, internal contradictions, sudden transitions from realism to phantasy, neologisms and anachronisms. These phenomena would be considered strange by those who seek in literature a representation of empirical reality in congruity with human logic. But for the ironic work, aiming at pointing up the tensions between reality and perception, language and logic, fiction and experience—these strange literary phenomena are essential. As we shall see later, the romantic irony of **Edo and Enam** transcends the limited ironies of point of view, plot and characterization. The generic incongruities, the narrative digressions and the informational discrepancies in the story serve not only the ironic treatment of the unreliable narrator, the schlemiel protagonist and the arbitrary plot progression, but also the reflexive irony of the story itself. The narrative instabilities contribute to the reader's insecurity, forcing him to re-examine the validity of his intellectual predispositions and preconceived notions about the text. In the following pages we shall examine the limited ironies of **Edo and Enam,** and the way in which they lead to the story's radical self-irony, or romantic irony.

2. THE IRONIC POINT OF VIEW

In order to detect the ironic point of view in **Edo and Enam,** we must first distinguish between, on the one hand, the narrator and the implied author, and on the other, the protagonist and the narrator. It is important to note that **Edo and Enam** consists essentially of two stories; that of the nameless narrator and that of Gamzu, his half-blind friend. The construction of a story within a story points up the parallels between the diegetic and meta-diegetic stories. the improbable coincidences informing Gamzu's tale, reflect on the coincidences reported by the narrator, and the synthesis of phantasy and realism in the latter highlights a similar synthesis in the former. The concentric narrative structure intimates that underlying the stories about the hymns of Enam and the enigmatic language of Edo is a story about the act of story-telling and the nature of human language in general. But before we deal with the far reaching implications of the ironic point of view, we must regress to the issue of the limited scope of the unreliable narrator who transmits the story to the reader.

The limited perception of the unnamed narrator is adumbrated in the first chapter, dramatizing the encounter between him and the Greifenbachs. Despite the obvious nervousness of his friends, the egocentric narrator refrains from inquiring about their discomfiture, apparently, because he has trouble formulating the right question. Even after they admit that in view of their incumbent voyage to Europe, they are worried about poachers who may take over their house in their absence, the narrator continues to ignore their problem, concentrating instead on what interests him; his idol, Dr. Ginath who happens to be the Griefenbachs' tenant.

> My heart beat fast as I heard this; not because of the Greifenbachs, but because they had spoken of Ginath as a real person. Since the time when the name of Ginath became world-known, I had not come across anyone who could say he actually knew him.

The Greifenbachs' subtle though desperate attempts to call the narrator's attention to their predicament crash against the narrator's obtuseness and egotism. These become all the more preposterous when the text intimates that the narrator admires Dr. Ginath for his fame and for the sheer controversiality of his findings. His unreserved praise for Dr. Ginath betrays his dilettantism and naive credulity, further undermining the validity of his point of view.

> Even with his first published article, "Ninety-nine Words of the Edo Language," Ginath had drawn the attention of many philologists; when he followed this up with his "Grammar of Edo," no philologist could afford to ignore him. But what made him truly famous was his discovery of the Enamite Hymns. To discover ninety-nine words of a language whose very name was hitherto unknown is no small achievement, and a greater one still is the compilation of a grammar of this forgotten tongue.

The narrator seems to be more interested in the history of Ginath's academic career, and the growth of his reputation (had drawn the attention of many philologists . . . made him truly famous), than in the genuine value of his findings. His description of Ginath's research is laudatory but too general and glib to win the reader's trust (no small achievement . . . a greater one). The suspicion of the reader, which is aroused by the fictional names of "Edo," the new-found language, and "Enam," the esoteric hymns, is not abated by the narrator's effusions. It is further corroborated by the fact that Gervaryahu and his daughter, Gemulah are said to have invented a private language for their own purposes.

The narrator's reliability is further undermined by his fallacious reasoning. For example, he rejects outright the possibility that "a European person like Ginath" should be able to dress like a traditional "hacham" a possibility, which is later vindicated by the narrative evidence. His gullibility and relentless veneration for Ginath, is contrasted with the critical and somewhat cynical attitude of Greifenbach towards the "science" of history and scholarship in general:

> I'm not in the habit of expressing my views about matters on which I'm no expert, but I think I can say this: in every generation, some discovery is made that's regarded as the greatest thing that ever was. Eventually, it's forgotten, for meanwhile some new discovery comes to light. No doubt that goes, too, for the discoveries of Dr. Ginath.

The narrator demonstrates a similar gullibility in his dealings with Gamzu. He praises Gamzu as a "scholar" who "had seen the world, had voyaged to distant lands, and reached places where no traveler had been before", and continues to accept his friend's highly suspect visits to the Greifenbachs' house at face value. Lured by Gamzu's exotic stories, the narrator forgets to pursue the obvious question; what is Gamzu doing in the middle of the night by the Greifenbachs' door? Although he expresses astonishment and even a modicum of suspicion when Gamzu "happens" to come by the Greifenbachs' house on the following night, he fails to press Gamzu for a more reasonable excuse for his repeatedly coincidental nocturnal visits. The narrator fails to challenge Gamzu when the latter explains that he came out to the Greifenbachs' house, having found a full-proof cure for his moonstruck wife. The narrator proceeds to accept Gamzu's far fetched explanation, despite its blatant incongruity with Gamzu's previous account about Gemulah, according to which, Gemulah suffers from an incurable malady and must not be left alone.

The distance between narrator and reader is created mostly by the incongruity between what the first considers important and what the latter wants to know. Towards the climax of the story, the narrator describes his encounter with Ginath and Gemulah in a most confusing way, mixing phantasy and realism and not bothering to clarify or explain the mysterious event:

> I looked around me, and saw Gamzu standing behind the door; I wondered what on earth he was doing there. The palm of a hand reached out and touched the door. Before I could decide whether what I saw was really seen or not, the door opened halfway and the light in the room shone out brightly. It drew me and I looked inside.

The narrator does not pursue the questions he raises during this mysterious scene, and the scene that follows in Ginath's room. The narrator does not account for Gamzu's eavesdropping behind Ginath's door or for the half-phantastic half-realistic description he offers to the reader. Not only does he refrain from elucidating ambiguities, he compounds them whenever he can. Mostly, he pursues trivial questions, leaving the most important ones unanswered. Thus, he describes his final encounter with Gamzu after the death of Gamulah and Gamzu, but he does not bother to supply additional details about the circumstances of the couple's tragic death. Instead he offers the reader bits of rumor and gossip, which only muddle the already incoherent picture. The reader is more frustrated than satisfied by this inept narrator.

But the unreliable narrator is only one aspect of the ironic point of view. The implied author who flaunts the narrator's unreliability whenever possible, seems to enjoy the reader's confusion as well. This situation, transcends the limited irony of point of view, in which the author and the reader collude as accomplices behind the narrator's back. The irony generated by the incongruity between the reader's and the author's stances has far-reaching repercussions. Unlike the limited irony of point of view, directed at the unreliable narrator, this irony unleashes questions relating to the nature of human perception, the

fickleness of fictional literature and the disturbing similarity between dream and reality. By leaving the identity of Gemulah (moonstruck woman or imaginary character) the nature of the magic leaves (simple tobacco leaves or leaves endowed with mystical powers) and the problem of Ginath and Gemulah's death (accident or suicide) unanswered, the implied author manages to destabilize not only the narrator's but the reader's point of view as well. One implication of these ironic instabilities is that the human perspective is by nature inadequate and insufficient, and that the complexities and absurdities encountered in our daily lives transcend the limits of human comprehension. Thus, the limited irony directed at the unreliable narrator of *Edo and Enam* grows in ever wider circles to encompass the reader and the implied author himself, who invalidates his own point of view by playing up the unresolvable discrepancies of his own story.

The ambiguities in *Edo and Enam* do not have to be resolved or elucidated: they form an integral part of the meaning of the story; they function as generators of irony which is directed at the unreliable narrator, the implied author and at the reader at the same time.

3. THE IRONIC PLOT

As noted above, there are two basic plots in *Edo and Enam*: the metadiegetic one, unfolds in Gamzu's descriptions of his travels; the other plot revolves around the narrator's experiences at the house of the Greifenbachs.

Despite the considerable differences between the stories they share similar ironic plot-structures, foremost among which are: the irony of coincidence and the irony of events. The irony of coincidence characterizes most of Gamzu's life. For example, an innocent visit at an old bookstore ultimately determines his future career. As a poor *yeshivah* student, Gamzu is coincidentally introduced to the hymns of Yehudah Halevi, Consequently, he trades all his possessions for the book. Inspired by Halevi's poetry, he seeks out other hymns. His relentless search for ancient hymns transforms him from a yeshivah student into a book-peddlar. His new job becomes a vocation; his search for books and manuscripts brings him to distant lands and turns him into one of the most celebrated bibliophiles in the world. His travels lead him to an exotic town, where he meets his future wife Gemulah, the daughter of a tribe leader. Another coincidence puts him in possession of a most rare manuscript, and by sheer coincidence he loses the magic leaves, which his father-in-law entrusted to him—the only means by which he can control the peregrinations of the moonstruck Gemulah.

The irony of coincidence controls the central plot of the story as well. The narrator arrives at the house of the Greifenbachs, with no previous planning, "following his legs" in his words. Although, he does not intend to spend the night at the Greifenbachs' house, he fulfills thereby his promise to keep an eye on their house during their absence. Gamzu's coincidental arrival at the house, is even more astounding, since he does not know the Greifenbachs, and had no way of knowing that he would meet his friend there. Gamzu describes his visit at the Greifenbachs' as a pure coincidence:

> 'Forgive me', he said, 'for suddenly bursting in on you. Just imagine, I came home after the evening service at the synagogue to get my wife settled for the night and found the bed empty. I went off in search of her. 'Going to the south, turning to the north, turning turning goes the wind, and again to its circuits the wind returns'. Suddenly I found myself in this valley without knowing how I came to be here. I saw a house; I felt drawn to enter it. I knew there was no point in doing this, but I did so just the same.

If the coincidental nature of Gamzu's visit is suspicious, his second visit, which takes place in the same place, and under similar circumstances is even more so. Although the narrator tells Gamzu that he will spend the following evening at home, he returns to the Greifenbachs' because the water supply in his neighborhood has been cut off. But Gamzu does not even have this alibi. His explanation harps again on the theme of coincidence: "I did not go to your home and I did not think of coming here . . . I came . . . but not intentionally". His second visit is all the more puzzling since, his first one was motivated by his search for his wife, whereas this time, he leaves her alone, at home, on a moonlit night, well aware of her susceptibility to these particular circumstances. Yet, on this night, Gamzu happens to find Gemulah, in Ginath's room, by sheer coincidence! The narrator does not seem disturbed by this set of coincidences. His speculations, however, point up the unlikelihood of the coincidental explanation: "When had he returned, when had he gone to his room? He must have come back while Gamzu and I were sitting in Greifenbach's room, and the woman must have gotten in through the window".

The frequent use of coincidence in a literary plot construction is often ascribed to the artist's laziness, or to poor narrative craftsmanship. But the coincidental plot also creates an ironic effect. It points up the arbitrary nature of daily life. The coincidental linkage of the literary plot dramatizes the absurd nature of life which unfolds by fits and starts, rather than causality and reason. This is the underlying nature of the ironic plot.

The ironic plot also contributes to the distance between the reader and the characters. Although the implied author refrains from giving the reader a fully coherent picture of the represented events, he intimates that the characters' interpretations of the events are aimed at hiding their true nature. The fact that Gamzu ends up finding his wife at the Greifenbachs' house, implies that his repeated visits to the house were not purely coincidental, and that he may have been motivated by a deep-seated suspicion concerning the relation between Gemulah and Ginath, and the place of their secret encounters. Similarly, the text implies that the death of Gemulah and Ginath is occasioned by suicide, rather than coincidence as surmised by unsuspecting onlookers:

> . . . eyewitnesses say that last night a gentleman went out of his room and saw a woman climbing up onto the roof. He rushed up to save her from danger, the parapet collapsed, and they both fell to their death.

Having been previously apprised of Gemulah's wish to be buried beside Dr. Ginath, the reader has reason to suspect that Gemulah may have jumped rather than fallen off the roof in a desperate attempt to put an end to her miserable liaison with her oppressive and hateful husband; and that of her lover, Dr. Ginath, joined her, once again, not by coincidence. While the presentation of the plot as a set of arbitrary incidents, linked by sheer coincidence satirizes life as an absurdist play, lacking order or reason, the presentation of the plot as a set of causally linked events, misconstrued by the characters as coincidental, satirizes life as a chain of gruesome comedies staged by a diabolical director.

The second major plot pattern in the story consists of the irony of events. This irony is generated by the incongruity between a character's expectations and the represented events. It appears in both the metadiegetic and the central plot. In the first, Gamzu receives the rare manuscript of the ancient hymns, just when he gives up hope for attaining them. In another instance, just when he loses his hope to ever revisit Gemulah he is employed by two unknown parties, to be sent on a mission which unexpectedly brings him back to Gemulah's village. When he does not expect any affection from Gemulah, she is warm and friendly, after their marriage, she turns cold and bitter. Gevariahu, Gamzu's father-in-law, who "goes up to the mountaintop to learn from the eagles how they renew their youth" is attacked by an eagle and dies of his wounds. His desire to prolong his life hastens his death. The irony of events appears frequently in the central plot as well, underlying trivial, as well as tragic incidents. The narrator who goes to the Greifenbachs' house, in the hope to find peace and tranquility, is awakened in the middle of the night by an unexpected visitor. Thieves break into the narrator's house precisely when he finds himself in charge of Gamzu's savings. The irony of events reaches a climax in the description of the Greifenbachs' return from their trip. The narrator deludes himself believing that: "when the Greifenbachs return to Jerusalem, they will find everything in order". On the night prior to their return, Ginath and Gemulah find their death by falling from the top of the Greifenbachs' roof. The irony is intensified by the narrator's coincidental encounter with the happy couple, on his way back from the funeral of Gemulah and Ginath. The cheerful attitude of the Greifenbachs is contrasted by the narrator's mechanical response:

> Greifenbach saw me and called from inside the automobile, 'How nice to see you! How really nice! How is our house getting on? Is it still standing?' Mrs. Greifenbach asked, 'Has nobody broken in?' 'No', I answered, 'no one has broken in'. Again she asked, 'Did you get to know Ginath?' 'Yes', I said, 'I got to know Ginath'.

The ironic tension stems from the incongruity between the unsuspecting questions, and the sinister implications of the automatic answers. The house is physically sound, nothing happened to it, but from its roof, two people jumped, and were killed. Strangers did not break into the house, but the narrator's own friend and his wife entered the house, under the most bizarre circumstances. The narrator indeed met Ginath, but neither he nor the Greifenbachs will ever be able to see him again. At this point, the irony of events is sharpened by the dramatic irony which allows the reader an awareness of the incongruity between event and expectation while withholding it from the characters.

The cumulative effect of the irony of coincidence in conjunction with the irony of events transcends the limited scope of the ironic plot. As pointed out above, it delineates not only the laughable and tragic character of the story's specific plotline but the incommensurability of human reason and life's vicissitudes in general. It ridicules the gap between human intention and the machinations of fate. In addition, it underlines the contrived nature of the fictional narrative, which most non-ironic works are careful to hide. The emphasis on coincidence exposes the artificial and artful nature of the fictional plot. It challenges the reader's suspension of disbelief forcing him to become self-conscious. It undermines the narrative's illusion of reality and its superficial claim to authenticity. This is the contribution of the ironic plot to the romantic irony of *Edo and Enam*.

4. THE IRONIC CHARACTERIZATION

Gamzu the protagonist, is introduced by the narrator as a dedicated scholar who "had become in his prime the attendant of a sick wife, who it was said, had been bedridden since their wedding night." Although the narrator concedes that this information is largely based on rumor, he affirms that:

> . . . it was certainly a fact that he had a sick wife at home, that there was no earthly cure for her, and that her husband had to nurse her, wash her, feed her and attend to her every need. Nor was she grateful for his self sacrifice, but would beat him and bite him and tear his clothes.

As the story progresses, however, this favorable introduction of Gamzu undergoes radical changes. To a large extent, the ironic characterization of the protagonist is based on the discrepancy between the narrator's laudatory introduction and the dramatization of Gamzu's words and actions. Gamzu's stories about his wife expose him as a romantic dreamer, in love with an image of a young girl, "an angel", "a star"—rather than as a responsible husband. His contradictory presentation of Gemulah as a bedridden hysterical woman and as a moonstruck wanderer who cannot be kept at home, reveals his own muddled perception of his wife. The scene which takes place in Ginath's room, reverses the roles of victimizer and victim as first presented; here Gamzu plays the possessive and violent husband, whereas Gemulah emerges as helpless and defenseless wife:

> Gamzu suddenly rushed in and clasped the woman's waist with his arms. The woman drew back her head from him and still in his embrace cried out . . . Gamzu put his hand over her mouth and held on with all his might. She struggled to escape from his arms, but he held her tight . . . With that, her strength left her, and were it not that Gamzu still held her she would have fallen. And once Gamzu had grasped her, he did not let go of her until he took her up in his arms and went away, while Ginath and I looken on.

The interchange between Gamzu and Gemulah reveals a troubled relationship between a jealous husband and an alienated wife who is desperately in love with someone else. Gemulah's answer to Gamzu's legal claim on her person implies that their marriage is but a legality; they have not even consummated it sexually: "I am not any man's wife. Ask him, has he ever seen me naked?" This state of affairs throws a different light on Gamzu's presentation as a dedicated and selfless husband. It shows him rather as a tyrannical owner [in a footnote, the critic points out that the Hebrew term "ba'al" means both "owner" and "husband"], forcefully imposing himself on his wife and holding her prisoner. Retroactively, his romantic descriptions of his first encounters with Gemulah become suspect. What first appears as an amusing anecdote, namely, his physical seizure of Gemulah right before their marriage, assumes tragic dimensions; the reconstructed picture, from Gemulah's point of view, indicates that the girl never wished to marry the old invalid in the first place, and that if not for her father's untimely death, she would probably have married her fiance Gedi ben Ge'im.

But there are ironic indicators in the story, which subtly invalidate Gamzu's point of view, even prior to the dramatic scene which exposes him unequivocally. These indicators are planted in Gamzu's narrated monologue, undermining the message of his words by deforming the style of his speech. The most obtrusive ironic device in the following example is the cumbersome sentence structure:

> There sat Gamzu and rolled himself a cigarette and talked about the magic properties of charms, whose virtue is superior to that of drugs; for the drugs we find mentioned in ancient books cannot for the most part be relied on, since the ways both of nature and of man have changed and with these changes the effect of the drugs too has altered. But the charms have undergone no change and still retain their first nature and condition, because they are yoked together with the stars, and the stars remain just as they were on the day when they were first hung in the firmament.

The cumbersome syntax of the narrated monologue reflects the questionable logic of Gamzu's abstruse ideas about the superiority of charms to drugs. The excessively complex syntactic unit is a common device in parody.

Gamzu's speech is heavily studded with biblical and talmudic references which are more often than not inappropriate or extraneous. Describing his peregrinations in Jerusalem, in search for his missing wife, Gamzu uses

Ecclesiastes 1:6 in order to describe the futility and aimlessness of his effort: "Going to the south turning to the north, turning turning goes the wind and again to its circuits the wind returns." The original meaning of the verse involves the unchanging regularity of cycles, the rational aspect of existence. Gamzu, however, uses this verse in order to illustrate the opposite: the fact that his life is ruled by sheer coincidence. Gamzu never misses a chance to indulge in casuistic interpretations of scriptures. His exegesis, however, complicates and confuses the original text. For example, Gamzu interprets the personal pronoun, "for his sake" (lema'anehu) in reference to music and song, in order to use the biblical verse containing this word as proof for his astrological theology concerning the relationship of God to the planets. Inspired by his own sophism, Gamzu fails to realize that his far-fetched interpretation is contradictory; on the one hand, he states that God creates everything for His sake, and on the other, that He does it for His chosen people, Israel. Gamzu's undiscriminating use of grammatical, pseudo-scientific and anagogical approaches to the classical Jewish texts, may well illustrate the untenability of the traditional exegetic method (pilpul) which was ridiculed by Y. L. Gordon, Mendele Mocher Sforim and other *maskilim.* Furthermore, by parodying Gamzu's complex exegesis, the text alludes to exegesis in general, including that of the present story. Gamzu's heavy-handed interpretations, demonstrate that the more one tries to explain, the more one risks imposing his own preconceived notions on a given text.

The internal contradiction is one of the most effective ironic weapons because, as David Worcester puts it: "Irony is never so sweet as when a character seems to defend his cause with consistency, but in reality gives it completely away" [*The Art of Satire,* 1940]. The internal contradiction undermines the validity of Gamzu's ideological standpoint on several occasions. On the first evening in the Greifenbachs' house, Gamzu defends religiously all the Jewish biblical scholars; "You know my opinion, that no Jew is capable of saying anything for which the bible gives no support, and especially that which is contrary to the plain meaning of the text." On the following evening, however, Gamzu lashes out at the Jewish scholars who "Have they not made our holy Torah into either one or the other (folklore or subject matter for scientific research . . . E.F.)?" At this point, Gamzu seems to forget that were it not for the folklorists he criticises so virulently, he would lose his main source of income. Another ideological contradiction refers to his opinion of modern medicine. During his first encounter with the narrator, Gamzu states that the healing power of charms surpasses that of drugs. On the following evening, however, he affirms the opposite, that charms are nothing but outdated drugs. Despite his declared distrust of modern physicians, he checks into a modern hospital in Vienna. He insists that for medical purposes he trusts only those who "purified their body in the Torah", yet, he is prepared to send his wife to a modern asylum. As an inveterate bibliophile, Gamzu presents himself as strictly interested in ancient books. "I do not look at books which are less than four hundred years old". But he betrays himself unwittingly when soliciting eagerly the narrator's opinion on Dr. Ginath's books, thus implying that he does indeed read modern secular books.

All these internal contradictions indicate that Gamzu pretends to be what he is not. He strives to present himself as a traditional Jew, fully committed to his religious heritage, its sources, laws and spirit. He pretends that modernity is a meaningless ephemeral phase which has hardly affected his life. But the truth peers through his numerous self-contradictions. Despite his lengthy excursus on the planets' ability to control human fate, he presents his own life as a series of coincidences, rather than predetermined events. He rejects modern medicine, but is forced to use it; he attacks secular Judaica scholars, yet uses their academic pursuit as a major source of income.

The discrepancy between his pietistic outlook and his actual life is especially poignant regarding his relationship with his wife, Gemulah. Gamzu presents it as a romantic fairy-tale with biblical trappings. But the factual contradictions in his story expose it as a wishful dream. Thus, he tells the narrator that Gemulah was given to him in matrimony, by her father, Gevariahu a whole year before the *actual* marriage. (Heb. 370) On the other hand, he confesses that he had to steal or abduct Gemulah, a few days prior to their marriage, because he knew that she was promised to Gedi ben Ge'im (Heb. 378). If Gemulah was Gamzu's lawful fiancée for a whole year, why did he have to abduct her before their marriage? Gamzu tells the narrator that on the night before his marriage Gevariahu gave him magic leaves with which to control Gemulah's moonstruck wanderings. Forgetting this detail, he recounts on the following evening, that Gevariah was mortally wounded prior to the marriage ceremony and completely incapacitated throughout the festivities. These inconsistencies indicate that Gamzu either deludes himself or deceives the narrator.

Gamzu romanticizes his first encounter with Gemulah using hyperbole and conceit.

> Gemulah was then about twelve years old, and her graciousness and her voice were more beautiful than any beauty in the world . . . When she burst out singing, her voice would blossom like the voice of Grofith, the bird, whose voice is sweeter than that of any creature in the world.

The fictional name of "Grofith", reinforces the effect created by the fairy-tale formulas employed by Gamzu. Gemulah is "perfect as the moon", her eyes are "sparks of light", and her face "like the morning star". The parallelistic style of description used by Gamzu is strongly evocative of the *Song of Songs,* which reinforces the literary impact at the expense of realistic authenticity. Gamzu's descriptions suggest that he does not really know his wife, and that he was more enamored of his own projections than with the woman herself.

Gamzu's descriptions of Gemulah's father as an invincible and majestic tribal hero are also anachronistic. His references to Gemulah's village invoke an ancient and primitive civilization, without giving any specific information which may identify the place:

> My wife is from another region, from the mountains. At first, her ancestors were settled beside the good springs, where the pasture was also good. But their neighbors made war on them, and they retaliated and drove them back.

When he tells of his journey from Gemulah's village back to Jerusalem, Gamzu uses, instead of dates or numbers, biblical numerical formulas. His hyperbolic style is reflected in his name whose root in Hebrew (g z m) means "to exaggerate". Gamzu's exaggerated descriptions, his glib generalizations and numerous inconsistencies expose the untenability of his story, especially where it pertains to Gemulah. The fairy-tale formulas Gamzu employs arouse the suspicion that his story about Gemulah's exotic tribe, its outlandish customs, her heroic father, the fiance who intended to capture her—are fabrications rather than facts.

Gamzu's most obtrusive self-betrayal pertains to his contradictory account of Gemulah's sickness. On the first evening he confirms that his wife is bed-ridden. His explanation for her sudden disappearance from home is that she is moonstruck:

> Every night on which the moon shines brightly, my wife gets up and goes wherever the moon leads her.

In his archaic, and formulaic style, Gamzu insists that there is no power in the world which can prevent Gemulah from leaving the house:

> Even if I hung on the door seven locks and locked every lock with seven keys and threw every key into everyone of the seven seas of Palestine, my wife would find all of them, open and go.

On the following evening, however, Gamzu announces that despite the bright shining moon, he left his wife at home, safely tucked in bed. To the astonished narrator he explains that he found "a medicine" capable of controlling his wife's movements. The wondrous medicine consists of a wet cloth placed under the bed. Gamzu explains that he has not used this device all this time, because "heaven made him forget it" as punishment for neglecting the *yeshivah,* in which he learnt of this "medicine". The effectiveness of Gamzu's new found "medicine" is demonstrated shortly afterwards, by Gemulah's appearance at the Greifenbachs' house . . .

Despite the narrator's sporadic misgivings and doubts, he seems to trust his interlocutor. Not once in the course of the narrative, does he suggest that Gamzu must be prevaricating the truth, to conceal the shameful fact that his wife carries on an affair with Ginath. This, however, does not prevent the reader from suspecting that the protagonist weaves a long yarn in order to hide the fact that he reached the Greifenbachs' house while searching for his wife, rather than by sheer coincidence. When the narrator hears footsteps in the adjacent room, Gamzu reassures him that "there has not been a sound or the slightest suspicion of one." When it becomes clear to the narrator, from his interlocutor's strange posture ("his head bent to one side and an ear turned towards the wall") that the latter is intently listening to sounds coming from the other room, Gamzu again denies it ("I can hear nothing nothing at all"). When Gamzu clearly hears his wife's voice from Ginath's room, his face changes "until at last all color left it, and there remained only a pale cast that gradually darkened, leaving his features like formless clay." Yet, when asked by the narrator about the cause of his sudden unease, Gamzu reassures the narrator that he had merely been fooled by his senses. Finally, when Gamzu's diversive strategies succeed, and the narrator dozes off, he sneaks imperceptibly towards Ginath's room. Having woken up, the narrator searches for his friend, and when he is about to give up hope he sees Gamzu standing behind Ginath's door. When Gamzu jumps into the room and seizes Gemulah by force, it becomes clear that his self-righteousness has been nothing but a sham strategy. But the text refrains from direct judgment. Gamzu's ironic characterization is consistently mediated by his own self-betrayal.

5. THE ROMANTIC IRONY

The ironic characterization of Gamzu accounts for many enigmas in *Edo and Enam*, but not for all of them. The question concerning the true nature of the language of Edo, and the hymns of Enam remains unanswered. Is the language that the narrator overhears an authentic one, or is it fabricated? What is the meaning of Gemulah's song, "yiddal, yiddal, yiddal, va pah, mah"? What is the source of the neologism "Grofith"? What is the function of the repeated letters gimel (g) and ayin (a) which appear in the beginning of the characters' names?

Most critics tend to explain each of the jarring elements separately. But despite the ingenious explanations, it seems that *the effectiveness of these linguistic oddities depends on their inexplicability and that their clarification destroys the impact they create.* The cumulative effect of the neologisms and the alliterated names create a sense of strangeness within a familiar context. The strange words disrupt the automatic flow of language and force the reader to switch his attention from meaning to sound. The nonsensical words stress the arbitrary nature of language, which consists of signifiers whose relationship to their signified correlatives is determined by convention rather than logic. The problematization of language is crucial in the context of *Edo and Enam*, which deals with a mysterious language, both authentic and jocular, factual and fantastic. The authenticity of the language of Edo should remain questionable because the story as a whole pertains not only to this particular language, but to the inherently ambivalent nature of language in general.

Similarly, the names *G*erhard, *G*reda, *G*reifenbach, *G*avriel, *G*amzu, *G*inath, *G*ideon, *G*emulah, *G*edi-ben-*G*eim and

Gevariahu are intended to break the narrative flow and point up their own arbitrary and artificial nature. The emphasis on the phonetic element of the character's name highlights their fictionality, the fact that they are linguistic products, word constructions. This effect functions as a sudden smear of silver on a window; the spectator can no longer see *through* it, he is forced to contemplate his own reflection, in what has become a mirror.

This effect dramatizes one of the central themes of the story, embedded in the very structure of the work which is based on a story within a story. For beyond the validity of Gamzu's story lies the larger theme of the artistic illusion of reality. The gullible narrator of *Edo and Enam* resembles to a large extent, the unselfconscious reader, who considers the story as a reflection of reality, and who fails to notice its reflexive irony. Gamzu, the imaginative fabulator, who mixes at will, legends and facts, resembles the author himself, who deliberately combines realism and phantasy, confusing the reader and laughing heartily at his own mischievousness.

The theme of fiction as a composite of realism and phantasy appears in the conversation of the narrator with the Greifenbachs in chapter I, which constitutes the prelude to the story. When Gerda jokingly refers to Ginath as having created a girl for himself, Gerhard explains that "She's thinking of the legend about the lonely poet". The narrator reminds his friends that the legend pertains to Rabbi Solomon Ibn Gabriol who was said to have created a woman out of wood. The king, believing the woman to be real, falls in love with her, but when he finds himself rejected by her, the artist reveals to him her inanimate nature. This Jewish version of the Pygmalion story may be construed as a quintessential version of our self-reflexive story, because it includes the major ambiguities characteristic of *Edo and Enam*. Like the woman in the legend, Gemulah is presented as realistic and imaginary at the same time. The Greifenbachs, who do not suspect her real presence in Ginath's room, assume her to be his own creation. Gamzu presents her as an angel, and a moon-struck woman, who is also physically sick. The narrator himself, does not clarify much by describing her as wrapped in white in a moonlit room, and emitting sounds in a strange language. The author implies that all three points of view are defective but avoids further clarifications and the reader is left with his own conjectures. Yet, the ambiguous identity of Gemulah as part real part fictional dramatizes the essence of the literary work of art.

Like the poet in the legend who exposes the real nature of his creation for the sake of the enamored king, our author exposes his work's artificiality to the involved reader. Both artists dispel the illusion they create. The creation of Solomon Ibn Gabriol is made of wood; that of our author—of words.

Beyond the poems of Enam, this story deals with the problem of fictional art in general. To ascertain the historical authenticity of the Enamite hymns is tantamount to establishing the genealogy of the wooden woman. The radical irony of the story's point of view, plot and char-acterization dramatizes the predominant theme of *Edo and Enam*. The structural and linguistic oddities in the story require contemplation not explanation. They are not flaws to be corrected by scholars, but effective devices serving the story's romantic irony. Their effectiveness depends on their ability to resist the critical attempt to domesticate them. In the case of *Edo and Enam,* the reader's ability to absorb the impact of the mystifying text rather than clarify it will allow him to gain a better understanding of the story.

David Aberbach   (essay date 1984)

SOURCE: "Passivity in Agnon," in *At the Handles of the Lock: Themes in the Fiction of S. J. Agnon,* The Littman Library, 1984, pp. 31-59.

[*In the following excerpt, Aberbach studies the meaning underlying the passivity of characters in Agnon's short fiction.*]

No characteristic of the Agnon hero is more pervasive, more problematical and deeply rooted than his passivity. In his contact with women and men, whether they are relatives, friends, acquaintances, or officials, his passivity shows itself in his indecisiveness, his failure to act or to complete his actions, his willingness to wait aimlessly, his malleability, "femininity", and masochism, his blind submission to authority of all kinds, and in his tendency to believe in predestination. In its extreme forms the passivity of the Agnon hero manifests itself in physical paralysis, and in his difficulties in taking a woman sexually.

The problem of passivity is one of the acute critical problems in Agnon. It no doubt helps to explain why Agnon is so often disliked by young Israelis: they have little patience for him. The nature of the problem can be appreciated even by those who are otherwise fascinated by Agnon's genius. Of Agnon heroes, Baruch Hochman writes [in *The Fiction of S. Y. Agnon*], "Their inherent passivity—their incapacity to engage in passionate struggle—oppresses the reader and, in the end, makes for a lack of conviction as to the integrity of the total vision." Perhaps it is unfair to suggest an overall "lack of conviction", but few critics would deny that Agnon heroes are inherently passive, and, at times, oppressively so.

Agnon's very style is peculiarly passive. [In *Massot al Sippure S. Y. Agnon*] Baruch Kurzweil has written of its "quiet genius", contrasting it with the tension in the action. It has none of the blood and thunder of Biblical Hebrew. Agnon's Hebrew has affinities with Yiddish, the language of the Diaspora, inturned, often oblique, and seemingly unaggressive. In a manner hitherto unrealized in Hebrew, it is subtle, sharpwitted, ironical, and psychologically complex. It expresses an intense Yiddish sensibility, a product of the east European village, or *shtetl*. Eighteenth-century *shtetl* culture, "when Torah ruled Israel" [Agnon], was apparently the world into which Agnon would have been born had he been given the choice.

To a limited extent, the passivity of the Agnon hero is typical of the Jewish Diaspora. This quality is found also in the poetry of Chaim Nachman Bialik, like Agnon an artist of the Diaspora, and is attributed by Mary Catherine Bateson [in *Mosaic,* Spring, 1962] to historical circumstances which "had cut the Jews off from any possibility of cultural and individual assertion vis-à-vis the Gentile world in which they lived. They had reacted to this by shaping their personal and community behaviour in terms of a feminine idea, symbolized by the Shekhinah; they dwelt in the passive world of memory and tradition." Critics sometimes explain the passive yearning of the Agnon hero for a hopelessly distant beloved as an allegory of the yearning of Israel for the Shekhinah. [In *S. Y. Agnon*] Harold Fisch writes of *A Simple Tale,* "Hirshl's love for Blumah is clearly the age-old, sad and hopeless love of Israel for that divine presence which once dwelt in the Temple whose destruction is mourned on the Ninth of Av." Rechnitz's idealization of Shoshana in **Betrothed** and Gamzu's longing for Gemulah in **Iddo and Enam** have been explained in the same way.

Agnonesque passivity is also a sign of the individual's helplessness in an alienating society. As in Kafka's works, this helplessness shows itself in universal situations involving contact with bureaucracies. In some of Agnon's stories, as in *The Trial* and *The Castle,* "The chains of tormented mankind are made out of red tape" [Gustav Janouch, *Conversations with Kafka*]. In **"HaTe'udah"** [**"The Certificate"**], the narrator finds himself in a crowded office trying to get a form: "I too was pushed, first to one official, then to another. I bowed my head in submission hoping that they would turn to me and ask what I wanted. They paid me no attention, and needless to say they asked me nothing." Submissiveness to impervious authorities is found also in the story **"HaBayit"** [**"The House"**], "I am a quiet man and have nothing to do with law courts. Even things for which others raise a hue and cry for in court I yield. Experience has taught me that things are stronger than I." Perhaps the most Kafkaesque of all Agnon's works is **"Hefker"**: the narrator is arrested for no reason and detained overnight. Curiously, he feels an almost childish pleasure at being controlled in this way, "And so I stood and I did not move. This status was good, like every status which excuses us from deeds."

The sheer persistence of the hero's passivity suggests, however, that deeper causes are also involved. From Hemdat in **"The Well of Miriam"** (1909) to Herbst in the posthumously published *Shirah*—both of whom resemble Agnon himself—the hero is invariably a passive type. Hemdat's decision to go to Palestine, for instance, is not his own "Hemdat did not decide his actions. He was blown by every passing gust of wind . . . He said to himself, you'll have grass growing on your chin before you go to Zion." Only under the threat of his being drafted into the Austro-Hungarian army, his family, not he, decides that he must leave the country. Agnon, too, left Galicia to go to Palestine in 1907 in order to avoid the draft, not primarily out of Zionist idealism (although this played an important role—he could have gone to America). Hemdat's character is a younger version of Herb-

st's. [In "Motif HaTzara'at be-*Shira* ve'Ad Olam'," in *S. Y. Agnon: Mehkarim uTe'udot,* edited by Gershon Shaked and Raphael Weiser] Gershon Schocken writes, "By nature Herbst is a passive man, with no small measure of infantilism."

Kurzweil was the first to note that Agnonesque passivity is often a form of regression to childhood:

> Ya'akov Rechnitz in **Betrothed,** Hirshl Horowitz in *A Simple Tale,* Yitzhak Kummer in *Yesteryear,* are all passive types who evade reality, and are enveloped within themselves. In all that they do the same fixed pattern is manifest—to renew the constellation of their early childhood, to alter reality, as it were, in the direction of the world of their childhood.

Kurzweil's claim that this immaturity is evident in "all that they do" may be exaggerated, but he is right to suggest that these characters have not grown up. However, he does not try to explain why, neither does he emphasize that this immaturity in various guises and degrees is found throughout Agnon's works.

Kafka's writings furnish a clue to this failure to achieve maturity. In his "Letter to his Father", Kafka states time and again that his father's overbearing nature has stifled his self-assertiveness. In consequence, he is frozen in the filial state, unable to launch out into life, remaining dependent upon his family. The nightmarish quandaries of Kafka's creations, such as Joseph K., when attempting to deal with authority, reflect the problem with the father. Kafka goes so far as to say: "My writing was all about you." Parental control which is inconsistent, unpredictable, always in the superior position, occasionally terrifying in its harshness, has this result in later life, Kafka writes in *Resolutions*:

> . . . perhaps the best resource is to meet everything passively, to make yourself an inert mass, and, if you feel that you are being carried away, not to let yourself be lured into taking a single unnecessary step, to stare at others with the eyes of an animal, to feel no compunction, in short, with your own hand to throttle down whatever ghostly life remains in you, that is, to enlarge the final peace of the graveyard and let nothing survive save that.

Kafka's analysis of his condition is borne out and elaborated by Charles Rycroft, the British psychiatrist, who writes of passivity, as Kafka does, as a form of defence and adaptive behaviour in response to overbearing parental control. This state of affairs was particularly common in the Victorian society into which both Agnon and Kafka were born:

> . . . the long biological childhood of human beings which is still further prolonged by the social conventions which allow parents to retain a measure of financial and legal control over their children for some years after they are physically mature, creates a situation in which conflicts of will inside the family—including the Oedipal rivalry

between father and son and mother and daughter—may be resolved by the child habitually adopting a submissive attitude which persists into adult life, and which forms the basis of the hysterical defence. The tendency of children to adopt the submissive role must have been enhanced in the Victorian era, when many parents invoked God as the source of their authority and considered it their religious duty to break their children's will.

The submissive response to situations of rivalry and competition is responsible for neurotic passivity in men. In situations in which it would be appropriate to be assertive and forceful, neurotically passive men habitually present themselves as feeble, ingratiating, and ineffective. In such men the anxiety induced by competitive situations and by taking responsibility arises not only from the present trial of strength but also from two other sources; the struggle for power with whichever parent dominated them, and fear lest the aggression, which was repressed when they adopted the submissive attitude, should return from repression. In the last resort such men are more frightened of their own aggression than they are of that of others.

[*Anxiety and Neurosis*]

As Agnon himself, on the testimony of those who knew him, was a somewhat withdrawn and passive man (though outwardly he could give the impression of being extremely gregarious), observation and analysis of the theme of passivity in his works are relevant to understanding the man, though this is not our primary aim. Like the narrator of *BeHanuto shel Mar Lublin* [*In Mr. Lublin's Shop*] who says, "I am not a man of deeds, and if I don't do anything I don't say I have done," Agnon said of himself, "I am not a man of deeds, and if I were given the opportunity by Heaven, almost certainly I would choose the spirit, not the deed." Many of Agnon's stories are first person narratives, and there is much clearly autobiographical material. A great deal is disguisedly so. Agnon's parents and grandfather, he admitted, are depicted frequently. The theme of submission to authority, whether exercised by men or women, counterbalanced, however, by the subtle denigration of authority, might stem, as it certainly does in Kafka's case, from harmful and overbearing family influences.

The structure of Agnon's early family is, therefore, a possible key to understanding the passivity motif, and the pattern of relationships which he depicts between men and women. Professor Dov Sadan, of the Hebrew University, Jerusalem, has said [in a personal communication to the critic, Aberbach] that Agnon's passivity helps to explain why men in his works play a passive role. Agnon apparently inherited this trait from his father, Shalom Mordekhai Czaczkes, who was, likewise, a passive man, and before his marriage, an impoverished scholar and poet. Esther, Agnon's mother, was the daughter of Yehudah Farb, a tough and wealthy fur merchant who wanted her to marry a scholar. Shalom Mordekhai had a reputation as an expert on Maimonides, the medieval Jewish philosopher. Although he was poor, his scholarship made him eligible for the hand of Esther Farb. (The account of the marriage of the passive, impecunious Barukh Meir to Tzirel

Klinger, the daughter of a wealthy merchant in *A Simple Tale,* has some parallels to this marriage). Esther had inherited her father's strength of personality. From her children's viewpoint—Agnon was the eldest of five—she must at times have seemed the dominant figure in this marriage. The money all came from her side of the family, and the entire family lived for several years in the house of Yehudah Farb. The father was often away on business (he had entered the fur trade of his father-in-law). For these reasons among others, the mother had a disproportionate influence over her son.

The earliest poems which Agnon could recall writing expressed longing for an absent father, and a feeling of being 'carried away' by an assertive female:

> When I was a child of six or seven, my father, of blessed memory, went to the fair in Lashkowitz. My longing for him made me despondent all the time. One evening I came home from *heder* [school for religious education of Jewish children] and my longing overwhelmed me. I leaned my head against the wall and wept. A cry tore from my heart, "Father, father, where are you?" Instantly a second cry joined it, "I have loved you deeply" [in the Hebrew these lines rhyme]. I was astonished at the poem which had come from me by accident. This was my first poem in Hebrew. After a while I began to write many poems and stories. To me they seemed lightweight in comparison with those two lines which I had rhymed out of longing for my father.

[*From Myself to Myself*]

In this account of the birth of his creative gift, Agnon may hint at a wish not only for his father to come home, but also to be a real and strong father, not a passive, ineffectual one.

The absence of the father may have heightened the bond between the mother and her firstborn and favourite son. Also, from her early adult life the mother apparently had a heart ailment of some sort, and Agnon had a special responsibility for taking care of her. Particularly in view of her illness and the fact that there were four children after Samuel, he may have suffered certain privations or distortions in his affectional bond with her. Yet, despite her illness—and perhaps partly because of it—the mother, by virtue of her strong personality and her love for her son, seems to have been a dominating influence in Agnon's childhood. Another early work of his foreshadows the many stories in which a woman takes the initiative with a submissive man:

> When I was about nine, I wrote a ballad about a boy who went to light candles on the eve of *selihot* [prayers said by orthodox Jews before and during the High Holy Days] as was the custom among boys in my youth. A mermaid carried him off. This was the second poem I wrote, after the poem of longing when father was away.

[*From Myself to Myself*]

Agnon's idealized portraits of his father in stories such as **"HaMitpahat"** [**"The Kerchief"**] are misleading, according to Professor Sadan. The mocking ambivalence towards his heroes more accurately conveys Agnon's feelings both for his father and for himself. Pious *Luftmenschen* such as Manasseh Haim may be dearly loved by the storyteller, but they are targets of his satire. It may be significant that 1858, the year when Manasseh Haim, the hapless *schlemiel* in *And the Crooked Shall Be Made Straight,* sets out on his travels, is approximately the year in which Agnon's father was born. A certain disillusionment with the father can be detected in curious details such as that in **"The Kerchief"** when the father comes home from his travels, the big, strong-seeming man, with gifts for his family. These gifts are worthy of praise, but the narrator adds a note of qualification, "Who praises things which get broken or lost?" An equally tiny detail which might indicate resentment towards the father—for his character, perhaps, or for being away too frequently—appears in *A Guest for the Night.* The narrator visits the house in which he lived as a child, "According to my reckoning, I am the same age as my father, of blessed memory, when he lived here with us." Recognizing Agnon's preference for subtle hints in describing situations of conflict, the phrase "when he lived here with us" rather than "when we lived here" seems extremely suggestive. Agnon's use of the seemingly innocuous phrase might betray his criticism of and condescension towards his father. The house was not his, and he had been chosen as a husband not by his wife, who might have preferred to marry for love, but by her father, in whose employment he was often away from home. At any rate, Professor Sadan has said, Agnon "hated passivity" and wanted badly to create strong and active characters. He failed to do so. His work was too strongly anchored to his behavioural pattern (this, too, could be an aspect of the name "Agnon"). As he could not help but give expression to his passivity in his fiction, all his major characters are, to some extent, projections of Agnon himself.

Agnon's marriage followed a pattern similar to his parents' marriage. His wife, like his mother (both were named Esther), was a strong-willed woman from a wealthy and scholarly home. She carried the brunt of responsibility for raising the children and taking care of the home. Professor Sadan has confirmed that the portrait of Henrietta in *Shirah* is based upon Esther Agnon, and that Agnon, like Herbst, tended to neglect his family in favour of his work. Agnon seems not to have been a good father to his son Hemdat (perhaps in the same way as his father did not provide him with a model of strength and masculinity), and after much friction between son and father, Hemdat left home.

Agnon shared with Kafka not only the trait of passivity, but also a failure, in certain respects, to grow up, perhaps partly for the reasons given by Charles Rycroft above. His own immaturity . . . is reflected in that of his characters. Agnon's wife, according to Dr. A. Y. Brawer, treated him like a child. She once told him, "Agnon is a child, stubborn like a child." Many of Agnon's acquaintances have expressed a similar view. There is room for conjecture, therefore, that when Kurzweil, who knew Agnon intimately, writes of the childishness of the Agnon hero, he also has Agnon in mind.

An anecdote about Agnon—possibly apocryphal—illustrates the autobiographical basis of the passivity motif. Standing in the editorial office of the Israeli newspaper *Ha'Aretz,* Agnon held an envelope in one hand and a stamp in the other. In complete helplessness he waited. Finally, someone came over, took the stamp, licked it, and stuck it to the envelope. Out of absurd scenes such as these *The Book of Deeds* is made. Kafka, who had similar experiences, tells a self-mocking story of his passivity. He was in his thirties with a doctorate in law. Sitting by the river in Prague, he was asked, as if he were a small boy, to take a man in a rowboat. He did so, filled with pride and a sense of worthiness at being of service, and was thoroughly disappointed at not receiving a tip.

Family causes of Agnonesque passivity such as those described in Kafka's "Letter to His Father" are clear in *A Simple Tale.* This is Agnon's only novel telling of a youth growing up at home. The influence of his parents, especially his mother, ensures his clinging dependence upon them, and cripples his ability to act for himself. Hirshl is "not kneaded from the dough of men of action". Otherwise, he would marry Blumah in defiance of his mother's will. Instead, he is like putty in her hands. Just at the moment when he begins to think, "is it not possible to change anything?", his mother catches him. In a tone of false commiseration she insists that "a man's world is not given into his hands". Starkly the narrator tells us, "now that she was treating him lovingly, his heart became soft as wax which can be moulded into any shape one wants".

This malleability leads to disaster after he marries Mina. He is driven to the brink of madness. In synagogue, he takes wax from a candle and kneads it in his hand:

> He hid his hand in his pocket so that no one would see him kneading. The wax fell from his hand and he kneaded himself. He was frightened. He had kneaded himself without feeling it. Perhaps his fingers had lost the sense of touch. Perhaps he had died.

By moulding him and depriving him of life, Hirshl's mother has caused him inturned, masochistic rage—the kneading of the self, the numbing of the senses, the signs of incipient madness. In view of Hirshl's low self-regard and his failure to assert himself as the man of the house, it is little wonder that his marriage collapses. In the throes of madness, he has nightmares of slaughtered cocks. These are a symbolic expression of his sexual inferiority. The cock represents masculinity and sexual assertion. Its slaughter suggests the reverse—passivity, inferiority, and sexual impotence.

In common with Kafka's characters and with Kafka himself, Hirshl's difficulty is that he cannot break away from the inferior position of being a son and achieve independence and manhood. His dependence upon his parents stems from their manipulation of him, and from their own immaturity. They did not marry for love, and the atmosphere at home is not loving, but depressive. Hirshl breaks down under the strain of acting against his impulses in order to satisfy his parents. His position is all the more frustrating as he cannot openly go against or criticize them precisely because of his dependence upon them. He is tragically aware of his dilemma: ". . . as long as I am dependent on father and mother there is no hope that I can correct anything". As a victim of learned helplessness, he knows that "as long as father and mother have authority over me I cannot change my ways". Hirshl despairs of changing his life for the better:

> The truth is this: a man is not judged by his deeds. Others have power over us. Yesterday they wanted this, today they want that. This or that way, the truth seems to lie with others. You shrink in your own eyes as you shrank in theirs.

Hirshl illustrates his sense of filial inferiority during his recovery in Dr. Langsam's asylum. He draws pictures of himself and his father rather than of his wife and child, "Hirshl should have drawn a picture of his wife and son, but as he was small in his eyes, he drew a picture of his father to show himself how big father was and how small he was".

A sense of smallness, of not being "a man of deeds", and even the welcoming of situations that "excuse us from deeds," are common in Agnon's works. . . . [The] egocentricity of the Agnon hero is probably rooted in his feelings of inferiority. The final story in *The Book of Deeds*, "HaMikhtav" ["The Letter"] closes with a Kafkaesque scene dramatizing the narrator's smallness. The narrator, a writer living in Jerusalem, stands alongside of Mr. Klein, a parent-figure and a "man of deeds" who has returned from the grave: "It was hard to stand before a man who once was kind to me but now ignored me. I turned my face away from him. He stood up over me with his cane. I was afraid and made myself very small." Like Hirshl in his drawing, the writer diminishes himself beside the authority figure. Kafka's *The Trial* has a scene in which the manufacturer and the deputy manager discuss a transaction in front of K.'s desk: ". . . as the two of them leaned against his desk, and the manufacturer set himself to win the newcomer's approval, it seemed to K. as if two giants of enormous size were bargaining over his head for himself." Again, Kafka's "Letter to His Father" comes to mind "You were so huge, a giant in every respect."

Filial smallness in Agnon's case was probably felt more in relation to his grandfather and mother than to his father. In his writings, women as well as men tower over the protagonists. In *Betrothed,* for instance, Rechnitz's difficulty with Shoshana lies partly in his inability to overcome a sense of inferiority towards her:

> There are some people whose silences are awesome; we imagine their minds to be full of great thoughts which keep them from communicating, and this makes us shrink in their presence, believing that they hold in their hands the keys of all wisdom. Yet if we consider the matter well, we shall find that their silence grows out of overweening pride and that they don't surpass us by so much as the breadth of a parrot's claw. It is only because we shrink that they tower above us. And why do

we thus belittle ourselves before them? This calls for investigation but I have no time for it.

Agnon, however, had little time for anything else. He spent his life exploring this question and interconnected ones, though not with the desperation of Kafka.

As Agnon in early manhood reacted against traditional Judaism, it is understandable that many of his works should be so preoccupied with the non-observance of the traditions.

—David Aberbach

The main signs of passivity, such as not doing what is planned or what ought to be done, the anguished hesitation, the confusion and indecisiveness, and the excruciating guilt that accompanies the failure to act, are found most emphatically in the twenty stories grouped under the somewhat ironic heading *The Book of Deeds.* The "deeds" at times appear scarcely worth the telling. In themselves they are unheroic and mundane, and they usually remain unfinished. Yet, they mean a great deal to the narrator who tells of them with quiet, extraordinary care. They stir up in him almost invisible upheaval. At times they bring to mind the conflicts of J. Alfred Prufrock ("Shall I part my hair behind?/Do I dare to eat a peach?") and the tramps in *Waiting For Godot.* The guilt and indecision in these stories often seem absurd. Most people perform such deeds without mishap. Questions such as whether to eat or to post letters, found in **"Pat Shlema"** [**"A Whole Loaf"**] are ludicrous to those who attach no symbolic significance to them (the self-mockery in *The Book of Deeds* suggests that the narrator is well aware of this).

The world of *The Book of Deeds* is exceedingly lonely. The stories are full of encounters with people, but without warmth. Often they give rise to guilt. The narrator is almost always in an inferior position, psychologically, to those whom he meets. As in Hirshl's case, family troubles appear to be at the root of his discomfiture (most of the stories date from the 1930's, when *A Simple Tale* was written). The narrator's parents figure in two of the stories (**"El haRofe"** [**"To the Doctor"**], **"HaPanim laPanim"** [**"The Face and the Image"**]). His grandfather plays an important role in **"HaNerot"** [**"The Candles"**], **"Ha' Autobus ha' Aharon"** [**"The Last Bus"**], and **"HaMikhtav"** [**"The Letter"**]. All of these stories are about guilt. The extremity of guilt aroused by trivial encounters, such as that between the narrator of **"A Whole Loaf"** and Yekutiel Ne'eman can be best explained in terms of "internalization"—the figures encountered, on one level represent the parents or grandfather of the narrator. Further observations of Charles Rycroft cast light on this side of Agnon's work:

The emotion of guilt is evoked by actions—and in some people even by thoughts—which offend against whatever authority or authorities the individual identifies himself with—or has *internalized*. Internalization is the technical term for the process by which the individual constructs a mental representation of the outside world and of the people in it and thereafter reacts to these mental representations as though they had some of the force and reality of the external figures themselves. . . .

[The sense of guilt] indicates the existence of a conflict between two parts of the self, one of which, the egotistic part, says "I want to" while the other, the internalized authority, says "I ought not to"; or, alternatively, "I did" and "I ought not to have". This conflict is not necessarily neurotic. . . .

However, as the sense of guilt is only evoked in situations of conflict, it tends to be evoked more frequently and intensely in persons who have internalized their authorities out of fear than in those who have internalized them out of love. The person who has been brought up by parents who have enforced their will and instilled their values by fear is more likely to be plagued by a sense of guilt than those who have been brought up kindly and have incorporated the values of authority figures whom they have loved and admired. The former bears a grudge against authority and wishes unconsciously to defy it, however much he may consciously subscribe to its values. His whole attitude toward values is, indeed, corrupted by a conflict between a wish to defy authority as such and a fear-inspired need to submit to it, which stands in the way of his ever making a genuine moral judgment or stand. This conflict tends to produce a vicious circle, since his defiance will make him frightened and increase his need to submit and his submission will increase his hostility and make him defiant. In severe cases this conflict leads to the condition known to psychiatry as obsessional neurosis, in which the patient feels compelled to think or to do things which are totally foreign to his conscious conforming personality; every thought and action becomes an agony of ambivalence and indecision and every relationship a battleground between defiance and submission. Poised on a caricature of moral conflict, he may lose all capacity for action.

[*Anxiety and Neurosis*]

Genuine moral conflict—indeed, any passionate struggle—is singularly lacking in Agnon's writings. Instead, one finds this "caricature of moral conflict" between two parts of the self, the true self, and the internalized authority, the false self. This conflict lies at the heart of *The Book of Deeds*. In these stories, most of the narrator's plans and intentions lose the name of action, ending in irresolution, or in paradoxical solutions: at the end of **"The Certificate"**, the narrator has still not obtained a form for his relative; after his ordeal in **"A Whole Loaf"**, he has still neither eaten nor delivered the letters; he has not called a doctor for his father in **"To the Doctor"**; and in **"The Face and the Image"**, he has not visited his ailing mother. **"HaTizmoret"** [**"The Orchestra"**] contains a cluster of deeds not done: writing letters, having a bath, giving a relative a concert ticket, going to the barber in preparation for the New Year, asking the Dayan, the re-

ligious judge, a question. The one thing "accomplished" by the narrator—going to a concert—was not intended. In this story, typically, the narrator is constantly in a state of transition towards a goal which he never reaches. . . . [The] difficulties of the hero are characteristic of the schizoid personality, who, faced with the caricature of conflict, loses his capacity for action.

In other stories, similarly, it is inaction which prevails. At the end of **"Laila min haLelot"** [**"The Night"**], the narrator has not gone to the concert as he has planned, or helped his relative; the tailor in **"The Garment"** has not finished the garment; Adiel Amzeh in *Forevermore*, like Herbst in *Shirah*, has not completed his scholarly work; the narrator of *In Mr. Lublin's Shop* has still not brought provisions or bathed before the Sabbath. In many of Agnon's stories the projected deeds are not what the narrator wants to do—in this sense they are foreign to him—but rather they are what others want him to do, or what he thinks they think is right. He moves like an anxious puppet across the cluttered stage of his conscience. His need to act involves an "agony of ambivalence and indecision". That his deeds remain undone suggests that in some cases he does not want to do them. His failure to act can, paradoxically, be an act of defiance against internalized authorities. This exacerbates his guilt. His passivity is not only a wound, but also a weapon.

In the stories **"To the Doctor"** and **"The Face and the Image"**, the parents themselves are the victims of the narrator's difficulty in taking positive action. As he does not succeed in calling a doctor for his father and in going to see his ailing mother, it is possible that he does this "accidentally on purpose". Unconsciously, he may not wish to help them or see them as he resents being fixed in the inferior, filial state, and he blames them for his psychological troubles. It may be that he uses his impotence to achieve an omnipotence of sorts, expressed through his defiance of authority. The narrator's failure to deliver the letters of Yekutiel Ne'eman in **"A Whole Loaf"** might also reflect an undercurrent of subversiveness in his character. The extremity of guilt could indicate a conscious or unconscious awareness that his failure is a defiant act. The same unwillingness to send letters is found in **"Knots Upon Knots"**. The narrator, on meeting Samuel Emden, feels guilty at not having replied to a letter of his. (The authority figure Emden is clearly an inner object as the historical character, a famous rabbi, was named Jacob Israel Emden, not Samuel, which is Agnon's own name.) Similarly, in **"The Orchestra"**, the doorman, whose letters the narrator has not answered, has the same features as the Dayan. He, too, can be seen as an internalized authority. Again, the narrator subtly defies authority—a defiance implicit in the fact that he goes to the concert on the night of Rosh Hashana—and again he suffers agonies of guilt.

As Agnon in early manhood reacted against traditional Judaism, it is understandable that many of his works should be so preoccupied with the non-observance of the traditions. His hero is a modern Tantalus, reaching for the fruit of religion, but never clutching it. A dream of

Agnon's, which might have formed the basis for a story in *The Book of Deeds,* illumines the religious indecisiveness in his works:

> Last night I dreamed that I was in a strange place among unknown people. I am hungry. They prepare a sumptuous meal for me. I'm eager to eat. Then I remember that it is the night of Tisha B'Av. But everyone is eating, so perhaps it is only the seventh of Av. I decide to eat. At the last moment I hold back. Maybe it is the Ninth of Av.
>
> [David Canaani, *S.Y.Agnon Be'al Peh* (Agnon in Conversation), 1971]

Most of the stories in *The Book of Deeds* take place on an important day in the Jewish calendar. Almost invariably, the narrator is remiss in fulfilling his religious duties. **"A Whole Loaf"** is set at the close of a Sabbath, but as the narrator has not eaten all day (and it is infernally hot), it has the force of Yom Kippur, without real atonement or forgiveness. The sending of the letters could, on one level, represent what his family, the "internalized authorities", expect of him—the preservation of the tradition of Moses (Yekutiel and Ne'eman are both names given to Moses.) He is, in a sense, their messenger, but he accepts his duty not out of love, but out of guilt and fear.

The Book of Deeds has been singled out by Professor Dov Sadan as "the most important biographical document" of Agnon's, and, indeed, Professor Gershom Scholem has said [in a personal communication with the critic, Aberbach] that the manuscript of these stories indicates beyond a doubt that they were based upon Agnon's own dreams. One of the clearly biographical motifs is the letter which does not reach its destination. Agnon told of a letter which he had written to his father in 1912. This letter never arrived. The incident later gave rise to the guilty feeling that he had not carried out the obligation to honour his father. **"Ma'ase ha'Ez"** [**"The Fable of the Goat"**], which can be read as an innocent children's tale, also reflects breakdown of communication between son and father. It anticipates stories in *The Book of Deeds,* especially **"A Whole Loaf"**. The defiance of authority in Agnon's case manifests itself in a reaction against orthodox Judaism and in a crisis of faith. Agnon apparently felt strongly that he did not "deliver the letters" entrusted to him by his family. Mrs. Emuna Yaron, his daughter, has said that Agnon as a young man was regarded as an *iluy,* a prodigy. His father and grandfather wanted him to become a rabbi. They were disappointed by his literary ambitions.

Another dream of Agnon's, which might also have inspired a tragicomic story in *The Book of Deeds,* illustrates his feeling of unworthiness and passivity. In the dream he went back to Buczacz and was asked by the elders of the community to take the job of rabbi and deliver a sermon:

> When the time came to go to the synagogue and speak, all my bones were shaking for fear of the congregation. What in the name of God was I going to talk about? For I hadn't a thing to say; but since I had promised I couldn't

go back on my word. I went to my grandfather's house and took a volume of the Talmud from the bookcase—it was tractate Megillah—and I began to study, looking for something new to say in public. Not only didn't I find anything new, but I didn't even understand what I was studying. Just as I was struggling with the Talmud, some of the town leaders came by to bring me to the Great Synagogue. I was dragged after them until we arrived. I wrapped myself in a prayer shawl and turned to the holy ark. I asked for a passage from the Bible or a saying of the rabbis to begin my sermon. In the meanwhile, I forgot why I was standing there and I forgot that the whole town was waiting expectantly to hear my sermon. I stood like this for a year, or two, or three, and not a passage from the Bible fell to my lips and no saying of the rabbis. I began to cry. I woke up because of my crying. When I found myself lying in bed, I knew that it was a dream.

> [S. J. Agnon, *From Myself to Myself*]

Despite the semi-farcical side of this dream, Agnon's paralysis in trying to fulfill a rabbinical role could reflect the unrealized hopes of his family and the community in which he grew up—as well as his own hopes—that he would be a rabbi. His family's expectations were all the greater as Agnon had distinguished rabbinical ancestors. This was a source of hardship as well as pride:

> When I was a child of six, a relative visited our house for a family wedding. He enumerated to me all my ancestors going back to Rabbi Samuel Edels. Why did he do this? After all, I was only a little boy and I didn't understand what he was saying. It was so that he could add, "And you play wildly with children in the street".
>
> [Canaani]

When Samuel returns to the house where he grew up, in *A Guest For the Night,* he remembers childhood inhibitions of a similar order:

> When did I stop playing ball with the girls? Once I was running after the ball, a little girl behind me. I touched her hand and blushed, I knew there was something sinful in it. I went away and played by myself. One day my teacher saw me and said, "What's the sense of a boy playing ball? If you want the ball, why do you throw it away? If you throw it away, why do you run after it? Because your evil impulse incites you—and if that's the case, don't listen to it'.

Inhibition in play might foreshadow sexual inhibition in later life. Sexual difficulties figure throughout Agnon's major fiction. With Jewish girls the hero tends to be passive. Gentile girls arouse religious compunctions. The narrator of *Thus Far* has an affair with a Gentile girl. One evening, after taking her home, he meets an acquaintance who, in response to his greeting, replies cryptically, "When Balaam tried to destroy Israel he stirred up the Moabite women among them". The narrator confesses: "Imagine to yourselves a man taking leave of a Gentile woman and meeting someone . . . who mentions the story of Balak and the daughters of Moab—how frightened he was". Agnon told of his involvement with a Gentile actress in Berlin during World War One (*Thus Far* is set at the same time and place). She was to come to his room one night, and his conscience assailed him, "'You, of holy stock, of the grandchildren of Abraham, Isaac, and Jacob, are about to become impure'. I was gripped by fear and strong emotion". He gave instructions that the woman was not to be admitted, and bolted his door.

As we have seen in the previous chapter, virtually none of Agnon's love stories tell of deeds leading to a satisfactory ending. Rather, they are unresolved at the end. Problems such as those in **The Book of Deeds** often seem to be invested with the emotional significance of major problematic relationships between men and women. In some cases, they are displaced effects of these difficulties, defending the narrator like the tempest in *King Lear* which does not allow the king "to ponder / On things would hurt me more" (1. iv. 24-25). In sexual affairs, Agnonesque passivity shows itself most startlingly. **"The Lady and the Pedlar"**, which, significantly, is placed immediately before **The Book of Deeds** in Agnon's *Collected Works,* is the height of passivity. A Jewish pedlar named Joseph is given shelter in winter by a mysterious lady, Helena. He does not know that she intends to fatten him up, slaughter him, and eat his flesh. After months together, the craving comes upon her. She steals into his room with a knife. But he has gone to the woods to pray. In a frenzy, she turns the knife on herself. When Joseph returns, she is half dead from knife wounds:

> He bent down to her. She stuck her teeth into his throat and cried, "Pui, how cold you are, your blood is not blood but ice water." The pedlar took care of the lady for a day and two days and another day. . . . On the fifth day she gave up the ghost and died.

One of the extraordinary things in this scene, apart from the woman being a vampire (this is a frequent hazard in gothic horror stories), is that Joseph puts up no resistance and seems masochistically to welcome her blood sucking. The denouement is a condensation of the dynamics of relations between men and women throughout Agnon's works. Even if they are hurt by women—perhaps especially if they are hurt—they remain passively dependent upon them.

Esther Fuchs   (essay date 1985)

SOURCE: "Wherefrom Did Gediton Enter Gumlidata?— Realism and Comic Subversiveness in 'Forevermore'," in *Modern Language Studies,* Vol. 15, No. 4, Fall, 1985, pp. 64-79.

[In the following essay, Fuchs focuses on the protagonist—both his characterization and behavior—in For-evermore (Ad Olam) in order to reveal "the underlying irony of the story, which is its most salient feature."]

1. INTRODUCTION

S. Y. Agnon's story **Ad Olam** (**Forevermore**) has stirred much critical controversy over its ideological meaning.

[In *Pesher agnon,* 1968] Meshulam Tochner sees the story as a polemic against modern Biblical criticism and modern Hebrew literature. [In *Hasifrut,* Vol. 1, No. 2 (April-May 1968)] Eddy Zemach claims that the story argues against secular Judaism. [In *Sipurei ahavah shel shai agnon,* 1975] Hillel Barzel maintains that the story demonstrates the transience of secular political statehood by displaying the way in which "one secular civilization is destroyed by another." Despite the considerable differences between these interpretations they all agree that the story is a vehicle for an ideological message, and that the "overt text" is of secondary importance. The allegorical method of interpretation underlying these analyses focuses on the intention of the author and the meaning of the story but ignores the *form* of the story, e.g., the way in which the hero is characterized and the structure of the plot.

Since in narrative fiction, or for that matter, in any work of art form and content are inseparable, the ideological-allegorical approach misses not only the aesthetic impact of the form, but the meaning generated by it. The critic who concentrates on the ideological implications of the story to the exclusion of its other elements runs the risk of imposing his own preconceived ideas on the work. Criticizing Tochner's approach to Agnon, Dan Miron gives expression to this problem by asking, "Did the research precede the conclusion, or was it the conclusion which determined the research?" [*Moznayim,* Vol. 27, Nos. 5-6 (April-May 1968)]. In the case of ironic works, such as **Ad Olam,** neglect of the formal aspect incurs far-reaching repercussions because it prevents the critic from noticing the incongruity between, for example, the point of view of the protagonist and that of the implied author. Most of the interpretations mentioned above indeed identify these distinct points of view; hence the interpretations ascribing to Agnon anti-Zionist or anti-secular conceptions. Furthermore, because of the obsessive concern with ideology, the ironic treatment of the protagonist and his field of research—the central metonymy of the story—was all but missed. It is ironic indeed that a story dedicated to questioning meaning and undermining the validity of academic research and logic in general should be presented as a rational-ideological allegory. By focusing on the two largely neglected aspects of characterization and the structure of the central metonymy, the present analysis will demonstrate the underlying irony of the story, which is its most salient feature.

2. THE CHARACTERIZATION OF THE PROTAGONIST

Adiel Amzeh, the protagonist of the story, enjoys a considerable popularity among critics. He is presented as a tragic hero who reaches the highest human destination: liberation from material constraints and a true dedication to the spiritual and moral goals of life. The mythical stature of the hero endows the story with high points not found in Agnon's other stories, which fail to offer an equal "epic, mythic and archaic development" of their heroes. Adiel Amzeh is praised not only for his moral stature but for his scholarly achievements as well, in stark contrast to Agnon's other scholars and scientists. Furthermore, Amzeh is presented both as the author's alter ego—his direct mouthpiece—and as the symbolic embodiment of the Jewish people.

The enthusiastic reception of Adiel Amzeh considers his actions *in vacuo*. It disregards the context and motivations of his praiseworthy behavior. A man who joins a leprosarium elicits immediate admiration because one supposes that only a humane motivation can inspire him to do so. But this is not Amzeh's reason for joining the suffering lepers. The unanimous critical applause also ignores the *manner* in which Amzeh performs his supposedly humane actions, as well as the way in which the author characterizes him.

Despite his central role in the story, Amzeh is characterized as a type rather than a full-fledged character. The expositional material gives little information about his past or about any activities that are not directly related to his research. Amzeh exemplifies the type of the monomaniac, obsessed by his work and completely controlled by it:

> The years during which he worked on his research made him a slave to his work, controlling him from the early hours of the day till bedtime. Everyday, immediately on waking up, his legs dragged him to his desk, and pen and papers, and his eyes, if not absorbed in mental pictures and visions would fix themselves in the books or photographs or maps of Gumlidata or in the maps of the battles which destroyed Gumlidata.

The syntactic structure of this excerpt emphasizes the idea that Amzeh is a slave to his work by presenting him as a direct object in both complex sentences (made him, controlled him, dragged him). His actions are described synecdochically: his legs, his eyes act for him. The synecdochic description emphasizes the physical, rather than volitional aspect of his actions, so much so that the protagonist seems more like a mechanical automaton than a human being. The mechanization of the human produces a comic effect, as explained by Bergson [in "Le Rire," *Oeuvres,* 1959]:

> The attitudes, gestures and movements of the human body are risible to the extent that this body makes us think of a simple mechanism . . . We laugh whenever a person gives us the impression that he is a thing . . . we laugh at any arrangement of acts and events which gives us . . . the illusion of life and the clear sensation of a mechanical agency.

Although Amzeh deals with an activity that requires intellectual concentration and emotional involvement he is presented as a mechanical object activated by the very thing he is expected to control—his work. The author could have created empathy for the protagonist had he explained Amzeh's attachment to the history of Gumlidata, psychologically and/or intellectually. But he does not do so. Amzeh's obsession with Gumlidata continues to be just that: an arbitrary involvement with an outlandish

topic. The description of Amzeh's writing and erasing, adding and subtracting adds to this impression of arbitrariness:

> At times he would add to *what he wrote* on the previous day, and *at times* he erased in one day *what he wrote* in many days. Similarly at night, often after going to bed, he would get up and return to the desk and check what he wrote, *sometimes with* a nod and *sometimes with* satisfaction and *sometimes* laughing at himself and his mistakes which caused him to investigate further and re-examine and correct.

The repetitions in this excerpt reinforce the repetitive actions of writing and erasing, rewriting and rechecking. This presents Amzeh's actions as circular and reversible, just like his going to bed and getting up. By omitting specific references to what is written and erased the author succeeds in presenting Amzeh's actions as vacuous motions, nothing more than insipid and mechanical gestures. Repetitiveness, reversibility, and circularity are rudimentary ingredients in all comic actions.

The compulsive behavior of the protagonist could have turned him into a tragic hero had he been aware of his absurd situation. Amzeh is capable of laughing at his silly mistakes, but he is incapable of perceiving the overall inanity of his life. The causal link between action and consciousness can turn a clown into a victim, as Unamuno says [in *The Tragic Sense of Life,* translated by J. F. Crawford, 1954]. Amzeh remains a clown because he is unconscious of his ridiculous conduct. In one of the climactic points of the plot, when Amzeh finds out that the wealthy Gerhard Goldenthal is interested in publishing his book on Gumlidata, the protagonist's conduct changes abruptly: "Suddenly he changed entirely and became like those famous scholars, who neglect their research work for the sake of the honor that people who do not deal with research give them." The radical change in Amzeh's attitude is comic because it is abrupt and arbitrary; it signifies the opposite of all the values associated with him previously. The sudden reversal contributes to the characterization of Amzeh as an automaton. The mechanical and obsessive manner in which he previously worked now typifies his anxious anticipation of his visit with Mr. Goldenthal: "And so he sat and glanced at his book and looked at the mirror, and glanced at the watch and checked his clothes and examined his movements, for he who seeks the presence of a rich man must take pains to look graceful in his clothes, and graceful in his face and graceful with his movements." Amzeh's new obsession with his appearance highlights the arbitrary quality of his previous obsession with his work. The series of synonymous verbs—look, glance, check, examine—intimates that Amzeh's activities are inherently static and bring about little progress. Despite the new direction of his obsession, the manner in which he acts does not change. It remains compulsive, mechanical, unconscious. This reversal foreshadows the arrival of Ada Eden, the old nurse from the leprosarium. When the nurse first appears, inconveniently right before the scheduled appointment with Mr. Goldenthal, Amzeh apologizes for not being able to pay attention to her. But when he hears of the book "which has become rotten with age and tears" he changes his mind. He offers her a seat and implores her to continue talking about the extraordinary book at the leprosarium, and when it finally becomes clear that the ancient book is indeed related to Gumlidata, he decides to join the nurse on her way back to the leprosarium. *It is clear that Amzeh acts out of academic curiosity, not out of altruistic compassion for the poor, segregated, and ailing people.* We are confronted with an insatiable desire to accumulate information, which is vastly different from a Kierkegaardian leap into transcendence, as some critics believe it to be. Amzeh's questions revolve around the book, not the lepers: "What did you hear of that manuscript? How did it end up with you? You made me curious, madame, curious hungry for knowledge, practically like a psychoanalyst."

Amzeh's attitude does not change even after his arrival at the leprosarium. His interaction with the lepers is not motivated by his will to alleviate their suffering but by his excitement over the things he finds in the book. The book is the aim, the lepers function at best as an audience with whom to share his discoveries: "And when he discovered something appropriate for everybody he entered the hall and gathered its residents and said to them brothers and friends sit down and I shall read for you."

The only time Amzeh cries is not at all related to the anguish of the lepers, but to the heroic act of the city scribe who, despite the danger to his life, continued to write the history of Gumlidata even during the final attack on the city. The protagonist joins the leprosarium for purely egotistical reasons; he does it in order to find out more information about Gumlidata, the ancient city he has been investigating for twenty years.

Still, the author could have diminished the ironic distance between Amzeh and the reader by describing the subjective perspective of the protagonist. Even the most irrational actions can be justified if their cause is understandable. It is evident, however, that the author does not wish to justify his monomaniac protagonist. The descriptions of Amzeh's excitement over the ancient manuscript focus on his facial features, not on his feelings. This is his reaction to Ada Eden's news: "Suddenly his face changed and his voice changed and his mouth became distorted and he burst into a stuttering laughter." When he sees the ancient book in the leprosarium: "He stared at it till his eyes grew as big as half of his face and he did not stop staring at it till he jumped to open it." When the lepers warn him not to touch the book with his bare hands and tell him about the dangers of contagion, the author adds sardonically; "I do not know whether he heard or did not hear. I know this: that his eyes grew till they stretched over his face and a part around his face." The description of Amzeh's physiognomical expressions deploys the technique of caricature which exaggerates a certain facial feature beyond recognition and distorts normal proportion. Amzeh's exaggerated response to the book contrasts with his indifference to the lepers, whose sufferings ought to have elicited at least some reaction in the visitor. The

caricatural description reflects the preposterous incongruity between reality and Amzeh's reaction.

The parody of Amzeh's speech increases further the ironic distance between him and the reader. Through repetition, digression, and cumbersome syntax the author manages to undercut Amzeh's run-on speech:

> I will tell you approximately about the matter; for twenty years I have dealt with the research of the history of that city; there is no piece of paper which mentions the city's name which I have not read, *if* I were a king I could reconstruct the city and rebuild it just as it was before its destruction, *and if* you want I will tell you about all the trips I take through it—I walk *in its* markets *and its* busy alleys, *and its* streets *and its* roads *and its* palaces *and its* temples. Oh, my good nurse the headache—from the trips I take there, and *I also know the order of its destruction, and I know how they destroyed it, and also* the name of every troop which worked on its destruction, *and how* many were killed by sword *and how many* died of hunger *and* thirst, *and how many* perished in the plague which followed the war, except for one thing that I do not know, from which *side* entered the troops of Gediton the hero, *whether from* the *side* of the great bridge which used to be called the Bridge of Courage or *whether* they came indirectly from the *side* of the valley of Aphardat, the Valley of the Cranes—the plural of crane is Aphardat in the language of Gumlidata, and not ravens *or* chestnuts *or* galoshes as linguists, such as Mr. X and Mr. True Advisor, Professor Y *and* all the other professors, whose pictures you saw in the illustrated newspapers when they received medals and honorable titles from the royal court.

This enormous period, which includes numerous inadequately punctuated complex and combined sentences, reflects the confused and desultory thought processes of the scholar. From the topic of his research, he goes on to describe the thoroughness of his research, mentions in passing the headaches caused by his imaginary trips in Gumlidata, elaborates on the trips he takes, returns to the things he knows concerning the controversial grammatical form of a certain word in the language of Gumlidata, while throwing in a disparaging comment about his colleagues. The incompatibility of these issues emphasizes the absurdity of lumping all of them into one prolonged period. The incongruity between the tragic destruction of the city, which seems to be the most troublesome issue in the period, and the academic problem that haunts the scholar (from which side did the enemy enter) reflects the skewed academic perspective that gives priority to knowledge over human suffering. Gumlidata's destruction is one of the many things Amzeh *knows* about the city and so it becomes preipheral, conceding the central place to Amzeh's eruditions ("there is not a piece of paper . . . I have not read . . . if I were a king I could reconstruct the city . . . and I know the order . . . and also the name . . . and how many were killed . . ."). For the running theme in this run-on period is what Amzeh knows and does not know about the city of Gumlidata. The subject is Amzeh, not Gumlidata. But the scholar's attempt to prove his superior knowledge by tediously enumerating the city's sites ("its markets, its busy alleys, and its streets and its roads . . .") and the macabre listing of the forms of destruction and death ("and I know how they destroyed it . . . and how many were killed . . . and how many died . . . and how many perished") undercuts the thrust of his speech because it reduces Amzeh's erudition to an insipid series of petty details. The reduction reaches the point of absurdity when it lists the plural forms of the word "crane," which Amzeh affirms to be "Aphardat," not "ravens," "chestnuts," or "galoshes." Not only is this linguistic discussion completely irrelevant to the main subject, but the incongruity among the terms as well as the phonetic incompatibility of the singular and plural formations overreaches all the other inanities in the speech. The repetition of conjunctions (if, and, whether, or), nouns (trip, side, destruction), and pleonastic constructions ("I also know the order of its destruction, and I know how they destroyed it") underlines the extraneous and trivial quality of Amzeh's knowledge. Above all, the numerous digressions in the jumbled speech point up the illogical nature of the professor's thought processes, presenting him as a buffoon rather than a serious scholar.

Amzeh's monologue alludes to the only causal link between the character and his academic curiosity. This curiosity remains an enigma because the emotional or psychological motives for it are still unclear. Amzeh's insatiable thirst for additional information on Gumlidata is his exclusive motivation throughout the story. As a monomaniac, Amzeh exemplifies what is, according to Auden, the quintessential comic character: "The comic butt of satire is a person who, though in possession of moral faculties, transgresses the moral law beyond the moral call of temptation, . . . The commonest object of satire is a monomaniac" [W. H. Auden, "Notes on the Comic," *The Dyer's Hand and Other Essays,* 1962]. The author satirizes Amzeh by creating a grotesque incongruity between the context of his life and his perception; there is no correlation between the suffering of the lepers and Amzeh's unabated passion for Gumlidata. He further distorts the relationship between reality and the hero's perception by exaggerating Amzeh's interest in Gumlidata while trivializing his objects of interest. When Amzeh takes his imaginary trips in the city he "talks with the dogs of its temples about their prices." Had Amzeh held his imaginary discussions with Gumlidata's ministers about the city's political predicament, had he argued with its philosophers about Gumlidata's religion, the reader might have forgiven and perhaps even admired the scholar's exclusive obsession with his city. The ironic effect is produced by the incongruity between Amzeh's seriousness and the identity of his imaginary interlocutors—dogs.

Amzeh does not change in the course of the story. His obsession with Gumlidata continues unabated after his arrival at the leprosarium. Not even the sight of the most wretched of human sufferers brings about a change in his limited perception of the world. Amzeh remains a monomaniac throughout the story, a flat and static type. His inability to change turns him into the stock character of comedy. Amzeh's rigidity illustrates Bergson's theory of the mechanical man as the typical comic butt. The capacity to change, develop and adapt to new circumstances is quintessentially human. The mechanical object must be moved by external forces in order to change and, even then, the change is not substantial. Despite the traumatic experience Amzeh undergoes he remains the robot described at the beginning of the story. The ironic emphasis on the mechanical activity of Amzeh is echoed in the ending, which defines the learning as "wisdom." "He would sit and discover secrets which were unknown to all the learned men of all generations, till he came and discovered them. And since these things are numerous and wisdom wide and there is much in it to investigate and examine and understand, he did not leave his work and did not budge from his place and sat there forevermore." Amzeh, who was on the verge of launching a brilliant academic career with the publication of a book he had been working on for twenty years, finds himself in a leprosarium by sheer coincidence and continues to live there "forevermore." "Wisdom" is said to have taken hold of him, compelling him to isolate himself from humanity and discover secrets that were unknown and will remain unknown "forevermore." What is the "wisdom" which overpowers the protagonist? What are the "secrets" he keeps? Does this "wisdom" justify Amzeh's sacrifice? The answer is alluded to in the nature of the central metonymy.

3. GUMLIDATA AS METONYMY

The city of Gumlidata is perceived by most critics to be a metaphor. Tochner maintains that the city of Gumlidata represents the Jewish tradition, the idolatrous city of Samaria, and modern secular Judaism. Amzeh's book on Gumlidata symbolizes for Tochner the secular research on the history of Judaism as well as modern Hebrew literature. The internal contradiction included in this interpretation does not prevent Tochner from concluding that Agnon "does not hesitate to hint" that the creations of the modern secular scholars are a product of "the destruction of tradition, the loss of the authority of the Torah and the pursuit of foreign values." This perception turns the story into a moralistictheological parable in which the author expresses "his rebellion against and revulsion from what is accepted and rooted in the taste and thought of the secular generation.

This interpretation is arbitrary, not only because Gumlidata is made to represent opposite things (traditional Judaism and secular modern culture), but also because there is nothing in the story of Gumlidata to suggest that it deals with Judaism at all, either as history or as philosophy. What in *Ad Olam* alludes to the Jewish identity of Gumlidata? Furthermore, if Amzeh is to represent Agnon, why is he shown to disregard the lepers' community (traditional Jewry)? Even if we accept the arbitrary logic of this allegorical interpretation we are confronted with an illogical conclusion, namely, that Agnon both supports and rejects modern secular culture. And if this is so, why does Tochner insist that Agnon "does not hesitate" to reject it?

A similar allegorical orientation brought other critics to the conclusion that the putrid, puss-covered ancient book of Gumlidata, to which Amzeh dedicates the rest of his life symbolizes the holy Torah. In addition to the problems already pointed out, it is unlikely that Agnon who according to this interpretation decries modern secular culture in favor of the Jewish tradition would use a repulsive object to symbolize the holy Torah. By perceiving Gumlidata as metaphor, the allegorists lose sight of its metonymic function: to serve as an indirect means of characterization. The allegorical orientation of the critics also ignores the satirical contours of the metonymy, an oversight that results in exalting what is in fact tacitly deprecated in the story. Thematically, the author satirizes Gumlidata by emphasizing the themes of sex and bestiality in Gumlidata's culture. These ingredients are familiar themes in satire because they highlight the mundane and physical aspects of human existence. The description of Gumlidata's social and cultural life manipulates both themes interchangeably:

> For it was customary in Gumlidata and its suburbs that when a woman became pregnant and it was not known by whom, her relatives would wait for her to give birth to the baby and then come and take the baby and bring it to the beasts, and they would look for a beast which gave birth at the same time and throw the baby to the beast, and take the beast's baby and bring it to the mother to be nursed with the milk of her breasts. If they do not find a beast's baby, they bring her the young of a tame animal. They took special care with the great ladies, "Gevtaniyot" in their language, for if she [the lady] gave birth, and no one knows [to whom] they would kill the baby and bring her a beasts's baby, because it is not dignified for the daughters of the great to nurse a simple woman's baby, and to have their good blood mixed with the blood of common people.

The outlandish custom of Gumlidata whereby human babies are exchanged for the young of animals implies that this culture is unable to differentiate between human life and animal life, deeming the two of equal importance. Furthermore, the custom that sanctions the murder of a child born of a lady and a common man reveals that human life is inferior to animal life, and that no means are spared to perpetuate social inequality by preventing the fusion of "the good blood" with the "blood of the common people," This description demonstrates that Gumlidata was not less barbaric than the Goths who destroyed her, and her destruction was no great loss to civilization.

Sex and animals appear as the major features that bring about the final destruction of the city. Both are embodied in the character of Eldag, the little Hun girl, captured by the soldiers of Gumlidata and forced to serve as the old king's concubine. After several failed escapes, Eldag determines to undermine her enemies by ruse. She changes her conduct, showing the king "secrets of love and feats of love which he did not know with any boy or girl." Free to roam through the city, the captive finds out that the city's wall by the Valley of the Cranes is shaky. Receiving for a gift a priestly garment with the shape of the Valley of the Cranes, she hangs it on the neck of her playmate a young wild ass and leads the ass toward the opening in the wall. When the wild ass arrives at the camp of the besiegers, Eldag's father deciphers the hint and the enemy storms the city through the Valley of the Cranes. Gumlidata's animal cult and sexual mores, as well as the king's self-indulgence, are operative in the city's final destruction by its enemies. The cumulative evidence culled from the different stories about Gumlidata undermines the initial description of the city as "a great city, the pride of mighty nations." This laudatory evaluation of Gumlidata reflects Adiel Amzeh's bias, not reality. But can we refer to Gumlidata as reality at all?

Amzeh's persistent search for Gumlidata is undercut by a pervasive use of verbal grotesque in reference to Gumlidata. The verbal grotesque is created by the alliteration of 'a (ayin) and g (gimal); "'Esrim shana 'asak 'Adiel 'Amzeh beheqer ta'alumot Gumlidata shehaita'ir gedolah ga'avat goyim 'a sumin, 'ad she 'alu gedudei hagotim va 'asauha 'aremot 'afar ve'et 'amameha 'avdei 'olam." (For twenty years Adiel Amzeh worked on the research of the mysteries of Gumlidata, which was a great city, the pride of mighty nations, till the troops of the Goths attacked it and turned it into heaps of ashes and her people into slaves.)

The pervasive alliteration of 'a and g was perceived by most critics analyzing the story. Some suggested that this extraordinary phenomenon is not significant while others see it as a primary allusion to the covert meaning of the story. Gavriel Moked, for example, suggests that the letter 'a signifies spiritual characters, such as 'Adiel, 'Amzeh, and 'Ada 'Eden, whereas the letter g stands for the concrete and materialistic entities, for instance the city of Gumlidata.

But this explanation pertains only to part of the phenomenon, to the alliteration of the different proper names appearing in the story. It does not deal with the alliteration of the series of nouns, verbs, and adjectives recurring throughout entire passages.

The alliteration, like the assonance and consonance and the rhyme, is a phonetic means that serves to intensify meaning through sound. These devices are most frequent in poetry, where language serves not only as a window through which to observe reality, but as a mirror in which language itself is reflected. In prose narrative the phonetic aspect normally fulfills a peripheral function. This is especially true in the realistic story that pretends to "imitate" reality and present it just as it is. *Focusing on the phonetic aspect of words in the realistic narrative increases the reader's awareness of the fact that a story is essentially made up of words that call attention to the fictive nature of the work.*

The employment of phonetic devices in a realistic story creates a paradox involving the basic principles of the narrative work of art as well as the process of reading, because the author presents the reader with a narrative sign that is supposed to be realistic and yet appears to be fictional. The alliterated words function both as carriers of meaning and as phonetic constructions. In this manner the automatic association between signifier and signified is undermined: the relationship between word and meaning, language and reality, the narrated story and the narrating process becomes highly problematical.

The verbal grotesque functions as an effective satirical weapon. By giving precedence to sound over meaning, the satirist ridicules the meaning of the things he conveys through words. The pervasive alliteration of *'a* and *g,* especially in the passages relating to Gumlidata satirizes Gumlidata's history and culture. The fictive names of Gumlidata's numerous gods, most of which start with a *g* (Gomesh, Gosh, Gotz, Goah, Goz, Gomed, Gihor, and 'Amol), ridicule the city's outlandish cult. The elaborate name of the city's ruler, Graf ("count") Gifyon Glaskinon Gatra'al ("poison cistern") of the house of Gayra'al ("poison valley"), alludes sarcastically to the rigid caste system of Gumlidata. The alliterated neologisms (gaza'im, gavtan, gandarfus, eygal, geyhaim, gorgeranim, gnognanim, golshaniyot) parody the language of Gumlidata. I do not believe that these neologisms create an authentic "atmosphere of archaic sources" [Tochner, *Pesher agnon*]. It seems to me that they produce the opposite effect: the absence of signified referents and the repetitive letters constitute common devices of the verbal grotesque. A similar effect is created by the references to the grammar of the language of Gumlidata:

> The plural of crane is Aphardat in the language of Gumlidata, and not ravens or chestnuts or galoshes . . . for really a raven in their language is Eldag and in plural Elgadata, for d and g when they appear together in the plural change reverse their order, and what are chestnuts and galoshes in Gumlidatic language, I do not know.

The verbal grotesque is created by the arbitrary rules of Gumlidatic grammar. There is no phonetic or typographical correlation between "agur" (crane) in the singular and "Aphardat" (cranes) in the plural. This plural formation bears no similarity to the formation of "Algadata" from "Eldag." No consistent rules can be discerned. There is no semantic correlation between "orev" (raven), "armonim" (chestnuts), and "ardalayim" (galoshes). Their mutual relationship and their relevance to the context is arbitrary. The alliteration of the letter *'a* (ayin) highlights a phonetic similarity between them, but this only reinforces the semantic gratuity of the collocation and creates a comic effect. The constant repetition of the letters *'a* and *g* at the beginning of names and words relating to Gumlidata implies that the entire vocabulary of the Gumlidatic language consists of words starting with either *'a* or *g,* thereby emphasizing its limited scope, arbitrary nature, and strange sound.

But the verbal grotesque does not only function as a satirical weapon against Gumlidata's culture, history and language. It points out not only its outlandishness but also its fictitiousness. The critical attempt to explain the fictive neologisms counteracts the effect and function of the verbal grotesque. By searching for specific meanings for the specific neologisms the critics "dissolve the for-

est into trees," as Leo Spitzer puts it [in *Linguistics and Literary History—Essays in Stylistics,* 1962]; they normalize and neutralize a literary phenomenon whose primary purpose is to unsettle the reader by alluding to the possible unreality of the world it evokes.

The ancient book of Gumlidata is also presented as ridiculous and fictive. This book, for which Adiel Amzeh sacrifices his life, is "soiled with old puss, and even the contaminated abhorred it . . . and it seemed that it was not written on parchment but on the skin of a leper, and not with ink but with puss." In addition to its repulsive appearance, the book contains questionable data. It is described by Ada Eden as "the chronicles of Gumlidata, and its tyrants to be read by king Alarich so that he hears of its exploits and the courage of its great men." The book of Gumlidata then, was written by the leaders of the city, not by an objective historian, and for political purposes, not in order to leave behind a factual account of its history. The "tyrants of Gumlidata" deployed this book as propaganda material against their main enemy, Alarich, the king of the Goths. The polemical purposes of the book invalidate its reliability as an authentic historical source. Furthermore, the story of the city's destruction "was written on the last page of the book that the city's scribe attached to the end of the book." Since this story describes the activities in the camp of the Huns and the Goths, situated outside the walls of the city, the obvious question is how could the city scribe report the events that took place in the enemy's camp? It will be remembered that the description contains a verbatim report of the dialogue between Gediton the hero and Gihol the prankster. How did the city scribe find out the information he offers at the end of the book? The description of the city's final demolition compounds the problem. If there is truth in the scribe's testimony according to which the Goths "set fire to the city, and cut down in their anger infants and babies, boys and old men and women, . . . no living being remained," how could he report these bleak events unless he was spared himself? If the scribe survived the destruction, like Eldag and the king's grandson, he ought to have mentioned it; if not, somebody else must have added the description of the city's final destruction without actually witnessing it. It is possible that one of the lepers added an imaginary ending, exonerating Gumlidata of its failure to resist the Goths by fabricating the story of Eldag's betrayal and exaggerating the Goths' insidiousness and ruthlessness. Either way, the factual validity of the ancient book, particularly the story of its final destruction is highly questionable. Our protagonist, however, fails to show the slightest sign of caution. On the contrary, he considers the book to be the ultimate authoritative source on Gumlidata.

Amzeh's gullibility indicates that his twenty-year-old research on Gumlidata also consists largely of questionable historical reconstructions. If the supposedly original book of Gumlidata contains undocumented, if not fabricated data, it stands to reason that the reconstruction of the city's history prior to its destruction must be based on mere speculation. This does not prevent our scholar from dedicating twenty years of his life to reconstituting the long-destroyed city with great precision. The author ridicules Amzeh's scholarly work by enumerating the endless details that went into the reconstructive effort:

> Gebhard Goldenthal was prepared to publish the book, Adiel Amzeh's book, although the publication of such a book is very expensive, because of its numerous maps and because of its numerous colors; for the writer colored them with different colors, one color for the city's general view, and one color for its temples, and one color for its altars, and one color for Gomesh and Gosh and Goah and Goz its gods, and one color for its mothers, and one color for its infants and fetuses, their bellies' loads, and one color for Gomed the great, and for Gihor and Amol the pillars of the cult, and one color for the rest of their workers, the priests and priestesses, not to mention the prostitutes born to the ladies and the prostitutes whose fathers are slaves and their mothers are ladies, and the female and male cult prostitutes and the dogs—for everyone has a separate color according to his skin according to his garment, and according to the pay and the price and the work of his labor.

This massive period, consisting of a single main clause, and seven subordinate clauses (one concessive, two causal, and four relative) baffles the reader and complicates the issues involved in Amzeh's work rather than clarifying them. The major parodic device consists of lumping together incongruous subjects: inanimate objects, human beings, animals, and gods. Temples, altars, and gods appear alongside slaves, fetuses, and prostitutes. The fusion of the spiritual and the bestial, the elevated and the degraded, pretends that there is no real distinction between these incongruous elements. By combining all these elements in one enormous period, the author parodies Amzeh's book, which lists things without offering the necessary differentiation or evaluation. The tedious repetition of the word "color" dramatizes the insipid monotony of what appears to be a colorful book. What is the point in coloring both people and sites in separate colors without attempting to draw more substantial distinctions between them? The scholar fastidiously distinguishes between prostitutes born to ladies and those whose mothers are ladies and fathers are slaves, but he fails to differentiate between dogs and gods, or altars and human beings. Everything is subjected to the systematic examination of objective scholarship via color differentiation. The parodic treatment of Amzeh's work satirizes indirectly the academic approach to history (even the humanities in general), which sacrifices common sense for objectivity and avoids value judgments in order to uphold a scientific posture.

Amzeh's fastidious attempt to find out from which side the troops of Gediton entered Gumlidata illustrates the obsession of certain historians with details at the expense of principles. Amzeh sacrifices the rest of his life in order to ascertain a strategic detail. The incongruity between the trivial detail and Amzeh's serious approach becomes preposterous when we keep in mind that this strategic detail is ascertained on the basis of the last page in the book of Gumlidata, whose dubiousness has already been established. The ironic distance between

author and protagonist becomes all the more obtrusive in light of the author's patent affirmation that trivial details, such as the direction of his protagonist's entrance, do not concern him:

> I do not know through which gate he entered and how long it took him to gain an entrance permit . . . And since I am not well versed in details and I do not like speculations, I am abandoning the conjectures and returning to the facts.

Adiel Amzeh sacrifices his life in order to verify from which direction the hero, Gediton, entered Gumlidata. Our author ignores wherefrom his own hero entered the leprosarium. This contrastive analogy reflects the ironic distance between author and protagonist. But the irony works not only vis a vis Amzeh; its effect is much more radical. The author's abrupt reference to himself discloses the fact that although he knows much about his protagonist, there are many details he does not know. The author's unexpected intrusion makes the reader aware not only of the information the author lacks, but that which he supposedly has. The authorial reference to "speculations" versus "facts" appears to reassure the reader of the validity of the narrative material, but this reassurance is ironic because the very act of enunciating the assurance undermines its effectiveness. The reader realizes that the "facts" the author is invoking are fictional ingredients of a fictional tale. These facts are no more reliable than Amzeh's findings on Gumlidata. Thus the ironic odyssey of our author comes full circle—the reader who has been gloating over Amzeh's misconceptions is stung by the recognition that he is a victim of irony.

4. REALISM AS FICTION—THE ROMANTIC IRONY OF "FOREVERMORE."

Our protagonist, Adiel Amzeh, does not wonder about the identity, purpose, and authority of Gumlidata's city scribe. His response to the story of Gumlidata is one of empathy and identification; when he reads the story of the city's final destruction, he begins to cry. The scribe himself also identifies with the material he describes. He never admits that his story is not all fact. Not so the author of **Ad Olam**: several times in the course of what appears to be a realistic story, he intrudes with irrelevant or digressive remarks, calling attention to his subjective point of view. Anticipating the fact that Amzeh's patron, Gebhard Goldenthal, will neither meet Amzeh nor publish his book, the author intrudes abruptly with the following remark to the reader:

> A pity this rich man did not see him Amzeh for if he did he would have seen that there is even a lovelier appearance than silver and gold. You see my friend for the sake of a moralistic lesson I present in advance the point of the ending.

The abrupt transition from an objective and omniscient to a subjective and personal authorial point of view jolts readers out of their complacency. They now become privy to the way in which the author manipulates the narrative material (anticipation) as well as the readers' own attitudes (by teaching them a moralistic lesson). By pointing up his authorial disadvantages ("I do not know through which gate he entered . . . I do not know whether he did or did not hear . . .") the author is undermining his reliability. By inserting technical comments regarding the narrative process of creation (". . . I will tell what the dead letters told, and I will tell briefly what is told there at length . . .") the author implies that the reality confronted by the reader is fictional and artificial, that it is made of words and literary constructions. The artist seems to be poking fun at himself as well as at the reader.

Seen from this perspective, the verbal grotesque parodies not only the metadiegetic story of Gumlidata but the entire story of **Ad Olam**. Because the verbal grotesque distorts the link between signifier and signified it also parodies the means by which the author communicates with his reader. The neologisms that are inserted into conventional linguistic contexts and the alliterations of conventional words sever the automatic link between a word and its assigned meaning, thereby highlighting the essentially arbitrary link between sound and sense, which constitutes the rudimentary foundation of all language. The frightening-comic effect of the verbal grotesque in **Ad Olam** dramatizes for readers the precariousness of their own position as readers of a fictional tale, mediated by an arbitrary language. Readers soon realize that the troublesome *'a* and *g* recur not only in the names of Gumlidata's heroes but also in the names of "their" story. In essence, *'A*diel *'A*mzeh, *'A*da *'E*den, and *G*ebhard *G*oldenthal are not different from *'E*ldag, the hero *G*editon, and the king *G*ifyon *G*olaskinon.

The limited irony directed at scholarly pretentiousness, the "science" of history, and the monomaniac obsession with one's work expands in **Ad Olam** to encompass the precariousness of fictional writing, of art, and of language. If we construe **Ad Olam** as an ideological "historiosophical" allegory about Judaism and Zionism, then most of the disquieting elements in the story will naturally be considered as superfluous and oppressive "riddles serving a private myth" [Baruch Kurzweil, *Masot al sipurei shay agnon*, 1975]. If, on the other hand, we approach **Ad Olam** as a work of art, these riddles become essential, for they make the reader aware of the tensions between fiction and fact, word and meaning, perception and reality. The riddles of **Ad Olam** may be frustrating to those who search for ideological reassurances; they are indispensable to readers who prefer far-reaching questions to restrictive answers.

Lev Hakak (essay date 1986)

SOURCE: "Sexual Symbols in 'Another Face' by S. Y. Agnon," in *Hebrew Annual Review*, Vol. 10, 1986, pp. 95-108.

[*In the following essay, Hakak offers a Freudian interpretation of "Another Face" ("Panim aherot"), claiming that sexual symbols pervade the story. Note: The title of the story, here translated as "Another Face," is also known as "Metamorphosis" (see Leon I. Yudkin, 1974).*]

> Michael was grateful to her for her not interpreting his dream according to Freud and his School.
> S. Y. Agnon, **"Another Face,"** Dec. 12, 1932, edition, *Dabar*

1. INTRODUCTION

Sexual Symbols play an important role in S. Y. Agnon's short story **"Another Face"** (1976, 3, pp. 449-68). These symbols accompany the progress in communication between Toni and Michael and thereby enrich the reader's aesthetic experience of the short story. The author dramatizes the couple's emotional world by projecting it upon concrete objects which function equally as symbols and as objects.

Sigmund Freud views many parts of the physical world as symbols of sexual activity or desire. A brief glance at the things and settings emphasized in **"Another Face"** reveal many objects to which Freud has assigned sexual significance: a parasol, hat, flowers, a garden, to name some of the more prominent. It may be argued that different readers may relate in different ways to Freudian symbology in the story. The reader may interpret the attitude of the narrator to these symbols as complex and ambivalent and as one which goes beyond the Freudian symbology; the reader may even argue that the narrator employs these symbols as virtual parody; or he may argue that the narrator employs Freudian symbols as defined by Freud. While the effect of these symbols may be viewed in different ways by different readers, ignoring the existence of these symbols may lead to erroneous interpretation because it is one of the means of characterization in the story. The existence of the phenomena is objective, the effect is subjective. Pointing to Freudian symbology will lay the foundations for various approaches as to the effects of these symbols. I agree with Barzel (1975, p. 61) who thinks that "undoubtedly, Agnon was well-versed in Freudian symbology and knew how key symbols of his story would be interpreted."

The presence of many of the sexually charged objects in **"Another Face"** indicates the presence of symbols. According to the Freudian approach, objects belong to one of two groups, the masculine and the feminine. This strict duality seems to some to be imposed by a mind psychologically predisposed to find and to unveil universal sexuality. Symbolic interpretation confined to sexuality may, in fact, be a degenerate form of symbolism. Nevertheless, **"Another Face"** demands that the reader take these symbols into account in interpreting the story and its central relationship. Various elements make it necessary to understand the sexual symbols in the story: the context of marital tension and sexual attraction; the frequent usage of explicitly Freudian objects; the encouragement of the reader in the story to see these objects as being more than simple objects; and the fact that some ideas in the story which seem flat or difficult become emotionally loaded and intelligible only when these objects are read as sexual symbols. These elements and others—such as the associative power and the centrality of these objects in the story and the sexual tension evoked by the interrelations of these symbolic objects—all support my contention as to the necessity of understanding the sexual symbols in this story. Other symbolic meanings for these objects are possible. My focus, however, is to read the text in the heretofore ignored light of Freudian sexual symbolism.

The first edition of **"Another Face"** was published on Dec. 12, 1932, in Dabar, by which time Freud's ideas were already well known in intellectual circles. Between 1913 and 1924 Agnon lived in Germany. Several of his short stories (**"The Doctor's Divorce"** and **"Fernheim,"** as well as **"Another Face"**) are set in German-speaking countries and concern themselves with crises within marriage. During his time in Germany, Agnon had close access to the ideas of Freud while he was writing the story. Indeed, as Barzel (1975, p. 64) points out,

> Certainly one should not relate to Agnon the exclusive following of one psychological approach or another, out of an attempt to imitated it. On the other hand Agnon knew well the spirit of Vienna and was influenced by the modes of thinking, and also by the ways of symbology of Freud and his followers.

Freudian interpretation has been successfully applied to Agnon's work by scholars such as Aberbach (1984) and Shryboim (1977). Agnon originally dedicated the story of **"Another Tallit"** to Max Eitington, who was a loyal disciple of Freud, and who organized in 1933 a Palestinian Psychoanalytic Society.

It is noteworthy that when **"Another Face"** first appeared in Dabar in 1932, it included the following passage which Agnon later omitted: "after (Michael) finished telling her his dream . . . (Toni's) . . . eyes became somewhat wet. Michael was grateful to her for her not interpreting his dream according to Freud and his School." By telling us why Michael was grateful, the narrator simultaneously reminds us of Freudian symbolism, with which he is obviously acquainted. Toni's eyes becoming wet is a statement to which Freud (1953, 5, pp. 358, 359) would give a Freudian significance, Feldman refers to the "sexual" connotations of the key-motif in Agnon's **"A Quest for the Night,"** and she thinks that Agnon is quite explicit in his use of dream symbolism, to the point that "he almost challenges the reader to go beyond the obvious in his search for an integrating reading" (1985, pp. 266, 267).

This paper does not intend to be conclusive regarding all the objects and situations that may be interpreted sexually in **"Another Face."** My intent is to point out a possible interpretation of Agnon which may enrich the reader's experience of Agnon's short stories and novels. Some critics hinted in passing at the possibility of giving a

sexual interpretation to some objects in Agnon's **"Another Face."** I intend to demonstrate that this possibility is much more substantial than Agnon criticism has so far considered it to be. Freudian symbols become a device to portray characters and their inner life and relations through an interplay between the conscious reader and the narrator on the one hand and, on the other, the characters who are (in the final version of the story) unconscious of the implications of some of their actions and objects.

2. THE CHARACTERS' PERSONAL EFFECTS

Agnon emphasizes various personal effects that Toni and Hartmann carry with them. Toni's dress, parasol, handbag, and bottle of scent, and Michael's hat, cigarettes, cigars, and cigar-knife, for example, become prominent in the short story. Freud deals in his work with some of these objects. It is noteworthy that, according to Freud himself (1953, 5, p. 685), these symbols are not confined to dreams; objects such as umbrellas ("the opening of this last being comparable to an erection" [5, p. 354]) and knives may stand for the male organ. (5, pp. 358-59; also p. 380 and pp. 683-84).

One of the objects that is mentioned in Agnon's **"Another Face"** is the parasol. The reader first notices the parasol when Dr. Tanzer and Svirsh, the two single bachelors who lust for Toni, welcome her as she leaves the judge's house:

> Svirsh took the parasol, hung it from her belt and, taking both her hands in his, swung them affectionately back and forth (1967, p. 4).

Svirsh's swinging back and forth of Toni's hands and his hanging her parasol from her belt denote sexual feelings. In this context it is noteworthy that the narrator makes frequent reference to parts of the body such as hands, thumbs, arms, mouths, lips and tongues (1953, 5, p. 359). Freud contends that the male's organ may be represented by his hand or foot, the female's by mouth, ear or even an eye. Undoubtedly, hands and arms are sexually significant in the short story. Indeed, Svirsh's and Tanzer's confident gestures (1967, pp. 4, 6) indicate merely selfish lust; for Toni is to them an object of sexual fantasies; Michael's graceless and uncertain gestures (pp. 4, 16, 17, 19), though, combine sexual desire and love. In portraying Toni as a good listener, the narrator describes her active silence: she listens, she looks, she thinks (p. 8). But her hand and arm motions are activated by men; she is passive. In other of Agnon's love stories, there are substantial obstacles to fulfilling love; but Tanzer and Svirsh do not constitute such an obstacle at all. Svirsh's lust is explicitly depicted by the narrator through the use of Free Indirect Speech and the symbolic use of Toni's parasol. Later (p. 11), in a moment of mutual attraction between Toni and Michael, Michael was busy dealing with his hat while Toni was busy fussing with the parasol. And Michael, desiring his ex-wife, makes gestures in the air as Toni, desiring her ex-husband, pokes the ground with her parasol (p. 17). Barzel (1975, pp. 63-64) correctly finds the parasol to be a male object while the ground is a female one. Toni's act with the parasol moves Hartmann because it reflects his own erotic excitement. Toni and Michael then arrive at an inn where they decide to dine. Michael is worried that his wife is aware of his sexual thoughts. He "took her parasol, laid it on a chair, placed his hat on top of it . . ." (p. 23). Hartmann's unconscious wish is that he will be able to accomplish his desires as simply as he was able to put his hat on Toni's parasol. At dinner, Toni's appetite (p. 24) represents her love for Michael and her frustrated desire for him. But Hartmann rejects her again: he "got up, took his hat and said: 'Let's go'" (p. 32). This time Hartmann does not deal with the parasol himself: "The waiter came up and handed Toni her parasol . . ." (p. 32). One concludes that Tanzer, Svirsh, Hartmann and Toni express hidden desire as they handle the parasol, and it indeed plays the same role as Freud's umbrella.

The appearance of a parasol in the story is often coupled with the appearance of the hat. Freud states that "a woman's hat can very often be interpreted with certainty as a genital organ, and moreover, as a man's" (1953, 5, pp. 355-56; see also pp. 360-62). The reader first notices the hat in **"Another Face"** when Svirsh and Tanzer are defeated by Michael. "Waving his hat, [Tanzer] walked off . . ." The word in Hebrew is *henip,* which can be translated as "waving" or "lifting" the hat. Tanzer doffs his hat and admits the loss of the sexual object. Now Toni and Michael are left alone. Michael is attracted to his ex-wife, and he is embarrassed: "He crumpled his hat and waved it about, smoothed its creases, crumpled it again, put it back on his head, and passed his hands over his temples down to his chin" (Agnon, 1967, p. 6). These helpless gestures with the hat, coupled with Michael's self-conscious avoidance of her eyes, indicate Michael's strong longing and sexual desire for his ex-wife. In another moment of confusion, when Hartmann is thinking about his separation and divorce, the narrator describes his feelings and his gestures: ". . . he removed his hat, mopped his brow, wiped the leather band inside his hat and put it back on his head" (p. 10). The hat serves as a refuge for Michael, who has a hard time facing his new status as a divorced man, and represents his desire for his ex-wife. Michael now learns that he cannot accomplish this desire as simply as he was able to put his hat on Toni's parasol (p. 23).

Critics have noticed the parasol and the hat; however, they have ignored their sexual implications. Goldberg (1963, pp. 213, 217, 218), Tochner (1965, p. 32; 1968, p. 99), and Kenani (1977, p. 491) emphasized the awkward, hopeless, repetitive and confused nature of Hartmann's unconscious gestures with his hat. Rivlin (1969, pp. 120-21) thinks that the parasol is Toni's support and protection. Tochner is aware of the longing and sexual desires between Toni and Hartmann (1968, p. 98), but does not substantiate his claim. Barzel (1982, p. 59) thinks that the parasol is "a combined expression of canopy, defense and erotic symbol." While I am not in disagreement with these statements, it seems to me that the sexual roles of the hat and the parasol are important to the

interpretation and the enjoyment of the text. The characters do not act out of conscious sexual urges; they do not ask themselves why they do what they do with the hat or the parasol. However, the narrator and the reader "must" be aware of those urges.

Additional phallic symbols in the story are cigars, cigarettes, a pipe and a cigar-knife. The story describes Michael's efforts during a frustrating marriage to find a satisfactory substitute for love. Michael tries friendship, reading books, and smoking "cigarettes first, then cigars" (Agnon, 1967, p. 14) as a means of fulfilling his unsatisfactory life. On the day of the divorce, Toni and Michael go the fields from the town to an inn. In a moment of attraction to Toni, Michael thinks about smoking (p. 18), but now he is self-conscious and the cigarette cannot satisfy his desires. After dinner Michael "took out a cigar and trimmed it with his knife then took out a pack of cigarettes and offered one to Toni. They sat opposite one another, the smoke they made rising and mingling . . . Toni parted the smoke with her fingers and went on smoking contentedly" (p. 28). Unlike the lonely, isolated smoking at home during their marriage, now Hartmann and Toni in a moment of good feeling and positive communication, smoke in a way which is satisfying for them both, and their smoke mingles. Michael's knife should not be disregarded (Freud, 1953, 5, pp. 358-60; also pp. 380, 683-84); nor should we ignore the fire of the phallic symbols of the cigar and the cigarettes (5, pp. 384, 395).

It is heavily symbolic and rather humorous that Michael, who was so desirous of his ex-wife, had to leave her room in the inn, in which there was "a broken horn with a bridal wreath on it" (Agnon, 1967, p. 36). Michael's desires for a renewed marriage end at this stage with a "broken horn." When the old man stated that there was only one room free, "Toni blushed. Michael crumpled his hat and said nothing" (p. 36). We have a detailed description of the way the innkeeper deals with his pipe prior to suggesting that Toni will sleep in the only available room and Michael on the billiard table.

Toni's blushing, Michael's crumpling of his hat, the innkeeper's knocking the pipe against the table (which "represents the approximate shape of the male organ" [Freud, 1953, 4, p. 86]), the innkeeper's putting his thumb into the pipe's bowl—all of these are sexually significant acts. There is one attractive woman and two lonely men. I disagree with Barzel (1975, p. 58), who claims that Toni's blushing is due here to her bashfulness and not to her erotic attraction to her husband. Simirman (1962, p. 18, 21-22) recognizes Michael's desire for his ex-wife, arguing, though, that the closer Michael gets to his ex-wife the more distant she becomes. I disagree with Simirman's analysis of Toni's feelings, in that it ignores the mutual attraction indicated by Toni's blushing and Michael's playing with his hat. Michael starts his life as a divorced man by sleeping on a public gaming table (billiard table), made for a game composed of balls, holes, and sticks rather than in the bed, once consecrated to him and his wife by marriage. His grotesque position is indicative of the fact that his sexual desires cannot be resolved without resolution of his relationship. There is another table in the story: When over dinner Michael started telling Toni his dream, sharing his intimate thoughts with his ex-wife, he put the cigar down (Agnon, 1967, p. 38) while communicating with his wife. Now that his wife is asleep and he is alone again, he thinks again about smoking, a thought that is encouraged by the thick cigar under the table, which itself is a symbol of a woman (Freud, 1953, pp. 355, 374, 376, 381).

In a moment of mutual attraction and self-awareness between Toni and Michael, Toni wets her hands, which is another act with a Freudian (1953, 5, p. 403) meaning: "Toni opened her handbag, took out a bottle of scent, and sprinkled her hands with it" (Agnon, 1967, p. 18). Freud calls attention to hollow objects such as handbags. According to Freud, "Boxes, cases, chest, cupboards and ovens represent the uterus . . ." (1953, 5, 354; also p. 373, regarding "purse").

When Toni and Michael returned to the garden of the inn, their attraction is mutual as Kenani pointed out (1977, p. 492), and it is reflected by the landscape described as they walk in the field after dinner.

Several times in the story Michael "wanted to take off his jacket and wrap it around Toni" (Agnon, 1967, p. 34). The original Hebrew text speaks of *me il,* which is a "coat" or "overcoat." Michael's awareness of Toni's being cold is coupled with his erotic attraction to her, and the overcoat becomes a male symbol here (Freud, 1953, 4, pp. 186, 204; 5, p. 365).

In the opening sentence of the story, the narrator mentions Toni's brown dress (Agnon, 1967, p. 4). He later draws attention to it in erotic contexts (pp. 12, 14, 22, 26, 34). Her dress stimulates Michael's thought about her nakedness.

3. THE FIELDS AND THE GARDEN

After their divorce Toni and Michael walk in the fields from their town to a garden of an inn. The setting is rich with Freudian meaning: they are sitting at a table in a garden near a gate; the garden is full of birds and fruit trees; they discuss rooms, dancing and an oven. On their way to the inn, Toni thought (p. 20) that the light of the inn was a firefly. The lights of the firefly are the courting strategies of the female and male fireflies. On their way to the inn, Toni is chilled by the wind:

'Are you cold?' Hartmann asked anxiously.

'I think I see people coming.'

'There is no one here,' said Hartmann, 'but perhaps . . .'

They should not be touching each other after their divorce, a transgression against Jewish law (see *Mishna Gittin* 8, 9, and also Rivlin, 1969, p. 110). Toni evades Michael's inquiry about her being cold, then she points

out a tall person: "A man with a ladder came towards them." Toni blushes now not because Tanzer is taller than Hartmann, as Kenani contends (1977, p. 492), but because of the erotic atmosphere, strengthened by the ladder as a Freudian element (1953, 5, p. 355). At this time, Toni and Hartmann do not communicate verbally. However, this interchange does not seem to be a failure in communication, but rather a display of timidity about their sexual attraction.

Ewen (1971, pp. 292-93) thinks that here Toni and Michael become distanced. Toni's lowering her eyes and blushing and the abortive conversation are taken by Ewen as an example of a "dialogue" without any real communication. This opinion seems to stem from ignoring the intense attraction and sexuality between Hartmann and Toni. Indeed the sexual excitement that marks this part of the story (Agnon, 1967, pp. 20-22) is unmistakable, when one pays attention to the sexual symbols and situations: Hartmann's anxiety regarding Toni being chilled by the wind, her indirect answer, his incomplete sentence, the tall man with the ladder who lit the lamp, Toni's blushing and lowering her eyes, Hartmann's smiles, the boy and the girl, and Toni looking at her ring and remembering that she is no longer married to Hartmann and that physical contact is now forbidden between them. The narrator here draws our attention to the progress in understanding the attraction between Michael and Toni, not to the alleged regression in their newly developed communication. Because of such moments, the reader understands that Toni and Michael have discovered another face in themselves, in their relations, and in each other as man-husband and woman-wife. After walking in the field, Toni and Michael see a restaurant (p. 22):

> A little later they came to a garden which was fenced
> on three sides. The gate was opened and to the right of
> it shone a lamp. Some smaller lanterns in the shape of
> pears and some apples hang from the trees in the garden.

We are then introduced to a girl who pulls at her skirt when they enter the garden of the inn, and Hartmann thinks that the girl is red-haired and freckled. Talking about the girl (pp. 22, 24) as red-headed with freckles is a way to evade his sexual thoughts about the girl and his wife. The girl appears again when she passes by "carrying a basket of plums with both hands. The juice of the overripe plums exuded an odor of cloying sweetness" (p. 26). Unlike Simirman, (1962, pp. 17, 19), it is my opinion that Hartmann's desire is for his wife, and not just any woman.

Freud discusses gardens (1953, 5, p. 346), fruits (1953, 4, p. 287; 5, pp. 372-73), gates (5, p. 346), trees, wood, etc., as well as keys and locks (5, p. 354) as sexual symbols. When Toni and Michael first enter the garden, "which was fenced on three sides," its "gate was open" (Agnon, 1967, p. 22). After they leave the inn, they come back to it and "Hartmann pushed the gate open and they went up the stone steps" (p. 34). He is full of erotic desires for his wife and her garden, hoping to consummate their renewed relations by sleeping with her. In this context the stone steps and the act of ascending them also have

Freudian significance; the shape of apples (1953, 4, p. 287) or of pears (4, p. 372). As Hartmann anticipates his meal in the inn's garden, it is clear that he is feeling the demands of his sexual appetites as well, he expects "fresh dishes" (Agnon, 1967, p. 24). The sexual connotation is that Toni has now become "fresh" in his eyes.

Leiter (1970, pp. 63-64) refers to various paragraphs in the story, such as the boy running with a lighted stick, the gesture of Hartmann with his thumbs, the flowers, the falling from the mount, and the wire, and he traces them to the Talmud (*Berakot* 51-53, 53a, 55b; *Gittin* 66a, 81, 90b). This seems to me a significant contribution to understanding the story without lessening the weight of the sexual symbology.

A bird plays an interesting role in this story. While Toni and Michael were eating, they listened to a song of a bird. Toni's face grew prettier, and Hartmann covered his knees with his napkin (Agnon, 1967, p. 24). Now they are content and attracted to each other. The bird's song is indicative of Michael's sexual excitement (Freud, 1953, 5, pp. 583-84). However, when Hartmann later thinks that divorcing his wife was a clever act, he listens neither to his wife's question about the bird nor to the "bird"; nor does he need to cover his knees any more. In Hartmann's dream the "frozen birds" (Agnon, 1967, p. 30) represent a breakdown in warmth and communication in the family.

Toni and Hartmann walk back toward the city. They come close to a river (p. 32), and the river now plays a role in the story: the stream lulling in its bed, the cry of the bird of prey, the echo reverberating through the ear, the waves raising themselves up and falling back exhausted, the stream rocking itself wearily—all this rhythmic motion happens in a moment of mutual desire between Toni and Hartmann. In general, nature in the story is described in a way which reflects the moods and relations of the characters.

We also meet the girl who sold Michael a bunch of asters (p. 10). The reader is told that Toni had always been fond of asters (pp. 24, 26). The flowers are cared for when Toni and Hartmann communicate and are attracted to each other, and they are thrown into the grass (p. 32) when Hartmann starts having negative thoughts about his wife and decides to leave the garden. Freud mentions flowers in various places and points out "that sexual flower symbolism . . . symbolizes the human organs of sex by blossoms . . . It may perhaps be true in general that gifts of flowers between lovers have this unconscious meaning" (1953, 5, p. 376).

4. THE DREAM AND THE MOUND

After dinner in the garden of the inn, Hartmann tells Toni about his dream. Various objects play an interesting role in the dream: the apartment, the dance-like walk of the landlady, the oven, the bedrooms, the study, the birds, the windows, and the walls. Coffin (1982, pp. 187-98) took into account Freudian notions in her important analysis of the dream. She pointed out the erotic aspects of the dream, including objects which are associated with sexual feminine attributes and are identified as such by Freud. Band has already explained this dream, as well as other central aspects of the story (1968, pp. 251-60).

Freud refers to rooms, apartments and houses in many places. "Rooms in dreams are usually women" (1953, 5, p. 354). Freud writes that an oven is representative of the uterus (5, pp. 354, 634), "the 'smooth' walls are men . . ." (5, p. 355).

It seems reasonable then to interpret the landlady in the dream as representative of Toni. In the bedroom, Hartmann had an oven (Toni). Only by completely sharing his life, including his work, with his wife could Hartmann feel the warmth of the "oven" outside the bedroom. His ambivalent attitude toward Toni finds an expression. Toni's defects may simply be in Hartmann's mind. In his dream, he understands that he has a nice apartment (wife, woman, Toni—"*'Ištô zô bêtô. Mah dîrā? 'Iš vĕ ištô.*") ("his wife is his home", and "what is home?" "It is a man and his wife") and he does not need to "change it for another" (Agnon, 1967, p. 30), i.e.—for divorce and another marriage.

Hartmann's desire to climb the mound may be interpreted by Freud (1953, 5, pp. 406-7, 410) as a sexual desire. Now Hartmann remembers an event from his childhood: he once climbed a mound, then slipped and rolled down to the bottom; "his limbs had felt relaxed" (Agnon, 1967, p. 42). Kenani (1977, p. 499) claims that this depicts Hartmann's longing for death. It seems to me that Hartmann simply longed for the womb (see Freud, 1953, 5, pp. 399-400). Now that he remembers his childhood, Hartmann is seized by a fear of falling. His panic is portrayed by content, by repetition of words, and by syntax which affects the fast rhythm (Agnon, 1967, p. 40). But he quickly understands that the fear of falling has had a stronger impact on his life than the actual falling would have had, and he now sees dangers and risk in proportion; he does not have to live as egocentrically as before, and he will no longer be paralyzed by fear.

Freud (1953, 5, p. 356) discusses wooded hills and the symbolic landscape which includes a path into a thick wood leading up to a hill of grass and brashwood (5, p. 366). In discussing dreams of falling, Freud finds connection to anxiety and to erotic desires (5, pp. 394-95).

Now that Hartmann can relate to his fears in a rational manner, there is a chance for him to communicate better; and, indeed, after understanding his dream of the mound, he starts seeing Toni in his imagination (Agnon, 1967, pp. 42-44). The arm, the red face, the asters, the parasol, the fingers, and the cigarette smoke are all united in a romantic way. The story ends with good memories, compassion, and attraction between them with the optimistic indication that Toni and Hartmann may again be husband and wife. Perry and Sternberg (1968, pp. 286-387) think that only someone who is "thirsty for sensation" can be interested in the question of what happened to this marriage. Many sensitive readers, however, concern themselves with this question. The ending is undoubtedly a renewal of the family. In Agnon's *A Guest for the Night* (1967, pp. 391-92; 1968, p. 418), the narrator says: ". . . one day (Hartmann) gave his wife a divorce, but as they left the rabbi's house he fell in love with her again and took her back." Fictional characters are talked about by the characters in other works of fiction as if they are part of reality, and the author presumes that he is addressing a reader who is intimately familiar with the author's entire work. Hartmann was not a Cohen. I am not in agreement with Leiter, who thinks that "Hartmann's dream of reconciliation is foredoomed" (1970, p. 61) and that "symbolic night" settles over the relations of Toni and Michael (pp. 61, 64). The crisis forced Hartmann to re-evaluate his relations. In the closing paragraph, Hartmann's face gets red merely thinking about his pretty wife. All her "shortcomings in no way detracted from her" (Agnon, 1967, p. 42). Several actions and objects (asters, parasol, fingers, cigarette smoke) which we perceived as erotic are now combined in Hartmann's mind as sources for his attraction and his compassion to Toni.

5. CONCLUSION

By paying attention to sexual symbols in **"Another Face,"** we gain a better capacity to enrich ourselves. We, of course, presume that the characters in the last version of the story are unconscious of the symbolism of their actions and their surroundings; however, their repressed wishes achieve a certain satisfaction through these symbolic patterns. Symbols help the reader to understand the characters' unconscious motivations, enrich the reader's aesthetic experience of the work and fulfill the demands of the text. Some of Agnon's other works will similarly yield rich layers of meaning to the reader who considers their clear sexual symbolism. It is my contention that while Agnon's works are not rich with explicit sexual scenes, they are loaded with sexuality and sensuality which are alluded to in various powerful ways. Sexuality can be understood in Agnon's works only by looking closely at actions, motions, objects, and settings. If this symbolic interpretation is done, the reader will find Agnon a sensuous author, expressing human sexual urge and giving it an expression which requires the imagination and the understanding of the reader.

Works Cited

Aberbach, David. 1984. *At the Handles of the Lock.* Oxford.

Agnon, S. Y. 1932. *"Panîm 'aherôt."* In *Dabar* Dec. 12, 1932.

———. 1957. "Metamorphosis." Translated by I. Schen in "A Whole Loaf," pp. 139-62. Ed. S. J. Kahn. New York.

———. 1966. "Metamorphosis." In *'Ôrôt: Journal of Hebrew Literature,* 1: 11-41.

———. 1967. "Another Face." In *Modern Hebrew Stories.* pp. 2-45. Ed. Ezra Spicehandler. Bantam.

———. 1968. *A Guest for the Night.* New York.

———. 1970. "Metamorphosis." In *Twenty One Stories,* pp. 111-34. Ed. Nahum N. Glatzer. New York.

———. 1976. "Panim 'aherôt" in *Kol kitbê Šemûel Yôsep 'Agnôn* vol. 3, pp. 449-68. Tel Aviv.

———. 1976. *Ôreah nata lalûn* in *Kol kitbê Šemûel Yôsep 'Agnôn.* 4 Vol. Tel Aviv.

Amir-Coffin, Edna. 1982. "A Dream as a Literary Device in Agnon's Metamorphosis." *Hebrew Studies.* 23: 187-98.

Band, Arnold. 1968. *Nostalgia and Nightmare.* University of California.

Barzel, Hillel. 1975. *Sippûrê 'ahaba šel S. Y. 'Agnôn.* Tel Aviv.

———, ed. 1982. *Šemûel Yôsep 'Agnôn: mibhar Ma'amarîm 'al yesîratô.* 'Am 'Obed. Tel Aviv.

Cirlot, J. E. 1962. *A Dictionary of Symbols.* New York.

Eben-Zohar, Itamar. 1965. *'Iyyûnîm besiprût.* Jerusalem.

Ewen, Joseph. 1971. *Haddaialôg besippûre S. Y. 'Agnon vedarkê issûbô.* *Hassiprût* 3: 281-94.

Feldman, Yael S. 1985. "How does a Convention Mean? A Semiotic Reading of Agnon's Bilingual Key-Irony in 'A Guest for the Night'." *Hebrew Union College Annual* 56: 251-69.

Freud, Sigmund. 1953. *The Standard Edition of the Complete Psychological Works of Sigmund Freud.* Vols. 4 and 5. London.

Goldberg, Leah. 1963. *Panîm 'aherôt lešay 'Agnôn, 'omanût hassippûr,* pp. 204-22. Tel Aviv.

Golomb, Harai. 1968. *"Haddibbûr hammešullab—teknîka merkhazît Bapprôza 'el 'Agnôn: lefî hassippûr panîm 'aherôt."* *Hassiprût,* 1/2: 251-62.

———. 1968-69. *"Panîm merubbôt: 'al yahase haggômlîn ben hassippûr panîm 'aherôt le-'Agnôn Ubên kotartô."* *Hassiprût* pp. 717-18.

Hakak, Lev. 1973. *"Moṭîb hattarnegôl besippûr pašût le-'agnôn."* *Hassiprût.* vol. 4: 713-18.

———. 1976. *'Al haddibbûr hassamûy bemika'el šellî le'amôs ôz.* *Bissarôn* 324: 249-52, 263.

Harael-Fish, A. 1971. *Hammesapper kehôlem bekitbe 'Agnôn, 'iyyûn hašva'atî.* *Bikkoret Uparšanût* 4-5: 5-10.

Kenani, David. 1977. "Hartmann 'ô haharada," *Mibbayît,* pp. 69-95. Reprinted in: *Šemûel Yôsep 'Agnôn—Mibhar ma ma'amarîm 'al yesîratô,* pp. 481-500. ed. Hillel Barzel, 1982. Tel Aviv.

Leiter, Samuel. 1970. "The Face Within the Face—A Reading of S. Y. Agnon *Panim Aheroṭ*" in *Judaism,* 19: 59-65. Reprinted in: *Selected Stories of S. Y. Agnon,* pp. 183-91. ed. by Leiter, Samuel. New York.

Perry, Menahem and Meir, Sternberg. 1968. *"Hammelek bemabbat 'irônî: 'al tahbûlôtav šel hammesapper besippûr davîd ubatšeba' ubište haplagôt latte'aoria šel happrôza."* *Hassiprût,* 1/2: 286-87.

Preminger, Alex, ed. 1965. *Princeton Encyclopedia of Poetry and Poetics.* pp. 833-36. Princeton.

Rivlin, A. 1969. *Mapteah dîdaqtî lehôra'at Hassippûr Haqqasar.* Tel Aviv.

Šofman, Geršon. 1968. *Kol kitbe G. Šofman,* Tel Aviv.

Shryboim, Debora. 1977. *Halômôt umabba'aîm demûye halômôt bayyesîrôt hassiprûtiyyôt šel 'Agnôn.* Dissertation, Tel Aviv University.

Simirman, David. 1962. *'Al šeloša missippûre 'Agnôn. 'Iyyûnîm.* Jerusalem.

Tochner, Mešullam. 1965. *Sûrôt ve'emsa'îm 'aestetiyyîm besippûre 'Agnôn.* Jerusalem.

———. 1968. *Pešer 'Agnôn.* Ramat-Gan.

Yair Mazor (essay date 1986)

SOURCE: "S. Y. Agnon's Art of Composition: The Befuddling Turn of the Compositional Screw," in *Hebrew Annual Review*, Vol. 10, 1986, pp. 197-208.

[*In the following essay, Mazor uses the stories "Between Two Cities" ("Ben sete 'arim") and "Two Scholars Who Lived in Our Town" ("Sne talmide hakamim sehayu be 'irenu") to demonstrate that Agnon sometimes employs puzzling narrative structure and plot development as conscious strategies.*]

1. Preamble

A remarkably intriguing aspect in S. Y. Agnon's art of composition is that in a considerable number of his works, the reader is confronted by a strikingly confusing organization. As the story's plot seems to reach its climax and move toward its denouement, and all the conflicts of the fictional world face resolution, an unexpected, intrusive plot development is presented, which disrupts the natural concluding momentum of the piece and forces seemingly arbitrary continuation. The confused reader is forced to surmise that the writer (or implied author, following W. C. Booth, *The Rhetoric of Fiction* 1961) has clumsily violated his own aesthetics by inserting unrelated material into his story and consequently upset the story's composition, undermined its integrity, and subverted its coherence. Furthermore, the flimsy nature of the casual sequence is not exposed in the overture of the piece itself. Many of Agnon's stories deliberately lead the reader astray. Significant portions of the piece's expositional sequence goad the reader to assume a traditional plot causality. Only in a relatively late stage of the text continuum does the reader realize that he has been mislead; the commencing causal order is found to be only a thin veneer that conceals a "deep structure" which deviates from the surface causality, forming a disengaged sequence. But once the reader becomes thoroughly familiar with the nature of Agnon's structure, ideology and aesthetic rationale, however, he realizes that his *prima vista* was, in fact, erroneous; it was just a conscious authorial ploy perpetrated by Agnon. An examination of the composition in the piece and its literary motivation sheds new light upon the alleged compositional fallacy, which is an adroitly performed device that generates sophistication for the piece.

It is the aim of this paper to examine this attractive aspect of Agnon's compositional *ars poetica* through a close reading of two of his stories, ***"Bên šetê 'arîm"*** ("Between Two Cities") and ***"Šnê talmîdê hakamîm šehayû be 'îrênû"*** ("Two Scholars Who Lived in Our Town").

2. "Between Two Cities"—A Tale of Two Compositional Systems

In examining this story's composition, the apparent looseness of which is caused by the disruptive intrusion of an unexpected turn of plot, it is essential to summarize the fictional features of the two allegedly conflicting parts of the story. The story opens with a tale of two small towns located in a region in Bavaria. Both of the towns have the same name, Katsenau. One of them is rather grey and oppressed, a working-class town of little splendor. Among its population is a small Jewish congregation, consisting of shopkeepers. The other town is much more appealing, being a resort town famous for medical baths and springs that attract many people, especially in the summer. The distance between the two towns is not great, and many Jewish people from the less-attractive Katsenau indulge themselves on Sabbath by walking to the more attractive twin town. Here they escape their labors for a short while and enjoy the refreshing air and the animated beauty of the woods.

One day, during World War I, Isidor Shaltheiz, a Jewish teacher from Frankfurt, arrives in the resort of Katsenau for a vacation. He soon becomes idle and restless. He begins spending his hours walking, and one day he arrives at the neighboring, poorer Katsenau. This Katsenau is not as alluring as the resort-Katsenau, but its faded features are compensated for by the kindness of its Jewish congregation. When these generous people find out that the recuperating teacher has a family in the big city that is deprived of the good food they can easily provide, they give him parcels stuffed with delicious food to send to his family. (The fact that the recuperating teacher is pampering himself with dainties and idleness while his family lives in destitution is later poignantly juxtaposed.) One day, during his journeying between the two cities, the bored teacher begins to count his footsteps, trying to pass the time between meals. While counting his footsteps, the teacher realizes that the distance between the two cities exceeds the bounds of the Sabbath limit (in Hebrew: *Tehûm Šabbat*)—the prescribed distance Jewish people may not exceed on the Sabbath without violating the sacred laws of the Sabbath. The teacher feels that it is his duty to notify the Jewish congregation in Katsenau that their refreshing weekly walks to the baths of Katsenau should be strictly prohibited since they constitute a severe religious transgression. Subsequently, the Sabbath walks cease and the few enjoyable hours the hardworking Jewish people have are taken away. The teacher continues to relish the luxury of his daily walks and to accept food from the Jewish people, while they have lost their one pleasure in life. At this point, the story's woeful conclusion seems to be reached. The plot's climax, which is a typical anti-climax of the teacher's recompensive discovery, passes; the peripety has been committed and the plot moves toward its turning point. Still, an unexpected surprise awaits the reader.

The story does not end. Instead, it develops a continuation with a new channel. This unanticipated development becomes even more surprising as the reader learns that the new episode does not proceed from the previous events. On the contrary, its content seems to have no connection to the story's previous fictional trends. Thus, the impression of a loose composition seems a judicious criticism.

The unexpected addition deviates from the story's plot by concentrating on the grief-filled misfortunes that the war caused the people of the two cities. The vicissitudes of war, mentioned only obliquely in the story's first part, become prominent in the second. Thus, the excessive addition is, in fact, a major thematic element of the story's second part which has been anticipated in the first portion of the story. Hence, it may be considered a foreshadowing integrative element which knots the two detached story parts.

In the second part of the story, the reader becomes acquainted with the aggravating distress of the baker's family. The family's only son has volunteered for the war, despite his physical limitations; he was severely injured and lost both legs. From this point in the story, the blemished leg, or the *Oedi-pus* (in Greek, swell-foot), acts as a leading element in the story. The sister of the baker's wife lived in resort-Katsenau, but because of the amassed daily troubles, the two sisters are deprived of getting together. Here one encounters another integrative element that glues the story's parts together. In both the story parts, the short distance between the two cities is important and seems longer, because of the disturbing occurrences associated with the distance. Thus, the short distance between the two cities is extended far beyond its geographical measure. The two sisters decide to meet in the forest midway between the two cities. Once the reader is acquainted with the symbolic meaning of the forest in Agnon's works (for instance, Hershel, the chastised lover in *Simple Story* [*Sippûr pašût* in Hebrew] goes insane in the forest), he is aware that the forest usually symbolizes a place of impending danger or a pessimistic outcome. The fact that a dog's bark is echoing in the entangled thicket as the meeting is about to take place reinforces the premonition of doom; in Agnon's writings, evil is associated with the figure of the dog (note, for instance, the prominent role of the mad dog in *Temôl šilšôm* [*Yesterday Heretofore*]). When the baker's wife reaches the meeting place in the forest, she is disappointed because her sister has not yet appeared. Although her sister does arrive at the end, her anxiety is indeed well-founded.

Suspense in Agnon's *ars poetica* is manifested by the flood of late buses, postponed trains and tardy streetcars demonstrated in **"The Doctor and His Divorced Wife,"** *Šîrah*, **"The Last Bus"** and many other works. These suspenseful incidents are always associated with neglected opportunities, agonizing misadventures, crumbling relationships or other misfortunes.

It has been noted that references to the deficient leg are central to the story's second part. The leg motif extends to the sisters as well. The sister who is waiting in the forest runs impatiently to and fro or stands as if her legs are chained to the ground. It appears that almost all the legs' potential functions are enumerated in Agnon's description of her: "She was *stepping* to and fro, *returning* and *standing,* as if her *legs were bound* to the ground, and she didn't know why she was *standing* there and not *running* toward her sister as her heart was *running* and pining toward her."

Similar descriptions, saturated with references to legs, are repeated as the two sisters meet: "Were those her *legs* that were *running*? It was her heart that was *running* and her *legs* followed it." There are even more references to legs in the short, added chapter, but the most significant is the one that closes the story: "The day was fading . . . the two sisters were standing in mute silence. At last one turned in her place and the other turned in her place and between them the forest's trees blackened until the stars came out and lit the way for the two sisters . . . who just parted from each other for many days . . . as one walks to one side and the other walks to the other side."

The gloomy atmosphere that permeates the scene is excessively oppressive and not likely to be overlooked by the reader. Consequently, the leg references mentioned in this closing paragraph of the story are evidently "oedipal". Once the reader couples the leg references portraying the sisters' grim fortune with the opening reference to the soldier's felled legs, he is in a better position to diagnose the meaning of the disfigured leg metonym in the story's addition; it is a symbol of the character's woeful distress.

In contrast with many of Agnon's other stories in which the leg metonym functions as a symbol of an erotic deterioration (see Yael's limping leg in **"The Hill of Sand"** [*"Gib'at hahôl"*]; the lame woman in Hartman's dream in **"Different Faces"** [*"Panîm aherôt"*]; Manfred's torn and ripped shoes in *Šîrah*; the wooden leg of Mintshey, the rejected lover in *Simple Story* [*Sippûr pašût*] and more), Agnon deletes the sexual connotations of the legs metonym in **"Between Two Cities"** limiting its reference to human misfortune. Thus, Agnon's literary fabric is not arbitrary. He attentively selects and, in this case, remolds his symbols to adjust to the alternating literary needs.

However, the metonym of the leg, inserted in a context of distress, acts as a benchmark of the story's seemingly clumsy addition. Yet, Agnon's capacity to remold a common symbol with a new meaning in order to harmonize with new subject matter does not initially seem to account for the disrupted composition of the story or the disturbing gulf between its parts. But the fact is that it does, indeed.

The leg metonym has already been alluded to as the integrative element which binds the two story parts. The major source of the Jewish congregation's distress is caused by the sudden divulgence that the resort-Katsenau is beyond the Sabbath limit, and consequently the enjoyable walks to it on the Sabbath are forbidden. The unexpected prohibition of these walks means the town's people are deprived of even the humblest chance for pleasure in their hard lives. The act of walking is an obvious reference—though indirect—to the leg metonym. Thus, the misfortune of the Jewish community in the story's first part is conspicuously attached to the metonym of the marred leg. Furthermore, the story's second part is sprinkled with references to the marred-leg metonym (the amputated legs of the soldier, the two sisters' restlessly running legs, their feeling that their legs are confined to the ground, their sombre walking in two different directions) and the major thematic trends also relate the the marred-leg metonym (the agony of the baker's wife because of her only son's felled legs, and the deficiency of the two sisters' capacity to meet with each other despite the short distance between their two cities). All these factors make the analogous strands between the two parts of the story very tight.

In both parts of the story, the metonym of the marred leg permeates the heart of the characters' agony. The characters are deprived of their only feeble chance to gain life's joy: the prohibited Sabbath walking between the two cities conspicuously foreshadows the sisters' inability to walk between the two cities. Hence, the absence of a causal connection between the two parts of the story is fully compensated for by a cogent, analogous connection: the dominant thematic trend of each part is metaphorically reflected by that of the other. The integrity of the complete story is deftly maintained. Beyond the seemingly clumsy surface of loose organization, a sound inner unity is very much *in esse*.

The analogous metaphorical relationship between the two parts of the story is not limited to its composition; it is also harnessed to the major ideological goal of the story, which is the perpetual anguish that clings to human disunion. The two components of the analogous equation, the Jews' prohibited walk between the two cities in the first part and the sisters' avoided walk between the cities in the second, are both reflections of anguish caused by human disharmony.

The second part of the story, then, does not deviate from the trend of the first. On the contrary, it acts as a mirror that radiates and enriches the first part with another angle of presentation. The two parts of the story are actually identical sides of the same thematic coin, two literary standpoints for the same idea. The authorial ploy has been pulled off; the first impression of a disrupted composition is replaced with a dexterously spun organization. Thus, the tale of the two cities is a tale of two systems—one is anchored in the story's compositional structure and evokes a delusional impression of loose organization, while the other system is concealed in the story's foundation and solidifies both parts through a well-intertwined analogy. The story benefits from a sense of controlled harmony which helps its artistic integrity.

The conflicting trends of the two compositional systems prevent an undesirably rigid and mechanical relationship between the story's two parts. The deviation from a strict analogy, on the other hand, made possible by the seemingly loose compositional system, supplies the story with a rhetorical flexibility by bridling its tightness and inhibiting artificial impact. Consequently, a well-measured authenticity prevails in the story.

3. "Two Scholars Who Have Lived in Our Town": One Plus One Make One

Like **"Between Two Cities," "Two Scholars Who Have Lived in Our Town"** is founded upon two parts which

seem at odds with each other—the second part deviating from the first in terms of plot and focus. As in the previous case, the writer adds a second part which seems to display poor craftsmanship. This second part seems to disrupt the first part and, consequently, violate its coherence and subvert its integrity. But a close reading of the thematic trends within the story's two parts shows that the first impression of an unorganized piece is incorrect. The initial perception of a redundant and shaky composition, caused by a superfluous patch, gives way to a well-constructed composition.

The first part of the story is devoted to the tense conflict between two celebrated scholars, Rabbi Moshe-Pinchas and Rabbi Shlomo, in a small Jewish congregation. The differences between these two scholars is apparent in every facet of their beings. Rabbi Moshe-Pinchas is unattractive and has a coarse physique; he is moreover exceedingly meticulous, sullen, irascible and demonstrably unsocial. Rabbi Shlomo appears as the alter ego of Rabbi Moshe-Pinchas. Rabbi Shlomo is attractive, tolerant, highly social, tender and affable, and he possesses amicable manners. The unbridgeable gulf between them is reminiscent of the differences between Shammai and Hillel. [Shammai and Hillel were two leading scholars who conducted the Sanhedrin, an assembly of 71 ordained scholars, which was the supreme court and legislature during the Roman regime period in Israel during the last years of King Herod's reign and after his death (4 B.C.). Shammai gained his fame for being extremely severe in judgment, while Hillel gained his fame for his tolerant consideration.] Yet, despite their differences, a solid friendship thrives between them. Moshe-Pinchas' personal barrier prohibits others from getting close to him, but it seems to fade around Shlomo. Perhaps their differences yield attraction; perhaps their reciprocal scholarly excellence is the basis of their friendship. For whatever reason, the friendship between Moshe-Pinchas and Shlomo is evident.

However, friendship requires a delicate balance, and the relationship between Moshe-Pinchas and Shlomo deteriorates drastically. The cause of this decline seems fairly trivial, but it is sufficient to destroy their friendship forever. Oddly enough, the amicable Rabbi Shlomo seems to cause the clash. At the peak of a Talmudic debate, Moshe-Pinchas intones his arguments in a tempestuous manner, raising his voice and waving his arms furiously; this casts him in a rather ridiculous light. Attempting to pacify and calm down the agitated Moshe-Pinchas, Shlomo used an idiomatic expression which might be considered teasing. It is obvious that Shlomo has not intended to insult Moshe-Pinchas. On the contrary, he probably thought that a touch of humor would be a delicate way of sparing Moshe-Pinchas any embarrassment. But Moshe-Pinchas is profoundly hurt and perplexed; he blushes, holds his words, and returns dejectedly to his seat. After that moment, he refuses to speak to Shlomo. Despite the divine commandment, Moshe-Pinchas bears a grudge and seeks to take vengeance.

Countless attempts by Shlomo to gain Moshe-Pinchas' forgiveness are rejected; his constant appeal falls on deaf ears. The rift between the two prominent scholars, which occurs early in the plot, casts a shadow upon the subsequent events of the story's first part. Moreover, the unresolved split not only leaves its grim mark on the rest of the occurrences in the story's first part, it seems to mold the characters in this grief-ridden state. For instance, when Shlomo is elected to serve as the chief rabbi of a neighboring Jewish congregation, Moshe-Pinchas disrupts Shlomo's scholarly acceptance speech with insults, attempting to contradict Shlomo's arguments and to shame him. But Shlomo does not take vengeance. On the contrary, he continues to laud Moshe-Pinchas' scholarly virtues in an effort to win his forgiveness. Still, his mulish adversary denies and rejects him.

The feud between the town's two venerable spiritual leaders inspires all the events in the plot of the story's first part. Thus, Moshe-Pinchas turns down an appealing offer to serve as a chief rabbi in a neighboring Jewish congregation when he learns that Shlomo has recommended him. Also, Shlomo is invited to serve as a chief rabbi in his hometown, but he turns down the tempting offer since Moshe-Pinchas' signature can't be obtained for the commission.

Moshe-Pinchas' animosity toward Shlomo also produces a well-designed thematic composition. Occurrences involving Moshe-Pinchas and Shlomo are intermittently mentioned, always calling attention to their unmended quarrel. For each event that happens to Shlomo which is caused by his bitter antagonist, there is a counteroccurrence that happens to Moshe-Pinchas which is effected by his grudge against Schlomo.

This well-coordinated equation of theme and composition is underscored by another equation in the story's first part, the inverted character pattern—a pattern founded upon a chiasmic motion. Shlomo's success is balanced inversely by Moshe-Pinchas' deterioration. As Shlomo ascends, becomes more esteemed, respected and famous, Moshe-Pinchas descends, declines and ultimately is excommunicated. The conflict between the two equations of the story's first part—a well-coordinated balance versus a chiasmic-reverse balance—defines an important thematic-ideological function as it evokes a sense of a split that reflects the split between the distinguished scholars, a split which injects a biting gloom in both their lives, drains their spiritual potency, and consequently deprives their congregations of full inspiration. Thus, the split between the two equations radiates the essence of the story's prevailing idea—the devastating power of a senseless feud and the powerful role of irrationality in human life.

The conflicting nature of the two equations is of rhetorical merit also, as it evokes a sense of authentic flexibility and prevents an undesirably rigid and mechanical effect. Thus, an effective dialectical pattern is obtained. On one hand, the two equations reinforce the composition of the story's first part as they yield compositional firmness. On the other hand, the conflicting trends of these two equations block a rigid stiffness by deviating from the tight compositional firmness.

The withdrawal of Moshe-Pinchas from the story's arena seems to violate the composition of the story and dismiss the story's major conflict—its dramatic essence. Moshe-Pinchas' death should move the story toward its conclusion. The nature of the split between the two scholars produces a paratactic sequence. From a theoretical standpoint, Moshe-Pinchas' enduring hostility toward Shlomo could produce an endless, horizontal sequence that lacks an ascending principle capable of extricating the plot from the sequential momentum and channelling it toward a climax. Theoretically, more and more fictional components (occurrences between Moshe-Pinchas and Shlomo) could join this horizontal continuum without drawing it closer to a climactic resolution. In this vein, Moshe-Pinchas' death plays the role of *deus ex machina,* or redeeming element which relieves the plot of its enduring momentum, disrupts the paratactical continuum and propels the plot toward its conclusion. The lack of a natural, inner extricating mechanism to deliver the culminating point of the fictional sequence is fully compensated for by the invasion of this external component, forcing a finale upon the plot by disregarding its most fundamental trend.

In spite of this, the story does not climax with Moshe-Pinchas' death, but evolves into an extended continuation. Furthermore, this unexpected continuation seems to abuse a leading thematic track in the story's first part. Shlomo's undeniably firm authority in the story's first part is severely shaken in the second. Though he is far from being completely powerless, he is certainly enfeebled. Thus, continuing the story after it seemed to reach its ultimate conclusion, and by patching a second part which violates a major thematic trend in the first part, appears questionable and upsetting. However, as with the story previously discussed, this impression of a poor composition is unjust: the seemingly botched composition is prudently motivated by sense, idea and well-wrought aesthetics.

The demise of Shlomo's authority seems to be an outgrowth of his reluctance to abandon justice for the sake of the brazen demands of the congregational members who wish to dominate and exploit weaker members. More than once, Shlomo is exposed to the impudence of the sanctimonious disputants, who openly display their disfavor and seek to subvert his position by insolent brawls. Yet Shlomo refuses to compromise his moral values.

Oddly enough, this grave situation comes into existence after Shlomo's arch rival, Moshe-Pinchas, has passed away. One would expect that Shlomo's foes would fade since his mighty adversary is no longer there to support their impertinence. Still, they are most insolent. Their denigration is no more than a delusion which will be fully deciphered in light of the comprehensive interpretation of the story, as the underlying knot between its two conflicting parts is united.

The relative demise of Shlomo's authority seems to be translated into compositional concepts. As already mentioned, the story's first part exhibits a compact, solid composition.

In the second part of the story, the undermining of Shlomo's authority is expressed by the crumbling of the composition. Attempts by the powerful, dissatisfied rivals to demolish Shlomo's authority, moving demonstrations of Shlomo's gracious attitude toward the late Moshe-Pinchas' family, the decline of Shlomo's health and his refusal to act as a chief rabbi in his old hometown are all plot fragments that bespeak a shattered, fragmentary composition.

Thus, the deterioration of Shlomo's authority is piously mirrored in the compositional layer, which widens the seemingly unbridged gulf between the story's two halves. Another difficulty is that as long as Moshe-Pinchas lived, Shlomo's other adversaries didn't dare threaten him. A strong support for Shlomo could easily have been raised. But once this support, Moshe-Pinchas, was no longer available, the opponents of Shlomo mysteriously began to offend and insult him.

The nature of this engimatic paradox challenges the reader to decode its concealed rationale. Accordingly, this paradox is the clue to solving the riddle of the perplexing relationships between the story's parts. The reciprocity evoked by two adversary forces engaged in a perpetual conflict produces a balanced parallelogram of forces, which is related in both thematic and compositional strategies of the story's first part. But when Moshe-Pinchas passed away, the tightly balanced parallelogram of forces is nullified. This parallelogram's nullification earns a literary reflection in the story's second part: the well-coordinated theme and composition that characterize the story's first part are countered by a fragmentary theme and composition in the story's second part. The splintered theme and composition of the story's second part flows from the ending of the story's first part—Moshe-Pinchas' death, which upsets the parallelogram of forces. Hence, the story's unity is dexterously maintained by a causal mending of its two parts. The story's seemingly disparate parts generate a solid integrity: one plus one makes one. The aesthetic features of a literary work of art may inform its ideological message. The bisected portrait of the story presents two polar positions in an ageless conflict that everlastingly haunts human life. The conflict may manifest itself as embittered, mordant, caustic, and yet somehow impressively august, like the conflict between Shlomo and Moshe-Pinchas in the story's first part. On the other hand, the conflict may manifest itself as mean-spirited, loathsome and ignominious, like the conflict inflamed by Shlomo's impertinent rivals in the story's second part. The pattern of everlasting human conflict is the constant; the variable is the specific human expression of those engaged in the conflict.

In this vein, the halved portrait of the story aims to portray the essence of *la condition humaine*; it draws together the potential, different poles of the eternal human conflict—the lofty and the base. As in the previously examined story, the first impression of a remissly patched composition does not lead one astray in vain: it draws the reader's attention to the aesthetic and ideological undercurrents of the piece. Agnon's befuddling turn of the compositional screw is highly shrewd indeed.

Naomi Sokoloff   (essay date 1988)

SOURCE: "Passion Spins the Plot: Agnon's 'Forevermore'," in *Tradition and Trauma: Studies in the Fiction of S. J. Agnon*, edited by David Patterson and Glenda Abramson, Westview Press, 1994, pp. 9-26.

[*In the following essay, Sokoloff asserts that the plot of* Forevermore (Ad 'olam), *which features "repetition, circularity, episodic fragmentation of narrative line, and disconnected events," is intended by Agnon to lend irony to the ostensible progress made by the protagonist.*]

Agnon's **Forevermore (Ad 'olam)**, a short story riddled with ironies and contradictions, features as its protagonist a scholar who has single-mindedly devoted twenty years to researching the history of an ancient city, Gumlidata. Having completed his work and finally found a publisher for his study, Adiel Amzeh suddenly discovers the existence of a previously unknown manuscript on his topic. Held in the possession of a nearby leper colony, this document beckons Amzeh, who yearns to clarify a puzzling detail about the final siege of the city. Renouncing his long-awaited opportunity for public recognition, the scholar repairs to the leper house and examines the manuscript. Reading and rereading with rapt fascination, Amzeh remains among the lepers forevermore.

A noble quest for knowledge despite adverse circumstances, or a foolhardy loss of perspective? Both interpretations have been offered to account for Adiel Amzeh's actions. The claim for purity of vision, which draws its inspiration from a traditional midrashic image, relies in part on a perception of the Jews in their devotion to Torah as an isolated people, degraded in exile, and spurned among the nations. Many critics, indeed, have seen in this story an allegory built around the protagonist's name, which means "this people, an adornment to God." The letters *'ayin* and *gimmel,* which appear recurrently as initial letters of names, have been seen as dividing the characters into groups of good and evil figures. Also working for the positive interpretation of Amzeh's predicament, a number of explicit comments made by the narrator and the secondary characters lend credence to the idea of noble sacrifice. Wisdom herself, personified, whispers in Amzeh's ear, "Sit my love, sit and do not leave me." But then again, is this a figure of purity or an emblem of seduction luring the scholar to false values?

A number of compelling factors counteract the pro-Amzeh arguments. First, the book that Amzeh pursues is not holy scripture, but rather description of a highly repugnant, idolatrous society devoid of redeeming spiritual values or law. Further deflecting power away from the sympathetic reading is Amzeh's characterization, which more closely resembles caricature than hagiography and which shows him to be ludicrously obsessed by an idée fixe. Moreover, those letters so crucial to distinguishing good from bad are sometimes scrambled, like the virtuous and wicked qualities of the characters themselves. Finally there is no pat distinction and no simple allegory so much as there is a nagging sense of undecidability. Every noble sentiment thus is in some way eventually undercut. My discussion . . . will focus on one aspect of the text, elements of plot, to support an ironic assessment of Adiel Amzeh. This approach to the protagonist lost in endless reading ultimately fosters a metanarrative reading that emphasizes the nature of texts, narrative impulses, and reading itself.

As Peter Brooks has pointed out in *Reading for the Plot: Design and Intention in Narrative,* plot is the principle of interconnectedness that, by linking discrete incidents, episodes, and actions, helps confer coherence onto those narrative components of a text. Plot is often conceived of as the outline, or armature, of a story; it is not, however, a static organization but a structuring operation actuated by reading and elicited by meanings that develop temporally through sequence and succession. Brooks observes that the term "plot" in English enjoys a semantic range that can include the idea of order and also indicate the concept of shaping or formulating as a dynamic activity. Plot may mean:

1. a small piece of ground, a measured area of land
2. a ground plan, as for a building; a chart or diagram (hence also the verb "to plot"—for example, to plot a graph)
3. a secret plan to accomplish a hostile or illegal purpose
4. a series of events, the action in a narrative drama.

The first two definitions are based on an idea of boundedness, demarcation, of marking off and ordering. The third suggests plot as scheme or machination, and it may have something in common with the first two categories insofar as to adopt a stratagem is to set out or delineate a particular course of action. In any event the last kind of plot, the literary term, combines the possibilities implied here of design as both pattern and intention. Plotting as Brooks is concerned with it is what "makes a plot 'move forward,' and makes us read forward, seeking in the unfolding of the narrative . . . the promise of progress toward meaning."

An overriding feature of the primary plot in *Forevermore* is digression, that is, the series of interruptions that prevent the central character from achieving his stated goal of publishing his research. Amzeh is waylaid first by Adah Eden, a nurse who collects magazines for the lepers. A visit from her delays his attending a decisive meeting with his financial benefactor, Gebhard Guldenthal. Then he dallies to hear a story she recounts about how the Gumlidata manuscript arrived in the hands of the lepers. From there he goes to the leprosarium and, as he reads, his publishing hopes indefinitely deferred, the contents of the manuscript are recounted at length and thus deflect the reader's attention, along with Amzeh's, away from the entire story line about the protagonist's life. A large number of Agnon narratives feature comparable antiprogressive patterns. Repetition, circularity, episodic fragmentation of narrative line, and disconnected events prevail in texts as diverse as *The Bridal Canopy* and *The Book of Deeds,* and the thematic implica-

tions that accompany this formal feature vary in various texts. In *Forevermore,* this kind of narrative design provides ironic plot. The main character perceives the events of his life as a kind of progress, but the reader, by contrast, does not. The fiction therefore offers a regressive plot masquerading as progressive because the protagonist views it as such. In the poem "Modern Love," to which my title alludes, George Meredith wrote, "Passions spin the plot." Amzeh's passion for futile and directionless study here spins his plot into an antiplot, inverting the very concept of plot from the normal sense of forward-moving action to one of disruption and deflection. Early on in the story Agnon succinctly sums up the oddity of Amzeh's life in a sentence that anticipates the deviation of narrative line to come and calls attention to matters of plotting. Articulating the assumption that time progresses in linear fashion and that progress of events is expected to accompany this advancing motion, the text notes that such is not the case with Adiel Amzeh. "Yatsu shanim ve-sifro lo yatsa," it remarks—that is, years went by and his book didn't appear, but literally, years went out and his book didn't come out. The same verb, *y-ts-a,* to leave or go out, is used twice to emphasize the scholar's anomalous lack of progress.

In short, this plot structure creates a pattern of distractions and interruptions that lead finally to a misguided subordination of social ties to an abstract ideal. The central constellation of tensions set up in this way—between action and inaction, text and the context of its transmission—is brought out and adumbrated by other aspects of the plot. The stories within the story, which constitute two of the major distractions in the primary plot, raise questions related to those addressed by that same overarching plot and the narrative as a whole.

The first embedded narrative, concerning how the book on Gumlidata arrived in the lepers' hands, is presented as part of Adah Eden's conversation with Amzeh. In brief it goes like this: When the Goths destroyed Gumlidata, they captured a nobleman who possessed a copy of the city chronicles. Shortly thereafter the captive contracted cholera and his captors abandoned him to die. Taken in by some itinerant lepers, the man was at first dismayed to find himself in their company. Later, however, he came to be grateful for the refuge they provided him. Joining their community, he recounted to them the glories of Gumlidata. After their deaths his book was acquired by succeeding generations of lepers, who passed it down through the ages. The function of this inserted narrative is clearly to provide a parallel to Amzeh's own experience. In a sense the events narrated anticipate his end: In each case a story survives, a book continues to exist—but at the cost of an individual's life, which is repressed and buried in the isolation of the leper colony. The immediate narrator, the nurse, attributes a positive value to her tale. "Men live and die," she concludes, "but their instruments remain and live on." In this fashion she sets up an interpretation that might be applied also to Amzeh. In effect, however, her evaluation helps build toward the concluding irony of the story. Any comparison of her tale with the experience of the protagonist produces a false analogy: The count's life depended on the lepers, but Amzeh does not go to the leprosarium to save himself. Even had the detail he sought out been a crucial one with which to validate his entire research, it would not have demanded urgent attention and might have waited till the following day. The reader, then, must judge Amzeh by weighing his loss more than his gain.

The second frame story, the account of Gumlidata's siege, provides another parallel to the main plot, but this is even more pointedly an alternative to, than an echo of, Amzeh's fate. Here the Hun girl Eldag has been captured and held in Gumlidata, forced to serve as a concubine to the aging, repulsive Count Gifayon, Glaskinon Gitra'al of the house of Giara'al. She cannot abide the old man's "groaning and drooling" or "the nauseating smell of the city and its sacrificial altars." Consequently she tries repeatedly to escape but fails. Eventually, though, when she relinquishes her attempts to flee and grants the count exceptional sexual favors, she gains the trust of her captors. Due to their relaxed watchfulness, she even finds opportunity to roam about the city alone. One day she takes a wild donkey to a particular place where a small breach has opened in the city wall. She has clothed the animal with a bizarre garment made of calves' eyes, called an Izla, which happens in its shape to resemble the Valley of Cranes—the very place where the walls' foundations are weak. Sending the beast through the opening, Eldag surmises that her father will associate the animal with her. Originally she was lost when riding on a donkey, and he should realize, therefore, that this is a signal for him and his allies, the Goths, to commence their attack. Subsequently this does indeed happen; the invaders enter Gumlidata through the shaky fortifications, destroy the city, and save the girl.

Most significant about this account is that it is a story of captivity and an attempt to break out of enslavement. Unlike Adiel Amzeh, Eldag comes up with a workable plot, a scheme to save herself from slavery. As an instance of action and attainment, it stands in stark contrast to the distractions and digressions that cripple the scholar—a figure who is described as a "slave" to his work. This is also a segment of text that recovers various senses of plot mentioned earlier. The girl schemes as she takes the initiative to bring about a turn of events; her plot, moreover, is enacted at a particular portion of ground that is plotted out, as it were, on the Izla—the garment that functions as a kind of map for the Goths because it is shaped like the Valley of Cranes. These varied definitions of plot converge here to provide a counterpoint to Amzeh, who is not capable of carrying out a plan or breaking out of the narrow strictures of his life. He welcomes enclosed space; his universe is his house, and within that house, the book he has been writing constitutes his entire reality. At the end he trades this limited existence for the even narrower confines of the leper house, and he fails to reach out to a wider sphere of living by publishing his findings. (It should be noted that *le-hotsi la-or*—to publish—in the Hebrew means literally to bring out to light, so this phrase contributes to the opposition between enclosure and openness that functions throughout the story as a central thematic element.)

The Eldag episode then serves fundamentally as an example of a well-conceived, forward-moving plot and as a stimulus for speculation on how Amzeh might better have lived his life. In the classical novel, the subplot often suggests a different solution to the problems worked through by the main plot; it may serve as a way of illustrating and warding off the danger of short circuit, of too easy a solution, and in this way assure that the main plot will continue through to the end. Here, by contrast, in a profoundly ironic text, this secondary, subordinate plot shows what the character might have done right. It presents the short circuit of decisive action that would ward off disabling distractions.

As this episode helps put into relief tensions between digression and linear plot, distraction and decisive action, it also emphasizes the central issue, discussed previously, of communicative circuit. The Eldag tale concentrates on communication. The Hun girl escapes enslavement, not through action alone, but by getting a message to her people, and so breaking out of her isolation. Her ingenuity at creating signs capable of conveying an urgent missive (the iconic reproduction of the valley in the form of the Izla/map, the transformation of the donkey into a visual message), undermines the conclusion Adah Eden reaches that story takes primacy over the teller. On the contrary, the act of transmitting and reaching an audience proves to be indispensable. The very fact that the story within a story functions as a principal organizing structure of the overall plot is significant in its own right. The nature of a frame story is to provide a context that subsumes another and serves as a referential framework for it. Any move from inner to outer tales suggests a movement of reference from fiction to reality, or from the remote to the immediate, and it also puts into relief the act of storytelling as a contractual relationship between narrator and narratee.

In **Forevermore,** concern with the process of transmitting narrative takes on overt prominence because of the central thematic opposition set up from the start: public recognition versus the worth of scholarship, the text itself and its audience. Here, by telling a story within a story, Agnon calls attention to the notion that narration is a preeminently social act that confers currency on stories society accepts as negotiable instruments. In other words, people listen to narrative, fictional or factual, which they perceive as meaningful and worthy of recognition. To survive, a story must have a listener. The manuscript about Gumlidata was making no impact on the world except in a severely circumscribed milieu. When Adiel Amzeh comes along, he functions dramatically as the one who, by reading, makes this story come to the attention of the current reader. By the same token, Adah Eden's anecdote about the count reminds the reader of much the same thing—it brings knowledge of the manuscript out into circulation, wider by one, than it had before. Her frame story, moreover, does not lead so much to information about the siege as to another narrative frame: how the count told his tales to others and under what circumstances. He had trouble preserving the story and succeeded only at the cost of limiting his audience to the lepers.

The doubling of frame story within frame story can easily bring the reader not to Adah's conclusions—that the teller is less significant than the tale—but to a sense of regress. What remains invariable is the telling and the dependence of the tale on the teller.

Agnon is . . . a writer whose work throughout is marked by its preoccupation and fascination with the past.

—*Naomi Sokoloff*

Amzeh's essential problem is precisely that he fails at communication. This doesn't bother him, because he thinks he is engaged in something more worthwhile: the attainment of verifiable historical truth. He believes that the web of words in which he is tangled will lead him to fact and to decisive answers. However, his unquestioning faith in referentiality is misplaced. Ultimately the story about Gumlidata is of doubtful factuality. It is based on a book of chronicles, written to perpetuate a glorious, heroic version of events from the Gumlidatan point of view. Furthermore, both the narrator and Adah Eden say that everyone in the city died during the conquest, and this information puts into question the authority of the scribe or storyteller transmitting any account of those events.

The obtrusive use of *'ayin* and *gimmel* in the text as initial letters of multiple words complements this understanding of Amzeh's convictions as poor judgment and misguided faith in referentiality. The bizarre repetition of the letters has the pronounced effect of highlighting and reinforcing the artifice of the work as a whole. Heightening an emphasis on sound, the author calls attention to the words themselves that make up the text and disallows any perception of language as simply a medium to convey an extratextual reality. In this way Agnon deliberately imposes fictionality on all levels of the narrative and, significantly, on the chronicles of Gumlidata. Therefore, whereas Amzeh believes that his sources and research represent historical, empirical inquiry into facts about the phenomenal world, the reader realizes the all-encompassing textuality and antimimetic nature of his endeavor.

These issues come into play pointedly at a moment of crisis. When Adah Eden disrupts Amzeh's plans to meet with his patron, the scholar begins to stutter. That is, his words are broken off in the middle. Consequently her interpretation is met with yet another kind of breakdown that recapitulates in miniature the overall pattern of the plot: Once more, interruption is accompanied by emphasis on communicative failure. The stammering suggests Amzeh's surprise, of course, but it also suggests more. The new information introduced by the nurse, the revelation of new evidence about Gumlidata, serves as an indi-

cation that the scholar's work so far has not been firmly based in social fact or even well informed of all the pertinent existing evidence. Indeed, it is hinted, his book is itself a kind of empty language or stammering. Highlighting this impression Agnon plays on the root *g-m-g-m* (to stutter) as Amzeh's stutter draws attention to the same letters in *Gum*lidata. Similarly the narrative calls attention to the interplay of *'ayin* and *gimmel* at a moment when the root *'-l-g* (to stammer) appears repeatedly. This portion of the story also deals with translation and in so doing contributes to much the same conclusion. Based on conjecture and rearrangements of letters, not grounded in empirical proof, the scholar's theories prove to be largely a play of sounds, signifiers without established connection to signifieds. In short, his research has been exposed as an edifice of words, a verbal construct or fiction. However, instead of recognizing it as such—thanks to Nurse Eden's intervention—and reevaluating his entire enterprise, the protagonist dashes off to the leprosarium to acquire yet more information of dubious factuality. Lost in a world of endless learning, generating more and more readings and interpretations, Amzeh never escapes the circle of signs into historical fact. Intellectually he remains trapped in the prison house of language.

Making his predicament even worse, the communicative circuit he has neglected for the sake of this questionable pursuit of truth does not simply dissipate and disappear. The entire issue of communication reinscribes itself in the story at this point because the protagonist cannot operate in a social vacuum. Rather, he trades a healthy context for a more restrictive and devastating one. Amzeh, who fails to finish composing his version of Gumlidata's history because of constant revising, rereading, and reconsidering, at the end is faced literally with decomposition; he is threatened with contamination by that manuscript, which has been handled by generations of lepers. Disintegrating, falling apart from handling by generations of lepers, this writing more closely resembles pus on skin than ink on paper. In a grotesquely graphic conception of the transmissibility of narrative, Agnon here presents text as contagion.

The ending to **Forevermore** must be understood then to deviate from expectations of narrative conclusion as outcome and closure. The outcome of events, of course, yields a failure to come out, and the result is also to undermine any sense of resolution. On the one hand, the character's fate seems like an emblem of closure par excellence. Enclosed in the leper house, Adiel Amzeh stays there forevermore, temporally and spatially sealed off from the demands of society that he shunned. The "ever after" of fairy tale and folklore, the convention of the perfect happy ending, remains the last word here. (The final sentence reads: ". . . he did not put his work aside and did not leave his place and remained there forevermore.") And yet this denouement does not represent a state of renewed equilibrium, a restoration of an original positive circumstance enriched by interim adventures, events, and obstacles overcome. Instead Agnon presents a built-in contradiction: a character who, in search of ennobling wisdom, lives a degraded existence, and who, finding an answer he sought with difficulty, has nonetheless missed out on essentials and been seduced by trivialities. In short the result here is an ongoing state of irresolution and finality without termination, a state that suggests an abdication of closure.

This conclusion is directed toward misreading by the narrator, who sees Adiel Amzeh's end as fortuitous. Learning, the narrator claims, "bestows a special blessing on those who are not put off easily." This evaluation should not be taken at face value, though, not only because of Amzeh's straitened circumstances, but also because the narrative as a whole puts into relief the limitations of this narrator's vision and the artifice with which he imposes meaning onto events. His comments here, for example, draw attention to the fact that he has set up a particular design for the story from the start. As a result the text heightens attention once again to narrators, in conversation with an audience, as ones who design plot. *Forevermore* thereby detracts from the vision of story as something independent from the context of its own formulation. For example, this dynamic is evidenced most clearly by an aside the narrator makes, to the effect that had Gebhard Guldenthal seen Adiel Amzeh at work, he might have observed the radiance of a man truly devoted to wisdom. These parenthetical remarks end as the narratorial voice says, "But you see my friend, for the sake of a little moralizing, I have gone and given away the ending at the very beginning of my story." Only ostensibly has he given away the denouement—that is, that Amzeh will choose pursuit of knowledge over public recognition. In actuality, as has already been said, the ending turns out to be considerably more complex. The effect of the narrator's comment, then, is simply to point out that this figure has a particular meaning or moral in mind for his story (to wit: Wisdom is more precious than worldly success). The narrator makes evident his role as someone who shapes a text, who tries to tell a tale in order to convey a particular message and design.

The treatment of the ending is especially important because the moment of closure is a highly sensitive one in the structure of narrative. If plot grants meaning over time, endings enjoy special status as the legitimizing authority on which beginnings and middles depend for their retrospective meaning. Readers assume that the end of a story will confer understanding on what has come before, and they read in confidence that what remains to be read will restructure the provisional meanings of what has already been read. For this reason it is possible to speak of the "anticipation of retrospection" [Brooks, *Reading for the Plot*] as a chief tool in making sense of narrative. In his consciously anticipatory comment, Agnon's narrator makes this dynamic explicit and lays bare the armature of his narrative. The author, Agnon, thereby also puts into relief the artifice of his own construction of narrative, while calling attention to the very issue of narration as a dominant concern in the text as a whole.

These remarks have taken us, then, from reading along with Adiel Amzeh in order to discover the "whodunit" of Gumlidata's last days (that is, who laid the siege and where) to a metanarrative reading that focuses on the nature of texts and narration. The first kind of reading—reading for the plot in a simplistic sense—is often assumed to be primary in fiction. To be sure, readers of fiction always read at least in part to do detective work, to construct a hypothetical *histoire* (that is, the narrated events) out of the available *discours* (the narration of events). This is the reason [literary theorist Tzvetan Todorov] assigns privileged status to the detective story as a genre.

In that genre the work of detection is overtly present for the reader, and it serves to reveal the as-yet-unrevealed story of a crime. The two orders of the text, inquest and crime, clearly illustrate the distinction between *discours* and *histoire,* and this kind of fictional pattern therefore lays bare the nature of all narrative. Agnon's *Forevermore,* though, suggests that reading as detective work is not enough; it is necessary but not sufficient. As the story clearly delineates Amzeh's limitations in his strategies for finding knowledge (that is, in his own detective work), *Forevermore* as a whole provides an alternative model of texts and reading as a path to gaining wisdom. The reader is challenged to ask why the fiction is built the way it is and what it conveys thereby, rather than to give weight first and foremost to narrated events. If we read for the plot, that is, to find out what happened to Adiel Amzeh, we miss out on the strategies of deferring and digressing, the crucial structures that put into relief important facets of characterization here and that in themselves contribute fundamentally to a thematic focus on textuality.

The story in effect offers an allegory of reading. In a sense all fictional texts are about reading at some level, and many guide us toward the conditions of their own interpretation. This work by Agnon more directly than many other texts raises these questions, because it explicitly concerns a search for meaning, authority, closure, narratability, referentiality, and audience. As such it invites the reader to be aware that one should not take narrators naively at their word, that it is important to be aware of the fact of narration, of who tells what to whom and why.

These ideas move us beyond the formalism of describing narrative organization to the issue of narrative desire: desire as a central thematic focus and desire as impetus for narrating. The two phenomena converge in *Forevermore,* for this is a narrative replete with multiple narrators, circumstances of narration, and motivations to narrate: there is the count who told his story of the siege to express his gratitude to the lepers, and the nurse who, though a comically bumbling, rambling narrator and a dilatory agent of digressive plot, tells her tales to highly effective, pragmatic ends (by distracting Adiel Amzeh she succeeds in getting him to turn aside from his appointment with Guldenthal and donate magazines, books, almost his entire library to the leprosarium); there is Amzeh who suffers a pathological inability to get his story out; finally there is the author, who tells his own tale via digressions, distractions, and multiple narrators, at once dramatizing Amzeh's distractability, identifying with his protagonist's vagaries, and warning against them. The essential question then arises: why this complexity, why the indirection, the subtleties, the obfuscation? Agnon's text turns on the fundamental irony that an author who creates a caveat against the unreliability of narrators and their hidden motives should create such a slippery narrative, deliberately teasing his readers into oversimple and mistaken interpretations.

Partly this art must be seen as the expression of a personality that needs distance from people, that seeks always to be sly, elusive. Deceits and ironies, hallmarks of Agnon's fiction, in *Forevermore* dramatize and stylistically recreate the thematic emphasis on unreliable narration. In part, also, we should note that the undecidabilities of the text force the reader, like all narrators, to write a story, making sense out of the available evidence. Leaving the reader with the burden of decoding baffling events, reconstituting them in an interpretation, the text in this way generates a reenactment of tensions that are its own essential concern. The resulting story, the reader's story, must always be formulated with some uneasiness.

Lest my own reading of this text seem too pat or pretend to account for all the puzzling elements of *Forevermore,* let me take note of yet another odd, disquieting irony. Perhaps the greatest undecidability of all, a condensation of previous tensions between in and out, text and world, occurs at the end of the text at the important moment of possible closure. Amzeh, locked away in the leprosarium, finds that other scholars have begun to publish his ideas and hypotheses. Though his book never reached the hands of the living, since no material objects are allowed to leave the leper house, somehow the information has leaked out. The narrator explains the phenomenon this way: "When a true scholar discovers a thing that is right, even if he himself is isolated and hidden away in the innermost chambers of his house, something of what he had found reaches the world." This explanation again insists that transcendent truth is a supreme value that works its way out to society. Another reading is also possible. It could be that the ideas that occurred to Amzeh were not so special and occurred to others as well. In that case his life has been a waste, his sacrifice unnecessary. It may be, too, that the manuscript he pursued was not truly indispensable for his work. Given all the evidence up to this point, I am inclined toward the ironic reading of Adiel Amzeh, but I do not discount the possibility that at this point the text may begin to deconstruct itself. The impasses of meaning here threaten to dismantle the binary oppositions of transcendent truth/contextualized discourse that have guided my discussion till now. Perhaps the final details of the fiction collapse the categories of understanding fundamental to an ironic reading of the scholar's sacrifice.

By way of conclusion I would like to suggest as well that this text, in its production of complex and intricate plot, which to a large extent concerns plotting, is revelatory of Agnon, the author himself, as a shaper of narratives. Agnon is a writer known for his many tales—some personal and some collective or religious—that attempt to recover a lost world. Many exhibit nostalgia for a more traditional time or for childhood and a religious milieu that have disappeared. In this regard, to some degree, the author resembles his protagonist. By no means a ridiculously simplistic, laughably monomaniac Amzeh, Agnon is nonetheless a writer whose work throughout is marked by its preoccupation and fascination with the past. In *Forevermore* that whole kind of enterprise is reconsidered. Self-conscious about the issues at stake—the pitfalls attendant on a passion to recuperate the past in writing—the author both reveals and conceals himself at once, simultaneously exposing a dream and protecting it, announcing his cynicism and masking it with pieties.

Presenting the ludicrous scholar to provide comment on the function and possibilities of writing as a means to restore lost worlds, *Forevermore* therefore also offers a perspective on Agnon's brand of artistry, whose point of departure is the lack of sacred texts in modern life. This is an art that Agnon saw as an outgrowth of, but an inadequate substitution for, religion. Imaginative tales cannot pretend to replace sacred writing, but the telling of them becomes significant in an effort to maintain textual tradition, to draw on the sources, and to keep a genuinely Jewish Hebraic influence alive. Not a return to the past, such writing does justify the artist as a shaper of community. So, although the allusive reference to Ecclesiastes, "for whom do I work?", echoes with futility for Adiel Amzeh at the end of his story, for Agnon himself the question can be answered somewhat more positively, perhaps with doubt but without the same profound sense of grief. The author's complex relationship to his narration and plot construction in *Forevermore* clues the reader in to these issues, and this consideration of plot may serve as a point of departure to recuperate and reintegrate some of those major aspects of the text mentioned at the outset of this chapter but not specifically dealt with here: the uses of allusion, the confusion of sacred and profane in the imagery of the story, the deliberate but inconsistent invitation to allegorical reading, which fosters puzzlement about what kind of hermeneutics to pursue in explicating the text. The metanarrative reading is not incompatible, for instance, with an understanding of *Forevermore* as a satiric look at modern scholarship or secular fiction. Agnon may be expressing his reservations about both those endeavors as they grasp at excavatory knowledge—archaeological or historical—rather than seeking out the sanctity and spirituality imbued in tradition. Viewing this story from the angle of plot is also not incompatible with an understanding that the text expresses a frustrated search for meaning. While Amzeh ascertains trivial answers to ease trivial dilemmas, his bigger problems go unsolved, and the perplexing uncertainties of the text as a whole defy easy answers. Because of the disallowing of simple allegory the narrative functions here—much in the mode of many Kafka narratives—as *aggada* without *halakha,* lore in search of law. All of these considerations, as they emerge out of careful examination of plot in *Forevermore,* may help illuminate Agnon's contradictory relation, as a modern writer, to tradition.

Miri Kubovy (essay date 1989)

SOURCE: "The Doctor's Dilemma: The Nature of Jealousy in Agnon's 'The Doctor and His Divorcée'," in *Hebrew Studies*, Vol. 30, 1989, pp. 41-7.

[In the following essay, Kubovy provides a psychological analysis of the protagonist's jealousy in "The Doctor and His Divorcée."]

There are many different interpretations of the story **"The Doctor and His Divorcée."** The story has been analyzed for spiritual, religious, social, and psychological meanings. I will concentrate on the psychological aspects of the story, focusing especially on the nature of jealousy and the interplay among its various components.

In this story a doctor meets a nurse named Dinah and is attracted to her particularly because of "that blue-black in her eyes," "and that smile which drove me wild with its sweetness and its sorrow." Eventually they marry. But the source of Dinah's sorrow remains hidden from him until, after long and persistent questioning, she reveals to him that she has had relations with another man in the past. After this revelation the image of the wife's former lover never leaves the doctor; indeed, he becomes increasingly obsessed with it. This obsession ultimately leads Dinah to conclude that a divorce is inevitable. The bulk of the story is the doctor's confession in which he contemplates his relationship with Dinah and the jealousy that finally leads to the divorce. Ya'akov Bahat and Hillel Barzel [*Al Hamishmar,* August 1, 1958, and *The Love Stories of Agnon,* 1975, respectively] believe that the doctor's excessive jealousy is the motivation for the divorce. But, as I shall seek to demonstrate, the text contains strong indications that jealousy is only the surface motivation for his behavior. I hope to point out structures of emotion and human behavior that offer a more complete explanation for the doctor's conduct in the story.

From the very beginning the doctor is attracted to the hidden source of Dinah's sorrow. He is obsessed with having it revealed, and he beleaguers Dinah with questions trying to understand this mysterious presence. After the secret of Dinah's affair is revealed, the story is largely motivated by the doctor's irrational preoccupation with the figure of her former lover. The figure of the lover becomes a destabilizing element in a triangular relationship in which the principal couple shifts and reverses. At the outset, the doctor and Dinah are the principal couple. However, as the story progresses we witness a reversal. The doctor and the lover become the principal couple, and Dinah becomes a subordinate figure who connects the two men. The doctor is ambivalent both towards Dinah and the lover, and it becomes increasingly difficult to determine the dominant relationship within the triangle. "I watch him and study him," says the doctor, "as though I could learn what rubbed off on him from Dinah and what rubbed off on her from him—and from devoting so much attention to him I was acquiring some of his gestures." And further on: "I returned her embrace and we stood clinging together in love and affection and pity, while all that time, this fellow never left my sight. . . ."

From their wedding night on, every time the doctor is in an intimate situation with Dinah, he is compelled to think or talk about the former lover and to include him in the moment. At the beginning of the story the lover is a completely abstract figure who does not belong to the realistic world of the doctor and Dinah. By the end of the story, the lover is transformed from an intangible presence to a concrete figure. The significant interaction takes place between the two men, and the figure of Dinah is relegated to the background. The image of the lover haunts the doctor incessantly: "From then on that man was never out of my sight, whether my wife was present or not. If I sat by myself, I thought about him, and if I talked with my wife I mentioned him. . . . But in the kiss of reconciliation I heard the echo of another kiss which someone else had given her. . . . When I wanted to be happy with my wife, I would remember the one who had spoiled my happiness, and I would sink into gloom."

Every contact with Dinah brings about the appearance of another man. Consequently, the doctor holds Dinah responsible for his obsession and the suffering caused by his attacks of jealousy. Yet, in reality, the doctor's jealousy of Dinah is also a disguise for his passionate preoccupation with the lover. The doctor cannot acknowledge this attraction, and he denies it by attributing it to his wife, who at this point is completely indifferent to the lover. The doctor is attracted to the lover, but he also hates him because he "doesn't leave him alone." Since he cannot reconcile this ambivalent relationship, the doctor can survive his inner turmoil only by denying his impulses and projecting his fantasies onto Dinah and the lover.

Both the lover and Dinah are passive characters. Most of the thoughts, feelings, and actions the doctor attributes to them are projections of his own emotions and creations of his own imagination. In some cases they serve as a defense against his own feelings towards the lover, protecting him from his own lust by attributing it to Dinah and the lover. The same pattern of inversion and projection occurs in a dream that the doctor has about the lover:

> "One night this fellow came to me in a dream: his face was sickly and yet just a little—just a little—likeable. I was ashamed of myself of thinking evil of him, and I resolved to put an end to my anger against him. He bent down and said, 'What do you want from me? Is the fact that she [*sic*] raped me any reason for you to have it in for me?'."

Unfortunately, the translation in the edition cited is marred by a mistake in a crucial pronoun: in this context the Hebrew [phrase in the final quoted sentence] means "you raped me." The translation, "she raped me," distorts the original meaning.

The essence of this story, as of many of Agnon's other stories, is distilled in a dream. This dream epitomizes the ambivalent structure of the doctor's jealousy by reflecting the violent force of his homosexual attraction and his equally forceful denial. He finds the patient's face both attractive and repulsive, "sickly" and "likeable." He masks his attraction with aggravated jealousy and, at the same time, is ashamed of his ill will towards the man. Ultimately, repression, guilt, and shame are transformed into the aggression and paranoia that are projected through the dream images of rape and accusation.

When the relationship between the doctor and the lover becomes concrete and the doctor has a chance to express his attraction, he keeps the lover unnecessarily in the hospital and seduces him with alcohol and "all sorts of luxuries." He allows the lover to smoke, in violation of hospital rules, and gives him extra food. In this, as in many of Agnon's stories, food has sexual significance, specifically in the scenes between the doctor and the lover. Other scholars have observed Agnon's use of food as a sexual symbol. Gershon Shaked, for example, claims [in *Omanut haSippur shel S. Y. Agnon,* 1973] that throughout Agnon's work food and eating habits are a displacement of erotic or sexual relationships. [In *The Dynamics of Motifs in S. Y. Agnon's Works,* 1979] Yair Mazor identifies seventeen instances in which food is used in the **"The Doctor and His Divorcée"** and considers this frequency as grounds for constructing a textual structure of meaning around food. He argues that food is the central principle of the story, and he divides Agnon's references to food into "positive eating" and "negative eating." According to Mazor, the fact that Dinah and the doctor are related only to the "negative scenes" foreshadows the failure of their marriage. Although Mazor observes similarities between the doctor's attitude toward Dinah and his attitude toward the lover, he does not discuss the doctor's ambivalence—his repulsion and attraction—towards them, nor does he analyze the doctor's general patterns of behavior in relation to the eating scenes.

The doctor feeds the lover his *own* food and works systematically on stuffing and fattening him. He virtually force-feeds him. Yet this excessive feeding is accompanied by a strong feeling of revulsion: "I looked at the double chin he had developed. His eyes were embedded in fat, like those of a woman who has given up everything for the sake of eating and drinking." Through the act of excessive feeding the doctor seeks both to express and resolve his conflict. Force-feeding is a way to penetrate and control the lover's body. But it also transforms the desired object into something shapeless, repulsive and less threatening because it looks feminine. A mixture of attraction and repulsion also accompanies the "extraordinary amount of care" that the doctor lavishes on the lover. He treats him frequently, "whether he needed it or not," and praises his body. Under the disguise of these treatments the doctor is able to touch the lover's body, but he denies his evident attraction through disproportionate protestations of revulsion: "I offered him my fingertips to shake . . . and immediately I wiped them on my white coat, as though I had touched a dead reptile. Then I turned my face away from him as from some disgusting thing, and I walked away."

Suspicion is another side of the jealousy the doctor feels. He accuses the lover of being the man "who brought ruin down" on him and of wrecking his wife's life. His anger surges within him and he becomes furious. In moments of lucidity the doctor knows that his suspicion is unfounded and that the lover is innocent; yet he cannot overcome his anger. This realization and his inability to change his behavior make him even angrier. When he cannot arrest his hatred and anger he invents far-fetched reasons to justify them. The greater the jealousy, the greater the anger; the greater the anger, the greater the guilt and the greater the need to rationalize it. This vicious circle of jealousy and anger hastens his self-destruction: "I have already searched all her books and found nothing . . . and that made me still angrier, for I was pretending to be decent while my thoughts were contemptible."

In Freud's "Some Neurotic Mechanisms in Jealousy, Paranoia, and Homosexuality" [in *Sexuality and the Psychology of Love*], we find a theory of jealousy and its characteristics that is particularly relevant to **"The Doctor and His Divorcée."** Freud states that there is an element of identification with the rival in every case of jealousy. There is a sense in which a person would like to be in the place of his rival, or in some way to be his rival. People "project outwards on to others what they do not wish to recognize in themselves." At the beginning of the story, the doctor doesn't even know the lover, yet he wants to believe that the lover is a special person. "To delude myself I imagined that he was a great man, superior to all his fellows." It seems to him that there is a connection between them, and that the lover reflects his own image. The doctor sees himself as if it were he who was in the body and in the gestures of the lover; he cannot separate the two: "from devoting so much attention to him, I was acquiring some of his gestures." This identification, according to Freud, could have erotic implications—homosexual when the rival is of the same sex. Like the doctor in our story a man might be excessively sensitive to the possibility of unfaithfulness in his wife, blowing out of all proportion all sorts of details (like Dinah's relationship prior to her acquaintance with the doctor) in order to deny his own homosexual tendencies. "As an attempt at defence against an unduly strong homosexual impulse, it may in a man be described by the formula: I do not love him, *she* loves him" [Freud].

This reading of the doctor's character coincides with David Aberbach's observation that:

> Many interrelated aspects of the Agnon character suggest a predisposition to homosexuality: . . . fear of and difficulty with women, his feeling of sexual inferiority, confusion about sexual roles and identities, and his apparent susceptibility to sexual inadequacy. Partly because Agnon was an orthodox Jew . . . he could not deal straightforwardly with this theme. When hints of homosexual impulses or behavior emerge, the reaction is usually abhorrence and flight. Nevertheless, certain peculiarities of Agnon's work—obscure dreams and fantasies, for example of sex changes or of men on top of one another, and mysterious patterns of relationships

with men and women—are more explicable if considered with the possibility of latent homosexuality in mind.

> . . . the Agnon hero is in constant search, not of peers but of a strong man as a model for emulation. [One type of this man] is the lover, or the former lover of the hero's beloved, whom he apparently adulates as a success in sexual relationships, where he usually fails dismally.

> [*At the Handles of the Lock*, 1984]

In **"The Doctor and His Divorcée,"** the process described by Aberbach gains a dimension of jealousy and works in two directions. The rival is the object of desire with whom the doctor identifies, and at the same time the rival is the hated enemy who robs the doctor of his happiness and brings about his loss and destruction.

The changes from hate to love and back are based on the doctor's inherent ambivalence towards the lover. Freud claims that ambivalence, like paranoia, serves the purpose of a "defense against homosexuality." Freud argues that "Since we know that with the paranoiac it is precisely the most loved person of his own sex that becomes his persecutor, the question arises where this reversal of affect takes its origin; the answer is not far to seek— the ever-present ambivalence of the feeling provides its source and the unfulfillment of his claim for love strengthens it. This ambivalence thus serves the same purpose for the persecuted paranoiac as jealousy serves for our patient—that of defense against homosexuality."

At the end of the story both Dinah and the doctor reach the conclusion that divorce is their only way out of the dilemma. The doctor is incapable of resolving his conflict: he cannot live with his ambivalence towards the attractive-repulsive man through his beloved-hated wife. After the doctor tells his wife of the dream in which the lover accuses him of having raped him, it is clear to Dinah that her relationship with her husband is hopeless. She says: "Whether I want it or not, I am prepared to do whatever you ask, if only it will relieve your suffering— even a divorce." The doctor eventually agrees: "Now I thought, however you look at it, there is no way out for us, except a divorce." But the conclusion offers no resolution. There is a penultimate moment in which true awareness seems to hover on the brink of the doctor's consciousness. But it is immediately suppressed through the familiar mechanisms of jealousy and suspicion: "Before long I saw with my own eyes and I grasped with my own understanding what at first I had not seen and I had not grasped. At once I decided that I would grant Dinah the divorce. We had no children, for I had been apprehensive about begetting children for fear they would look like him."

Gershon Shaked (essay date 1989)

SOURCE: "The Genres and Forms, the Novella, and the Short Stories," in *Shmuel Yosef Agnon: A Revolutionary Traditionalist,* translated by Jeffrey M. Green, New York University Press, New York, 1989, pp. 167-241.

[*In the following excerpt, Shaked identifies five primary types of short stories written by Agnon.*]

The Fantastic Folk Tale

A thorough study of even one story belonging to each of Agnon's genres is beyond the scope of this study; thus, I have chosen to analyze five so-called poles from the entire work, beginning with the short folk story **"Three Sisters."**

"Three Sisters" was first published in 1937 and is typical of Agnon's fantastic tales. It is outstanding in its brevity and tight structure. Its source is a ballad of social commentary ["The Song of the Shirt" by Thomas Hood (1799-1845)] that reached Agnon from English literature through Isaac Leib Peretz's Yiddish translation. What characterizes **"Three Sisters"** is the extreme modification of the motif, the social message of which has been raised to balladic-mythical significance.

"Three Sisters"

Three sisters lived in a gloomy house, sewing linens for others from morning light to midnight, from the end of Sabbath to Sabbath eve never moved from their fingers either scissors or needle, and the sigh never ceased from their heart, not on hot days nor rainy ones. But blessing came none from their work. And what dry bread they found was never enough to sate their hunger.

Once they were occupied making a fine dress for a rich bride. When they finished their labor, they remembered their sorrow, that they had nothing but the skin on their flesh, and that too was growing old and weak.

Their hearts filled with sorrow.

One sighed and said, "All our days we sit wearying ourselves for others, nor have we even a scrap of cloth to make ourselves shrouds."

The second one said, "Sister, don't invite misfortune."

She too sighed till she shed a tear.

The third wanted to say something too. As she started to talk, a blood vessel burst in her mouth and splattered, soiling the dress.

When she brought the dress to the bride, the rich man came out of his salon. He saw the stain. He scolded the seamstress and dispatched her with obloquy. And needless to say, he did not pay her.

Alas, if the second had spit blood, and the third had wept, we could have washed the dress with her tears, and the rich man would not have become angry. But not everything is done in timely fashion. Even if everything were done in timely fashion, that is, if the third one had wept after the second spat blood, there would still be no true consolation here.

The stylistic fabric of this story in Hebrew is quite rhythmical, bringing out the balance both within and between the sentences. The author heightened the emotional effect by sonorous means and through the use of rhetorical strategies, such as the anaphora ("from . . . from") and antitheses in the sentence structure ("morning . . . midnight"; "hot . . . rainy"), and also in the strategy of gradual intensification (skin "growing old and weak"). The story would merely be pathetic if its content were not based on a series of ironic antitheses.

The legendary elements of the story are conspicuous, for none of the figures is characterized. They are formulaic characters—as the number three is itself formulaic—acting in an eternal time (for example, dawn to midnight; from the end of the sabbath to the eve of the following sabbath; and rain and shine). The eternal act of sewing connects these sisters to the three sisters of Greek mythology who knit the threads of destiny.

The story is based on a tale of social protest about three sisters in their poverty, a rich bride, and a cruel rich man who does not pay the sisters' wages. However, Agnon broadened the scope of the tale. In the dialogue, which pierces through the eternal time frame, each of the sisters laments her bitter fate—one in words, one in tears, and one in blood. Yet sighs do not change fate; indeed, they make it worse. The order of the world does not depend on the social situation but on chance or on a blind force, which also brings suffering to humanity. The decree does not strike only the poor and destitute but penetrates the depths of the human situation. At the end, in ironic fashion the narrator responds to his "story" with aphorisms taken from Ecclesiastes 3:11—the sense of which are reversed. A change in the events would not change the situation, which is fundamentally bad. The ballad—the high point of which is the burst blood vessel and the culmination of which is the meeting with the rich man—is thoroughly and ironically epitomized in the remarks of the narrator. Thus, here is a structure based on folkloric components—contrasts between light and dark, the dialogue, the depiction of time, and the characters who are emblematic of the fates. Yet the content is modern, describing the human condition.

This particular story is not exceptional. When compared to other folk tales, both long and short, told by Agnon (for example, **"Agunot: A Tale," "The Tale of the Scribe," "The Dance of Death," "The Dead Girl,"** and **"The Tale of Rabbi Gadiel, the Infant"**), it shows the author's tendency toward formulaic characterization and tight, dramatic plots advancing toward a climax that is a crisis—or a decree of fate—that is close to the world of imagination, myth, and universal significance. What is lacking in detailed visual description is made up by rhythms, intertextual mythical references from various cultures, and rhetorical intensification. Most of these texts are intense and tightly wrought. Their components do not simply interrupt the act of reading or break the linear continuity; rather, they deepen them.

The story is based on the parodic deautomatization of the folk tale. Peretz's version of this story is already an ironic retelling of the story about the three sisters waiting for a groom. Agnon made use of this motif and gave it a positive folk conclusion with "the rooster—ex machina" in *The Bridal Canopy* but not in **"Three Sisters,"** in which he placed greater emphasis on the ironic aspect of the situation, denying any chance for the fortunate conclusion commonly found in folk tales about poor young girls. The source of evil is not the social struggle but rather the human condition. Man is thrown into a world where arbitrary powers rule without mercy. In this story, through the use of a traditional literary device—that is, the standard structure of a folk legend—Agnon described an absurd existential situation. Parody is one of the typical devices used by the revolutionary in his war against the tradition or in his attempt to reveal its vacuousness.

The Realistic Story

One would expect Agnon's realistic stories to be the opposite of his folk tales. In contrast to a plot and characters that lack specificity—the purpose of which is to make an emotional and ideological point—here is a plot derived from reality and peopled with well-depicted characters, all of which represent a full realization of literary structures. Agnon's first stories in the Land of Israel, such as **"The Hill of Sand,"** were written in this fashion, as were later ones, such as **"Metamorphosis," "The Doctor's Divorce," "Fernheim,"** and **"Between Two Cities."**

"Ovadia the Cripple" (1921), which tells the story of an errant maidservant betrothed to a miserable cripple, borders on naturalism. After a flirtation with the son of her employers, the maidservant sleeps with another servant and becomes pregnant. When her crippled fiancé returns from the hospital, he finds her with a bastard in her arms.

The crippled fiancé is a pathetic figure taken from melodramas and is reminiscent of Victor Hugo's Quasimodo or Mendele Mokher Seforim's Fishke the Lame. Knut Hamsun also wrote a story about an innocent cripple, Minutte, in *Mysteries*. The mistreatment of Minutte recalls the sadistic tormenting of Agnon's Ovadia in the dance hall. The wayward servant girl is also a rather familiar melodramatic figure (see Gerhard Hauptmann's *Rose Bernd* [1903] and Peretz Hirschbein's *Miriam* [1905]). The relationships among the oppressed and miserable were a favorite topic in naturalistic literature. By exploiting this topic, naturalistic literature appealed to the basic instincts of its readership. The danger in depicting such characters is excessive sentimentality; and, in fact, the richness of the material can be its own undoing.

The problem confronted by authors who use such material, which can border on cliché, is how to give the details new meaning, how to motivate the plot, and how to specify its message. Agnon solved these problems through structure. The story takes place first in the consciousness of the hero, Ovadia the Cripple, and then in the dance hall, where Ovadia finds Shayne-Seril dancing and where he is tormented by the young men. Afterward, the paths of the two characters diverge. Ovadia goes to the hospital, and Shayne-Seril returns to her master's home. In the end, the author brings them back together. The hero leaves the hospital and finds that his betrothed has taken another lover.

A conspicuous line in the plot is the effort to forge a hidden link of cause and effect between Ovadia's deeds in the hospital and those of Shayne-Seril in her master's house. The fact that Ovadia does not leave the hospital somewhat determines the girl's fate, just as Shayne-Seril directly causes Ovadia's two failures. Thus, the relationship between the cripple and the sensual girl is based on mutual culpability; social circumstances and the characters' personalities are the root of the evil. The sages said, "Everything is predictable, and the choice is in our hands." But here everything is predictable, and people have very little freedom of choice. The fateful bond between the pair is presented ironically, both in the protagonists' thoughts and in the connections among the chapters. The hidden text, which expands the significance of the story, is revealed mainly in structural ways, such as links and gaps among the components of the story and the explanation of the heroes' fate.

One does not customarily look for a hidden text with multiple meanings in a naturalistic story. However, it is not Agnon's wont to go completely without hidden meanings. The story also implies intertextual connections that expand its significance; however, this expansion is not allegorical. The male protagonists, Ovadia and Reuven, allude only indirectly to biblical figures, although the story has affinities with the portion of the Bible beginning with "Vayishlah" [Genesis 32:4]. The Book of Ovadia, for whom Agnon's character is named, is read in the synagogue on the sabbath when that portion of the Bible is read. Indeed, upon examining the text from Genesis, one finds many indirect parallels with **Ovadia the Cripple."** Just as the patriarch Jacob was maimed in the thigh by the angel, so, too, is Ovadia a cripple. In Genesis, Reuben violates his father's marriage bed and sleeps with Bilhah; similarly, Reuven, the redhead in Agnon's story, violates Ovadia's marriage bed. The hidden parallels between Ovadia and the patriarch Jacob and between the biblical Reuben and Reuven in the story have yet another aspect, suggested by the passage from the prophet Ovadia—which deals with the bitter war between Israel and Edom, the descendants of Esau. If the people of Israel are the seed of Jacob (or Ovadia), then red-headed people are the descendants of Esau. Jacob epitomizes the spirit; and Esau, the one who is enslaved to his instincts, epitomizes flesh and blood.

Agnon does not intend the connection to the tradition to indicate that the characters should not be taken as they are. On the contrary, the story's protagonists are just what they appear to be. However, the instinctual struggle waged in the story is enhanced by the biblical connotations, which are partially parodic and partially archetypal. Those connotations do not (to use the elder Israeli critic

Dov Sadan's phrase) create "a story within the story." Rather than make the story of Ovadia more profound, the biblical comparison mocks the hidden archetype—that is, Jacob, the "plain man dwelling in tents" [Genesis 25:27]. The two forces, flesh and spirit—the hands of Esau and the voice of Jacob—are presented here in an ironic, sarcastic light—the latter in its hopeless impotence and the former in all its naked coarseness. The references do not intensify and expand but rather limit and dwarf the stature of the protagonists. That is to say, the structure and the texture (the hidden text) are meant to alter and deepen the naturalistic materials.

Moreover, toward the end the author brings the story to a climax, giving it a new and broader meaning. The tale does not merely recount the story of a couple that has been over-whelmed and crushed by eros and thanatos, as well as by the hypocrisy of bourgeois society, but goes beyond the exposure of the victims. Here is the final passage of the story:

> Ovadia's mouth was open, his tongue like an immovable rock, and the sweets in his hand kept melting and melting. The baby suckled with pleasure at his mother's breast, with a still small voice. Ovadia took the candies with his right hand and the crutch with his left. The baby stretched and removed one hand from the teat, and Shayne-Sirel's anger was still not appeased. Ovadia feared to give her the candies and bent down and laid them on the infant's palm.

The reader might have expected that Ovadia would turn on his heels and leave the mother and her child to their sighs. But Ovadia does not. He feels that Shayne-Seril is not guilty. Apparently, in such affairs there are neither sinners nor guilty parties but merely creatures in need of mercy. The story is cruel and naturalistic and is cleared of all sentimentality by the author's sarcasm, but it concludes with a catharsis of human compassion. Different faces are brought to light. Agnon does not convey compassion via the shortcut of sentimentality but rather by following the path of woe.

"Ovadia the Cripple" is an example of Agnon's delicate handling of coarse naturalistic material, just as **"Three Sisters"** is an example of his ability to craft an entire world within a balladlike dewdrop without portraying actual human situations. The two stories illustrate the concept of fate from different points of view. The characters in the balladlike story accept and submit to fate, while the characters in the naturalistic story find a humane way of overcoming it. In the folk tale, depiction is formal and restricted; hence, the function of the intratextual features is expanded. In the realistic story, the description is detailed and extensive, thus limiting the function of those features; and allegorization is prevented despite them.

"Ovadia the Cripple" may also be seen from another viewpoint. Agnon writes ostensibly as a believer to a readership of believers, as a typical bourgeois to a bourgeois audience. According to customary laws, Shayne-

Seril's baby was born out of wedlock; thus, judged by the standards of the Jewish bourgeoisie he is a social outcast from every point of view.

Agnon's comic point of view is, to a large extent, anarchical. He does not advocate social reform or changes in the system; rather, the entire state mechanism seems fundamentally ridiculous to him.

—Gershon Shaked

However, Agnon turns the moral tables here. Toward the end of the story he creates an effect of moral deautomatization, which is also an effect of literary deautomatization. The child, according to this view, need not be ostracized and cast out because Ovadia, although he is not the biological father, gives the child the candies—thus, accepting moral responsibility. This is not in keeping with the naturalistic school's material world of flesh and blood, although the protagonists are portrayed throughout most of the story according to that world's basic assumptions.

The naturalistic story receives a moral and spiritual dimension from the world of grace. In contrast to the bourgeois morality based on genetic rules and regulations, a humanistic ethos is portrayed, based on relationships of grace, mercy, and responsibility—all of which contrast with traditional bourgeois values. Agnon once again shows himself to be a traditional revolutionary both in form and in content.

The Abstract Story: The Humorous Feuilleton

The comic perspective is central in Agnon's work. He exploited every possible variety of comedy—from social satire, in **"Of Our Young People and Our Elders,"** to farce, in **"With the Death of the Saint"** and **"The Frogs."** Agnon even employed Rabelaisian grotesquery in **"Pisces"** and **"At Hemdat's."** Most of the comic stories tend to hyperbole, thus intensifying the sense of realism, although a few are stripped bare.

One example of stark, comical abstraction is the feuilleton **"On Taxes"** (1950), included in *The Book of the State.* It is an abstract story without reference to place or time, to real characters, or to human situations. Furthermore, the protagonist is not an individual but rather a collectivity—that is, the state. The fictional situation with all its ramifications provokes laughter because it evokes official bureaucracies everywhere. It is taken as a comic hyperbole, a mechanism for its own sake beyond any actual need or purpose. In the story an imaginary state is about to go bankrupt, which leads to a strike threat by the offi-

cials. From the very first the bureaucracy is characterized as a superfluous body, creating work where there was none but to no purpose: "The grumblers quipped and mocked, saying, 'What work will the bureaucrats stop doing? Perhaps they'll stop their idleness and thumbtwiddling.'"

Meaningless activities are reiterated in various contexts. Committees are constantly being formed, each merely a comic synonym of its predecessor. Agnon's technique is to amass details that do not advance the plot, showing that every action is merely repetition and that the entire plot is superfluous:

> They formed a new committee. Since the active intellect is active equally in every person, that committee proposed what the first committees had proposed, aside from the bill for expenses, which was slightly different from the bills of the first committees, since in the meanwhile the cost of living had risen by several points.

The coincidental and arbitrary turning point occurs when salvation comes to the state in the form of the cane, upon which taxes had not yet been imposed. The cane deflects the course of events, giving the plot a goal. In the author's words: "However the state was fortunate. Even in a trivial matter, its luck held. It happened that a certain elderly member of the House of Lippery-waggers forgot his cane."

That turning point provokes a chain reaction: taxation of canes, discussions of the form of taxation, a black market in canes, legislation obliging people to carry canes, the importing of wood from abroad, the burning of wood, the transfer of the ashes from the site of the fire to the sea, and finally the importing of finished canes—a precipitous decline in which each event pulls down its fellow. Since the actions do no one any good, the author intervenes to repair a fault but cannot do so. His attempt comes to little more than adding fault upon fault, a comic snowball showing with increasing clarity that action does not improve matters but simply drives them round and round to no purpose, until the cycle itself attains a value of its own.

Since everything done in the state is foolishness, only that which is not done is intelligent. The state is itself evil. The author is weary of an other-oriented society whose only force is verbal, taking its own social organization as a value in itself. The story does not relate to people; it is not people who pervert the world. The root of evil does not lie in the Weichsls and Deichsls or Mundspiegels who populate **"Of Our Young People and Our Elders"** but rather in the House of Lippery-waggers, the tax bureaucracy, and the state itself. Moreover, the bureaucrats, so long as they are not connected with the bureaucracy, are like anyone else—trivial people who would not harm a fly, collectors of jokes and scissors who serve in high positions. However, as soon as they put on their official hats, they are liable to do damage:

> So the Treasurer sat there with the members of the Committee with a cordial expression and a smile on his

face, not passing over a single prominent figure in the state without telling a joke about him, one of those jokes that people amuse themselves by telling. He said, "Most likely these will commemorate our colleagues rather than their actions, even though their actions are one long joke." He kept talking that way until the members of the Committee recalled why they had come. They raised their voices and spoke to him. Immediately his bright countenance altered, his lips twisted, his nose swelled, his ear-lobes turned black, and he looked entirely like a state official. If we didn't know him, we could not discern that he was capable of understanding a joke.

Here, the comic element is impersonal. The fictional world is detached from actual social materials and is presented as a bare skeleton. It is funny because the schematization of phenomena exposes their vacuity better than would a concrete description. The abstract scheme removes the coincidental, human, and individual element from the world, and everything is frozen. The world is driven like a mechanism without direction, a comic wheel revolving upon itself without significance. The reader is left without air to breathe. Even the narrator, who appears as an objective chronicler called "the author of *The Book of the State,*" has no human reality.

Agnon's comic point of view is, to a large extent, anarchical. He does not advocate social reform or changes in the system; rather, the entire state mechanism seems fundamentally ridiculous to him. The story might be aimed at the political establishment of the State of Israel, which had just been born and already had managed to erect its own bureaucracy. (This story was printed in *Haaretz* in 1950!) However, it applies to any bureaucratic system in any place at any time. Agnon saw bureaucracy as a mechanism that feeds on itself and expands at the citizen's expense without any regard for common sense. This is an anarchical work written in a classical style.

Even when writing a satirical piece with comic abstraction of social reality, Agnon remained faithful to himself. Here, too, he played the role of a revolutionary who, using irony tinged with sharp sarcasm, destroys the most sanctified establishment in any society—the bureaucracy, which feeds upon itself, and the people's representatives, who make the parliament (which Agnon called "the house of lippery") into an institution that acts in its own behalf and supports itself with meaningless jabber and pointless laws.

This sort of work has various artistic limitations. Agnon's tendency toward an abstract worldview and toward situations merely hinted at is evident in his earliest writings. It is a style that appears in various proportions in different works. The better the equilibrium between the concrete and the abstract, or the specific and the universal, the more significant is the work. Agnon's abstract writing, in its many forms, is limited to a single meaning. This is because its components are not sufficiently concretized but rather are presented as abstractions or as a series of allegorical keys; thus, the situations are not open to more than one interpretation. The paradox is, of course, that the abstract texts are much more closed and

unequivocal than are the concrete and ostensibly realistic ones. These techniques, which were supposed to reflect the modern formal revolution explicitly, are not always as open-ended and multivalent as Agnon's more conservative, traditional techniques.

In Agnon's traditional techniques, the modern "revolution" is implicit and alluded to in intertextual parodies and in minuscule stylistic and compositional shifts and deviations from traditional literary conventions. If any sin may be laid at the door of Agnon's work, it is the sin of abstraction. He exerted a negative influence on younger writers primarily because they seized upon the abstract and unequivocal aspects of his work.

The Abstract, or Nonrealistic, Story

The tendency toward abstraction is found mainly in the so-called modern stories that Agnon began publishing in the early 1930s, which ultimately were collected in *The Book of Deeds.* That book was Agnon's attempt to satisfy modern man's need to express a new realm of experience. Such an expression might simply have been a vital need for Agnon himself and represented a fulfillment of tendencies that had existed within him almost from the first (see, for example, **"Agunot: A Tale"**). In any case, I do not consider *The Book of Deeds* to be the finest of his works, although its influence on younger writers has been greater than the influence of his realistic fiction.

I will take the example of **"Quitclaim"** (in Hebrew, **"Hefker"**), published in *Haaretz* in 1945, which follows the pattern typical of *The Book of Deeds.* Generally, the narrator is the hero. The pattern is a kind of journey ending in a dead end or in an unexpected reversal; and, since all the stories appear in a single collection, each sheds light on the others.

At first we seem to be reading a story about a man who has made an appointment to meet a friend in a café. He lingers for a long time and later tries to go home. Since he seems to have missed the last bus, he goes by foot, enters a cul-de-sac, and becomes entangled with an eccentric character who apparently summons him to judgment. Finally, for no reason at all and with no explanation, he appears before a strange judge. The judge does not judge him, and he sets out once again. On his way, he notes another group of Jews who apparently also are waiting for their trial. The overt text is neither plausible nor logical; the circumstances are extremely surprising and bizarre. The story has no meaning unless the reader attempts to descend to its deepest depths and rescue the latent text.

A detailed analysis shows the story's message to be that the lower and upper worlds, which are not depicted in the overt text, are controlled by powers that do not permit a person to choose his own path. The protagonist vacillates from crisis to crisis and is forced to seek his way, but the inner obstacles are beyond his strength. Not only can he find no shelter in his own home, he also cannot resolve whether he has behaved properly.

That meaning is implicit in the name of the story, **"Quit-claim,"** which suggests a world where the law has been abnegated, without judge or judgment. It is a world in which the holy and the profane and laughter and dread are intermingled. The plot is not bound by realistic cause and effect but is instead held together by bits and snippets having the same cohesive power or meaning—that is, a unified atmosphere. The inner journey of "that man" passes through various emotional stations and reaches the destination intended from the start.

I will now analyze in detail one of those stations along the way to show how the general meaning of the story crystallizes within the reader. Here is a central passage in which the protagonist stands before the mysterious judge to pay the forfeit for a sin he has not committed:

> He asked me nothing but sat before his desk and took up pen and ink and paper and started writing. In the room it was quiet and the smell of kerosene wafted up from the heater. Only the sound of the pen scratching the paper was heard. If the pen does not break and the paper does not tear, he will never stop his writing. I stood in my place and thought to myself, hasn't the middle of his mustache turned white in the meanwhile? The middle of his mustache had not turned white, but its two ends were befouled.

This text is interesting because of the relationship between the overt text and a latent one. Earlier in the story, Agnon used expressions in reference to the judge that recall attributes of the Creator found in "The Song of Honor," a kabbalistic hymn incorporated in the sabbath liturgy.

"Quitclaim"	"The Song of Honor"
I saw before me a man, neither young nor aged.	And Thou art held to be aged and youthful.
Gray was sown on it at both its ends.	The hair of Thy head is gray and black.
And in the middle of the black mustache . . . He stood and donned a miter with several ends.	He donned the miter of redemption.

Such a comparison seems to indicate that God is the hidden hero, latent in the figure of the judge. The figure in the overt text might also be a parody of the latent figure, by means of which the oxymorons attributed to the Creator are illuminated from a new point of view. Traditionally, the oxymoron is a way of expressing the ineffable greatness of God. This story, however, reveals a contradictory aspect of the oxymoron—that is, the eternal ambivalence of the highest judge, who lacks unequivocal answers to man's questions. In the description of the God-judge, the grotesqueness, characteristic of the previous passages, reaches a peak. The God-judge, a central figure in the story, throws the narrator-hero's world into such confusion that he is unable to reach any decisions.

When the narrator stands there like a pupil before his master or a sinner before his judge, the authority figure can be perceived as either comic or threatening. The ambiguity rests on the relationship between the overt text and the hidden one, a reciprocity that exists throughout and determines the special character of these stories.

What is the typical method of Agnon's abstract stories? As noted, the structure is based on the plot of a journey. The hero wanders through space. However, that space is not concrete but is rather the metaphorical embodiment of the soul or of a metarealistic world. Hence, the journey is not situated in historical or chronological time; it is the time of the soul, in which anterior and posterior are merely various stages in the hero's development. Such a method is closely related to expressionistic techniques, in which reality does not exist in itself; there are merely expressions of the fragmented ego or the ego's outcry.

The plot of the story knows neither causality nor probability but rather elliptical connections, which are both intratextual and intertextual. The materials that permit the discovery of the connections among the various links are given as the latent content of the overt text, and they are revealed to the interpreter as he or she fills the gaps through semantic, rhetorical, and structural analyses.

I have noted already that the overt text may be a parodic substitute for the subject hinted at by the latent text (the judge, the Lord of the Universe). The contrast sometimes reaches grotesque dimensions, as, for example, when the feeling of dread seems justified in the latent text but is comical and unfounded in the overt text. The relationship between what is implied in the two levels of expression is typical of the grotesque in these texts.

The latent text emerges for the reader both through a metaphorical understanding of the physical settings (for example, the cul-de-sac appearing in this story) and also through the accretion or extension of motifs as later ones shed light on those that came earlier. Thus, for example, the handkerchief (in the sense of a scarf or a shawl) appears in **"Quitclaim"** as the garment in which the narrator-protagonist wraps himself, not wanting any connection with the world about him.

All of these factors indicate that the world depicted is not anchored in reality but rather in a realm including far more than what the narrator-hero, who presents the story to the reader, is capable of interpreting for himself. The world of the story is a kind of psychological pattern. It could be interpreted as a repressed reality (in psychoanalytic terms), or as a metareality (following various metaphysical systems), or as a world of archetypes (according to Jung). In any case, the determining factor is the material representing multisemantic relationships between the latent subject and the overt one.

Naturally, one must realize that in fiction of this sort characterization declines in importance, and the protagonists cease being portrayed as unique individuals. As in folk tales, the character in the abstract story has a largely formal function. Even when the author gives names to his characters, they do not exist in their own right but must be taken as anonymous embodiments of emotional and identional elements of the psyche. Their appellations are likely to be allegorical, hinting at the latent text—the broad cultural connotation. But in such a case, one must understand the character from various points of view—that is, according to the meaning implicit or implied by the character's name (for example, Yekutiel = God shall acquit me and Ne'eman = faithful; both of these are epithets of Moses in midrashic literature, and they are used in Agnon's **"A Whole Loaf"**) or through the cultural links derived from the epithets (such as in "The Song of Honor").

Although the story is told by a narrator-hero, a consciousness with a psychological structure, he functions within the story without comprehending his context. In his journeys, the narrator-hero encounters various characters that seem to be superfluous to the logic of the plot. Through the use of chance appearances, the "I" encounters projections of himself, which become aspects of the structure of the relationship between him and the emotional factors that comprise the work's internal structure. The parallel between microcosm and macrocosm gives these emotional factors metarealistic significance; as a result, the interpretation of the story is transferred from the psychological level to an abstract level and thus to metaphysical concepts and values.

Since Agnon's fiction of this type attempts to present the realm in which problems exist rather than the realm in which they are solved, the parodic technique of multiple meanings is an appropriate one. Agnon portrays an ambiguous world that is filled with anonymous heroes and settings and is studded with epigrams and generalizations. The symbolic coloration of the elements leads us to interpret them as though the author sought to identify the Everyman in his story with every person outside of the story, and that the author attempted to provide a complete exposition of what is known as the human condition. That is to say, he presents his own inability and the inability of Everyman to give unequivocal ratification to the content of the work or to any values as a general truth. Human alienation, the solitude of his generation, the opacity of reality, and the impassivity of the powers that be are the subjects of the story.

If this assumption is correct then the form of the story fits its subjects, and the latter are suited to the form. This story is the most extreme instance of the embodiment of the modern worldview in Agnon's oeuvre. Here, Agnon also used intertextual techniques related to the cultural tradition. The intertextuality is generally parodic in effect; it is extreme and, in most cases, leads to grotesque results. The messages of these texts are ambivalent. However, it is not the kind of ambivalence that portrays something and its opposite at the same time but an ambivalence that disorients the addressee. Despite the traditional style and the intertextual connection to a latent traditional text, the story exposes the social and moral anarchy of modern man.

Agnon was quite conscious of the "writerly" effect of these stories. The dreamlike codification demanded an "analytical" decodifier. The signifiers in these texts do not have determinable signifieds but are quite multivalent and have, of course, no definitive referent. Moreover, they do not have any informant-analysand in presentia who could provide the reader with further information by bringing up "unique" connotations and associations in reference to specific signifieds—by excluding irrelevant information and including relevant data. The result is that the analyst-addressee (the reader) has to fill the "empty" semantic units, using paradigms and semantic connotations alluded to in the text or drawn from the addressee's own life experience. In addition, the addressee must fill in missing links and gaps, sometimes using analytical (that is, Freudian) techniques.

The addressee must "rewrite" the text to the best of his or her abilities in the areas of explication, elucidation, and interpretation. In a sense, the text "wants" to be and actually becomes a "writerly" text. As a result of this demand upon the addressee, the circle of potential readers is diminished. The author expects his readership to be composed of analytical readers who act as critics or of critics who act as analytical readers.

Nonetheless, this type of story does not represent Agnon at his greatest. His powers are most impressive in stories where reality is mingled with what is beyond, in the private and collective spheres, as in the novellas or in the short stories, such as **"Three Sisters"** and **"Ovadia the Cripple"**—one of which is built mainly upon sonorous, rhythmic, and stylistic effects; whereas the other is based on scenes and concrete situations. The best of Agnon's nonrealistic stories are those with an element of the concrete, such as **"The Overcoat,"** *Edo and Enam,* and **"From Lodging to Lodging."**

Between Abstract and Concrete: Stories
Conveying a Philosophy of History

Several of Agnon's stories can be interpreted in many ways and operate simultaneously on several levels of meaning; these include **"The Overcoat," "From Lodging to Lodging,"** *Edo and Enam,* and *Forevermore,* stories that are both existential and sociohistorical. Of course, the main meaning is existential, and the historical stratum is not a chronicle but rather the penetration to the roots of a situation through mythical writing. The mythic character of these stories, particularly *Edo and Enam* and *Forevermore,* tilts them toward a bond with traditional texts, which convey themes bearing on a philosophy of history.

"The Covering of Blood," included in the posthumously published *Within the Wall* (1975), constitutes the final link in that chain of stories. The existential level is less pronounced in **"The Covering of Blood"** than in the earlier stories, and the emphasis is placed on the historical stratum. This long short story may be regarded as a social survey of the history of the Jewish people in past generations. It is a general summation by the author, who looks at the past and anticipates the future. The traditional revolution reached its peak in these stories. In them, Agnon concretized the social and historical significance of the revolution that contained its own end within it. The revolution destroyed the tradition and, in the process, sowed the seeds of its own destruction.

The narrator-witness is confronted with the life stories of the three protagonists: Hillel, Adolf, and the old American. The three men are uprooted from Europe; two end up in the Land of Israel and one in America. They are not victims of the Holocaust; however, they are victims of the Jewish history that is epitomized by the Holocaust.

Hillel, an ordained rabbi, never is appointed to a rabbinical post because of baseless hatred within Jewish society, and even the post of ritual slaughterer is given to him as a favor rather than by right. Jewish society rejects him because it no longer believes in the values of the Torah and prefers material values. When he is exiled to the United States, his leg is amputated because Gittele-Frumtshis, the owner of the slaughterhouse, demands that he work day and night—not even releasing him to break his fast after the seventeenth of *tammuz*. Hillel is the victim of Jewish society in two versions of its exile, the European and the American (the latter is a kind of exacerbation of the former).

Adolf, a sergeant in the First World War, saves Hillel from death but is a victim of events between the two wars. He eats with Gentiles and lives with their women; assimilation makes him need their favors. He drifts from place to place and meets with destruction everywhere, until he emigrates to the Land of Israel. There, too, he is a beggar.

The old American reaches the New World as a child. He serves as a cantor's assistant until he marries a wealthy woman. Then he goes through a miniature holocaust: his daughter commits suicide after being deserted by the gentile singer who has gotten her pregnant, and his son is murdered by his friends after joining a band of thieves. The old man is bereft and solitary, undone by the assimilation of the second generation in the new place of exile.

The Holocaust is in the background, melding the three into a single figure that represents different aspects of the surviving remnant. The main character, Hillel, is a kind of Job whom the Lord does not bless in his later years. Both of Hillel's wives die because of the war, as do all of his children. He never has any possessions. In his confessions to the narrator-witness, there is a touch of a reproach directed on high. By choosing the name Hillel, Agnon asserted a connection between his character and the historical personage: the ancient rabbi who founded a school called the House of Hillel and who tempered the letter of the law with mercy. It was a later sage by the same name, Hillel, who said: "The Jews have no Messiah because they already devoured him in the days of Hezekiya." The reproaches of Hillel the sage, like those of Hillel in the story, are directed chiefly against the Jews who gobbled up their Messiah, both in

earlier times (represented by the quarrel between the Hassidim and the Mitnagdim) and in the time of the State of Israel. National redemption brought no change. Rather than redemption replacing exile, exile usurped the place of redemption. The ordained rabbi became a slaughterer, and the slaughterer became a beggar. Hillel is now without the House of Hillel.

In the course of the story, Hillel mediates between the two other characters: Adolf, who saved Hillel from death in the First World War, and the old American, who saves him from starvation after his leg is cut off on the seventeenth of *tammuz* in Gittele-Frumtshis's slaughterhouse.

The irony, or rather the grotesquery, of history is shown mainly in Gittele-Frumtshis's slaughterhouse, where Hillel says the benediction over the slaughtering and is covered with blood. The implicit parallel in the written language is the legend about the prophet Zechariah, who was slaughtered by the Jews and whose blood bubbled up and could not be covered until Nevuzaradan came and slaughtered ninety-four thousand residents of Jerusalem on the blood of the prophet. That event took place on the seventeenth of *tammuz* (an unlucky day in the personal life of Agnon's Hillel). According to tradition, that is the day when the first tablets were broken, when the walls of Jerusalem were broken through, and when an idol was placed in the Temple. Such linguistic and cultural allusions also point to Bialik's poem "On the Slaughterer." Perhaps one is justified in viewing the hundreds of chickens that are slaughtered while multitudes of Jews were being murdered overseas as part of the ceremony of repentance. (The owner of the slaughterhouse sends Hillel eighteen dollars as compensation for his leg.) The parallel creates an unusual link between reward and punishment. Hillel's "blood" will not be atoned for until the Jews are slaughtered. Gittele-Frumtshis operates an assembly line of slaughter; she presses for increased productivity, her heart bent on gain. Jews eager for money lost sight of what was happening across the ocean. The dreadful "hand in hand" (the subtitle of the story) shows that the Jews are bound up with each other, creating a strange and grotesque kind of logic—a justification of fate, which is not sufficiently justified. It is almost possible to say that the technique of analogy ("hand in hand") is no longer a literary stratagem here but has become the ironic and grotesque subject of the story.

Analogy is an important device in most of Agnon's writings and serves various functions in his works. For example, in *A Guest for the Night,* he uses analogy to depict the disintegration of society despite the common fate of the individuals within it. In **"The Covering of Blood,"** ironic analogy is an expression of Agnon's ironic view of history. The parallels among various phenomena that affect the social group shed ironic light both on the group itself and on the ironic author—the hidden entity, the master of history who creates phenomena so different and yet so similar. The writer's revolutionary irony is directed against both the Master of the Universe and the chosen people, whom He chose above all other nations. Another ambiguous parallel, as though blaming the Jews themselves for the Holocaust, is the name Adolf given to the Jewish sergeant:

> Hard days came to him. He had no choice but to beg from door to door. At any rate he praised himself for not doing what Hitler did and standing at the doorways of convents for the bowl of sauce they handed him.

Adolf is a fornicator. A number of gentile women give birth to his progeny, and he suspects that the destroyers of the Jewish community are descended from him. Adolf confesses to Hillel, who describes the state of affairs to the narrator-witness:

> I found him very depressed. I asked him what had happened to him, and he told me he had dreamt that a certain heathen of Hitler's party had struck a Jew and killed him cruelly, and that Jew was his nephew, and the heathen was the son of the lady who had had him by Adolf. In the daytime as well he sees all kinds of visions, and most of them are related to the results of that sin.

It is as if the victim created his murderer. But the ambivalent relationship to basic situations is created not only through the context of the names but principally by a parodic view of extraliterary situations, which are shown in a new light in the text. For example, the heroes frequently are caught in predicaments with no way out, and only saviors from the outside can rescue them from starvation and death. Their rescue offers neither consolation nor salvation. Rather than bringing redemption to the rescued, it brings profit to the rescuers, as when the slaughterer saves Hillel from starvation in order to exploit him (to keep a place open for his grandson) and when Gittele-Frumtshis behaves similarly. The story becomes a parody of the Jewish efforts at rescue between the two world wars. Even basic Zionist values, such as the ingathering of the exiles, are seen in a new light. The two immigrants—the survivors—do not journey to the Land of Israel of their own free will. Adolf is brought to Palestine by mistake. He is asked to serve as a translator for a circus, although he knows no Hebrew; he wanders about the country as a beggar without finding a place for himself. Hillel is sent to the Land of Israel at the expense of a rich American, but the ingathering of exiles does not bring unity. Here, art—as parody always has—distorts extraliterary motifs. As the reader compares fiction to reality, the meanings of the motifs are altered.

What is achieved through the intra- and intertextual connections, by means of the parodic use of extraliterary states of affairs, also is achieved through several fundamental symbols of the story: the severed leg, the hurdy-gurdy, the monkey, the parrot, and the dollars. Hillel's leg was not cut off when he was a child; a prince's coach did nearly run him over; and he was saved by a poor Jewish porter. His leg was not severed when he was buried in a landslide during the First World War; then, Adolf, another poor Jew, saved him. Only after ending up in Gittele-Frumtshis's slaughterhouse is his leg cut off because of her lust for wealth. All of the tension between rescue and rescue for the purpose of profit is exposed by the fate of Hillel's leg. The leg's value decreases progressively in the Land of Israel: an automobile destroys the rubber leg, and a wooden one takes its place (the gift of the Fair Measures Brotherhood); and holes turn up in the leg because a mad Hassid has done something with it. As the value of the leg decreases, so, too, does the value of Hillel's dollars. The state takes the dollars intended for the survivors of the Holocaust and derives profit from them.

Another central symbol is the hurdy-gurdy. Adolf receives the instrument from a beggar in Europe. He wanders through Austria with it and then brings it to the Land of Israel. The hurdy-gurdy plays the song of the sons of Korah (a rebel who opposed Moses) at the gates of the underworld ("Moses is one and his Torah is one"), but the song no longer expresses actual values. There is only the hidden echo of a not-so-splendid past. What remains is the hurdy-gurdy as a symbol of wanderings, to which the "Gypsy" monkey and the parrots are joined. The wandering Jews, Adolf and Hillel, have inherited a Gypsy legacy of aimless roaming.

In contrast to Agnon's decoherent stories, **"The Covering of Blood"** is not broken off but actually comes to a conclusion. The end attempts to predict the future of the native Israeli generation, as though returning to the question posed in *A Guest for the Night*.

The heroes of **"The Covering of Blood"** are alone. The American branch of survivors has no posterity. The children commit suicide or are murdered because they have assimilated. Yet Hillel is not alone in the way that Adolf, whose illegitimate sons are the murderers and destroyers, is. The only son and inheritor is Adolf's nephew:

> I do not recall whether I mentioned Adolf's sister's son. Adolf told me he was the Adolf from a certain city, all of whose Jewish inhabitants were killed by Hitler, to the last man, and of those who went to the Land of Israel, some died of hunger during the First World War and others were killed by the Arabs' shells during the conquest of the land. Adolf had one sister whose second marriage was to a Hebrew teacher, and she had a son by him. The boy's father, his sister's husband, that is, died, leaving her nothing. She raised the son in poverty, by dint of hard work, and every penny she saved she spent on his education. When he got older he joined the youth movement, and in the end he settled in the Land of Israel and promised his mother he would bring her. He arrived in the Land of Israel close to the time of the war between the Jews and the Arabs. He took part in the war, was wounded, and recovered. After the war he went to a kibbutz and became a tractor driver. One day the Syrians crossed the border, seized him, and took him prisoner. Since that time no one has heard anything of him.

According to Agnon, because the Jews of the Land of Israel did not change, even in their own country, their fate is liable to be like that of the Diaspora Jews. Regarding both the children of the American father and those of Hillel, we could say in the most general fashion that the fathers are sour grapes, and the children's teeth are set on edge. But in the case of Adolf's nephew, we are stunned. There is no proportion between the sour grapes and the setting on edge of teeth. The narrator is himself astonished at that strange fate, just as he wonders over and over again whether there is any connection regarding reward and punishment between the behavior of an individual and the fate of the nation.

The fate of Adolf's nephew, the last remnant of a destroyed family, remains obscure. Hillel is waiting for the young man, who might not be alive. If he is alive, his life might not be worth living, considering the inheritance left for him by his Uncle Adolf—that is, things from the Diaspora and symbols of Gypsy life: the hurdy-gurdy, the monkey, and the parrot. That, of course, is a harsh vision. It is a prophecy of agonies that do not purify; it is exile with no redemption.

The only light in that darkness is Benyamin, an American boy whose soul yearns for Torah and who has settled in the Land of Israel to study with Hillel. Perhaps that is the final life raft: the Torah, which is independent of place or time and exists beyond the dialectic of exile and redemption and holocaust and rebirth.

In this story, abstraction and concrete illustration are intermingled. Each episode—Hillel during the war, Hillel in the slaughterhouse, Adolf in the Land of Israel—is detailed and stands by itself. However, the connections among the episodes and the paradigmatic, or intertextual, links with various cultural materials give the story its meaning as a statement of a philosophy of history. The technique of the multifaceted parallels is an adequate correlative for the subject: what happened to the Jews, "hand in hand," in different historical settings. We have here an actualization of history that has become fantastic, or else a grotesque illumination of real situations that seem to compete with each other in their deformation.

This long short story more or less sums up the thematics of the traditional revolution: On the one hand, it describes the dead end in which the Zionist revolution culminated after inheriting the inner crises of the traditional society—as shown by the life and wanderings of Hillel and Adolf. However, on the other hand, the story shows clearly that, according to Agnon, the Zionist revolution did not bring a balm to cure the protracted ills of the Jewish people. In the Land of Israel—where the revolution took place, where everyone believed that "all hopes would be fulfilled" (to quote a famous song of the Second Aliya), and where the "Divine Presence would also dwell"—the revolution did not bring the longed for results. This story seems to show that the solution to the inner paradoxes of the revolution that destroyed the tradition might be a strange return to the *roots of the Jewish tradition*—before it was established in any traditional or secular institutions. That return, which could be a way out of the morass, is embodied in the figure of the young American Jew who comes to the Land of Israel to combine the study of Torah and working the land. The Torah, in its purity, might be one way out of the situation with no way out. The narrative situation in **"The Covering of Blood"** resembles the situation in *A Guest for the Night*, and I

believe that the analogy was a conscious one. Here again, the narrator-author is an addressee-witness to Hillel's story or confession. In turn, Hillel is the addressee and witness of Adolf's story. These are two modern interpretations of the myth of Job—recollections of the suffering of two individuals who happen to be victims of the last fifty years of Jewish history. Like Job, they have lost their loved ones and their possessions. The two storytellers are victims of the collective history of their community. The addressee is similar to the "guest" in *A Guest for the Night*—that is, an aesthetic involved/noninvolved spectator. His guilt is the "implied" blame of Job's companions, who bear witness and listen to Job's complaints but who were mere bystanders, seeing Job's afflictions and doing nothing but misunderstanding and misinterpreting them intellectually.

The implied author's goal and message is the transference of the implicit guilt feelings of the narrator as addressee to the implied readers. In the act of reading, the readers become witnesses and spectators for the primary and secondary narrators of the story. The implied authors demand that the readers take responsibility upon themselves for the miseries inflicted upon their brethren. The readers also belong to the social circle (Jews in America and Israel) that, in the literary model, was at least partly responsible for the suffering of the victims and the survivors. Moreover, I believe that Agnon indicates that any survivor must accept some responsibility for the miracle of survival while his or her group was victimized. This is the meaning of the stories of Hillel and Adolf, and this is their significance for the narrator, for their addressees, and for the narrator's addressees as well.

Based on the inner logic of the plot, **"The Covering of Blood"** is also one of Agnon's most ambiguous and grotesque stories. For example, Adolf, the pursued, is given the first name of Hitler—the arch pursuer. Between the two a bizarre synonymity is created. The story also ends in deep despair, with a strange prophecy for the future of the Jewish state—the children of which are liable to inherit the Gypsy heritage. However, with the motif of Benyamin, Agnon concludes one of his last stories—apparently written in the 1960s—in a manner similar to the author of Ecclesiastes, the most pessimistic of the twenty-four books of the Hebrew Bible. There, it is written:

> The end of the matter, all having been heard: fear God, and keep His commandments; for this is the whole man. For God shall bring every work into the judgment concerning every hidden thing, whether it be good or whether it be evil.

Lippman Bodoff (essay date 1993)

SOURCE: "Kabbalistic Feminism in Agnon's 'Betrothed'," in *Judaism,* Vol. 42, Fall, 1993, pp. 423-34.

[*In the following essay, Bodoff interprets* Betrothed *as a symbolic tale in which the modern Jew (represented by the protagonist Jacob) is torn between Hebraism (in the figure of Shoshanah) and the appeal of the secular worldliness (as symbolized by Jacob's travels, career, and involvement with gentile women).]*

INTRODUCTION

The struggle to provide and maintain a Jewish identity as the core of Israeli culture, in the face of the chasm in Jewish life opened up by modernity between the self and reason at war with community and faith, is an underlying theme in much of Agnon's work. He simultaneously developed this theme and reflected it in his writing technique, by using modern literary approaches to character analysis and plot development, together with traditional Jewish symbols, allusions and subtexts. Nowhere is his concern about the importance of maintaining the Jewish core in Israeli life—indeed, in the lives of Jews everywhere, but even, perhaps, especially, in Israel—than in his two novellas, *Edo and Enam* (1950), and *Betrothed* (1943).

Betrothed, written in the midst of the Holocaust, sought to provide some reassurance that, somehow, the bones of Jewish tradition would yet live—or, more precisely, magically come alive again in the *Yishuv,* in the newborn Jewish homeland of *Erez Yisrael.* The reassurance is conveyed in *Betrothed* through the mystical doctrines of kabbalah, that portray history as the pre-destined process of the liberation of the sparks of Divine holiness temporarily captured in a world of evil, and their ultimate reunification with the Godhead through a spiritually redeemed Israel (Jacob in the story) united with the *Shekhinah* (Shoshanah in the story). But Agnon adds a strong dramatic touch to his novelistic treatment, pitting the spiritual, feminine *Shekhinah* of kabbalah against six secular, lovely, but lethal, spiritually debilitating young women of the *Yishuv,* in a cosmic battle for the soul of Jacob. The latter, in context, is made into an anti-hero; while ambitious and dedicated to his own professional advancement, he remains passive, uninterested and even oblivious of the spiritual battle around him.

SUMMARY OF THE STORY

As children, living in the European *Galut,* Jacob and Shoshanah (before *Betrothed* starts) had sworn eternal faithfulness to each other while playing together at the home of her parents, who had reached out to Jacob when his mother died in his youth. Their betrothal is consummated in a ceremony in which she cuts off a lock of her hair and his, and burns the hair, and they both consume the ashes. As the novella opens, Jacob is a young man living in the Land of Israel. His *aliyah* was funded by Shoshanah's wealthy father, Ehrlich, but started as an educational and career opportunity rather than as an expression of any Zionist idealism by either of them. Jacob has remained in the *Yishuv* as a teacher at a university, where he does research in the dead plant life of the Mediterranean, an activity "remote from the interests of the Jewish settlements"; not surprisingly, his cultural interests run to Hellenism rather than Hebraism.

He lives in a secular city, Jaffa, where each person is busy "pursuing his own ends." and associates with a circle of six similar secular young women; together, they become known as the "Seven Planets." Oddly, there is not even the hint of any sex or romance between Jacob and any of them, despite their variety of origins, physique and personality. They spend time together in the homes, streets, and beaches of Jaffa, on the Mediterranean, under what seems like a remote, unseeing, star-filled sky— bonded to nature, happy together in an innocent, almost childlike way, in a cyclical, unchanging existence, with no evident goals, cares or concerns. Jacob is passive to them, and to the land and its culture.

Agnon usually provides non-realistic, even miraculous escapes from the historical abysses and dead-ends faced by Jewish ideals and traditions, when his characters are confronted or mocked by the stubborn realities of modernity.

—*Lippman Bodoff*

Suddenly, Jacob learns that Shoshanah and her father are coming to Palestine for a brief visit, at the end of a long, worldwide trip that has taken them to many countries, before returning home to Vienna. Meeting Shoshanah for the first time as an adult, after many years, he immediately senses a permanent attachment to her—based more on their mutual childhood covenant than on any special feelings that she now engenders. But he feels undeserving of her, and unhappy, without knowing why. Shoshanah seems jealous of his six girl friends—particularly of Tamar, to whom Jacob has been most physically attracted (although Shoshanah had no evident way of knowing this)— and insists that Jacob repeat his childhood vow of faithfulness and marriage. But their future as a couple is clouded. First, there are her continued bouts of somnolence, interrupted only by a rewarding tour of the *Yishuv*—in which she is impressed by the rebuilding of the land and language of the Jewish people, while her father continues to view it as a place for the old, for retirement and death. Second, Shoshanah's and Jacob's outlooks are fundamentally different. He values his freedom and his career, and looks at the world optimistically, as a place of opportunity. She sees herself as separated from the world, a world which humans have nothing "to be proud about." Third, Jacob is offered an attractive new position in America, and he quickly decides that it's time to move on, even if this means leaving Palestine and Shoshanah.

At this point, Shoshanah falls into a virtual coma; her doctor's scientifically based prognosis is that she will die unless she returns promptly to Vienna for some unspecified treatment. Jacob finds out about her illness and, this one time revealing a religious sensibility, prays: "Oh

God, . . . save *me* in Your great mercy" (emphasis added). Yet, he is determined to go to America. To deter him, Tamar attempts to seduce Jacob, but they are interrupted by the rest of the women, who succeed in moving the action, one last time, to the seashore, under the stars. They determine that one of them shall marry Jacob and go to America with him—the victor in a race that reverses the Greek practice: the girls will race for the man. The night and the rite capture the passive Jacob into seeming acquiescence at his coming captivity. Just when it appears that Tamar is about to win the race, Shoshanah appears and overtakes the pack, captures her human prize, and crowns herself with the garland of seaweed which the girls prepared for the victor.

STORY ANALYSIS

The battle of the contending forces of tradition and modernity in Jewish history is portrayed in **Betrothed** through the Jewish community in the Land of Israel, as it struggles to create a new homeland for the Jewish people. Agnon praises those who love the land and its people, who come to the land, work the land, and stay in the land—for whatever reason or motive. The Yemenite Jews have difficulty in reconciling Biblical texts with the world of reality, but—unlike Jacob—they continue to live and work in Israel, and to study Torah and obey its commandments. The Russian Jews are enthusiastic and passionate to the point of incivility, and the Sephardim are unsociable and superior—but both are loyal to their People and their Land. Yet, while the return to the Promised Land has required the destruction of the passivity, the defeatism—indeed, even the traditional faith—of most of Diaspora Jewry, Agnon recognizes that there can be no justification for the return unless the new Israel, represented by Jacob, inherits the tradition of Jacob's ancestors—represented, as we shall see, by Shoshanah. Even her secular father, Ehrlich, is able to discern that she and Jacob are eternally tied together, as he says to Jacob after the latter has decided to leave Shoshanah and the Land of Israel:

> "Let me put it to you this way. Suppose I am holding on to some valuable object, which I am about to return to its *rightful* owner. Suddenly, the object slips from my hands before it has reached the owner and there we are, both left empty-handed; I who had it in my grasp and he who reached out to take it" (emphasis added).

But that eternal bond, that alone can give a reborn Jewish people an identity, is threatened by secularism, on two fronts. First, is the battle for Jacob's loyalty to the Land, represented by the invitation from New York that he go there to become a full professor and occupy an academic chair that has been established in his honor. Second, is the looming battle for Jacob's spiritual and cultural loyalty between Shoshanah and the six maidens—indeed between Shoshanah and the entire secular ambiance of the story, from Vienna to Jaffa, from her father to the "Seven Planets," from ancient sea to modern university. Both battles are ultimately a battle between Judaism and Hellenism, for Jacob's soul. Given his secular training and

career, and a life that is not rooted in Jewish tradition, it seems inevitable to Agnon that secular Judaism means the death of Judaism and ultimately of the Jewish people.

Thus, Jacob's response to the call of New York to his career is single-minded and unreserved acceptance. His decision to leave, and Shoshanah's resultant sickness, produce another challenge, one last attempt by the six maidens to capture Jacob as a husband for one of them, if not for the land and its people. For them, the issue is who will go with Jacob to America. Looking out from the shore to a passing ship, too far to permit a perception of its direction, "to Jacob and his companions it made no difference where the ship was headed." For them, as for Ehrlich, travel is the goal, to see the world; all places and cultures are equal. Leaving the Land of Israel is no different than coming to it, if there is no special meaning to *Erez Yisrael*.

We are now ready to understand Shoshanah, and her role in the battle for Jacob's soul—a battle between Past and Future, Religion and Nature, Spirituality and Science, Hebraism and Paganism, Jewish tradition and Greek and Roman culture, God and Nature, the three-century old Death of Religion and its rebirth. For Agnon, however, there is more to the tale than just that clash; at stake is *the inevitability of its resolution*—an inevitability that Agnon represents for us in the symbols that permeate **Betrothed**.

Jacob is seemingly a permanent part of a secular circle which Agnon describes, in the words of the Jaffa community, as the "Seven Planets." These, in turn, represent the kabbalistic concept of the seven lower *sefirot*, or emanations of God, which represent the Divine in the material, observable universe, and guide its destiny. The three uppermost *sefirot* are *Keter* (the "*ein sof*" or eternal Godhead), and *Hakhma* and *Binah* (wisdom and intelligence), the two forms of knowledge in their male and female aspects. Together they make up the three upper *sefirot* that man cannot even approach. But through Torah, and the kabbalistic understanding of its symbols and commandments, man may comprehend and achieve the essence of the seven lower *sefirot*: *Tiferet* (beauty or compassion) (Jacob and the People of Israel); *Hesed* (love) (Abraham); *Gevurah* (power) (Isaac); *Nezah* (endurance) (Moses); *Hod* (majesty) (Aaron); *Yesod* (foundation) (Joseph); and—the tenth and most mystical of the *sefirot*—*Malkhut* (kingdom) (David). The last *sefirah* is not limited, however, to David. Indeed, in Lurianic kabbalah it stands for the *Shekhinah*, the feminine, merciful aspect of God that must combine with *Tiferet* (Jacob) and ultimately with the Godhead itself, with *Keter*, in order for the world to operate in harmony and thereby be redeemed and returned to its original perfection, the perfect unity of God. Shoshanah, in Jewish tradition, is the *Shekhinah*. Thus, the history of the universe becomes, in kabbalah, a spiritual process of world redemption, in which the *Shekhinah* is the catalyst. Somehow, Shoshanah must become part of Jacob's circle of seven—and transform it by her presence and union with Jacob from seven secular "planets" to seven holy *sefirot*. Because of this Divine

Plan, comprising the subtext of **Betrothed,** harmony will come, and redemption is inevitable.

The Israeli critic, and my revered teacher, Gershon Shaked, has recognized the importance, for Agnon, of the miraculous in explainning Jewish history and its eternality. He argues that Agnon usually provides non-realistic, even miraculous escapes from the historical abysses and dead-ends faced by Jewish ideals and traditions, when his characters are confronted or mocked by the stubborn realities of modernity. Agnon generally provides

> . . . a miraculous and non-rational counter-plot, deriving from irrational realms. . . . These works do not end happily, with reconciliation, but rather with acknowledgement of the dead-end, the gap between the powers at odds with each other. . . .

What emerges from a general examination of the plots of these novels is that Agnon argued that only by means of irrational counter-plots (or a rational one contrasting with an irrational act based on nostalgia, the return to the doomed *shtetl*) can this generation grapple with the conflicts it confronts. According to the nature of things and logic, recent generations of Jewish society have reached a cul-de-sac, and each generation, everywhere, is threatened with devastation. One might possibly say that the final lesson of Agnon's view of history and society is that the society exists by virtue of miracles, and if we do not depend on miracles, we have nothing to depend on.

> ["By Some Miracle: S.Y. Agnon—the Literary Representation of Social Dramas," *Modern Hebrew Literature,* Spring/Summer, 1986]

Jewish tradition is rich in the symbolic importance of the *Shekhinah* and its metaphor, *Shoshanah* (or rose). The Midrash speaks of the *Shekhinah* as the Divine Presence, an aspect—and more particularly the feminine, daughter, sister and bride, aspect—of the Godhead, to which (a male) Israel seeks to cleave. It also equates that term with *Knesset Yisrael*—the Jewish people in its ideal (feminine) form, which claims (a male) God as hers alone, as Shoshanah claimed Jacob when they were children. Their mutual oath in **Betrothed** is like a modern double ring ceremony; each is dedicated to the other—"*Dodi li, v'ani lo,*" as we read in *Song of Songs,* the canonical love duet and love longings between God and Israel as they eternally search for each other in the streets of Jerusalem. The Midrash speaks of Israel, the *shoshanah* of God, as a "rose among the thorns," in that, like Agnon's Shoshanah, it withstood foreign cultures while in *Galut,* preserving the purity of Jewish belief, of Jewish monotheism and spirituality.

Agnon does not leave Shoshanah's status, as a player in a cosmic process, to our imagination or speculation. He does more than simply provide her with a name with traditional connotations. He endows her dramatically with redemptive qualities. She is a *Galut* girl who—unlike Jacob—has not lost her Jewish pride and identity despite the past secular ambience of her family and country. Though a latecomer to the Holy Land, she knows where she belongs when she gets there.

The *Shekhinah* (Shoshanah) has been in *Galut,* where our tradition tells us it went to accompany and preserve Israel in its wanderings among the nations (B. *Meg.* 29 a). It has always sought to remain close to Israel, just as Shoshanah and Jacob, although having different parents, lived together in Vienna as part of one family. Shoshanah and the People of Israel were, from the beginning of exile, betrothed, as God took Israel for His bride on Mount Sinai. It was an oath taken to last until redemption, and the final unity of the People of Israel with the *Shekhinah,* in the Land of Israel.

But, as the *Zohar* represents, they have become separated, and, wandering from land to land, she is now tired, sleepy, although still able to withstand long voyages. Agnon's imagery reminds us of *Song of Songs,* where Shoshanah (there representing the Jewish People [2:1]), describes herself as "asleep, but my heart is awake" (5:2). She can endure separation and endless travel among the nations away from Jacob as long as she is not permanently rejected by him. She is prescient (recall her meeting with Tamar), suggesting powers that are more than mortal, the powers of spiritual insight. Indeed, when Jacob and Shoshanah first meet, as adults, in *Erez Yisrael,* Shoshanah speaks optimistically of "the resurrection of the dead," a concept which the secular Jacob emphatically rejects. For Shoshanah, there is more to history than man's perception of reality; for Jacob, there is only reality, the lessons of science. Her response, as if sensing that there will soon come a time when resurrection of the dead will have to be a reality for both of them, is described in the following way by Agnon:

> At that moment Shoshanah seemed to hover (*merahefet*) over those blue distances she had spoken of. Then, suddenly, she answered Jacob's gaze. She took out her handkerchief, wiped her eyes, opened them and looked at him with absolute love. After a while she said, "I am going to close my eyes and you, Jacob, are to kiss me on the eyelids."

> Jacob's own eyes filled with tears. With the tears still there, he placed his lips on her wet lashes.

Later, when Jacob is about to be enveloped in a pagan marriage rite orchestrated by the six maidens, this kiss and its remembrance will save him, protecting him from an enveloping, consuming alien embrace. We should note Agnon's use of the word "*merahefet,*" hovering, to describe Shoshanah's spirit, with its connotation of the Divine Spirit, from the opening lines of Genesis.

Shoshanah is not close to her father, who is secular; and Agnon suggests that his love for her is less as a daughter than as an heirloom, a treasured object of which one is proud, behind glass or in a portrait, but which is not a part of one's active life. She remains aloof from foreign cultures and uncontaminated by them. For Shoshanah, her childhood oath with Jacob is a lasting one. She loves the Land of Israel, as we see in her joy at her father's decision to settle in *Erez Yisrael,* and at the use of the Hebrew language as the language of prayer and daily life by her reborn People in a reborn Land. Shoshanah identifies Hebrew with the *sidur,* the language of prayer, that brings man in direct contact with God. Unlike Jacob, she believes in personal rebirth—personal resurrection—one of Maimonides' thirteen fundamental creeds of Judaism.

Agnon never lets us be certain of what the verdict of history will be, which is to say, whether history and not God will really write the final text of his story.

—*Lippman Bodoff*

Jacob, like her father, shares neither her spirituality nor her faith. Indeed, she is the only protagonist in the story with a belief in, and an attachment to, Jewish land, liturgy, ritual, history and theology. Neither her father, nor Jacob, nor the "six maidens," show a loyalty to these values. It is her full acceptance of Jewish tradition that differentiates her from the others, that separates the *Shekhinah* from the other, opposite, forces contending for Jacob's soul. These forces include the locus of the story—multi-national, secular Jaffa, which Agnon points out was established by Japheth, father of Indo-European nations and cultures, and the Greek and Roman traditions and values of Western civilization. Jacob still clings to them; Shoshanah easily sheds them.

To realistically portray Jacob as both Shoshanah's beloved *and* the object of her spiritual battle for him, Agnon insightfully makes Jacob merely a passive, easily diverted, symbol of Hellenism. His life represents not Eros and instinct, as in the case of the six maidens who surround him, but knowledge and science—not Dionysus but Apollo. As we have seen, the key to the meaning of Shoshanah's relationship with Jacob is provided by the kabbalah and its imaging of the cosmic process of redemption. Significantly, for Agnon, it is Shoshanah who must pursue and capture the passive Jacob, who is incapable of overcoming his desire to pursue, alone, a secular scientific life—despite his instinctive understanding that without Shoshanah he is nothing.

At the beginning of the story, the *Shekhinah* and Israel have become separated; we recall her words in *Song of Songs, "ani yeshena, v'libi er,"* "I am asleep but my heart is awake," and we read about Shoshanah's initial intermittent dazedness, sleepiness, and her glazed, uninterested look as she waits unsuccessfully for Jacob to choose her over her spiritual adversaries, and bring redemption to the world. She has been this way since he left her years ago to find his individual fulfillment. Meanwhile, Jacob has been bound up in a life from which every element of Jewish tradition has been lost. But, soon after Shoshanah's arrival in Palestine, she has Jacob reaffirm his

oath of loyalty to her, to the *Shekhinah,* which he does without hesitation or reservation, although—as his actions show—still without real love and total commitment.

From that moment on, Shoshanah is alert, active—even enjoying material pleasures. Yet, Shoshanah is still unhappy as she contemplates the future, knowing from her past European, Viennese experience that life even together with Jacob will be difficult in a hostile, warring world, in which evil is so powerful. Shoshanah's sadness is not a private death wish, but the real concern of someone who is aware of Jewish suffering, foreseeing that so much hardship is in store for them in the real world.

In contrast, Jacob is optimistic about the future, which he can see only as a vibrant young man, and not as a Jew threatened by the cultures that surround him. "Both of us are young enough, with all of our life before us." It is Jacob, the modern man of science and reason, who is unrealistically optimistic, who—caring only about himself—cannot accurately see where a world without spirituality is heading. But Shoshanah, sensitive to Israel's tradition and history, despairs, because she is concerned that the future may not be "any better than the life that lies behind." The depth of Agnon's own despair in the middle of the Holocaust is represented by the despair of the *Shekhinah* itself, even as it contemplates renewed spiritual union with Israel, in the Land of Israel.

Jacob, because of his estrangement from Judaism, now is twice tempted to betray Shoshanah. First, he accepts the offer to become a professor in a New York university, without thought or regret. Shoshanah presumably learns about Jacob's decision when the rest of Jaffa learns about it, as they do very quickly. Only then does she succumb to a new kind of sleep, seemingly permanent and just short of death, an illness both real and metaphysical, as she is about to be abandoned again by Jacob.

But the lure of a new, voluntary *Galut* in New York is not the only temptation facing Jacob. A far more serious test immediately awaits him, a test to which Shoshanah herself must respond, lest the Divine Plan for redemption go awry. For the six maidens now make one last effort to capture Jacob permanently, which is to say, to exclude the *Shekhinah* permanently from their community, and from ever marrying Jacob. It begins as Tamar comes to see him in his room for the first time—Tamar, whom Shoshanah perceived as the true obstacle to her spiritually and physically uniting with Jacob and entering the "circle of seven," as Jewish tradition envisions, and thereby changing its essence from natural "planets" to spiritual *sefirot.* It is Tamar to whom Jacob has been most attracted physically and with whom he has most nearly formed a physical attachment. It is this Tamar—whose name connotes a dark moral aspect in Jewish tradition—who now appears, asking Jacob for advice on two strangely contrasting career paths, which now become understandable in their symbolism. The first alternative is for Tamar to go to Europe and become a doctor (a traditional and honorable career for a Jew) and thereby leave room for Shoshanah to join the circle of seven. The second, is for

Tamar to remain in Israel and take up sculpturing (symbolic of graven images) and the beauty of form, a cultural symbol of Paganism and Hellenism, with their emphasis on strength and beauty. As we shall see, Tamar's appearance in Jacob's room, ostensibly for career advice, is a ruse for arousal. Tamar is out to become, and is about to become, the wife of Jacob—which will permanently exclude Shoshanah from the "planets," destroy the reunification of the Divine *sefirot,* and bind Jacob forever to all that Tamar represents.

In short order, Tamar is joined by the other five girls, and there soon commences an unmistakably pagan, Greek rite under the stars, at the water's edge of Jaffa. They encircle and dance around Jacob, reminiscent of the psalmist's remark, *"sabuni gam sevavuni"* ("they compassed me about"), in describing the encirclement of Israel by its enemies. Soon, the girls decide to emulate the Greeks and have a race, with the winner—the "mighty runner"—to be crowned by Jacob and given to him in marriage. Jacob is described as in a state of being "carried beyond himself," as he had been all those other nights that he and the six maidens had walked by the sea under the stars feeling at one with the mighty beauty of nature around them—heaven and earth, land and sea—"which had become a single whole."

But, adds Agnon, so that the reader keeps the invisible Divine role in mind, "this [unity of nature] was contained in yet another greater whole that no eye could see." Indeed, while Jacob now "put[s] Shoshanah entirely out of his mind" and is completely in the power of the maidens and the outcome of their rites, Agnon has not forgotten her: "Her memory formed a circle around his heart, like the golden lashes around her eyes as she slept," the lashes that she had earlier insisted that Jacob kiss, with evident prescience.

The race commences, with the one who proves to be the most "mighty," not the one whom Jacob truly loves, to be his bride. Here, Agnon presents a powerful irony. Jacob, who prides himself on his independence and freedom, has now become the object of capture and enslavement by those who symbolically represent precisely those values and virtues he has most sought in life. His enslavement will be symbolized by his being crowned by the victor with the very seaweed, the subject of his professional excellence, that symbolized that freedom and independence. To compound the irony, his enslavement is about to be achieved by Tamar, who is about to win the race, and with it Jacob, and thereby change a destiny that, of course, cannot be changed, because for Agnon there is a "greater whole that no eye could see." We know that Tamar wants to win the race and Jacob, because Agnon is careful to point out that she *overtakes* first Rachel and Leah, then Mira, Asnat and Raya, who had alternately taken the lead. Indeed, it is now evident from this effort that winning Jacob was her objective when she came to his room, ostensibly to discuss career choices.

Shoshanah suddenly appears, in her white nightgown, "like a maiden suddenly alarmed in her sleep," alarmed because history is about to be irrevocably changed, because a destiny foretold in Jewish tradition is about to be permanently altered, nullified. She almost literally rises from the dead and wins Jacob's hand, crowned by the garland of seaweed prepared by her adversaries, which recalls her garland when, as children, she and Jacob first vowed their eternal union. She triumphs not because such an outcome is rational, but because for Agnon she is an instrument—the crucial instrument—of God's Divine plan for Israel. Harmony has been restored to history through the Divine Plan as understood by kabbalah.

Agnon's imagery of a near-death Shoshanah saving Jacob, the assimilated Jew, from extinction, re-enacting a pre-ordained cosmic process, points to an important message. Shoshanah can never be re-united with Jacob unless she pursues him, because the modern pull of acculturation makes him incapable of permanently identifying with and choosing either Shoshanah or her opposites. For him, as Gershon Shaked suggests, [in "Portrait of the Immigrant as a Young Neurotic," *Prooftexts,* January, 1987], they are all sisters, each other's and his, and so he cannot independently unite with any of them without help. But, Agnon inverts the kabbalistic tradition of the *Shekhinah* waiting for an impatient lover, the *ze'ir anpin,* to symbolize how difficult the process of redemption will be. In the modern world, man cannot rely on a kabbalistically foretold destiny; only a miracle, wrought by those who believe in miracles and embrace those who do not, will suffice.

HOW DOES IT END?

Agnon never lets us be certain of what the verdict of history will be, which is to say, whether history and not God will really write the final text of his story. For, at the end of **Betrothed,** we are told that this is the end of the story "for the time being." On what does the outcome depend? That we are not told. In the end, perhaps, it is for each of us to answer that question, by our faith, or our actions, perhaps both. Is Israel safe, even within the Land of Israel, if its culture, indigenous or imported, is a secular culture without religious content? For the hideous possibility of Israel permanently exiled in its own land, **Betrothed** provides the healing balm of the possibility of a faith that such a permanent separation is impossible between Jacob and his eternal, historic, covenanted companion, Shoshanah. Such an exile, resulting from the permanent incompatability between the *Shekhinah* and Israel, would be contrary to God's plan in Jewish tradition, which provides the underlying text for this story.

There remains the question of whether there is a possibility, as some critics suggest, that the ending of **Betrothed** is a parody of Jewish tradition, a sick joke played at Jacob's expense. Is **Betrothed** a story of *Thanatos,* symbolized by Shoshanah capturing Jacob in a final deathly embrace, or as I have suggested—a symbolic tale of hope for a Judaism and a Jewish people saved at the last minute from the deathly embrace of Hellenism and assimilation?

There does seem to be a sharp contrast, as Shaked suggests, between the *Shoshanat Ya'akov,* the Shoshanah of

Jacob in the Jewish tradition (in the Purim poem established by the Great Assembly in the 5th Century, B.C.E.) who is *zahala ve'sameha,* happy and joyous, and the almost always sad, sleepy, and death-obsessed Shoshanah of Agnon's novella. Yet, it is difficult to support the view that Agnon is parodying the tradition—giving us a story ending in death and not life (or ignoring Jewish tradition altogether, as a minority suggest)—rather than employing it, as I argue, as a serious subtext for **Betrothed.** To adopt the parody view, one would have to believe that Agnon adopted in **Betrothed,** while the Holocaust was raging, the critique of traditional Judaism by the anti-Semite Nietzsche as the life-denying way of life, *par excellence.* One would have to believe that Agnon embraced in **Betrothed,** while Jewry's religious sages were being murdered, the anti-religious, secularist-nationalist views of such as A. D. Gordon, M. J. Berdiczewski and Ahad Ha'am. This is too radical a view for Agnon; it is not his way. I believe, therefore, that Shoshanah is seriously and not ironically symbolized, and her sadness and death obsession are not meant to ridicule the *Shekhinah* of Jewish tradition but to reflect on its historic crisis and describe its ultimate redemption. But there are additional historical and textual reasons that may be adduced.

Betrothed was written in 1942-43, when Hitler still occupied most of European Russia and most of North Africa, and was close to seizing Palestine and the rest of the Middle East, when the Holocaust had become known as an actuality if not in its full dimensions of 6 million Jewish dead. Shoshanah has a right, as it were—without symbolizing *Thanatos*—in a work written to be read by readers living in the awesome eye of Hitler's racial devastation, to envy the dead and to foresee tragedy lying ahead for her and for Jacob. Yet, she seeks and obtains Jacob's commitment to marriage and a future life together, and looks forward to it; she praises the rebirth of Hebrew and the Jewish people in the *Yishuv*; and she literally jumps for joy when learning that she and her father will live in *Erez Yisrael.* These are not the indications of a person that craves death, but of a sensitive, aware, realistic person who spiritually and ideologically wants to live and achieve her destiny, even while—on a realistic and rational level—she recognizes how difficult Jewish life can be.

And there is the concluding personal observation by Agnon at the end of **Betrothed,** where he tells us that, because Shoshanah and Jacob were betrothed to one another through a solemn vow, he has titled the work *Sh'vuat Emunim,* the vow of those who are faithful (to God? to each other? to both?) and not, as "at first we had thought to call it, 'The Seven Maidens'." The concept of covenant between Jacob and Shoshanah overcame the secular, ambivalent, ironic concept of seven maidens (i.e., the inappropriate combination of the *Shekhinah* with her spiritual antagonists). For, without Jacob, there is no special content to "seven maidens"; they would merely symbolize seven women fighting for the loyalty and love of a man. But, because of the childhood oath sworn by Jacob and Shoshanah, symbolizing the covenant at Sinai between Israel in its historic youth and God, the title—

and the story's significance—had to be restated as the "Vow of the Faithful."

The tale will, indeed, continue, as Agnon has noted, but the chasm between Jewish dreams and Jewish realities—and the modern chasm between what our minds believe and our souls perceive—will ultimately be bridged, as **Betrothed** reassures those with faith in Jewish destiny and redemption.

Nitza Ben-Dov (essay date 1993)

SOURCE: "The Web of Biblical Allusion," in *Agnon's Art of Indirection: Uncovering Latent Content in the Fiction of S. Y. Agnon,* E. J. Brill, Leiden, Netherlands, 1993, pp. 135-52.

[*In the following excerpt, Ben-Dov contends that a buried layer of biblical allusion in "The Dance of Death, or the Lovely and Pleasant" belies the overt meaning of the story.*]

> *Agnon's scriptural and talmudic resonances and nuances, his historical and textual layers, his allusive and elusive echoings and patternings, are so marvelously multiform, dense, and imbricated that he is daunting even to the most sophisticated Hebrew readers.*
>
> —Cynthia Ozick
> "Agnon's Antagonisms"

. . . . .

In this [essay], we shall be concerned exclusively with examining how the multiplicity of meaning so integral to Agnon's style, which makes it difficult for his readers to retrace a situation, utterance, motif, or even the plot of his narratives without sensing that the concealed exceeds the revealed, owes much to the linguistically allusive dimension of his stories, hidden in which are elements whose importance is often greater than that of more visible surface features.

The connotative riches of Hebrew, a language encompassing three thousand years of literary creativity and a great network of intertextual commentaries and references, have been used for fictional purposes by many modern Hebrew authors, but by none with the narrative cunning of Agnon. Intertextual allusions in Agnon's work create complex layers of meaning through their evocation, often by means of a single word or brief phrase, of entire passages from antecedent texts. They are, however, commonly overlooked not only by readers of his work in translation, which cannot possibly reproduce such effects, but also by many Hebrew readers, who lack the traditional Jewish education needed to follow the recondite hints of Agnon's language. Even those readers who make the effort, aided by dictionaries, concordances, and so on, to trace Agnon's many literary allusions to their source often miss the subtleties, narrative implications, and parody that contribute to the tension between the explicit and implicit which is the essence of his artistry.

Most of Agnon's fictional works are composed of all the many linguistic strata of Hebrew, from the Bible and on through the Mishnah, the Talmud, the midrash, the prayer-book, the medieval Hebrew poets, the rabbinic commentaries, and the Hasidic tales of Eastern Europe. Only two are quarried exclusively from what the Israeli writer Amos Oz has called the Hebrew language's "biblical bedrock" ["Thoughts on the Hebrew Language," in *Under This Blazing Light* (Hebrew), 1979]. One of these is the novella *In the Prime of Her Life*; the other is the collection *Tales of Poland,* a short story from which called **"The Dance of Death, or the Lovely and Pleasant"** will be the focus of the present [essay]. By means of this story I hope to show how Agnon's extraordinarily subtle use of the Hebrew tradition of intertextuality can endow a narrative with a hidden meaning, a meaning even which is a contradiction of the apparent surface meaning. Thus, allusion performs a function analogous to dream-imagery in opening unsuspected perspectives through a strategy of indirection.

Before examining **"The Dance of Death,"** however, I would first like to say a few . . . words about the use of biblical language in *In the Prime of Her Life.* I have contended that the critical consensus that this novella ends on a note of desired consummation is mistaken, and that the real theme of *In the Prime of Her Life* (as of all Agnon's love stories) is not fulfilled but disappointed love. What I wish to do now is demonstrate how this claim can be substantiated by a close reading of two biblical allusions that, occurring in a passage at the beginning of the novella, harbor within themselves the covert content of the entire work. . . .

Agnon had obvious mimetic reasons for composing *In the Prime of Her Life* entirely in biblical Hebrew, for his narrator Tirtza Mintz is a woman of a traditional Orthodox Jewish upbringing who has been schooled in the Bible but not in Rabbinics. A closer reading of the story, however, reveals that purely aesthetic considerations determined the choice of its language too. The laconic style of biblical prose, which mutes emotive voices and screens dramatic feelings, fits the solemnly tempered tone and melancholy atmosphere of the novella. The grim mood of the story's opening; the growth of its heroine in the shadow of her mother Leah's premature death; the girl's love for Akavia Mazal, Leah's first and only romance; Leah's chronic illness which Tirtza reenacts in the form of acute lovesickness; Tirtza's ultimate marriage to Akavia, a man far beyond her years, who spends his days recording local history and unearthing ancient tombs; and finally, the death wish with which the story ends as Tirtza, now pregnant, feels her unborn child quicken in her womb—all of these are effectively captured by the use of scriptural language.

The very first encounter between Tirtza and Akavia illustrates the quiet power of biblical allusion in this complex love story. At the end of their year of mourning for Tirt-

za's mother, Tirtza and her father take a walk together to Akavia's home, which is located at the edge of town. Akavia, a scholar-poet and antiquarian, has been asked to compose the epitaph for Leah's tombstone. Tirtza narrates:

> At that time my father stopped saying the mourner's prayer. And he came to me and said, "Come, let us go see to a tombstone for our mother." And I put on my hat and gloves and said, "Here I am, father.". . . We took a long route around the town. My father put his hand in mine and said, "Let us go this way."

> As we reached the end of the town, lo, there was an old woman digging in her yard. And my father greeted her and said, "Please tell us, good woman, is Mr. Mazal here?" And the woman set aside the spade with which she had been digging and answered, "Yes, sir, Mr. Mazal is at home." And my father put his arm in mine and said, "Come, my daughter, let us go in."

To the Hebrew reader who knows his Bible, this description immediately brings to mind two scriptural episodes: the binding of Isaac and Saul's quest for his father's asses. We are alerted to the first of these the moment Tirtza says *hineni,* "Here I am," which is Abraham's response to God when he is called upon to sacrifice Isaac. Subsequently, this scene from Genesis is suggested several more times in the course of the passage, as in the long, circuitous walk Tirtza and her father take (Abraham and Isaac walk for three days to reach the place of Isaac's sacrifice) and in the frequent use of the verb "to go," as when Mr. Mintz, using a grammatically archaic form, tells Tirtza, "Let us go this way" (*nelkha-na shama,* a clear echo of Abraham's *nelkha ad koh,* "We will go yonder"). By using such language Agnon intimates that Tirtza, like the biblical Isaac, will passively undergo an extraordinary ordeal at the hands of her elders, who will sacrifice her upon the altar of their own emotional needs.

The second biblical allusion in this episode is implicit in Mr. Mintz's query, "Is Mr. Mazal here?" the unusual Hebrew phrasing of which *ha-yesh ba-zeh mar Mazal?* occurs only once in the Bible. This is in I Samuel 9:11, where Saul and his servant, who are seeking the prophet Samuel in order to inquire about Saul's father's lost asses, ask some maidens they meet at a well, "Is the seer here?" (*ha-yesh ba-zeh haro'eh*). In the Bible, of course, especially in the Book of Genesis, an encounter between a young man and a maiden at a well is a frequent prelude to betrothal, and there is thus a special significance in Tirtza's encounter being with an old woman. The age of Mazal's servant presages Tirtza's future romance with a man twice her years and implies that her fate will be radically different both from that of Saul, who sets out in search of his father's asses and discovers a kingdom, and from that of the Patriarchs, who discover youthful love at a well. Unlike them, Tirtza is entering an aged world of excavated antiquities, an eccentric realm over which there hovers a spirit of death.

In the Bible itself, these two episodes have no verbal or thematic relationship. Even in Agnon's tale, they function in opposite ways. Tirtza and her father's walk to Akavia's home directly parallels the biblical story of the binding of Isaac and thus takes on a mythic or epic quality. In contrast, the story of Saul's search for the asses that results in his unexpected elevation to the monarchy is inverted in *In The Prime of Her Life*: whereas Tirtza thinks she is setting out on a romantic adventure when she goes to meet Akavia Mazal, her mother's youthful love, she is in fact taking a first step toward entrapment in a mundane, oppressive marriage. The Saul allusion, therefore, is ironic; it contrasts the destiny of Agnon's characters with those of the great heroes of the Bible. As [is the case] in *In The Prime of Her Life,* part of the difficulty in interpreting Agnon's allusive language lies precisely in deciding when it is "mythic" and when "ironic," when it reinforces certain apparent meanings or implications in the text and when it undermines them. In addition to the many other kinds of indeterminancy in Agnon's fiction that have been discussed in these pages, this one too must be taken into account in any close reading.

This technique of compound scriptural allusion is commonly used by Agnon in his *Tales of Poland,* a slim, early volume that has been commonly considered by critics to be little more than a minor exercise in the literary recasting of Jewish folk materials. In the following analysis of one of these tales, **"The Dance of Death,"** a story only four pages long, I hope to show how Agnon's choice of specific biblical allusions is always deliberate and thematically significant; how even small and seemingly inconsequential markers whose significance appears to be localized are part of a larger design; how this design interweaves these components so that a coherent and surprising interpretation of the text is made possible; finally, how, even when such coherence is achieved, the many-sided indeterminacy that is . . . characteristic of Agnon's work, is preserved and even intensified.

At first glance, **"The Dance of Death"** has a strong thematic resemblance to apparently similar stories in the literature of the 19th-century Hebrew revival which make use of Jewish martyrological materials both to immortalize Jewish suffering at the hands of a cruelly anti-Semitic world and to challenge traditional Jewish assumptions of a benevolent Providence that guides Jewish fate. A careful stylistic analysis of **"The Dance of Death,"** however, demonstrates how far removed in fact it is from such stories, whose thematics it restates for its own deeply ambivalent ends. In Agnon's tale, the center of gravity is subtly shifted from questioning the reliability of Providence to questioning the reliability of the Jewish soul itself. The many binary relationships that exist in **"The Dance of Death"**—Gentile and Jew, Jew and God, human responsibility and human passion, law-giving and law-receiving, life and death, sin and punishment, retribution and atonement, man and woman, daughter and father, individual and community, rich and poor, Jewish past and Jewish future—can support various readings of the text, of which that suggested here is only one of many possibilities. Moreover, **"The Dance of Death"** was written by Agnon in several versions, including an original Yid-

dish one called *Der Toytntantz.* In each of these versions the focus shifts slightly, but I believe that the "deep" meaning is the same in all of them, and it is this meaning, as it is most acutely revealed through the use of biblical language, that concerns me in the last version examined here.

Agnon apparently composed his *Tales of Poland* in biblical language in order to stress the antiquity and consolidation of the Jewish community in Poland and to suffuse it with a glow of nostalgia in which fantasy and history coalesce. Moreover, as in *In the Prime of Her Life,* the biblical language of these tales fits the romantic and morbid aspects of the themes of unrequited love, desperate yearning, and tragic death that permeate them. In the case of **"The Dance of Death, or Lovely and Pleasant"** we already know from the story's title and accompanying epigraph from II Samuel 1:23 ("Lovely and pleasant in their lives, and in death were not divided") that we are dealing with a story heavily steeped in scriptural allusions. On the surface, these allusions seem to do little more than Judaize what is essentially a brief gothic romance. The story begins with a short introductory passage in which the narrator describes a peculiar local phenomenon:

> On the edge of Poland, on the outskirts of a small town, there stands a very old synagogue. Beside this synagogue is a stone mound some four cubits high, sprouting with blood-red grass. Weddings are not held there. The voices of joyous grooms are not heard there. And none of the priestly descendants of Aaron tread upon that mound unto this day.

The tale is an explanation of this phenomenon. A lovely, chaste bride and her groom, a young man of surpassing erudition and piety, stand one day beneath a wedding canopy outside the main synagogue of the city. Suddenly, the festive ceremony is disrupted by the appearance of a man on horseback, identified as the local Count. As the Count reaches the canopy, the bride's exquisite beauty unleashes a paroxysm of desire within him. He brandishes his sword, strikes the groom a mortal blow, kidnaps the bride, and rides off with her to his castle. In order to "arouse the wrath of vengeance," the townspeople bury the groom, enshrouded in his blood-stained nuptial raiment (*kittel*), at the site of the canopy. Subsequently, in the castle, the bride's life is also cut short: one day when the Count is out hunting, she vividly recalls the scene of her wedding day, asks her ladies-in-waiting to dress her in her wedding gown, and thus adorned, she dies. The Count returns to find her lifeless and buries her in a Christian grave on Christian ground. But the lovely and pleasant bride and groom, torn asunder on their wedding day, reunite and embrace after death. Every day of the year, "in the secret of the night," the bride's grave opens and "a veiled woman arises . . . [and] with anguished steps she walks toward the Great Synagogue. Then from his grave rises the dead groom whose blood was spilled beneath the canopy. In the secret of the night he stretches forth his arms, draws his bride to his heart, and together they dance the dance of death." "Therefore," the narrator concludes, "the priests do not tread on that mound and weddings are not held there unto this day."

And so, "lovely and pleasant in their lives," the groom and his bride are, like Saul and his son Jonathan in David's lament, not divided in death. True, the analogy is inexact, since the bride and groom of **"The Dance of Death"** do not die on the same day like Saul and Jonathan; yet this discrepancy is resolvable, since the abducted bride is likened to a dead person. The townspeople mourn over her no less than over the groom, and the words used to describe her abduction—"and the bride was not there, for the Count had taken [*lakah*] her"—are those used for the death of Enoch in the Bible: "And Enoch walked with God, and he was not, for God took him" (Genesis 5:24). In a similar vein, alluding to the Book of Job, the narrator comments: "What could they [the wedding guests] do? The Lord gave and the Lord hath taken away. They had not come to a wedding feast but to accompany the dead on their last journey." Further on in the text too, the bride's death in the castle is identified with the groom's at the wedding: like the groom in his *kittel,* she breathes her last in her white wedding gown, and the Count's arrival at that exact moment in his blood-drenched hunting garb brings to mind the murder beneath the wedding canopy.

If, however, one continues to pursue the analogy suggested by the story's epigraph, it becomes problematical. Saul and Jonathan, the Bible tells us, were "lovely and pleasant in their lives," whereas the bride and groom of our story are parties to an arranged match who hardly know each other up to the moment of their wedding. Indeed, Agnon's narrative clearly implies that the match may not even have been to the bride's liking: it has been arranged, we are told, by her father, a wealthy and distinguished member of the community, who found his daughter "a man *after his own heart*" (emphasis added). At the very least, this seems to mean that the bride was not consulted about the match; at the most, that she was unhappy with the husband chosen for her.

Agnon's inversion of the analogy with David's lament does not end here. Its greatest irony, when the lament is read in the light of our story, lies in David's plaint, "Ye daughters of Israel, weep over Saul, who clothed you in scarlet, with other delights; who put on ornaments of gold upon your apparel." This clashes with the story in that the bride has dressed for her wedding in a plain white dress because she has been forbidden anything fancier by the laws of the Jewish community of Poland. The community has put a ban on expensive wedding clothes because they "consume the wealth of Israel," that is, lead to competitiveness that poorer families can ill afford. Indeed, on the story's overt level, this decree, or rather, the bride's father's opposition to it, may well be what brings on the tragedy. Because the father is annoyed that he cannot parade his wealth at the wedding, he petitions the authorities to waive the ban especially for him—and his hubris in doing so, it is hinted, which persists after his request is rejected (even under the wedding canopy, we are told, "he was clearly unhappy with the ban on [fine] clothing"), is punished by Heaven with the Count's frightful deed.

The bride's entire family is so obsessed with the matter that when the Count is first galloping toward them in the distance their initial reaction is, "Look, the head of state [that is, of the Jewish *kehillah*] has sent us a special messenger to allow us to wear silk clothing." (Oddly, only the bride seems unperturbed by the prohibition.) Immediately, however, a darker note is struck by the words "a man on horseback," literally, "a rider on a horse," which evoke the phrase in the "Song of Sea" (Exodus 15:1) used to describe the Egyptian cavalry in pursuit of the fleeing Israelites. Indeed this is not a bearer of good tidings but a menacing figure who will transform the wedding day into one of everlasting woe. In another moment the groom's blood-stained robe will present the family's materialistic concern with fine clothing in a different perspective.

If the father and his guests are not at first aware of the approaching horseman's identity, is there anyone who is? Let us look closely at the passage describing his approach:

> Then the groom took the wedding ring, and the groom put the ring on the finger of the bride and said, "Behold, thou are sanctified unto me," and all the guests and all those assembled cried, "Mazal tov!" And the groom broke a glass in memory of the Temple, and the marriage contract was read, and the women . . . struck up a dance. And they took two braided breads and clapped them against each other while one woman cried, "O groom like a king," and another answered, "O bride gracious and beauteous," and everyone called out, "Mazal tov, mazal tov!" The bride lowered her pure eyes to the ground. Who was riding on his horse? Like the shadow of a great rock, so his shadow fell between her and the groom.

We have seen before how in Agnon's works a few seemingly innocent words can contain a clue that leads us to revise our reading of an entire text. Such are the sentences, "Who was riding on his horse? Like the shadow of a great rock, so his shadow fell between her and the groom." In whose mind or minds do these thoughts take place? If in everyone's, they are not particularly significant. But we must pay attention to the fact that between them and "everyone" ("everyone called out, 'Mazal tov, mazal tov!'") another consciousness, the bride's, has been interposed ("The bride lowered her pure eyes to the ground"). The reaction to the horseman, then, would seem to be hers alone—and if it is, we are being told something of the utmost importance: unlike the rest of the gathering, the bride has an inkling of who the mysterious rider is and of what his arrival portends. Why else indeed would she perceive his shadow as falling "between her and the groom?" (That this is her subjective perception and not that of the guests is further demonstrated by the fact that she and the groom are standing so close together that there would be no room for an actual shadow to be cast between them even if the rider—as does not seem to be the case—had halted his mount directly in front of them.)

It is at this point that Agnon's use of biblical allusion is revealed in its full artistry. The phrase "the shadow of a great rock" has a decidedly ominous ring to it and would seem to be no more than a reflection of the bride's dark premonition that something terrible is about to happen—*unless* we happen to know its origin. This is Isaiah 32:1-2, in which we read: "Behold, a king shall reign in righteousness, and princes shall rule in judgment. And a man shall be as a hiding place from the wind, and a covert from the tempest; as rivers of water in a dry place; as the shadow of a great rock in a weary land." For Isaiah, who is speaking about a sun-ravaged countryside where shade is a boon, "the shadow of a great rock" is not something to be feared. It is *a positive and protective image,* no less than "a covert from the tempest" or "water in a dry place." With this observation we are compelled to reassess **"The Dance of Death"** in its entirety.

Therefore, if the biblical allusion here is context-incorporating—and we have seen that in Agnon it invariably is—its clear implication is that the bride *welcomes* the approaching horseman, who is for her "a prince ruling in judgment" come to rescue her from an unwanted marriage to a husband chosen by her father against her will. Her "pure eyes," it now appears, have not been lowered to the ground in modesty at hearing herself praised with the ritual phrase of "bride gracious and beauteous," but rather in the knowledge of what is about to take place, for her abduction is something that she and the Count have planned together.

Once aroused, our suspicions concerning the bride's relations with the Count prior to her wedding deepen when we realize that the sentence describing her abduction, "The bride was not there because the Count had taken her," can admit alternate interpretations. Overtly, this allusion to the biblical verse that tells of Enoch's unusual and preternatural death seems aptly to represent the unique situation of the abducted bride as one who hovers between life and death threatened by both corporeal and spiritual annihilation. But we must also remember that before his death, the Book of Genesis tells us, Enoch "walked with God," that is, was especially intimate with Him. Read contextually, therefore, is not our story implicitly informing us that, before being "taken" by him, the bride's relationship to the Count was of a similar nature?

A Jewish bride who, before her wedding, has an illicit romance with a Christian Count and connives with him to be snatched from under the wedding canopy—not only does such a reading of **"A Dance of Death"** seem improbably subversive even for Agnon, an author incorrigibly fond of inverting the surface meaning of his own narratives, it also seems irreconcilable with the rest of the story. For if, contrary to all appearances, the first half of **"The Dance of Death"** is not about violated innocence but rather about sexual defilement and treachery, what are we to make of the story's second half, which tells us that the bride and groom are eternally united in death? How can such a union be possible if the proposed reconstruction of affairs up to the wedding drama is correct?

The answer, as a close reading will reveal, is that **"The Dance of Death"** is a story not only of concealed crime,

but also of concealed repentance. If one reads the story on its overt level, of course, there is no need for the bride to repent because she has done nothing wrong. Read for its allusive content, however, its concise account of her penitence is once again full of surprises.

That the bride of **"The Dance of Death"** *does* repent after being taken to the Count's castle can be shown by a comparison of two passages, the one cited above describing her abduction and a second in which, before her death in the castle, she remembers this scene. It is noteworthy that in her recollected version most of the particulars—the wedding ring, the breaking of the glass, the reading of the marriage contract, the dancing women—are missing. At this remove from the event only the significant details are recalled:

> She remembered the days of her youth, her wedding day when she stood to the right of the groom near the Great Synagogue. A rider gallops on his horse, gallops toward the canopy. The best men clap hands and sing, "O groom like a king" and the bridesmaids clap loaves of braided breads and sing, "O bride gracious and beauteous." And everyone assembled calls out, "Mazal tov." Who rides on his horse, his shadow weighing on her heart like a great rock? The canopy trembles over her head and its poles fall to the ground. And with that she collapsed, for her heart was stricken.

Let us begin by considering the opening phrase of this passage, "She remembered the days of her youth" (*vatizkor ne'ureha*). Since there is a linguistic allusion here to Jeremiah 2:2, "Thus saith the Lord, I remember the kindness of thy youth [*zakharti hesed ne'urayikh*], the love of thy espousals," there is surely significance in the fact that the word "kindness" is missing from the bride's recollection. Unlike the God of Jeremiah, who lovingly remembers His relationship with Israel in the desert, compared to a period of betrothal, the bride has no fond memories of the period of her own betrothal, which was forced upon her by her father. Now, however, reliving the day of her wedding, her perspective has changed radically. No longer does the shadow of the Count lie shelteringly *between* her and the groom; rather, it now weighs *on her heart,* transforming the Count himself, the "great rock," from a protective to a crushingly burdensome presence. Nor, it would seem, can she bear to remember the moment of lowering her "pure" eyes, which is also not mentioned. Indeed, no one but she knows how impure she has been—nor was her impurity ever greater than at the very moment she appeared to be modestly looking at the ground. "She remembered the days of her youth": the God of Jeremiah is willing to forgive Israel its transgressions, but can she be forgiven?

"And she collapsed, for her heart was stricken"—a logical conclusion to a painful process of recollection. Plainly put, the bride dies from extreme physical and emotional exhaustion. Here too, however, a complex of biblical allusions calls this simple reading into question. The pivotal sentences announcing the bride's death are borrowed from a passage in the Book of Samuel that describes the death of the high priest Eli and his sons. More precisely, the account of the bride's death parallels that of Eli's daughter-in-law, the wife of his son Phineas, who dies in childbirth upon learning of the capture of the Ark of God by the Philistines and of the death of her husband and his father. Occurring in both the biblical account and Agnon's tale, the Hebrew verb *va-tikhr'a,* "And she collapsed," has the root *k.r.'a,* which possesses the primary meaning of kneeling or going down on one's knees, but can also signify going into labor. Here are the two texts, first the modern and then the ancient:

> And she collapsed [*va-tikhr'a*] for her heart was stricken. And as she lay dying, the women attending her said, "Thy Lord has returned from the hunt." She did not answer or give heed. And she said, "Let them bring my wedding gown that I wore when I first came hither." And they brought her the wedding gown that she wore when she came to the castle.

> [**"The Dance of Death"**]

> And she collapsed [*va-tikhr'a*] and gave birth, for she was stricken with labor. And as she lay dying, the women attending her said to her, "Fear not, for thou hast brought forth a son." But she did not answer or give heed. And she named the child Ichabod [i.e., Inglorious], saying, "The glory has departed from Israel," because the Ark of God was taken and because of her father-in-law and her husband. And she said, "The glory has departed from Israel, for the Ark of God is taken." (I Samuel 4:19-22)

In the Bible, Phineas's wife is a symbol of national consciousness in the wake of national destruction. Going into sudden labor when she hears the catastrophic news of the capture of the Ark and the death of her family, she finds the catastrophe of Israel even greater than her own personal calamity and—dying in childbirth—names her son Ichabod to commemorate the dishonor of her people. If we continue to regard Agnon's biblical allusions in **"The Dance of Death"** as contextual, must we not then infer that the bride of his tale is pregnant with the child of the Count and dies, acknowledging her disgrace, while giving birth to an adulterous son?

This possibility is less far-fetched than it may seem to be at first glance; in fact, an early story of Agnon's entitled **"ha-Panas"** (**"The Lamp"**) confirms that it is precisely what he had in mind! Written when Agnon was still in his teens, **"The Lamp"** is structured as a bedtime story related by a mother to her son, in the course of which he is told by her:

> Once upon a time, under a marriage canopy, there was a Count who murdered a groom and stole his bride. He led her to his chambers and there he lived with her. It is said that a grandson and heir to the family converted and studied the Torah in the old House of Study next to the Great Synagogue. And so that the convert would not walk in darkness as he went to the House of Study, a lamp was lit.

Of course, if the bride of **"The Dance of Death,"** who is quite obviously a later version of the bride of **"The**

Lamp," has a grandson, she has a son or daughter too! In eliminating any overt reference to such a child in **"The Dance of Death,"** Agnon clearly did not wish to eliminate the child from the narrative, for in that case he would not have chosen to describe the death of the bride in language parallel to that concerning Phineas's wife. His intention was rather to conceal the child's existence within the covert network of meanings of **"The Dance of Death,"** whence it may be extracted only by probing the story's pattern of biblical allusions in depth. Does Phineas's wife die from the shock of the terrible tidings or from a complication in childbirth? The Bible does not offer an unequivocal answer but rather emphasizes the coincidence of both factors. Similarly, the death of the bride in **"The Dance of Death"** can be seen as the result of both physical and psychological factors, a fusion so complete that it is impossible to determine which one of the two is the cause and which the result of her suffering. Do the pains of a fatal labor make her repent what she has done? Or is it rather a penitent awareness of sin that induces labor? And if the latter, does she deliberately choose death as her atonement? Just as the attendants of Phineas's wife assume that the delivery of a newborn son will gladden their stricken mistress, so the abducted bride's ladies-in-waiting assume the news of the Count's return will gladden her, but the recognition that she has sullied the honor of Israel renders her, like Phineas's wife, oblivious to their message of consolation.

The conclusion to **"The Dance of Death"** develops the parallel with the biblical story of Eli even further by means of an additional linguistic allusion. The last sentence of the tale—"Therefore the sons of Aaron do not tread on this mound of stones, nor is the wedding canopy placed upon it unto this day"—returns us to its beginning, in which the narrator tells us that he is going to explain why, on a certain mound of stones, weddings are never performed and "the priestly descendants of Aaron do not tread." Of course, since according to Jewish law priests are forbidden to have contact with the dead or even to enter a cemetery, the presence of the groom's grave under the mound is enough to explain this prohibition. It is not, however, the only explanation. On the concealed level of biblical allusion there is a second one, which is suggested by yet another verse in the Book of Samuel's account of Eli's death. After the Holy Ark has been captured by the Philistines and triumphantly displayed in the temple of their god Dagon, Dagon's idol miraculously falls down before it—in grieving commemoration of which, the Bible tells us, the priests of Dagon do not "tread on the threshold of Dagon in Ashdod unto this day" (I Samuel 5:5). The allusion to this verse in **"The Dance of Death"** would appear to suggest that in Agnon's story too the desecrated spot is avoided because the enormity of the misfortune that took place there cannot be forgotten or forgiven. Despite the bride's efforts to erase the memory of her life with the Count, she can never wash away the stain of her ignominy. Just as the elders of Israel failed to foresee the consequences of their decision to bring the Ark to a war with the Philistines, so the bride had no sense of the disaster that her plot with the Count would wreak upon the innocent groom. It is a deed beyond expiation, and when she delivers a child of dishonor, she suffers, dies, and remembers her sin every night as she joins her groom in the dance of death.

And yet as is always the case in Agnon's stories, every interpretation bears its own contradiction. The Book of Samuel makes clear that the national dishonor brought about by the Philistines' capture of the Ark of God is only temporary. By felling the idol of Dagon, the God of Israel manifests his supremacy; the Holy Ark is later returned to the Israelites with great pomp and ceremony and the Ashdodite priests' ritual avoidance of the threshold is in fact a tribute to the triumph of the Hebrew God. By analogy, therefore, the abduction of the bride in **"The Dance of Death"** and the dishonor she brings upon herself are but temporary too; although she is buried in alien soil, she arises from her grave every night to join her groom, her people, and her God. The sacred custom of the priests with respect to the site where she has both betrayed and asked forgiveness of her groom is a testament to her moral victory in casting off her sin and returning to the God of Israel.

This, then, is the key to understanding **"The Dance of Death."** The bride does not rise from her grave each night because she has forgotten her love for the Count and wishes to dance an erotic dance with the groom. Rather, her dance is a celebration of religious and moral triumph, a point reinforced by the story's biblical title. In the light of the great disaster of their defeat, both personal and national, whatever conflict existed between King Saul and his son Jonathan in their lifetime (and indeed, the Bible tells us that it was severe) disappears from view; they will forever be remembered as having been lovely and pleasant in life as they were in death. So, separated by murder and reunited by contrition, will the bride and groom of **"The Dance of Death."**

I have proposed here an interpretation of **"The Dance of Death,"** based on a close reading of its biblical allusions, that is—I hope, at least to some readers—surprising but coherent and based upon reasonable evidence. With all this, is it "valid"?

The quotation marks around "valid" provide, I think, a large part of the answer. Obviously, if there is no such thing as "correctness" in the interpretation of literary texts in general, but only a graded plausibility of possible readings, this is even truer of Agnon, who—as we have seen in the course of this study—delights in indeterminacy and multiple significances. It is certainly possible to read **"The Dance of Death"** as I have proposed doing here. It is also possible, however, to read it conventionally, as the tale of an innocent Jewish bride abducted by a cruel Gentile and reunited with her husband after death. Indeed, both readings are not merely possible. *Both,* although they are to all appearances mutually exclusive, are forced upon us not only by the conflict between an overt level of the story that seems to tell us one thing and a covert level that seems to tell us the opposite, but by deliberately planted contradictions *within* the covert level itself.

In Agnon's story, immediately after the announcement of the bride's abduction, "And the bride was not because the Count had taken her," comes the sentence, "The maiden cried out [*tsa'akah ha-na'arah*] and there was none to save her." Of course, if we wish to interpret **"The Dance of Death"** in the nonconventional manner that I have suggested, the bride's screams are to allay suspicion. The problem is that here too we have an unmistakable echo of biblical language. The allusion is to Deuteronomy 22, where we read (verses 23-26), "If a maiden that is a virgin be betrothed unto a husband and a man find her in the city and lie with her [without her crying out] . . . ye shall stone them with stones that they die; the maiden, because she cried not. . . . But if a man find a betrothed maiden in the field, and the man force her and lie with her . . . unto the maiden thou shalt do nothing . . . for . . . the betrothed maiden cried and there was none to save her."

The point of the biblical law is clear: if a betrothed young woman is violated within earshot of other people who do not hear her cry out, she is presumed guilty of having participated willingly in the act; but if she is violated "in the field," that is, out of earshot, she is presumed innocent on the assumption that she screamed and was not heard. To read this allusion intertextually, therefore, would appear to compel the conclusion that the bride of **"The Dance of Death,"** who screamed and was heard by all the wedding guests, is innocent after all! But is it so? We have already seen that many of Agnon's biblical allusions are "inverted," that is, point not to a correspondence but to a discrepancy between the biblical situation and the situation in the modern story. How can we be sure that this is not the case here too? How can we know, for that matter, whether *any* biblical allusion in this or any other Agnon story is consonant or dissonant, a mythopoetic strengthening or an ironic undermining of the apparent meaning of the text?

Is not this an interpretive impasse into which Agnon has knowingly led us, not only in **"The Dance of Death"** but in all his writing? . . .

Agnon rarely means what he seems to be saying—there are always other possibilities of interpretation lying in wait to surprise us. And because so much is conveyed through indirection, we are implicated as readers in a incessant process of inference, in the course of which new discoveries do not rule out previous or additional *aperçus,* even if they appear to contradict them. Agnon, in sum, has devised a fictional technique that seeks to match the complexity and constant overdetermination of human psychology and the insoluble dilemmas of moral judgment. I have tried in my analyses to adopt a reading mode which comprehends the fullness of this play of indeterminacy without investing it with the status of an exclusive exegetic principle. . . .

I would now maintain that, just as what appears secondary or marginal in Agnon's narratives is not always so, so those purportedly minor or irrelevant works of his that have thus far escaped serious critical attention are not necessarily undeserving of it. Indeed, in scrutinizing them one sometimes discovers that they display Agnon's artistic technique in sharper relief than the familiar narratives.

Naomi B. Sokoloff (essay date 1994)

SOURCE: "Expressing and Repressing the Female Voice in S. Y. Agnon's *In the Prime of Her Life,*" in *Women of the Word: Jewish Women and Jewish Writing,* edited by Judith R. Baskin, Wayne State University Press, 1994, pp. 216-33.

[*In the following essay, Sokoloff offers a feminist reading of the novella* In the Prime of Her Life.]

While the last fifteen years have witnessed an upsurge of interest in feminist critical thought and literary interpretation, few attempts have been made to explore the implications of gender as a thematic concern in modern Hebrew texts. Yet Hebrew warrants special feminist examination because of its exceptional history as a holy tongue that for many centuries was studied almost exclusively by men. It was only the major cultural upheavals and transformations of the Jewish Enlightenment and Zionism—sources, as well, of the Hebrew linguistic and literary renaissance of the last two centuries—that led to significant changes in women's social and intellectual roles. The inevitable tensions between a male-dominated tradition and modern cultural change have left their mark on literary representations of women in Hebrew writing by men, even as they have fostered a singular set of obstacles and stimuli for the creation of a female literary tradition in modern Hebrew literature. In light of these considerations, *In the Prime of Her Life* (1923) invites a feminist rereading, since this novella by Shmuel Yosef Agnon, Nobel Prize winner and preeminent Hebrew novelist of the first half of the twentieth century, is centrally concerned with the sounding and silencing of female voice.

Much of the feminist critical agenda has aimed at documenting ways in which female figures have been represented by men, as well as ways in which women have spoken back, representing themselves through their own vocal self-assertion. Agnon's novella, which features a female narrator, a young woman who marries her mother's former suitor and recounts her life story in the form of a written memoir, raises questions of interest for both modes of reading. Consequently, even as *In the Prime of Her Life* represents women through the filter of male perceptions, the text poses as a woman's account of her own experience and so calls attention directly to women's expression and language.

In this fiction such issues develop explicitly through insistent treatment of tensions between suppressed and emergent voices. Though critical appraisals have been curiously silent on this matter, Agnon in effect structures the entire novella around a series of verbal exchanges and keen thematic attention to talk. Virtually every paragraph centers on obtrusive reference to or citation of conversations, interior monologues, and varieties of written messages. In this way the text endorses the primacy of linguistic acts as plot actions that regulate matters of will, power, and social relations. It is noteworthy, too, that the representations of language, like the social conflicts they imply or convey, are marked by sexual difference. Just as men and women behave differently, so they express themselves differently, and their uses of words illuminate contrasting privileges and predicaments. The novella in this way highlights the protagonist's attempt to make herself heard by stating her convictions and expressing her own desires. This is not to say that the text necessarily applauds her efforts. At times it clearly decries them. Agnon himself was by no means a feminist nor an advocate of women's liberation, and he sometimes casts his character in a distinctly unflattering light. The narrative nevertheless maintains an intense scrutiny of women's voices, and for this reason feminist theory may provide a productive critical framework for examining *In the Prime of Her Life,* illuminating aspects of the text that have been overlooked, underestimated, or marginalized by critics.

From the start, *In the Prime of Her Life* concentrates on the silence of a female character, Tirza's ailing mother, Leah. In the process the text associates subdued voice with death and confinement. Describing the period of Leah's declining health, the opening paragraph relates: "Our house stood hushed [*dumam*] in its sorrow and its doors did not open to a stranger." The next paragraph reiterates and augments this introductory announcement: "The winter my mother died our home fell silent [*damam*] seven times over." Both passages play on the Hebrew root *d-m-m,* recalling the sounds of the title and the first sentence of the novella: "In the prime of her life [*bidmi yameha*] my mother died." *Demi,* "silence," functions in this last phrase to signify "in the prime" of her days. Submerged within it, too, heightening its ironic nuances, is reference to blood (*dam*). These lines thereby connect silence with the snuffing out of vitality in a young woman who died too soon. Subsequently the narrative illustrates the cruelty of Leah's fate by relating another image of suppressed language: letters Mother received from her true love, Akaviah Mazal, have been kept under lock and key for years. She opens them, it is recounted, only to destroy them, burning them in a room whose windows are locked tight. In this stifling setting of enclosure and repression, smoke rises in an allusion to the sacrifice of Leah's true desires.

After her death, Father's arrangements for the inscription on Leah's tombstone reconfirm the entire pattern of her life as silenced and suppressed desire. To understand this episode we should remember the feminist claim that patriarchal culture has often defined woman according to its needs rather than hers; it has also frequently represented females as passive beings unable to produce their own meanings. In this way, as Susan Gubar argues, men have attempted to create woman through masculine discourse, and women, serving as secondary objects in someone else's scheme of things, have been perceived as blank pages on which to write and be written [Gubar, "'The Blank Page' and the Issues of Female Creativity," in *New Feminist Criticism,* edited by Elaine Showalter, 1985]. In Agnon's story, these descriptions are apt; men have been writing the script for Leah all her life. Not allowed to sound her wishes, she has been denied intentionality. Most importantly, her father marries her to the wrong man, one who is better off financially and considered more socially desirable than the suitor she herself prefers. As a result she dies at an early age, her heart physically and metaphorically weakened because deprived of love. Through the incident of the tombstone Agnon creates a startling, culminating illustration of this phenomenon. The woman, her spirit extinguished, has been transformed into an object, her identity reduced to a name carved in stone. It is pointed out, moreover, that her husband thinks more about her epitaph than about her. Though he is genuinely and deeply aggrieved at the loss of his wife, in choosing the lettering for the grave he "all but forgot" the woman. The writing, his defining of her, eases his pain. To Mintz's credit he does reject a highly formulaic epitaph, one which Mr. Gottlieb has prepared, in favor of one more meaningful. The first inscription is very clever; it is based on an acrostic of Leah's name that also incorporates the year of her death into every line of the poem, but there is nothing personal in it. Recognizing this shortcoming, the husband opts for something more authentic. He goes to Mazal, the former beau and author of those now burnt love letters, to commission a second inscription. Though it is finally too late, and though he acts only through an intermediary who is a man, Mintz makes at least some concession toward acknowledging his wife's suppressed desires and inner life: her ardent feelings for Mazal.

Tirza, the daughter, who is at once the narrator and the primary focus of the narrative, establishes her own significance in opposition to these actions on the part of the men. Her initial introduction of herself, for example, in the first paragraphs of the story, serves as a celebration of her mother's voice: "Lying on her bed my mother's words were few. But when she spoke it was as though limpid wings spread forth and led me to the Hall of Blessing. How I loved her voice. Often I opened her door to have her ask, who is there?" While the rest of the paragraph insists on suffocation and enclosure, rendering the mother's thoughts inaudible, Tirza here emphasizes aperture (the outspread wings and the open door) along with sound, self-assertion, listening, and response. These emphases evolve into question about Tirza's identity ("Who is there?") and so constitute an affirmation of her own presence.

Tensions between the suppression and emergence of female voice develop further as the plot unfolds into a story of the daughter's search for independence. Tirza sets her heart on marrying Akaviah Mazal, falls ill in a kind of duplication or reenactment of her mother's final illness, and, surviving this, convinces her father that she and Mazal should be wed. The assertion of her desires, as a recuperation of her mother's lost life, progresses through any number of verbal encounters that disclose identifiably distinctive masculine and feminine aspects. When, for example, Mrs. Gottlieb invites Tirza to spend the summer at her home, the narrator recounts: "My father readily agreed, saying 'Go now.' But I answered, 'How will I go alone?' and he said, 'I will come and visit.' Kaila stood dusting by the mirror and she winked at me as she overheard my father's words. I saw her move her lips and grimace in the mirror, and I laughed to myself. Noticing how my face lit up with cheer my father said, 'I knew you would heed my words,' and he left the room."

This passage could be a textbook illustration of sociolinguistic observations on female verbal behavior. Women, because of the more vulnerable status they occupy in many societies, often tend to avoid language that threatens or endangers the stability of relationships. Consequently, they rely heavily on a range of politeness strategies meant to deflect attack and help maintain interpersonal equilibrium. These include attentiveness, approval, flattery or indirectness, the use of honorifics, appeals to a higher law, generalizations, and excuses of exigence. In the passage cited, Tirza, too, is deferential because of her subordinate position. Accordingly, she restricts her comments to a question. Despite her unhappiness about the plans for the summer, she leaves the father's decision open and does not impose her own mind or views on him. The housekeeper likewise avoids straightforward declaratives. Trying to convince Tirza to agree with her father and respect his desires, Kaila expresses herself only by indirections and distortions. Tirza, aware of the preposterous incongruity of her servant's actions, laughs with amusement at the linguistic inequity prevailing in this exchange. Only fourteen, she does not yet take her own powerlessness quite seriously. She remarks innocently in the next paragraph: "Kaila, God be with you, speak up, don't remain silent, please stop torturing me with all your hints and riddles." For this she is reprimanded and reminded of the gravity of the situation: this trip is for the father's well-being, not hers, and would she but look at him closely she would realize that he is lonely and needs the opportunity to visit the Gottliebs in the country. In short, Kaila first acts on the conviction that she mustn't express herself directly, and then, when pressed, conveys this same message more overtly to Tirza. The girl's personal desires must remain unspoken. As a result of all the indirectness, Mintz for his part misreads Tirza entirely. "I knew you would heed my words (*lishmoa' bekoli*)," he says, thus reinscribing her back into his code of understanding. Using an expression typical of biblical discussions on obedience to God, he reinforces his patriarchal authority and reconfirms his failure to appreciate the inner thoughts of the women in his life.

Other incidents as well contrast the discourse of men and women, demonstrating an imbalance of power between them. For instance, the matchmaker who comes to visit talks at great length, making tiresome chitchat and keeping Tirza a captive but courteous audience. Tirza's father, for his part, unselfconsciously exercises strategies to dominate conversations. Not only does he direct talk to his own preferred topics (generally, his personal misfortune due to Leah's death); he also extends his own words to encompass everyone: "We are the miserable widowers," he laments, and Tirza comments, "How strange were his words. It was as though all womankind had died and every man was a widower."

In addition to these scenes in which Agnon neatly contrasts masculine communicative prerogatives with the women characters' cautions and insecurities about speaking, on other occasions male characters explicitly impute negative qualities to or give misogynistic interpretations of female speech. In an embedded tale recounting Mazal's past, Leah's father is quoted as chiding his wife for engaging in "woman's talk"—that is, talk he deems to be idle and impious. A comparably condemnatory comment surfaces when the doctor comes to visit the Mintz family after Mother's death. Remarking that the daughter has grown and that she has on a new dress, he asks if she knows how to sew. Tirza responds with a maxim, "Let another man praise thee, and not thine own mouth." Restricting herself to a nonassertive stance, this character offers a formulaic reassurance of the male interlocutor's initiative in conversation. All the same he responds by saying, "A bold girl and looking for compliments." What the man takes as an act of boldness is more properly an evasion of confrontation and a highly reticent hint at a topic the daughter is actually eager for others to acknowledge: her budding sexuality, her own growing up which has been overlooked because everyone is preoccupied with mourning. This incident, like the scolding Leah's father gives his wife, underscores attention in the text to the characters' stereotypic notions of women's speech and to a conviction that female expression should remain sharply circumscribed.

In a pivotal scene concerned with these issues, Tirza at first submits to the discourse of men characters. Quelling her own impulses, she molds her expression to conform to their expectations. However, the episode quickly becomes a turning point, a moment of rupture in which she attempts to emancipate herself from male-dominated patterns of verbal interaction. This happens when Mintshi Gottleib, her hostess, discloses that Akaviah and Leah were once in love. Tirza, struck by melancholy and confusion, is then approached by Mintshi's husband, and the following exchange ensues: "'Look, our friend is boring a hole through the heavens,' Mr. Gottlieb said laughing as he saw me staring up at the sky. And I laughed along with him with a pained heart." Afterwards, although she has humored him, Tirza remains deeply troubled by Mrs. Gottlieb's revelations about the past and she cannot let the matter rest: "Night after night I lay on my bed, asking myself, 'What would now be if my mother had married Mazal? And what would have become of me?' I knew such speculations to be fruitless, yet I did not abandon them. When the shudders which accompanied my musings finally ceased, I said: Mazal has been wronged. He seemed to me to be like a man bereft of his wife yet she is not his wife." Shortly after that her ruminations resume:

> How I loathed myself. I burned with shame and did not know why. Now I pitied my father and now I secretly grew angry at him. And I turned my wrath upon Mazal also. . . . Sometimes I told myself: Why did Mintshi Gottleib upset me by telling me of bygone memories? A father and mother, are they not man and woman and of one flesh? Why then should I brood over secrets which occurred before my time? Yet I thirsted to know more. I could not calm down, nor could I sit still for a moment's quiet. And so I told myself, if Mintshi knows what happened surely she will tell me the truth. How though will I open my mouth to ask? For if I but let the thoughts come to mind my face turns crimson let alone when I speak out my thoughts aloud. I then gave up all hope. More I could not know.

Tirza's lengthy internal monologue offers an explicit meditation on her fears of speaking up. In its very length the passage itself is an act of verbal self-assertion—a muffled voicing of her anxieties, to be sure, but at least a way of formulating and sounding her preoccupations in her own mind. Here once more the character's remarks consist of questions rather than declaratives or imperatives, but, in contrast to her earlier silences and deferential reserve, these questions are angry and searching. Language, moreover, serves specifically as a way of constituting a self. Probing her origins, Tirza asks overtly, who am I? and ponders what she might have been had her mother married somebody else.

This character's progress toward self-expression is subsequently impeded but then also spurred on by her engagement, engineered by the matchmaker Gotteskind, with a young man in whom she takes no interest. Recoiling at the prospects of an arranged match, Tirza dreams that her father has married her off to an Indian chief and that her body is "impressed with tattoos of kissing lips." If, as feminist criticism has argued, the female predicament entails the imposition of a male cultural script onto woman, a writing of her that determines her sexual life and social status, in this passage we find a graphic image of a woman whose destiny is being inscribed directly onto her body. The verbal and sexual power so prominently featured in *In the Prime of Her Life* as part of the male domain converge in this scene. They are presented through a single dramatic symbol of female disempowerment: the mouth, locus of both kisses and speech, appears here as tattoo, sealing the young woman's dreaded fate of being married off by force to someone entirely foreign and alien to her. This episode makes Tirza all the more determined to have Akaviah Mazal, whom she perceives as the true object of her desire.

As she pursues Akaviah and so expresses her own will, Tirza again resorts to speech characterized by indirection and generalization. She does so, though, with a new flare. According to accepted protocol, she cannot easily speak with her beloved. Mazal is not only older than she; he also becomes her teacher when, turning sixteen, Tirza begins attending a teachers seminary. With increasing daring she devises pretexts for making conversation with Akaviah. To reach him she pretends that a dog has bitten her hand, and so, under the guise of soliciting compassion and protective care, she dupes him into allowing her to reveal her erotic intent. (As many readers have noted, the dog in Agnon's texts is frequently an indicator of uncontrolled sexuality and also of madness, that is, of impulses threatening to the accepted limits of society.)

Tirza's most extreme declaration of desire occurs when societal constraints are further removed. During her illness, at the height of feverish delirium, she etches the name "Akaviah Mazal" many times into her mirror. She also writes Akaviah a letter, noting, "You shall dwell in my thoughts all day." In both instances the young woman is trying to write him, to inscribe him, into her inner self or subsume his signature into the image of herself which she receives from the mirror. In this way Tirza attempts to reverse that early pattern, epitomized by the episode with the tombstone, in which the men inscribed Leah's name in their discourse. It is significant that she does this at a time when she is sick and suffering delusions. Literary equations of woman's rebellion with madness have been noted recurrently in feminist criticism. At times, too, feminist interpretations have considered this identification of aggression or self-assertion with insanity as an attempt to discredit female protest. Tirza's temporary derangement conforms in part to such a pattern; her daring is a function of illness and irrationality. Agnon's text, however, is subtle in its judgment of her. The scene serves less as an attempt to trivialize Tirza's situation than as a sensitive acknowledgment of how profound are the disorders that plague the entire family and culminate in the events of the daughter's life. Yet, by contrast with those gravely disturbing matters, her efforts at self-expression do come to seem of diminished seriousness. What remains certain is that, opening a Pandora's box of emotional troubles, this character courts disaster. Something has gone fundamentally wrong in this home, and Tirza's sickness is highly overdetermined. Not only the occasion for speaking out, the fever is an expression of psychic dis-ease. Tirza invited a chill by wearing inappropriate attire (a summer dress in winter), and her illness then is instrumental in manipulating her father's (and perhaps Mazal's) sympathy. That this partially unwitting ploy is effective results from the susceptibility of the older generation to emotional blackmail as well as from their complicity, their willingness to arrange a new marriage to settle old scores. Each for his own reasons agrees to the match. Therefore, because of the complicated interpersonal context in which Tirza's development takes place, *In the Prime of Her Life* is only in part the story of a young woman's rebellion against social mores; beneath the surface there is another agenda, one in large measure pessimistic about the ability of a young woman to free herself of patriarchal imperatives.

Tirza's name has been understood as both "will" (*ratson,* from the Hebrew root *r-ts-h*) and "pretext" (*teruts,* from the root *t-r-ts*). A range of meanings delimited by these concepts underlies the events of her life and complicates the rather straightforward examples of incipient self-assertion brought forward in the first half of this essay. At issue, most crucially, is the protagonist's dangerous psychic involvement in the events of the past and in the unresolved tensions of her parents' youth. Her reliving of Mother's life turns out to be less a renewal than a repetition of mistakes, and in this light determination becomes a pretext for passivity and determinism. Agnon explores these matters by combining attention to mother/daughter relations—a central topic in current feminist criticism—

with one of his own major thematic preoccupations: struggles between individual will and forces beyond the control of the individual, be those explained as destiny, divine intervention, or the workings of the unconscious.

Many critics have claimed that Tirza's recreating of her mother's life enacts a variation on the familiar Agnon theme of the love triangle. The young woman marries a father figure and continues to yearn for her father's company, even as Mazal marries the daughter instead of the mother he loved. Leah similarly married Mintz instead of her beloved, and Mintshi, enamored of Mazal, married Gottlieb and buried herself in ceaseless activity. Each case creates a three-some that interferes with the attainment of intimacy or displaces love from one object of passion to a dissatisfying substitute. What has not been sufficiently recognized and stated, though, is the degree to which Tirza's problems are those of an adolescent, specifically a female who must deal with the death of her mother, and the connection between these issues and that of emergent voice.

Adolescence is a time of gradually letting go, of loosening bonds with parents in preparation for making choices of all sorts, but most importantly erotic. As Katherine Dalsimer notes, [in *Female Adolescence: Psychoanalytic Reflections on Literature,* 1986], this withdrawal from parents accounts for the unique place this stage of life occupies in psychoanalytic writing. Deemed at once to be a time of possibility and aperture, it is also an age of pain. Because tensions present since earliest childhood are reactivated in adolescence, this is a moment of awakening that permits new resolution to old conflicts. At the same time, pulling away from parents is felt subjectively by youngsters as a profound loss or emptiness not unlike mourning. The actual death of a parent, occurring at this juncture, inevitably heightens that inner loss experienced in the normal course of growing up. It can also influence the reworking of psychic conflicts essential for the young person to attain new maturity. If all deaths are greeted by the living with some degree of denial, the impulse to disbelieve the finality of the loss proves that much more intractable for children or teenagers. Unchallenged, unmodified by day-to-day experience, such wishful fantasy may prove even more difficult to abandon and may result in further magnified esteem for the lost figure.

Tirza's life is decisively affected by just such a turn of events. Matters are complicated further, because she is female. The field of psychoanalysis has increasingly recognized the enduring nature of a daughter's relation to her mother. In adolescence there is heightened need for mother as the individual who provided crucial primary intimacy, and much as was true in the earliest days of childhood, the daughter often looks to her mother as a mirror through whose approval and disapproval she can recognize, define, validate, delimit, and forge herself. Tirza Mintz moves toward maturity with difficulty, for in her case the pull to identify with the mother is at once unhealthily strong and also exacerbated by Leah's death. Tirza's father, for his part, cannot compensate for the mother's absence. He is singularly unable to provide his daughter the mirroring she needs because he is deeply self-absorbed, preoccupied always with his mourning and his business dealings. Not only does he misread his daughter, as in the passage examined earlier; in addition he overlooks her awareness of her own emerging womanliness. When, for instance, concerned with her appearance, she puts on festive new clothes, his reaction of surprise leads her to feel deeply guilty; though the mourning period has passed, she comes to perceive her attentions to herself as a failure of devotion to Leah. As she moves one step toward embracing life, he encourages her to prolong mourning for her mother. Tirza notes explicitly: "In my grief I said, my father has forgotten me, he has forgotten my existence." This passage alludes neatly to the two kinds of grief the reader can identify in Tirza's adolescent experience: she suffers a natural loss of intimacy, a withdrawal between parents and children, but this is a blow intensified many times over by the physical death of the mother. Both are made worse by the father's self-centered reactions.

It is in this context that Tirza tries to realize the fantasy of reenacting and revising her mother's life; she wishes to redress the (perceived) wrong done Mazal, even as she would like to reverse her mother's romantic disappointment, and so she tries to make the crooked straight (that is, *letaretz*—"to straighten"—a word that again recovers the sound of the protagonist's name). She attempts, too, to preserve a memory, to deny Leah's absence, and to find validation of herself as a woman. The implication raised by this set of circumstances is that, though Tirza believes she is pining away for love of Mazal, in effect and at a deeper level she attempts to hold onto childhood and maternal intimacy. That highly important psychic business of adolescence, the need to develop autonomy, is retarded and distorted by confusion of her own identity with that of her mother. The tragedy of this excessive attachment is then compounded by the incestuous quality inherent in the solution Tirza seeks out: her marriage to Mazal. Altogether, Tirza's adolescence, far from an emancipation, has become a subjugation to the parents' past and to her continuing need to imitate her mother. In a chilling scene Tirza, now pregnant, foresees for herself an early death parallel to Leah's. Part of this fantasy, moreover, is that she prays for a daughter—to take care of Mazal. This eventuality would result yet again in a displacement onto another of the maternal role; her wish hints that Tirza wants less to be a mother than to implore someone else to do some mothering.

The full extent of the protagonist's tragedy becomes apparent, like many other developments in the narrative, through the treatment of dialogue, talk, and matters of voice. For example, one of the first signs that Tirza has made a serious mistake in pursuing Mazal occurs early on in their courtship. She feels attracted to him precisely because she expects she can confide in him. Overcome with ennui at the seminary she notes, "I saw there wasn't a person to whom I could pour out my heart; and I then said, I will speak to Mazal." Her projected scenario does not materialize. Welcoming her into his house, Akaviah latches onto her as a listener and, telling her his life

story, doesn't allow her to get a word in edgewise. Tirza, instead of speaking up, is drawn into his discourse. It is the long ago that remains dominant here, and not Tirza's newly emergent young life. It is significant that Mazal's monologue is presented as a long interpolated sequence in the novella; the very status of his speech as embedded narrative indicates that it is essentially extrinsic to Tirza's story, yet absorbs her attention and displaces the novella's focus from her present onto the past. Subsequently, in another scene that relies on pointed reference to voice, Tirza's description of her illness testifies to the increasing intensity of her problems. She has come more and more to resemble her mother. The text observes, "My heart beat feebly and my voice was like my mother's voice at the time of her illness." A similar remark appears, too, when her marriage fails to bring her the happiness she had expected. Pregnancy precipitates a crisis of depression that confirms and clarifies the nature of Tirza's discontent. She has not progressed to a mature autonomy, and when her father brings presents for the new baby, the mother-to-be speaks as if she were herself the child: "'Thank you, grandfather,' I said in a child's piping voice."

This scene also makes strikingly clear that forces operating in Tirza's life invalidate, alter, or bring additional layers of meaning to her vocal self-assertions. Noting, "The child within me grows from day to day," the text here recalls the first description of Tirza listening to her mother's voice, which stated "I was still a child." Though the young woman is not aware of it, the reference to the child within may include Tirza as much as her offspring. Here, as throughout the narrative, what is said aloud is quite different from what the characters mean. If at first woman's speech is indirect, a kind of deferential duplicity determined by relations of power and powerlessness, later on words also function in another way to both conceal and reveal. They contain hidden significations, and Tirza at times unknowingly discloses deep motivations she herself would not recognize. For such reasons voice cannot in any simple sense be synonymous with will. While Tirza's early attempts to make herself heard were intended to help her wield some power, it becomes clear in the course of the text that her unconscious desires, deeply powerful ones, exceed and elude the goals she has defined and willed for herself. Nor does the birth of her child signal joy; her final melancholy is one more manifestation of the crooked that cannot be made straight.

At the end of *In the Prime of Her Life* the question of voice reasserts itself, complicated by such matters. Tirza seeks out a new kind of expression by composing a memoir. This fact has several implications. On a simple dramatic level, the effort to chronicle is plausibly motivated by Tirza's adolescence. Given the enlarged self-preoccupations typical of teenagers, keeping a diary is a natural activity for this time of life. In Tirza's case such writing is a more formal attempt at the task begun earlier in the story: to constitute a self through language, to puzzle over her life and ask, who am I? (For Tirza this self-definition is crucial if she is not to subsume her identity totally within that of someone else.) That she is a female brings additional meaning to this act. She is, after all, a figure who has sought and is still seeking to assert her own voice in a society which discourages outspokenness by women. She turns, significantly, to the form of writing often favored by women: the diary or memoir not intended for publication but meant to provide an outlet for emotion and a forum for self-expression. Her purposes of self-definition and self-expression are stymied, though, because she finds herself unhappily trapped in a situation much larger than her own imagined script of events. Since other powerful forces are at play, and since even her public speaking up has led her to an all-encompassing, seemingly preordained pattern of relations, writing serves as a last resort, a way for her to seek solace and not as a way for her to arrive at an unambiguous enunciation of identity. As her persistent unhappiness and continuing restlessness lead her to one last act of speaking out, she brings the uncertainties of her stance to the fore in her closing comments: "Sometimes I would ask myself to what purpose have I written my memories, what new things have I seen and what do I wish to leave behind? Then I would say, it is to find rest in my writing, so did I write all that is written in this book." Caught between the new and the old, she is left still searching for a context for her own voice, establishing it—only ambiguously—in a private realm of writing.

Yet Agnon's purposes extend beyond Tirza's private female predicaments to his concern with larger collective issues. Throughout the history of Hebrew writing, female figures have often served to symbolize an entire reality or the Jewish people as a whole—from the desolate widow of Lamentations, to the personification of Zion as beloved in medieval poetry, to A. B. Yehoshua's contemporary psychohistories of Zionism. While Agnon deals in depth with Tirza's personal tale specifically as a woman's experience, he also uses her to alert readers to a series of questions, both historical and linguistic, connected with national rebirth. Tirza lives in an East European shtetl at the turn of the century. From an enlightened family, she receives a Hebrew education that is unusual for a girl of this time. As Agnon, at various junctures in the novella, brings out the theme of Enlightenment and transformations of tradition, there emerges a parallel between his protagonist's individual efforts to revive the past and the communal effort to create a Jewish cultural renaissance and to forge a rebirth of the Hebrew language. Tirza's psychological dilemmas—especially her struggle for a context in which to make her own voice heard—parallel the struggle of the Hebrew language to achieve a new audience and new vitality. In addition, attention to Tirza's Hebrew schooling makes for a specific dramatic situation, in this sociohistorical milieu, that turns questions about women's social roles into an integral part of the collective issues treated here. It is a novelty for a woman to have the opportunities Tirza has—to study and to insist on her own wishes in rebellion against her father's plans for her marriage. Her audacity becomes possible in a climate that has begun to encourage human beings to shape their own future. Within that context, where the question of individual freedom looms so large, Agnon examines the possibility of freedom for a woman whose expected lot in life is very different from that of the men around her.

Two major thematic concerns thus coincide and enrich one another in *In the Prime of Her Life*: the return of what has been repressed, and the repression of female voice. The past of the mother resurfaces even as the daughter's early inclinations reemerge in adolescence with destructive force. Agnon's use of a woman's struggle for emancipatory language, together with the portrayal of the female adolescent as partially emergent voice, effectively symbolizes and conveys the drives at once present and absent in these lives. Tirza takes remarkable initiatives, but they become enmeshed in cultural and historical circumstances that irrefutably oppose her willfulness.

In *In the Prime of Her Life* it is the past both personal and mythic that fatalistically overshadows the future, leaving Tirzah Mintz Mazal incapable of determining her own fate. Yet, while he does not champion her cause, Agnon does pay serious attention to female predicaments and grants them credence as a legitimate topic for literary art, bringing remarkable insight and what can only be described as a brilliant synthesis of themes, narrative strategies, and stylistic sensitivities to his representation of a woman's voice. While designed to serve his own artistic aims, the treatment of women's speech and silence in this narrative renders *In the Prime of Her Life* exceptionally responsive to feminist readings.

FURTHER READING

Bibliography

Band, Arnold J. Bibliography and Appendixes. In *Nostalgia and Nightmare: A Study in the Fiction of S. Y. Agnon*, pp. 453-524; pp. 525-56. Berkeley: University of California Press, 1968, 563 p.

> Extensive bibliography of works by and about Agnon. The secondary bibliography consists entirely of works published in Hebrew.

Kabakoff, Jacob. "S. Y. Agnon's Works in English Translation." *Jewish Book Annual* 25 (1967): 39-41.

> Identifies English-language translations of more than 30 stories by Agnon in anthologies and such journals as *Ariel, Commentary, Jewish Heritage,* and *Mosaic*.

Criticism

Band, Arnold J. *Nostalgia and Nightmare: A Study in the Fiction of S. Y. Agnon*. Berkeley: University of California Press, 1968, 563 p.

> Contains discussions of Agnon's early Hebrew and Yiddish stories, as well as his fantasies, folktales, mythic narratives, and gothic stories.

Coffin, Edna Amir. "The Dream as a Literary Device in Agnon's 'Metamorphosis'." *Hebrew Studies* XXIII (1982): 187-98.

Examines "the function of the dream sequences in 'Metamorphosis' ['Panim Aherot'], as well as their effect on character development and on reader response."

Cohen, Carolyn. "Worlds Lost and Found." *Commonweal* 123, No. 7 (April 5, 1996): 36-8.

Reviews *A Book That Was Lost, and Other Stories,* highlighting the tales "Agunot," "A Book That Was Lost," and "The Sign." Cohen observes that "the pleasure in reading these stories comes from their humor and irony."

Gross, John. "The Art of Agnon." *The New York Review of Books* (November 3, 1966): 10-11.

Review of *Betrothed* and *Edo and Enam.* Gross comments on the poetic and allusive qualities of Agnon's writing and states that these stories, though ostensibly pessimistic, are ultimately affirmative.

Hochman, Baruch. "'The Whole Loaf': Tales of the Modern World." In *The Fiction of S. Y. Agnon,* pp. 158-84. Ithaca, N.Y.: Cornell University Press, 1970.

Discusses the short story collection *The Book of Deeds* and the novellas *Thus Far, Betrothed, Edo and Enam,* and *Forevermore,* focusing on Agnon's depiction of solitary individuals suffering "psychic and spiritual isolation" in the modern world.

Hoffman, Anne Golomb. "Inclusion and Exclusion: Three Stories." In *Between Exile and Return: S. Y. Agnon and the Drama of Writing,* pp. 105-22. Albany, N.Y.: State University of New York Press, 1991.

Examines the relationship between traditional Hebrew texts and Agnon's stories "Upon a Stone" ("Al even ahat"), "The Sense of Smell" ("Hush hareah"), and "The Document" ("Hate'udah").

Kaspi, Joseph. *A Study in the Evolution of S. Y. Agnon's Style.* Chicago: Spertus College of Judaica Press, 1969, 168 p.

Detailed study of Agnon's stylistics, supplemented by tables and statistical findings.

Leiter, Shmuel. "The Face within a Face." *Judaism* 19, No. 1 (Winter 1970): 59-65.

Attempts to demonstrate that Agnon's use of symbolism in "Panim Aherot" ("Metamorphosis") transforms this story of "two unimaginative people" into art.

Miron, Susan. "Catastrophe Always Looms." *The New York Times Book Review* 100 (May 21, 1995): 37.

Favorable review of *A Book That Was Lost, and Other Stories.*

Patterson, David, and Glenda Abramson, eds. *Tradition and Trauma: Studies in the Fiction of S. J. Agnon.* Boulder, CO: Westview Press, 1994, 226 p.

Includes essays on the stories *Forevermore,* "The Hill of Sand," "The Doctor's Divorce" ("Ha-rofe u-gerushato"), and "Friendship" ("Yedidut"), and the collection *The Book of Deeds.* The essay on *Forevermore,* by Naomi Sokoloff, is reprinted in the preceding pages.

Rosenberg, Israel. *Shay Agnon's World of Mystery and Allegory: An Analysis of 'Iddo and Aynam'.* Philadelphia: Dorrance & Company, 1978, 143 p.

Attempts a scholastic explanation of the mysterious elements and hidden meanings of *Edo and Enam.* The preface states that "a substantial knowledge of Agnon's writing is impossible to have without a profound knowledge of the Jewish sources, both in the written Torah and in the oral Torah (the Talmud), in the so-called religious literature and the various Responsa literature."

Roskolenko, Harry. "In These Tales, God Is Everywhere." *The New York Times Book Review* (May 10, 1970): 10.

Reviews *Twenty-One Stories.* Roskolenko perceives that "so much of Agnon's words deal with God, praise for God, for one's parents—and the family of Judaism living in pious precincts, good deeds, memories of antique ways."

Shaked, Gershon. "Midrash and Narrative: Agnon's 'Agunot'." In *Midrash and Literature,* edited by Geoffrey H. Hartman and Sanford Budick, pp. 285-303. New Haven, CT: Yale University Press, 1986.

Asserting that Agnon's fiction can be fully understood only in the context of the literary tradition to which the author refers, Shaked uses the story "Agunot" to demonstrate that the "creative power" of Agnon's tales "arises from the constant tension between the text itself and the sanctified or semi-sanctified literary tradition . . . which it invokes."

Sholem, Gershom. "Reflections on S. Y. Agnon." *Commentary* 44, No. 6 (December 1967): 59-66.

Considers the relationship of Agnon's fiction to Hebrew language and literature and to the modern history of the Jewish people.

Wiesel, Elie. "A Dream of the Past." *Book Week* 4, No. 3 (September 25, 1966): 8.

Reviews *Two Tales: Betrothed & Edo and Enam.* Wiesel contends that both stories in this collection "begin as realistic narratives that lead slowly into a dreamlike spell that confounds and dissolves the normal categories of time and space, of reality and fantasy, life and death."

Yudkin, Leon I., ed. *Agnon: Texts and Contexts in English Translation: A Multi-Disciplinary Curriculum, Bibliographies, and Selected Syllabi.* New York: Markus Wiener Publishing, 1988, 300 p.

Includes essays on the stories *Ad Olam (Forevermore),* "Yedidut" ("Friendship"), and "Tallit Aheret."

Additional coverage of Agnon's life and career is contained in the following sources published by Gale Research: *Contemporary Authors,* Vols. 17-18, 25-28 (rev. ed.); *Contemporary Authors New Revision Series,* Vol. 60; *Contemporary Authors Permanent Series,* Vol. 2; *Contemporary Literary Criticism,* Vols. 4, 8, 14; and *Major 20th-Century Writers.*

Gina Berriault
1926-

American short story writer, novelist, and scriptwriter.

INTRODUCTION

Berriault is best known for brief short stories in which she utilizes detached, economical prose to empathetically but unsentimentally portray a wide variety of characters in crisis situations. Unable to enact change on their own behalf or to articulate their feelings of loss, despair, and loneliness, Berriault's protagonists often suffer in isolation. Addressing psychological, emotional, and existential concerns, Berriault's stories frequently examine such subjects as lack of intimacy, reality and illusion, failed familial and sexual relationships, and unrealized expectations. Berriault's stories are collected in *The Mistress, and Other Stories* (1965), *The Infinite Passion of Expectation* (1982), and *Women in Their Beds* (1996), the latter of which won the 1997 Book Critics Circle Award for fiction and the 1997 PEN/Faulkner Award.

Biographical Information

Berriault was born in Long Beach, California, to Russian Jewish immigrants. She grew up during the Depression, and her father, who worked as a marble cutter and later as a writer, was not always able to secure employment. Her mother went blind when Berriault was fourteen years old, an event that Berriault has suggested influenced her writing. When Berriault was young, she loved reading books, and she started to write her own stories when she was in grammar school. After graduating from high school, Berriault worked various jobs, including clerk, waitress, and news reporter. She first attracted attention as a writer in 1958 when seven of her stories were collected in Scribner's *Short Story 1*. Berriault was awarded a fellowship from the Centro Mexicano de Escritores in Mexico City, where she lived and wrote in 1963. During the 1960s, she also wrote articles for *Esquire* magazine. Berriault has taught creative writing at San Francisco State University and Ohio University and received an appointment as a scholar at the Radcliffe Institute for Independent Study.

Major Works of Short Fiction

Berriault's first short story collection, *The Mistress, and Other Stories,* includes fifteen stories, most of which were previously published in magazines. Often set in the San Francisco Bay area in California, the stories examine such subjects as grief, despair, loneliness, and sexual conflict. "The Stone Boy," for example, centers on a nine-

year-old boy, Arnold, who ostensibly shows no remorse for accidentally shooting and killing his brother. Because Arnold is unable to show his grief, he is virtually shunned by the community and everyone in his family except his grandfather. "The Diary of K. W." is the story of a sixty-three-year-old woman who has no friends or relatives, is unable to keep a job, and is dying of starvation. Written in diary form over several weeks, K.W.'s musings reveal that she was once married and successful but is now so immobilized by fear, loneliness, and poverty that she is unable to ask for help. Another story in the collection, "Death of a Lesser Man," examines the ambivalence an attractive young woman feels toward her terminally ill, older husband as she contemplates the possibility of taking a lover. *The Infinite Passion of Expectation* gathers twenty-five pieces written over a span of more than two decades, with twelve of the stories previously appearing in *The Mistress, and Other Stories.* "Myra" focuses on a young black woman who, passionately in love with her husband, continues to clean, cook, and care for him despite his indifference toward her and her pregnancy. "The Infinite Passion of Expectation," the title of which is taken from a work by Danish philosopher Søren Kierkegaard, tells the story of a young waitress whose seventy-nine-year-old psychologist asks her to marry him. When she denies his request, he calls her "cold" and tells her "you will never be loved." *Women in Their Beds* contains thirty-five stories, many of which were first published in magazines and journals. Like her previous collections, this volume focuses on a wide variety of characters and experiences. "Who Is It Can Tell Me Who I Am?", for example, centers on a dapper librarian who believes a young drifter he has befriended plans to kill him, and "Stolen Pleasures" features a poor young girl who becomes preoccupied with her wealthy friend's piano.

Critical Reception

Berriault's short stories have not received much critical attention, but some commentators speculate that with the publication of the award-winning *Women in Their Beds,* her work in the genre will begin to generate the wide critical and popular recognition it deserves. The critical reaction Berriault has received, particularly early in her career, has been mixed, with some critics describing Berriault's stories as overly pessimistic and her prose style as too precise and intellectual. Some reviewers have also faulted the brevity of her stories, sometimes negatively referring to them as "miniatures" or "watercolors." Most critics, however, have commended her convincing and unsentimental depiction of the emotional and psychological hardships of her characters. In particular, critics have praised what they have called her amazing range of characters, noting that she is able to convincingly write from both male and female viewpoints and that her characters come from all social, ethnic, and economic backgrounds. Despite past ambivalence toward Berriault's work, some critics continue to assert that Berriault's short fiction will become increasingly appreciated and influential. Andre Dubus, for example, has called *The Infinite Passion of Expectation* "the best book of short stories by a living American author." Similarly, Gary Amdahl has stated that Berriault, "having written so beautifully and so consistently for nearly forty years, ought to be as familiar to us as Toni Morrison and John Updike."

PRINCIPAL WORKS

Short Fiction

The Mistress, and Other Stories 1965
The Infinite Passion of Expectation: Twenty-Five Stories 1982
Women in Their Beds: New and Selected Stories 1996

Other Major Works

The Descent (novel) 1960
Conference of Victims (novel) 1962
The Son (novel) 1966
The Lights of Earth (novel) 1984

The Stone Boy (screenplay) 1984
Afterwards (novel) 1998

*This work is an adaptation of Berriault's short story "The Stone Boy." It was released by Twentieth-Century Fox and starred Robert Duvall and Glenn Close.

CRITICISM

Charles Poore (review date 1965)

SOURCE: "Books of the Times: The Moment of Truth Doesn't Need Stretching," in *The New York Times,* September 11, 1965, p. 25.

[*In the following mixed review of* The Mistress, and Other Stories, *Poore discusses the length of Berriault's stories and comments on her characterization and originality.*]

The trouble with many short stories is that they are too long. Their advertised brevity is inauthentic. A point a reader grasps in two minutes gains nothing by being nested in words for half an hour.

That, I think, is why short story collections, by and large, are said not to sell. There are exceptions, of course, as we all know well. One, in fact, should be Gina Berriault's *The Mistress and Other Stories,* on our table today. Current short story garlands, however, are usually pretty safe from predatory borrowers. They numb in short doses. Yet they numb, nevertheless. A novel by a gifted author can be taken at a gallop. A bookful of his briefer tales may turn out to be a singularly slow motion steeplechase.

Authors and their publishers are alert to that hazard. Not rarely, they subtly subtitle a sheaf the "selected" tales of the writer. Would they put out a volume called the "selected" scenes from a long novel that has elsewhere been published in full?

Well, yes. Much more rarely, though. And in such cases the thing is called a "condensation," or an "abridgment," or whatever. The truncation, then, is a venture in capsulated culture.

No one needs to apply such stunting measures to Gina Berriault's stories. You usually know from the start whether you want to go on. The one called **"The Diary of K. W.,"** for example, gets nowhere in particular, and gets there rapidly, in a bitter crone's progress.

The title story, **"The Mistress,"** has just one lamentable point to make. A discarded high-spirited doxy is revengefully eager to let a boy know she once held his father's wayward affection. She does so, in the cruelest way.

Murder, Miss Berriault shows us, has many forms and devices. It is seemingly explicit in **"The Stone Boy,"** where a life ends in a shooting accident. How much of an accident was it? we are left to ask. At that point, the explicit and the implicit merge in shadows.

It is hard to believe that any writer, in our passing day and age, could do much with the bit about the melancholy housewife romantically moping over her Bohemian fling in Paris. It's threadbare. It's passé. But read Miss Berriault's "Death of a Lesser Man," and you'll see that life can be pumped into that antique vein.

—*Charles Poore*

She does not stay for our answer. She is on to another event in another place. Always Miss Berriault displays a splendid gift for cutting her characters' gains—or losses—according to the point of view, with quick endings.

Not O. Henryesque Surprise! Surprise! endings, either. Her music, as T. S. Eliot liked to say, is successful with a dying fall.

The scene is often California. There are several stories about the San Francisco Bay area, where the fiery contemporary spirit has lighted notable conflagrations lately. Uppergrade beatniks, middlegrade beatniks, and the true beatniks of desperation are all over the place.

Miss Berriault swiftly fields their antics, their poses, their despairs. She shows us people who fight for what they want. Whether they deserve it or not becomes an irrelevancy in justice's scales. It is burningly germane to her stories.

The man or woman is always self-revealed. Assists are generously supplied by other characters. Offhand, it is hard to believe that any writer, in our passing day and age, could do much with the bit about the melancholy housewife romantically moping over her Bohemian fling in Paris. It's threadbare. It's passé. But read Miss Berriault's **"Death of a Lesser Man,"** and you'll see that life can be pumped into that antique vein.

"So they don't talk Robbe-Grillet or Camus," her exasperated consort says, insisting that she go to a provincial party. And in **"Felis Catus,"** a sad-sack evader of everyday responsibilities only wants to get sick enough to give up his job and write forlorn explications of modern art. The moony yearning to meet someone who has been in a Fellini movie or knows Beckett is crisply anatomized under Miss Berriault's razory words.

Her effects pour out in amazing combinations. Here, for example, she is about to describe a man literally throw-

ing a fit. While she's at it, she satirizes a way of life. Look:

"In the midst of seven friends eating pickled mushrooms, cheeses, smoked oysters . . . and drinking Danish beer from tall green Mexican glasses in an apartment of red Naugahyde furniture and black shag rugs . . . his eyes rolled up . . ."

So do ours, so do ours. Our eyes roll down again, though, when we come to another setting, in another story, where people live in hunger and want. And there is a synthesis, of sorts, when a girl from a slum is given patronizing work in the world of black shag rugs and Danish beer in tall Mexican glasses.

Richard Kostelanetz (review date 1965)

SOURCE: "Isolation Is the Norm," in *New York Times Book Review,* September 19, 1965, p. 54.

[*In the review of* The Mistress, and Other Stories *below, Kostelanetz praises Berriault's portrayal of psychological and emotional concerns but faults her prose and depiction of male characters.*]

Gina Berriault at her best creates portraits of complex feelings; she is adept at swiftly evolving a convincing character. Her prime virtue is an extraordinary capacity to empathize with a wide variety of isolated people and then to convey in fiction her knowledge of their minds.

As a collection of stories, *The Mistress* demonstrates the breadth of her psychological range. It encompasses a young boy who feels no remorse for accidentally killing his brother but considerable embarrassment at being caught naked (**"The Stone Boy"**); a young wife who, once she has her own nose shortened, develops a passion for men with lengthy beaks (**"Anna Lisa's Nose"**); a young girl who realizes that she looks upon her institutionalized father with a disinterested eye (**"The Bystander"**); a 63-year-old woman with no friends or relatives, who is unable to hold a job (**"The Diary of KW"**); a mistress who, upon meeting her former lover's son, discovers she has more feeling for the boy's mother than her past paramour (the title story). Save for bits of hokum here and there, these portraits are deft and true.

In my favorite, **"Death of a Lesser Man,"** one of the two stories not previously published, Mrs. Berriault perceptively evokes the ambivalences of an attractive young woman toward her kindly, ailing, aged husband and the possibility of taking on a lover. Mrs. Berriault's talent is less sure with male characters, as in **"Around the Dear Ruin"** and **"Nights in the Gardens of Spain."** Strangely absent from the book is her most successfully realized male narrator, the traveling salesman of **"Something in His Nature"** originally published in *New World Writing* in 1955.

The brilliance of her knowledge accents her deficiencies in another aspect of fictional art—style. Her prose is generally dreary and often prolix. Her sentences are too frequently clumsy; she hardly ever executes a sharp line or an elegant turn of phrase. Then, too, the stories are prosaic in form—even the "diary" structure is a bit old-fashioned by now—and, unlike the best contemporaries in the short form, she makes little attempt to exploit the mode itself for original patterns and perspectives.

Thus, her work seems at first less interesting than it really is. Her style bores before her material attracts. Mrs. Berriault's sensitivity and wisdom are commendable—but fictional art requires knowledge and beauty too.

Dorrie Pagones   (review date 1965)

SOURCE: "Foredoomed Failures," in *Saturday Review,* Vol. XLVIII, No. 46, November 13, 1965, pp. 104-05.

[*Below, Pagones provides a mixed assessment of* The Mistress, and Other Stories.]

Gina Berriault's *The Mistress and Other Stories* is so good a book that it ought to be better. Reading several of the stories at a time is to be avoided, like looking too long at splendid scenery; one marvels while stifling a yawn. Gina Berriault is a formidably intelligent, observant, and analytical person, but indispensable though these qualities are, they are not enough to give her prose what the landscape lacks—the ordinary breath of life.

For all that, these fifteen stories are worth anyone's while. Miss Berriault takes a thoroughly pessimistic view of human nature, using as a prefatory quotation José Ortega y Gasset's opinion that "Every life is more or less a ruin among whose debris we have to discover what the person ought to have been." No one behaves as he should, and even supposing anyone did, it is quite clear, as the title of one story puts it, that "All Attempts Will End in Failure." Everyone fails, from the mistress of the title story, who is appalled to discover, years after the passing of her great love affair, that "the person in her memory who affected her the most was not the one she loved the most but the one she had understood the least."

In **"The Diary of KW"** an old woman loses her job as a school cafeteria helper because "it occurred to me that food was abominable and that . . . if they went on eating their hot lunches every day they would only be preparing themselves to suffer, they would only grow up to suffer." The parents obtusely fail the child in **"The Stone Boy,"** and the child inevitably fails the parent in **"The Bystander."** Most frequently of all, men and women fail each other, like the white woman and Negro man, former lovers, of **"Lonesome Road."** When he accidentally meets her in the park with her children he is unable to wave casually at them in parting "because his pity for her, the pity that he had failed to experience in the time of his love, forbade him small and amiable signals."

There are plenty of other kinds of failure here, as many as there are stories. Since no one particularly cares to think of his life and all other lives as foredoomed fiascoes, the temptation is to say that Miss Berriault has overdone it, that she is being academic about life. But if her book is, in any sense, a failure, it is better than many successes.

Belle Pomer   (review date 1966)

SOURCE: "Clean Cuts," in *The Canadian Forum,* Vol. 46, June, 1966, p. 70.

[*In the following evaluation of* The Mistress, and Other Stories, *Pomer compares Berriault's work to that of American writer Mary McCarthy and praises Berriault's examination of human motivation.*]

[*The Mistress, and Other Stories*] contains a small masterpiece called **"Death Of A Lesser Man"**. Not since [American writer] Mary McCarthy's *Ghostly Father, I Confess* have I read such a fascinating dissection of a certain aspect of the female personality. The subject of Miss McCarthy's study was the kind of woman who needs to reassure herself constantly by securing the attention of every man she meets; in **"Death Of A Lesser Man"** the heroine's nature is strongly narcissistic. Gina Berriault is knowing and she is exact—in all the twistings and turnings, the shades of feeling and motivation, the impingement on one another of fantasy and reality.

Miss Berriault's stories have been published in *Mademoiselle, Scribner's, Paris Review, Harper's Bazaar, Saturday Evening Post, Contact, Esquire* and *San Francisco Review.* As this list suggests, her style and approach are fashionably sophisticated. The humans she so shrewdly observes are mostly inhabitants of California; they include rural and urban, old and young, Negro and white. Several of these stories—**"Myra"**, **"Around The Dear Ruin"**, **"The Stone Boy"**—are first-rate. **"Anna Lisa's Nose"** and **"Felis Catus"** are clever, funny and cutting. I also liked the slighter **"Nights In The Gardens Of Spain"**.

One always quarrels, I suppose, with the arrangement of a collection; it is a puzzle to find that so many of them put their worst foot forward. The title story of this volume makes a weak beginning, and since reading a number of stories by one person can produce a cumulative effect, **"The Mistress"** would probably stand a chance of appearing less superficial if placed elsewhere. It is followed, however, by a more promising story and then by several of the very good ones. Miss Berriault cuts cleanly through defenses and self-delusions to lay bare the ego and human motivation. This exposure will make some people cringe, but I think it would be safe to say that anyone who likes Mary McCarthy's fiction will read this collection with pleasure.

Review of *The Mistress, and Other Stories*:

Gina Berriault prefaces her *The Mistress, and Other Stories* with an aphorism by Jose Ortega y Gasset: "Every life is more or less a ruin among whose debris we have to discover what the person ought to have been." Miss Berriault is an apt delineator of ruin. Her characters, in a great many of the stories, are desiccated intellectuals—gray people, inhabiting gray rooms, reporting to and fatigued by gray jobs. . . . Berriault is a writer of substance and quality who brings precious, strange perceptions to somber, dour lives.

Kirkus Reviews, *Vol. 33, No. 12, June 15, 1965.*

Edith Milton   (review date 1983)

SOURCE: "Lives That Touch without Intimacy," in *New York Times Book Review,* January 9, 1983, pp. 28-9.

[*In the generally positive review of* The Infinite Passion of Expectation *below, Milton praises Berriault's focus on characters who are "caught in emotional ambiguities and contradictions," but calls the stories in the collection "oddly cerebral."*]

Gina Berriault has been writing novels and short stories for some 25 years. And the 25 stories collected in *The Infinite Passion of Expectation* are without exception nearly flawless miniatures in her particular mode. They always descend below the surface of the events and phenomena out of which they are woven, but they descend only minimally, so that their observations stay easily within the perceptions of the characters and the reader is given the illusion not merely of looking at alien lives but of moving through alien sensibilities. In story after story, Mrs. Berriault focuses on lives that touch each other without intimacy. She magnifies the banal instances that are her fiction's raw material until we see a series of worlds in close-up, anatomies as simultaneously repellent and magnetic, exotic and familiar, as a Chuck Close portrait.

In particular she is a virtuoso in the sort of claustrophobia from which Jean-Paul Sartre built his play *No Exit*; the emotional climate, I mean, that develops when two or three characters with conflicting fears and expectations jostle against each other in a rather small space. In the book's title story a young woman with no money, no friends and no capacity for hope becomes the temporary housekeeper of an old man who is rich, optimistic and intellectually and sexually vital. With nothing before her except a long life, she locks herself away; for him, who has everything and wants more, existence is already receding. Their lives confront and contradict each other. In **"The Mistress"** a woman and the son of her former lover meet at a party and exchange clashing memories of a time that to her meant love and to him misery. In **"Myra"** a bride is still passionately in love with her young hus-

band, who, already grown used to her, wants simply to take her for granted and be left alone.

The characters of these stories, almost without exception, are humble people caught in emotional ambiguities and contradictions that have paralyzed them and made it easier to live in dreams or the past than to confront the present world. Often, in fact, their longing for the past and their illusions about the future reduce them to shadows. The middle-aged woman who is the protagonist of **"Bastille Day"** drifts into a bar where the ghosts of her youthful rebellions and ideals lie in wait for her, as unrealized and disappointing as the great events enshrined in the celebration of July 14. Claudia in **"Death of a Lesser Man"** dreams of love and intellectual adventure, but the freedom that these imply seems quite as deadly to her as her role in the futile progress of a polite marriage. In **"The Stone Boy"** a child accidentally kills his brother and is so numbed by this catastrophe that he can only react to it as if nothing had happened. In **"Nights in the Gardens of Spain"** a guitar teacher finds momentary solace for the insufficiencies of his daily life, not in his own music or that of his students, but in a borrowed recording.

The rewards for most of Mrs. Berriault's people are, in fact, usually brief and borrowed and often illusory. A large part of her characters' existence is spent rear-ranging their expectations, adjusting what they see and feel to what they had hoped to see and feel, which was quite different. A son explores his contradictory responses to his father's mental illness; mothers and children walk a delicate tightrope between the child's ignorance and dependence and the adult's confused loyalties and responsibilities. The most poignant story of the collection and my favorite is **"The Diary of K. W.,"** in which an old woman dying of starvation listens to the sounds of the happy life in the apartment above hers, too shy and too conditioned by isolation and self-denigration to ask for help.

Although most of these stories take place in or around San Francisco, the experiences they represent are amazing in their variety: from bar nights to discussions of Camus, from the routines of farm chores to the hand-to-mouth improvisation of the urban ghetto. These are particular worlds drawn from the specific witness of the characters themselves.

And yet in some way difficult to describe, Mrs. Berriault's fiction remains oddly cerebral. Her characters' inner voices seem always to move toward generalization. "He was the parent who breaks down under the eyes of his child," the narrator of **"The Bystander"** says of his father, ". . . while the child stands and watches the end of the struggle and then walks away to catch a streetcar." That exquisite, aphoristic ending also seems disturbingly at odds with the gritty, down-at-heels realism of the story's characters and setting. The heroine of **"Death of a Lesser Man"** thinks about the man who has been following her and who she is afraid may attack her: "The obscene dolt must have stolen away her dream of herself in the future, the dream that was only a memory of herself in the past. . . . The intruder must have stolen away the past and the future." Surely an incredibly subtle insight for a woman who is both choked with fear and distressed by incongruous stirrings of sexual excitement.

The characters of these stories, almost without exception, are humble people caught in emotional ambiguities and contradictions that have paralyzed them and made it easier to live in dreams or the past than to confront the present world.

—Edith Milton

In one of the longer stories in the collection, **"The Search for J. Kruper,"** a lionized writer of autobiographical schlock heads into the Mexican wilderness to find his antithesis and idol, the great J. Kruper, who "forgot the self that bore a name and became all others." J. Kruper is, one assumes, Mrs. Berriault's own ideal of authorship, and the aim of her fiction, like his, is forgetting the self and becoming all others. But as the story wryly notes, the self is not easily forgotten and, far from obligingly becoming all others, often subverts all others to become the self instead.

In fact, it is hard to escape the author's voice in these stories: Their diction is sophisticated, their prose bristles with astute observation. An occasional witty quirk of syntax seems to grant control to the inanimate and the abstract: "She heard his breath take over for him and . . . carry on his life"; "The silence she ought to have kept overcame me." I suppose I may be quibbling over what is merely a shrewd exploitation of grammar to define human helplessness, but the mannerism adds to the sense that these pieces are more about the pattern of people's lives than about the people, that they develop less from the integral needs of their characters than from the ideas they have been created to contain.

The 25 stories of *The Infinite Passion of Expectation* are limited, then, by the control of their author's intellect. But within those limits they work brilliantly. None really moved me, none jarred my complacent prejudices or stirred my compassion; but there is not a story among them that is less than elegant, less than perfectly observed, perfectly resolved fiction.

Gina Berriault with Bonnie Lyons and Bill Oliver (interview date 1994)

SOURCE: An interview with Gina Berriault, in *The Literary Review*, Vol. 37, No. 4, Summer, 1994, pp. 714-23.

[*In the following excerpt from an interview, Berriault discusses such subjects as how she became a writer,* *contemporary American fiction, her writing style, and the major themes in her works.*]

[Bonnie Lyons and Bill Oliver]: *How do you think your childhood reading affected you as a writer?*

[Gina Berriault]: That little girl who was me was a restless spirit, confined in a classroom and yearning to be out and roaming, either in the landscape or in her own imagination, and that restlessness was channeled into reading. I read more books than any other student in grammar school, roaming everywhere the persons in the stories roamed; I was those persons. Among the earliest books was *Water Babies* (that one belonged to the family across the alley and I remember climbing in through their kitchen window when they were away on vacation, reading it over and over, sitting on the floor in a corner) and George MacDonald's great-hearted books, especially *At the Back of the North Wind* about a poor family and their love for one another. That deepened me. I began to know who I was, and that kids in poor families were worthy of books about them. And A.A. Milne, who wakened in me a delight in dialogue, an intuitive ear for what goes on between us and our beloved small animals—conversations of pretend naivete and subtle wit, that can make a child feel she knows more than adults think she knows. And later, in the novels of I. Zangwill, who wrote about Jewish families in Europe, I found a secret kinship, and I found that Jewish persons were worthy of being in novels. No one, all through my school years (except for a teacher who must have felt a kinship with Hitler) suspected that I was Jewish, and I must have been one-of-a-kind in that small California town. An insatiable reader, I began early to write my own stories, because, when you find yourself enthralled by their marvelous manipulation of language, when you find your wits sharpened, your heart stirred, your conscience revealed, then those writers become your guardian angels. They bring you to see your own existence as valuable—why else would they write their stories for you?—and they seem to be giving you their blessing to write your own. They seem to be blessing all children, even those who can't read a word.

Do you remember how you actually began writing?

My father was a free-lance writer for trade magazines and he had one of those old, stand-up-high typewriters. So I began to write my stories on it.

So you began writing when you were very young?

Yes, I began to write on that typewriter when I was in grammar school. I also wanted to be an artist and an actress. A drama teacher in high school offered to pay my tuition to an excellent drama school, but just at that time my father died and it was necessary for me to support my mother, brother, and sister. I never had any formal training as a writer, either.

Do you remember anything specific about how you taught yourself to write?

I simply wrote and wrote, and I was an avid reader. One thing I'd do was put a great writer's book beside the typewriter and then I'd type out a beautiful and moving paragraph or page and see those sentences rising up before my eyes from my own typewriter, and I would think "Someday maybe I can write like that."

You mean you'd type the words of someone else's story?

Yes, to see the words coming up out of my typewriter. It was like a dream of possibilities for my own self. And maybe I began to know that there was no other way for that sentence and that paragraph to be and arouse the same feeling. The someone whose words were rising from that typewriter became like a mentor for me. And when I went on with my own work, I'd strive to attain the same qualities I loved in that other person's work. Reading and writing are collaborations. When you read someone you truly love, their writing reaches your innermost self. You're soulmates.

How old were you when you did that experiment with your father's typewriter?

In my teens. I did it a few times. You shouldn't do it more than a few times because you must get on with your own.

Could you talk a bit more about how you began writing and publishing?

My experiment with my father's typewriter was going on at the same time I was writing my own stories. Rejection cards and letters with hastily scribbled encouragement helped to convince me that I existed. I remember a letter from an elegant, slick magazine, asking me to make a change or two and offer the story again. I did that, and when it was returned I cried for hours. By that time my parents had lost their house and the orange tree and the roses, and I wanted to earn enough with my writing to buy a farm for them. (I'd always wanted to live on a farm.) My father died before I could be of any help to him with my stories.

Elsewhere you mentioned that your mother began to go blind when you were fourteen. Could you talk about how that affected you as a person and as a writer?

As I wrote in my essay for *Confidence Women,* my blind mother sat by her little radio, listening to those serial romances and waving her hand before her eyes, hoping to see it take shape out of the dark. That could be a metaphor for my attempt to write, hoping to bring forth some light from out of the dark. I haven't yet.

How much formal education did you have?

After high school I took over my father's job. Then after work I'd roam through the Los Angeles public library and pick out whatever names or titles intrigued me. Having no mentor to guide me through that library, I just found writers by myself.

Do you regret not having a mentor?

My father was mentor for my spirit, I can say, and there were others from whom I learned about the world. I regret not having a formal, organized education. I wish I'd studied world history, philosophy, comparative literature, and I wish I'd learned several languages. Really, there is no excuse for my lack of those attainments, of that intellectual exploring, except as it is with every unschooled person—the circumstances of each one's life.

You don't say you regret not having gone through a creative writing program. Suppose a young writer wrote to you and said, "I admire your work and I want to write. Should I get a degree in creative writing?" What would you say?

I'd tell that person to learn more about everything, to rove, to be curious, and to read great writers from everywhere. If there's a true compulsion to write, a deep need, that person will write against all odds. And if that person enters a creative writing program, it would be for the purpose of learning how to shape what's already known and felt. Sometimes, when I taught workshops, I was glad I hadn't subjected myself to the unkind criticism of strangers. There's so much competitiveness, concealed and overt, among those who want to be writers and those who are writers. In Unamuno's *Tragic Sense of Life* he speaks about poets' desperate longing to be remembered, to be immortal. I think that concept of immortality is long past, long gone from our consciousness. Such immense change going on in the world, so much that will be irretrievable. So now the vying with one another is only for present gain. When I asked the students if they'd read this-or-that great writer, most had read only contemporary writers, and if the ads and the reviews praised those writers, the students accepted that evaluation. Ivan Bunin, for example, has been almost forgotten, and what a writer he was!

Speaking of contemporary writers, whose work do you admire?

Nabokov, Primo Levi, Jean Rhys—aren't they contemporary still? And to go a little further back, but still within my view contemporary, Chekhov, Turgenev, Gogol, Bunin. They are my first and last deep loves. I liked Raymond Carver's first collection best. Those stories were like underground poetry. He must have felt that the reader possessed an intuitiveness like his own, and picked up on the meaning, just as with poetry.

Isn't that a way of taking your reader as equal?

And when you take the reader as your equal, your work isn't affected or false. You establish that collaboration, that shared intuitiveness.

In your career there's a big gap between The Son *and* **The Infinite Passion of Expectation.** *Why?*

That's a question that should never be asked. It opens a wound. What can a writer say about gaps and silence? The question can't be answered because the answer involves the circumstances of a lifetime and the condition of the psyche at one time and another. How can a writer possibly answer it without the shame of pleading for understanding of one's confusions and limitations and fears? You call it a gap, but that's the time between publications. There is no measurable gap. I never ceased writing, but I destroy much of what I write or I can't work out what I want to say and I put the piece aside. The longing to write and the writing never cease. When I taught to make a living, evenings and years were given over to guiding students through their own imagination, to the neglect of my own. And there's the disbelief, so often at my elbow as I write, that I can write at all.

Do you see yourself primarily as a short story writer rather than a novelist?

Oh, yes. When my first stories were published, there was a lot of enticement from editors to write novels. But I wish I'd written twenty stories to one novel, instead. Short stories and some short novels are close to poetry, with the fewest words they capture the essence of a situation, of a human being. It's like trying to pin down the eternal moment.

Many critics have praised your work for the extraordinary variety of characters and settings, including characters of various races and classes. Do you think your life experience was important in developing that wide scope?

I never thought I had a wide scope. The way to escape from the person who you figure you may be is to become many others in your imagination. And that way you can't be categorized as a regional writer or a Jewish writer or a feminist writer, and even though you may be confined by the circumstances of your life, you're roaming out in the world, your imagination as your guide. I haven't roamed far enough.

You've said, "Between the lines of every story, readers write their own lines, shaping up the story as a collaborative effort." As the writer, are you concerned about controlling or directing the reader's lines, with the question of a "correct" interpretation?

Of course the writer wishes to compel and persuade and entice and guide the reader to a comprehension of the story, but there's no such thing as a "correct" interpretation of a piece of fiction. That's demanding a scientific precision of the writer. Each reader's interpretation originates in his or her life's experiences, in feelings and emotions of intensely personal history. You get more from what you read as you grow older, and your choices change, and, wiser, you bring more to that collaborative effort.

How about screenplays?

They're so mechanical to write, and you must leave out the depths you try to reach when you're writing your stories. A screenplay is a simplification and an exaggeration at the same time. By contrast, if you slip in a false note in a story, the whole thing falls. But a film can be packed with other persons' demands upon it, become a falsification of the writer's original idea, and then be hailed as one of the year's best—the usual. What makes a film work are the magnified, publicized, idolized actors moving around up there on the screen. And because the influence and the gain from movies are made to seem more real than from your obscure small stories, so many young writers think it's the highest achievement in life to write a movie script.

Were any of the interviews you wrote for Esquire *in the Sixties memorable to you? To whom did you talk? In addition to your story* **"God and the Article Writer"** *did they have any lasting influence or effect?*

Whom did I interview? I interviewed the topless dancers, the first nightclub topless dancers, not first in the world, of course, but in San Francisco. I remember that an editor at *Esquire* asked me to write an article; they had published some stories of mine, and he said that fiction writers write better articles. So I offered the idea of the topless dancers, who had only recently stepped out onto the stages in North Beach. His "Okay" sounded tentative to me, and so I was very surprised when he phoned a few weeks later wanting to know where the article was. I had only a week in which to research and write, and I got it to them in time. Synchronicity is at work when you're writing an article. Pertinent things—overheard conversations, random meetings—are attracted by your task as by a magnet, and the article shapes up in a surprising way. That's not always the case, but it happens. Then an editor at *Esquire* asked me to interview someone or two who were fallen from the heights and so I found a very elderly couple, man and wife, who had been Broadway entertainers in their youth, and, in their shabby apartment, I looked through their piles of old newspaper clippings and photos; I was moved. I interviewed the student at Stanford who was a leader of demonstrations opposed to the Vietnam War, and I interviewed the men who were the firing squad executioners in Utah, the last firing squad that wasn't, after all, the last. They all wanted anonymity—shame, I suppose—and the photographer took their picture together in silhouette, dark, against a yellow sunset, out in a field. Since I am an outsider, an observer at heart, not an interrogator, I'm not facile at asking people about themselves. And protective as I am of my own secret self, my own personal life, I am reluctant to inquire of others, even though I find that some others don't mind at all telling about themselves. Pride intervenes, too; you feel subservient, at times, to the person you're interviewing, and it was this attitude, this uneasiness, this feeling of being an intruder, that brought about the story **"God and the Article Writer,"** wherein the lowly article writer transcends himself by becoming one with God. It's a bit of a satire and it amused me as I wrote it.

In the more than thirty years you've been writing and teaching, what do you think has been the most significant change in fiction?

One thing that dismays is the cruel pornography of recent novels and how they're considered an honest probe of these desecrating times. What's inspiring is the work of more Black writers and Hispanic writers, and the availability of the small presses and quarterlies. But most of the short stories in most of the large circulation magazines seem about the same as they always were—about the middle class, their mishaps and misapprehensions. An elitism in a vacuum. There's no sorrow and no pity. We're far from writers like Steinbeck and Dos Passos and Nelson Algren. I remember reading *In Dubious Battle* all through the night, I remember just where I was and what period of my life—like a vivid fragment. There's been an intimidation of writers in this country. We write to be acceptable. Some things I wanted to write about, I haven't because I was afraid I wouldn't be published, and writing has been and is my livelihood. I supported myself and my child with my writing. I like to believe that I never misled and that I wrote truthfully, but I've always felt the presence of anonymous and not-so-anonymous authority.

Do you think there is a connection between the superficiality you find in so much writing today and the fact that many writers are academically trained and remain in academia as teachers?

It may be that superficiality results from covert or implicit censorship of our work. The academe isn't to blame, I think. Some very fine writers, prose and poetry, are teaching in universities to keep a roof over their heads and to find pleasure in teaching. Superficial writers seem to make a good living and don't need to teach.

Right now, a first person, present tense style is very popular. How do you feel about it?

I imagine that the first person, present tense is the easiest way to write. But to me it seems to contain the most emptiness. It brings a sense of immediacy, and with immediacy you think you've got hold of the truth and the real, and so there's a touch of satisfaction about it, a conceit. Just recently I was looking at Sebastiao Salgado's book of photos, *An Uncertain Grace,* and there was a short introduction by Eduardo Galeano, who wrote "Salgado shows us that concealed within the pain of living and the tragedy of dying there is a potent magic, a luminous mystery that redeems the human adventure in the world." When I read that I thought that's what great writers have always done. Salgado lived in Africa with those suffering people and he lived in Central America. He was right there, where the truth and the real and that luminous mystery are found. It can all be found in this country.

Do you see yourself as a woman writer or as a writer who happens to be a woman? And has your gender affected your career at all, caused you any difficulties?

I've known and still know a fear of men's judgments and ridicule and rejection. At the same time I've been acutely aware of the oppression and abuse and humiliation that men endure and struggle against, the same that women endure and now know they don't have to endure. In other words, I'm a humanist, I guess.

How do you think of your work in relationship to the Women's Movement?

Most of my stories, early ones and later ones, are about women. My wonder and my concern over women are present always in the natural course of my writing.

When you look at your own work, do you think there are recurring themes?

I don't look over my past work, or I don't like to. I want to look over my future work. If there is a recurring theme, it's an attempt at compassionate understanding. Judgement is the prevalent theme in our society, but it's from fiction we learn compassion and comprehension. In Gogol's great story, "The Overcoat," there's a description of the poor copying clerk's threadbare overcoat, how the cold wind got in across his back. I don't know why those lines move me so much, except when you visualize how the cloth has worn out without his knowing until suddenly one day he's surprised by that cold invasion—isn't that a description of an entire life? That copying clerk is always ridiculed and insulted by the younger clerks. I guess that in my work, in my way, I attempt to rouse compassion for those who are called demented or alien or absurd or ridiculous, for those who are beyond the pale. . . .

It seems to me that although your writing is never propaganda, it is indirectly quite political and that you see social or political engagement as essential to serious literature. Do you agree?

Engagement is the only word you need, because it explains why some of us must write. And political engagement is essential to serious literature as design or perspective or materials are essential to any work of art, but only as an integral part of that engagement, that dedication.

What do you make of the idea, popular in some circles today, that writers should only write about people like themselves, people of their own ethnicity, class, gender, and sexual preference?

How limiting that is—to write only of your own ethnicity, class, gender, sexual preference. Your imagination is left to hang around the sidelines. Say that you're crammed in at a restaurant table with your ethnic friends or friends of the same preferences as yourself, all speaking the same language, and you notice someone, a stranger, out on the street, who's glancing through the window, and your eyes meet his, and you want to get up and go out and say to that stranger, "Don't I know you?"

Publishers Weekly (review date 1996)

SOURCE: A review of *Women in Their Beds: New and Selected Stories,* in *Publishers Weekly,* Vol. 243, No. 6, February 5, 1996, p. 77.

[*In the review below, the critic favorably reviews* Women in Their Beds.]

Whether focusing on yuppies or drifters, social workers or Indian restaurateurs, heroin addicts or teenage baby-sitters, Berriault (*The Lights of Earth*) writes with great psychological acuity and a compassion that comes always from observation, never from sentimentality. These 35 short stories [*Women in Their Beds*] have been published in magazines ranging from the *Paris Review* to *Harper's Bazaar*; 10 of them are here issued in book form for the first time. In **"Who Is It Can Tell Me Who I Am?"** the dapper Alberto Perera, "a librarian who did not look like one," fears that the young drifter who has befriended him, wishing to discuss the Spanish poetry he carries in his pockets, is out to kill him; but the drifter is only trying to understand how—both literally and philosophically—to live. A 79-year-old psychologist woos a young, pragmatic waitress in **"The Infinite Passion of Expectation."** When she meets his ex-wife and witnesses the selfishness spawned by a life spent in deferment, she flees. In the clever **"The Search for J. Kruper,"** an extremely famous and narcissistic novelist, noted for writing grand, poorly disguised autobiographical confessions, learns of the possible whereabouts of one of the few remaining living novelists as famous as he, a recluse who betrays nothing of himself in his writings. Each story is constructed so gracefully that it's easy to overlook how carefully crafted Berriault's writing is. Her lilting, musical prose adds a sophisticated sheen to the truths she mines.

Tobin Harshaw   (review date 1996)

SOURCE: A review of *Women in Their Beds: New and Selected Stories,* in *New York Times Book Review,* May 5, 1996, p. 22.

[*In the following review of* Women in Their Beds, *Harshaw praises Berriault's imagination but faults her characters' inaction.*]

As an alternative to those trivial compendiums of literary opening passages sold near bookstore cash registers, how about a collection of last lines from Gina Berriault's very short stories, [*Women in Their Beds: New and Selected Stories*]. Consider this stand-alone triumph: "He lay facedown under the tree and bit off some grass near the roots, chewing to distract his smile, but it would not give in, and so he lay there the entire day, smiling into the earth." Or: "She heard his breath take over for him and, in that secretive way the sleeper knows nothing about, carry on his life." Ms. Berriault is nothing if not consistent. In these 35 stories, one struggles to find a sentence that is anything less than jewel-box perfect. And the author uses her gift for language to do more than show us the world through her characters' eyes; we are also forced to think about it from their point of view—no small feat for someone who favors third-person narration. These are complex characters, and although many stories run

only a few pages Ms. Berriault never falls back on clichés: an aging male librarian, for example, is no shrinking violet; instead, he sports "a Borsalino fedora" and "English boots John Major would covet." Most of Ms. Berriault's characters are caught at moments of divergence: in **"Soul and Money,"** a lapsed Communist confronts God and Mammon in Las Vegas; in **"Lives of the Saints,"** the son of a famous religious artist undertakes his own sort of pilgrimage, visiting his father's works, and discovers that life is more lasting than art. Yet in the smooth flow of Ms. Berriault's writing, few of these people manage to register the emotional pitch needed to transcend their crises. It is not a matter of stoicism; instead, most seem dizzyingly unaware of the option to act on their own behalf. Thus the stories, so exquisite to wend through, leave one a little cold. Like their characters, they seem trapped by the perfection of Ms. Berriault's prose.

Julia B. Boken on Berriault's fiction:

Gina Berriault identifies with no school or cult of writing. The stories, whose locale is often northern California, are peopled with a remarkable array of characters, happenings, and insights, all woven into a style that is subtle and deceptively simple. The themes usually focus on the pain that comes from inevitable loss, the dark night of the soul, failed relationships, spare language that makes communication almost impossible, families torn asunder, death causing guilt to the living, the indefinability and essence of love, and the abandonment of hope. Through her keen insight, imaginative art, and finely honed craft, Berriault creates a world of flawed people. Most of them succumb to burdens that are often self-inflicted. Yet some survive and prevail, if only because they are suckled by "the infinite passion of expectation." Berriault portrays the human condition with astute psychological probing and an imagination and texture of language that promise to ensure that her novels and short fiction will continue to be popular.

Julia B. Boken, in Dictionary of Literary Biography, *Volume 130, Gale Research, 1993.*

Gary Amdahl   (review date 1996)

SOURCE: A review of *Women in Their Beds,* in *The Nation,* Vol. 262, No. 25, June 24, 1996, pp. 31-2.

[*In the positive review of* Women in Their Beds *below, Amdahl states that the publication of this work will bring Berriault the wide recognition she deserves.*]

In the absence of a certain peculiar force, the American short story declines swiftly toward the uniform. This may be true of all human endeavor, but in the case of our short fiction, the degenerate form has been made to seem the acme of the art. The teaching of it is liturgical, the writing pious and intolerant of deviation, the reading devotional, the publishing straight-faced. It has been one of the most relentlessly banal decades in the history of

U.S. literature, but, I'm happy to say, it's over: A collection of new and selected stories by Gina Berriault [*Women in Their Beds*] (serious readers in the late fifties and early sixties will know this name—she wrote three novels and a volume of stories by 1966, another novel and collection after that—but most will not) is good enough not only to be read enthusiastically, reviewed widely and cheered wildly but to inspire as well, and to be as broadly influential as, perhaps, Ray Carver was (the one guy who could do what he did; and I don't mean to imply that Carverism—Raymond as Jesus with Tobias Wolff the Pope presiding over a bureaucracy of celibate workshop directors—is the only thing wrong with short fiction). If she does get the wide notice she deserves, it will have been a long time coming: Having written so beautifully and so consistently for nearly forty years, she ought to be as familiar to us as Toni Morrison and John Updike.

How she does what she does is less easy to say than that she does it magnificently. It is, for instance, difficult to quote her. She does not indulge in fits of "me" language connected by ligamentary plot development. Each sentence is as good, as subtly evocative, as poised and full of import and pleasure as the next. Nevertheless, from **"The Island Ven,"** in which a terribly ill woman visits the Tycho Brahe museum on an island in the Baltic: "a picture of the Astronomer composed itself for her eyes and for her hand someday: up in his observatory, the young Brahe, his face lifted to that brilliancy, to that inescapable portent, its reflection floating in his eyes, and in the gems on his plump fingers, and in the waters of a fountain, and on every leaf turned toward the heavens." And this, from **"Stolen Pleasures,"** a poor young girl's contemplation of her wealthier friend's piano: "The piano, a huge, flat, forbidding face, until her best friend, Ellsworth, across the alley, sat down before it, lifted the long upper lip, baring the long rows of black and yellow teeth clamped together in an unsightly grin, and with nervous fingers picked out cajoling sounds that meant Please, piano, piano, open up a happy future for me, for me, piano, please, for me, for me."

Berriault's imagination and her prose (both are cause and effect at once) are as carefully ambitious and elaborate as Henry James's, her meanings and rhythms as closely allied as Cynthia Ozick's. She reminds me too of Barry Hannah, not so much in the prose itself—Berriault makes a virtue of calm, while Hannah makes one of fever—but in the sense they both give of being somehow unable not to write: A sentence appears before them, and the world spills out of it. Finally it's Chekhov she most calls to mind: Her characters, for the most part, are entrancingly anonymous.

So much current fiction depends on a very narrow understanding of character. Blurb after blurb, review after review, we are assured we will encounter characters we really care about. We will identify with these people because they are just like us. We will bond with them, and share. Berriault, on the other hand, creates characters whom we emphatically do not recognize—or whom we recognize, rather, only in ways that have nothing to do with superficial similarities. (I have had that experience! I have known those mixed feelings!) Describe them how you will—a struggling actress doing social work in a hospital in the little story; a fussy, overly cautious dandy librarian in **"Who Is It Can Tell Me Who I Am?"**; a classical guitarist at mid-life in **"Nights in the Gardens of Spain"**; a fired school food-service worker in **"The Diary of K. W."** (one of my favorites)—these are people we do not know, just as we do not know any but an infinites with fraction of the people we see each day. They are not likable, "nor are they unlikable."

Whether or not certain kinds of novels and stories train readers in the sympathetic imagining of others' lives—from which spring the civic virtues of tolerance and concern for the welfare of all—can be debated. What is incontrovertible is that Berriault writes real fiction.

—Gary Amdahl

Ozick once wrote of Chekhov that when "his characters strike us as unwholesome, or exasperating, or enervated, or only perverse (especially then), we feel Chekhov's patience, his clarity, his meticulous humanity," and this applies perfectly to Berriault as well. She deals with the inner lives of the perforce invisible, and sees no need to force familiarity upon us. One of the most notable features of her work is the absence of categorization, of description by quick (lazy) reference. There are no brand names, trademarks, franchises, buzz words or jargon here, no free rides on fads, no trading on popular issues or current affairs. No one is "alcoholic" or "abused," much less "recovering." Even age, race and gender are more elusive than you expect them to be. This is not slacker fiction or cyberfiction or domestic fiction, not K Mart realism or minimalism, not magic realism, not post modernism, not avant-pop. It's not multicultural in the corporate sense, it's multicultural, if you will: not monocultural, not balkanized and not exclusive.

Which is not to say the work is not direct, detailed, specific: "Anonymous" does not mean "general" (or "downtrodden" or "neglected" or "residing on the margins of society"—inner lives do not recognize class distinctions), as this quote should make clear:

> The Judge's voice was cleaving its way through the soiled air, asking legalese questions and informing each of his destination, which asylum, what refuge. Like a scene in any number of plays, where an assassin or a priest comes to tell the prisoner what his future looks like, this was a scene in a debtors' prison for those who couldn't pay back all that civilizing in vested in them. She'd been in even closer proximity to this Judge. A

wedding reception at the Stanford Court Hotel atop Nob Hill, where she'd carried trays loaded with prawns and oysters up to that buttoned-up belly. Over in a few minutes, this orderly dispersal of the deranged. The Judge left and she followed at a discreet distance, noting his brisk sort of shuffle, a slight uncertainty of step that carne from sitting in judgment for so many years. If she were ever to play a high-court judge on the stage in the park, she'd stuff a bed pillow vertically down her front and take those small steps, the uncertainty in the head repressed all the way down to the feet.

Fiction has never been so poorly read, poorly understood and poorly represented as it is right now: made up, not true, diverting, entertaining, escapist, therapeutic—this is mock fiction, imitations of a thing easily imitated (by the carefree).

Consider the following, from **"The Light at Birth,"** in which a woman, renting a room on the ocean, apprehends the last moments of a very old woman one floor beneath her:

> She was wakened in the night by the strangers at the old mother's garden party. Visions of light and of luminous strangers in that light, that was what the dying saw. She knew who they were, those strangers. They were the first of all the many strangers in your life, the ones there when you come out of the dark womb into the amazing light of earth, and never to be seen again in just that way until your last hours. She got up and walked about, barefoot, careful to make no sound that would intrude on that gathering of strangers in the little room, below.

While it may seem a lot to ask of some short stories, **Women in Their Beds** could conceivably vindicate the art, and thereby participate in the saving of the Republic. Whether or not certain kinds of novels and stories train readers in the sympathetic imagining of others' lives— from which spring the civic virtues of tolerance and concern for the welfare of all—can be debated. What is incontrovertible is that Berriault writes real fiction.

The epigraph of her previous collection, *The Infinite Passion of Expectation,* is from Neruda: "and that's how we are, forever falling / into the deep well of other beings." Berriault does not imitate, cater, affect or position. She deepens reality, complements it and affords us the bliss of knowing, for a moment, what we cannot know.

FURTHER READING

Berriault, Gina. "Almost Impossible." In *The Confidence Woman: Twenty-six Women Writers at Work,* pp. 127-32. Atlanta: Longstreet Press, 1991.
   Discusses the nature of writing, focusing in particular on her students' reactions to her short stories.

Theodore Dreiser
1871-1945

American short story writer, novelist, playwright, journalist, critic, and essayist.

INTRODUCTION

After the publication of his novel *An American Tragedy* in 1925, Theodore Dreiser was generally considered the United States's greatest living author. He received early encouragement from the influential critic, H. L. Mencken, and his novel *Sister Carrie* (1900) enjoyed a warm critical reception in England, though its poor sales in the United States drove Dreiser to clinical depression. Dreiser wrote thirty-one short stories, and many of these were revised and collected in two volumes: *Free and Other Stories* (1918) and *Chains* (1927). Dreiser pioneered Naturalism in the United States along with Stephen Crane, Frank Norris, and James T. Farrell, all of whom maintained that men and women had very little agency in their lives, and that their fate was determined largely by such ungovernable forces as biology, economics, and society.

Biographical Information

Dreiser's formative years were marked by poverty and personal struggle; he was one of thirteen children whose lives were strictly governed by their father, a staunch Catholic who steadfastly adhered to the conservative doctrines of his faith. Largely because of his early experiences, Dreiser came to view the world as an arena for struggle and survival. He left his family home in Terre Haute, Indiana, when he was sixteen, and eventually began a journalism career, moving to Chicago, St. Louis, and Pittsburgh. In New York, Dreiser's brother Paul, a successful Tin Pan Alley song writer, helped him achieve the editorship of *Ev'ry Month,* and Dreiser published his first story in that magazine. After his sixteen-year marriage to Sara Osborne White ended, Dreiser lived with his distant cousin, Helen Richardson, whom he eventually married in 1944. Following a long illness, Dreiser died in Hollywood on December 28, 1945, leaving his novels *The Bulwark* and *The Stoic* unfinished.

Major Works of Short Fiction

Perhaps more so than with his novels, Dreiser tended to revise his short fiction nearly obsessively, and those pieces which he collected for his two volumes of stories were almost all rewritten after their first appearance in magazines. Scholars have singled out several of Dreiser's stories as worthy of re-evaluation: "Free," "McEwan of

the Shining Slave Makers," "The Lost Phoebe," "Chains," and "Marriage—For One." "Nigger Jeff," however, became Dreiser's most widely-anthologized story, and, like many of his short works, was based upon actual events. In this case, the plot revolves around the criminal trial and eventual lynching of an alleged rapist. This early story, written in 1901, evidences a common theme in Dreiser's fiction: his concern with legal justice, and his contention that all men and women are driven by primal instincts.

Critical Reception

Of his initial attempts as a short story writer, Dreiser wrote: "After every paragraph I blushed for my folly—it seemed so asinine." Known for his long, ponderous novels, the short story form at first appeared alien to Dreiser, and editors rejected many of his stories even when he was at the height of his popularity. While some scholars have lauded Dreiser's willingness to explore grand themes in the short form, many more have maintained that his literary talents were uniquely suited to the long novel form and that his writing style was far too loquacious and circuitous for shorter narratives. Even so, commentators have praised Dreiser's stories for their departure from the conventions of highly-plotted fiction. Moreover, Dreiser's works significantly influenced the realistic narratives by such authors as Stephen Crane, Kate Chopin, Jack London, and Ernest Hemingway.

PRINCIPAL WORKS

Short Fiction

Free and Other Stories 1918
Twelve Men (sketches) 1919
Chains, Lesser Novels and Stories (short stories and novellas) 1927
A Gallery of Women (sketches) 1929
Fine Furniture 1930
The Best Short Stories of Theodore Dreiser 1947

Other Major Works

Sister Carrie (novel) 1900
Jennie Gerhardt (novel) 1911
The Financier (novel) 1912
The Titan (novel) 1914
The "Genius" (novel) 1915
Hey Rub-a-Dub-Dub (essays) 1920
A Book About Myself (autobiography) 1922
An American Tragedy (novel) 1925
The Stoic (novel) 1947

CRITICISM

H. L. Mencken (review date 1918)

SOURCE: "Dithyrambs Against Learning," in *Theodore Dreiser: The Critical Reception*, edited by Jack Salzman, David Lewis, 1972, pp. 313-14.

[*In the following review of* Free and Other Stories, *which was originally published in* Smart Set, *Vol. 57, in November, 1918, Mencken asserts that the most successful of the stories in the collection are constructed as chapters of novels, and that the works which are self-contained, more traditional short stories are failures, because Dreiser's writing style does not lend itself to this form.*]

The eleven pieces in **Free and Other Stories,** by Theodore Dreiser, are the by-products of a dozen years of industrious novel-writing, and are thus somewhat miscellaneous in character and quality. They range from experiments in the fantastic to ventures into realism, and, in tone, from the satirical to the rather laboriously moral. The best of them are **"The Lost Phoebe," "The Cruise**

of the *Idlewild,"* **"The Second Choice"** and **"Free."** The last-named is a detailed and searching analysis of a disparate marriage that has yet survived for forty years—an elaborate study of a life-long conflict between impulse and aspiration on the one hand and fear and conformity on the other. Here Dreiser is on his own ground, for the thing is not really a short story, in any ordinary sense, but a chapter from a novel, and he manœuvres in it in his customary deliberate and spacious manner. **"The Second Choice"** is of much the same character—a presentation of the processes of mind whereby a girl deserted by the man she loves brings herself to marriage with one she doesn't love at all. Those of the stories that are more properly short stories in form are less successful; for example, **"A Story of Stories," "Old Rogaun and His Theresa"** and **"Will You Walk Into My Parlor?"** The true short story, in fact, lies as far outside Dreiser's natural field as the triolet or the mazurka. He needs space and time to get his effects; he must wash in his gigantic backgrounds, and build up his characters slowly. The mountebankish smartness and neatness of the Maupassant-O. Henry tradition are quite beyond him. He is essentially a serious man, and a melancholy. The thing that interests him most is not a deftly articulated series of events but a gradual transformation of personality, and particularly a transformation that involves the decay of integrity. The characters that live most brilliantly in his books, like those that live most brilliantly in the books of Conrad, are characters in disintegration—corroded, beaten, destroyed by the inexplicable mystery of existence.

In the midst of many reminders of his high talents, Dreiser's worst failing as a practical writer appears with painful vividness in this book. I allude to his astonishing carelessness, his irritating slovenliness. He seems to have absolutely no respect for words as words—no sense of their inner music, no hand whatever for their adept combination. One phrase, it would seem, pleases him quite as much as another phrase. If it is flat, familiar, threadbare, so much the better. It is not, indeed, that he hasn't an ear. As a matter of fact, his hearing is very sharp, and in his dialogue, particularly when dealing with ignorant characters, he comes very close to the actual vulgate of his place and time. But the difficulty is that this vulgate bulges beyond the bounds of dialogue: it gets into what he has to say himself, unpurged by anything even remotely resembling taste. The result is often a series of locutions that affects so pedantic a man as I am like music on a fiddle out of tune, or a pretty girl with beer-keg ankles, or mayonnaise on ice-cream.

Sherwood Anderson (essay date 1918)

SOURCE: Introduction to *Free and Other Stories*, The Modern Library, 1918, pp. v-x.

[*In the following introduction to Dreiser's* Free and Other Stories, *Anderson offers a laudatory assessment of Dreiser's literary achievements as well as of his personal integrity and commitment to honesty in his writing.*]

Theodore Dreiser is a man who, with the passage of time, is bound to loom larger and larger in the awakening æsthetic consciousness of America. Among all of our prose writers he is one of the few men of whom it may be said that he has always been an honest workman, always impersonal, never a trickster. Read this book of Dreiser's, **Free and Other Stories,** and then compare it with a book of short stories, say by Bret Harte or O. Henry. The tradition of trick writing began early among us in America and has flowered here like some strange fungus growth. Every one knows there are no plot short stories in life itself and yet the tradition of American short story writing has been built almost entirely upon the plot idea. Human nature, the strange little whims, tragedies and comedies of life itself, have everywhere been sacrificed to the need of plot and one reads the ordinary plot story of the magazines with a kind of growing wonder. "Is there no comedy, no tragedy, no irony in life itself? If it is there why do not our writers find it out and set it forth? Why these everlasting falsehoods, this ever-present bag of tricks?"

One is sometimes convinced, in thinking of the matter, that, among most of our prose writers, there is left no feeling at all for life, and the prose writer, at least the tale teller, who has no feeling for life is no artist. There is the man or woman who walks beside me in the street, works beside me in the office, sits beside me in the theatre. What has happened in the lives of all these people? Why do our writers so determinedly spend all their time inventing people who never had any existence—puppets—these impossible cowboys, detectives, society adventurers? Are most of our successful short story writers too lazy to find out something about life itself, the occasional flashes of wonder and strangeness in life? It is apparent they are. Either they are too lazy or they are afraid of life, tremble before it.

But Theodore Dreiser is not afraid. He does not tremble. Often I have thought of him as the bravest man who has lived in America in our times. Perhaps I exaggerate. He is a man of my own craft and always he has been a heroic figure in my own eyes. He is honest. Never in any line he has ever written will you find him resorting to the trick to get himself out of a hard situation. The beauty and the ironic terror of life is like a wall before him but he faces the wall. He does not mutter cheap little lies in the darkness and to me there is something honorable and fine in the fact that in him there is no lack of courage in facing his materials, that he needs resort to tricks of style to cover.

Dreiser is a middle-westerner, large of frame, rather shy, brusque in manner and in his person singularly free from the common small vanities of the artist class. I often wonder if he knows how much he is loved and respected for what he has done by hundreds of unknown writers everywhere, fellows just trying to get ground under their feet. If there is a modern movement in American prose writing, a movement toward greater courage and fidelity to life in writing, then Theodore Dreiser is the pioneer and the hero of the movement. Of that I think there can be no question. I think it is true now that no American prose writer need hesitate before the task of putting his hands upon his materials. Puritanism, as a choking, smothering force, is dead or dying. We are rapidly approaching the old French standard wherein the only immorality for the artist is in bad art and I think that Theodore Dreiser, the man, has done more than any living American to bring this about. All honor to him. The whole air of America is sweeter to breathe because he had lived and worked here. He has laid a foundation upon which any sort of structure may be built. It will stand the strain. His work has been honestly and finely done. The man has laid so many old ghosts, pounded his way through such a wall of stupid prejudices and fears that today any man coming into the craft of writing comes with a new inheritance of freedom.

In the middle-western country in which Dreiser grew to manhood there could have been no awareness of the artist's obligations. How his own feet found the path they have followed so consistently I do not know. One gets so little from his own writings, from those little flashes by which every artist reveals himself in his work, that helps toward an understanding of his fine courage. Grey smoky hurried towns, Terre Haute, Indiana, Chicago, St. Louis, and the other places wherein he worked and lived, a life of hard work for small pay in dreary places. Twain had at least the rough and tumble heartiness of western life, the romance of the old Mississippi river days, and as for the eastern men who came before Dreiser, the Hawthornes, Emersons (and one is compelled to include the Howellses) they grew out of a European culture, were the children of a European culture, a fact that no doubt advantaged them while it has been of so little help to the Americans who are seeking masters to aid them in finding a life and a basis for a culture of their own.

Our earlier New England writers knew Europe and Europe knew them and accepted them as distant cousins anyway, but in Terre Haute, Indiana, in Dreiser's day there, when his own life was forming—if any of his fellow countrymen of that day and place ever crossed the sea I dare say they went to the Holy Land and came back with a bottle of Jordan Water. The only knowledge they had of the work and the aims of European artists was got from reading that most vulgar of all our Mark Twain's books, *The Innocents Abroad.* The idea of an artist, with all of the strange tangle of dreams and hopes in his brain being also a workman, owing something to his craft and to the materials of his craft, would have been as strange to the Terre Haute or the St. Louis of twenty-five years ago as a camel sitting and smoking a pipe on the court-house steps.

And it was out of such a grey blankness (from the artist's point of view, at least) that the man Dreiser came and he came alone, making his own path. What a figure he has made of himself, always pounding at the wall of stupidity before him, throwing aside always the cheap triumph to be got by trickery, always giving himself fully and honestly to the life about him, trying to understand it, never lying to himself or to others. One thinks of such a life and is appalled.

Theodore Dreiser's nature is the true artist's nature . . . He is the workman, full of self-respect, and—most strange and wonderful of all for an American writer—full of respect for his materials, for the lives of those who come close to him, for that world of people who have come into life under his pen.

—Sherwood Anderson

There is that story we have all heard of the young Dostoevsky, when he had written his first book, *Poor Folks*. He gave the manuscript to a writer friend who took it home and read it and in the middle of the night drove to the home of a publisher, filled with excitement. The two men sat up together and read the manuscript aloud and then, although it was four in the morning drove through the wintry streets to the young writer's lodgings. There was joy, excitement, happy fellow craftsmen, even tears of joy. A new and great writer had come into Russian life. What glad recognition. It was like a wedding or a birth. Men were happy together and you may imagine how the young craftsman felt.

That happened in Russia and in America Dreiser wrote his *Sister Carrie* and it was published and later buried out of sight in the cellar of a publishing house, for some ten years I believe, and might have been there yet but for the fighting impulses of our critics, our Hacketts, Menckens and Dells. Some woman, a relative perhaps of some member of the publishing firm, had decided the book was immoral and today one reads with wonder, seeking in vain for the immorality and only made glad by its sympathetic understanding of life.

Theodore Dreiser, whose book *Free and Other Stories* is now included in the famous Modern Library series, has lived out most of his life as a comparatively poor man. He might have grown rich had he but joined the ranks of the clever tricksters or had he devoted his energies to turning out romantic sentimentalities. What amusing and clever men we have had in his time, what funny fellows, what masters of all the tricks of writing.

Where are they? What have they given us?

And what has Dreiser given us? A fine growing and glowing tradition, has he not, a new sense of the value of our own lives, a new interest in the life about us, in offices, streets and houses.

Theodore Dreiser's nature is the true artist's nature, so little understood among us. He is no reformer. In his work, as in the man himself, there is something bold, with all the health of true boldness, and at the same time something very finely humble. He stands before life, looking at it, trying to understand it that he may catch its significance and its drama. He is not always crying, "Look at me! See what I am doing!" He is the workman, full of self-respect, and—most strange and wonderful of all for an American writer—full of respect for his materials, for the lives of those who come close to him, for that world of people who have come into life under his pen.

As for my trying to make in any detailed way an estimate of the value of the man's work, that is beyond me. The man has done, is doing, his job, he has fought his way through darkness into the light and in making a pathway for himself he has made a pathway for us all. Because he had lived and worked so honestly and finely America is a better place for all workmen. As for his work, there it stands—sturdy, strong, true and fine and most of all free from all the many cheap tricks of our craft.

And as for the man himself, there he also stands. One knows Dreiser will never stoop to tricky, second rate work; cannot, being Dreiser, ever so stoop. He is, however, not given to advertising himself. He stays in the background and lets the work speak for the man. It is the kind of fine, honest work that is coming to mean more and more every year to a growing army of sincere American craftsmen.

Henry Longan Stuart (review date 1927)

SOURCE: "As Usual, Mr. Dreiser Spares Us Nothing," in *Theodore Dreiser: The Critical Reception,* edited by Jack Salzman, David Lewis, 1972, pp. 504-06.

[*In the following review of* Chains, *which was originally published in* The New York Times Book Review *on May 15, 1927, Stuart dismisses the collection as tedious and carelessly written.*]

One of those clever Frenchmen whose perceptions every one is glad to remember, but whose names every one is resigned to forget, has told us that, in literature, all styles are permissable except one—the boring style ("sauf l'ennuyeux"). No critic with any self-respect, it may be stated at once, is likely to take shelter behind any such aphorism. In the first place, it strikes at the root of his own reason for being. In the second, it leaves the judgment of what is possible or impossible writing too nakedly at the mercy of an individual appetite for coarse fare. People exist, some of them very finicking over their own production, who make no shame in owning to an occasional relish for the corn beef and cabbage of letters. It is not by what readers will resign themselves to on occasion, but by what they would be content, at need, to live with, that a standard of taste is to be judged.

Even Mr. Dreiser's most ardent admirers, one presumes, would be prepared to admit some very serious disabilities in their idol. To begin with he has no perceptible sense of humor. The spark that can be struck out by the contact of two minds moving on different planes of intelligence and which is the most fertile source of the ludicrous, is out of his ken. He writes with no appreciable relish, being perhaps the most eminent drudge among our native practitioners. Syntax is continually presenting him with difficulties, as whom does it not? But instead of solving them as they arise with the contrivances out of which style is hammered, he has recourse to sorrowful expedients that Ring Lardner at his happiest could not better.

Yet it would be both unjust and absurd to deny that with all these faults goes an equipment that many a felicitous writer must envy. His patience is untiring. No one has written more convincingly of a man or woman thinking and brooding, because no one can more naïvely and convincingly cling to the trail of a thought, discarding nothing, selecting nothing, but following each sad convolution into its innermost recesses and blindest alleys. In this respect he has all the candor of George Moore, whom one suspects he follows in his own leaden-footed fashion, without the occasional frivolity of the Irish master. And only a prodigious memory, a faculty for impressibility that never lets the sharp edge of what has once been observed be dulled, can account for his uncanny power of so taking over the sensory apparatus of his characters that one cannot read his criminal trials without sharing in some degree the vertigo of the man in the dock, nor his murders without every silly, vulgar hue and cry registering upon exasperated nerves, nor of death in a tunnel accident without feeling the slime and ooze and drip underfoot and overhead.

One is hardly well started on *Chains,* a series of fifteen "lesser novels and stories" by the author of *An American Tragedy* without being plunged in a sea of slovenly writing. **"Sanctuary"** is the story of a sensitive tenement child born amid foul smells and fouler language, who falls into prostitution, is "reformed" in a home conducted by gentle nuns, leaves it to become the prey of a pimp and bully, and creeps back to it convinced that what has been assigned her as punishment is really the only condition under which life is possible. As we read it wonder grows that it can be humanly possible, talent apart, for any practicing writer to advance to where Mr. Dreiser had advanced, while retaining a construction and syntax that would bring down the blue pencil in any composition class in a high school. Worse even than the flaws in syntax are vulgarities of diction repeated over and over again so unbelievable in a writer of the slightest distinction that one asks one's self whether Mr. Dreiser may not perhaps be hovering on the brink of a new literary experiment and striving to convey banality of mind by banality of phrase.

> . . . One of those suave masters of the art of living by one's wits, with a fortune of looks, to whom womanhood is a thing to be taken by an upward curl of a pair of mustaches, the vain placement of ringed locks, spotless

and conspicuous linen, and clothes and shoes of a newness and lustre all but disturbing to a very work-a-day world.

Where all is so precious it is an ill task to pick out any one gem of language, but surely "all but disturbing" deserves mention.

"Chains," the story which gives the collection its title, affords Mr. Dreiser's talent its happiest chance. The musings of an elderly and doting husband, returning to a young wife whom he has married in an afterglow of passion and against all sense and reason, are retailed for us with unsparing deliberation. No one of the illusions at which men snatch under such circumstances to allay the intolerable bitterness of jealousy fails to find a place. The strange faculty of jealous and hapless lovers gradually to build up for themselves a picture of what they suspect, image upon image, and at the very moment that the phantom is taking on reality to recoil and fly back to the old drug of self-deception, has never been more convincingly identified. On this one essay Mr. Dreiser, it seems to us, might base a claim to be not only an investigator but to some extent a pioneer in a field that might be called sentimental pathology. . . .

It is not likely that *Chains* will unsettle the reputation of the author of *An American Tragedy* with those who hold a belief in his excellence an article of national faith, nor improve it with those who believe his reputation to be a victory won by sheer bulk and persistence and regard the place given him as not much short of literary imposture. Every writer has the faults of his qualities. What is most exasperating about Dreiser's faults is that they are not a part of his qualities at all. They are gratuitous ugliness and slovenliness, poor literary manners that have been suffered to persist (just why is his own secret) from prentice days, and to mar a thought which is, on the whole, fine, austere and pitiful. Their danger resides in the bad example they afford through the very eminence of the man who insists on practicing them. Nothing worse could happen to the American novel, already subject to danger enough at careless and disingenous hands, than a belief that genius can dispense with taking pains.

H. L. Mencken   (review date 1930)

SOURCE: "Ladies, Mainly Sad," in *American Mercury,* Vol. 19, February, 1930, pp. 254-55.

[*In the following review of* A Gallery of Women, *Mencken faults Dreiser's wordplay and narrative style, but praises his ability to capture the essence of his characters. Mencken asserts that* A Gallery of Women *is "not quite as interesting" as* Twelve Men *because "women themselves are considerably less interesting than men."*]

A Gallery Of Women is a companion to *Twelve Men,* published in 1919. There are fifteen sketches, each dealing with some woman who impinged upon the author at some time in the past; if the collection is not quite as interesting as its forerunner, then that is probably because women themselves are considerably less interesting than men. Not one of them here is to be mentioned in the same breath with Dreiser's brother Paul, the shining hero of *Twelve Men,* or with Muldoon the Iron Man, who plainly posed for the stupendous Culhane. Perhaps those who come closest to that high level are Regina C——, who succumbs to cynicism and morphine, and Bridget Mullanphy, almost a female Culhane. The rest are occasionally charming, but only too often their chief mark is a pathetic silliness. What ails most of them is love. They throw away everything for it, and when they can't get the genuine article they seem to be content with imitations. And if it is not love, real or bogus, that undoes them, then it is some vague dream that never takes rational form— of puerile self-expression, of gratuitous self-sacrifice, of something else as shadowy and vain.

Dreiser draws them with a surety of hand that seldom falters. He is at his best in just such character sketches, and he has a special skill at getting under the skins of women. In all of his books, indeed, the matter chiefly dealt with is female vagary, and to its elucidation he has brought an immense curiosity and no little shrewdness. As I have said, men are naturally more interesting, if only because they show a higher variability, but women remain more mysterious, and hence more romantic. Why should Regina C——throw herself away as she does? Why should Esther Norn waste her devotion upon men who have no need of her, and set no value upon her? Why, indeed, should old Bridget Mullanphy stagger through life in shackles to her loafer of a husband and her abominable daughter? The common answer is that there is something noble about that sort of immolation, but Dreiser is too wise to make it. He simply sets forth the facts as he has seen them, and leaves the philosophizing to less conscientious sages. He sees into all these women, but he would probably be the last to claim that he really sees through them. They remain figures in the eternal charade, touching always but inscrutable to the last.

Dreiser's writing continues to be painful to those who seek a voluptuous delight in words. It is not that he writes mere bald journalese, as certain professors have alleged, but that he wallows naïvely in a curiously banal kind of preciosity. He is, indeed, full of pretty phrases and arch turns of thought, but they seldom come off. The effect, at its worst, is that of a hangman's wink. He has been more or less impressed, apparently, by the familiar charge that his books are too long—that his chief sin is garrulousness. At all events, he shows a plain awareness of it: at one place he pauses in his narrative to say, "But hold! Do not despair. I am getting on." The point here, however, is not well taken. He is not actually garrulous; he always says something apposite, even though it may be obvious. What ails him is simply an incapacity to let anything go. Every detail of the human comedy interests him so immensely that he is bound to get it down. This makes, at times, for hard reading, but it has probably also made Dreiser. The thing that distinguishes him from oth-

er novelists is simply his astounding fidelity of observation. He sees every flicker of the eye, every tremor of the mouth, every change of color, every trivial gesture, every awkwardness, every wart. It is the warts, remember, that make the difference between a photograph and a human being.

Every detail of the human comedy interests him so immensely that he is bound to get it down. This makes, at times, for hard reading, but it has probably also made Dreiser.

—*H. L. Mencken*

Most other American novelists of his generation have been going downhill of late, but Dreiser seems to be holding on pretty well. The youngsters coming up offer him nothing properly describable as serious competition. They all write better than he does, but they surely do not surpass him in the really essential business of their craft. As year chases year, such books as *Jennie Gerhardt* and *The Titan* take on the proportions of public monuments; they become parts of the permanent record of their time; there is a sombre dignity in them that will not down. The defects that are in them are defects that are common to all latter-day American fiction. They may be imperfect, but they remain the best we have.

Howard Fast   (essay date 1947)

SOURCE: Introduction to *The Best Short Stories of Theodore Dreiser,* edited by Howard Fast, Ivan R. Dee, Inc., 1989, pp. 1-5.

[*In the following essay from a collection that was originally published in 1947, Fast asserts that "Dreiser has no peer in the American short story," and argues that the key to Dreiser's success as a short story writer lies in the author's tremendous capacity for compassion in creating his narratives and characters.*]

One evening recently, a group of us set about making, for our own amusement, a list of the finest short stories in the world. Actually, they were by no means the finest— there are no real absolutes in art—but rather a reflection of personal taste and preference; yet, it was curious how much unanimity of opinion there was—or perhaps not so curious, when you consider what universal and ageless appeal a rich and well-rounded tale has.

One of the rules of this game was that a person bringing forth a story the others did not know had to tell it, and it was revealing how many stories, bright in our memories, failed utterly in the telling. While at the time of reading, these tales had evoked a certain mood and emotion, the substance did not stand up with time. Flesh and blood were absent; the type of story called a "casual" by the editors of *The New Yorker* magazine, is just that: a casual, a glimpse of life that lacks form and meaning. For a story to last, it must hold up in telling; it must partake of something of the richness and complexity of life, the action, reaction and interaction of the human beings who make up our society. More than by the story-teller's art, mood and emotion must be determined by the characters themselves, by what they do to each other and by what society does to them.

Concerning this last, I know of no better example in American story telling than Theodore Dreiser. Certainly, we are a land not poor in story-tellers, and, with the possible exceptions of Russia and France, the short story has nowhere else developed to the height and richness it has here. But for all of that, Dreiser has no peer in the American short story. If his short stories are not yet sufficiently known his own genius is to blame; for his monumental novels overshadow them—perhaps rightly so, perhaps not. As fine as his novels are, they do not attain the artistic wholeness of his short tales; and I say this along with the opinion that no American has ever equalled Dreiser in the field of the novel.

Among the moderns, there is almost no one capable of writing tales like these. The best of today is pallid and non-human when compared with Dreiser's compassionate searchings; the average of today is another medium, outside the pale of comparison.

Now, this is much to be said of any writer, and wherein is the key? It is not enough simply to state that Theodore Dreiser was a unique genius of American letters; that he was, indeed, but, more than that, he was a man born at a certain time and in a certain place, and moulded by time and place, so that he could become the articulate and splendid spokesman for that time and place. The turn of the century, the coming of age of American industrialism, the withering away of the independent farmer, the onrush of imperialism, the first great world conflict, the rise of the labor movement, the movement for women's rights, the disillusionment and moral wreckage that followed World War I, the brief intellectual renaissance that spread like a flame across America, the mighty yet earthbound heroes of his native Midwest—all of these in turn and together reacted upon a man who was large enough to receive them and understand them, a man who was a curious mixture of pagan and Christian, provincial and urbane, a great mind and a great heart, turned by the endless search for the truth into a splendid artist.

The key to Dreiser the artist is compassion, the compassion of a Hugo or a Tolstoy. I can think of no tale of his wherein hatred or contempt or cynicism is the theme motif, either primarily or secondarily. His understanding was wide and extraordinary, and where he could not understand he presented the bare facts, as a historian might, leaving the explanation to time. How he pitied those—

and their number is legion—whom society had trod on, ground down, distorted and perverted!

In **"Phantom Gold,"** for example, and in **"Convention,"** he takes human wreckage and somehow extracts from it all the dignity and beauty of which life could be capable. It is not that he is charitable in his appraisal, but rather that he gives, as does Charlie Potter in **"A Doer of the Word,"** of himself.

A friend of mine met Dreiser in the street one day, and seeing that Dreiser's eyes were filled with tears, asked whether something terrible had happened, some personal tragedy? Dreiser shook his head; he had been unaware of the tears; he had simply been walking along, watching the life he saw, reflecting on it. He was that sort of man. In all my reading, I know of no better statement of the love of one brother for another than Dreiser gives in **"My Brother Paul."** It is an incredibly sweet and gentle tale, yet never does it partake of the saccharin of the cheap, of the vulgarly sentimental. A singular love of his fellow man, along with direct sincerity, gave Dreiser the prerogative to go where all others feared to tread.

Combined with this, there was a flair for fancy, an imagination that literally soared. How little those who call Dreiser "earthbound" understand of him! It was no earthbound mind that sent McEwen down among the shining slave makers, so that he might do battle with the ants, and thereby come to understand the wondrous variety and complexity of life, the goodness of it, and the eternal value of comradeship.

Through all his stories, the theme of brotherhood runs as a constant. He saw no lonely existence for man; man was a part of the whole, and if that was taken away, there was little reason for man to exist; over and over again this theme recurs, in **"The Lost Phœbe,"** in **"Marriage—For One,"** in **"My Brother Paul"**—and to a degree in all the other tales. Yet he did not write preachments; the very idea of writing a preachment would have repelled and disgusted him; his stories are filled with men and women and children, with the ebb and flow of life, the color and taste of it. There is no revengefulness in him, no hell fire. He sees life as it is; he would want it different; but until that time when life is different, the task is to know why it is what it is.

And what of his writing?

As I have said, I believe that Dreiser practiced his craft better in his short tales than in his novels. Most of these tales are superbly written; he had none of the staccato fears of the modern school. If the need dictated, he wrote leisurely, comfortably, in well-turned and thoughtful sentences. In evoking a mood, in painting a pastoral scene, in baring the soil and contour of his own beloved Midwest, he has no master; nor has he a master in describing men and women—not their surface features, but the essential and deep-rooted conflicts in their egos. He painted not with the quick, nervous brush of today, but in large planes and solid masses.

Occasionally, too, he told a story with such delightful zest, such light mastery, that the reading of it is a rare adventure. His two stories of Arabia, **"Khat"** and **"The Prince Who Was a Thief,"** are of that category.

I don't know whether or not Dreiser was ever in Arabia; in **"Khat,"** he evokes a very real image of Arabia, however, and I was affected nostalgically in terms of my own Arabian memories. Yet the point here is that Dreiser, in these two tales, writes not of Arabia, whatever of the setting he may use, but of the wonderland that some writers create, the land wherein a casual wayfarer may come upon the Sire de Maletroit's door, or again upon the four directions of O. Henry's roads of destiny. In both tales, his protagonist is essentially the same, the professional beggar and story-teller who is too old to be of any use. In **"Khat,"** the old entertainer finds every gate closed to him, the world walled up, barred, and shut off, a cynical, colorful world, yet somehow not so different from our own.

In **"The Prince Who Was a Thief,"** there is a story within a story, an ageless romance told by the old mendicant with priceless skill, humor, verve—but one which brings him only half the price of bed and board, leading him to remark:

> By Allah, what avails it if one travel the world over to gather many strange tales and keep them fresh and add to them as if by myrrh and incense and the color of the rose and the dawn, if by so doing one may not come by so much as a meal or a bed? Bismillah! Were it not for my withered arm no more would I trouble to tell a tale!

Rarely is Dreiser's tongue in his cheek, but when it is his wit is gentle and beguiling. And meaningfully enough, in all his stories, he laughs only at someone who practices his own trade: the making and the telling of tales—and, of course, the selling of them, since even story-tellers must eat.

I imagine that the moral there was very close to him. He was a giant in a world of Philistines, and the level upon which he practiced his art was beyond the sight, much less the comprehension, of the critics of his own day—yes, and of this day, too. Like Melville, he had little enough gain from his writing; but, again like Melville, he remains in a process of growth. His stature will increase with the years—and his wise, searching tales will be read and re-read.

James T. Farrell   (essay date 1956)

SOURCE: Introduction to *The Best Short Stories of Theodore Dreiser,* World Publishing Company, 1956, pp. 9-12.

[In the following essay, Farrell praises Dreiser for his achievement in the short story form and for his "healthy pessimism."]

Theodore Dreiser was a good storyteller and this collection contains some of his best stories. Due to the fact that his novels are so powerful and caused so much controversy, his stories have been neglected by critics. But among them are some of the finest and most moving short stories written by an American in this century.

Dreiser saw a struggle between instinct and convention, and this was a major motif in both his novels and his stories.

—James T. Farrell

In these tales there is variety of scene and range and depth of emotion. The emotions of mismated married people; the crazed feelings of a simple Midwestern old farmer who has lost his Phoebe, the partner of his life; the greed for gold of an illiterate farmer and his equally illiterate family; the despair of an Arabian beggar who approaches his end, poor, ragged, and despised; the feelings of Dreiser himself for Paul Dresser, his song-writing brother; the words and personality of a New Englander who lives by the Word of the Bible; the superstitious feelings of an Irish immigrant who works as a sand-hog under the Hudson River—here is range and variety. Dreiser paints and re-creates a broad human scene and, in each instance, he reveals his probing, searching mind, his ability to assimilate and make use of many details, and a compassion for humanity, its dreams and tragic sufferings, which is linked up with a sure insight into the nature of people.

During his entire literary life, Theodore Dreiser sought for a theory of existence. His mind seems constantly to have been filled with "whys." Why was life? Why was there this human spectacle of grandeur and misery, of the powerful and the weak, the gifted and the mediocre? Why did men drive and struggle for the prizes of this world—sometimes with little more than a jungle morality? And his fiction was a revelation of what he saw and how he felt about these questions. He found no answers, and most certainly he avoided cheap answers as he did the cheap tricks of commercial and plot short story writers. He was a deeply serious and brooding man, and in his writing he treated his characters with seriousness. They became intensely human in their dreaming, aspiring, and struggling as well as in their unhappiness, bewilderment, and moments of tragedy.

Dreiser saw a struggle between instinct and convention, and this was a major motif in both his novels and his stories. He saw how convention and conformity frustrates men and women. Here in this volume, there are several stories which deal with this subject matter. **"Free,"** the story of a gifted architect with definite artistic ability and of his dying wife dramatizes the frustrating role of convention in the life of a man with singular gifts. All of his life, Rufus Haymarket has been loyal and faithful to his wife in deed and action. She has controlled and dominated their social life. He has sacrificed his own impulses and many of his tastes in order that she will be happy. And when she lies dying, he dreams of freedom. He gazes out of the window of their apartment on Central Park West in New York City, thinks over their common life together and of his many frustrations. With her he has not found happiness or fulfillment. But she will die and then, for a brief span of years, he will be free. He is troubled by such thoughts. He does not want to have to think in this manner. But he has missed so much, a love that would be deeply satisfying, a life less bound by conventional tastes and values, and his need for freedom is rooted within him. And then his wife dies. Then he is free. But he realizes the meaning of his freedom. "Free! . . . Yes—free . . . to die!" This is a story of futility, but it is told with such sympathy and compassion that it acquires emotional force. Its simple tragedy becomes awesome, almost mysterious in the way that tragedy in real life is sometimes awesome and full of mystery. There are other stories of unhappy marriages, **"Convention," "Marriage for One,"** and **"The Shadow."** These, again, are marked by a sympathy and understanding on a parallel with these same qualities that endow **"Free"** with such depth of feeling.

Along with **"Free,"** there are two other Dreiser stories in this volume that have already become acknowledged classics, **"The Lost Phoebe"** and **"Nigger Jeff."** Henry and Phoebe lived together on their farm for forty-eight years. Their love had changed into a condition of habit and mutual need. Then, Phoebe died. Henry lived alone, and in time his mind became deranged. Day after day, he tramped the countryside searching for his lost wife. He could not accept the fact that she was dead—she had merely gone away. He would find her. The memory of Phoebe when young returns to him vividly. His search is not for the old woman who died, but for the young girl who had been his bride: his search is for dreams long since faded. He dies in deranged happiness, seeking the beautiful young Phoebe he knew years ago. In this story, it is as though life itself were speaking to us through the author. And it is a tale not only of the sad end which comes to us in old age; also, it is a tale of a lost dream, a dream that once endowed life with a beauty that was akin to poetry. Time, the enemy of all men, has eaten away beauty and rendered dreams obsolete. And yet the dreams remain. Dreiser's handling of this theme is truly poetic.

"Nigger Jeff" is a sympathetic and vivid account of a lynching. The main character is a reporter from a big city newspaper (undoubtedly a St. Louis journal) who is sent into a country district to cover a story where there might be a lynching. The description of the lynching, and the account of its impact on the young reporter, is presented so vividly and movingly that we feel that we are on the scene ourselves. And the "cruel sorrow" of the colored mother whose son has been hanged by a mob can only bring a choke in our throats. The young reporter says, in the last line of the story, "I'll get it all in!" Dreiser did get it all in and this means the human feelings, the terribleness of human sorrow that is caused by such a lynching.

> **Every story in this book bears the mark of genuineness and caliber. In every story, there is respect—deep respect for human beings.**
>
> *—James T. Farrell*

Totally different is **"My Brother Paul,"** Dreiser's account of his older brother. The feeling he had of brotherly affection is finely and sensitively revealed. Also, the story is quite genuinely nostalgic. It creates the Broadway atmosphere at the turn of the century so well that I found myself longing to have lived in that era and in Paul Dresser's world. Often, Dreiser has depicted emotions of greed, and he has described how human beings can destroy one another. Here, he writes of generosity of feeling, of manly affection, of kindness and helpfulness.

But every story in this book bears the mark of genuineness and caliber. In every story, there is respect—deep respect for human beings. Great art reveals the importance of human feelings and emotions. This is what Dreiser achieved. He cut beneath the surfaces of conventional attitude and sought, painstakingly, carefully, and sensitively to see human beings as they are and to render and re-create them truly but with sympathy.

We all must come to terms with time and death. Growth and maturity are evidenced in the way we make our terms with these. Dreiser's lifelong quest for a theory of existence was bound up with his own answers to time and death, his own willingness to face them in a spirit of moral bravery. This is one of the sources of his pessimism. It is a healthy pessimism, and when we encounter it we can gain a deepened sense of and respect for life. And these fifteen stories are but some of the works which Dreiser left us in his own quest and journey through the world. They tell us of men and women dreaming, struggling, and becoming caught in tragic bewilderment; they create a sense of wonder about those feelings which are the common clay, the common ground, the common elements of our humanity. Often they are somber, but their somberness breaks out in a revelation of that wonder and mystery of life which Dreiser felt so deeply.

Theodore Dreiser was a great writer of our century, and these tales of his fully bear the mark of his greatness, his sincerity, and his genius. Written years ago, they remain vital today. They belong to our literary tradition and they should long stand among the major short stories written in twentieth-century America.

Charles Shapiro (essay date 1962)

SOURCE: "The Short Stories: No Lies in the Darkness," in *Theodore Dreiser: Our Bitter Patriot*, Southern Illinois University Press, 1962, pp. 114-23.

[*In the following essay, Shapiro examines several of Dreiser's short stories, asserting that while some of them are effective literary achievements, Dreiser's style was more suited to the novel form.*]

Students usually get an unfortunate and inadequate introduction to Dreiser's fiction, for though his talent lies in the lengthier form of the novel, he too often is presented as a short-story writer. Assorted collegiate anthologies sandwich his contributions between the shorter efforts of Henry James and Ernest Hemingway, and it would, in truth, take a truly dedicated reader to be inspired to sample more of Dreiser's work.

Much of Dreiser's effects in his novels depends on a steady, cumulative emotive presentation, small, pointed, meaningful additions which add to the formal action of the fiction. The short stories too often read, not as complete architectonic units within themselves, but as compressed, dehydrated novels. In these cases the famed Dreiserian defects bulge out. Pompous, essentially show-off expressions are trotted out for no specific purpose. In **"Free,"** for example, at an inappropriately dramatic moment we have the following: "It was a mirage. An ignis fatuus." Superficial, sophomoric psychologizing is abundant. "They were amazing, these variations in his own thoughts, almost chemic, not volitional, decidedly peculiar for a man who was supposed to know his own mind—only did one, ever?" Worst of all are the stretches of clumsy, overwritten prose, much too typical of the magazine fiction of the time. A child dies, and "little Elwell had finally ceased to be as flesh and was eventually carried forth to the lorn, disagreeable graveyard near Woodlawn." As for the father: "How he had groaned internally, indulged in sad, despondent thoughts concerning the futility of all things human, when this had happened!" And these lapses, lamentable in Dreiser's realistic tales, become absurd in his feeble efforts at fantasy (such as in **"McEwen of the Shining Slave Makers," "Khat,"** and **"The Prince Who Was a Thief"**).

Though a few of the stories are of interest (especially two of the three we will look at—**"Nigger Jeff,"** and **"The Lost Phoebe"**) there is little to support James T. Farrell's contention [in the introduction to *The Best Short Stories of Theodore Dreiser,* 1961] that they rank among the best written in America during this century or Howard Fast's belief that Dreiser has "no peer in the American story" [*Best Short Stories*]. It is interesting that Sherwood Anderson, who wrote the introduction to a 1918 edition of Dreiser's stories, never becomes specific with his judgments. His tribute is a general one, in praise of a man "who with the passage of time is bound to loom larger and larger in the awakening consciousness of America," who is brave, and who was no trickster. Most important of all, he sees Dreiser the hero

of an American movement aiming "toward courage and fidelity to life in writing," and notes that "the beauty and the ironic terror of life is like a wall before him but he faces the wall" [Introduction to *Free and Other Stories*]. Certainly Dreiser is, as always, sincere and honest, boy scout virtues which are not, in themselves, enough for a writer. Only in a very few controlled, shorter works did he manage to approach the strength of his better novels.

Howard Fast was right in commenting that Dreiser "painted not with the quick, nervous brush of today, but in large planes and solid masses." This slabbish quality is probably best seen in **"Free,"** a flashback tale which depressingly plunges us into the study of a seemingly successful architect whose wife is dying and who realizes, to his horror, that life, for him, was but a series of pitiful compromises. "Like the Spartan boy, he had concealed the fox gnawing at his vitals. He had not complained." Now he complains, and with a vengeance.

A longer story than most of Dreiser's, **"Free"** has a structural unity, an action based on the wife as the symbol for the architect's essential lack of nerve.

> But even that was not the worst. No; that was not the worst, either. It had been the gradual realization coming along through the years that he had married an essentially small, narrow woman who could never really grasp his point of view—or, rather, the significance of his dreams or emotions—and yet with whom, nevertheless, because of this original promise or mistake, he was compelled to live. Grant her every quality of goodness, energy, industry, intent—as he did freely—still there was this; and it could never be adjusted, never. Essentially, as he had long since discovered, she was narrow, ultra-conventional, whereas he was an artist by nature, brooding and dreaming strange dreams and thinking of far-off things which she did not or could not understand or did not sympathize with, save in a general and very remote way. The nuances of his craft, the wonders and subtleties of forms and angles—had she ever realized how significant these were to him, let alone to herself? No, never. She had not the least true appreciation of them—never had had. Architecture? Art? What could they really mean to her, desire as she might to appreciate them? And he could not now go elsewhere to discover that sympathy. No. He had never really wanted to, since the public and she would object, and he thinking it half evil himself.

Rufus Haymaker (other names in the narrative include Elwell, Ethelberta, and Ottilie) is vague in his anger, never really focusing on specific targets and less intense than the middle-aged heroes of, say, Sherwood Anderson, Thomas Wolfe, or William Faulkner. It is a formless rage aimed, not at his wife, his spoiled children, or even American society, but at heavy, Dreiserian fate. "Cruel Nature, that cared so little for the dreams of man—the individual man or woman." If ever there was a tale nakedly revealing the naturalistic movement's effect on the American writer, this is it. "Almost like a bird in a cage, an animal peeping out from behind bars, he had viewed the world of free thought and freer action."

Perhaps the ruminations and outbursts of Haymaker have relevance to Dreiser's own peculiar marital troubles; in any case they do betray some of the blatantly adolescent attitudes about sex which marred *The "Genius,"* "Think of it! He to whom so many women had turned with questioning eyes!"

After a long chronicle of repressions and chances missed, Haymaker looks into a mirror. The theme of the story is recapitulated. "The figure he made here as against his dreams of a happier life, once he were free, now struck him forcibly. What a farce! What a failure!" And summarizing it all, the meaning of his failure, he wonders just what he had missed. With his wife's death he will be free; but it is too late. He is free only to die. What has happened here is that a novel is compressed into shorter form. We never understand even a small part of Haymaker, his life or his development; in consequence his problem, stated over and over, is essentially meaningless as it doesn't involve a defined character. Dreiser misuses the short-story form here, and **"Free"** unfortunately becomes a parody of his poorer novels.

While **"Free"** is an artistic failure, **"Nigger Jeff,"** which at first seems just one more protest tale of a lynch mob and its victim, develops into a well-structured, meaningful story centered on the reactions of a bewildered young city reporter who faces organized violence for the first time. The action lies in our discovery of how Elmer Davies reacts to the horrifying event and what he discovers about America and himself.

Davies is introduced as "a vain and rather self-sufficient youth who was inclined to be of that turn of mind which sees in life only a fixed and ordered process of rewards and punishments." At first he believes in the justice of the forthcoming lynching and is concerned only with the story he must write. Arriving at Pleasant Valley he notices the white houses "and the shimmering beauty of the small stream one had to cross in going from the depot." Throughout the narrative Dreiser, as Crane before him, will inject descriptions of the placid countryside, almost as direct counterpoint to the frightening events taking place. As the mob hurries on, "the night was so beautiful that it was all but poignant . . . and the east promised a golden moon." Again: "Slowly the silent company now took its way up the Sand River Pike whence it had come. The moon was still high, pouring down a wash of silvery light." At the lynching "the pale light over the glimmering water seemed human and alive." And as Davies sits, watching the dangling form, "the light of morning broke, a tender lavender and gray in the east. . . . Still the body hung there black and limp against the sky, and now a light breeze sprang up and stirred it visibly." Finally, after the body is cut down, it is placed in a small cabin and Davies watches the rapist's mother weeping over her son Jeff. "All the corners of the room were quite dark. Only its middle was brightened by splotches of silvery light."

Along with balancing the transcending wonders of nature with the human agonies, Dreiser also details Davies' petty dealings which are necessary to his reporting assignment.

He is forced to haggle and connive. These three elements: the powerful landscape, the tragedy played out in front of it, and the reporter's small movements have their effects on Davies. His attitude towards life is different. "The knowledge now that it was not always exact justice that was meted out to all and that it was not so much the business of the writer to indict as to interpret was borne in on him with distinctness by the cruel sorrow of the mother, whose blame, if any, was infinitesimal."

[In his *Theodore Dreiser: Apostle of Nature,* 1970] Robert Elias feels that in his stories Dreiser restates "his belief that nature must prevail . . . the subject of each story served to show that individuals were limited by circumstances or feelings for which only an inscrutable and indifferent nature appeared to be responsible. Men and women, created in one image, could not make themselves over in any other, and if there was a solution to their predicaments, no one knew it." Perhaps. But man can learn. **"Nigger Jeff"** ends with the reporter's crying out his new ambition, as a man and as a writer. "I'll get it all in!" In no sense does Jeff become a Joe Christmas, for Dreiser, unlike Faulkner, did not write a complicated allegory of modern man's betrayal. He simply told of one man's discovery; and this tale, carefully constructed, is a strong and moving work.

Dreiser's strangest story, **"The Lost Phoebe,"** had a curious publishing history. Though completed in 1912, four years elapsed before it was finally accepted for publication. Even Dreiser's champions were shocked by the tale. In a letter to Dreiser, H. L. Mencken noted: "Nathan is so full of the notion that this '**Lost Phoebe**' lies far off of the Dreiser that we want to play up that I begin to agree with him" [*Letters of Theodore Dreiser,* 1959].

"The Lost Phoebe" relates the pathetic wanderings of an aged, lonely farmer who is unable to accept the reality of his wife's death. For seven years he stumbles around the countryside, kept up by "spiritual endurance." Finally, one night, he believes he truly sees his late wife, younger, more beautiful. "He had been expecting and dreaming of this hour all these years, and now as he saw the feeble light dancing lightly before him he peered at it questioningly, one thin hand in his gray hair." Old Henry Reifsneider chases the phantom over a cliff. "No one of all the simple population knew how eagerly and joyously he had found his lost mate."

This depressing story does have its rough moments. The steady, dreary chronicle is too often interrupted with the familiar Dreiserian asides, especially forced commentaries on the simple nature of his protagonists. And at times Dreiser, the pseudo-scientist, interrupts: "That particular lull that comes in the systole-diastole of this earthly ball at two o'clock in the morning." But the story is successful, combining a lyric quality epitomized in the title and the descriptions of the landscape, with the hard facts of farm life.

> They had lived here, these two, ever since their marriage, forty-eight years before, and Henry had lived here before

that from his childhood up. His father and mother, well along in years when he was a boy, had invited him to bring his wife here when he had first fallen in love and decided to marry; and he had done so. . . . Of the seven children, all told, that had been born to them, three had died; one girl had gone to Kansas; one boy had gone to Sioux Falls, never even to be heard of after; another boy had gone to Washington; and the last girl lived five counties away in the same State, but was so burdened with cares of her own that she rarely gave them a thought. Time and a commonplace home life that had never been attractive had weaned them thoroughly, so that, wherever they were, they gave little thought as to how it might be with their father and mother.

The petty details of farm life are noted, and the minor quarrels of the elderly couple are presented in some detail. F. O. Matthiessen is quite correct in calling this Dreiser's most poetic story, yet it is the artful juxtaposition of the dreary, daily existence with the later mystic quality of the search that makes the tale so successful [*Theodore Dreiser,* 1973]. We feel we are face to face with pain and truth, just as we were with **"Nigger Jeff,"** and this is truth given us by an accomplished artist. As Sherwood Anderson noted [in his introduction to *Free and Other Stories*], "If there is a modern movement in American prose writing, a movement toward greater courage and fidelity in writing, then Theodore Dreiser is the pioneer and the hero of the movement."

My study, while facing some of the critical questions which inevitably arise in any discussion of Dreiser's work, deals, for the most part, with the themes present in his novels. There are, however, some qualities evident in all his books, qualities of spirit rather than tone, subject, or artistry. Man's courage in the face of tragedy, the bitterness, the sadness of America is usually at the heart of most of his fiction. Such an attitude towards life, of course, could slop over into a maudlin sentimentality if it were not for Dreiser's sense of wonder, his sympathy for and amazement at the way his characters operate, and survive. In this he is close to Faulkner. There is an energy and fierce sense of purpose common to both novelists.

I have concentrated on Dreiser's novels, but he was also the prolific author of poetry, plays, short stories, and nonfiction. The less said about his poetry and drama, the better. Dreiser simply wasn't a poet or dramatist. His shorter works of fiction contain many of the attributes of his novels, though very few come close to *An American Tragedy* or *The Bulwark.* Dreiser needed a large canvas. His nonfiction, especially his autobiographical works, have never been adequately dealt with, and I believe it is in this area that new studies of Dreiser will be most needed. The University of Pennsylvania recently issued an edition of Dreiser's collected letters, and this material will undoubtedly focus attention on biographical matters. *Dawn,* Dreiser's account of his early life, especially deserves revival and re-evaluation.

In the field of his novels most of the criticism has been in the nature of violent attacks or spirited defenses. As Dreiser comes to be an accepted part of American literary history, however, there will be more scholarly and critical, and less polemical, attention paid to his work. Indeed, such a trend is already established; we have begun to assess and appreciate the various aspects of Dreiser's achievement as a novelist.

And this achievement, I believe, marks him as one of our best novelists, a rare man who was able to make art out of his vision of life. Admittedly, Dreiser still bothers many readers. Perhaps Alfred Kazin is right when he observes that we often don't know how to react to Dreiser because a sense of contemplativeness, wonder, and reverence is at the center of Dreiser's world: "It is this lack of smartness, this puzzled lovingness for the substance of all our mystery, that explains why we do not know what to *do* with Dreiser today" [Introduction to *The Stature of Theodore Dreiser,* 1955].

But this refers to emotive reactions which are qualified by the time in which we live. If we often are unable to know how to handle our reactions to Dreiser, we can certainly appreciate these important chronicles of our American experience. For as Randolph Bourne said of Dreiser [in *Stature of Dreiser*], "his faults are those of his material and of uncouth bulk, and not of shoddiness. He expresses an America that is in process of forming. The interest he evokes is part of the eager interest we feel in that growth."

Donald Pizer   (essay date 1969)

SOURCE: "Theodore Dreiser's 'Nigger Jeff': The Development of an Aesthetic," in *American Literature,* Vol. XLI, No. 3, November, 1969, pp. 331-41.

[*In the following essay, Pizer examines three versions of "Nigger Jeff" to illustrate how Dreiser's artistic emphasis in his writing moved from sentimentality toward moral polemics.*]

Thanks to the work of Robert H. Elias and W. A. Swanberg, we are beginning to have an adequate sense of Dreiser's life. But many aspects of Dreiser the artist remain relatively obscure or unexplored—in particular his aesthetic beliefs and fictional techniques at various stages of his career. An excellent opportunity to study Dreiser's developing aesthetic lies in the existence of several versions of his short story **"Nigger Jeff."** The extant versions of this story reveal with considerable clarity and force Dreiser's changing beliefs concerning the nature of fiction.

Dreiser's first attempt to write a story about the lynching of a Missouri Negro is preserved in an unpublished University of Virginia manuscript called **"A Victim of Justice."** Although **"A Victim of Justice"** is clearly a work of the 1890's, it is difficult to date its composition precisely. The narrator of the story begins by noting that he has recently spent "a day in one of Missouri's pleasant villages." While visiting a Potter's Field, he recalls a rural Missouri lynching that he had witnessed "several years since." This opening situation is the product of a number of events of the mid-1890's. Dreiser was a reporter on the St. Louis *Republic* in the fall of 1893, and it was during this period that he observed the lynching on which the story is based. In addition, on July 23, 1894, Dreiser wrote for the Pittsburgh *Dispatch* an article entitled **"With the Nameless Dead"** in which he described an Allegheny County Potter's Field. A few weeks later he visited his fiancée, Sallie White, who lived in a small town near St. Louis. Dreiser's only attempts at fiction before the summer of 1899 occurred in the winter and spring of 1895 when he wrote several stories after leaving the New York *World* and before becoming editor of *Ev'ry Month*. In view of these facts, it is possible to speculate that Dreiser wrote **"A Victim of Justice"** in early 1895 and that he combined in the story his memory of the 1893 lynching, his July, 1894, article (from which he quoted several passages verbatim), and his visit to Missouri in the summer of 1894.

The next extant version of the story is a manuscript in the Los Angeles Public Library entitled **"The Lynching of Nigger Jeff."** This manuscript served, with minor changes, as the text for the November, 1901, publication of **"Nigger Jeff"** in *Ainslee's Magazine*. Encouraged by his friend Arthur Henry, Dreiser had begun writing stories in earnest during the summer of 1899, and he later recalled [in a letter to H.L. Mencken dated May 13, 1916] that **"Nigger Jeff"**—that is, the Los Angeles Public Library-*Ainslee's* version—dates from this period. The fourth version of the story is Dreiser's revision of the *Ainslee's* version for inclusion in his *Free and Other Stories*, published in August, 1918. Since the changes in this last version are primarily additions to the *Ainslee's* text, and since this added material is not in the Los Angeles Public Library manuscript, the revision can be attributed to the period shortly before the appearance of *Free*, when Dreiser collected and revised his stories for republication.

There are thus three major versions of **"Nigger Jeff."** Although none of these versions can be dated exactly, each can be associated with an important segment of Dreiser's career. The Virginia manuscript of the mid-1890's reflects the Dreiser depicted in *A Book About Myself*, the young journalist who was viewing much of the tragic complexity of life but understanding little of it. The *Ainslee's* publication represents the Dreiser of *Sister Carrie*. The story has been rewritten by an author with a characteristic vision of life and with a distinctive fictional style. The 1918 publication suggests a writer whose ideas have become increasingly self-conscious and polemical, the Dreiser of the essays of *Hey Rub-a-Dub-Dub* (1920) and the Dreiser who was eventually to devote a large portion of his later career to philosophical inquiries. The three versions, in short, span the principal periods of Dreiser's career, and their differences can tell us much about Dreiser's developing aesthetic.

Although the three versions of **"Nigger Jeff"** differ in a number of important ways, all have the same basic out-

line. A young man is sent in early spring to investigate reports of a possible lynching in a rural Missouri community. He discovers that a farmer's daughter has been attacked by a Negro and that the farmer and his son are in pursuit of the Negro in order to lynch him. The Negro is apprehended by a local peace officer, however, and is taken to another village for safekeeping until the arrival of reinforcements. A mob gathers, overpowers the peace officer, and returns with the Negro to its own community, where he is hanged from a bridge. The following day the investigator visits the home of the Negro and views his body.

Dreiser's earliest version of this story, **"A Victim of Justice,"** is told in the first person and uses a frame device. The story opens with the unidentified narrator visiting a Potter's Field near a small Missouri town. After much soulful lament over the "strange exigencies of life" that have brought the denizens of the graveyard to their mournful fate, the narrator is disturbed by the "grieving orisons" of an elderly woman. Before he can question her, she departs. But she has stimulated still further his moody reflections on the "wounding trials of life," and it is on this note that he introduces his recollections of the lynching. He begins by explaining that he was "commissioned to examine into the details" of the incident, but he does not identify himself as a reporter. Nor do we have a sense of his involvement in the action of the story. His narrative "voice" is principally an omniscient authorial voice, telling us about the lynching (often in summary form) but devoid of personal participation. The story concludes with the second half of the frame device. The narrator describes the Negro's lonely grave on a hillside, a burial place marked by a wooden cross. "Day after day it stands, bleak, gray, desolate, a fitting emblem of the barren life now forgotten, wasted as sparks are wasted on the night wind." Again the narrator broods over the vicissitudes of life, though his melancholy is lightened somewhat by the thought that nature is ever-beautiful even in this forsaken spot.

"A Victim of Justice" has three major themes. The first is suggested by the ironic title of the story and by several authorial comments. The Negro (named Jim in this version) is the victim of the "hasty illegalities" and "summary justice" of the mob. The second theme involves a more generalized sorrow over the fate of most men, a theme which arises out of the narrator's "mediations" in the graveyard. Dreiser's lugubrious exploitation of the conventional rhetoric of injustice and melancholy suggests that both themes have their source in the traditional literature of sentiment. Jim is a "poor varlet," and the graveyard scene echoes the diction and sentence structure of a Hawthorne or an Irving. Life is sad, Dreiser says, and he asks us to share this sentiment by imitating the prose of writers known for their ability to evoke melancholic moods. The third theme of the story is that of the powerful human emotions that arise out of the lynching itself—the quest for vengeance by the father, the resoluteness of the peace officer, the terror of the Negro. In a sense these emotions constitute a suppressed or unacknowledged theme, since they are extraneous to the explicit themes imposed upon the story by the narrator. The peace officer could have been a coward and Jim brave and unflinching, and the narrator would still have been able to enclose the story within his reflections on injustice and melancholy. These reflections may be apt responses to a lynching, but Dreiser's failure to integrate them into the account of the lynching itself implies that he has indeed imposed them on his response. His "true" response is "buried" within the narrative of the lynching, for Dreiser at this point was unable to articulate his response—that is, he was unable to recognize what moved him in the lynching. Thus, though he depicted the lynching as a moving event, he confused the nature of his response with those "deep" emotions readily available to him in traditional literary forms.

The *Ainslee's* version of **"Nigger Jeff"** omits the frame sections. The story, now told in the third person, focuses on the experiences of a young reporter, Eugene Davies, who has been sent to look into a possible lynching. It is a beautiful spring day and the insouciant, self-confident Davies undertakes his assignment with relish. Arriving in Pleasant Valley, he is drawn into the events of the lynching as he pursues his story. Davies is at first a passive observer of these events. But when the blubbering, terrified Jeff is seized by the mob, the reporter uncontrollably "clapped his hands over his mouth and worked his fingers convulsively." "Sick at heart," he accompanies the mob back to Pleasant Valley. The hanging itself stuns him into a deep torpor. By the close of the story, when he encounters Jeff's weeping mother, he has viewed a wide range of character and emotion—the competent, strong-willed sheriff, the cowardly mob, the father intent on vengeance, and above all the terrified Jeff and his heartbroken mother.

In **"A Victim of Justice"** Dreiser mentioned the grieving mother early in the narrative but not afterward. In **"Nigger Jeff"** he reserved introducing her grief until the final, climactic scene of the story, a scene which is present only in brief summary form in the earlier version. As Davies views Jeff's body, he hears a noise in the room.

> Greatly disturbed, he hesitated, and then as his eyes strained he caught the shadow of something. It was in the extreme corner, huddled up, dark, almost indistinguishable crouching against the cold walls.

> "Oh, oh, oh," was repeated, even more plaintively than before.

> Davies began to understand. He approached lightly. Then he made out an old black mammy, doubled up and weeping. She was in the very niche of the corner, her head sunk on her knees, her tears falling, her body rocking to and fro.

On leaving the cabin, Davies "swelled with feeling and pathos. . . . The night, the tragedy, the grief, he saw it all."

"'I'll get that in,' he exclaimed, feelingly, 'I'll get it all in.'"

Dreiser has thus shifted the axis of the story. Unlike **"A Victim of Justice,"** in which the narrator presents us with a response to a lynching, **"Nigger Jeff"** dramatizes a growth in emotional responsiveness by the principal viewer of the action. The narrative is now primarily an initiation story—the coming into knowledge of the tragic realities of life by the viewer. And since the viewer is a reporter who will attempt to "get it all in," the story is also the dramatization of the birth of an aesthetic.

Despite his reputation as stylistically inept, Dreiser was capable of a provocative and moving verbal symbolism.

—Donald Pizer

Briefly, the conception of the theme and form of art symbolized by the "it" in the last sentence of **"Nigger Jeff"** contains three major elements, each rendered in dramatic form within the story. These are: a belief that two emotions in particular pervade all life; a belief that these emotions are often found in moral and social contexts which lend them a special poignancy; and a belief that these emotions adopt a certain pattern in life and therefore in art. Let me discuss each of these beliefs more fully, beginning with the central emotions of life as Dreiser depicts them in this story.

One such emotion is sexual desire. It is the first flush of spring, and Jeff, a poor, ignorant Negro, attacks a white girl—a girl who knows him and whom he meets in a lane. "Before God, boss, I didn't mean to. . . . I didn't go to do it,'" he cries to the mob. Although sexual desire may not lead to the destruction of such figures as Frank Cowperwood, it is nevertheless a dominant, uncontrollable force in almost all of Dreiser's principal male characters. Hurstwood, Lester Kane, Eugene Witla, and Clyde Griffiths are at its mercy. In addition, the "it" of the final sentence includes the unthinking love and loyalty which exists within a family and particularly between a mother and a child. When Davies arrives at Jeff's home after the lynching, he asks the Negro's sister why Jeff had returned to his cabin, where he had been captured by the waiting sheriff.

> "To see us," said the girl.

> "Well, did he want anything? He didn't come just to see you, did he?"

> "Yes, suh," said the girl, "he come to say good-by."

> Her voice wavered.

> "Didn't he know he might get caught?" asked Davies.

"Yes, suh, I think he did."

She stood very quietly, holding the poor battered lamp up, and looking down.

"Well, what did he have to say?" asked Davies.

"He said he wanted tuh see motha'. He was a-goin' away."

The son come back to say good-by to the mother, the mother mourning over the son's body—here is emotion which in its over-powering intensity parallels the sex drive itself. It is the force which binds the Gerhardt family together, which is the final refuge of Clyde Griffiths, and which creates the tragic tension of Solon Barnes's loss of his children. In **"Nigger Jeff"** this force appears not only in the relationship between Jeff and his mother but also in the figure of the assaulted girl's father. Although Dreiser depicts the mob as cowardly and sensation-seeking, he respects the motives of the father. Both victim and revenger and caught up in the same inexplicable emotional oneness which is a family.

"Nigger Jeff" thus contains two of the most persistent themes in all of Dreiser's work—the power of desire and the power of family love and loyalty. Davies's awakening to their reality can be interpreted as Dreiser's declaration of belief in the dominance of these emotions in human affairs. Indeed, in his later autobiographies Dreiser depicted these emotions as two of the principal inner realities of his own youth. His ability to identify himself with these emotions as early as **"Nigger Jeff"** is revealed by a sentence omitted in *Ainslee's* but present in the Los Angeles Public Library manuscript of **"The Lynching of Nigger Jeff."** Immediately following "The night, the tragedy, the grief, he saw it all," there appears in **"The Lynching of Nigger Jeff"**: "It was spring no less than sorrow that ran whispering in his blood." The sensuality of youth, the family love taking its shape in sorrow—these appear in Dreiser's work as complementary autobiographical themes until they coalesce most fully and powerfully both in *Dawn* and in *An American Tragedy.*

The second major aspect of Dreiser's aesthetic contained in the final "it" involves the moral and social context in which these emotions are found. Like most of Dreiser's characters, the principal figures in **"Nigger Jeff"** have little of the heroic about them. Even the sheriff loses his potential for such a role once he is easily tricked by the mob and complacently accepts its victory. Jeff himself is described at the moment of his capture by the mob as a "groveling, foaming brute." But the major figures in **"Nigger Jeff,"** despite their often grotesque inadequacies, feel and suffer, and the young reporter comes to realize the "tragedy" of their fate. To Dreiser, tragedy arises out of the realities that nature is beautiful, that man can desire, and that a mother or father can mourn. These realities do not lend "nobility" to Dreiser's figures; like Jeff, they are often weak and contemptible despite their fate. But their capacity to feel combined

with their incapacity to act wisely or well is to Dreiser the very stuff of man's tragic nature. The realization which the young reporter must "get in" thus involves not only the truths of lust and of mother love but also the truth that the experience of these emotions gives meaning and poignancy to every class and condition of man.

The third aspect of the aesthetic symbolized by the final "it" concerns the pattern assumed by the two principal emotions of the story. Most of Dreiser's novels involve a seeker or quester—sometimes driven by desire, sometimes by other motives—who finds at the end of the novel that he has returned to where he started: Carrie still seeking beauty and happiness; Jennie once again alone despite her immense capacity to love; Cowperwood's millions gone; Clyde still walled in; Solon returning to the simplicity of faith. It is possible to visualize Dreiser's novels as a graphic irony—the characters believe they are pushing forward but they are really moving in a circle. Dreiser occasionally makes this structural principle explicit by a consciously circular symbol, such as the rocking chair in *Sister Carrie* and the street scene in *An American Tragedy*. **"Nigger Jeff"** contains a rough approximation of this pattern. The passions which have driven the narrative forward in its sequence of crime and punishment are dissipated, and Jeff returns to where he has started both physically and emotionally. That is, the bleak room in which he rests and his mother keening over his body represent the permanent realities of his life and his death. He, too, has come full circle.

Despite his reputation as stylistically inept, Dreiser was capable of a provocative and moving verbal symbolism. This quality appears in his use of "beauty" in connection with Carrie at the close of *Sister Carrie* and in his use of "life" in the next to last paragraph of *The Bulwark* ("'I am crying for *life*'"). These otherwise banal abstractions represent the complexity and depth of experience depicted in the novels concerned, and they are therefore powerfully evocative. The word "it" at the close of **"Nigger Jeff"** has some of the same quality. The word symbolizes a deeply felt aesthetic which Dreiser never explained as well elsewhere, just as he never discussed "beauty" and "life" in his philosophical writings as well as he dramatized their meaning for him in his novels.

The *Free* version of **"Nigger Jeff"** omits almost nothing from the *Ainslee's* text. Aside from stylistic revisions, the changes in the *Free* version consist of additions, many of which merely flesh out particular scenes. Some of the additions, however, extend the themes of the story in two significant ways.

One such extension is revealed in Dreiser's addition to the first sentence of the story (here and elsewhere the added material appears in brackets):

> The city editor was waiting for one of his best reporters, Elmer Davies [by name, a vain and rather self-sufficient youth who was inclined to be of that turn of mind which sees in life only a fixed and ordered process of rewards and punishments. If one did not do exactly right, one did

not get along well. On the contrary, if one did, one did. Only the so-called evil were really punished, only the good truly rewarded-or Mr. Davies had heard this so long in his youth that he had come nearly to believe it.]

By the next to last paragraph of the story, Davies has come to realize that "[it was not always exact justice that was meted out to all and that it was not so much the business of the writer to indict as to interpret]." In these and similar additions Dreiser has extended the nature of Davies's initiation. In the *Ainslee's* version, Davies's growth is above all that of his awakening to the tragic nature of human experience. The *Free* version associates this awakening with his conscious awareness that moral absolutes are based on naïveté or inexperience and are inapplicable to the complex realities of life. In a sense even **"A Victim of Justice"** contains an aspect of this theme, since Dreiser in that version noted the injustice of the "summary justice" of mob rule. But in the *Free* **"Nigger Jeff"** this theme is both more overt and more central. Its presence in this enlarged and emphatic form suggests Dreiser's increasing tendency throughout the later stages of his career (beginning about 1911) to associate the function of art with the explicit inversion of conventional moral and social beliefs. It is during this period that Dreiser the polemicist (as revealed in *Hey Rub-a-Dub-Dub*) and Dreiser the novelist combine to produce *An American Tragedy,* in which the putative reader is placed in the position or Davies. Like the naïve beliefs of Davies, the reader's faith in the American dream of success and in the workings of justice is destroyed by encountering the reality of a tragedy.

A second major extension of theme in the *Free* **"Nigger Jeff"** occurs in the scenes following the capture of Jeff by the mob. As Davies accompanies the mob on its way to hang Jeff, he reflects that

> [both father and son now seemed brutal, the injury to the daughter and sister not so vital as all this. Still, also, custom seemed to require death in this way for this. It was like some axiomatic, mathematic law-hard, but custom. The silent company, an articulated, mechanical and therefore terrible thing, moved on. It also was axiomatic, mathematic.]

After the hanging, Davies sits near the bridge and muses: "[Life seemed so sad, so strange, so mysterious, so inexplicable]." These additions reflect two of the principal areas of Dreiser's philosophical speculation during the last half of his career. On the one hand, he believed that every phase of life is governed by law. During the period from approximately 1910 to the late 1920's he often, as in the *Free* **"Nigger Jeff,"** associated this law with the harsh extermination of the weak. Dreiser the mechanist called this law an "equation inevitable" in *Hey Rub-a-Dub-Dub*. But by the end of his career Dreiser the quasi-pantheist had come to call it "design" in *The Bulwark* and to associate it primarily with beauty and with cosmic benevolence. His particular conception of law at various stages of his later career, however, is perhaps less important than his enduring search for a principle of mean-

ing which would encompass the cruelty and the beauty, the destructiveness and the continuity, which he found in life. On the other hand, Dreiser affirmed throughout his later career a belief in the essential mystery at the heart of life. Both attitudes-the search for meaning and the belief in mystery-are present in *Hey Rub-a-Dub-Dub,* in which the often doctrinaire mechanistic philosophizing is counterbalanced by the subtitle of the work: "A Book of the Mystery and Terror and Wonder of Life." And both are present in *The Bulwark,* in which Solon's discovery of the principle of design is inseparable from his discovery of the mystery of life. In his *Free* version of **"Nigger Jeff"** Dreiser has thus expanded his aesthetic to include not only an explicit ironic reversal of moral certainties but also a dramatization of the vast philosophical paradoxes underlying all life. Davies's discovery of what art must do—"[to interpret]"—now has a conscious philosophical element which was to play an ever increasing role in Dreiser's career.

The various versions of **"Nigger Jeff"** which I have been discussing incorporate Dreiser's principal beliefs about the nature of art. From the imposed sentimentality of **"A Victim of Justice"** to the moral polemicism and incipient philosophizing of the *Free* **"Nigger Jeff,"** the three versions reflect much that is central in Dreiser's thought and in his practice as a writer. No doubt there is room for qualification of some of the generalizations about Dreiser's developing aesthetic which I have drawn from this study of the three versions of **"Nigger Jeff."** Nevertheless, there is much to be said for the attempt to deduce a writer's beliefs about art directly from a creative work dealing with the nature of art rather than from his literary criticism. For Dreiser, there is a special need for this kind of attempt, since most of his overt comments about art are either vague or overpolemical. Moreover, we are coming to realize that Dreiser is not only a writer of stature (as Alfred Kazin has maintained [in *The Stature of Theodore Dreiser,* 1955]) but also of finesse (as Ellen Moers believes [according to "The Finesse of Dreiser," *American Scholar* XXXIII, Winter, 1963-1964]). He is a writer, in other words, whose stories and novels in their various revisions can often be explored for the complex intertwining of permanence and change characteristic of the creative work of a major literary figure.

Arthur Voss (essay date 1973)

SOURCE: "The Short Story in Transition: Stephen Crane, Jack London, Edith Wharton, Willa Cather, and Theodore Dreiser," in *The American Short Story: A Critical Survey,* University of Oklahoma Press, 1973, pp. 157-82.

[In the following excerpt, Voss surveys several of Dreiser's short stories, and maintains that while the short story form did not lend itself to Dreiser's particular writing style, "few other short-story writers have written more powerfully and movingly on the theme of entrapment."]

Born in Terre Haute, Indiana, of German stock, Theodore Dreiser (1871-1946) was a journalist in his late twenties, who had worked in St. Louis, Chicago, and Pittsburgh when he began to write fiction. He was unfavorably regarded for a number of years by many readers and critics because of the uncompromising naturalism and alleged immorality of *Sister Carrie* (1900), suppressed after publication by the publisher and not reissued until 1907, *Jennie Gerhardt* (1911), and later novels. It was not until the 1920's, by which time he had published his best-known novel, *An American Tragedy* (1925), that he attained a substantial measure or popularity and prominence.

Dreiser's earliest short stories, written at about the same time as *Sister Carrie,* are notable for their variety but are a good deal less impressive than that novel. **"When the Old Century Was New"** is a somewhat stilted historical narrative laid in New York City at the beginning of the nineteenth century. **"McEwen of Shining Slave Makers"** is an allegory with a deterministic theme, in which a man falls asleep on a park bench and dreams he is an ant fighting with his tribe against another tribe of ants. The conflict, characterization, and setting of the much more realistic **"Old Rogaum and His Theresa"** are handled convincingly, although Dreiser perhaps overemphasizes his point that if the strict old German father had not relented after locking his rebellious teen-age daughter out of the house one evening when she does not come in as soon as he calls, she would have been compromised by the young tough she has been meeting on the street and would have suffered the fate of other young girls for whom such a situation had been the first step in becoming a prostitute. **"Nigger Jeff,"** based on a lynching which occurred during Dreiser's early newspaper days in St. Louis, has less impact than later lynching stories by Erskine Caldwell and William Faulkner but achieves considerable force by focusing on the reactions of a somewhat naïve young reporter whose belief that justice prevails is destroyed by the event.

Free and Other Stories (1918) contains these early stories and seven others. Two or three of the latter are little more than journalistic pieces. Dreiser employed the manner of O. Henry in **"A Story of Stories,"** an entertaining account of the rivalry between two newspaper reporters. Very different is the poetic tone and poignant situation of **"The Lost Phoebe,"** in which an old man suffers from a hallucination that his dead wife is still alive. Also moving without being sentimentalized is the plight, in **"The Second Choice,"** of the working girl who is thrown over by the man she loves. There is likewise little hope for happiness for the young husband in **"Married,"** a story which appears to reflect Dreiser's own unhappy first marriage. A musician married to a farm girl, whose background prevents her from sharing his aesthetic interests, the husband increasingly feels their incompatibility, but because of her devotion and her obvious fear that she will lose his love, he cannot bring himself to leave her. In **"Free,"** also, a sense of duty has long tied a much older man to a woman whose attitudes and values he could never agree with, even though he

deferred to them. Should he not, he reflects, have ignored convention and left her? Yet his wife had tried to do her best according to her lights, and he reproaches himself for hoping that she will die now that she is seriously ill. She does die, and he is free, but, ironically, free only to die also. "Now the innate cruelty of life, its blazing ironic indifference to him and so many grew rapidly upon him."

The retrospective method of narration in "Free" has certain drawbacks. When a character is made to review past actions in his mind, the story is likely to seem tedious and lacking in dramatic quality, and if the actions are a cause for regret there is a danger that the character will be made to seem too sorry for himself. Yet Dreiser manages to a considerable extent to make a virtue of the method. The very weight of the slow-paced, sometimes repetitious, relentless accumulation of details bearing on the situation of Rufus Haymaker gives power to his story.

Dreiser was so preoccupied with the theme of unhappiness in marriage that he also treated it in seven of the fifteen stories collected in *Chains, Lesser Novels and Stories* (1927). Like **"Free,"** three of them—**"Chains," "The Old Neighborhood,"** and **"Fulfilment"**—are retrospective in their telling, repeat its tone of irony and futility, and emphasize that life traps and deludes us. More like some of Sherwood Anderson's stories are **"Convention"** and **"Marriage—For One."** In the first story, of which Dreiser said, "I set it down as something in the nature of an American social document," a man is unfaithful to his dull, drab wife. When the wife sends herself a box of poisoned candy, attempting to make it appear that it came from the other woman, the affair is exposed and brought out in the newspapers. What concerns the narrator is the effect this incident has on the husband, who is so bound by convention that he can easily abandon the mistress whom he had loved to go back to his wife. He is a psychological mystery to the narrator, who is left feeling "cold and sad." In the second story the narrator is profoundly moved by "the despair, the passion, the rage, the hopelessness, the love," of a man whose wife has left him. The other stories in *Chains* either are journalistic pieces written to entertain or treat themes which Dreiser had developed to better advantage in his novels. **"The Victor"** is a miniature companion piece to *The Financier* (1912) and *The Titan* (1914), Dreiser's two lengthy novels of unscrupulous financial dealings, being the history of a shrewd and ruthless financier who becomes a multimillionaire oil king. **"Typhoon"** and **"Sanctuary,"** stories of girls betrayed by faithless lovers, are reminiscent in some respects of *Jennie Gerhardt* and *An American Tragedy.*

Twelve Men (1919) and *A Gallery of Women* (1929) are other collections of Dreiser's shorter pieces, but they are not properly short stories. The former is made up of sketches of actual persons who were Dreiser's friends and acquaintances, while the latter contains descriptive portraits—partly factual, partly fictional—of the personalities of various kinds of women. Dreiser once said, in explaining why he did not write more short stories, "I need a large canvas." His novels and stories seem to confirm that this statement was usually true, though certainly not in every instance. The comment of one critic that Dreiser was never at home in the short story does not give us a fair picture of his shorter work. It has obvious limitations—an almost relentless and sometimes tiresome imposing of his deterministic philosophy on the reader, a lack of psychological penetration into his characters, and stylistic lapses—yet Dreiser succeeds nevertheless in leaving an impression on us, and few other short-story writers have written more powerfully and movingly on the theme of entrapment.

Don B. Graham   (essay date 1977)

SOURCE: "Dreiser's Ant Tragedy: The Revision of 'The Shining Slave Makers'," in *Studies in Short Fiction,* Vol. 14, No. 1, Winter, 1977, pp. 41-8.

[*In the following essay, Graham compares two versions of "The Shining Slave Makers" and notes how Dreiser stressed the struggle for life and "humanistic" values in the latter version.*]

In 1900 Theodore Dreiser wrote a long letter to Robert Underwood Johnson, the associate editor of the *Century,* protesting his decision not to publish Dreiser's "ant tragedy," a short story titled **"The Shining Slave Makers"** [*Letters of Theodore Dreiser,* 1959]. The letter championed imagination and emotional power over rigid adherence to scientific fact. Far from overturning Johnson's decision, Dreiser was obliged, upon receiving a second letter from Johnson, to apologize for his charge that no literary editor had read the story [*Letters*]. Sometime later, *Ainslee's Magazine* accepted the work and published it in June, 1901.

The "allegory" that Johnson disliked and refused to publish begins with a frame opening in which a man named Robert McEwen, sitting beneath a tree on a hot summer day, discovers an ant on his trousers, looks for others, and kills one on the walk. Fixing his attention then on an ant moving erratically to and fro, McEwen feels himself suddenly amidst a new world where, as he gradually realizes, he is an ant himself. A series of encounters with other ants ensues. One ant alludes to the coming war with the Sanguineae and predicts a famine. A second, Ermi, refuses to share some bread with the now ravenously hungry McEwen. A third, also hunting for food, angrily refuses to offer McEwen aid. Then McEwen comes upon the third ant again, who, dying from a wound inflicted by a falling boulder, offers his bread to him. After eating and resting, McEwen watches as four enemy warriors attack Ermi. He rushes into the fray on Ermi's behalf, and together they defeat the enemy. The comrades-in-arms return to Ermi's home where McEwen observes the ants' daily life and is caught up in their plans for war. He participates in a raid on a weaker tribe, the Fuscae, and exults in the fighting. In the next fight, an all-out battle with the Sanguineae, McEwen does not fare well however-

er. Wounded to the point of death, he closes his eyes to die, only to awaken, in the frame conclusion, back in the place where the revery began and restored to his former human status.

When Dreiser put together his first collection of short fiction, *Free and Other Stories* (1918), he included the 1901 story under the title **"McEwen of the Shining Slave Makers."** He made other changes as well. The *Free* text contains approximately 169 instances of revision, including changes in punctuation, diction, syntax, and the addition of passages, some of which are over 150 words in length. Although many of these revisions are primarily stylistic modifications with little substantive effect, the added passages are of a different order and have important consequences for the conceptual movement of the story. The new material, which contains Dreiser's discursive commentaries and amplifications and which perforce affects both characterization and theme, makes comparison of the two versions a necessary act of criticism.

Comparison also helps resolve an interpretational conflict regarding the meaning of **"The Shining Slave Makers."** The question of whether the story presents a positive or negative vision of experience has led critics to opposite conclusions. According to Robert Elias, for example, **"The Shining Slave Makers"** expresses Dreiser's social Darwinism: "an allegory of life, in which the struggle to survive is carried on blindly, uncritically, and in which strength rather than notions of good and evil determines one's fate" [*Theodore Dreiser, Apostle of Nature,* 1970]. Ellen Moers, however, reads the story quite differently: "**'The Shining Slave Makers'** is a celebration of the capacity for feeling in humble creatures—their sensitivity being perhaps more highly developed than that of the man who coldly observes and carelessly destroys them [*Two Dreisers,* 1969]. Elias' view, as Moers demonstrates and as he confirmed to her, is but half of a satisfactory interpretation. From the *Ainslee* text one can array a quantity of evidence supporting a social-Darwinist reading and at least an equal quantity supporting an anti-social-Darwinist reading—that is, in the first view the ants are warriors; in the second, they are brothers. Moers' interpretation is a necessary corrective of Elias', but it seems clear that what she says of **"The Shining Slave Makers"** exaggerates the story's commitment to the positive values discovered among the ants. In fact, when she seeks to prove that McEwen "awakens at the end . . . to marvel at the oneness of life," she quotes from the *Free* text which, as she points out in a note, "underline[s] the mood of melancholy wonder with which Dreiser always surveyed parallels between man and the simplest organisms." Precisely, except that Dreiser in 1918 was more inclined to write of melancholy wonder than he was in 1899. Conflating the two texts blurs their essential differences in meaning: in the second Dreiser kept and even intensified the degree of struggle necessary for survival (Elias) and clarified, emphasized, and made unmistakable the degree of "humanistic" values observable among the ants (Moers). The added material clearly reveals this pattern emerging.

The first addition to the *Ainslee* text occurs in the seventh paragraph. Up to this point in both versions we know that Robert McEwen, lolling on a summer day, has observed some ants; has casually killed one; and has suddenly found himself in an "unknown world, strange in every detail." The paragraph in the *Ainslee* text concludes with "Only the hot sun streaming down and a sky of faultness blue betokened a familiar world," whereupon the story moves directly to McEwen's next act: "Then McEwen set out and presently came to a broad plain, so wide that his eye could scarce command more than what seemed an immediate portion of it." But the *Free* text contains new commentary between the "familiar world" and the movement to the plain. Dreiser has added:

> In regard to himself McEwen felt peculiar and yet familiar. What was it that made these surroundings and himself seem odd and yet usual? He could not tell. His three pairs of limbs and his vigorous mandibles seemed natural enough. The fact that he sensed rather than saw things was natural and yet odd. Forthwith moved by a sense of duty, necessity, and a kind of tribal obligation which he more felt than understood, he set out in search of food and prey and presently came to a broad plain, so wide that his eye could scarce command more than what seemed an immediate portion of it.

This passage seems almost to be a response to the *Century* reader of eighteen years before who had complained about the handling of the transformation from man to ant, arguing that Dreiser should have made the ant female and dropped the human name McEwen. Dreiser replied by wondering about the archetypal audience in Indiana: "What, pray, does the Elkhart, Indiana, reader care whether McEwen was a male or a female so long as he fulfilled the dramatic requirements of the situation and held his interest?" [*Letters*]. In the revision Dreiser underscores the odd and unusual metamorphosis while at the same time he tries to ground the miraculous change in something more concrete than the fanciful prerogatives of allegory. He tries, in fact, to give McEwen a more credible psychology.

The key phrase in the new passage is *tribal obligation,* a concept which becomes the focus of the altered psychological presentation of the man-ant. The concept works perfectly in expressing necessity in a positive way. Under the pull of tribal obligation McEwen learns to act for the benefit of others. Several lengthy additions develop this growing understanding of McEwen's ant-hood in relation to tribal identity. In one new passage, for instance, McEwen, hearing a dying ant pronounce the word *tribe,* remembers a past in which he himself was a member of a "colony or tribe" governed by "the powerful and revered ant mother" (*Free*). This knowledge leads him to gather food for other ants and to merge his individualism with the common good. On another occasion the death of a fellow ant produces in McEwen an atavistic memory of having seen "so many die that way" (*Free*). His tribal identity receives climactic force in his effort to save the life of his friend Ermi. The *Ainslee* text conveys the action swiftly and without attributing motive: "McEwen gazed, excited and sympathetic. In a moment he sprang forward

and rushing upon the group, landed upon the back of Og, at whose neck he began to saw." The *Free* text, however, contains an intervening explanation which stresses motive: ". . . but a moment later [he] decided to come to his friend's rescue, a feeling of tribal relationship which was overwhelming coming over him."

Part of McEwen's new psychology is a more intensified capacity for violence and war. Tribal loyalty means not only peaceful support but martial defense as well. In the last and fiercest battle of the story, the one which results in McEwen's "death," he is shown in the revised version to share the group excitement in a way that he does not in the original. The *Ainslee* text reads:

> Ever and anon new lines formed, and strange hosts of friends or enemies came up, but McEwen thought nothing of it. He was alone now—lost in a tossing sea of war, and terror forsook him. But he was very calm.

And the *Free* text:

> Ever and anon new lines were formed, and strange hosts of friends or enemies came up, falling upon the combatants of both sides with murderous enthusiasm. McEwen, in a strange daze and lust of death, seemed to think nothing of it. He was alone now—lost in a tossing sea of war, and terror seemed to have forsaken him. It was wonderful, he thought, mysterious—.

Here one sees a participatory interaction between McEwen and the warring ants and an important individual perception by McEwen alone: "It was wonderful, he thought, mysterious."

This sense of wonder and mystery emphasizes a motif that is one of the most characteristic touches of Dreiser in 1918. He added such speculative notes to several stories in the *Free* volume. The vague suggestiveness of impenetrable philosophical meaning evident in such lines as the final one of the quotation above, becomes the dominant mood of the story's close. The frame at the end, which returns McEwen to his human state, combines philosophical bewilderment with the now familiar psychological fluidity of McEwen's mental processes. The *Ainslee* frame begins with a brief paragraph restoring McEwen to the human city:

> McEwen opened his eyes. He was looking out upon jingling carriages and loitering passersby. He shut his eyes again, wishing to regain a lost scene. A longing filled his heart.

The *Free* text expands this paragraph into three:

> McEwen opened his eyes. Strangely enough he was looking out upon jingling carriages and loitering passersby in the great city park. It was all so strange, by comparison with that which he had so recently seen, the tall buildings in the distance, instead of the sword trees, the trees, the flowers. He jumped to his feet in astonishment, then sank back again in equal amaze, a passerby eyeing him curiously the while.

"I have been asleep," he said in a troubled way. "I have been dreaming. And what a dream!"

He shut his eyes again, wishing, for some strange reason—charm, sympathy, strangeness—to regain the lost scene. An odd longing filled his heart, a sense of comradeship lost, of some friends he knew missing. When he opened his eyes again he seemed to realize something more of what had been happening, but it was fading, fading.

Three kinds of detail have been added. One simply amplifies the contrast between the urban setting and the miniature jungle of grass where McEwen formerly was. A second kind stresses psychological verisimilitude by revealing McEwen's confusion and rational attempt to explain his previous dreaming state. The third amplification contains another familiar motif, the value that McEwen discovered among the ants—comradeship and friendship.

The second and closing paragraph of the frame incorporates another lengthy addition which illustrates in both method and content Dreiser's process of revision. The *Ainslee* text reads:

At his feet lay the plain and the ants. He gazed upon it, searching for the details of an under-world. Only a few feet away in the parched grass, lay an arid spot, overrun with insects. He approached it, and stooping, saw thousands and thousands engaged in a terrific battle. Looking close, he could see where lines were drawn, how in places, the forces raged in confusion, and the field was cluttered with dead. A mad enthusiasm lay hold of him, and he looked for the advantage of the Shining Slave Makers, but finding it not he stood gazing. Then came reason, and with it sorrow—a vague, sad something out of far-off things.

The *Free* version reads:

At his feet lay the plain and the ants with whom he had recently been—or so he thought. Yes, there, only a few feet away in the parched grass, was an arid spot, overrun with insects. He gazed upon it, in amazement, searching for the details of a lost world. Now, as he saw, coming closer, a giant battle was in progress, such a one, for instance, as that in which he had been engaged in his dream. The ground was strewn with dead ants. Thousands upon thousands were sawing and striking at each other quite in the manner in which he had dreamed. What was this?—a relevation of the spirit and significance of a lesser life or of his own—or what? And what was life if the strange passions, moods and necessities which conditioned him here could condition those there on so minute a plane?

"Why, I was there," he said dazedly and a little dreamfully, "a little while ago. I died there—or as well died there—in my dream. At least I woke out of it into this or sank from that into this."

Stooping closer he could see where lines were drawn, how in places the forces raged in confusion, and the field was cluttered with the dead. At one moment an odd mad enthusiasm such as he had experienced in his

dream-world lay hold of him, and he looked for the advantage of the Shining Slave Makers—the blacks—as he thought of the two warring hosts as against the reds. But finding it not, the mood passed, and he stood gazing, lost in wonder. What a strange world! he thought. What worlds within worlds, all apparently full of necessity, contention, binding emotions, and unities—and all with sorrow, their sorrow—a vague, sad something out of far-off things which had been there, and was here in this strong bright city day, had been there and would be here until this odd, strange thing called *life* had ended.

The revised version is a microcosm of Dreiser's techniques and themes. We observe him making inner-sentence modifications and adding new passages. In the first paragraph he changes the unfortunate "under-world" of *Ainslee's* to "lost world," which better conveys the emotion and avoids the connotation of hell or inferiority. Familiar detail about the number of warriors and ferocity of battle recalls McEwen's war experience among the ants. Further, McEwen is moved to philosophical speculation by what he sees. Typically, the speculation is ambiguously unresolved. A series of questions poses the essential problems of (1) which, if either, existence has significance and (2) what life is if ants and men are equally under the sign of passional necessity and conditioning.

The second paragraph also recapitulates the revised characterization of McEwen, as we see him confounded once more as to whether he dreamed the ant life and death or not. His final observation balances the ambiguity nicely: "At least I woke out of it into this or sank from that into this." We can say for certain that McEwen of the *Free* version takes a great deal longer to wake up than he does in the *Ainslee* text and that the dream will remain with him appreciably longer. In the first version McEwen has had a dream; in the second, his dream, its import, and the very process of dreaming become symbolic of all existence.

The third paragraph substantiates the "mad enthusiasm" of the *Ainslee* text by inferentially connecting the present slaughter with the carnage McEwen has witnessed in his ant-life. After exhibiting McEwen's inability to determine whether his tribe is winning, the revised paragraph extends his reaction far beyond the quick return of "reason" and the "vague, sad something" of the *Ainslee* text. McEwen is "lost in wonder," one of the prototypical stances of the Dreiserian hero. What is true of the ants on their darkling plain, McEwen is convinced, is true of his human sphere. When Dreiser modifies the "vague, sad something out of far-off things" of the *Ainslee* text with this crucial clause—"which had been there and was here in this strong bright city day, had been there and would be here until this odd, strange thing called *life* had ended"—he is insisting upon a continum between ants and human beings. The *Ainslee* text, *in toto*, is a dream allegory that leaves its hero finally quite distant from the content of the dream; the *Free* text is a study in psychological verisimilitude and evolutionary correspondences that involves the hero more deeply and more permanently in the content of the dream. Thus the change in title reflects what textual comparison shows: the focus shifts from the ants to McEwen of the ants.

Along with **"Nigger Jeff"** and **"The Cruise of the 'Idlewild'"** Dreiser's ant tragedy is one of those stories in *Free* that repays close attention. To understand Dreiser's social thought, his fictional use of science, and his sense of craft, it is imperative to study the process of revision. What his story said at the turn of the century may not in fact be what it is saying in 1918; and, as we have seen, its manner may not be the same either.

Yoshinobu Hakutani (essay date 1978)

SOURCE: "The Making of Dreiser's Early Short Stories: The Philosopher and the Artist," in *Studies in American Fiction,* Vol. 6, No. 1, Spring, 1978, pp. 47-63.

[*In the following essay, Hakutani traces the common belief that Dreiser's thought was inconsistent—romantic, realist, mystic simultaneously—to the early short stories.*]

In the summer of 1899, shortly before the writing of *Sister Carrie,* Theodore Dreiser tried his hand at the short story, his first concentrated effort to write fiction. Whatever technical devices he might have conceived, or whatever technical difficulties he might have encountered in producing his first short stories, the disposition of mind which lay behind and shaped these stories must have grown out of the disposition of the previous years. In fact, as a newspaperman in the early nineties, Dreiser felt severely restricted. He often detested the city editor's control over his selection of news material and his interpretation of it before the draft of an article was sent to press.

There is a great deal of information in *A Book About Myself* concerning the restrictions imposed by the press. But an article Dreiser wrote as late as 1938 still poses a question of the difference between literature and journalism. In this article Dreiser recalls a routine assignment while he was a young reporter in St. Louis. He was to interview an old millionaire about the city's new terminal project, and naturally he expected to meet a forceful experienced businessman. Unexpectedly, however, Dreiser met a pathetically aged and feeble man who thought of his success and power as useless. During the interview the old man could only say to Dreiser: "My interest in all these things is now so slight that it is scarcely worthwhile—a spectacle for God and men. . . ." Upon his return to the city desk, Dreiser asked the editor whether he should write about the old man's age. "No, no, no!" the editor almost shouted. "Write only his answers. Never mind how old he is. That's just what I don't want. Do you want to queer this? Stick to the terminal dope and what he thought. We're not interested in his age." "No doubt," Dreiser reflects, "the vast majority of the people thought of him even then as young, active, his old self. But all this while this other picture was holding in my mind, and continued so to do for years after. I could scarcely think of the city even without thinking of him, his house, his dog, his age, his bony fingers, his fame." Dreiser then concludes:

Those particular matters about which the city editor had asked to know concerned, as I now saw, only such things as were temporary and purely constructive in their interest, nothing beyond the day—the hour—in which they appeared.

Literature as I now saw, and art in all its forms, was this other realm, that of the painter, the artist, the one who saw and reported the non-transitory, and yet transitory too, nature of all our interests and dreams, which observed life as a whole and drew it without a flaw, a fact, missing. There, if anywhere, were to be reported or painted such conditions and scenes as this about which I had mediated and which could find no place in the rush and hurry of our daily press.

Then it was, and not until then, that the real difference between journalism and literature became plain.

["Lessons I Learned from an Old Man," *Your Life,* Vol. 2, January, 1938]

Compared with such an experience, his editorial and free-lance work (1895-1900) was less inhibited in the expression of ideas. It is true that as editor and "arranger" of *Ev'ry Month* (1895-97) Dreiser was not always in command of its material; he complained of the limitation imposed by the publisher and of the necessity to cater to the predilection of readers. In his free-lance articles his freedom in selecting topics, of course, became much greater. There is no doubt that by the time he became involved in magazine work, particularly his free-lance writing, the kind of restriction he suffered in his newspaper experience had become less severe.

During this period Dreiser managed to express himself on the concepts that had been latent in his mind for a long time. It is clear that when he first read Herbert Spencer's work, he absorbed the technical theories of Spencerian determinism as he confessed in *Ev'ry Month.* Seeing the proof of determinism in his own experience, he ignored Spencer's inherent theory of unending progress and chose to believe that man was a victim of natural forces. Dreiser's conclusion then was that "man was a mechanism, undevised and unrelated, and a badly and carelessly driven one at that." More significantly, he declared with an implication of pessimism,

I felt as low and hopeless at times as a beggar of the streets. There was of course this other matter of necessity, internal chemical compulsion, to which I had to respond whether I would or no. I was daily facing a round of duties which now more than ever verified all that I had suspected and that these books proved. With a gloomy eye I began to watch how the chemical—and their children, the mechanical—forces operated through man and outside him, and this under my very eyes.

[*A Book About Myself,* 1922]

Whatever else he might have been in these years, Dreiser was a thoroughgoing determinist. He observed behavior in terms of natural laws: the complexities of individual life were to be explained by physical and chemical reactions.

Despite the pessimistic conclusion at which he arrived in his interpretation of deterministic theory, it is still possible to find optimism in his belief that there is an inward, driving force, which is pushing mankind upward and onward. It is important here to point to three related quotations from *Ev'ry Month*. First, as Dreiser wrote with a sign of optimism, Spencer showed "how life has gradually become more and more complicated, more and more beautiful, and how architecture, sculpture, painting and music have gradualy [sic] developed, along with a thousand other features of our life of to-day." Secondly, he expressed his latent hope: "We will be concerned with making things good, and with living so that things shall be better . . . there will be naught but hope, unfaltering trust and peace" [Vol. 3, No. 2, Nov. 1, 1896]. Finally, he quoted a Western journal as saying: "The world is not going downward to ruin, as the writer would have us believe. Everything in this splendid country has an upward trend, despite the wail of the cynics" [Vol. 3, No. 4, Jan. 1, 1897].

Such an apparent discrepancy in Dreiser's thoughts that can be seen in the period preceding the writing of his early fiction may account for a disharmony in his mind reflected in his novels. His critics, of course, have noticed this disharmony in discussing his fiction. R. L. Duffus, an early critic of Dreiser, felt that his mind was not all of a piece, and regarded him as romantic, realistic, and mystic all at once. As many critics have already pointed out, his reasoning was not reliable. He leaped to conclusions, generalized too easily, failed to examine narrowly enough. James T. Farrell remarked:

> He accepted as science generalizations based on the ideas of nineteenth-century materialism. From these he adduced a deterministic idea, and this, in turn, was represented as biologic determinism. In *The Financier* and *The Titan* this biologic determinism is usually explained by the word "chemisms." Paradoxically enough, Dreiser's appeal to "chemisms" is made quite frequently in specific contexts concerning motivations of characters, where we can now see that the real rationale of these motivations can be most satisfactorily explained by Freudianism. Often his "chemisms" are overall generalizations of impulses of which the character is not aware. In this respect Dreiser asserted a biologic determinism, which, in terms of our present state of knowledge about man, is crude.

> ["James T. Farrell Revalues Dreiser's *Sister Carrie*," *The New York Times Book Review*, July 4, 1943]

This observation, perhaps, not only holds true of *The Financier* and *The Titan* but also is significant in revealing the loose formulae that Dreiser understood as laws. It must be added in this connection that Dreiser himself admitted to the existence of discrepancies in his fiction. In reply to the question as to what motives were important in writing his fiction, he said, "From time to time I have had all the motives you list and many variations of the same. In connection with a work of any length, such as a novel, I don't see how a person could have a single motivation; at least I never had."

In the making of his first stories, therefore, Dreiser might have had discrepant, or even contradictory, thoughts. Significantly enough, **"The Shining Slave Makers,"** Dreiser's first fictional effort, submitted to the *Century Magazine* late in 1899 and subsequently rejected by its editor, is an allegory embodying a deterministic world view. What Dreiser tells by way of this allegory is reiterated in another short story, **"Free,"** with which **"The Shining Slave Makers"** and the other early stories were later collected in a volume. Speaking for the plight of Rufus Haymaker, the protagonist of **"Free,"** Dreiser makes this statement:

> One of the disturbing things about all this was the iron truth which it had driven home, namely, that Nature, unless it were expressed or represented by some fierce determination within, which drove one to do, be, cared no whit for him or any other man or woman. Unless one acted for oneself, upon some stern conclusion nurtured within, one might rot and die spiritually. Nature did not care. . . . All along he had seen what was happening to him; and yet held by convention he had refused to act always, because somehow he was not hard enough to act. He was not strong enough, that was the real truth— had not been.

> [*Free*]

In the second short story, **"Butcher Rogaum's Door,"** Dreiser dramatizes a conflict between parent and child in much the same way as Stephen Crane deals with it in *Maggie*. Unlike the first two stories, the other stories in this group seem to mirror a considerable optimism and hope for man's condition. In **"Nigger Jeff"** the protagonist recognizes how a helpless man, a victim of natural forces within him and a prisoner of hostile forces in society, encounters his tragedy, his death. But this story by no means paints a hopeless predicament for man; man is also destined to ameliorate. **"Nigger Jeff"** ends with the hero's proclamation of his new ambition and hope not only for himself as an artist but for all men. And somewhat blatantly, in **"When the Old Century Was New,"** the fourth story, there is more social optimism than Darwinism, so that Dreiser looks upon life as an easy struggle for Utopia rather than as a bitter struggle for survival.

It is also important to recognize that Arthur Henry, who later urged Dreiser to work on *Sister Carrie,* influenced him to write these stories. What philosophical influences Henry exercised on Dreiser during their friendship, especially before Dreiser wrote the early stories, are hard to define clearly. His letters show that Henry warned Dreiser against the dangers inherent in the contemplative disposition that Dreiser as editor revealed in the "Reflections" of *Ev'ry Month*. At that time Henry contributed essays entitled "The Philosophy of Hope" and "The Good Laugh" to Dreiser's magazine. Criticizing his despairing mood with a suggestion of optimism, Henry argued that Dreiser should turn to creative writing rather than pursue further his editorial work. So Henry, in the summer of 1897, invited him to visit the house at Maumee, Ohio, which Henry and his wife had bought, and suggested that they work together on various projects.

Because of further involvement in his work on *Ev'ry Month* and of his later venture into free-lance writing, Dreiser's visit to Maumee was postponed until the summer of 1899.

In the meantime, Dreiser and Jug (Sara Osborne White) were married in December 1898 in Washington. It was Henry again who, calling upon the newly wedded couple in their New York apartment, insisted that he write fiction. However, as late as 1898 Dreiser was not at all enthusiastic about becoming a novelist. As he told Mencken later, he had a desire to write drama in these years. But Henry, seeing short stories in him, finally forced him to work on a story:

> I wrote one finally, sitting in the same room with him in a house on the Maumee River, at Maumee, Ohio, outside Toledo. This was in the summer of 1898 [1899]. And after every paragraph I blushed for my folly—it seemed so asinine[.] He insisted on my going on—that it was good—and I thought he was kidding me, that it was rotten, but that he wanted to let me down easy. Finally HE took [it], had it typewritten and sent it. . . . Thus I began[.]

The theme of **"The Shining Slave Makers,"** as might be expected from Dreiser's current preoccupation with the deterministic philosophy, is the survival of the fittest. The setting of the story soon moves from the human world to the world of ants. As Dreiser describes the environment and the action of the inhabitant, the ants' world is bizarre and fantastic yet turns out to be the same world with which he was familiar. It is characterized by self-interest, greed, and the struggle for power.

"It was a hot day in August," Dreiser begins his tale. "The parching rays of a summer sun had faded the once sappy, green leaves of the trees to a dull and dusty hue." The observer of this spectacle is a man named Robert McEwen, a sensitive and sympathetic student of life much like Dreiser himself. McEwen, taking leave of the drudgery of the busy city life, comes out to take a seat under a soothing old beech tree. And for a while he sinks into his usual contemplative mood. Suddenly his meditation is interrupted by an ant crawling on his trousers. Shaking it off and then stamping on another running along the walk in front of him, McEwen now finds a swarm of other black ants hurrying about. At last, when one more active than the others catches his eye, McEwen follows its zig-zag course while it stops here and there, examining something and considering the object's interest value. Suddenly, with a drowsy spell, McEwen discovers himself in an imaginary world in which, during a famine, the black ants are at war with the red ants.

Some critics have noticed a similarity between the setting of this tale and one of the interpolations Balzac makes towards the end of *The Wild Ass's Skin*. Balzac's passage reads:

> Who has not, at some time or other in his life, watched the comings and goings of an ant, slipped straws into a yellow slug's one breathing-hole, studied the vagaries of a slender dragonfly, pondered admiringly over the countless veins in an oak-leaf? . . . Who has not looked long in delight at the effects of sun and rain on a roof of brown tiles, at the dewdrops, or at the variously shaped petals of the flowercups? Who has not sunk into these idle, absorbing meditations . . . ?

In Balzac's story, however, its character, Valentin, is weary of his life and yet feels desperate at the thought of his approaching death. In order to divert his thoughts, Valentin tries to observe nature, thereby consoling himself with the equation of man and natural beings. "The leading idea of this human comedy," Balzac writes, "came to me first as a dream. . . . The idea came from the study of human life in comparison with the life of animals." Balzac's vision, in his writing of *The Wild Ass's Skin,* is that of a human biologist. In writing **"The Shining Slave Makers"** Dreiser is not viewing man's life in terms of animal life. Rather, as in Thoreau's ant war in *Walden,* Dreiser is looking at ants in terms of man.

In its outline the first feature story he wrote for the Pittsburgh *Dispatch,* **"The Fly,"** had the same intention as **"The Shining Slave Makers,"** though less developed in its treatment than the short story in question. In **"The Shining Slave Makers,"** the first ant that encounters McEwen in the dream interrogates him in a friendly manner but in a selfish tone: "'Anything to eat hereabout?' . . . McEwen drew back. 'I do not know,' he said, 'I have just—' 'Awful,' said the stranger, not waiting to hear his answer. 'It looks like famine. You know the Sanguineae have gone to war.' 'No,' answered McEwen, mechanically." McEwen, upon seeing another ant carrying a crumb as large as the ant's body, asks the ant where it has found the crumb. "'Here,' said Ermi. 'Will you give me a little?' 'I will not,' said the other, and a light came in his eye that was almost evil."

With vivid dramatic force this situation projects a jungle-like world. More interestingly, McEwen, who is now a member of the same tribe, the black ants, cannot secure help from the ants of his own family. Needless to point out, the persistent, reciprocal warfare among members of the family is more evocative of life in the animal kingdom than it is of the world of civilized man. Ironically, Dreiser intended to project an image of the survival of the fittest, not in the world of men but in the world of ants.

Dreiser's major motif here is man's selfishness as it is illustrated by the ants' behavior toward their fellow beings at the time of a strife:

> "All right," said McEwen, made bold by hunger and yet cautious by danger, "which way would you advise me to look?"
>
> "Why, any way," said Ermi, and strode off.
>
> . . . . .
>
> He eagerly hailed the newcomer, who was yet a long way off.

"What is it?" asked the other, coming up rapidly.

"Do you know where I can get something to eat?"

"Is that why you called me?" he answered, eyeing him angrily.

"Certainly not. If I had anything for myself, I would not be out here. Go and hunt for it like the rest of us."

"I have been hunting," cried McEwen, his anger rising. "I have searched here until I am almost starved."

"No worse off than I or any of us, are you?" said the other. "Look at me. Do you suppose I am feasting?"

This is, to be sure, an allegory of life, but more importantly it is an allegory of Dreiser's own struggle in the past. In the newspaper experience of the early nineties, Dreiser viewed "life as a fierce, grim struggle in which no quarter was either given or taken, and in which all men laid traps, lied, squandered, erred through illusion" (*Book*). One ant's angry reply to McEwen, the newcomer, "Is that why you called me? . . . Go and hunt for it like the rest of us" is reminiscent of the very scene of the survival of the fittest that Dreiser witnessed in the office of Pulitzer's *World* when he managed to be on the staff of the paper in the cold winter months of 1894-95. In that newspaper office, as Dreiser later remembered, the men working under Pulitzer appeared to him like tortured animals. They were concerned only with themselves, and whenever Dreiser as fellow reporter asked them a question or favor, he would be stared at by them as if he were an idiot or a thief. This motif in **"The Shining Slave Makers"** is not contrived to fit the doctrine of survival but is based on an actual experience.

Later in the story, when another ant is facing death, the compassionate McEwen attempts to offer him aid, but the ant, now overwhelmed by his own despair and resignation, declines. McEwen now realizes how helpless a creature can be under these circumstances. He cannot but simply look silently on the ant. "The sufferer," Dreiser remarks, "closed his eyes in evident pain, and trembled convulsively. Then he fell back and died. McEwen gazed upon the bleeding body, now fast stiffening in death, and wondered." Dreiser's inference on the scene is clear cut: man, just like an insect, is powerless against those incidental forces that always surround him. This scene also resembles the aftermath of a train accident Dreiser reported a few years earlier in St. Louis. He then asked, viewing the dead bodies which were twisted and burned beyond recognition, "Who were they? The nothingness of man! They looked so commonplace, so unimportant, so like dead flies or beetles" (*Book*).

When a war breaks out between the black slave makers and the red Sanguineae (in Theoreau's ant war, between the black imperialists and the red republicans), McEwen, of course, sides with the black ants, but finally meets his own death. Dreiser seems to be telling himself: join the crowd, fight for the crowd, die for the crowd. The struggle for survival continues without purpose or a goal in sight. Only the fittest will survive; death alone is safe. After McEwen finally returns to reality, he is now possessed by a "mad enthusiasm." He tries to figure out the advantage of having met his recent comrades, the Shining Slave Makers, but, Dreiser writes, "finding it not he stood gazing. Then came reason, and with it sorrow—a vague, sad something out of far-off things."

By projecting a serious and significant human dilemma onto minute sub-human life, Dreiser achieves detachment. But, in the allegory, though detached from the violent scene in which the struggle for survival is carried on, he can look at McEwen somewhat in the same way that McEwen looks at these ants in the insect kingdom. In this way he does not reduce his life experience to a mere objective show but dramatizes it from a clumsy but instinctively derived point of view. By the solid material behind the theme and plot, the story became a powerful expression of his preoccupation at the time.

What Dreiser had to say in his first piece of fiction was exactly what brought about its rejection by the editor who first read the manuscript and returned it to the author with a letter protesting the "despicable philosophy." If this were the way the young author thought about man's life, the less he wrote about it the better. The editor thought that Dreiser was saying that men are cruel and deceptive just as nature is. The editor's reasoning was that Dreiser enjoyed these qualities of man—the brutal, the deceptive, the violent—and that Dreiser was, therefore, dangerous to human society. However, Dreiser, who was blazing in those years with a strong passion for society and fellow men, was still lined up against them.

Despite this slap from the timid and conventional editor-ambassador, Dreiser was soon to discover an ally. **"The Shining Slave Makers"** was accepted by *Ainslee's Magazine* for publication and Dreiser probably took this acceptance as an encouragement for the continuing adherence to his own philosophy. He then wrote **"Butcher Rogaum's Door," "The World and the Bubble," "Nigger Jeff,"** and **"When the Old Century Was New,"** and had all of them published. In **"Butcher Rogaum's Door,"** Dreiser again justifies the value of Spencerian determinism. The events of the story happen with the mechanical consistency of the so-called "chemisms." The story is a study of an incident which Dreiser sees as inevitable, granted the incipient *milieu* in which the character is placed.

The plot first develops with the tension between an old father and his teen-age daughter, who has begun to be allured to the street lights and the boys loitering outdoors on summer evenings. As the title suggests, the door to Rogaum's apartment above his butcher shop on Bleecker Street, New York City, becomes significant. Old Rogaum tries to exhort against her going out after dark. But adolescent Theresa, awakening to a burgeoning sexual feeling, now wants "to walk up and down in the as yet bright street, where were voices and laughter, and occasionally moonlight streaming down"; thus she cannot help disregarding her father's discipline. The stubborn German father's last resort is threatening to lock her out, and indeed one night the determined old Rogaum does lock her out when she fails to return by nine from dallying with her young friend. At the door Theresa overhears her father talking savagely to Mrs. Rogaum, "Let her go, now. I vill her a lesson teach." Rattling the door again and getting no answer, she grows defiant. "Now, strangely," Dreiser observes, "a new element, not heretofore apparent in her nature, but, nevertheless wholly there, was called into life, springing in action as Diana, full formed. The cold chill left her and she wavered angrily." She walks back to George Almerting. The night deepens, no sound of Theresa, and Rogaum starts searching for her. Returning in fear and without success, he sees at the door a young woman writhing in unmitigated pain as a result of her having drunk acid in a suicide attempt. Rogaum at first mistakes the woman for his daughter Theresa. However clumsy the coincidence Dreiser devises to suggest Theresa's possible fate, this story in the simple truth of its setting and characters mirrors the world Dreiser had grown to accept. The suicide, like Theresa, was once locked out, but Theresa, unlike the suicide, is never to become a prostitute or suicide or both like Crane's Maggie. Theresa obviously was written about as though she were one of Dreiser's own sisters. He was portraying the life of the people he knew by heart and what they could have become.

Fortunately, Theresa comes back safely, unlike the girl who sees a tragic end. But this was exactly his own family, since the religious old father, strict with the wanton daughter, locked her out one night and then worried, so that when he regained her unharmed, he refrained from beating her as he had intended. In the story Dreiser, as elsewhere (*Dawn, Jennie Gerhardt, The "Genius," An American Tragedy*) treats the father with a sympathetic tone. A too Calvinistic German butcher, Rogaum emerges as a strangely appealing and rather pathetic figure. As in another of Dreiser's short stories, **"Typhoon,"** the father is a German immigrant with a heavy accent and has a moderately prosperous small business. The children in the Dreiser family, and indeed those in the Gerhardts' and Griffiths' families, attempted to run away from their oppressive poverty-stricken household. The chief difference between the Rogaum family and the other families is that it is not poverty stricken. But here Dreiser's emphasis is upon the inability of parents to understand not only the social desires, in this case money, but the natural desires and inclinations of their children.

Mrs. Rogaum, "a particularly fat, old, German lady, completely dominated by her liege and portly lord," is warmhearted but is in no position to advise her daughter. Dreiser's image of the mother is a significant departure from that of a modern American mother. This is exactly the scene of the family he knew in his youth. Thus Dreiser delineates not so much the social conditioning of his individuals, as critics maintain, but the historical complexities that make understandable the uniqueness of each individual's experience.

The city life to which Theresa is attracted is also important historically. Dreiser is here interested in the American family of the 1890s, as in *Sister Carrie* and *Jennie Gerhardt,* which was changed and perverted by artificial lures. Theresa, like the children of the Dreiser family, is discontented with family ties and enchanted by the outside forces which sever her from the family. This is the same situation in which Dreiser describes Carrie's approaching the city in the summer of 1889 with the same "wonder and desire" he himself had felt in approaching Chicago two summers earlier. The role of the parent in the family structure was diminishing; the truth of this becomes obvious when the family of Dreiser's fiction is compared with that of the present day. And this change, while important in the values of the children, was devastating in its effects on the parents.

In **"Butcher Rogaum's Door,"** concepts of individual morality are bound to the larger, overall concept of man in a society where the artificial restraints of social position are removed and where the chemical urges of the blood are observed and respected. If Theresa could become enthralled with the lures of the city and meet a fine young man with "a shrewd way of winking one eye" within the boundary of her household, she would not have gone out to the streets at night. Dreiser's point is that evil in man results not so much from an inherent tendency for evil in the individual as from the unreasonable and often unjust demands in society—in Theresa's case, the father, his customers, the police, and the townsmen in Bleecker Street. She is, first of all, the result of a home environment which has alienated her from life, so that when she faces its risks and might possibly be betrayed, it is the society that has provided such a *milieu* which is to blame. Likewise, whoever might exploit Theresa is not so much the result of a limitation of character as the result of society's failure to develop necessary virtues in the would-be exploiter. These are represented less as the natural virtue of the passively innocent than as the qualities of aggression, selfishness, deceptiveness, competition, which Dreiser perceives as the law of nature. In this sense **"Butcher Rogaum's Door"** is analogous to his first story, **"The Shining Slave Makers."**

In both stories the image of life Dreiser presents is necessarily colored by a rather pessimistic frame of mind in accord with the philosophy of the gloomy determinism that accounts for human conditions. This is, perhaps, most obviously shown at the end of **"The Shining Slave Makers,"** where McEwen's vision of life as he is awakening from his recent dream is tinged with sorrow. This is also shown in the story of Rogaum and Theresa, but in this story the sense of sorrow is somewhat lightened by the hopeful tone Dreiser gives to the outcome of the incident. The story, of course, does not say that one should not lock out his daughter at night lest a dire fate befall her. Nor does it say that Theresa has learned a lesson so that she will not wander off at night again. For the author does not believe that man's life is only at the mercy of fate. Old Rogaum has learned that he must not be too harsh toward his daughter because he now recognizes the necessary demands of a young woman.

In the second story, then, Dreiser was to tell the reader that such a conflict between father and daughter can be adjusted. Man's unreasonable environment being ameliorated, man can learn. In **"Nigger Jeff,"** the third story, Dreiser was yet to weave this sign of hope into patterns of action with architectonic skill. As a result, he achieved in the texture of the story a cumulative effect of no little significance. Because his two earlier stories derive from his own experiences (the characters in them are like himself, his family, and the people he knew, and the incidents are those he saw) his expression is spontaneous and markedly consonant with the feelings deeply rooted in his heart. Also in **"Nigger Jeff"** he was to express such congenial feelings as he remembered from an incident that occurred in his newspaper experience in St. Louis. The story develops around a report of an apparently nefarious rape; it is not simply an illustration of man's conduct observed in terms of the deterministic philosophy but rather the process of revelation a newspaper reporter goes through. One day he is sent out by the city editor to cover the lynching of a Negro rapist. The reporter, Eugene Davies, much like the young Dreiser in St. Louis, is portrayed as a naive youth. On that day, a bright spring afternoon, Davies "was feeling exceedingly well and good natured. The world seemed worth singing about." But, after learning the circumstances of the rape, the Negro's behavior, his family's grief, and above all the transcending beauty and serenity of nature in contrast with the human abjection and agonies, Davies realizes that his sympathies have shifted. This reporter, then, is not simply the obtuse observer, a mystery story character who watches the plot unfold. He is the perceiving center; he recognizes that the world is not neatly dichotomized as black and white. The action of the story takes place in the hero's reaction to the dreadful violence and in his understanding of American society and himself as artist.

One of the most salient technical devices displayed in this story is the contrast in the images of man and nature. Although in the beginning the reporter is convinced that Jeff is guilty, he grows increasingly less certain. Even before he reaches the site of the lynching, he takes note of "the whiteness of the little houses, the shimmering beauty of the little creek you had to cross in going from the depot. At the one main corner a few men [a part of the mob] were gathered about a typical village barroom." As the mob hurries on with the horror impending, the "night was exceedingly beautiful. Stars were already beginning to shine. . . . The air was fresh and tender. Some pea fowls were crying afar off and the east promised a golden moon." Again, a contrast of the light and the dark is maintained in a later scene:

. . . The gloomy company seemed a terrible thing. . . .

. . . He was breathing heavily and groaning. His eyes were fixed and staring, his face and hands bleeding as if they had been scratched or trampled on. He was bundled up like limp wheat.

. . . Still the company moved on and he followed, past fields lit white by the moon, under dark, silent groups of

trees, through which the moonlight fell in patches, up hilltops and down into valleys, until at last the little stream came into view, sparkling like a molten flood of silver in the night.

As Davies watches the limp body plunging down and pulling up with the sound of a creaking rope, in the weak moonlight it seemed as if the body were struggling, but he could not tell. . . . Only the black mass swaying in the pale light, over the shiny water of the stream seemed wonderful.

. . . The light of morning began to show as tender lavender and gray in the east. Still he sat. Then came the roseate hue of day, to which the waters of the stream responded, the white pebbles shining beautifully at the bottom. Still the body hung black and limp, and now a light breeze sprang up and stirred it visibly.

On the one hand, the hero clearly recognizes the signs of evil indicated by "the struggling body," "the black mass," and "the body hanging black and limp." On the other, the images of the dark are intermingled in Davies' mind with those of the light that suggest hope: "the weak moonlight," "the pale light," "the shiny water of the stream," "the light of morning," "tender lavender and gray in the east," "the roseate hue of day," "the white pebbles shining beautifully at the bottom." As the story progresses toward the end, the images of good increasingly dominate those of evil, a pattern already revealed in this scene.

Later, visiting the room where the body is laid and seeing the rapist's sister sobbing over it, Davies becomes aware that all "the corners of the room were quite dark, and only in the middle were shining splotches of moonlight." For Davies, the climactic scene of his experience takes place when he dares to lift the sheet covering the body. He can now see exactly where the rope tightened in the neck. The delineation of the light against the dark is, once more, focused on the dead body as Dreiser describes it: "A bar of cool moonlight lay across the face and breast." Such deliberate contrasts between the light and the dark, hope and despair, suggest that man has failed to appreciate "transcending beauty" and "unity of nature," which are really illusions to him, and that he has only imitated the cruel and the indifferent which nature appears to symbolize.

At the end of the story, Davies is overwhelmed not only by the remorse he feels for the victim but also by his compassion for the bereft mother he finds in the dark corner of the room. "Davies," Dreiser writes, "began to understand. . . . Out in the moonlight, he struck a pace, but soon stopped and looked back. The whole dreary cabin, with its one golden door, where the light was, seemed a pitiful thing. He swelled with feeling and pathos as he looked. The night, the tragedy, the grief he saw it all." The emphasis of the story is not, therefore, upon the process of the young man's becoming an artist; it is upon the sense of urgency in which the protagonist is compelled to act as a reformer. With his final proclamation, "I'll get it all in," the hero's revelation culminates in a feeling of triumph. Although, to Dreiser, man appears necessarily limited by his environment and natural feeling, Dreiser asserts that man can learn.

> **Unlike other literary naturalists, Dreiser attempted to discover an ideal order in man's life as he does in these stories.**
>
> —*Yoshinobu Hakutani*

"**Nigger Jeff,**" in disclosing true social conditions, can be construed as a powerful expression of Dreiser's hope for the better in American society. And it is quite reasonable to suppose that all this time there was in Dreiser as much optimism in viewing life as a struggle for Utopia as there was pessimism. For among his earliest short stories the last, "**When the Old Century Was New,**" though generally considered inferior, is clearly more a wistful Utopian picture than the others. He reconstructs one day in the spring of 1801 in New York City after the turn of the century. In such a world there is no misery, no struggle; the gulf dividing the rich from the poor is unimportant, and the friction between social classes is totally unknown. William Walton, a dreamer, taking a day off from his business engagement, strolls down the social center of New York. There he notices the celebrities of the city, even Thomas Jefferson and "the newly-elected President" Adams.

Walton is also Dreiser himself; Walton, too, like Dreiser with Jug in New York, is accompanied by his fiancée:

> Elatedly they made their way to the old homestead again, and then being compelled to leave her, while she dressed for the theatre, he made his way toward the broad and tree-shaded Bowery, where was the true and idyllic walk for a lover. . . . Here young Walton, as so many others before him, strolled and hummed, thinking of all that life and the young city held for him. Here he planned to build that mansion of his own—far out, indeed, above Broome Street.

Unlike Walton, however, Dreiser cannot help noticing "the aristocracy, gentry and common rabble forming in separate groups." Although Walton at heart feels optimistic toward the new century, Dreiser at his side could not escape the prospect of misery and oppression. Dreiser observes with a touch of satire that Walton "had no inkling, as he pondered, of what a century might bring forth. The crush and stress and wretchedness fast treading upon this path of loveliness he could not see." F. O. Matthiessen can legitimately call "**When the Old Century Was New**" only a sketch "with nothing to distinguish it from other paper-thin period pieces." But it is worth noting that even in such a slight piece of fiction

there is Dreiser's dramatization of the American success story with his world of changing cities, where new careers and new fortunes are made daily. Despite the gloom hovering under the deterministic theory of life at his disposal, there was in his mind during this period much joy and optimism that influenced his writing.

Robert E. Spiller, in the *Literary History of the United States,* maintains that Dreiser's short stories "in theme and treatment add little to an analysis of the novels and may be compared to a painter's sketches." But these pre-novel short stories are, nonetheless, closely related to his early novels. In subject matter these stories are studies on the conditions of men and women in society, sometimes as individuals and at other times as groups. Man tends to be a victim of forces not only within him but about him. Dreiser, moreover, views men not only as social individuals but also, as in "**Butcher Rogaum's Door,**" as historical individuals. Much can be learned from the pages of *Sister Carrie* and *Jennie Gerhardt* about the nature and structure of American society and the American family in the years before the turn of the century. But, delineating the growth of cities, exhibiting the forceful lures of city life, and emphasizing the conflict between convention and individual demands, Dreiser shows one of the basic motifs of his early novels in such stories as "**Butcher Rogaum's Door**" and "**When the Old Century Was New.**"

His early stories, like the ant tragedy developed in "**The Shining Slave Makers**" give him a congenial means of expression, primarily because they contain characters, whether in an allegory or a historical romance, like Dreiser himself, personages he knew or events he remembered from his experience. It is arguable that Dreiser's early short fiction would have been more significant had he not been influenced by many of the specific technical concepts of the Spencerian world. More important for the argument here is that, as an artist, Dreiser transcends these technicalities and writes fiction with living individuals, whose personalities express their historical *milieu* and do not reflect merely the abstract motivations of "chemisms." This is, perhaps, why Eliseo Vivas has observed: "Fortunately the sincere artist magnificently contradicted the self-taught materialist and found a purpose that, had he been consistent, he could not have found. . . . And if life's meaning is something sad or tragic, in Dreiser's own life, in his enormous capacity for pity, we find an example of a man who, through his work, gave the lie to his own theories." What prompted Dreiser to write fiction was his overwhelming desire to understand human beings. Unlike other literary naturalists, Dreiser attempted to discover an ideal order in man's life as he does in these stories. In this sense, he is more an idealist than a pessimist. And his understanding of humanity often goes beyond the deterministic philosophy he learned from Spencer.

This ambivalence in Dreiser's thoughts in the making of the early stories gave rise to his practice of applying the theory of determinism as well as designing his stories with a historical, and often personal, significance. This is why consistency in these stories is nearly impossible. Even though his characters tend to be controlled by circumstances, the focus of the stories is upon the individual and the moral consequences of his actions, as shown by Eugene Davies in **"Nigger Jeff."** Dreiserian characters are sometimes larger than the author's occasional philosophy, and then they are able to speak for themselves. Dreiser the philosopher only gets in their way; Dreiser the artist remains true to them. In the end the interest of the story lies not in his mind, but in his heart. Hence, his frequent tone of optimism, mingled, as it frequently is, with his pessimism, can be reasonably accounted for.

Yoshinobu Hakutani   (essay date 1979)

SOURCE: "The Dream of Success in Dreiser's *A Gallery of Women*," in *Zeitschrift Fur Anglistik und Amerikanistik,* Vol. 27, No. 3, 1979, pp. 236-46.

[*In the following essay, Hakutani examines Dreiser's treatment of women characters in* A Gallery of Women, *paying particular attention to the character's dream of success.*]

I

Although Theodore Dreiser is often regarded as a pioneer among modern American novelists for the characterization of woman, very little critical attention has been paid to *A Gallery of Women* (1929). Upon its publication, this collection of fifteen semifictional portraits was compared to his *Twelve Men* (1919), a well-received volume of biographical portraits. Despite his disclaimers to the contrary, Dreiser did not have the same intimate knowledge of his women as he did of his men. Undoubtedly Dreiser portrayed women whom he had come across in his career, but his portraits lack conviction. Critics agree that the best portraits in *Twelve Men* are those of his brother Paul and his father-in-law Arch White, or men like Peter McCord and William Louis Sonntag, Jr., both most inspirational in his early journalism. Dreiser's readers had thus expected as much authenticity in *A Gallery of Women* as in *Twelve Men,* but they were disappointed. And yet later readers still persisted in the same expectation. Considering *A Gallery of Women* as the companion volume to *Twelve Men,* F. O. Matthiessen, for instance, looked for Dreiser's technique in differentiating women characters but concluded that such skills "deserted him when he tried to handle details that must have seemed to him more intimate" [*Theodore Dreiser,* 1951].

But the comparison was grossly unfair. The cool reception that has attended *A Gallery of Women* might have resulted not so much from Dreiser's treatment as from his subject-matter. Readers in twentieth-century America have shown a tendency to minimize the importance of woman in fiction. Only recently have Kate Chopin's short stories attracted serious attention; *Sister Carrie* was

suppressed for seven long years. Such a tendency is hard to understand, for in the late nineteenth century the public accepted as a matter of course the greater freedom in the selection of themes in fiction than before. Needless to say, James' *The Portrait of a Lady* (1881) is a monumental work concerned with the problem of an American woman. A realist like Howells, too, responding to the libertarians' attack on the socially enforced misery of marriage, successfully treated a divorce for his subject in *A Modern Instance* (1882). In modern times, there has been no question about American novelists' willingness to deal with the woman question.

> **What distinguishes** *A Gallery of Women* **from a book like** *Twelve Men* **is that Dreiser's attitude toward his material is more psychological than social.**
>
> **—*Yoshinobu Hakutani***

The difficulty, however, lies with the reading public. Ironically, even H. L. Mencken, Dreiser's staunch supporter, dismissed *A Gallery of Women* as a work inferior to *Twelve Men*:

> . . . if the collection is not quite as interesting as its forerunner, then that is probably because women themselves are considerably less interesting than men. Not one of them here is to be mentioned in the same breath with Dreiser's brother Paul, the shining hero of *Twelve Men.* . . . The rest are occasionally charming, but only too often their chief mark is a pathetic silliness. What ails most of them is love. They throw away everything for it, and when they can't get the genuine article they seem to be content with imitations. And if it is not love, real or bogus, that undoes them, then it is some vague dream that never takes rational form—of puerile self-expression, of gratuitous self-sacrifice, of something else as shadowy and vain.
>
> ["Ladies, Mainly Sad," *American Mercury,* Vol. 19, February, 1930]

Moreover, what disappointed many early readers was the lack of variability they felt in Dreiser's characterization. For a reviewer who had expected to find as great a variety of preoccupations in women as in men, *A Gallery of Women* left the impression that "Mr. Dreiser believes there is one kind of women—the one who is over-troubled with sex" [Rollo Walter Brown, "Fifteen Women," *Saturday Review of Literature,* Vol. 6, February 8, 1930]. But this is far from true, for many of the heroines are not even remotely concerned with sex. Ernita, for example, is an American revolutionary who has voluntarily joined the communist movement in Siberia and is not at all tormented by sex. If she is over-troubled by her life, it is not because of sex, but because she immerses herself in the ideology of communism. If Dreiser's ideal woman calls for an equilibrium of mind and heart, Ernita serves as an example of the woman who lacks heart. After an unwilling experience with what Dreiser calls "free love", in which she fails to satisfy herself, Ernita finally decides to return to her lawful husband. She confides to Dreiser: "I walked the floor, suffering because of my mind—this unescapable Puritan conscience of mine". In Dreiser's denouement, Ernita, if anything, is "under-troubled" with the problem of sex.

The same holds true of the portraits of the fortuneteller Giff and an invincible ghetto woman named Bridget Mullanphy. Both are the types that are untroubled with sexual problems of any kind, and they are the ones who survive the most persecuting tyranny of life itself. In that world, however, as one critic observes, Dreiserian women are temperamental rather than intellectual; "so inevitably, as they strive to escape a dilemma not truly of their own making, they fare badly" [John J. McAleer, *Theodore Dreiser: An Introduction and Interpretation,* 1968]. This dilemma destroys an ill-prepared woman like Esther Norn, who lets her lovers exploit her. But such a predicament is not what distresses other women in the same book. Under the circumstances, stoic women such as Bridget and Albertine fare magnificently because they are the types of women that Dreiser knew are endowed with unusual strength of character. Their success in life, furthermore, is demonstrated in terms of the qualities of mind and heart that make those of men glaringly inferior and shameful.

Whether heroines in *A Gallery of Women* fare well or not thus depends upon their individual merits and faults. For some, their lovers are wealthy and only seek sexual enjoyment in them; for others, their lovers are sexually content but only interested in their money. Being women, they are all subjected to various predicaments, but their ultimate success or failure in life is determined not by their circumstances but by themselves. In case after case, Dreiser's portraits suggest not a seemingly meaningless and ferocious struggle for existence, but an affirmation of individual worth. Always sympathetic with his heroine's potential as an individual being, Dreiser strives to present her in the best light. In their quest for success, Dreiser's women are unmistakenly drawn here to emphasize their own special needs for fulfillment. In brief, his intention was not a rehash of social determinism.

Thus, what distinguishes *A Gallery of Women* from a book like *Twelve Men* is that Dreiser's attitude toward his material is more psychological than social. The character traits that fascinated him in *A Gallery of Women* are not defined in terms of the social patterns that determined the characters in *Twelve Men.* The idiosyncrasies of Dreiser's women seemed more internal to him than those of men. This was perhaps why Mencken, commenting on Dreiser's difficulty with *A Gallery of Women,* argued that women in general "remain more mysterious and hence more romantic". Even though Giff appeared strangely nebulous in her intellectual outlook, or Olive Brand seemed only vaguely motivated by her sexual freedom, Dreiser did not fill in his abstract moral equations

with the kind of realistic detail expected of a naturalist writer. Rather, he left the mystery inscrutable to the last.

Dreiser's attempt to be a "romantic" writer, however, did not result in ambiguities in his characterization. He made the best of his material, and of his knowledge about woman. He was persistent in search of truths about feminine temperament and what he understood to be woman's fate. His method was thus analytical, and to some of the portraits he adopted a psychological, if not consistently psychoanalytical, approach. For revelation of feminine secrets, Dreiser was occasionally preoccupied with Freudian theory, which was already fashionable in the 1920s. But here, too, Dreiser was curious rather than convinced, openly experimental rather than theoretical. Dreiser's open-mindedness about his subject and treatment in *A Gallery of Women* was thus indicated by his mention of the project as early as 1919. "God, what a work!" he told Mencken, "if I could do it truly—The ghosts of Puritans would rise and gibber in the streets" [*Letters of Theodore Dreiser,* 1959].

II

One of the major themes that bind together the various portraits in *A Gallery of Women* is the American dream of success. Dreiser's women regard themselves as protagonists in their battle for success among male antagonists. In many of the stories, however, the heroine craves for success in her profession not so that she can rise superior to men, but so that she can achieve pride and peace of mind as an individual. By the time Dreiser planned to formulate these portraits, the dream of success for men had been so finely engrained in American life that it had become an essential part of the American psyche. Dreiser was only expected to modify this tradition as it would have applied to women. Unlike the characterization of the hero in a success story—in which the author's avowed emphasis was on the man's natural survival tactics in society—Dreiser's focus in *A Gallery of Women* was upon the heroine's personal motives and actions rather than the social and economic forces that would also determine her life.

Despite the variety of women portrayed in the book, and its length, the details of social and familial contexts that mark a Dreiserian novel are indeed scarce. This is a clear departure from Dreiser's use of imagery and symbolism derived from the concrete details of the character's reality—streets, houses, rooms, furniture, and clothes—as in *Sister Carrie* or a short story like **"The Second Choice"**. Instead his portraits abound in verbal impressions, conversations, confessions, points of view, and abstract authorial explanations of various kinds. The successful portraits are those in which Dreiser effectively structures these details to show how his heroines are trying to fit their temperaments to their struggles despite repeated failures. In particular, Dreiser's primary interest lies in an exposé of the intricate and complex relationships which a woman writer, painter, or actress holds with her husbands, lovers, and gigolos. In the most successful of his portraits, such as **"Esther Norn"**, Dreiser's denouement creates pathos, since the heroine's "pursuit of happiness" is constantly hindered by the turn of the events that stem from her own errors in judgment.

Dreiser's portraits of the women professionals derive in large part from his own experiences in Greenwich Village in the twenties. He was fascinated by their lives, as he says at the beginning of each tale, because they were young and beautiful and they appeared intellectually competent. But as the story develops, the narrator—in most cases Dreiser himself—gradually informs the reader with some hesitation that the woman in question lacks the qualities of mind necessary for the realization of her dream. Clearly, Dreiser is dealing here with a "second-rate" personage in a particular profession. It is interesting that Dreiser as a magazine writer in the 1890s was convinced of the gift and originality attributed to many a woman professional—artist, writer, composer, lawyer, musician, singer. Perhaps Dreiser of the twenties was a much more severe critic of woman's abilities than Dreiser of the nineties.

In any event, *A Gallery of Women* as a whole suggests that the dream of success in fields like art and writing could be realized only by independent, strong-willed women. This implication does have some relationship with Dreiser's latent prejudice against woman's intellectual abilities. In 1916 Dreiser told his first biographer, Dorothy Dudley Harvey, a graduate of Bryn Mawr, that he had found it difficult "to name one woman of any distinction or achievement out of the twenty-five years of that institution" [Dudley, *Dreiser and the Land of the Free,* 1946]. Later in "Life, Art and America", included in *Hey Rub-a-Dub-Dub,* Dreiser thus declared:

> There is not a chemist, a physiologist, a botanist, a biologist, an historian, a philosopher, an artist, of any kind or repute among them; not one. They are secretaries to corporations, teachers, missionaries, college librarians, educators in any of the scores of pilfered meanings that may be attached to that much abused word. They are curators, directors, keepers. They are not individuals in the true sense of that word; they have not been taught to think; they are not free. They do not invent, lead, create; they only copy or take care of, yet they are graduates of this college and its theory, mostly ultra conventional, or, worse yet, anæmic, and glad to wear its collar, to clank the chains of its ideas or ideals— automatons in a social scheme whose last and final detail was outlined to them in the classrooms of their alma mater. That, to me, is one phase, amusing enough, of intellectual freedom in America.

What ultimately prevents Ellen Adams Wrynn, one of the heroines in *A Gallery of Women,* from becoming a successful painter is the lack of independence and freedom in her character. Although Dreiser emphasizes at the outset how this "young, attractive, vigorous, and ambitious" blonde will benefit the free spirits and creativity associated with the bohemian life of the Village, he predicts that "her enthusiasm would not last the numerous trials and tribulations of those who essay illustration and painting in general" (*Gallery*). Ellen marries Walter

Wrynn, a young broker, for "the delight of sex as well as the respect and material prosperity and social advancement that sometimes went with marriage for some". The marriage is obviously doomed and Dreiser uses Jimmie Race, a novice in painting much like Ellen, to serve as a foil to Walter. Dreiser's argument is that there is nothing wrong with a young woman's—much less an artist's— being a "varietist". More significantly, Ellen's problem is caused by her attitude toward sex; she takes sex lightly and lets her success dream pre-empt her desire for fulfillment. Despite her innate beauty and intelligence, she deliberately seeks the habits and mores antithetical to those one must acquire as an artist. For the benefit of her husband, she functions merely as a form of "sex worship"; for Race, her first lover, she remains a listener to his sophormoric discourse on art and poetry.

Ellen's static personality, shown by the lack of spiritual communion with her sexual partner, is also reflected in her work. Though she travels to Paris and studies first hand the Post-Impressionists by living with one painter after another, she fails to he recognized for her work. One of her most influential lovers and mentors is a Scotish painter, Keir McKail, whose workmanship gives a clue to what is lacking in hers. While Dreiser admires the exotic color and thought in her painting, he notices the internal solidity behind the paint in McKail's work. "Naturally", Dreiser comments, "he avoided with almost religious austerity any suggestion of the sterile eccentricities that spoiled so much of the work of others . . . whereas beneath her surfaces was no real depth".

Another flaw in her character is reflected in a rigid and extreme relationship she establishes with her lover. She either dominates him or lets herself be dominated by him. Domination, in Dreiser's scheme for this story, means some compensation for the one who is dominated. Thus Ellen, dominated by McKail, learns a great deal from him about painting, and her workmanship improves. The irony is that from the other men she has dominated, she gains nothing but what she does not need for purposes of her art. From her husband she gets his physically strong manhood and their unwanted child; from Race, his complaints and lectures on abstract subjects. The most significant point is that Ellen lacks an independently motivated discipline of art. This initial deficiency in her character is proved by the fact that as soon as McKail leaves her, her workmanship declines and she is once more doomed to be a failure.

Another heroine in *A Gallery of Women* who fails in her career is an Hollywood actress named Ernestine De Jongh. She later commits suicide in New York at twenty-nine. At the close of the story, Ernestine relates to Dreiser another tragic story in which an actress she knew in Hollywood went downhill and committed suicide. Dreiser listens to her observation that Hollywood actresses "counted the years from sixteen to twenty-eight as the best of those granted to woman. After them came, more than likely, the doldrums" (*Gallery*). Ernestine's account here not only points to the age phobia from which many women in that profession suffered but more significantly reveals the lack of confidence underlying her own character. As in Ellen Adams Wrynn's career, Ernestine always ecounters the problem of identity. She is an actress as anyone recognizes, but she does not take advantage of her own beauty and "sex appeal"—the undeniable asserts in her that Dreiser emphasizes.

Dreiser's women professionals like Emanuela and Ernestine share their common family backgrounds that are intellectually stifling and detrimental to their growth and development.

—*Yoshinobu Hakutani*

The most serious problem Dreiser discovers, however, in Ernestine's career as in that of any other woman here is the lack of development in her character. It is true that Ernestine's becoming the mistress of Varn Kinsey, a poet and an altruistic intellectual of the community, enables her to reject the tinsel world of Hollywood. She recognizes through him, for example, that the order of the day in Hollywood is an orgy of self-satisfaction totally oblivious of art and creativity. And yet she deliberately seeks fame and power in that world by succumbing to an incompetent director whose main interest is in sexual orgies rather than in film-making. Despite her gift and ingenuity, she always remains secondary to a leading actress. Ironically, "she was looked upon as rather serious . . . and directors desired and required types which were all that youth and beauty meant but without much brains. In Dreiser's assumption, then, she is neither brilliant nor ignorant; she is neither accomplished nor innocent. Like Ellen Adams Wrynn, Ernestine is denied possible success because of a dilemma: although she has sufficient intelligence to reach the top of her profession, given the guidance of a lover like Kinsey, she can never reach her goal, nor is she content to take a secondary role in her profession.

In Dreiser's conception of the success dream, the lack of flexibility and growth in the woman's training for her profession has a direct corollary to the degree of her failure. Ernestine's failure, unlike Ellen's, is tragic not because of her suicide, but because there has been less interaction in her relations to her lovers than in the case of Ellen. The problem Ernestine faces in her life with Kinsey is thus more serious than that of Ellen in her relations with McKail. Ellen can gain artistic insights from her domineering lover; for Ernestine, however, her lover's dictatorial demeanor does shut off the channels of intellectual and artistic influence which she desperately needs. Even though Ernestine, like Ellen, displays her sympathy and admiration for her lover's noble spirits, she must dictate her own code of behavior and thus ruin her meaningful relationship with him. This naiveté is also

evident in her sexual life. Ernestine's attitude toward sex is immature, for her beauty and physical appeal are used only for self-satisfaction and for mercenary gain. Dreiser suggests that she is guilty of isolating her sexual life from the meaningful communion between man and woman. For she makes sex the touchstone of her own pleasure and, in particular, her vanity in quest of success.

Ernestine's attitude toward sex thus contrasts with Albertine's. Albertine is a strong-willed but graceful woman—a wife, a mother, and the mistress of a sculptor. Dreiser admires Albertine because she is capable of making sex grow beyond the realm of the physical. For her, unlike Ernestine, sex represents a search for human relatedness, a way out of her otherwise meaningless social and economic struggle. Besides saving herself from loneliness and isolation, she gives birth to an illegitimate child whose identity is kept only to themselves. Ernestine's way of life, on the contrary, is sterile. For Ernestine, the call of sex is not transformed in character since it is not supported by a genuine feeling of love and responsibility. In short, Ernestine's sexual life neither enriches her life nor improves her talent as an actress.

The weaker qualities of mind and heart exhibited in the failures these heroines have faced in their careers can be related to their backgrounds. Except for Esther Norn, all of the women in search of success in their chosen fields come from wealthy, conservative families. In the case of Emanuela, her family's Puritan heritage—despite her broad education in literature—has made her sexually frigid for life. Failing to seduce her at a crucial point in their relations, Dreiser bluntly tells her: "You're suffering from an inhibition of some kind against sex, your normal relationship to men and life" (*Gallery*). Isabel Archer in *The Portrait of a Lady,* who seems to live with a fear of over-sexed men, is nevertheless capable of feeeling the power of sex as shown in her final encounter with Goodwood. If Isabel is considered a morally and sexually independent spirit, as she is by most critics, Emanuela in *A Gallery of Women* is clearly a pathological case. At the final moment in her encounter with Dreiser—who has by then lost all his passion for her—she confesses: "Oh well, you may be right, I don't know. I'm not going to try to explain or adjust myself now". Ernestine De Jongh's background is equally conservative and affluent: she is the daughter of a prosperous dairyman in America's northwest. Although she is not sexually inhibited as Emanuela is, her family education has not helped her become a free spirit. The irony in her life is that her most esteemed lover is involved in many liberal causes—woman suffrage, child labor, and publication of radical magazines.

Thus, Dreiser's women professionals like Emanuela and Ernestine share their common family backgrounds that are intellectually stifling and detrimental to their growth and development. Esther Norn, on the other hand, does not come from such a family, but she is handicapped in another way. Losing her mother in her youth, she was raised by her father. Because he was often unemployed, as in many of Dreiser's stories as well as in his own life, Esther was forced to subject herself to a series of menial jobs. Like Sister Carrie, she manages to obtain a small part in a play and thus begins her career to realize her dream. She falls in love with a young poet of the Village—"an on-the-surface eccentric and clown or court-jester". As this relationship wears off, another self-styled poet, Doane, comes into her life. Though she marries him. Doane turns out to be financially dependent upon her. The significant point in her character, however, is that her actions of sacrifice for the benefit of her husband are not caused by his inability or unwillingness to secure a livelihood for them, but derived from her own upbringing. The reader is constantly reminded of the fact that Esther's father, like her lovers, has always been what Dreiser calls a "loafer" and "woman-chaser". This image in her girlhood was so strongly imprinted in her mind that she takes her father's way of life for that of all men. Unlike Hurstwood, who falls a victim in a similar predicament, Doane can instead prey on Esther. For example, Doane encourages Esther, his lawful wife, to be sexually involved with a theatre manager so that she may succeed on the stage. Dreiser's advice against such an adventure for Esther's sake suggests that not only is Doane a moral coward, but also that she is destined to be a failure as well.

In *A Gallery of Women,* then, the loss of self-confidence an heroine suffers in seeking success seems to result partly from her early life. The respective backgrounds of Esther and Ernestine, for example, represent two extreme cases of family influence. Esther's life is perverted by the ever-present parasitic way of life led by her father; Ernestine's is misdirected by the cloistered existence in her early life. Each in her own way struggles to lead an independent life in spite of the earlier influences and experiences which are detrimental to her new spirit. Some women, such as Ellen, come close to the realization of their dreams. In fact, Ellen does reach a point of excellence in her career. But she cannot maintain that excellence, let alone go beyond, without the help of a superior artist and philosopher who also serves as her lover.

This pattern of failure, however, applies to Dreiser's heroines who are deliberately seeking success in the professions formerly monopolized by men. There are no such dreams cherished by women like Bridget and Albertine. Bridget, a wife and mother, is the virtual head of a household inhabited by her drunken husband, an old daughter with an illegitimate child, and relatives: and yet she succeeds in putting her family together and survives with dignity. Albertine is the loyal wife of a businessman who is bankrupt and charged with a fraud, but she too survives the ordeal and successfully raises her children. For the woman whose function in life is to be a wife and mother, her dream of success is survival. But for the woman whose dream is to achieve success in a man's world, she is necessarily handicapped, and no matter how bravely she pursues her goal she fails to reach it.

Why is it that a woman professional fails in America despite her promising potential? Dreiser attempts to answer this central question in *A Gallery of Women.* The international critic of women who appears in **"Ernestine"** describes American women in a lengthy commentary:

> These American girls are astonishing, really. They are not always so well equipped mentally, but they have astounding sensual and imaginative appeal as well as beanty and are able to meet the exigencies of life in a quite satisfactory manner, regardless of what Europe thinks. . . . By that I mean that your American girl of this type thinks and reasons as a woman, not as a man, viewing the problems that confront her as a woman, studying life from a woman's viewpoint and solving them as only a woman can. She seems to realize, more than do her sisters of almost any other country to-day, that her business is to captivate and later dominate the male, with all his special forces and intelligence, by hers, and having done that she knows that she has bagged the game. Now I do not count that as being inferior or stupid. To me it is being effective.

However, what is finally lacking in a woman like Ernestine De Jongh is a stable and independent philosophy that transcends the narrow confines of feminine mentality. Dreiser's prediction, stated before her story unfolds, is that she is "too much inclined, possibly, to look for worth in others—too little to compel it in herself". Dreiser's conclusion, therefore, is just opposite of the European observer's view: the way in which an American woman of Ernestine's type is prepared in her quest for success is simply *not effective.*

III

There is no doubt about Dreiser's compassion for these ill-prepared heroines in *A Gallery of Women,* just as one is reminded that Dreiser has shown more sympathy for Jennie Gerhardt than Carrie Meeber. *A Gallery of Women,* moreover, exhibits a consciously developed pattern in which the less self-reliant the heroine is the higher price of injury she has to pay for the battle of life. Because she is not mentally well equipped, she develops a tendency to rely on men for spiritual and financial securities. Because she has a limited vision and understanding of her lover's worth, she can be swiftly exploited by him. All this happens to Ernestine, Emanuela, and Ellen with equal intensity.

The most complex pattern Dreiser weaves into the success stories in *A Gallery of Women* is that of Esther Norn. It bears a structural resemblance to *Sister Carrie.* Both women, under twenty, start out in a huge, friendless city, looking for employment but in vain. Then they are both rescued by men. Esther's first lover is, like Drouet, a good, carefree man "in search of pleasure and things to interest him", and he maintains a bachelor apartment on the borders of the Village. Esther's second lover is Doane, who is, like Hurstwood, more sophisticated than his rival in every way. Once Esther and Doane are married, Doane's infatuation with Esther wears off and Doane, like Hurstwood, becomes financially dependent upon his wife who can make more money in the theatre. Unlike Carrie, however, Esther lets Doane take advantage of her livelihood. The third man who appears on the scene for Esther is a liberal social worker named J. J. As in Carrie's relationship to Ames, Esther is greatly fascinated by J. J.'s intellectual abilities but avoids any emotional, much less sexual, involvement with him. The most important difference between the two heroines is obvious: while Carrie is "bright" to begin with and able to cultivate a free spirit in her development, Esther is not.

The most serious failing Dreiser finds in the women who cherish the dream of success is their dependence upon men.

—*Yoshinobu Hakutani*

Dreiser's conception of the success dream in *A Gallery of Women* is thus crystalized in the story of Esther Norn. For Esther figures as a clear antithesis to what Carrie stands for in a woman's struggle for success in the modern world. Esther is not motivated by honorable intentions as Carrie is; financially Esther becomes the mistress of her fate as Carrie does not. From the beginning Esther falls in love with a well-intentioned rich man only for security, but she does not possess a temperament, a vital spirit, that must serve as proof against the wheel of life. As her consumptive health well demonstrates, her striving for success is set back by every change of fortune; Esther is the type of woman that cannot fulfill ever higher potentialities of being. Each of her affairs, unlike Carrie's, does not serve to facilitate her emotional and artistic growth. Even when Doane becomes unemployed and his character begins to degenerate, she fails to take over and dominate him. She has none of Carrie's resourcefulness and eagerness to face up to and venture into all that life has to offer. Most pathetically, while Carrie at the end of the novel is on her way to "success" in her profession, Esther dies in a sanatorium only wondering about her husband who has long neglected her.

The most serious failing Dreiser finds in the women who cherish the dream of success is their dependence upon men. This idea which pervades *A Gallery of Women* is based on Dreiser's conviction that success attends only those truly liberated women who can resist men's intellectual and economical influences. Marguerite Tjader, who perhaps knew Dreiser more than anyone else living today, writes [in *Theodore Dreiser: A New Dimension,* 1965]:

> Women's characters and experiences interested Dreiser endlessly. He loved to question them about themselves, their impressions, their reactions to this and that. He was never tired of studying the likes and dislikes that made up, what was to him, the mystery of feminine behavior. . . . Women were tremendously stimulated by him, because he always wanted to build them up to whatever superior qualities they might have, wanted them to be their best, most daring, selves.

At the same time, he had come to be afraid of making commitments to any woman who might want to depend on him too much.

Such testimony by a woman reader clarifies the places of various heroines in Dreiser's feminism. A woman of Esther's type that immediately reminds us of Jennie Gerhardt is a battered heroine of beauty and gentleness, thus generating our pity and sympathy. But the character of such a woman is decidedly inferior to the contrasting stature of Carrie, whom Dreiser calls a "little soldier of fortune" (*Sister Carrie*). Carrie is better armed for the battle of life, can outlast any man placed in a similar predicament. And, in the end, even after breaking the conventions of society—in which "All men should be good, all women virtuous"—by becoming the mistress of one man after the other, she is still too strong to suffer any anguished pangs of remorse as a Jennie or an Esther is not. It is understandable that genteel American readers could swallow neither Carrie's success at the close of the novel nor her indifference to society's so-called "moral" laws. From the standpoint of liberated women, however, Dreiser's ending of *Sister Carrie* could have elicited nothing but their admiration and respect. Given a male point of view, on the other hand, it is not difficult to understand why the stories of Jennie and Esther can bring in the reader not only compassion but a deluded sense of relief and satisfaction.

Vinoda (essay date 1983)

SOURCE: "Don Juans and 'Dancing Dogs': A Note on Dreiser's *A Gallery of Women,*" in *Indian Journal of American Studies,* Vol. 13, No. 2, July, 1983, pp. 147-55.

[*In the following essay, Vinoda suggests that Dreiser's portrayal of women in* A Gallery of Women *is far from being as woman-affirming as other critics have argued, presenting women primarily as physical objects and defining them mainly in terms of their relationships with men.*]

American society was not ready to receive Dreiser's *Sister Carrie* (1900) and *Jennie Gerhardt* (1911) when they appeared, since the portraits of women presented in them were far ahead of the times: the female protagonists in them were shown to adopt unconventional social means in their struggle for success and fulfilment. As F. O. Matthiessen has argued [in "A Picture of Conditions," *Sister Carrie,* 1970], contrary to the prevailing ideology concerning projection of women in fiction, Dreiser created characters who deserved punishment but who were set free in a manner that outraged his contemporaries; worse still, he did not even regard them sinful for their transgressions. Many contemporaries of Dreiser, like Sherwood Anderson and Dorothy Dudley, are said to have hailed him for his forward-looking views on women, although his books were often published without enthusiasm and some were even sought to be suppressed ["A

Picture of Conditions"]. Dreiser was aware of his unconventionality himself:

> The world, as I see it now, had trussed itself up too helplessly with too many strings of convention, religion, dogma. . . . Is it everybody's business to get married and accept all the dictates of conventional society—that is, bear and rear children according to a given social or religious theory? . . . And, furthermore, I am inclined to suspect that the monogamous standard to which the world has been tethered much too harshly for a thousand years or more now is entirely wrong. I do not believe that it is Nature's only or ultimate way of continuing or preserving itself.

> [*A Book About Myself,* 1922]

The moral and ethical agnosticism of this confession should sound the key-note to many of the attitudes and assumptions that manifest in his fiction especially in regard to woman and her relations with man. Dreiser's views naturally appeared anarchistic to the nation founded by Puritans. His writings aroused a great deal of antagonism as they were unlike anything written before.

The American novel has traditionally reflected the sexist bias emphasizing the role-conception of woman as a home-keeping private creature who must be dependent, submissive, pure and loyal; transgression and violation of the social degree were generally punished in American fiction. Wendy Martin has effectively demonstrated that American novelists from Susanna Rowson through Hawthorne to Hemingway have enacted in their tales the lives of fallen women who, like Eve, have paid for their sin through dependency, servitude and ignoble death. Contrary to this image Dreiser's fictional women reject the social norm, declare their independence and venture forth in pursuit of higher ambitions. Their asocial placement has predictably offended the Puritan sensibility of his contemporaries. However we will be amazed to find, on closer examination, that these women do not always seem real in their unconventionality. Matthiessen's perceptive observation that Dreiser robs Carrie of warmth and that "she is never a woman in love" should be a pointer. This weakness of *Sister Carrie* points today to a much larger artistic failure—a failure on the part of Dreiser to follow the situation of his fictional women to its logical end by endowing them with a psychology that makes them truly liberated. The artistic failure, then, would turn out to be a failure of imagination. From this study it will be seen that Dreiser, thwarted by a sexist bias, created women who are not as liberated as they are mistaken to be.

Dreiser has often claimed to see life as it really is from a detached distance, but after Wayne C. Booth, George P. Elliot and such others we know today that there is no such thing as absolute detachment and that writer's judgment of facts is always implicit in his fictional transmutations. The author as "meddler" could be accordingly seen in the particular situations and events in Dreiser's fiction where his assumptions about women clearly suggest themselves. This study attempts to crystallize these assumptions from the examination of a limited number of fairly representative stories to which women are cen-

tral. The stories I examine here are all included in *A Gallery of Women* which Dreiser scholars have significantly included in the category of "non-fiction" or "sketches." If the account of Dreiser's secretary, William C. Lengel, could be relied upon, the "sketches" of women in *A Gallery* were all based upon Dreiser's knowledge of real life figures [Introduction to *A Gallery of Women,* 1962]. The flimsy fictional garb given to the narrator-spokesman-painter of these portraits has furnished me a further reason for choosing *A Gallery* for study here since the attitudes crystallized from them would be even more authentic than those elicited from pure fiction.

William C. Lengel was probably unaware of the devastating irony of his words when he said that in Dreiser America found a genius whose fiction presents "evidence of one man's mastery of 'the eternal feminine'." Lengel seems to have meant that Dreiser's portraits of women transcend limitations of time and that they are of universal interest. But Goethe's phrase "eternal feminine" [in *Faust*] applied to Dreiser is really misplaced since Goethe attributed an upward influence to the female. Goethe was in a long tradition of mythology, poetry and religion where woman has been glorified as transcendence (as opposed to immanence), as the divine grace, as Beatrice guiding Dante in the beyond, as Laura beckoning Petrarch to sublime heights of poetry, as harmony, Reason, as Minerva, as glorified substance (and not flesh) to be adored, as an eternal being Virgin Mary representing pity, tenderness, and so on. Lengel unwittingly evokes all the associations surrounding this feminine mystique by applying the resonant words "eternal feminine" to the women in Dreiser's *A Gallery,* but he seems to be swayed off his feet by his personal admiration for Dreiser. In truth Dreiser deflates the myth of the eternal feminine by projecting an image of the female whose terms of being do not extend beyond the fact of her gender appeal to the male and who is never allowed to achieve the dignity of interacting with man's world in the way she aspires. To be sure, Dreiser's much vaunted realistic method might claim that in man's world woman's presence is directly felt in desire, in embrace and love, but Dreiser could never conceive that from even a commonsensical point of view there is more to woman's being than this. Aspiring women of whom we see many in *A Gallery* do nothing more than try to define their existence in relation to man; they never aspire away or apart from man as if such a thing does not exist. There were indeed women like Elizabeth Cady Stanton, Margaret Fuller and Anne Bradstreet in America and it was not as if Dreiser was unaware of such women. In fact one of the stories of *A Gallery,* **"Olive Brand,"** mentions the rebel woman Emma Goldman who was his contemporary. Paradoxically, Dreiser received much undue praise for being unconventional although his projections of woman were not unconventional enough: they were far from being such revolutionaries as Emma Goldman. In fact Olive Brand appears in the story of that title as an activist writer who is said to have participated in labor strikes and met Emma Goldman, but she is nevertheless shown to end up as the Muse of a failed writer called Jethro whom she desired to inspire to good writing. The story thus betrays its own promise and conception.

It has never been sufficiently recognized that women in Dreiser's stories do not transcend their physicality since they are essentially creations of a "hedonist, a voluptuary and a varietist" [Lengel]. As a consequence we find in the tales an unresponsiveness to the self-generated moral issues; they even reveal a double standard that men have always adopted in their relations with women. Worse still, the "center of consciousness" in the stories approves of this double standard. The source of this double standard morality, it seems to me, could be traced to Dreiser's views said to be "loose in formulation, and inconsistent . . . his theory of the relativity of morals is as inconsistent as it is challenging" [*Literary History of the United States: History,* 1963]. In a way the stories reflect what Lengel observed of Dreiser the man:

> He displayed a casual indifference towards women. He was a hedonist, a voluptuary and a varietist—but *he did believe in a double standard.* While he was a free agent and let his fancies roam, the girl who was the temporary object of his affection had to be, as Caesar's wife, beyond suspicion (italics added).

It may not be unfair to speak here of the author's own attitude to women, especially when the evidence of the stories points beyond their fictional frame and reinforces Lengel's personal observations. It would indeed be methodologically wrong to state these personal attitudes first because that might prejudice the discussion of the stories. But the evidence presented in the next few pages will be seen to refer back to what Mark Schorer called the "author's secret world of value" regarding women ["Technique as Discovery," *Critical Approaches to Fiction,* 1966]. It is, however, possible to consider the evidence independent of the external support and arrive at the same conclusions as those we arrive at after reading Lengel's personal observations.

Most stories in *A Gallery* are patterned to show relationships between men and women which are governed by more or less similar assumptions and attitudes. Women in them generally take to unconventional professions—unconventional for those times—while uncommitted men are continually on the look out for sexual adventures. The ambitious pursuit of these sexually liberated women generally forces them out of their rigidly puritanical backgrounds and leads them to challenging occupations: they struggle for success as writers, movie stars, actresses, intellectuals, painters, and so on, but eventually are thwarted by the relations they bear to men. For in the course of their search they meet what Dreiser repeatedly calls "varietistic" men. It would be interesting to note that the word "varietistic" is often used in the stories without a trace of disapproval. In fact loyalty and marriage appear to be despised bourgeois virtues for these men. Women's higher search in these stories, then, is generally matched by the libidinous search of the men. Paradoxically however the writer's heavy hand seeks to present

the Don Juans as saviors of these women. As it turns out fulfilment for the woman often defines itself as nothing more than a sexual liaison with a man of taste and culture or with a man of superior achievement in the field in which she aspires.

In **"Ellen Adams Wrynn"** Ellen at first has a "foolish" notion that marriage was necessary for woman, but two or three years after her first marriage she realizes that it is a "reprehensible illusion or mistake." Soon she dispenses with the "silly business of wife and mother and social flutterings," leaves the child to the care of her in-laws never to think of it again, and goes off with a painter, Jimmie Race because she believes at that time that Race satisfies her artistic craving, her need for "spiritual depth and sincerity." Eventually Race gives way to Mc-Kail when she realizes that he lacks "material strength which she could truly respect." In McKail she finds vigor, liveliness, aggressive masculinity, sincerity, superior artistic skill and talent, iron will and so on. Her art flourishes while she is with him, her paintings partaking of the nature she admires most in him. As the narrator suggests, Ellen reaches the highest success in her painting career while working under McKail's shadow:

> At any rate in the case of McKail and Ellen, it had been as plain as anything that artistically and emotionally she was his slave. . . . As an artist Ellen rested on McKail as on a rock, and from heavy but sure physical base took her flight.

On his part McKail does not take seriously either her art or her as person. The narrator makes this clear: "And I could see that at last and probably *for good* she was dominated by one who was not likely to take her too seriously, not he." Ellen finds artistic success and personal happiness while under McKail's powerful influence, but when he abandons her for another fascinating woman she loses grip on her life and art. She withers like a wilted flower; her success seems to derive from Mc-Kail's superiority as a man and as an artist although, however, she or any woman in her place makes little difference to his own professional success. The assumption here is that Ellen and McKail represent, as the narrator explains, the "essentially masculine and feminine" and that woman's growth and success needs man's superior strength while the man himself *can* find his destiny quite independently. The narrative further assumes that male and female natures are distinctly antithetical and that however socially liberated the latter is, it is essentially physical and sensuous, as opposed to the mental or intellectual. These assumptions become explicit especially in the narrator's interpretations of Ellen's paintings which relate, rather subjectively, the various phases of her life with the paintings of those periods:

> There was a certain homey femininity about her which puzzled me. For how came this unity of something extremely feminine with these quite powerful and almost gross canvases on her walls? For they were not only *lush* and *fecund* and *floreate*—canvases which might well spring of an aphrodisiac mood—but broad and

comprehensive and strong . . . broader and more comprehensive, more colorful and imaginative than anything which came from McKail. Yet, with all this, an exceedingly *soft, feminine,* and even *sensuous* voice and manner, a body that suggested graceful rhythms of flesh: eyes, arms, shoulders, neck, cheeks, all speaking of *harmonies physical rather than mental* (italics added).

In this description the narrator defines not merely Ellen's difference but that of what he regards as distinctively feminine. That such a bold, free and apparently independent minded Ellen should manifest this essentially female nature "puzzled" the narrator. But the narrator succeeds in seeing in Ellen's paintings the qualities of female of which he has definite notions. Ellen should represent the female in spite of her unfeminine worldly success; in spite of her proven ability to pursue her artistic ambitions without leaning on a man, she must achieve success only under the shadow of a superior man. These notions are borne out by her art as well as her life. So Ellen must fail when McKail abandons her. Had it not been for Dreiser's inability to conceive of success for woman independent of man's redeeming support, Ellen at the end of the story would not be looking for a substitute for McKail, for "some one man of force or distinction or both in the walk of arts."

More or less similar assumptions have given shape to the lives of women in the stories, **"Ernestine"** and **"Emanuela."** Like Ellen, Ernestine preferred career to marriage, and her restlessness for higher achievement goads her, in much the same way as does Ellen's to abandon the comfort and security of marriage in her challenging search for success as an actress. Much against her first man's pleasure Ernestine accepts even the corruptions of Hollywood in order to get opportunities of acting in films. On his part Varn Kinsey, her first man, decides to leave her because he was "too vigorous and interesting a man to share the favors of any woman, however attractive, with another, and that was what success in this work [in Hollywood] for Ernestine appeared to mean." The narrative here coolly glosses over Kinsey's hypocrisy either when he swindles large sums from charity collections or when he practices duplicity for a while living with his wife (a woman of "ability and charm who was a painter and illustrator") as well as Ernestine. If anything, the moral center of the story seems to approve of him as the ideal whose absence in Ernestine's life creates an inconsolable emptiness at the height of her success in Hollywood. What is especially significant in this story is that Ernestine, like Ellen, could not live without man's nutritive love and security in spite of her liberating worldly success.

"Emanuela" too shows the life of an intellectual woman going to seed for want of love and union with man. The narrator's opening description of what he regards as unfeminine intellectuality should anticipate the hollow conclusion to the life of the woman intellectual. It surprises the narrator that woman's life should find a meaningful context other than that of man's 'love':

How could any one so beautiful, so voluptuously formed, be so indifferent to every eligible and likable youth within her ken? No visible emotional interest in any one! Only thoughts, lofty thoughts. . . .

It appears incongruous that so much beauty should be so coldly intellectual; it is shocking that the woman intellectual should reject femaleness as the primary condition of her being. After such rejection what can be expected of her? What is essentially wrong in this perspective is that woman's being is seen opposed to intellectuality. Why should a woman be imagined as an intellectual if she should at all be damned for being frigid unless intellectuality is held responsible for it in some way? The basic question is whether woman would be unsexed, Lady Macbeth like, if she takes over what has been a man's province? If Dreiser faced this question Emanuela at the end would not feel that her life was wasted because she neither married nor gave herself to the narrator:

Oh, what's the use of life anyhow? I used to think I understood what it was about, but now I know I don't. And I'm indifferent or not suited to it any more I guess. I should have married or given myself to you. I know that now, but just knowing what life is really like now doesn't help me. It's too late, I guess.

Of all the other stories of *A Gallery* **"Emanuela"** is perhaps the most explicit in positing the view that nothing at all would make a woman's life complete if she does not find her man.

Man, however, is not similarly placed in Dreiser's worldview. For his men do not see love as the beginning of responsibility—not in the narrow sense of taking on the burdens of marriage, family, etc.—but as what Dreiser elsewhere termed "an intellectual sublimation" of lust [*Hey Rub-A-Dub-Dub,* 1920]. To understand a self-confessed immoralist like Berenson it would be necessary to know Dreiser's views on sex stated plainly quite early in his literary career:

What is actually true is that via sex gratification—or perhaps better, its ardent and often defeated pursuit—comes most of all that is most distinguished in art, letters and our social economy and progress generally. It may be and usually is "displaced," "referred," "transferred," "substituted by," "identified with" desire for wealth, preferment, distinction and what not, but underneath each and every one of such successes must primarily be written a deep and abiding craving for women, or some one woman, in whom the sex desires of any one person for the time being are centered. "Love" or "lust" (and the one is but an intellectual sublimation of the other) moves the seeker in every field of effort.

[*Hey Rub-A-Dub-Dub*]

This attitude seems to explain the conduct of many such men as Dan of **"Rella,"** Doane of **"Esther Norn,"** McKail of **"Ellen Adams Wrynn,"** and so on. "Varietism" in sexually liberated women, of course, is welcomed, but the way it affects men and women is shown to be radically different. McKail of **"Ellen Adams Wrynn"** and Varn Kinsey of **"Ernestine"** are men to whose success their women contribute little; they continue to thrive in their chosen vocations even after separation from their women. The women, however, lose all sense of direction in life when abandoned by men. This double standard, already referred to earlier, is even more obvious in the story, **"Albertine."** In this Berenson seduces the faithful housewife Albertine in the name of gratifying her finer longings for culture and art. Eventually when an illegitimate child is born he complacently thinks that he had done her a good turn because she wanted a child by a man of culture:

> . . . she [Albertine] had wished that she and I might have a child. And now here it was! And should she, for want of a little courage, throw away this opportunity? Never! *Besides, then and always she would have something of me with her, something of me that she could love and be happy with, and that long after I was gone—as soon I would be, never fear!* . . . Yet all things considered, and particularly since Albertine wished it [the child], I was not opposed. *For this was not the first instance of the kind. Others. Others. But not without the consent and wish of the woman in each instance. I never forced any one to go it alone, to do what they did not wish to do* (italics added).

Berenson's "love" knows no commitment and for him Albertine is only one woman in a series. His "varietism," however, cannot be extended to Albertine since that would upset him, as indeed he is when he hears that she is attracted to another man during her tour of Europe. If he expected Albertine to be like him—i.e. without loyalties—he would not feel enraged on hearing about her involvement with Stetheridge. In anger he flails and flagellates all womankind along with Albertine for its weakness for "brains and taste . . . as well as an exceedingly grand manner." Far from feeling guilty for betraying his best friend by taking on his wife, Berenson feels revulsion for being betrayed by her when in fact his own value system allowed such a free "love." Varn Kinsey of **"Ernestine"** similarly refuses to share Ernestine with the movie producers when he had himself lived with her while still married to a woman of charm. The irony in this story is that it is Ernestine who in spite of her sexual amorality has loved Kinsey deeply enough to carry with her the emptiness created by him to the willed end of her life. The "center of consciousness" in these stories, as in others, no doubt sympathises with these women but at the same time it does not seem to disapprove of the wantonness of the men.

The point that needs special emphasis is that the finer longings of women, as in the case of Albertine, become a mere pretext in these stories for bringing them close to men like Berenson, just as the liberating aspirations of women turn out to be a helpful ground on which Dreiser's Don Juans enact their erotic fancies. **"Olive Brand"** and **"Emanuela"** provide yet another pattern where women aspire to a life of intellect, but one of them ends up as what Cynthia Ozick calls the "Muse," the inspirer of man, and the other finds her life sterile for not being similarly useful to man.

A truly liberated woman, then, has no place in Dreiser's gallery of women. His inability to imagine a woman for whom man is only a part of her aspirations has consistently thwarted him in presenting convincing portraits of women in these stories, although they have been traditionally admired for wrong reasons. The reason why Hurstwood sounds more convincing than the central figure Carrie could now be attributed to the sexist bias in Dreiser's imagination. Carrie succeeded in offending the sense of propriety of his contemporaries, but her portrayal prefigured the sexist bias so obvious in *A Gallery*.

Lawrence E. Hussman, Jr. (essay date 1983)

SOURCE: "The Marriage Group," in *Dreiser and His Fiction: A Twentieth-Century Quest*, University of Pennsylvania Press, 1983, pp. 113-25.

[*In the following essay, Hussman illustrates how in his "marriage group" tales, which Hussman argues are the best of Dreiser's short stories, Dreiser explores his thematic struggle between self-interest and self-sacrifice.*]

In a series of short stories that first appeared in various magazines, Dreiser examined in detail the mostly harmful effects of marriage on both husbands and wives. Like Chaucer's "marriage group," the set of tales told by certain of the Canterbury pilgrims, Dreiser's stories focus on the need for balancing the interests of the parties to the marriage contract. For Dreiser, however, such balance is at best achieved only temporarily by two parties whose needs mesh at a given time. Since needs are constantly changing, the delicate balance cannot be sustained without the continual compromising of personal dreams and desires, but that effort at accommodation inevitably diminishes either the husband or the wife or both. The stories in Dreiser's "marriage group" turn on the conflict between one's duty to oneself and one's obligations to another which marriage imposes. They play an important role in Dreiser's continuing existential search, framed by his fiction, for ethical moorings. In the give and take of marriage, he found a paradigm of the larger conflict between self-interest and self-sacrifice that is at the center of all social relationships.

"Married," which first appeared in *Cosmopolitan* in September 1917, was an episode dropped from the manuscript of *The "Genius"* and some-what altered for separate publication. The most autobiographical of the "marriage group," it concerns a concert pianist named Duer and Marjorie, his wife of several months. The conflict in the story arises out of the differing values that the two bring to their marriage. Duer (patterned after Dreiser) is a connoisseur of the New York studio life, a man with a rich and volatile artistic nature, while Marjorie (patterned after Sara White) is a conventional and conservative farm girl from Iowa. The first indication of trouble in this marriage occurs when Marjorie becomes jealous of the women invited to the studio—women with "their radical ideas, their indifference to appearances, their semisecret immorality." Since she is thoroughly grounded in the doctrine of "one life, one love," she cannot understand her husband's attraction to such women, and when she reproves him for being flippant with one of them at a studio gathering, Duer begins to see the dimensions of his mistake in marrying. He dreads his wife's increasing censure and control, an encumbrance that was not in evidence before their marriage. But mindful of the concessions demanded by marriage and already disposed to compromise out of a sense of guilt for having failed to be faithful to his engagement vows, he chastises himself for being too free, for laughing and singing too boisterously. Dreiser's meaning is clear. With each such adjustment, freedom is eroded and personhood diminished.

When Duer and Marjorie are invited to a dinner party at the Plaza, they are thrust into the company of social types different from the artists. They meet a music critic, a museum curator, a wealthy opera sponsor, and their wives. Marjorie is attracted to these men with their airs of impressive business achievement and their wives whose interests cluster about children and housework. After the dinner, Marjorie comes to feel that Duer should choose such solid people for his friends. She believes that if he were limited to this sort of society, he could be remade into a "quiet, reserved, forceful man"—her idea of the perfect husband. But he cannot give up his artistic friends, and when he neglects her at a studio party, the first marital crisis ensues. Marjorie, having been "unable to hold her own in the cross-fire of conversation, unable to retain the interest of most of the selfish, lovesick, sensation-seeking girls and men," throws herself on Duer's pity, pathetic in her humiliation. Seeing that she is "feeling neglected, outclassed, unconsidered, helpless," which is "more or less true," he is led by his compassion for her to falsely deny that he finds her dull and conventional. Dreiser attributes Duer's lie to the demand in such a situation for "kindness, generosity, affection, her legal right to his affection." In a speech reminiscent of Ames's attempt to bolster Carrie, Duer tells Marjorie that she is "emotionally great" beyond the hopes of the studio types and that no common soul could have such depth of feeling. Duer partly believes what he says, for the quality that had originally attracted him to her had been her emotional side, developed through her closeness to nature on the prairie farm. But unlike Carrie, Marjorie has no artistic talent through which to channel her emotions, and Duer reflects that her self-portrait of dullness had been just. With sad resignation, he looks forward to the necessity for reassuring her with lies: "He would always be soothing and coaxing, and she would always be crying and worrying."

"Married" explores not only the tragedy of temperamental incompatibility of husband and wife, but also several of the negative aspects of what has recently come to be called the "closed marriage." Marjorie's jealousy of Duer's female friends, her assumption that she owns her husband, her unwillingness to allow him to be himself, her attempts to fit him into a mold of her own design—all of these things contribute to the undoing of the rela-

tionship. Instead of loving Duer for what he is, for his ability to function in his artistic circle, she loves him in spite of his interests and friends. His response is predictable—not an increase in love but a demeaning pity spurred by guilt and the first questioning about whether he has ever loved her at all. But neither Duer nor Marjorie is cast as the villain of the piece. The wife's point of view is as sympathetically portrayed as the husband's, the simple virtues of Midwestern life as admirable as Eastern sophistication. This inherent fairness was one of the reasons that Sherwood Anderson was so taken with the story. But if Duer and Marjorie come off reasonably well, the institution of marriage does not. The tragedy is that the structure of marriage often traps two very different people in a situation they are incapable of handling or escaping. Marriage calls for a legislated self-sacrifice which few spouses can achieve without a residue of resentment. Marjorie cannot understand or tolerate Duer's social dreams. Duer's very recognition of his obligation to be compassionate to and understanding of Marjorie detracts from the freedom that alone can purify those virtues.

"The Second Choice" appeared in *Cosmopolitan* in February 1918. This story concerns a woman named Shirley whose commonplace life is uplifted by the arrival of a brilliant and attentive suitor named Arthur. For a while they enjoy an idyllic affair together, and his buoyant personality and passionate nature put all of Shirley's previous acquaintances in a demeaning perspective. But Arthur's visits become less frequent and finally he writes to her that he is taking a job in Java and that he is too young to marry anyway. The romantic world Arthur had created suddenly crashes around her, and she is forced to consider marriage to Barton Williams, a "stout, phlegmatic, good-natured, well-meaning" and essentially boring admirer, whom she had been keeping at a distance while Arthur was seemingly available. Since marriage is "her only future," she decides to take up with Barton again, but she cannot expunge the memory of what it would have been like to be married to Arthur or cease her conjecture about what would happen if Arthur returned to find her married to Barton. After reviving her relationship with Barton, she feels that she has been forced by something beyond her control to sever her ties to the romantic past. When the train taking her to her suburban home passes over a river whose destination is the sea which she and Arthur had loved so much, her infinite longing is stirred: "Oh, to be in a small boat and drift out, out into the endless, restless, pathless deep! Somehow the sight of this water, to-night and every night, brought back those evenings in the open with Arthur at Sparrows Point, the long line of dancers in Eckert's Pavilion, the woods at Atholby, the park, with the dancers in the pavilion—she choked a sob." When she arrives home she watches a neighbor preparing dinner in her kitchen while her husband reads the newspaper on the front porch, and she contemplates the flow of sad, gray years that lie ahead of her with Barton: "'My dreams are too high, that's all. I wanted Arthur, and he wouldn't have me. I don't want Barton, and he crawls at my feet. I'm a failure, that's what's the matter with me.'"

"The Second Choice" concerns the tragedy of marriages of compromise, which most seem to be. Seldom, if ever, do two souls who share the same dreams with equal intensity marry one another. The implication in the story is that Arthur's aspirations were larger than Shirley's, just as Shirley's were larger than Barton's. Arthur wants the world, Shirley wants love and marriage, and Barton wants only Shirley. Caught in the middle, Shirley will be forced by society's irrational insistence on marriage—she capitulates to Barton in order "to save her face before her parents, and her future"—to compromise before she becomes too old to make any match at all. Dreiser's point is that a marriage based on such self-sacrifice cannot bring fulfillment to anyone.

"Free," first published in the *Saturday Evening Post* in March 1918, is Dreiser's finest story and one of the most compelling in American literature. A long narrative concerning the thoughts of a sixty-year-old New York architect during his wife's medical crisis, **"Free"** describes the conflicts of a man caught between his dreams of personal fulfillment and the obligation to forego those dreams for the good of his family. The architect, ironically named Haymaker, has devoted over forty years of quiet desperation to his conventional, socially sensitive wife and to his children, all the while lamenting the fact that he has never had the kind of woman that he really desires. The story opens with Haymaker, his eyes "weary and yet restless," brooding over the news from his wife's physician that she is in imminent danger of death because of a heart lesion. His wife's condition has revivified his longing to be free, to spend his last few years doing only what he really wants to do. But this longing is balanced by his recognition of his selfishness, and throughout the story he vacillates, alternately wishing his wife will die, and being ashamed of his thoughts. Haymaker is described like other Dreiserian drifters, "wondering if time, accident or something might not interfere and straighten out his life for him, but it never had." The drift is caused by the paralyzing curse of the thinking person—the ability to see all sides of a given situation. The more he longs to be free of his wife the more tender and compassionate toward her he becomes, all the while sacrificing his own fulfillment in his wish to see her and the children happy. But outside his home the call of desire induces in him the infinite ache, and on the way to his office, he longs to be one of the bustling young businessmen possibly destined for a rendezvous with a charming young wife. The spires of the city skyline evoke in him his unextinguished hope. He does not recognize that the young men he envies are doubtlessly headed for their own marital tragedies and that the city is a seducer dealing in doomed dreams. Instead, Haymaker longs still, even though he remembers that his marriage to his wife so many years before had been an ideal love match—that she had appeared to him "a dream among fair women." But like Dreiser, he had been unable to marry immediately, and between the first promise and the marriage, his point of view had been altered by larger experiences. Nonetheless, he had married because of his belief that "an engagement, however unsatisfactory it might come to seem afterward, was an engagement, and binding." His duty to go through with the marriage had been compounded by his duty to stick by it for the rest of his life, acting as if he were satisfied.

Of late, however, Haymaker had begun to wonder what the compensation for a life of such sacrifice might be. He sees in the possibility of his wife's death a last chance at fulfillment with a woman who could truly understand him, but his conscience will not allow him even now to contemplate with equanimity such a denouement. Haymaker has insight into his own futility and recognizes the remedy: "Unless one acted for oneself, upon some stern conclusion nurtured within, one might rot and die spiritually. Nature did not care. 'Blessed be the meek'—yes. Blessed be the strong, rather, for they made their own happiness." One such strong personality is Zingara, another architect and former friend of Haymaker's who had never married and had become a distinguished success in his field. Despite the fact that earlier Haymaker's wife had disapproved of Zingara's poverty and had forbidden Haymaker to associate with him, Zingara had pursued his profession indifferent to what might be said about him. But Zingara's life is meant to show that even those who live free cannot make their own happiness. He has spent his last years a "dreamy recluse," the equally sad destiny of those who, refusing to submit to fatal compromise, find themselves alone.

After Haymaker's wife's rally and relapse, which induce in him a variety of emotional responses ranging from hope to sorrow that she might not recover, she does, in fact, die. Haymaker is finally free, but a glance into a tall pier mirror tells him that his freedom has come too late, for he is "old, weary, done for!" The story ends with Haymaker musing on the innate cruelty of life: "'Free! I know now how that is. I am free now, at last! Free! . . . Free! . . . Yes—free . . . to die.'"

"Free" is perhaps the most brutally honest story about the married state ever written. Haymaker's marriage, undertaken in a state of youthful idealism and transient sexual attraction, is portrayed as a tragic mistake, compounded with each passing day of self-sacrifice and burning longing to be free. But clearly, the architect's life would have been blighted even had he left his wife years earlier, because the guilt he would have felt over his failed obligation and responsibility would have allowed him no peace of mind. This is made clear at the end of the story when Haymaker, finally released by his wife's death, reproaches himself for having caused her to die with his thoughts: "So then his dark wishing had come true at last? Possibly his black thoughts had killed her after all. Was that possible? Had his voiceless prayers been answered in this grim way? And did she know what he had really thought? Dark thought. Where was she now? What was she thinking now if she knew? Would she hate him—haunt him?" Mrs. Haymaker's reach beyond the grave at the conclusion of **"Free"** may well have influenced Steinbeck's classic short story "The Harness." In that piece, the devoted husband and farmer Peter Randall, whose life is defined by his ministering to his sickly wife, decides at her death that he will cut himself loose from his past and live a new life unencumbered by care. But like Haymaker, he discovers that his self-denial has become so ingrained that he cannot change, and he is led to remark ruefully that his wife "didn't die dead."

Dreiser's analysis of Haymaker's sacrifices in **"Free"** is not altogether negative. He does not disparage the intimate feelings the architect has displayed toward his wife during their marriage. There is no reason to regard them as anything but genuine. The compassion and tenderness he shows for his wife is as close to love as one can approach in marriage, which is an institution based on the denial of the most fundamental law of life—the law of change. In stories like **"Free,"** Dreiser uses marriage as a stage set within which the conflict between man's desire for both freedom and structure, for personal fulfillment and loving dedication to another, for the many and the one is played out with no resolution forthcoming. **"Free"** is especially disturbing since its considerable length allows for a full exposition of the crippling ambivalence that is the inevitable outcome of marriage for the man or woman who is introspective. In *The "Genius,"* Dreiser had imagined himself confronted with the premature death of the wife he no longer loved. In **"Free,"** he showed what life is like for the many who lack the courage to end a marriage that has been frustrating or disappointing.

"The Lost Phoebe" first appeared in *Century* magazine in April 1916. One of the most frequently anthologized of Dreiser's stories, it is also atypical in that it deals with a happy marriage. It concerns an old farmer named Henry Reifsneider, whose wife of forty-eight years, Phoebe Ann, has just died. Henry and Phoebe Ann had been devoted to each other, and when death separates them, Henry slowly loses his grip on reality until he hallucinates his wife back among the living. Spurred on by a vision he believes to be Phoebe Ann, the farmer is finally led over the edge of a cliff to his own death. Some readers have been tempted to see in this poignant story Dreiser's underwriting of the doctrine of "one life, one love," but it should be remembered that he attributes this enduring marriage to a want of imagination in both Henry and Phoebe Ann: "You perhaps know how it is with simple natures that fasten themselves like lichens on the stones of circumstance and weather their days to a crumbling conclusion. The great world sounds widely, but it has no call for them. They have no soaring intellect. The orchard, the meadow, the corn-field, the pig-pen, and the chicken-lot measure the range of their human activities." Hence: "Old Henry and his wife Phoebe were as fond of each other as it is possible for two old people to be who have nothing else in this life to be fond of." In its rustic subject matter, **"The Lost Phoebe"** is as anomalous among Dreiser's works as *Ethan Frome* is among Edith Wharton's. But the story evokes the devotion of a simple man in such a moving manner that it deserves the critical attention it receives. And in it Dreiser reveals that if he could not devote himself exclusively and unlongingly to one woman, he could see beauty in the lifelong devotion demonstrated by Henry Reifsneider. **"The Lost Phoebe"** foreshadows the treatment of marital fidelity in *The*

Bulwark, wherein Solon and Benecia Barnes abide in commitment and peace.

"Chains" first appeared under the title **"Love"** in the *New York Times* in May 1919. A long stream-of-consciousness narrative, it recreates the thoughts of a businessman named Garrison during a train trip from a convention city to his hometown. The subject of his thoughts is Idelle, a woman half his age to whom he has been married for three years and to whom he is "chained" through his irrational need. He had met her by chance in the office of a physician friend of his, and he had fallen in love with her because she was so beautiful and because she reminded him of a former lover. In Garrison's mind, Idelle turned out to be like her predecessor in many ways—restless, selfish, cruel, and varietistic. **"Chains"** explores the resistless attraction some men have for women whom they know or perhaps wish can only hurt them. Garrison is portrayed as conservative and society-minded, but also as a self-destructive fool with a weakness for beauty and a need to show off a younger woman to his envying associates. The more Garrison gives to the relationship, the more he believes Idelle has heartlessly toyed with him. As the train carries him closer to his home, he rehearses all of his wife's lies and assorted transgressions (perhaps inventing some of them and perversely enjoying his own torture), and he resolves to leave her if she does not meet him on his arrival as promised. When he gets to the house he discovers that she has left him a note asking him to join her at a friend's house party. Intent on following through with his plan to leave, Garrison packs his bags but decides to join his wife at the party instead, unable to break the bonds of his peculiar passion. While Garrison is on the train, his stream-of-consciousness is frequently interrupted by the sights and sounds along the way. At one point, his musing is appropriately disturbed by "the crashing couplings" of the train cars, for this is the story of the helplessness of a man who may be seen as the self-willed victim of his own "crashing coupling."

Wray, the subject of **"Marriage—For One,"** a story which first appeared in *Marriage* magazine in 1923, tries purposefully to avoid making the kind of mistake that ruins Garrison's later life in **"Chains."** With his "clerkly mind," he methodically sets out to find "a woman of sense as well as of charm, one who came of good stock and hence would be possessed of good taste and good principles." She must be liberal and intelligent as well—in short, someone whom he can regard as his equal. And he takes care to seek out a woman he could genuinely love. Soon he meets a stenographer who seems to fit his requirements except that she has a rather conservative religious background. Unbeknown to her parents, Wray sets about remaking her in a more liberal mold. He succeeds in developing in her an interest in books and art to the point where he deems her worthy to marry him. Soon after the wedding, however, she comes under the influence of several "restless, pushing, seeking" New York women who so embellish her education in books and the arts that she begins to regard her husband as excessively narrow. When she leaves Wray, he is left to contemplate the ashes of his dreams until, on the advice of the narrator of the story, he induces his wife to return on her terms and convinces her that they should have a child. This proves not to be the solution, however, since the intellectual gap remains. Before long, the wife has found a more suitable man, and the Wrays have separated permanently.

It remains for the narrator of the story to gloss Wray's attempt at playing Pygmalion. When Wray comes to him for advice, he is hesitant to provide it because he realizes that "the mysteries of temperament of either [Wray or his wife] were not to be unraveled or adjusted save by nature—the accidents of chance and affinity, or the deadly opposition which keep apart those unsuited to each other." He concludes that the couple had represented "two differing rates of motion, flowing side by side for the time being only, his the slower, hers the quicker." The more Mrs. Wray had come to despise her husband, the more her husband had loved her, and the narrator is "shaken" by this irresolvable situation. The story ends with the narrator brooding over "the despair, the passion, the rage, the hopelessness, the love" which the situation bespeaks: "He is spiritually wedded to that woman, who despises him, and she may be spiritually wedded to another man who may despise her." In Dreiser's world, feeling within marriage is almost never reciprocal because men and women constitute "differing rates of motion," which by their very nature seldom "flow side by side" and only during brief interludes. The mutual needs that must be addressed if marriage is to fulfill both partners demand a brittle balance between giving and receiving which is nearly impossible to sustain.

"The Shadow," originally entitled **"Jealousy,"** appeared in *Harper's Bazaar* in August 1924. The story is divided into two parts. The first is written from the point of view of Gil, a man who fears that his wife, Beryl, is guilty of infidelity because of his fleeting glimpses of a person he takes to be her in various suspicious situations. He eventually decides on the basis of circumstantial evidence that she is having an affair with a violinist, but her denials lead him to doubt the justice of his accusation. In the second part, the same situation is described from Beryl's point of view. We learn that she has indeed had an affair, but with a novelist named Barclay whose realistic portrait of a woman much like herself had inspired her to write to him. Her motivation is familiar. Gil is a clerk "with a clerk's mind and a clerk's point of view," whose love for Beryl exceeds her love for him. Beryl's dissatisfaction with the marriage is fueled by her husband's propensity to be "too affectionate and too clinging." She had married him primarily because he was "rather handsome" which had "meant a lot to her then." She had realized her mistake "only after she was married and surrounded by the various problems that marriage includes." Like the wife in **"Marriage—For One,"** Beryl had quickly grown past her husband. She gives up her affair and resolves to stay with him only because she realizes that if her indiscretion is discovered, she will lose her right to her three-year-old son, whom she loves deeply. Thus, the price she pays for her child is a married life of repressed hostility. The story ends on a note of Dreiserian irony as Beryl remem-

bers that in Barclay's novel, which had drawn her to him, "the husband had gone away and the architect had appeared."

If Dreiser's portrait of the institution of marriage in the fiction of his middle career was almost uniformly depressing, he was sometimes able to see some advantages in the married life, as he demonstrates in one of his unpublished essays, "Rebellious Women and Marriage." The essay was produced after he had been totally immersed in the question of individual responsibility while writing *An American Tragedy*. It sets out to examine the modern woman's restless absorption with rights and freedom and the strain this puts on the traditional marriage. It begins with an analysis of the moral situation at the moment, an analysis in which Dreiser offers a self-revealing explanation of the temptations of modern society: "I myself think that in the matter of our emotions and our morals many of us are at loose ends. We are perhaps too much shaken by the passing of dogma, if not convention and most certainly we are considerably loosened by not only the vastly increased opportunities for social contacts and exchange, but the amazing and arresting lures to the same." But he cautions those who want sexual freedom: "one thing is sure and that is that apart from such passing pleasure or entertainment as there may be in either polygamy or polyandry or the varietistic attitude in general there is little or no genuine romance." The reason is: "Romance centers around two and two only." Although the so-called varietist does not consciously recognize his need, he is always desperately searching for real romance, which is necessary for personal peace: "without that capacity for love of one and one only—or a genuine understanding of and so harmony with one other, how is any single individual to be content, let alone happy in marriage." Dreiser goes on to say that he approves of divorce, but only as a necessary instrument through which the unhappily married person can renew the search for the one partner who can bring peace and bliss. But he is quick to point out that his recognition of the necessity of divorce does not lessen his respect for marriage: "I am for more marriages of an enduring character where they can be built on genuine understanding and sympathy and so mutual helpfulness—none more so." The rest of the essay constitutes some gratuitous advice to married couples, admonishing them to work at preserving their marriages. He suggests trying "all forms of compromise" before ending a marriage because, "as the years roll on, both sexes are certain to find that more and more they require a certain personal as well as social stability which they can never find in varietism and without it they are likely to prove mental as well as emotional tramps of the road—hoboes." The effort expended in sustaining a good marriage is worthwhile because: "In the long run—the later and soberer years—how wise and even beneficial will seem the compromise." Dreiser seldom wrote in this vein before *The Bulwark*, but another instance occurs in the sketch of a woman he had known, fictionalized as **"Reina"** in *A Gallery of Women*. He portrays the profligate Reina as a lazy loafer married to a "workaholic" and excoriates her for taking no pains to fulfill her half of the couple's marital vows. But even in "Rebellious Women and Marriage," Dreiser recommends that if a person finds himself in a union in which there is no romance, he should immediately "move and seek the real thing." Indeed, in the midst of his discussion of the strengths of marriage, Dreiser interjects a set of questions that implicitly and contradictorily applaud his own proclivities and undercut his whole argument: "Have you the strength of the varietistic life? The real courage? If not,—then what?—." The essay clearly demonstrates his characteristic need for the one and the many in his sexual relations—a need that he was never to outgrow. Throughout his life, he longed for and actively pursued the tempestuous exhilaration of sexual variety at the same time he desired the emotional stability of monogamy. Whatever attitudes Dreiser expressed about marriage in his essays, his fiction remains the repository of his deepest feelings about this as well as most other subjects. The short stories of the "marriage group" reveal that "genuine understanding and sympathy and natural helpfulness" within the married state are extremely rare. When two people join in a sanctioned and sustained relationship in Dreiser's stories, they form an unstable compound—each striving for control, seldom intersecting spiritually, socially, emotionally; changing and growing at differing rates; never achieving the elusive balance between giving to and receiving from the other that could create harmony and happiness. This unstable compound is inevitable since most marriages result from short-lived sexual passion or temporary individual dreams or social pressure. The many personal tragedies that follow are owing, not only to the relative inaccessibility of divorce in Dreiser's day, but also to the fact that divorce does nothing to ease the inevitable guilty self-questioning which often leaves permanent emotional scars.

Ironically, however, Dreiser achieved a harmonious and happy wedding of content and form in his short stories about marriage. The expression of certain writers' ideas is better suited to one genre than another. Sherwood Anderson, for example, was a master of the short story. But the ideas in his novels, stretched beyond the requirements of the single moment of character illumination, did not hold up well. On the other hand, Dreiser's lumbering style and gigantic, brooding imagination were best suited to the form of the novel. Not often was he able to narrow his focus and effectively encase his ideas within a short story. By far his most successful ventures into the shorter form were the stories in the "marriage group." They allowed him to concentrate on the dialectic which was at the very core even of his most sprawling and sometimes directionless novels—the dialectic between giving and getting, observable in the microcosm of marital relationships. His next novel would dramatize his deepest soundings yet of the human heart, torn between desire and responsibility.

Joseph Griffin   (essay date 1985)

SOURCE: "Dreiser's Later Sketches," in *The Dreiser Newsletter*, Vol. 16, No. 2, Fall, 1985, pp. 1-13.

[*In the following essay, Griffin surveys the character sketches collected in* Twelve Men *and* A Gallery of Women, *as well as the uncollected stories known as the "Black Sheep" series.*]

In 1919 and 1929 respectively Theodore Dreiser published his two collections of character sketches *Twelve Men* and *A Gallery of Women.* Several months before the publication of the latter on November 30, 1929, his six-part serialization of **"This Madness—An Honest Novel about Love"** began appearing in *Hearst's International-Cosmopolitan. Twelve Men* and *A Gallery of Women* were constituted for the most part of pieces that had already appeared in periodicals; **"This Madness,"** essentially a series of three sketches of women with whom Dreiser had intimate relationships in his early middle age, contained material not published before. Together these three collections comprised thirty character sketches. Their number suggests Dreiser's healthy interest in the genre; their generally favorable critical reception indicates that he had achieved considerable success with something of a bastard form. After 1929, however, Dreiser's output in the genre fell off radically. During the last fifteen years of his life he returned to the form only in two brief bursts of activity, and, with one notable exception, did not maintain his earlier standard. Between 1933 and 1945, nine sketches appeared under Dreiser's by-line: three during the thirties (two in the *American Spectator* and one in *Esquire*), and six, at least two of which were ghost-written, as an *Esquire* series in 1944-45.

It was the sketches in *Twelve Men* that established the genre, at least as Dreiser conceived of it, and against which his subsequent work would be measured. Characteristically, Dreiser's subjects here are men whom he had known personally or to whose personality he had been drawn by hearing about them through third persons. Patently biographical in orientation, the sketches are autobiographical—Dreiser invariably leaves himself in the picture—as well as fictional—he plays freely with time, place, and other detail so as to construct not so much portraits that are factually accurate as ones that, though recognizably modeled on men of his acquaintance, become new creations on the pages. In his choice and conception of subjects Dreiser is drawn by an enigmatic quality, which he renders and does not seek to solve. His attitude in the sketches is one of puzzlement and wonder at the human enigma: his is more than merely a narrative and observing presence, but an emotionally responsive and often philosophizing one as well.

Dreiser set a high standard in *Twelve Men* and reviews were generally laudatory. Some comments, such as H. L. Mencken's "rotund, brilliantly colored, absolutely alive," were especially flattering [review of *Twelve Men,* in *New York Sun,* April 13, 1919]. Reviews pointed explicitly to the variety of subjects presented: the fact that nearly all the sketches came in for special attention as the particular favorite or favorites of one or another reviewer attests to their broad appeal.

One is not struck as favorably by *A Gallery of Women* as a collection as by *Twelve Men.* Although several individual sketches equal or approach the high quality of Dreiser's male portraits, there is a sameness about the pieces, even though they picture women of different ages, backgrounds, avocations and occupations. Dreiser's frequently cited comment to Mencken in 1919 when the sketches for *A Gallery of Women* were in their preparatory stages suggests that he saw these pieces as being of a mold:

> For years I have planned a volume to be entitled *A Gallery of Women.*
>
> God, what a work! if I could do it truly—The ghosts of Puritans would rise and gibber in the streets.
>
> [*Letters of Theodore Dreiser,* 1959]

Although the portraits turned out not to be nearly as sensational as Dreiser predicted, nevertheless their grounding in the central theme of the liberation of the American woman gives them a certain homogeneity. Observations by Yoshinobu Hakutani in his close study of *A Gallery of Women* encourage the notion that Dreiser sought more to startle than to portray unique women: "Despite his disclaimers to the contrary, Dreiser did not have the same intimate knowledge of his women as he did of his men. Undoubtedly Dreiser portrayed women he had come across in his career, but his portraits lack conviction" ["The Dream of Success in Dreiser's *A Gallery of Women*," *Zeitschrift fur Anglistik und Amerikanistik,* Vol. 27, July, 1927]. "Dreiser . . . privately admitted that *A Gallery of Women* was clearly more fictional than otherwise and that at its planning stage it was not equated with *Twelve Men.*"

Reviewers of *A Gallery of Women* commented on the similarity among Dreiser's subjects and on the fictional quality of the sketches, often labeling them "short stories." There was, also, frequent allusion to Dreiser's strong presence in his work: at least two publications, *Vanity Fair* and *Book League Monthly,* titled their reviews of the book "A Gallery of Dreiser." The reviewers, generally, were not as complimentary as they had been with *Twelve Men,* and according to Hakutani, Dreiser's readers, "who had expected as much authenticity in *A Gallery of Women* as in *Twelve Men,* . . . were disappointed."

At the same time as he was preparing the contents of *A Gallery of Women* for publication, Dreiser was at work on his serialized novel, **"This Madness"**; indeed, there is evidence that one of the studies that became a major portion of **"This Madness"** was originally meant for *A Gallery of Women.* Louise Campbell, who was typing manuscripts for Dreiser in the summer of 1927, states that of the fifteen sketches that were to constitute the latter, **"Sidonie"** [which was published as installments 5 and 6 of **"This Madness"**] was to be one. Although **"This Madness"** was billed and presented as a novel by *Hearst's International-Cosmopolitan,* its contents and presentation have more in common with the sketches in *A Gallery of Women* than with an extended piece of Dreiser fiction. Dreiser had difficulty setting up **"This Madness"** "with the continuity it lacks now and which I am sure you realize it should have for present purposes," as William

Lengel, an editor at *Hearst's* told him. "Each of these stories quite naturally winds up a complete episode and stands by themselves. Be a good fellow won't you, and at the end of Aglaia write a couple of paragraphs that will lead into Althea and do the same thing at the end of Althea leading into Sidonie," Lengel directed.

In his choice and conception of subjects Dreiser is drawn by an enigmatic quality, which he renders and does not seek to solve.

—Joseph Griffin

Dreiser did little to repair the seams in **"This Madness,"** but what does give the serialization considerable cohesiveness despite this is the sustained presence of the autobiographical narrator. Early in Part IV, the second half of **"Elizabeth,"** Dreiser writes "I could fill a volume with brief pictures of many, but they would be too much alike to be interesting." In fact, the problem with **"This Madness"** is that even the three women who are the major subjects are not very interesting—not so much because of what they are themselves as because of the use Dreiser puts them to. For Aglaia, Elizabeth, and Sidonie, and the minor women who fill the gaps in Dreiser's life, become little more than case examples of the work's underlying philosophy, "the knowledge that my nature was not given to a single affinity or fever. I could not hold fast to one only" [**"This Madness"**]. *Hearst's* played up the shock value of the series. Editor Ray B. Long wrote in a blurb promoting **"This Madness"** in the issue preceding its first episode: ". . . in it, Theodore Dreiser reveals the impulses and the results of love with a candor that will surprise you, may shock you, but will so impress you that you'll never forget it."

It is difficult to assess the reception of **"This Madness"** since there were no reviews. It would not be surprising to hear that, despite Long's enthusiasm, and Dreiser's own commendation, cited by the editors in a preamble to the fifth installment: "You people may not realize it, but in **'This Madness'** you are publishing the most intimate and important work so far achieved by me," the series did not create the deep impression so ardently desired by its author and publishers. The flaws noted about *A Gallery of Women* were multiplied many times over in **"This Madness,"** particularly the lack of variety, the grinding at a thesis and the too pronounced presence of the narrator, Dreiser himself. It is a fact that after he published **"This Madness"** and *A Gallery of Women* in 1929, Dreiser produced no sketches of women until 1944, and the one that appeared under his by-line then may not have been his own. While the reasons for Dreiser's virtual abandonment of sketches of women must remain speculative, it is possible that he was leery about returning to this form because of negative criticism of *A Gallery of Women* and **"This Madness"** and of himself as their author.

Dreiser's brief return to sketch-writing during the early thirties began with two appearances in the *American Spectator,* "a literary newspaper" of which he was one of the founding editors. According to its prospectus the *American Spectator* sought to publish "the type of critical reaction which ignores the conventionalist, the moralist, the religionist, and favors the unaccepted and the misunderstood as opposed to the accepted and understood" [Marguerite Tjader, *Theodore Dreiser: A New Dimension,* 1965]. It wanted articles of 1000 or 1200 words and paid contributors at the rate of a cent a word (although as an editor Dreiser was also eligible for ten per cent of the profits).

Dreiser's sketch **"Townsend"** appeared in the June 1933 *American Spectator.* Although far in excess of the 1200-word limit, **"Townsend"** is nevertheless too brief to develop a portrait in the tradition of the *Twelve Men* sketches. Walter Townsend, when Dreiser first meets him, is an ambitious young clerk who aspires to a high position in the world of finance, whose heroes are Vanderbilt and Rockefeller. For a time Townsend advances to better-paying jobs and more prestigious positions, but his progress is slow and, finally, very limited, and as Dreiser recalls his later contacts with him—which have been at intervals of several years—he records his subject's inevitable decline. Finally, he hears of Townsend's lonely death: victimized by the Depression, left a widower after his wife's premature death, and out of contact with his married daughter, he passes away in a rooming house, leaving a half-written note to Dreiser requesting that he call. Dreiser has recorded the limited rise, and fall of Townsend rather than rendered it. The sketch's length does not allow for that multiplication of anecdote that had given the *Twelve Men* pieces their vitality. **"Townsend"** is, finally, another example of that favorite Dreiser theme of the American victimized by the dream of success—this one not developed much beyond the type.

Dreiser's second publication of a sketch in the *American Spectator* was in the December 1933 issue, a short time before he severed his editorial association with the newspaper out of dissatisfaction with its orientation. **"Winterton"** is more in the *American Spectator* spirit of "favor[ing] the unaccepted and misunderstood as opposed to the accepted and understood" than **"Townsend"** and, though not a great deal longer, is a more successfully achieved portrait than its predecessor. Here Dreiser has gone beyond the generalizations of **"Townsend"** and fleshed out his picture of Winterton with more anecdotal detail.

Dreiser's acquaintance with Stanley Winterton dated back to the time of his own attempts to make it in the newspaper business in New York in the 1890's. A newspaper columnist noted shortly after the sketch's appearance that "it brings up memories of events that tally with [Dreiser's] story and suggest that he has again written close to

his material" [Harry Hansen, "The First Reader," *New York World Telegram,* Vol. 25, November, 1933]. Winterton is the Sunday editor of the New York *Express* Metropolitan Feature Section with whom Dreiser has attempted to place material. Dreiser becomes intrigued by the enigmatic personality of the man, on the one hand the professional "slowly but surely achieving a place for himself as a Sunday editor of real awareness and selective skill," on the other hand the human being not particularly favored by nature with physical attractiveness or ease of manner, unsure in his contacts with women, "marked for frustration" in fact. Winterton's frustrations become evident when Dreiser notices his penchant for collecting "French Follies posters by Cheret, Grasset and Willette, drawings and etchings by Rops, Beardsley and Boucher together with endless nudes, photographic as well as semi-pornographic, by various young Americans of the time," and for entertaining gullible juvenile girls in his studio. Quite possibly framed by someone about whom he has published unfavorable comments, Winterton becomes one of Comstock's victims: "his quarters are raided, his books and pictures are seized, and he is accused of corrupting the morals of minors" and of "a statutory offense, third degree." The charges hold up, Winterton is jailed, and upon his release after a shortened sentence, escapes to anonymity in the west, his career ended.

Stanley Winterton is, like Walter Townsend, a pathetic figure. Dreiser grants him no stature; he is seen entirely as victim, first of an ungenerous Nature, then of Comstockery, and finally of the indifference and cowardice of the members of his own profession, who do or say nothing in his defense. Given the limitations of his subject, and the *American Spectator* word ceiling, Dreiser's portrayal of Winterton is effective enough. More importantly, it seems to have prepared the ground for **"Mathewson,"** a much fuller study of another frustrated newspaperman, one Dreiser knew as a young journalist in St. Louis.

Rejected initially by *Liberty,* **"Mathewson"** was serialized in the May and June 1934 numbers of *Esquire,* a magazine in which Dreiser made several appearances during the first decade of its existence. Correspondence shows that Arnold Gingrich, *Esquire*'s founder and editor, actively solicited manuscripts from Dreiser, and explained thoroughly why he made cuts and changes in accepted material. **"Mathewson"** benefited from Gingrich's editorial skill and generous word allowance, and Dreiser accepted *Esquire*'s $200 for each part (although he had requested $300).

Dreiser's acquaintance with Wilson Mathewson was a brief but intense one: he had known him during the period between November 1892 and March 1894 when he worked in St. Louis for the *Post-Democratic* and *Republic.* Introduced to Mathewson in the course of his professional duties—as acting city editor, Mathewson gives Dreiser an assignment at one point—Dreiser is taken immediately with his "gentility, apprehension, sensitivity, speculation and more, brooding and very likely poetic thought. How different from the broad, solid, sullen, conventional, contentious" newspaper editors of his experience [Dreiser, **"Mathewson"**]. His fascination with Mathewson increases as he learns from his fellow journalists and then sees at first hand the squalor of his living conditions and life style: his lodgings in a rundown part of the city, and his drinking and drug addiction. Thus Mathewson has the stuff of which the best Dreiser sketches are made, the enigmatic quality, "the mystery of character," to use Robert H. Elias's term. Part of the Mathewson appeal is related to his writing, particularly to an essay about Zola that has appeared in one of the St. Louis dailies. The essay reinforces Dreiser's sense of the compelling ambivalence of Mathewson: "in the office . . . he had seemed so frail, so pale and retiring, whereas in this article, smooth and stylized to no small degree, he conveyed a genuinely stirring mental force and acumen." Yet the mystery about him remains unsolved.

It is a dramatic chance meeting that he has with Mathewson that draws back the veil and allows Dreiser some glimpse into his subject's make-up. Mathewson's drunken outburst on this occasion startlingly expresses his concept of a senseless world and his confronting of it:

> "Look at 'em!" (And once more waving a feeble hand.) "Ignorant! Dirty! Useless! Eating and drinking and loafing, and, and, reproducing themselves. For what? For what? So's there'll be more of 'em to eat and drink an' loaf an' reproduce. An' they're supposed to be sober. An' I'm drunk. An' everybody else that wants to eat and drink and . . . reproduce themselves in St. Louis an' everywhere. You're sober. An' I'm drunk. An' you want to reproduce. An' I don't. An' I want to think. An' they don't—or can't. An' they're sober. An' you're sober. An' I'm drunk. Ha! Ha!"

Dreiser's subsequent meetings with Mathewson—he becomes something of a confidant for Mathewson—reveal the tortured psyche, the brilliant mind capable of deep insight into the human predicament but without the resources, emotional or physical, to cope with the consequences of that insight. When Dreiser hears of his friend's suicide, he registers no surprise. Nor does the reader. The outcome is entirely credible given the nature of Mathewson's dilemma.

With **"Mathewson"** Dreiser repeats the early success of the best sketches in *Twelve Men*. The autobiographical element is kept in control and secondary to the biographical focus on the subject; the delineation of the subject is particularized by anecdotal and background detail. Most of all, the subject himself, especially in his embodiment of profoundly human tensions, engages the reader's sympathetic interest. It is this last element especially that distinguishes **"Mathewson"** from **"Winterton."** Whereas Stanley Winterton may elicit interest he remains a *cause celebre*. Wilson Mathewson, for all his apparent misanthropy, is a deeply caring person. His sensitive plea on behalf of the widow of the deceased engineer, his baby-sitting for his widowed landlady (so out of character for a hard-boiled newspaperman), and his feeding of the mouse in his room all establish his essential warmth.

Marguerite Tjader, who typed the **"Mathewson"** manuscript for Dreiser, was much taken by the sketch, in particular by the special revelation it made about the Dreiser she knew. As she recalled in 1965,

> It was so different from the political, combative work he had been doing, that I was transported into another world—to the plane where Dreiser, the creative mystic, brooded over the fate of men. . . . This sketch was a sort of memorial dirge for [Mathewson] almost a tone-poem of the defeat of a human life through supersensitivity. It was what Dreiser . . . at times felt his own life might have been, had there not been that other side of his nature, the positive, materialistic, sensual side, loving the earth and violence. . . . This was the first Dreiser I had known, the brooding philosophical mind partaking of the woes of humanity without the political violence, the constant fight that seemed to be in him. Now in all the welter of action, he had been writing this.

After **"Mathewson"** Dreiser did not return to sketch-writing for another ten years, and then only in a minor way. Taking advantage of his long-standing ties with *Esquire* he wrote Gingrich in October 1943:

> This is to advise you that I have just thought of a *series idea* which may interest you. For, annoyed by the highly moral as well as spiritual characters and deeds of the most unforgettable characters in the Literary Digest [Dreiser meant the *Reader's Digest*] it suddenly occurred to me that *your* readers might be interested in a series of *Unworthy Characters*. . . . I do not mean criminal or wholly worthless or intentionally evil creatures—but rather men and women—young and old—who are mostly their own, not the public's worst enemies and who frequently serve to amuse one and another of us.

He went on to say that he had several subjects in mind that could be "arrestingly drawn in fifteen hundred or two thousand words" [*Letters*]. Gingrich promptly accepted the idea and the project was underway, but Dreiser was to go about producing the series in novel fashion.

Over a year before, in July and August of 1942, Dreiser had been visited in Los Angeles by an old friend from Canada, Sylvia Bradshaw. Learning that she had worked for a literary magazine during the thirties and had at one point entered a writing contest, Dreiser encouraged her to take up writing seriously. "He urged me," recalls Sylvia Bradshaw, "to begin writing some character sketches of persons I knew well in Maine. I managed to get several done" [Bradshaw, "Reunion," unpublished]. Now, with *Esquire*'s order for six sketches, to be called *Unworthy Characters* or *Baa! Baa! Black Sheep*, he wrote Louise Campbell explaining the concept behind the series and wondering if she would contribute to it:

> I've been thinking that you might have some characters, male or female, who as described by you might fit the series, only and also they have to be signed by me. And they can only be 2000 words long. The amount offered me is $300—and of that I would see that you get $100. And I would have to retain the privilege of editing the same.
>
> [*Letters*]

Both Sylvia Bradshaw and Louise Campbell submitted more than one sketch for the series and at least one sketch written by each of them was published as part of it.

The six sketches of the Black Sheep series, as it was finally called, appeared in consecutive issues of *Esquire* beginning in October 1944, each under Dreiser's by-line and each labelled "semi-fiction." The editorial caption "Introducing a series of unregenerate characters, each a bad piece of work, ranging from worthless to pernicious," appeared under the title of the first installment. Of the six sketches, **"Black Sheep No. Three: Bill"** and **"Black Sheep No. Four: Ethelda"** were written by Sylvia Bradshaw and Louise Campbell respectively: correspondence shows this clearly as does Sylvia Bradshaw's recollection of events. It has been suggested, as well, that "Of the other four sketches, the prose style of numbers one, five and six resembles Dreiser's while that of number two does not" [Pizer, et. al., *Theodore Dreiser: A Primary and Secondary Bibliography*]. **"Black Sheep No. Two: Otie,"** a one-page lacklustre account of a young Chicago woman whose purpose in life is to "spar with the law," in the words of the editorial caption, has nothing to recommend it; it is doubtful Dreiser would have turned out anything so irrelevant. Of the remaining three, the least remarkable is **"Black Sheep Number One: Johnny,"** while **"Black Sheep No. Five: Clarence"** and **"Black Sheep No. Six: Harrison Barr"** have a certain appeal. None of the Black Sheep sketches reaches anywhere near the standard achieved in *Twelve Men, A Gallery of Women* and **"Mathewson."**

The subject in **"Johnny"** is the parasitical father of three sons who have achieved considerable success, and it is through information furnished by two of the sons that Dreiser constructs his sketch. Initially, **"Johnny"** lacks focus: much of the narrator's attention is given to the subject's father—and mother-in-law and sons. When Johnny is finally centered on, one wonders why, for the character is not made engrossing or even interesting. Dreiser's problem here was surely the concept behind the series: he was temperamentally unable to commit himself to the portrayal of a subject he could not take seriously.

The same criticism can be made of **"Harrison Barr,"** although the fact that the sketch is firmly set in Greenwich Village during the twenties and that Dreiser observed and met the subject personally give it more vitality than **"Johnny"** has. Barr has struck Dreiser's attention because he manages to live off succeeding waves of aspiring writers by creating the grand hoax that a play has to be written for the magnificent set he, as a designer, will create. But if Harrison Barr has more potential for effective characterization than Johnny has, the possibility is not realized, no doubt because of a lack of commitment to the subject as well as to space constrictions.

"Clarence" is the most readable of the Black Sheep pieces. Dreiser has written not so much a character sketch as a modern morality or parable. What begins as an examination of Clarence McGaven, an over-confident young

movie executive, develops into a contemporary exemplum of the pride-cometh-before-the-fall maxim. There is a directness and purposefulness about **"Clarence"** that is not found in the Black Sheep series generally. It is as if Dreiser, acknowledging his incompatibility with the underlying principle of the series and being unwilling to put himself through the motions any longer, redirected **"Clarence"** into something he could live with.

Dreiser's interest in producing sketches and in having others write about people they knew under his by-line did not end with the publication of the Black Sheep pieces, although he seems to have abandoned the idea of picturing disreputable characters. Writing Louise Campbell in September 1944, after the *Esquire* Black Sheep series had been arranged for, he proposed: "If you think of another character yarn, let me see it. My agent Duffy says that he could sell one that had a touch of pathos—something that would arouse a feeling of pity at the same time that it had the feeling of reality." Later he told her about his plans to publish a book called *My Natal Health,* in which writers would describe characters who "made or filled their lives between ages six and twelve" [*Letters*]. None of these projects saw print and effectively the Black Sheep sketches were the last Dreiser wrote in the genre.

Marguerite Tjader has told a fascinating story about Dreiser and the **"Mathewson"** manuscript. The following incident occurred after she had completed the typing and was turning over manuscript and typescript to Dreiser:

> He put away his new script and carbons, and holding out the original, looked down at me: "Here—Do you want this? You can keep it—" He was looking at me with that intense gaze which had in it, unpredictably, a wild challenge.
>
> "No, I don't particularly want it," I said. . . .
>
> His eyes darkened like skies before a storm. Without a word, he savagely tore the thick pile of papers and threw them into the waste-basket.

Marguerite Tjader's story can serve as a dramatic symbol of what happened to Dreiser the sketch-writer in the middle of the thirties: he tore up the script. The symbol can also serve a larger purpose: the falling off in the quality of the sketches after **"Mathewson"** corresponds generally to a diminution in the quality of Dreiser's short stories written during the same period as well as to an abandonment of new work in the novel.

Joseph Griffin (essay date 1985)

SOURCE: "Later Stories: 1929-1938," in *The Small Canvas: An Introduction to Dreiser's Short Stories,* Fairleigh Dickinson University Press, 1985, pp. 111-27.

[*In the following essay, Griffin discusses the stories that came after the publication of* Chains: *"Fine Furni-*

ture," "Solution," "Tabloid Tragedy," "A Start in Life,"
and "The Tithe of the Lord."]

Two years after the publication of **Chains,** Dreiser's short
fiction was in the magazines again with the two-part serialization of a story entitled **"Fine Furniture"** in *Household Magazine,* a Topeka, Kansas, monthly of excellent
quality, according to [Frank Luther] Mott [in *A History of
American Magazines,* 1938-68]. Available as early as
1923, this story was rejected by nine magazines between
1923 and the time of its acceptance. On 2 April 1929,
Household's editor, Nelson Antrim Crawford, wrote
Dreiser's agent, George T. Bye, expressing the hope that
Dreiser would publish the story in his magazine. Crawford felt that a Dreiser appearance would give his small-
town readership fiction of high quality, and apologized
for the small stipends he was forced to pay in contrast to
the big-city slicks. In fact, *Household* paid Dreiser $1,000
for **"Fine Furniture."** It gave him a new audience as
well: Bye wrote Dreiser in 1931 relaying Crawford's
enthusiasm about the positive response the story had
received and his hope that Dreiser would submit another
short story. The year after its publication by *Household
Magazine,* **"Fine Furniture"** appeared again, this time
as Number 6 in the Random House Prose Quarto series
in a limited edition of 875 copies.

Although it shares with an early Dreiser story, **"Old
Rogaum and His Theresa,"** the use of a happy ending,
"Fine Furniture" stands apart from the bulk of the short
fiction in its preoccupation with a theme that, although
serious, is without depressing or tragic implications. If
Dreiser ever gave in to the demands of the slick magazine editors—and *Household Magazine* was a country
slick—it was in this story of marital conflict resolved.
"Fine Furniture" has a glibness not generally seen in
Dreiser fiction. The story is told in a chatty—at times,
even breezy—way that tends to impart a note of mock seriousness. The following passage, with its Greek chorus
effect, expressing the collective view of Opal's fellow
workers about her, illustrates the story's mock-serious tone:

> But whether understood by Mr. Broderson or not, the
> other waitresses about the camp were not long in fathoming
> the mystery. Who was this upstart, anyway? Why the
> better clothes? the Renton airs? Upon our united words!
> Why hadn't she stayed at the Calico Cat? Up here to
> catch a man as sure as anything, because she couldn't
> get one down there! And that man, as it soon appeared,
> none other than Broderson, as fine and innocent a logger
> as was anywhere to be seen. And earning one hundred
> and fifty dollars a month. And this upstart now trying to
> steal him from the older (in point of service) waitresses
> who naturally had a prior claim on him.

In effect, then, the informality is more than simply that.
With its overlay of mock seriousness it draws attention
to the social pretentiousness that is the story's main
concern.

At times the mock seriousness becomes parody. The
following passage describes Opal's reaction to a suggestion by her husband that her fine furniture is something

less than an asset in the lumber camp: "Boo-hoo! To think
that she should have married a man that didn't want her to
have anything nice around the house, an' just after she
had married him, too! Boo-hoo! To think that she should
have gone to all the trouble of trying to get the nicest
things for him, an' that would make his dirty old camp
pleasanter for him, an' then that he should tell her he
wished she hadn't done it an' that she was not as good as
that cheap little Mrs. Saxstrom because she happened to
be the wife of the superintendent! Boo-hoo!" The passage is too exaggerated to be taken as a literal rendering
of Opal's consciousness; it is rather the parody of her
reflections. The purpose of the parody here is to draw
attention to the pettiness of Opal's argument and thus to
expose her pretentiousness as expressed in her overt striving for social position.

Opal's status seeking is seen in terms of her background,
especially of those facets of her experience that suggest
for her the possibility of transcending her prosaic world.
In her response to two sets of places—two towns and
two restaurants—she reveals her desire for upward mobility. Her contrasting views of Renton, a city of 25,000
and a railway junction, and MacCumber, "a dreary hole"
of 800 people, "the central provisioning point for some
four or five logging camps," establish her desire to escape drab surroundings and a demeaning existence. But
within the framework of the Renton-MacCumber contrast is another contrast that more pointedly high-lights
Opal's wish to transcend, that between the two restaurants where she has worked as a waitress—the Calico Cat
in Renton and McSpeer's Restaurant in MacCumber. The
latter was "nothing more than a long counter" run by "a
fat greasy nobody . . . as greasy and odorous as his kitch-
en." On the other hand, the Calico Cat, like Renton itself,
resonates in her mind with excitement, color, and glam-
our because of its appearance and associations. Here "the
fine young men in Renton, with their hair oiled so nice
and laid so flat" came "with their best girls to sip ice
cream sodas and sundaes, talk of Spokane and Seattle.
Yes, indeed, some of them had been to both places. And
some of them had cars. After eating lunch or dinner, these
boys and girls on occasion would leisurely make their
way to a waiting roadster outside and buzz off. To what
paradise? To what dreamland?" But it is the Calico Cat's
interior that inspires her to attempt to take tangible hold
of the world for which she years so deeply:

> The tables and chairs of the Calico Cat were delicate-
> legged and grey-stained, scattered most gracefully about
> a room that was papered in grey. The walls were
> ornamented with candle-shaped electroliers supporting
> oval pink silk shades which glowed exactly like some
> bright, delicious candy. And there was a handsome grey
> rug on the floor. The front section held a really splashous
> candy counter on one side—all glass and gilt—and on
> the other side a fripperous soda fountain of grey marble,
> with leather-upholstered stools in front of it. Grandeur
> indeed! And the windows were graced with net curtains
> of a delicate, creamy hue, with a blue calico cat rampant.

"Fine Furniture" is really the story of Opal's attempt
to transport the Calico Cat to a Washington lumber camp,

of her attempt to transcend the drabness of the world she is used to by insulating herself with reminders of an enchanted world. In her bedroom will hang "blue chintz or lace curtains, a la the Calico Cat," and "the interior of the cabin was rehung with electroliers similar to those that adorned the walls of the Calico Cat." But her fantasy world collapses in the face of the exigencies of lumber camp existence and she realizes finally that her demands for a better life must be delayed somewhat. Marital tension is resolved and disaster averted. Fine furniture, ironically the cause of the upheaval, is put aside until a more appropriate time. Thus the happy ending, an important ingredient of the story's slickness.

What dictates the slickness of **"Fine Furniture"** is its subject matter. If Dreiser's style here is untypical it is because he is concerned with a less than gripping human problem. If Opal initially shares with her frustrated sisters, Madeleine Kinsella, Ida Zobel, and Shirley of **"The Second Choice,"** and desire for a more colorful and meaningful existence, **"Fine Furniture"** is not primarily an analysis of this frustration as are **"Sanctuary,"** **"Typhoon,"** and **"The Second Choice."** The major concern of **"Fine Furniture"** is rather to examine certain repercussions of the dream achieved. Opal's problems are not ultimately debilitating but minor and solvable. The flippancy into which the informal tone often lapses is a sign of Dreiser's lack of real involvement in his story. [John J.] McAleer's mention of the fact that **"Fine Furniture"** is an exception to Dreiser's usual clumsiness with dialogue [in *Theodore Dreiser: An Introduction and Interpretation,* 1968] is perhaps significant in the context of these remarks. It might be interpreted to suggest that when confronted with trivial themes Dreiser is capable of embellishing his fiction with style and polish. Conversely, it may be legitimate to conclude that, when he is engrossed with examples of significant human misery, Dreiser's smoothness and slickness are set aside in favor of the more powerful, if clumsier, form that seems to derive directly from his forceful themes.

Dreiser continued his flirtation with the women's magazines in the story **"Solution,"** published in the November 1933 issue of *Woman's Home Companion,* during the thirties an enormously successful monthly with a circulation of between two and three million. Among the usual women's features, this magazine carried four or five short stories in each issue. During the twenties and thirties, the fiction of many of the best American and British writers had appeared there, including the work of Willa Cather, Sherwood Anderson, Ellen Glasgow, Sinclair Lewis, Arnold Bennett, and John Galsworthy. The publication of **"Solution"** by *Woman's Home Companion* was something of an honor accorded Dreiser, for the story appeared in a special anniversary number of the magazine.

With **"Solution,"** Dreiser was again molding a story that seemed to suit the prescriptions of the popular magazines. While pursuing its author's investigation into the varieties of the man-woman association, an investigation that occupied so much attention in *Free and Other Sto-*

ries and *Chains,* **"Solution"** is without the ultimately tragic orientation of earlier Dreiser love stories. The boy-girl relationship, thwarted so often in earlier stories by either callous or ambitious young men and women, and eventuating in either living or fatal tragedy, usually for the young women, here, after an extended period of severe stress, resolves itself satisfactorily for both the principals as well as for their loved ones. But it is not only the presence of a solution that qualifies the story as untypical of Dreiser, but the manner in which the solution is effected. **"Solution"** in fact, has closer affinities to Dreiser's last novel, *The Bulwark,* than it has to the body of his fiction as a whole.

"Solution" begins and ends in the house of the patriarchal Isaac Salter, small-town Greenville's "principal and certainly . . . most honest and helpful general storekeeper." And although Salter's physical presence is not frequent in the story, he is a dominant figure in terms of the fashion in which he exerts active influence on the lives of the principals as well as in the extent to which his philosophy of life permeates the story. Possessing some of the rigor and sense of convention that characterize other Dreiser short-story fathers—Rogaum of **"Old Rogaum and His Theresa"** and William Zobel of **"Typhoon"**—come most quickly to mind—Salter tempers these qualities with sentiments of love and forgiveness which are allied in him to a sensitivity to the beauty and sense of mystery his motherless daughter Marjorie brings to his life. The arrival of his young daughter from school strikes him thus, for example: "What a mystic dreamful thrill it gave him in the midst of his weighing of butter and cutting of bacon and sacking of potatoes, to hear her voice, see her dancing gestures, her dainty dress! Carefully and prayerfully he watched her development, so beautiful to him, seeing her future as innocent, happy, virtuous, until some day she should marry some boy who must meet the approval of himself and Deborah and who because of his worthiness of Marjorie, would inherit Salter's store, his house and whatever possessions he should have at the end of his days or even earlier." At the same time Salter and his sister, Deborah, are conscious that Marjorie is "restless, curious, mischievous and headstrong" and are "at loss for diplomatic and at the same time effective control" of her. What distinguishes Salter from the likes of Rogaum and Zobel is the fact that his "effective control" is moderated by his diplomacy. Whereas the two earlier fathers lack flexibility in dealing with their willful daughters, his sense of Marjorie's intrinsic human worth and his pain at seeing her potential thwarted motivate him to bring his Christian principles to bear on her desperate situation.

Perhaps the character to whom Salter comes closest in all the Dreiser short fiction is Mother St. Bertha of **"Sanctuary,"** the superior of the House of Good Shepherd, who offers Madeleine Kinsella unpatronizing and unqualified Christian love. A practicing Presbyterian, "one of seven vestrymen" of his church, Salter pays more than lip service to his religion. The story's early details of his honesty and helpfulness as a storekeeper are entirely consistent with the integrity and love with which he deals with his daughter's plight. It is he who initiates the restoration of peace between the Stone family and his own, thereby, literally, opening the door to his granddaughter's father and making possible the story's closing scene: "And so Walter and Marjorie married and living in the home of Isaac Salter. And in the evening when the day's work was over. Salter and Walter Stone returning to the old gray house. And then, when dinner was upon the table, Salter bowing his head and reciting: 'Oh, Lord, make us thankful for all Thy mercies and gifts, past, present and to come. We ask Thee in Jesus' name, Amen. Marjorie pass the bread. Walter, how is that new Ringold house coming along?'"

"Solution" dramatizes the conflict between Salter's Christian ideals and the pleasure-seeking preoccupations—centered largely in the sexual attraction—of the younger generation, as they are embodied in Marjorie and her friends. Marjorie, attempting to escape the drabness that characterizes her life in her father's house, engages in all of the frivolities her beauty and thoughtlessness make her heir to. Maturing in taste she eventually recognizes the charm of sober Walter Stone, "the archness of his smile, the unconscious droop of heavy lids and thick lashes over his deep-set contemplative slate-blue eyes; the thickness of his light brown hair; his trim figure and graceful hands; but, above all, his natural poise and courtesy which could not be shaken apparently either by beauty or by jest." Conscious after some time that Walter does not reciprocate her feelings for him, and aware of the power her beauty exerts, she very deliberately sets out to seduce him, with the intention of forcing love and marriage. Her seduction attempt is successful, and she becomes pregnant, but she learns that she has miscalculated Stone's willingness to absorb blame. Hence Marjorie's dilemma and the story's complicating circumstances.

The solution of Marjorie's plight and the resolution of the story bring sharply into focus the moral orientation of "Solution." That resolution is, in part at least, the result of a recognition and acceptance on the part of both Marjorie and Walter of past culpability. Whereas Marjorie had for a long time tended to see her seduction of Walter as unequivocally motivated by love, she ultimately recognizes it as inspired by "that fatal infatuation which had moved her to betray him." Whereas Walter has steadfastly denied responsibility for the impregnation of Marjorie on the basis that she herself had wholly inspired the occasion, moved by Marjorie's repeated and disinterested attempts to comfort him upon his return from the war an amputee, he finally realizes that he must share her guilt. At the same time, circumstances have a large part to play in the story's resolution: an obvious advantage accrues to each of the two young people—not to mention to old Salter—by virtue of the fact that they do take one another. Yet it does not appear to be Dreiser's intention to look upon the young couple's reconciliation with a cynical eye; rather, the emphasis is on the all-forgiving love that motivates Marjorie's attempts to revive the relationship. And Walter's acceptance is based on the realization that "without love, and above all and more than all,

without such love as this, its fullness, strength, self-renunciation," his future is grim indeed.

All of this suggests a new Dreiser; "Solution" represents an about-face from the anticonvention position Dreiser invariably took. Here, Salter's, and Greenville's, values are vindicated: unbridled behaviour is seen to be disruptive and peace is restored when conventional moral values are applied. However, there are disquieting elements about "Solution" that raise legitimate questions concerning Dreiser's commitment to his new stance and indeed, about his intentions with the story. "Solution" is suffused with a joylessness that persists to the end—even after things come to a satisfactory conclusion. Some of this joylessness is the result of the emphasis on grayness. Grayness frames the story and recurs within as well. Thus "The old gray faded gabled wooden house," rendered sad as the story begins because of the death of its chatelaine, is the same "old gray house" to which Salter and his new son-in-law return after their daily work. Marjorie first approaches Walter "in the windy grayness of a raw March Saturday morning" later, she ceases her pleas that he marry her on a day of "cold gray fading dusk" and after his departure for the war lives "an almost nun-like existance within the walls of the old gray covered house."

Then, too, there is the story's narrative tone. Told retrospectively, "Solution," especially from the time of Walter's return from the war, is characterized by a sort of grand inevitability, as if, given the circumstance of Walter's visible physical handicap, things must irrevocably move towards a foregone conclusion. Such a paragraph as the following, describing a visit to Walter by Wanda, his one-time fiancée, carries this note of inevitability:

> And so more strange days in which anxious and curious people thought and acted variously. Wanda, for instance, calling on Walter in a dubious mood and recoiling at the sight of his empty sleeve in his right-hand pocket, his emaciated body, and so alienating Stone at once and forever. And after her none other than old Salter, only not directly to Walter but to his father.

In this paragraph, composed entirely of sentence fragments, either present or past participles are substituted for verbs. The effect is as of events perceived as having moved swiftly along as if everything were *fait accompli*. Enhancing the effect of paragraphs similar to the sample is the frequent use of such paragraph openings as "And so," "And then," "And after that." The joint impact of these devices is what gives the closing portions, especially, of "Solution" their particular flavor.

What significance is to be placed on these apparent contrarieties in "Solution"? Is it possible that Dreiser was writing for two audiences at once? Was he deliberately giving the *Woman's Home Companion* readership what it wanted while imposing on the story a suggestive dimension that would cause at least perceptive readers to question his pat solution? Do the ambiguities in the story reflect Dreiser's inability or unwillingness to commit himself unreservedly to a revised vision of life? Clearly, given the context of **"Solution,"** these and similar questions are relevant ones, if not easily answered. On balance, however, it must be said that the major thrust of **"Solution"** is towards an affirmation of conventional American moral values.

The month following the appearance of **"Solution"** saw the publication of another Dreiser short story; **"Tabloid Tragedy"** was carried in the December 1933 issue of *Hearst's International-Cosmopolitan,* the magazine that had published **"The Wages of Sin"** nearly a decade before. The prepublication correspondence regarding this story—it had borne in manuscript form the enigmatic title **"It Is Parallels That Are Deadly"**—is of considerable interest for it brings into focus the question of Dreiser's apparently changing attitude about resisting the requirements of magazine editors. A dramatization of the tension within a married man caught up between his duty to divulge the truth about a murder to which he has been witness and the pressure on him to protect his own reputation and that of his girl friend, **"Tabloid Tragedy,"** as published, ends with the man cut adrift by both wife and paramour—hardly the stuff of slick magazine fiction. *Hearst's* editor, William Lengel, apparently told Dreiser's agent, Bye, that he would have preferred a happier ending, for Bye's letter of 17 March 1932 informed the editor that he had talked to Dreiser about changing the ending and felt confident that he could persuade him to do so. Dreiser's penciled addendum on a copy of this letter appears to confirm Bye's assumption that Dreiser might be prevailed upon to change the ending: "Dear Will: This is silly. Bye asked if the ending could be changed. It could in two ways—by returning to his wife, by reconciliation with the girl. In final book form the story will stay as written." Then on June 13, Dreiser wrote from El Paso to an aide: "Airmailed Lengel to-day new ending for **"It Is Parallels That Are Deadly,"** also wired him. If he is not quite satisfied have him change it to suit himself, and mail me through you, final copy of revision."

It is reasonable to assume that **"Tabloid Tragedy"** "[stayed] as written" even in its magazine form. If Lengel ultimately did prevail on Dreiser to change the ending, one staggers to think what the original ending must have been. As it is, it is dark indeed:

> [Thompson's] one inescapable and painful thought was: "I tried to do good, didn't I? And just see how I am rewarded. Just see! That little difference in time that I couldn't explain has made this enormous difference in my life. Whatever else I am, I am no murderer, and these other people are. I was trying to do good. And they, by lying, have got away with evil. If I reestablish myself it is going to be a long, slow fight. These people murder and yet here is Tony in his garden and Frank in his restaurant." Thompson walked on confused, irritated, disillusioned, toward the new life he was going to try to make.

"Tabloid Tragedy"'s concluding paragraph suggests a familiar Dreiserian dilemma. Thompson, having found himself in a predicament in which each of the two obvious solutions he might choose will produce its own distasteful repercussions, attempts to extricate himself by inventing an alibi and finds not only his life ruined as a result but his attempt at seeing justice done thwarted as well. It is the delineation of Thompson's dilemma that is clearly intended to be the *raison d'être* of **"Tabloid Tragedy."** The editor's preamble on the title page bears this out:

> Suppose you saw a murder committed?
>
> Suppose you were a married man, and with you was a young woman not your wife?
>
> *Should you permit the perpetrators of that crime to go free so as to protect the name of that young woman? Or should you go to the authorities and tell what you saw?*
>
> That was the problem confronting the man in this powerful story.
>
> What he did and what happened to him truly make another "American Tragedy."

However, the American tragedy of Thompson vies for attention with the sensational tragedy that is conventionally the fare of the tabloid newspapers. The examination of the protagonist's inner turmoil is forced to share attention with the story of the murder of Luigi Del Papa, the ensuing investigation and trial of Frank and Tony Palmeri, and their subsequent release. As in his early **"A Story of Stories,"** where he is taken up with reporting interesting factual detail, Dreiser becomes so absorbed with describing the mildly lurid details of Rosie Palmeri's extramarital antics, Tony's—and his brother Frank's—response to her carryings-on, and the precourt and courtroom examination and cross-examination, that he loses sight of his major subject over extended portions of the story. At least in retrospect, Dreiser seems to have been conscious of the double impact **"Tabloid Tragedy"** had. His secretary, answering an inquiry about Dreiser's source, wrote, two months after the story's appearance: **"TABLOID TRAGEDY** really combines two cases which were matters of newspaper comment—the married man and the girl, and the Italian family's difficulties. It simply occurred to Mr. Dreiser that both phases might very easily have been involved, in real life, in one tragedy, and he wrote **TABLOID TRAGEDY** which combines the two." As for the *Hearst's* editors, their presentation of the story highlighted its more spectacular features. The title is spread across the top of two pages in large type and framed by cuts of first pages of tabloid newspapers carrying such blaring headlines as MURDER, KILLERS, and SLAYING.

Assuredly the diffusion of interest detracts from the overall effectiveness of **"Tabloid Tragedy"** as a psychological study. And there are other, and more serious, problems as well. Clearly, the narrator is in sympathy with Thompson and praises his refusal to deny his role in the process of justice. Compared to Marcella, who is "hard," "cold and calculating," he is "impulsive and generous"; compared to the townspeople, who first applaud his act of heroism and then condemn his tactlessness, he is a model of persistence and single-mindedness. But at the same time Thompson is a man whose faults cannot easily be glossed over. If he can excuse his philandering by "[believing] the whole trouble of his life sprang from his wife, who was so cross and faultfinding that he couldn't enjoy himself around his home," the facts remain that he is a liar and a perjurer and that he has induced Marcella to lie and to perjure herself—facts which he seems never consciously to acknowledge as faults. And although his "Whatever else I am, I am not a murderer" betrays a certain vague acknowledgment of his human foibles, he is completely blind to the implications, for himself, of his statement, "And they by lying have got away with evil." Dreiser's discarded title for the story, **"It Is Parallels That Are Deadly,"** has particular application here. The parallels that are fatal to Thompson are those that are unperceived by him; the kind of blindness that renders Thompson unaware of his own lies reveals a soul hardened to deception. To the end Thompson remains "thoroughly convinced that he had been betrayed by his life's finest impulse." It is clear that Dreiser wishes to make this point of Thompson's self-deceit; it is questionable that he renders it altogether effectively. The side of Thompson that is "generous" and courageous is not reconciled with the side of him that is unprincipled and deceitful. We are not sure how he is to be seen—in the same way that we are not sure whether the story is to be seen as a study of interior tension or a feature story from a tabloid newspaper.

There is, furthermore, in **"Tabloid Tragedy,"** a narrative fuzziness characteristic of much Dreiser short fiction. For one thing, the omniscient narrator speaks in many voices, and one is not always certain which voice is meant to predominate in a given instance. A case in point is the narrator as a morally conscious voice who attempts to enlist the reader's sympathy by making him a confidant. The story begins with its direct appeal to the reader, phrased in the imperative mood ("First think of moonlight, romance, illicit love"), pursues a chatty tone in many places ("And so now what of Rosie Palmeri and Tony Palmeri and Frank Palmeri and the late departed Luigi Del Papa? Well, just this") and reverts occasionally to the direct address of the reader ("The reader may guess how feverish and really fatal it all was . . ."). This voice is strongest in the following paragraphs when, having described the lovers' witnessing of the murder, it obtrudes with a sort of "voice over" effect on the action:

> But with what thoughts! That murder! Their indifference! For was not Thompson strong, and still young? And might he not have prevented this? But no! There had been this social thing, this social fear, the prospect of their own characters jeopardized that had held them dumb and numb.

> And then Thompson seated at the wheel of his car, its lights still dark, listening, and then backing swiftly out and into the main road, but turning in the opposite direction. And without one wish on the part of either to

see the body. Whose was it? In what condition now? How mangled? Or was there yet life? And they were running away. God! Both were running away. Yet it was Marcella who first said: "Oh, I hope we don't meet anyone. Think! Think! Oh, how terrible!"

Here one is aware of the moral voice but not always sure when it begins or ends and gives way to the conscience-stricken inner voices of Marcella or Thompson.

The imprecision and diffusion of **"Tabloid Tragedy"** militate against its effectiveness. If "What [Thompson] did and what happened to him truly make another 'American Tragedy,'" as the editorial preamble claims, **"Tabloid Tragedy"** is a far cry from Dreiser's 1925 novel in terms of both emotional intensity and artistic execution.

"Start in Life," a piece that appeared a year after **"Tabloid Tragedy,"** is reflective of Dreiser's tendency, especially toward the end of his career, to blur the distinction between the short story and the personal sketch. Carried in the October 1934 issue of *Scribner's,* one of the quality group of magazines in which Dreiser had long sought to place his fiction, **"A Start in Life"** had been through hard times. It had been rejected by *Cosmopolitan, Collier's, Saturday Evening Post, Woman's Home Companion* (despite the editor's previously stated request for a story), *American Magazine, Delineator,* and *Pictorial Review. Collier's* rejected the story, wrote Dreiser's agent, Maxim Lieber, because it lacked mass magazine appeal. And despite Dreiser's insistence that he would not take less than $500 for it, he had to accept the *Scribner's* offer of $275.

"A Start in Life" is structured as the first-person narration of one not directly involved in the action he is describing but intrigued by the nature of certain developments in his protagonist-subject's life. It is less a dramatic presentation than a recapitulation, given at such intervals as the paths of subject and narrator cross, of segments of the subject's life. Direct discourse is kept to a minimum; when it does occur it is usually to render brief parts of conversations held between the narrator and his subject or the subject's wife, and it projects more a tone of scientific interest than a feeling of personal involvement in the subject's extremely painful predicament. As such, it most closely resembles Dreiser's earlier story **"Marriage—for One,"** and is in sharp contrast to other stories of first-person narration, notably **"Convention,"** for example, where the narrators are not merely listeners and recounters but become dramatically involved, either actively or psychologically, in the events they detail. **"A Start in Life"** is the examination of a character that intrigues Dreiser and what strongly suggests that it is more fact than fiction—despite the label on the *Scribner's* cover and the editorial caption, "A Story by the Author of 'An American Tragedy'" on the title page—is the identification of the narrator as "Mr. Dreiser" by one of the characters.

Dreiser's subject in **"A Start in Life"** is Nelson Peterson, a Swedish American from "the Dakotas" who comes to New York to fulfill a "very considerable and . . . arresting ambition" to write. The story is the history of how that ambition is brought to fruition. That history is related in the words of the narrator who, although not passionately taken up in the plight of his subject, is nevertheless fascinated by a life that provides insight into the nature of artistic development. The detached stance of the narrator is frequently reflected by a choice of word and phrase that is calculated to play down the potential involvement in his subject's dilemma and resolution of it. At one point he remarks of Peterson: "Curiously enough, as I noted, he was not so much pained and irritated at any time by the difficulties of life as he was by a gnawing doubt as to his own talent for creative writing." Later, commenting on Peterson's girl friend, he says: "What came to the surface, and soon, was the interesting psychological fact that Amalie also was a writer . . .". And, referring to the new Peterson, he says: "My conclusion was that I was facing a man who was facing a second choice and doing his best to make himself like it." Words and expressions such as "curiously enough," "noted," "the interesting psychological fact," "my conclusion," in the context, give the narrator's recapitulation the tone of an intriguing case history.

Beyond this, certain facets of descriptive detail seem calculated to impose more of an atmosphere of reality than would normally be found in a piece of fiction. The following description of the contents of a country school library is a case in point: "There were books there, also the village, as well as an occasional Minneapolis or St. Paul paper, and these, plus some magazines and weeklies—*Cosmopolitan, Saturday Evening Post, Collier's*— all had made him conscious of the great world without." Here the mention of three magazines places a documentary note on the passage and one recalls Dreiser's earlier practice of fictionalizing even the most patently autobiographical stories—**"A Story of Stories,"** for example, his short fiction version of three chapters from *A Book about Myself,* where he changes the names not only of the two reporters competing for a news story but of their two newspapers as well. Because of such documentary touches and because of the tone of scientific interest, the reader is not altogether surprised to find, in the third last paragraph of **"A Start in Life,"** the hitherto unnamed narrator referred to as "Mr. Dreiser."

Dreiser repeated the first-person narrative structure he used in **"A Start in Life,"** but in much more sophisticated fashion, in his last published story, **"The Tithe of the Lord."** Available as early as 1934, this story appeared in the July 1938 issue of *Esquire,* the new but immediately successful men's magazine which sought "a breadth of editorial pattern" and published the very top rung of contemporary writers, including Thomas Mann, Hemingway, and Fitzgerald [Theodore Bernard Peterson, *Magazines in the Twentieth Century,* 1956]. Once again Dreiser's hopes for remuneration were far in excess of what he actually received. In 1934 he wanted *Liberty* to pay $1,500; four years later he accepted *Esquire's* $300 stipend.

If the appearance of a religious story in *Esquire* seems inconsistent with that magazine's hedonistic reputation—

Esquire actively sought from other magazine editors manuscripts by well known writers "that seemed too daring or too different for them to use"—it can be attributed both to the appeal of the Dreiser byline and to editor Arnold Gingrich's stated editorial policy: "We wanted always to feel that the reader could never feel sure, as he turned from one page to the next and from one issue to the next, of what might be coming up" [Peterson]. **"The Tithe of the Lord"** must surely have surprised *Esquire's* fashionable clientele. Although superficially a "man's" story, with it combines, trusts, big businessmen, and bankers, it articulates themes that are essentially philosophical, moral, and religious rather than entrepreneurial and financial.

The central situation of **"The Tithe of the Lord"** is described in a two-paragraph preamble to the story, printed on the title page and probably written by an editor:

> Sitting there, cold and helpless, on a park bench, the thought intrigued Benziger. "Suppose I do just that . . . make a bargain with the Lord? Supposing, here and now, I should try to make such a contract? Would it work?" Would the Lord, for instance, prosper him as He had prospered his father, he who was now so miserable, so at odds with the world? Assuming there was a Lord, and that He really acted in behalf of those who, like him, had sinned, would He forgive him his early errors? Restore him to a decent social position; make him as well off as he was before? Would He?

> Then and there he decided he was going to try it. He was going to make a deal with God, or whoever it was that ran the world, just as he would make a deal with anyone in the business world. If God would help him to get over this despair so that he could get work and get on his feet again, he would, from then on until his death, *devote ten per cent of everything he should gain to helping those who needed help worse than he did.* Furthermore, he would leave women alone. Or better yet, get married, and be helpful—and faithful—to one woman.

The story is, in fact, the account of the cause of Benziger's decision, as indicated in this preamble, and of its aftermath: with the exception of a few passages in which the narrator, Lamborn, a man who is "identified with shipping interests," refers to his own contacts with Benziger, **"The Tithe of the Lord"** is told via the direct words of Lamborn's two informants, Kelsey, an architect, and Henneberry, a banker. Lamborn is almost exclusively listener, "allowing" first Kelsey and then Henneberry to inform him about the two significant periods of the subject's life and then reproducing their respective stories largely verbatim.

Kelsey's function in the story is almost exclusively a narrative one. His recounting of Benziger's life is chronological and in summary form up to the critical time of Benziger's conversion. After cursory description of Benziger's family background, his rise to business success and leadership, his wife's suicide, and his subsequent personal deterioration and business failure, Kelsey engages in a detailed account of the circumstances surrounding his friend's change of heart. It is clear from the emphasis given by Kelsey to Benziger's conversion—and by Lamborn as well, for it is he who ultimately "selects" what will constitute the story—that it is this event that particularly intrigues them. And if after his account of Benziger's conversion Kelsey vanishes, except in the memory of Lamborn, he has set the state for ensuing events.

Years later, as Lamborn listens to the rendering of the second half of Benziger's life history by Henneberry, he thinks: "Like Kelsey before him [Henneberry] seemed to me to be talking in order to solve something for himself." One senses that Lamborn's interest in Benziger is motivated by the need "to solve something for himself" as well. Henneberry's recounting of the details of Benziger's second deterioration and of his death is much more interpretive than Kelsey's and as such impels a dialogue between himself and Lamborn, the nature of which is at the heart of the significance of **"The Tithe of the Lord."** Henneberry, characterized by Lamborn as "in the main . . . your typical conservative, cautious, semi-religious banker," tends to interpret Benziger's fall as evidence of Divine retribution. He says to Lamborn: "While I am not a member of any faith, I do belive in a God and in His control in some mysterious way of the affairs of the world. While I cannot personally say whether Benziger deliberately broke this agreement or whether the breaking of it was, as you seem to think, forced upon him, I still believe if he did break it and did believe deeply in the significance of it, it is probable that it might have affected him in some way." Lamborn's view, similarly, reflects his philosophy of life. He says of Benziger: "While he did not very much believe there was a God, he kept fulfilling his agreement just in the event there should be one, and of course his conscience was clear as long as he did. But not being sure of this mysterious Thing, as soon as he stopped fulfilling the agreement he was haunted by the whisperings of his conscience." However, the dialogue, and the story, ends in an accommodation, as the closing paragraphs indicate:

> "In other words," said Henneberry, "you are not a religious man."
>
> "Not in the accepted sense of the words, no."
>
> "Well, I am," he said. "You call it conscience, but to me conscience is God, or the only thing we know of as God, our guide. And when we go against that, we go against Him."
>
> "So be it," I said. "And it may be that both of us are talking ofone and the same power."
>
> "I think we are," he said.

Whatever philosophical differences they suggest, both the positions expressed here reflect acknowledgement of and allegiance to a transcendent force that makes moral demands on men. Benziger, by virtue of his early home training, has been schooled in the Protestant work ethic, has repudiated it, accepted it again out of expediency, and, unable to live up to its prescriptions, has failed. Unlike other Dreiser entrepreneur-subjects, notably the Frank Cowperwood of *The Financier* and *The Titan,* Benziger bends to the requirements of conventional morality, however tenuous they are for him at times. More significantly, the story's three narrators, all members of the business establishment themselves, judge Benziger according to norms of conventional morality. What is more, they leaven their judgement with understanding and sympathy. Even Henneberry, the most orthodox of them, is more impressed with Benziger's charitable accomplishments than he is disenchanted with his misdemeanors.

The narrative method in **"The Tithe of the Lord"**—the most complex in the Dreiser fiction canon—is entirely consistent with the story's desired emphasis. If Benziger is in a sense the subject of **"The Tithe of the Lord,"** the story is not primarily about him but about the response he creates in Lamborn and Henneberry and, to a lesser extent, in Kelsey. Lamborn sees Benziger only rarely; most of his knowledge of the man comes at second hand. Moreover, the crucial discussion of Benziger between Lamborn and Henneberry takes place some years after his death. Thus, a distance is maintained assuring an impartial view, a view that recreates Benziger less as a person than as an object lesson. Then, too, the reader sees Benziger, for the most part, two persons removed; he is effectively far away in time and, in a sense, in place, the subject of the narrator's curiosity and conversations more than an entity in himself.

In fact, Benziger serves to vindicate the transcendent view of life held by Lamborn and Henneberry. He serves also as an exemplum of a morality that is essentially Christian. The circumstances of his life and of the lives of those who are associated with him familially and entrepreneurially, implicitly and explicitly illustrate the validity of integrity, forgiveness, love, and service. Thus, the reconciliation of Benziger with his father is seen in the light of the parable of the Prodigal Son, the destructive effects of adultery are recognized, and the integrity of the family unit is upheld. Affirmed also are honesty in business dealings, the care of down-and-outers, the adoption of children, the selflessness of a wife who hurries to the deathbed of an unfaithful husband. A far cry all this is from Cowperwood's dictum, "I satisfy myself."

"The Tithe of the Lord" is reminiscent of Dreiser's earlier story, **"The 'Mercy' of God."** There, two friends engage in dialogue about the plight of a young woman who, unable to attract men, has slipped into a state of fantasy in which, mercifully, she is assuaged from her anguish. And although the account of the woman's life takes up the greater length of the story, as does the Benziger account in **"The Tithe of the Lord,"** **"The 'Mercy' of God"** is, again like **"The Tithe of the Lord,"** a story in which a potentially dramatic series of episodes becomes merely the launching pad for a philosophical/

religious discussion. But if Dreiser's narrative method is essentially the same in the two stories there has been a considerable evolution in the nature of the resolution of the dialogue. Against the wistful skepticism of the narrator's closing lines in **"The 'Mercy' of God,"** "Truly, truly . . . I wish I might believe," Dreiser now gives us the agreement of his two conversers as to the existence of a benevolent transcendent force.

Unquestionably the cluster of stories Dreiser published after *Chains* reflects a consistent change of attitude toward a more reconciled view of the human predicament: this is revealed in the substance of **"Fine Furniture," "Solution," "A Start in Life"** and **"The Tithe of the Lord"** as well as in the tone of each of them with the exception of **"Solution."** As for **"Tabloid Tragedy,"** if it is a more traditional Dreiserian tale, there is surely significance in the fact that its author was not unwilling to allow changes to his story that would give it a more optimistic coloration. However, these five stories do not show Dreiser the short fictionist at his best. Like that portion of E Scott Fitzgerald's fiction written after the Jazz Age or of the fiction of John Steinbeck written after the Great Depression, Dreiser's later stories lack the spark of the best earlier ones; they are generally competent and interesting but no longer passionate and engrossing.

FURTHER READING

Bibliography

Boswell, Jeanetta. *Theodore Dreiser and the Critics, 1911-1982.* Metuchen: The Scarecrow Press, 1986, 305 p.
 A partially annotated bibliography of selected works by and about Dreiser.

Pizer, Donald, Richard W. Dowell, and Frederic E. Rusch. *Theodore Dreiser: A Primary and Secondary Bibliography.* Boston: G. K. Hall & Co., 1975, 515 p.
 A comprehensive bibliography of works by and about Dreiser.

Criticism

Asselineau, Roger. "Theodore Dreiser's Transcendentalism." In *The Transcendentalist Constant in American Literature,* pp. 99-114. New York: New York University Press, 1980.
 Exposes Transcendental elements in Dreiser's fiction.

Graham, D. B. "'The Cruise of the Idlewild': Dreiser's Revisions of a 'Rather Light' Story." *American Literary Realism, 1870-1910* 8, No. 1, (Winter 1975): 1-11.
 Explores Dreiser's revision process.

Graham, Don. "Psychological Veracity in 'The Lost Phoebe': Dreiser's Revisions." *Studies in American Fiction* 6, No. 1 (Spring 1978): 100-05.

Notes changes in style, syntax, and diction that Dreiser made to his story "The Lost Phoebe" between its publication in *Century* in 1916 and in *Free and Other Stories* two years later.

Griffin, Joseph. "Dreiser's Short Stories and the Dream of Success." *Etudes Anglaises* 31, No. 3-4 (July-December 1978): 294-302.
 Identifies short stories in which the theme of success plays a prominent role, noting that "what makes Dreiser's stories unique is that, while recognizing the lure as false, they nevertheless attest to its tremendous impact in American life."

———. "'When the Old Century Was New': An Early Dreiser Parody." *Studies in Short Fiction* 17, No. 3 (Summer 1980): 285-89.
 Purports that the early story "When the Old Century Was New" is a social parody or satire rather than a feeble attempt at popular, romantic fiction, as many critics have assumed.

———. "Dreiser Experiments with Form: Five Stories from *Chains.*" *English Studies in Canada* 8, No. 2 (June 1982): 174-86.
 Documents the use of experimental narrative devices in five of Dreiser's short stories found in the collection *Chains*: "Chains," "Fulfillment," "The Shadow," "The Hand," and "The Victor."

———. "'Butcher Rogaum's Door': Dreiser's Early Tale of New York." *American Literary Realism, 1870-1910* 17, No. 1 (Spring 1984): 24-31.
 Discusses "Butcher Rogaum's Door" as an experimental work within the context of Dreiser's first "Maumee" stories.

———. *The Small Canvas: An Introduction to Dreiser's Short Stories.* Rutherford, N.J.: Fairleigh Dickinson University Press, 1985, 172 p.
 Comprehensive overview of Dreiser's short fiction.

Hakutani, Yoshinobu. *Young Dreiser: A Critical Study.* Rutherford, N.J.: Fairleigh Dickinson University Press, 1980, 228 p.
 Examination of Dreiser's early life, focusing on his youth, journalistic work, and his career as a magazine editor in an effort to demonstrate the significance of these experiences in the shaping of his early short stories and *Sister Carrie.*

Lingeman, Richard. "Summer on the Maumee." In *Theodore Dreiser: At the Gates of the City, 1871-1907,* pp. 210-20. New York: G. P. Putnam's Sons, 1986.
 Provides biographical and historical details regarding the composition of five short stories written by Dreiser during one summer in Maumee—"McEwen of the Shining Slave Masters," "Old Rogaum and His Theresa," "Nigger Jeff," "The World and the Bubble," and "When the Old Century Was New"—and offers plot synopses of the stories.

West, Ray B., Jr. "Fiction and Reality: The Naturalists." In *The Short Story in America: 1900-1950,* pp. 28-58. Chicago: Henry Regnery Company, 1952.

Considers Dreiser's stories within the context of his brand
of social Darwinism, paying particular attention to "Typhoon"
and "The Lost Phoebe."

**Additional coverage of Dreiser's life and career is contained in the following sources
published by Gale Research:** *Concise Dictionary of American Literary Biography, 1865-
1917*; *Contemporary Authors,* Vols. 106, 132; *Dictionary of Literary Biography,* Vols. 9, 12,
102, 137; *Dictionary of Literary Biography Documentary Series,* Vol. 1; *DISCovering Authors*;
DISCovering Authors: Canadian; *DISCovering Authors: Most-Studied Authors Module*;
DISCovering Authors: Novelists Module; *Major 20th-Century Writers*; *Twentieth-Century
Literary Criticism,* Vol. 10, 18, 35; and *World Literature Criticism.*

George (Palmer) Garrett
1929-

American short story writer, poet, novelist, critic, and editor.

INTRODUCTION

A prolific author of short fiction, novels, poetry, and literary criticism, Garrett has been lauded both for the diversity of his works and for the breadth of his literary talent. Although most of the critical attention he has received has been focused upon his novels, which include *Death of the Fox* (1971), Garrett's short stories and novellas have been hailed by critics for their masterfully written and dynamic narratives, as well as for their insightful social commentary. Garrett's short stories have appeared in numerous periodicals and have been collected in several volumes, including *King of the Mountain* (1958), *Cold Ground Was My Bed Last Night* (1964), and *An Evening Performance: New and Selected Short Stories* (1985).

Biographical Information

Garrett was born in Orlando, Florida, on June 11, 1929, one of four children of George Palmer and Rosalie Toomer Garrett. Garrett's father was an idealistic and widely-respected attorney who fought such intimidating entities as the Ku Klux Klan and large railroad companies. His maternal grandfather, Colonel William Morrison Toomer, was a capricious Southern aristocrat given to ostentation and wild spending sprees. Two of Garrett's siblings, both sisters, survived, but Garrett's older brother died at birth, and according to Garrett remained what he called "a haunting presence" in his life; Garrett has questioned whether his deceased brother's "presence" has motivated his preoccupation with duality in his fiction. Garrett was reared as an Episcopalian, and his religious beliefs have informed many of his works.

In 1946 Garrett graduated from the Sewanee Military Academy and in 1947 he graduated from the Hill School; he went on to earn a bachelor's degree in English at Princeton University in 1952. Also in 1952, Garrett married Susan Parrish Jackson, with whom he had two sons and a daughter. Following his graduation from Princeton, Garrett served for two years in the Free Territory of Trieste and in Linz, Austria, as a member of the United States Army Active Reserves. Garrett earned a master's degree in English at Princeton in 1956, and although he began his doctorate studies in the late 1950s, he did not complete his doctorate in English at Princeton until 1985. While continuing his writing career, Garrett has served as an educator at a number of colleges and universities since 1957, including Wesleyan University, Rice University,

Hollins College, the University of South Carolina, and the University of Virginia.

Major Works of Short Fiction

Garrett's short stories vary tremendously in terms of plot, characters, and settings, but in general concern a changing contemporary society in which an established social and personal order is giving way to uncertainty and confusion. As W. R. Robinson commented, Garrett's short stories are marked by an "energy . . . in the rush of action and fury of emotion, impelled by passion and culminating in violence, which characterize his narrative technique, and in experiments with point of view, tense, character types, and plots—resulting from Garrett's persistent quest to tell the true story about change." In his first collection of short fiction, 1958's *King of the Mountain,* the final five stories, which are grouped under the title "What's the Purpose of the Bayonet?", are semi-autobiographical and reflect Garrett's army experience. Treating the themes of morality and order versus disorder as manifested in the military arena, the "Bayonet" stories are recounted by anonymous narrators who undergo an assortment of harrowing experiences and learn about the pain and brutality that underlie everyday human life. In the last story, "Torment," the narrator witnesses the savage beating of a group of prostitutes by police in Linz and concludes: "The things God has to see because He cannot shut his eyes! It's almost too much to think about. It's enough to turn your stomach against the whole inhuman race." The other stories in this first collection present a variety of themes and viewpoints, including "The Rivals," which details a father-son relationship, and a group of stories titled "Four Women" that present realistic narratives from the perspective of women characters.

The stories in *In the Briar Patch,* Garrett's 1961 collection, which includes such titles as "The Gun and the Hat," "Thus the Early Gods," and "The Last of the Spanish Blood," are all set in the South, which is presented as a symbol of a defeated empire in which kindness and compassion are requisite qualities for survival. In the title story, a young boy observes the predicament of a black soldier named Leroy, who after being revealed as a deserter, uses the same strategy employed by folktale character Br'er Rabbit to avoid the "briar patch," that is to avoid being sent back to live in the poverty he escaped by joining the military. *Cold Ground Was My Bed Last Night* contains a novella of the same title and nine short stories, including "The Old Army Game," which treats corruption in the military. Published in Great Britain in 1969, *A Wreath for Garibaldi and Other Stories* collected some of the stories that had previously appeared in *Cold Ground Was My Bed Last Night,* including the title novella from that volume, which was also featured, under a new title "Noise of Strangers," in Garrett's next volume of short fiction, *The Magic Striptease* (1973). *The Magic Striptease* also included two other novellas, *The Satyr Shall Cry* and an eponymous novella that relates a humorous tale revolving around the main character Jacob Quirk, who possesses the ability to change into other people as well as into inanimate objects.

In his 1985 collection, *An Evening Performance: New and Selected Short Stories,* Garrett included "A Record as Long as Your Arm," which, as William Peden termed it, "begins as apparently another romp in a cuckold's bedroom [and] ends in a maggoty, blood-spattered, vomit-stained basement." Garrett followed *An Evening Performance* with 1992's *Whistling in the Dark: True Stories and Other Fables,* a volume that includes autobiographical and fictional elements, which, Garrett asserted, "turned out to be about my memories and how other people's memories blend into your own. . . . Memories distort and change with time, so it also has to do with the different ways we remember things." The book contains widely varying stories, fables, memories, excerpts from lectures, and poetry, in which Garrett comments upon the creative process, as well as on the human condition.

Critical Reception

Garrett has been highly praised by critics for his works in all genres, but his novels have received the most notice. Nevertheless, Garrett's short fiction has been critically acclaimed since the time he began publishing it; in a review of his first collection, *King of the Mountain,* Paul Engle commented: "Garrett is exactly the sort of writer getting his start who deserves wide support, just the kind who will enrich the life of the country with his writing." Commentators have responded favorably to the insight and intelligence displayed in Garrett's short stories and novellas, and have applauded his economy with words, as well as his ability to depict characters and situations with clarity, accuracy, and compassion. Although most critics agree that Garrett's brand of short fiction is unique and not closely related to the style of any particular American writer, he has been characterized as a Southern writer and has been compared—in terms of the effectiveness and quality of his writing rather than for its style or subject matter—to such writers as Flannery O'Connor and Ernest Hemingway. Noel Perrin asserted that Garrett's writing "has a cleanness, a clarity, an utter *thereness,* that I have encountered only a few times in my life. One of those times was when I first read Hemingway; another came with Willa Cather. If you think I mean to compliment George Garrett by putting him in such company, you are right. . . . [H]e is in their league." Garrett has received numerous accolades for his works, including the T. S. Eliot Award for creative writing, which he received in 1989, and the PEN/Malamud Award for short fiction, with which he was honored in 1991. In addition to these two prizes Garrett has received several fellowships, grants, and literary awards.

PRINCIPAL WORKS

Short Fiction

King of the Mountain 1958
In the Briar Patch 1961
Cold Ground Was My Bed Last Night 1964
A Wreath for Garibaldi and Other Stories 1969
The Magic Striptease 1973
To Recollect a Cloud of Ghosts: Christmas in England
   1979
An Evening Performance: New and Selected Short Stories
   1985

Other Major Works

The Reverend Ghost (poetry) 1957
The Sleeping Gypsy and Other Poems (poetry) 1958
The Finished Man (novel) 1960
Abraham's Knife and Other Poems (poetry) 1961
Which Ones Are the Enemy? (novel) 1961
Garden Spot, U.S.A. (drama) 1962
Sir Slob and the Princess: A Play for Children (drama)
   1962
The Young Lovers (screenplay) 1964
Do, Lord, Remember Me (novel) 1965
The Playground (screenplay) 1965
Frankenstein Meets the Space Monster [with R. H. W.

Dillard and John Rodenbeck] (screenplay) 1966
For a Bitter Season: New and Selected Poems (poetry)
1967
Death of the Fox (novel) 1971
The Sounder Few: Essays from "The Hollins Critic"
[editor with R. H. W. Dillard and John Moore] (essays) 1971
Welcome to the Medicine Show: Flashcards / Postcards /
Snapshots (poetry) 1978
Enchanted Ground: A Play for Readers' Theater (drama)
1981
Luck's Shining Child: A Miscellany of Poems and Verses
(poetry) 1981
The Succession: A Novel of Elizabeth and James (novel)
1983
The Collected Poems of George Garrett (poetry) 1984
James Jones (biography) 1984
Poison Pen; or, Live Now and Pay Later (novel) 1986
Understanding Mary Lee Settle (criticism) 1988
Entered from the Sun (novel) 1990
Eric Clapton's Lovers and Other Stories from the Virginia Quarterly Review [editor with Sheila McMillen]
(short stories) 1990
My Silk Purse and Yours: The Publishing Scene and
American Literary Art (criticism) 1992
The Sorrows of Fat City: A Selection of Literary Essays
and Reviews (essays and criticism) 1992
Whistling in the Dark: True Stories and Other Fables
(essays, nonfiction, memoir) 1992
The King of Babylon Shall Not Come Against You (novel)
1996

CRITICISM

Kenneth Eble (review date 1958)

SOURCE: A review of *King of the Mountain,* in *Western Humanities Review,* Vol. 12, No. 2, 1958, p. 193.

[*In the following review, Eble provides a mixed evaluation of* King of the Mountain.]

"I shall never finish a symphony," Brahms wrote. "You have no idea how it feels to hear behind you the tramp of a giant like Beethoven." Such a candid admission applies to all artists whose creativity is shaped not only by their own hands but by the hands of one or more of their predecessors. For American short story writers, the tramp of the giant has likely as not been that of Ernest Hemingway. Since Hemingway, one might say, it has been impossible for a young writer to work within a range of style and subject matter which has been too clearly marked by the hand of the master. In Mr. Garrett's first story in this collection, **"The Rivals,"** a boy and his father square off in a manner as sharply defined as the way the bull-fighter faces the bull. In the stories about men and women the men are insensitive and sleep with other women; the women say "You bastard," and frequently cry; both are baffled by sexual relationships and

lace their conversation with "I don't know," or "You just don't know." The over-all impression one receives from this collection is that here is a writer of undeniable talent who has not yet found his own voice.

The stories throughout are extremely well-done. The technique, even when imitative, is of a high order. The mind behind the style is perceptive and at times penetrating.

—*Kenneth Eble*

Unlike some first collections of short stories, this collection makes little attempt to strike out in original directions either in style or matter. It is almost as if Mr. Garrett were a conservatory student writing out academic compositions in the manner of Haydn or Mozart or Chopin. In this respect the book is vexing even as it is impressive.

The stories throughout are extremely well-done. The technique, even when imitative, is of a high order. The mind behind the style is perceptive and at times penetrating. And derivative or not, such stories as **"The Seacoast of Bohemia," "The King of the Mountain,"** and **"Don't Take No for an Answer"** capture character, situation, and mood, and arouse the reader's feelings. This aroused response turns to a kind of disappointment when one can't rid himself of the feeling that these are re-pressings of old masters. Our age puts more stress upon originality of expression than many ages past. Imitation is, for us, a nasty word. Nevertheless, there seems some point in insisting that whatever model the artist uses and however much he draws upon the past, he must fashion for himself a voice which can be recognized as his own. It may be that Mr. Garrett, who is a poet as well as a short story writer and who is planning his first novel, is not yet ready to move toward establishing and refining his own distinct style. When he does, he will be able to draw upon a very impressive talent.

James Stern (review date 1958)

SOURCE: "With a Whimper and a Bang," in *The New York Times Book Review,* March 2, 1958, p. 4.

[*In the following review, Stern offers a highly favorable assessment of* King of the Mountain.]

This first book by George Garrett begins in innocence, with a boy's whimper, and ends in evil, with a bang.

Long before the bang comes you will know that the author is out of the top of the literary drawer.

Mr. Garrett is aware, as was the young Hemingway, of the attraction of the first person singular and the second plural ("Ask me why I pick that time and I'll tell you"), of the sense of immediacy and intimacy the confidential technique can produce, of the power it has, like the sudden use of Christian names, to engage your full attention. But Mr. Garrett is no mere charmer. In some twenty stories he says more, and more forcefully, than is commonly said in as many full-length novels. Every page of *King of the Mountain* rings true, and the author has some profound and terrible tales to tell.

The subjects of the stories can be roughly divided between father-son relationships and war, or rather the effects of war upon its survivors. Some stories are likely to make the middle-aged feel old. "Our generation," says the narrator of **"The Seacoast of Bohemia,"** which is Greenwich Village, "had come to life after the war." For Mr. Garrett, who comes from Florida, there have been two wars: the American Civil War and Hitler's war. For those to whom memories of the Kaiser's war are still very much alive, it may come as something of a shock to learn that Garrett himself is an Occupation veteran who will be 30 next year.

His is the generation that was conceived in the Depression, "that anxious time" when, in the center of Florida, the scene of the title-story, a child learned the meaning of bitterness by having to watch as a mob beat his father into a cripple for publicly criticizing the Ku Klux Klan. This story has something of the chilling violence, the authority and the power of the work of Robert Penn Warren and James Baldwin. That no Negro figures prominently in its pages, that no one is likely to guess the awful irony of its dénouement, only enhances the story's stature as a work of art.

Blurb writers are unpredictable people. Here only the first three stories are mentioned by name: the two very brief ones, about women, are perhaps the least memorable in the volume, while the third, a tale of courage and cowardice involving a boy and his father, is described as having "apparent in every word * * * the surge of adolescence within the boy." Readers allergic to surges should turn a deaf ear.

For most people, I think, it's the bang with which this book ends that will remain longest in the memory. These are Occupation stories appearing collectively under the title: **"What's the Purpose of the Bayonet?"** **"The Art of Courtly Love"** is about a D. P., a German refugee war-widow in Austria whom the American narrator is determined to seduce. Which he does. Only to discover that the woman has an Austrian lover. How the American then behaves makes reading only a few degrees less appalling than the behavior of Americans to Americans and Austrians to Austrians in the seven blood-and-terror pages that follow.

As indictments of war, of the military system, these three short tales talk very loud. Courage of a high order, moreover, was required to write them, for if you write in the first person, and as truly as Mr. Garrett, you are likely to be associated with your "I." But this author is out to fool no one. As the American lover says: "You can fool yourself quicker in a dozen ways than it takes to tell about it." And he knows that what he has said is a cliché.

Marvin Mudrick (review date 1958)

SOURCE: "Is Fiction Human?", in *The Hudson Review*, Vol. XI, No. 2, Summer, 1958, pp. 294-301.

[In the following excerpt, Mudrick provides a mixed review of King of the Mountain, *reserving his praise only for the story "What's the Purpose of the Bayonet?".]*

George Garrett is another writer who has read his homework in *Mademoiselle, Harper's Bazaar,* and *The New Yorker.* "They were sitting in a little *trattoria* beside the Arno," he says abruptly [in a story in *King of the Mountain*]; and the befuddled reader, not yet informed that the latest American Bohemia is the land of the Caesars, may be excused for wondering what a *trattoria* is—restaurant? restroom?—and whether the Arno is a cartoon or a celebrated Spanish dancer. S. J. Perelman makes his living (in *The New Yorker!*) by disposing of this sort of writing for all time: "The Patagonian *demi-vierges* were shaking their little *iabots.* . . ." In the *trattoria* story, the weak husband and the wise disillusioned wife move finally into a scene that Mr. Garrett has vulgarly parodied, at least in unconscious anticipation, straight out of *La Strada* with its chain-breaking strong man:

> While his companion passed the hat, the strong man sat in the street and looked at his legs, smiling a little. She turned away and looked at Harry. Poor Harry would never understand. Whatever she finally decided to do, Harry would never understand.

Nor, *carissima,* will Harry or the reader ever care, unless you say it in good English.

Mr. Garrett offers, also, several varieties of gripping psychodrama, one about a boy and his father who come through a pseudo-Hemingway test of courage with bathos unimpaired ("He was thinking, as he bailed, that maybe being a man would be like that, going ahead with something and doing it because you had to even when you knew what the outcome would be"), another a dreadful pseudo-Lawrence story about a professor's wife who falls for the new Italian (*sic*) gardener ("The leaves were burning slowly, going up in pale smoke, and he was whistling a tune she didn't know"), another a cornpone-and-metaphysics documentary *à la* R. P. Warren about a Southern politician, and a number of nondescript anecdotal pieces more or less obviously autobiographical and unworked. After all these, as if to prove everything else a mistake, comes the last and longest story in the volume, **"What's** the Purpose of the Bayonet?": a sardonic evocation of the hells available for inspection to a soldier of the Occupation of Europe, culminating in the scene of the beating of the whores by Austrian police—

> The women were all crying and screaming and begging and praying. The cops were running around in circles like sheep dogs. They'd beat at random and then spontaneously single out an individual and beat her down to the floor, the truncheons blurring with fury and speed. Some of the cops had their shirts off. One or two were naked themselves. They had wild, crazy faces like men hopped up on dope. One man sat on a table where the record player was, changing the records, smoking and just watching.

The purpose of the bayonet is, as the story reminds us, to "Kill! Kill! Kill!"; in this hallucinated story an American soldier takes the time to observe, off duty in the halls of hell, the privileges and consequences of his vocation.

Wallace Stegner   (review date 1958)

SOURCE: A review of *King of the Mountain,* in *Saturday Review,* Vol. 41, No. 24, June 14, 1958, p. 38.

[*In the following review, Stegner responds positively to* King of the Mountain.]

Counting as separates the twelve vignettes which are grouped under the titles **"Four Women," "Comic Strip,"** and **"What's the Purpose of the Bayonet?"** there are twenty stories in George Garrett's first collection, ***King of the Mountain.*** They are enough to mark him as more than a writer of promise. In seriousness, intelligence, economy, in their knack for people and places and their ear for talk, above all in the illusion of reality upon which, Henry James said, all the other values of fiction helplessly depend, these are stories to compel respect.

Born in Florida, educated at Princeton, tested by the Army of Occupation in Europe, and now teaching at Wesleyan University in Middletown, Conn., Mr. Garrett reflects in his stories most of his experience except the pedagogical. His themes here are the uneasy relationships between fathers and sons, the muffled struggle between aspiration and resignation in the young, the brutality and soullessness of army life, and the frustrated sexuality of women.

I find him least persuasive on women. However, there is an admirable objectivity in Mr. Garrett's handling of his themes, even when he assumes the first personal singular. Sometimes he poses problems so coolly or in such balance between two characters that it is hard to tell where he himself stands. In the title story, one of the best, a small-town Southern lawyer bucks the Ku Klux Klan at the risk of his life, when no one else will do so. Much later, commenting on that checkered political career, his son remarks that "it took a narrow-minded, petty demagogue with a wild desire to be a martyr to stand up for

law and order at that time . . . This isn't an age for heroes. When we get a hero he's a caricature."

Or he is an incompetent or an accident. The disenchanted ex-bohemian of **"The Seacoast of Bohemia"** reflects on a poet friend, incompetent in every way, who got a medal in Korea: "It probably takes a poet or a madman to be a hero anyway." Mostly Garrett's characters are sadists, drunks, goof-offs, or failures, not heroes. "A man is what he is and he doesn't have to apologize for it," says the Princeton student of his drunken father in **"A Hard Row to Hoe,"** and another boy in **"The Lion Hunter"** remarks that "if you have to spend all your time being what people want or think you are, you'll never find time to find out who you really are."

Perhaps it is Mr. Garrett himself airing those quasi-existential, quasi-quietist, limp, and uncommitted opinions. I hope not, and I think not, because under his presentation of these characters, as under his presentation of the demoralized army, is what I take to be a controlled anger, a moral conviction. I take him to be with the poets and madmen.

J. A. Bryant, Jr.   (review date 1963)

SOURCE: A review of *In the Briar Patch,* in *The Sewanee Review,* Vol. LXXI, No. 1, January-March, 1963, pp. 115-22.

[*In the following excerpt, Bryant offers a highly favorable review of* In the Briar Patch.]

George Garrett, a young writer whose publications in verse and fiction should leave no doubt about the high quality of his gift, seems to share O'Connor's attitude toward the short story. The rough spots that characterize even the best of the stories in this collection testify to his ability to let a story discover itself; for if Garrett's stories are sometimes not quite finished, they are also never finished off. The title story, **"In the Briar Patch,"** wanders somewhere along the road that stretches between Br'er Rabbit's "Please, Br'er Fox, don't throw me in de briar patch" and Hamlet's "rather bear those ills we have / Than fly to others that we know not of." It takes shape in the consciousness of a small boy, whose naïveté has preserved for him the independence of his elders' self-made mantraps and who can thus appreciate both the principle that Br'er Rabbit acts upon in the tar-baby tale and something of Hamlet's apprehensiveness about trying his luck in a strange world. This enables him to understand the plight of a young Negro soldier named Leroy whom his father has caught intimidating the household maid and turned over to the police. Leroy, it turns out, has been using the device of A. W. O. L. to move freely between the Army and the world of colored folk, two briar patches that he knows well; and he earns the little boy's admiration when he uses the rabbit's stratagem to persuade the civil authorities to turn him back to the military. Yet from his own protected position, the boy also has the insight to sympathize with his frustrated parent, who senses Leroy's victory and happiness but has long since lost the capacity to comprehend either.

Garrett's portrayal of the wisdom of innocence appears again and again in these stories: in a young girl, who, without instruction, acts out the timeless pastoral of love-making by trading buttermilk for kisses; in the simple-minded mountaineer who learns the knack of getting gifts from the sophisticated people who give him rides; in a young boy who in ignorance, innocence and wonder shelters and feeds a runaway lion. This last story, called simply **"Lion,"** is symbolic of what Garrett seems to be doing in much of his work. One of the mottos that he places at the beginning of his collection, a passage from the Bible, says the same thing: "Let brotherly love continue. Be not forgetful to entertain strangers: for thereby others have entertained angels unawares." To Garrett the incident, the man, the lion, all are strangers and all are to be entertained, not because they are angels or even because they may turn out to be; but simply because brotherly love needs to continue. In short, Garrett's humility before the object and his respect for it seem to be the important reasons for his writing. He loves the lion because it is there, not because it can ever conceivably prove useful. He tames nothing. He protects and feeds everything. That is why his stories, even the roughest of them, seem to have an additional capacity for growth, and why the best of them are unmistakably alive.

T. A. Hanzo (essay date 1965)

SOURCE: "The Two Faces of Matt Donelson," in *The Sewanee Review,* Vol. LXXIII, No. 1, Winter, 1965, pp. 106-19.

[*In the following excerpt, Hanzo examines Garrett's treatment of the human condition in* Cold Ground Was My Bed Last Night.]

George Garrett's stories exhibit [a] kind of concern for the moral predicament, though not for the difficulties or impossibilities inherent in the acceptance of ethical norms. Garrett tells the story in **"The Old Army Game"** of the tough First Sergeant who is in all of us. Sergeant Quince, who teaches Sachs the stupid game, is the old Nick himself. We go on to the Professor in **"My Picture Left in Scotland."** He envies the talent of the bright young Jewish student, lusts after the nubile, stupid young thing, and then returns to his house, the slave of an intellectual, slothful woman. The moral ruin is everywhere, from the violence of **"Texarkana Was a Crazy Town"** to the debased language of Madison Avenue in **"Man without a Fig Leaf."** Fergus McCree, the modern poet, sums it up in this latter story: "Everything is all wrong." One consequence is that no one may be himself; the anguish would be too visible, as the victim in **"The Wounded Soldier"** finds out. Or as does the wife of the academic returning from sabbatical in **"More Geese than Swans."** Mary discovers that Sam Browne, the bachelor gossip who tells the tale of an awkward and trivial love affair, is merely a vicious man.

Garrett's ear is always sensitive to this undertone of malevolent energy. The reader's interest, of course, always turns to the quality of the perception which discerns and assesses it. At one point, in **"Bread from Stones,"** Garrett faces this necessity and gives the narrator a self-consciousness which perceives the more serious evil that a lack of judgment might produce: "The truth is I really didn't care what Raymond did with himself. But when I think about it, it seems worse somehow than caring strongly one way or the other." The title story, **"Cold Ground Was My Bed Last Night,"** develops this theme; Ike Toombs has, as he believes, divested himself of every care or want, so that nothing will hurt or touch him. But out of a perversity in his nature or in Sheriff Jack Riddle's, the malevolence strikes, without reason, beyond human care or the lack of it, and he is sent to be tried for a crime he did not commit and for which he will certainly hang. The truth is the last in Garrett's catalogue of the possible evils that befall vulnerable man. Nothing—not love, not money, and not innocence or passivity—will save him. The universal condition is a subjection to an incomprehensible hostility, the cold ground of an essentially inhospitable world.

Ike Toombs, like Fergus McCree, is crippled, suffering, and victimized. What their passion declares or redeems, however, is not clear, and that uncertainty, one supposes, is the moral burden of these fictions. Indifference rules choice, and uncertainty beclouds the value of suffering. Taylor and Hawkes have appreciated in their own ways the same dilemma, but their esthetic response to it is more poised. For Garrett the fictional realization tends to be confined to a kind of self-exposure: Ike and his foolishness, the Professor in **"My Picture Left in Scotland"** and his slavery to his wife, the truck-driver of **"Texarkana Was a Crazy Town"** and his affection for a Negro. The fictional technique expresses the realization by holding off its moment in a sequence of incidents whose lack of interior relationship corresponds somehow to the sense of indifference as to moral choice. The story, as though in thrall to the moral disorder it examines, seems deliberately to insist on the fortuitousness of its own principle of selection. Again in **"Cold Ground Was My Bed Last Night,"** and as a final example, the role of Deputy Larry Berlin seems at times integral to the action and at last negligible.

George Garrett with Charles Israel (interview date 1973)

SOURCE: "Interview: George Garrett," in *South Carolina Review,* Vol. 6, No. 1, November, 1973, pp. 43-8.

[*In the following excerpt, Garrett discusses various aspects of his writing in general and his literary career in particular.*]

[*Israel*]: *What do you think are the major problems faced by the beginning writer in our time?*

[Garrett]: I'll dodge that one a little. All serious writers, with a few exceptions, are in the same boat. Each book is a beginning. Look at this. Wright Morris and Philip Roth, for example, are in the position of starting a new thing everytime. The mechanics of the literary marketplace are such that a Wright Morris, who is probably our greatest living producing novelist, has done in effect a series of first novels. So all serious writers are beginners. Robert Penn Warren is an exception. And the problem is that it is sometimes more difficult for the old-timer beginner than for the first-shot-out beginner. The first shot out is on a clean slate. You don't have a track record.

But, here we go, here are two of the biggest problems facing beginning writers. First, it is extremely difficult now under any circumstances—much more difficult than ten years ago—to get published. There are large numbers of very good manuscripts bouncing around the United States, and if you're optimistic, you'll believe that those good manuscripts will find a home. But the only way for that to happen is for the writer to survive, to preserve his manuscript, to fight it through. It's analogous to the difficulty of the American poet at the time Frost was coming along. It took him twenty years to get his first book. This problem is compounded by two things: there are more good young writers around than ever, and simultaneously, there are fewer places to publish them. Right now is the only time in this century that we have had a significant backlog of good unpublished book manuscripts in this country. Second, most student writers have been doing poems and stories. These are what they have time to do in their kinds of lives. It is probably true, as Frost says, that a person can have his lyric voice at twenty. Many of these manuscripts by young writers are lost in the shuffle of college and graduate school. Most who persist are magazine poets, and this turns them away from producing coherent books. I do have the idea, as a parenthesis, that college literary magazines will get increasingly important—starting now—because they have the money to survive. . . .

I read that George Garrett is a Southern writer. Does that expression—Southern writer—have any meaning for you?

That handle probably had meaning to writers themselves a long time ago in terms of the specific place they wrote about most times. I don't think we're quite out of that. I've seen in my lifetime at least three or four times when distinguished scholars and elder writers have announced that the Southern Renaissance is over; then out of the Southern schools come bunches of young writers who haven't heard that it's over. The region has family characteristics that prevail. They are general characteristics. In the most recent generation of Southern writers, for example, there is a certain approach to language, a certain formalism. Most Southern poets, I believe, have been formalists. Poetry has always been on the topmost rung of the Southern literary hierarchy. It was OK to be a nutty poet; it was bad to be Erskine Caldwell. A drunken poet in Macon, Georgia, was OK because he was writing poetry with a capital *P*. Because that is so, it would be

impossible to conceive of a Southern William Carlos Williams playing with the colloquial and the everyday. Take James Dickey, superb poet; he's in the grand school of Southern Poetry. Poetry with a capital *P*. The poet as the Supreme Maker. So we have a different attitude toward Southern fiction. The Southern fiction writer begins with the liberated sense that he is working in a slightly inferior form. He thinks that its materials are not the great universal bones of Poetry. This means that the Southern fiction writer is open to varieties of spoken language as distinct from poetry. The prose fiction of the South has an enormous range as compared to the prose fiction of other regions of the country. Even at his most literary, the Southern fiction writer doesn't go too long on a high tone. Even Miss Eudora loves to drop into the colloquial. They love variety of speech, from public rhetoric to the rhetoric of movies and the pop culture. The Southern young writer, for example, who is using pop culture in much the same way as the urban writer—I call him an urban character sometimes because of this—is more at ease with it, less pedantic about it. Less stuffy than the urban writer. . . .

When you sat down and had your idea for the three novellas coming out soon, **The Magic Striptease,** *did you have an audience in mind?*

No, just myself as audience. I couldn't have done it any other way. If I were what some one has called a "public novelist," I would have aimed at a particular audience. If you're a playwright like Tennessee Williams, though, you must think in terms of an audience every time. I am a private novelist, it seems.

You know, don't you, that you're now considered a South Carolina writer?

That's all right with me. I see much more literary activity here than when I first came. There are Barry Hannah and Mark Steadman and Bob Sorrells at Clemson, and Bill Fox is a South Carolina writer. It's funny about Clemson. They have a great gathering of writers there without having a formal writing program. Maybe all that just grew out of the red clay soil like kudzu. . . .

About the physical act of writing. Do you write on top of a refrigerator?

I'm too short for that. For screenplays and dramatic pieces, I compose on a typewriter because it's easier to tell what you're doing and where you are in that form, but *Death of the Fox* and most of my fiction was done several times over in longhand and two or three typescripts. Look at the short paragraphs in *Death of the Fox.* They're short because I can cover a page in forty or fifty longhand words. . . .

Auden says that writing is not a horse race and that writers and critics shouldn't enter into their jobs feeling that it is a horse race. Still—if you had to name the three or four most influential twentieth century writers, the most influential ones on recent American literature, who would they be?

I'd say the Joyce-Proust-Mann trinity, plus William Faulkner in terms of amount of work. Faulkner was a great reshaper of fiction. I think new beginnings were opened up by these pioneers. They didn't end anything. They certainly did not kill the novel. They *started* something. But the problem with the horse race is how many entries are there? . . .

This is a personal question. What do you find funny?

This interview for one thing. I find it very difficult not to find everything that surrounds us, including our own aches and pains, pretty funny. This new book I've finished, *The Magic Striptease,* two thirds of it was written in reaction to the sixties, and those two thirds are grotesque comedy. It's really hard to sustain any seriousness when you're writing about the sixties, I guess.

You call this large portion of **The Magic Striptease** *grotesque comedy. Is it also satiric?*

Yes, it's possible to have satire, I believe. But satire shouldn't be so comfortable as to confirm the prevailing prejudices of the group to whom it is addressed. That's the danger of satire for our generation. As far as satire goes, we haven't advanced much from *Babbitt.* Most recent satire I read is still whipping philistines. I don't know if you're satirizing anything when you describe the building of great concrete plazas and then make a case for the tree. A more interesting form of satire might be not to make a case but to think of all the things that can be said *against* trees. You could do a good satirical piece on a corrupt Johnny Appleseed.

A part of this problem is that we have no big open debates anymore. We're warned against being divisive if we want a real debate. It's only in our generation that we've begun to say that things are unthinkable. Nothing is unthinkable. And it profits a democratic country and it profits a literary artist to start thinking the unthinkable. Without debate there is not much possibility for genuine literary satire.

Susan Heath (review date 1974)

SOURCE: A review of *The Magic Striptease*, in *Saturday Review/World,* Vol. 1, No. 9, January 12, 1974, p. 52.

[*In the following review, Heath offers a laudatory assessment of* The Magic Striptease.]

George Garrett's latest work [*The Magic Striptease*], a tidy fictional threesome, shows him to be a refreshing and casual yarn spinner of no little imagination. Distinctive in matter and manner, ranging in mood from comic to grim, these vignettes might have been written by different authors, except for the constants of Garrett's realistic, imaginative dialogue and dazzling quick-sketch portraiture.

The title story is a comic-strip fable brimming with magic and secret laughter that tells of one Jacob Quirk, an invet-

erate mimic so enamored of the concept of human freedom and man's ability to change that he devotes his life to the perfection of his mimetic art and, ultimately, to self-transformation. The extent of his vagaries limited only by his own imagination, Quirk buttons himself into bodies and peels them off at will as he pursues the rich varieties and subtleties of human experience.

Predictably, he soon comes to an enigmatic end, and we are left with the bareskin message of his magic striptease: "In whatever shape and form one finds himself, the only possible contentment accessible to a human being is to be at peace with oneself and rejoice at being alive."

Garrett calms down in **"Noise of Strangers,"** a gentle sketch in counterpoint of a small-town sheriff and a small-time drifter rubbing shoulders in a dusty, landlocked Florida town. Framed by suffering and self-delusion, it is a subtle and disquieting portrayal, in a mood quite contrary to the frolicsome spirit of its companion pieces.

In the final story, **"The Satyr Shall Cry,"** Garrett has created "a movie soundtrack in various tongues and voices" that is a delightfully frothy recreation of a frenetic, improbable evening of revivalist preaching, whoremongering, tent burning, robbery, and murder. The jumble of happenings is gradually illuminated as the bevy of religious zealots, pubescent psychopaths, and just plain well-meaning folk juggle their testimonies. It is an engaging tale of humorous circumstance, and a fitting capstone that will leave the reader high on the art of this raconteur.

David Tillinghast (essay date 1976)

SOURCE: "George Garrett," in *South Carolina Review,* Vol. 9, No. 1, November, 1976, pp. 21-4.

[*In the following essay, Tillinghast analyzes Garrett's writing style and surveys several of his works, including* The Magic Striptease.]

Offhand observations often reveal truths about people and the times. When I was a child it was quite common to witness someone strolling along the street whistling a tune. No one whistles (or strolls) today.

Whistling is an unconscious gesture, usually a positive signal that everything is satisfactory. We all recognize, however, that there's little worth whistling about anymore. And each has his own way of handling this disheartening fact. Some refuse to confront, some maintain indifference, and some avoid despair by adopting the pitying, most damnable emotion, cynicism.

To me it is encouraging that someone who has the burden of seeing the truth in life so much more accurately than most of us, and feels it more poignantly, takes none of these approaches. George Garrett's very appearance gives him away. There is honesty in his eyes; a brightness, a glance suggesting a sense of humor, a steadiness that identifies him as a man who possesses a correct picture of this existence we find ourselves in: "sometimes neat and soft / as a puff of smoke / more often unkempt / extravagant and formless" (from an early poem, "Forsythia"). There is always the notion with this man that something can be done, and that when a resolution is reached it will be worked out by man himself in terms recognizable and meaningful.

George Garrett delivers the goods. He is a writer whose realistic statement dispels illusions yet encourages hope, as in the poem for his sons: "Nothing of earned wisdom I can give you / . . . I am a foolish father like all the rest, / would put my flesh, my shadow in between / you and the light that wounds and blesses."

Garrett refuses to become one of those writers who produce to public specification. "For the aim of these," he states in the introduction to *For a Bitter Season*, his third book of poetry, "is to make the poet, whether a prophet or charmer, into a respected and respectable citizen. At the moment of Truth the Priests and the Pharisees, like the King and the Procurator and even the dancing Princess, arc conspicuously absent. Under the circumstances, it seems better to kneel in the shadow with the rest of the common soldiers and shoot craps, better in fact to crap out and lose all when the prize is beyond all price."

This acknowledgement accounts in part for his many experiments in prose, his three books of poetry, a children's play, as well as movie scripts for Hollywood and television. That he doesn't depend on a once successful formula is admirable and risky. For example, the stance he takes in *Death of the Fox* produces a flavor Elizabethan enough to deliver the reader into the age, but not to abandon him there—a crafty technique that allows the reader to maintain proper distance without losing interest and without becoming immersed, thus to forfeit perspective: just involved sufficiently to care about his subject matter and be thankful he isn't part of it.

Other innovations of style in *Death of the Fox,* such as sentence fragments and archaisms which provide the effect of immediacy, work successfully and fall in proportion to purpose. Of course, the greatest risk of all lies in attempting to write an historical novel in the first place. At the outset the author is already aware that he won't be taken seriously by scholars of the period or historians, and that he will be ignored by the popular reader confronted with such depth and exposition. Nor will the commercial reader have any idea of the research required to blend historical facts and imagination into a readable narrative.

The nerve to experiment is part of a writer's charm. We are naturally drawn to someone who takes a chance. Each of the narrators, seven or eight of them in all, in Garrett's experimental third novel, *Do, Lord, Remember Me,* contributes to the total plot through a monologue of his own that has no truth in it. Yet finally the whole narrative takes shape for the reader. Not only does the technique make sense after the reader participates and learns the rules of the game, but each of the fabricating narrators reaches a point of development as well.

Perhaps this impulse to experiment also accounts for the unfinished quality of some of Garrett's work. But George Garrett is not an average writer. He does not see life only as it relates to literature or to public appeal. *The Magic Striptease,* his latest book, three novellas under one cover, is so outlandish and mischievous that the reader really questions its intention, but again the imagination of the author fascinates—especially in the book's first novella, about a man named Jacob Quirk, who can change himself into another person, and not simply another flesh and blood human being, but a character in fiction. Ridiculous, extravagant, and successful, *The Magic Striptease* fulfills the basic requirement of all good fiction: the reader wonders what in the world is going to happen next—and keeps flipping the pages. And it is not the least bit inconsistent with George Garrett's versatility that the hilarious *Magic Striptease* follows right on the heels of the sober *Death of the Fox.*

Of course every type of writing calls for a different style, and often these changes (necessary to accommodate purpose) flirt with disaster. In *Death of the Fox* one sometimes finds himself irritated by more supportive material than he can reasonably suffer. He feels that he wants more narration, less information; he is uneasy in the presence of a quantity of material that would appear impossible ever to carry out to a proper resolution. But the prose is engaging, and at the end of the book the reader leaves with a satisfaction that he suddenly, strangely though gratefully, understands could never have been his had he not been required to encounter and endure the shock and frustration. At the end of *Death of the Fox* the reader is content: something has ended.

Sometimes Garrett's poetry, in its flash, seems a bit quick, not resolved sufficiently to suit our sensibilities:

> I am amazed. I wonder
> even in a dream,
> what the image with my face
> will ever be able to answer.
> Awake, I'm usually tactful
> and much too often polite.
> I wouldn't know what to say
> if somebody popped that question.
> In dreams at least I'm definite.
>
>   (from "Anthology")

It is the truth in statement, though, the accuracy of the word arrangements, and the familiarity of the images (they are close to home) that convince. The responses the poetry provokes are deep and honest ones. The images work because they call forth feelings the reader didn't know he had, or more significantly, had forgotten he had. The suggestions the images and statements make connect.

Still it is difficult to explain the appeal of the poetry, for it is rarely polished sufficiently to feel comfortable settling in with on a rainy afternoon. It is lyrical, sometimes graceful, often rough; yet one feels this is the way he would have it—he knows that he is in the hands of someone who has been there, who has the equipment to register the happinesses and disappointments of life as we know it (without the imposition of clever nuances and dead-end mannerisms) as he could never do. He finds himself faced with human emotions that matter:

> Now that was a long time ago.
> And now I know them for what they were . . .
>
> Still I would have them back.
> Let them be wooden and absurd again
> in all the painted glory that a child
> could love. Let me be one of them.
> Let me step forward once more awkwardly
> and stammer and choke on a prepared speech.
> Let me bring gold again and kneel
> foolish and adoring in the dirty straw.
>
> ("The Magi")

Poetry such as this reflects the understanding of a man of travel, experience, and friends. The poet has other things to do than dicker with words on a page, and this is part of the reason that he can size up a situation so correctly.

The reader feels that the solid word choices, mostly nouns, which construct the images are the right ones for him. They are delivered and set up for him so that the background he brings to the poem will take it from there: now they are his. He is grateful to be associated with a poet who doesn't heed the modern obligation to try to reduce an image to its core. Possessed of a genuine tenderness, the poetry is as honest as the man behind it.

It is tone that is most likely to be the key to the man. A tone of concern, without the denying pessimism that cuts the heart out of significance, underlies all the work of George Garrett, a legitimate concern indicative of hope, hope of a moral quality. This is why Sir Walter Ralegh is Garrett's man, to return to his greatest work, *Death of the Fox.* It is right that the two men should be associated, because, as did Ralegh, George Garrett represents amid the limitations and disappointments of our society, a spiritual hope, an example of dignity in a period that hardly any longer knows the meaning of the word. Sir Walter Ralegh maintained a courageous poise in an age that was losing it all—just as George Garrett does today, though he knows that he is casting in the dark.

George Garrett with Allen Wier (interview date 1977)

SOURCE: An interview with George Garrett, in *Transatlantic Review,* No. 58/59, February, 1977, pp. 58-61.

[*In the following interview, Garrett explains his approach to writing.*]

George Garrett is a friend and helper to many of his fellow writers, a kind man who has been generous with his time and his energies, a warm, wild, funny man, a great storyteller, a vital person. A list of all his publications would take fifteen pages. In addition to books edited, articles, book reviews, poems and stories in periodicals, he has published four books of poems, five books of stories and four novels: The Finished Man; Which Ones Are the Enemy; Do, Lord, Remember Me; Death of the Fox. *He also wrote* Sir Blob and the Princess: A Play for Children, *and the original story and the screenplay for the film,* Frankenstein Meets the Space Monster. *He has taught at Rice, Wesleyan, University of Virginia, Hollins College, University of South Carolina, Florida International University, and Princeton. He helped found* Transatlantic Review *and was for some years its poetry editor.*

[Wier]: *We were talking earlier about readers. How a reader, over a period of time, comes to anticipate what different writers are going to be doing in their books. When you write how much do you try to anticipate your reader? Do you have in mind an ideal reader, ideal reactions, etc.?*

[Garrett]: You can only think of *one,* which was a startling discovery to me. It's a very obvious, basic thing. In most of the literary forms you're only addressing one person, because only one person can read the book at a time. This is one of the really great distinctions between a book and any other form of narrative. The book has all the strengths of direct, intimate conversation with one person. And, so, yes, I think of a reader, but I suppose different readers at different times. I'd like to please myself as reader, but more than that I have in mind an ideal reader who's a little more sensitive, a little smarter than I am. In this sense this imaginary reader has a share in the creation of the story. Part of my job is to engage and charm and delight that imaginary human being to the extent that the human being will participate in the dialogue and that makes the book, the poem, the story, possible. Which doesn't mean, of course, you're trying to please everybody, or any numbers of readers. There cannot be a numbers game finally, because after you get published it becomes *purely* a numbers game and is meaningless. Ego gets involved when someone says "I've got thirty thousand readers." But it is important for young writers to get published so they have the occasion to meet that *one* imaginary reader. After that it's only arithmetic and the difference between one and thirty thousand is very very small.

What would you like to accomplish as a writer? What do you see for yourself, at some time, when you look back at your work? Do you ever think about that?

I don't think about it directly, but it is a very good question and one that's very pertinent to some other things I'd like to talk about. Unconsciously it has an effect on me. I deal with young writers a lot, and I know that what they want is clearly different from what I want at this point. Now I'm not talking about accomplishment, recognition, that sort of thing—all that is like love and sex, there's never enough. And you remain subject to gusts of hungers of one kind or another. You hope you're mature enough to recognize, ah, I'm being victimized by a gust of hunger or desire—but you hunger for different things, even in terms of the relationship to the work.

We talk about prize fighters at a certain point ageing out of the game, and this is not because their reflexes are really slower at age thirty, which a lot of trainers will tell you is not really true, and, besides, it's a hard thing to prove. In a certain kind of technical way, prize fighters should reach their peak in the first five years of their thirties, but, by thirty most of them are finished. So the thing used to be to say "They're not hungry any more, laziness has set in, they've gotten complacent." But I don't really think that's true. I think they're just not hungering for the *same* things, and, therefore, they aren't really fit competition for the younger fighter. And there's a connection here—the older writer has other aims and hungers, new ones he didn't know existed before. His hungers are not the same as the younger writer's.

All of us probably would profit from going back and taking a basic writing course and doing sonnets and villanelles again, however traumatic it might be, like learning to skip rope and punch a bag again, but—and this is an exciting thing about writing—such skills as I have acquired are only applicable to the books that I have already written. I don't know if they are applicable at all to the books I would like to write in the future. That's kind of disappointing to realize. I understand Eliot's poems, "Ash Wednesday", and "Four Quartets", in those terms much better than I did ten or fifteen years ago. The psychology of it, when he keeps coming back to what do you do with what you did, is a running theme in there as far as the literary part of it is concerned.

Since this is so, since the movement is in some way forward into undiscovered country, and since you don't know if any of your skills have fitted you for this, it's a challenge and a total, empty, scary kind of thing. I somewhat envy writers who haven't happened on a certain skill, or are able, apparently without being unhappy, to continue to do the same thing and perhaps do it better as time goes on. I'm not sure whether I could, now, do some of the things I did before. I don't know, even if it were a matter of life and death, if I could once again muster those particular skills, the combination of skills and desire, that I had for those works. But I console myself with the notion that necessarily I'm a perpetual beginner, that maybe this is less unusual than one thinks, that it is close to the process of what happens to things in life, that it's a way of being alive, because once we settle for one of those fixed situations we're always looking for—that's a kind of death. The *energy of life,* whatever else, is constantly new, is constantly begin, begin, begin, begin. I used to think fourteen books ahead. I've forgotten what most of those are because they were really fourteen of the same kind of books, and I picked one. Now I'm thinking, at most, one and a half books ahead, and there's a dreadful desert beyond that, and I think what if, at that point, that's it, and I can't think of anything else. I can think of thousands of things to do, but none which interests me sufficiently to do well. I don't know if this is just a gradual

diminution of my own ability or if it's the right thing, but I'm stuck with it. At least you see it in the other arts and it may be a very commonplace experience. It's said over and over, and this shows up in his journals and letters, that after each of Beethoven's great symphonics and then the quartets that he had been so totally committed to that particular piece of work that he had these long periods in which he said he didn't believe he'd ever do another piece of music.

I abstractly dream of an ideal for all writers, and that's to feel totally empty. The guy who saves it hasn't pushed himself to the edge. I used to run the quarter mile, I was never any good at it in terms of times, but the ideal at any distance other than the 100 or 220 was to breast the tape precisely one step before the step which would carry you into unconsciousness. Not to fall down unconscious early, not to fall down unconscious at all, because you hit the finish line precisely one step before that. I think that's the writer's dream, and thus the worldly wise and the sharp and the shrewd, I guess, are those who have never had a kick left at the end of the race. They've run a good time and have plenty left and they'll run again. But there's something deeply unsatisfying about that, no matter how fast you are, something very unsatisfying if you've never pushed yourself to your limit. And that's what I want for myself. Of course it may not look like that to the reader, it shouldn't, it should look like a good race or a good dance or anything else. Ideally it shouldn't call attention to itself, it should look graceful.

Drape yourself with chains, then dance so that they don't clink.

Right, that precisely the aim. But for yourself, for the writer, it should be that one breathless second away. That's what you're pushing for all the time. Nobody ever gets there, or very few. And a great irony is that they are the only ones who know it, if they're any good.

Then, in a sense, after you've done a particular piece, even something, or, maybe, especially *something as big as* Death of the Fox, *twenty years of work, once it is done it doesn't, in this one sense, matter anymore?*

It doesn't matter at all.

Do you lose interest in it and start moving forward?

That's right. Oh, I'd be lying if I said I wasn't pleased that some people liked it, I'd be foolish to say that, though I like the new book more, whatever the new book is. I'm hoping the new book, the next one, will be for me—I'm not worrying about readers or the publisher—for me I hope it will be a better experience, better and *different.*

William Peden   (essay date 1978)

SOURCE: "The Short Fiction of George Garrett," in *Ploughshares,* Vol. 4, No. 3, 1978, pp. 83-90.

[*In the following essay, Peden surveys Garrett's short fiction, praising the author's writing skills and treatment of universal themes.*]

George Garrett has written four volumes of short fiction along with about thirty uncollected pieces including **"A Record As Long As Your Arm,"** which appears in this issue of *Ploughshares.* He's had his share of praise along the way, but not as much as his short fiction warrants. In a very real way, he's been a story-teller all his life, talking them before he could read, he tells me in some very recent conversations via cassette and the United States Postal Service. The most important single influence on his early stories was Chaucer, which really isn't very surprising when you consider the variety and exuberance of Garrett's canon.

An experimenter and an innovator for years before the much-publicized fictional "breakthroughs" of the Sixties, Garrett is constantly searching for form and method, for the right, the inevitable, marriage between subject matter and structure. **"A Record As Long As Your Arm,"** for example, was begun as a relatively brief story, then re-written as a chapter in an uncompleted novel, and then as a novella. At certain stages of his career he's worked simultaneously in the novel, poetry, and film as well as the shorter fictional forms. "Messing around," trying not to repeat himself, Garrett wrestles with the angel; exploring the relationship between places and people: setting has always played a dominant role in his fiction. ("It is the place that makes all the difference.") Reading Kipling, Stevenson, Maupassant in his father's library, then during his student days at Princeton, reading Hemingway, Faulkner, Dos Passos, Fitzgerald, he was finally turned on by Chaucer; "being slovenly"; rewriting; trying to make his fictions move and breathe, to capture the feeling and pace of the spoken language, the sense of something taking place at the moment, in the here and now.

King of the Mountain, Garrett's first collection, was published in 1957; ten stories mostly appearing in little magazines like *Folio, Coastline, The Husk, Perspective,* and characterized by the variety and technical expertise that were to be the hallmarks of all his subsequent fiction. The stories range in time and place from his native Florida to Trieste in the 1950s; in mood from the comic to the somber; in subject matter and method from the conventional story that opens the collection (**"The Rivals,"** a testing between a father and his son, looking good in there or not looking good a la Hemingway; compact, moving, much praised by critics including Eudora Welty, though she didn't like some of the others because of the prevalence of "ugly talk") to the five semi-related impressionistic fictions of the last piece, **"What's the Purpose of the Bayonet?"**, which is highlighted by an almost Dante-esque depiction of a group of whores being beaten up by some Austrian police.

Despite this variety (the arrangement from the conventional to the non-conventional is, of course, intentional), the *King of the Mountain* fictions have a lot in common. They're similar in their concern for the average individ-ual: Garrett's characters for the most part can be called folk heroes of the usual, the "non-commissioned officers" of society, theirs "isn't an age for heroes." They're involved in the usual business of living and dying: a group of young people in Greenwich Village on the eve of the Korean War when "we bit into life and life was as sweet as a ripe apple" (**"The Seacoast of Bohemia"**); a Princeton undergraduate awaiting a visit from his alcoholic, lowborn father (**"A Hard Row to Hoe"**); another young man reflecting on the time his father, now dead, took him to see *Death of a Salesman* (**"The Lion Hunter"**); a group of G. I.'s playing cards and reminiscing about women (**"Don't Take No for an Answer"**).

> The most important single influence on his early stories was Chaucer, which really isn't very surprising when you consider the variety and exuberance of Garrett's canon.
>
> —*William Peden*

Most of the *King of the Mountain* fictions grow out of a situation that produces a confrontation, a clash of personalities and concepts, a testing, a proving. Some of Garrett's characters fail in this testing, yet survive in one way or another. Others fail and are destroyed. Still others pass the immediate testing but, paradoxically, fail. Don't search too hard for an answer, Garrett implies: there are no easy answers to anything. So despite the quick pace of his stories, and the frequent and always effective use of the first person narrator which lends credibility to situation and at the same time accentuates the surface buoyancy and humor of much of his work, George Garrett's house of fiction has as many dark rooms as sunny ones, and there are maggots in the basement. Child or adult, man or woman, intellectual or mindless man in the crowd, they are alike in their vulnerability: close kin all to the strong man of the story of the same title: They're "lonely out there . . . alone and almost naked."

Similarly the thirteen stories of *In the Briar Patch*, 1961, among the most interesting of which are several concerning teen-agers or young adults. The opening piece, like the first story of *King of the Mountain,* is relatively conventional in both subject matter and technique, and (not coincidentally, I am sure) is entitled **"The Test"**: three boys have made an improvised diving helmet; they skip their high school commencement exercises to test it, one of them drowns. But the real story doesn't begin until after the drowned boy's funeral, in a series of reversals and contrasts involving another kind of testings-and-adversary-relationships between the two survivors and their parents:

All you people with so much *imagination.* You have all these wonderful schemes and ideas. You don't care what the risk is. And that's all right for you. But somebody has got to watch after you all the time. And when you're all finished . . . somebody has got to come along and start to clean up the mess. . . . You people are like babies. . . ."

The same can be said of **"The Last of the Spanish Blood,"** with its naive narrator ("I wasn't a child any more and not a man either") and his hot-blooded older cousin, and its literally smashing confrontation between them and a bullying cadre of white trash. Still another kind of confrontation/contest/test occurs in a remarkable story, **"A Game of Catch,"** which climaxes in a manic game on a windswept, deserted beach involving a young woman and two brothers, one of whom "was just out of the State Asylum." (This scene *demands* to be choreographed; I hope some one will do it sometime).

Like the skilled playwright he has been and is, Garrett constantly makes effective use of contrast. Contrast of mood, situation, and highly individualistic characters ranging from freaks and grotesques to squares and straights in **"Time of Bitter Children,"** a blending of suspense and comedy involving a former professional boxer-turned-hitchhiker and one of his 'victims'; in **"An Evening Performance,"** a woman high-diver, her manager, and a hard-nosed, tight-fisted citizen of the small Florida town where the woman is planning to perform; in **"Goodbye, Goodbye, Be Always Kind and True"** (the title, in case anyone doesn't recognize it, is from a Sunday School song), a disabled World War I veteran (who rigs up a remarkable group of mannequins near a new highway to the Florida beaches) and three pairs of motorcycle freaks who would be very much at home in *Star Wars*. And, perhaps most effectively of all, in what I think is my own personal favorite among all of Garrett's stories (a preference that I doubt most readers would share), **"The Gun and the Hat."**

Red Leland, a Florida farmer worn out by years of hard work and tribulation, buys a pistol to kill John Pengry, a local eccentric and grade school teacher, who, Red thinks, had ridiculed his son, a child "you could hardly call . . . a boy at all . . . it was something wrong with his glands." The ensuing confrontation between Red and Mr. Pengry on the doorstep of the Pengry home is a classic—Pengry, dressed in his long-dead mother's pink silk dressing gown and wearing his great grandfather's Confederate officer's hat, a hat altered by successive generations of the Pengry women, bedecked with ribbons and tassels and feathers—and Red, one hand brandishing the pistol, the other clutching his son's hand. Pengry does not even recognize his pupil.

"'Little boys all look alike to me,' Pengry stammers. 'I apologize . . . I'm not really responsible. Go ahead and shoot me if you want to, but I won't take off this hat'."

Back in the truck, Red breaks down. The fat child reaches over, pats his father with his soft white hand.

"'Don't mind, Daddy. . . . It don't make no difference to me'."

A small, spontaneous act of love in what could be a dark void, but like Shakespeare's candle it generates a lot of light.

During a reading at a writers' conference last summer, Garrett said that he was beginning to feel that only the comic mode is viable in today's world, and it is with such a meld of the serious and the comic (or rather the comic presentation of the serious that has characterized so much English and American fiction from Chaucer through Fielding and Mark Twain to Aldous Huxley and a host of others) that Garrett has found, or been found by, as his most effective narrative voice.

[Garrett] can tickle you to death with a feather or stun you with a single blow, elbow you into submission, fascinate you with his footwork, shed your blood without your even being aware of it.

—*William Peden*

This same juxtapositon, along with Garrett's virtuosity, characterizes the stories and the title novella of *Cold Ground Was My Bed Last Night*: he can tickle you to death with a feather or stun you with a single blow, elbow you into submission, fascinate you with his footwork, shed your blood without your even being aware of it.

The collection is highlighted by a Kafka-esque parable, **"The Wounded Soldier."** An unnamed veteran with a hideously war-wounded face is bribed-coerced-bullied by a "High-Ranking Official" to remain in hospital; his appearance, the Official points out, "would only serve to reawaken the anguish of the civilian population" and "cause a considerable cooling of patriotic ardor . . . and a noticeable decline in enlistments." Finally, however, the soldier, masked, leaves in spite of the warnings of the Head Nurse, the only compassionate human being in the Establishment:

> . . . you'll be back here in no time beating on the door with bloody knuckles, begging them to get back in. You don't understand people. They are the worst things in the whole creation. They will smell your blood like sharks and go mad. They'll kill you.

In a series of events including the soldier's tour as a clown ("In the daylight he could see the audience and they knew it and refused to laugh. Only when they were in the safety of the dark would they give themselves over to . . . laughter") *and* an operation, Garrett strips the bandages from the reader's eyes, leaving him, like the acrobat of **"Four Women,"** alone and naked, to contemplate his own wounds and ponder, like another disabled soldier (the old man in **"Goodbye, Goodbye"**) a "shared truth." And a shared truth always "needs a disguise. Laughter will do.

Otherwise, like Adam and Eve without the wit of fig leaves, the naked truth would shame to the quick."

In marked contrast, we have the comedy of **"The Farmer in the Dell,"** Chaucerian in its gusto, *Sartor Resartus*-circa-the-1960s in its implications, the mock epic of a shy and modest schoolteacher, his fleeting bathroom encounter with the wife of his best (indeed, his only) friend, culminating in the schoolteacher's naked flight through town and its aftermath.

And a different variation of Garrett's preoccupation with nakedness, **"Man Without a Figleaf."**

And a pair of acidly urbane dissections of Academia: **"My Picture Left in Scotland,"** which should be required reading of all creative writing students *and* their teachers, and **"More Geese than Swans,"** as effectively low-keyed an execution as anything Garrett has ever written.

To say nothing of the frequently-anthologized **"The Old Army Game,"** with its unforgettable portrayal of Sergeant Quince.

Despite their differences, Sergeant Quince, Professor Dudley, and creative writing academician Sam Browne are brothers under the skin:

Schmucks all.

Professional, hard core, dedicated, unredeemable schmucks.

So very different, these *Cold Ground* fictions, yet united by Garrett's artistry and his continuing preoccupation with what the late Elizabeth Bowen so aptly termed the problem of human unknowableness.

A Wreath for Garibaldi, published in London in 1969, contains half a dozen stories from the preceding volume, and four previously uncollected pieces. The title story has never been one of my favorites, though I'm not exactly sure why. But the story of slow-witted, awkward Henry Monk's return to his home place with his German war bride, **"My Pretty Birdie, Birdie in My Cage,"** is Garrett at his best, highlighted by a remarkable skinny-dipping scene when the women of the community turn savagely upon the German ("These were the ones who knew too well how beauty fades and what a long time there is to live afterward, gnawing the memory of its haunting visitation like a bitch gnawing a sour bone") following which Henry remains unaware that only now, after their own holocaust, "they could freely offer him . . . his rightful place in the only world they knew or care to believe in."

"A Record As Long As Your Arm" is a remarkable tour de force, the swan song, I assume, of John Towne, who has appeared in several uncollected stories, most recently in **"P. S. What's Octagon Soap?"** in the *Texas Arts Journal.* Once again, we are in familiar Garrett country: two young professors, and their wives, in an unnamed

New England college. Familiar, too, are Garrett's hallmarks: adroit manipulation of narrative elements, expert use of the first person narrator, marvelous dialogue, and the bringing together of the serious and the comic, the silly and the truly dreadful, which he counterpoints as skillfully, say, as Kafka juxtaposes the familiar and the surreal; the passage from one kind of world to another takes place so skillfully that the reader isn't aware of where he's being taken until he's already there.

> **There may be some American short story writers who are consistently producing better stories than George Garrett's, but I can't think of their names.**
>
> —*William Peden*

Thus, in **"A Record As Long As Your Arm,"** what begins as apparently another romp in a cuckold's bedroom ends in the maggoty, blood-spattered, vomit-stained basement of . . . But why give away the denouement of this remarkable story. . . . ?

Beneath the clowning and the vaudeville, the quick shots, the breezy tongue-in-cheek narration, George Garrett is consistently preoccupied with universal problems—good and evil, hypocrisy and truth, looking good in there or not looking good in there. A moralist disgusted by the disgusting aspects of the society of the man without a figleaf, Actaeon gnawed by his own hounds, first cousin to Housman's stranger and afraid in a world he never made, a world of "fine avenues and boulevards where . . . meanwhile . . . in back rooms, in hidden corners, behind blank smiles, all over the world people are suffering and making other people suffer. . . . It's almost too much to think about."

There may be some American short story writers who are consistently producing better stories than George Garrett's, but I can't think of their names.

Mary Peterson (review date 1980)

SOURCE: A review of *To Recollect a Cloud of Ghosts,* in *North American Review,* Vol. 265, No. 1, Spring, 1980, p. 69.

[*In the following review, Peterson provides a synopsis and favorable review of* To Recollect a Cloud of Ghosts.]

This is a wonderful book—quite literally, full of wonder. The occasion is Christmas in England, 1602-1603. The narrative begins its fine curve through the countryside from London, when an annual procession moves to the vast palace and grounds of Whitehall. As Queen Elizabeth I comes home, so does the season: the candles and flowers, Yule Log, fire and light and evergreens, rich cloths and tapestries, the Lords and Ladies of the Court. But this Christmas is to be the last for the aged Queen, and for the ghosts of her memory.

All the rituals of the season are observed. The dances are danced; the poems read; the supper eaten. Then Elizabeth is presented with her New Year's gifts—the treasure at the center of the story.

Garrett renders the jeweled lists of gifts in perfect counterpoint with memories of the "great and the powerful, the fortunate and privileged and celebrated." But also the soft and weak, the faithless.

Memories cloud the Court. The young women who attend the Queen can't understand or even believe in the nasty old woman and her dreams. They are dreamers of the future, who care nothing for these "lost names and the old portraits of her forgotten suitors of one time and another." But Elizabeth is wiser than they are.

She paid for many of the gifts herself. She was not universally loved. Yet she is still the necessary cameo center of this yearly celebration, where there is (still) mystery: of change, of death, this year certainly, but also of her people's need to believe and to hold sacred. Of the necessity of faith.

> [She believed] that the future, whether good or ill, belonged to God alone and could be no more examined and questioned than God Almighty can be. Believed therefore that in this world doubt alone is the appropriate and accurate posture towards the future. Believed, then, all the more firmly because of the depth of her doubts, that faith alone is the accurate and appropriate response to what must be, can only be, doubted.

They are all, except the Queen herself, hostage to the future.

The Queen retires; the narrative curves away. To the servants and Lords and Ladies, who worry over the next reign. To the great men of the City, the men of the Guilds, who sing and dance to the music of change. To the countryside.

For now, Christmastide has been kept in England. "According to old traditions and customs. Which, since they solve no riddles of the past nor answer any questions put to the future, must be, then, old or new, wholly of the present, only of the here and now. . . . Thus we celebrate our own joy and folly, our own vision and our ignorance." As, in its striking final image, this story celebrates them.

George Garrett (essay date 1982)

SOURCE: "Plain and/or Fancy: Where the Short Story Is and May Be Going," in *The Teller and the Tale: Aspects of the Short Story*, edited by Wendell M. Aycock, Texas Tech Press, 1982, pp. 133-41.

[*In the following essay, Garrett comments on the short story, examining the history of the genre and predicting its future.*]

In his Harvard commencement speech of 1978, a speech which outraged a good many prominent people, Alexander Solzhenitsyn made a pertinent remark concerning what he had noticed about intellectual life in the United States:

> Without any censorship in the West, fashionable trends of thought and ideas are fastidiously separated from those which are not fashionable and the latter, without ever being forbidden, have little chance of finding their way into periodicals or books or to be heard in colleges. Your scholars are free in the legal sense, but they are hemmed in by the idols of the prevailing fad. There is no open violence as in the East; however a selection dictated by fashion and the need to accommodate mass standards frequently prevent the most independent-minded persons from contributing to public life and give rise to dangerous herd instincts that block successful development.
>
> ["A World Split Apart," *Vital Speeches*, September 1, 1978, p. 681]

Solzhenitsyn's remark provides a good point of departure. But we can begin to describe the present only if we can define its characteristic differences from the past. Our culture concentrates a great deal of energy and attention on just this effort: getting to know the past, especially the recent past. This task would seem to be easy because so many texts and images and artifacts remain. There are even people to talk to who were there and are here, people who should have viable perspectives worth sharing.

Yet recent history, including literary history, is marred not only by faulty, slovenly understanding and interpretation, but also by an excess of factual inaccuracy and crude distortion. We, writers and society at large, permit liberties and license in dealing with the recent past which we would never tolerate in any study directed toward the middle ages, Classical Rome or ancient Greece. The closer we get to our own time, the greater the distortion. For instance, nothing in film, documentary or specialized, comes even close to expressing the basic truths of the Vietnam War. Ironically, the only way to reassemble the truth is by and through the poetry and fiction about the war which has been published or is coming along. But this assembling must be done with the understanding that most critics and reviewers are unaware even of what has already been published on the subject, including some superb short stories. Still worse, those critics who are aware deliberately ignore all but the few bits and pieces which confirm their preconceived opinions. *Published material* is even more highly selective and more distorted. Beyond considerations of quality—quite aside from any considerations of quality—the materials published on that extremely controversial time must necessarily conform closely to *somebody's* preconceptions of the events and their meaning in order to find a way into print. Unfortunately Solzhenitsyn is right. The contemporary critical mindset favors novelty. Since the so-called new slant must somehow conform to the basic theoretical clichés and the historical consensus, novelty becomes, purely and simply, a matter of style.

The recent past can be rearranged to fit any theory. Precisely because there are so many facts, images, texts, and artifacts available and since an act of selection must be made (which one is important or worthy of attention and which one is not), it is quite easy not merely to select, but to *preserve* those aspects of the past that one wishes to preserve and, in effect, to nominate for oblivion all that one does not approve of. Even print technology conspires against us. The warehousing and storage of books is already a problem. But so is paper. The life of a contemporary commercially published book is estimated at only fifty years. Already a great many books are disintegrating. All will follow after. Some will be saved, copied and stored by other means. What a fine way to dispose of what is *irrelevant,* what is out of fashion. I am told that the Soviets are literally and continually changing the pages of their encyclopedias and newspapers to make them fit present policy. Our way may prove just as effective. Paradoxically, this acid-ridden, biodegradable, rapidly disintegrating paper is still so valuable that it has shortened the life of many books that are not enormously and immediately successful. Many books that were once remaindered are now pulped for the sake of that valuable paper. Ironically those texts which may have the best chance of surviving are those on fancy broadsides and especially those in typescript or longhand, done on the highest quality paper.

Oral history may become increasingly influential as literacy declines. But too often the authenticity and authority of the speaking voice overrides our considerations of its accuracy and honesty. The clichés of the evening news are made authentic, given legitimacy by the newscaster's persona (even as the clichés of modern fiction are given substance by their inclusion in a significant anthology). And tape recordings are, like film and video tape, easy to manipulate, by erasure, by editing and rearrangement. This kind of editing is already commonplace and accepted in broadcast news (both radio and TV) and in documentary film. There is no reason to imagine that even honorable custodians of oral history will not edit it to advantage.

I will illustrate my next point with a brief quotation from the "Prologue" to [Sara Davidson's 1977 book] *Loose Change: Three Women of the Sixties*:

> In that time, that decade which belonged to the young, we had thought life was free and would never run out. There were good people and bad people and we could tell them apart by a look or by words spoken in code. We were certain we belonged to a generation that was special. We did not need or care about history because we had sprung from nowhere. We said what we thought and demanded what was right and there was no opposition.

"We did not need or care about history because we had sprung from nowhere." This deliberately cultivated ignorance of the past cannot be overlooked for its import to our survey of the past.

Now, where, in terms of my chosen topic, do these observations about the past and present take us? What is the state of the contemporary short story? We may begin by pointing out some positive signs.

Like the old-fashioned postman who was not stayed from the swift completion of his appointed round, the writer of stories does not seem deterred or dismayed by the climate of the times and his knowledge or ignorance of it. The stories keep coming. And, in my opinion, many, many of them are very fine.

As the number of *national* places for short stories has dwindled and diminished, the importance of the quarterlies and little magazines has grown; and the number of little magazines, coming and going quickly as always, has greatly expanded. Although there are not nearly enough places in which the writer of short fiction may show and tell, there are a great many. The extremely limited national showcase for stories has resulted in a near (if not perfect) equality among little magazines. One can find excellent, exciting work in even the most humble and obscure of them. And on the next level of book publication of story collections, even though the commercial publishers have backed away from more than minimal support, there are a growing number of university presses and small presses publishing short fiction. Some of these, both magazines and small presses, have gained government support for their activities. There are also prizes and contests and so forth (like the AWP contest Gordon Weaver ably managed) to encourage both writers and publishers.

It is true that many of the older, more mature and experienced fiction writers, who certainly could be writing short stories, do not do so much (except in the forms of excerpts from novels in progress). They refrain from writing short stories mainly because, as "professionals," not many of them can afford the time. So, except for a few prominent regulars, there is a loss of contribution from the mature professionals. (Such is not the case in poetry where we have some very fine poets, still working, who have passed into old age.)

But coming out of the proliferating creative writing courses and programs at both graduate and undergraduate levels are many very gifted and often very well-trained beginning writers. They are mostly young, but not always. And the story writer of today has, at his disposal, a wealth and variety of examples, *models,* barely imagined by the earlier generations. There is not merely the assimilation of the stories of the past, but also the stories, past and present, of the whole world, coming in translation. Ideally these models should extend the range of narrative possibilities for the writer and encourage a more open and varied fiction than we have yet known in America. Since the publication of stories is not *directly* profitable for most writers, there seems a certain purity of purpose and quality, which used to be reserved for lyric poets.

Thus far the present situation looks fairly positive. All this energy, all this activity must surely come to something. As optimistic Americans we have to believe that there will be, as if by Newtonian physics, some commensurate reaction. Surely in spite of difficulties, the future for short fiction looks good, if not exactly rosy.

Or does it? Is even the present as vital as I have described it? Let me work backward through the same positive points I made.

Purity of Purpose

The pressures on the writer to get work published, especially if the writer is a teacher, are enormous. The jostling competition for place and space is just as rough and ready as it would be if large, direct rewards were involved. Because of the pressures and the sense of competition, the opportunities for dishonesty and corruption are frequent and, in my best judgment, more and more frequently seized on and rationalized.

Richness and Variety of Models and the Influence of Available Translations

It is my experience that the young and beginning American writers do not even begin to take advantage of all the available examples they could learn and profit from. The majority are poorly read, except for anthologies and for the work of a very few, very well-known and highly-regarded writers. In other words, they approach literature in more or less the way they approach popular culture (records, for example), depending on the star system. They have neither the time nor the inclination for discovery of their own. They are a perfect audience, then, for the literary status quo, being committed to the maintaining of it, in the hope that, somehow, some room may yet be found for them.

Despite all the unquestionable richness and variety of models at their fingertips, the beginning writers, out of almost invincible ignorance on the one hand and an urgent desire for recognition and reward on the other, have reduced their narrative choices, their "options," to a bare minimum, thus becoming, from the outset of their writing careers, profoundly conservative. Even a great deal of the so-called experimental fiction is more derivative and less adventurous than it ought to be.

Little more may be said for the influence of translation. We have some wonderful translators among us, and they deserve recognition. But a great many of our poets and story writers who imagine that they are influenced by foreign literature in translation have less than a whiff of the original language to fuel them. And they are generally ignorant of the culture from which the literature grew.

Furthermore, the competition and pressure for recognition mitigates against either much variety or adventure. If the young writer wants to be *recognized,* he has to be published. To be published, the work must seem to possess *recognizable* qualities to one or more editors, who have limited time and energy and are overwhelmed with manu-

scripts. Once again we must return to Solzhenitsyn's observation. Recognizable quality is, then, by definition, *something they have seen before.* Once recognized, and in order to maintain this visibility, the artist, whether he is John Updike, Bernard Malamud, Donald Barthelme or a brand new writer, is strongly encouraged to imitate his own style.

Having made these observations about recognition, I must suggest a paradox. Editors naturally get bored with this situation in which everyone's turf and boundaries are as tamely well-defined as the plots of land in some suburban development. It is easy to feel jaded, to imagine that they have seen it all. So there is, in fact, some modest effort, within the already stated and very limited terms, to "discover" new and different talent. (The results are usually no better than "new improved Blue Cheer with lemon borax," *that* kind of thing.) What is discovered—whether it is good or bad in itself is irrelevant—is recognizable in technique and acceptable in content, but different from the conventional in some conventionally superficial way— like tone of voice.

I have just mentioned content. I don't want to waste a lot of time on the subject (and anyway Solzhenitsyn said it all), but it should be understood that the *substance* as well as the style is involved in the editorial and critical recognition of quality. The very process we have developed in the publishing business would lead, even in ideal circumstances, to an ideological conformity bordering on totalitarian rigidity. Most of what filters through in fiction, non-fiction and poetry merely serves to confirm the intellectual consensus, that is fashion. Contemporary literature has to be fashionable (recognizably so) in content as well as form. Therefore, most contemporary American fiction, short or long, and poetry, is forced to handle ideas on about the level of flashcards and feelings with the same depth as Top Forty Tunes. Instead of dancing to any tune in the world, most American writers are content to caper in the leg irons and handcuffs of fashion.

One final note about *recognizable qualities.* Since recognition is a crucial factor, it follows that the recognition of the writer himself, as personality, as celebrity, can be the essential difference between one writer and another, between success and failure. The color and charisma of personality and appearance become as important as the literary work itself. This is not surprising, but what is, is that the whole sense of literary and historical context in which "major" figures grow and thrive is lost. Ironically, one can be surprised to rediscover the truth. Novelist and poet Fred Chappell, in a recent newspaper commentary about a new anthology, *Contemporary Southern Poetry,* notices something we all tend to forget or ignore:

> A curious thing is that in this anthology the big guns make no grander bangs than the smaller ones. Here James Dickey does not appear as a giant among pygmies. . . . Crowded in with his peers, Dickey is simply an equal among equals, and one begins to realize how much his personal flamboyance has contributed to his national acclaim.

Creative Writing

I have professionally and consistently supported the teaching of creative writing. But there are a couple of problems worth mentioning. First, so many of the graduates of creative writing programs, especially the larger ones, go directly into the teaching of creative writing themselves. This fact is neither good nor bad, as such, but certainly has the dangerous potential of enforcing an academic climate and reinforcing the status quo, creating a kind of *beaux arts* school of fiction and poetry. Another problem derives from the competition among schools and programs for status, for their own kind of recognition. This competition can and does lead to variations on the old-school-tie syndrome, which can and does manifest itself editorially and critically, adding one more inducement to intellectual dishonesty.

The Old Pros

All of these conditions serve to make the withdrawal of so many mature fiction writers from the short story form all the more serious in its consequences. They alone seem to be in a position to take really adventurous directions, to exercise free choices, and to set examples that might be helpful for the apprentice and journeymen writers. It is good to have John Cheever and Eudora Welty (and now again Truman Capote) writing short fiction. But what a pleasure and a consolation it would be to have more stories by the likes of Wright Morris, Robert Penn Warren and Shelby Foote. Something of the formidable rigor of the system we live under may be inferred from the fact that we seldom get new short fiction from our old masters.

Growth and Proliferation of Small Presses and Little Magazines

It is hard to find fault with this phenomenon. And yet, we *do* have a history, and we *can* make comparisons. When Fitzgerald and Faulkner and Hemingway and all the others were publishing their stories, they dealt by and large with well-funded profit-making institutions—*Liberty, Colliers,* the *Saturday Evening Post,* the old *Esquire.* Today, among the mass magazines that publish fiction, only *The New Yorker* and *Playboy* have the kind of financial base to claim that kind of independence. But it is worth remembering that *The New Yorker* was alive and kicking then, too, and didn't publish Faulkner or Hemingway or Fitzgerald or Steinbeck or Sinclair Lewis.

Anyway, the chief quarterlies and the university presses are dependent on the institutions that support them. The little magazines and small presses are, of course, non-profit enterprises. That is more a description of reality than a legal category. None of them will ever make a profit. Most will seldom, if ever, break even on individual works. Thus they are, one and all, dependent upon the whimsical circumstances of private charity or, increasingly, on government support. Thus, we have the whole knotty problem of the relationship, in this country and at this time, of our government to

the arts. Whatever stand one takes, whatever position or party one cleaves to, he will have to admit that there are real dangers involved in government support of the arts.

Finally, little magazines and small presses are run by amateurs and dilettantes, who publish much more poetry than short fiction, and more short short fiction than long short fiction. If one dabbles editorially in the arts, he can publish many more poets than story writers.

Well, there's the present, as I see it. Is there any cause for optimism? What are the future prospects? For one thing, the sheer number of writers of short fiction delights me, if only because statistically a certain number, however small, are bound to produce adventurous and interesting work, often in spite of themselves and certainly despite the system.

There is finally the matter of history. Ignoring history, the high priests and celebrants of the literary establishment have sought to manipulate the present and to control the future. History proves, not rarely but invariably, that the latter is impossible and that the former (manipulation of present reality to suit one's interests and preconceptions) can indeed be accomplished and often successfully enough to be satisfactory (*as in our own era*). But there is one absolute truth—the present becomes the past. As soon as that happens, a new establishment is created. History proves that every new establishment, *even if it is wholly hereditary,* will leave the dead to bury the dead, will promptly ignore the immediate past, or will seek to review and rewrite it. If the former, then it all came to nothing anyway. What is ignored cannot be celebrated. If the latter, then writers of history will be called in. And one of the things that historians uniformly despise is the discovery that others have tried to do their work for them in advance.

Perhaps it will be the honor and pleasure of some future story teller to remind them of the undeniable truth, out of our deepest past, of the only future we and they, one and all, can be certain of. Here is how David, the King and Psalmist, chose to say it (in the 49th Psalm):

> Though they thought well of themselves while they
>   lived, and were praised for their success,
> They shall join the company of their forbears, who
>   will never see the light again.
> Those who are honored, but have no understanding,
>   are like the beasts that perish.

Josephine Jacobsen (review date 1985)

SOURCE: "Stories From a Lifetime," in *Washington Post Book World,* Vol. XV, No. 37, September 15, 1985, p. 5.

[*In the following review, Jacobsen applauds* An Evening Performance, *referring to "Noise of Strangers," the final story in the collection, as "a contemporary classic."*]

The short story is popularly supposed to be having a re-naissance. Those who never envisaged or foretold its death, and who are familiar with the brevity of popular rebirths, are little impressed by this announced resurgence. Good short fiction has continued to appear in the better literary magazines and university quarterlies which have always been, as George Garrett points out in his preface, a haven for good stories. They have been stories of great variety, strongly experimental, socially oriented, or deal-ing head-on with basic human emotions, behavior and needs.

The stories of George Garrett belong to the last of these groups, but he brings to them the formidable resources of his work in poetry, and of the off-beat historical fiction of *Death of the Fox* and *The Succession*. The dangers for a short-story writer inherent in being also a poet and nov-elist are very real, and one of the major victories of this splendid collection is that those dangers have been avoid-ed; there is no "poetic prose"—although there is plenty of poetry in the stories—as there are none of the lulls and detours which the novel can afford.

Of his stories, Garrett says, "I stand by them one and all with a full awareness that many of them are less than they might be, and none, not one, is as good as it ought to be. . . . Meantime, this is what I have and who I am."

What he has and who he is is a gift for all of us. These [stories in *An Evening Performance*] are stories never taped down and finished off with a stitch. They are open-ended: these people lived before the story began, and most of them will continue their complex and often des-perate lives after its final word. One of Garrett's special triumphs is that, while he opts for the traditional ac-tion of moving human beings from here to there, show-ing their changes in the process, he also forces the reader to imagine something beyond the printed conclusion. Certainly that is a characteristic of the finest kind of short story.

Army life looms large in the book and is responsible for a number of Garrett's funniest (he is very, very funny when he chooses), most vivid and most appalling stories. One of the themes of the book—perhaps its central theme—is the grimness of self-discovery, its unfore-seeable, irrevocable quality. Just as pride, loyalty, cour-age, and that battered word, compassion, are seen as the touchstones of what is most valuable and essential in human nature, so cruelty, treachery and brutality are seen as the interior enemy—the unrecognized but ever-present possibility that any human may inflict or suffer shame. Here cruelty in a variety of forms is seen to be conta-gious as any plague; applied to the helpless, it can kindle its replica in the most unlikely spot.

In these stories, there is always a double level: the one on which we like to, and tend to believe we do, live, and the one below it, secret until brought suddenly into con-sciousness. "I was sick of walking about the fine av-enues and boulevards of this world where you walk with your head up, strut if you want to like a god, and

meanwhile all the time there's an invisible world breed-ing and thriving. In back rooms, in hidden corners, be-hind blank smiles." This, from a series of four short piec-es grouped under the title **"What's the Purpose of the Bayonet?"**

Garrett is fascinated by the fringe figures who have in their oddity or loneliness something of the mythical: the circus-woman, grifter, lion-tamer, clown, prisoner, hobo, or, as we unctuously express it, "the physically disadvantaged."

A word which frightens Garrett is "purity"; not purity in the sexual sense, but in that of an unflawed field of snow, a desert of printless sand, with no record of the blunder-ing human foot. Humanly speaking, such purity is either an illusion, dangerously held, or a mask worn so long and tightly that the features beneath it have changed secretly beyond recognition. Though the writing is perfectly straight-forward, every story carries with it what Garrett refers to as "the old sad weight of complexity." A nurse who wit-nesses the onslaught of a violent crime and refuses to become involved, loses her capacity for sympathy, first with herself and then with her patients. Full of contempt for them, she addresses herself furiously to becoming a popular and valued nurse. "She felt a sense of exhilara-tion . . . she saw herself wielding a knife she had not owned before."

It would be all wrong to give the impression that the overall impact of the book is grimness. On the contrary, humor is not only everywhere present, but a number of the stories, including some of the most sobering, are hi-larious. A number are concerned also with the nature of justice and its virtual impossibility as humanly applied. In the section headed "In The Briar Patch," the epigram from Isaiah reads in part: "We look for judgment but there is none. . . . But if the achievement of justice is dubious, the search remains vital. It is when the spirit of resistance to cruelty, to smugness, to injustice dies that all is over; resistance is all."

"That's how real resistance goes on," Garrett writes, "and its strength is directly proportionate to the num-ber of people who can let themselves be taken to piec-es, piece by piece, without quitting too quickly. It is an ugly business and there are few if any wreaths for them."

Wisely, the book closes with a long story, **"Noise of Strangers,"** which it is no exaggeration to refer to as a contemporary classic. To describe it would be to injure it, but it deals, brilliantly, with the possibility of justice, and its chances. The story moves easily, rich in detail, superb in characterization, to a conclusion that the reader is not likely to forget. In it Garrett's strengths are at their height: atmosphere, characteriza-tion, dialogue, scope. Read three or four times, it in-creases its force. It is very sad, and very funny, and has the kind of gritty pathos which makes it a small masterpiece. Alone, it would be, as we say, worth the price of admission.

Greg Johnson (review date 1985)

SOURCE: A review of *An Evening Performance,* in *the New York Times Book Review,* October 6, 1985, p. 28.

[*In the following review, Johnson provides a mixed assessment of* An Evening Performance.]

Though best known for his historical novels—*Death of the Fox* and *The Succession*—George Garrett has also produced a large body of short fiction encompassing the American experience of the last 30 years. The stories collected [in *An Evening Performance*] describe the conflicts of adolescence, romantic and domestic turmoil, life in small Southern towns, academic life and wartime experiences, and they range in manner from the naturalistic to the near-farcical. Never less than workmanlike, solidly traditional in form, Mr. Garrett's stories frequently sound the theme of human cruelty. "Human beings are the foulest things in all creation," says a character in **"Wounded Soldier,"** while the boy-narrator of **"The Last of the Spanish Blood"** is made to confront his own potential for evil and violence. **"What's the Purpose of the Bayonet?,"** a powerful story of wartime, ends by indicting "the whole inhuman race." This abiding misanthropy does, however, allow for the saving grace of humor. **"Bread From Stones,"** an amusing tale of a feckless gigolo, also forms a tiny critique of the American dream. Perhaps the best story in the volume, **"Texarkana Was a Crazy Town,"** tells of a likable former soldier who finds "real life" much more fearsome and wondrous than anything he had encountered in the military. With few exceptions, the stories seem defiantly "unfashionable" in style. In our age of pared-down realism, Mr. Garrett's flaws as a writer—a fondness for elaborate similes, an occasional straining after poetic effects and a general prolixity—are particularly noticeable. Especially in the earlier pieces, the reader often must cut through a wilderness of verbiage to get to the heart of the story. As a whole, however, this volume displays a fitful but genuine power and shows Mr. Garrett as a master of this distinctive form.

Peter La Salle (review date 1986)

SOURCE: A review of *An Evening Performance,* in *Studies in Short Fiction,* Vol. 23, No. 2, Spring, 1986, pp. 205-06.

[*In the following review, La Salle characterizes the stories in* An Evening Performance *as compelling and well-written.*]

Surely the only ill effect of the critical acclaim granted George Garrett's big, haunting novels about Elizabethan England (*Death of the Fox* in 1974, and *The Succession* in 1983) was that it seemed to eclipse the fact that he has waged a long and important career in the genre of the short story, where for the last thirty years he has been chronicling in detail how Americans live.

Which is why *An Evening Performance* is so welcome. Gathered here is work from his four story collections as well as a half-dozen new or uncollected stories. The appearance of the book is even more significant because two of those earlier collections were released in smaller printings by university presses, and almost all of the stories originally appeared in literary magazines or quarterlies, as opposed to large-circulation publications.

Voice constitutes the essence of these pieces about Army life, university life, suburban life, and, most often, rural Southern life. Behind the probing of the characters of these always complex everyday people is an authorial tone that is compassionate and humorous, gentlemanly and constantly astonished. And at the heart of each piece *is* a story—a story being something that needs to be told, and also something that has apparently been forgotten in the current vogue for short fiction of icy understatement about chicly bored characters who pretty much do nothing. To read a Garrett story is to have somebody whisper to you "Listen," and you do.

In the title story, a woman high-diver comes to a run-down town to perform her shabby sideshow, an event that strangely changes the outlooks, even the dreams, of the inhabitants. In **"Don't Take No for an Answer,"** a soldier brags to his buddies with tales of how he took advantage of a dowdy, lonely woman, having a high time of it as she bought him drinks and clothes and never feeling a qualm—he claims. In **"A Game of Catch,"** three friends drive out to a beach in Florida; one young man is just out of an institution, another is deep into a business career, and the young woman with them is self-conscious of even appearing in a bathing suit, though she lets herself be talked into embarrassingly undressing in front of them while they continue to go on with a mad game of catch on the deserted sand, ignoring her.

I was struck by how often the words "gun" and "ghost" turn up here. The two almost define the success of this fiction—the suspense suggested in the first, the airy mystery of all experience itself suggested in the second.

Do read this book, and "Listen."

George Garrett with Richard Easton (interview date 1990)

SOURCE: An interview with George Garrett, in *New Orleans Review,* Vol. 17, No. 4, Winter, 1990, pp. 33-40.

[*In the following excerpt, Garrett discusses contemporary literature and explains various aspects of his own approach to writing.*]

Celebrate the sixty years of author George Garrett, a national treasure. As artist, George Garrett has always had the courage to go beyond mastered skills to explore new genres and techniques. He is novelist, poet, short story writer, essayist, and satirist. With patience and humility he has become the very model of how to cultivate insight and craft throughout a career to achieve master works. In the rich narrative portraits and historical detailing of his critically acclaimed Elizabethan novels *Death of the Fox* (1971) and *The Succession* (1983), Garrett discovered worthy tapestries to display his diverse talents. In the autumn of 1990 he will publish the third of these Elizabethan works, *Entered from the Sun*. This novel centers on the sordid end of playwright Christopher Marlowe.

George Garrett has also been selfless in sharing his knowledge of the traditions and craft of writing. Currently he serves as Henry Hoyns Professor of Creative Writing at The University of Virginia. As a familiar in literary and academic circles, his generous sharing of his wit and wisdom has become legend. In this interview he reveals his astute grasp of the contemporary literary scene as he talks of his own quest to create works worthy of the audience and experience he so loves.

[Easton]: *What's the primary work of a successful artist?*

[Garrett]: Artists, I think, by definition are more explorers than exploiters. The one thing that artists who are still alive and growing are most anxious to do is this: not to recall a series of habitual gestures. Yet it is the habitual gesture in the artist, a familiar if obsessive pattern, that is easiest for the contemporary critic to deal with.

Do you sense a tension now between the successful creative personality and the literary critic?

The critics of contemporary literature are an industry in a sense. They have a vested interest in establishing and maintaining some kind of canon. This is precisely the opposite goal of most writers. Obviously, though, there is a complicated symbiotic relationship. Those writers today who are successful in conventional terms owe a certain amount of their success to having found a niche in the critical hierarchy. They, therefore, are also in cahoots with publishers, critics, everybody working together to maintain an establishment and a canon.

In the development of the present-day American short story certain writers are thrust forward as representative—for instance, Ann Beattie, a fine person and a fine writer, and the late Raymond Carver. But I don't think either one of them is what the critical establishment believes them to be. Raymond Carver published several books of stories. They can be described critically; they are interesting. But the stories are not the only things that Americans are doing with short fiction. Beattie has published three or four books of stories. Her stories have a kind of trademark, but they are not the only exciting things that are happening with the short story. Once critics decided that they were good, they went on record as saying that any story of the eighties is a variation of an Ann Beattie or a Raymond Carver story.

But many writers are going in a wonderful diversity of directions. One of the big things a writer has to fight is the insistence of critical pigeonholes. Probably we would be commercially better off as writers if we developed some obsessive, little gimmicky idea to write a story. Anything that doesn't fit the approved critical patterns ends in a vacuum somewhere. The result is that what in fact is happening on the American scene is not being described by the critical apparatus. There is, then, a serious dichotomy between artistic and critical activity. But ironically they both feed each other. I think that if a Martian came down to describe what's happening on the American short story scene, he would find an enormous diversity of activity, quite belying the official description of only four or five basic types of stories being written in the 1980s. I think that's basically nonsense. It's gotten quite serious over the years because we have a great many talented but disaffected writers who don't fit a critical description.

Yet, you have been very successful in the academic and literary worlds. Are you saying that there is an overt tension between artists who need to do something new, to cut new territory in genre and technique, and critics who want the familiar gestures?

The tension is there. One of the great ironies for me is [that] over the long haul there has been a decline of overt hostility. Maybe it was better when we were actively hostile toward each other. Now, it's kind of you go your way and I'll go mine, and, perhaps, we'll quarrel.

Do you think then that the atmosphere for fostering creativity is improving in the U.S.?

There's a lot more artistic activity that is supported under the umbrella of educational institutions than was the case, and that is probably all to the good. There's a lot more opportunity to do what used to be called studio work, and that would apply to writing as well. The value of that is clear in undeniable facts; for instance, we furnish most of the world's symphony musicians. Travel to Frankfurt, and it's mostly American kids performing in concert halls. We have our great conservatories. This is our position in the world, and, I think, the same thing is true in most artistic fields. I'm not sure that the study of periods and characteristics does much good, though, because the models are inaccurate descriptions. The more I know what is happening the less I am able to describe it. I am quite stunned with people who seem quite confident that they can. I can only believe that they have shut their eyes to a lot that is happening artistically.

You've been involved in so many college and university writing programs, you must be optimistic about their effect on young writers.

For better or worse, the last generation in America not to go to college very much was the generation of Hemingway, Faulkner, and Steinbeck. The last two generations, 99.9% of all American writers have been graduates of colleges anyway. A great many passed through writing programs because by college age they had some interest in writing. Some of them chose creative writing courses because it gave them a certain amount of time in the context of formal education to work. Also, as a studio person there are lots of things that can be learned. You can't learn the things that make great writing, but you can learn lots of things that make for good writing and speed up the process of self-learning.

What about the academic establishment controlling the studio and therefore stifling the spirit of rebellion?

I do believe that the Iowa Writer's Workshop has become quite rigid and academic. It's the model of what is supposed to be good, but it cannot be because everybody who comes out of it sounds just alike. One of the founders of the Iowa Workshop was R. V. Cassill, who had a lot to do with getting writing programs into major institutions and smaller ones. He created the organization The Associated Writing Programs. For some years he ran it out of his basement with his wife as secretary—they were it! Nobody was very interested, but slowly it came along and today it has over two hundred institutions as members. He sort of dropped out and let it go its own way. A couple years ago, after a fifteen-year hiatus, he was invited to speak at a national convention as founder, first president, etc. He shocked them all by saying, "Well, we have now proven our point, and the advantages of the writer being associated with institutions are now outweighed by the disadvantages. I think we ought to disband the whole thing and pack it in. The writers should get out of the institutions at this point." I think he's speaking about programs that prepare people who go directly into teaching and advance themselves by publication in just the same way that straight academics can. The rigidity really came from within the workshops rather than from the outside—from the writers themselves who ran it. They became respectable within the academic community. They demanded respectability from their students, and the results of that have not been altogether auspicious.

Cassill, however, is a famous gadfly. He would have to agree that what we have created isn't a bad thing on the whole. I was talking with the people at Hollins about this—many people from the program are teachers now. The situation in Europe was set up against the United States, and in the debates the United States came off better than Europe because in Europe, once you get yourself certified as a writer you do not have the opportunity to go to work for the patronage of a university or a college. One is subsidized by the state, which has happened less and less. And what can a writer who is subsidized do— none of those writers are making any money from their books in Europe to speak of; they make it over here if their books get translated. If your whole living depends on the good will of the state, it seems to me you are in a more dangerous position of selling out everything than someone who can, at least, leave one institution for another. We have, at least, as much freedom as baseball players. We can battle to improve our situations and we can also have the situation in the U.S. of dropping out completely or dropping out from time to time from the whole institutional patronage system. The whole situation is more anarchistic, but it's probably better than the Eu-

ropean situation. For one thing, the European states can't afford very many writers.

Do you think U.S. writing has generally become less international in concerns and techniques in the last decades?

That's a hard one to answer because we have more consciousness of what is happening in Europe and world literature than we ever had. Lately, we have many things not being translated. Even so, we have more consciousness. We are influenced. We have numbers of American writers who can't read a word of Spanish being deeply influenced by Garcia Marquez's writings, as far as they understand them. So on the one hand we aren't turning inward, but many Europeans and others feel our people are becoming self-engaged navel watchers.

Are there any influences that you would point to in the creation of your Elizabethan novels?

Fielding, I think. I've read a lot of Fielding, once upon a time. And Chaucer.

How about Hawthorne?

Well, I find "The Custom House" passage in the *Scarlet Letter* very useful. I've read it a great many times.

While writing the Elizabethan novels, were you trying to be original—the restless explorer?

No. I liked to read some of the very good novels about the Elizabethan period that I'd heard about and some of the bad ones. I liked to do a study of those novels. And I wanted to do a trilogy. Ford Maddox Ford did a trilogy. The originality of the forms derives from the inability to compress the material into a conventional form. I would have rather done them more simply.

What led you in these directions?

Well an element popped into my mind while you were talking. I wanted something that nobody else could adapt into a movie. Actually, there's a funny story about this. Somebody hired Frederick Raphael, the screenwriter for *Darling,* and gave him a very large sum of money to do the screenplay for *Death of the Fox.* I don't know what it was, but it was a good deal more than the total earnings of the book will ever be. He took a year off and wrote a script which I've been told that I really ought to read because it is so beautiful it would bring tears to my eyes. But I was told it's unfortunate that it can't be made because it would cost fifty million dollars to shoot.

So you were conscious of preserving and extending the genre of the novel?

Well, I hope so. I know how to adapt novels into screenplays. With these novels something could be done—total wrecking crew activity—but something could be done that wouldn't be the same. I wanted something not translatable to the screen. Non-translatable. I've succeeded—so far.

Were you aware that you were moving away from the minimalist treatment?

I very much see that now. For awhile I thought they knew something the rest of us didn't. One big change in my understanding of the minimalists [came about when] I went out and bought a tape of a collection of stories to listen to on a car trip. Two hours into the trip I realized that they are very special when they work. They are very small, delicate pieces, but they don't open doors. Back to back they numb you. That's a danger. I want to understand because I have a personal friend, Ann Beattie. She's very adroit with them. Minimalist stories in the hands of Carver were a series of gestures. I'm really interested in writers who explore more than that. I guess that's a characteristic of Southern writers.

Some have suggested your narrative techniques imitate William Faulkner's.

Well, in the technical way, that is the kind of relationship with Faulkner I don't have. I honestly do think and I wouldn't be afraid to say that some writers are sort of copycats. For instance, Styron imitates Faulkner's language and rhythm and everything else but doesn't really get to the heart of it. He creates a loud Faulknerian blast. There are some others like William Humphrey who went through a Faulknerian phase. Faulkner has had a tremendous influence, but, I think, most of the influence is stylistic. I don't think there's a lot of stylistic influence in my books except in a couple [of] places in early books when I was trying to indicate there was a fiction: somebody telling a story and getting Faulknerian in style, hoping that a reader would react to the obviousness that something bogus was happening, a fiction. It would be the arranged fiction rather than the series of actual events.

I think I learned a lot technically from him, particularly from his handling of time. We had some similar experiences too. Both of us—he much more than I—worked in the movies about the same ages in our lives, and I can understand what that did to him. It's really the effect of working in film. First, you learn to make certain kinds of moves with the narrative. At the same time he rebelled against its limitations and qualities. He did anti-cinematic things—like trying to explore what you can do with the texture of prose which cannot be done with the camera. At the same time, you have picked up little devices like speed writing structure and relationship of parts. So, I would say I hope I haven't been influenced in a copycat way but I would admit he has been an enormous influence on me. He was amazing. Do you know that no two books—twenty-five novels—are alike at all. They seem alike because they are all in the same style, but each narrative organization is different. He seemed to get bored with settling in and doing books the same way. I think of him as a kind of restless explorer. He never stopped long enough to throw up a cabin or anything. I think Faulkner opened dozens of doors for American writers rather than

closing off things. I don't think he ever closed a door. Some think he burned up a lot of subject matter forever. Certain aspects, his generation's view of things, he used—more efficiently than people will be able to later. I think it is only in the minds of the critics that they say the Southern subject has been exploited and mined and there's nothing but tailings left. I think that is not true.

I began searching your earlier novels and short stories for some sign of the historical interest evident in your later Elizabethan novels. But your earlier prose works are portraits in the realistic mode. Had you experimented with the creation of historical fiction before the completion of these novels?

Actually I have a couple of places. There were four or five short pieces published which I originally thought were going to be part of *The Succession* but never made it. They inevitably had the shape of stories because they had to. A couple of them were identified as excerpts but don't appear in the finished novel.

I perceive a thematic relationship between the earlier realistic fiction and the Elizabethan works: your fascination with the effects of people's dealing with authority and aggressiveness, of the effects of war, of the self-images people create, of the humor they use to survive, of the complicated mysteries of life that never daunt but challenge them. But will you comment on what led you to create the rich style and narrative structure evident in your Elizabethan novels?

The style and language are radically different. The language of my stories has always been more vernacular, more colloquial than any of my other prose forms except, maybe, one novel done in the first person, a G.I. novel *Which Ones Are the Enemy?*

The re-creation of Elizabethan characters, then, somehow freed your powers of language and imagination?

I've found it difficult all my life to do much with something which other writers don't seem to have much difficulty, to do much with what might be called a high style or moderately elevated style while dealing with mundane twentieth-century life. At least when I was writing about the past, I was able to exercise a style that I couldn't permit myself when writing about present-day domestic life. The necessity of creating a style and language for a distant period is very hard. I see by writers from all over the U.S. both eloquent and elegant accountings of life as we live it now. I have trouble doing that while keeping a straight face. I can't do it. I am trying to think of someone offhand who does—Updike, for example. I have great admiration for what he seems to achieve, and I manage to keep a straight face while reading him. The lavish and lush language—the effect could be comic very often. I have difficulty writing in any kind of lavish style about motels.

There are trends in commercial publishing, for instance Gore Vidal's *Burr* and *1876,* which I think are some of the best of his novels. I reviewed *Lincoln,* and I liked it very much. I do think in almost every case Vidal's main thrust is just to take a popular assumption and turn it upside down. Lincoln emerges as a slick politician rather than as the icon of our society. The same thing with Burr. I like Vidal's books; I like the fact that they're not too deep.

I never really thought about this, but the model for my historical writing is Shelby Foote, who wrote what's probably the single biggest piece of prose narrative of our lifetime: the three volume history of the Civil War. He also had written a lot of excellent pieces of fiction before he wrote that. He greatly disapproves of the distortions of fact necessary for interesting historical fiction where the facts are known. That's one of the reasons—and a point of conscience—that I admire his work so much. He makes a good case that you should not really write novels about Lincoln. You should write narratives about him. Then you can deal with the facts and not introduce them. He truly disapproved of Styron's *Nat Turner,* not for any reason except that it distorts the facts of Nat Turner's life.

As far as I can interpret, Foote likes my books and has been very kind about them. One of the things that justifies my dealing with Elizabethan life and fiction is that a lot of the facts are not known and never will be. The people were very conscious of this. Another thing, it was an age which in the absence of television people created images—they dressed up in a quarter of a million dollars worth of clothes. They were fictional characters creating their own little narratives and dramas. It is, therefore, not unjust to treat them in a fictive cast because that's the way they lived. But if you wanted to write about the eighteenth century or the Old West, the facts are not in doubt and there is a closer relationship to what

is presented and what is, so what can be identified as truth is different.

Publishers Weekly (review date 1992)

SOURCE: A review of *Whistling in the Dark,* in *Publishers Weekly,* Vol. 239, No. 22, May 11, 1992, p. 64. [*In the following brief review, the critic provides a favorable assessment of* Whistling in the Dark.]

Much is enjoyable and uplifting in this farrago of memoir, fable, poem and essay, most of which previously appeared in such journals as *Kenyon Review* and *Virginia Quarterly Review.* [In **Whistling in the Dark**] Garrett, author of novels, poetry, short fiction, biography and criticism, strides down the paths his narratives take him with careful, assertive writing. In the reflective pieces, he often allows himself the heroic poise of inspirational rhetoric. As he tells of wartime experience and legacy, the noble character of his tribe (be it defined as blood relatives or Anglo-American white men), the two one-eyed (literally) coaches from his days at the Sewanee Military Academy and Princeton, or anecdotes from other halcyon days of academe, the prose has a lithe, muscular glow. Some readers will find this glow self-serving, even pompous. Garrett's style often rides clipped, declarative rhythms that are almost Hemingwayesque, and aspects of his material—war, Europe, pugilism—demand comparison to Papa. The book's second section, "Doing the Literary," indulges in backhand criticisms of certain literary figures' callowness or cowardliness, and authorial confidence begins to smell like mean arrogance. Yet for all its too readily stereotyped material and minor irritations, Garrett's voice is powerful and articulate.

Additional coverage of Garrett's life and career is contained in the following sources published by Gale Research: *Contemporary Authors,* **Vols. 1-4;** *Contemporary Authors Autobiography Series,* **Vol. 5;** *Contemporary Authors New Revision Series,* **Vols. 1, 42;** *Contemporary Literary Criticism,* **Volumes 3, 11, 51;** *Dictionary of Literary Biography,* **Vols. 2, 5, 130, 152; and** *Dictionary of Literary Biography Yearbook,* **Vol. 83.**

Conrad Ferdinand Meyer
1825-1898

Swiss novella writer, translator, and poet.

INTRODUCTION

A writer of both poetry and prose, Meyer is best known for his eleven historical novellas, which fictionalize the lives of such figures as Charlemagne, Henry II, Thomas Becket, Dante, and Louis XIV. His novellas are noted for their complex structure, objectivity, and attention to detail. According to W. Silz, Meyer "has no peer . . . in the artistic reanimation of history."

Biographical Information

Meyer was born in Zurich to a cultivated and wealthy family. He was a lively and healthy child until the age of six, when a bout of illness seemed to profoundly affect his personality. He became moody, alternating between tantrums and listlessness, and began to isolate himself from society. The death of Meyer's father in 1840 further affected his mental outlook; his preoccupation with death and loneliness were themes that would appear in his novellas and poetry. In his teens, Meyer tried his hand at painting and Romantic verse, but had little success. It was later, after travels to Italy and France, where he immersed himself in history, architecture, and art, that he began to develop his sense for description and historical stories. While it was the poem *Huttens letzte Tage* (1871, *Hutten's Last Days*) that first brought him fame, Meyer considered himself principally a writer of fiction. With the publication of *Das Amulett (The Amulet)* in 1873, he began his career as a writer of novellas; he wrote ten more novellas between 1874 and 1891. In the last years of his life, Meyer suffered from deep depression and possible senility, but he managed to complete his last novella, *Angela Borgia,* in 1891. He died suddenly of a heart attack in 1898.

Major Works of Short Fiction

Many critics contend that although Meyer wrote about great historical figures and events, he drew inspiration for his work from his own life, in particular his feelings of isolation and rejection by society. The author once claimed, "The mediocre saddens me because it coincides with something analogous in myself; therefore I desire the grandiose so intensely." Thematically, Meyer's novellas reflect a pessimistic worldview, as they generally concern crime, revenge, love, hate, justice, and death. Even Meyer's one humorous novella, *Der Schuss von der Kanzel* (1878), is set amidst the horror and devasta-

tion of war. Meyer's novellas are noted primarily for their technical strengths. Edward M. V. Plater asserted that the "highly conscious and intricate style" of Meyer's novellas requires for the "reader to approach his work with the greatest care, if he is to enjoy all the subtleties of his complex narrative art." Meyer frequently employed a framework device, through which he told a story within a story. For example, *Der Heilige* (1880, *The Saint*), which utilizes fictional details to relate the life of Saint Thomas Becket, features a narrator, Hans, who recounts Becket's story within the context of his own life. Another novella, *Georg Jenatsch* (1876), relates the story of the Swiss national hero who liberates his country while sacrificing his ideals. Written in three parts, it demonstrates Meyer's use of ambiguity and objectivity, as well as his ability to condense vast amounts of historical material into prose.

Critical Reception

Critical reaction to Meyer's novellas has been varied. They were popular with the readers of his day, and Meyer lived to see many of his works go through numerous editions. Even so, early critics often faulted Meyer's stylized manner. E. K. Bennett observed that when Meyer "has to deal with passion in his works, he does not find the natural expression for it, but uses a mannered, forced style, which . . . merely chills the reader." Many commentators have attempted to interpret Meyer's novellas from a psychological viewpoint, asserting that the use of historical settings in his novellas allowed him to escape the reality of his time and own life. More recently, critics have been drawn to the technical complexity of Meyer's novellas, observing that his shifting narrative perspectives accommodate modern feelings of skepticism and relativism. They further contend that Meyer's work foreshadows the psychological writing of the twentieth century.

PRINCIPAL WORKS

Short Fiction

Das Amulett [*The Amulet*] (novella) 1873
Georg Jenatsch: Eine alte Bündnergeschichte [*Jürg Jenatsch*] (novella) 1876
Denkwürdige Tage: Zwei Novellen (novellas) 1878
Der Heilige [*The Saint*] (novella) 1880
Kleine Novellen (novellas) 1882
Die Hochzeit des Mönchs [*The Marriage of the Monk*] (novella) 1883
Das Leiden eines Knaben [*A Boy Suffers*] (novella) 1883
Die Richterin [*The Judge*] (novella) 1885

Die Versuchung des Pescara [*Pescara' Temptation*]
(novella) 1887
Angela Borgia (novella) 1891

Other Major Works

Zwanzig Balladen von einem Schweizer [*Twenty Ballads Written by a Swiss*] (poetry) 1864
Romanzen und Bilder [*Romances and Pictures*] (poetry) 1869
Huttens letzte Tage [*Hutten's Last Days*] (poetry) 1871
Engelberg (poetry) 1872
Gedichte (poetry) 1882

CRITICISM

Donald Douglas   (review date 1930)

SOURCE: "True Romance," in *New York Herald Tribune,* Vol. 6, No. 34, May 4, 1930, p. 2.

[*In the following review of an early English translation of* The Saint, *Douglas lauds the novella for its romantic elements.*]

Embedded like imperishable gems in a hidden fastness, the romances of Meyer have long lain hidden from English discoverers. Perhaps there is no German writer so difficult to translate; and the translation can only be done by one whose English matches the rich, subtle and complicated prose of Meyer's German. It is not a labor of love, but a labor of genius, and in the present translation there is love, no doubt, but there is not even skill, for Professor Hauch makes Meyer sound like Sir Walter Scott—of all funny people! None the less one must welcome the inauguration with a clamor of golden trumpets, for perhaps it may mark an era when one of the finest historical novelists in the world is gradually revealed to nations who fancy that the Germans of the nineteenth century wrote nothing but incomparable lyric poetry and incomprehensible philosophy.

Indeed, the translation of *Der Heilige* will afford pleasure to many to whom *The Monk's Marriage* and *The Page of Gustavus Adolphus* and *Jurg Jenatsch* will forever remain closed and secret books unless some publisher can induce a writer of genius to take time off from his own novels and give Meyer a garment of English prose that will reflect the glorious and many-colored tapestry of romances as far away from the maundering stuffiness of Walter Scott as they are from the irresistible but shallow-pated Dumas. There is no possible use in telling any one the "plot" of *The Saint.* It is about Thomas Becket and Henry II, and it is told by "John the Crossbowman," who was present at the crucial scenes of that difficult and almost mythical encounter. Like most of Meyer, it is all done by indirection; and the indirection throws a prismatic light upon the mysterious drama of human beings. Dumas would have told a straight story of credulous ro-

mance. Undset would have gone profoundly and a little drearily into the wages of sin. Weyman and Sabatini, . . . but enough, quite enough.

Meyer is concerned largely with the inexplicable, and therefore Meyer is concerned with the true romance. His characters are themselves puzzled by the inscrutable characters of great men; and therefore his romances are very much like the profound gulf of night caped with illusory stars. The gemmed cadence of his prose is not a deception, but a revelation of the darkling and interwoven souls of Becket and Pescara and Gustavus Adolphus. His inaccessibility from English readers stems not only from his style. The translator has to feel and think as Meyer feels and thinks; and that kind of person is usually much too busy writing his own work. After all, one cannot be too severe on Professor Hauch, whose translation sounds like Meyerbeer trying to rewrite "Parsifal." How in goodness is one to translate a pharse like "Dante hielt inne"?

Unfortunately, those who have never read Meyer in German will think that *The Saint* is just another Walter Scott gone wrong. None the less one greets its appearance with the hope that it may usher in some not too far-off divine event when Meyer's novels will irradiate the English world in the radiance of the great sun.

E. K. Bennett   (essay date 1934)

SOURCE: "The Psychological Novelle: Conrad Ferdinand Meyer." In *A History of the German Novelle: From Goethe to Thomas Mann,* Cambridge University Press, 1934, pp. 215-30.

[*In the following essay, Bennett discusses the defining characteristics of Meyer's short fiction.*]

If [Paul] Heyse may be described as the aesthete and mass-producer of the Novelle, the Swiss poet Conrad Ferdinand Meyer is the aesthete and virtuoso. Meyer, like Heyse, lacks that rootedness in the bürgerliche life of his time—though in a different way. He is an observer of life rather than a partaker in it. This attitude to life in both poets gives to their work something of the exotic, something which is remarkable by its variance from the normal type—in the scientific sense the quality of a freak product. Both poets, standing outside the Bürgertum, within the limits of which [Gottfried] Keller, [Theodor] Storm and [Adalbert] Stifter found inspiration and security, are representatives of that aesthetic individualism of the end of the nineteenth century which was the outcome of the liberal conception of the individual in his relation to society, and led to the dissolution of the Bürgertum of which it was itself the outcome; just as in the realm of economic life the principle of liberalism led to the dissolution of the Bürgertum in the emergence of socialism.

In Meyer's Novellen the dissimilarity to the prevalent type, the uniqueness, is more apparent than in the Novellen of Heyse, for the very good reason that Meyer possesses as a poet a personality much more marked and original than that of Heyse. One thing may be observed with regard to Meyer. He tends in so far to return to the classical type of Novelle, in contrast to the type which had become characteristic for the writers of Poetic Realism, in that he shifts the social plane of his characters up into the bürgerlich-aristocratic world instead of keeping to the 'kleinbürgerliche' world which was the special province of Keller. The same thing may be observed of Paul Heyse, the characters of whose Novellen except in his occasional excursions into stories of peasant life, are inhabitants of the world of education and culture. It is permissible to find in the two types of Novelle—the Romance and the Germanic—a difference which is inherent in the spirit of the Mediterranean and of the Northern peoples; and to see precisely in Keller and Meyer, the two writers of the neutral territory of Switzerland, the representatives of the two cultures: the Germanic bürgerliche and the Romance aristocratic culture. Living in the same town as Meyer, Keller is directed towards German ideals in literature. Meyer, in spite of the fact that he writes in German (his correspondence is mostly in French), is directed towards Romance ideals in literature.

A further contrast may be observed between Keller and Meyer: Keller can make use of everyday mediocre subject matter because of his strength; Meyer must use incidents which contain the big historical gesture because of his weakness. Keller, secure in his rootedness in Bürgertum, need not assert himself with an impressive gesture; Meyer, floating in his Ästhetentum, must conceal his weakness and insecurity behind the heroic pose, the flamboyant setting. The two writers are exact antitheses: Keller is 'lebensbejahend'; Meyer is 'lebensfürchtend'. Keller writes out of his wholehearted acceptance of life in every form, whether it reveals itself to him as history or breaks upon him as contemporary event; Meyer writes out of his fear of actual life, his inability and conscious inability to deal with it, and lives only vicariously in the characters of grand format which he sets upon his stage. Meyer writes: 'The mediocre saddens me because it coincides with something analogous in myself; therefore I desire the grandiose so intensely'. Keller neither feared 'the mediocre', nor was he aware of it within himself, and if he had been he would have been unconcerned about it. Meyer takes refuge in the past because he is afraid of reality, i.e. the present. As he himself says: 'the past gives me a feeling of peculiar calm and greatness'. In one important respect therefore his works differ from the classical Novellen much more than those of Keller do: his subject matter is never taken from contemporary life, is never gossip raised to the level of literature—as Keller's subject matter often is, and as that of the original type of Novelle usually was. It is always taken from the historical past, and places important historical characters upon the stage.

All this is so closely connected with the personality of Conrad Ferdinand Meyer as a human being, that it becomes necessary briefly to say something of his personal history. The son of very cultivated parents, he was an example of that lack of vitality which often accompanies an over-refinement: a similar case is that of the Novellist, Eduard von Keyserling. From his boyhood Meyer revealed a timidity in the face of life which was unquestionably pathological, and developed in course of time to such an extent that he spent some time in a mental home. The whole of his poetic activity as a writer of Novellen lies between the years 1870 and 1890, after which year he succumbed again to mental disorder. Timidity in the face of life is the key to his poetic activity, as it is with [Franz] Grillparzer; as it is in a certain sense with [August] Platen. Both Meyer and Grillparzer seek refuge from life in the vicarious life of their art, but in a different way. Grillparzer disguises his weakness under the form of some superior quality; Meyer leaves it as weakness but sets up an heroic façade in front of it.

Like Platen, Meyer found his way to his own particular expression through contact with the art of Italy; but whereas Venice acted as the open sesame upon Platen's imagination and determined the form of his poetry, with Meyer it was the art of Rome. With both poets art overshadows life both as a source of inspiration—as the stimulus to write—and as the source of their subject matter. Both of them give a rarefied form of life—a stylization of it, in the sense that the life they represent is not seen at first hand but already moulded by art, preeminently by the plastic arts. Thus Meyer's Novellen are full of reminiscences of paintings or sculptures, and he frequently has recourse to the description of an imaginary picture in order to present a psychological situation, to symbolize an event.

Meyer wrote in all eleven Novellen—if *Jürg Jenatsch* be included as a Novelle, though it may perhaps more correctly be classed as a novel. The subject matter of all of them is taken from the historic past—they are historical in a sense in which Storm's Chroniknovellen are not historical, in so far as they deal actually with characters who are known to history, or with situations which are illuminating for Kulturgeschichte. Further the subject matter is predominantly taken from the period of the Renaissance, if the term be stretched so as to include that whole period in European history in which the individual is beginning to assert himself and rebel against the constraint imposed by church or tradition or state. Of the eleven Novellen the one which deals with the earliest historical period is *Die Richterin* (1885), in which the scene is laid partly in Rome, partly in the Rhaetian Alps at the time of Charlemagne, who himself appears as the *deus ex machina*. The latest period which Meyer presents is the eighteenth century in *Der Schuss von der Kanzel* (1878), the weakest of his stories, in which he presents an 'original' who is somewhat akin to Salomon Landolt in Keller's *Landvogt von Greifensee*. In between these two extreme dates lie *Der Heilige* (1880), which deals with the conflict between our English King Henry II and Thomas à Becket; four Novellen treat of the Italian Renaissance in the strictest sense: *Plautus im Nonnenkloster* (1882), of which the narrator is the Italian humanist Poggio; *Die Hochzeit des Mönchs* (1884); *Die Versuchung des Pescara* (1887); and *Angela Borgia* (1891). *Das Amulett* (1873) has as background the French wars of religion in the sixteenth century; *Jürg Jenatsch*

(1876) the history of the Grisons early in the seventeenth century; whilst *Gustav Adolfs Page* (1882) has its action in Germany during the Thirty Years' War; and *Das Leiden eines Knaben* (1883) takes place at the court of Louis XIV. With the exception of *Der Schuss von der Kanzel* there is not a single Novelle in which one of the more famous characters of history does not appear; and there is probably no single writer who has, in so restricted a range, placed so many famous people before his readers: Charlemagne; Henry II and Becket; Dante, Can Grande della Scala; Ezzelino di Romano; Cosmo de' Medici, Poggio; Lucrezia Borgia; Vittoria Colonna; Coligny and Montaigne; Gustav Adolf and Queen Christina of Sweden; Louis XIV, Madame de Maintenon—all of them characters of unusual vitality and originality and active participation in the life of their time. And immediately the doubt arises whether any poet who was not a Shakespeare could possibly have breathed life into all these gigantic figures, so various in their ways, yet all of them so bursting with energy, with vital force. It is true that many of them appear only episodically: Dante merely as the teller of the story of the faithless monk; Can Grande della Scala as the listener to it; Louis XIV and Madame de Maintenon as the listeners to a story which their court physician tells them to beguile an autumn evening. Yet one feels that there is a certain arrogance on the part of a poet who undertakes to present so large a number of the world's greatest personalities in work of so small a compass.

Two things come up for discussion here in the choice of Meyer's characters. First the difference between the dramatist and the Novellen writer. It is quite true that only a superhuman poet like Shakespeare could have dramatized such varied but vital supermen; but a writer with much less creative power can use them as characters in a Novelle. The reason is that the dramatist must conceive them from within, must live them and let their actions be the outcome and expression of their inner life; but the Novellist, who is concerned in the first place with the event and not with the action, can record their gestures, their appearance, their characteristic attitude and so give an image of them seen from outside rather than from within. And if the reader ask himself in reading these Novellen whether Meyer has really penetrated into the characters of Dante and Can Grande and Louis XIV—the answer is 'No'. They are not really there as living characters at all but as theatre 'supers', going through all the gestures associated with the characters they represent, but not living inwardly. Secondly, in spite of all this parade of supermen and superwomen, of heroes and Kraftnaturen, the characters whom Meyer really presents to us from within are all weaklings and beings whose life is moving in uncertainty and doubt and the shadow of disaster: the unstable monk in *Die Hochzeit des Mönchs*; the feeble-minded youth in *Das Leiden eines Knaben*; the conscience-tortured Stemma in *Die Richterin*; the general suffering from a mortal disease in *Die Versuchung des Pescara*; Henry II and Thomas à Becket both seen from a semi-pathological point of view, both wounded in their most vulnerable feelings, in *Der Heilige*. The grand gesture, the historical setting, the heroic attitude is façade with Meyer; the threatened insecure building behind it is

the reality, the real Meyer. And this gives to all Meyer's work that sense of conflicting elements, which prevents it from making the effect of an organic unity. It is fundamentally weakness masquerading as strength: uncertainty and insecurity disguised by the bold gesture. Form and subject matter are nearly always in conflict, except perhaps in the one Novelle, *Das Leiden eines Knaben.*

It is usual to speak of Meyer's Novellen as being specifically historical Novellen—and this is superficially true. But essentially Meyer was concerned not so much with the historical event and setting as with the ethical problem which was incorporated in the event of each Novelle.

—E. K. Bennett

The duality in Meyer's personality comes out in many ways; even in spite of his weakness and timid withdrawal from life there is an element of strength in him. It is by sheer strength of will that he forces his way out of the darkness of mental depression into the light of day in which he can achieve something: and every single work of his is an achievement, something wrested from the forces that threaten to submerge him. And he proposes to himself always the most difficult problems of form, as though to test his will power, his ability to the utmost: the subtle conflict between king and prelate is related by a simple-minded crossbowman. Meyer could hardly have made it more difficult for himself than by mirroring the psychological workings of the mind of Becket in the consciousness of the Swiss soldier who tells the story; and the technique of *Die Hochzeit des Mönchs,* with Dante himself as the story-teller, is more complicated than that of any other framework story.

The characteristic form for Meyer is that of the framework Novelle—just as for Storm it is the Erinnerungsnovelle; for Keller the cyclical framework story; for Heyse the Bekanntschaftsnovelle. Meyer himself writes: 'The tendency to use the framework is quite instinctive on my part. I like to keep the object at a distance from myself or more correctly as far as possible away from my eye' [*Briefe C. F. Meyers,* 1908]. The type of framework Novelle which Meyer uses may be defined more closely as that of the virtuoso framework, for he tends by the choice of the person who tells the story, or the situation in which it is told, to make his task as difficult as possible, so that the effect is rather that of difficulties triumphantly overcome, of a *tour de force,* the skill of which amazes though it may not necessarily delight. As an instance of this virtuosity of technique the framework Novelle *Die Hochzeit des Mönchs* may be considered in detail. The scene is the Court of Can Grande della Scala at Verona. The Duke and his courtiers are gathered round the fire when Dante, the exile, enters and asks for hospitality, which is granted him. The company is engaged in relating instances of sudden changes of vocation with good or evil results, and Dante is bidden to contribute a story. He agrees, saying that he will develop his story from an epitaph which he read on a tombstone years before in Padua. Translated from the Latin it runs: 'Here lies the monk Astorre with his wife Antiope: Ezzelin had them buried'. Now the form of the Novelle is that of a narrative set in the past and seen as something completed. If therefore Dante had related his story in such a way that he said: 'I know what happened; as a matter of historical fact, it was thus and thus'; then the result would have been the normal type of framework Novelle. But Meyer hits upon a more ingenious method than this: all Dante knows is the fact expressed by the epitaph; he makes up the story as he goes along, so that what we are listening to is not a piece of the past completed and laid aside; but a piece of the present going on before our eyes and not yet completed. But that is not enough for Meyer: he adds to the ingenuity of the form still further; the characters in the story which Dante tells are fitted on the characters of the persons present to whom he is telling the story. He takes his listeners and makes them the actors in his drama, adapting the characters of the personages of his story to what he considers to be the characters of the persons before him. The word drama is here used deliberately, because this Novelle of Meyer's stands on the very frontiers between narrative and dramatic poetry, confusing and interchanging them in a way which is both paradoxical and perverse and outdoing in ingenuity anything that the Romantics did in this line. Epic poetry deals with the past; the drama creates a fictitious present. The characters in *Die Hochzeit des Mönchs* exist both in the past and the present. The virtuosity of this method is astonishing. When the butler enters the circle of courtiers (in the framework) Dante immediately uses him as the major-domo in the story he is telling, his peculiarities of speech and gesture being transferred to his equivalent in the Novelle. Further, Dante acknowledges and at the same time annuls the presence of the court jester, in the framework, by obliterating him with a gesture in the Novelle, ' "ich streiche die Narren Ezzelins" unterbrach sich Dante mit einer griffelhaltigen Gebärde, als schriebe er seine Fabel, statt sie zu sprechen, wie er tat'. Again: in the court circle are sitting two ladies; the wife of Can Grande, a woman of commanding presence, and—as is suggested though not openly stated—the mistress of Can Grande, a woman of more facile charm. Suggested too, but only suggested, is the jealousy of the wife for the mistress. In the Novelle the monk hero forsakes his affianced bride, whom Dante endows with the personality of Can Grande's wife, for a woman who is modelled on the personality of Can Grande's mistress; and is murdered by the rival whom she has supplanted. But Meyer's ingenuity goes no further than this, though it may well be asked what would have become of the form if he had made use of the trick, so common in the drama, of making the characters of the play step out of its framework and become living persons; if at the point in the story at which Diana stabs Antiope, the wife of Can Grande had also stabbed her rival.

This Novelle of Meyer's is not cited here as an example of perfection in the Novellenform, but merely as an example of extreme virtuosity and ingenuity in the manipulation of technique, in what appears to be the rather perverse pleasure of Meyer in setting himself technical conundrums and solving them. Technical skill can go no further than this; but the result partakes too much of the nature of a *tour de force* for it to be entirely satisfactory as a work of art. If Meyer's command of technique in this Novelle be compared with an equal mastery in Goethe's Novelle, the difference between an arbitrary and a legitimate use of technique will be apparent. In Meyer's Novelle technique has become in modern slang a 'stunt'—always a sign of decadence in art, since it exists for its own sake and not as something subservient to the significance of the work. Herein it may be said that Meyer approximates to the cult of sheer artistry, of *l'art pour l'art,* which was the ideal of the last years of the century.

But Meyer's sense of form was in reality far less genuine and sure than the ordinary historian of literature asserts. No doubt there is a certain surface brilliance about it as in the technique employed in the narrative here and in *Der Heilige*—and this brilliant overcoming of technical difficulties, this bravura effect, blinds the reader to the fact that the inner form is often very faulty and that which ought to be a single unity is in reality a confusion of two separate themes. In this very Novelle, *Die Hochzeit des Mönchs,* two themes are imperfectly welded—two themes which are not necessarily connected at all: the theme of the monk who forsakes his vows, and the theme of the faithless bridegroom. The renegade monk is not at all necessary to the second half of the story: the bridegroom who abandons his bride for another on the eve of the wedding. Similarly in *Der Heilige,* the real theme, the conflict between King and Prelate, is entirely falsified by the episode of Becket's daughter Grace whom the King abducts, thereby causing her death. In *Die Richterin,* the real theme, that of a woman whose present life is disturbed by the memory of a past crime, is obscured, during a great part of the Novelle, by the theme of brother and sister love. In all three of these works the inner form of the story is not impeccable but indeed very faulty. In fact, in his form as well as in his subject matter, there is with Meyer a good deal of façade, concealing the inherent weakness and dualism.

As there is in Keller's Novellen a loading of the form with detail—an overloading perhaps—but still an enrichment by reason of the living quality of the detail; so in Meyer's works there is a similar overloading of his form with historical detail, which does not in any way contribute to the convincingness of the theme, but merely clogs with the weight of mere learning. This is particularly noticeable in *Das Leiden eines Knaben,* in which Meyer bolsters up his main narrative with continual references to the historical and literary conditions of the time. Thus the reader is informed that Madame de Maintenon, who is merely the listener to the story, is a granddaughter of Agrippa d'Aubigné; he is reminded of Madame de Sévigné, of Molière's last performance in *Le Malade Imaginaire*; that le Duc de Saint Simon is writing *Mémoires,* and that

Condé won battles for Louis XIV. This is merely another instance of that quality in Meyer which leads him to overdo everything and produces an excess of ingenuity, an excess of strength, an excess of learning, an excessive mannerism of style. Keller wrote once, defending the sober quality of his own style: 'Es liegt mein Stil in meinem persönlichen Wesen: ich fürchte immer manieriert und anspruchsvoll zu werden, wenn ich den Mund voll nehmen und passioniert werden wollte'. Meyer was a man and a poet without passion, an observer of, not a participator in life. When he has to deal with passion in his works, he does not find the natural expression for it, but uses a mannered, forced style, which aims at producing the effect of plasticity, but in reality merely chills the feeling of the reader.

It is usual to speak of Meyer's Novellen as being specifically historical Novellen—and this is superficially true. But essentially Meyer was concerned not so much with the historical event and setting as with the ethical problem which was incorporated in the event of each Novelle. His Novellen are in the first instance Problem-novellen—just as those of Paul Heyse were—with the possible exception of *Das Leiden eines Knaben.* He himself wished to be recognized as a Problemdichter, to be appreciated as the describer of conflicts of the soul: he wrote in a letter: 'Je n'écris absolument que pour réaliser quelque idée'. 'Certaines profondeurs de l'âme où j'aimerais descendre.' He resented praise of his work which stressed his power of resuscitating the past, because this was to him of secondary importance as compared with the problem of conscience which was the real theme of his stories. The proof of this inherent method of his—the proceeding from the problem to the characters and events and setting by which it was to be rendered 'anschaulich'—can be gathered from the fact that he made various attempts to 'place' the problem incorporated in his Novelle *Die Richterin,* and tried Sardinia and Sicily for settings before he finally decided upon the Rhaetian Alps at the time of Charlemagne. The essential content of all Meyer's Novellen is the ethical problem, a problem of conscience. With regard to the last of his Novellen, *Angela Borgia,* he writes: 'Cette nouvelle est à proprement dire l'histoire de la conscience'. And if it be asked for what reason he places these problems in historical settings, the answer is given in his own words [in a letter to Félix Bovet, January 14, 1888]:

> Je me sers de la nouvelle historique purement et simplement pour y loger mes expériences et mes sentiments personnels, la préférant au Zeitroman, parce qu'elle masque mieux et qu'elle distance davantage le lecteur. Ainsi sous une forme très objective et éminemment artistique, je suis au dedans tout individuel et subjectif. Dans tous les personnages du Pescare, même dans ce vilain Moroni, il y a du C.F.M.

The statement calls to mind Friedrich Schlegel's description of the Novelle, that it is particularly suited to render a subjective mood indirectly and as it were symbolically because of its natural tendency to objectivity. Meyer's Novellen form a singularly striking example of this, one in which at first sight the subjective and objective elements are an exact antithesis, and weakness, insecurity and doubt are concealed beneath the heroic attitude and the sculptural gesture.

The real Conrad Ferdinand Meyer has only lately been discovered. Earlier biographers and critics of his work drew attention rather to the heroic façade than to the insecure dwellings it fronted and concealed. It seems a truer estimate of him to recognize that this too, with its strong, self-reliant, active and vital characters, is a wish-fulfilment of the real Meyer, who suffered under all the spiritual problems of a declining age.

Meyer's contribution to the development of the German Novelle was too original, too personally individual to have any real influence upon the genre as such. Moreover the German Novelle as a genre had exhausted its utmost possibilities in the works of Keller; every possible aspect of it had already been exploited and Keller's Novellen represent the summit of the development. Conrad Ferdinand Meyer's Novellen at the close of that development, like the stories of Kleist at the beginning, are too individual to be assimilated to any traditional form. Every writer of Novellen no doubt contributes certain individual features and enlarges the possibilities of the genre thereby; but not every kind of individual characteristic can be assimilated or is such that a later writer can profit by it. Kleist and Meyer are individual writers, whose specific qualities cannot easily be assimilated to the tradition of the genre, and their contribution compared with that of Keller, for instance, may be described as morbidly individual. Another writer of Novellen whose works are open to the same criticism is E. T. A. Hoffmann. All three writers have a certain originality which marks them out from other writers of Novellen and impresses them upon the memory and the imagination. Though their works considered singly may or may not conform to Heyse's theory and supply the 'Falcon', yet as a whole they have a more strongly marked silhouette, make a more vivid impression than that which is received from the works of other writers who have been discussed. Though they are less central and lie more on the periphery than the works of Keller, for instance, they attract more attention and seem to possess a greater positive quality than his. The reason is that, compared with the balance and harmony, the equal distribution and completeness of Keller's work, they obtrude some characteristic which is developed at the expense of the harmonious whole.

The Novelle is a bürgerliche genre. It reached the summit of its development, realized its essential form as a German genre in the works of writers like Stifter, Storm and above all Keller, writers standing within the confines of that literary movement known as Poetic Realism, which was the most characteristic expression of German Bürgertum of the middle of the nineteenth century. The critic von Lukacs in his book of essays, *Die Seele und die Formen,* writes: 'In the middle of the last century there were still in Germany, especially on the periphery, towns in which the old Bürgertum still remained strong and living, the Bürgertum which is the greatest contrast to that of to-day. Of this Bürgertum these writers were begotten, they are its genuine, great representatives. . . . Their works are the historical monument of Bürgertum'. Heyse and Meyer are no longer representatives of that Bürgertum, but individualists living outside of it. Heyse's individualism moves only on the surface of life, belongs to the world of fortuitous and irresponsible contacts—the world of hotels and railway carriages; and already in his works the cosmopolitanism of the twentieth century announces itself. Meyer's individualism is of that morbidly psychological nature which isolates the subject from the society which surrounds him. Both of them—Heyse in his cosmopolitanism, and Meyer in his susceptibility to the spiritual problems of his age—were representatives of the disintegrating forces from without and within, which were undermining the Bürgertum with its established mode and accepted code of life.

Colin Walker   (essay date 1967-68)

SOURCE: "Unbelief and Martyrdom in C. F. Meyer's *Der Heilige*," in *German Life and Letters,* Vol. 21, 1967-68, pp. 111-22.

[*In the following excerpt, Walker discusses the major themes of Meyer's* Der Heilige *and traces the religious development of the novella's protagonist, Thomas Becket.*]

Critics will never agree whether the death of Meyer's Thomas Becket is the innocent martyrdom of a genuine convert, whether it is the act of an unbeliever taking revenge on King Henry for the death of his daughter Gnade, or whether the truth lies somewhere between these two extremes. Meyer himself indicated that the Novelle was 'absichtlich mehrdeutig', and he allowed his readers complete freedom of interpretation on the basic enigmas of Becket's passivity, his conversion, and his desire for revenge. His own comments on the work, while extremely illuminating, are so varied and contradictory that one could find some support among them for almost any conceivable interpretation of Becket's character. For instance one cannot immediately accept his unequivocal assertion that Becket remains an unbeliever after he has become Archbishop of Canterbury, for the text and Meyer's other comments are by no means unequivocal on this point. Therefore the following interpretation is not an attempt to provide generally acceptable solutions but offers some suggestions about crucial aspects of Becket's religious development.

Becket's initial paganism can be attributed largely to his Saracen blood and to his experiences at the Moorish court of Cordoba (and perhaps also in Aquitaine). It is conveyed to the reader through his actions (or assumed actions), his usually enigmatic pronouncements and, equally important, by the images and motifs Meyer associates with him.

Becket is a deacon of the Church, yet he is ostentatiously worldly, revelling in Oriental colour and splendour, with no regard for the dark asceticism of the cloister. As a devotee of Greek sculpture he is neither Saracen nor Christian, but a forerunner of Renaissance paganism. He has also a modern humaneness which sets him apart from the medieval barbarism of his Christian contemporaries. Indeed for the narrator Hans the main evidence for Becket's unbelief seems to lie in his reaction against superstition, as in his defence and rescue of the 'witch', Black Mary. His distaste for cruelty and bloodshed is evident in his refusal to have a crucifix in the chapel of Gnade's woodland castle, or to allow hunting on his estates, or again in that incongruous episode where although a cleric he fights in Henry's war and yet throws away in horror a sword covered with French blood. Nevertheless he can threaten death to his servants with just as much glibness as Henry, and he admits that as Chancellor he has been guilty of 'Gewalt, Bestechen, Wortbruch', and other crimes too horrible to mention. Becket is humane, then, in that he is fastidious and enlightened, but he is no more a saint than his Christian associates or antagonists.

His fatalism has roots in Saracen astrology, which he studied in Cordoba, and it is fairly safe to link it with that of the Arab astrologer whom Hans met in Granada and who believed in a universe so fixed that all human and divine choice was excluded, so that there was no room even for the wrath or the grace of God. Becket says that he and Henry are linked by their stars, and that Gnade is guided by her star, and he appears to believe at times in a Providence whose plans for the world cannot be upset by the vain strivings of men. Yet his Providence is personal and does avenge the wrongdoings of mankind. Thus Becket refuses to take action against the traitor Fauconbridge—'Es regen sich unter dem Tun eines jeglichen unsichtbare Arme. Alles Ding kommt zur Reife, und jeden ereilt zuletzt seine Stunde'. However, it would be wrong to see this as the principle governing his outlook throughout the Novelle. If that had been his consistent policy he would not have remained Chancellor for long, and it is clear that Meyer has introduced this incident largely to foreshadow Becket's later passive attitude to the King. When he is Chancellor his passivity is by no means complete, for although his Providence may ensure the eventual downfall of evildoers it does nothing to protect the innocent, and the invisible arms which rescue Hilde from Gui de Malherbe or free Black Mary from her prison are surely those of Becket's henchmen, in the latter case of Hans himself.

Although basically pagan Becket does make some concession to Christianity. His daughter Gnade in her idyllic castle gives him refuge from the cruelties of his world—he tells her 'heidnische Märchen, die den grausamen Weltlauf zu einem süssen Abenteuer verfälschen', and he allows her no such symbols of Christian suffering as a crucifix, missal or saint's image—but he has not had his child brought up wholly as a Muslim. Rather he has given her a reverence for the divine within a framework of very limited and painless Christianity. Like her foster-father Calas they both pray the 'Our Father', no doubt in Arabic.

Becket may well believe in a divinity governing the universe, but the objects of his adoration are all on the earthly plane. His real gods are his daughter, the epitome of earthly beauty and innocence, and also the majesty and power of the king whom he serves.

The narrator speculates why Gnade is so called:

> Ob der gnädigen Bekehrung seiner eigenen so getauften Mutter zu Ehren, oder einer heidnischen Anwandlung nachgebend, weil Grazia wohl die himmlische Gnade bedeutet—die Gott uns allen schenken möge!—aber ebensogut die feinste Blüte menschlicher Art und Anmut.

The second explanation must surely carry greater weight. We may safely assume that Gnade is the daughter born to his Moorish wife Princess 'Sonnenschein', who died at the birth. Under such circumstances it is hardly likely that in the name Gnade he wished to commemorate his mother's conversion from Islam.

Hans calls Gnade Becket's 'Heiligtum', he himself calls her 'Mein Einziges, mein Alles!' When Hans sees him riding through the forest to meet his daughter he likens him to a knight on pious pilgrimage to the Holy Grail. But the clearest indication of Becket's religious devotion to his daughter is that scene in the chapel where he lies mourning beside her body:

> Aber da war kein Kruzifixus und kein ewiges Licht, und statt eines heiligen Leichnams unter dem Altar lag in einem Schreine vor demselben, ebenso reich geschmückt, die tote Gnade.

We learn that Gnade submits to the King because of her predominantly Saracen blood—'Der König ist [den sarazenischen Weibern] an Gottes und des Gesetzes statt und mehr als Vater und Mutter'—and Becket's servility and loyalty are also attributed to his Saracen heritage. It is difficult to determine exactly the Chancellor's attitude to the King in the first part of the Novelle. At first he appears to have had some respect and affection for his master, but because of Henry's licentious and irresponsible mode of life these feelings have turned to contempt. Yet he still tells Gnade that respect and obedience are due to the King, and his attitude to him could be summed up in the words with which he finally accepts the Archbishopric—'Was du verhängst, das geschehe!' One certainly cannot say that he has much opinion of Henry the man, but his service of the King, the power which such service brings, and the royal favour in which he stands—these come only after his relationship with Gnade as the supreme values in his life. . . .

Let us now consider the significance of sun motifs in *Der Heilige*.

We have already seen how Becket treasures his daughter Gnade above all else. Perhaps this is because she is a living reminder to him of his wife, Princess 'Sonnenschein'. He, Prince 'Mondschein' and half-Saxon, may be more at home under the northern skies of England, this 'gegen Mitternacht gelegenen Insel', but he wishes to see his daughter live 'nicht unter diesem feuchten Himmel, sondern jenseits des Meeres, in einem sonnigen Lande von mildem Sitten'. Nor is she suited, he tells her, for life in the cloister—'du hast keine Sünde zu büssen und Licht und Sonne nötig'. Meyer also indicates that she is a child of the sun by the fairy-tale castle in which she is enshrined and which is first introduced to us glistening under the rays of the setting sun, by the shining gold band which holds her hair, by the golden spheres playing in the fountain of her castle courtyard, and finally in the scene where she lies dead in the chapel, a figure of unearthly beauty, robed in garments of gold and bathed in sunlight.

Becket also experiences 'Gnade' in that other relationship which takes the place of a relationship with a personal God, though here it is 'Gnade' in the sense of royal favour. Once again Meyer resorts to sun imagery. When Hans first enters service at Windsor Castle he is told of the terrible deaths of the Norman kings—'Aber was tut's? Glänzende Sonnen gehen blutig unter'. Henry, with his 'blauen unbeschatteten Augen' burning like two flames, is also a man of the sun, but in the sense that he embodies earthly vitality and power, rather than kindliness and beauty. He is one of those of whom Meyer writes in *Unter den Sternen*, who '. . . in der Sonne kämpft, ein Sohn der Erde'. Thus we find that in the early stages of their relationship—'der Kanzler der einzige Sachse war, der im Sonnenlicht der königlichen Gnade wandelte', and we also learn something of Becket's attitude to this favour—'dieser sonnte sich wie eine schlanke, weisse Schlange in den Strahlen der fürstlichen Gunst'.

Of course there can be no suggestion that Becket himself is a sun-worshipper, or a man of the sun. He has none of the pagan vitality of Frederick II. And he is after all Prince 'Mondschein'; Meyer characterizes him repeatedly with moon images. He does have an intellectual's devotion to the naive children of the sun, although any original devotion to the person of the King is soon soured. He draws religious sustenance from his secular relationships, and Meyer has emphasized this through a secular use of the concept of grace. This is then reinforced by the association of grace with the supremely pagan motif of the sun.

Therefore I believe that the primary symbolical meaning of the figure of Gnade lies in the secularization of the Christian concept as an indication of Becket's essential paganism. I cannot agree with Lily Hohenstein's suggestion that the corruption of Gnade symbolizes Henry's rejection of God's Grace and thus the unforgivable sin against the Holy Ghost. No matter how heinous his crime may be, and although he does rebel against God by breaking His law, there is no suggestion in the Novelle that Henry consciously opposes God; rather he continues to regard himself as a humble Christian. In any case the equation of two such sins is theologically impossible, as can be seen from Christ's words (Matthew xii. 31)—'Wherefore I say unto you, all manner of sin and blasphemy shall be forgiven unto men; but the blasphemy against the Holy Ghost shall not be forgiven unto men.' Henry's seduction of Gnade is a *mortal* sin, as

Hans says, a sin that occasions the wrath of God and indeed the withdrawal of Grace, but also one that *can* be forgiven after due repentance and penance. As we shall see, Becket later offers Henry the opportunity for such forgiveness.

When Gnade is killed the sun all but goes out of Becket's life. In spite of his continued loyalty to the King his contempt for him has now turned into seemingly implacable hatred, and he is waiting passively for his daughter's death to be avenged. He seems even more convinced of the fundamental suffering that is the lot of man—'sunt lacrimae rerum', he tells Henry—and he turns for help to the 'geduldige König der verhöhnten und gekreuzigten Menschheit', to Christ. The scene where Hans overhears Becket's prayer to the crucifix is of the utmost importance for the interpretation of his religious development, and the prayer must be taken as completely sincere, for this is one scene where Becket believes he is unobserved, and all the masks have fallen away. He addresses Christ in Arabic, perhaps because Christ, too, was Oriental, perhaps because Arabic has been the language of his private devotion. In any case it is clear that committal to Christ now takes the place of devotion to Gnade. He feels drawn to the crucifix, from which his 'verwöhnten Augen' had hitherto been repelled. But it is a tragic Man of Sorrows whom he reveres, not the Risen Saviour. Christ died for man's salvation, he says, to bring peace into the world, and yet nothing has changed and the world is still a realm of suffering. Yet he resolves to follow Christ, and prays: 'Verscheuche den Geier des unversöhnlichen Grams, der mein Herz verzehrt! . . . Damit ich in deine Stapfen trete . . .'.

It is not clear just how he regards Christ at this turning-point in his religious life. He appears to waver between devotion to Christ the man—'der Nazarener', 'der Andere', 'der Gekreuzigte'—and Christ the God, the 'himmlisches Gemüt', who is divine not because of the teaching of the Church or because of a work of salvation, but because of His powers of divine (i.e. super-human) love and forgiveness. And one important consequence of this new communion with Christ is Becket's policy of making the burdens of the Saxons more tolerable, though he manages this without arousing the opposition of the King or of the Norman barons.

When the King is so gracious as to appoint him Archbishop of Canterbury, in part compensation for the death of Gnade, he shrinks from this office and the conflicts of conscience he knows it will bring him. It soon appears that his fears were justified and in his new asceticism and forthright championing of the Saxons we cannot distinguish between genuine personal devotion to the Prince of Sorrows, the new master in whose hands the King has placed him, and defiance of Henry as an expression of his uncontrollable hatred. There may be much truth in Bertram de Born's accusation: 'Du glaubst der Liebe zu dienen, aber der Hass ist der mächtigere'.

Christ becomes the sole recipient of his devotion, and he gives back to Henry the Chancellor's seal—'dies Pfand

deiner übergrossen, unverdienten Gnade, die mich lange Jahre beglückte . . .'.

Becket now also appears to move towards a more orthodox relationship with Christ. He speaks of Him as his brother, but also as his master; when the King asks him whom he serves he points upwards in ecstasy. He seems to see Christ more definitely now as a God, less as the man on the cross, his equal. He suggests that in protecting the refugee Saxons he is doing God's will—he now has some belief in a Christian God, at least in a divinity whose ethical nature is to be equated with Christ's.

Yet his conversion has involved him in a tragic paradox: his prayer to the crucifix has made it plain that if he is to follow Christ he must strive to forgive Henry and reach a reconciliation with him; at the same time it is his duty as Christ's disciple to promote the welfare of his Saxon flock, a policy which makes reconciliation impossible (and which may be subconsciously motivated by hatred).

This personal tragic conflict is almost resolved when the King and Archbishop meet in hope of agreement. At first all seems finally lost when Becket shrinks from the kiss of peace, but with exemplary self-domination he then moves to the fulfilment of his Christian discipleship—in a remarkable speech which must be quoted extensively. First he doubts if his master the Nazarene, who kissed the traitor Judas, could have touched the lips of one who had corrupted His child. Then he continues:

> Und da er zugleich ein Gott ist, wie die Kirche lehrt, so kann er den Mord seines Lammes nicht vergeben ohne eine schwere und völlige Sühne, weil er sich selbst, das heisst die Gerechtigkeit, die sein Wesen ist, nicht zerstören kann. Und ich, der ein Mensch aus heidnischem Blute und nicht so gelassen bin, als ich scheine, ich soll über mich bringen, was mein Meister nicht vermocht hätte! Und doch, es soll geschehen. Aber um ein Lösegeld, Seele gegen Seele!

He specifies the penance a few moments later: 'Ich vergebe dir den Tod Gnades und deine Lästerung, wenn du meine Brüder, die Sachsen, freigibst und fortan göttliche und menschliche Wege wandelst!' Here the confusion in Becket's Christology is complete. Although he earlier associated the Christ of the Gospels with perfect justice he now first excuses his own weakness by saying that even Christ the Nazarene *could not have* made the gesture of forgiveness. But Christ the God, the Essence of Justice, *can* forgive—at the price of atonement—and Becket himself will forgive Henry in Christ's name. It may be thought that the parenthesis 'wie die Kirche lehrt' in fact shows his detachment from the doctrine of Christ's divinity, yet it is only by complete commitment to Christ the Lord and Judge that Becket has been able to find an answer to his prayer to the Prince of Sorrows that he may be released from the hatred consuming his heart. After this momentary confusion and this new identification with Christ the unclear distinction between Christ the Nazarene and Christ the God disappears.

The offer to Henry and his identification with Christ the Judge have marked the end of his passivity, if indeed his opposition to Henry in the form of protection of the innocent Saxons could ever properly be called passive. Now he has decisively intervened. Admittedly divine vengeance would be averted as a result of Henry's atonement, but it is Becket who has taken the initiative: his offer of help and forgiveness is the prerequisite for the reconciliation and thus for Henry's salvation: 'Über dir schwebt eine andere als meine Rache. Ich sühne sie dir. Ich schirme dich'.

[In *GRM,* Vol. XXXVI, 1955], Werner Oberle concludes that Becket's gesture represents 'höchste Ironie', that he expects the King's refusal. I cannot share this view, largely because of the reason stated above—to forgive Henry was Becket's most sincere desire—but also because of the fervour with which he urges Henry to accept. The King wavers towards acceptance, and Becket seems genuinely dejected at the refusal. If Henry had agreed to this penance Becket's own tragic conflict as a disciple of Christ would have been removed, for Henry would have been forgiven and the welfare of the Saxons ensured.

The opportunity is denied him. The offer is rebuffed, and Henry forbids Becket on pain of death (a significant innovation of Meyer's) to set foot on English soil. Becket seems broken. He says he will return to his flock which has been deprived of its shepherd, and he welcomes the prospect of martyrdom as a release from his burdens.

Becket is now determined on martyrdom, for the King has destroyed all hope of accommodation. Just as Becket emulates Christ as Judge in his offer of reconciliation dependent on Henry's atonement, and sees himself as the agent of divine forgiveness, so too he emulates Christ as Judge in his act of martyrdom, and sees himself as the agent of divine punishment. In the final scene in the cathedral he is not just the martyr imitating in word and gesture the Passion of his Lord the Nazarene, he is also like Christ in majesty, Christ the Judge. Such is the transformation from the humble servant of his flock that Hans scarcely recognizes him. When the four knights enter— 'Der Bischof hatte sich bei ihrem Eintreten in seinem Stuhl emporgerichtet, und ich wunderte mich über die Erhabenheit seiner Gestalt, aus welcher jede Schwäche gewichen schien'. Hans does not dare to look on Becket's face, 'weil ich fürchtete, der Dreifaltige habe in seinem Leibe Einzug gehalten und blicke majestätisch aus seinen Augen'. Becket has told the knights that he received the archbishopric 'Aus den Händen meines Königs zu seinem Gericht'. This is now the moment of final judgment.

I find it difficult to share the view of W. A. Coupe [in *GLL,* Vol. XVI, 1963] that in his martyrdom Becket maintains both passivity and innocence. One can certainly see in his desire to return to his Saxon flock one of the main motives for his defiance of Henry's warning, but if a peaceful death had been his chief concern he would have stayed in France. When back at Canterbury and faced with the prospect of martyrdom he could well

have fled, for there was good enough precedent for it— one need only think of St Paul. Even Becket himself had once fled the country 'wie ein Verbrecher'. Flight would have been quite legitimate if Becket had felt that he would be more useful to his flock alive and in exile again rather than dead and crowned as a martyr. If nothing could be gained by escape then of course he could not be blamed for staying and undergoing martyrdom—that is if these were the only considerations. However, flight in this instance could have meant safe-conduct to one of his persecutor's castles, an opportunity he angrily rejects. This is a most important innovation by Meyer: Henry recants his angry words and orders that Becket should be protected from the knights who plan to murder him. When Hans informs Becket of this he refuses to listen. He has already decided that his death at Henry's command is the will of God and insists in spite of Hans's protests that it is the will of the King. Hans accuses Becket of deliberately trying to ruin the King, and Becket rounds on him with words recalling Christ's reply when St Peter tried to dissuade Him from entering Jerusalem—'Hebe dich von hinnen, du Schalk und böser Knecht, denn du bist mir ärgerlich!' It is difficult to deny completely the justice of Hans's charge or of his anger at Becket's reply. This does not necessarily mean that the Archbishop wishes the King's soul to be damned, since we do not know how real such a concept would be to him, but since he has no answer to Hans's accusation it is hard to escape the conclusion that Becket has determined that the guilt of the murder should be on Henry's head, and that this, as well as the consequent strife within the kingdom, should be fitting punishment for the crime Henry has refused to expiate. He probably feels that the justice of Christ is working itself out through him, but he has made a calculated decision. Meyer has given him a choice of alternatives which rules out a passive attitude.

If a martyr's desire for martyrdom is licit then his self-sacrifice does not in itself make him responsible for his persecutor's guilt, for the guilt is permitted and not intended, just as Christ permitted but did not intend the guilt of Judas Iscariot (as Dr Coupe points out). If, however, a prospective martyr hears that the persecutor does not desire the death and in fact offers protection against those supposedly acting in his name, then the martyr has the moral obligation to ensure that he remains alive. If he insists on the execution he is doing more than permitting the guilt of the persecutor; he is consenting to it. He is acting as the negative secondary cause of that guilt and indeed of his own death.

The primary end of martyrdom must be glorification of the Faith, of God and His Church. Martyrdom desired for its own sake or out of world-weariness is illicit and sinful. Martyrdom welcomed as a means of punishing the persecutor must be doubly so. If the Pope had heard the testimony of Hans, if he had known the cruel reality instead of the pious legend (and if he had left out political considerations), it is doubtful if Becket would have become a saint. Dr Coupe suggests that if we judge Becket by his acts alone, then he is indeed a saint, but it is not just the acts which make the saint nor the death alone which makes the martyr, but the faith for which he lives and dies. His motives must be pure beyond doubt.

Throughout the Novelle Becket spurns the Latin Church, and he is clearly an unbeliever if judged by the Christian standards of his day—evidently no great fault in Meyer's eyes. He can scarcely be called an unbeliever in the modern sense, for there seems little doubt that he believes that Christ is God. But he is modern in that the core of his religion is ethical. Christ is not really worshipped for His own sake, only in so far as He is the divine embodiment of suffering, love and justice.

Becket's type of religious development does not stand alone in Meyer's work. In **Angela Borgia,** for instance, Don Giulio is also a Hellenist, 'ein in der Sonne Atmender', a pagan, however, of a more sensualist variety. When blinded he is bereft of the sun and of the life of the senses, but through his suffering and with the help of Angela Borgia he attains to a Christ-like existence. Becket also strives to emulate Christ, and he comes to identify his own feelings with his master's. His life becomes increasingly Christ-like, but in his death he takes it upon himself to exercise that vengeance which is the Lord's. It is his tragedy that in his overweening ambition to emulate Christ he probably falls victim to just that human frailty of vengefulness that he has striven through Christ to overcome.

Mattingly on the artistry of *The Saint*:

Not even Flaubert has ever recaptured more successfully the color and spirit of the past than has Meyer in **The Saint,** his short novel about Thomas à Becket, now translated. The medievalism of the tale is not a matter of museum study, of archeology dragged in by the heels, but of imaginative penetration to the inner character of the epoch. Every attitude of his actors has at once the naïve, fantastic angularity, and yet the convincing humanness and vigor, of a *laisse* from a *chanson de geste* or of a twelfth century window at Chartres. By bold invention and adaptation of the divers threads of legend and of history, Meyer has woven a surprisingly unified story. With the aid of the tale which ballad readers will recognize as that of young Bicham and Shusy Pie, he provides Becket with a Saracen mother and a Saxon father, following in this a late legend, and by making the Chancellor the father of fair Rosamund, he supplies a motivating link between his early services to Henry II and his later opposition.

Garrett Mattingly, "A Halo for a Saint," in
The Saturday Review of Literature,
July 5, 1930, p. 1172.

Lee B. Jennings   (essay date 1970)

SOURCE: "The Ambiguous Explosion: C. F. Meyer's *Der Schuss von der Kanzel,*" in *The German Quarterly,* Vol. XLIII, No. 2, March, 1970, pp. 210-22.

[*In the following essay, Jennings offers a psychoanalytical interpretation of Meyer's novella.*]

Der Schuss von der Kanzel is at once the least pretentious of Meyer's Novellen and the one which best captures the contemporary tone of bourgeois realism. Yet in reading it we have the feeling of moving in an uncanny private world of the author amid submerged fears and portents; it is the type of story which, despite its overt claim to prosaicness and innocuousness, seems to demand some degree of psychological subtlety in its interpretation. Indeed, Meyer, while hardly a spontaneous writer, seems unable to edit out a strong component of the unconscious in his works. His statements of artistic purpose are notorious for their lack of insight into his true strengths and weaknesses. Sigmund Freud was struck by the accurate portrayal of the mechanics of repression, with respect to an incest theme, in Meyer's **Richterin** and there is some reason to think that this encounter was instrumental in the birth of psychoanalysis. It is safe to assume that Meyer's outstanding psychological insight in this case was more the result of personal affinities than of his observation of other persons. Meyer writes, in general, as Freud's patients spoke: in urbanely acceptable transformations of unacceptable horrors. The suggestion that Meyer, even in his best years, displayed "neurotic" symptoms may offend some of his admirers; it should not, since his claim to be wresting significance from chaos and nothingness is thereby strengthened. It is time again to cast doubt on the comfortable fiction of the healthy author writing for healthy readers, a fiction which makes little allowance for spiritual depth. If literary study needs protecting, it is not from intimations of morbidity, but from preconceived ideas of health.

There are, of course, powerful arguments against psychological approaches to literature. They are said to shift attention from the work to the author-as-person. If they admit to psychoanalytic influence, they are thought to be wholly bent upon uncovering unconscious motivations, which, aside from being difficult to prove, are also difficult to distinguish from conscious ones. While these objections actually seem most applicable to the cruder attempts of Freud's disciples in the 1920's and 30's, they must be taken into account. Perhaps it would be helpful to take the standpoint that, although it would indeed be futile to seek out unconscious motivations exclusively, it is likewise foolish to think that one will be so fortunate as to be able to deal entirely with conscious motivations in connection with a phenomenon as complex as a work of art. Then, too, certain questions arise: Can the work really be cleanly severed from the author? Is the elusiveness of unconscious elements really sufficient excuse for ignoring them? Does not strict *Werkimmanenz* eliminate consideration not only of the author's unconscious tendencies, but of his conscious intent also? If our answer to the last question is affirmative, then we might have all the more grounds to be skeptical of Meyer's direct or implied claim to be presenting a constructive, optimistically tinged world picture, and our estimation of his humor must be determined more by the quality of our laughter than by any protestation of light-heartedness on his part. *Werkimmanenz,* while it provides a valuable technique, must be practiced consistently or not at all; it cannot be used to justify a Gottschedian rationalism in the face of the creative act.

It is clear that Meyer is made uneasy by his own attempts at fanciful humor, which began as a cloak for unsavory matters and then somehow became unsavory themselves.

—Lee B. Jennings

The following consideration of **Der Schuss von der Kanzel** does not conform to the prevalent notion that interpretations must be total revaluations, exhaustive and artfully wrought. It is intended rather as an admittedly partial treatment supplementing the existing body of critical opinion. It will proceed on the assumption that the author's statement or implication of intent should neither be accepted unquestioningly nor totally ignored. It is assumed, further, that authors' minds, like those of other persons, operate according to certain ultimately or generally determinable patterns, on levels other than the strictly conscious. Finally, while we cannot hope, in the absence of more concrete information, to uncover all, or even most, of Meyer's basic irrational motive factors, it is our contention that any partial revelation of them can only be regarded as a gain. We shall assume, in other words, that the body of psychoanalytical literature has not failed to reveal some patterns in the operation of the mind at different levels; that most thought does, indeed, tend to move on different levels; that literature, as a product of mind, is not devoid of these patterns; that its aesthetic merit is by no means endangered thereby; and that, on the whole, one stands to gain more by being aware of the existence of such patterns than by repudiating them.

When we turn to Meyer's actual statements about **Der Schuss von der Kanzel** in his correspondence, we find, as it happens, a curious strain of dissatisfaction and uneasiness. He repeatedly refers to it as a potboiler and bagatelle, a work undertaken against his better judgment and outside his real sphere of competence; he is even annoyed afterward at the praise it has received. The vehemence of the statements suggests that he is protesting too much, and a closer examination of them shows that his feelings about the work are highly ambivalent. Far from going about his task offhandedly, he is quite absorbed in it, while at the same time somewhat awed at the "craziness" of his prankish fantasy which comes to light:

> Ich bin gegenwärtig verschollen bis ich meine Novelle beendigt habe, worin ich mich völlig vergaâ mit der ich aber, bei anhaltender guter Stimmung, in dieser Woche

zu Ende zu kommen hoffe. Es ist tolles Zeug, das mir eigentlich nicht zu Gesichte steht.

To be sure, he attempts to give the impression that the "craziness" was injected intentionally for reasons of practical craftsmanship; he reports having told the potential publisher: "ich hätte von Zürchersachen nur diess *geringe* Sujet und ich müsste es toll behandeln, sonst werde es gemein." Similarly: "Ich hoffe, der ernste Hintergrund wird dem tollen Zeuge wohlthun. Es war gar nicht leicht und brauchte eine feste Hand, die Novelle so zu halten, dass sich kein Vernünftiger daran stossen kann."

The stimulus for these defensive remarks seems to have been a series of complaints by literal-minded, pious, and patriotic readers regarding the treatment of Swiss historical figures, especially General Werdmüller. Such unpleasantnesses even make Meyer wish he had not written the "Teufelsnovelle," and they cause him to request of his editor "eine Andeutung über den Humor, wie er auf alle Gesichter dasselbe groteske Licht fallen lässt," in connection with a projected foreword. In another, almost identical, passage he speaks of "barokke Beleuchtung" his overt purpose is to assert that he is singling out no one personage or faction for exaggerated treatment or caricature, but we can discern also the realization that he is creating a special kind of world, one governed by a strained and fanciful humor.

Meyer's own remarks thus detract somewhat from the idea of an innocuous literary joke, and they make us wonder whether the rather forcible application of humor has helped render palatable other injudicious things besides those mentioned as being inherent in the historical subject matter. It is clear that Meyer is made uneasy by his own attempts at fanciful humor, which began as a cloak for unsavory matters and then somehow became unsavory themselves. Perhaps his discomfort stems from the fact that his own inner tensions, being afforded no opportunity for sublimation in this "lowly" genre, threaten to expose themselves. This would explain the often-cited remark to Wille:

> Sie schlagen den "Schuss" entschieden zu hoch an, ohne die Nötigung des gegebenen Wortes wäre die Posse ungeschrieben geblieben. Mir individuell hinterlässt das Komische immer einen bittern Gesehmack, wahrend das Tragische mich erhebt und beseligt.

A parallel may be seen in the case of Theodor Storm, who, in his Novelle *Der Herr Etalsrat,* likewise decides upon a tone of boisterous, drastic, fanciful humor, which he also refers to as "grotesk," explicitly in order to deal with an aesthetically (or otherwise) questionable theme, and he likewise ends by making the work a vehicle for his own anxieties.

Der Schuss von der Kanzel, in its serenely humorous and idyllic aspect, has been taken as an expression of Meyer's new-found domestic happiness. No doubt there is an ironic self-portrait, or perhaps a caricature of a discarded former self, to be glimpsed in the inept suitor

Pfannenstiel. Furthermore, the setting of the story, the peninsula "die Au" (the site of Wertmüller's estate), was also the site of Meyer's proposal of marriage. It is very likely, however, that Meyer's marital bliss was far from undisturbed, in view of the interruption of his long-standing attachment to his sister and the obvious disquiet he reveals everywhere in regard to erotic matters. In a poem on his betrothal, left unpublished during his lifetime (perhaps wisely so), we are struck by the air of gloom and moribundity that threatens to assume dominance over the assertion of fulfilled life:

> Kennst du, Kind, im Sterngefunkel
> Noch das Eichendunkel?
> Noch das Eiland unbelauscht,
> Dran die Welle rauscht?
>
> Dort im Abendlicht vor wenig Wochen
> Ward ein Wort gesprochen—
> Zwei Verarmte macht' es ewig reich—
> Doch du wurdest bleich.
>
> Dort im Abendlicht vor wenig Wochen
> Ward ein Bann gebrochen,
> Dass der Quell des Lebens überquoll,
> O wie voll, wie voll!

The story, revolving as it does about the paradoxical situation of the pistol shot in a sanctified place, has the skeletal sparseness of a Boccaccio tale, but with noticeable idiosyncrasies. The vicar Pfannenstiel, a scholarly young man lacking in self-assurance, calls upon General Wertmüller, a notorious rugged individualist bordering, it seems, on schizoid eccentricity, who, though at heart good-natured, cannot resist a prank. In the eyes of his pious neighbors, the General is probably damned, if not actually in league with the Devil. Pfannenstiel has been warned to expect merciless harassment from him. The General, feeling that it is time to put his house in order, has mellowed somewhat and would not be averse to performing an act of benevolence, providing it could be combined with some lusty piece of mischief. He dismisses, understandably, the unassuming Pfannenstiel's petition for the chaplainship of a remote military unit. However, he sees also that some powerful motive must underlie such a peculiar request, and he correctly surmises that an attachment to his goddaughter Rahel is behind it all, and that a bit of skulduggery on his part might put things right by facilitating the desired marriage. Rahel's father, a pastor and cousin of the General, has a nearly disgraceful weakness for firearms. Through crafty maneuvering, the General first presents him with an exceptionally hard-firing antique pistol and then surreptitiously substitutes its hair-triggered companion piece. As expected, the clergyman cannot refrain from trying the mechanism, and a loud report ensues just as he is exhorting the congregation to praise God with loud acclaim. The scandal is so great that he must relinquish his holy office—and his daughter—to Pfannenstiel. The baffled congregation is sworn to silence in return for being bequeathed a long-coveted piece of land. Soon afterward, we are told the General has died of a sudden and mysterious illness in the midst of his new campaign; the stage is returned, so to speak, to the grand events of history.

The pistol shot is the focus of the story. It is awaited by the reader with almost unpleasant suspense and serves as a wondrous immediate resolution of most of the story's problems, a purge of various anxieties. The humor is clouded; there is a strange air of the infantile about the whole affair. Nevertheless, the pastor's passion for firearms is more acceptably rechanneled; the General is able to dispose of his worldly goods in a constructive way while bolstering his pretensions to omnipotence by means of a consummate prank; and while Pfannenstiel is not directly involved, the symbolic reflection of the psychic development taking place within him is unmistakable.

Pfannenstiel's problem, in the General's estimation, is a lack of elemental masculinity ("männliche Elementarkraft") that prevents him from winning the girl he loves in the face of rather insignificant obstacles. She eventually makes it clear that she accepts, or perhaps prefers, him the way he is, but meanwhile Pfannenstiel has himself become aware of a certain deficiency in this area, which he vaguely associates with ineptness in the use of firearms. The General, in one of his more malicious outbursts of teasing, has tried to persuade Pfannenstiel to rush to his sweetheart and entreat her to flee with him, and to threaten suicide if she refuses. Pfannenstiel does not take this suggestion seriously, but he does have a dream in which he carries this proof of manliness to its fatal conclusion. Though one must be on guard against the tendency of Freud's early adherents to assume a fixed language of sexual symbols, it is evident that the firing of a gun is here closely associated with Pfannenstiel's emergent virility, while yet standing for the punishment that awaits the emergence.

From a psychoanalytical point of view, to be sure, it would be difficult to say without further evidence whether the gunfire in church—the libidinous discharge in a sanctified place—is indicative here of a wholesome incipient genitality or perhaps of recalcitrant, regressive anal tendencies. Nevertheless, it seems not incompatible with our understanding of the story to surmise that one or the other pattern, or perhaps both, may exist as an overtone to the more obvious train of motivated events. The role of General Wertmüller cannot be regarded as entirely benevolent to Pfannenstiel's psychic growth. His insistence, however playful, upon self-destruction as the only alternative to successful wooing is only too suggestive of Meyer's frequent pairing of erotic love and death in general; it is consistent, however, also with the role of a fatherly guardian of familial purity, the senior partner of an Oedipal relationship. On the morning after his dream, Pfannenstiel leaps a fence and visits his beloved in a wild-eyed, disheveled state; but soon we leave the couple in a scene of domestic bliss, or perhaps tedium, with her sewing onto his coat the buttons that the General, in his importunate "button-holing," had detached. Pfannenstiel, indeed, feels that he has attained a lattice-enclosed paradise on earth: "Nun kam es über ihn wie Paradiesesglück. Licht und Grün, die niedrige Laube, das bescheidene Pfarrhaus, die Erlösung von den Dämonen des Zweifels und der Unruhe!"

Meyer, while hardly a spontaneous writer, seems unable to edit out a strong component of the unconscious in his works. His statements of artistic purpose are notorious for their lack of insight into his true strengths and weaknesses.

—Lee B. Jennings

There is thus a real and symbolic resolution of conflicts, but one which somehow remains less than satisfactory. The shot in church calls forth no relief on the part of the outraged congregation. Their enforced secrecy is ironically described as the reverse of the acclaim which Wilhelm Tell's feat enjoyed, a remark which favors the seeking of Oedipal implications (since the Tell-shot represents a unique and fabled reversal of the Oedipal situation). The General seems to have used the near-sacrilegious gunfire to maintain his sovereignty as the dangerous, arms-bearing symbolic father, the discourager of virility in others. He has engineered the disgrace of a fumbling quasi-father (the pastor), who then retires into the woman's world of domesticity with his equally inept successor. Pfannenstiel, when first questioned as to his identity by the General, can only mutter: "Ich bin der Vetter . . . des Vetters . . . vom Vetter," thus stamping himself as a denizen of the world of uncles and cousins, not that of fathers and sons. His very name (notwithstanding the fact that it is the name of a nearby mountain) suggests a ludicrous appendage, not to mention the repeated motif of torn-off buttons (Pfannenstiel's colleague has come from an interview with the General "mit abgerissenen Knöpfen und gerädert").

Meyer, perhaps unwittingly, has embarked upon a bawdy Aristophanean comedy based on the disgrace of the inept male, i.e., symbolic castration. Being basically ill at ease with bawdiness, he is unable to maintain the corresponding tone for long, especially when it comes to the restoration of a main character to respectable status. This is possible only by a general renunciation of heroism in terms of the lowered horizons of Biedermeier resignation and self-irony. The comedy of the eunuch is replaced by the exploits of the little man, content in the end to return to his slot in the contemporary social structure. The moderate success of Pfannenstiel then serves to transform the laughter of contempt into the benign chuckle of sympathy reserved for one's inferiors; the procedure in Keller's *Kleider machen Leute* is similar, in that the tailor is rehabilitated only after renunciations of his high aspirations, that is, his aspirations to be like us.

Certain details of the story, which stand out strangely from the realistic narrative, render these symbolic considerations more plausible. As Pfannenstiel approaches the General's isolated domain we note an air of enigma and magic, not without sinister overtones. His companion, a neighboring pastor, warns him of the General's blasphemous nature and fiery diabolical pastimes. Pfannenstiel defends his undertaking in terms that suggest a determination to communicate with the unconscious: "Ich will es ein bisschen mit der Torheit versuchen, die Weisheit hat mir bis jetzt nur herbe Früchte gezeitigt." There is the hint of an underworld voyage in the boat trip across to the uncanny realm: "Schon warf das schweigsame Eichendunkel seine schwarzen Abendschatten weit auf die schauernden Gewässer hinaus." (After his arrival, Pfannenstiel's initial feeling of being in a bad dream gives way to that of an apprehensive but intrepid bather about to plunge into the water.)

The ferryman can be persuaded to go on only with difficulty in the face of the harassments of the General's Moorish servant, a good-natured primitive who revels in shouting imprecations ("Swineund!"), as it seems, ubiquitously across the water through a megaphone, to the indignation of God-fearing citizens. Conceived along similar lines—namely, as a signal that a more primal realm is being entered—is the figure of a Turkish girl seen at a window of the General's estate. Implausibly enough, this painted semblance of an exotic temptress is taken to be a flesh-and-blood person by passing boatmen. The apparition haunts Pfannenstiel's dreams—those same dreams in which the pistol shot reaches fateful proportions. The idea that some profound feminine archetype is working its way toward Pfannenstiel's consciousness is heightened by the transformation of the Turkish girl into his beloved Rahel. Even before he falls asleep, he is fascinated by the hushing gesture of the painted girl, which he takes to signify: "Come, but be silent," perhaps an invitation to explore the recesses of his own mind, or to do so without arousing the paternal guardian. The author tells us, in fact, that something heretofore unrecognized rose to the surface of Pfannenstiel's mind at this time, something to which he dared not yet give a name: a burning desire and the blissful possibilities of fulfillment: "Es tauchte etwas ihm bis heute völlig unbekannt Gebliebenes in seiner Seele auf, etwas, dem er keinen Namen geben durfte,—eine brennende Sehnsucht, die glückselige Möglichkeit ihrer Erfüllung." Negative feelings, however, are not easily removed from this arousal of slumbering eroticism, and we read further of a thrice-repeated cycle of desire, wickedness, and repentance.

Despite the rather inconclusive results as far as the hero is concerned, we can observe here a remarkable, probably instinctive, pre-Freudian understanding of the fact that erotic desire may be attached to different types of objects and may go through progressive changes in the development of an individual, and that such changes may be heralded in such partially disguised forms as dreams.

Not only Eros but also Thanatos sends representatives into the General's eerie realm. He himself is a man consecrated to death, and like the numerous characters of this type in other works of Meyer he takes on some features of the Grim Reaper himself. It is not difficult to glimpse in him also the archetype of the trickster, in Jung's words "a minatory and ridiculous figure" who "stands at the very beginning of the way of individuation, posing the deceptively easy riddle of the Sphinx." This is, for Jung, a variant of the Shadow, the elemental inferior aspect lying just below the surface of any personality— a regressive figure, but one sometimes presaging greater awareness of the contents of the personal unconscious. General Wertmüller seems to play such a role, especially when taken together with his barely civilized servant. He acts as a mischievous protector of Pfannenstiel, but also as a guardian of Orphic mysteries. His surface benevolence is constantly threatened by eruptions of diabolical trickery. His face is likened to a grotesque mask, he is compared to an Egyptian god, his goddaughter refers to him as a kobold or troll, and when he conceives of his plan his laughter is echoed "in so geisterhafter und grotesker Weise, dass es war, als hielten sich alle Faune und Panisken der Au die Bäuchlein über einen tollen und gottvergessenen Einfall."

Also, it cannot be reckoned merely as the scurrilous whim of a man used to facing death that the General keeps a uniformed skeleton standing watch before his bedchamber. Through Pfannenstiel's eyes, we apprehend in the face of this figure that the fight for psychic identity and independence calls for an encounter with the specter of death, a recognition of one's mortality that, if successful, will dispel the preoccupation with mortality. The threat-and-promise of libidinal release that gives the story its peculiar tone is undoubtedly bound to this incipient awareness, most probably as the result of a lingering unconscious conviction on the author's part that eroticism is punishable by death. It is doubtful that Meyer himself succeeded in taking the step toward a more mature recognition of mortality; but then it is also a matter of some conjecture whether any poet can afford to do so without sacrificing his art.

On the whole, we may say that Meyer almost unwittingly avails himself of the framework of an unprepossessing humorous interlude in his production to present, symbolically, certain psychological insights that could have been formulated otherwise, on the basis of existing knowledge, only with great difficulty. Apparent sexual conflicts appear, veiled but near the surface. They press for an eruption into consciousness and threaten fusion with the specific, overt, but somewhat de-eroticized theme of male inadequacy (a theme that appears trite only to the post-Freudian reader). Meyer thus approaches, by virtue of his peculiar symbolic method, a directness in dealing with sexual matters seldom equaled among his contemporaries. Even the radicals of midcentury, such as Gutzkow, are painfully self-conscious in erotic matters. In the conservative camp of Biedermeier-Poetic Realism, as in English Victorianism, the question is neatly avoided by two mechanisms: assimilation and demonization. Sex is assimilated into the confines of orderly and polite society in its approved (marriage-oriented) form by means of

the fiction that it is not problematic and that, out of gentility, one chooses not to discuss it (whereas in fact one dare not); and to the extent that it cannot be assimilated, it joins antisocial and disruptive elements to become the familiar bugbear of lasciviousness. Keller, for example, arrives at a statement of healthy eroticism in *Romeo und Julia auf dem Dorfe,* but one feels that the relaxing of constraints there is made acceptable only by the impending death of the characters. In *Frau Regel Amrain und ihr Jüngster,* on the other hand, a theme patently impinging on the erotic sphere, a mother's education of her son toward his masculine role in society, is treated with more typical indirectness, masculinity being regarded clearly as a socio-economic matter rather than a biological one. Still, in fairness to Keller, it must be said that he generally contrives, through an adroit use of symbol and suggestion, to convey an affirmation of eroticism slightly in excess of the prevailing quota.

Meyer's link with such authors as Keller, Stifter, and Storm, however, is tenuous at best, and in view of his predilection for unfettered heroes who live in the grand style, we should not expect to find the customary bourgeois restraints in his work. Yet in the case of his most erotically obsessed major character, the monk Astorre, there is a suggestion of bourgeois demonization in his mind-clouding, tainted passion, especially since it is unclear to what extent the short-lived heroic hedonism of the protagonist is to be commended. In general, there is a pronounced erotic strain in Meyer's works, but the forms assumed by it make a curiously stunted impression. The reasons for this pattern are probably to be sought more within Meyer's psyche than in external factors such as the literary demands of particular works (though an aesthetically fortunate union of the two is not ruled out). Thus, aside from the literary merits, under certain circumstances, of comparisons between love and death, it is ominous in terms of Meyer's psychic well-being that he makes them so often. The incest theme in **Die Richterin** has been the object of speculation as something perhaps not unrelated to personal problems of the author. Meyer's attachment to his sister, in any case, was a strong one, and his paranoid denunciation of her in his final mental illness points up the profundity of the problem.

Der Schuss von der Kanzel can scarcely be regarded as an innocuous document of marital bliss on the part of a man with an easy grasp upon maturity. It is one of the records left by a man straining toward normal libidinal development, and we may expect the product, whatever its merits, to show traces of the struggle. It is in the area of character development that we may expect such matters to be most directly dealt with, for character development is, after all, a question of the channeling of psychic energies. It is noteworthy that Meyer's later works, for better or worse, lack the urge observed here toward moderation and psychic integration within the "healthy" region. They pursue instead the fates of bizarre and heroic characters somewhat outside the pale of ordinary society and dominated by extreme active or passive principles—unfettered heroes and abject martyrs, with a curious air of morbidity and impotence about even the more energetic ones. Perhaps Meyer became unable to conceive a life of grandiosity without the taint of monstrosity, an understandable development in view of the standards of his day and a tendency which others were to carry still further near the turn of the century.

When he does conceive of harmonious social integration, as we have seen, it is in terms of recognizing one's limitations and being content with one's station in life—that is, agreeing that one's true being does not go beyond the role assigned by society. Meyer here seems to underwrite the General's admonition to Pfannenstiel: "Wozu sind die Geleise bügerlicher Berufsarten da, als dass Euresgleichen sie befahre? Ihr wisst nicht, welcher Schenkelschluss dazu gehört, um das Leben souverän zu traktieren." On the other hand, he is affirming the right of the exceptionally vital and strong individual to defy the social leveling process. Meyer's essential difference from the Poetic Realists may lie in his Faustian suspicion that the psychic development of the individual is inseparable from questions of libido and that it follows inner laws rather than being necessarily compatible with the prevailing social system.

The resulting conflict receives a turbulent, inconclusive direct expression in *Die Hochzeit des Mönchs,* historically displaced, to be sure, and with the complication of personality deterioration on the part of the protagonist simultaneous with his self-realization. In *Der Schuss von der Kanzel* the conflict is more dimly rendered, and the fiction of harmonious resolution is allowed to prevail, in keeping with Meyer's tendency to see the domain of humor as a stagnant pool apart from the mainstream of life and history. In *Jürg Jenatsch* Meyer had attempted to portray the exceptional person who changes history (though his treatment turns out to be somewhat unproblematic); and it is only fitting that in *Der Schuss von der Kanzel,* this later, more static examination of a single segment of Swiss history, the dynamic figure of Jenatsch has become legendary and diabolical for the likes of Pfannenstiel. Wertmüller's role is that of a lesser demon who renders the apocalyptic specter of change into something assimilable for the average person. Meyer's condescension toward that average person may well constitute self-irony; he, too, is a Pfannenstiel, for whom the threat of inner revolution is fearsome enough.

Thus, the willingness to acknowledge psychological symbolism of the kind elucidated by psychoanalysis, while it has not really cast much light on Meyer's personal mental problems (that was not our aim), has at least raised some questions about the work itself, questions not without pertinence to its style and structure. It is of course possible to interpret a work without considering the author's intent or motivation. Often, however, attempts in this direction merely seize upon the author's overt statement at the expense of the numerous covert and half-unwitting ways in which he may be signalling the reader. It has often been claimed that psychological approaches are one-dimensional, that they stunt our understanding of the work by stressing only one aspect of it. The possibility seems to exist, however, that, if followed cautiously, such approaches may instead add a dimension to our insight.

Edward M. V. Plater   (essay date 1975)

SOURCE: "The Figure of Dante in *Die Hochzeit des Mönchs,*" in *MLN,* Vol. 90, No. 5, October, 1975, pp. 678-86.

[*In the following essay, Plater determines the significance of the narrator, Dante Alighieri, in the novella and finds connections between Dante, the protagonist of the story, Astorre, and Meyer.*]

Die Hochzeit des Mönchs is perhaps the most demanding of Conrad Ferdinand Meyer's novellas. Here Meyer seems to have stretched the possibilities of the genre to its limits. He himself ruefully stated in reference to the complex interlacing of story and frame in this novella that he had created "ein non plus ultra." The evaluation of Meyer's actual achievement with this novella depends, of course, on the recognition of all the features that contribute to its complexity. One such feature which has not yet been fully understood is Meyer's use of the great Italian poet, Dante Alighieri, as fictional narrator.

Before Dante begins his story of the monk's wedding, he announces to his listeners his intention to take the characters for it from their midst, using their names and physical features but leaving untouched their inner beings. That this intention springs from an ulterior motive is suggested by the manner in which it is announced, namely "mit lächelnder Drohung." [In *DVLG,* Vol. XII, 1966] Michael Shaw, whose interpretation of Meyer's Dante goes further than any other to date, argues convincingly that Dante's use of his audience as models for his story is a "carefully calculated insolence." By means of this device Dante gives vent to his annoyance with certain members of his audience and retaliates for humiliations he has been subjected to at the Veronese court. He thus becomes a protagonist himself in a subtle plot of his own making, which competes with the story within the frame for the reader's interest.

The members of Dante's audience having counterparts of the same name in his story, such as Burcardo or Gocciola, know exactly with whom they are to identify and therefore cannot fail to understand any impertinence Dante might direct at them through their counterparts. The most prominent member of Dante's audience, his host Cangrande, does not, it is true, furnish the name for any character in the story Dante tells, but he is present in Dante's story nevertheless, having in fact two counterparts with whom to identify. One of these is Astorre, whom Dante places in his story between the namesakes of Cangrande's wife Diana and the temporary object of his attentions, Antiope. The other is Ezzelin, whose physical features in *The Divine Comedy* Dante admits to having modelled after his host. By encouraging Cangrande to identify with Ezzelin, Dante subtley suggests that his host's wisdom and power are less than absolute. One indication that Cangrande realizes Dante's impudence is his reaction to Dante's indirect rebuke of him for keeping a fool at his court. "Er [Cangrande] versprach sich im stillen, bei erster Gelegenheit mit Wucher heimzuzahlen." The extent of Cangrande's awareness of the effrontery, however, remains uncertain, since this question depends on how much Cangrande does in fact identify with his counterparts, counterparts who do not share his name.

What Cangrande—and, for that matter, everyone else in the audience—does not seem to realize is that Dante too is present in his story and that he uses his presence there to intensify his chastisement of his host. Ernst Feise, in his discussion of the interrelationship of frame and story, has pointed out the correspondence between Dante and Ezzelin: "Die Vermutung ist kaum abzuweisen, dass Dante in der selbstherrlichen Art des Schicksalsspielers Ezzelin mit seiner eignen Kunst, die Fäden seiner Marionetten zu leiten, andeuten wolle." Ezzelin is, to be sure, a tyrant, who exercises close surveillance and control over the lives of his subjects. His ineffectual attempts to avert disaster, however, reveal him to be a mere instrument of fate, who, as Cangrande is to understand, has little real power. Dante, on the other hand, takes great pains to impress upon his host the extent of his own power as a poet. For example, when Cangrande interrupts to ask Dante whether he really believes that the Emperor Frederick II called Moses, Muhamed and Christ charlatans and that Petrus de Vinea was innocent of treason, Dante indicates with a shake of his head that he does not. Yet, as Cangrande points out, he has condemned the Emperor in *The Divine Comedy* to the sixth circle of hell and permitted the traitor to protest his innocence. Dante's arbitrary exercise of the poet's prerogative in these matters does not fail to impress his host: "Dante, mein Dante . . . du glaubst nicht an die Schuld und du verdammst! Du glaubst an die Schuld und du sprichst frei!"

Dante, who is described upon entering the novella as resembling a "Parze oder dergleichen," also emphasizes his great power throughout his narrative by constructing a chain of events heavily dependent on chance and, as Ernst Feise has suggested [in *Monatshefte*, Vol. XXX, 1938] by manipulating his characters in a thoroughly peremptory manner. He thus tells his host indirectly that his sovereignty, the sovereignty of an artist over his creation, in contrast to the sovereignty of a secular prince, is truly absolute. The "carefully calculated insolence" which Michael Shaw refers to is, then, double-edged, for Dante uses his character Ezzelin not only to expose with impunity his host's limits and shortcomings but also to sing his own praises.

Once one recognizes this complex and shrewd subterfuge, one quite naturally wonders whether Dante might also be employing it in connection with his host's other counterpart in the story, the monk Astorre. Shaw points out that Dante encourages his host to identify with the monk in order to impress upon him through the contrast with Astorre's rare love for Antiope the shabbiness of his "Zweiweiberei." The question remains as to whether there is any justification for regarding Astorre as Dante's counterpart too and, if so, whether Dante gains in stature from a comparison with the monk, as he does from a comparison with Ezzelin.

The most obvious basis for identifying Dante and Astorre with each other is the great loves of their lives, Astorre's love for Antiope and Dante's love for Beatrice, which he celebrated in *The New Life* and *The Divine Comedy*. According to Dante's own account he was smitten by an overwhelming love for Beatrice upon their first meeting, when both were only nine years old. He states that from that time forth love ruled his soul, but that he exercised self-restraint by tempering his emotions with reason. Though Dante no doubt saw Beatrice subsequently many times from afar, their second encounter did not take place until nine years later. On this occasion she spoke to him for the first time, addressing him with a salutation. This had such an effect on him that he believed he beheld "the very limits of blessedness." It was this meeting which is said to have ignited the spark of Dante's poetic genius.

It is not difficult to find parallels here to the beginning of Astorre and Antiope's love. Astorre, too, is smitten by love on first seeing Antiope, at the execution of her father. He too is unable from this time forth to dismiss her from his thoughts. And like Dante, Astorre checks his desire by exercising self-restraint. The second encounter between Astorre and Antiope does not take place nine years after the first, as did Beatrice and Dante's, but nevertheless a rather long period of time does elapse—three years—before they meet again. And it is, as it was with Dante, this second encounter which has such a momentous effect on Astorre's life. To be sure, it does not ignite the spark of poetic genius, it does not inspire great poetry in celebration of his beloved, but it does, by setting the stage for Antiope's humiliation at the engagement ceremony, arouse Astorre's compassion and so cause his love for her to burst forth in its full vitality and move him to abandon all self-restraint. Moreover, just as Dante spiritualized his love for Beatrice, placing her among the blessed in the presence of God and making her his guide through Paradise, so he endeavors to raise Antiope up (though with reservations, it is true, for he also suggests certain frailties of her character), to transform her beyond human bounds into a blessed figure, particularly in the description of her sitting at the window, enveloped in an aureole of light from the setting sun. Her disheveled hair is said to resemble the points of a crown of thorns and her languishing lips are said to imbibe heaven. Here we witness almost the apotheosis of Antiope into the figure of "der neuen Vicedomini," a title that fittingly describes Beatrice's place in *The Divine Comedy*.

The temptation to identify Dante with Astorre is made even more irresistible by the resemblance that Dante's betrothal bears to the monk's. Just as Astorre is forced by his dying father to agree to wed Diana, whom he does not love, so Dante Alighieri was "gloomily betrothed about three years after he first met Beatrice to "der ungeliebten Gemma Donati." Dante's father, it is said, was ill at the time and apparently wished to put his son's affairs in order before he died.

The establishment of Dante as one of Meyer's major symbols further increases his significance in the total design of the novella. Meyer's success in investing him with a highly personal meaning without compromising his credibility as a character in the novella is an impressive achievement.

—*Edward M. V. Plater*

All of these parallels between Dante and Astorre, while providing justification for regarding the monk as Dante's counterpart in the story within the frame, also answer affirmatively the question as to whether Dante benefits from a comparison with the monk. For in contrast to the ignoble and destructive course of self-abandon that Dante has the hero of his story follow, Dante's own reaction in similar circumstances—his acceptance of his father's will and his inspired celebration of his beloved—was both noble and productive. Thus, as he did in his use of Ezzelin, Dante again risks provoking his host with double-edged insolence; for while Dante compares favorably with the monk, Cangrande, as pointed out earlier, does not.

There exists still another connection between Dante and Astorre, one which, though rooted in the fictional world of the frame, goes far beyond the scope of Dante and his audience, leading ultimately to the inner world of Meyer's personal symbolism. I am referring to the specific association of Dante with monkhood. One factor which encourages this association is Dante's own connection with the monastic brotherhood to which Astorre belongs. Dante was to become a Franciscan monk but left the order before completing his novitiate.

The argument for regarding Dante as a monk figure is further strengthened by a subtle parallel between the fictional narrator and Astorre that begins with the monk's forced departure from the monastery. This echoes Dante's emergence from his room because of the neglect of the servants, who had failed to provide him with a fire in spite of the cold November evening. The "hochgelegene Kammer" from which Dante emerges is, like the monastery, a quiet place for contemplation; and it is to this place that the poet withdraws to devote himself to the visions of his poetic world. Cangrande's remark that he had overheard Dante earlier scanning verse in his room encourages this interpretation.

It is Dante, it will be recalled, who introduces on this evening of storytelling the idea of the *forced* abandonment of monastic life, thus giving a special twist of his

own to a theme that had already been treated by at least two other members of the group, the theme of the renegade monk. Within the fictional world of the frame the negligence that forces Dante from his room may well have given him the inspiration for this innovation. But whether or not Dante is to be thought of as conscious of the parallel between Astorre's leaving the monastery and Dante's leaving his room, the highly conscious and deliberate author Meyer surely was, when he made the new variant of an established theme conform to Dante's own immediate circumstances. And it is, of course, Meyer's awareness that matters when one is considering the highly personal symbolic content of the novella.

The parallel includes, moreover, not only what Dante and his counterpart leave but also what they enter. The secular world of passion, jealously, and ambition, in which Astorre suddenly finds himself, echoes the "sinnlichen und mutwilligen Kreis" into which Dante solemnly and haughtily steps. Here too, within the small circle of Dante's audience, are examples of the ambition, jealousy, passion, and frivolity that Astorre encounters when he leaves the monastery. This aspect of the parallel is also expressed by means of related imagery. The contrast between the coldness of Dante's room and the warmth of the fire blazing on the hearth round which the members of the court are gathered is echoed in Dante's story by, for example, the shaded lane, "bis zum Schauder kühl," which runs along the wall ringing the monastery, and the burning rays of the sun, which the monk encounters when he leaves the grounds of his palace for the first time since having renounced his monastic vows.

The significance of Dante as a monk figure becomes apparent upon consideration of the implications of the extended parallel just traced. This parallel suggests a definite kinship not only between the figures in this novella, Dante and Astorre, but between the poet and the monk as choices of existence, between the solitary hours which the poet spends nurturing his poetic vision and the seclusion into which the monk withdraws in order to devote himself to matters of the spirit. It further suggests that only outside the monk's chaste cell or the poet's cloistered study does real life lie, the life abundant with all its passions and intrigues.

Of course, this parallel between Dante and the monk must not obscure the fact that very important differences exist. Although Dante enters "den sinnlichen und mutwilligen Kreis," which represents life, he remains largely aloof from it. He becomes involved only to the extent that he contributes a story to the evening's entertainment and gives vent through his story to certain resentments he harbors against members of his audience. Yet the ambitions, passions and frivolity that typify these people have little appeal to him. He smiles only once during the entire evening. Thus, unlike his counterpart, who yields to his awakened sensuality and in the end is swept to his destruction by the "alles mitreissenden Strom der Welt," Dante, having paid with a story for his seat by the fire, leaves the circle of life and climbs the stairs again to his cold and solitary room:

"Er schritt durch die Pforte, welche ihm der Edelknabe geöffnet hatte. Aller Augen folgten ihm, der die Stufen einer fackelhellen Treppe langsam emporstieg." This echoes the lines in *The Divine Comedy* spoken by Beatrice, the symbol of Divine Truth, leading Dante to the presence of God: ". . . my beauty, which, along the steps of the eternal palace kindleth more, as thou hast seen, the higher the ascent . . ."

All of these observations are consistent with the findings of Heinrich Henel, who points out [in *The Poetry of C. F. Meyer*], although in reference to Astorre, that the renegade monk is one of Meyer's recurrent symbols and that it expresses the conflict between his "desires for seclusion and for active living, between spiritual and worldly impulses." Henel also discusses the specific association of monkhood with the life of the *poet*. He cites two of Meyer's poems in which the motif of monkhood is applied to the poet's vocation, to his dedication to "an inner world of poetic vision." Although Henel does not refer to Dante in this connection, the evidence indicates that Meyer's fictional narrator should be added to this small group of exponents of the monastic life of the poet.

The establishment of Dante as a symbolic monk figure, however, seems to give rise to a contradiction, for how, one might ask, can he and Astorre, who react so differently to the life abundant, both symbolize the conflict in Meyer between desires for an active life and for seclusion and contemplation? Part of the answer is that Meyer's attitude toward the life abundant was not simple and easily definable, but encompassed rather a range of feelings. Moreover, Dante's symbolic significance is more specific than Astorre's, for, as already suggested, he is to be associated primarily with Meyer's attitude toward the rewards and sacrifices of the poet's vocation, whereas Astorre is to be viewed in the larger context of the conflict in Meyer between the active versus the contemplative life. Obviously, the withdrawal from active living in order to write is only a part of the reflective, self-communing life of a poet.

Thus Astorre, by virtue of his fierce resistance to renouncing his monastic vows in spite of his lingering, though repressed, sensuality, and by virtue of his subsequent headlong plunge into secular life and the violence that ensues, suggests a complex of feelings consistent in their turbulence and intensity with the emotional conflict that Meyer experienced in his twenties, preceding his difficult break with his long dream life. This conflict between longings for solitude and reflection and longings for a full, active life left a lasting impression on the poet's psyche. The fictional Dante, on the other hand, seems to express, in his annoyance at having to leave the solitude of his room, the brevity of his excursion into the life abundant, the basic aloofness he maintains there, and his return to seclusion at the end of the novella, his creator's dedication to the poet's vocation. One cannot, of course, separate entirely Meyer the man from Meyer the poet and must, therefore, consider both monk figures together, and indeed the monk figures in all of Meyer's works, in order to arrive at a reasonably accurate impression of the feelings that comprise the author's attitude toward the active versus the contemplative life.

The figure of Dante, then, is of greater importance in the total design of *Die Hochzeit des Mönchs* than has heretofore been noted. His campaign of insolence turns out to be even subtler than previously realized, for he gives to his critical thrusts at his host a double-edged effect through his own surreptitious presence in his story, in not one, but two of his characters. This shrewdly perpetrated insolence adds considerably to the fascination which the narrator holds for the reader as a portrait of a great historical personage. Moreover, the establishment of Dante as one of Meyer's major symbols further increases his significance in the total design of the novella. Meyer's success in investing him with a highly personal meaning without compromising his credibility as a character in the novella is an impressive achievement. This complex figure, then, is, to use Meyer's own words regarding the interlacing of story and frame, though in a positive sense, "ein non plus ultra" and must be given major consideration in an evaluation of the novella as a whole.

George F. Folkers   (essay date 1976)

SOURCE: Introduction to *The Complete Narrative Prose of Conrad Ferdinand Meyer, Vol. I: 1872-1879*, translated by George F. Folkers, David B. Dickens, and Marion W. Sonnenfeld, Bucknell University Press, 1976, pp. 11-27.

[*In the following essay, Folkers provides a stylistic and thematic overview of Meyer's novellas.*]

Conrad Ferdinand Meyer (1825-1898) is a prominent figure in German literature and one of the most important of the Swiss writers. He was the son of a prosperous family in Zurich, and his maturation reflects the problematical intellectual climate of post-Napoleonic Europe and the age of positivism, a climate by nature hostile to literary endeavors because of its materialistic orientation. Meyer succeeded in forging an expositional technique which not only was comprehended and appreciated by his contemporaries, but which also transcends its time to remain artistically valid to the twentieth-century reader of perception and sensitivity. This is Meyer's literary achievement.

Meyer's background prepared him for his literary calling while it condemned him to failure in ordinary middle-class terms. Steeped in the classical traditions and the history of Europe, his work has the profundity that distinguishes the best in German literature from the time of the Renaissance to the present day. Meyer was bilingual in German and French; during his youth he seriously considered a career as a teacher of French and was intimately familiar with French literature. This interest accounts for Meyer's cosmopolitan quality, which contrasts strongly with the decisively parochial character of other great nineteenth-century authors—Theodor Storm, Fritz Reuter, even Meyer's great compatriot, Gottfried Keller, who almost without exception favors a Swiss locale for his narrative work. Meyer was the first German symbolist writer, and his work has been described as the precursor of psychological writing in the twentieth century; both the Austrian dramatist Arthur Schnitzler and the psychiatrist Sigmund Freud had a high regard for Meyer's work.

Meyer's prose production was somewhat limited in quantity (eleven novellas) but of the highest quality. All are historical—that is, all are set in relatively remote times. His technique of exposition reveals an intuitive grasp of the historiographic techniques of Ranke without ever degenerating into chronicles. . . . Meyer was a superb master of the *Rahmenerzählung,* the technique of the tale within the tale, and is distinguished by an objective, dispassionate attitude toward his subject matter. His aloof attitude, his detached posture go so far that his stance can be described as ambivalent; that is, Meyer's position in and toward his work is so neutral—so clinical—that both antagonist and protagonist frequently appear in similarly positive light. Best illustrations of this ambivalence are the figures of Thomas Becket and Henry in *The Saint*; the same ambivalence can also be discerned in *Pescara's Temptation* in the characters of the field marshal Pescara and his tempter, the chancellor Morone, who is endowed with great patriotism—for C. F. Meyer a very positive trait. In other instances Meyer takes a figure regarded traditionally or historically as an essentially negative one and rehabilitates him, so to speak, by imbuing him with some positive characteristic and by attributing to him a constructive effect on the course of history. The best example of this is *Jürg Jenatsch.* In his depiction of the historical Jenatsch, Meyer shows that he is not merely rewriting a fictionalized account and not just attempting to illustrate history; rather, he is assuming a stance of ambivalence to render more relative to history in its totality the role played by the nature and character of the title hero. In this manner the true spirit of a phase of history and its relation to the present can be evoked. The dynamic quality of the effective forces in historical events can be intimated by employing this approach to the protagonist and antagonist in the drama of human events.

Another example of Meyer's ambivalent attitude toward figures in history is his characterization of Azzelino da Romano in *The Marriage of the Monk.* Here Meyer's narrator, Dante, carefully qualifies Azzelino's reputation for cruelty and is supported in this by Cangrande. Perhaps the most striking example of ambivalence is the scene in which Cangrande questions Dante about a statement attributed to Emperor Frederick II, that the three great prophets of history, Moses, Mohammed, and Jesus, had deceived the world in matters of faith.

A stylistic technique favored by Meyer to emphasize his ambivalence is proposing two opposite motivations for a given act. This technique can be discerned throughout his prose works, but a few examples in which it is especially apparent may serve to demonstrate, as in *The Saint*:

> My father was avoided by his clan . . . when he, *to evade his creditors and to save his soul,* attached the cross to his doublet and went to the Promised Land. [Italics mine]

Or in *A Boy Suffers*:

> Père Tellier was gone. *Was it that he had not believed* Argenson's whispered insinuation and had simply used the opportunity to escape from us? *Or had he believed* it and still let the one driving spirit of his order overcome the other, pride over ambition? [Italics mine]

Or in *The Marriage of the Monk*:

> 'I have come to warm myself at your hearth', said the stranger half solemnly, half disdainfully, and he did not demean himself by adding that the lax servants, either by *design* or by *carelessness,* had failed to light a fire in the upstairs guest room, despite the frostiness of the November night. [Italics mine]

This passion of Meyer's for objectivity, this skeptical attitude toward the validity of any single phenomenon, this constant attempt to explain things in context and not in a dogmatic way—be it even the smallest, secondary motivation for an act by a minor character—this urge to emphasize the ambivalence of truth, is symptomatic of Meyer's view of reality. In the zenith of positivism, in an era that sought truth precisely in denying those things communicated to us by means other than the senses, Meyer intuitively sensed the limits of the positivist perception; he intuitively realized the complicated relationships between the obvious, the apparent, the external in phenomena and the unseen, the invisible yet immensely powerful elements in all phenomena and events. Therefore, Meyer's vision of reality, his interpretation of truth, had to include all these elements, expressible and inexpressible. To permit this all-inclusiveness, he had to maintain his ambivalent objectivity.

A second central characteristic of Meyer's prose is the representation of contending polar forces reflected in the decisive events or commanding figures of history. For instance, antagonisms and inherent hostilities of a particular time and place which led to explosive calamities often form the background of his works. An example of this can be seen in *Jürg Jenatsch,* where local patriotism and Protestantism in Graubünden vie with the expansionist imperialism and Catholicism of France and Spain. The struggle between these two forces is mirrored in, and has a devastating effect upon, the hero, who, in turn, brings about the most important developments in the action. Background and character are so carefully interwoven that each is relative and dependent upon the other. Other examples of the same device are to be found in *The Amulet,* in which the background and main action are provided by events leading to the Saint Bartholomew's Day Massacre, and in *The Saint,* which depicts happenings leading to and resulting from the murder of Thomas Becket.

These two characteristics, ambivalence and polarity of forces, impart to Meyer's work a pervading sense of ambiguity which he deliberately intensified by giving many novellas paradoxical titles.

It can be said in summary that Meyer's style is characterized by its ambivalence and ambiguity, by its tendency to involve the reader's imagination in the formulation of meaningful forms and evocative images, thereby eliciting from the reader a dynamic contribution to the development of the plot.

—George F. Folkers

As already noted, Meyer borrowed themes for his work from the great events of history, modifying historical facts freely to serve his own purposes, but always remaining true to the spirit of the time and era represented. To insure accuracy in matters pertaining to local color, Meyer consulted the art historian J. R. Rahn with reference to *The Saint* and *Pescara's Temptation.* The collective effect of this procedure is such that in the words of the critic W. Silz, "He has no peer . . . in the artistic reanimation of history."

Of special importance to Meyer was the problem of form. Earlier critics frequently reproached Meyer for employing history as a basis for his art, in that history gave the poet an already completed scheme and point of view. It is unfair to make this a basis for reproaching Meyer. By borrowing from historical concepts already formed, Meyer was able to use more of his creative energy to impose his own idea of form on the subject. By means of this form, Meyer attempted to suggest the interrelatedness of all aspects of existence; he did this not as a philosophical program, for the determinism and positivism of his era would not accept such a transcendental concept in philosophical terms, but, rather, by indirect means. Also, Meyer was a poet, not a philosopher. In employing plot structures and their pertinent sociological concepts already formed by history, Meyer had at his disposal material which was no longer completely formless. It had a vaguely suggested outline imposed upon it; it could lend itself as an abstraction to be expanded in detail by the poet to achieve his artistic goal, which he himself formulated as being to suggest the connection of the individual's existence and strivings with those of the human race and the individual's longing to be a part of a larger, more significant whole. By employing this outline provided by history, Meyer was free to concentrate on the dynamics of the event in question and on the motivations of the personalities he created. He could stress those characteristics of the outline which accommodated the ultimate effect which he desired, eliminating those details that detracted from a grasp of the larger picture.

Thus, in the process of molding motif and theme, ambivalence and polarity, ambiguity and paradox into an artistic unity, Meyer imposed artistic form upon the schematic outline offered him by history. In doing so, he achieved his artistic goal: to reflect, in a complex of external, visible, objective images, by means of the interaction of these images with the forces of history, his subjective feeling and intuitive understanding of the nature of life itself. To realize his goal, Meyer reduced to a bare minimum that element which would tend to distract from the desired collective effect—namely, the individual, personal, and therefore momentary factor. The sought-after collective effect is the impression of the unity of all aspects of existence, the totality of member parts to form an organic, harmonious whole. It is in a subliminal awareness of this unity of existence that one is able to bear the pain in existence. Art and history offered Meyer the means of conveying an impression of this unity. Meyer's works, therefore, reflect not only human reason but also the total force of the human personality; they evoke the notion of "soul".

In his works, Meyer did not ignore the fact that life consists of a mingling of that which is base and noble; he accepted and reaffirmed this fact in the quality of relativity, thus tacitly recognizing the essential equality and interdependence of all entities, traits, characters—base and noble. Meyer's understanding of relativity is different from the relativism of his era, for this relativism was amoral in character. Relativism, to be sure, recognized the equality of all attitudes and views, but this from a position of positivism, from a point of view which rejects and denies all transcendental values. For Meyer, existence must be viewed in its totality, the past being a part of the present and the present bearing in it the seeds of the future. Past, present, and future are for him links of an endless chain, a system, perhaps, to be likened to Leibnitz's monads; but the chain remains capable of development, of change, of reflecting in a dynamic way the influences of varying forces. An outgrowth of this conviction is the dichotomy that pervades his work. Meyer's notion of dichotomy is intimately associated with his views of the anthropocentric idea, a concept fundamentally important to nineteenth-century positivism. This positivism was inclined to see man as the measure of all things.

Meyer tended to be skeptical of the then-popular anthropocentric idea, the notion that man is the center of the universe and the measure of all things. From his own personal experience, Meyer was only too acutely aware of the limitations of the human personality. For this reason, he wrestled with the transcendental ideas of the world's religions throughout his life.

Meyer depicts the human condition as basically almost incurably dichotomous. The only way to overcome this division, the inner conflict that comprises the human condition, is through a force that lies beyond the human being: the transcendental power of the Ineffable. For Meyer, the anthropocentric idea is illusory and deceptive.

In recognizing and trying to capture the quality of continual movement and change in his works, Meyer made them essentially dynamic—that is, he lodged in them the potential for contention, for conflict between opposing forces. He endowed them with possibilities for tension, for action and reaction, for growth, for change. Thus, each of Meyer's prose works is an attempt to represent the harmony of existence in terms of relative and dynamic elements in the ever-recurring cycle of life. Each is an attempt to evoke the impression of the logical totality in all aspects of existence.

> **Meyer imbues all human attitudes and all expressions of the forces of life with a sense of irony, for there is no absolute of any kind either visible or implied. Everything within the realm of representation remains limited, circumscribed, ephemeral, subject to change, fluctuating.**
>
> *—George F. Folkers*

Thus, it can be said in summary that Meyer's style is characterized by its ambivalence and ambiguity, by its tendency to involve the reader's imagination in the formulation of meaningful forms and evocative images, thereby eliciting from the reader a dynamic contribution to the development of the plot.

In Meyer's employment of a variety of narrative techniques to evoke his view of the totality of existence through the interaction of a plethora of influences and forces to produce continual evolution and change, development and growth, it is possible to discern, in general, three stages or phases in the structure of the Meyer novella as it emerges from the dynamic interaction of relative forces.

The first of these phases is the exposition, the delineation of the realm of representation. The first picture in the narrative frame of *The Saint* conveys the impression of nothingness by means of slowly falling snow on a vacant countryside. The appearance of a horseman is presaged by the sound of hoof beats in a covered bridge; his identity is also so gradually revealed as he enters the city of Zurich that the reader's anticipation is keenly whetted. This exposition rests on the principle of form emerging from chaos, of substance and warmth evolving out of nothingness and cold. The entire presentation depends on contrasting opposites; it is dialectic in nature. Furthermore, Meyer reveals the character of his narrator to us through the medium of Hans's interaction with other people; we learn his name and his profession from the tradesmen of Zurich who call greetings to him from their shops and the streets. Thus, Hans blends in with his surroundings; in a way, he is an inconspicuous part of the background, being, as he seems, only a simple traveler.

Yet he is different, for he is called the Englishman, and, in contrast to the stay-at-home citizens who call to him, he is shown to be a man widely traveled. Thus, the dialectic nature of the exposition continues, adding bit to bit and increasing the inventory of the contrasting elements—i.e., the men of the city with its women, the two chief churches which house the male and female religious communities, and so forth. An intermediate high point is reached in Hans's encounter with the old canon Burkhard, who plays a key role in the exposition as Hans's auditor. It is from Burkhard that we learn the central theme of the novella, the nature of Thomas Becket's sanctity. Characteristically for Meyer, the theme is brought out in conversation with Hans—that is, the dialectic arrangement of personalities is continued. In Hans and Burkhard, the reader witnesses two approaches to the problem of Becket's sanctity. Burkhard, the man of intellect and a priestly functionary, is perplexed by Becket's enigmatic character. Burkhard's rationalist approach to the question of Becket's sanctity yields only confusion. Hans, the seemingly simple tradesman, the man of action, and, therefore, to all appearances Burkhard's opposite, is no less perplexed by this question. The question itself is quite alluring to all men, for it suggests an absolute concept, a highest instance in human affairs, a point of achievement that is not qualified by other forces in life, since it stands above and beyond life. The essentially ambiguous results of Burkhard's inquiries and Hans's attitude toward his experience with Becket the man suggest that this realm of sanctity, this metaphysical area, is unexplored by human beings; perhaps it is even unexplorable. The essence of the question is mystery, and the only way to investigate it, as Meyer seems to suggest in his exposition, is by involving all aspects of the human personality in experiencing what sanctity might constitute. A truly cognizable appreciation of the quality of sanctity seems unattainable. As Hans says, "These are difficult, inexplicable matters!" Man must relive the experiences and the events to grasp them in their many-faceted significance. Meyer aids the reader in doing this by causing Hans to relive the events for the benefit of Canon Burkhard.

Meyer's novella *The Marriage of the Monk* opens with a simple sentence: "It was in Verona." Here the point of departure is the opposite of that in *The Saint,* in which the movement was from the cold nothingness of a blizzard to the warmth of the Canon's living room; here we begin with the description of a blazing fire and a huge hearth and move to the semi-circle of persons standing around the blaze to warm themselves. Again the identity of the figures involved is only gradually revealed: "In front of a great fire . . . there lay . . . a group of young courtiers . . . of both sexes . . . and an equally youthful lord and two ladies glowing with youth . . . the prince was . . . called Cangrande." Even from this brief description we see the tendency toward dichotomous grouping. The dichotomy is heightened by the appearance of a grave, older man, whose bearing and mien contrast sharply with those of the young ruler and his retinue. Even as was the case with Hans in *The Saint,* the identity of the old man is not immediately revealed; it is from the lips of Cangrande that we learn the new arrival is none other than

Dante, the renowned poet and exile of Florence. As in *The Saint,* in which the theme of the novella is determined by the Canon, here the general topic is suggested by the group gathered about Cangrande's hearth: "Sudden change of profession with good, bad, or ridiculous results" Ascanio tells the old poet. Dante, who is to serve as the narrator in this novella, further qualifies the nature of his tale: "If for example a monk, not at his own initiative . . . not because he had failed to recognize his true character, but to please another . . . becomes unfaithful to himself, violates vows made to himself more than the vows he made to his church. . . ." Thus, the dynamics of this story seem to be the opposite of the line of change in *The Saint*; in *The Marriage of the Monk,* the development would seem to be from the state of a monk to that of a worldling, whereas in the other novella the apparent direction is the opposite, from the condition of a heathen to that of a hero of the Church. Also, whereas the narrator Hans in *The Saint* purports to relate events that he actually experienced, the narrator Dante acknowledges from the outset that he is developing the story as he goes along, using as its inspiration the epitaph of an old tombstone which reads in Latin: "Hic jacet monachus Astorre cum uxore Antiope. Sepeliebat Azzolinus." The Latin inscription presents another dichotomy; to be understood by the others it must be translated into the vernacular, a task which Cangrande accomplishes. He suggests thereby that his novella will be more than just a means to while away an idle hour; his novella will have some relevance to life. This is also intimated by the reaction of Cangrande's wife, the duchess, whose indifference to the proceedings begins to fade, and by the eagerness of the entire company to hear Dante's story. Dante's preparation has a similar effect on the reader.

In Meyer's humorous novella *The Shot from the Pulpit,* delineation of the realm of representation is accomplished by the reader's witnessing the conversation of two Swiss divines as they descend from a terraced vineyard. The two men, Rosenstock and Pfannenstiel, incorporate opposite principles both in their physical appearance and in their view of reality. The pastor, Rosenstock, is unimaginative, a trifle biased and one-sided, devoted to comfortable living, and inclined to obesity, whereas the seminarian Pfannenstiel is shown to be a dreamy, more than a little impractical person, tolerant and unprejudiced, but also unemployed. As his colleague is distinguished by his corpulence, Pfannenstiel stands out because of his emaciated appearance. The topic of their conversation is the discussion of a proposed solution to Pfannenstiel's difficulties in adjusting to his environment, difficulties which stem from his fondness for General Rudolf Wertmueller's godchild and Pastor Wilpert Wertmueller's daughter, Rahel. For the pragmatic Rosenstock, Pfannenstiel's solution—to seek a position as chaplain with Wertmueller's mercenary troops—is "void of reason." The central problem of the novella is revealed in stages in this conversation, in this dialogue between two opposite types, in Rosenstock's attempt to refute Pfannenstiel's proposal and Pfannenstiel's defense. In this way, the chief characters of the novella—the two Wertmuellers and Rahel, as well as certain facets of their nature—are in-

troduced. Here again we come to know each personality by stages, first from the external, superficial point of view of an outsider, of an absolute spirit, Rosenstock; later we gain a completely different impression in viewing the interaction of the characters one with another.

In each of these expositions, and indeed all of his expositions, Meyer attempts to show us the relationship of two forces in their interaction, one with the other, rather than their individual identity and inner essence in a stereotyped, dogmatic way. Thus, he evokes a different appreciation of these forces. Meyer shows us that the place of the so-called omniscient author is not *above* everything that happens, but, rather, in the midst of events. In this way, the author becomes the instrument of his art. In this way, the artist suggests the linking of great, and to outward appearances, at least, irreconcilable elements with one another. Thus, Meyer imbues all human attitudes and all expressions of the forces of life with a sense of irony, for there is no absolute of any kind either visible or implied. Everything within the realm of representation remains limited, circumscribed, ephemeral, subject to change, fluctuating. By means of this style of composition, Meyer leads the reader to an appreciation of that state of unrest which was central to his dynamic view of reality. Thus, the reader is led to a deeper concern for general actualities; he acquires an eagerness for a skeptical investigation of relationships and a new capacity to comprehend these relationships in a novel, a more creative, and a more revealing way. In place of the rigid structure of the absolute view typical of the omniscient author, the reader visualizes a dynamic and flexible quality in the structure of existence.

To gain an appreciation of Meyer's expository prose, it is necessary to consider briefly the time which he lived in and which exercised influences on his art. Meyer's life spans the latter three quarters of the nineteenth century; his literary production falls roughly into the years comprising the latter three decades. This entire period was a time of tremendous change and transition, a period of flux and upheaval during which all the traditional values, hallowed by generations of acceptance, were subject to intense scrutiny and criticism by men such as Feuerbach and Nietzsche in the realm of philosophy, Strauss in religion and biblical criticism, Vischer in aesthetics, and many others. It was a time of the "Revaluation of all values," in Nietzsche's expression. It was the period which saw the propagation of the ideas and ideals of the French Revolution, which also saw the rise of capitalism, and which experienced the industrial revolution, the emergence of positivism and materialism, the technical triumphs of the empirical method applied by the rapidly developing natural sciences. It was a period not only of dynamic transition; it was also a time when, in the opinion of many observers, man was gaining progressive control over his environment, when man no longer seemed to be at the mercy of the forces of nature. It was a time of increased confidence in man's eventual ability to control the natural forces around him by learning to understand them. Of necessity, these developments exercised an influence on man's view of life, the human condition, reality. The essentially transcendental quality of the then-dominant and traditionally accepted artistic viewpoints—classicism and romanticism—the tendency of these points of view to seek an absolute verity in terms of the ideal, invalidated them as an adequate means of interpreting the human condition in view of the progressively positivist, empirical, materialist trend in the thinking of the nineteenth-century European, for the very concept of the ideal was itself open to question. The classicists' vision of the emergence of the ideal, an absolute in aesthetic terms, and the romantics' goal of combining all the possibilities of human existence, were both incapable of expressing the new experience of life and reality. The new attitude toward reality placed increasing confidence in sensory perception and was ever more aware of the multitude of possibilities in life. The new view of reality saw its greatest hope in the law of cause and effect, which had proved so fruitful when applied to technology. All these trends were by nature hostile to the essentially visionary, even metaphysical quality of the classicist and romantic view of the world. The artistic forms chosen by the earlier authors to convey this view were therefore outmoded.

In his maturation as an artist, Conrad Ferdinand Meyer intuitively realized the need for new modes of expression better suited to the contemporary view of reality. Responding to all these trends in his environment, Meyer departed from the current allegorical symbolic mode of representation. He adopted a mode by which the inner action of a constellation of figures and forces evokes not the comprehension of the ideal in absolute terms, but, rather, an appreciation involving the totality of human perception—rational, emotional, sensory—of the multiplicity of the options open to the human being, the possibilities latent in life, the mosaic pattern of these options and possibilities, the essential validity, the equality of all of them, and the mystery inherent in the total life process. It is in the affirmation of *the mystery of life* that Meyer differs from the positivists.

Contrary to the opinion of those who see Meyer's works as a mask of his personality, Meyer did not intend primarily to express himself by projecting the characteristics of his ego in prototype heroes to illustrate the destiny of the individual within the framework of time. Rather than this, Meyer shows his belief to be that literature offers a means of representing the reality of the structure of life as it really is by conveying the mystery of life. No one individual, no character or single human being, is capable of dominating the picture; but, rather, a constellation of forces and action, the reaction and interaction of these forces, comprises the impetus for life. Even though Meyer made use of the events of history to embody and to exemplify his view of the universal mystery of the world and life, to impart, as it were, a fleeting glance at God in His immanence and at the never-ending development and change of existence, Meyer's true interest was not in the past, but, rather, in his own time, in the present. The figures and action of the past offered him convenient media for expressing his view of the eternal questions of human life.

Characteristic of Meyer's exposition is his use of the frame technique. By means of the frame, Meyer reveals in stages that have the most significance to the reader in terms of apparent cause and effect, in terms of the positivist views of the world in his day, the constellation of forces at work in a particular segment of history and of the options from among the myriad available which are most illuminating to a proper appreciation of the problem at hand. Central to this appreciation is a proper understanding of a human being's role in the midst of forces and the dilemma of choice which these forces pose. This understanding is at variance with the determinist view of existence, a view that sees the individual solely as a product of his heredity, environment, and biological urges. Meyer's frame serves the vital function of filtering and organizing the many possibilities into manageable proportions so that an appreciation of his total effect is realized. Perhaps this is best illustrated in *The Marriage of the Monk,* where Dante serves as narrator, where he consistently narrows the topic so that it is limited to one circumstance, enacted by a relatively restricted number of participants taken from the circle about Cangrande's fire. Meyer suggests this in his formulation of Dante's procedure: "His tale lay before him poured out in abundance; but his disciplined will was in the process of selecting and simplifying his material."

By means of the frame, Meyer creates the illusion of time and history, and he evokes determining social and political presuppositions, such as the struggle over investiture in *The Saint* or the separation of the function of the two highest virtues—justice and mercy—in *The Marriage of the Monk.* Thus, Meyer achieves poetic irony—that is, he maintains a constant flexibility of perspective to disclose various aspects of the central problem of the novella and of his characters. Thomas Becket is seen in the Moslem surroundings of Cordova and the Christian realm of England. The nature of his travels is described in negative terms by Hans's Saxon mentor and with legendary overtones by the Mohammedan storyteller in Cordova. The circumstances surrounding Astorre's dropping of the smaller of the two wedding rings in *The Marriage of the Monk* are presented in two different ways by Dante and Antiope Canossa's Maid Sotte—her name means "foolish" in French. Rudolf Wertmueller's *ménage* is variously described by Pastor Rosenstock and by the boatman Blaeuling in *The Shot from the Pulpit.*

Meyer's frames compel the reader to be thoroughly involved in the novella, as Cangrande's duchess in *The Marriage of the Monk,* for example, is engrossed in Dante's tale; yet he also urges the reader to assume an objective attitude, a detached, contemplative frame of mind in keeping with the tone set in his own composition. His poetic intention culminates in his creation of characters and actions that reflect his own experience of life—namely, that life is constantly shifting, growing, developing, changing; that the forces of life are actually relative, not absolute. Meyer reveals a fundamental structure in human destiny, but a structure which is not rigid, which is always in the process of changing. It is a structure which suggests the dialectic of the past and the present uniting to evolve the future.

For Meyer, existence must be viewed in its totality, the past being a part of the present and the present bearing in it the seeds of the future.

—George F. Folkers

The novella *The Amulet* actually gives the reader three separate stages of development in terms of the framing of the introduction. The first of these is the short retrospective action involving Schadau and the elder Boccard. Another scene which also has an anticipative effect, Schadau's frenzied battle with Franz Godillard concerning the merits of the Spanish commander Alba, is a microcosmic example of the macrocosmic catastrophe of the Huguenot Massacre. The third is the seemingly irrational outburst of Wilhelm Boccard, otherwise the soul of tolerance and calm in discussing religious matters, at Schadau's slightly disparaging remark about the cult of the Virgin Mary. Thus, Meyer illuminates the problem of an absolute attitude toward religious or political questions from three perspectives, each suggesting that emotional acceptance of an absolute and exclusive view can wreak havoc on human relationships. The tendency to view or seek absolutes in life as guides engenders pride, spite, and hatred, forces that contribute to the disintegration of human relationships and even of life itself.

In employing and exploiting the frame technique to the fullest extent, Meyer uses his art in a manner analogous to the scientific method; he shows the reader essentially the complexes of phenomena that can be perceived through the senses, but, in the process of increasing perceptivity, the reader intuitively begins to apprehend more than sensory organs or reason alone convey to him.

The second structural phase of the Meyer novella is a delineation of the scope of the options open to the individual within the framework of the realm of representation. The second phase also suggests a threat to the balance, to the harmony in the constellation of forces, a harmony which, in Meyer's view, is essential to the preservation of life itself. The forces at work are presented explicitly.

In *The Saint* we will note that these forces are the intellectual-spiritual element embodied in Thomas Becket and the physical-material aspect in the king. At the beginning of Hans's sojourn in the English court, the king and his chancellor are shown to be equal and interdependent personalities; both accept and acknowledge the importance of the other in the common task of governing the Anglo-Norman realm. Both harmonize with their oppo-

site number. Yet, even at the outset, there is an intimation of potential rivalry and hostility between the two. Thus, even though a balance and harmony prevail between the two entities, the polarity of their natures contains an inherent, hostile element, which requires only a catalyst and the proper ignition to trigger a destructive rivalry.

The Marriage of the Monk presents the contending forces in the shape of Astorre Vicedomini, the monk, the man of mercy, whose entire makeup is compassion and the capacity for love, and of Ezzelin the Tyrant, the representative of justice as the governor of Padua. The offices of mercy and justice are conceived in Dante's tale as being separated. Despite this separation, Ezzelin recognizes at the beginning of the action the contribution of the office of mercy. Astorre has a similar regard for Ezzelin. The element which threatens the harmonious relationship between the polar elements in this novella is Diana Pizzaguerra's short temper. It is Diana's outburst of temper that inspires the elder Vicedomini to urge Astorre to renounce his monastic vows in order to replace his brother Umberto, drowned in the accident on the Brenta. Diana's unbridled emotion plays a fateful role on two later occasions in the novella, as we shall presently see.

In *The Amulet* the polar forces represented are the two interpretations of Christianity, Calvinism and Catholicism, depicted in the persons of the two Swiss mercenaries Hans Schadau and Wilhelm Boccard. The same is reflected on a larger scale within the French state in the Catholic majority and the edict of toleration which apparently permits the Huguenot émigrés to return to France and to exist as a minority party. The great hope in the hearts of the Huguenot leaders for averting a civil war caused by religious tensions is to channel the energies of the entire nation toward a common goal—the conquest of the Netherlands from France's Spanish rival.

In *The Shot from the Pulpit* the contending polar forces are the two eccentric Wertmuellers—the unorthodox general and the pastor afflicted with a passion for firearms—opposite the conventional villagers of Mythikon, whose spokesman is the church elder Krachhalder. The factor suggesting the possibility of hostility between the two groups is the villagers' suspicion of the general's unconventional interests and preoccupations, as described by Pastor Rosenstock to Pfannenstiel. The ever-present possibility of a public scandal because of Pastor Wertmueller's addiction to guns, which is a source of continual worry to his daughter Rahel, is another manifestation of this same factor.

Concurrent with the confrontation of these polar forces is Meyer's ambivalent representation of them. Both elements are provided with justification for their behavior so that responsibility for the collapse of harmony between them, the harmony which is essential to the preservation of life itself, is equally distributed. This can be seen in detail in the instance of *The Saint,* where, although Hans heaps blame on the king's head, Meyer's intention clearly is to show Henry's innocence and regret in Grace's death. In *The Marriage of the Monk* there is a similar distribution of responsibility for the catastrophe at the end of the story. The elder Vicedomini's insistence on Astorre's quitting the monastery is motivated by the enumeration of the loss of his other sons and in the Old Testament interpretation of God's blessing on mankind as enunciated by Isaschar, Vicedomini's Jewish physician. Even Diana's outbursts of temper are justified in terms of her psychological set, of which she gives Astorre warning, and the provocation first of Olympia Canossa in insulting her parents, then of Antiope herself when trying to reclaim the fateful betrothal ring.

Similarly, the responsibility for the outbreak of hostility between the Calvinist and Catholic elements in *The Amulet* is distributed to suggest equal culpability in both parties. Schadau's duel with Count Guiche in spite of express orders from Admiral Coligny for all Calvinists to avoid such incidents suggests this; the clever Montaigne's complaint to Senator Chatillon and to Schadau that the Huguenots created resentment for themselves among their compatriots by isolating themselves from the rest of the population reinforces the impression of Meyer's intention to qualify the position of both elements. Meyer emphasizes the relativity and interconnection, the interdependence and interaction, of both factions by this distribution of culpability.

The problem is somewhat different in *The Shot from the Pulpit* because of the positive outcome of the story. Here the essential equality of all factions is intimated in the distribution of shortcomings in each character. Examples are Pfannenstiel's clumsiness, Rudolf Wertmueller's humiliating defeat in the siege of the Catholics, and the ironic description of Krachhalder's piety. There is even implicit criticism of Rahel for her uncritical acceptance of the villagers' attitude toward both Wertmuellers. Thus, none of these characters is without human failings; none of these personalities can lay claim to absolute justification for his actions or criticize others with impunity. All are co-equals in the unfolding plot. All are interdependent, and, what is significant in connection to the positive outcome of the story, all recognize their dependence. Even the one-sided Rosenstock, for example, acknowledges the community's need of the general's good will and shows a willingness to compromise his zeal to prosecute and punish an alleged blasphemy. Wertmueller's support, financial and otherwise, is important to the Protestant congregations in these areas; his conversion to Catholicism would represent a setback to the worldly interests of the Protestants. Similarly, General Rudolf Wertmueller is aware of a human dependency on his godchild Rahel because of his love for her. This, in turn, makes him concerned about the villagers' feelings toward his practical joke at the expense of his cousin the pastor. His concern finally makes him responsive to the appeal, made by Krachhalder in the interest of the congregation, for his generosity in the matter of deeding over the portion of his forest property adjoining the church's. It is this network of interdependence which makes Wertmueller's daring scheme involving the exchange of pistols possible in the first place. Mutual good will is an essential element. The recognition by all factions of their mutual dependence one upon the other is the factor which forestalls a tragic outcome in the story. By means of this representation Meyer conveys to the reader a realization of the relativity of all aspects of existence. No one element of life is superior to or independent of the others. For this reason there can be no absolutes in life. As Meyer himself says, we human beings are characterized by a basic dichotomy in our nature; absolutes in human affairs suggest a unity, a wholeness that does not exist.

The third phase in the Meyer novella is the representation of the consequences of that dichotomy which permeates human existence and which is reflected in the polarity of forces that is central in Meyer's prose. The final consequence is the disintegration of all the positive and human manifestations of life. Friendship is one; an example of its tragic disintegration is the final scene of *The Marriage of the Monk,* in which Astorre and Germano, who had been childhood friends, first become rivals for the hand of Antiope Canossa, then actually succeed in killing each other in an irrational frenzy. Another such manifestation is the family; an example of its tragic dissolution is the outbreak of hatred among the sons of King Henry, ostensibly because of Becket's resigning as the royal tutor. This results from the incipient isolation of the king and chancellor in *The Saint.* The destruction of the scions of the Vicedomini, Pizzaguerra, and Canossa families at the conclusion of *The Marriage of the Monk* is another example. The threatened collapse of the social order and, indeed, of the state itself is suggested in *The Saint,* when the sovereignty of the Normans over the Saxons is challenged in Becket's one condition for a reconciliation with the king—the release of the suppressed Saxons from the control of the Norman barons; in *The Marriage of the Monk,* when patrician hegemony is threatened in the final scene of the novella by the disillusionment of the people with the aristocrats because of Ezzelin's charitable judgment of Astorre and Antiope; in *The Amulet,* when anarchy explodes in the annihilation of the bourgeois Huguenots by the aristocratic and proletarian Catholic faction. Even in Meyer's humorous *The Shot from the Pulpit,* dissolution of the governing constellation of forces is suggested in the pastor's retirement and in the general's death, an event which qualifies the happy outcome.

Even though Meyer shows us interacting forces reflected in human actions and seems to deal with tangible, material concepts when demonstrating these forces, even though the secondary motivation for the disintegration of the constellation of forces is rendered visible, still the ultimate cause, the primary motivation, is shrouded in mystery. In *The Saint,* for example, Hans and the king find the path by which they entered the forest blocked by the sudden thunderstorm, so they have to seek a different exit. This results in the fateful discovery of the Moorish fortress. The discovery initiates the chain of events culminating in Becket's murder before the altar of Canterbury's cathedral. But what causes the thunderstorm at this particular time and under these circumstances? The result of Ezzelin's ride along the river Brenta is plainly visible in Dante's description, and it forms the impetus for the various events leading to the death of Astorre, Antiope, and Germano in *The Marriage of the Monk*. What force drives Ezzelin to ride at this site and at this hour? What motivates Germano to play his practical joke on Astorre—lifting him onto a spiritied horse which runs away with him—just as Astorre is about to reclaim the ring dropped by Antiope Canossa? Why do circumstances place Antiope, who unknowingly exercises a strong influence on Astorre's subconscious mind, on the crowded bridge at precisely this moment? In each instance the answer that suggests itself is coincidence. Yet, the role played by coincidence in these instances is too crucial to the denouement to be an adequate explanation; nothing of such central importance can be ascribed to mere chance in the work of a painstaking and conscious artist like Meyer, who invests such meticulous planning in the structure of his works. Ezzelin's interpretation of this influence in *The Marriage of the Monk* as fate, as doom, is too rigid and inflexible a view of it when one considers its quality in *The Shot from the Pulpit*. Here Rudolf Wertmueller plays with this influence in the lives of the people dearest to him; by understanding the nature of the constellation of the forces, possible because of his personal involvement with all the central characters, Wertmueller seems able to manipulate the prime mover. He succeeds in his manipulation where the elder Vicedomini, in *The Marriage of the Monk,* fails, because Wertmueller's tampering is for altruistic reasons; Vicedomini's meddling is the expression of egotism and selfishness. Still the question remains: What driving power is behind the constellation of forces?

The disintegration of all the manifestations of life, such as friendship, family, society, state, is basically tragic because it is brought on by the exclusivity of the individual, the inclination toward an absolute attitude. This quality intensifies the dichotomy that is at the core of the human condition, leading to the final dissolution of the constellation of forces. Yet, paradoxically, the capacity for the absolute position is also a humanizing factor. It is Becket's unconditional love of his daughter Grace, bordering on idolatry, that saves Becket from being an automaton functioning solely for the state. Astorre's capacity for genuine human warmth and love makes him the real hero of Dante's tale. Boccard's comradely devotion to Schadau makes him the most appealing figure in *The Amulet*. Rudolf Wertmueller's affection for Rahel and Pfannenstiel, for the old pastor, and even for the villagers of Mythikon is the rehabilitating factor that completely negates Rosenstock's resentful comments about the old general. In the deaths of each of these characters, which is the final result of the disintegration of the constellation of forces, there is the suggestion of a fulfillment, a self-realization that contrasts sharply with the loss of life involved. Hans's most vivid recollection of Becket's murder is "a dying, smiling face." Astorre, when he expires, is brought to rest next to his beloved Antiope. Boccard's dying gesture after being felled by the shot from Schadau's lost pistol is to press his medallion of Our Lady of Einsiedeln to his lips. Of Rudolf Wertmuel-

ler it is said, ". . . at the stroke of midnight he coughed out his peculiar soul," a description which suggests the defiance typical of him even in his dying breath.

There are always survivors of the disintegration of the manifestations of life in Meyer's novellas: Hans and Sir Rollo live to tell the tale of Becket and Henry in *The Saint*; Ezzelin and Ascanio survive the tragedy in *The Marriage of the Monk*; Schadau and Gasparde escape the purge of the Huguenots in Paris and return to Switzerland to establish a home and family in *The Amulet*. Pfannenstiel and Rahel presumedly do likewise in *The Shot from the Pulpit*. Thus, this disintegration is not total. The loss of stability and of effective laws does not necessarily result in complete chaos or final defeat for mankind. Although the dissolution is tragic for the individual, this loss of stability is a prerequisite for ushering in new growth, development, and change. The old, outmoded structures and relationships—the spent and exhausted constellations—must make way for the new. This dynamic process is one of the mysteries of existence. The seemingly convulsive and destructive events marking eras of change are actually also the birth pangs that signal the arrival of fruitful periods of transition and development in human affairs.

The condition of flux that Meyer depicts in this third phase of his novellas is also the nature of all post-Medieval or Renaissance periods. In his character as a well-read student of history and in his capacity as a poet, Conrad Ferdinand Meyer realized the repetition of such periods in the ebb and flow of history. He recognized the similarity of circumstances in his own era to those of earlier periods, and he discovered in the framework of history a medium for the expression of his own dynamic and relative view of existence, of the condition of man. The framework of history also offered him a convincing way to suggest the connection of the individual's existence with the aspirations of mankind in general—past, present, and future. In so doing, Meyer intimates that the force which Ezzelin calls fate, doom—the driving power behind the visible constellation of forces—is a guiding, constructive Intelligence that makes a harmonious whole, a unity of all events and disparate, individual fates.

In conclusion: Each of Meyer's prose creations has an existence of its own as an artistic entity. Each follows its own laws of form to an outcome that is tragic in the full meaning of the word. Each is conceived as a dynamic, vibrant work of art, for each is, to borrow a concept from Alexander Calder, a "moving construction", a "mobile". This result Meyer accomplishes by constructing visible, interacting, relative figures and forces. Thus, it may be fairly said that form *is* content in a unique way for Conrad Ferdinand Meyer.

Dennis McCort   (essay date 1978)

SOURCE: "Historical Consciousness versus Action in C. F. Meyer's *Das Amulett*," in *Symposium*, Vol. XXXII, No. 2, Summer, 1978, pp. 114-32.

[In the following essay, McCort discusses the stylistic techniques Meyer utilizes to achieve realism in Das Amulett.]

It has been long in coming, but due recognition is finally being accorded Conrad Ferdinand Meyer's earliest novella, *Das Amulett.* As sometimes happens with works whose artistry is subtle, critical evaluation has come full circle. Deemed a triumph on publication for its integrity of plot structure, in the critical canon of our own century the novella fell to the status of an apprenticeship-exercise, faulted variously, even contradictorily, for awkward organization, strained symbolism, hedging on questions of destiny versus free will, and outright fatalism. Sporadic attempts to "rehabilitate" the work, from the mid-thirties through the late fifties, finally issued in a groundswell of positive revaluation in the late sixties and early seventies, a full century after its appearance.

The irony of the critical picture as it now stands is that contemporary critics who have taken a close look at the text of *Das Amulett* and found it meritorious are in no more agreement as to the source of that merit than were the earlier critics with regard to its defects. The confusion seems to revolve around a basic uncertainty over the light in which Meyer intends us to regard his Calvinist hero, Hans von Schadau. [In *Revue des Langues Vivantes,* 1968] D. A. Jackson stresses "the distinction to be made between Schadau's [bigoted] mental consciousness and Meyer's own," and argues that "Forty years after the massacre [of St. Bartholomew's Day], Schadau is as blind as he was at the time. His creator Meyer has no love for him." [In *Conrad Meyer's Epik,* 1973] Gunter Hertling, on the other hand, tries to persuade us that Schadau does indeed outgrow his religious fanaticism and that Meyer is really portraying "die Wandlung eines orthodoxen Protestanten zum toleranten Menschen, dem die Gnade Gottes teilhaftig wird," replete with autobiographical resonances. Consistent with this more charitable view of Schadau's character is Paul Schimmelpfennig's interpretation [in *GR,* 1972], according to which Schadau's spontaneous acts of generosity toward those proscribed by his faith—his uncommitted uncle, the old Catholic Boccard and the areligious Bohemian fencing-master—gradually undermine his narrow Calvinist precepts, ultimately enabling him, during the civil crisis, to "appeal to Boccard to help save Gasparde 'im Namen der Muttergottes von Einsiedeln,'" this last "a clear manifestation of heightened spiritual flexibility." Finally, George W. Reinhardt takes a completely different tack [in *GQ,* 1972], viewing Schadau and the novella as a whole, along with the lyric, "Die Karyatide," as Meyer's vehicles for an indictment of "French bloodlust as manifested by the Massacre of St. Bartholomew as well as by the excesses of the French Revolution and the Commune of 1871." Between the lines Reinhardt would have us detect Meyer's need to rationalize his own enthusiasm for the *Realpolitik* of the new *Reich.* Showing the French Catholics as demoniacally possessed fanatics "enables the moral absolutist in Meyer to accept the Franco-Prussian War as a Manichean struggle between the armies of light and darkness."

Reinhardt's political extrapolations show the interpretative extremes to which the puzzling character of Schadau can give rise. The question remains: How are we to take Meyer's hero? As reminiscing first-person narrator, is he essentially the same hardheaded partisan he was forty years ago; or have the atrocities he has lived through, committed by both sides in the name of religion, made him more aware of the mindless, mechanical nature of fanaticism? Any interpretation of *Das Amulett* hinges on the question of whether Schadau has learned from the experiences he relates to us. At the risk of compounding the confusion of critical voices, but also with the hope of resolving it, I offer an interpretation of the novella centered on a scene almost all the various readings acknowledge as revelatory of Meyer's intent but which I believe has eluded correct interpretation up to now: Schadau's vision during his night of imprisonment in the Louvre. Close examination of this scene and its function within the novella's inner form will show that the meaning of *Das Amulett as literature* has little to do with pronouncements against religious bigotry—or any other moral issue—and everything to do with the portrayal of the characters' varied levels of historical consciousness in relation to their respective roles in contemporary events. This interpretation opens upon a discussion of some of the intellectual issues surrounding Meyer's artistic conception and calls for a general comment on the quality of realism in the novella which such a reading discloses.

The scene in question is brief: Boccard, whose loyalty to Schadau as a fellow Swiss overshadows religious differences, has locked Schadau in his room in the Louvre to protect him from the impending massacre of the Huguenots. Schadau is unaware of his countryman's friendly motives and suspects him of betrayal. The shock of imagined betrayal jolts Schadau into a crisis of doubt and panic. Perhaps the king has gone mad and turned against the Huguenots. Could his warm affection for Admiral Coligny have turned to bitter hatred within a few hours? Worried over these matters and over his unexplained lateness at home, where his new bride, Gasparde, awaits him, Schadau sees his darkest fears confirmed as he peers out through the bars of an elevated window at three sinister figures on a balcony just above him: King Charles, his brother, Duke of Anjou, and Catherine de Medici, the queen mother. The first shot rings out and Schadau witnesses Catherine's "benediction" of the massacre: "'Endlich!' flüsterte die Königin erleichtert und die drei Nachtgestalten verschwanden von der Zinne." Schadau's panic mounts to fever pitch as he realizes his utter helplessness in a situation involving grave danger to his wife: "Das Haar stand mir zu Berge, das Blut gerann mir in den Adern." Reduced to the desperate situation of a trapped animal, whose instincts of rage and fear merge in the single all-consuming urge to escape, Schadau flails away in vain at the heavy oaken door and the barred window.

To understand the true significance of the vision that Schadau is to have later during this agonized night of incarceration, we must take careful note of the distraught quality of his emotional state at this point, especially its physiological manifestations: "Das Haar stand mir zu

Berge, das Blut gerann mir in den Adern. . . . Ein Fieber-frost ergriff mich und meine Zähne schlugen auf ein-ander. Dem Wahnsinne nahe warf ich mich auf Boccards Lager und wälzte mich in tödlicher Bangigkeit." Hair raised, blood coursing, chills, chattering teeth, convul-sions, a sense of impending madness—these are symp-toms of a body operating on an emergency level and poised for survival action but to which every path of action has been blocked. Meyer does not present such physio-logical details simply as strokes of sensationalism to intensify the melodrama; rather, they form an essential prelude to a mode of escape Schadau would never have thought to attempt deliberately—escape from his own body into a sphere of metaphysical truth.

Curiously, Schadau, who is recording these events some forty years after their occurrence "so mein Gemüt zu erleichtern," tells us nothing of the few hours between his convulsive "tödlicher Bangigkeit" and this exosomat-ic deliverance. Perhaps the unnarrated interval, during which his consciousness could only have congealed into a numbed despair, is too painful to recall. It may also indicate a transitional nimbus between normal conscious awareness and the limpid breadth of vision to come. In any case, toward dawn it yields to an event that defies all known natural law. Inexplicably, Schadau finds himself back up at the barred window. Peering through, he wit-nesses a dialog on the folly of religious fanaticism be-tween the goddess of the Seine and a caryatid supporting the balcony just outside his room. There are several in-dications in the text that Schadau's experience of these extraordinary beings is not meant to be taken as merely a dream of gratuitous "vision" of the *deus-ex-machina* sort, but as an actual out-of-the-body experience (OOBE) leading to metaphysical insight. This phenomenon, akin to satori, mystical release, and similar ecstatic states of consciousness, only gradually is coming to be understood by psychologists; but OOBE's have been spontaneously happening to people both in life and in literature from time immemorial. Robert Crookall's landmark *Study and Practice of Astral Projection* contains hundreds of "ac-counts of people who claimed temporarily to leave the body, to be conscious apart from it, and to 'return' and recount their experiences." Similarly, Charles Tart, in *States of Consciousness,* discusses "people [who] report existing at space/time locations different from that of their physical bodies, or being outside of space/time al-together." Meyer provides sufficient clues to indicate that Schadau's perception of the caryatid and the river-goddess occurs in just such a state of consciousness apart from his physical body. That Schadau's experience is not simply a dream or a "vision" but a bodiless waking state of expanded consciousness has important implications for Meyer's central purpose: showing the dichotomy within his major characters between historical awareness and decisive action.

One of the typical features of OOBE's is that they are only partially remembered, or remembered as dreams (Crookall). In recalling his experience, Schadau is hesi-tant to label it a dream, even though his reason has no other convenient category for it. He is intuitively aware

of its uncanny nature, since he admits he had drifted "in einen Zustand zwischen Wachen und Schlummern, der sich nicht beschreiben lässt." This hypnagogic or twilight area of consciousness, when one is no longer awake but not yet asleep, is most conducive to the occurrence of an OOBE, especially when one is self-preoccupied and ob-serving oneself "in the process of falling asleep" (Crook-all). Schadau is not merely self-preoccupied but obsessed with the desperate impotence of his incarceration. Un-consciously he is seeking the only way out of his prison left to him. The complete frustration of a life-and-death need to get to another location can nudge the psychic body loose from its moorings in the physical body. With-out explaining how he got there, since he himself does not know, he says simply: "Ich meinte mich noch an die Eisenstäbe zu klammern und hinaus zu blicken auf die rastlos flutende Seine." This is no dream, any more than his first glimpse through the barred window at the Machi-avellian triumvirate, earlier on. Dreams, even "Fieber-träume," occur during sleep. To assume Schadau capable of attaining sleep in his present predicament is to fly in the face of the most elementary logic of emotions. Moreover, as in reality, dreams in Meyer's fiction—wit-ness Pfannenstiel's erotic dream in *Der Schuss von der Kanzel* or Leubelfing's guilt-ridden nightmares in *Gustav Adolfs Page*—are intimate expressions of a character's deep-rooted wishes and fears. By contrast, Schadau's vi-sion is oddly impersonal; it strikes us as less psycholog-ical manifestation than metaphysical revelation. And he is not directly involved in it at all, but simply witness to a dialog between two larger-than-life entities that take no notice of him. One is led to conclude that Schadau's consciousness has left his body. While his physical body remains on Boccard's bed in cataleptic stupor, the psy-chic body in which his consciousness is now draped drifts up to the barred window just beneath the ceiling. Ironi-cally, the cell from which Schadau is liberated is not the object of his violent protestations but the mortal coil that entwines all men, obscuring the clarity of vision Schadau now attains.

In this radically altered state of consciousness, Schadau is present at a most enlightening scene between the god-dess of the Seine who has just risen from its waves, "ein halbnacktes, vom Mondlichte beglänztes Weib," and "eine Steinfrau, die dicht neben mir die Zinne trug, auf welcher die drei fürstlichen Verschwörer gestanden." Complain-ing of the procession of blood-drenched corpses staining her waters, the river-goddess expresses her annoyance in decidedly un-godlike language, "Pfui, pfui!" and asks her "Schwester" the reason for all the killing: "Machen viel-leicht die Bettler, die ich abends ihre Lumpen in meinem Wasser waschen sehe, den Reichen den Garaus?" The caryatid whispers in response, "Nein . . . sie morden sich, weil sie nicht einig sind über den richtigen Weg zur Seligkeit." At this point Schadau notes, "ihr kaltes Antlitz verzog sich zum Hohn, als belache sie eine ungeheure Dummheit . . .".

Within the context of Schadau's OOBE it is impossible to know with certainty whether the river-goddess and the caryatid exist subjectively or objectively. Meyer does not elaborate on their mode of existence. They may be archetypes from Schadau's unconscious, projected outward onto the embattled cityscape, since the inner barriers between the conscious and unconscious mind are lifted with release from the body during an OOBE. On the other hand, they may be veridical hallucinations, i.e., objectively valid astral beings that existing a dimension outside the normal space-time continuum and can only be perceived from within that dimension. It is also well to bear in mind that the subject-object distinction is regarded by mystics as an illusion of conventional consciousness so that the whole question of ontology may be inappropriate. In any case, their function within the narrative remains the same and it is a more complex function than has been assumed generally. Critics have focussed exclusively on the caryatid's ironic remark, accompanied by mocking grimace, about the stupidity of religious fanaticism, identifying this as Schadau's profound insight and/or Meyer's own point of view. They have failed to see that Schadau's perception is here clairvoyant and must be regarded in its entirety as a *Gestalt*. Reducing it to a propositional statement about religious fanaticism robs it of its vibrant symbolic resonances, both concretely visual and abstract intellectual. This means missing the function of the entire scene within the novella as a whole. It is essential to note that, whatever their ontological status, the river-goddess and the caryatid manifest themselves to Schadau as intimately related entities. "Flussgöttin" addresses "Steinfrau" as "Schwester." If we take this sibling form of address, in whatever sense the river-goddess may intend it, as a clue to a dialectical relationship between the two, then Schadau's profound insight takes on a decidedly different cast from the usual interpretation of his moral transcendence of religious bias. In fact, we move out of the moral sphere altogether and into the metaphysical or cosmological. The river-goddess is the spirit of changing social forms, of transitions from old to new orders. Her bloody stream is the violent flux of historical cataclysm. She is the upstart, the trouble-maker, and speaks appropriately in the street idiom of the revolutionary. Her movement is as inevitable as the flowing of the Seine itself. The caryatid is the solid bulwark of cultural tradition. She is not, as Hertling claims, the "Trägerin des Louvredaches," but the bearer of the balcony "auf welcher die drei fürstlichen Verschwörer gestanden," hence the "bedrock" ("*Stein*frau") of the established order. Though opposites, these historical forces are nevertheless "Geschwister," each eternally evolving out of the other in dialectical interdependence. Seen together, they embody allegorically not merely the struggle of the Huguenots, bound by particulars of time and place, to broaden the scope of the rigid Catholic establishment, but the very cosmology of historical movement itself. Meyer portrays a similar symbiotic relationship between change and tradition or movement and stasis in the famous lyric, "Der römische Brunnen."

It is not only in their visual aspect that the river-goddess and the caryatid symbolize history as dialectical movement. The very form of their verbal exchange, the question and answer, is also dialectical on the level of logic

or thought process. Meyer was certainly no Hegelian; his historian-mentors were, among others, Ranke, an outspoken opponent of Hegel, Burckhardt and Michelet. Still, the dialectical principle, whether in the triadic form given it by Hegel or otherwise, was part and parcel of nineteenth-century intellectual life, and the notion of the extension of this principle from the realm of thought and language into nature and history was in Meyer's time an internationally popular one. It had its ancient origins in such thinkers as Heraclitus and Proclus and its nineteenth-century exponents, even apart from Hegel and the German romantics, in Coleridge, Emerson and the French philosopher, Victor Cousin. Meyer, a voracious reader in French history and philosophy, may well have read Cousin's Hegelian *Introduction à l'histoire de la philosophie,* although there is no evidence that he did. In any case, he makes creative use of the dialectical idea by having the verbal exchange between "Flussgöttin" and "Steinfrau" imply through its dialectical form an extension into the metaphysical process of history, which the two figures visually symbolize.

If, then, we view this scene as Schadau's attainment of metaphysical rather than moral insight, if his epiphany is the realization, not that fanaticism is evil, but that history will take its inevitable course, using human conflict as its vehicle of self-realization, then the caryatid's sarcastic response to her "sister" 's question is a comment on the inability of most mortals in their shrouded consciousness to perceive the true pattern of history rather than a preachment against the moral deficiencies of human character: "'sie morden sich, weil sie nicht einig sind über den richtigen Weg zur Seligkeit.'—Und ihr kaltes Antlitz verzog sich zum Hohn, als belache sie eine ungeheure Dummheit . . .". It is human ignorance that the caryatid mocks, not evil behavior. It is man's remoteness from the cosmic perspective, not his malevolence, that makes him an object of "the laughter of the gods." The distinction between the metaphysical and the moral is crucial, because on it rests the entire matter of Meyer's thematic and formal intent in *Das Amulett.*

Schadau's insight into the cosmic pattern of history, accessible only in a bodiless state of clairvoyance, is the most dramatic sequence in a novella whose inner compositional principle is the problem of discontinuous levels of historical consciousness. It is Meyer's artistic preoccupation with this problem of human consciousness, cast in its contemporary historistic mold, and not his moral interest in indicting human bigotry, that provides the key to *Das Amulett.*

The rich vein of irony inherent in Meyer's theme becomes apparent the instant Boccard enters the room, for it is at this point that Schadau loses the cosmic vision attained during his OOBE. Boccard's sudden entrance dispels the vision and forces Schadau's consciousness back into his body: "In diesem Augenblicke knarrte die Türe, ich fuhr auf aus meinem Halbschlummer und erblickte Boccard." Immediately it is evident that Schadau has lost the significance of this rare experience, since he implores Boccard for information regarding the violent events whose underlying meaning he has just penetrated more deeply than anyone else: "'Um Gotteswillen, Boccard', rief ich und stürzte ihm entgegen, 'was ist heute nacht vorgegangen? . . . Sprich! . . . Ist das Blutbad beendigt?'" Re-entry into the body has resulted in contraction of Schadau's consciousness from the dispassionate, Olympian perception of universals to impassioned, self-interested concern for specific details, above all, concern for his wife: "Jetzt zuckte mir der Gedanke an Gasparde wie ein glühender Blitz durchs Gehirn und alles andere verschwand im Dunkel." The irony of this last clause is that the first-person narrator is telling us more than he knows. Unlike the reader, he himself has no inkling of what "alles andere" involves. Looking back on this episode from a temporal remove of forty years, as Jackson says, Schadau "is as blind as he was at the time." Jackson errs, however, in concluding from this that "His creator Meyer has no love for him," i.e., that Meyer's chief concern is to portray a hero whose lifelong moral intransigence he can condemn. Schadau's "blindness," even forty years after the massacre at the time of narration, is less moral than metaphysical. The function of the initial frame chapter, in which he displays a singular lack of sympathy for the wretched condition of the old Catholic Boccard, is to show that his Calvinist partisanship is as much a shroud over his perception of historical movement in old age as in his youth. Having occurred on a bodiless plane of existence discontinuous with embodied consciousness, (his momentary God's-eye view of history) has had no broadening effect on his historical myopia.

In the frame chapter, we also see how Schadau's retention of his narrow Calvinist outlook into old age has assuaged his guilt over the death of his Catholic friend, Boccard, who had helped him and Gasparde escape the massacre. Observing the old man's frugality, he remarks with a sneer, "Rafft und sammelt er doch in seinen alten Tagen, uneingedenk dass sein Stamm mit ihm verdorren und er seine Habe lachenden Erben lassen wird." Only a rigid Calvinist convinced of the hand of providence in Boccard's death could regard the old man's pathetic situation with such disdain. On the ride home after concluding his business with old Boccard, Schadau is overwhelmed by a flood of memories: "die Bilder der Vergangenheit [stiegen] vor mir auf mit einer so drängenden Gewalt, in einer solchen Frische, in so scharfen und einschneidenden Zügen, dass sie mich peinigten." But it is not the need to confess and expiate on guilt that induces Schadau to record past events "so mein Gemüt zu erleichtern," since his religion has provided him with a convenient rationalization for any guilt. Schadau's need for relief is really a need for bodily release, a need to recover and assimilate the lost vision of his OOBE, which has left an indelible imprint on his unconscious. The tragic irony of his "narrative search" is that it yields no result beyond recollection of a "dream" that took place upon his lapse "in einen Zustand zwischen Wachen und Schlummern, der sich nicht beschreiben lässt." His admission that his descriptive powers fail to do justice to this condition indicates his vague inkling that there is more to the phenomenon he is about to relate than his memory is

able to get at. The visual and auditory components of the OOBE are recalled and related. But the immediacy of metaphysical truth and the entire paranormal significance of the event are irrevocably lost to a reminiscing narrative consciousness that remains shrouded by the body.

In its historical setting and its implicit reference to various traditional configurations of the out-of-the-body experience, *Das Amulett* certainly reveals Meyer's strong intellectual ties to the past. Paradoxically, however, it is this very retrospective attitude that makes the novella a distinctly contemporary work of fiction.

—Dennis McCort

The split between mind and body, consciousness and action, grasping the pattern of history and participating in that pattern—this is the thematic and formal principle of *Das Amulett*. It appears in stark dichotomous outline when we place Schadau's OOBE, his sole moment of enlightenment, next to any number of incidents occurring before and after it that portray his historical vision as severely myopic: his duel with Guiche and its profound political repercussions to which he is blind; his confident dismissal of his landlord's fear of bloody reprisals against the Huguenots in Paris: "'Habt keine Angst', beruhigte ich, 'diese Zeiten sind vorüber und das Friedensedikt gewährleistet uns allen freie Religionsübung'"; his Calvinist scruples, resurfacing only moments after his vision, about appealing to Boccard for help "Im Namen der Muttergottes von Einsiedeln!", an appeal he can bring himself to make only after all others have failed; or his bigoted coldness toward old Boccard's misery forty years later.

Implicitly *Das Amulett* poses the questions: Is there some goal-directed pattern informing the chaotic events of history and, if so, under what conditions can men perceive this pattern? Meyer depicts an optimistic answer to the first question but a pessimistic one to the second. The dialectical relationship between the river-goddess and the caryatid reveals history's telic pattern of movement, but Schadau's capacity to perceive this truth only in a condition in which he is impotent to act on it, i. e., out of his body, dramatizes the tragic darkness of conventional human consciousness. After Hegel and Darwin, the problem of discerning general laws governing historical change was one no serious writer of historical fiction could avoid. Tolstoy, for whom Meyer often professed admiration, wrestled with it in *War and Peace* (1869), which appeared at the time Meyer was resuming work on *Das Amulett*. In his paragon of historical novels Tolstoy poses the problem of human historical consciousness in terms that could serve as the perfect thematic abstract for Meyer's novella. Grimly the "omniscient" narrator declares: "nowhere is the commandment not to taste of the fruit of the tree of knowledge so clearly written as in the course of history. Only unconscious activity bears fruit, and the individual who plays a part in historical events never understands their significance. If he attempts to understand them, he is struck with sterility." This is precisely what happens to Schadau during his night in the Louvre. Up to now he has been a blind participant in the pattern of historical events. In killing Guiche, he unwittingly triggered the outbreak of violence against the Huguenots. There he was an *actor* on the stage of history. But as disembodied witness to the cosmic dialog, he is a *seer*, and in seeing, he is "struck with sterility," for his insight is conditional upon the loss of the only instrument through which historical actions can be realized—the body.

The tragic split between grasping and making history is epitomized in Schadau. But, to one degree or another, it is a shaping principle of the other characters as well. The wise scholar, Chatillon, whose sense of history has matured far beyond the partisan squabbling of Schadau and Boccard, is to that extent impotent to act. Historical actions in **Das Amulett** are impelled by narrow factionalism, by more or less unquestioning commitment to either religious cause. Chatillon is isolated by his capacity to achieve an overview of the conflict, to see it in its historical inevitability as a *Gestalt*. His broadened consciousness depletes his motivation to act on behalf of his Huguenot comrades. Despite a firm intellectual commitment to their cause, "doch bewahrt er," as Brückner says, "seiner Natur gemäss den Abstand von den Dingen." His niece, Gasparde, recognizes and accepts his deep-rooted pacifism out of love, though she has no inkling of its source. It is Schadau, and not her uncle, to whom she turns for help against the insulting Guiche: "Ich mag dem lieben Ohm bei seiner erregbaren und etwas ängstlichen Natur nichts davon sagen. Es würde ihn beunruhigen, ohne dass er mich beschützen könnte."

Chatillon's tragic death at the hands of the rioting Catholics is also, at least partially, a result of what Tolstoy means by the sterility of understanding. No one could have sensed the explosive situation in Paris more acutely than Chatillon. Yet he takes no steps to protect Gasparde and himself from danger. His ostensible reason for staying in the city is that he wants to renew a commitment to his fellow Huguenots that he has failed in the past to uphold by deeds. Even here, however, his words betray rather doom-ridden resignation than commitment to decisive action: "ich stand nicht zu meinen Glaubensgenossen, wie ich sollte; in dieser letzten Stunde aber will ich sie nicht verlassen." The perspicacious Montaigne senses something of this when he chides the old man good-naturedly: "Alter Junge, du betrügst dich selbst, wenn du glaubst, dass du aus Heldenmut so handelst. Du tust es aus Bequemlichkeit. Du bist zu träge geworden, dein behagliches Nest zu verlassen selbst auf die Gefahr hin, dass der Sturm es morgen wegfegt." But Chatillon is

far from deceiving himself. To the contrary, the tragic irony implicit in his ominous words "in dieser letzten Stunde" is that his heightened awareness transcends even itself: he realizes that his own awareness has rendered him impotent to act, even in order to survive.

Other characters in the novella may also be seen as variations on the inverse proportion between historical consciousness and action. Montaigne and Schadau's uncle both resemble Chatillon in their libertarian social attitudes formed from a broad overview of historical currents. Also like Chatillon, their heightened consciousness keeps them aloof from the scene of action. Montaigne, a freethinker, has left Paris by the time violence erupts, and Schadau's uncle spends his years in scholarly seclusion on the lake of Biel in Switzerland, well out of range of the religious cold war being waged in the cantons. Gasparde and Boccard bring up the opposite end of the consciousness-action spectrum. Though she has little interest in doctrinal matters, Gasparde is a devout Huguenot and shares responsibility with Schadau for the fateful action taken against the hated Catholic Guiche. In using Schadau as her instrument to avenge an insult magnified out of all proportion by her own religious prejudice, she becomes in turn an instrument of the process by which history manifests itself. Boccard is a superficial hotblood little given to conscious reflection. His actions are impulsive, motivated as they are by two unexamined and at times even conflicting biases—religion and nationalism. His resentment of Schadau's Calvinism is mitigated only by his loyalty to Schadau as a fellow Swiss. Aiding Schadau during the massacre he does not reach out to a human being in need but makes a concession to a Swiss compatriot who, in desperation, finally patronizes his superstitious devotion to the Virgin of Einsiedeln. It is "isms" that automatically determine Boccard's attitudes and behavior. His is a darkened consciousness that reduces him to the status of a pawn in the conflict of historical forces. For this reason, he is Chatillon's antipode.

One other character, or rather fictional presence, is vital to the theme of levels of consciousness and to the form of the novella. Between title and first chapter Meyer inserts himself as translator of Schadau's memoirs with the announcement: "Alte vergilbte Blätter liegen vor mir mit Aufzeichnungen aus dem Anfange des siebzehnten Jahrhunderts. Ich übersetze sie in die Sprache unserer Zeit." Commentators have noted the function of this device as a means of enhancing the verisimilitude and quasi-historical authenticity of Schadau's chronicle. Beyond this, however, the fictional translator serves as a transcendent consciousness, a disinterested point of view located in both a literal and a figurative sense over and above the work, encompassing the limited visions of the characters and, together with them, forms a hierarchy of historical consciousness. This perspectivistic hierarchy constitutes the novella's inner form. One might visualize it metaphorically as a set of Chinese boxes of awareness ranging from the all-enclosing historical vision of the author-translator-(hence) reader through a median area of enlightenment provided by Chatillon, Montaigne and

Schadau's uncle down to the smallest, innermost boxes of myopic partisanship evidenced by Boccard and Gasparde. Schadau, as the central character who experiences a radical, though temporary, transformation of consciousness through his OOBE, moves from the innermost to the outermost box and back to the innermost. His momentary elevation to the God's-eye-view of the translator imbues the inner form of the novella with tragic dynamism, for his inevitable return to the body is a return to his role as blind instrument of the self-actualizing process of history.

Meyer's portrayal of historical consciousness over against action as a tragic polarity reflects the strong ambivalence he must have felt toward the prescriptive ideals of his "historian-father," Leopold von Ranke. Meyer read nearly everything Ranke wrote, and we know from his letter of May 4, 1868, to his good friend, the Swiss historian Georg von Wyss, that he had consulted Ranke's *Französische Geschichte, vornehmlich im sechzehnten und siebzehnten Jahrhundert* (1852-54) as a source for his depiction of the St. Bartholomew's Day Massacre in ***Das Amulett.*** However, it is less Ranke's historical studies than his historiographical principles that are relevant here. In *Über die Epochen der neueren Geschichte* (1854) Ranke poses a formidable challenge to the historian: "Die Gottheit—wenn ich diese Bemerkung wagen darf—denke ich mir so, dass sie, da ja keine Zeit vor ihr liegt, die ganze historische Menschheit in ihrer Gesamtheit überschaut und überall gleich wert findet. . . . vor Gott erscheinen alle Generationen der Menschen gleichberechtigt, und so muss auch der Historiker die Sache ansehen." Later, in a letter to King Max II of Bavaria (Nov. 26, 1859), Ranke speaks of the ideal that "darin liegen [würde], dass das Subject [i. e., the observer of history] sich rein zum Organ des Objects . . . machen könnte." Intellectually, Meyer subscribed to this ideal state of historical consciousness in which all bias falls away as the historian becomes the pristine mirror ("Organ") in which events are reflected. As Karl Fehr points out, it is precisely such an Olympian posture of "historisch-pragmatische[r] Objektivität" that Meyer adopted from Ranke and claimed for himself as author of ***Das Amulett.*** But Meyer's underlying ambivalence toward this ideal, particularly his doubting man's capacity to perceive the pattern of contemporary history in which he is himself swept up and then with wisdom to act on that perception, is seen in the tension between intellectual assent and artistic intent in ***Das Amulett.*** While Meyer, as historical novelist temporally removed from his subject, can answer the Rankian challenge, his protagonist Schadau can only do so by relinquishing his sole instrument of historical action, his body. In an ironic sense, it is only as a bodiless consciousness that either author or protagonist can penetrate the metaphysical meaning of the conflict between Catholics and Huguenots. Obviously Meyer, for whom these events are past, can have no physical impact on them; his relationship to them is limited to the rarefied sphere of authorial consciousness. By the same token, Schadau, though a contemporary to the conflict, is no less impotent to act during his moment of illumination. And his actions after that moment has passed show

no trace of that illumination. Both author and character are caught up in the mind-body split.

> **It is probably fortunate for us that Meyer never fully exorcized his own demons of doubt. If he had, the corpus of realistic fiction might well have been the poorer for it.**
>
> *—Dennis McCort*

Even Meyer's intellectual assent to Ranke was not unwavering. Although able in his better moments to affirm a divine consciousness that both viewed and permeated history in its totality, he as often questioned his own capacity, and by extension man's, to rise above the constraints of ego and identify with its cosmic vision. Thus in a letter to his cousin, Friedrich von Wyss (July 27, 1866), recalling the beauty of an Alpine landscape: "so sage ich mir, dass derselbe Meister, der dies geordnet hat, auf dem ganz anderen Gebiete der Geschichte gewiss auch seine, wenn auch für mich verborgenen Linien gezogen hat, die das Ganze leiten und zusammenhalten." This concept of immanent justice, a suprarational sense of the inherent rightness of events which Heinrich Henel has aptly called "a manifestation of mystic thinking in the realm of ethics," is the informing principle of Meyer's philosophy of history. It is just such immanent justice, the inexorable working-out of the mysterious "verborgenen Linien" of historical evolution, that Schadau glimpses in the dialog between river-goddess and caryatid. The pity is that it is only for a flickering instant of transfigured consciousness that Schadau can, as Henel says of Meyer the lyricist, "surrender to powers (both without and within him) that are mightier than his reason and larger than his conscious self." It was Meyer's ambivalence toward Ranke that generated the esthetic impulse to ***Das Amulett,*** his attraction to Ranke's ideal of godlike historical consciousness and his simultaneous skepticism of man's ability to grasp those historical currents, and in grasping to shape them, "larger than his conscious self," in which he is bodily embedded. The simple, unalterable fact of the physical grounding of consciousness in the present would prevent man forever, whether as historian, novelist or otherwise, from fashioning for that present something Stendhal, with reference to the novel, called a "mirror of life," reflecting, as it "journeys down the highway," the "blue of the skies and the mire in the road below."

In a larger sense, the ephemeral quality of Schadau's insight reflects Meyer's nostalgia, the nostalgia of a self-designated "Kind[es] des neunzehnten Jahrhunderts" who felt himself an exile in his own time for a bygone era before the all-embracing mystico-metaphysical world views began to be eclipsed by the piecemeal truths of an objective science. Although it is impossible to cite direct sources from this longed-for past for Meyer's portrayal of the out-of-the-body experience, or even to know whether he had any specific antecedent in mind, it is a fairly simple matter to identify various conceptions of the phenomenon from the recent and remote past which he doubtless encountered in his lifelong study of history and literature. One could point to the Platonic view of the body as the temporary prison of the incorporeal, conscious component of man; or the out-of-the-body experiences reported by the Swedish theosopher, Emanuel Swedenborg; or the allegory of Homunculus, the incandescent entelechy in quest of a body in *Faust II.* Meyer was well acquainted with these and other philosophical, mystical and artistic permutations of the mind-body mystery. In his historical sketch of eighteenth-century Swiss town life written for the *Zürcher Taschenbuch* in 1881, "Kleinstadt und Dorf um die Mitte des vorigen Jahrhunderts," he relates an anecdote about an out-of-the-body experience involving the wife of a close friend of the young Lavater that had provided the inspiration for Lavater's first literary success, *Die Aussichten in die Ewigkeit* (1768-78).

Even in his own experience Meyer the "realist" seems to have had at least a nodding acquaintance with mystical states of consciousness. During his recuperation from a nervous disorder in the pietistic asylum at Préfargier in 1852, he had employed some mystical technique or other as a means of establishing distance between himself and his illness. This momentary rising to a less ego-bound perspective on one's own oppressive situation—one way of describing what happens to Schadau—is mentioned in a letter to A. Meissner of November 24, 1877: "In meinen ganz schlimmen Zeiten [at Préfargier] habe ich mich oft mit etwas bescheidenem Mysticismus gefristet und ihn—in kleinen Dosen—probat gefunden d.h. über die Unterwerfung unter das Notwendige . . . hinaus suchte ich im Schicksal, wie es falle, etwas zu lieben." Meyer does not say whether these "mild doses" of mysticism were self-administered during the hypnagogic moment between waking and sleeping, as is the case with Schadau, but we do know from Henel's searching study of Meyer's lyrics that this transitional phase of consciousness, this threshold to an awareness far superior to either waking or dreaming, had a special significance for the poet: "The dream states which Meyer describes [in the lyrics] are complicated by the fact . . . that both the subconscious and the conscious mind are active in them. They resemble the moment just before waking up, when reality intrudes upon the sleeper's visions, when he tries to 'get a grip on himself,' and when he is painfully aware of two worlds." Schadau, of course, is not on the verge of waking up but, conversely, sinking into a kind of numbed hysteria, "in einen Zustand zwischen Wachen und Schlummern, der sich nicht beschreiben 'lasst'." Functionally, however, the two conditions are the same, each a potential point of entry to a sphere of awareness lying above and beyond the normal waking-sleeping zone. All that is needed to reach this sphere is an impetus, which for Schadau assumes the form of a profound frustration of his need to escape that pushes him out of the waking-sleeping zone into a bodiless state of metaphysical illumination.

Perhaps the most intriguing speculation on possible prototypes for Schadau's OOBE is occasioned by the fact of Meyer's strong attraction to St. Paul. Although Meyer never overcame his ambivalence toward the dogmatic aspect of Christianity, his admiration for the aggressive confidence with which Paul pursued his mission was unwavering. Through the spring and summer of 1860 in Lausanne, Meyer steeped himself in Paul's letters and in the *Acts of the Apostles,* intending to write a biographical sketch of the apostle. The sketch was never realized, but the effects of Meyer's intense preoccupation with this charismatic personality were deep and durable. The influence of Pauline thought on *Das Amulett,* completed over a decade later, has been observed by Schimmelpfennig. It is an influence that extends even to the language that Meyer has issue from Schadau's mouth. Whether Meyer resumed his study of Paul's letters during the writing of the novella or knew them well enough to paraphrase them in the novella from memory, we do not know. In either case, it is not unreasonable to suppose Meyer was also familiar with Paul's concept of the psychic or spiritual body: "there are bodies that belong to earth and bodies that belong to heaven. . . . If there is such a thing as a natural body, there must be a spiritual body too" (I Cor. 15: 40, 44). And in following the exciting account of Paul's conversion in *Acts* 9, Meyer may well have had a lingering impression of an episode strongly resembling an OOBE related in the previous chapter in which we are told that Philip, after baptizing a eunuch, "was carried off by the spirit of the Lord, and the eunuch did not see him any longer; he went on his way rejoicing. As for Philip, he was next heard of at Azotus" (Acts 8: 39-40).

In its historical setting and its implicit reference to various traditional configurations of the out-of-the-body experience, *Das Amulett* certainly reveals Meyer's strong intellectual and emotional ties to the past. Paradoxically, however, it is this very retrospective attitude that makes the novella a distinctly contemporary work of fiction. Through Schadau's out-of-the-body experience, Meyer looks back wistfully to a time when it was still possible to conceive of the world and history as making metaphysical sense. But the futility of Schadau's moment of total historical consciousness, the immediate loss of something gratuitously attained, echoes a most contemporary nineteenth-century dwindling of faith in man's capacity to perceive himself as part of what Fritz Martini calls "einen gemeinsamen Bedingungs- und Ordnungszusammenhang des Lebens." The fading of a transpersonal vision of life, of a world whose ordering principle emanates from a center beyond the narrow constructs of individual consciousness, lies at the core of German realism. Meyer's portraits of characters who stand at either end of the consciousness-action spectrum, characters who act without awareness or are aware but impotent to act, reflect his own and his era's increasing perception of human behavior as little more than a stimulus-response mechanism, and of historical awareness as having no impact on historical reality. In Schadau's out-of-the-body experience it is as if Meyer is lifting his hero up above the stifling miasma of his belief-system by the scruff of the neck and demanding he see, at least for once in his life, a transpersonal pattern of wisdom informing his own narrowly partisan actions. Through Schadau, Meyer objectifies and symbolically dramatizes his own crisis of metaphysical doubt. But the atmosphere in which the river-goddess and caryatid reside is too heady for Schadau, and the author must soon allow him to be pulled down by the weight of an ego-bound consciousness rooted in the body.

The transitory character of Schadau's historical vision shows it to be an example of what Richard Brinkmann calls the "hypostasierte Ganzheiten" or reconstructed cosmologies from an earlier, more idealistic era that are built into many works of German realistic fiction. Thus do realistic authors take pains to elaborate the limited, perspectivistic nature of their characters' consciousnesses and proceed then to sew these tight pockets of awareness onto the comforting mantles of metaphysically ordered worlds, worlds that are, however, more products of nostalgic longing than confident conviction, worlds, as Brinkmann says, "die nicht aus der erfahrenen Tatsächlichkeit abgelesen sein wollen, sondern nach denen das in der Erfahrung isolierte Einzelne normativ angerordnet wird." Schadau's out-of-the-body experience symbolizes the spiritual need of an author who has "Gottvertrauen, so viel ein Kind des neunzehnten Jahrhunderts haben kann," to get beyond a historistic world view that is merely hypostasized to one that is manifestly real. It is probably fortunate for us that Meyer never fully exorcized his own demons of doubt. If he had, the corpus of realistic fiction might well have been the poorer for it.

Manfred R. Jacobson (essay date 1979)

SOURCE: "The King and Court Jester: A Reading of C. F. Meyer's *Das Leiden eines Knaben*," in *Seminar*, Vol. XV, No. 1, February, 1979, pp. 27-38.

[*In the following essay, Jacobson considers the significance of the relationship between the characters of King Louis XIV and Fagon in Meyer's novella.*]

The frame of *Das Leiden eines Knaben* is dominated by Louis XIV and Fagon—antagonists whose very special relationship and interaction give this *Novelle* both its form and its meaning. The frame is a kind of dramatic dialogue and subsumes the interior tale as both an extended argument within the dialogue and as a part of the subject matter of the dialogue. The specific subject of the dispute between Louis XIV and Fagon is whether Père Tellier, the priest who has just been chosen father-confessor to the King, is the villain Fagon alleges him to be. Louis doubts Fagon's claim that Tellier murdered a young boy and the interior tale, the story of Julian Boufflers, is, on one level at least, presented by Fagon as evidence to substantiate his accusation. While the question of Tellier's guilt is certainly important, in itself it is also the

point of departure for a confrontation on questions of more universal significance. Likewise, the story of Julian Boufflers is not without interest or merit when read independently. However, while the bulk of the work is devoted to telling his story, it does not stress the boy's psychology or delve into the workings of his stunted mind as much as it stresses the reaction and attitude of others to him. Its true significance lies in its role within the larger context of the frame.

Louis XIV and Fagon are introduced in turn in the first few pages of *Das Leiden eines Knaben* The *Novelle* opens with the words 'Der König,' giving Louis a preeminence of place that not only is commensurate with his station and historical importance, but also properly, although perhaps surprisingly, places him at the centre of the story. Louis is shown in old age and in a very private situation. He has just entered his wife's chambers and thrown open a window, letting in cold air which causes her to shiver. This is the entire content of the first paragraph. The prominent position of this act and the language in which it is couched suggest that it has special significance. The King is described as 'für die Witterung unempfindlich,' suggesting in this context an insensitivity to more than just the climate. Since Frau von Maintenon is his wife and consort of many years, one would expect the King to be aware of and sufficiently concerned about her fragile constitution to have foregone his own desire for fresh air. By introducing this seemingly trivial incident at the outset of the *Novelle,* we are led to wonder what to expect of the King's attitude to his subjects.

The King has come to tell his wife an amusing story, as she divines from his expression. He does so succinctly, describing how Fagon, during the presentation of Père Tellier, whispered an insult at the priest. The King repeats the insult twice, and is inconsistent, once using the term 'Nichtswürdiger,' the second time 'Niederträchtiger.' This variation in the King's narration of the episode reveals that he refuses to repeat the actual insult for he considers it too crude and therefore replaces it with more moderate expressions. The King's commitment to decorum implicit here is made explicit further on in the passage and in fact becomes one of several motifs sustained throughout the story.

After the King concludes his anecdote, a servant arrives with two candelabras which illuminate the room and reveal Fagon standing in the doorway eavesdropping. He angrily corrects the King's expurgated anecdote, adding that he had spoken only the truth. The word 'truth' occurs again a little further on in the same paragraph, and a concern for the truth is thereafter associated with Fagon, as the counterpart to the King's commitment to decorum. Fagon also confirms Madame de Maintenon's suspicion that his insult must have been occasioned by something more important than Tellier's display of false humility. It is here that Fagon accuses Tellier of having murdered a noble lad and identifies him as Julian Boufflers. The King expresses his disbelief, calling Fagon's assertion a fairy tale. In a beautifully ironical reversal of roles Fagon euphemizes his own original assertion: "Sagen wir: er hat ihn unter den Boden gebracht," milderte der Leibarzt höhnisch seine Anklage.' This is an obvious ironic allusion to the King's earlier attempt to find more moderate words for the insults Fagon flung at Tellier. And thus Fagon is suggesting that the rewording of the original accusation, although it is only a euphemism for the first, will none the less be more palatable to the King. This implies Fagon's belief that the King is all too willing to sacrifice the truth to decorum. From the very outset, then, the King's tendency to euphemize reality is contrasted with Fagon's apparent preference for the truth. A discussion ensues which ultimately leads into the narration of the story of Julian Boufflers.

The introductory pages of the *Novelle* already hint at a rather unusual relationship between Louis and Fagon, for Fagon dares to behave in a very impertinent and familiar manner without apparent fear of retribution. This relationship between King and subject may be explained if one considers Fagon as having been cast in the role of court jester. It is in fact possible to enumerate a surprising number of attributes that Fagon has in common with the traditional court jester. For this purpose it will be useful to cite a brief standard description:

> Zur Hofnarrentracht gehörten Narrenkappe, Hofnarrenzepter (eine Rohrkolben-order lederne Keulenform), übergrosser Halskragen auch Schellen. Zum H. machte man mitunter Männer von verkrüppeltem oder zwerghaftem Wuchs, hauptsächlich aber solche mit kritisch-satir. Witz, die unter der Maske der Torheit ein Zerrbild ihrer Zeit zu entwerfen fähig waren; als lustige Räte unterhielten sie die Hofgesellschaft und genossen dafür 'Narrenfreiheit.' Gelegentlich gewannen sie auch politischen Einfluss als fürstl. Ratgeber.

Fagon's physical appearance presents us with the first similarity to the jester as described above. His deformity is stressed several times. The first of these references is an extended and impressive description, not accorded anyone else in the *Novelle*: 'eine wunderliche Erscheinung, eine ehrwürdige Missgestalt: ein schiefer, verwachsener, seltsam verkrümmter kleiner Greis, die entfleischten Hände unter dem gestreckten Kinn auf ein langes Bambusrohr stützend, das feine Haupt vorgeneigt, ein weises Antlitz mit geisterhaften blauen Augen. Es war Fagon.' His bamboo cane topped with a golden knob reminds one of the *Hofnarrenzepter*. [The author states in a footnote: The *Hofnarrenzepter* was often also a cane or much like a cane.] It is not only that we know him to be in possession of such a cane, but the cane is mentioned so frequently that it becomes a fixed part of our image of him.

More important than these physical similarities, however, is Fagon's position at court. He is allowed certain liberties in the presence of or directed against the King which would not go unpunished if attempted by anyone else: 'Frau von Maintenon wusste, dass der heftige Alte, wenn er gereizt wurde, gänzlich ausser sich geriet und unglaubliche Worte wagte, selbst dem Könige gegenüber, welcher freilich dem langjährigen und tiefen Kenner sein-

er Leiblichkeit nachsah, was er keinem anderen so leicht vergeben hätte.' His *Narrenfreiheit* is made explicit in Fagon's request for three liberties before narrating his story, which is ostensibly meant to entertain the King and Maintenon. He is in possession of a finely honed satiric wit, and he meets the condition of creating a caricature of his time. Finally, it may be said that the entire narrative is an effort to advise the King, completing the portrait of the court jester.

The similarities between Fagon and the court jester are too many to be discounted as accidental or insignificant. While I am inclined to believe that they are intentional, it does not seem very important whether in fact Meyer consciously endowed Fagon with these characteristics. In speaking of the painter Mouton's Pentheus sketch, Meyer himself allows for the likelihood that this insightful and prophetic drawing was produced, 'in dumpfer Genialität.' This criterion may be applied to Meyer as well, for the subconscious plays a role in the creativity of both 'primitive' and sophisticated artists alike. What is important, however, is the nature of the traditional relationship between a jester and his master, especially if the jester is a 'wise fool,' as Fagon most certainly is. Such a relationship is usually based on a considerable amount of mutual good will, in spite of a necessary tension between the two parties. If the master, in this case Louis XIV, is afflicted with some kind of self-delusion, it is the fool's mission to exorcise it or, in literary tradition, at least to expose it to the reader or audience. In ***Das Leiden eines Knaben*** the interior tale will be Fagon's weapon in unmasking Tellier and also functions as a mirror, holding up and exposing to the King and the reader his insensitivity, abrogated responsibility, and blindness to the significance of his power.

The introduction of Saint-Simon just before the narration of the interior tale begins serves to bring out the real issue on which Fagon wishes to engage the King. Meyer acknowledges that the *Novelle* was inspired by Saint-Simon and draws heavily on his account of the reign of Louis XIV. Both Saint-Simon's and the *Novelle's* accounts are intimate, gossipy, and often critical of Louis. Saint-Simon is introduced for the immediate reason that he, too, had a connection to Julian, in that he dubbed him 'le bel idiot.' More important, however, is that mention of Saint-Simon and his activities disturbs the King: ' "Nichts mehr von Saint-Simon, ich bitte dich Fagon," sagte der König, die Brauen zusammenziehend. "Mag er verzeichnen was ihm als die Wahrheit erscheint. Werde ich die Schreibtische belauern? Auch die grosse Geschichte führt ihren Griffel und wird mich in den Grenzen meiner Zeit und meines Wesens lässlich beurteilen. Nichts mehr von ihm. Aber viel und alles, was du weisst, von dem jungen Boufflers. Er mag ein braver Junge gewesen sein. Setze dich und erzähle!" ' The salient aspect of this passage is that the King's words contain an implicit distinction between the 'grosse Geschichte,' which, he seems to feel, will judge him fairly and positively, and the kind of history dealing with more intimate or private matters that Saint-Simon is engaged in writing and which the King expects to be critical of him and his reign. He clearly places greater stock in the 'grosse Geschichte' which he thinks will vindicate him. It should be pointed out that, while his annoyance with Saint-Simon is great, he makes a point of his refusal to stifle him: 'Werde ich die Schreibtische belauern?' However, he also fails to make any meaningful connection between the 'grosse Geschichte' and what we may call the 'kleine Geschichte.' The story which Fagon is encouraged to tell and which is the content of the interior tale parallels Saint-Simon's efforts and clearly falls into the category of the 'kleine Geschichte.' But, as we shall see, Fagon does not accept the assumption that *grosse* and *kleine Geschichte* are unconnected, but instead wishes to demonstrate that they are in fact inextricably intertwined.

The traditional relationship and distinction between the historian and the court jester might also be mentioned here: 'for what a chancellor refuses to say and a court Chaplain may not say, a jester and a historian will. The latter tells us what has happened, a jester what is happening now.' Seen as only the story of Julian Boufflers, the interior tale properly belongs to the historical past, and the outcome is made known before the tale is even told. Seen as an integral part of Fagon's dialogue with the King, however, it exposes what is current in Louis's realm, and also points to the future.

The three characters of the frame have rather different expectations of the story that is to follow. Madame von Maintenon is clearly relieved that she has found a means of entertaining the King. The King also expects to be entertained, but for him the story which earlier had seemed unpromising ('Ludwig zuckte die Achseln. Nichts weiter. Er hatte etwas Interessanteres erwartet') has now become more interesting because it promises to be flattering to him: 'Und wäre er wie bei dem Ende des Kindes zugegen gewesen, wie es in der Illusion des Fiebers, den Namen seines Königs auf den Lippen, in das feindliche Feuer zu stürzen glaubte . . .' . Fagon must already know that his story is going to be more than just a means to while away a few hours, for before he begins he requests his three liberties:

> 'Sire, ich gehorche,' sagte Fagon, 'und tue eine untertänige Bitte. Ich habe heute den Père Tellier in Eurer Gegenwart misshandelnd mir eine Freiheit genommen und weiss, wie ich mich aus Erfahrung kenne, dass ich, einmal auf diesen Weg geraten, an demselben Tage leicht rückfällig werde . . . In ähnlicher und verschiedener Weise bitte ich mir, soll ich meine Geschichte erzählen, drei Freiheiten aus—' 'Welche ich dir gewähre,' schloss der König.

The actual story satisfies Maintenon's hope that it entertain the King, for he becomes sufficiently enthralled by it to postpone his dinner in order to hear it to the end. Being a man of strict habit, this is sufficient testimony to his unusual interest in the tale. Fagon has succeeded in holding the King's interest by repeatedly placing him at the centre of the tale, thereby appealing to his vanity: 'Allein Fagon las in den Zügen des Allerchristlichsten nichts als ein natürliches Mitleid mit dem Lose des Sohnes

einer Frau, die dem Gebieter flüchtig gefallen hatte, und das Behagen an einer Erzählung, deren Wege wie die eines Gartens in einen und denselben Mittelpunkt zusammenliefen: der König, immer wieder der König!' While the King's centrality to the interior tale may have been intended by the narrator to hold his attention, its ultimate purpose is of a different kind altogether. It is a carefully developed motif that has been adumbrated in the first sentence of the *Novelle,* and underscores the King's responsibility for conditions at court and in all of France. Thus, Fagon's unflattering and extremely critical descriptions of the court and the country become oblique criticisms of the King.

Fagon, in keeping with the proper role of the court jester, has exposed Louis's flaws both to the King himself and to the reader, while none the less consistently underscoring his stature and centrality in the story.

—*Manfred R. Jacobson*

This admixture of compliments and criticisms is very much in the tradition of the court jester: 'The three compliments and the three truths, or rather insults, have survived to this day in the game of forfeits.' While Fagon's three liberties are explicitly identified as such, corresponding compliments are not as obvious. However, there are three different levels of compliments, the first two of which do occur in conjunction with Fagon's liberties. The King is called a model of decorum for Fagon and all of France. Fagon equates the King with the sun: 'Hat Mouton die Sonne unserer Zeit gekannt? Wusste er von deinem Dasein, Majestät? Unglaublich zu sagen: den Namen, welcher die Welt und die Geschichte füllt—.' Finally, the King is said to be the only one with the power to undo the humiliation that must necessarily lead to Julian's death: 'Erzählt alles der Majestät. Sie wird Julian die Hand geben und zu ihm sprechen: "Der König achtet dich, dir geschah zu viel! und der Knabe ist ungegeisselt." Ich gab ihm recht. Das war das Beste, das einzig gründlich Heilsame, wenn es nicht zu spät kam.' The use of the three liberties or insults negates the compliments and exposes the King's flaws.

The first liberty is used after Fagon tells of a kind of conspiracy by the Jesuits to neglect and thereby damage Julian Boufflers in order to avenge themselves on his father. The King expresses his incredulity and Fagon becomes enraged, charging that force is being used to convert the Huguenots to Catholicism. It is this charge that costs him his first liberty: ' "Diese Frage," erwiderte der König sehr ernsthaft, "ist die erste deiner heutigen drei Freiheiten. Ich beantworte sie. Nein, Fagon. Es wird, verschwindend wenige Fälle ausgenommen, bei diesen Bekehrungen keine Gewalt angewendet, weil ich es ein für allemal ausdrücklich untersagt habe und weil meinen Befehlen nachgelebt wird." ' Fagon's reaction is described by the third person narrator: 'Entsetzen starrte aus seinen Augen über *diesen* Gipfel der Verblendung, *diese* Mauer des Vorurteils, *diese* gänzliche Vernichtung der Wahrheit. Er betrachtete den König und sein Weib eine Weile mit heimlichem Grauen.' Fagon, therefore, is horrified by the King's blindness and unwillingness to see or admit the truth. It is not the details of the tragic fate of a boy that are at issue here, but the facts of history. The King's blindness is seen as a direct function of his vanity, and prevents him from exercising his power responsibly.

The second liberty is used up by introducing the uncourtly Mouton into the tale. Interestingly, it is Fagon himself who suggests that the introduction of Mouton means the expenditure of a liberty, and only later do we discover that the King must have concurred. The reason why the introduction of Mouton is offensive to the King is not, as Fagon seems to suggest, his uncourtly appearance and manners, nor even his ignorance of the glory and achievements of Louis and his reign. Rather, it is offensive because the King realizes he has been introduced to suggest an invidious comparison between the values of the King and his court and those values Mouton represents—a kind of natural decency and independence which point up the petrification, sterility, and meanness that are actual characteristics of the reign of the Sun King.

The third liberty is used up when Fagon confesses that he suggested to the Jesuits that the King may have been Julian's natural father in order to secure the preferential treatment which the somewhat retarded boy so desperately needs. While this lie was told with the best of intentions, it is the only instance in which Fagon is shown as transgressing against the truth and, therefore, deserving of censure. However, the King is not incensed by the lie; rather he would have wished Fagon to compound it in the name of decorum: ' "Fagon," sagte der König fast strenge, "das war deine dritte und grösste Freiheit. Spieltest du so leichtsinnig mit meinem Namen und dem Rufe eines von dir angebeteten Weibes, hättest du mir wenigstens diesen Frevel verschweigen sollen, selbst wenn deine Geschichte dadurch unverständlicher geworden wäre." ' The King's commitment to decorum is therefore again shown as fostering untruth.

Fagon, therefore, in keeping with the proper role of the court jester, has exposed Louis's flaws both to the King himself and to the reader, while none the less consistently underscoring his stature and centrality in the story. Yet what does this have to do with the suffering and destruction of Julian Boufflers to whom so much attention is devoted? Clearly, Fagon seems somehow to hold the King responsible for the boy's demise, yet alternative sources of responsibility, which have been understood by other critics as the sole or at least primary causes of his death, are suggested within the text. Both Fagon and fate have been understood this way. Fagon in fact does accuse himself of negligence, while the strange incident con-

cerning Mouton's sketch suggests that fate is at work. However, both of these alternate sources of responsibility are in a sense dependent on or connected with the King. Fagon's responsibility consists essentially in hesitating to act swiftly by taking Julian out of school and sending him to join his father at the front. It is, however, considerations of decorum, in a sense the king's values, that restrain him from acting: 'Wenig fehlte, ich schlug ihm vor: ohne weiteres eines meiner Rosse zu satteln und stracks an die Grenze zum Heere zu jagen; aber dieser kühne Ungehorsam hätte den Knaben nicht gekleidet.'

As far as fate is concerned, it is the King himself who, in a real sense, has been shown as the fate of the age. This is underscored by his very centrality to the *Novelle,* particularly the interior tale—he is the dominant presence without ever making an actual physical appearance, and it is his values which determine Julian's fate. Julian, like his mother, is dumb, beautiful, and in possession of many moral virtues. The crucial difference between the two is that she, the wife of a strong-willed husband, is given no responsibilities that are beyond her means, is completely accepted, even admired, by the society of the court, while her son, the offspring of France's greatest military hero, is expected to cut an impressive figure at court, yet in fact seems destined to be an object of universal scorn or pity. Fagon is able to understand both mother and son, appreciate their virtues, and show true compassion for their limitations. The King, however, rejects the boy out of hand, while he has nothing but praise for the mother who once adorned his environment. His attitude, then, is reflected in the attitude displayed by Marshal Boufflers—the blindness and insensitivity he, too, shows his own son. Most important, however, is the explicit assertion that Louis had the power to prevent Julian's demise. The story of Julian Boufflers, then, illustrates the king's ultimate responsibility for the *kleine Geschichte.*

The frequency and importance of parallelism and antithesis in Meyer's works is generally recognized, and examples of each occur quite often in this *Novelle.* One of many clear-cut examples of parallelism is that between Louis XIV and Marshal Boufflers. The particular instance cited above indicates at least two things: that the King's attitude and values are reflected in his subjects and that Louis never really understands the significance of what happened to Julian, in contradistinction to W.D. Williams's view where he suggests that Marshal Boufflers recognizes the wrong he has done. In fact Marshal Boufflers does not know the full story that implicates Tellier. The parallelism King/Marshal Boufflers signals that the King will not really understand either, and therefore will not understand his responsibility.

The tale that Fagon has been telling is in the realm of the *kleine Geschichte,* dealing with seemingly trivial matters. Furthermore, it treats events that occurred in the past—the destruction of Julian and the immediate responsibility of Tellier for his death. However, Fagon uses the past to castigate the follies of the present, and to suggest that the individual fate of a retarded boy may reflect the sickness of an entire society. Finally, towards the end of the interior tale, we learn that Fagon's purpose in its telling is not simply to condemn Tellier for the past, or to block his appointment, for Fagon seems to know that Louis will not reconsider his choice of father-confessor. Rather, he also wants to warn or advise the King of the danger to the future of his reign in elevating Tellier to a position of such importance and influence. The third-person narrator indicates that Fagon's foreboding is justified: 'Nicht dass er sich schmeichelte, Louis werde seine Wahl widerrufen. Warnen aber hatte er ihn wollen vor diesem Feinde der Menschheit, der mit seinen Dämonenflügeln das Ende einer glänzenden Regierung verschatten sollte.' Furthermore, the knowledgeable reader is specifically aware that under the influence of Tellier Louis will revoke the Edict of Nantes leading to the open persecution of the Huguenots and ultimately to the destruction of the Bourbon monarchy. Fagon's prophetic warning concerning the danger in elevating Tellier to a position of influence is borne out by history, just as Mouton's prophetic sketch suggesting Tellier's destruction of Julian Boufflers is borne out by the interior tale.

Tellier, then, not only links the past, the present, and the future, but he also illustrates the connection between *grosse* and *kleine Geschichte*. Fagon knows, the reader learns, and Louis fails to see that his disregard of Tellier's abuses in the realm of the *kleine Geschichte* may have overwhelming consequences for the kind of history he considers significant. In general he fails to learn that what seems inconsequential from a larger historical perspective may in fact have drastic ramifications.

The closure of the frame is somewhat perplexing. The delirious Julian dies, phantasizing that he is on the front fighting for the King. The interior tale is now concluded and the frame closes with the sentences: 'Fagon hatte geendet und erhob sich. Die Marquise war gerührt. "Armes Kind!" seufzte der König und erhob sich gleichfalls. "Warum arm," fragte Fagon heiter, "da er hingegangen ist als ein Held?" ' Thus it is confirmed that to the very end the King fails to see that Fagon's tale is anything more than a moving account of the demise of a rather pathetic boy. The perplexing aspect of the closure is Fagon's expressed attitude towards Julian's death. His remark that Julian was not pathetic because he died a hero's death is difficult to take at face value and his apparent cheerfulness in uttering it is even more difficult to explain. The remark is probably ironic—a thrust at the King. Fagon's cheerfulness is then an expression of his pleasure at having gotten away with another liberty. He has failed to exorcise the King's folly, but as a wise fool in the literary tradition he has succeeded in his primary mission, in the only matter still left open—making the reader aware of the follies of the past and how they affect the future.

Edward M. V. Plater   (essay date 1979)

SOURCE: "Alcuin's 'Harmlose Fabel' in C. F. Meyer's *Die Richterin*," in *German Life and Letters*, Vol. 32, No. 4, July, 1979, pp. 318-26.

[*In the following essay, Plater explores the function of Alcuin's fable within* Die Richterin, *asserting that Meyer succeeded in "suggesting not only an important scene later in the narrative but also the general background of the story and the basic plight and motivation of the main characters."*]

Little has been written about the passage near the beginning of **Die Richterin** that describes the region in which the title character lives. Yet with this passage Conrad Ferdinand Meyer provides, as he frequently does in his novellas, a comprehensive prefiguration of the story that follows. In response to Charlemagne's question about the region of Rhaetia, Alcuin, the director of the famous Palace School, speaks first of the roads and paths that lead across the mountainous region and the bewildering network of interconnected valleys, which fable has populated with dubious shapes and nebulous horrors. In the ghostly light of the snow-covered peaks 'ringlet sich die Schlangenkönigin, wie verlockt von einer Schale Milch, einem blanken Wasser zu, gegenüber, aus einem finstern Borne, taucht die Fei und wehklagt. . . . Sie ahnt das ewige Gut und kann nicht selig werden. Dahinter, zwischen Schnee und Eis, in einem grünen Winkel, weidet eine glockenlose Herde und ein kolossaler Hirte, halb Firn halb Wolke, neigt sich über sie.'

These words, which Alcuin refers to as a 'harmlose Fabel' that loses its force at the first sign of human habitation, seem intended merely to establish a background of rugged, uncharted nature and of mystery and pagan superstition for the story that unfolds. Yet certain echoes of them later in the novella caution against dismissing them as part of the atmosphere and nothing more. There is, first of all, the writhing serpent on the cap of the vial of poison that Stemma has had in her possession ever since the disappearance of Peregrin fifteen years ago. This tiny etched figure provides a possible link between Stemma and the serpent queen of Alcuin's description, which, as if enticed by a saucer of milk, weaves its way toward a smooth body of water. A tentative interpretation might be that just as the serpent queen seeks calm water, so Stemma, subconsciously at least, longs for the inner peace which her conscience denies her.

The narrative offers many hints that Stemma does indeed suffer from a guilty conscience. Granted she may feel no remorse at having poisoned the man whom her father had forced upon her; yet it is reasonable to assume that the injustice of her own impunity is a constant source of uneasiness to her, at least below the threshold of her consciousness. After she had secured her position following the death of the Comes and the birth of her daughter, she went through a period of sleepless nights during which she often sat near Palma's bed and fidgeted with the vials containing the poison with which she had killed her husband and the antidote with which she had saved her own life. To play with these vials until daybreak became an obsession with her. Since then, to be sure, she has conquered this obsession and, so it would seem, has succeeded in suppressing her feelings of guilt. Her inner unrest, however, has not subsided completely.

Though it is true that even before she murdered the Comes she exhibited a judicial bent for settling disputes, her grim preoccupation since then with solving the most unusual and complicated crimes and her untiring efforts to apprehend and punish the guilty suggest a more than natural concern for justice, as if she felt constantly compelled to justify to herself her own exemption from punishment.

Stemma's purpose in sending for Wulfrin is to secure her daughter's future, which she hopes to accomplish by obtaining Wulfrin's assurances, now that he has reached his majority, that he will not claim Palma's inheritance after Stemma's death on the pretext that Palma is not the legitimate heir. Yet the question arises why this woman in the full bloom of life is so eager to put her affairs in order. Is she perhaps weary after fifteen years of having to keep her secret? Does she subconsciously long for death as a release from the pretense and the mockery of justice that she has felt forced to engage in for her daughter's sake? The evidence of a guilty conscience cited thus far would seem to indicate that this is so.

As the story proceeds, other considerations begin to weigh heavily upon her conscience. The interview in which Stemma's childhood playmate Faustina confesses to a crime almost identical to her own must stir up in her long suppressed feelings of guilt. And Faustina's sincere repentance and demand that Stemma sentence her to death as punishment for her crime must intensify these feelings of guilt in Stemma, since she herself has committed the very same crime and yet has firmly resisted making a confession.

One indication that Stemma's conscience has been affected by the interview is the fact that she gets out the vials again with which she used to fidget during the sleepless nights following the death of the Comes. Another indication is the vision that she experiences after her talk with Faustina, in which the fainthearted youth, whose child she was carrying when she was forced to marry Wulfrin's father, appears and lays claim to Palma. Stemma's attempt to destroy the vial of poison, and with it the only evidence of her crime, and her denial to the apparition that she ever submitted to him, as well as her scornful smile for the Comes whom she sees in her imagination sitting in the reeds and puzzling over the possible cause of his death, all indicate, to be sure, that she fully intends to go on keeping her secret; yet the very fact that she reverts to her old habit of playing with the vials and experiences this vision betrays a conscience disquieted by the past which the interview with Faustina has revived.

New pressure is brought to bear on Stemma's conscience when Wulfrin insists on making public confession of his love for his presumed sister and demands that Stemma judge him. After attempting to reason with him she agrees, reluctantly, to this demand. The prospect of Wulfrin's public disgrace and death by fire (the punishment for incest) cannot fail to have an impact on Stemma's conscience, since she knows that Wulfrin is innocent of the sin of which he accuses himself and that all that is needed is a word from her to clear up the misunderstanding. Furthermore, the uncompromising personal honour exhibited by Wulfrin confronts Stemma with an example of moral integrity that must also prod her conscience. Still she seems determined to keep her secret, as indicated by the vision which she experiences after agreeing to Wulfrin's demand that she judge him. She sees in her imagination a large woman of awesome beauty sitting with a slate across her knee and apparently seeking the solution to some question. Stemma, believing her to be after her secret, cries out defiantly: 'Das bringst du nicht heraus! Du findest keine Zeugen!' The blast of Wulfrin's horn, the 'Wulfenhorn,' which precipitated this vision, is followed by a second one which appears as an answer to her defiant cry, a shattering summons to confess: 'Ihr antwortete ein erschütternder Ruf, der aus allen Wänden, aus allen Mauern drang, als werde die Posaune geblasen über Malmort.' These blasts and the third and final one, which finally throws Stemma into such a state of anger and confusion that she rushes down to the courtyard and confesses her crime to a figment of her imagination (the likeness of the Comes on the lid of his stone coffin), come to symbolize her conscience at work. According to legend the horn has the power to force the wife of its owner to confess any sins she may have committed in her husband's absence; and although Stemma was able to defy its supernatural power fifteen years ago when she poisoned the Comes, she cannot resist its phychological power now.

The last and greatest challenge to Stemma's conscience, however, comes as she sees the health of her daughter, who had overheard her confession to the imagined ghost of the Comes, gradually being destroyed by the horrible secret she now must share with her mother. But only when Palma, who has refused all nourishment since having learned her mother's secret, appears on the brink of death, does Stemma finally relent and agree to make a public confession of her crime. It is true, the most immediate and compelling reason for this decision is to save Palma, whom she loves more than anything and for whose sake she had poisoned the Comes and had kept it a secret all these years. Yet her conscience plays a part in the decision too. Palma's abhorrence unto death of her mother's crime and her own, albeit completely innocent, role in it (Stemma had said to the stone image of the Comes that the unborn Palma novella was responsible for his death) and her steadfast insistence on impartial justice set an example of incorruptible goodness that cannot help but intensify Stemma's sense of guilt. Indeed, the accumulated force of all these factors, from the subconscious feeling of guilt revealed in Stemma's unflagging pursuit of lawbreakers to her daughter's sheer inability to suffer the affront to her pure and incorruptible nature, contributes to her decision to confess and her desire to atone for her crime.

If we return now to our point of departure for this discussion, namely the serpent queen in Alcuin's fable, we may conclude that this supernatural figure is, after all, an apt representation of Stemma's situation and behaviour in the story. The serpent's attraction to the calm water as if to a saucer of milk symbolizes Stemma's longing for inner peace.

The interpretation receives further support from the symbolic meaning that attaches to milk in the novella. In the scene at Pratum Gracious spoons milk from a bowl for Palma, but she prefers the wine with which Wulfrin has just drunk a toast to them. The wine becomes associated here with the passionate feelings stirring in Palma and Wulfrin and the violent outburst of Wulfrin's pent-up emotions, while the milk comes to represent the absence of ardent physical passion, or to put it mildly, sexual calm. This is, to be sure, a different kind of calm from that which Alcuin's 'Schale Milch' represents—the context has created a new connotation—yet the basic meaning remains and thus supports the association of the saucer of milk with the inner peace that Stemma desires.

In this connection the pagan fable takes on a Christian meaning. At the end of the novella the offering of a prayer for the soul of Palma's mother brings to mind the singing of a mass for the soul of Charlemagne's father in the first chapter. The novella begins, in fact, with a verse from this mass. The verse invokes the saints Peter and Paul. Paul is the patron saint against poisonous snakes, and according to legend, when he was beheaded at Rome, milk flowed from his veins. Milk is, of course, a universal antidote for poisoning. The saucer of milk in Alcuin's fable, then, could represent, as an antidote to the deed that has been poisoning Stemma's conscience, the inner peace that comes from adherence or resubmission to the law propagated by Paul as the apostle to the Gentiles. Some statements pertinent to Stemma's situation appear in Paul's letter to the Romans, where he speaks of impartial justice: 'Therefore thou art inexcusable, O man, whosoever thou art that judgest: for wherein thou judgest another, thou condemnest thyself; for thou that judgest doest the same things'; 'Or despisest thou the riches of his goodness and forbearance and longsuffering; not knowing that the goodness of God leadeth thee to repentance?'; 'For there is no respect of persons with God'; and Thou that makest thy boast of the law, through breaking the law dishonourest thou God?' In other words, Christian teaching, suggested by the saucer of milk, holds out the promise to Stemma of inner peace as the reward for confession and atonement. To be sure, this is not clearly formulated in her mind; it is reflected only in her unconscious longing for inner peace.

Stemma's public confession, however, is not the end of her ordeal. After confessing she asks the Emperor to judge her, but he replies that she should judge herself. 'Nicht ich,' sagte sie, wendete sich zu dem Volke und rief: 'Gottesurteil! Wollt ihr Gottesurteil?' . . . Da sprach die Richterin feierlich: 'Erstorbenes Gift, erstorbene Tat! Lebendige Tat, lebendiges Gift!' und hatte den Kristall aus dem Busen gehoben und geleert.' She takes poison confident that it will kill her and believing it is God's judgement that she die in precisely this manner. To understand this properly one must go back to the incident in which she had attempted to destroy the vial of poison with which she had murdered the Comes by crushing it beneath her heel but had inadvertently destroyed the vial containing the antidote. She had immediately discovered her mistake and placed the remaining vial beneath her heel to dispose of it in the same way. The crystal, however, had resisted the pressure of her weight, and she had picked it up again to hurl it against the wall. Yet with her arm already raised to throw it she had stopped, out of fear that she might awaken her daughter, or, as Meyer enigmatically adds, 'mit einem andern Gedanken barg sie es sorgfältig in dem weiten Busen ihres Gewandes.' There is no way of knowing for sure what this other thought might have been. Perhaps it was some vague presentiment prompted by the talk she had just had with Faustina that stayed her arm. In any case, when she later proclaims the judgement of God, she apparently has this incident in mind and now regards the curious oversight as the working of God's will. Moreover, she welcomes this sign of God's will, for she realizes that, were she to continue to live, she would never find inner peace. She would be haunted by the example set by Faustina and by the fact that she had been willing to permit Wulfrin's public disgrace and death and the destruction of Palma's happiness (even though it was to insure her daughter's future security). Only her death by the judgement of God can restore to her the peace which the saucer of milk and the calm water of Alcuin's fable symbolize.

'Der kolossale Hirte' and 'die glockenlose Herde' in Alcuin's fable suggest the general context in which the events of the novella take place. They bring to mind the Biblical references to the Lord as a shepherd and the faithful as His flock. The fact that the flock is without bells suggests that the process of taming and domestication has not been completed. This corresponds in general to the situation in Rhaetia, where even though Christianity has made significant inroads into the region and the consciousness of its people, old superstitions and pagan beliefs still persist and marauding and murder and other acts of violence have been plaguing the countryside for years.

Both the shepherd and his flock are echoed specifically in the scene in Chapter III in which Palma and Wulfrin rest at the edge of a mountain lake. In this scene the snow-capped mountain that towers majestically above Palma and Wulfrin and reaches to the clouds corresponds to the colossal shepherd. The identification rests upon Alcuin's description of the shepherd as half perpetual snow and half cloud. The 'glockenlose Herde' which the colossal shepherd tends has its counterpart in the natural landscape of the scene too, in the boulders strewn about the shore of the lake. Alfred Zäch mentions the possibility that Meyer might have had Lüscher lake in mind when he wrote this scene and offers a description of the lake by Dietrich Jecklin, which he cites as a possible source. Jecklin's use of the word 'Brüllen' to describe the echo that results when the wind blows through the peculiarly shaped formations which rise up from the ground around the lake supports the identification of the boulders with a 'glockenlose Herde.'

The symbolic meaning of the snow-capped mountain and boulders, though related to the meaning of the colossal shepherd and the flock without bells, is not identical to it, for the latter is determined by reference to the Bible and by the general background of the entire story, while the former is determined by the specific scene at the shore of the lake. The main point of this scene, a private interlude experienced by Palma and Wufrin when they stop to rest on their way to Palma's betrothal to Gnaden-reich, is to show how hopelessly attracted to each other the alleged siblings are. And it is the nature of their love that determines the specific variation in the meaning of the shepherd and flock that is to be associated with the boulders and the snow-capped mountain.

Alcuin's fable serves as a striking reminder of the highly conscious and intricate style characteristic of Conrad Ferdinand Meyer and of the special need of the reader to approach his work with the greatest care, if he is to enjoy all the subtleties of his complex narrative art.

—Edward M. V. Plater

Love has both a physical and a spiritual dimension, and Palma's love for Wulfrin is no exception. She is, after all, at the age of adolescence, and the sexual energy stirring in her young body naturally seeks an outlet. But Palma is, at the same time, the epitome of childlike innocence. She is somewhat wild, to be sure, but that is simply part of her irrepressible youth. She appears in Wulfrin's eyes as an angel such as one might find depicted in the intricate letters of a costly psalter. Her angelic quality is also suggested as she sets out with Wulfrin and Gabriel for Pratum. She is described as climbing as if on wings; her breath comes freely and she remains fresh and cool like a bubbling spring in the burning sun, as if she were unhampered by the weight of physical reality, like an unembodied soul. In fact, butterflies fluttering about her head are intended to suggest this idea; they are frequently used by Meyer to symbolize the soul. The author even has Wulfrin exclaim later, as he beholds Palma in his mind's eye: 'Meine Seele!' Palma, though a character of flesh and blood, is the soul of goodness and innocence, and thus she is not aware of the sexual nature of her love for Wulfrin. In her heart the feelings of a sister for a brother and the feelings of a woman for a man merge into one overpowering love. We read in the scene by the shore of the lake: 'Palma umfing den Bruder in Liebe und Unschuld.' This innocent, childlike aspect of her love for Wulfrin is suggested by the spiritual, unearthly quality of the mountain peak that rises above them and is covered with eternal snow.

Wulfrin's love, on the other hand, lacks the childlike innocence of Palma's. He soon becomes aware of the elemental desire stirring within him and struggles to subdue it. In the scene by the shore of the lake, however, in an unguarded moment the fiery intensity of his love breaks forth: 'Wulfrin . . . ging unter in der Natur und wurde eins mit dem Leben der Erde. Seine Brust schwoll. Sein Herz klopfre zum Zerspringen. Feuer loderte vor seinen Augen . . . .' This strong physical side of his attraction to Palma is suggested by the heavy, earthbound nature of the large boulders. Thus the symbolic meaning which the scene imparts to the mountain peak and the scattered boulders is a variation of the dualism of the Christian spirit on the one hand and the violence and lawlessness of the Rhaetians on the other, a dualism which is symbolized by the colossal shepherd and the flock without bells.

The image of the fairy in Alcuin's fable, who is disconsolate because she has a vague inkling of eternal bliss but cannot attain it—'sie ahnt das ewige Gut und kann nicht selig werden'—prefigures the plot interest revolving round Palma, who almost to the very end of the story suffers the unhappiness and frustration of unfulfilled love. The fulfillment of her love for Wulfrin is the unattainable bliss of the fairy, unattainable because of the fiction that Palma and Wulfrin are sister and brother.

Specific passages later in the narrative support the identification of Palma with the fairy. One of these is the description of the mountain lake. Its dark, clear water over which a wall of rock casts a giant shadow is analogous to the dark well, the 'Finstern Borne,' in which the fairy languishes. This analogy is further strengthened by Wulfrin's playful remark that the lake might be inhabited by a water spirit. The lake holds a strong attraction for Palma. She regards it, in fact, as *her* lake and has been looking forward to showing it to her brother. Thus it becomes linked with Palma in a way akin to that in which the well is associated with the fairy.

The fairy's lamentation is echoed by a recent experience of Palma's at the shore of the lake, an experience, as she relates, which made her weep and sore at heart: 'Jetzt prangt und jubelt der Schneeberg, . . . aber nachts, wenn es mondhell ist, zieht er bläulich Gewand an und redet heimlich und sehnlich. Da ich mich jüngst hier verspätete, mache sich der süsse Schein mit mir zu schaffen, lockte mir Tränen und zog mir das Herz aus dem Leibe.' The moonlight, the intimate and longing manner in which the mountain 'spoke' to her, the tears, and the heartache all indicate that this experience had to do with love, with Palma's awakening womanhood, with feelings which she in her childlike innocence did not and still does not understand.

On the present occasion, however, Palma feels, as she sits beside Wulfrin at the edge of the lake, a sense of bliss similar to that for which the fairy longs. A cloud formation described by the author as a 'himmliches Fest' passes over the snow-capped mountain peaks, and figures become discernible that resemble friends or lovers inclining toward each other. As these figures threaten to dissolve, Palma cries out: ' "Bleibet! oder gehet nur! . . . wir sind Selige wir ihr! Nicht wahr, Bruder?" und sie blickte mit trunkenen Augen bis in den Grund der seinigen.'

The scene, however, ends on a dissonant note when Wulfrin, horrified by the water's reflection of him holding his sister in his arms, jumps to his feet and hurries away. With this Palma is returned to a state of frustration and unhappiness, which corresponds to the state of the woeful fairy.

The connection between Palma and the fairy is further reinforced by the parallels in the pagan story of Byblis and Caunus contained in a book belonging to the library at Pratum. According to Ovid Byblis loved her brother Caunus and followed him through many lands, hoping that he would return her love. Finally she gave in to despair and wept inconsolably. From her tears arose an eternal spring. The parallel to Wulfrin and Palma's relationship is obvious and is made inescapable by the fact that the figures in the illustration to the story even resemble in physical appearance the alleged siblings. The eternal spring produced by Byblis' tears calls to mind the well mentioned by Alcuin, thereby reinforcing indirectly the connection between Palma and the woeful fairy.

Another passage which supports the identification of Palma with the fairy is the one in which Palma, whom Wulfrin threatened to throw into the raging river current if she should cross his path on the way home from Pratum, encounters her presumed brother and pleads with him: 'Bruder, Bruder, was habe ich an dir gesündigt? Ich kann es nicht finden! Siehe, ich muss dir folgen, es ist stärker als ich! . . . Töte mich lieber! Ich kann nicht leben, wenn du mich hassest! Tue, wie du gedroht hast!' Palma, in sensing that her happiness depends on the affection of her presumed brother without realizing that she is in love with him, resembles the fairy, who also has only a vague idea of what it is she longs for ('Sie ahnt das ewige Gut').

In still another passage Wulfrin is overcome with remorse and compassion for Palma, whom he knocked unconscious the day before when he pushed her away from him. He now realizes that he loves her and pictures her in his mind's eye: 'Er sah sie mit allen ihren Gebärden, jedes ihrer süssen und unschuldigen Worte nahm Gestalt an, er schaute in ihre seligen Augen und in ihre wehklagenden. Jetzt füllte er sie, die sich weinend und schmeichelnd mit ihm vereinigte, und wusste, dass sie noch lebte und atmete.' Both words used here to describe the alternating moods expressed in Palma's eyes, 'selig' and 'wehklagend,' were used in Alcuin's fable to describe the fairy. Indeed the very process by which Wulfrin recalls the scenes with Palma from the preceding day encourages the identification of Palma with the fairy of Alcuin's fable, for the process is essentially the same as that exemplified by the description of the fairy. Wulfrin objectifies in his mind's eye the words which Palma had uttered: 'jedes ihrer süssen und unschuldigen Worte nahm Gestalt an.' That is, he vividly recalls the postures, gestures, and facial expressions which accompanied her

words and expressed their meaning in concrete form. This process of objectification is precisely the narrative principle underlying the prefigurative function of the disconsolate fairy. Meyer uses the image of the fairy to express in concrete form the unhappiness and frustration that Palma experiences in the unfolding story. The only difference is that Wulfrin makes use of natural, logical externalization (gestures and expressions), whereas Meyer uses figures and forms that have no immediate, causal connection with Palma. Nevertheless both objectify Palma's situation and her dominant feelings. In fact the entire fable related by Alcuin with its symbolic figures and landscape exemplifies, as this investigation has revealed, this same process of expressing abstract thoughts and feelings in concrete form. This process, as critics have pointed out, is basic to Conrad Ferdinand Meyer's method of writing. What is particularly impressive about the case at hand, however, is that the author succeeded in such a seemingly straightforward, 'harmless' passage comprising just sixty words in suggesting not only an important scene later in the narrative but also the general background of the story and the basic plight and motivation of the main characters. Thus Alcuin's fable serves as a striking reminder of the highly conscious and intricate style characteristic of Conrad Ferdinand Meyer and of the special need of the reader to approach his work with the greatest care, if he is to enjoy all the subtleties of his complex narrative art.

Herbert Rowland   (essay date 1985)

SOURCE: "Conscience and the Aesthetic in Conrad Ferdinand Meyer's *Plautus im Nonnenkloster*," in *Michigan Germanic Studies,* Vol. XI, No. 2, Fall, 1985, pp. 159-81.

[*In the following essay, Rowland analyzes the interweaving of structure, motifs, and narrative perspective in Meyer's novella.*]

Conrad Ferdinand Meyer's ***Plautus im Nonnenkloster*** has been called [by Alfred Zäch, in *Conrad Ferdinand Meyer: Dichtkunst als Befreiung aus Lebenshemmnissen,* 1973] "ein Kleinod der Novellenkunst . . . in formaler Hinsicht makellos, höchst reizvoll als ästhetisches Spiel und doch nicht ohne menschlichen Gehalt . . ." Significantly, this praise is lavished more on the form than on the content of the work. Indeed, Meyer's story of an Italian humanist who delivers a codex of Plautine comedies and a vital Swiss girl from a convent has generally been regarded as superficial. The tenacity of this view is due in part, perhaps, to the author's own apparent assessment of the tale, which he once described as "ein Novellchen, das zwar nicht viel zu bedeuten hat, aber solid gebaut ist." In any case the work has received far less individual scholarly attention than many other *Novellen*, including the formally less felicitous ***Die Richterin.***

While stressing the formal success of ***Plautus,*** Meyer also adverted to a more substantive aspect of its content:

"In den drei Figuren sind die drei hist. Bedingungen der Reformation, in komischer Maske verkörpert: Die Verweltlichung des hohen Klerus" (Poggio), "die Verthierung der niedrigen Geistlichkeit" (Brigittchen), and the "ehrliche [n] Fond in der deutschen Volksnatur (Gertrud), ohne welchen die Reformation eine Unmöglichkeit gewesen wäre." Certain recent critics, not content with the author's historical emphasis, have placed the tale squarely in the context of his whole lifework, seeing it in a surprisingly complex expression of the relationship between conscience and the aesthetic. These scholars are also unanimous in their perception of a decidedly negative criticism of the humanist Poggio and his aestheticism. They are at one in their assertion of a fundamental criticism of the aesthetic on the part of Meyer's implied narrator and thus in the work as a whole. At the same time, they are divided on the specific nature and presentation of Poggio's experience and conduct, which, of course, have a decisive bearing on the total statement of the work.

This lack of consensus stems largely from a failure to account adequately for the central complex of theatrical motifs and to relate it to the structure of the plot and implied narrator's usage of irony. Accordingly I propose to take a closer look at Meyer's complex of motifs and plot as they develop over the internal story as well as the narrative perspectives provided by both frame and internal stories. Such an approach uncovers a more positive attitude toward Poggio and the aesthetic than that allowed by recent critics, indeed, an intimate, if still problematic, relationship between art and morality in Meyer's work.

At the beginning of the frame story the narrator relates that a group of cultivated Florentines has assembled around Cosimo de' Medici for an evening of conviviality. However, it is not Cosimo, but Poggio whose gray hair is conspicious among them and whose eloquence rivets their attention. Together with his age and polished conversation a strangely mixed expression of cheerfulness and sorrow distinguishes him from his companions. Thus, Poggio is immediately set apart from the rest of the company and with good reason. As secretary of the Florentine Republic and, earlier, of five popes, as author of the popular *Facetien* and discoverer of Plautus' comedies, he has grown old in the service of state, Church and art. In addition to these distinctions, he has also suffered a well-known personal misfortune. All of his sons, while highly gifted, have become ne'er-do-wells. One even committed an act bordering on theft which not only cost Poggio a serious financial sacrifice but also cast the shadow of disgrace over his old age.

The contrast between Poggio and the other Florentines grows sharper when Cosimo asks him to tell a *Facezia inedita.* Thoroughly familiar with the witty and racy *Facetien,* based on experiences of the author's youth, Cosimo can now enjoy only the "schlanken Wendungen einer glücklichen Form," but can no longer experience curiosity and surprise. He seeks to entice him by adding that the circle of friends will understand the most subtle allusion and pardon the boldest jest. "Erzählend und schlürfend,"

moreover, Poggio will forget his sorrow. Poggio jokes initially in the spirit of the group, but his reluctance to return to those "Possen" and "Jugendlichkeiten" is clear. For, as harmless as they may have been at base, his open-mindedness and easygoing philosophy of life appear to have degenerated in his son to profligacy by some uncanny law of progression.

At this point, Romolo accuses Poggio of preaching, referring to the fact that it is he who has given the comedies of Plautus back to the world. Poggio thanks him for the reminder and promises to regale his listeners with a *Facetie* entitled *Der Fund des Plautus.* However, a scoffer interjects that he should call it the *Raub des Plautus* instead. Unperturbed, Poggio expresses the hope that his tale will both entertain his companions and rid them of the notion perpetuated by the envious that he had stolen the codex. He goes on to say that his *Facetie* has to do with two crosses, a heavy and a light one, and with two barbarian nuns, a novice and an abbess. Ippolito interrupts him in glee over the prospect of hearing more of the "treuherzigen germanischen Vestalen" who filled the baths on the Limmat in an earlier letter from abroad. But Poggio says that he had exaggerated, adding that the youth, as an admirer of ingenuousness, will enjoy his barbarian nun nevertheless.

Through the contrast between Poggio and his companions Meyer develops the theme of conscience and the aesthetic from the very beginning of the work. The Florentines reveal an Epicurean attitude toward life and its artistic representation and experience all but devoid of any existential or ethical dimension. As Cosimo's words suggest, they have reduced the episodes of Poggio's youth as well as the creation and reception of art in general to the level of pleasurable, even frivolous form and to a means of escaping the problems of life. For Romolo, somber experiential substance and instruction have no place within the purview of art. Ippolito completely overlooks the potential seriousness of a story dealing with religious symbols and figures. Even the scoffer's objection to the title of the *Facetie* appears to stem more from cynicism than from moral indignation, as the smiles following Poggio's mild protest imply.

Now, Poggio is highly sensitive to the importance of entertainment in art and life. After all, he is the author of the formally sophisticated, risqué *Facetien.* Just as he had exaggerated the nuns in his letter from abroad, he may well have excluded the present story from the collection in consideration of his readers' taste. And now he responds to the reminder of his social responsibility by eschewing further mention of his private concerns. It is small wonder that the Florentines treat him as a most illustrious member of a group of kindred spirits.

Nevertheless, Poggio distances himself subtly from his friends and their views and, in the process, from his own past. He refers to the tales of his youth as farces which Cosimo may relish but which he himself no longer savors. Furthermore, he relates the context of his story in a parody of the verbose argument typical of the opening of Italian novellas such as his own. His tale of a simple, barbarian nun may well entertain Ippolito, but not, as he knows, in the way his young friend expects. Here, Poggio creates distance by means of irony. For through the fate of his sons he has apparently sensed that the attitudes of his companions and his youth are somehow unequal to the exigencies of life and art. On the other hand, he has learned that they are entirely capable of prejudicing his integrity. In his *Facetie,* therefore, he intends at once to please and instruct his audience, to do justice to the demands of conscience and the aesthetic and at the same time to defend his rectitude in an entertaining fashion.

Despite Poggio's implicit appeal to Horace's time-honored concept of the poet, the subjective aspect of his edificatory intent immediately renders his endeavor open to doubt. And his friends' reservations toward his character are not at all without foundation. The narrator relates that Poggio is not only a statesman, artist, and humanist but was also a cleric who exchanged his collar for a wife and family. He allows Poggio to disclose without a blink that he was quite prepared to adorn truth in order to please his readers. By endowing him with an ambivalent countenance, moreover, he suggests that Poggio is fundamentally divided within himself. Just as Poggio distances himself from other Florentines, the narrator steps back from his protagonist. Accordingly, the reader must anticipate Poggio's tale with a certain degree of skepticism.

Poggio indeed seeks to resolve seeming antitheses—entertainment and instruction, art and life, conscience and the aesthetic. This is at least in effect the intention of Meyer and his narrator as well. Whether the nature and results of the two enterprises are ultimately the same, however, remains to be seen.

In Poggio's tale, as in the frame story, the thematic constellation of conscience and the aesthetic is established at the very outset. Poggio is in Constance to participate in the ecumenical council called to unify and reform the Church and to elect a new pope. Contrary to what one might expect of a man of the cloth, however, he divides his idle hours "zwischen der Betrachtung des ergötzlichen Schauspiels, das auf der beschränkten Bühne einer deutschen Reichsstadt die Frömmigkeit, die Wissenschaft, die Staatskunst des Jahrhunderts mit seinen Päpsten, Ketzern, Gauklern und Buhlerinnen zusammendrängte,— und der gelegentlichen Suche nach Manuskripten in den umliegenden Klöstern." Significantly, the Constance of the council presents itself to Poggio as theater, as comedy, with a delightful, contradictory mixture of the highest and lowest, the best and worst of society. Similarly, it is a codex of Plautine comedies that he learns is in a nearby convent and determines to obtain. Indeed, he leaves Constance to search for it despite the rapidly approaching papal election.

Poggio's questionable enthusiasm controls more than two-thirds of the entire tale. He sets out for the convent in exuberant anticipation, hearing "die Musen und die Englein" singing—one of many passages in which he mixes elements of antiquity and Christianity. To pass the time

and "aus Menschenliebe," he gives his tristful companion, Hans, a number of riddles to solve, in which biblical figures play quite human roles. On learning that Hans's melancholy and eventual tears stem from his beloved's imminent entry into the convent, he exclaims in delight, "Bei dem Bogen Cupidos . . . ein unglücklich Liebender!", as if having unexpectedly discovered some lost romantic comedy. He listens, to be sure, as Hans relates the circumstances surrounding his engagement to Gertrude and her inexplicable decision to take the veil. Yet, afterward, he simply inquires about the character of the abbess, his philanthropy apparently not extending to charity.

Poggio experiences his first encounter with Brigittchen and the *Scheinwunder,* like Constance, as comic theater. Indeed, the "Szene" on the cloister meadow is depicted in much the same way as the earlier one, if in greater detail. Laymen and monks, peasants and noblemen, ballad-mongers, gypsies, and prostitutes—again, a colorful mixture of the high and low and the good and evil of society— surround a group of nuns who, in turn, encircle a tattered soldier blowing a trumpet, the abbess, and a gigantic cross. However, the tone of this scene is markedly different. The spectators stand "in den traulichsten Stellungen"; each attempts to bear the cross and fails to the shouts and laughter of the others. Brigittchen dances around like one possessed, inspired like the rest by the convent wine, and praises the miracle of the cross like a circus barker. Poggio describes her as a "Hanswürstin" and the whole scene as a "possierlichen Vorgang." And, indeed, it is portrayed like some pagan ritual in low comic form, a bacchanal in which the cross takes the place of the phallus. Poggio finds the whole "Ärgernis" repugnant, all the more so when Brigittchen challenges him mockingly to lift the cross with his own weak arms and, alerted by an inept predecessor, accuses him of dishonest intentions.

Seeking refuge from the laughter of the crowd, Poggio enters the nearby church and finds Gertrude kneeling before the statue of a powerful woman struggling under the weight of an immense cross and aided by a smaller female figure. Asked to interpret the image, Gertrude says that it represents a duchess of long ago, the founder of the convent, and the Virgin Mary. According to tradition, the woman had poisoned her husband and escaped secular justice owing to her high station. Eventually despairing of her salvation, however, she took vows and underwent a long period of atonement. In hopes of a sign of forgiveness, she had a cross made which even the strongest man could scarcely lift and sought to bear it during her investiture. The Virgin indeed lightened it upon her shoulder and, as we learn later, has since favored every novitiate in the same manner.

Gertrude then explains her decision to renounce Hans and take the veil. As a young girl, she had promised herself to the Virgin for her twentieth year if the Virgin would heal her hopelessly ill mother. Since her mother indeed recovered and her vow has come due, she is now preparing to fulfill it. In the meantime, it is true, she has fallen in love with Hans. She often thinks that the Virgin would not hold an innocent child to its word and would likely have cured her mother without obligation. While the sinful duchess was happy in the convent, moreover, she herself would be sick at heart: "Trägst du mir das Kreuz, so erleichtere mir auch das Herz," she prays, "sonst gibt es ein Unglück . . .". Nevertheless, she intends to keep her pledge, for "Handel ist Handel . . . Ehrlich währt am längsten . . . Ohne Treu und Glauben kann die Welt nicht bestehen."

On hearing Gertrude's simple but earnest and foreboding story, Poggio suggests with a cunning smile that a clever girl could extricate herself from the matter by slipping and admires her youthful arms "mit künstlerischem Vergnügen." When she leaves in indignation, he sits down in the confessional, his mind on Plautus rather than Gertrude and her plight. He then realizes in sudden exultation that the miracle of the cross must in fact be a sham. While conceding that the duchess Amalaswinta may well have borne the heavy cross with the strength of despair and fervor, he is convinced that the abbesses have since substituted a much lighter *Gaukelkreuz* for it. Based on this conviction and the discussion of monastic reform in a commission of the council on which he sits as secretary, he contrives his own scheme to wrest the codex from Brigittchen. Meanwhile, he locates the convent library and enters, "nicht anders als wäre ich ein verliebter Jüngling und beträte die Kammer Lydias oder Glyceras . . . und hätte ich . . . die Komödien des Umbriers gefunden, ich bedeckte sie mit unersättlichen Küssen." Once again, Poggio expresses his excitement through an allusion to romantic comedy, this time with more explicitly erotic overtones. His ardor is dampened, however, when he finds "nur" rituals and liturgies among the books. His only "Beute" is a copy of St. Augustine's *Confessions,* which he has always loved because of its captiousness.

Poggio gives little better account of himself in the scene that follows. Brigittchen surprises him with the volume under his robe and accuses him of planning to steal the "Pickelhering" or "Possenreisser," which she hopes to sell in order to buy a barn or wine press for the convent. Inspired by the "Nähe des versteckten komischen Dichters," however, he assumes the mien of a Church father, unfolds a stately innkeeper's bill, and pretends to read a decree condemning immoral reading and false miracles in the nunneries. Brigittchen turns pale but, drawing on her own admirable presence of mind, as Poggio calls it, praises the council's reformatory zeal and feigns compliance by handing him the most evil book she can think of—his own *Facetien.* Beginning to hate the abbess, Poggio threatens her with death at the stake, should the miracle prove spurious, and ultimately intimidates her into revealing the counterfeit cross. However, an involuntary exclamation of admiration for its artistry gives him away. While conceding defeat and promising to give him the codex, Brigittchen laughs cynically, as if to say, "Wir alle wissen, wo Bartolo den Most holt, wir sind Schelme allesamt und keiner braucht sich zu zieren."

Poggio's growing disgust and longing "nach dem unschuldigen Spiele der Muse" lead him to put a quick and char-acteristic end to the affair. He determines to spare Brigittchen, both to uphold the reputation of the Church, as he says, and to prevent his own exposure. He makes her vow to burn the false cross, only, however, after the forthcoming performance of the miracle, which, "aus Klugheitsgründer," he dares not prevent. On receiving the codex, he rushes her away and locks himself in his room. When she returns and, fearing discovery, demands the key to the chamber concealing the *Gaukelkreuz,* he says that he does not have it, which, while literally true, is false insofar as he knows where it is. Allowing her to lament like a soul in Purgatory, he luxuriates "im Himmel des höchsten Genusses . . . in hochzeitlichen Wonnen."

At this point in Poggio's story, which precedes a decisive turn in the plot, it will be useful to pause to reflect and expand upon our observations. The relationship between conscience and the aesthetic manifests itself primarily through the symbolic usage of theater. As Poggio's descriptions of Constance and the bacchanal and response to his fellow man attest, the theater is a cipher for a fundamental mode of experience and action. He observes the spectacle in Constance, refuses to be drawn into the exhibition on the meadow, and stands aloof from Hans and Gertrude and their concerns. That is to say, Poggio typically witnesses the unfolding of events and character from the psychological and emotional distance of a spectator. He extorts the codex from Brigittchen by means of what amounts to an improvised comic intrigue. His is an intuitive, spontaneous nature; his riddles occur to him "aus dem Nichts," while he hides the key to the chamber with the counterfeit cross "ohne bestimmten Plan." Poggio's experience of life from an inner remove and instinctive behavior are intimately related. Involved more with himself than with the world and the people about him, he acts, if at all, not on principle but on his own interest according to the demands of the moment and with ethically questionable results.

Poggio is not so different from Brigittchen as his condescension toward her suggests he thinks. To be sure, she is "ein garstiges, kleines Weib." Through her drunken display on the meadow she makes a travesty of herself and the cross. Discovering Poggio in the library, she gropes about his robe in an unseemly manner and later, on hearing the tittering whispers of her nuns, takes leave of him with an oath on her virginity. Accepting the rationalization of her predecessor and confessor, she ingenuously seeks to justify the pseudo miracle as a symbol of the initial difficulty and later ease of a pious life and asserts in one breath that she has committed no wrong and that as a child she too had once been honest. On the other hand, she is a masterful administrator. Like the abbesses before her, she views the *Scheinwunder* as the financial salvation of the convent and has indeed restored it and her nuns to prosperity, which lends her deception an at least tangentially religious and quite considerable human justification. Here is a solid, if unenlightened and secularized faith.

Poggio, for his part, is doubtless morally superior to Brigittchen in one central respect. He clearly recognizes the hypocrisy of the false miracle and scorns her specious attempt to vindicate it. At the same time, his scorn is compounded not only of righteous indignation but of quite human anger over her witting and unwitting assaults on his own virtue. And, of course, he is not free of hypocrisy himself. He laughs up his sleeve over the earnestness of the Church fathers' discussion of abuses in the nunneries, yet affects such solemnity in his plot to get the codex. He is often no more concious of his sanctimony than the abbess. After recounting his expression of admiration for the counterfeit cross, he adds that he was extolling not the fraud, but the art expended on it, unaware that they amount to the same thing. His revulsion over the bacchanal is attributable in part precisely to its crass, unaesthetic nature. However, there is something distinctly pagan and orgiastic about the manner in which he pursues and enjoys the Plautus-codex. Poggio's aestheticism and Brigittchen's materialism are but two different aspects of the same, broad secularization of religion and morality and are related to each other symbolically through the false cross. At different levels of sophistication, the humanist's improvisational theater is at least as questionable as the nun's partly unintentional burlesque and, in view of his treatment of her, is certainly more inhumane.

The dubiety of Poggio's aesthetic mode of existence is most evident in his initial encounter with Gertrude. Her religiosity and morality are of coarser fabric than his, it is true. While he concedes the plausibility of the legend of Amalaswinta, she states uncategorically, "Sie ist wahr!" She displays naiveté befitting her peasantry in her rationalizations with the Virgin and use of folk sayings to explain her decision to take the veil. There is a stubborn individualism about her matched only by her powerful ties to everyday life. However, the rough texture of her faith and ethics is their very strength. Owing to it, she is quite willing to undergo the ordeal of the cross at the cost of total self-denial and at the risk of self-annihilation. Far from representing egoistic casuistry, as has been claimed, her unsophisticated reasoning heightens the probity of her resolution to honor her vow. She is the only one of the three major characters in the work who is spared Meyer's irony. Like the rude statue in the church, in front of which Poggio first sees her, she is "etwas in seiner Weise Schönes." According to her measure of humanity, she offers a model of faith and integrity before which Poggio pales. He discerns only her sturdy physical beauty and is prepared to sacrifice her to preserve his dignity and that of the Church. While she readies herself for a heavenly wedding which may mean her destruction, he revels in the sublimely carnal ecstasy of aesthetic gratification.

Poggio reveals himself to have been a man of the Renaissance cast entirely in the mold of Cosimo and the other Florentines—devoted to the culture of antiquity and possessed of a cavalier attitude toward the Church and its sphere of concern. For him, life is a theater in which one may enjoy the comic plot from the balcony, perhaps even perform for a time, and then return to one's seat as one likes. Should it momentarily contradict its nature and

intrude upon one's tranquility, one can flee into the purer comedy of art. This, of course, is precisely what happens in the first part of Poggio's story. The circumstances of his acquisition of the Plautus-codex form an essentially self-contained farce with beginning, middle, and end—a kind of *Verwechslungskomödie* complete with *Zwillingsmotif* in small. At the same time, this portion of the story represents the first act of quite another piece. It is no accident that Poggio responds to Hans's tears with an allusion to romantic comedy, for Hans and Gertrude, like the young lovers of the genre, encounter an obstacle to the fulfillment of their love. However, the typical blocking character, an intransigent parent, is eliminated prior to the beginning of the action through the timely death of Hans's malicious stepmother. The obstacle that rises in her place is of a different and far more formidable sort—conscience, Gertrude's own unbending moral character, compounded by the immorality of the abbess' deception, which threaten to make a tragedy of the piece. Poggio, already acting out of a self-indulgent scenario more demanding than he anticipated, is totally indifferent to the development of a drama for which his experience has so ill prepared him. By the conclusion of his intrigue to obtain the codex, his attempt to vindicate his honor has grown more complex than at the outset and is very much in jeopardy.

Despite all shortcomings, Poggio's aestheticism discloses positive potential. On entering the church following the scene on the meadow, he finds Romanesque arches and vaults, rather than the fashionable Gothic, and regains his clear and peaceful state of mind. He is thus able to be moved by the despair and pity expressed on the faces of the statue. In the midst of his intrigue he sees the real cross leaning against a wall, "so gewältig . . . als hätte heute erst eine verzweifelnde grosse Sünderin es ergriffen und wäre darunter ins Knie gesunken, die Steinplatte schon mit der Stirne berührend in dem Augenblicke da die Himmelskönigin erschien und ihr beistand." Unlike Constance and the bacchanal, the legend of Amalaswinta evoked by the cross strikes Poggio with dramatic immediacy. Unable to lift it an inch, he senses the absurdity of the sacrilege all the more and grows firmer in his resolve to find the hidden imitation. If all-pervasive and subject to cultural chauvinism, Poggio's aesthetic sensibilty makes him receptive to religious and moral values as well as to art and is capable of spurring him to corresponding action.

We saw earlier that Poggio's aestheticism is accompanied by a certain rational skepticism. While Gertrude expresses naive faith in the miracle of the cross, Poggio states that it *could* be true and seeks a logical explanation for it. His skepticism is double-edged, however, for it concedes possibilty at the same time as it questions actuality. He says of the miraculous, "Ich denke . . . lässlich davon, weder abergläubig noch verwegen; denn ich mag die absoluten Geister nicht leiden, welche, wo eine unerklärliche Tatsache einen Dunstkreis von Aberglauben um sich sammelt, die ganze Erscheinung . . . ohne Prüfung und Unterscheidung entweder summarisch glauben oder eben so summarisch verwerfen." To the extent that it remains accessible to the undemonstrable, his skepticism is entirely compatible with his intuitive, aesthetic nature. And, indeed, Poggio describes the miracle as a combination of "das Unbegreifliche" and "Betrug," his procurement of the codex as the result of a "Verschwörung von Gelegenheiten." In fact, a number of apparent coincidences leads to his acquisition of the comedies: the chance proximity of the council to the cloister and presence of the codex there, the accidental manner in which he surmises its location, the fortuity of Hans's becoming his traveling companion, the existence of a counterfeit cross and a commission concerned with false miracles and illicit reading, and Brigittchen's giving him his own *Facetien,* which prompts him to redouble his efforts to settle the matter. After telling of his hiding the key to the chamber with the false cross, Poggio says, "So aber tat ich . . . auf die Einflüsterung irgend eines Gottes oder einer Göttin." Despite the obligatory allusion to antiquity, he at once foreshadows things to come and implies the possible working of divinity in this conspiracy of opportunities. His aestheticism and skepticism are thus open both to religious and moral values and to the possibility of their transcendental foundation.

The scene which brings a decisive turn in Poggio's story is structured initially by the same contrast between conscience and the aesthetic observed earlier. Poggio digresses momentarily to comment on the significance of the newly secured codex: "Ein an das Licht tretender Klassiker und nicht ein dunkler Denker, ein erhabener Dichter, nein das Nächstliegende und ewig Fesselnde, die Weltbreite, der Puls des Lebens, das Marktgelächter von Rom und Athen, Witz und Wortwechsel und Wortspiel, die Leidenschaften, die Frechheit der Menschennatur in der mildernden Übertreibung des komischen Zerrspiegels—während ich ein Stück verschlang, hütete ich schon mit heisshungrigen Blicken das folgende." Having finished the first piece, he pauses to rest his eyes and becomes aware of a group of girls outside singing the refrain, "In das Kloster geh'ich nicht, / Nein, ein Nönnchen werd' ich nicht . . . ." He knows full well that they are taunting Gertrude and even pictures her in the sacristy preparing for her heavenly wedding. Asking rhetorically, "Doch was kümmerte mich das?"; however, he turns to the next work and once again abandons himself to orgiastic pleasure.

All the same, his attitude soon changes radically. Falling into a restless slumber, he finds himself surrounded by familiar comic figures, among them a braggart soldier and a pair of young lovers. But then, "unversehens—mitten unter dem lustigen, antiken Gesindel stand eine barfüssige, breitschultrige Barbarin, mit einem Stricke gegürtet, als Sklavin zu Markte gebracht, wie es schien, unter finsteren Brauen hervor mich anstarrend mit vorwurfsvollen und drohenden Augen." Poggio starts from his sleep in fright to hear a monotone invocation passing over into a stifled groan and then into a violent cry from the nearby church. Telling himself that something must have come over Gertrude while he was reading, he goes to the sacristy and finds her before the cross pleading with the Virgin to spare her: "Mir schaudert vor der Zelle

. . . Was mir taugt . . . ist Sonne und Wolke, Sichel und Sense, Mann und Kind . . . ." Poggio can still smile at this very human confession to the Intemerata, but his smile suddenly dies on his lips. For Getrude leaps to her feet and continues, "Lass mich unter deinem Kreuze sinken, es ist mir zu schwer! Erleichterst du mir's aber auf der Schulter, ohne mir das Herz erleichtern zu können, da siehe zu . . . dass sie mich eines Morgens nicht mit zerschmettertem Schädel auflesen!". Faced unexpectedly with the unequivocal possibility of Gertrude's suicide, Poggio responds immediately, "Ein unendliches Mitleid ergriff mich, aber nicht Mitleid allein, sondern auch eine beklemmende Angst"—all the more so when he recognizes approaching madness in the way she plaits her loosened braids and varies the little girls' refrain in an unnatural child's voice: "In das Kloster geh' ich ein/ Muss ein armes Nönnchen sein . . . ."

At this point, the "Optimus Maximus" uses Poggio as his instrument and bids him save Gertrude at any cost. Turning "in freier Frömmigkeit" to the virgin goddess called Athena by the ancients and Mary by his contemporaries, he prays, "Wer du seist . . . die Weisheit, wie die einen sagen, die Barmherzigkeit, wie die anderen behaupten,—gleichviel, die Weisheit überhört das Gelöbnis eines weltunerfahrenen Kindes und die Barmherzigkeit fesselt keine Erwachsene an das törichte Versprechen einer Unmündigen. Lächelnd lösest du das nichtige Gelübde. Deine Sache führe ich, Göttin. Sei mir gnädig. Having promised the abbess to have no further contact with Gertrude, Poggio determines to suggest the truth to her "in antiker Art" by performing three symbolic actions so clear that even an unsophisticated peasant girl could understand them. As if unaware of her presence and employing comic language and gestures, he cuts a notch in the cross and then intimates both the lightness and location of its false counterpart. Recognizing the first signs of flaming anger in her expression, he returns to his room and enjoys the sweet slumber of a good conscience.

Poggio's dream assumes a form closely resembling his descriptions of Constance, the scene on the meadow, and the comedies of Plautus. For it presents explicitly or by implication the same varied mixture of social and moral types—the same microcosm of life—depicted in the earlier passages. Gertrude's appearance as a reproachful slave girl brought to market to the laughter of the ancient mob may at first seem to introduce a new, darker element into this world. However, the shadowy side of life is at least implicit in the heretics, charlatans, and prostitutes in Constance as well as in the passions and impertinence of human nature and the market laughter typical of Plautine comedy. And it is manifest in the scene on the meadow, where the cross is exhibited in an expressly carnival atmosphere accompanied by Dionysian overtones. Here, the cross together with all it stands for—utmost personal integrity, self-sacrifice for higher principles, the salvation of humanity—is debased, as it were, enslaved and put on the block for essentially materialistic ends. In Poggio's dream, life and art merge into a theatrical whole in which their full range of possibilities, their tragic as well as comic potential, becomes transparent. And through the inner truth of dream the cross and Gertrude undergo a metaphorical union which imposes their common, if peculiar, sanctity and jeopardy on Poggio with pressing urgency. Poggio and his conscience are awakened with a jolt, for the imperiled sacredness of Christianity as well as human life has taken on a congenial aesthetic form. The *visual* drama of his dream and then the *sound* of Gertrude's cry of despair rouse him from his characteristic indifference and at the same time turn the plot of his story in a new direction.

In its nuanced interweaving of motif, structure, and narrative perspective *Plautus im Nonnenkloster* is indeed a formal tour de force.

—Herbert Rowland

Content earlier to leave Gertrude to her fate, Poggio now actively seeks her in the sacristy of the church. And there, the stark reality of her desperate situation bursts upon him with full force, for through the sight and sound of her latently suicidal "Ringkampfe mit der Gottheit" she presents him with living drama. If stirred in different ways and degrees by the statue in the church and the slave girl of his dream, he now reacts to Gertrude, the vital human being, with pity and fear, the traditional categories of audience response to tragedy. In the same heightened state of receptivity he sees her braiding her hair, hears her singing her refrain, and thus perceives the onset of madness in her. At this moment, aesthetic form and living experience converge to imbue Poggio with a keen sense of the existential fullness of another individual. Similarly, they infuse him with an acute awareness of the exigencies of conscience and art, for they compel him to act and, what is more, to do so within an entirely aesthetic mode. As suggested by the allusion to the *commedia dell'arte* in the name of his cutler, Pantaleone Ubbriaco, Poggio's three symbolic actions *in antiker Art* correspond to the three acts of comedy in general and represent an intrigue much like the one executed against the abbess. While acting earlier on largely egoistic motives, however, he now proceeds altruistically in the spirit of Gertrude and the cross.

The obstacle to the union of the young lovers indeed proves formidable and potentially tragic, for in concert with Brigittchen's deception Gertrude's moral integrity, the very best within her, threatens to become her ruin. By thwarting the abbess' intrigue with one of his own, however, Poggio holds out the prospect of a comic resolution. In this, the climax of the work, his aesthetic relationship to life reveals itself capable of embracing and overcoming tragedy as well as comedy, both in himself and others.

Poggio's inner life at the confluence of antiquity and modernity does not permit him to put a clear label on the ultimate source of his inspiration. The expression *Optimus Maximus* refers to the greatest Good of both ages and to the traditional final instance of neither. In turning to the goddess called Athena by the one and Mary by the other, he again mixes elements of the two cultures. His piety is indeed *frei,* for he identifies with both eras and more with their values than with their institutions. Piety it is nonetheless, and in his own way Poggio prays just as earnestly as Gertrude. If unable to disclose the specific shape of the absolute, his mode of experience enables him to recognize its existence and to draw upon its substance. And whatever their particular origin, the wisdom and mercy both embodied by Athena and Mary, by the mitigating exaggeration of ancient and modern comedy and the cross of Christianity, suggest a fundamental identity of the values of the two worlds as a positive force in human affairs. Poggio has good reason to sleep well, for he has loosened the bonds not only of Gertrude and the cross but of Plautus and the broad moral spirit of art as well. His mode of life is not only open to conscience, but is also capable of being filled by it.

The scene depicting Gertrude's ordeal evinces the same emotional intensity as the preceding one but has an entirely different tone. While dressing for the ceremony, she dons the crown of thorns so forcefully that blood spurts forth and runs down over her forehead. "Ein erhabener Zorn, ein göttliches Gericht" blaze from her eyes and begin to frighten the nuns assisting her. "Jetzt," in Poggio's words, "entwickelte sich alles rasch wie ein Gewitter." Finding the cross given her unmarked, Gertrude smashes it jubilantly on the floor of the sacristy and gets the true one from the chamber that normally conceals the Gaukelkreuz and which due to Poggio's deception the abbess has been unable to lock. Lifting it to her shoulder in triumph, she ignores the wailing abbess and her nuns and sets off with the words, "Jetzt, Muttergottes, schlichte du den Handel ehrlich!" She then enters the choir before an immense assembly of clergy, nobility, and peasantry waiting breathlessly in the spacious nave. Much as Poggio had earlier imagined Amalaswinta's procession, she attempts to continue with all her might, but slowly sinks under the weight of her burden and finally crashes unconcious with it onto the floor to the collective sigh of all present.

In view of the feverish pitch and pace of these events, what follows represents a drastic change. On regaining her senses, Gertrude discerns Hans in the silent crowd and asks whether he wants her as his wife. Receiving an affirmative reply, she joins him in the nave and disappears together with him. Initially entranced and then nonplused, the people in the crowd now argue furiously over the unexpected invalidation of the miracle, the men condemning the abbess and the women denouncing Gertrude. When Brigittchen begins to retort in kind, the faces of the clergymen reveal "eine vollständige Stufenleiter von einverstandener Schlauheit bis zu der redlichsten Dummheit." Informed meanwhile of developments in Constance, Poggio ends the "Ärgernis" by announcing the election of the new pope and intoning a *Te Deum*. Afterward, the crowd disperses and all hasten to the city, where, as Poggio says, "der nach Beendigung des Triregnum urbi und orbi gespendete Segen dreifach kräftig wirken musste." On leaving the convent, the Plautus-codex under his arm, Poggio encounters the thrifty Brigittchen carrying the pieces of the false cross in a large basket and congratulates her ironically "zu der Lösung des Knotens." She tells him to go to the devil together with the other Italian rogue, whereupon he himself returns to Constance.

After announcing the end of his story, Poggio relates that on the trip back to Italy he met Hans and Gertrude together with their child as the proprietors of an inn. He now presents Cosimo with the codex and offers his *Facezia inedita* as a supplement. He intended, he says, to bequeath it to him in his will but gives it to him now for fear that his sons might not respect his last wish. Cosimo accepts the gifts with the words, "Ich danke dir für beides, deinen Plautus und deine Facetie. Skrupellos hast du sie gelebt und ausgeführt, jung wie du damals warest. Als ein Gereifter hast du sie uns erzählt mit der Weisheit deiner Jahre." He then raises a fine chalice enclasped by a laughing satyr and toasts Poggio and his blonde barbarian. Here, amid drinking and laughter, the conversation turns from Plautus to the "tausend gehobenen Horte und aufgerollten Pergamente des Altertums und auf die Grösse des Jahrhunderts."

Gertrude's procession presents itself in the theatrical manner of the earlier mass scenes, from Constance to Poggio's dream, but ensues with inner necessity from the foregoing dramatic climax. She gives the crowd "das ergreifende Schauspiel" of her struggle from the "offener Bühne" of the choir in the church. Poggio says of her triumphant collapse, "Das war die blutige Wahrheit, nicht der gaukelnde Trug." For a brief but extended and intense moment he and the others watch her as if transfixed. As soon as she returns to Hans and everyday life, however,— that is to say, as soon as the denouement to which Poggio refers is complete—the spectators return to a state of normalcy as well. Only moments before sighing as one, the people in the church now offer the same varied, contradictory picture as in earlier scenes. And Poggio, who made a comic resolution of the tragic conflict possible, can now say, "Verlache mich, Cosimo! Ich war enttäuscht." Indeed, he, too, reverts to his former self. Much as in his intrigue against the abbess, he uses his priesthood consciously—"Ich fühlte mich als Kleriker"—to end the renewed *Ärgernis,* likening the termination of the *triregnum* and the new pope's blessing to the conclusion of some unholy comedy, he again speaks flippantly of religious affairs. Moreover, he once again treats Brigittchen in a manner ill-becoming his office.

In view of this reappearance of moral laxity in his conduct one is justified in asking whether or to what extent Poggio has succeeded in his attempt to vindicate himself and to unite conscience and the aesthetic. Has he truly been affected by the experience of his youth and become a mature man, as Cosimo states? A return to the narrative perspectives discussed earlier will prove instructive.

Poggio distances himself from his companions and past at various points in his tale as well as in the frame story. After relating Gertrude's account of the original miracle, for example, he states that she used not his words, but rather simple, crude ones, which could not be translated into cultivated Tuscan without becoming churlish and grotesque. He then adds, "und das, Herrschaften, würde hinwiederum nicht passen zu dem grossen Ausdrucke der trotzigen blauen Augen und der groben, aber wohlgeformten Züge, wie ich sie damals vor mir gesehen habe." While betraying something of his cultural chauvinism, Poggio also implies that his sophisticated language is itself incapable of capturing the inner truth of Gertrude's uncultivated German and personal presence. Later, he introduces his comments on the miraculous with the words, "Ich weiss nicht, mein Cosmus, wie du vom Wunderbaren denkst." Now, the text provides no incontrovertible evidence regarding Cosimo's position on the miraculous. Given his worldliness and Poggio's prefatory concession, however, one must assume that he is not sympathetic to it. Here, as in the previous passage, Poggio sets himself apart from his companions and at the same time seeks to make them receptive to his actions and the uncommon events of his story.

In both instances Poggio interrupts his account to address his listeners from the narrative present. Accordingly, his insight into cultural relativity and liberal view of the supernatural characterize him at the moment of narration as well as in the narrated past. Since both attitudes are occasioned or at least reinforced by his experience in the convent, moreover, narrated past and present appear to be directly related. That is, the two passages bridge the gap between past and present and suggest a development of character. Yet, other narrative interpolations contradict this notion. On expressing his excitement over the prospect of discovering the Plautus-codex, Poggio says, "Dass ich darüber den Schlaf verlor, das glaubest du mir, Cosmus, der du meine Begeisterung für die Trümmer einer niedergegangenen grösseren Welt teilst und begünstigst!" And when admiring the "Italianate" artistry of the counterfeit cross, he states, "da ich für den Ruhm meines Vaterlandes begeistert bin, brach ich in die Worte aus: 'Vollendet! Meisterhaft!'" Again speaking from the narrative present, Poggio displays the very solidarity with his friends that the earlier passages appear to vitiate or refute.

While these passages neither confirm nor belie a direct relationship between past and present or a change in Poggio's character, others prove more illuminating. Just before Poggio's narration of the climactic events in the church we read, "'. . . Mein gelehrter und ruhmbedeckter Freund,' unterbrach sich der Erzähler selbst, gegen einen gravitätischen Mann gewendet, welcher . . . sich trotz der Sommerwärme mit dem Faltenwurfe seines Mantels nach Art der Alten drapierte, 'mein grosser Philosoph, sage mir, ich beschwöre dich, was ist das Gewissen?'" Asking rhetorically whether it is universal, he himself responds that it is not and offers the example of Pope John XXII, who in the midst of his evil needs awoke every morning more cheerful than he had gone to sleep the night before.

He then continues, "Nein, das Gewissen ist kein allge-meines und auch unter uns, die wir ein solches besitzen, tritt es, ein Proteus, in wechselnden Formen auf. In meiner Wenigkeit z.B. wird es wach jedes Mal, wo es sich in ein Bild oder in einen Ton verkörpern kann." By way of il-lustration he recounts a recent experience at the court of a petty tyrant, where during an evening of conviviality on the balcony of a tower he had heard the sigh of a prisoner below. He concludes by saying, "Weg war die Lust und meines Bleibens dort nicht länger. Mein Gewis-sen war beschwert, das Leben zu geniessen, küssend, trink-end, lachend, neben dem Elende. Gleicherweise konnte ich jetzt das nahe Geschrei einer Verzweifelnden nicht ertragen."

Here, as in numerous other passages, Poggio puts his listeners at arm's length. By posing his question hyper-bolically to the philosopher among them, whose mien and attire already relate him to the *dottore* of comic tradition, he subtly discredits them all and sets himself up as an authority. At the same time, he unintentionally reveals his own limited qualification to judge in matters of conscience. To be sure, he recognizes that conscience is not universal and manifests itself in different ways in different people. He also realizes that in his own case it assumes aesthetic forms. However, he is blind to the corollary that, when unable to take on such forms, it remains dormant in him and delivers him over to the caprice of situational ethics. Even when roused, his illus-tration indicates, it does not always lead to moral action. While the prisoner's misery weighs heavily on his con-science, he simply leaves the court without attempting to help. This interpolation and its implications clearly ex-plain Poggio's contradictory behavior during his stay in the convent. When he is under the immediate influence of Gertrude and her overwhelming drama of conscience, his own conscience awakens and compels him to act according to its demands. Before and after his encounter with her, however, when life appears to him as unsubstan-tial form, his conscience remains inert, and he acts with, at best, questionable moral integrity. Connecting past and present in a generalizing manner, moreover, the interpo-lation demonstrates that Poggio has undergone no basic development of character. With regard to conscience and the aesthetic, the graybeard is essentially the same as the young man.

Another narrative intrusion suggests the fundamental rea-son for this state of affairs. After expressing his disap-pointment over the outcome of events in the church, Poggio says, "Eine kurze Weile hatte die Bäuerin vor meinen erregten Sinnen gestanden als die Verkörperung eines höhern Wesens, als ein dämonisches Geschöpf, als die Wahrheit wie sie jubelnd den Schein zerstört. Aber was ist Wahrheit? fragte Pilatus." Poggio proceeds un-wittingly from the tacit assumption that truth and art are of the same order of being and, therefore, that an aes-thetic mode of experience is capable of capturing truth in personification or other artistic form. However, his dis-appointment and whole experience in the cloister imply on the contrary that art, while providing an avenue to truth, is not identical to it and cannot make a permanent

possession of it or its moral imperative. Poggio's equiv-ocal behavior and basically static character derive not only from his limited access to conscience, but also from the problematic relationship between art and morality itself.

The results of Poggio's endeavor to vindicate himself are as ambiguous as the morality of his conduct. Certainly, he does not steal the codex in the customary sense of the word, but the sophisticated coercion through which he obtains it amounts ultimately to a kind of theft. On the other hand, it is precisely this dubious behavior that leads to his encounter with conscience and frees the moral spirit of art from crass materialism. He breaks his word to the abbess by divulging her artifice to Gertrude, but at the same time liberates the cross and Gertrude from sanctimony and inhumanity. It is not fortuitous that the codex and the cross, linked metaphorically with Gertrude, are both presented as hidden treasures coming to light.

Poggio obviously has no answer to Pilate's question. He neither penetrates absolute truth nor fully comprehends the relative truth of his personal experience. Thus, his view of himself as the instrument of divinity indeed ap-pears hubristic. However, the exposure of the false mir-acle and Gertrude's fulfillment in family life, like that of Keller's Beatrix, are surely truths pleasing to both God and man. Like the council on a large scale, Poggio re-stores the integrity of the church in one of its many small corners and enables Gertrude to bear "das eheliche Kreuz" commensurate with her measure of humanity. Despite his shortsightedness, he therefore implements the design implicit in the *Verschwörung von Gelegenheiten.* For a grand moment, he probes the limits of his own measure of humanity and in fact succeeds in uniting conscience and the aesthetic. If he still finds his *Jugendlichkeiten* basically innocuous and remains largely insensible to their ramifications, he nonetheless has grown wiser insofar as he is able to articulate a fundamental mode of existence previously experienced naively and in the un-canny law of progression at least dimly recognizes its metaphysical questionability and his own cross. By pre-senting his tale as a supplement to his *Fazetien,* he seeks to compensate for the extra vagences of his youth. In a broad but very real sense, his narrative posture is thus justified and he indeed vindicates himself. Perhaps for all these reasons, both positive and negative, his story wins the approval of Cosimo and the other Florentines, with whom he has so much in common after all. He both entertains and edifies them to the degree that they are educable and he is capable.

Meyer's implied narrator is more successful than Poggio in the attainment of his goals. After the opening frame, to be sure, he appears to retreat into total anonymity to return briefly only at the end of the work. In reality, however, he stands in the wings throughout the internal story and not only maintains but increases his initial dis-tance from his material. He allows Poggio to present his tale as a drama which he both performs and recounts and thereby objectifies the events themselves and Poggio's twofold relationship to them. In the process, he provides himself and his reader with a detached and consistent point of view from which to observe the explicit levels of narration. From this vantage he allows the numerous discrepancies within each level and between the two to emerge and permits his reader to assume his own ironic attitude toward the subject matter. Accordingly, he puts the reader in a position to enjoy and learn from his aesthetic experience in a different and far more comprehensive way than Poggio's audience and to know more than Poggio himself.

The narrator's success extends beyond his narrative strategy to his primary attempt to resolve the problem of art and morality. Viewed strictly in terms of his own contribution, certainly, Poggio proves to be less than a totally reliable ally. Yet, to concentrate on his shortcomings would be to disregard the spirit and structure of the work. While the decisive scene in the church remains an episode in his life, it furnishes the dramatic climax and formal apex of the work, without which the entire edifice would collapse. Despite all qualifications, it is the narrator's affirmation, through Poggio, of art as a means of experiencing the actualizing conscience that determines the dominant tone and structural center of the work.

Moreover, the narrator's success is not dependent on Poggio's. Indeed, he presents Poggio's aestheticism as but one of many forms in which conscience may appear and contrasts it with two others which reveal strengths as well as weaknesses. Brigittchen's religiosity is materialistic to a fault but retains a degree of justification in its hard-nosed pragmatism, necessary for the survival of the Church as an institution. Gertrude's faith is adamantly personal, yet remains exceedingly admirable in its unshakable integrity. Thereby, the narrator suggests that a certain relativity obtains among the three—and, by extension, all—expressions of conscience, both in the abstract and as historical phenomena. The morality of the major characters, as representatives of these expressions and the cultural currents of the fifteenth century, is contingent in part on their frame of reference, and what is moral within one may be immoral within another. More important than the antitheses themselves is the "Zusammenschau der Gegensätze." This is not to say that the narrator makes no distinctions. He obviously has little sympathy for the abbess. And in the contrast between Poggio's decadent issue and Gertrude's fruitful marriage he intimates both a personal and supranatural judgment. However, Poggio's leading role in a drama both poetic and implicitly trascendent testifies amply to his significance within the system of values established in the work. The narrator's criticism does not penetrate to the core of Poggio's existence, but touches only its extremes. Precisely by demonstrating the impotence as well as the power of art through an artistic medium, Meyer and his narrator achieve a union of conscience and the aesthetic, a union less pretentious than Poggio's, but enduring due to its foundation in the author's perception of the nature of things.

In its nuanced interweaving of motif, structure, and narrative perspective *Plautus im Nonnenkloster* is indeed a formal tour de force. And in its treatment of the problematic relationship between art and morality it can lay claim to thematic consequence. Yet, recognition of this theme should not beguile one into misprizing the very force that gave it expression. The Florentines' celebration of the greatness of the century at the end of the work is tinged with irony, to be sure. However, the satyr embracing the chalice, symbols of Poggio and Gertrude and of art and conscience, laughs perhaps less at those who overestimate the value of art than at those who underestimate it.

Tiiu V. Laane   (essay date 1990)

SOURCE: "Static and Dynamic Images as Thematic Motifs in C. F. Meyer's *Die Versuchung des Pescara,*" in *Michigan Germanic Studies,* Vol. 16, No. 1, Spring, 1990, pp. 44-67.

[*In the following essay, Laane explores the variety of imagery used in* Die Versuchung des Pescara.]

Conrad Ferdinand Meyer's commitment to impart pictorial force to language is well known. Profoundly influenced by Romance literature with its accent on plastic form and sharp contours, and awed by the monumental grandeur of Michelangelo's statues which transmute emotion into compelling visual representations, Meyer found a locus for these ideals in Friedrich Theodor Vischer's teachings which emphasize the concretization of ideas. Gestures in Meyer's novellas become symbols of the inner man; scenic settings and costumes represent an obsession to unite the tangible in objects with their felt meanings. The metaphorical dimension of language is exploited to a degree rarely found in German literature. "In der deutschen Literatur empfinde ich einen Mangel," Meyer declared to Fritz Kögel, "das ist nicht scharf genug gesehen, nicht sinnlich herausgestellt, es ist unbildlich verschwimmend. . . . Die Gleichnisse und Bilder im Deutschen sind schwach, sie erhellen und beleuchten nicht." In his own work, intricately formed patterns of imagery are developed into a refined and recondite intellectual medium and impart to his prose its characteristic flavor. They set him apart among the poetic realists of his period.

In no other of Meyer's novellas does imagery occur in such quantity as in this late work, his third Renaissance novella, *Die Versuchung des Pescara* (1887). It is Meyer's most formalized work in which even minutiae of fictive reality—objects, paintings, colors—assume symbolic significance and in which form is submitted to extreme stylization. Metaphorical language bears the same visual and symbolic intensity. Images permeate the language. Concrete objects mutate into other concrete objects or are transmogrified into animation. Pale abstractions take on substance. In all, there are more than three hundred images in *Die Versuchung des Pescara,* which translate into more than two per page. If one considers that many of the images are extended, that is, they are developed into prolonged pictures, one readily sees why the pictorial effect of the novella is at first overwhelming. In part, the bravura of Meyer's metaphorical language is demanded by the opulence of the historical setting, the elegant courts and castles of Italy. It reflects also Meyer's highly cultured taste and sense of "Grosser Stil" and monumentality, which he declared were in his blood. The elaborate pictorial structure has drawn, however, much criticism. Meyer's publisher Haessel advised Meyer not to expect a large reception for his work: "Dazu ist der behandelte Gegenstand zu herb und leider wieder so kunstvoll zusammen gebaut,—ich fürchte den Vorwurf der Künstlichkeit!—dass sich nur wenige finden werden, die sich mit Liebe in Ihr Buch vertiefen." Modern critics have found the enormous pictorial force of the work at times unpalatable. Meyer himself was quick to rise up in angry self-defense. . . . "J'ai lu, dans la Biblioth. Univer., que je 'continue d'exploiter ma veine,'" he wrote to Felix Bovet on January 14, 1888 upon reading that his novella was yet another tour de force. "On ne saurait s'exprimer avec moins de vérité, car je n'écris absolument que pour réaliser quelque idée, sans avoir aucun souci du public et je me sers de la forme de la nouvelle historique purement et simplement pour y loger mes expériences et mes sentiments personnels. . . . Ainsi, sous une forme très objective et éminemment artistique, je suis—au dedans individuel et tout subjectif." Stylistic brilliance was clearly not Meyer's aim, rather the expression of his most fundamental thoughts. The "eminently artistic form," which encompasses his use of elaborate and richly embroidered metaphorical language, is not parasitic, rather a means to epitomize the inner meaning of his novella. In the hands of this most conscious of artists, images play a part in the very fabric of the work.

In probing the metaphorical coloring of *Die Versuchung des Pescara,* one begins to discern significant patterns in what seems at first pictorial chaos. Clusters of imagery inundate the prose at times, yet the language is almost devoid of it in other instances. Some characters speak in bursts of metaphor; the hero does not. The key to Meyer's intent lies in the modifications he made in the historical events of the story. The novella is based primarily on Leopold Ranke's account of the final days of Fernando Avalos, the Marquis of Pescara (1489-1525), a general in Spanish service who won an important victory over France in the battle of Pavia in 1525. Half Italian and half Spanish, he was asked to become the commander of an Italian league against the Spanish Emperor Charles V and to establish an Italian state free from Spanish rule. The historical facts clearly suggest a fundamental struggle between loyalty and betrayal. The historical Pescara, in fact, joined the collusion but then carried out the emperor's orders and suddenly died, most likely of wounds received at Pavia. Meyer, after originally toying with the idea of treating the theme of "Willensfreiheit," strips the historical matter of its dramatic potential and focuses on the fact that Pescara is dying and, unknown to the conspirators, is beyond temptation. The heart of the novella becomes a static condition where potentially there could have been action. "Pescara hat nur wenig Handlung, nureine Situation," says Meyer in a detailed commentary on the novella. "Die Täuschung seiner Versucher und das allmälige Hervortreten seiner tödtlichen Verwundg. Er ist vorwiegend lyrisch." Meyer then continues to elaborate on the "grossen Momente" of the work:

> 1. Die männlich-rührende Ergebung des Helden in sein Loos.

> 2. Die Veredlung seines Characters (karg, falsch, grausam) durch die Nähe des Todes.

> 3. Die Aufregung und die leidenschaftliche Bewegung einer ganzen Welt um einen "schon nicht mehr Versuchbaren."

> 4. Die Fülle von Zeitgestalten. Sehen Sie nur die beiden spanisch en Typen (der D. Juan-typus und der Loyola-typus).

> 5. Die Symbolik. Das sterbende Italien bewirbt sich unwissentlich um einen sterbenden Helden.

Critics have repeatedly referred to these "grossen Momente" in analyzing the symbolic intent of the novella. They have not fully recognized, however, the degree to which movement around a person who has reached a state of rest (the "leidenschaftliche Bewegung") governs the inner structure and thematic matter of the narrative. The novella is governed by static and dynamic configurations. Structurally the work may be likened to a hurricane which swirls around an eye of quiet. At the center stands Pescara who is dying. An array of subordinate characters surround him in a whirlwind of activity. Unknowing of Pescara's imminent death, they try to entice, even coerce, him to betrayal. Thematically seen, the hero represents death, for Meyer a state of rest and equilibrium where man escapes from the unsolvable conflicts of life and is without suffering. It is the state of "Leidlosigkeit" so often portrayed in Meyer's poems. In contrast, the subordinate characters, representations of the Machiavellian excesses of the Renaissance, symbolize in the author's pessimistic view the brutality and immorality of life, a state of frantic activity which in the end is illusion.

That this basic dichotomy of motion and rest represents the fundamental philosophical core of the novella is substantiated by a second significant change that Meyer made in the historical material. In fashioning the figure of Morone, Pescara's chief antagonist and the principal conspirator, Meyer exercised telling poetic license. In historical accounts Morone appears as a personage of noble background, a brilliant but amoral lawyer who performed duties at the various courts of Italy. Meyer's Morone becomes a figure of low birth, a blend of idealist and fool, who manipulates his way into kingly circles and who in every aspect, moral and physical, represents movement. Morone's face is in continual motion and he gestures so wildly that others call out to him not to gesticulate "wie ein Rasender." Movement lies at the essence of his amoral character and governs his twirling thoughts and emotions. The idea of motion, particularly when contrasted with the stasis of the hero, is so insistent, that one senses that one has arrived at an underlying narrative pattern which is symbolic of the meaning of the entire novella. Viewed within this context, the seemingly overwhelming imagery in *Die Versuchung des Pescara* takes on new meaning and cohesion. Harnessed to give powerful aesthetic representation to the thematic matter of the novella, a kaleidoscope of metaphorical language underscores in contrapuntal manner, both through content and form, Meyer's dualistic view of existence. Images are interwoven throughout the narrative like complex arabesques and play a vital role as a cohesive force in shaping the inner structure of the novella. Dynamic images of life, images of energy and motion, underscore again and again the grandiose but illusory quality of existence. Static images of death, images of equilibrium and rest, probe the core of the novella, a center where man has reached fulfillment.

By far the largest number of images in *Die Versuchung des Pescara* gives visual and emotive impact to the negative pole of Meyer's antithetical theme, that of worldly corruption. Profoundly influenced in his later years by Jacob Burckhardt's work, *Die Kultur der Renaissance in Italien* (1860), with its view of the Renaissance as an age of amoral, power-hungry individuals, Meyer poses the lonely, ethical man, a bearer of the most modern agnosticism and nihilism, against this great tableau to give voice to the theme of the novella. The Renaissance was for Meyer, as for Nietzsche, who also learned from Burckhardt, "great" in an aesthetic rather than a moral sense. Meyer viewed it as an era of brutal excesses and decadence which both fascinated and repelled him. In *Die Versuchung des Pescara* he submits the epoch to biting irony in stressing through imagery its iridescent, but morally dubious character. Transcribed into terms of motion and rest, the Renaissance represents chaos which the author pits against harmony and quiet. The sheer numerical weight of images of earthly corruption reflects the boisterousness of life and ultimate illusion. Meyer places them into narrative description where the images comment on the basic personality traits of the characters and serve, at times, as incisive authorial value judgment. Swirling metaphorical language also colors the speeches of the subordinate characters, who represent "types of the Renaissance," patterned after that great but morally dubious archetype, Machiavelli. These images form a vibrant negative pole which Meyer poises against the silence of death. In their pictorial and decorative grandeur, images of earthly corruption reveal Meyer's fascination with the aesthetic side of the period. Their capacity to manipulate and their strident rhetoric depict the questionable morality of "Realpolitik." Through the voice of Pescara, Meyer offers an alternative which he consecrates through simplicity and eloquence of picture.

In transmuting the theme of wordly illusion and deception into imagery, Meyer resorts to his favorite technique, the leitmotif, to establish a clear metaphorical link between certain realms of experience and dominant ideas in the novella. Two major leitmotifs of imagery interlace the narrative to portray a world of pretense and evil.

Theater images, a familiar motif in Meyer's novellas, underscore again and again the concept of the human condition as a bitter comedy or tragedy. War, the most brutal of man's activities, stares "wie eine Maske mit leeren Augen." Pescara, dying, expresses toward the end of the novella his weariness of the "menschliche Komödie." Subordinate characters don masks and cloaks to win support for their interests. Morone, the protean master of masks, goes to the closet of his imagination to pick a suitable costume to influence his listeners:

> Schnellen Geistes wählte der Kanzler unter den Truggestalten und Blendwerken, über welche seine Einbildungskraft gebot, eine hinreichend wahrscheinliche und wirksame Larve, um sie seinem beweglichen Gebieter entgegenzuhalten und ihn damit heilsam zu erschrecken.

In Meyer the very identity of a person is a mask which is deceptive and impenetrable. Conjecturing about Pescara's true motives, Moncada, a Spanish nobleman, wonders: "Eine Maske . . . eine durchdachte Maske. Welch ein Antlitz verbirgt sie?" Pescara himself adopts an ironic stance as he urges Morone to assume the mask of Machiavelli while the Chancellor attempts to justify the dubious morality of betrayal. Pescara compares Morone's efforts to win his allegiance to the conspiratorial league to a theatrical performance. It is given a title and attended by an audience:

> "Herrschaften," sagt er [Pescara], "hier wurde Theater gespielt. Das Stück dauerte lange. Habt Ihr nicht gegähnt in Eurer Loge?"
>
> Da schlug der Bourbon in plötzlich umspringender Stimmung eine gelle Lache auf. "Trauerspiel oder Posse?" fragte er.
>
> "Tragödie, Hoheit."
>
> "Und betitelt sich?"
>
> "Tod und Narr," antwortete Pescara.

While the motif of the worldly masquerade is traditional, Meyer, a master of revitalizing conventional analogies, makes the extended metaphor memorable by fashioning it as an ironic exchange between characters and by placing it prominently at the end of a chapter to give it further emphasis.

Imagery dealing with games and playing, the second principal leitmotif in the novella, forms an extension of Meyer's theater imagery. Cards, dice and chess recur as motifs to underline metaphorically that life and human interaction are a pretense, a game in which one person tries to outwit the other. Action lies again at the root of the analogies. "Wie wirst du spielen, Pescara?" ponders one character. "Man blickt uns in die Karten," frets another. The game of politics runs like a persistent thread throughout the novella, filtering down even to dead metaphor which Meyer imbues with new significance. War is a game of dice or a cunning game of chess. Images provide analogies for the relationships between characters. Significantly, Meyer first introduces Pescara through the use of a symbolic picture where the General is depicted playing a game of chess with his wife Victoria. Meyer forces the reader to ponder along with the subordinate characters as to whether Pescara will participate in worldly intrigue. Translated into the realm of the animal kingdom, game imagery becomes the tormenting and deadly game of cat and mouse. The motif is first associated with the cruel and sensual Don Juan, Pescara's nephew, one of the Spanish types of the Renaissance. The imagery reflects Meyer's virulently anti-Catholic bent to associate Spain with particular cruelty. Using personification, Meyer lets Don Juan envision Pescara caressing and subjugating a sensuous Italy and then tossing her away like a wanton woman. "[O], er wird mit ihr spielen wie die Katze mit der Maus!" he calls out, making a snatching motion with his hand, a typical Meyerean gesture. Other characters echo this motif later, imprinting it on the reader's mind. Pescara's physician Numa, fearing the Spanish side of Pescara, begs Pescara not to play a "grausames Spiel" with his beloved Italy. "Ich spiele mit Italien, sagst du?" responds Pescara. "Im Gegenteil, deine Landsleute, Numa, spielen mit mir: sie heucheln Leben und sind tot in ihren Übertretungen und Sünden." The image is an ironic reversal of the motif of the deadly game between cat and mouse. While a mouse simulates death in an attempt to save its life, the Italians here pretend to be alive, when, in fact, they are morally dead, as is their collusion to overthrow the emperor.

Subsidiary motifs interlace with these images of playing and play-acting to underline and elucidate the over-arching themes and to impress them on the reader's mind. The motifs are many, yet are drawn together thematically in that they portray a world of frantic action. Strong characters manipulate the weak like wax puppets; evil stretches out its roots like a giant tree which must be torn out to eradicate the malignancy. The idea of spinning portrays worldly action. Events turn on a wheel of fortune and encircle the man of action. Making use of repeated harsh "r" sounds to imitate the roar of a storm, Meyer gives pictorial form to the idea of events whipping and tossing man by combining wheel and storm imagery. Fire imagery adds an element of danger:

> ". . . ich glaube nicht, dass mein Italien untergeht, denn es trägt Unsterblichkeit in sich; aber ich möchte ihm das Fegefeuer der Knechtschaft ersparen. Gib acht, Söhnchen: ich lese zwischen deinen Augen, dass du noch eine Rolle spielen wirst in dem rasenden Reigen von Ereignissen, der über meinen lombardischen Boden hinwegfegt."

Elsewhere Meyer develops the idea of storms by depicting man being tossed about on the waves of life. Powerful individuals like Luther, he tells us, can stand firm against "den aufspritzenden Gischt des Jahrhunderts." Images of dirt and filth focus in on the unsavory nature of human dealings. Politics are likened to the mercantile—concepts of buying and selling—to describe human interaction. Pescara views political maneuverings as "ein schmutziger Markt und sein Weib dürfe nicht einmal die

helle Spitze ihres Fusses in den ekeln Sumpf tauchen." War leads "zu der roten Lache einer Schlachtbank." No realm of society escapes condemnation. Meyer submits the Catholic church to particular irony: "Unsere kluge Kirche öffnet ihre Buden und legt verständig ihren Vorrat an guten Werken zum Verkauf aus." Popes are belittled through imagery. Pope Clemens is compared to a cunning sailor; Pope Julius thunders like Zeus on a cloud, only to crash down in Hades.

Chasm imagery, which depicts characters falling into an abyss, a realm of lies and deception, develops Meyer's pessimistic evaluation of existence further. The images play with the idea of imbalance, the precariousness of existence, darkness and danger. In a striking extended metaphor, Italy is first compared to a morass which is hollowed out by its own morally corrupt excesses. Then Meyer associates it with a malicious woman, who is seemingly beseeching, but is actually trying to "pull away solid ground from under Pescara" in order to force him to jump into a chasm. The ethically indifferent Morone is seen as an "Abgrund von Lüge, in welchem der Blick sich verliert." The human condition leaves man chronically poised at the edge of the precipice. The danger may also take the form of treacherous quicksand. In an image which becomes the basis of dialogue, Pescara warns Morone of the perils of disloyalty:

> "Fusset Ihr auf diesem Undanke des Kaisers und auf diesem Grolle Pescaras, so tut keinen Schritt weiter: Ihr würdet in den trügerischen Boden versinken."

> "Da fusse ich nicht."

Snake and poison imagery symbolize betrayal. Meyer focuses in on the twisting and turning of snakes to refract the idea of spinning from yet another angle. A certain fascination with evil, a sign of Meyer's love-hate relationship with the Renaissance, emerges from the pictures. Morone becomes enthralled by a painting of the coat of arms of the Sforza family, a gruesome and twisting wreath of snakes, brought to life by the "süsse" Leonardo da Vinci in a "Spiel einer grausamen Laune." Pescara turns to snake metaphor to give voice to his negative view of betrayal. He has learned that defaming letters have been disseminated about him to coerce his defection from the emperor. He has sent these letters to the Emperor. The reader learns about Pescara's action for the first time in this image which serves to summarize events:

> "Ich habe vorgebeugt und die arglistigen Schriften wie in einen Käfig eingesperrte Schlangen dem Kaiser überliefert. Habet Ihr Eure Finger auch in dieses Gift getaucht, Morone?"

The image of the basket of snakes depicts grisly motion. The repeated "s" sounds imitate the hissing of snakes and synecdoche focuses in on the evil, the poison of betrayal. Elsewhere disloyalty takes the shape of slithering fogs and mists or flicks like a tongue from under the earth's surface. The latter motif is associated with Bourbon, the archetypical betrayer, whose undulating and volatile moods reflect his tormented conscience.

Images are interwoven throughout the narrative like complex arabesques and play a vital role as a cohesive force in shaping the inner structure of the novella.

—Tiiu V. Laane

As can be seen from the examples cited, Meyer's metaphorical language of worldly corruption partakes linguistically of a grammar of movement. Most frequently the image is located in a verb, with the verb metaphor serving as the originator of the image, changing nouns implicitly into something else. Verb metaphor also supports other types of analogies, helping to fashion highly graphic pictures charged with inner movement. Language is transmuted into action. The technique is a favorite one of Meyer, who equated movement with beauty. In *Die Versuchung des Pescara,* however, verb imagery appears in greatest number and highest ratio of all of his novellas. Here analogies of action assume a higher significance, becoming bearers in linguistic form of thematic matter. All manner of metaphoric transformations strike Meyer's imagination. At times, a simple metaphoric verb transmutes one thing into another. Don Juan, for example, "pants for prey" thereby mutating into an animal; the papal seat "spits out heresy" thus becoming a gigantic monster. Complex verb metaphors, each of which makes use of a more intricate relationship between metaphorical verbs and other elements of the sentence, far outnumber simple verb metaphors in fashioning detailed pictures of action. In an ironic image, which reflects Meyer's condemning attitude toward dreams of temporal grandeur, he plays with the idea of Victoria's vanity by turning loyalty to the state into a corpse and then describing how Victoria steps over it: "Sie schritt mit einer geraubten Krone wie die erste Tullia, nicht über den Leichnam des Vaters, sondern über die gemeuchelte Staatstreue . . . ." Betrayal is a distorting vapor and repulsive fog which creeps into each and every relationship of a betrayer, making him hideous.

As can be seen, verb metaphor lends itself well to personification, and Meyer uses it frequently to animate the inanimate and to mutate one thing into another. As touches of cultural milieu, images in the Renaissance tradition attribute actions to personified abstractions like death, virtue and justice: death lowers its torch and snuffs it out, or it knocks at marble portals. Virtue marches forth in person. In the same tradition, particular actions are attributed to ready-made personifications such as gods and demons, which are changed anthropomorphically.

Morone thus envisions the goddess of victory, betrayed by the Spanish emperor at Pavia, marching forth and choosing out Pescara to lead the fight for a free Italy. Meyer depicts Italy, a symbol of the Renaissance in its beauty and moral decay, in leitmotif fashion to paint a canvas of grand proportions. Italy throws itself defenselessly at Pescara's feet, and lies in painful chains. Seemingly innocent, she maliciously hollows out the ground from under Pescara to try to force him to jump into a chasm of betrayal. She offers her bridal ring to him but is in fact a prostitute who must learn virtue in chains.

Frequently Meyer harnesses similes to his verb metaphors to add visual impact. A striking simile depicts Luther, a dynamic force in the course of history, bracing himself against the events of his time. Sound adds to the richness of picture:

> ". . . er vollzieht, was die Zeit fordert, dann aber—und das ist ein schweres Amt—steht er wie ein Gigant gegen den aufspritzenden Gischt des Jahrhunderts und schleudert hinter sich die aufgeregten Narren und bösen Buben, die mittun wollen, das gerechte Werk übertreibend und schändend."

The image is a typical Meyerean allegory, a story that unfolds before the mind's eye. The gigantic Luther, who in the simile calls to mind the colossus of Rhodes, first stands firm against the foaming battering of his time, a metaphor of the ocean. The hard "g" sounds and repeated sibilants onomatopoetically repeat the chopping and frothing of waves. Luther then tosses aside the insignificant men of his generation, the fools who dare to meddle in great events. Always sensitive to the pitch and quality of vowels, and to the character of consonants, Meyer—though considered primarily an "Augenmensch"—finds a wealth of opportunity in assonance and alliteration in creating his tableaux charged with inner movement. Metaphorical adjectives serve as a pithy way to animate the pictures further. The image "foam of events" is enlivened by the adjective "spraying." Similarly Meyer speaks of "der verröchelnden Republik" and of "einen in Monddämmerung kriechenden Hinterhalt," turning the abstract concepts into animate beings.

Noun metaphors, the most complex of metaphors grammatically, make up about one half of the images in *Die Versuchung des Pescara.* Almost all of these analogies, images depicting various modes of worldly activity, receive support from verb metaphors, being prolonged into optically clear pictures in which a series of actions unfold. Making use of parallelism to equate a chasm with Pescara's secretive soul, for example, Meyer first pairs the abstract term (the soul) with the noun metaphor (the chasm). Then he prolongs the analogy with verb metaphors to create an image of manipulation:

> So schaukelte Pescara sein Weib über dem Abgrund und dem Geheimnis seiner Seele und hinderte sie, Fuss zu fassen, die mit dem ganzen Ungestüm ihres Wesens Boden suchte, den Sieg erstrebend, den zu erringen sie

nach Novarra geeilt war. Auf immer neuen Wegen verfolgte sie das Ziel von welchem Pescara sie ferne hielt.

The idea of Pescara's lofty vantage, his wife's helplessness in the face of it, and a certain degree of playful cruelty give shape to the image. Movement is also intrinsic to noun metaphors which make use of the different types of genitive links to associate the proper term or "tenor" with the metaphoric term or "vehicle" (e.g. "Gesicht der Zeit," "rasender Reigen der Ereignisse"). These types of noun metaphors usually depict a functional relationship in addition to a sensuous relationship between tenor and vehicle (e.g. in the image "rasender Reigen der Ereignisse" the events *are* the roundelay, both of which spin). Motion is thus present in the idea of the noun metaphor itself. Meyer develops these images by adding metaphoric verbs to intensify action:

> . . . [sie flehte], dass Rom und Italien nicht versinke in das Grab der Knechtschaft.

> ". . . ich möchte ihm das Fegefeuer der Knechtschaft ersparen. . . . [I]ch lese zwischen deinen Augen, dass du noch eine Rolle spielen wirst in dem rasenden Reigen von Ereignissen, der über meinen lombardischen Boden hinwegfegt."

In the images above, the metaphor expresses the identity of the tenor and vehicle (e.g. the "Fegefeuer" *is* the "Knechtschaft"). Images which express attribution depict even more specific actions. By assigning a quality to a proper term (e.g. in the image "Gesicht der Zeit" the capacity of seeing is attributed to time, thus turning "Gesicht" into a face), especially by means of a verb plus a preposition which expresses exactly what one thing is doing in, with, or out of another, Meyer creates intense dynamic formulations. The formula is used as a main means of personification. Vanity is thus endowed with arms which she uses to squander her earthly possessions. A cloak is wrapped around the shameless exhibitionism of Italy to give her more dignity. At times, noun metaphors simply replace a proper term with a more poetic one. Verbs again support the noun metaphors. A colorful array of imagistic heroes, gods and half-gods from Greek mythology and Roman history capture the flavor of the Renaissance. Pescara is Achilles who "zürnt im Zelte. "Der garstige Leyva," Pescara's crude but loyal general, and Pescara's wife Victoria are "Mars und Muse" who both feel insulted by betrayal.

As can be seen, each of the images of worldly corruption cited above embroiders a picture of movement within the content of one analogy. Others become dynamic in development. The original analogy, produces through some association a new analogy and then yet another in a kind of chain-reaction. A sequence of images thus pushes the narrative forward, intensifying and propelling the sense of action. The intrigant Nasi uses such an image to describe his plan to coerce Pescara to join the Italian league. He will bribe a disreputable poet to write and circulate letters about Pescara which will proclaim the probability of Pescara's betrayal of his emperor:

> "Ich will ihm eine sehr starke Summe senden, und ihr werdet euch über die Saat von schönfarbigen Giftpilzen verwundern, die über Nacht aus dem ganzen Boden Italiens emporschiesst: Verse, Abhandlungen, Briefwechsel, ein bacchantisch aufspringender, taumelnder Reigen verhüllter und nackter, drohender und verlockender Figuren und Wendungen, alle um Pescara sich drehend und um die Wahrscheinlichkeit und Schönheit seines Verrates."

The images are charged with association and compress complex thought into vivid pictures. The movement of mushrooms springing from the ground suggests the image of dancing figures. The beauty of the colorful mushrooms leads Meyer in association to naked circling bacchanalian characters. The dancers are threatening and dangerous, as are the poisonous fungi, yet they are alluring as are the colorful mushrooms. The moral ugliness of betrayal is clear, yet it entwines with enticing expediency. Once again ethical decay and aesthetic voluptuousness symbolize visually Meyer's mixed feelings about the Renaissance.

It is important to note that Meyer's dynamic images are not only found in narrative description, but are placed into the speeches of his Machiavellian subordinate characters. Meyer was well aware of the efficacy of metaphor in the delineation of characters, and used images vivid in movement, both in structure and thought content, as signs of the outlook and temperament of the subordinate characters who view the world as an every-changing scene of conflict. Laden with pictorial force, these images become rhetorical devices by which one character attempts to capture the imagination of the other and thereby to sway him. A whirlwind of verbal activity surrounds Pescara. Meyer ascribes some of his most rhetorical metaphorical formulations to the speeches of the secondary characters who as a group serve as a foil against Pescara. They have a compulsion, even as Meyer himself, to give concrete shape and outline to their thoughts and use imagery consciously to give vivid and dynamic form to their impassioned feelings. A higher percentage of emphatically rhetorical imagistic formulations occurs in *Die Versuchung des Pescara* than in any other of Meyer's novellas except for his last work *Angela Borgia*. The subordinate characters employ images for hyperbole, periphrase, repetition and syllogistic argument. They build crescendos, retards and climaxes in a manner found in Renaissance tracts. Having been schooled in rhetoric, they love to display their metaphors and use the most clear and emphatic grammatical formulations to achieve emotive power. Highly rhetorical pictures of action unfold. Nasi's image of the poisonous mushrooms, as we have just seen, is formulated first as a declaration and then a visually intense variation: "Ich will ihm eine sehr starke Summe senden . . . die Saat von schönfarbigen Giftpilzen. . . ." Then Nasi adds an apposition, a clarifying "that is," strengthened by a colon, for explicit rhetorical intensification of picture: "Verse, Abhandlungen, Briefwechsel, ein bacchantisch aufspringender, taumelnder

Reigen verhüllter und nackter, drohender und verlockender Figuren und Wendungen . . .". The demonstrative formula of imagery, making use of either the definite article or "diese" to specifically point out the image, serves characters for imagistic repetition:

> "Hier ist ein Sieg davonzutragen, grösser als der auf dem Schlachtfelde. . . . Ich sehe sie vor mir, diese Königin der Tugend, die Priesterin, die das heilige Feuer hütet, die Erhalterin der Herrschaft, und, hosianna! ganz Italien wandelt hinter ihren Schritten, lobpreisend und frohlockend!"

Copula, the most direct and emotionally strong type of rhetorical analogy, occurs in highest percentage in *Die Versuchung des Pescara* of all of Meyer's novellas. In this type of figure of speech the tenor and the vehicle are equated point blank with the verb "to be" to proclaim identity:

> "Ich bin Italien und liege zu deinen Füssen: erhebe mich und nimm mich an deine Brust!"

> "Dieser Mensch ist ein Abgrund von Lüge, in welchem der Blick sich verliert."

Such dynamic images serve as climaxes in speeches of high emotional impact. In a particularly striking example, the Florentine Guicciardin uses such an analogy for calculated effect as he builds his rhetorical oration to his listeners. Meyer provides no less than five exclamation points to indicate the intensity of Guicciardin's emotions. The Italian's speech culminates in an image. In Meyer the characters are attentive to each other's metaphorical language and are verbally responsive to it. Many images, as we have seen, even become the subject of dialog. Pushed to the extreme, the intensely rhetorical dynamic analogies become a sign of the hollowness of language per se. This happens in the idiom of Morone, Pescara's chief adversary, whose imagery becomes empty theatrics. Here Meyer reaches for the tool of linguistic irony to suggest that human communication and interaction are intrinsically false and without meaning.

In many ways Morone is the novella's most interesting character. His figure serves, as we have seen, as the clue to the static and dynamic configurations of the narrative. His highly excitable and many-faceted character resonates with movement. Morone's physical mannerisms—rolling eyes, grimaces and gestures—are so pronounced that other characters become disturbed, even irritated, by them. They call out repeatedly: "Lass die Grimassen, Narr!"; "ich kann nicht sprechen, wenn Eure Gebärden so heftig dareinreden." Even in disguise Morone is readily recognized by his vehement movements. Images of motion portray the Chancellor's twirling thoughts and emotions. His ideas "wimmeln wie in einem Ameisenhaufen" and brew as if in a witch's kettle. Morone is capable of the noblest and basest emotions, and as a true man of the Renaissance, springs to either extreme as expediency demands. Analogies of jumping depict his volatile nature

and his amoral flexibility. "Von den steilsten Dächern herabrollend, kommst du wie eine Katze immer wieder auf die Füsse zu stehen," proclaims Duke Sforza, Morone's master, in envious wonderment. Guicciardin, too, sizes up Morone's character: "Ein Phantast wie du, Kanzler, mit den unbändigen Sprüngen deiner Einbildungskraft ist dazu da das Unmögliche zu erdenken und auszusprechen." Morone is the embodiment of the actor, a Proteus, a black magician who adopts whatever mask necessary to achieve his political aims. He picks out suitable costumes from the "closet of his imagination" to impress his listeners and changes his cloaks as quickly as his concepts of morality. Morone is the mastermind of the Italian league, at once noble and eloquent in his love of Italy and possessed by the dream of national unification. At the same time, he is a caricature of Machiavellian "Realpolitik," "der tolle Kanzler," the "Narr," "Buffone," "Gaukler," who carries his "klassischer Bocksfuss unter der Toga."

For Morone, the master rhetorician, imagistic language is the most expedient way to fulfill his goals, and he uses it consciously, actually altering it for calculated effect. In speeches early on in the novella, Morone's idiom is very much like that of the other characters. Images occur, but not with more frequency than in the speeches of the other characters. When adopting the role of the tempter, however, his idiom changes radically. It becomes highly rhetorical and laden with dynamic images which accumulate to build emotional climaxes. The other characters respond to this according to their own dispositions. Realists like Guicciardin are not emotionally swayed. "Genug deklamiert!" he calls out as Morone begins to laud the concept of the Italian league too ecstatically. On the other hand, rhetoric completely wins over the highly imaginative and temperamental Victoria. Morone builds his oration to her by creating an allegory which appeals to her "altertumstrunkenes Auge." Emotive and culturally laden images play upon her vanity. Movement characterizes the analogies. Morone first paints a picture of the grand triumphal parade of the century and the revolving wheel of fortune. Victoria is the "Königin der Tugend, die Priesterin, die das heilige Feuer hütet." She will lead the jubilant processional and throw herself in front of Pescara, exhorting: "Ich bin Italien und liege zu deinen Füssen: erhebe mich und nimm mich an deine Brust!" The vivid pictures couched in rhetorical phraseology overwhelm her feelings and appeal to the poetess in her who is keenly attuned to the melody and rhythms of language. Morone's temptation is as much linguistic as philosophical. Highly emotional himself, he joins Victoria in moving to a rarefied atmosphere beyond the realm of truth and reality. Meyer sums up Victoria's reaction with irony in a passage which parodies the temptation of Christ:

> Victoria senkte die Augen, denn sie fühlte, dass sie voller Wonne waren und brannten wie zwei Sonnen.

> Da sagte der Kanzler: "Ich habe Euch ermüdet, edle Frau, die Augen fallen Euch zu. . . ." Und der Listige trat in die Nacht zurück, die sich inzwischen auf die ewige Stadt gesenkt hatte.

In contrast to Victoria, Morone fails in his verbal temptation of Pescara. Endeavoring to get the General to switch allegiance, Morone begins his oration once again by painting an allegorical canvas of a magnificent processional. He envisions the goddess of victory of Pavia, having been insulted by the Spanish emperor, leading Pescara into battle on behalf of the Italian league. "Mein Pescara, welche Sternstellung über dir und für dich! Die Sache reif und reif du selbst!" As Morone's emotions come into full swing, he begins to leap from metaphor to metaphor, carried away by the momentum of his own language. A world of gigantic deeds and actions awaits Pescara. Morone implores Pescara to play along in the grandiose happenings:

> "Eine entscheidende Zeit, ein verzweifeltes Ringen, Götter und Titanen, Freiheit sich aufbäumend gegen Zwingherrschaft, die Welt heute noch Bewegung und Fluss, morgen vielleicht zur Lava erstarrend! . . . Zuckt dir die formende Hand nicht danach? . . . Blick auf die Karte und überschaue die Halbinsel zwischen zwei Meerfarben und dem Schnee der Gebirge! Befrage die Geschichte: ein lebendiges Geflecht, oft gewaltsam zerrissen und immer wieder zusammenwachsend, von Republiken und Fürsten, mit zwei alten Feinden, zwei falschen Ideen, zwei grausamen Chimären, Papst und Kaiser! Siehe den ausgestreckten Finger Gottes, daran sich ein neue Menschheit emporrichtet: eine sich selbst regierende und veredelnde Menschheit ohne höchstes Amt, weder weltliches noch geistliches, ein Reigen frei entwickelter Genien, ein Konzert gleichberechtigter Staaten—"

Morone's style, a combination of rhetorical question, exhortations and analogies, is impossibly inflated. Images of spinning and motion—melting lava, nations twisting and turning like a living wickerwork, God's outstretched finger creating a new humanity, a roundelay of superior men, a concert of states—are heaped to a degree where they can no longer be visualized. As their proliferation becomes irrational and the Chancellor reaches the point of hysteria, Pescara takes Morone by the hand, saying: "Fliege mir nicht davon, Girolamo!" Dying and beyond temptation, Pescara sees Morone's language, a symbol of the unrealistic folly of the Italian league itself, clearly for what it is: empty theatrics. Language per se, Meyer tells us, is a sham. Human interaction is futile and hollow. At the end Morone becomes the fool, a jumping "Paillasse" who is led away straddled backwards on a donkey, roaring at his own misery. The scene represents the pinnacle of Meyer's irony.

If one now contrasts these images of excess, hollowness, and feverish activity with the cluster of images which typifies Pescara, a dramatic difference can be noted. In the first three chapters of the novella, Pescara's own idiom remains terse and relatively unadorned and is characteristically tinged with irony. Metaphorical language making use of dynamic formulations swirls around Pescara, conjecturing about his motives and character. These images are spoken, however, by other characters who—typical Meyerean figures—can not probe the center of the hero's consciousness. Victoria laments that even though she knows the least of her husband's gestures, facial expressions, and habits by heart, his mind and soul remain full of closed doors and chambers which prevent her from reaching him. The image aptly conveys the plight of all the other characters who find the hero's nature unfathomable. Pescara is a "Sphinx" whose motives remain shrouded in mystery. He seems, in fact, to be playing a game with the other characters. The General is introduced into the novella in a picture which portrays him playing chess with his wife. Meyer describes him dangling her over an abyss, his secretive soul, and intentionally preventing her from reaching solid ground, the truth of his motives. Meyer, who loved the ambiguous hero, the "what if" of situations, can not resist casting oblique perspectives on his protagonist. He spoke of a "geheime Basis" of the novella. "Vielleicht unterlag Pescara, ohne die Wunde." Characters make metaphorical suppositions as to whether Pescara, too, isn't a cunning man of the Renaissance.

From the first, however, Meyer associates Pescara with death and the reader becomes gradually aware that Pescara's stance is different from that of the subordinate characters. Unknown to the others, Pescara is dying. Death has sharpened his perception of political maneuverings and made him aware of the futility of human action. Pescara's characteristically ironic language reflects this superior vantage which merges with that of Meyer the author. Death images, at times thematically interwoven with play images—as in the extended metaphor of death and the fool, or the reference to Pescara playing chess with his wife "blass wie der Tod"—occur at regular intervals to cast light on Pescara's inner state. Pescara's bitter lucidity about the brutal nature of human activity overlaps with Meyer's own pessimistic attitude. In a scene that is crucial to the meaning of the story, the crust of Pescara's irony breaks and an elegiac mood overcomes him. A series of lyrical images expresses his acceptance of death and his view of it as a benefactor who will deliver him from moral conflict. Character and author merge to hallow the release from earthly existence. Images paint a picture of beauty, rest and quiet. In contrast to the profuse and often strident analogies of the other characters, these images are few. Their form is characterized by utmost simplicity. Many are simple similes, which Meyer elevates through eloquence of language and symbolic intent. When Pescara finally clarifies his true motives, he reaches for a simile to tell his wife that he has been fully aware of the political maneuverings. Not only the thought content of this critical image, but also its acoustical shape encapsulates the static and dynamic configurations of the novella:

> "Ich sah die Versuchung lange, ich sah sie kommen und sich gipfeln wie eine heranrollende Woge, und habe nicht geschwankt, nicht einen Augenblick, mit dem leisesten Gedanken nicht."

With the tonal and rhythmic thrust of a poem, the image of the wave repeats the motif of the tossing ocean seen earlier in the novella. The rhythm of the language peaks three times as the metaphorical wave, the temptation, builds to engulf Pescara. Pescara, however, prevails as the wave washes away to nothingness, represented by the threefold retard at the end of the simile. "Meine Gottheit . . . hat den Sturm rings um meine Ruder beruhigt," says Pescara, responding imagistically to the motifs of storms and struggle seen previously in the story. The lilting rhythm of the analogy and the repeated sonorous "r" sounds unite sense and sound to convey the picture of a man at peace. The motif of the boatsman with oars at rest is a familiar death symbol in Meyer's poems and novellas where it depicts a state of equilibrium, a sense of welcome release and mood of unconcern in the face of temptation and intrigue. The quietness of Pescara's death, a blend of pseudoreligious fatalism, escapism and resignation, resembles the realm of sleep and dreams where the contradictions of existence disappear and where a secretive, dark and gentle god saves man from irresolvable contradictions. As death now makes its appearance to Pescara and he struggles for his life and breath, he becomes for his wife like a dream, a bloody winter sun which has set with splendorous finality. The glow of the setting sun associated with blood symbolizes death at the moment of life's greatest magnificence, a concept which fascinated Meyer. Riding together for the last time to a cloister where Victoria is to await Pescara's summons, Pescara and Victoria enter a world of silence:

> Kein Windhauch und nicht der leiseste Versuch einer Wolkenbildung. Keine Lerche stieg, kein Vogelsang, es dämmerte ein stilles Zwielicht wie über den Wiesen der Unterwelt.

The verbless first sentence of the image, followed by the short clauses of the second, retard all action. The repeated sibilants and the lingering "i" sounds evoke breathless silence. The image conjures up a time when light hangs in balance and no motion or sound disturbs the uncanny stillness. The scene in its nakedness is intensely visual, the mood almost surrealistic in its suspended animation. The images of grinding action which have traversed the novella like vivid bits of cinema, portraying turbulent life, give way. Pescara is filled with a sense of streaming calm, "das Fluten der Ewigkeit." "Ich bin jenseits der Kluft," states Pescara, posing an antithesis imagistically to the motifs of precarious instability and danger. "Was soll dieser Sturm?" he asks his wife as they view a painting depicting human activity. "Alles in rasender Tätigkeit." Death, a "Todesengel," will cut through the unsolvable knot of his existence. Death is Pescara's "Befreier," the "Schnitter" who brings down what has come to fruition. His dark "Beschützer" means him well, believes Pescara, and will take him tenderly from here. "Wohin? In die Ruhe." When Pescara dies, the novella closes with a simile of sleep which hallows his release from the conflicts of existence:

> Pescara lag ungewaffnet und ungerüstet auf dem goldenen Bette des gesunkenen Thronhimmels. Der starke Wille in seinen Zügen hatte sich gelöst, und die Haare waren ihm über die Stirn gefallen. So glich er einem jungen, magern, von der Ernte erschöpften und auf seiner Garbe schlafenden Schnitter.

The image is rich in association. The background of the golden bed is reminiscent of the setting sun of Meyer's harvest poems where it pours down over reapers when they return from their toils. It envelops them in a heavenly halo and consecrates their life's work even as the golden glow of the bed does here. Rest and peace dominate. Bathed in warm golden light like the yellow of ripened fields of grain or the golden background of old religious paintings, action is frozen at this epiphanic moment as in a painting, more beautiful than life itself. Suffering and tempestuous emotion are distilled into an aethetic form which objectifies pain and, by doing so, transcends it. The image, the final sentence of the novella, climaxes the images of death. In number they are few, yet in their intensity and symbolic value, they bring us to the thematic core of the novella.

Meyer's method is conscious. He was not what Bruneau terms an "inspired imagist" whose imagery grows from intuitive and visionary perceptions, but rather a "chimiste" whose creation is tempered by a rational process. By chiseling consistent and pronounced metaphorical patterns to contrast life and death, Meyer creates a substructure which counterpoints the dramatic structure of the novella. Images become symbols which far transcend their individual existence. Functionally, dynamic metaphorical language serves as an instrument of actual temptation which the protagonist rejects. Through the juxtaposition of realms from which images are drawn, as well as their tone and distribution, Meyer also fashions a political allegory of an entire era and reveals his ironic attitude toward the Renaissance. Above all, the complex metaphorical arabesques, crystallizations of repose poised against vibrant pictures of action, become instruments of probing and analyzing complex experience. Firmly attached to the dominant themes, static and dynamic images play a compelling part in conveying the meaning of the novella and deepening its artistic effect. They become symbols of metaphysical and moral values. "Vor dem Tode erschrecke ich nicht," wrote Meyer, "warum auch? Habe ich ihn doch—nach meinen Kräften—verherrlicht in den Gedichten und im 'Pescara'." Images weave a rich tapestry of Meyer's fundamental mode of vision and provide the poignant symbols for his view of life and death.

Deborah S. Lund (essay date 1992)

SOURCE: "Of Doubtful Virtue: The Virago in C. F. Meyer's *Angela Borgia*," in *Seminar*, Vol. 28, No. 3, September, 1992, pp. 208-21.

[*In the following essay, Lund contends that the character of Angela Borgia "fails as a figure in the novella because of her unyielding 'masculine' strength of character."*]

Conrad Ferdinand Meyer's last novella, ***Angela Borgia***, first published in 1892, has long suffered at the hands of scholars and critics. It is frequently neglected as unworthy or untypical of Meyer's oeuvre, and has, when studied, been found to contain a series of flaws, often attributed to the waning artistic powers of the author. Uffe Hansen's exhaustive study [*Conrad Ferdinand Meyer: "Angela Borgia." Zwischen Salpêtrière und Berggasse,* 1986] has redeemed the novella in many respects by uncovering Meyer's true intent in writing it, namely to document through the medium of historical fiction developments in the science of psychology (particularly hypnosis) during the last decades of the nineteenth century. Hansen's extraordinarily well-documented and well-argued study accounts for the flaws without trying to diminish their impact on an aesthetic evaluation of the work. His is the most detailed study of the novella to date and will very likely continue to be unmatched in Meyer-scholarship.

Nonetheless, this [essay] will add observations on an aspect of the novella which Hansen overlooks and which bears extension to other fictional-historical texts, namely the discursive mixing which occurs when the historical text and the (author's) historical context are culturally incompatible. This discursive mixing is clearest in the figure of Meyer's paradoxically peripheral heroine, Angela Borgia.

According to the historical sources consulted by Meyer, Angela Borgia ought to have been an ideal heroine. She was a figure of noble stature, of moral purity and integrity, of physical beauty and of an inner strength which would enable her to hold firm while opposing the corruption of the Italian Renaissance. The juxtaposition of Angela with her cousin Lucrezia—"2 Frauen, eine mit zu wenig, die andere mit zu viel Gewissen"—might have achieved this integral aspect of Angela's characterization. Hers was to be a nature of constancy and straightforwardness in contrast to a time of "unverschämter Wahrheit und gründlicher Lüge." Indeed, each time Angela appears in the novella, Meyer reiterates in slight variation the initial description of his heroine:

> [. . .] mit einem zarten Flaum auf den Wangen und dem Feuer ihrer Augen, [entwickelte sich in Angela] eine gewisse ritterliche Tapferkeit, nicht nach dem duldenden Vorbilde ihrer weiblichen Heiligen, sondern mehr nach dem kühnen Beispiel der geharnischten Jungfrauen, die in der damaligen Dichtung umherschweiften, jener untadeligen Prinzessinnen, die sich der Schwächen ihres Geschlechtes schämten und welche zu handeln und sich zu verteidigen wussten, ohne dabei die Grazien zu beleidigen.

> So erwuchs Angela kraft einer edeln Natur zu einem widerstandsfähigen und selbstbewussten Mädchen, zu dem, was das Jahrhundert in lobendem Sinne eine Virago nannte.

Unfortunately, Meyer's heroine is never characterized any further than in such superficial descriptions. In fact, other figures in the novella, by reacting negatively to the virago-type and undermining the unequivocally positive image outlined above, seem to work against the creation of a positive heroine. Rather than portraying an ideal

Renaissance woman, Angela is in the end more nearly an illustration of the later Enlightenment view that a woman who acquires the qualities of a man—no matter how positive—loses her own.

As will be shown, the actual Angela of Meyer's text, as compared with the apparently intended Angela based on the positive understanding of the Renaissance virago, is a victim of the inevitable historicity of thought; that is, Meyer and the major nineteenth-century historians who served as his sources could not help but conceptualize the Renaissance and its virago in the context of late nineteenth-century discourse. Meyer thus inevitably creates a fairly typical image of a beautiful, sensitive woman in love with a man; yet this very nineteenth-century type fails as a figure in the novel because of her unyielding "masculine" strength of character. Angela is finally defined by two mutually exclusive stereotypes—a masculine ideal applied to a woman in the figure of the virago, and a Kantian ideal of the feminine. She is ultimately the unsuccessful intermingling of two disparate cultural discourses (Renaissance and Victorian) which express directly opposing views of what a virago is and how she fits into the society around her.

Angela Borgia was completed in 1891, only months before Meyer's final mental breakdown, and, as noted above, has been discussed in scholarship chiefly for its failures. These are several: the language is not as finely honed as in Meyer's earlier work, leaving it somewhat more awkward in syntax and more burdened with superfluous adjectival modifiers than in earlier prose. This has been understood to be a function of the time constraint under which Meyer worked as he realized his health was failing. Related to this are narrative inconsistencies regarding such elements as the chronology of events, and the motivation of characters. In addition, the narrator is heavy-handed in the interpretation of each carefully inserted symbol within the context of the narrative, denying them the usual multiplicity of meaning lending depth to any reading of the work. The two most obvious examples of such narrative meddling—untypical of Meyer, who usually left his symbolic moments ambiguous—are the statue of the cupido whose broken wings and strewn arrows illustrate the taming of Lucrezia Borgia's passions in marriage; and the red cross on Angela Borgia's brow resulting from the pressure of her forehead on the bars of Don Giulio's prison window. Pater Mamette interprets this last symbolic image for the benefit of Lucrezia (and the reader) in the final chapter of the novella.

Finally, the major puzzle in the minds of the critics has been Angela Borgia herself, cousin and handmaiden to the notorious Lucrezia Borgia. While providing a central impulse to the action of the novella, Angela is not the focal point of narrative interest. She is caught between two more compelling figures, in whose lives she plays more a punctuating than a central role. Angela is a curious mixture of poorly developed heroine and *Nebenfigur,* and as such confuses the expectations of the reader. While all of these reasons for the novella's awkwardness, and in some instances, flatness, are basically valid, they retreat before the fundamental obstacle, which emerges clearly here and in Meyer's other historical novellas, namely the difficulty of rendering history in fiction.

Meyer's story-line, which provides the context for the inner contradiction of Angela's character, is a loose interweaving of two plot strands. One concerns Angela's cousin, Lucrezia Borgia, and the other, Don Giulio d'Este, the depraved younger brother of Alfonso, Duke of Ferrara. Angela accompanies Lucrezia to Ferrara immediately following the latter's marriage—her third—to Don Alfonso.

Lucrezia's new life begins in Ferrara, away from the corruption of her father's papal court and the equally corrupt influence of her brother, Cesare. Yet her struggle to extricate herself from her family's political intrigues continues and is central to one line of action in the novella. Lucrezia's intellect, her skill in politics, her wariness in intrigue, her understanding of human weakness and her ability to manipulate it, prove to be the more fascinating to Meyer and effectively obliterate Angela from the first third of the novella.

The narrator emphasizes repeatedly Lucrezia's intellectual superiority, which is augmented—and mitigated—by her enchanting beauty and a peculiar quality of innocence. This innocent appearance sparks the interest of the men around her, who are aware of her corrupt and violent past, and they are drawn to her in a literally fatal attraction. She is "schuldig schuldlos, wie die liebliche Frauenschwachheit ist." She embodies the inner ambiguity of the feminine myth: her strength lies most clearly in her weakness, and it is to this treacherous weakness that men succumb.

The critical person to come under Lucrezia's spell is Herkules Strozzi, the chief judge in Ferrara, whose "love-sickness" is diagnosed by Bembo, still another victim of Lucrezia's beauty and intellect:

> Du bist weit gefährlicher krank; denn dein Übel entspringt auf dem Gebiete deines stolzen und eigenwilligen Geistes. Dein strenger Rechtssinn verdammt das, was dein Auge beglückt und das Feuer deines Herzens entzündet. Das ist dein Widerspruch und dein Irrsal. Der Richter wird entflammt für die von ihm Gerichtete.

Lucrezia enlists Strozzi to aid her in helping her brother, Cesare—who escapes from his Spanish captors at the mid-point of the novella's action—regain his political foothold in Italy. Her desire to remain true to Alfonso is overwhelmed by the literally hypnotic hold her brother has over her. The struggle to extricate herself from these psychological bonds is the focal point of this line of action, and is successfully resolved only when news of Cesare's death reaches her.

The other plot strand involves Don Giulio d'Este, the youngest and most decadent brother of Lucrezia's husband, Alfonso. Don Giulio's entrance onto the scene coincides with the arrival of Lucrezia and Angela in Ferrara, when he is released from the Duke's dungeons as part of a general amnesty celebrating Alfonso's marriage to Lucrezia. Angela's reaction to her first glimpse of Giulio is typical of her subsequent behaviour in the novella—she cries out before all the townspeople of Ferrara: "Schade, jammerschade um Euch, Don Giulio! Fürchtet Gottes Gericht!" She is unable to contain her moral outrage and sorrow that such beautiful eyes should be the windows of a corrupt soul. With this cry—echoed by the people of Ferrara—she falls in love, and gives the impetus for a fateful series of events in Giulio's life.

Angela's love for Giulio becomes obvious to Cardinal Ippolito, another brother of Alfonso and Giulio, in the early part of the novella. Ippolito, in his turn, is in love—with Angela—and, in a fit of jealous rage inspired by Angela's impulsive praise of Don Giulio's eyes, causes the latter to be blinded. Recognizing herself as the innocent impulse behind this terrible crime, Angela repeatedly attempts to atone for a sin she did not commit. Yet each of her attempts to free herself from an undeserved guilt results in plunging Don Giulio deeper into already tragic circumstances. Her despairing declaration of love drives Giulio to attempt the revenge he would not otherwise have sought. For this he is sentenced, together with his brother and co-conspirator, Ferrante, to death. Though reprieved on the point of being executed—thanks to Ippolito's guilt-ridden intervention—he must spend the rest of his life imprisoned in Alfonso's dank dungeons. There is, however, a final resolution achieved in Angela's secret marriage to Giulio. In his many tribulations, Don Giulio experiences a religious purification of soul which culminates in the realization of his love for Angela, for his "geliebtes Unglück."

These two plot strands are finally joined in the fast-paced closing chapter of the novella, in which Angela's secret marriage to Giulio comes to light, where a long-standing conflict regarding disputed lands is settled peaceably, and other minor intrigues which were present in the background throughout the novella are resolved. These parallel plot strands, which periodically intersect, are nonetheless poorly integrated. Each could stand, in fact, on its own, although the peripheral presence of Angela serves to join them at intervals.

There are several factors leading to Angela's secondary status in the novella. The main problem lies in the dichotomy of Angela and Lucrezia. The logical method of characterization would appear to be to contrast these two figures, thus allowing the disparities to emerge more sharply. However, Lucrezia benefits here more than Angela. This is implicit in Meyer's letter to Friedrich Wyss (Aug. 22, 1891), where he states that the subject of the novella was to be:

> 2 grosse Frauen, die eine mit zu viel, die *zweite* mit zu wenig Gewissen, *diese* keine Geringere—noch Bessere—als Lucrezia Borgia, die es mich brannte, den Professoren (Gregorovius) aus den Händen zu nehmen u. in alle ihre authentischen Frevel wieder einzusetzen.

Similarly, in a letter to Emil Milan (Aug. 30, 1891):

Ein schwerer Gegenstand: Keine Geringere—noch Bessere—als Lucrezia Borgia mit dem Pendant einer anders gesinnten Verwandten (zu wenig und zu viel Gewissen).

From these letters, among others, it is apparent that Lucrezia is the focal point of Meyer's interest, whereas Angela is not even referred to by name. What might have been an effective contrast of two very different natures simply lacks the necessary balance between the figures; Lucrezia takes centre stage. The contrastive characterization fails, and Meyer's enduring interest in exposing and exploring the condition of guilt in his figures fails to materialize in this work. It may also simply be the case, as Meyer's sister, Betsy, speculated in an unpublished review, that Angela is just too pure:

Es ist sicher, die komplizierte Natur mit Verbrecheranlage ist interessanter als die einfache. Die gerade Linie, das ungebrochene Licht ist, menschlich geredet, nicht schön. Reine Naturen sind, fürcht ich, poetisch nur zu verwerten, wenn sie sich verirren, sich selbst untreu werden, darunter leiden und dafür büssen müssen.

In another more important way, Angela is overshadowed by Lucrezia in the very domain in which she ought to excel, namely as a Renaissance virago. Angela is not obviously a virago in the sense that she is educated beyond the usual standard for women of her time. Her claim to this distinction lies more in her warrior-like, *manly* virtues. This contributes to a problematic aspect of her character, since she is admired—at least from the standpoint of the narrator—for her moral courage, but not for her intelligence. Here, too, Angela loses substance in the comparison with Lucrezia. The more infamous Borgia possesses a wit and cunning which are admired in and of themselves by statesmen of equal intelligence and power, such as Ippolito d'Este, and these qualities are enhanced by her physical beauty. Angela, in juxtaposition with Lucrezia, seems naive, inflexible, impulsive, in short simply *emotional* in her courageous morality, and this, too, compromises her designation as a virago in the positive sense of the word. She thus lacks inner consistency, which can be understood as a result of a narrative ambivalence regarding what a virago might be. In addition, Angela suffers from a peculiar stasis which is emphasized by her reintroduction nearly half-way through the novella by a minimally varied repetition of the introductory description:

Unter dem durchsichtigen Himmel eines Herbsttages ritt auf einem der [. . .] Waldwege, die nach Pratello [Giulio's estate] führten, eine Amazone, schlank von Wuchs und untadelig im Sattel, welche, wie aus einem Rittergedicht entsprungen, auf Abenteuer fuhr.[. . .] In den feurigen, von flatterndem Kraushaar beschatteten Augen wohnte Wahrheit und auf dem weichen Mund neben einem kindlichen Zuge der Trotz der Liebe, ja eine gefährliche Entschlossenheit.

Since Angela had virtually disappeared from the action of the novella, the narrator had little choice but to intro-duce his heroine as the exposition and development of the second plot strand involving Don Giulio d'Este were laid out. However, even here, there is little opportunity for her development as a figure, particularly since the tragedies in which she unwillingly participates (the estrangement of Ippolito and Giulio, leading rapidly to the blinding of Giulio, and later, in direct causal relation to Ippolito's treacherous crime, the attempted revenge and coup d'état of Giulio and Ferrante) are not her own, and so motivate little inner development in her character. In fact, the narrator devotes more space to the psychological exposition of both Ippolito and Ferrante, than he does to the characterization of his heroine. Thus, Angela, a victim of innocent guilt—*schuldlos schuldig,* to reverse the paradoxical formulation describing Lucrezia—poses an interesting puzzle. Not only is she displaced in her title role as heroine and overshadowed in the comparison with her cousin, but she is cast in inconsistencies, which render her narrative development problematic.

The elements which are essential to her are her warrior-like posture, her love of truth, and her grim determination to adhere to her inner moral standards. The statuesque figure of the Amazon is never developed beyond this *type,* and has no psyche of any depth or contour. Angela remains flat and undefined except as she is presented to us in the description of her in the saddle. The descriptions of her are qualitatively ideal, not concrete, and her stasis as virago is further emphasized on those occasions when she does participate in the action of the novella and is permitted to voice her thoughts. These few utterances do not lend profile to the figure, nor do they reveal anything of an inner conflict in response to the tragedies and intrigues around her.

Lucrezia, Ippolito, Herkules Strozzi, Giulio and others all suffer her direct moral reproach at some point in the novella, and each responds in anger and frustration at the irritating naïveté of her rebuke. The consistency with which these outbursts are described is noteworthy. The knitted brow, the earnest eyes, the *Empörung,* accompanied by a favorite epithet ("Schmachvoll!") add one more aspect to Angela's monotonous appearance. As Giulio is about to be condemned for consipiracy, Angela cries out:

O ihr Lügner und Heuchler! [. . .] Wenn jemand gerichtet werden soll, wahrlich so bin ich schuldiger als Don Giulio!

And later in the same scene, she addresses Ippolito, who has come to beg clemency for Giulio to assuage his own guilty conscience, with equal vehemence:

Trittst du immer der Gnade in den Weg, Widersacher! Beruhige dich, du wirst Blut trinken! Hier ist keine Gnade . . . Hier ist die Hölle! . . . Um dich, mit dir, in dir war die Hölle von Anfang an! Ist es doch ein Wort des Heilands, das dich zum Greuel trieb!

In a final example, Angela reproaches both Lucrezia and Herkules Strozzi, as Lucrezia encourages Strozzi to flee Ferrara and the punishment of Alfonso for love of her:

Da empörte sich die stille Angela gegen diese
Verführung—selbst zum Guten, zur Rettung.

"Richter", wandte sie sich mit heissen Wangen gegen
Strozzi, "esist schmachvoll, da Ihr zaudert. Fort aus
Ferrara! Wie? ein Mann,den die Jugend als ihr Vorbild
bewundert, ein Lehrer des Rechts, hat nicht die Kraft,
mit dem Bösen zu brechen und den Zauber eines armen
Weibes zu fliehen!—Errötet!"

Strozzi's reaction, "Was träumt diese da von Gut und
Böse? [. . .] Was phantasiert sie von Recht und Unre-
cht?", relativizes Angela's relentless morality and, in effect, discredits her purity of spirit as the whithered heart
of an old maid. He continues:

Du aber, Mädchen, schweige! Was verstehst du von
Liebe! Eine, die den Liebsten blendet—einkerkern lässt—
seinen Kerkermeister nicht besticht—sich nicht in seine
Arme schleicht—nicht sein Weib, seine Magd wird—
was weiss eine solche von Liebe!

Strozzi seriously undermines here the positive value attributed to the virago, Angela, and he is not the first of
the male figures in the novella to do so; even Giulio
claims before his tragic blinding that "Wuchs und Gebärde dieser Virago sind nicht mein Stil." What ought
to have been an ideal heroine according to the consistent
narrative descriptions becomes a figure who gives rise
to scorn in her fellow characters and ambivalence in
the reader. Although Angela is presented in a consistently positive fashion, and is praised for her courageous
morality, her words have the monotony of a shrew despite the noble sentiments expressed. At the core of this
narrative ambivalence is the concept of the Renaissance
virago.

Jakob Burckhardt's *Kultur der Renaissance in Italien*
was an important source for Meyer in much of his work
on the Renaissance, and quite definitely coloured his view
of that period. One early twentieth-century critic of
Meyer's Renaissance view, Franz F. Baumgarten, casti-
gated the obsession of both Nietzsche and Burckhardt
with the Renaissance and asserted that their love of the
Renaissance grew out of a disenchantment with the life
of the *Gründerzeit* [in *Das werk Conrad Ferdinand
Meyers. Renaissance-Empfinden und Stilkunst,* 1920].
Baumgarten characterized this as "eine Haltungslosigkeit,
ein Alles-Versuchen und Nichts-Können, das Gegenteil
einer organischen Kultur." He diagnosed the "Renaissance-
ism" of the late nineteenth century as an offspring of
historicism which was in its turn born of "[d]as schlechte
Gewissen und die Kultursehnsucht des XIX. Jahrhunderts,"
and claimed that the Renaissance is merely a construct,
not an actual historical epoch. "Erst die Zeit der Renais-
sancebegeisterung und der Renaissancenachahmung hat
die Renaissance entdeckt: früher kannte man weder Namen noch Begriff."

Whether or not Baumgarten's vehement critique holds
true is a question which goes beyond the scope of this
discussion, but it does indicate how problematic any evaluation of an historical epoch must be. Obviously, such an
evaluation is necessarily determined by the context within which one—historian or critic—pursues the investigation at hand, and thus any conclusions to be drawn inevitably bear the stamp of the perspective from which judgment is pronounced. This vulnerability of the concept of
objectivity is illustrated in Meyer's virago, whose essence he drew almost word for word from Burckhardt. In
Burckhardt's text we find a revealing complex of cultural
equivocation regarding the standards by which women are
defined and evaluated:

Das ruhmvollste, was damals von den grossen
Italienerinnen gesagt wird, ist, dass sie einen männlichen
Geist, ein männliches Gemüt hätten. Man braucht nur
die völlig männliche Haltung der meisten Weiber in den
Heldengedichten, zumal bei Bojardo und Ariosto zu
beachten, um zu wissen, dass es sich hier um ein
bestimmtes Ideal handelt. Der Titel einer "virago," den
unsere Zeit für ein sehr zweideutiges Kompliment hält,
war damals reiner Ruhm.

The positive view of the Renaissance virago—i.e., as interpreted by nineteenth-century historians—seems at least
superficially to have been incorporated successfully into
Meyer's virago-heroine. Yet the relativization of the virago-
title in Burckhardt's text by the subtly pejorative use of
"männlich" and the phrase: "den unsere Zeit für ein sehr
zweideutiges Kompliment hält," could not have escaped
Meyer's attention. His male figures, such as Herkules
Strozzi, fit quite neatly into the nineteenth-century mould
in their negative reaction to Angela. Meyer's own cultural context and its accompanying discourse thus prevented
Angela, as a virago, from being a postive image.

That the complimentary nature of the virago had undergone a negative reevaluation and redefinition in the span
of time from the Renaissance to the late nineteenth
century is evident in both Burckhardt's text above, and
in Ferdinand Gregorovius's historical treatise on Lucrezia Borgia. Gregorovius remarks there with much less
delicacy:

Eine gelehrte Frau, vor welcher heute Männer mehr
Grauen als Respekt zu haben pflegen, nennen wir, zumal
wenn sie Bücher schreibt, einen Blaustrumpf. In der
Renaissance nannte man sie eine Virago.

In each of the above passages we can see the confrontation of cultural values representative of two different
historical epochs. The Renaissance accepted traditionally
masculine virtues as admirable in women and thus arrived
at the virago, an unambiguously positive figure. The virago was one representative of an overall androgynous, i.e.
humanist view of the time that virtue, while having masculine and feminine components, was not exclusively in
the possession of men or women. Positive characteristics, while being considered typically masculine or feminine, were ideally the property of *both* men and women.
For example, "[f]or a man to be fully human meant that he
had accepted his own obligation to cultivate the feminine
virtues and recognized the masculine virtues in women."

Today, however, the common dictionary definition of virago has degenerated to a "quarrelsome loud-mouthed woman; shrew." During the Enlightenment as well as during the reaction against Enlightenment thought (*Empfindsamkeit*), the "Amazon" or virago was much more a target of mockery than an object of admiration. At the time Meyer wrote his novella, the weight of definition had certainly shifted towards "shrew" as opposed to a Joan of Arc-figure, making it very difficult for a female character endowed with "masculine" courage and moral fortitude to be received favorably, not to speak of the inherent difficulties of portraying such a woman—at least from a male perspective. This ambivalence of view is evident in Angela Borgia.

In the description of Angela cited above, Meyer combines two mythic dimensions of women separated by three hundred years of history. The untarnished virgin of noble, i.e. manly, soul ("welche zu handeln und sich zu verteidigen wussten") is combined with that indefinable feminine essence ("ohne die Grazien zu beleidigen")—*das ewig Weibliche*. Such an introduction might seem to promise a central figure rich in inner conflict and strength of character such as one finds in Meyer's earlier novellas (e.g. **Gustav Adolfs Page, Jürg Jenatsch**), and seems to be reflected by the choice of name. Angela Borgia, though a historical figure, represents in her fictional rendering a synthesis of the two enduring myths of women postulated in the scholastic literature of the Renaissance, namely the truly *angelic* virtue of which only women, being closer to nature, were capable, as well as the depths of sin—epitomized in the Borgia family—to which only a woman could descend. This paradox, exemplified in her name, contributes to the ambiguity of the figure, whose positive qualities of fortitude and moral strength constitute a distinct disadvantage, despite any implication to the contrary on the part of the narrator. Perhaps not surprisingly, in light of the development in nineteenth- and early twentieth-century thought on sexual roles, these positive qualities become negative because a woman possesses them. Angela's failure as a heroine is, thus, in part due to the cultural-historical incompatibility of Meyer's images. The historical backdrop of the Renaissance is coloured by the mind-set of the nineteenth century.

We find a similar situation with regard to a heroine in Meyer's first novella, **Clara,** completed in 1856, but first published posthumously. Here, too, we find two women, the sisters Franziska and Clara—one beautiful, sweet, but not quite virtuous, the other competent, strong and eminently moral—set in opposition to one another in such a way that the comparison falls out negatively for the more competent older sister, Clara. The similarity of the constellation of characters and the implementation of the same contrastive characterization in these two novellas suggest that cultural (male) ambivalence was a determining factor in the depiction of these female figures and that this was a problem which occupied Meyer—consciously or unconsciously—throughout his career as an author. In this early novella, he writes:

Man sagt, die Liebe öffne das Herz und fessle den Geist. Nie war Claras Geist klarer und durchdringender gewesen. Im Gegensatz zu Bettino, den selbst in männlichen Wissenschaften sein leichtes Naturell immer auf die Oberfläche zwang, stand sie überall gleich auf dem Punct der Sache, wo diese zusammenhieng und beherrschte dann leicht das Einzelne. [. . .] Diese grausame Überlegenheit erschreckte Bettino, der gern glänzte und belehrte. Auch ängstigte ihn ihre Schönheit.

Clara, in the end, must relinquish Bettino to her younger, less terrifyingly virtuous sister, and enters a cloister. Though the problems are very different in this early novella, Clara's virago-like qualities reveal a direction which Angela's might have taken, had she been anything but a Renaissance figure. Lodged in a more forgiving historical context, Angela retains some of the positive aura attributable to her moral superiority, and escapes the later stereotypical fate of the cloister.

In the Renaissance the virago was a positive figure *because* she was in possession of masculine virtues. We saw this aspect emphasized in Burckhardt's description of the virago (*männlich*). To discount her for that which was praised in men was essentially a logical inconsistency. For the Renaissance, as noted above, virtues and vices may have been described in terms of male or female, but they could be possessed by either men or women. Nonetheless, the virago was an exceptional being; the majority of women were considered less exceptional. [In *The Renaissance Notion of Women: A Study in the Fortunes of Scholasticism and Medical Science in European Intellectual Life,* 1980] Ian Maclean asserts that women in the Renaissance were generally conceived in terms of two extremes: completely sinful or capable of attaining peaks of virtue not accessible to men, the latter type being in the minority. The nineteenth-century historians cited here—Gregorovius and Burckhardt—essentially agree with this view and were of the opinion that the Renaissance virago—however difficult it may be for historians to pinpoint her "essence"—was an entirely positive figure, in opposition to the majority of the female sex, which was viewed in an entirely negative light.

Both Burckhardt and Gregorovius, however, show that for them the virago was no longer contained in the inventory of positive feminine types. Other aesthetic ideals had developed for women which were applicable *only* to women. When applied to men, they could only be negative qualities, just as masculine virtues could no longer be a positive addition to the feminine. The development of the separate feminine category explains in part why the virago in Meyer's text is finally something of a *Zwitterwesen* which could not command unequivocal admiration or approval.

Angela is thus something of a lost soul because she does not fit unequivocally into any one of the aesthetic categories prescribed for women. She is perhaps too good, as noted above, due to the narrative attempt to counterbalance the inevitable nineteenth-century association of the virago with a shrew. She is willful, unrelenting in judgment, incapable of seeing any goodness in Lucrezia's weakness, and intolerant of any deviance from moral uprightness. When she loves Don Giulio in spite of his debauchery, she is horrified at herself, and condemns herself to misery, indirectly and inadvertently imposing the same upon him. Angela is unbending and thus lacking in humanity, such that her love for Don Giulio—both immediate downfall and eventual salvation for him—is unconvincing in the context of the narrative. She is more to be feared than to be pitied as she is portrayed, and this is confirmed again and again, as each time her impetuous forthrightness and honesty plunge Don Giulio further into his brother's disfavour and further from happiness.

The nineteenth-century censure of such virago-like women comes through strongly in each outburst of moral outrage and in the male reaction to them described above. In addition, her love for Don Giulio, instead of being a redeeming quality within the nineteenth-century context, is shown only as a weakness, undermining the positive Renaissance evaluation of the virago. Thus Angela is a paradox of negativity in the novella of which she is the *Titelheldin*: her feminine weakness found in her blind love for Don Giulio is evaluated negatively against the masculine standards of the virago, while her courage and moral strength are deemed inappropriate in the context of her beauty and femininity. Angela is thus not only a victim but a product of a double standard.

FURTHER READING

Burkhard, Arthur. *Conrad Ferdinand Meyer: The Style and the Man.* Cambridge: Harvard University Press, 1932, 225 p.
Critical and biographical study.

Burkhard, Marianne. *Conrad Ferdinand Meyer.* Boston: G. K. Hall & Co., 1978, 175 p.
Comprehensive overview of Meyer's life and work.

Grinstein, Alexander. *Conrad Ferdinand Meyer and Freud: The Beginnings of Applied Psychoanalysis.* Madison, Conn.: International Universities Press, 1991, 399 p.
Provides a psychoanalytical analysis of Meyer's work.

Hardaway, R. T. "Dreams and Visions in the Works of C. F. Meyer." *The Journal of English and Germanic Philology* XXXI, No. 1 (January 1932): 84-91.
Explores Meyer's use of dreams and visions in his short fiction.

———. "C. F. Meyer's *Der Heilige* in Relation to Its Sources." *PMLA* 58, No. 1 (March 1943): 245-63.
Identifies the source material for *Der Heilige* and elucidates how Meyer altered these sources.

Hart, Gail K. "The Facts of Fiction: C. F. Meyer's Dismantling of Facticity." *Seminar* XXVI, No. 3 (September 1990): 222-36.
Maintains that Meyer's historical novellas are examples of

"realistic realism"; that is, his fictions "are apparently similar but essentially different" from historical events.

Holub, Robert C. "The Narrator of Realism: Orientalism in C. F. Meyer's *Der Heilige*." In *Reflections of Realism: Paradox, Norm, and Ideology in Nineteenth-Century German Prose,* pp. 152-73. Detroit: Wayne State University Press, 1991.
Discusses the xenophobic nature of *Der Heilige*.

Jackson, D. A. "Dante the Dupe in C. F. Meyer's *Die Hochzeit des Mönchs*." *German Life and Letters* 25, No. 1 (October 1971): 5-15.
Explores the autobiographical aspects of the novella.

Jacobson, Manfred R. "The Motif of the Hunt in C. F. Meyer's *Der Heilige*." *Forum for Modern Language Studies* 16, No. 1 (January 1980): 46-52.
Determines the symbolic meaning of the hunting motif in the novella.

Klenze, Camillo von. "Realism and Romanticism in Two Great Narrators: Keller and Meyer." In *From Goethe to Hauptmann: Studies in a Changing Culture,* pp. 130-55. New York: The Viking Press, 1926.
Contrasts Meyer's life and work with that of Gottfried Keller.

Komar, Kathleen L. "Fact, Fiction, and Focus: Their Structural Embodiment in C. F. Meyer's *Der Heilige*." *Colloquia Germanica* 14, No. 4 (1981): 332-41.
Examines stylistic aspects of *Der Heilige*.

Laane, Tiiu V. *Imagery in Conrad Ferdinand Meyer's Prose Works: Form, Motifs, and Functions.* Germanic Studies in America, No. 47. Berne, Ind.: Peter Lang, 1983, 258 p.
Analyzes the imagery and linguistic forms in Meyer's novellas.

Lund, Deborah Sue. *Ambiguity as Narrative Strategy in the Prose Work of C. F. Meyer.* New York: P. Lang, 1990, 207 p.
Asserts that the ambiguity or "equivocation" in Meyer's novellas reflects the turbulent and transitional nature of his era.

Plater, Edward M. V. "The Banquet of Life: Conrad Ferdinand Meyer's *Die Versuchung des Pescara*." *Seminar* VIII, No. 2 (June 1972): 88-98.
Views the description of the biblical fresco as a symbolic motif in the novella.

———. "'Der Schöne Leib' in the Prose of Conrad Ferdinand Meyer." *Seminar* XIV, No. 4 (November 1978): 255-67.
Discusses Meyer's use of objectification in his novella.

Reinhardt, George W. "Two Romance Wordplays in C. F. Meyer's *Novellen*." *The Germanic Review* XLVI, No. 1 (January 1971): 43-62.
Explores the function of puns in *Die Hochzeit des Mönchs* and *Das Leiden eines Knaben*.

———. "The Political Views of the Young Conrad Ferdinand Meyer: With a Note on *Das Amulett*." *German Quarterly* XLV, No. 2 (March 1972): 270-94.

Assesses the changing political climate of Switzerland during Meyer's early literary career and describes him as a political moderate.

Schimmelpfennig, Paul. "C. F. Meyer's Religion of the Heart: A Reevaluation of *Das Amulett.*" *The Germanic Review* XLVII, No. 3 (May 1972): 181-202.
    Refutes the idea that Meyer's novella is simply a melodramatic and immature first work, contending that it shows depth and coherence.

Swales, Martin. "Fagon's Defeat: Some Remarks of C. F. Meyer's *Das Leiden eines Knaben.*" *The Germanic Review* LII, No. 1 (January 1977): 29-43.
    Examines Fagon's role as failed narrator in the novella.

Williams, W. D. *The Stories of C. F. Meyer.* Oxford: Clarendon Press, 1962, 221 p.
    Full-length critical study of Meyer's novellas.

Additional coverage of Meyer's life and career is contained in the following source published by Gale Research: *Dictionary of Literary Biography,* Vol. 129.

Emilia Pardo Bazán
1851-1921

Spanish short story writer, novelist, essayist, and historian.

INTRODUCTION

Emilia Pardo Bazán achieved fame in her time for her unconventional views concerning art. She introduced Emile Zola's naturalism to Spanish letters, although she herself rejected many of naturalism's principles. A prolific author in many genres, Pardo Bazán published over five hundred short stories during her career, in addition to twenty novels and a significant amount of nonfiction. Her works are noted for their psychological insight and realism, although their innovative artistic tenets are what have made Pardo Bazán one of the most important woman authors of pre-twentieth-century Spain.

Biographical Information

Pardo Bazán was born on September 16, 1851, in the province of Galicia, a region treated with great passion in her works. She was born in the village of La Coruna, a coastal town that reflected cosmopolitan as well as traditional influences. Her father was given the title of Count in 1871, and her family socialized with the aristocratic elite of society. Pardo Bazán married Jose Quiroga in 1868, and later traveled with him throughout Europe, meeting many of the leading intellectual and literary figures of the day, including Victor Hugo. She gave birth to a son, Jaime, in 1876, and a daughter, Blanca, in 1879, when she also published her first novel, *Pascual López.* Her literary productivity accelerated, and she began publishing many works, including the influential collection of essays, *La cuestion palpitante* in 1882. In the 1880s Pardo Bazán wrote most of her short stories, including the collections *Cuentos de Marineda, Cuentos nuevos,* and *Cuentos de amor.* King Alfonso XIII made Pardo Bazán a Countess in 1907, and she campaigned fiercely to be included in the academic establishment of the nation. In 1910, she became Advisor of the Ministry of Education and six years later a professor at Central University of Madrid. She died on May 12, 1921 in Madrid.

Major Works of Short Fiction

The majority of Pardo Bazán's short stories were written between 1879 and 1890. A devout Catholic, her short fiction is deeply moral. At the same time, she embraced many contemporary artistic theories, which prompted widespread controversy during her life. Also controversial was her frequent usage of a male narrator. Pardo Bazán's stories are generally divided into two categories; her early tales are lively and dramatic, while her later, more psychological and often pessimistic fiction is marked by "barrenness" and "spiritual isolation," according to Porfirio Sanchez. The majority of her works focus on characters rather than action. Most concern such broad themes as love and death, although some stories delve into such daring subjects as incest.

Critical Reception

Many critics have sought to interpret Pardo Bazán's short fiction, usually drawing from her many essays and novels for support. Others have focused on how her fiction evolved over time. The majority of critics, however, have been most interested in Pardo Bazán the woman, her contribution to Spanish literature in general, and her role in world literature in particular. According to John W. Kronik, "An insatiable intellectual curiosity and all-encompassing cosmopolitan drive that sought out—for approval or for rejection—whatever was interesting and new beyond the Pyrenees were trademarks of the Countess for which she was both praised and attacked by her contemporaries and for which subsequent critics have bestowed recognition of her."

PRINCIPAL WORKS

Short Fiction

La dama joven 1885
Insolación [*Midsummer Madness*] 1889; expanded edition, 1923
Cuentos escogidos 1891
Cuentos de Marineda 1892
Cuentos nuevos 1894
Arco iris 1895
Novelas ejemplares 1895
Cuentos de amor 1898
Cuentos sacro-profanos 1899
Un destripador de antaño y otros cuentos 1900
En tranvía: Cuentos dramáticos 1901
Cuentos antiguas 1902
Cuentos de la patria 1902
Cuentos de Navidad y Reyes 1902
Cuentos del terruño 1907
El fondo de alma 1907
La sirena negra (novella) 1908
Sud exprés 1909
Belcebú: Novelas breves 1912
Cuentos trágicos 1913
Cuentos de la tierra 1923

Cuadros religiosas 1925
Short Stories 1935
Pardo Bazán 1945
Cuentos 1984
Las setas y otros cuentos 1988
Cuentos completos. 4 vols. 1990

Other Major Works

Jáime (poetry) 1876
Pascual López, Autobiografía de un estudiante de medicina (novel) 1879
Un viaje de novios [*A Wedding Trip*] (novel) 1881
La cuestión palpitante (criticism) 1883
La tribuna (novel) 1883
El cisne de Vilamorta [*Shattered Hope, or The Swan of Vilamorta*] (novel) 1885
Los pazos de Ulloa [*The House of Ulloa*] (novel) 1886
La madre naturaleza (novel) 1887
Al pie de la torre Eiffel (essays) 1889
Una cristiana [*Secret of the Yew Tree, or, A Christian Woman*] (novel) 1890
Por Francia y por Alemania (nonfiction) 1890
La prueba (novel) 1890
La piedra angular [*The Angular Stone*] (novel) 1891
Adán y Eva: Doña Milagros (novel) 1894
Adán y Eva: Memorias de un solterón (novel) 1896
El saludo de las brujas (novel) 1897
El tesoro de Gastón (novel) 1897
El niño de Guzmán (novel) 1899
Misterio [*The Mystery of the Lost Dauphin (Louis XVII)*] (novel) 1903
La suerte (play) 1904
La Quimera (novel) 1905
Cuesta abajo (play) 1906
Verdad (play) 1906
La literatura franscesca moderna. 3 vols. (nonfiction) 1910-14
Dulce dueño (novel) 1911
El porvenir de la literatura después de la guerra (lectures) 1917
El lirismo en al poesía francesa (nonfiction) 1923

CRITICISM

John W. Kronik (essay date 1966)

SOURCE: "Emilia Pardo Bazán and the Phenomenon of French Decadentism," in *Publications of the Modern Language Association of America,* Vol. 81, No. 5, October, 1966, pp. 418-27.

[*In the following essay, Kronik describes Pardo Bazán's acceptance of some elements of Decadentism and rejection of others.*]

The fourth volume in the series of studies that Emilia Pardo Bazán had entitled *La literatura francesa moder-na* was to bear the caption of *La decadencia.* In the three previous volumes the Countess had followed the evolution of the French literary process of the nineteenth century from romanticism to naturalism, and in the last she planned to gather old notes and new ideas into an analysis of end-of-the-century trends. She never brought this project to fruition, but she did leave dispersed among her many other critical writings her ideas and interpretations touching on this phenomenon that she labeled variously "la decadencia" or "el decadentismo."

Pardo Bazán did not commit herself to a specific definition of decadentism anywhere in her writings. It is clear, however, that she gave the word a broad literary base. In terms of time, she limited the apogee of decadentism to the years approximately between 1880 and 1915. Within this period, she labeled all the general literary currents as decadent, without tracing subtle dividing lines among the sundry "isms" then extant. She did not, for example, divorce symbolism from decadentism. On the other hand, she did appreciate the social-historical phenomenon of decadence and the literary one as events that were at the same time causally related and endowed with independent life and traits. She observed and understood the first and commented on the second, offering in the course of her writings on the topic her vision of the development and character of French decadentism as well as a series of judgments of it. In the process she revealed some of her own strengths and prejudices as a critic.

Always of a relativistic bent, Pardo Bazán drew a connecting line between literary decadence and non-literary events of the day. Then, when focusing exclusively on literary matters, she continued to construct her assessments on a foundation of historical evolution. The world of letters, as she understood it, reflected the social group from which it stemmed, and she pointed out that the society of which decadent literature was a product suffered the same weaknesses as the writings. She stated the matter succinctly [in *Porvenir de la literatura después de la guerra,* 1917] in these words:

> Y como quiera que detrás de cada ideal está un vasto mar de sentimientos, y el sentimiento no quiere morir, la literatura reflejó esta protesta, y apartándose de la muchedumbre, se refugió (más o menos sincera en sus quejas y aislamientos) en la vida interior, artística y sentimental—cosa de iniciados, sin popularidad alguna—. En una hora de decadencia, fué decadente, y no podía ser otra cosa. En un mundo moralmente enfermo, fué morbosa, mostró lesiones generales de todo el organismo. Los caracteres de esta literatura, dificiles de precisar porque carece de la unidad sistemática de las escuelas, fueron el misticismo, el simbolismo, el satanismo, el sadismo, el sobrenaturalismo, la poetización de lo nefando, la magia negra, el espiritismo, el hermetismo, el ocultismo, el erotismo cerebral, y hasta, literariamente, el gongorismo, y lo que, con gracia, se ha llamado el *oscurismo* . . .
>
> La literatura no es causa, sino efecto y expresión social. Sería error ver en las escuelas y en los excelsos escritores decadentistas, que los hubo, al principio, culpa

muy grave. Mirando atrás se ve mejor hasta qué punto la literatura es obra del período en que se produce, y de los anteriores . . .

Pardo Bazán saw in the collapse of the Second Empire and in its defeat at the hands of Prussia at least a partial cause for the decadence evident in French letters thereafter [as noted in *La literatura francesa*]: "Las lesiones internas causadas por el desastre no contribuyeron poco a la aparición de los desequilibrados, diletantes, escépticos, pesimistas satíricos, melancólicos, devotos de la nada y de Satanás." There was a weakening of the spirit, a lack of regenerative impulse, a denial of nationality, a failure on the part of society to formulate the ideals that it wished to substitute for yesterday's ideals. Naturally, the literary consequence of this miscarriage of a vain last effort at national splendor had been germinating for some time, and Pardo Bazán traced to the very beginnings of the period what she called the "germen morboso" of nineteenth-century French literature. The three decades of decadentism's flowering were simply a fated heir, the victim of a consuming process that Pardo Bazán viewed not as a natural death or the inevitable end of a literary current, but as a congenital disease leading to disintegration and anarchy and which she dubbed, with combined horror and admiration, "un bello caso clínico" endowed with "dolorosa magnificencia" [*La literatura francesa*]. The forebears and disseminators of decadence in literature were of course the romantics.

Pardo Bazán habitually referred to the years falling approximately between 1820 and 1850 as the "momento romántico de escuela," insinuating thereby the existence of a future moment that would also be classifiable as romantic though not as a school. At one time she arrived at a tripartite classification of the post-romantic era, in whose successive phases—1) transition from romanticism to naturalism; 2) naturalism; 3) neoidealism, decadence, and anarchy—she perceived a rapid decomposition of the surviving elements of romanticism that, nonetheless, withstood annihilation and persisted. Usually she simply called the final phase neoromanticism, a term by which she seemed to imply not a rebirth, but a modified revivification built on a latent continuity of values in decline. Thus she ranked Mallarmé and Verlaine and all the symbolists and other decadents, despite their anti-Hugo posture, among the descendants of Hugo insofar as the poet laureate of romanticism had preceded them in looking upon words not just as representations of ideas, but full of musical, pictorial, sensual values. In the suggestivity of the language used by Lamartine, in the mysterious rhythm of his sentences, in his voluptuous languor and imprecision, Pardo Bazán also saw roots of the esthetic to which the decadents were to aspire. Barbey d'Aurevilly, with his Manichean conception of reality, was another spiritual ancestor of the group; and even in some of the poems of Béranger, whom she thought of as a preromantic, Pardo Bazán encountered ideas later exploited by "el neorromanticismo decadente"; while George Sand, with her implacable insistence on the theme of love—"este virus que desorganiza y corrompe la literatura francesa"—was to blame in a measure for the literary

decadence that brewed during the age of romanticism and became the salient feature of neoromanticism [*La literatura francesa*].

Pardo Bazán thus saw a positive element in the literary decadence that grew out of the decay of society's high ideals; namely, the stuff that for its very repugnance drew the decadents to it also aroused in them, in the end, sentimental, spiritual, Catholic tendencies.

—John W. Kronik

In more general terms, Pardo Bazán considered both romanticism and the decadent movements as temporary interruptions of the typically French proclivity toward classicism, which she evidently interpreted in the light of a social orientation: the classicists wrote not for themselves, but for the general culture of an age. Had the romantics not mended their ways after a time, she said, the public would have abandoned them just as it later abandoned the romantic offshoots that took the forms of decadentism. The Countess was treading on tenuous ground with these generalizations, and she later softened or at least drew exceptions to them; but she was of course correct to the extent that the writers of both periods—though in highly different degrees—did not make it their guiding principle to operate within the domain of reason, but rather on the basis of lyric impulse. For the romantics and the symbolists and even for later heirs of the movements, such as Valéry, this impulse resulted in a solipsistic philosophy that denied the naturalistic view of the outside world as a force imposing itself on the individual and, instead, allowed the self full freedom to impress its image onto exterior reality and actually to shape and determine its form. Understanding this, Pardo Bazán maintained that nineteenth-century lyricism was a phenomenon of individualism, more specifically a protest on the part of the rebellious individual against the formulas of society.

Pardo Bazán of course recognized fully that romanticism and what she called neoromanticism were not the same thing despite the existence of the individualistic impulse as their common denominator. Differences in motives, orientation, and expression placed the artists of the two periods in separate fields of the lyric spectrum. The symbolists, for their part—their strong lyric impulse notwithstanding—were far too calculating in their artistic paths to be set at one with the romantics of earlier in the century. The sophistication of Verlaine and others of his group distinguished them from their predecessors, who were not so careful to avoid the pitfalls of rule by sentiment. In some instances the writers of the decadence were actually no less vociferous than those of the generation before them in their rebellion against romanticism, particularly against aspects of it such as the cults of nature and ideal love. Nonetheless, though sentimentalism was not one of their driving forces, the "finde siècle" groups did draw inspiration from the romantics, and despite sharp differences their connection with romanticism after the interlude of positivism is undeniable. It must be said to the credit of Pardo Bazán that the link she established between the two periods in question by no means resulted from a moment of critical aberration on her part. Not only did she show acute observation in certain matters of detail, but she was in consonance with critics of our own day who, delving more deeply into the problem, have tended to view the entire nineteenth and twentieth centuries as a cultural development of romanticism and romanticism itself as a dynamic force that has not yet been superseded.

When Pardo Bazán set out to evaluate the literary phenomenon of French decadence, she immediately fell victim, in spite of the strength of her personality, to an unavoidable play between her inclinations as a private individual and her obligations as a critic. The cosmopolitan and the traditional were forces that drove her at all times in conflicting directions. This was the case many years earlier when she launched, in her much-cited *La cuestión palpitante,* an exposition of French naturalism, even though she could never wholly embrace its scientific implications; and the same dual impulse still guided her in her later years when she confronted the problem of decadence. Thus, she was unable to stifle her indignation at the general aspects of the decadent trends that offended her sense of propriety, and she decried the element of humbug in them. Yet, she did reserve praise, on the one hand, for those of their traits that aroused her sympathy and, on the other, for those writers among them—admittedly few in number—who showed both talent and sincerity.

Surprisingly perhaps, the realm in which the Countess was willing to grant the decadents the most concessions was in the matter of form. Her heart had always gone out to the esthetic of "poésie pure," and the writer whose name literally dotted her critical writings and who fared well at every turn was Théophile Gautier. Though she felt partial to the author of *Voyage en Espagne* for the homage he had paid her native land, what Pardo Bazán esteemed most in *Mademoiselle de Maupin* and in Gautier's poetry was the pictorial element, the delicacy and intensity of the style. She saw in Gautier a master of poetic artifice in whose impassive and impersonal art she relished the perfection of form, the picturesque, evocative descriptions, the defense of beauty in the face of the threat imposed by science. Though she did not apply the formula to her own work, she was in sympathy with Gautier's esthetic fanaticism and his Hellenic concept of precise plastic beauty, and she was willing to be known as a "ferviente devota del 'estilista impecable'."

In admiring Gautier, Pardo Bazán admired a decadent, and in praising especially the qualities of his language, she was sanctioning a central feature of decadentism and its

allies: the search for the rare, refined, and artificial, the expression of what was theretofore unexpressable, the worship of created beauty as a transcendence of nature. When dealing with writers like Gautier or Verlaine, Pardo Bazán readily warmed to the rhythmic phrasings of their prose and to their verses designed to please the senses. In fact, she credited romanticism with a stylistic renovation of poetry in that it disposed of the alexandrine and restored fresher, more lightsome meters, and she traced a marked improvement in the quality of French versification from the days of Musset, through Gautier, Baudelaire, and others, to those of Richepin, in the process of which, she said [in *Por Francia y por Alemania,* 1890], "el artificio métrico ha llegado a ser un dechado de perfección." Nothing in her writings justifies any suspicion that Pardo Bazán saw a weakening of this perfecting trend in the hands of the decadents and symbolists who were contemporaries of Richepin. This is not to suggest that she preserved any patience for what she regarded as the symbolists' willful obfuscation of ideas through language, but she did in more than one instance declare herself in favor of the symbolists' conception of poetic expression. Speaking of the symbolists as if she were dealing with a neo-baroque resurgence, she declared them to be the inevitable concomitant of an enervated age shackled to the gods of formalism, ultrarefinement, glitter, and extravagance. Yet, filtering through the meshwork of censure, gentle or captious as the occasion demanded, came Pardo Bazán's unselfconscious recognition of the metrical perfection of French poetry and of the far greater originality exercised by French than by Spanish poets of the day. She was, then, receptive to concentration on form provided that the impulse was esthetic and the result artistic, that is, in her eyes perfect and elevated.

Much as she admired its vehicle of expression, when the time came to evaluate decadentism in general terms, Pardo Bazán could not help standing in moral judgment over it. She simply did not like the attitudes of these writers whose convictions clashed with her own. As early as in *La cuestión palpitante,* she pointed out that the younger generation of the period sat in obedience to an eclectic drive that often impelled it to seek out what was strange in preference to what was beautiful. The decadents, as she saw them, liked to cry "no" to the world purely for the pleasure to be derived from open defiance of established mores. This to her constituted a waste of energies and resulted in an art whose porousness created an abyss between it and its respondent and at its worst degenerated into an incomprehensible show of superficiality. Pardo Bazán, into whose lines one can often read a certain predilection for classicism despite her love of specific romantics or symbolists, could not condone the obscuring tactics of the decadents, and she decried their perversities, their states of exaltation, their search for inspiration in immorality, their subversion of ethical standards.

In partial explanation of the decadents' failings, the Countess had recourse once more to the growth of individualism. She viewed the individualistic impulse not only as a phenomenon linking romanticism and post-romantic decadentism, but as a potent force that exercised a nefarious effect on man and his habits, and his habits included his art. Speaking of the earlier of the two periods and pointing an admonishing finger at the example of Nerval and his "locura romántica," she explained that he was a victim of the extravagance of the romantic moment. When its doctrine touched lesser figures, rather than the vigorous, exceptional ones like Hugo, Lamartine, and Vigny, it reaped as its only fruit ineptness in art and in life. Had romanticism been a healthy force, she continued, it would have given life to all men. But a doctrine that emphasized the self and eclipsed everything else, that knew no sacrifice, could not spread health and strength. Romanticism's emphasis on the freedom of the individual, on an esthetic that allowed each author the right to unlimited flights of the imagination and to the imposition of his own will, was a case of unbridled license that served as a stimulus to immorality while it reflected the essential evil, disillusionment, and iconoclasm of the age. The same moral interdiction applied inevitably to romanticism's heirs, for the tenets of egocentrism, wrote Pardo Bazán [in *El lirismo en la poesía francesca,* 1926], also suffused "todas las nociones morales y hasta intelectuales que observamos en la decadencia, último brote del romanticismo individualista, y consecuencia la más lógica de esa enfermedad del ensueno, del amor propio, de eso que se ha llamado el mal del siglo." Romanticism propelled the individual into unprecedented importance in the literary terrain, and as this impulse became intensified, the unbridling of instincts became dogma to a whole generation. And so the process, as Pardo Bazán saw it [in *El lirismo*], continued: "Con la sanción de los instintos desaparecen las responsabilidades; con la sanción de los instintos las categorías morales dejan de existir. Y esto es lo que va a predominar en el desenvolvimiento de la literatura y de la poesía rimada, hasta llegar a proponer, en tiempos más recientes, como ideal la perversidad, y como criterio de belleza la misma corrupción de las almas, refinada artísticamente. Esto será, en gran parte, lo que se llama decadentismo." Pardo Bazán clearly did not wish to conceive of man beyond the limitations that social law imposed on him. By her standards, man, whether an artist or not, was not only responsible to a group, but could find his best means of expression within the confines of the ethical structure of that group. She was, however, careful to emphasize that this individualistic moral decay did not have its seeds in French letters, but in life, which had suffered the worst of immoralities, worse even than sexual laxity: the decay and abasement of society's great collective ideals. The next moment then logically found the artist, now an emancipated being, suggesting the artistic and moral postures that contemporary and future generations were to adopt. The accuracy of this last observation was attested to by the entourage of lesser lights that clung to the giants of symbolism and mimed the standards and practices of individuals rather than of society.

Pardo Bazán naturally did not deplore the very existence of the decadent trends in literature. Rather, she centered her proscriptions on decadentism's excesses and insincerities. She joined those who assailed the "desbordamientos literarios" now and then evident in French literature but was not so ready to assault the decadent factions as such. Reporting one day on a Provençal folk festival that she had witnessed and enjoyed, she concluded [in *Por Francia . . .*] that such wholehearted simplicity was atypical of France: "La gente del Mediodía se asemeja más bien a la espanola de ciertas regiones que a los *decadentes y enervados,* o que hacen profesión de serlo, de París." *Que hacen profesión de serlo* are the key words here. They indicate Pardo Bazán's revulsion at what she considered a pose within young French literary circles and at the emptiness and falseness of their artistic gesturings. She seemed to find comfort—and not always mistakenly so—in the conviction that these experiments, which she dismissed as farcical, displeasing, and uninspired, would have no repercussions in the world.

Pardo Bazán was not blind to the fact that, with the ever-increasing anti-democratizing inclinations in art and the greater emphasis on an esthetic vision, the growth of new currents was inevitable. If one of the forms that modern art wished to take was what so many of her contemporaries, French and Spanish alike, used to call "the literature of perversion," so be it. But let the artist beware lest his perversion be a mask instead of an emanation from the soul. Fraudulent practices in literary creation Pardo Bazán would not admit, and she entertained the perfectly sensible notion that a poet must obey his own poetic impulses. If, then, a poet in being a decadent was sincere, she could not condemn him and would censure him, rather, if he were to deviate from his decadent inclinations in order to follow a path of poetic expression less suited to him, in which case his production would be false and affected. Thus, in an obituary article about Catulle Mendès, she lamented the practice among gifted and skillful writers of prostituting their art by molding it to please an inferior and perverted segment of contemporary society. She felt that art whose aim was to surprise and overpower might gain immediate success, but no matter how much effort was put into it, if the ingredients of artistic sincerity and loyalty were absent, its glory could not be lasting. "Tal es la suerte de los que en vez de despertarse pensando en sí mismos, en las formas de arte que sienten y aman, se despiertan (y acaso no han dormido) discurriendo de qué ignotas regiones traerán la pimienta y la mostaza que más sutilmente estimulen los paladares fatigados y botos." The artist is under no obligation to shy away from a scabrous exterior, but through it he must arrive at an element of human essence, and this is possible only if he truly expresses his own being ["La vida contemporánea," *La Ilustración Artística,* Vol. XXVIII, 1909].

The consequence of this personal critical assessment of decadentism on the part of Pardo Bazán was that she directed her disapproval at the untalented and uninspired mass of writers but reserved praise for those among them who showed exceptional gifts. Again and again she drew clear distinctions between the masters and the followers, the true artists and the pretentious rabble, the chieftains of the sect and the pseudoartistic exhibitionists. One problem, as she put it, was that beginning with the last two decades of the past century few vigorous literary minds arose to replace the titans of old. Those were the days of "esas relativas esterilidades en que brotan un sin-número de lindos arbustos, y ningún árbol alza majestuosa copa" [*La literatura francesa*]. She scoffed at the idea that this artistic decadence (here strictly in the sense of decay) had anything to do with the chronological phenomenon called "fin de siècle" or that it was attributable to the neo-idealistic canons. She saw it simply as a case of substitution of figures of lesser stature for outstanding literary personalities whose death left a vacuum behind them. New names and new works did, of course, fill the scene in startling quantities, and there was even no dearth of originality. But the originality then in evidence often reached extravagance and delirium and amounted to discoveries that were insignificant. The host of new writers, who sometimes did possess greater potential artistic ability and refinement than the more powerful masters to whom they owed their existence, generated a literature that was the product of calculating reflection, of a critical spirit rather than of unconscious genius and spontaneous inspiration, and hence it turned out to be wearisome and labored.

These remarks, to repeat, pertained to the quantitative force, to what Pardo Bazán liked to call "el séquito" or "la cola" of the newer literary options, not to the notable exceptions, whom the Countess always admired and read with pleasure. The strict leaders-followers dichotomy to which she adhered thus explains why Pardo Bazán viewed as neither surprising nor contradictory the appearance at the same moment and even within the same genre of distressing aberrations on the one hand and compositions of unquestionable durability, worthy of unmitigated acclamation, on the other. The renovating spirit of the age obviously was an additional explanatory factor. It is important to note the curious detail, put forth on more than one occasion, that the Countess accorded to the exclusive gifted minority privileges that alarmed her when she saw them infiltrating and poisoning the lower levels, who interpreted them wrongly and imitated them awkwardly. Interestingly, she applied this criterion not only to the literary impulse, but to social standards as well and at least in theory distinguished between the rights of the superior person and those of the inferior one who never emerged from his anonymity in the social aggregate. Consequently, Pardo Bazán was able to sing the praises of a poet like Paul Verlaine while at the same time heaping abuse on the mass of symbolist parasites whose skills were more modest and whose depositions were less honest.

Among the host of decadent writers and even among the select few who had gained her sanction, Verlaine was the one who drew from Pardo Bazán the most unwavering esteem; and the work of his that succeeded best in satisfying her demands was *Sagesse*. There was a reason for these inclinations. Despite her appreciation of the formal attributes of the art of the symbolists and their predecessors, she failed to see their vision of the poem as something hermetic, something that was its own justification as an artistic entity. Although she did not expect art to be doctrinal, she leaned towards literature with whose con-

tent she was able to step into communication. Thus, while she ranked Mallarmé among the masters and recognized his gifts as an innovator and technician, when she placed Mallarmé and Verlaine side by side, she felt constrained, in the final analysis, to confess a preference for the latter, who in her view reached more deeply into the soul and expressed himself with greater clarity. And she chose to focus on *Sagesse* because that was where she felt the connection between poet and artistic expression to be most manifest, much more so, for example, than in the pictorial nostalgia of *Fêtes galantes*. Without abandoning her sensitivity to artistic considerations, she displayed even greater enthusiasm when the content of a work coincided with her own predispositions. Ronald Hilton has pointed out [in "A Spanish Francophile: Emilia Pardo-Bazán," *RLC*, Vol. XXVI, 1952] that as Pardo Bazán's attitude toward the French became more favorable, she tended to stress the Catholic tradition in French literature. So one finds her defending Verlaine as one of the nineteenth century's admirable Catholic poets.

In reference to another poet [Hégésippe Moreau], whom she chided for bemoaning his wretchedness while rejecting every opportunity to overcome it, she suggested that the vague malaise and lack of will which she recognized as a state of mind prevalent among romantics and their successors could have been alleviated had they sought regeneration in religious faith. The poet in question did so on occasion, particularly towards the end of his life, and in other writers of the century, too, Pardo Bazán could point to at least a periodic and personal quest for religion as a consoling antidote to a prostrating character and comportment. In fact, she singled out Chateaubriand's *Génie du Christianisme* as the work that heralded a religious rebirth after a period of doubt and pragmatism, and she showed that even the latest currents of decadentism were suffused with a religious preoccupation. "De estos caracteres," she wrote of the decadent postures [in *Porvenir*], "nacieron tendencias sentimentales, y un catolicismo, no diré que tal cual lo aprobaría un obispo algo escrupuloso, pero catolicismo al fin, opuesto al racionalismo y mirando al materialismo con náusea y horror." It is of the utmost importance—and perhaps surprising—that, her own orthodoxy notwithstanding, Pardo Bazán welcomed expressions of religious concern that were clothed in thoroughly unorthodox garb. Thus, while most of her countrymen recoiled with horror at the few samples of Satanism that had come to their attention, the Countess discovered in it a healthful spiritual concomitant, for which she sought and found an explanation, one that was by no means unwarranted: Satanism, with its admixture of transgression and religious inclination, corresponded to a need of the moment, a need that had been expressed earlier by Musset and was to be reflected later in Verlaine. When the last remaining ideal in this age of ferment—the ideal of love—also finally crumbled, then there inevitably arose, said Pardo Bazán, "el misticismo que nace de la sociedad [sic; *read* saciedad] y de la vanidad del goce, de la imposibilidad de llenar con el goce el abismo del corazón." This was, in other words, a sort of inverted mysticism born of fatigued senses and driving pleasure that assumed the typically nineteenth-century character of "la falta de fe religiosa, unida al anhelo desesperado de recuperarla, o por lo menos, a la nostalgia del tiempo en que el alma reposaba en ella, y la añoranza continua de ese reposo, único capaz de reconciliarnos con el destino y con el vivir" [*El lirismo*]. In a series of comments that she made about Barbey d'Aurevilly, it became evident that Pardo Bazán did not limit her definition of a Catholic to the timid, seraphic, optimistic individual that many liked to imagine. She conceived of the religious sentiment, manifesting itself through Catholicism, as something rich, fruitful, and varied. Baudelaire, Barbey, Richepin, and Verlaine belonged to that exciting group—"los católicos que podemos llamar de la cáscara amarga"—whose Catholicism came to light in their terrified attraction to sin and in their horror of and fascination with sacrilege but whose religious sentiment was no less palpable for having emerged from corruption. "Todos los conflictos del alma humana se resumen en el pecado y el arrepentimiento," wrote the Countess [in *La literatura francesa*], who was stirred by the emotion, virility, and suggestiveness of the confessions of the sinner who was conscious of his wrongdoing and had a sense of responsibility.

Since Verlaine's religious poetry had the motif of remorse at its core, Pardo Bazán could easily accept the aberrations that he, as a decadent, incurred. *Sagesse,* the volume of verses in which Verlaine voiced all his despondency and contrition, fulfilled both the esthetic and spiritual demands that Pardo Bazán placed on her readings, particularly in the years when her natural inclinations, fanned more than a little by her contacts with Russian literature, directed her increasingly towards the currents of Christian neospiritualism. In this context she defined Verlaine as a reprobate Catholic poet as sincere in his repentance as in his recurrent transgression. To her, the verses in *Sagesse,* truly mystical, were the most exquisite fruit of the modern muse, and they prompted her to mention Verlaine in a breath with St. Francis of Assisi and St. John of the Cross. Verlaine's bittersweet revelations of the wretchedness of his soul inspired Pardo Bazán, so she avowed, to a greater understanding of the natural order and to a more profound contemplation of the eternal. His moments of deeply felt religious emotion, alternating though they did with intervals of moral disorder, coupled with his consistent clarity of expression, placed Verlaine high on Pardo Bazán's list of preferences. In her eyes, Verlaine was a Catholic, a mystic, and a sublime versifier—and none the less so for having been a decadent.

Pardo Bazán thus saw a positive element in the literary decadence that grew out of the decay of society's high ideals; namely, the stuff that for its very repugnance drew the decadents to it also aroused in them, in the end, sentimental, spiritual, Catholic tendencies. Moreover, there is perceptible in the chronology of the Countess' repeated concern with the problem of decadence a certain shift, not in the consistency of her attitude, but in focus. With the passing of years, her attacks on decadent aberrations waned, and in a significant lecture that she delivered in Madrid near the end of her career on 5 December 1916

(*Porvenir de la literatura después de la guerra*), she chose to emphasize the salutary features of decadent literature, such as its mystical undercurrent. She espoused the theory that a period of illness carries within it the seeds of rejuvenation that are destined to germinate as a period of convalescence, a theory that Ramiro de Maeztu likewise sustained when he expressed his not entirely original idea that national decadence, in distinction to old age in a man, is a process that repeats itself infinitely. So Pardo Bazán was able to write in her lecture: "Como artista, antepongo a la utilidad la belleza. Reconozco todos los peligros de aquel individualismo romántico que emancipó la personalidad, que reclamó para el artista y el escritor la libertad de afirmarse contra todo y contra todos; reconozco igualmente la exaltación ilimitada de tal principio en el segundo romanticismo neoidealista; pero también reconozco que son bellos [los dos romanticismos] y que en tales evoluciones hubo un germen vital. No fué época muerta."

In an individual whose predilections tended towards Lamartine, Hugo, Chateaubriand, and especially Musset, the unsaddling effect of the decadent esthetic is easy to understand. What is surprising is that in the course of her diagnostic confrontation with decadentism Doña Emilia's staunchly Catholic morality was not more deeply offended than it actually was. Though on many occasions, as we have indicated, she was unable to overcome her personal prejudices, she remained always conscious of the critic's need to do so; and it must be said in her favor that in the final analysis, when she was confronted with the task of determining a work's intrinsic literary merit, she was usually able to view it within an esthetic framework unmarred by any recalcitrance stemming from ethical considerations. In a commentary on Barbey she herself insisted on the equitability of her judgments: "no confundo las censuras del orden puramente moral con otras que en mi entender, son las únicas que pueden dirigirse a un escritor en concepto de tal: las que se relacionan con deficiencia de aptitudes" [*Al pie de la torre Eiffel,* 1890]. She showed later that her social convictions did not, in effect, deprive her of admiration and "involuntaria simpatía" for first-rate artists of whose behavior she might have disapproved [*El lirismo*]. For this reason she was able to see beauty in Gautier, Baudelaire, and Verlaine. The only qualification one must make is that, though she could separate it from literary merit, Pardo Bazán could never completely lose sight of moral purpose and was guided by it at least unconsciously in some of her moments of warmth towards decadentism, as when she praised Barbey for the originality of what she termed his "satanismo católico." Yet, just as in the specific case of Richepin she was careful to underscore her aversion to his political ideas, religious impiety, and personal nihilism while lauding the daring originality of his poetic inspiration and expression, so too on a general scale did she deplore the lack of ideals and values of an age while at the same time as a critic she could appreciate the accomplishments of the art produced by that age. When she abandoned the esthetic posture, she was more likely to lapse into vituperation, but her strictly literary yardsticks were sound. Only because of the objectivity of her critical vision was she able to write in the lecture already cited: "Yo temo ser antisocial cuando, no obstante todo lo que en contra de ella se ha escrito, la fase decadente de la literatura me interesa en lo hondo, y siempre hallo en sus mejores documentos algo que hace vibrar mi espíritu."

An insatiable intellectual curiosity and an all-encompassing cosmopolitan drive that sought out—for approval or for rejection—whatever was interesting and new beyond the Pyrenees were trademarks of the Countess for which she was both praised and attacked by her contemporaries and for which subsequent critics have bestowed recognition on her.

—*John W. Kronik*

Pardo Bazán is to be commended not only for having brought to her discussions of decadentism a high degree of critical objectivity often achieved at the expense of her personal leanings, but for the very fact that she took the time and interest to dwell on the decadent trends at all. An insatiable intellectual curiosity and an all-encompassing cosmopolitan drive that sought out—for approval or for rejection—whatever was interesting and new beyond the Pyrenees were trademarks of the Countess for which she was both praised and attacked by her contemporaries and for which subsequent critics have bestowed recognition on her. Never a slave to the demands of modesty, Pardo Bazán once said of herself: "Yo agradezco a Dios que me haya dado gusto comprensivo, sensibilidad dispuesta para asimilarme todas o, por lo menos, muchas y muy variadas manifestaciones de la belleza artística" [*Retratos y apuntes literarios,* published earlier in her *Discurso en la velada que la ciudad de Salamanca consagró a . . . Gabriel y Galán,* 1905]. Her self-assessment was correct. She was quick to attack the neophyte who in his critical haste failed to think independently and rushed capriciously and ebulliently into an embrace with whatever was novel, but she was equally reproachful towards those who condemned new currents without taking the time to examine them. She defended doctrines as diverse as classicism, romanticism, naturalism, and decadentism because in all of them, amidst a quantity of erroneous ways, there existed, as she put it, a soul of esthetic truth.

Wide though the Countess' knowledge and contacts were, in no national literature was she as well versed as in French literature. One of her contemporaries went so far as to characterize her as "par l'esprit et par la culture, une véritable Parisienne" [Enrique Gómez Carrillo, "Mme. Pardo Bazán à Paris," *Mercure de France,* LX, 1906].

She first visited the French capital when she was just under twenty and returned innumerable times thereafter, occasionally for extended stays. She attended literary gatherings there, became personally acquainted with many of the important writers of the day, and read voraciously the works of both major and minor figures. Most important of all, perhaps, she felt akin to French intellectual society and judged its forms of expression simultaneously as a Spaniard and as a cosmopolite.

Pardo Bazán's critical approach based on evolution—the method of Brunetière and others of her time—now is generally regarded as antiquated. Occasional contradictions in her essays, attributable in large measure to the immediacy of the impressions derived from her wanderings and the eclecticism of her literary interests, render more difficult the task of systematizing her thought. In addition, she was neither sufficiently methodical nor consistently dispassionate enough to leave behind her a body of definitive judgments on the decadent trends with all their aims, shortcomings, and achievements classified in an orderly, scientific fashion. Pardo Bazán was in some respects more a journalist and chronicler than a literary critic. Nevertheless, whatever the limitations and weaknesses of her critical method, it must be recognized that many of her opinions have not lost their validity. She was a perspicacious phenomenologist, and her judgments were marked by such equilibrium and discernment that her conclusions can even today be considered interesting and astonishingly accurate and original.

With her comments on French decadentism Pardo Bazán contributed both to posterity and to the contemporary scene. Those among the succeeding literary generation who denied the procedures and ideas of Pardo Bazán and her generation had to read and understand their works before they could issue a legitimate protest, and in so doing they naturally learned much from their forebears. Those who read the Countess' articles and books or heard her lectures did not have to turn to Darío to make a first discovery of the beauties of symbolism. The impact that Pardo Bazán exercised on her contemporaries through her importation into Spain and proclamation of foreign literary fashions was significant. Pardo Bazán explained what was happening in Parisian literary circles of the moment. She introduced new names to her Spanish readers and was one of the earliest to write of important artists, like Verlaine, who were to gain prominence later on. She centered attention on them not only after the turn of the century, but in the preceding ten years. She was open to decadentism, as she was to other currents, at a time when contemporary critics like Valera and Menéndez Pelayo turned a deaf ear to it and even Clarín was fearful and skeptical. Pardo Bazán laid before her educated countrymen the traits and precepts of the decadent mode and told them what she thought of it. Decadentism never did gain an avid following in Spain, and its detractors were still vociferous in the twentieth century (Unamuno was a notable case in point); but the inroads that the worthiest elements of the esthetic of decadence were to make into Spanish literature, poetry in particular, did so with forceful assistance from Pardo Bazán.

Porfirio Sánchez   (essay date 1969)

SOURCE: "How and Why Emilia Pardo Bazan Went from the Novel to the Short Story," in *Romance Notes,* Vol. 11, 1969, pp. 309-14.

[*In the following essay, Sanchez describes Pardo Bazán's shift in artistic focus toward short fiction.*]

Emilia Pardo Bazán published her first novel, *Pascual López, autobiografía de un estudiante de medicina* in 1879, and her last of twenty novels, *Dulce dueño* in 1911. Between 1879 and 1890 she published ten of her twenty novels and only nine of over five hundred short stories. In what here will be called her second period of writing, that is from 1900 to 1919, Pardo Bazán dedicated more and more of her time each year to the short story and less to the novel. During these last years she wrote close to three hundred short stories and only four novels. The last eight years of this period were dedicated solely to the short story.

It is obvious that Emilia Pardo Bazán did go from the novel to the short story in her creative development, as her own literary production indicates, but was this change something that happened haphazardly, or was it part of her artistic growth? This is what we shall try to demonstrate here.

Emilia Pardo Bazán's novelistic and short story production demonstrate two distinct procedures. Her early works, written from 1879 to approximately 1900, parallel the practice of Galdós and Pereda, as emphasis is placed on a pretended close observance and faithful portrayal of everyday reality. Usually centered around a not clearly delineated protagonist or narrator, these first works are fraught with colorful descriptions of Galician landscape as a background and with unrestrained literary realism. Julián, the priest that comes to *Los pazos de Ulloa* is met by the following view on the morning after his arrival: "El valle ascendía en suave pendiente, extendiendo ante los pazos toda la lozanía de su ladera más feraz. Viñas, castañares, campos de maíz granados o ya segados y tupidas robledas se escalonaban, subían trepando hasta un montecillo, cuya falda gris parecía, al sol, de un blanco plomizo. Al pie mismo de la torre, el huerto de los pazos asemejaba verde alfombra con cenefas amarillentas . . ." In this first period (between 1879 and 1900), the life motif is predominant, and there is a strong dramatic environmental relationship between the character and his surroundings. An illustrative title of her first period is *La Madre Naturaleza,* or the life motif, where the animal quality or instinctive nature of the individual is dominant. Examples of her last period are either *La quimera* (1905) or *La sirena negra* (1908), where the death motif prevails. The thematic difference in Pardo Bazán's entire period of literary creativity can also be seen by comparing two of her characters, Pedro Moscoso in *Los pazos de Ulloa* and Gaspar de Montenegro in *La sirena negra.* The predominant theme in relation to Pedro Moscoso, as in most of her earlier works, is that of man and his environment, of his actions and reactions as he moves

through a friendly or monstrous milieu. Pedro Moscoso is depicted in a semianimalistic stage, very much concerned with all the animal functions, such as reproduction, gestation, breeding, feeding, drinking, hunting, etc. This same Pedro Moscoso will first have an illegitimate son (son of the instinct), before he gets married to another woman whom he selected under the guidance of reason. Of the two unions, the instinctive is the successful one, inasmuch as it produced the son he wanted. By his lawful wife he has a daughter, which to him was indicative of failure since he is thus denied a legal heir to his name. In the sequel to *Los pazos de Ulloa* the reader will witness the complete triumph of matter over mind, the incest of the half-brother and sister brought on by the sensuous environment that surrounds them. In reference to Gaspar de Montenegro on the other hand, one can note that Emilia Pardo Bazán's philosophical attitude and many elements of her style are anticipatory of twentieth-century literary themes and techniques. She adopted and refined what she had learned of the use of psychological analysis and quixotic symbolism, to develop a narrative technique employing the multivalent subjective attitude and the figure of the contemplative hero which are found today in prose fiction. She presented the so-called "resigned" hero and the truly "resigned" hero, who withdraw from life instead of facing reality.

Writers like Pardo Bazán or Pereda have been taken to task for burdening their pages with an excess of tedious minutiae. [Emilio] González López compares her unfavorably in this respect with some fellow Galicians [in *Emilia Pardo Bazán, novelista de Galicia,* 1944]. It is quite evident that doña Emilia was very generous with details, especially in her earlier novels about Galicia, following what she had learned in Zola's books, although never reaching his extremes. But it is not only the amount but the kind of descriptive detail that gives these scenes their special meaning, their lyrical perspective. This poetic quality in the works of Pardo Bazán is indeed extremely important if one is to get the correct perspective of her entire literary development. This is precisely the stylistic change that she developed as a result of her thematic change. In her earlier and later works she made extensive use of similes in her descriptions, but there is a big difference in the terminology used in each period to present those similes. In her novels of the first period she usually compares people to homely and earthy objects, such as the following examples will illustrate. In *Los pazos de Ulloa* the wet nurse brought there was "una muchachona de color de tierra, un castillo de carne: el tipo clásico de la vaca humana." (I, 230) In *La Tribuna,* the hands of the woman who work in the cigar factory were "manos nudosas como ramas de árbol seco." In the similes of her later works she compares people to beautiful things, such as flowers and precious stones. This increased tendency towards the poetic in her later works also parallels her preference at that time for the short story. This lyrical tendency in the style of Pardo Bazán's final period of writing is further substantiated by the author's recurrent use of nouns, verbs and adjectives in groups of three, which further enhances the lyrical quality of her later works. This technique of triple enumeration is almost nonexistent in her earlier novels. In *La Quimera* (1905) one can see the following example: "El Cordero místico, manso y herido; nerviosos ataques, ahogos y asfixias pasajeras; es un destino humano, corto, intenso . . .".

In her earlier works . . . the drama is played on a verdant stage streaming with life, but in her later works, the blackness and barrenness of the settings place the spiritual isolation of the protagonist in relief.

—*Porfirio Sanchez*

With the writing of her last three novels (*La Quimera, La sirena negra,* 1908, and *Dulce dueño,* 1911), Emilia Pardo Bazán, by choice, changed over to the short story, a genre which she was to continue for eight more years after her last novel.

The majority of the short stories of Pardo Bazán, and especially those that have some small object, act, or look as the central part of the plot, are illustrative of some of her best short stories.

Some critics say that the *theme* of a good short story can be summed up in one sentence. This is rather an artificial canon of criticism, yet valid in the sense that most good short stories are based on some motif from past literature or from life itself. The situations and the actions depicted in the motifs of literature contrive to illustrate a moral dealing with some aspect of human experience or character: greed, gratitude, selfishness, ingratitude, patience, improvidence, industry, or any other expression of life itself. Each one has good artistic unity with no long descriptions, with practically nothing that is irrelevant or does not contribute to its total meaning. The action in each is direct and immediate, with the small object or act in each instance suggesting further events and intensifying the reality.

So it can be seen that the *motivating theme* that gives the short story as well as the novel its structure, will usually have as its center a combination of human traits, reactions, and experiences, with the one exception; the short story can and often does revolve around one small object, whereas in the novel this is rare. Emilia Pardo Bazán, as a critic of Taine says: "En la vida diaria todos procedemos como Taine, y de las pequeñeces deducimos cosas serias" [Emilia Pardo Bazán, *La literatura francesa moderna—El Naturalismo, Obras Completas,* V. 3, n. d.]. It was about "pequeñeces" that Pardo Bazán wrote her best short stories. In fact, of her last two hundred and seventy-three short stories, at least one hundred and twen-

ty-five are developed on one of the points mentioned above. In each one the author gives the reader just enough of an idea, presents just enough information concerning the forces behind the chain of events, to enable the reader to accept what appears to be a simple story. Part of the *plausibility* here is the result of the restraint on the part of the author, something she preferred not to do in her first period of writing.

Thus with *La Quimera* and *La sirena negra,* Emilia Pardo Bazán will complete a long evolutionary process going from the novel to the short story. Because of this change, in her later works, Pardo Bazán becomes very conscious of her style and thematic development, where her main characters are now, as one critic says, "no longer of real flesh and blood; they are schematic, shadowy, unnatural, pathological" [C. C. Glascock, "Two Modern Spanish Novelists: Emilia Pardo Bazán and Armando Palacio Valdés," *University of Texas Bulletin,* n. 2625, July 1, 1926]. In the later novels and many of the stories of Pardo Bazán, action, character, and narration are all subordinated to one theme, that of time and death and the relations of these two to that of the individual personality. Because of deliberate avoidance of detailed, realistic descriptions of the exterior reality in her works, the drama of personality will now be played on an empty stage, or, at least, against a very general one. Illustrative of this aspect are some of her short stories like: **"El fuego"**, 1900; **"El pozo de la vida"**, 1905; **"Un solo cabello"**, 1907; **"El sino"**, 1910, and **"Arena"**, 1912.

In her earlier works, as was mentioned earlier, the drama is played on a verdant stage steaming with life, but in her later works, the blackness and barrenness of the settings place the spiritual isolation of the protagonist in relief. It also underscores their almost complete incapacity for objectifying external reality due to their orientation toward internal or subjective reality. In her last three novels there is an analysis of one person in each, and in each case the individual is the narrator of his own life. And, just as in the short stories, the theme predominates over the aspects of time and background, the character is no longer observed in relation to his environment. In her final period, Pardo Bazán will be concerned with only one firmly outlined *case,* one character, one thing, or one act taken in isolation from society at large and, in so doing, will be going along with the current literary movements of that time, with novelists who concentrated on the psychology of their characters rather than on the external action. This is evident in her last three novels and in the majority of her short stories.

Thomas Feeny (essay date 1977)

SOURCE: "The Child as Redeemer and Victim in Pardo Bazán's Short Fiction," in *Revista de Estudios Hispanicos,* Vol. 11, 1977, pp. 425-32.

[*In the following essay, Feeny explores the symbolic significance of children in Pardo Bazán's short fiction.*]

A study of the characters in Pardo Bazán's short fiction reveals the inordinate significance she attaches to the role of the child. Repeatedly she portrays him as redeemer of man or as victim, either of society or of destiny. In an attempt to shed light on the author's particular vision of the child, I shall consider several of her many works that cast him in the role of redeemer or victim.

Through his birth, his existence, and his death will the child prove to be man's savior. In the short novel *La sirena negra* Gaspar, a wealthy voluptuary disillusioned with an existence he finds inane, feeds on thoughts of death. But his grim obsession fades as the young boy, Rafaelín, comes into his life. Awakening Gaspar's latent paternal instinct, the boy obliges him to become less self-concerned, to draw nearer his fellow man. That Pardo Bazán holds foster parenthood in highest regard is clear from even a cursory study of this and other writings. She addresses the subject most directly, however, in **"Allende la verdad,"** where she states: "todo eso de la 'voz de la sangre,' forma del instinto, es una baja leyenda fisiológica; que los hijos se engendran en nuestra psiquis mejor que en una matriz, y creer ser padre es igual a serlo . . ." Contending he is more than father to Rafaelín, Gaspar asserts: "El chico es más mío . . . que si lo hubiese engendrado materialmente."

Rafaelín twice redeems Gaspar. Though it provides him the will to live, the first redemption proves temporary, for after raping the child's governess in a moment of rage, he plans suicide. It appears that Death, whose life-long fascination for him the boy has briefly dispelled, will win after all. But Pardo Bazán's concern here is with salvation. Granted, had she omitted the last two chapters, the boy's goodness would still have saved Gaspar; these chapters, however, give impact to the novel's outcome and, more important, allow the author to strengthen the parallel between Rafaelín's relationship to Gaspar and Jesus' relationship to man. Gaspar's permanent redemption results from the boy's accidental shooting, caused during the former's attempted suicide. Ironically, while foster paternity made him recognize himself as a part of society, only at the child's death, when he is no longer a parent, can Gaspar totally identify himself with mankind and be truly redeemed. Prostrate over Rafaelín's corpse, he understands he has been forgiven and thanks the child—"el Niño," who is both Jesús and Rafaelín—for the miracle of his redemption.

Similarly, in **"El niño de San Antonio,"** it is a dead boy who finally saves his embittered father. The latter, overwhelmed by his sole offspring's death, has come to feel "misoteísmo: mala voluntad contra Dios y sus santos," who ignored his pleas to spare the child. Only the discovery of a statue of St. Anthony without the traditional babe in arms but with his finger raised toward heaven allows the man to accept his son's fate and regain his faith.

Also in this collection are two tales in which a child's life, not death, works redemption. In **"El martirio de Sor Bibiana"** a nun offers her own flesh to save a boy's arm and in doing so recovers her faltering faith. Clearly, the author views this child as the sister's redeemer, bringing redemption through life, the unscarred existence she has ensured him. **"La penitencia de Dora"** also treats a holy woman's salvation resulting from her sacrifices for another's son. St. Teodora struggles to keep alive an unwanted baby; ultimately he proves her savior, for his presence in her life enables her to make a true act of penance and attain sainthood. This plot parallels that of **"La salvación de don Carmelo"**; here, a drunkard priest takes in an abandoned baby. Certain he is the boy's father, the villagers slander him and mock the child. But at the priest's death, despite his misspent life, he gains heaven solely because of his protection of the boy and the trials this single good act brought him. In this tale the child, at first society's victim, is in the end the redeemer of the wayward priest.

In *Cuentos nuevos* Pardo Bazán stresses the redemptive powers of birth. Whether an adopted baby or one just conceived, his prospective arrival into a childless home brings hope to the barren women of **"La estéril"** and **"Vida nueva."** Similarly, in **"Allende la verdad"** the author has her protagonist long for "vida nueva," in his case the fatherhood he hopes will reform his errant life.

Related to Pardo's vision of the child as redeemer is the frequent portrayal of him as victim, either of adults or of destiny. Those children of the first category at times undergo inhuman brutalities. Blood and gore abound in **"Un destripador de antaño"**: the author presents Minia, a young orphan named for the holy martyr, as a "víctima propiciatoria," destined to suffer quietly. Her relatives' abuses only encourage the child's piety. With a display of savagery rare in Pardo Bazán, the story culminates in the girl's butchery.

In **"Sobremesa"** (*Cuentos nuevos*), unable to feed her five children, a destitute widow strangles them. Pardo injects a particular pathos into the execution of the eldest daughter; on realizing death, alone, can protect her, "la chiquilla, convencida, alargó el pescuezo y se dejó estrangular sin defenderse." The author indulges in irony and social comment, both in the short-witted professor's indictment of the widow for not having saved her money and also in the very choice of title, **"Sobremesa"**; the implication is that this woman's tragedy, and by extension the plight of all the poor, serve as little more than after-dinner conversation for the upper classes.

Pardo's compassion for hurt children pervades these writings. In **"Accidente"** she openly pities the undersized boy, "desmedrado y consumido," who strives to earn a few cents through his toil at an excavation site. By carefully detailing the need for his meager pay at home, his pride in doing a man's work, and the strain on his young body, Pardo Bazán arouses the reader's sympathies and adds poignancy to the child's death in the cave-in. This ending comes as no surprise, for the author often reveals her story's outcome in the opening pages. In *La sirena negra,* for example, as early as the second chapter she indicates Rafaelín will die and twice later alludes to his impending death. Not unaware of what some might consider a literary flaw, rather Pardo seeks, in *Sirena* and elsewhere, to suffuse the atmosphere with the inevitability of the child's death and thus point up his preordained role as redeemer or victim.

During her lifetime Pardo Bazán was often accused of writing like a man. This charge stems in part from her daring to treat forbidden or unseemly themes, such as incest, from her preference for a male narrator in many of her writings, and probably from her occasionally antagonistic personality that offended certain of her contemporaries.

—*Thomas Feeny*

These stories portray children victimized by adults or society. Among those tales that present the child as victim of destiny is **"Responsable"** (*Cuentos de la tierra*). Through carelessness a boy allows his brothers and sisters to set their hut afire; realizing his negligence, he rushes into the flames to perish with the others. Though Pardo does mention the boy's poverty, her emphasis is on his innate sense of duty that results in his immolation. Convinced he is the son of "un señor," the child believes he hears his father's voice urging him into the blaze. Here Pardo displays a keen note of irony, since the boy's father has no knowledge of his existence.

Also depicting the child as victim of destiny are two tales of striking similarity, **"La niña mártir"** (*Cuentos nuevos*), and **"Jesusa."** In each story the title character is the sickly young daughter of rich, middle-aged parents who try in vain to protect their sole offspring from death. One finds in these tales a number of similar passages, such as the descriptions of the care and luxuries lavished on the two girls; Pardo apparently seeks to contrast this extravagance with the deprivations of the poor. Also much on her mind are the miserable straits of the homeless child, for although neither story deals directly with such children, she makes pointed mention of them within the first two paragraphs of both tales. In **"La niña mártir"** she reviles the stereotypic "sañuda madrastra," whose brutality drives the child from his home. And in **"Jesusa"** she sardonically observes that "cualquier fruslería" in the home of Jesusa's parents would feed and clothe a poor child for a year. Yet at the stories' outcome we see her intention is not, after all, to plead for the poor but to show that the wealthy, too, have their sorrows. Accepting injustice as inherent to the worldly order, Pardo Bazán does not strive for social reform. To her mind, for rich and for poor, only God's mercy offers peace.

At each tale's end, both girls at last symbolically escape the protective cocoon that has isolated them from the world. In **"La niña mártir"** this break is represented by the opening of the window in the sick room, an act that seems to make the dead child smile. Jesusa's escape comes just before her death. Innocently convinced that if she imitates the poor in their sufferings, God will give her health, she begs her mother to lay her uncovered on the straw beside Jesus in a miniature manger set up in her room. At once joy fills the child's face and she dies. Thus the author implies these children, ever denied all contact with others, are in the end incorporated into the human totality. This ultimate fusion with the rest of mankind echoes Gaspar's redemption in *Sirena*.

During her lifetime Pardo Bazán was often accused of writing like a man. This charge stems in part from her daring to treat forbidden or unseemly themes, such as incest, from her preference for a male narrator in many of her writings, and probably from her occasionally antagonistic personality that offended certain of her contemporaries. Yet in her biography of Pardo [called *Vida y obra de Emilia Pardo Bazán* 1962], Carmen Bravo Villasante states the author's femininity and maternal orientation were dominant facets of her character; and we find, in fact, in most of those writings where she portrays children, her intensely maternal nature is most apparent. It is, for example, clearly a mother's compassion Pardo shows those young souls forever consigned to nothingness in **"La Noche Buena en el Limbo"**: "Asombraba y entristecía considerar tal floración de capullos helados antes de abrirse, tanto fruto verde tronchado por el granizo, tanta cuna vacía, tanta desesperada madre (*Cuentos nuevos*)." That Pardo Bazán inevitably chooses a child for the role of redeemer or victim reflects her maternal outlook.

Baquero Goyanes has suggested [in *El cuento español en el siglo XIX* 1949] that among Spanish *cuentistas* of the last century, the frequent appearance of the child might well denote "un deseo de pureza, de sencillez" on the part of the author. Yet youthful candor is often violated, as we have seen, and not only in Pardo's writings. Clarín's *Pipá*, for example, the graphic account of society's callous destruction of a young boy, represents, in effect, the obliteration of innocence. Like Clarín, Pardo is aware the child, in his vulnerability the natural prey of evil, readily lends himself to the role of victim.

Since most of the adults who people Pardo Bazán's pages are frustrated, psychotic, or otherwise disturbed, in her quest for purity and guiltlessness, traditional requisites for the role of redeemer and victim, the author must turn elsewhere. Her religious education no doubt leads her to envision Jesus as the supreme example of persecuted innocence. But, although Jesús the man was crucified, and as victim brought redemption, uppermost in her thoughts appears to be the image of Jesus the child. Recall that in *La sirena negra* she has Gaspar speak of "el Niño que hizo el milagro . . ." Thus Pardo's search for innocence, together with her maternal and religious orientation, would account for her choice of the child to serve as victim and redeemer.

Thomas Feeny (essay date 1978)

SOURCE: "Pardo Bazán's Pessimistic View of Love as Revealed in *Cuentos de amor,*" in *Hispanofila,* Vol. 64, 1978, pp. 7-14.

[In the following essay, Feeny reviews the stories collected in Pardo Bazán's Cuentos de amor.*]*

On examining Emilia Pardo Bazán's collection of short stories intitled **Cuentos de amor,** the reader might well wonder at the exceedingly grim view of love the author reveals in these tales. For although the theme of love is touched upon in nearly all of the forty-three stories, it will almost never be that of joyous or blissful love. Rather, Pardo Bazán chooses to write about love unfulfilled (**"El viajero," "Más allá"**); or love betrayed (**"La perla rosa," "Así y todo . . . ," "Sor Aparición," "¿Justicia?"**). She prefers the themes of unrequited love, treated in some depth in **"El dominó verde,"** or aberrant love that inflicts pain and death (**"A secreto agravio," "Los buenos tiempos," "Delincuente honrado"**). Though there are starry-eyed lovers, they appear singly, never in pairs. Men and women are, for varying reasons, unable to make each other happy. One cannot, in fact, easily say which sex fares worse in these tales. For while Pardo displays a penchant for etching weak male characters, resounding failures in matters of the heart, she also fancies scheming women who employ their sexual allure solely for personal gain.

Despite her contention that literature, like life, should depict both "lágrimas y risas, el fondo de la eterna tragicomedia del mundo" [Preface to *Un viaje de novios,* 1919], within the pages of **Cuentos de amor** one finds Pardo invariably emphasizes the most tragic aspects of love. In an effort to account for the disillusion and cynicism that suffuse these stories, let us examine them in some detail.

The first two tales, **"El amor asesinado"** and **"El viajero"** set the tone of the collection. The former deals with a woman's rejection of love, personified by a Cupid-like child. She flees from him and finally strangles him, only to discover in doing so she has brought about her own death. **"El viajero"** recounts a woman's abandonment by love. Pardo's choice of the traveler to symbolize love indicates the transitoriness she ascribes to that emotion. Although, owing to the fantastic quality of these stories, her pessimism does not strike one as extreme, it increases as she treats more realistic situations. In a few tales, such as **"El corazón perdido"** and **"Mi suicidio,"** the author displays a mildly ironic humor rather rare in her writings. In the first, the narrator attempts to restore a lost heart to the woman who has mislaid it, but though all those he finds are without a heart, none will claim it. When finally a young girl accepts his gift, she dies from an excess of sentiment. Despite Pardo's light touch, the clear implication is that woman, heartless in the literal sense, is equally so in the figurative.

The irony in **"Un corazón perdido"** becomes more evident in **"Mi suicidio."** Here a recent widower, planning suicide because of his grief, discovers his late wife, whom he thought perfect, was unfaithful. Rather than shoot himself, he shoots her portrait. He is but the first of several in **Cuentos de amor** deceived by their wives. Noteworthy, however, is the author's procedure for pointing up the irony of the outcome. Early in the tale, by means of the protagonist's reminiscences while studying his wife's portrait, Pardo leads the reader to understand the dead woman was in all ways a model spouse. Then compromising letters appear, and the reader finds he, like the husband, has been misled. This literary practice of idealizing an initial situation that eventually proves far from ideal, can, of course, lend an ironic twist to the denouement. But in this collection the practice becomes so frequent as to lose its effectiveness. First appearances cease to mislead when they become immediately suspect. More than coincidental, however, is that just as in **"Mi suicidio,"** the initial idealized situation of tales like **"Los buenos tiempos," "El encaje roto," "¿Justicia?"** and **"A secreto agravio,"** depicts the joy of apparently happy couples; that their bliss proves fleeting or illusory reveals Pardo's disillusion with love's permanency. In fact, in **"Los buenos tiempos," "A secreto agravio,"** and **"Así y todo . . ."** one member of the pair ends up slaughtering the other.

The irony that characterizes the author's jaundiced view of love in the early stories turns to bitter cynicism in **"El dominó verde,"** Pardo reveals her thoughts on unrequited love when the protagonist, scorning his former beloved's affection, asserts: "Mas no es culpa nuestra si de este barro nos amasaron, si el sentimiento que no compartimos nos molesta y acaso nos repugna, si las señales de la pasión que no halla eco en nosotros nos incitan a la mofa y al desprecio, y si nos gozamos en pisotear un corazón, por lo mismo que sabemos que ha de verter sangre bajo nuestros crueles pies."

Granted it is possible the character speaks for himself and not for the author; yet the length and acrimony of his attack, not entirely justified by the events of the story, make one suspect Pardo Bazán has let her own skepticism show through. In discussing the importance of observation to a novelist, she writes: "La novela es traslado de la vida, y lo único que el autor pone en ella es su modo peculiar de ver las cosas reales" [Preface]. Although she is talking about analysis and the novel, it would follow that to the short story, as well, an author must bring his particular way of viewing things. And if his view of love and lovers is essentially bleak, then in his treatment of these subjects the pessimistic note will predominate.

Even when a happy outcome would be most plausible, Pardo Bazán purposefully shuns it. Consider **"Martina,"** for example. Though there is no obstacle to the lovers' marriage, almost as an afterthought the author somewhat unconvincingly dispatches the lady off to a convent that she might not die of happiness—"morir de felicidad"—at her beloved's side. When, on rare occasion, Pardo shows herself at all generous to those in love, she does so begrudgingly. In **"Más allá,"** upon the lovers' death their two souls become one. But since his is earmarked for purgatory and hers for heaven, as a single entity they can enter into neither region. Thus they are denied forever the peace of "la eterna bienandanza."

Although nearly all the tales of *Cuentos de amor* **reveal Pardo Bazán's cynical view of love, of special interest are a number that, within the limits the short story allows, present psychological studies of people whose afflictions are related to love.**

—*Thomas Feeny*

Another thought frequent in Pardo Bazán's writings and doubtlessly related to her disillusion is that time must inexorably take its toll. This is particularly evident in **"Primer amor," "Sor Aparición,"** and **"Cuento soñado."** In the first tale, the repulsive old aunt who sprays her young nephew with spittle as she cackles at him contrasts starkly with the seductive woman in the photo taken years before. Sparing no details in her description, Pardo appears to share the boy's revulsion at time's handiwork. And in **"Sor Aparición,"** the portrait of the withered nun, with her "cara de una amarillez sepulcral, su temblorosa cabeza, su boca consumida" contrasts with the description of her as a young, passionate girl, an "asombro de guapa." In these tales one laments the fading of youthful beauty. Similarly, when the aged queen of **"Cuento soñado,"** worn with the cares and duties of her office, returns to the scenes of her childhood, the author describes her as overwhelmed by the irretrievable loss of "la juventud, la ilusión, la misteriosa energía de los años primaverales," whose passing has left her faded and weary.

In her essays and criticism Pardo Bazán frequently declares her fiction teaches no lesson. "Aborrezco las píldoras de moral rebozadas en una capa de oro literario," she writes in the preface to *Viaje de novios.* Yet in a number of her short stories there is a subtle moral, for the author, with obvious relish, repeatedly demonstrates that in matters of love often man's best efforts are doomed to naught. In **"La perla rosa"** the generous husband indulges his unfaithful wife but fails to win her affection. The industrious shopkeeper of **"A secreto agravio,"** on learning of his wife's betrayal, sets fire to his hard-earned business and to his spouse and her lover. And despite his most sincere endeavors to preserve a single illusion about woman's capacity for purely spiritual love, the protagonist of **"La última ilusión de Don Juan"** ends up totally disenchanted.

Evidence of Maupassant's influence on her short stories appears in *El naturalismo,* one of Pardo's several volumes of criticism on French literature. Admiring his

objectivity, she also extols "la forma, . . . lo límpido de la prosa, su naturalidad." In praise of his short stories, she writes: "No son meramente de gorja: hieren otras cuerdas dramáticas, dolorosas, irónicas: la lira humana." As we have seen, the sense of the ironic and emphasis on man's tribulations she admires in Maupassant because they are so much a part of life abound in her own short stories.

Maupassant chose the short story, Pardo Bazán declares, as most suited to his temperament, and in this genre he succeeded in expressing "su concepción de la vida—, pesimista, sensual y cruel." These comments alone may explain why Walter Pattison [in *Emilia Pardo Bazán,* 1971] and other critics attribute much of the pessimism in Pardo Bazán's short stories to Maupassant's influence. It is well, however, to note her remarks in *El naturalismo* concerning other French decadent writers. Having speculated that the early symptoms of Maupassant's ultimate madness had for many years intensified his pessimism, she adds that personal anguish likewise affected the gloomy outlook of a number of his contemporaries: "La tensión e hiperestesia nerviosa de los Goncourt, causa probable de la temprana muerte del menor; la epilepsia de Flaubert; el agotamiento que excesos de la mocedad determinaron en Daudet y que le obligaron a intoxicarse con morfina; la crisis de misticismo modernista de Huysmans, a quien conocí tan enfermo del estómago—y hablo de novelistas únicamente—, arrojan sobre este período, en mis recuerdos, una sombra de desolación íntima, más oscura que la melancolía romántica."

Thus, while Maupassant's influence may well account for much of the disillusion in her short stories, Pardo does acknowledge that the physical and mental sufferings of other French decadents, many personal acquaintances, also worked to cast a grey pall over her recollections of the era.

Although nearly all the tales of *Cuentos de amor* reveal Pardo Bazán's cynical view of love, of special interest are a number that, within the limits the short story allows, present psychological studies of people whose afflictions are related to love; in this category falls **"El dominó verde,"** already discussed. Also included is **"Delincuente honrado,"** whose title character proudly boasts of having redeemed his honor by butchering his young daughter whom, in his madness, he has confused with his unfaithful wife. In **"Un parecido"** the protagonist suddenly realizes that despite the uncanny resemblance between the woman who has rejected him and her half-sister, who loves him, the latter has no appeal since she can exist for him only in her resemblance to his first love. **"El fantasma"** deals with the amorous fantasies of an unstable, sensitive woman wed to a prosaic husband. Her excessively romantic nature has her choose as her fictitious paramour a typical Don Juan figure, "un perdido y un espadachín." The author's attitude toward the wife's hallucinations bears mention; she neither pities nor mocks the woman's delusion but rather maintains a cool detachment while sketching in the details of her illness. Under gentle attack, however, is the foolish sentimentality of the story's narrator. Referring to his "fatuidad de muchacho" and "petulancia juvenil," he feels only embarrassment on recalling his youthful ardor for the wife. Thus, once again, romantic love fares ill at Pardo's hands. The wife's passion is, after all, absurd because her affair is pure illusion; and the young man, in retrospect, views his rapture as mere puerile infatuation. Pardo Bazán's contention, it appears, is that the only genuine sentiment is the stolid husband's devotion to his distraught spouse, an emotion, in the final analysis, more protectively fraternal than conjugal.

In **"La culpable"** Pardo recounts the trials of a loving woman ridden with remorse for having run off with her fiancé before their marriage. Her socially conscious parents, preoccupied with public opinion, never forgive her brief moral lapse. And although, to amend the past, she vows to be a perfect wife, her husband rejects her devotion and plays upon her guilt complex. Magnifying the gravity of her error, she attempts to atone through complete self-effacement. She endures her husband's philandering in silence, convinced she has no moral right to reproach him. In this story Pardo portrays the wife as victim of her "amante corazón," that leads her to risk reputation for love. The author details at length the bitter anguish the woman's sense of unworthiness inflicts upon her. For, though she is guilty in society's eyes and, ironically enough, in the eyes of the man who is the cause of her sorrows, it is her own exaggerated sense of guilt that finally destroys her life.

Although in **"La culpable"** Pardo maintains less detachment than in **"El fantasma,"** and openly sympathizes with the stricken wife, still the author regards the woman's tragedy as inexorable. For it is not merely that she has given her affection to an unworthy man; no one, neither husband nor parent nor child, Pardo implies, could banish the wife's torturous sense of guilt. On her deathbed she receives divine pardon. But, Pardo carefully points out, this does not content the dying woman. She begs her husband's forgiveness. The hypocrisy of his kiss, given as a sign of pardon, illustrates Pardo's contention that man's forgiveness is totally without meaning.

In **"Saga y Agar"** a middle-aged man, his ardor for his wife cooled, becomes involved with his adopted daughter. Here the author traces the evolution of idylic conjugal love into passionless fraternal affection, as well as the evolution of fatherly love into illicit rapture. Pardo's customary dire view permits those involved no lasting happiness, for the tale ends in abandonment and death.

There are in this collection two tales that show striking similarities in their portrayal of woman's guile and cunning in amatory affairs. In both Pardo shows not only does love often fail to bring anything resembling happiness, but on occasion it leads to crime, disgrace and death. In **"Afra"** what immediately attracts the narrator to the title character is not a conventional beauty but the cold, imperious sexuality she radiates. Inquiring about her, he discovers she is suspected of having murdered her best friend, the fiancé of the man Afra desired. Particularly

chilling is her calculating *sang froid*; on learning of her friend's engagement, she conceals her jealousy and helps select the wedding gown. Then the two girls go bathing and though the sea is rough, Afra, an excellent swimmer, urges the other into the surf, where she drowns.

Far more revealing than the bare facts of the tale's plot is Pardo's treatment of her heroine. As a murderess, she must suffer; her punishment is rejection by her beloved, who goes off. Yet, probably because the author is so taken with the woman's determination and capability, qualities Pardo herself possessed in abundance, she really does not treat Afra harshly. On the contrary, there is more than a hint of admiration in the description of Afra's strange power over men and haughty manner shown all would-be suitors.

The title character of **"La Bicha,"** so named for her snake like appearance and evil reputation, draws men to her with a challenging sensuality much like Afra's. Expelled from a society ball as an unwelcome guest, **"La Bicha"** resolves to seek vengence on the organization's president. Employing all her meretricious allure, within five months she is secretly wed to him. As with Afra, Pardo Bazán seems to revel in depicting the woman's craft and boldness. After her disgrace, feigning remorse, she appears at the president's home to beg his forgiveness. Through tears and flattery, she soon seduces him. With their marriage, her revenge is complete; his young daughter dies and **"La Bicha"** dominates him ruthlessly.

One finds in the early pages of **"La Bicha"** explicit evidence of Pardo Bazán's dim view of romantic love's possibilities for happiness. In a quasi-serious tone the author, through her spokesman, an elderly widow, points out the irony that although man seldom complains about parents or children, whom he cannot, after all, choose, he is never content with servant or spouse, his own choices. Then by way of preface to her tale, the widow announces she will recount a story that proves man is quite unable to select a suitable partner, hence his inevitable marital grief.

Pardo's position regarding Afra and **"La Bicha"** is curious. Like the unfaithful wife of **"Así y todo . . ."** who, having murdered her husband, weds an "acaudalado caballero" and lives in luxury, Afra and **"La Bicha,"** though portrayed as evil, ultimately conquer. Although Pardo does intimate Afra's disposal of her rival constitutes a bitter victory, **"La Bicha"** apparently escapes quite unscathed. The author's attitude verges on approval, not of the women themselves, but of their strength and audacity. While Pardo's gentle or submissive female character often must suffer resignedly (**"La culpable," "La novia fiel," "Sor Aparición"**), the forceful, astute woman frequently wins out over adversity and over man in particular.

Mary E. Giles has written that, at least in Pardo Bazán's latter novels, she shows the influence of the modernists' predilection for "exploring the psychology of their characters" ["Pardo Bazán's Two Styles," *Hispania,* 48 (1965)] While C. C. Glascock does not relate Pardo's increasing preoccupation with psychological portraits to the modernists, he does find in her latter writing much evidence "she has deeply studied abnormal psychic phenomena," and terms her heroes of this period "schematic, shadowy, unnatural, pathological" [*Two Modern Spanish Novelists: Emilia Pardo Bazán and Armando Palacio Valdés,* 1926]. These critics are referring primarily to the intense, soul-searching studies of Pardo's last novels (*La quimera,* 1905; *La sirena negra,* 1908; *Dulce dueño,* 1911). But as early as 1891 in "La novela novelesca" the author conveys her extreme interest in the psychological novel. She hesitates to undertake that type of work at this time for fear the Spanish public would reject novels that were, in essence, "estudios científicos-psicológicos" [*Nuevo teatro crítico,* 1891]. She is far more willing, it seems, to experiment within the realm of the short story. Thus, although Pardo's major successes in psychological portraiture appear with the new century, one can find in her *cuentos* of the 1890's a foreshadowing of that later writing.

That Pardo Bazán chose to attempt psychological sketches in her short stories would not, in itself, account for the overriding gloom of *Cuentos de amor.* Hopefully, a psychological study dealing with love need not be despairing in tone. But as Walter Pattison points out, not only in her three latter novels, but "even as early as *Mother Nature*" (*La madre naturaleza*—1887), Pardo Bazán appears to feel that "compared to divine love, human love is vile . . . Nature, which operates through instincts, draws people together through sex, which we may idealize into Love." Our study of **"La culpable,"** I feel, bears out this observation. Unable to take solace in God's pardon, the wife must have the insincere forgiveness of her shallow spouse.

Pardo Bazán's own marriage proved unsuccessful; both Blanca de los Ríos and Carmen Bravo Villasante, perhaps Pardo Bazán's most thorough biographer, intimate she was profoundly disappointed in love. One can, of course, only speculate on the effect the unfortunate outcome of her marriage had upon her view of sensual involvement. Clearly, however, her cynical attitude toward that type of emotion in *Cuentos de amor* may, at least in part, explain that in her final novels it is not love for another human but divine love that will ultimately afford one his salvation.

Thomas Feeny (essay date 1980)

SOURCE: "Illusion and the Don Juan Theme in Pardo Bazán's *Cuentos de amor,*" in *Hispanic Journal,* Vol. 1, No. 2, 1980, pp. 67-71.

[*In the essay below, Feeny explores the use of a Don Juan figure who does not take advantage of his prey in three of Pardo Bazán's short stories.*]

Within Pardo Bazán's collection of short stories, *Cuentos de amor,* we find three very brief tales with essential-

ly the same theme: the failure of a Don Juan figure to take advantage of possible prey. Despite this similarity of theme, in her handling of this material the author projects two rather different images of herself. Here and elsewhere in her fiction, Pardo Bazán appears torn between the tendency to approach her characters' trials and grief sentimentally and her penchant to treat them with utmost detachment and even irony. Possibly both attitudes, despite their differences, are genuine facets of her nature. In this study we shall examine and compare Pardo Bazán's varying treatments of the Don Juan in *Cuentos de amor* and consider how they relate to her belief in man's vital need for hope and illusion, a contention paramount to each tale.

In the first story, **"La última ilusión de don Juan,"** sentimentality abounds. The author states in her opening paragraph that although superficial people usually insist Don Juan has no true sentiment, no sincere emotions, poets like herself realize that in fact he is the most sentimental of beings. The account goes on to detail the platonic relationship between the legendary lothario and his lovely young cousin, a paragon of virtue and innocence. Throughout, the author strives to humanize her hero, to rescue him from the realm of mere stereotype in order to prepare the reader for the story's outcome. She mentions, for example, that more than once Don Juan would return from a tryst wearing a smile on his lips solely to "mascar la hiel de un desengaño—porque también don Juan los cosecha."

While humanizing Don Juan, Pardo Bazán chooses to exaggerate her portrait of the girl, "la virgen de Murillo," "la mansa paloma," and thus to relegate her to simple caricature. Probably the author does this to render plausible Don Juan's fear of soiling through mere contact someone so pure. At any rate, this purity proves contagious. The great lover's "casta consagración" to his cousin eventually persuades him never to see the girl again for fear of finding her "desmejorada y cambiada por el tiempo." The reader senses without Pardo Bazán's ever saying so that somehow Don Juan's very salvation depends upon his preserving this illusion. In time, of course, it is shattered. His cousin writes to him that she is to be married, a possibility Don Juan cannot comprehend. With her frequent ironic touch, Pardo Bazán has the girl wed not for love but for money, and Don Juan is destroyed.

All who have studied Pardo Bazán are aware of Zola's influence upon her, an influence most evident in at least several of her novels. Still, Pardo Bazán never accepted Naturalistic determinism in full; man's spiritual side, she contended, could never be dismissed. Thus we find that in reviewing Zola's *Le Docteur Pascal,* she insists on the inevitability of "la perpetua aspiración de nuestras almas, siempre doloridas y tristes, siempre orientadas hacia el ideal . . ." ["'El Doctor Pascal,' última novela de Emilio Zola," *España Moderna,* Sept. 1893]. When Don Juan's last illusion has vanished, he gives himself over to erotic sadism. Yet clearly his need for illusion has won him all the author's sympathies. For he, she claims, is "el verdadero soñador" who, as always, must suffer when confronted by those who would compromise their dreams.

> Both in literature and in temperament, Pardo Bazán was ever the realist. Just as *Cuentos de amor* reflects her bleak negativism regarding the potentialities of romantic love, so too similar pessimism suffuses her assessment of other possibilities open to man.
>
> —*Thomas Feeny*

Equally sentimental and subjective is Pardo Bazán's portrait of Trifón, the would-be Don Juan of **"Desquite."** Her pity for the wretched cripple is apparent in the first line, as she observes that he "tuvo la malaventura de no morirse en la niñez." Trifón's promising musical career that seems to offer some hope of compensation for his handicap soon reaches an impasse. Echoing the theme of **"Ultima ilusión,"** the author again implies that in order to survive, man must have faith and hope; when Trifón finally realizes he will never surmount his deformity, never gain any measure of respect, Pardo Bazán openly sympathizes with him: "La pérdida de ilusiones tales deja el alma muy negra, muy ulcerada, muy venenosa." At this point the author is not simply laying the groundwork for the cruel change about to take place in Trifón, but also establishing that whatever metamorphosis he might undergo, it will not be a true part of his personality but rather the result of vicious circumstance. Increasingly embittered, Trifón, vows revenge upon the world and soon sets out to seduce the innocent girl to whom he gives music lessons.

"Candorosa y . . . sentimental," the child closely resembles the ingenue of **"Ultima ilusión."** As such she is no match for the artful cunning of her would-be seducer. In detailing the craft and calculation Trifón uses in his relentless campaign to break down the girl's moral fiber, Pardo Bazán shows him no mercy. He becomes the very embodiment of evil. Similar exaggeration characterizes the author's portrait of the girl, depicted as *amor virginal* first faced with carnal temptation. Thus far Trifón has done his wooing incognito and by letter. Pardo Bazán keeps the reader in suspense as he wonders how the deformed wretch will manage to seduce the girl without finally allowing her to set eyes on him. The literary language as well as the plot might indeed seem more appropriate to a romantic writer than to one usually associated with Spanish naturalism. Consider her description of the "noche de desvelo, zozobra, llanto y remordimiento" that precedes the girl's decision to surrender her virtue. Equally Romantic language imbues the description of the final scene; Trifón arrives at the girl's gate in a "carruaje sin faroles"; the night's darkness is "de boca de lobo," a masterful choice of words that has the reader envisage the young virgin about to be swallowed up by an evil beast. Pardo Bazán's sentiment gushes full force when, beside him in the darkened coach, the child tells her unknown lover what the poor outcast "no habia escuchado nunca" and he bursts into weeping. The purity of her trust has left him unable to profit from it. Trifón has the driver return the astonished girl to the safety of her home.

In both **"Ultima ilusión"** and **"Desquite,"** Pardo Bazán's penchant for sentimentality dominates her fondness for irony. This is not so in **"Remordimiento,"** however. Speaking through the narrator who is visiting the Vizconde, a once famous Don Juan, Pardo Bazán establishes her ironic tone in the very first paragraph. She relates that after having squandered his relatives' patrimony as well as his own on wanton pleasures, the old rogue happened to be blessed by an odd stroke of fortune that now allows him, despite the sins of his youth, to enjoy his old age with "un criado para cada dedo."

The very title, **"Remordimiento,"** reflects an irony that becomes clear only at the tale's conclusion. Early in her interview the narrator convinces herself there must exist some chink in the armor of this apparent personification of Evil triumphant: "¿No tendrá un remordimiento, no habrá realizado un acto de abnegación, una obra de caridad?", she asks herself. The question is not mere rhetoric. Rather, it reveals Pardo Bazán at her artful best as she moves to reinforce the irony embodied in the title. For by painting the Vizconde in the darkest of colors, by underlining his "absoluta carencia de sentido moral" and terming him a "negrero del amor," she has managed to plant some small seed of doubt in her reader's mind: Can any man be so evil? one asks. Thus when the author wonders aloud if the blackguard does not know some regret for his past life, it is precisely due to her total condemnation of him that the reader *expects* a sign of remorse on his part. Pardo Bazán has her audience's close ear as the Vizconde tells his story: how years before, his young niece, despite all his efforts to discourage her, had become so swept up in sensual passion for him that she offered to become his mistress. Although aroused by her enticements, the Vizconde had refused, sought out a suitable husband for her, and forced the marriage. At this point the idealistic visitor inserts: "¡Ya me parecia!— exclamé entusiasmada.—Una acción generosa, bonita! ¡Si no podia menos!" But the Vizconde at once demurs: "Una acción detestable," he retorts, for within the year the girl was dead for love of him. The full force of Pardo Bazán's irony lies in the final revelation that, while the old reprobate *does* acknowledge remorse, it is not at all of the type the woman had expected. His single regret is his failure to take his niece up on her proposition, a failure he feels certain brought on her early death. The Vizconde's ultimate conclusion: "Nadie debe salirse de su vocación y la mia no era conducir a nadie al sendero del deber y la virtud."

In discussing Pardo Bazán, [Miguel de] Unamuno, a great admirer of hers, observed that in her writing a reader could tell immediately that the author was a woman, "precisamente en cierta afectación de masculinidad a que no puede escaparse a pesar de su gran talento" [*Ensayos II,* 1966]. In support of Unamuno's contention, we recall the chilling climax to Pardo Bazán's **"Un destripador de antaño"** [*Obras completas,* n.d.]. Here she conceals all trace of what Unamuno would regard as femininity in her coldly objective account of the savage butchery of the peasant girl. Undoubtedly this analytical, often unfeeling, detachment that frequently characterizes Pardo Bazán's response to her characters' tribulations owes much to the Naturalistic school. Yet, as we have seen in **"Ultima ilusión"** and **"Desquite,"** at times she appears most compassionate toward her characters' plight. To appreciate how very far from the confines of Naturalism Pardo Bazán would occasionally stray, one has only to read the pathos-ridden conclusion to **"Jesusa."**

It would be rash to insist from this brief study that either Pardo Bazán's cold detachment or her marked sentimentality indicates her true nature. What we can conclude, however, is that even when treating essentially the same theme, her approach is not predictable. Although the plot of the sardonic **"Remordimiento,"** which has the young girl perish because of frustrated passion, could easily lend itself to the same sentimentality the author has shown in the other two stories, in this latter tale she chooses to resist any emotional response to the situation.

Yet in the final analysis **"Remordimiento"** does have much in common with **"Ultima ilusión"** and **"Desquite"** besides the unconsummated relationship between the Don Juan character and the girl. A far more telling bond linking these stories is that each reveals Pardo Bazán's confirmation of man's great need to cherish illusions, no matter how tenuous they may be. As she implies in **"Ultima ilusión,"** man has the right to "mirar al cielo cuando el peso de la tierra le oprime." Thus when Don Juan finally loses his last illusion, he disintegrates. And in **"Desquite"** when Trifón, long able to nurture the hope of overcoming his physical defects through his art, must at last recognize he is without talents to compensate for his handicaps, he gives himself to evil. (That he can ever be a successful malefactor is itself a kind of illusion—though of a different sort—as his final tearful change of heart shows.) Even in **"Remordimiento"** the need for man to preserve his illusions is still evident; here, however, it is not the Don Juan figure but rather the author herself, speaking through her narrator, who evinces distinct reluctance to surrender her belief that deep within the Vizconde lies some element of remorse for his past sins.

But in **"Remordimiento,"** one might well ask, because the female narrator obviously speaks for the author, when Pardo Bazán mocks the former's efforts to find a saving grace in one who is ostensibly all bad, is Pardo Bazán not in fact mocking her own need for illusion? Admittedly the author seems inclined to self-parody in depicting the visitor's over-eagerness to ascribe some resultant good to the old man's actions, a good he flatly denies. But while here Pardo Bazán may seem to deride her own ingenuousness, **"Remordimiento"** still shows a basic

consistency. Both in literature and in temperament, Pardo Bazán was ever the realist. Just as **Cuentos de amor** reflects her bleak negativism regarding the potentialities of romantic love, so too similar pessimism suffuses her assessment of other possibilities open to man. For in all three of our tales, Pardo Bazán's underlying statement is only that man must possess illusions. As the outcome of each story indicates, nowhere does she imply these illusions will be realized.

Lou Charnon-Deutsch   (essay date 1981)

SOURCE: "Naturalism in the Short Fiction of Emilia Pardo Bazan," in *Hispanic Journal,* Vol. 3, No. 1, Fall, 1981, pp. 73-85.

[*In the following excerpt, Charnon-Deutsch explores the influence of Emile Zola on Pardo Bazán's short fiction.*]

Naturalism was debated in Spain even before translation of Zola's works appeared, but it was not until Emilia Pardo Bazán published her controversial *La cuestión palpitante* (1882-83) that critics began lining up in earnest on either side of the issue which bore so many sociological and ethical overtones. The series of articles that make up *La cuestión* failed to convince the Spanish readership that the experimentation being carried on by Zola and his followers was of any aesthetic or moral value. What irritated Spanish readers of Zola (and a great deal of non-readers who gathered their secondhand information from periodicals) was the attitude towards determinism which the new school accepted as a cornerstone of its doctrine. Equally distasteful to the Spanish public was the use of vulgar language and accounts of brutality and sexual immorality. The more enlightened prose writers, such as Emilia Pardo Bazán and Leopoldo Alas, succeeded in eliminating what was truly unacceptable for the Spaniard and adopting the style and themes of Zola and his contemporaries while never wholly embracing their ideology. . . .

The countess Pardo Bazán was (until the end of the century when Blasco Ibáñez belatedly took up the cause) the movement's most zealous and outspoken defender and follower, even though both she and Zola understood the gulf that existed between French naturalism and her own particular brand of it, which some critics have since called *Catholic naturalism.* Because she was the self-styled leader of the movement in Spain, critics usually look to her stories for its characteristic manifestation. However, a careful examination of the major collections of stories published between 1885 and 1923 reveals that, despite the fact that many stories do show an unmistakable naturalistic gravity and purpose, she did not have, as some critics maintain, a period which was distinctively naturalistic. She chose instead to adopt an independent position vis-à-vis the French school, for she did not consider the story a proper vehicle to promote social change (although social comment is, in some pieces, very prominent) and she rarely overemphasized subject matter at the expense of technique.

Most critics assume, perhaps because it is so in the case of her longer fiction, that naturalism played a decisive role in Pardo Bazán's short fiction. Porfirio Sánchez claims that between 1879 and 1900 the countess' story publication paralleled that of Galdós and Pereda in its adherence to the "faithful portrayal of everyday reality" ["How and Why Emilia Pardo Bazán went from the Novel to the Short Story," *Romance Notes,* Vol. 11, 1969]. Yet it was during this period that she wrote some of her most romantic stories (see numerous examples in *Cuentos de amor,* 1898). Emilio González López states categorically that the countess is the most prolific writer of naturalistic stories of all times, and he stresses the predominantly naturalistic tone of *Cuentos de Marineda* (1892), *Cuentos nuevos* (1894), *Cuentos de amor* (1896), *En tranvía* (1901) and especially *Un destripador de antaño* (1900), of which he says, "lòs cuentos son trágicos, con personajes que, movidos por fuertes y primitivos instintos, terminan trágicamente" ["Doña Emilia Pardo Bazán y el naturalismo en la narrativa: *Los pazos de Ulloa, La madre naturaleza y Un destripador de antaño y otro cuentos,*" *Sin N (Asomante),* Vol. 7, No. 3, 1976]. It may be that Pardo Bazán wrote more such stories than did her contemporaries, but since she wrote more stories of every kind than most of them, the fact is misleading. Most of the five hundred or more stories she published between 1879 and 1921 are decidedly not naturalistic in any strict sense of the word, and apart from *El destripador,* it cannot even be said that in the above collections naturalism (technically considered) is the style of choice.

In the latter half of the nineteenth century authors of novels and short stories chose to plot the course of the action in contemporary settings with characters selected from the middle or lower classes. This was due partly to the influence of realists and naturalists such as Zola and Flaubert, but to a large extent the shift to a more mimetic fiction was an outgrowth of the *cuadro de costumbres,* whose success as a genre ran concurrent with and then waned as the artistic story's popularity increased in the late decades. Many of Pardo Bazán's stories do end tragically and do deal with contemporary figures and issues, but to call them naturalistic merely because they end in a certain manner is to confuse a plotting device for the literary movement itself and to overlook a basic trait of the nineteenth-century short story. Many artistic stories (whether naturalistic or not) end at the moment a lesson is painfully learned or a test failed, unlike fairytales and folktales which usually end in a manner rewarding to the hero, who profits from his lessons and who is rewarded with wealth, fame or love. In this respect the nineteenth-century story resembles the *exemplum* more than the folktale because it is concerned with the learning of a lesson rather than the reward for its having been learned.

All of Emilia Pardo Bazán's story collections appeared after the *Cuestión palpitante* began to occupy a place in the Spanish literary conscience. It is therefore not possible to judge the effect of the movement by studying collections prior to the 1870s. What I have done instead is to study and compare the individual works of each collection to determine if there was a predominantly naturalistic period in her production. It was found that, while Pardo Bazán wrote her novels in a style which progressed slowly from the strictest naturalism of *Los pazos de Ulloa* and *La madre naturaleza,* to a more spiritualistic period (*La sirena negra*), her stories over the decades show a mixture of romanticism and manners sketch, the starkest naturalism and most fanciful legend, devotional narrations and supernatural accounts. Furthermore, she did not feel it inappropriate to offer her public a mélange of all of these styles and forms in a single collection.

The selections of *Cuentos nuevos* (published in 1894, two years after the publication of *La nueva cuestión palpitante*) provide a perfect example of the eclectic nature of the author's short fiction. **"La hierba milagrosa,"** as the countess herself explains, is an adaptation of an *exemplum* taken from *Instrucción de la mujer cristiana* by Luis Vives, in which an angelic Albaflor protects her virtue by tricking her would-be seducer into killing her. **"El tesoro"** begins as a traditional folktale: the heroine is happy and gifted in every respect, except that she is cursed "allá en el más escondido camarín del pensamiento" with "una curiosidad." Leaving home one day she passes a cave and is confronted by a *brujo* (equivalent to the tale's donor) who gives her a box containing her innocence (the magic agent), as well as a warning (the tale's interdiction): the box is not to be opened under any circumstances. Inés' interdiction becomes her test. Unlike the hero of the folktale, however, she fails her test, opens the cask only to find it is empty, except for the words which suddenly appear on the cover, "cuando sepas lo que es la inocencia, será que la perdiste." At the end **"El tesoro"** contains a moral that sums up neatly what the argument has already illustrated. It is implied that Inés is now without her "innocence" as a result of her overwhelming curiosity. **"El tesoro"** and **"La hierba milagrosa"** are typical of the moral and religious stories that comprise a large portion of Pardo Bazán short works. They can in no way be considered naturalistic.

A number of stories in the same collection, perhaps the majority, are peopled with characters who are not figures of contemporary society, or who suffer spiritual rather than physiological needs. The *niña mártir* (from the story by the same name) is surrounded by every physical comfort imaginable. The narrator states her case by pointing out this fact:

> No se trata de una de estas criaturas cuyas desdichas alborotan de repente la Prensa, de esas que recoge la Policía de las cortes en las altas horas de la noche, vestidas de andrajos, escuálidas de hambre, ateridas de frío, acardenaladas y tullidas a golpes, o dislaceradas *[sic]* por el hierro candente que aplicó a sus tiernas carnecitas sañuda madrastra.

At issue is a spiritual as opposed to a physical deprivation. Society has become too wrapped up in sensationalism to recognize this type of martyr, as much a victim of her ambience as any other. The *niña* is a prisoner of overbearing love, protective. So complete is the heroine's isolation that she regards with envy the "desharrapados granujas" playing in the street—at least they are healthy and out of doors.

Were the martyr simply to die of her condition, and her death be described in awesome detail, this story might be considered naturalistic, even by a stricter follower of Zola's technique than Emilia Pardo Bazán. But here, as elsewhere in the countess' short works, some of the elements which contribute to the effect of the whole would appear hopelessly outdated to a naturalist author. For instance, to emphasize the approaching death of the child-martyr, death itself is personified in a somewhat frivolous manner:

> Entre tanto, la muerte, riéndose con siniestra risa de calavera, se acercaba a la señorial, y cenada mansión. Es de saber que no encontró ni puerta por donde pasar, ni siquiera por donde colarse, y hubo de entrar, aplanándose, por debajo de una teja, a la buhardilla.

Satisfied the metaphor serves to depict the insidiousness of the stalking foe, the narrator continues on a lighter note, following death through a keyhole, up a flight of stairs and into the doctor's pocket where it remains hidden behind his *fosforera*.

Thus, the reader is momentarily misled by death's playfulness, but the story's conclusion is no less tragic for the diversion. Like many a Zola subject, the heroine suffers a slow degeneration (in this case physical, as opposed to moral followed by physical) because she is unable to escape her environment. What is absent from **"La niña mártir"** is the naturalist's attention to detail and technical descriptions, an aseptic view of the situation which would render the stalking death a superfluous metaphor. So, while determinism plays a role in the story's outcome, the elaborative techniques do not in any way resemble those used by the naturalists.

Even what could be called Pardo Bazán's most realistic short works are not always devoid of impressionist techniques or sentimentality. **"Náufragas"** has barely a note of levity and is written in a direct and matter-of-fact manner, with an argument which fully anticipates the gloomy conclusion. It is also one of the better stories of the *Cuentos nuevos* collection, although not for that reason. But one cannot know from its exposition, an idealized luminous view of Madrid, that **"Náufragas"** will be any different from the romantic **"La paloma negra,"** or the sketch **"Cuatro socialistas"**:

> Era la hora en que las grandes capitales adquieren misteriosa belleza. La jornada del trabajo y de la actividad ha concluído; los transeúntes van despacio por las calles, que el riego de la tarde ha refrescado y ya no encharca. Las luces abren sus ojos claros, pero no es aún de noche; el fresa con tonos amatista del crepúsculo envuelve en neblina sonrosada, transparente y ardorosa las perspectivas monumentales . . .

Prosaic buildings and streets are rendered beautiful when bathed in light. The fragrance of the acacias inspires languid dreams and the faces of the city women appear evanescent in the dying light of the penumbra. Yet this same Madrid is about to engulf the impoverished widow and her daughter, who gaze in wonder at its beauty. The concern of the two *náufragas* is the preservation of their dignity in the face of adversity. While the story's ending is not, to a modern audience, terribly pathetic (the heroine's moral downfall is not even depicted), the story itself is so, because the young girl's aspirations are so out of touch with the realities of Madrid life. It is this contrast between ideals and what life has to offer which achieves the special effect of **"Náufragas."** In the case of the two country women, the high degree of moral rectitude is not complemented by a well-rounded education or even a native perspicacity: "Muy honradas, sí . . . ; pero con tanta honradez, ¿Qué?, vale más tener gracia, saber desenredarse." This indirect statement, voicing the sentiments of an erstwhile friend, seems to comprise the hard lesson the *náufragas* face in Madrid.

"Náufragas" is a very short story, with little space to describe the economic organization of the displaced family or detail their degeneration in progressive stages. The author has chosen instead to subordinate descriptions and exposition towards achieving effects of contrast, thereby heightening emotional response in the reader at the story's conclusion. In this respect it is typical of Emilia Pardo Bazán's stories in that it calls on the reader to imagine only in vague terms the adversity which would surely be documented in a longer narration or a novel, dwelling on the unobtainable good as well as the bleak reality. When the unmarried girl fails to procure a suitable position as a housekeeper, she will, it is implied, sell her favors in a beer hall. But nowhere, not even at the conclusion, is this openly stated. In the end the young girl merely decides to accept work in the beer hall. Resigning herself, she stammers, "En todas partes se puede ser buena," hiding her fear, and alerting the reader to the fact that the opposite is more likely to be the case. Here, as in so many of her short works, Pardo Bazán avoids the naturalist's tendency to depict the darker side of human relationships.

Victims of violence.

While most of Pardo Bazán's stories escape the naturalistic mold for one reason or another, others do not, and although the author shuns the use of pornography and examples of hereditary determinism, she is not above employing low speech and depicting acts of brutal violence and death. Furthermore, her frequent use of environment as a restricting or destructive force demonstrates she lent more credence to Zola's theories than it was her custom to admit when she spoke about determinism. In his careful thematic study of Pardo Bazán's stories Baquero Goyanes reviews several dozen of what are considered the countess' most naturalistic works. Of those which have as a setting the author's native Galicia, he writes, "Son narraciones breves, aguafuertes bárbaros y vigorosos. En casi todos ellos se advierte un clima de angustia muy peculiar en las obras de la autora. *[. . .]* Existe un personaje latente en estos cuentos que es la barbarie, encarnada en costumbres y tipos." The description fits the majority of stories mentioned in the section on rural naturalism. The "latent personaje" is better defined as a hostile environment working at counter-purposes to the goals of the protagonist. In most of her naturalistic stories the countess creates an external reality which determines rather than reflects the psychology of the characters. The mode for the action is the relationship between either a victim and an aggressor or aggressors, or a victim and his or her environment which, as Baquero Goynes infers, is bound by social conventions which are shown to cause people physical or psychological harm.

The typical narration depicts (often in scant detail) a series of acts which lead up to and follow an act of extreme violence or submission. Very often the violence is premeditated and results in a character's death, and usually it is perpetrated by one man or a group of men who injure or take the life of another man, although in several cases the victim is a woman (**"Madre gallega," "La capitana," "El indulto," "Ardid de guerra"**). Only rarely does a woman commit an act of violence against another woman (**"El destripador," "La mayorazga de Bouzas"**) and never is a woman's victim a man. The victim of violence is either a totally innocent person caught between opposing sides of a struggle or one who, because of age, sex, immaturity or some defect, is unable to protect himself or herself from harm. In a few cases the victim is guilty of some incriminating or imprudent deed, but the punishment tends to be unusually severe.

The underlying causes for physical violence and death may be attributed to a large range of emotions and sociological factors, such as murky regional politics (**"El nieto del Cid," "Ardid de guerra," "Madre gallega"**), revenge (**"La capitana," "La corpana"**), superstition (**"El destripador," "Curado"**) and greed (**"El destino," "Contratreta"**), to name a few. It is important to note that poverty is rarely the force behind an act of violence or unlawfulness. It is often indirectly involved; for example, the stepparents of **"El destripador"** are poor (though not destitute), but it is greed which is shown to be the force that propels the stepmother to kill her daughter. Poverty may play a role, but characters do not kill or rob because they are hungry. The stories where poverty is the issue have non-violent conclusions: the protagonist may struggle his way out of a difficult situation (**"El mundo"**), recall former poverty (**"El vidrio roto"**), come face to face with poverty (**"El disfraz"**) or succumb to it (**"Las náufragas"**).

Heredity does not play a significant role in determining a character's personality or demeanor. If anything, the author is careful to avoid the issue of physiological determinism, or she indirectly combats it by showing good sons born to bad parents or conversely, bad to good. For example, the foul and greedy parents of **"Los padres de un santo"** are blessed with a son who becomes a priest and afterwards a sainted martyr in Japan, while his parents remain all but indifferent to his plight. A hint of a relationship between barbarity of customs and physiognomy occasionally enters a description: when the cruel father of **"Las medias rojas"** notices his daughter wearing a pair of red stockings, his shocked face is described thus: "Una luz de ira cruzó por los ojos pequeños, engarzados en duros párpados, bajo cejas hirsutas, del labrador." For the most part, however, little comparison is made between personality, deeds and physiological phenomena.

More common is the question of fatality and free will which resolves itself differently from story to story. In **"La dama joven"** the heroine's decision to select a dull life over an eventful one is entirely determined by social and religious pressures. On the other hand, in **"Las desnudas"** (from the collection *En tranvía*), the narrator's stated purpose is to demonstrate that "bajo la influencia de un mismo terrible suceso, cada espíritu conserva su espontaneidad y escoge, mediante su iniciativa propia, el camino, bueno o malo, que en esto precisamente estriba la libertad." The story tells of a misfortune shared by five women, and each one's reaction to her disgrace. As a result of being paraded nude through the streets, one woman dies, another enters the convent, a third becomes a soldier and dies fighting the *liberales,* and a fourth a streetwalker, while the fifth lives "humilde y resignada" with her uncle on whose account she suffered such an outrage. The narrator hopes to show the diversity of reaction to misfortune. However, the story's outcome does not altogether contradict one character's contention that, like a rock obeying laws of physics, we fall inevitably into the *abismo*. It cannot escape the reader, as assuredly it did not the author, that although each woman reacts differently, not one of them obtains in her adult life what she had hoped for. It is implied that the girls are eager to marry: "a pesar de su fe no tenían vocación monástica, y entre los mozos incorporados a la partida del cura, más de una rondaba sus ventanas y pensaba en bodas." So, while each woman expresses a degree of individuality in her response to tragedy, no one of them rises above her hostile environment. The narrator's conspicuous affirmation, that no one reaction is alike, seems calculated to dispel concern or criticism over Pardo Bazán's naturalistic tendencies. But, a careful examination reveals that, in this case at least, the narrator's rhetoric runs contrary to the fatalistic logic of the text.

"La dama joven" and environmental determinism.

In the group of short stories reviewed above the characters seem unable to endure or maintain dignity in a harsh environment. But it is only in the longer works such as **"La dama joven"** that the process of subjugation and determination of will is woven into the narration without violence. Outside of **"Viaje de novios,"** where environmental circumstances as well as inherited characteristics come into play, **"La dama joven"** may be Pardo Bazán's most representative example of environmental determinism.

The initial situation resembles the beginning of several of Zola's novels *(Au Bonheur des dames, Le Rêve,*

L'Assomoir), which portray the struggle of a woman who has lost the support of her parents or husband. In this case two sisters, Dolores and Concha, orphaned since Dolores was thirteen, struggle to maintain their dignity and dream of an honorable marriage for the younger Concha. The moment of crisis arrives when the latter must choose between a career on the stage and a respectable, if somewhat dull, marriage to a cabinetmaker. Even though Concha herself voices the final consent to the loutish Ramón, her decision is, more than true assent, an acquiescence to the will of her sister, the parish priest and her fiancé, all of whom conspire to convince her to marry. Singly, neither one of the forces at work (the Church in the figure of Dolores' confessor, and social respectability, championed by the combined forces of Dolores and Ramón), would be able to sway Concha who, if left to her own devices, would opt for the theatre. It is implied that the cautious Dolores would have dealt too heavy-handedly with her spirited sister, thereby losing her respect. But behind the well-meaning Dolores, whose attitudes toward morality have themselves been determined by an unhappy experience with men, is the Church—a much stronger, more cunning and experienced force at work to shape Concha's future.

No overt criticism accompanies descriptions of Dolores' confessor-priest, but there are numerous clues to the sinister nature of his function and the probity of his advice in the context of the story. He is always described as an extension of his black confessional, a "jesuita sagaz," whose pious words cloak the plan that may or may not be leading to Concha's happiness. When from the confessional grate he sees Dolores enter the church, he rushes to dismiss the others who precede her in the confessional line, for he is anxous to play a role in Cocha's future. It is only the tip of the priest's nose that Dolores sees through the grate; he is perceived as a non-person, whose feelings and thoughts are translated through his nose:

> La punta de la nariz que Dolores veía al través de la reja se contrajo con severidad. Pero dilatóse al punto, como si la llenase el aura de una idea bienhechora. [. . .] La nariz se aguzó, y su fina punta pareció recalcar una suave ironía.

The priest's plan is to allow Concha an intimate tête-à-tête (her first) with Ramón the very night her impresario is to ask her for a final decision about joining the theatre. It is hoped that the intimacy of the moment will set Concha dreaming of wedding plans. Dolores is skeptical the plan will work, but as always bows to the yoke of her confessor's dictates, expressed once again by his nose:

> Dolores miraba atónita aquella nariz, severa por costumbre, y la desconocía viéndole tan tolerante, tan benignamente entreabierta. Sin embargo, no dudó: no había recibido allí jamás consejo alguno que no probase bien seguir.

In the last scene of the domestic drama all the forces at work in Concha's life converge to bend her will: Estrella, the *star* of the theatre where Concha works; Gormaz, her would-be agent; Dolores, serene and determined after her session with the priest; and the *novio,* in a position at last to set a wedding date. Added to these is the house Dolores and Concha share, the "habitación arregladita," beckoning with its "bienestar humilde," a symbol of duty, familiar protection and comfort.

It is Concha's misfortune that the scene of her decision is to be her home. Had it come in the theatre, there is little doubt she would have chosen to act instead of marry, for earlier, when Ramón threatens to break their engagement if she wears a low-cut dress on stage, she defiantly ignores his wishes. Outside the theatre she is anyting but self-determined. Her complete abnegation of will is reflected in the narrator's total omission of her thoughts and words during the last few scenes of the work. Nothing is directly or indirectly attributable to her until she says quietly, "Qué sé yo, lo que quiera mi hermana." In the end, the defenseless and unpotentialized *Concha* delivers herself into the hands of *Dolores,* to partake of life's sorrows. It is a great victory for moderation and mediocrity. Concha's future with the cabinetmaker seems secure. But the final statement belongs to the actress and agent, and leaves little doubt as to the more sinister consequences of Concha's decision:

> —¡Bah!—murmuró Gormaz—, ¡Y quién sabe si la acierta, hijo! A veces, en la oscuridad, se vive más sosegado . . . Acaso ese novio, que parece un buen muchacho, le dará un felicidad que la gloria no le daría.

> —¿Ese?—exclamó Estrella, cortando con las dientes la punta del puro—. Lo que le dará ese bárbaro será un chiquillo por año . . . , y se descuida, un pie de paliza.

From this it is clear Concha is being manipulated by forces beyond her power to contradict. Her powerlessness is reflected in the very narrative structure of the work. The determinism is carefully masked; Concha's decision is shown to be one which brings with it certain privileges of class and bourgeois security. It is a decision millions of women made every day, and it was probably seen by the majority of Pardo Bazán's readers as the *right* decision. Yet in the context of the story (when all the clues to the pressures of environment come to light after a careful analysis of character function) Concha's decision can only be interpreted as an act of submission and self-denial which will bring more happiness to those around her than to herself.

Information regarding the protagonist's circumstances is never broadly or dogmatically stated, nor documented in close detail. Instead, the pressures brought to bear on her are coded into the narration via a subtle series of clues such as those which divulge the nature of the priest's role. In Emilia Pardo Bazán's novel-length narratives there is proportionately more coding of the type she worked into **"La dama joven,"** as well as more documentation of the type Zola recommended. But among her shorter works literary naturalism seems not to have been the success it was in the novels.

The reasons for this extend beyond the influence of contemporary literary currents and the personal tastes of the author. The economy of the short story required more attention to style than the naturalist was often willing to pay, his primary purpose being to use art as a means of social statement. Only verifiable aspects of life were fit to be part of the *materia novelable.* By its very length the short story, like a poem, calls attention to its form. Pardo Bazán's best stories concern themselves with impressions and fantasies, special effects (in Poe's interpretation of the word) and, above all, the proper expression of these diverse elements in often less-than-straightforward terms. Pardo Bazán's naturalistic pieces are often burdensome because their pessimism does not allow for anticipation, either on the part of the character or the reader. Heroes are not created who wake to a reality which is an illusion or dream contradicted. The world as created in these stories is so bad, so predisposed to evil, that characters seem to work within their circumstances without illusions and therefore without hope. Since the story, as a form, is more end-oriented than the novel,' this predictability would be unbearable to most readers of short stories. It is perhaps for this reason that Pardo Bazán chose to offer her readers a mixture of styles when she gathered her stories into collections. To avoid being classified a naturalistic (or any other type) author, she made sure that what was stated or implied in one story was negated or forgotten in the next.

Carolyn Richardson Durham   (essay date 1989)

SOURCE: "Subversion in Two Short Stories by Emilia Pardo Bazán, in *Letras Peninsulares,* Vol. 2, No. 1, Spring, 1989, pp. 55-64.

[*In the following excerpt, Durham discusses Pardo Bazán's use of the grotesque to explain the status of women in society.*]

Although Emilia Pardo Bazán was admired by her contemporaries for the ability to write "like a man," she often used her work to address the concerns of women. Her ability to synthesize diverse ideas and literary currents characterizes her work from the time of her rise to prominence as the author of *La cuestión palpitante.* Her reputation as a pacesetter was further confirmed when she assimilated the structure of the grotesque into her short stories. The grotesque especially suited works dealing with the status of women. Two stories, **"Posesión"** and **"Los pendientes"** are typical of the literature produced by women writers in the nineteenth century.

Many of Pardo Bazán's ideas concerning women markedly diverged from what was commonly expected of the women of her time. As a feminist she shocked many people when she advocated increased economic and educational opportunities for women. It is understandable, therefore, that she hesitated to openly express some of her more radical ideas, evidently fearful of how such a challenge would be met by patriarchal Spanish society.

Instead she chose to present these ideas covertly, submerging her subversive ideas in a text that made them somewhat inaccessible. The strategies used for simultaneously hiding and communicating forbidden topics were not unique to Pardo Bazán. Such methods were used by other nineteenth century women writers including George Eliot, George Sand, the Brontë sisters, Mary Shelley, Jane Austen and Emily Dickinson.

It was common for women writers to use the fantastic as a mode of expressing their alienation. The fantastic was suited to this function because of its tendency to express "a desire for something excluded from the cultural order—more specifically for all that is in opposition to the capitalist and patriarchal order which has been dominant in Western society over the last two centuries" [Rosemary Jackson, *Fantasy: The Literature of Subversion,* 1981]. A certain ambiguity inherent in the fantastic makes it possible to vacillate in taking a clear position on an issue. Tsetvan Todorov explains [in *The Fantastic,* 1973] that a successful fantastic tale requires a certain complicity on the part of the reader. It obliges the reader to "consider the world of characters as a world of living persons and to hesitate between a natural and a supernatural explanation of the events described."

Pardo Bazán was also able to take advantage of the grotesque, another structure that demonstrated ambiguity. She was undoubtedly familiar with the rich legacy of the Spanish grotesque which manifested itself in the artistic works of Velázquez and Goya as well as in the literary works of Gracián, Cervantes, Quevedo, El Duque de Rivas, Espronceda and Bécquer. Her contemporary, confidante, and colleague, Benito Pérez Galdós, demonstrated skill in delineating grotesque characters. In addition, the grotesque enjoyed wide dissemination throughout Europe during the nineteenth century. Hugo wrote of the moral purposes of the grotesque in the "Preface" to *Cromwell.* Baudelaire's critical works on Poe's *Tales of the Grotesque and Arabesque* discuss the moral and social purposes of the grotesque. Several other nineteenth-century writers wrote grotesque works: Coleridge, Dickens, Melville, and Dostoevsky. The grotesque flourished during the nineteenth century, a time of pervasive change. It described a challenge to order, including the subversion of traditional modes of action and thought. This structure, like the fantastic, was well-suited to the concerns of women writers. . . .

The grotesque, however, deals with those themes that threaten us, particularly those that reflect the malevolent intervention of the supernatural. For example, certain animals are commonly used as grotesque motifs, particularly creeping animals and vermin. Symbols of death, such as skeletons, skulls and apparitions, likewise are commonly associated with the grotesque. Moreover, the malevolence of an external presence renders the universe strange and ominous. The grotesque, therefore, differs from the fantastic inasmuch as it inspires a fear of life. [Wolfgang] Kayser summarized the ingredients of this aesthetic category [in *The Grotesque in Art and Literature,* 1981].

We have observed the progressive dissolution that has occurred since the ornamental art of the renaissance: the fusion of realms which we know to be separated, the abolition of the laws of statics, the loss of identity, the distortion of "natural' size and shape, the suspension of the category of objects, the destruction of the personality and the fragmentation of the historical order.

Common to the structures of the fantastic and the grotesque is the theme of the double, which serves as an indication of the repressed desires of the individual. Described by Freud as a psychological manifestation, dualism of the personality was frequently expressed in nineteenth-century literature.

Over the course of the nineteenth century, fantasies structured around dualism—often variations of the Faust Myth—reveal the *internal* origin of the other. The demonic is not supernatural, but is an aspect of personal and interpersonal life, a manifestation of unconscious desire. (Jackson 50)

Women were frequently portrayed as either gentle, powerless angels or as evil, demanding monsters in nineteenth-century literature. Such representations, reflecting stereotypical thinking about the personalities of women, were often written by men. Strangely, women who wrote during this period also appeared to perpetuate these same cultural types. Often the true meanings of their works are not easily ascertained.

From Austen to Dickinson, these female artists all dealt with central female experiences from a specifically female perspective. But this distinctively feminine aspect of their art has been generally ignored by critics because the most successful women writers often seem to have channelled their female concerns into secret or at least obscure corners. In effect, such women have created submerged meanings, meanings hidden within or behind more accessible "public" content of their works, so that their literature could be read and appreciated even when its vital concern with female dispossesion and disease was ignored. [Sandra M. Gilbert and Susan Gubar, *The Madwoman in the Attic: The Woman Writer and the Nineteenth Century Imagination*]

Pardo Bazán, evidently aware of the conventions of the time, likewise used the traditional stereotypes to create a personal statement about the status of women that could be appreciated even if the reader was unaware of a hidden meaning.

Another way that women expressed their rebelliousness was by conferring their beliefs on the "mad double." This character enabled female authors to "dramatize their own self-division, their desire both to accept the structures of patriarchal society and to reject them" (Gilbert and Gubar). In other cases the double can manifest itself as another individual or as a supernatural being such as a ghost or demon. The emergence of a demon is a psychological manifestation of the division of the Self. Rosemary Jackson comments that Gothic tales such as those written by nineteenth-century writers Charlotte Brontë, Emily Brontë, and Elizabeth Gaskell often have themes similar to those of the grotesque in which ghosts or demons appear. In the Gothic, such tales often deal with the repression of women, and the ghost or demon reflects the division of a personality that has been repressed, unable to achieve self-expression otherwise.

Pardo Bazán's short story **"Posesión"** deals with a madwoman who claims to be possessed by the devil. The main character, Dorotea, seems to simultaneously rebel against and adhere to the dictates of Spanish society that would limit her life choices to being either a wife or a nun. When her cousin becomes a Carmelite nun, Dorotea becomes envious of her cousin's happiness. The nun successfully sublimates her desire into a religious experience:

Sucedió que una prima hermana mía, que acababa de vestir el sayal de las carmelitas y a quien yo solía visitar en su reja, comenzó a hablarme exaltadamente de sus nupcias con Jesús, de los éxtasis y deliquios que gozaba en brazos de su celestial Esposo y de lo despreciables que parecen en cortejo de tan divinos regalos, los amoríos y las aventuras de la tierra.

Dorotea does not find an equally acceptable way to sublimate her sexual desires. She rebels against what is expected of her by seeking the love of the devil, who appears to her as a handsome young man. While the priest of the story perceives that Dorotea has been possessed by the devil, Jackson's theory, in contrast, suggests that such a supernatural being originates due to society's imperative that women repress a part of themselves. Dorotea, therefore, attributes a sense of evil to her feelings and consequently experiences them as a devil that needs to be exorcised. Her description of a visit to the devil's headquarters shows the connection between sexuality and demonic possession.

Allí se apinaba una muchedumbre inmensa que reconocía la autoridad de mi señor, y bullía al pie de su trono una hueste de mujeres hermosísimas, cortesanas, reinas o diosas, desde la rubia Venus y la morena Cleopatra hasta la insaciable Mesalina y la suicida Lucrecia. Y como yo sintiese en el corazón la mordedura de los celos vi que las apartaba indiferente sin mirarlas y oi que decía: No temas, yo no soy como el "Otro", yo no me reparto . . .

Each of the women mentioned by name in this passage was known for her erotic allure. Venus was the goddess of love; Cleopatra was known for her power over the Roman leaders Marc Antony and Julius Caesar. The empress Mesalina was sentenced to death for her sexual infidelity. Lucrecia was raped by her husband's son. The presentation of these non-Christian women of erotic renown is a deliberate choice, descriptive of the nature of Dorotea's sins.

After reading **"Posesión"** one would conclude that Pardo Bazán, like other women writers of the nineteenth century, felt that one of society's problems was the repression of female sexuality, and in a broader sense, the repression of women in general. Therefore, although **"Posesión"** may be predicated on a religious experience, it is really about Spain's social realities.

Pardo Bazán recognized that this story of demonic possession was objectionable to the Spanish public, who criticized it strongly when it was first published. Nevertheless, she chose to republish it and other controversial stories in the collection **Cuentos sacroprofanos.** She explains that the source of the plot of **"Posesión"** is both authoritative and reputable in order to defend herself against criticism. She writes in the prologue of the collection:

> El asunto de *Posesión* lo hallé en un libro aprobado por la autoridad eclesiástica, perfectamente ortodoxo; y él que quiera saber a Salamanca. Había lindas ganas de arremeter contra *Posesión* lo mismo que contra *La sed de Cristo,* pero reprimieron los ímpetus caritativos, porque olfatearon que aquello tenía guardadas las espaldas, y no quisieron encontrarse enzarzados por arte de birlibirloque con algún Santo Padre o doctor de la Iglesia. La idea de *Posesión* casi huelga decirlo se basa en la conocida frase "El diablo es el mono de Dios." La perdición de Dorotea de Guzmán, alma elevada y altiva, la consigue Luzbel, no por medio de la grosera concupiscencia de la carne, sino tentando y extraviando su espíritu con apariencias de pureza y hasta de poesía.

By stating that demonic possession had a basis in church history and that it could be documented in specific church records, Pardo Bazán placed herself firmly within the bounds of orthodoxy. Closer examination, however, reveals that the details of the event described in **"Posesión"** emphasize the public censure of female sexuality and of those who resent the limited career choices available to women. The choice of details, as much as the selection of demonic possession as a topic, was deliberate. Like many fantastic-grotesque stories, this one expresses a cultural taboo. Nevertheless, it is possible for the reader to enjoy this tale without ever being aware that it deals with something other than religious matters.

The technique we shall call "fragmentation of the body" can be found in several short stories by Pardo Bazán. In such stories a part of the body that is severed takes on a life of its own. The part continues to serve its normal function, but with heightened intensity and total independence from the body of which it was once a part. Fragmentation of the body is common in grotesque works of literature and art.

Pardo Bazán writes of a body part that becomes independent in **"Los pendientes,"** a tale of fantastic horror exhibiting a subversive, covert meaning. The story tells of how Floraldo forsakes his beloved Claraluz for the charms of Mara, a dancer of gypsy and Jewish origin. When Mara demands a unique jewel as evidence of Floraldo's affections she suggests that he procure the sapphire blue eyes of Claraluz to be worn as earrings. Claraluz plucks out her eyes willingly, with just one admonition. If Mara should ever be unfaithful to Floraldo, the eyes will cease shining

and Floraldo will be required to come back to Claraluz. The potential of infidelity torments Floraldo. When, indeed, the shining eyes turn into two pieces of dull, opaque glass, Floraldo kills Mara in a jealous rage.

In **"Los pendientes"** the eyes take on a life of their own although severed from the body. They continue to see, but with heightened intensity and total independence from the body of which they were once a part. Such fragmentation of the body is common in grotesque works of literature and art. The precedents for fragmentation of the body date back to the time of the fifteenth century artist Hieronymous Bosch, whose works served as models for subsequent creators of the grotesque. Pardo Bazán, who wrote that Goya was the heir to the tradition of Bosch and Brueghel, was probably aware of Bosch's painting. "Millenium." This work, housed in the Escorial, includes independent body parts wandering through the landscape.

The transition from the human through the semi-human to the inanimate that characterizes the eyes/earrings of **"Los pendientes"** is common to the aesthetic of the grotesque. Hegel treated the transition from one realm of nature to another in his aesthetic writings, stating that such a transition symbolically joins the sensuous and the spiritual. Since the two women in the story represent spirituality and carnality respectively, the transition through which the eyes pass symbolically joins the two women.

Further examination of the grotesque motif of the eyes provides the key that will yield a still fuller significance of the story. The profuseness of symbols related to the eyes allows for a thorough interpretation. Among the outstanding attributes are the use of light and the underlying social and religious attitudes expressed in the story.

A profusion of references to light extends throughout **"Los pendientes."** Various bodies of light are compared to Claraluz and her effect on others: *lunas, astros, sol,* and *La blanca Febe.* Other references describe the light that she or her eyes emit: *fulgor, irradiación, lumbre,* and *claridad.* Several adjectives describe her eyes: *luminosos, brillantes, resplandecientes,* and *fulgurantes.* Various actions describe the glow that the eyes emit: *alumbrar, deslumbrar, destellar,* and *esplandor.* The references to light far exceed the mentions of darkness.

The physical, moral, and religious contrasts between Claraluz and Mara reinforce the division between light and darkness. Claraluz—the fair, blue-eyed, virtuous Catholic—triumphs over the exotic, evil, materialistic Mara of the burnished copper complexion and gypsy-Jewish heritage. While Claraluz is described as angelical, various epithets depict Mara, including "la hija de Satanás" and "la cava impúdica." The derogatory comments that the narrator makes about Mara's heritage are consistent with those made about Jews by Pardo Bazán in some of her other works. Brian Dendle comments [in "The Racial Theories of Emilia Pardo Bazán," *Hispanic Review,* Vol. 38, 1970] that Pardo Bazán frequently attributes despicable traits to

Jews, relying heavily on so-called genetic theory to justify her bigotry. Dendle states that "Although her anti-Semitism is based in part on religious prejudice, her racial theories are an important element in her naturalism; race is one form of heredity; it is scientific." One must bear in mind, however, that these racial and religious attitudes are expressed in order to create the dichotomy between the women. The concealed message suggests that racial and religious categories are insignificant when viewed in the light of other cultural considerations.

Pardo Bazán establishes Clara and Mara as doubles, opposites of the same spectrum and as such fragments of a whole personality. Clara is always aware of what Mara is doing. Such omniscience may be attributed to the fact that Clara and Mara are essentially the same person. The choice of the double as a narrative technique allows Pardo Bazán to challenge the categorizations and limitations placed on women by society.

Despite the initial presentation of Clara as the self-sacrificing, passive, powerless angel who waits patiently for her beloved, it soon becomes evident that there is more to Clara than is at first perceived. She is capable of foreseeing the future, predicting that Mara will betray her lover. She uses her eyes to manipulate the situation and eventually gains vague control. The cost of her triumph, however, is great. First she plucks out her eyes in order to keep watch over her carnal side, Mara. Clara's eyes go on living, serving to watch Mara, but when the carnal Mara betrays Floraldo, the eyes of Clara die. Clara sacrifices the lamp of her body and the mirror of her soul for Mara's transgressions. Indeed, when Mara betrays Floraldo, the light of Clara's eyes goes out, symbolically indicating Clara's spiritual demise. Likewise, when Floraldo kills Mara, he kills the carnal side of Clara as well. Therefore, the destruction of Clara and the death of Mara come about as a result of this episode.

The covert message of **"Los pendientes"** now can be more easily appreciated. Pardo Bazán shows that women have been reduced to fragments by a society that refuses to recognize their total personalities. Whether fair or dark, Christian or non-Christian, women are universally subject to society's restrictions and limitations. Defined as either spiritual (good) or as sensual (evil), women find that in killing one aspect of their personalities they destroy themselves totally. Sometimes they must sacrifice their very souls in the process of becoming objects (earrings) for the convenience and pleasure of others rather than subjects who take control of the action. While often restricted to a role of passivity or powerlessness, women, in general, like Clara, harbor extraordinary powers which can be channelled to accomplish one's desires.

The short stories we have examined go beyond merely stating Pardo Bazán's personal tastes. They attack fundamental beliefs that made the discussion of female sexuality a taboo subject. Early in her career Pardo Bazán learned that such disclosures would shock society because they were considered inappropriate for discussion by women. When she admitted to finding a man's legs attractive she scandalized some people. Such a statement was daring for the time, according to Ruth Schmidt, who states [in "Women's Place in the Sun: Feminism in Insolación," *Revista de Estudios Hispánicos,* Vol. 8, 1974]:

> Not only did she disturb her readers by expressing a woman's appreciation of a handsome male body, an improper revelation for a woman, but also by pointing out the inequality of society's expectations for men and women in other areas of life.

It is understandable that she later chose to use structures that obscure the forbidden topics, making it possible to discuss such matters and to disseminate her work widely. It is likely that if she had given these covert messages more prominence, her works would not have been widely circulated. The subversive nature of these stories allowed Pardo Bazán to make important statements about cultural expectations that affect women. Those who were unable to decipher the subversive content were, nevertheless, well entertained by masterfully constructed stories with engaging plots.

Francie Cate-Arries   (essay date 1992)

SOURCE: "Murderous Impulses and Moral Ambiguity: Emilia Pardo Bazán's Crime Stories," in *Romance Quarterly,* Vol. 39, No. 2, May, 1992, pp. 205-10.

[*In the following essay, Cate-Arries examines Pardo Bazán's frequent use of crime in her short fiction.*]

In an article published in *La Ilustración Artística* in 1909, Emilia Pardo Bazán writes somewhat wistfully of her secret desire to join the ranks of professional crime solvers: "Todos llevamos dentro algo de instinto policíaco; cuando leo en la prensa el relato de un crimen, experimento deseos de verlo todo, los sitios, los muebles, suponiendo que, de poder hacerlo así, averiguaría mucho y encontraría la pista del criminal verdadero." It is well known that the Condesa confined her restless powers of detection to her armchair; indeed, criminals and their victims fill a wide range of her short stories and novelettes. In this essay I propose to examine the implications of Pardo Bazán's recurring appropriation of crime as anecdote in her short fiction.

The most logical place to start the investigation is with Pardo Bazán's best-known crime story, the novelette **La gota de sangre,** published in 1911. So begin other critics who have tracked the Galician novelist's incursion into the realm of murder and mystery. Paredes highlights the short novel in his study of doña Emilia's detective fiction [*Los cuentos de Emilia Pardo Bazán, 1979*]. Anthony Clarke focuses his 1973 article, "Doña Emilia Pardo Bazán y la novela policíaca," on **La gota,** critiquing the Spanish work according to criteria based on British models of crime-solvers [*BBMP,* Vol. 49, 1973]. The narrator-protagonist Selva himself is constantly aware of

Sherlock Holmes's influence. Implicated in the murder of a wealthy businessman, Selva is framed in fact by the real assassin. To clear his own name and to bring the guilty party to justice, the accused takes it upon himself to solve the crime. Early on, the narrator acknowledges the pre-existing literary model that generates his own text, and motivates his decision to follow in the footsteps of the fictional amateur detectives that have gone before him: "Quizá me ha sugerido tal propósito la lectura de esas novelas inglesas que ahora están de moda, y en que hay policías de afición, o sea *detectives* por *sport*. Ya sabe Ud. que así como el hombre de la Naturaleza refleja impresiones directas, el de la civilización refleja lecturas." In a quasi-metafictional moment, Selva self-consciously attempts to assume the role he has learned through the mediation of literary forms: "Tenía yo que jugar un poco al *detective* y servirme de medios un tanto extravagantes, con espíritu de novela jurídicopenal." Later, stumped by the turn of events, he muses, "En mi situación, ¿qué haría un *detective* profesional?" His answer is lifted directly from the pages of fiction: don a disguise, affect an accent. By the end of the story, the narrator is so captivated by the British model of detection that he announces his intention of setting off to England to pursue his new-found profession, "a tomar lecciones de los maestros." The narrator's tale concludes with the promise of future escapades to be shared with the reader: "Traeré al descubrimiento de los crímenes elementos novelescos e intelectuales, y acaso un día podré contar al público algo digno de la letra de imprenta."

The next year, in 1912, the author does offer a similar detective story, **"La cana,"** in which another narrator-protagonist is framed for a murder. Again, using the same powers of deduction, the accused exonerates himself and aids police in the apprehension of the real criminal. But despite the expectations raised in the closing pages of **La gota de sangre**, Pardo Bazán's amateur sleuth Selva never reappears in subsequent publications. In fact, following the appearance of **"La cana"** in the collection **Cuentos trágicos**, doña Emilia completely abandons this type of detective fiction. In 1916, she refers to her disillusionment with the genre of crime stories which have become so popular in her day: "Fijémonos en que la característica de tales novelas policíacas es la acción, no como resultado de móviles psicológicos, sino por sí misma, como el salto sin finalidad del acróbata de circo" [*El porvenir de la literatura después de la guerra*, 1917]. Her rejection of crime literature that focuses on the criminal act itself was prefigured some 25 years earlier in 1894 in a curious prologue to Pardo Bazán's novel *Doña Milagros*. In the short allegorical preface, a convicted murderer meets his Maker, finding to his surprise that he will not be condemned to burn in eternal Hell: "¿Conque no soy asesino? ¿No soy criminal?" The booming voice of the Creator responds: "El hecho descarnado nada significa para mí. . . . El beso de Judás fue asesinato; el tajo de Pedro, que cercenó la oreja a Malco, fue caricia. Cuando Pedro desenvainó la espada, rebosaba amor por mi Hijo. Intenciones, motivos, pensamientos . . . Hechos, no. . . . El hecho es la cáscara de la realidad."

It is at this point that the critic tracking the case of Emilia Pardo Bazán's attraction to murder, mystery, crime and criminals realizes that she has been led down the wrong path by her reading of stories like **La gota de sangre.** By allowing herself to be seduced by the narration of the riveting criminal acts themselves and the ingenious solutions to the murder, she has failed to discover any meaningful clues as to why Pardo Bazán returns time and again to the scene of a crime in her short fiction. The detective Selva's own seduction in **La gota de sangre** by the murderer's beautiful accomplice, la Chulita, may provide the key to understanding the essential common denominator shared by the disparate criminal acts scattered throughout La Condesa's work. Selva gazes into the eyes of la Chulita, and glimpses the very heart and soul of crime reflected there: "No era la mujer y sus ya conocidos lazos y redes lo que causaba mi fascinación maldita; era la idea de que aquella boca estaba macerada en el amargo licor del crimen, en la esencia de la maldad humana, que es también la esencia de nuestro ser decaído y al morderla gustaría la manzana fatal, la de nuestra perdición y nuestra vida miserable . . .". Questions of original sin, humankind's fall from Grace, the struggle between the forces of good and evil, free will and the power of circumstance: this, then, is the stuff crimes are made of, at least according to Pardo Bazán's confabulation of them.

The Condesa first explored the potential ramifications for literature of the Catholic concept of original sin in her well-known treatise on Naturalism, *La cuestión palpitante*: "Sólo la caída de una naturaleza originariamente pura y libre puede dar la clave de esta mezcla de nobles aspiraciones y bajos instintos, . . . de este *combate* que todos los moralistas, todos los psicólogos, todos los artistas se han complacido en sorprender, analizer y retratar." The author recognizes that the twin imperative of human nature produces a particularly promising source of grist for the literary mill: "¡Qué horizontes tan vastos abre a la literatura esta concepción mixta de la voluntad humana!" A dozen years later, Pardo Bazán combines for the first time her elaboration of the concept of original sin with theoretical disquisitions about criminality in her *La nueva cuestión palpitante*. The new burning question of this most recent book concerns the legitimacy of current theories propagated by César Lombroso y Max Nordau. Pardo Bazán refers particularly to Lombroso's work—which includes the books *El criminal* and *El crimen político y las revoluciones*—explaining that his research has profoundly modified the concept of penal law. Both Lombroso's and Nordau's studies classify criminal, insane, or "degenerate" behaviour as products of physiological or pathological processes, and largely ignore the factors of free will, circumstance, and intention. Not surprisingly, the Catholic Spanish author dismisses such theories as being simplistic and reductive: "La salud y normalidad intelectual y física, que Lombroso considera como el genio algo concreto, positivo y absoluto, no es más que un estado transitorio, relativo, modificable. . . . Así como no existe hombre enteramente justo—ya sabemos que el mejor cae 7 veces al día—tampoco lo hay enteramente sano ni enteramente cuerdo." She rejects the proposed notion of the "criminal nato"—"Embriones de iniquidad, de *pecado* . . . no faltan en ningún hijo de Adán" (p. 1168)—and expresses a growing fascination with the external forces capable of producing deviant behaviour: "La embriaguez, el miedo, la cólera, el hambre, el orgullo ofendido, los odios, exaltan el instinto de acometividad y destructividad que reside en las profundidades del ser humano, y hacen de un hombre que parecía normal un insensato y tal vez un asesino."

For Pardo Bazán, the vehicle that allows her most dramatically to lay bare the often tenuous relationship between right and wrong, good and evil, is certainly the crime story. Here she may detect a glimmer of goodness in the darkest of souls; by the same token, seemingly innocuous acts may be charged with perversity.

—*Francie Cate-Arries*

In March of 1885, Pardo Bazán had discovered a powerful literary appropriation of this criminal transformation in Dostoyevsky's *Crime and Punishment.* The Spanish writer, by her own admission, was profoundly impressed by the psychological portrait of this "hombre que parecía normal" who acted upon murderous impulses. In *La revolución y la novela en Rusia,* she writes of Dostoyevsky's creation: "Horroriza que aquellos sentimientos tan bien estudiados sean humanos y todos los llevamos ocultos en algún rincón obscuro del alma; no sólo humanos, sino propios de una persona de gran cultura intelectual." In this novel, Pardo Bazán not only finds confirmed the lesson espoused by Catholic doctrine that no one is innocent: "Nadie es puro y perfecto; nadie deja de estar sujeto a flaquezas y miserias de la voluntad y del entendimiento también" [*La nueva cuestión palpitante*]. What she most admires is Dostoyevsky's masterful manipulation of moral absolutes: "Subvierte las nociones del bien y del mal hasta un grado increíble" [*La revolución . . .*].

It is in her own crime stories of violence, deceit, and death where Pardo Bazán will consistently call into question conventional notions of good and evil, criminality and socially condoned behavior. The author's ongoing experimentation with these issues in her fiction is especially evident in two radically different stories: **"En el presidio,"** published in 1916, and **"Crimen libre,"** of 1892. The narrator of **"En el presidio"** opens his story by painting a detailed picture of the hulking Juanote, the man convicted of a particularly gruesome murder. The lengthy, heavily naturalistic description of the prisoner appears at first glance to reduce him to little more than a sum of his animalistic parts: "De las orejas y de las manos mucho tendrían que contar los señores que se

dedican a estudios criminológicos. . . . En fin, dibujarían el tipo del criminal nato." But the narrator's interlocutor, the prison warden, offers an unexpected twist in the presentation of this brutal murderer. The warden explains that Juanote refused to comply with his accomplices' insistence that he kill the young boy who witnessed the murder. His act of kindness saved the boy's life, but jeopardized his own freedom when the youngster did indeed betray him to the authorities. The irony of Juanote's position is made clear; he is in jail "no por su crimen, sino por su buen sentimiento." The warden concludes his tale to the narrator by affirming the thin line separating criminals from the rest of society: ". . . las acciones de los mayores criminales, en lo habitual, no se diferencian tanto, tanto, de las del hombre normal, de bien."

The narrator of the second story **"Crimen libre,"** meets with two friends in the casino to pass the time by agreeing to "arreglar el Código y reformar la legislación penal." The narrator tells his listeners of a skating accident in which two young boys fall through the ice. A bystander strips and throws himself into the frigid water. He emerges with the boys to find that someone has stolen his trousers. The narrator explains the significance of the anecdote: "Existe un orden de crímenes que no puede estimar como tales la ley, y, sin embargo, revelan en su autor más perversidad, más ausencia de sentido moral que ninguna de las acciones penadas por el Código." Pardo Bazán's refusal to base a moral judgement solely on the act itself recalls the words of the prologue to *Doña Milagros* cited earlier: "Intenciones, motivos, pensamientos . . . Hechos, no . . . El hecho es la cáscara de la realidad."

The complexity of moral questions raised in Pardo Bazán's crime stories is further exploited by her treatment of "guilty" perpetrators of criminal acts and "innocent" bystanders affected by them. The often blurred boundaries drawn between the two groups are representative of general tendencies in nineteenth-century crime literature. Beth Kalikoff notes in her analysis of the evolution of Victorian murder stories: "Responsibility for murder moves closer and closer to the ordinary citizen or reader. . . . Responsibility for crime moves toward the hearth and, more distressingly, into the mirror" [*Murder and Moral Decay in Victorian Popular Literature,* 1986]. Indeed, both amateur detectives of *La gota de sangre* and **"La cana"** share an unsettling sense of complicity with the murderers that they track. Even as Selva—self-appointed "righter of wrongs"—endeavors to bring the guilty party to justice in *La gota,* he himself feels incriminated by his questionable liaison with the murderer's seductive partner in crime: "Acababa de comprometerme a salvar a la mujer, y mi compromiso me hacía, en cierto modo cómplice de los dos reos. . . . Una parte del pecado me correspondía ya."

The narrator of **"La cana"** is proven innocent of murder at the end of the story. But he is similarly overwhelmed by the disquieting recognition of his own moral shortcomings, and concomitant unwitting role in the crime. His lack of confidence in personal blamelessness echoes in the silence following his closing remarks:

"Yo no era asesino ni ladrón pero . . ." Yet another protagonist of the murder mystery **"Nube de paso"**—published with **"La cana"** in 1911—refers to the feeling of shared guilt that haunts the most "innocent" witnesses of crime: "Cien testigos afirmaban nuestra inculpabilidad, y, así y todo, nos quedó de aquel lance yo no sé qué: una sombra moral en el espíritu, que ha pesado, creo yo, sobre nuestra vida . . ."

Pardo Bazán's short story characters are not the only creatures called upon to confront their own moral accountability for others' socially deviant behavior. In various essays—most notably those addressing "crimes of passion"—the author points an accusatory finger at Kalikoff's "ordinary citizen or reader." In one of two such pieces, Pardo Bazán condemns society as a whole for essentially condoning the crime which she most vehemently denounces, the "crimen pasional": "Con este nombre especioso, se cohonestan las acciones más inicuas. . . . Y por esta simpatía, y esta excusa prevenida siempre para el llamado 'delincuente pasional' tiene razón Oliver, cuando titula su drama *El crimen de todos*. La sociedad, al prevenir al individuo la impunidad y hasta la aprobación cuando mata, es tan criminal como él; es, en efecto, cómplice, y casi diré que más culpada que el mismo autor de la fechoría." [Quoted by Paredes Nuñez]. The Catholic countess reminds her reader in "Coletilla a 'La cuestión palpitante'" that "la naturaleza humana está viciada por el pecado, y que no somos espíritus puros"; her meditations on crime are particularly informed by this fundamental belief.

In her study of the nineteenth-century Spanish story, Lou Charnon-Deutsch analyzes the evolution of the genre from its earliest treatment at the hands of the *costumbristas.* The narrator created by these authors, notes Charnon-Deutsch, "assumes that the difference between right and wrong is something graspable and translatable into fiction" [*The Nineteenth-Century Spanish Story: Textual Strategies of a Genre in Transition,* 1986]. The critic characterizes the later generation of Spanish *cuentistas* as writers in search of a dialectic, whose insistence is "less and less on the character's innate goodness or evilness, and more on the process that leads a character from innocence to corruption." For Pardo Bazán, the vehicle that allows her most dramatically to lay bare the often tenuous relationship between right and wrong, good and evil, is certainly the crime story. Here she may detect a glimmer of goodness in the darkest of souls; by the same token, seemingly innocuous acts may be charged with perversity. As armchair detective, la Condesa is hot on the trail of moral ambiguity, retracing the steps to that place where innocence and guilt, criminality and goodness intersect and overlap: at the scene of the crime story.

Peter P. Ashworth (essay date 1992)

SOURCE: "Of Spinning Wheels and Witches: Pardo Bazán's 'Afra' and *La bruja,*" in *Letras Femeninas,* Vol. 18, Nos. 1-2, 1992, pp. 108-18.

[*In the essay below, Ashworth details similarities between one of Pardo Bazán's short stories and the drama* La bruja, *shedding insight on Pardo Bazán's narrative technique.*]

Pardo Bazán's short story **"Afra"** begins in a theater where the narrator and his friend are watching a performance of *La bruja,* a zarzuela whose initial image is that of women spinning at their wheels and singing about their work while the men drink and play cards:

> Hilemos todas
> el copo suave
> y dando vueltas
> el huso baile.

This self-reflective image of the zarzuela as a tale spun and sung works its metaphorical magic on the village priest who calls for an end to the playing and spinning and for one of the women to tell a story. A woman named Rosalía volunteers, and her story, told in romances, the narrative form par excellence in Spanish poetry, is the first of many told in this musico-drama that is itself a narrative ball of yarns, a tall tale in the zarzuela tradition, set at the end of the 17th century and dealing with witches, love and the Inquisition. Rosalia's story, even further removed in time to the days when there was a kingdom of Granada, tells of a Moorish princess and the Christian who loves her. They are jailed by her father, but the Virgin helps them escape to Christian territory where they can be married. This fanciful tale reflects the main plot of the zarzuela that is to follow, whose richly intertextual relationship to Pardo Bazán's story is much more complicated and ironic, although no less concerned with the narrative act.

That **"Afra"** engages in an intertexual dialog with *La bruja* is borne out by the resonances in plot and characterization and even setting: woman is accused, woman has contact with foreign culture, woman swims in river or sea, main male characters are in the military, woman is ostracized and isolated, actions take place on the margins of Spain. But at least as strong as the similarities of plot and the marginality of places and women are the privileging of the narrative act and the tension and attraction between drama and fiction. As the dramatic text begins with a reference to narration, so Pardo Bazán's narrative starts in a theater; as the zarzuela foregrounds the narrative process, so the tale stages part of its action. And, finally, the short story's ironic inversion of the intertext is heralded within *La bruja* by the conversion of its protagonist from witch, branded as such by her society and by the title of the zarzuela she is in, to innocent normal woman. Doña Emilia's protagonist is never labeled explicitly as witch but is condemned by innuendo, and the reader must discover her innocence in the metafictional techniques and in the dialog between text and intertext. This witch may be roasted, but she is not for burning.

The unveiling of the zarzuela witch is as simple as telling the plot. This work by Ramos Carrión and Maestro Chapí antedates **"Afra"** by seven years and conforms to those characteristics typical of the genre: humor, costumbrismo, liveliness, popular spirit and a light tone en route to an inevitable comic ending. Set in Navarre at the time when Carlos II, el Hechizado, was reigning (or waning), *La bruja* offers an instance of the limits of the monarchy as ruling system and a critique of superstition and ignorance in the days of the Inquisition. The "bruja" of the title is the orphaned daughter of a nobleman who died in exile fighting against Anne of Austria. His daughter "haunts" the family castle as a way of living incognito in Spain, and, while fostering the witch image, she proves herself always a good witch; her charity and "magical feats" help several of the people of the village. She tells Leonardo, the hero, who spots her swimming in the river at night and falls in love with her, that she has been enchanted by a witch; he can break the enchantment by winning glory and honor. To prove his love and win hers, he enlists in the Army and goes off to fight in Italy. He returns triumphant, but she is arrested by the Inquisition and condemned to "reclusión perpetua," forced to profess as a nun to show her faith, although there is no proof of the accusations made against her. The rest of the comic intrigue involves getting her out of the convent and country to marry Leonardo and live happily ever after far from the clutches of the Inquisition and the repressive atmosphere of Spain.

Much more difficult is the job of unmasking the witch in **"Afra,"** for its plot, title, narrator and focalizer all implicate her. Newly stationed at Marineda, Pardo Bazán's fictive version of La Coruña, the soldier who narrates **"Afra"** goes to the opera in the company of a fellow officer, Alberto Castro, a native of Marineda. Faithful to the military code, the narrator is more interested in the young women than the opera, and he turns his glasses at intermission on those attending, eager to see if they live up to their reputation for beauty. He finds that theirs is a beauty of complexion. This superficial perception of women, of beauty only skin-deep, soon yields when he discovers one who stands out, one whose dramatic presence captures his dramatic imagination. It is Afra Reyes, as singular in appearance as in name. When Castro notices that Afra is the subject of his companion's gazes, he warns him not to become interested in her "sin que yo te avise y entere de su historia." Later, as they walk by the port, he explains that although no one has ever suggested that Afra's virtue is anything but beyond reproach—that is, she has no sexual *"historia"*—she nevertheless has another *"historia,"* which Castro is eager to give fictional form.

A naval officer, the cousin of Afra's best friend, Flora, came to town to court his cousin but gave the impression that he was interested in Afra. After learning that he intended to marry Flora all along, Afra, educated in the English fashion and accustomed to a regimen of physical activity, accompanied Flora on a long swim. Afra returned alone, explaining that Flora had floundered and then panicked at Afra's attempts to save her, pulling them both under water where Flora's head had struck the keel of a sunken ship. There were no witnesses, but the cousin's body washed ashore the next day with signs of a blow to the head. Since then Afra has not smiled. Castro, who began with a warning, ends with another: "el corazón del hombre . . . selva obscura. ¡Figúrate el de la mujer!"

A traditional or cursory approach to this story, such as that of Paredes Núñez in his *Los cuentos de Emilia Pardo Bazán,* reveals only a tale of jealousy and revenge, set among others in the same collection that deal with frustrated love, human passions and violence, relieved by an occasional touch of humor. The narrator's juxtaposition of Afra and the zarzuela's title suggests guilt by association and would allow Pardo Bazán's contemporary readers an interpretation that would not challenge the status quo. Within the text, Castro's clever and persuasive narrative will presumably suffice to steer the first-person narrator away from shipwrecking with this green-eyed siren. It would seem that he and Paredes Núñez both read their texts from such a traditional male perspective; the Inquisition and its accompanying superstitions have given way in the nineteenth century, but the patriarchal society that fostered them is still going strong. The foregrounding of the story within this story and the drama-opera-zarzuela lurking in the background suggest another interpretation and help Pardo Bazán, well known for her feminist views, point to a different reading of the two texts: Afra as woman and **"Afra"** as tale. Such a reading reveals in Afra a much more sympathetic character and in **"Afra"** a critique of the structures of that patriarchal society.

One of those structures that Pardo Bazán attacks in **"Afra"** is the narrative tradition that she inherits from male authors. Patricia Waugh in *Metafiction: The Theory and Practice of Self-conscious Fiction,* says of that tradition: "So, in metafiction, a convention is undermined, or laid bare, in order to show its historical provisionality: to show, for example, that the use of an implicitly male omniscient author in popular continuations of realism is tied to a specific ideological world-view which continues insidiously to pass itself off as 'neutral' or 'eternal' or 'objective,' and which has its historical roots in the late eighteenth and early nineteenth centuries." Pardo Bazán uses her fiction to make a metafictional comment on the state of the art of novel writing and the limits and problems it poses for a woman writing in her times and offers her reader one male spinning a yarn about a woman within a yarn told by another male. In my reading of **"Afra,"** the nameless narrator will stand for the author/implied author and his friend Castro for the narrator, who between them form this "implicitly male omniscient author" that dominates the fiction of Pardo Bazán's era. Needless to say, the real implied author of **"Afra"** has carefully distanced herself from these two and from their role in the narrative structure. Her challenge is to weave a feminine fabric from a masculine yarn spun on a patriarchal spinning wheel.

Just as the typical realist novelist went about observing his real world as the basis for the fictional heterocosm of his latest novelistic project, so does Doña Emilia's symbolic author sally forth in his guise as narrator of **"Afra."** He leaves his real world, that is his prior military post, for the fictional world of Marineda, whose name masks but does not destroy its correspondence with the historical world of nineteenth-century Spain. He represents the military, identifying his membership in the masculine fraternity of conquest and power. His first action is to go to the theater, the world of artifice. A believer in the referentiality of language, he has come to capture reality and not to examine fictional form. This preference for product over process leads him to ignore the opera, except for its highly suggestive title, and to look for material for his fictions, to conduct his witch hunt, among the real women attending the opera. This quintessential voyeur trains his opera glasses, his powerful capacity to observe his physical world, on one woman and now presents her to his readers through an external description of her appearance, based on male-determined notions of feminine beauty. But true to his novelistic trade and the demands of realistic fiction, he also penetrates beneath the surface and gives a psychogical portrait as well: "Aquella fisonomía, sin dejar de atraer, alarmaba, pues era de las que dicen a las claras, desde el primer momento, a quien las contemplaba: 'Soy una voluntad. Puedo torcerme, pero no quebrantarme. Debajo del elegante maniquí femenino, escondo el acerado resorte de un alma'." The glasses remind us, however, that it is an image, woman as object and not as subject, that he has brought closer. The glasses magnify but also exclude and distort, restricting his view; the woman herself is still distanced, and his view of Afra, Pardo Bazán seems to be warning us, will indeed be very limited. His curiosity is piqued, but his partner in narration will keep him from discovering the 'alma' hiding behind Afra's elegant surface.

Having found his character in search of an author, and one with an obviously interesting story to tell or be told, the soldier/author now needs a narrator. Afra may seem too formidable, too distant, maybe even reluctant to tell, but he finds a willing candidate right next to him, and the proximity is important, in his fellow male officer who is not only handy but likewise inhabits this fictional version of the real world. Castro cannot narrate from within the theater, the world of illusion, but wants to tell the story on the stage where it took place, the world of reality. He implies that he is no mere teller of tales, for his language will capture that reality; he is the historian seeking and speaking only the truth. In current critical parlance, he prefers mimesis to diegesis.

The stage on which he will reveal his truth is that archetypal giver and taker of life, the sea. The narrator, as befitting an officer and a gentleman, might have rescued a real woman floundering in a sea of masculine prejudice and gossip and placed her in his tale. Instead, he borrows not a life, but an archetype, not a rounded female personality, but woman as witch. This would-be historian freely mixes myth with history. [Patricia] Waugh refers to Simone de Beauvoir's categorization of this archetype as woman's most disturbing and most fascinating aspect and adds her own observation that this archetype presents "a heroine who at one and the same time fulfills contradictory male desires, is both apparent seductress and in fact virgin . . . who thus ultimately conforms to a male con-

cept of female contradictoriness embodied in the femme fatale" [*Metafiction: The Theory and Practice of Self-Conscious Fiction*, 1984]. These two males, both as fictional characters and as symbols of the male-dominated narrative structures that Pardo Bazán inherited, present a female type readily molded to masculine purposes and perceptions. Conveniently overlooked is the soul-mate archetype of the zarzuela who is only pretending to be a witch.

The rest of the narrative belongs to Castro, the focalizer who relishes this opportunity to tell as history the collective male-authorized version of how Afra qualifies for witchhood. His approach, reminiscent of some of Galdós's narrators, vacillates between affirming the truth of his history and undermining it as fiction. First he says that only God and the sea know the truth, that the rest is conjecture, even admitting that he may be wrong. Then he adds: "Pero hay tan fatales coincidencias; hay apariencias tan acusadoras en el mundo . . . que no podría disiparlas sino la voz del mismo Dios." Castro's voice is all too human, but his privileged position vis-à-vis his fellow officer lends his voice an apparent narrative authority that the careful reader must question. Castro never directly accuses, but his tale leaves no doubt as to what he thinks. In fictionalizing what is already a fiction, he loses any claim to historicity or narrative authority, an irony that surely escapes him. Since the narrator shows no signs of loss of faith in Castro, we have both an unreliable narrator *and* focalizer. The reader of the text must be more alert and perceptive than the hearer in the text.

To the metafictional suggestions of Castro's narrative, his story-within-a-story, Pardo Bazan adds a strong parodic thrust, particularly in the way that his beginning and ending relate to those found in contemporary short stories. He constructs a straightforward plot but ends it with the other half of the frame of hedging, self-protection and broad verbal winks with which he began and which are intended to convince his hearer, while allowing Pardo Bazán to warn her reader. She further alerts her reader with Castro's opening words: "no creas" and accepts Castro's closure as her ending, which allows her to parody the typical closures of late nineteenth-century short stories while leaving her own story ironically open-ended. Some of these techniques of closure are mentioned in a recent book on the short story in Pardo Bazán's Spain [called *The Nineteenth-Century Spanish Short Story*, by Lou Charnon-Deutsch, 1985]. The author points out that few of Clarín's stories "end without additional statements which reflect on past events or project forward to speculate about the protagonist's future. Some works must do this in order to fulfill the expectation created earlier when a question or enigma was posed but its solution delayed until the last moment." Castro seems familiar with this type of ending for he has certainly posed an enigma and then given a delayed solution. He reiterates the enigmatic nature of his protagonist with this rhetorical question: "¿Que si creo que Afra . . . ?", which both reflects on the past and anticipates the future, while allowing him to shift the onus of unravelling the enigma and the blame for it to his hearer. Of course, it also allows Pardo Bazán to undermine Castro's authority in his double role as male gossip and co-conspirator in the male-omniscient-author plot that **"Afra"** so deftly exposes.

The epilogue is a second common device to give closure, and Castro's penultimate paragraph functions as an epilogue: "Sólo añadiré que al marino, novio de Flora, no volvió a vérsele por aquí; y Afra, desde entonces, no ha sonreído nunca . . .". These suspension points are a favorite device of Castro the masculine narrator, and he manages six sets of them in the last page alone, part of a strategy to asseverate while demurring, to bestow authority on his fiction while undermining his protagonist. His epilogue trails off in the same gesture of complicity with his hearer and reader as his rhetorical question. He thus avoids directly answering the question while pointing smurkingly to the unavoidable conclusion.

The final step in his three-part effort to round off his closure is another reminder that the parodic purpose of these steps is different from that intended by the tellers within the tale. Charnon-Deutsch states: "To avoid limp endings or endings which trail off to no apparent purpose, nineteenth-century storytellers often made a point of packing their closing remarks with ironic meaning or emotion-seeking dramatics . . . to shock the reader into the realization of some truth or irony . . .". This seems to be Castro's purpose as he concludes with this "kernel of moral truth": "Por lo demás, acuérdate de lo que dice la Sabiduría: el corazón del hombre . . . selva obscura. ¡Figúrate el de la mujer!" Thus his final statement also serves as closure to the narrator's story, with similar intent and desired effect. But on the third level of closure, Pardo Bazán's parodic thrust cuts through the other two towards a different and highly ironic ending: Afra's story has come to an end without being told. The title proclaims this to be her story, and Castro presents it as history, but it is really his-story or their-story. Afra is here an absence, and what is offered as presence is a patriarchal pastiche made up of rumor, convention, innuendo, prejudices and fears. This witch has no voice. That is, she has no narrative voice except that briefly and indirectly allowed her by those who wield narrative control. This is, of course, Pardo Bazán's dilemma, too, as a woman trying to write her way out of or around the conventions of patriarchal discourse. Afra's protestations of innocence, perhaps as given to the police, are further filtered through Castro and the narrator, muted and muffled and hedged about with insinuations. The spy-and-tell methods of the Inquisition, which protected the identity of the informer, continued in force in the nineteenth century in chauvinistic social and narrative structures.

Pardo Bazán's reader, unlike Castro's, can hardly be content with the sense of this ending, especially after having been promised so much more by the nameless narrator in his description of Afra. His opera glasses foregrounded her, but his tale keeps her distanced. He prefers to leave the final word with Castro. Seen from this perspective, Castro's would-be punch line further undermines his authority and leaves him holding his fictional bag that he

has so self-satisfactorily emptied out and closed up. What was intended to "strengthen the symmetry of a story by complementing the opening situation or setting" now sends the reader scuttling back to the beginning in search of a character, beyond the exotic mystery woman adumbrated by Castro's account, to the real woman briefly seen through the glasses. The work's intertext helps to recuperate some sense of presence, some faint voice, as it resonates with Pardo Bazán's text. The masculine text, ironically, refuses to penetrate; it stresses the negative, superficial suggestions of Afra's name, African and marginated like the Moorish women in the tale from the zarzuela, and the narrator studies the surface of the women in the theater and offers only the surface of the zarzuela, its provocative title. But that title marks an intertext that invites the alert reader to dig below the surface of the masculine text and see beneath Afra's perplexing and vexing exterior. Such a reading serves to restore a sense of depth, balance and symmetry to the story and the woman, foregrounding the positive qualities of dignity and worth, power and presence, associated with her surname, Reyes.

Castro and the narrator, for all their complicity, do represent different and limited ways of perceiving and converting into fiction both reality and members of the opposite sex. The narrator conducts his pseudo-scientific observations through binoculars that deform as they magnify, leaving his subjects larger than life but still lifeless. He sees his narrative act as a way of analyzing Afra, and Castro's account is just another datum to be studied. He is less interested in the narrative process than Castro and prefers character analysis, although he confuses it with character assassination. When his spy glasses fail him, he can rely on his superior linguistic and rhetorical skills. Metaphorically, he first suggests Afra's burden of guilt: "su cuello delgado y largo, que parecía doblarse al peso del voluminoso rodete"; then with a simile he rejects her as unsuitable as a character in his fiction, or in his personal life, if she fails to measure up to his standards of female sexual purity: "porque sin amar a una mujer me gusta su pureza, como agrada el aseo de casas donde no pensamos vivir nunca." But if he is in charge linguistically, Pardo Bazán remains in firm control of the irony, and his carefully constructed case is shown to rest on as false and flimsy a foundation as his house metaphor, which is doubly suspect and offensive. He has, after all, constructed a fictional house for Afra, and yet he refuses to let her live in it. Both his metaphorical house and his metaphor need tidying up.

Castro's strength, *qua* narrator, is the act of telling, but he confuses product with process. Under the guise of saving his friend from the clutches of the local siren, he indulges in his favorite narrative game of converting half-truths and gossip into historical novels. Since it is historical truth he claims to seek, it is fitting that his optic be clear and free of distortions. He says, referring to her *pureza*, that Afra is "como el cristal." It is a glass, nonetheless, through which he sees darkly, if at all. Or, perhaps, sees clear through, missing the woman, all women, completely. She remains a game, a riddle or enigma that he cannot solve, a toy for his narrative play. His name, besides its more obvious military reference, subtly foregrounds his ludic spirit, his basic duality as man-child, soldier-gamester: *castro* is similar to hopscotch but with "las rayas dispuestas al modo de la situación de un *ejército encampado*" (Real Academia, 1984. Italics added). In this story that deals centrally with seeing and telling, it is ironic that this seer and teller, his own surname so at odds with itself, fails to note the oxymoronic implications of the names of the two female characters: Flora Castillo and Afra Reyes. In his arrested stage of development, he is content with his childish games and simplistic ways of perceiving things, at least things feminine.

As a corrective to such a limited all male perspective, the resonances between story and zarzuela serve important functions, assuring us that there is certainly more to Afra than meets the eye or ear in this tale. *La bruja*'s spinning wheels suggest an intertextual relation with yet another Spanish work of art in another medium. Just as Velázquez, in *Las hilanderas,* places the finished product of the tapestry in the background and foregrounds the creative process, the artist's tools and raw material, so has Pardo Bazán woven Afra's story on a distant tapestry and given privilege to the processes, materials and tools of her craft. Unlike Arachne, Pardo Bazán as weaver is not competing with the gods; she must weft against the warp and woof of male-determined fabrics and patterns.

Velázquez' spinners lead back to where this article started, like a turn of the spinning wheel that serves as my central metaphor. In the zarzuela, the priest calls for an older, experienced woman to tell a story:

> Como siempre, la más vieja
> que nos cuente una conseja.

The male authority does not get his way, for it is a young woman that tells a woman's story, prefacing her tale with an invitation and a warning to her listeners:

> Formad la rueda
> y oído atento;
> mucho cuidado
> que va de cuento

The ambivalence of the word *rueda,* referring to the circle of listeners and the spinning wheel, is echoed in Pardo Bazán's tale as she addresses her circle of readers and likewise seems to warn and invite: "mucho cuidado" when *he* spins *her* yarn; if her story is to be accurately told, there must be a woman at the wheel. Pardo Bazán's soldier-narrator receives Afra's story already twice told, all by male voices. Pardo Bazán's reader may be assured that this third male voice is no more authoritative than the other two. It would seem that the real tale is yet to be told.

But **"Afra"** is not a story of failure, nor a failed story. Pardo Bazán, too much the creative artist to be stifled by imposed masculine restraints, whether social or narra-

tive, has managed, by thematizing and parodying those restraints, to write around them and thus to tell Afra's story and her own, too. Afra's voice is heard, faintly in her own filtered account, but with increasing strength and authority through the parody, metafiction and intertext that are ample evidences of Pardo Bazán's firm hand at the wheel.

Joyce Tolliver   (essay date 1992)

SOURCE: "'La que entrega la mirada, lo entrega todo': The Sexual Economy of the Gaze in Pardo Bazan's 'La Mirada'," in *Romance Languages Annual,* Vol. 4, 1992, pp. 620-26.

[*In the following essay, Tolliver discusses the sexual meaning of the lover's gaze in Pardo Bazán's short story* "La Mirada."]

In Pardo Bazán's 1908 story, **"La mirada,"** a character identified only as a "señorito" makes the following pronouncement: "la que entrega la mirada, lo entrega todo." This comment encapsulates the complex dynamic of the gaze between men and women, for it clearly associates sexuality with the gaze, and both of these with notions of trade, surrender, power and control. **"La mirada"** explores this dynamic both on the level of story and in the structure of the narrative discourse.

"La mirada" employs a male autodiegetic narrator. From his room at the inn in the town of "M . . .", where he frequently travels on business, the unnamed narrator/protagonist makes a practice of spying on the young married woman across the street, whose bedroom window faces his. One day, he overhears a group of businessmen comment that although Tilde, the young woman, takes pleasure in perfecting her appearance, she does so for the gratification she receives from the envy of other women, and not in order to attract other men. In fact, she would not so much as look at another man. This pleasure is constrained, however, by her husband's miserliness, which limits her access to the tools of beauty. When the French jewel merchant mentions that he plans to make a business call on the young woman, the protagonist/narrator forms a plan: by taking the jewel merchant's place, he manages to visit Tilde in the very bedroom where he had so often watched her from across the street. Knowing her love of self-adornment and her husband's stinginess, he offers her a beautiful jeweled necklace, assuring her that she might pay for it on an installment plan. Her responsive look makes it clear that she understands that the payment will be in flesh, and that she accepts the terms. Years after the affair has ended, the narrator/protagonist visits the same town and finds that the woman "seguía pasando por inexpugnable, que ni con la mirada . . .".

Questions of surveillance and control are clearly at issue in this story. Foucault's theory of the function of the gaze as a controlling institutional force helps to clarify the imposition of power inherent in the anonymous narrator's surveillance of Tilde. In *Discipline and Punish,* [Michel] Foucault suggests that the institutional "panoptic" gaze of surveillance, of external control, eventually results in an internalized vigilance. He uses as a metaphor for societal control Bentham's model of the Panopticon, which he describes as follows:

> at the periphery, an annular building; at the centre, a tower; this tower is pierced with wide windows that open onto the inner side of the ring; the peripheric building is divided into cells, each of which extends the whole width of the building; they have two windows, one on the inside, corresponding to the windows of the tower; the other, on the outside, allows the light to cross the cell from one end to the other. All that is needed, then, is to place a supervisor in a central tower and to shut up in each cell a madman, a patient, a condemned man, a worker or a schoolboy. By the effect of backlighting, one can observe from the tower, standing out precisely against the light, the small captive shadows in the cells of the periphery.

Each prisoner is enclosed in an individual cell, constantly within the view of the supervisor but unable to see either the supervisor or other prisoners. The delinquent is thus under constant surveillance by an invisible authority and, equally importantly, shut off from contact with others. From this derives, says Foucault, "the major effect of the Panopticon: to induce in the inmate a state of conscious and permanent visibility that assures the automatic functioning of power. So to arrange things that the surveillance is permanent in its effects, even if it is discontinuous in its action . . . in short, that the inmates should be caught up in a power situation of which they are themselves the bearers."

Although not explicitly discussed by Foucault, patriarchy as an institution fits easily into the paradigm he suggests. His theory illuminates the way in which the patriarchal gaze of control is eventually internalized by the woman, so that she posits herself as object of this male gaze, relinquishing her own specular subjectivity. The voyeuristic narrator/protagonist of **"La mirada"** reproduces and emblematizes the gaze of patriarchal power under which Tilde lives her life.

Tilde dramatizes this dynamic, for she constantly examines herself in the mirror, exemplifying the way in which, as Irigaray suggests, "[woman's] entrance into a dominant scopic economy signifies, once again, her relegation to passivity; she will be the beautiful object." The autodiegetic narration of the story underscores Tilde's status as "beautiful object." Tilde sees herself (or at least she sees the artistic construction which she enacts upon her own body); the narrator/protagonist sees Tilde seeing herself. While the "outside world" is allowed only a view of the finished product, the narrator/protagonist is privy to the beautiful woman's self-construction, as well as the evolving product. Tilde's grooming constitutes the object of the protagonist's privileged, yet unauthorized, gaze:

> yo veía a la bella que, instalada ante una mesa cargada de frascos y perfumadores, contemplándose en el espejo,

> peinaba su regia mata de pelo color caoba, complaciéndose en halagarla con el cepillo, en ahuecarla y enfoscarla alrededor de su cara pálida y perfecta. Cuando acababa de morder las ondulaciones laterales el último peinecillo de estrás, sonreía satisfecha, alisando reiteradamente, con la mano larga y primorosa, el capilar edificio. Después se pasaba por la tez suavemente, la borla de los polvos; se pulía las cejas; se bruñía interminablemente las uñas con pasta de coral; se probaba sombreros, lazos, cinturones, piquetes de flores, encajes, que arrugaba alrededor del cuello . . . en suma: se consagraba largas horas a la autolatría de su beldad.

The description of Tilde's activities is so detailed that it is clearly based on much more than a cursory glance through her window: she arranges her hair in waves with combs made of "estrás," a glittery stone; she polishes her nails with "pasta de coral" and tries on "piquetes de flores." Later, when the time finally comes for what Tilde thinks is the industrialist's first encounter with her, the narrator is careful to emphasize the unauthorized knowledge he possesses even of Tilde's is wardrobe; she is wearing "una bata que yo conocía." If Tilde, in the conventional view of the narrator, devotes long hours to "la autolatría de su beldad," the narrator devotes equally long hours to surveillance, and judgement, of this "autolatría." The protagonist's observation is far from casual, then, and in fact is charged with an odd sort of voyeurism which allies itself closely with Foucault's surveillance of power, as well as with [Jacques] Lacan's conception of the voyeuristic gaze as projection of fantasy. [*The Four Fundamental Concepts of Psycho-analysis,* 1977].

The language which narrates the protagonist's surveillance uncannily evokes the Foucauldian interplay of power and knowledge, as well as the panoptic dynamic: "Desde mi observatorio se registraba de modo más indiscreto su tocador, y yo veía a la bella. . . ." "Y clavado a la ventana por el incitante espectáculo, encendida la sangre al profanar asi la intimidad de una mujer seductora, nacía en mí otra curiosidad, el ansia de conocer su historia, en la cual, sin duda, habría episodios pasionales, goces, penas, recuerdos. . . ." The use of the verb *registrar* is particularly revealing, associated, as it is, with searches and inspections. These associations are strengthened by the use of the noun *observatorio* to refer to the protagonist's room, and the combination of these images points toward a sort of surveillance remarkably similar to that made possible by Bentham's Panopticon. Even the impersonal form of the verb *se registraba* echoes the anonymity of the Panoptic guard.

The catoptric activities of the woman are presented by the narrator as a provocative spectacle ("incitante espectáculo") which clearly excites the protagonist's desire. But, curiously, this desire, although eroticized, is not framed as an exclusively sexual desire in the narrator's description of his own scopic activity. Rather, what excites Tilde's spectator is the unauthorized view he has managed to gain of what is meant to be a solitary, private activity: he surveys Tilde's dressing table "de modo más indiscreto;" his observation of her grooming activities enables him to "profanar así la intimidad de una mujer seductora." This privileged view, this special specular knowledge, arouses in the anonymous protagonist the desire for further "inside information," for knowledge of the "historia, en la cual, sin duda, habría episodios pasionales, goces, penas, recuerdos . . ." of this "mujer seductora." In short, this epistemological voyeur is erotically excited, not by the sight itself of a woman at her dressing table, but by the prospect of learning the secrets of her sexual history. The voyeuristic gaze of the protagonist/narrator here is thus intimately tied to power, for the view of the woman preparing herself as a "beautiful object" puts him in control of her secrets—the secrets of her toilette and, by extension, the secrets of her sexuality.

This intermingling of the notions of knowledge, power, and the cultural construction of sexuality, analyzed by Foucault in *The History of Sexuality,* informs the entire narrative discourse of **"La mirada."** The evocation of the myth of the Garden of Eden brings this interdependence to the forefront. When the industrialist proposes his trade of the necklace in return for Tilde's favors, he does so "con silbo serpentino al pie del árbol del Mal," it is Tilde's "sagacidad de Eva habituada a la adoración" which allows her to perceive the implications of the false jewel merchant's offer. It is interesting, however, that while the narrator imputes to Tilde the "sagacidad de Eva," the element of knowledge in the construction of desire is elided by the choice of the word "Mal" rather than the equally traditional "Ciencia" in the expression "árbol del Mal."

This idea of secret knowledge is, in fact, present throughout Pardo Bazán's short text. Not only is the protagonist invisible to the woman whose solitary activities he monitors, he is also unknown in the town, as he makes clear in the very first sentence of the narration: "Por asuntos de la gran Sociedad industrial de que yo formaba parte, hube de ir varias veces a M***, donde nadie me conocía, y a nadie conocía yo." Thus, unbeknownst to Tilde, he keeps a vigilant watch over her private moments. Likewise, the narrator/protagonist protects both his anonymity and his privileged position of knowledge by keeping secret his transgressive sexual liason with Tilde. This belies the common assumption that "en los pueblos relativamente pequeños no quedan ocultas esas cosas."

The protagonist is anonymous, not only to the townspeople and to Tilde, but also to the narratee. The narration is told in the first person, thus facilitating the anonymity of the narrator/protagonist, and nowhere does the narrator make his identity known to the narratee by such devices as use of his name in the reported speech of other characters. The narrator's reference to the town (M***) only by its first initial further emphasizes the privileged knowledge he has but which he withholds from the narratee, in keeping with the realist convention which propagates the illusion that the town actually exists but its true identify is being masked. This convention, and its attendant associations with the power of knowledge, is also employed when the narrator explicitly calls attention to his withholding of Tilde's last name from his narration: "el via-

jante francés en joyas . . . pensaba pasar a casa de la belle Madame . . . —aquí el apellido, que no entregaré a la publicidad—." The motif of sexuality as intimately connected with secret knowledge is, finally, emphasized even in the very last sentence of the story: ". . . al volver años después a M***, supe que la hermosa—siempre hermosa, pues parecía poseer un secreto y conservarse entre nieve—seguía pasando por mujer inexpugnable, que ni con la mirada . . .".

> **Throughout this short text, the gaze is explicitly posited as a reflection of the economic element of sexuality; the entire story is heavily framed in economic terms.**
>
> *—Joyce Tolliver*

This sentence is, in fact, most interesting in its ambiguity, which arises largely due to a double interpretation of the word "parecía." On the one hand, "parecía poseer un secreto y conservarse entre nieve" represents the townspeople's perception of Tilde's apparent eternal `youth; Tilde appears to the villagers of M*** to possess the secret *of* conserving her youthful appearance. That this might be a brief instance of free indirect discourse is supported by the use of the colloquial, popular expression "conservarse entre nieve." On the other hand, it is only too true that Tilde only *seems* to possess a secret; for the narrator has revealed her secret, in the narration which forms this story. And this secret is not, as the townspeople think, only the secret of maintaining a youthful appearance, but rather refers to the secret of Tilde's transaction with the protagonist/narrator. It is in the little conjunction "y" that these two perspectives, that of the townspeople and that of the narrator, come together. When the phrase "parecía poseer un secreto y conservarse entre nieve" is read as representing the villagers' perspective, the "y" could easily be substituted with the preposition "de" (with the possible minor modification of changing the article from indefinite to definite): "parecía poseer el secreto [de] conservarse entre nieve." But when the same phrase is interpreted as representing only the narrator's perspective, that "y" is crucial, for it separates Tilde's secret from her youthful appearance. While the narrator suggests a causal relationship, Tilde's secret is not in itself that of eternal beauty, but rather the secret of her proscribed sexual relationship. Tilde, then, *appears* to possess a secret (which in fact has been revealed to the narratee) *and* maintains her youthful appearance. The syntax of this intercalated clause thus emphasizes the connection between secret knowledge, which is a form of power (a power which the narrator steals from Tilde by telling her secret story), sexuality, and the primary criterion for assigning value to a "woman on the market": "beauty."

Yet the fairly conventional association between the last two categories, sexuality and beauty, is in fact surprisingly undermined by the imagery of coldness and lifelessness evoked in the expression "conservarse entre nieve." This expression echoes an earlier description of Tilde as "no solo . . . intachable, sino *glacial* e inexpugnable." Tilde's creation and presentation of herself as a desirable object is, then, very much related to sexual desire, but to the desire of others, of men. Indeed, Tilde seems to construct herself as the "passive image of virtual perfection," in Laura Mulvey's phrase, the woman who is the vehicle of the voyeur's pleasure ["Visual Pleasure and Narrative Cinema," *Visual and Other Pleasures,* 1989]. The narrator's language of panoptic control through secret knowledge already aligns him with Mulvey's formulation of the cinematic voyeuristic character, but in fact the protagonist's behavior goes beyond the control of the gaze: elements of aggression, even of sadism, permeate the narrative discourse.

Mulvey's essay, "Visual Pleasure and Narrative Cinema," seems particularly relevant to Pardo Bazán's story. It is with the narrative aspects of cinema that Mulvey associates the presence of this sadistic voyeuristic look in film. Further, the narrative situation of this story is remarkably similar to that of Hitchcock's *Rear Window,* which Mulvey takes as a prime example of the deployment of sadistic voyeurism in cinema. When Tilde visually signals her acceptance of the protagonist's offer to exchange her body for the jewels which she desires, the gaze itself is described by the narrator in explicitly violent terms:

> los puñales, buidos, crueles, de nuestro espíritu, se cruzaron en forma de ojeada larga y significativa . . . 'No ha delinquido ni con una mirada . . .' 'La que entrega la mirada, lo entrega todo.' Recordé esta frase del señorito, y al recordarla, me deslumbró más aún aquella luz diabólica que llegaba adentro, al fondo de mi ser de hombre apasionado, caprichoso, en la plenitud de la edad. . . .

The aggression and domination inherent in the classical metaphor of the gaze of love as twin arrows emanating from the eyes is exaggerated here, becoming positively "diabólico": the arrows are now cruel pointed daggers in this gaze which seals a carnal contract. The protagonist directs toward Tilde a look which exemplifies Mulvey's sadistic gaze, in which "pleasure lies in ascertaining guilt . . . asserting control"; it is Tilde's look itself which confirms the falsehood of the young gentleman's assertion that Tilde "no ha delinquido ni con la mirada." This element of violence in the protagonist's stance toward Tilde is, in fact, consistent throughout the narration. The first time the protagonist hears Tilde mentioned in the round table of businessmen which congregates in his inn, he is aroused in a way which is described explicitly in terms of aggression and domination: "Me alteré, como el cazador al sentir rebullir en el matorral la pieza que aguarda." Finally the protagonist's desire for knowledge of Tilde's amorous history, already excited by his visual invasion of her bedroom, may be satisfied; the imagery used clarifies the relationship between possession of this

knowledge and sadistic domination. Tilde, or, to be more precise, Tilde's story, is the protagonist's easy prey.

The sadistic element of the protagonist's desire to physically penetrate Tilde's chamber is further highlighted in the narration of what perhaps constitutes the climactic moment in terms of plot: "Me incliné y le tendí al mismo tiempo mis brazos y collar, abrochándolo tiránicamente a su garganta, tembloroso de enredarme los dedos en la regia mata de pelo y caoba, viva y eléctrica . . .". This moment captures the melding of power, control, aggression on the one hand and erotic desire on the other. The adverb *tiránicamente* makes explicit the sadistic nature of the protagonist's act, while the metonymic positioning of *collar* and *brazos* even suggests the image of a strangling. Finally, the narrator's surveillance of the beautiful woman across the street has culminated in the expression of his aggression, with the precious necklace almost fetishistically acting as the protagonist's arm, in both senses of the word.

These elements of domination on the part of the autodiegetic narrator would posit Tilde as a passive victim of the industrialist's scheme, and would, in fact, uphold the image of beautiful (and beautified) woman as a passive object of desire for men. Tilde would seem to embody an extreme representation of what Kaja Silverman refers to as "the alterity of the gaze," the notion that the affirmation of one's subjecthood always depends on the look of another ["Fassbinder and Lacan: A Reconsideration of Gaze, Look and Image," *Camera Obscura,* Vol. 19, 1989].

In fact, Tilde's lack of autonomy is emphasized by her confinement to the role of object within the narrative discourse itself. The plot is largely advanced by what the male characters say about Tilde. This discourse, which is, unvarying, presented directly, without narrative intervention, is quite extensive indeed, considering the text's brevity (three pages). The narrator even comments on the loquacity of these men who dedicate their conversation to a consideration of the relative availability or unavailability of Tilde's beautiful body ("al final de la plática, que aún se prolongó *verbosamente* . . ."). Tilde, in contrast, speaks but one word: "¿Cuánto?" This interrogative not only places Tilde as speaker squarely in an economic context, it also encapsulates her powerlessness relative to the false merchant, whose prerogative it is to name the price he wants for the coveted jewels.

From an economic perspective, Tilde's presentation as merchandise seems to be a perfect emblematization of "women on the market" [Luce Irigaray, *This Sex Which Is Not One,* 1986]. On the other hand, Tilde's aesthetic self-construction may be seen, alternatively, as an attempt to empower herself in the limited way allowed her, in a culture in which woman's body is treated as coin. By adorning herself, Tilde is increasing her own value in patriarchal culture, for the more beautiful she is, the more valuable she is (provided, of course, that she is always publicly designated as a particular man's property—a provision which is explicitly fulfilled in this story). Jenijoy La Belle's recent work on the literary motif of women who use the mirror to determine and discover their own identities is relevant here, in its suggestion of another possible motivation for Tilde's "mirroring" besides the conventional (masculine) imputation of vanity: Tilde, like many other female literary characters, uses the mirror to determine, and confirm, her own value in the dominant sexual economy [*Herself Beheld: The Literature of the Looking Glass,* 1988]. It is important, in this respect, that the one male character who comments on Tilde's situation is adamant that her preening is not motivated by any illegitimate desire:

> ¡Al contrario! Tilde no ha dado jamás que decir ni esto. . . . No niego que esté engreída con su hermosura; lo está y mucho; pero su única pasión es la compostura, el adorno. La disloca, más que hacer conquistas, que rabien las otras mujeres ante la elegancia. ¡Bah! Si en algo hubiese delinquido, aunque solo fuese en una mirada, se sabría. (. . .) Y la que entrega la mirada, lo entrega todo . . . Les repito a ustedes, y cualquiera se lo repetirá, que Tilde no sólo es intachable, sino glacial e inexpugnable.

Tilde wants (and deserves, says the young man of leisure) beautiful objects in order to enhance her own status as an object of consumption. She derives most of her pleasure from seeing the envy of other women—the envy that comes from having to recognize the superior value, the enhanced worth, of the product which Tilde has made of herself. This look which comes from other women, and which confirms Tilde's limited subjectivity, is devoid of power; it does not participate in the male gaze. It is the look of other products of consumption, of Irigaray's "commodities among themselves." Thus Tilde successfully turns herself into desirable—but, crucially, noncirculating—merchandise, a product which already has an owner. In this way, the element of explicit sexual power inherent in successfully eliciting the male gaze of desire is elided, and Tilde's attempts to empower herself are still set within a legitimate frame; her actions seemingly involve no transgression. It is the exposure of this hidden frame of the sexual economy which gives the narrator his secret power. And it is in the gaze that this evocation of desire, the creation of a limited subjectivity, and the economic converge.

Throughout this short text, the gaze is explicitly posited as a reflection of the economic element of sexuality; the entire story is heavily framed in economic terms. The narrator's employment in a "gran Sociedad industrial" is foregrounded in the very first sentence (even the very first clause) of the text, when the narrator informs us that it is, in fact, through his employment as an industrialist that he regularly visits the town of M*** and thus sees Tilde. It is, again, through his position of power in industry that the protagonist first hears of Tilde's situation, when his colleague, the jewel merchant, mentions that he plans to pay a business call on Tilde. Tilde is, thus, from the very beginning, presented in an economic context, as a potential consumer of the merchant's items of luxury.

Not only is the woman posited in economic terms, but the relation between the sexual and the economic is high-lighted. As Irigaray comments, "the passage into the social order . . . is assured by the fact that men, or groups of men, circulate women among themselves." It is a "señorito," who has the leisure time to travel to the village purely for pleasure, who explains that the jewel merchant cannot hope to make a sale with Tilde; her husband is too stingy. It costs a woman money to maintain the edifice of beauty she constructs, and this money must necessarily come from her husband, the man who has bought the rights to her body. That the husband's generosity ended with his wedding gift is significant. This presentation of marriage as a financial transaction emphasizes women's position as commodity exchanged among men, as does the passage in which Tilde's predicament is presented within, to use Irigaray's pun, a hom[m]osexual conversational circle. Tilde's story is a desirable commodity which the men exchange among themselves, in lieu of Tilde's body. In fact, not only is Tilde's story circulated, but Tilde herself is in fact handed over from one man to another, when the jewel merchant allows the protagonist to take his place, thus providing him with access to Tilde's bedroom. And, of course, the transgression which Tilde finally commits is to allow another man, the protagonist, to sexually take the place of her husband, whom the "señorito" refers to openly as her "dueño legal."

But Tilde's supposed unavailability, her removal from the market, is problematic; her "dueño legal" does not give his valuable object the care which she deserves. As the young gentleman exclaims, "*Tener* una mujer así, y sujetarla a una mensualidad exigua para sus trapos!" (my emphasis). The husband is "más tacaño que las hormigas"; "un sucio." He clearly is not satisfying his wife economically, nor, by implication, sexually. This association is suggested when the French jewel merchant wonders if perhaps the reason the husband withholds his money from Tilde is because "el esposo se entender [sic] mal con su dama, la cual es sí bonita y le trompará, *allons,* todo naturalmente?"

The narrator/protagonist, of course, is eager to usurp the husband's position, gaining entry, not only to her bedroom, but also to the secrets of her sexuality. The industrialist overtly buys Tilde's sexual favors, exchanging one "beautiful object" for another. The protagonist's reaction to his first glimpse of Tilde up close is expressed through an openly monetary metaphor: "¡De cerca era más divina aún la beldad! En su lotería se pagaban aproximaciones." When the protagonist shows her the jewels he supposedly wants to sell, he watches her, again, without her seeing him, thus duplicating the voyeuristic activity in which he had engaged from his own room: "No me veía; yo era para ella el escaparate, lo menos que secundario, lo accesorio." The narrator's metaphor of show-case or store window to describe his own role in this encounter is particularly appropriate here, with its associations with display of merchandise. The convergence of the sexual and the economic is expressed, again, when the narrator relates Tilde's tacit acceptance of the sexual contract: "El temblor del alma se filtraba al través de las vulgares ofertas comerciales . . . .". The terms of the sexual contract are inscribed in the one look which Tilde "gives" the narrator. (It is revealingly difficult to avoid the metaphor of trade when speaking about the gaze, so inextricably intertwined are the two notions in our culture!) Sex is presented explicitly as a financial transaction, finally, when the narrator summarizes his relationship with Tilde by remarking, "Me costó algo cara Tilde. A joya por entrevista . . .".

The sexual dynamics of the gaze are thus explored in considerable detail within the story and the narrative discourse of this remarkably rich text. But there is even more. The structure of the narrative perspective itself clearly replicates the voyeuristic stance of the protagonist/narrator toward Tilde. Due to the autodiegetic narration and the limited perspective that it implies, the narratee and implied reader are inevitably also cast in the position of voyeur. This effect reproduces the perspectival structure of traditional cinema explored by Mulvey. In this text, it seems that one must respond to Ann Kaplan's question [in *Women and Film: Both Sides of the Camera,* 1983] "Is the gaze male?" with a resounding "yes."

However, we must specify which narrative gaze is involved. In contrast to the straightforward fusing of protagonist's and camera's look (and gaze) which occurs in "Rear Window" or in "Vertigo," narrative perspective in **"La mirada"** functions in such a way as to undermine and subvert the narrator/protagonist's sadistic gaze. Obviously, any reading of this story must take into consideration the fact that it was published by Pardo Bazán at a time when she had already firmly established her position as foremost feminist critic of Spanish culture. But even leaving aside the context of the historical author, the narrator's deconstruction of his own specular discourse undeniably justifies a reading of the text as irony. As we have seen, the narrator's discourse is replete with elements of domination and sadism. But the narrator attributes to himself far more innocence than his own discourse reveals. He presents his surveillance of Tilde, for instance, as simple admiration: "pude, desde mi ventana, admirar la hermosura de una señora que vivía en la casa de enfrente." If there is indiscretion involved in this activity, it is, curiously, attributable only to the physical lay-out of the two buildings: "Desde mi observatorio se registraba de modo más indiscreto su tocador." The speaker's responsability is markedly lessened, in this sentence, through the use of the impersonal *se* construction, which relieves the human syntactic subject of any responsability for the action of the verb—a hedge which is, of course, undermined by the choice of the words "observatorio" and "registrarse."

The merging of sexual domination and economics also plays a part in the narrator's self-exculpation. The duplicitous manipulation inherent in the protagonist's plan to trade places with the French jewel merchant and thus gain entry to Tilde's bedroom is presented simply as a respectable business transaction, for the narrator informs us that the jewel merchant "me respetaba como a persona metida en altos negocios," a trust which was firmly grounded since "estaba muy hecho a distinguir la gente seria de los tramposos." This last sentence can only be read ironically, given the "trampa" that the protagonist proposes to the merchant. Finally, when the protagonist succeeds in his deception and manages to enter Tilde's house, he imputes to himself only the most innocent of motives: "Sólo esto me proponía: verla, respirar su hálito de ámbar, y que acaso nuestras manos se rozasen un momento al manejar las joyas . . .".

At the moment in the narrative when the protagonist actually enters Tilde's room, however, the pretense of innocence sharply begins to erode. The narrator still refers to himself as an "hombre apasionado, caprichoso, en la plenitud de la edad," nicely encapsulating the sort of "boys will be boys" excuse we still hear today for sexual misconduct and abuse. But now these innocuous qualities are framed in a context which marks them as ironically incongruous:

> 'No ha delinquido ni con una mirada . . .' 'La que entrega la mirada, lo entrega todo.' Recordé esta frase del señorito, y al recordarla, me deslumbró más aún aquella luz diabólica que llegaba adentro, al fondo de mi ser de hombre apasionado, caprichoso, en la plenitud de la edad. . . .

This use of "luz diabólica" echoes the earlier association of the protagonist with the devil as incarnated in the (obviously phallic) serpent of the Garden of Eden, and anticipates the climactic moment in which the protagonist "tiránicamente" fastens the necklace around Tilde's neck. By the last paragraph of the text, it has become abundantly clear that the narrator's discourse is not to be read "unidirectionally," to use [Mikhail] Bakhtin's term [*Problems of Dostoevsky's Poetics,* 1984]. The distance between the narrator's discourse and what Bakhtin calls the "ultimate semantic authority" is highlighted in the narrator's crude cynicism as he concludes, "Me costó algo cara Tilde. A joya por entrevista . . .". This sentence makes it strikingly explicit that the narrator has purchased Tilde's sex. Futher, the choice of the word "entrevista" as a euphemism for sexual exchange is now charged with ironic overtones, given its metonymic association of the sexual with the visual. This dissonance between narratorial discourse and authorial intonation invites the reader to join the author in stepping out from behind the male gaze. The resulting distance allows for an examination of the gaze itself, as the point of convergence of our notions of sex and economics.

This "hombre apasionado, caprichoso, en la plenitud de su edad," this industrialist who could never be confused with "los tramposos," but rather respected as a "persona metida en altos negocios," as "gente seria," is thus ultimately revealed as an ironic embodiment of the specular economy, in which women and their sexuality are commodities exchanged among men. Pardo Bazán adopts the voice, and the gaze, of this purveyor of "beautiful objects," but imbues them with her own parodic intonations, her own penetrating eye. She makes us see what Kaja Silverman, in a reference to Hollywood films, pointed out only recently: "The problem, in other words, is not that men direct desire toward women . . . but that male desire is so consistently and systematically imbricated with projection and control." **"La mirada,"** finally, represents an incisive commentary that anticipates contemporary theoretical constructions, not only of the gaze but also of woman's place in the sexual economy.

Robert M. Fedorchek (essay date 1993)

SOURCE: "Translator's Foreward," in *The White Horse and Other Stories,* Associated University Presses, 1993, pp. 9-13.

[*In the following excerpt, Fedorchek places Pardo Bazán in the context of some of her contemporaries.*]

An admired novelist and a respected critic, Emilia Pardo Bazán is also considered, by virtually all scholars and students of Spanish literature, one of nineteenth-century Spain's foremost short story writers. Others (Leopoldo Alas) can be more profound and some (Pedro Antonio de Alarcón and Armando Palacio Valdés) are considerably more gifted with a sense of humor, but few of her Spanish contemporaries have her range and none her volume. The critic Juan Paredes Núñez [in *Los cuentos de Emilia Pardo Bazán,* 1979] has been able to locate the staggering number of 580 stories, and states that even this figure is not definitive inasmuch as Pardo Bazán published not only in Spain, but also in numerous foreign newspapers and magazines.

If Nathaniel Hawthorne is an American short story writer who best depicts New England, and Guy de Maupassant a French short story writer who best depicts Normandy, then Doña Emilia Pardo Bazán is to be seen as a Spanish short story writer who best depicts her home region of Galicia. Situated in the northwestern corner of Spain, Galicia saw itself in the nineteenth century as remote, isolated from the central government, and cut off from Castile by forbidding mountains. It was and is the garden of Spain, a lush, verdant land of valleys and woods, fields and dairy farms, streams and estuaries; a land blessed with the bounty of the ocean, which surrounds it from Vigo in the southwest to Ribadeo in the northeast. Galicia is a land steeped in history: La Coruña, the capital city where Pardo Bazán was born in 1851, the port of departure for emigrants to the New World; Santiago de Compostela, the ageless, universal city of pilgrimage; Orense, ancient city of gold (*oro*) panned from the River Sil; Lugo, a Roman city surrounded by ancient walls; Pontevedra, at the head of an inland bay. It is the land of *hórreos* (elevated rectangular granaries set on stone pillars) and *pazos* (manor houses of the gentry), of peasants who squeeze a living from the earth; it is the land where Pardo Bazán usually spent three or four months of the year, principally at her *pazo* in Meirás, not far from La Coruña; it is a land rich in customs and Catholic tradition, with a language more like Portuguese than Castilian.

Doña Emilia Pardo Bazán, the cosmopolite, the aristocrat, the socialite who resided most of her life in Madrid, was inextricably bound to the Galicia of her childhood and adolescence, but unlike her sister writer, the poet Rosalía de Castro, she chose Castilian, that is, Spanish, rather than Galician as her linguistic medium. Was she announcing to Spain that she was a regionalist but not a separatist (as many Galicians were, and are)? Did she wish to find a greater audience? Was she simply more "at home" in Castilian? We may never know what the choice *did* mean, but perhaps we can hazard guessing what it did *not* mean—a rejection of her roots. Quite the opposite: her love and knowledge of Galicia was central to her grasp of the universal, the heritage that equipped her to explore the gamut of human responses, for like all great writers her uniqueness—the "Galicianness" inseparable from her "Spanishness"—was her understanding of the land and people that nurtured her in order to represent the commonality of mankind.

Interested as she was in the reality around her, Pardo Bazán often found the subject matter of her stories in the mysteries and vicissitudes of life. Some tales are fictional accounts of actual occurrences or people (**"The Pardon," "A Galician Mother," "The Lady Bandit"**); others are a defense of women subjugated by a double standard (**"The Guilty Woman," "The Faithful Fiancée"**); a number focus on the figure of the rural priest (**"A Descendant of the Cid," "Don Carmelo's Salvation"**); one is highly symbolic (**"The White Horse"**) and qualifies Pardo Bazán as the godmother of the Generation of 98, the group of writers who exhorted Spain to rid itself of inertia, apathy and fixation on past glories in order to begin anew; several are like contemporary tales of suspense (**"The Cuff Link," "The White Hair"**); many reveal keen psychological insight (**"The Torn Lace," "The Substitute," "Scissors," "The Nurse," "Rescue"**); and her themes are fear, love, hatred, forgiveness, cruelty, poverty, necrophilia, repentance, homesickness, madness, and so on—that is, naked reality, bitter reality, and very often an ugly, vicious reality.

It can be said that Pardo Bazán's realities led her to a morbid realism, that her stories frequently highlight the perverse, the wicked, the cruel; it can also be said that many of her stories are punctuated with naturalistic detail or emphasis (**"The Gravedigger," "Consolation"**), not surprising in a writer who created a sensation in Spain when she published *The Burning Question* (1882-83), an introduction to and critical commentary on Zola's theories that earned her numerous enemies (who believed that she espoused in their entirety the French novelist's ideas) and precipitated the separation from her husband. Are we to conclude that she had a proclivity for blood, torture, cruelty, depravity, desecration, misery, and death? No, but as Carmen Bravo Villasante suggests [in *Vida y obra de Emilia Pardo Bazán,* 1973], there is a possible explanation for her attraction to the dark side of life: Francisco de Goya, the celebrated painter of the court of Carlos IV. In 1901 Pardo Bazán gave a lecture at the Fine Arts Center of Madrid entitled "Goya and Spanish Spontaneity." After remarking that some of the Iberian tendencies seen in his work are cruelty, bloodthirstiness, ferocity, and heroism conveyed through jarring contrasts of chiaroscuro, she singled out his etchings: "Monstrosity, insanity, brutality, violent dementia, perversity, torture, and black magic tempt and seduce him as an artist, even though he condemns all of it in verbal lashings that accompany the drawings as commentary" [Bravo Villasante]. If, like Goya, she was drawn to the gruesome in order to come to grips with it, she also, like Goya, condemned it. Representation of evil is not acceptance of it, much less approval. There can be little doubt of the affinity, indeed, parallel, between the two great Spaniards.

One of the indisputable giants of the nineteenth-century short story is Guy de Maupassant. Pardo Bazán met him (along with Daudet and Zola) in France and considered the author of "The Horla" the master of short story writers. Although he influenced her, most notably in psychological inquiry and careful attention to realistic detail, Pardo Bazán put her own stamp on her stories and developed a style *sui generis,* the most striking feature of which is brevity. The *short* of the English term "short story" suits her to a tee and describes admirably her tales. Rarely did she write stories of the length of **"Ball of Fat"** (she would have called them short novels or novellas); the vast majority average six or seven pages . . . **"Soft-Boiled Eggs,"** is a mere two pages.

The essence of her approach is to engage the reader as quickly as possible, certainly in the first paragraph, frequently in the first few sentences. Some aspect of a character or an episode is brought to light and the story unfolds rapidly. There are third-person narratives in which the author occasionally injects herself or her point of view; others are presented wholly in the first person, a few by the omniscient narrator, some by the "players." From time to time another technique used by Pardo Bazán is to have someone tell the story to her, and then as narrator she becomes the audience. When she is the disinterested or omniscient narrator, Pardo Bazán maintains distance from her sex to appear . . . what? As strong and detached as a man? As worldly as a man? It is entirely possible that some of her graphic descriptions were intended to blunt accusations of softness (i.e., femininity) that would be associated, foolishly, with a woman writer. Men are just as capable of maudlin outbursts and descriptions that ooze with sentimentality (and conversely are capable of the back-biting associated with women, as proven by Leopoldo Alas and Armando Palacio Valdés, her contemporaries). But when the time came to represent the plight of women—in terms of natural, understandable sexual needs and intellectual acceptance—Pardo Bazán wrote as a woman to capture the anguish and inferior status of her Spanish sisters.

Doña Emilia Pardo Bazán reflected the reality around her as well as the reality that she lived. Should she be called the Spanish Maupassant or should Maupassant be called the French Pardo Bazán? Should she be called the Spanish Chekhov or should Chekhov be called the Russian Pardo Bazán? Or should we speak of Turguenev, Hoffmann, Machado de Assis, Poe, Crane, Eça de Queirós, James, and . . . other nineteenth-century short story writers? In the end, such comparisons may be useful, if only to suggest that these writers have transcended their linguistic borders, that through translation their catholic and enduring vision has awakened human chords in a large part of the world.

Janet Pérez (essay date 1995)

SOURCE: "Subversion of Victorian Values and Idea Types: Pardo Bazán and the *Ángel del hogar,*" in *Hispanofila,* Vol. 113, 1995, pp. 31-44.

[*In the following essay, Pérez examines several of the stories collected in Pardo Bazán's* Cuentos de Marineda, *which she considers "ironic or otherwise subversive reactions to the Victorian ideal."*]

The mention of the word "Victorian" evokes a world unto itself, a closed world based largely on authority: God, the church, parents, elders, the upper classes. And Emilia Pardo Bazán was—among other things—a Victorian writer, born and raised during the long reign of Victoria Regina (1837-1901), who wrote her most celebrated works in the Victorian era. The canon has heretofore privileged those aspects of Pardo Bazán which might be deemed least Victorian, i.e., those classed as Naturalistic, yet she was something more—and something less—than a Naturalist, as recent studies have begun to elucidate.

Maurice Hemingway has termed Naturalism a "red herring" turning attention away from multiple and diverse facets of Pardo Bazán's work [*Emilia Pardo Bazán: The Making of a Novelist,* 1983]. Similarly, Darío Villanueva remarks that the tendency to view Pardo Bazán as representing a particular literary movement—i.e., as the principal disseminator of Naturalism in Spain—has worked to the detriment of broader and deeper understanding of her originality and talent ["*Los pazos de Ulloa,* el Naturalismo y Henry James," *Hispanic Review,* Vol. 52, 1984]. Comparing criticism of the Countess with that of her contemporary Henry James, Villanueva deplores the absence of a comparable scholarly approach to the works of Pardo Bazán. Marina Mayoral likewise contributes to amending earlier views of Pardo Bazán's masterpiece as exclusively Naturalistic. Via close reading and rhetorical analysis, she demonstrates the incorporation of stylistic features learned from Zola while arguing that "los planteamientos de la autora no eran naturalistas" [*Estudios sobre Los pazos de Ulloa,* 1988]. This contention is buttressed by Pardo Bazán herself in the seldom reprinted "Apuntes autobiográficos," an authorial introduction to the first edition of *Los pazos* omitted from subsequent printings. Presenting highlights of her intellectual history, the novelist provides a compendium of her emerging aesthetics up to 1886, discusses her intentions in writing *La cuestión palpitante* and specifies her discrepancies with French Naturalists.

Given the appropriateness and timeliness of rethinking canonical views of Pardo Bazán, it should prove useful to look at her as a Victorian writer, albeit sometimes a parodic one. As I have shown elsewhere powerful arguments exist for believing that the Countess knew the Gothic novel well enough to parody it, and many of her little-studied short stories can be illuminated by reading them as subversions of Victorian, patriarchal values and ideal types ["Naturalism and Gothic: Pardo Bazán's Transmogrifications of the Genre," *Studies in Honor of Donald W. Bleznick,* 1993].

Pardo Bazán's not inconsiderable intellectual independence has been often downplayed or overlooked, in part because of phallocentric stereotyping, in part because she often faithfully (if somewhat tongue-in-cheek) followed models of self-deprecation prescribed for Victorian writers—especially females—and in part because of human tendencies to remember or repeat only certain salient points. Thus, we are frequently reminded of Pardo Bazán's conservatism, her early Carlist sympathies, her abiding Catholicism and alleged aristocratic tendencies at the expense of countervaling elements. Her "Apuntes autobiográficos" mention, for example, that in her parents' home, the government was often criticized, that her uncle, General Santiago Pineiro was a "curious Voltairian," that her father had labored with the "honest progressive party, whose dream had been to reconcile religious interests with constitutional freedom," and that the coat-of-arms at the family residence, La Granja, was removed by one of her grandfathers, a "flaming liberal of the hottest variety, that is, a Mason." Among her family's associates were found liberal orators, constitutional politicians and Krausists, and her own readings included much contemporary philosophy. Regardless of her husband's conservative, patriarchal, Victorian attitudes, Pardo Bazán was clearly exposed to liberal influences in her formative years. Aside from the obvious contradiction between the postulation of any deep-seated and lasting conservatism and her participation in movements such as feminism and Naturalism, no matter how attenuated, she is clearly not only less conservative and orthodox than traditionally portrayed but a great deal more complex intellectually.

Daniel Whitaker's study of *La Quimera* identifies ingredients ranging from latent Romanticism and *costumbrismo* and Spiritualist influences to Decadentism, Modernism, and Pre-Raphaelist elements in addition to Naturalism and aspects of parody [*"La Quimera" de Emilia Pardo Bazán y la literatura finisecular,* 1988]. Another recent book on the writer observes that "For too long critical studies devoted to Emilia Pardo Bazán have been predominantly concerned with her role as principal disseminator in Spain of French Naturalism," and indeed, by focusing on Pardo Bazán's relationship to Zola, Hispanists have too often "examined" her work somewhat in the fashion of the three blind men who went to "see" the elephant [Francisca González Arias, *Portrait of a Woman as Artist,* 1992]. Not only is much examination limited to selected, discrete parts of her opus, but there have been few attempts, indeed, to view the writer either in an international context or as an eclectic composite of multiple, polyvalent, and occasionally conflicting influences.

Pardo Bazán was interested not only in Zola but in a broad range of contemporary French writers. During some two years, she frequented the Paris attic of Edmond Goncourt (whose works she translated). She was received by the aged Victor Hugo whose novels she had admired since childhood. In 1878, she read George Sand, and while staying at the Vichy spa during the fall of 1880 she read Balzac and Daudet, the Goncourts and Flaubert. She authored a history of *La literatura francesa moderna* in three volumes (I, El romanticismo; II, La transición; III, El naturalismo—volumes 37, 39 and 41 of her *Obras completas* [Madrid, 1910, 1911, 1914]) and death prevented her completing a fourth volume on "la decadencia." She read Romantic and contemporary writers such as Foscolo, Alfieri, Silvio Pellico and Manzoni in Italian, and later published an article on "El futurismo y Marinetti" in *La Ilustración Artística* [reprinted by C. Bravo Villasante in *Emilia Pardo Bazán. La vida contemporánea (1896-1915)*]. Pardo Bazán renewed independently her study of English and in 1878 read Shakespeare and Byron in the original, later moving on to Walter Scott, Bulwer-Lytton, and Dickens. She was sufficiently familiar with English detective stories to try her hand at the genre with modest success. Her major essay on Spanish women was first published in English by the British *Fortnightly Review* (winter 1889), possibly via the mediation of Giner de los Ríos. She also published a Spanish version of John Stuart Mill's *On the Subjection of Women* in her series, "La Biblioteca de la Mujer."

The "Apuntes autobiográficos" attest to her familiarity with the works of Narcís Oller (with whom she corresponded) and other contemporary fiction in Catalan. Her critical writings abound in references to Latin American writers and their works, as well as Peninsular writers past and present, and in 1892 she helped to organize the Congreso Pedagógico Hispano-Portugués-Americano. Pardo Bazán read and understood Gallego, and although she did not publish in that language, she attested to her enjoyment of Galician literature, especially poetry, and founded the Galician Folklore Society (1884). Her reading of Krause in translation led to discovery of Kant and inspired her to study German, with subsequent readings of Goethe, Schiller, Bürger and Heine. Despite subsequently abandoning her readings in German metaphysics, she was able to draw meaningful distinctions between the thought of Schelling, Fichte, Kant, Schopenhauer and Hegel. Although apparently she had no knowledge of Russian, she had more than a passing acquaintance with the Russian novel, discovered Dostoyevsky in Paris and gave lectures on contemporary Russian writers at the Madrid Ateneo in 1887 (published as *La revolución y la novela en Rusia, Obras completas* III [Madrid 1887], 760-880). Pardo Bazán probably knew more about contemporary European and world literature than other coeval Spanish (male) novelists combined.

Because she was largely self-taught, her vast erudition is insufficiently recognized, together with her great thirst for intellectual stimulation and the sense of intellectual isolation which led to her correspondence with numerous contemporaries from Giner de los Ríos (1876-1909) to Galdós and Menéndez y Pelayo, to mention only the best known. In her voluminous and wide-ranging correspondence, Pardo Bazán appears typically Victorian, but she differed from the norm in her openness to new ideas. "Most Victorians were not taught to cultivate open minds, to consider all sides of a question . . . They feared new ideas; they sensed danger and evil in change and innovation" [Morton Cohen, "Lewis Carroll and Victorian Morality," *Sexuality and Victorian Literature,* 1984]. Given her feminism and her knowledge of English, Pardo Bazán was almost certainly aware of the "New Woman" controversy of the 1890s, accompanied by fiction depicting feminine frustrations,

> demands for sexual equality and self-development for women and a challenge to the traditional Victorian marriage arranged for money and position, to the subservience of wives to their husbands, and even in some cases to the ideas of motherhood and a distinctively womanly human "nature" . . . in "New Woman" novels the usual consequence of the heroine's struggle for sexual and social independence is that she suffers "nervous disorder, disease and death" as a result of her opposition to the society she lives in. [Alan P. Johnson "'Dual Life': The Status of Women in Stoker's *Dracula,"* *Sexuality and Victorian Literature,* 1984]

Viewing *Los pazos* in this context, i.e., as opposing the "traditional Victorian marriage arranged for money and position," and "the subservience of wives to their husbands," provides another lens through which to view the Countess's masterpiece. Unquestionably, such a perspective suggests another hermeneutic option for that fiction of Pardo Bazán which is clearly not Naturalistic nor easily classifiable under other rubrics commonly applied to her writing. The present essay examines a handful of her short stories of the 1890s, primarily from the **Cuentos de Marineda,** testing the hypothesis that these tales can be illuminated and enriched by reading them as ironic or otherwise subversive reactions to the Victorian ideal type, *el ángel del hogar.*

Coventry Patmore's sugar-sweet portrait of the pure angel-woman of Victorian male fantasy, *The Angel in the House* (serialized 1854-63), achieved a currency far exceeding its literary merits. So enormous was its popularity that it became a byword for the paragon of feminine endurance, long-suffering perseverance and patience even in the face of tyranny and abuse. The poem appealed to sentiment (bathos was not without its public) and was opportune as pro-establishment propaganda enabling patriarchal society to indoctrinate successive generations of women in the belief that their sacrifice of liberty and personal aspirations to domestic encloisterment was somehow compensated by elevation to angelic status. Nina Auerbach's comments on the poem in *Woman and the Demon* reveal that the felicitous title entered popular discourse as "a convenient shorthand for the selfless paragon all women were exhorted to be, enveloped in family life and seeking no identity beyond the roles of daughter, wife and mother." The inextricably close relationship between the concepts of "angel" and "house" resulted in their virtual synonymity, a linking inadvert-

ently underscoring feminine confinement to the domestic sphere. Long-suffering heroines embodying emotional nurturance, natural graces and domestic virtues abound in Nineteenth Century Spanish fiction, as seen in works by "Fernán Caballero," Carolina Coronado, and Sinués y Navarro, as well as such masculine counterparts as Pereda and lesser novelists, most of whom reflect the Victorian commitment to gradually evolving affections rather than intense romantic passion. So entrenched was the patriarchal value system, buttressed by Victorian morality and traditional arguments for the marginalization and encloisterment of women, that the *ángel del hogar* had counterparts in Latin America, as noted by Francine Masiello, who devotes a chapter to "Angels in the Argentine House" [in *Between Civilization and Barbarism,* 1992]. Masiello affirms that "By enforcing woman's duties to the home and by emphasizing her empathic qualities, leading intellectuals molded an image of the Argentine spouse and mother to suit their projects of state."

While observers have rightly noted the differences between the status of women in England and Spain in the Twentieth Century, the Victorian era exhibited greater similarities between Spanish and English views of women's nature, role and "place." Almost certainly Patmore's poem had its Spanish admirers, for the coetaneous existence of a Nineteenth Century Spanish magazine for women entitled *El ángel del hogar* must be more than mere coincidence. That it was no aberration is clear from the contemporaneous publication of numerous family-oriented periodicals such as *La Defensa de la Familia, La Familia,* and *El Museo de las Familias,* cited in Pardo Bazán's short story, **"Linda,"** as among the outlets for a hack novelist. A plethora of sentimental magazines catering to female readers included *La Margarita, La Guirnalda,* and *El Pensil del Bello Sexo,* all functioning to reinforce the submissive, beautiful, self-abnegating, chaste and cloistered image. Given her involvement with periodical publishing and work with *Nuevo Teatro Crítico* (1891-93) plus her knowledge of English, Pardo Bazán cannot safely be presumed to have been ignorant of either these patently Victorian Spanish publications or their British counterparts, and her feminism compels hypothesizing that she knowingly parodied the *ángel del hogar.* The numerous instances of infidelity, domestic violence, spousal murders, abuse or neglect of women and children, emotional isolation and alienation of wives, and otherwise unhappy marriages in her fiction suggest that she did not unreservedly subscribe to the prevailing domestic ideology.

Calderonian concepts of honor, *machismo,* the cult of virginity and similar mores contributed to the entrenchment and prolongation of the traditional Spanish *encierro* (considered by some a derivation of the Moorish harem). Exclusion of the female from the public sphere in Spain, periodically strengthened by periods of resurgent, reactionary conservatism, was effectively revived by the Franco regime which not only promulgated its own version of the "Angel in the House," but passed legislation designed to perpetuate the separation of public and domestic space and confined women to the latter. Small wonder, then, that the cult of domesticity in Pardo Bazán's Spain outlived that of Victorian England, rendering her subversive stories eminently readable today.

Women and children were probably less idealized in Nineteenth Century Spain than were their British counterparts:

> Never since the Middle Ages had woman been worshipped for her innocence and for her goodness as she was [in England] in Victorian times . . . she and her sisters composed a breed of humanity closer to angels than men; they were models of virtue. They had no sexual appetites to plague them, and their instincts were unsullied. . . . Along with this cult of feminine purity came the cult of childhood innocence which the Victorians inherited from the Romantics. (Cohen)

However, as Hughes and Lund observe [in *The Victorian Serial*, 1991], "The congruence between domestic ideology and elements of serial reading could . . . take a less benign turn." Citing an early reviewer of *Angel in the House*, these authors point out that the concept of home as a kind of happy haven or refuge from the commercial world also "suggests the marginality of home, poetry and women to the world of men and business." Still less benign, the Spanish tradition of patriarchal authority over children (the right of *patria potestas*) was buttressed by assumptions that children are naturally or inherently evil and only rigid education and discipline might prevent scandalous behavior. Rousseau's notions to the contrary clearly had less impact in Spain than in England.

As was the case with the Victorian novel, Pardo Bazán's works contain numerous references to prostitutes, women led to the marriage bed like lambs to the slaughter, and marriages sustained by the extramarital samplings of errant husbands. "Fallen women, marital infidelity, the sterility of sexual relations are all insistent themes in the Victorian novel. But perhaps the most insistent theme of all . . . was the theme of sex and cash" [Jenni Calder, "Cash and the Sex Nexus," *Sexuality and Victorian Literature*, 1984]. Arranged marriages, marriages of convenience motivated by financial considerations, abound in Pardo Bazán's fiction, long and short. While many are mismatches, in general they are not more prone to failure than the romantic matches portrayed in her writing.

Despite evidence on Victorian prudishness and reticence, fear and hypocrisy on sexual matters, and the damage caused by Victorian sexual repression, novelists of the period did not skirt the problem of sexuality, although many resorted to euphemism, innuendo, and metaphor. Pardo Bazán seems to burlesque such prudishness in **"El mechón blanco"** (*Cuentos de Marineda*) when the Marquesa's nephew—a military officer—recounts allegations of infidelity against the Generala (information avidly desired by the prying gossips) using not the biblical or legal terms but "lo que usted sabe" to allude to adultery. The euphemistic accusation of "you know what" panders to the lewd imagination and encourages embellishment in subsequent retellings. This same story exem-

plifies the Victorian belief in fulminating punishment of sexual transgressions, as the Generala allegedly swore her innocence on the life of her daughter, after which the child fell ill, dying of meningitis within forty-eight hours, and causing the mother's white lock which attracts the morbid curiosity of her social circle. Pardo Bazán implicitly condemns idle, nosy gossip, adding an unusual second story, a sequel which takes up the thread a few years later. **"Cobardía"** portrays the suffering of the Marquesa's own son, subsequently connected by gossipers with the Generala and challenged to a duel. The latter tale clearly takes a stand against duelling, but leaves no doubt that such encounters often resulted from idle gossiping. In Victorian society, as in Spanish society traditionally, the woman "does not have the power to define herself as a good and modest woman; this power resides in the public sphere with those who, hidden behind the anonymous mask of 'public opinion,' will arbitrarily interpret her actions and appearance" [Bridget C. Aldaraca, *El angel de hogar*, 1991]. Although the Generala belongs to the upper class and her modest dress and discreet behavior coincide with the *ángel del hogar* paradigm, almost everyone (excepting the Marquesa's son Rodrigo) believes her guilty. Vaguely reminiscent of *El gran Galeoto* in presenting two (or three) people whose lives are ruined by "el qué dirán," the paired stories suggest that modesty, self-abnegation and some degree of encloisterment do not suffice to protect attractive women from idle gossip.

Not all of Pardo Bazán's relevant stories involve infidelity or allegations thereof; some depict an intellectually or sentimentally deprived female. **"Fantaseando"** sketches a bourgeois family's attendance at a theatrical performance. The housewife's confession that she dreams of being like the singing star provokes mockery from family and friends. Pilar "era un pájaro, un pájaro chusco y burlón, que se mofaba de sí mismo. ¡Dejarla a la pobrecilla explayarse! Mañana, desde las ocho, tendría que lidiar con la cocinera, atender a los chiquillos . . .". Not only do the *ángel del hogar* and her individual reincarnations lack the right to venture beyond domestic space, but social ridicule functions to prevent even fantasizing. "That virtue which is the antonym of the self-interest which rules the public sphere is acclaimed as the supreme female virtue: the negation of self, self-denial, renunciation, self-abnegation" (Aldaraca).

As Bridget Aldaraca has convincingly demonstrated in *El ángel del hogar,* the underlying ideology is essentially bourgeois in origin, applying less to the lower classes than to middle and upper-class women. It necessitated, first of all, a sufficient degree of economic security to allow for women of (relative) leisure, freed from the need to work as domestics or in factories, and as a bourgeois ideology, viewed the lower classes with disdain and distrust. Therefore, those stories of Pardo Bazán which relate strictly to the concept of the *ángel del hogar* deal, presumably, with the middle and upper-class family. However, a considerable number of her stories present lower-class women who are faithful, long-suffering and self-abnegating, yet are cruelly abused. Their "angelic" patience and long-suffering fidelity brings no reward, but occasionally dooms them. In **"El indulto,"** a poor laundress lives in terror that her husband, imprisoned after butchering her mother for the old woman's savings, will return and carry out his threat to kill his wife, Antonia, for identifying him as the killer. Royal pardons reduce his twenty-year sentence, and Antonia consults a lawyer to find if she can be legally protected: "¡La ley, en vez de protegerla, obligaba a la hija de la víctima a vivir bajo el mismo techo, maritalmente con el asesino!" The only possibility of avoiding that is separation:

> —Dice que nos podemos separar . . . después de una cosa que le llaman divorcio.
> —¿Y qué es eso, mujer?
> —Un pleito muy largo.

> Todas dejaron caer los brazos con desaliento: los pleitos no se acaban nunca, y peor aún si acaban, porque los pierde siempre el inocente y el pobre.

Subsequent discussion suggests that Antonia, even with money would have little hope of a divorce, as she must provide evidence (i.e., witnesses) of her husband's abuse and threats. The story proves especially interesting because the neighborhood women band together to help Antonia on several occasions, taking turns nursing her baby when fear and stress leave her unable to do so, and later helping to care for her son. One even offers to sleep in her house to protect her. But a false rumor circulates as to the husband's death, with Antonia's tearful joy and relief implicitly constituting one of Pardo Bazán's stronger statements on women's situation. Arriving home with her son after celebrating her reprieve by a long walk in the fresh air, Antonia finds the criminal waiting. He forces her to feed him and go to bed with him, and the following morning the neighbors "encontraron a Antonia en la cama, extendida, como muerta. El médico vino aprisa, y declaró que vivía, y la sangró, y no logró sacarle gota de sangre. Falleció a las veinticuatro horas . . ." Pardo Bazán denied having invented any part of this story, insisting that it was based upon a recent happening in "Marineda." Nevertheless, the rhetoric of the "retelling" is necessarily her own, as is the indictment of the disempowerment of women and their victimization by spousal abuse. Pardo Bazán saw clearly beyond the culpability of any individual abusive husband, challenging the laws promulgated by the phallocentric establishment while exposing the fallacy of notions that it sufficed to have an angel in the house for home to be a happy haven.

Another story reflecting feminine helplessness under prevailing social and legal conditions is **"Sobremesa,"** a case narrated by a marqués as an ethical puzzle. A poor woman in Madrid, abandoned by her husband, becomes a ragpicker to feed her five children, aged one to ten, but things go from bad to worse. At Christmas, she sells her only valuable possession, a goat, buys food and a few presents for a final celebration, then kills her children and attempts suicide. "Saved" by neighbors, she is sentenced to life in prison.

Al pronto, nadie comentó la historia del marqués, tan impropia de un amo de casa que obsequia a sus amigos. Por fin, el catedrático de Economía murmuró sentenciosamente:

> —No veo clara la conducta de esa mujer. ¿Por qué no ahorró los dineros producto de la venta de la cabra, en vez de malgastarlos en figuritas de Reyes y estrellas de talco? Con esos cuartos vivirían una semana lo menos. El pobre es imprevisor. ¡Ah, si pudiéramos infundirle la virtud del ahorro! ¡Qué elemento de prosperidad para las naciones latinas!

The author's implicit, ironic commentary, conveyed by the adverb, *sentenciosamente,* again indicts society—those who make the laws—rather than the irresponsible husband and father whose abandonment led to the tragedy. Elements of lachrymose sentimentalism inherent in the events of **"El indulto"** and **"Sobremesa,"** together with the melodramatic dualism of good and evil would have appealed to many Victorian readers, but any bathetic potential is undercut by Pardo Bazán's irony and sardonic brevity.

"Confidencia" suggests that total self-abnegation is not an unmixed blessing, even for the putative beneficiary. The narrator befriends Solís to learn the secret of his enigmatic depression, eventually hearing how the excessive attentions of the latter's mother drove him first to doing everything she might forbid, subsequently drinking to excess, and finally an outburst of violence when she attempted to put the drunken man to bed. He knocked her to the floor, her candle ignited her dress, and she died of the burns, not without first forgiving him. This final, angelic gesture has been driving him mad. Such saintly behavior, the writer implies, is neither normal nor human; few things are harder to live with than perfection. After stories exposing the dark side of the "angelic" domestic state from the woman's perspective, **"Confidencia"** suggests the dark side where men are concerned; at the same time, it provides yet another instance where womanly virtue is not rewarded, but leads directly to the untimely demise of the self-abnegating wife or mother.

Pardo Bazán utilizes a modern variant of the animal fable (recounting what appears to be an autobiographical anecdote) to illustrate further the negative effects of self-abnegation for the female. **"Piña"** concerns a lonely pet monkey, for whom the family buys a mate who proves to possess the worst *machista* traits:

> ¿Estaría aquel galán empapado en las teorías de Luis Vives, fray Luis de León y otros pensadores, que consideran a la hembra creada exclusivamente para el fin de cooperar a la mayor conveniencia, decoro, orgullo, poderío y satisfacción de los caprichos del macho?

The rhetorical question attests to the writer's familiarity with patriarchal theories concerning woman's inferior nature and role, and it is no accident that she alludes to two Spanish authorities still used to justify feminine oppression (Vives exhorts the prolongation of feminine innocence while fray Luis in *La perfecta casada* preaches continually against visiting, shopping, attending parties, gossiping, or merely being in the street and affirms that the unfaithful wife "no es ya muger sino alevosa ramera, y vilissimo cieno, y vassura la más hedionda de todas"). Piña's "marriage" is abusive from the outset: "La hembra ni siquiera intentó defenderse; agachó la cabeza y aceptó el yugo. No era el amor quien le doblegaba, pues nunca vimos que su dueño le prodigase sino manotadas, repelones, y dentelladas sangrientas." The use of the word *dueño* is clearly calculated, although Pardo Bazán does not specifically relate Piña to her human counterpart, the *mujer-objeto*. Having detailed Coco's "wife-battering" and Piña's passivity, the author observes.

> Era únicamente el prestigio de la masculinidad, la tradición de obediencia absurda de la fémina, esclava desde los tiempos prehistóricos. Él quiso tomarla por felpudo, y ella ofrecía el espinazo. No hubo ni asomo de protesta. Y Piña se moría.

The family which has simply observed eventually decides to intervene: "Nosotros habíamos desempeñado hasta entonces el papel de la sociedad, que no gusta de mezclarse en cuestiones domésticas y deja que el marido acabe con su mujer, si quiere, ya que al fin es cosa suya . . .". If the latter remark, and earlier use of *dueño,* provide too little indication of authorial attitude, Pardo Bazán also uses the words *tirano* and *verdugo* to refer to the "husband" and *la mártir* for the simian wife. The abusive relationship described has a name now, the "battered wife syndrome," but society's reluctance to intervene in "domestic matters" remains unchanged today.

Not only does the author burlesque and satirize traditional patriarchal and phallocentric justifications for unequal treatment of women, but she subverts the ultimate authority cited in such matters, the Bible, the creation myth, and (by extension and implication) the tradition of blaming Eve for Adam's fall. **"Cuento primitivo"** reorders the chronology provided in Genesis: God creates not the world but Adam first (explaining man's imperfections, i.e., God's lack of practice). The world and other things in it are created as Adam expresses a need or desire, and not until he is bored with everything, tired of tranquility, does God create woman:

> le fue sacando, no una costilla, como dice el vulgo, sino unas miajitas del cerebro, unos pedacillos del corazón . . . un algo de toda su sustancia; y como Dios . . . tomó de lo mejorcito, lo delicado y selecto . . . la flor del varón, para constituir y amasar a la hembra. De suerte que al ser Eva creada, Adán quedó inferior a lo que era antes, y perjudicado.

Adam first sees Eve as a celestial, luminous creature and is filled with wonder—until the day he wants the apple she has in her care. "Yo sé de fijo que Eva la defendió mucho y no la entregó a dos por tres, y este pasaje de la Escritura es de los más tergiversados. En suma . . . Adán venció como más fuerte, y se engulló la manzana . . .". Instantly, his view of things changes, and he begins to see Eve as evil: "en vez de creerla limpia y sin mácula, la

juzgó sentina de todas las impurezas y maldades . . . le echó la culpa de su desazón, de sus dolores, hasta del destierro que Dios les impuso." And Eve hears it so often that she ends up believing it:

> se reconoció culpada, y perdió la memoria de su origen, no atreviéndose a afirmar que era de la misma sustancia que el hombre . . . Y el mito genesíaco se reproduce en la vida de cada Eva: antes de la manzana, el Adán respectivo le eleva un altar . . . después de la manzana, la quita del altar y la lleva al pesebre o al basurero.

For obvious reasons, Pardo Bazán does not claim authorship of this feminist rewriting of sacred history, but attributes it (as she frequently does with feminist and social thesis tales) to a male.

Although numerous other stories shed light on the Countess's reactions to the *ángel del hogar,* the foregoing are representative. Pardo Bazán subtly mocks publications which purveyed the paradigm, as in the case of *El Museo de la Familia,* by suggesting that their contributors are hacks and the contents paraliterary; she exposes women's discontent with "angelic" confinement to domestic space, and indicts the power of public opinion and gossip to destroy a woman's reputation, regardless of private realities. Her works portray the "pampered" housewife's longing for self-definition and self-realization, even in those fortunate cases where no wife-battering or mistreatment occur. The writer documents numerous cases of wife abuse, neglect, and abandonment which have no connection to wifely virtue or character, implicitly demonstrating that by submissiveness, the female simply becomes an accomplice in her own doom. Pardo Bazán ridicules masculine claims to ownership of women, and parodies the appeal to scriptural authority, used for milennia to justify patriarchal oppression. Her own decision to abandon the constricting role of "Angel in the House" rather than accede to her Victorian husband's demands that she renounce her writing argues that, notwithstanding repeated allegations as to her conservatism and Catholic orthodoxy, Pardo Bazán was far from accepting either the model of the *ángel del hogar* or the arguments used to justify it.

FURTHER READING

Bieder, Maryellen. "Emilia Pardo Bazán and Literary Women: Women Reading Women's Writing in Late 19th-Century Spain." *Revista Hispanica Moderna* XLVI, No. 1 (June 1993): 19-33.

   Discusses Pardo Bazán's distancing herself from other women writers, as well as her refusal to play the self-effacing role expected of women writers.

Brown, Donald Fowler. "Conflicting Voices," in *The Catholic Naturalism of Pardo Bazán.* Chapel Hill: The University of North Carolina Press, 1957, pp. 145-55.

   Summarizes widely varying critical assessments of Pardo Bazán.

Giles, Mary E. "Impressionist Techniques in Descriptions by Emilia Pardo Bazán." *Hispanic Review* XXX (October 1962): 304-16.

    Discusses Pardo Bazán's use of stylistic devices derived from Impressionist paintings in her descriptions of both landscapes and characters.

Davis, Gifford. "Pardo Bazán, Juan Valera, and Literary Fashion." *Romance Notes* XI (1969): 315-21.

    Details a literary exchange between Pardo Bazán and Juan Valera, who disliked Naturalism and defended art for art's sake.

————. "Literary Relations of Clarín and Emilia Pardo Bazán." *Hispanic Review* XXXIX (October 1971): 378-94.

    Discusses the relationship between Pardo Bazán and her contemporary, who also espoused Naturalism.

————. "Catholicism and Naturalism: Pardo Bazán's Reply to Zola." *MLN* XC (1975): 282-87.

    Details Pardo Bazán's reaction to Zola's opinion of her work.

Feeny, Thomas. "Maupassant's `Lui?' and Pardo Bazán's 'La Calavera': A Possible Case of Influence." *South Atlantic Bulletin* 41, No. 4 (1976): 44-47.

    Presents a brief comparative study of these stories.

Goldin, David. "The Metaphor of Original Sin: A Key to Pardo Bazán's Catholic Naturalism." *Philological Quarterly* LXIV, No. 1 (Winter 1985): 37-49.

    Uses the concept of original sin as a way of reconciling Pardo Bazán's religious beliefs to Naturalist influences.

Hemingway, Maurice. "Grace, Nature, Naturalism, and Pardo Bazán." *Forum for Modern Language Studies* XVI (1980): 341-49.

    Questions traditional critical approaches to examining Pardo Bazán's Naturalism.

————. "Pardo Bazán and the Rival Claims of Religion and Art." *Bulletin of Hispanic Studies* LXVI (1989): 241-50.

    Weighs the influences of Catholicism's relation to individual and collective experience and to art on Pardo Bazán's perspective.

Hilton, Ronald. "Pardo-Bazán and Literary Polemics about Feminism." *Romantic Review* XLIV (February 1953): 40-46.

    Details Pardo Bazán's interest in the inclusion of women in academia.

————. "Doña Emilia Pardo-Bazán, Neo-Catholicism and Christian Socialism." *The Americas* XI, No. 1 (July 1954): 3-18.

    Explores Pardo Bazán's feelings about the political significance of Catholicism.

Oliver, Walter. "A Privileged View of Pardo Bazán's Feminist Ethos." *Romance Notes* XXVIII, No. 2 (Winter 1987): 157-62.

    Demonstrates through a series of Pardo Bazán's letters her opinion of feminism.

Pattison, Walter. "Short Stories and Criticism: Short Stories." In *Emilia Pardo Bazán,* pp. 92-7. Boston: Twayne Publishers, 1971.

    Details some of Pardo Bazán's devices for developing plot in her short fiction.

Pérez, Janet. "Winners, Losers, and Casualties in Pardo Bazán's Battle of the Sexes." *Letras Peninsulares* V, No. 3 (Winter 1992-93): 347-56.

    Examines Pardo Bazán's use of gender politics in her fiction to further the autonomy of women.

Tolliver, Joyce. "`Sor Aparición' and the Gaze: Pardo Bazán's Gendered Reply to the Romantic Don Juan." *Hispania* 77, No. 3 (September 1994): 394-405.

    Studies Pardo Bazán's symbolic interaction with the Don Juan figure in one of her short stories.

The Kreutzer Sonata
Leo Tolstoy

The following entry presents criticism of Tolstoy's no-vella *Kreitserova sonata* (1890; *The Kreutzer Sonata*). For further information on Tolstoy's complete works of short fiction, see *SSC*, Volume 9.

INTRODUCTION

The Kreutzer Sonata, a novella written during the clos-ing years of the 1880s, issues from the later period of Tolstoy's literary career, which followed his moral and spiritual crisis of the late 1870s and culminated in works of fiction largely defined by his moral preoccupations. *The Kreutzer Sonata* emphasizes Tolstoy's controversial view on sexuality, which asserts that physical desire is an obstacle to relations between men and women and may result in tragedy. Although the moral stance on sexual relations presented in *The Kreutzer Sonata* has been criticized as simplistic or severe, the novella also has been recognized as among the best examples of Tolstoy's art of storytelling. Russian dramatist and contemporary Anton Chekhov wrote: "You will hardly find anything as powerful in seriousness of conception and beauty of execution."

Plot and Major Characters

The Kreutzer Sonata opens as a third-person narrative by an anonymous gentleman making his way across Rus-sia by train. When the conversation among the passen-gers turns to the subjects of sex, love, and marriage, a lawyer claims that many couples live long, content mar-ried lives. But Pozdnyshev, another passenger, violently contradicts his statement and announces that he has mur-dered his wife in a jealous rage, a crime of which a jury has acquitted him. Citing that the deterioration of their marriage began on their honeymoon when they first be-gan a sexual relationship, Pozdnyshev reveals himself as a man with an insane sexual obsession—he links sex with guilt, regards it as a 'fall' from an ideal purity, and de-scribes sexual intercourse as a perverted thing. He tries to persuade his captive audience that all marriages are obscene shams, and that most cases of adultery are occa-sioned by music, the infamous aphrodisiac. This latter idea explains the title of the story, which is also a musi-cal composition by Ludwig von Beethoven. Pozdnyshev explains the circumstances that led to his tragedy: after marrying a pretty woman who bore him children, he came to hate but lust for his wife. One day a musician named Trukachevsky, accepting Pozdnyzhev's invitation to visit their house, accompanied Pozdnyshev's wife on the vio-lin while she played the piano. Convinced that the pair were having an affair, Pozdnyshev went into the country to attend the meeting of the local council, often recalling the look on their faces as they played the "Kreutzer So-

nata." He returned home early, thinking that he would find the lovers in bed and consequently kill them; instead he found them sitting in the drawing room after they had played some music. Enraged nevertheless, Pozdnyshev killed his wife after Trukachevsky had escaped.

Major Themes

Critics observe that *The Kreutzer Sonata* presents Tol-stoy's moral ideals through the medium of an artistic narrative, and that its principal theme is the corrupting power of sex and attendant jealousy. The novella summa-rizes Tolstoy's disgusted attitude toward sex, which he completely denounces, and reflects his new faith in cel-ibacy and chastity after his conversion to a radical Chris-tianity. The narrative is also said to manifest Tolstoy's belief that since Christ was not and could not be married, total chastity is the ideal state. *The Kreutzer Sonata* rests on the premise that carnal love is selfish and that unself-ish love needs no physical consummation. For Pozdny-shev and Tolstoy alike sex is repulsive and destructive, even in marriage. Pozdnyshev's story highlights this premise by suggesting that sexual love degrades a human being and results in hostility to others and to one's self.

Pozdnyshev also dismisses love, or what the world calls love as distinct from sensuality, as non-existent between the sexes. To him traditional marriage has lost meaning and represents a cover for vice, fostering misunderstanding, jealousy, lies, and criminal passions. Finally, the title suggests that music provokes lechery, especially in the context of Beethoven's sonatas, which are often characterized by their intensity of feeling and violent contrasts of mood and emotion. Overall, commentators find that *The Kreutzer Sonata* represents Tolstoy's iconoclastic renunciation of social institutions, accepted conventions, and the lifestyle of the cultured class.

Critical Reception

The initial reception of *The Kreutzer Sonata* generated a great deal of controversy, especially since some readers perceived Pozdnyshev's story as advocating free love. Censored by government and church officials, Tolstoy's novella circulated widely in manuscript, both in Russia and abroad, before it was published. Since then *The Kreutzer Sonata* has become one of Tolstoy's most read works, sometimes referred to as his "crowning achievement." However, many commentators have criticized the novella for its unrealistic plot, inconsistent method, and the unsound principles espoused by Pozdnyshev ("How would the human race survive?" they have asked), and others have criticized its aesthetic imperfections, noting Tolstoy's failure to connect diverse points and direct contradictions in Pozdnyshev's arguments. Attempts by such critics as Dorothy Green and Bettina L. Knapp to relate the structure of the story to the structure of Beethoven's sonata have been successful, and such critics as Ruth Crego Benson and John M. Kopper have approached the various aspects of sexuality in the novella, including the relations between men and women and the position of women in modern society. Above all, *The Kreutzer Sonata* is often discussed in terms of the author's personal life. R. F. Christian has described the appeal of Tolstoy's novella: "Few other novelists could have made compelling reading out of sentiments and arguments which are irritating and manifestly unjust. Few other novelists could have given pathos and poignancy to the ending of a story whose limits appear to be laid down by the advice proffered in its opening chapters: 'Do not trust your horse in the field, or your wife in the house'."

CRITICISM

Isabel Hapgood   (review date 1890)

SOURCE: "Tolstoi's 'Kreutzer Sonata'," in *The Nation*, Vol. L, No. 1294, January-June, 1890, pp. 313-15.

[*In the following review, Hapgood summarizes the plot of* The Kreutzer Sonata, *noting the novella's language, style, and construction, but disparaging its moral.*]

What are the legitimate bounds of realism? To what point is it permissible to describe in repulsive detail the hideous and unseemly things of this world, simply because they exist, when it is quite impossible to say what the effect will be upon thousands of people to whom such description conveys the first knowledge of the existence of evil? It has been proved that public executions, far from inspiring horror of the deeds which led to them, and deterring others from the commission of like deeds, through fear of the result thus presented, actually give rise to crimes copied after those which are thus brought to general attention. The same thing is true in the case of crimes which are minutely described in the newspapers. But books? On the whole, although a sensational realistic book may never reach as many people as an article published in the popular newspaper, it probably produces as much effect because of the weight and respectability which the binding and comparatively high price give to it.

One has occasion to reflect upon this topic rather frequently in these days of "psychological" romances; but it is not often necessary, I think, to meditate so seriously as one is forced to do over Count Lyoff Tolstoi's last story.

When I first reached Russia, in the autumn of 1887, I heard that Count Tolstoi was writing a new tale: it began on the railway, and a man murdered his wife, and it was to be of the searching psychological type exemplified by *Ivan Ilyitch.* So much seemed to be known in well-informed circles. I asked no questions when I made the Count's acquaintance a year later. But one evening last July, during a visit which I made to Yasnaya Polyana, at the Countess's invitation, the Count spoke to me of his story as being near completion, and asked me to translate it when it should be finished. I promised, and inquired whether it was in a condition for me to read. "You may read the last version if you like," he answered, "but I would rather have you wait." His wife showed me sheets of the fourth version, which she was then copying, and advised me not to waste time in reading it, as it was quite likely that he might suddenly see the subject in a totally different light, and write it all over again from that point of view. So I read nothing, asked no questions, and waited, being informed from time to time that the book was progressing. How many different versions were finally made, I do not know, but this winter one of these versions began to make the rounds in Petersburg. The solitary manuscript flew rapidly from hand to hand. I was warned, however, that it or any copy from it would be imperfect, incomplete, and not approved by the author, who was at work upon the final version. I contented myself with the verdict of those who were too impatient to wait, and who had not been promised the first complete copy, as I had been. That verdict was, "Shocking!" "Beauties mingled with horrors," and so forth. It was said that it was not allowed to be printed—the usual cry; but, as there is nothing religious or political in it, its morality must have been the cause of the prohibition, if true.

At length I received the first copy of the genuine story (the second went to the Danish translator), with the information that, although the substance was nearly identical with that of the version which had already been circulating, and which was said to be in process of translation into foreign languages, the execution had been so altered that "not one stone was left upon another" in some places, while in others whole pages, and even chapters, had been completely rewritten by the author. My copy was corrected by the author especially with a view to translation, and was, therefore, to be regarded as the only one sanctioned by him for rendering into other tongues, and this version is yet unattainable in St. Petersburg.

Why, then, do I not translate a work from the famous and much-admired Russian author? Because, in spite of due gratitude to Count Tolstoi for favoring me with the first copy, and in spite of my faith in his conviction that such treatment of such a subject is needed and will do good, I cannot agree with him. It recalls the fable of his countryman, Kriloff, anent the man who borrowed his neighbor's water cask, used it for wine, and returned it impregnated with vinous fumes to such a degree that the unfortunate lender was obliged to throw it away, after using every possible means, during the space of two years, to expel the taint so that the water should be pure once more.

"Too frank and not decent," was one of the Petersburg verdicts upon this *Kreutzer Sonata.* This is so true that, although thus forewarned, I was startled at the idea that it could possibly be beneficial, and, destroying the translation which I had begun, I wrote promptly to decline the task. It is probable that the author and his blindly devoted admirers will consider that I have committed an unpardonable sin. But they must remember that his "comedy," *The Realm of Darkness,* although it was acted in private, in high Petersburg society, and in public in Paris, has never been translated into English, so far as I am aware, at least. I yield to no one in my admiration for and appreciation of Tolstoi's genius, as displayed in certain of his works. I tried to get American publishers to bring out *War and Peace* and *Anna Karenin* in 1881, five years before American readers were treated to the mangled versions of those works through the French. They declined, and one noted Boston publisher said, with great frankness: "No one in Russia knows how to write except Turgeneff, and he is far above the heads of Bostonians." I predicted a change of opinion, and if I am now morally compelled to appear unfaithful to my own former admiration, my regret is certainly more deep and sincere than even the regret of those who merely repent their failure to grasp an opportunity for making money, or of those who, consciously or unconsciously, follow the literary fashion of the hour.

But I will turn to the book. After making due allowance for the ordinary freedom of speech, which has greater latitude in Russia (as elsewhere in Europe) than is customary in America, I find the language of the *Kreutzer Sonata* to be too excessive in its candor. At the same time I admit that if that subject was to be treated in that way, no other language would have answered the purpose. I mention this first because it is the first thing which

strikes the reader, and because it is also the special thing which hovers over the horrors of the tale with an added dread, and lingers long behind in the reader's mind, like a moral bad taste in the mouth. Next, the style and construction. The construction is good, as is usual with the author. The style errs in the direction in which all his books are faulty, viz., repetition. The unnecessary repetition of words or phrases occurs in his greatest works, while in the later, the polemical, writings, it has become greatly exaggerated. It forms a feature of this book, and although it gives strength at times, it is too marked on the whole. One must think that this tautology is deliberate on the author's part, since he is never in haste to publish uncorrected matter; but the result is harshness, which increases with every fresh work. Nevertheless, the book is well written. And the story? It is that of a man who kills his wife out of jealousy for a semi-professional violinist, who plays Beethoven's "Kreutzer Sonata" with her one evening.

The author begins by narrating how he is making a long journey by rail. In the compartment with him are a lawyer and a lady, masculine in appearance and attire, who converse, and a gray-haired man with brilliant eyes, who avoids all attempts to talk with him and utters a peculiar sound from time to time. A merchant and a clerk enter the railway carriage at one of the stations. A partly inaudible conversation between the masculine lady and the lawyer about some woman who has fallen out with her husband, leads the lawyer to remark upon the amount of attention which is being bestowed all over Europe upon the question of divorce, and to say that there was nothing of the sort in olden days. The merchant answers him that there were cases even in old times, but they were less frequent; and people had become too "cultured" nowadays. In the discussion which ensues, the merchant advocates the old-fashioned arrangement of marriages by parents, and strict government on the part of the husband, as most conducive to wedded happiness, alleging that love will come in due season. The masculine lady argues that it is stupid to join in marriage two people who do not love each other and then feel surprised if discord ensues between them, and that the day for such unions is past. The merchant maintains that the day for obeying the New Testament rule, "Let the wife fear her husband," will never pass away; that although unfaithfulness, which is assumed to be impossible on the part of the wife, may happen in other classes, in the merchant class it does not happen, and that the carouses of married men at the fair, which the narrator has heard him relating, and of which he reminds him, form a special topic which must be excluded from the discussion.

Here the merchant leaves the train, but the conversation is continued by the passenger with gray hair and brilliant eyes inquiring to what sort of love the masculine lady has reference. What is "true love," and how long must it last—a month, two days, or half an hour—when it has been defined as the preference for some one man or woman above all other men or women in the world? He contends that only in romances does this preference last for a lifetime, as per theory; whereas in real life it endures for a year, generally much less, and is felt by every man for every pretty woman; also, that this love is never mutual, and if it were, and if it lasted a lifetime on one side, it would not on the other. Identity of ideals, spiritual likeness, he does not admit as a ground for entering upon marriage. He gives a brief sketch of the manner, in his opinion, in which marriages are entered upon, winding up: "And the result of this is that frightful hell which makes men take to drink, shoot themselves, poison, and murder themselves and each other."

The lawyer, with a view to putting an end to the unseemly conversation, replies that "there are undoubtedly critical episodes in married life." Whereupon the speaker remarks: "I see that you recognize me. I am Pozdnisheff, the man with whom occurred the critical episode of murdering his wife." In fact, no one knows anything of him, but the lawyer and masculine lady change into another compartment as soon as possible, while Pozdnisheff offers to withdraw if his presence is disagreeable to the narrator. Finding that it is not, he offers to while away the night by relating the story of his life. I may remark here, in view of the above, that the author gives not a hint of his own opinion as to which is preferable, a marriage of love or a *mariage de convenance,* and also that some of the points suggested do not seem to be answered thereafter.

Pozdnisheff begins his tale with his introduction to evil at the age of sixteen. Shorn of digressions, his story would be brief. But the digressions attack many accepted views of things—or views which he says are accepted. The present order of society and life, modes of marriage, dress, and so forth, form the topics of these digressions. Pozdnisheff states that he has taken to analyzing the subject since his own life reached a climax in his crime. Many of these remarks I recognize as substantially identical with attacks on those subjects contained in all the author's serious writings. The sentence, "I never see a woman clad in ball attire that I do not feel like shouting, 'Police!' and ordering her to be removed as dangerous," closely corresponds to former utterances upon low-necked dresses and so on. He repeats former denunciations of higher education for women, but, astonishing to relate, instead of winding up with the moral that women should devote themselves solely to becoming the mothers of the largest possible families, he praises the Shakers because they do not marry, and declares that woman will only rise to a higher plane, cease to rule in underhand ways as an offset to oppression, and acquire her full rights, when virginity shall have become the highest ideal of womanhood.

I am tempted to a personal digression at this point. Count Tolstoi one day praised the Shakers in this manner before a table full of people. I was afraid to ask him his meaning, lest he should explain in detail, so I questioned his wife in private as to whether this new departure was not somewhat inconsistent with his previously advocated views on woman's vocation. She replied: "Probably it is inconsistent; but my husband changes his opinions every two years, you know." The explanation which I venture to offer is, that just at that time he was reading Mr. Howells's *An Undiscovered Country,* and that he is impressionable. At all events, however clearly one can understand from these too frank digressions what a man should not do, it is quite impossible to comprehend how he thinks a woman should dress, behave, and live.

Returning to the thread of his story, Pozdnisheff relates how he proposed for his wife after a very brief acquaintance, fascinated by her jersey, her well-dressed hair, and a boating excursion, and adds that, had it not been for the tailors who dressed her well, and the close jersey, etc., he should never have married. This does not agree with the statement that all through his vicious bachelorhood he had firmly intended to marry if he could find any one good enough for him. An interesting point here is that he shows his betrothed his bachelor diary, just as Levin shows his to Kitty in *Anna Karenin,* and with precisely the same effect, only less well told. The repetition of this incident and the probable rarity of such diaries seem to hint at a personal experience.

They are married. The description of the honeymoon and of their married life nearly up to the date of the final catastrophe is, like what precedes, unquotable. Suffice it to say that they quarrel promptly and continue to quarrel frequently and fiercely, eventually using their five children as moral battering-rams so to speak, against each other. This last is very well done. At about the age of thirty, his wife becomes plump and prettier, and begins to take an interest again in pretty clothes. His mad jealousy interprets this into a quest for a lover, though there are no proofs of such a thing even alleged. The description of his jealousy is, however, the best part of the book. Presently the object for jealousy for whom the husband has been on the lookout, makes his appearance in the person of a handsome young man, of good family, who has been educated in Paris by a relative, as he has no money, and who has become a very fine and semi-professional violinist. The young man comes to call on his old acquaintance, Pozdnisheff, on his return to his native land. Pozdnisheff instantly fixes upon him, in his own mind, as the fated lover. Nevertheless, or rather in consequence of this, he is unusually cordial, introduces the musician to his wife (quite unnecessarily), and begs him to bring his violin that very evening and play duets with her. The musician comes, behaves with perfect propriety, as Pozdnisheff admits, but jealousy causes him to see what he expects. He urges the musician to dine and play at his house on the following Sunday, still impelled by the fancies of his own disordered brain. The musician accepts; but, having called in the interim to decide upon the proper music to present to the company, he drives Pozdnisheff to such a pitch of unreason that the latter uses vile language to his innocent wife and throws things at her, whereupon she promptly retires and takes poison.

She is rescued, a reconciliation ensues, the dinner comes off, and the "Kreutzer Sonata" in the evening is a great success upon the violin and piano. But the husband's jealousy and imagination are all alive, and interpret every glance of the players to suit himself. On taking leave that evening, the musician bids Pozdnisheff and his wife a final farewell. Pozdnisheff is going to the country on business, and the musician says that he shall leave Moscow himself before the former's return, intimating that he shall not call upon Madame during her husband's absence. Pozdnisheff goes to the country in a tranquil frame of mind, but a letter from his wife, in which she mentions that the musician has called to fetch her the music he promised, sets his jealousy aflame again. He hastens back to Moscow, finds the musician eating supper with his wife, and murders her. On trial he is acquitted on the plea of "justifiable homicide," and when the narrator of the story meets him in the train, he is on his way to a small estate in one of the southern governments, his children remaining with his dead wife's sister.

The whole book is a violent and roughly worded attack upon the evils of animal passion. In that sense, it is moral. Translation, even with copious excisions, is impossible, in my opinion, and also inadvisable. The men against whom it is directed will not mend their ways from the reading of it, even if they fully grasp the idea that unhappiness and mad jealousy and crime are the outcome of their ways, as Pozdnisheff is made to say in terms as plain as the language will admit of, and in terms much plainer than are usually employed in polite society. On the other hand, the book can, I am sure, do no good to the people at whom it is not launched. It is decidedly a case where ignorance is bliss, and where uncontaminated minds will carry away a taint which a few will be able to throw off, but which will linger with the majority as the wine of the fable lingered in the cask meant for pure water. Such morbid psychology can hardly be of service, it seems to me, much as I dislike to criticise Count Tolstoi.

Donald Davie   (essay date 1965)

SOURCE: "Tolstoy, Lermontov, and Others," in *Russian Literature and Modern English Fiction: A Collection of Critical Essays,* edited by Donald Davie, University of Chicago Press, 1965, pp. 164-202.

[*In the following excerpt, Davie analyzes the central conflict between human intelligence and the will to act in* The Kreutzer Sonata, *observing Tolstoy's inconsistency of method.*]

In general, we regard *The Kreutzer Sonata* as a didactic tract disguised as a novel. Such tracts in disguise can be works of literary and artistic value. Perhaps they are necessarily of the second rank as works of art. But at least the novel of ideas is a thoroughly respectable literary kind, having methods and conventions proper to it. One may cite, in our day, the novels of Mr. Arthur Koestler. But is *The Kreutzer Sonata* a novel of ideas, of this sort? I think that it is not. It is a novel and a tract at once, or it essays to be both at once. It is both and neither. And the conventions which govern it are confused, so that the reader does not know "which way to take it." Nor, so far as we can see, was this ambiguity intended by the author. It is therefore a grossly imperfect work.

The scene in the railway-carriage is set, in the first two chapters, with pleasing skill. Thereafter, until chapter xxi, the initial convention is not altogether sustained; the reader begins to wonder why the scene should have been set at all. These chapters constitute the first part of Pozdnishchev's confessional monologue, and the sentences interjected from time to time, reminding the reader of the setting, seem only perfunctory. Still, this part is read, with no discomfort, as within the convention of the novel of ideas; and the reader hopes that the significance of the setting will emerge later. We infer, meanwhile, that the sentiments expressed by Pozdnishchev are not to be taken as being "in character," that the sentiments expressed are the sentiments of Tolstoy himself. In chapter xxi Pozdnishchev tells how he introduced into his home the man who was to cause him to murder his wife:

> I disliked him exceedingly from the first moment I looked upon him. But some strange fatal force moved me not only to refrain from repelling him, but to draw him nearer to me. What could be simpler than to exchange a few words with him, to bid him good-bye chillingly, and not to introduce him to my wife? But no; I must talk about his playing, and tell him that I had heard he had given up music. He said it was not so; that he had never practised more assiduously all his life than at that moment; and passing from himself to me, reminded me that I too had played in times gone by. To this I replied that I did not play now, but that my wife was a good musician. It is very curious! From the very first day, from the very first hour I saw him, my relations towards him were such as they could only have been subsequently to everything that occurred later on. There was something very strained in my intercourse with him; I took note of every word, every expression uttered by him or by myself, and invested them with a significance justified by nothing that I then knew.

It is very curious indeed. It is very curious that Pozdnishchev who in previous chapters has been so empirically reasonable, impatient of idealism and illusion, should here show himself as believing, not only in precise foreboding, but also in "some strange fatal force." He believes in these, moreover, against the run of the empirical evidence. There was apparent, as he says, nothing to prevent him from keeping his rival away. Yet in the earlier chapters the appeal was always to the empirical evidence, to milliners' shop-windows and the social usages of the Russian gentry, against any preconceived notions. If we are to believe, despite all appearance to the contrary, in "some strange fatal force," why must we not believe, despite appearances to the contrary, in the quite general existence of ennobling and permanent love between the sexes?

Three pages later, the "strange fatal force" reappears as "an invisible power":

> I could not help noticing all this, and I suffered horribly in consequence. And yet, in spite of this, or rather, perhaps, by reason of it, an invisible power compelled me against my will to be not only extremely courteous, but affectionate towards him. I am unable to specify the motive which prompted me to act thus; whether it was

to prove to my wife and to him that I was not actuated by fear, or to deceive myself, I cannot say; I only know that from the very first my relations with him were not natural and unaffected.

The "power," it is plain, the "fatal force," is inward. And it is "strange" and "mysterious" only because it cannot be rationalized, brought into consciousness. But the contradiction remains. Whence this inability to specify the motive? The sudden humility is suspicious after the downrightness with which Pozdnishchev specified the motive in the earlier passages of courtship and honeymoon and parenthood. For the remainder of the novel, however, this humility is maintained. In the wonderful passages which describe the murder itself, we gape at the fluctuating and mysterious complexity in the mind of the murderer:

> I knew very well what I was doing, and did not for a single second cease to be conscious of it. The more I fanned the flame of my fury, the brighter burned within me the light of consciousness, lighting up every nook and corner of my soul, so that I could not help seeing everything I was doing. I cannot affirm that I knew in advance what I was going to do, but the very moment I was doing anything, and I fancy some seconds beforehand, I was conscious of what I was doing, in order, as it were, that I might repent of it in time, that I might afterwards have it to say that I could have stayed my hand. Thus, I was aware that I was striking her below the ribs, and that the blade would penetrate. The moment I was doing this, I knew that I was doing something terrible, a thing that I had never done before, an action that would be fraught with frightful consequences.

And again:

> I recollect the indescribable horror of this state of mind, and I infer from it, and in fact I may add that I have a dim remembrance, that having plunged the dagger into her body, I instantaneously drew it out again, anxious thereby to remedy what I had done, to stay my hand. I then stood motionless for an instant, waiting to see what would happen, and whether it was possible to undo it.

I suppose it is this in Tolstoy which we especially admire; on the one hand, the effortless accuracy about the processes of thought (as here first the recollection, then the inference from the recollection, last the corroboration from dim remembrance); on the other, the shocking honesty about the endless irrationality of motive—"I instantaneously drew it out again, anxious thereby to remedy what I had done. . . . I then stood motionless for an instant, waiting to see what would happen. . . ." And indeed it is fine—we are persuaded once again about the complexity of the mental life, and about the irrationality of motive.

All the more, then, are we indignant, on turning back to the earlier chapters, to find motive over an enormous field of human experience reduced bluntly to one simple proposition:

Last spring a number of peasants were working in our neighbourhood on a railway embankment. The usual food of a strong peasant when engaged in light field labour consists of bread, kvass, onions, and this keeps him alive, active, and healthy. When he enters into the service of a railway company his food is porridge, and a pound of meat daily. This meat he gives out again in the form of sixteen hours' labour, driving a wheelbarrow of thirty poods, which is just as much as he is able to perform. We, on the other hand, eat game, meat, and fish, besides sundry other kinds of heat-giving food and drink. Now where, may I ask, does all this go? To produce excesses, abnormal excitement, which, passing through the prism of our artificial life, assumes the form of falling in love.

What we have learned from Tolstoy he appears never to have learned himself. Only in Tolstoy himself, he would have us think, are the processes of thought and the faculties of knowledge not muddled but naïve and clear. Only in himself, he implies, are the springs of action always reasonable.

But this is a monster. One really cannot believe that the man who knew so profoundly the minds of his fellows knew his own mind so little. There must be another reason why Tolstoy cheated the most valuable trait in himself, his plastic apprehension of irrationality and complexity. I think there is. For Tolstoy all thought was vicious, whether artistic or philosophical, so long as it did not lead to action:

> Music instantaneously throws me into the state of feeling in which the composer of it found himself when he wrote it. My soul blends with his, and together with him I am transported from one frame of mind to another. But why I am so ravished out of myself I know not. He who composed the piece—Beethoven, for instance, in the case of the Kreutzer Sonata—knew perfectly well why he was in that mood; it was that mood that determined him to do certain things, and therefore for him that state of mind has a meaning; for me it has absolutely none. This is why it is that music only causes irritation, never ends anything. It is a different thing if a military march is played, then the soldiers move forward, keeping time to the music, and the end is attained; if dance music is played people dance to it, and the object is also accomplished; if a Mass is sung I receive Holy Communion, and here, too, the music is not in vain; but in other cases there is nothing but irritation, and no light how to act during this irritation.

There is no disputing the puerility of this. The argument rests upon hypotheses about the mind of Beethoven in the act of composing, assumptions which are not, in the nature of the case, susceptible of proof. Nor can it be argued, I fear, that Tolstoy is aware of the puerility, that it is not his but his puppet's, Pozdnishchev's. This is a passage in which the plastic imagination breaks down, as in the earlier chapters, before the half-baked rationalist. What emerges, however, as the overriding preoccupation here, is the desire for art to prove its utility by leading to action. And since the passage was apparently crucial for Tolstoy in that it provides the title to the book, we are justified in supposing that what he says here of music he would have applied, with more or less qualification, to the other arts—to his own, for instance, the art of the novelist. There is corroboration of this in other pamphlets.

Tolstoy is not alone in supposing that . . . it was impossible to meet fully the claims of the will, demanding expression in action, and also the claims of the intelligence, demanding freedom and scope to analyze, weigh pros and cons, and scrutinize motive.

—Donald Davie

Now it is plain that passages of the kind we have admired from *The Kreutzer Sonata* do not lead to action. There is no need to argue a case that great art produces a stasis or an equilibrium, not a drive to the act. We need only say that we shall presumably be wary of intervening in any situation if that situation is presented as of great psychological complexity, and that we shall not be so wary if the issues are simplified for us. At bottom, the reason for inconsistency of method in Tolstoy is as simple as this. On the other hand, Tolstoy is not alone in supposing that, for the sophisticated individual of the nineteenth century, it was impossible to meet fully the claims of the will, demanding expression in action, and also the claims of the intelligence, demanding freedom and scope to analyze, weigh pros and cons, and scrutinize motive. On the contrary, this was a preoccupation common to most of the European Romantics. It was Shakespeare's Hamlet who talked of being "sicklied o'er with the pale cast of thought"; but it was Coleridge, the Romantic critic, who saw in this the problem debated in every line of the play. Tolstoy, again, was not alone in deciding that the rights of the will overrode the rights of the intelligence. Most of the Romantics had agreed, and it is this which lends color to the contention that Romanticism was antirationalist, that it worked by impulse and intuition, not by intelligence. There is no question, therefore, of looking for a "source" for Tolstoy's attitude. The spirit of his age led him inevitably to think in these terms, to see the claims of the analyzing intelligence in conflict with the claims of the will to act.

In terms of this conflict Tolstoy saw life; and in terms of this conflict he lived his life. The conflict in the living spills over into *The Kreutzer Sonata* and breaks that book into two. From other books, earlier than *The Kreutzer Sonata,* and later, the conflict was excluded. Or rather, the conflict is present, as the theme which is debated, as the terms of the vision which is presented; but it is not present as the agony which was lived. In *The Cossacks,* in *War and Peace,* in *Hadji Murad,* the conflict which

Tolstoy lived is kept separate from the conflict which was seen. In *The Kreutzer Sonata,* the conflict of the life distorts the conflict of the vision. When we discuss Tolstoy's narrative method and his style, we try to find out how the conflict of the life was kept out of the vision. In these, the great books, the conflict is seen as the conflict inside men, not in the first place as the conflict inside Tolstoy. We are concerned with Tolstoy the artist, not with Tolstoy the agonized titan. It has been said that this is impossible, and in general it is true. It is better to say, therefore, that we are concerned with Tolstoy's vision, not with Tolstoy's life, and with the means by which the vision was made independent of the life. The vision is not independent in *The Kreutzer Sonata,* and the novel suffers accordingly.

Dorothy Green   (essay date 1966)

SOURCE: "*The Kreutzer Sonata*: Tolstoy and Beethoven," in *Melbourne Slavonic Studies,* Vol. 1, No. 1, 1967, pp. 11-23.

[*In the following essay, originally delivered as a lecture in 1966, Green discusses the connections between* The Kreutzer Sonata *and Beethoven's musical composition, focusing on similarities of dramatic feeling and structure in both works.*]

The origin of this paper was a strong impression that there is a closer connection between Tolstoy's novel and Beethoven's music than is usually allowed for in criticisms of the book. The paper is also an attempt to counter a tendency to regard the book merely as an expression of a thesis. Before anything else, Tolstoy's *Kreutzer Sonata* seems to me a complete work of art, as much a thing made and existing in its own right as Beethoven's sonata, obeying the laws of a particular kind of literary form, as the sonata obeys those of a particular kind of musical form.

Criticism of this kind is bound to be impressionistic: it is obviously impossible to prove what a piece of music suggests to the mind of anyone but oneself, but it is hoped that the interpretation will be found to be inconsistent neither with the text of the novel, nor with that of the music. It would be absurd for one knowing no Russian to undertake any kind of verbal analysis and I have tried to draw conclusions which are independent of linguistic knowledge, and as far as possible, independent of a comparison of variant texts. There are nine of these altogether, bearing witness not only to Tolstoy's struggle for artistic excellence, but to the strenuousness of the argument he was conducting with himself. The finished work seems to me a triumphant solution to a dual problem.

Alexandra Tolstoy, in her biography of her father, tells us that he had begun and abandoned a story called *The Murderer of His Wife* in the 1870's. His English biographer, Simmons, says that on a hint given him by the actor Andreyev-Burlak, he had begun this tale of sexual love in

1887 and put it aside. Both agree that early in 1888 in the spring, occurred the incident which gave a new and final impetus to the story. Among the guests at the Tolstoy house in Moscow were the painter Repin, Burlak and Lysoto, a violinist. The violinist and Tolstoy's young son Sergei played Beethoven's *Kreutzer Sonata,* a performance which for some reason particularly moved Tolstoy. As we might infer from the novel itself, Tolstoy responded especially to the first movement and when one considers the ideas that come to the surface in the story, it is not hard to suggest why, as I shall try to show. Under the influence of the music, Tolstoy suggested that Repin should paint a scene inspired by it, a kind of back-drop, and that in front of this Andreyev-Burlak should read the story that Tolstoy would write, based on the sonata, or on the ideas it suggested to him. That is to say, his conception of the total experience "Kreutzer Sonata" shaped itself as a kind of miniature drama, with a background of unheard music; in reality, a miniature music-drama. Merezhkovski, who is usually so sensitive to Tolstoy's artistry, complains that the hero is 'reduced' to a voice: "a mere plaintive voice and a pair of eyes, glowing with feverish, half-crazy fire." With all due respect, this seems to me precisely the point, the essential element in Tolstoy's structural intention. The story makes its appeal, and was intended to make its appeal largely through the ear. The voice is the literary equivalent for the instruments; it has to carry the burden of the statement that Tolstoy reads, or hears, in the music. One's attention is constantly being drawn to sounds, for example, to Pozdnyshev's cough, or laugh, "like a sob." (One has to resist the temptation to formulate an analogy here, very strongly). The view that the story was designed to appeal to the ear has thematic justification also: the novel is cast in the form of a "confession." No other narrative method but that of the almost continuous speaker could have approximated to the music embodied in piano and violin, those two voices that strive through the sonata to become one. The main critical problem, then, resolves itself into trying to identify what the music of the story is saying. And this is where I find most of what I have happened to read about the novel in English unsatisfactory. Its relationship with Beethoven's music is ignored, the artistry of the story itself is dismissed and criticism is sidetracked into discussions of the merits and demerits of Tolstoy's ideas about sex, chastity, modern medicine, the relations between men and women and the position of women in modern society. To make matters worse, discussion of the ideas is confused by the publicity given to Tolstoy's personal life. They are never discussed for their own sake, but always in the light of his own application of them and in that of his relations to his own wife. Whether Tolstoy practised what he preached is in the long run irrelevant; a doctrine is not necessarily wrong because its advocate fails to practise it. And it is not at all certain that the intention of the story is to persuade one to follow a doctrine. Some of the confusion in discussion is Tolstoy's own fault. Essays like *An Afterword to the Kreutzer Sonata* distract our attention from the artistic organisation of the tale and encourage the view that he was more interested in propagating a belief than in creating a work of art. When an artist finds

his ideas being taken seriously, he is often tempted to become a kind of "doctrinaire-after-the-fact." Before writing the *Afterword,* it is important to remember, Tolstoy insisted to Obolensky that the views expressed in the story were the views of its hero. This seems to me an unassailable fact; there is nothing in the views themselves inconsistent with the dramatic situation set up in the novel. It is true, perhaps, that once he had written the story, Tolstoy became ambivalent in his attitude to it, unable to make up his mind whether he preferred it to be regarded as art or as sociology. Even at the second level, the usual discussions have done less than justice to the ideas in the book and it might be as well to have another look at them before going on to the more relevant artistic questions.

Two of the ideas at least are extremely important and highly relevant to our own situation. The fact that Tolstoy has tangled them up with notions of chastity that seem at first sight rather bizarre has tended to obscure their importance. In the first place, he raises that irritating question *What is it all for?* He is asking: "Do we raise children in order to raise children in order to raise children . . . ?" and so on, ad infinitum. This is a question of the same kind as "Do we train teachers to train teachers to train teachers . . . ?" These are the sorts of fundamental questions which are not supposed to be asked and which are always begged by writers on education or on family relationships. But at some stage in our history they are questions which will have to be asked, even though there must and should be uncertainty about the answer. The mere asking them acts as a corrective. Tolstoy irritates those who are obsessed with processes because he forces us to face squarely the fundamental question of purpose. Not only does he question the whole notion of child-bearing as an end in itself, but he points out the possibility that child-bearing may be an obstacle to the accomplishment of full adulthood; he reminds us that life on this planet must end, whether we subscribe to the religious or to the scientific point of view and that its limitation makes the accomplishment of life's purpose, whatever it may be, more urgent.

> 'You ask how the human race will continue to exist,' he said, having again sat down in front of me, and spreading his legs far apart he leant his elbows on his knees. 'Why should it continue?'
>
> 'Why? If not, we should not exist.'
>
> 'And why should we exist?'
>
> 'Why? In order to live, of course.'
>
> 'But why live? If life has no aim, if life is given us for life's sake, there is no reason for living . . . But if life has an aim, it is clear it ought to come to an end when that aim is reached . . .'

If the possibility of life on some other scale than the mere animal, life-for-the-sake-of-life, appears idiosyncratic, we should remember that it has been put forward by an outstanding scientist in our own day, Teilhard de

Chardin, as an evolutionary possibility. Moreover, scientific materialists who are overtly opposed to teleological views, frequently behave and write as if they held them.

> **Tolstoy reminds us that life on this planet must end, whether we subscribe to the religious or to the scientific point of view and that its limitation makes the accomplishment of life's purpose, whatever it may be, more urgent.**
>
> —*Dorothy Green*

The second idea which is fundamental to the structure of the novel concerns the changing role of women in human history, the full implications of which have hardly yet begun to be seen. Like George Eliot, Tolstoy perceived that this was no simple matter which could be adjusted by a few adroit social and political changes.

> 'If there is to be equality,' says Pozdnyshev, 'let it be equality!' 'Women's lack of rights arises not from the fact that she must not vote or be a judge—to be occupied with such affairs is no privilege—but from the fact that she is not man's equal in sexual intercourse and has not the right to use a man or abstain from him as she pleases— is not allowed to choose a man at her pleasure instead of being chosen by him. You say this is monstrous! Very well! Then a man must not have those rights either. As it is at present, a woman is deprived of that right, while a man has it. And to make up for that right, she acts on men's sensuality and through his sensuality subdues him, so that he only chooses formally, while in reality it is she who chooses.'

In spite of surface modifications, this picture is still substantially correct. Tolstoy goes on to paint a further and more vivid picture of the economy of the western world dominated by female consumer-demand, a picture which, to us, seems more accurate than when he drew it.

Both Tolstoy and George Eliot perceived that the real obstacle to the genuine independence of women lay partly in man's concept of woman and partly in her concept of herself. Tolstoy felt the concept to be the result of sexual drive in the male and held the male responsible. Eliot was perhaps more perceptive in grasping the fact that women are saddled with a physiological organisation ill-adapted to social change. But both pointed to the necessity for a woman to organise a meaningful life for herself without reference to a man. Tolstoy arouses resistance because his way of making his point is repugnant to a generation conditioned by Freudian thinking. The situation will change, Pozdnyshev says, "only when woman regards virginity as the highest state and does not as at present consider the highest state of a human being a

shame and disgrace." If we substituted the phrase 'single state' for 'virginity', we might feel less resistant, but only to a slight degree. The question Tolstoy is really asking is too revolutionary still for us to contemplate without passion: Is marriage now, as it once was, the best way of organising society, or has it outlived, in its present form, its traditional function? The attempt to commend the notion of woman as a free-living organism brings us up against the ideas about chastity that so many people find repellent and hysterical, especially when they identify Tolstoy too closely with his central character. But what Tolstoy is really doing is pointing out that our attitudes to this question are partly the result of conditioning and education. In this he is anticipating by about eighty years some recent thinking on the subject. It is in fact difficult to know how much of our sexual appetite is innate and how much is the result of tradition and outside influence. It is quite possible that a great many more people could lead happy, purposeful and celibate lives if the propaganda against doing so were not all-powerful at an early stage. Even now, a good many do, for religious reasons. And the lot of those who must do so, for other reasons, would be much easier to bear if they had not already been conditioned to regard it as unbearable. The conditioning of girls for motherhood begins very early. No-one thrusts a doll into a little boy's hands; he is usually asked what he *wants* to be when he grows up. But a little girl is told what she wants to be. The cynical commercial exploitation of sex-drive in our own day by the advertising world is evidence enough of the point Tolstoy is making: that wants and beliefs can be foisted on people to the point where it is impossible to conceive of any alternative.

A third fundamental question raised by Tolstoy, which again anticipates some very recent thinking on the subject is the increase in anxiety-states paradoxically brought about by advances in medical science, particularly in respect of the mother's attitude to her children. In every instance, what Tolstoy is attacking is some subtle form of propaganda, brain-washing, manipulation, or exploitation. Behind the whole argument is the detestation of the idea that one human being should be used by another for his own purposes.

Such, then, are the main general questions raised in the novel and by the novel, but it does not seem to me that these are what the story is about.

For one thing, they are reflections, meditations, the attempts at an intellectual understanding of his situation by a man who has been brought by a catastrophe to question the whole foundation of his life. Pozdnyshev raises the questions, but does not claim he has the answers; he is merely, in trying to make sense of his experience, shaking his and our own basic convictions. We have to try to set aside our knowledge that for a time Tolstoy himself preached complete chastity as the goal for human beings, though he modified his doctrines sensibly enough later on. The conclusions of the novel are Pozdnyshev's and given the kind of man he presents himself to be and the situation he is in, they are the kinds of conclusions which are natural and credible. He presents himself as insanely jealous, and sees the jealousy as the immediate cause of the disaster. The foundation of the jealousy, however, he detects in his 'swinishness'; that is, he attributes the jealousy to his innate sexual drive which causes him to view women as its goal, or object. The drive is 'swinish' because it has caused him to regard a human being as a thing, a thing which exists only for the purpose of gratifying him. Because he finds that the thing is not his exclusively, but has a being of its own, he kills it in a fit of jealous rage. When he becomes aware of the cause of his state of mind, he wishes naturally enough to obliterate the cause, to discredit the sexual drive.

> I wouldn't take a young man to a lock-hospital to knock the hankering after women out of him, but into my soul, to see the devils that were rending it! What was terrible, you know, was that I considered myself to have a complete right to her body, as if it were my own, and yet at the same time I felt I could not control that body, that it was not mine and she could dispose of it as she pleased and that she wanted to dispose of it, not as I wished her to.

When a man has been brought suddenly to realise the essential otherness of a human being, the truth that it has a sacred centre of self-hood which has no reference to his own, is it inconceivable that he should wish to destroy that impulse in his nature which has prevented him from recognising this otherness? The tragedy is that Pozdnyshev realised the otherness of his wife only when he destroyed her. Is it inconceivable that his horror at the deed his blindness has brought him to should tempt him to generalise his experience and hold it up as a warning? The generalisation, the articulate moralising, it should be noticed, occur in the story up to Chapter 18, before the advent of the musician into the narrative and the account of the disaster that ensued. That is, they are not allowed to break the unity of the central events, yet they are not only a consequence of these, but a preparation for our understanding of them. It is difficult to agree with George Steiner's objection (in *Tolstoy or Dostoevski?*) that the moral elements have become too massive to be absorbed into the narrative structure. They seem to me to have been placed in the narrative structure exactly where they ought to be.

But to come now to the connection of the novel with the music, to its artistic organisation.

Tolstoy's interest in music had developed early in his life and it is clear that he was particularly open to its influence. He regarded it, his daughter tells us, as a divine manifestation of the human soul; it heightened his creative powers and loosed a flood of images. One would expect Pozdnyshev to be conscious of its voluptuousness, and he tells us that he is. There is a reason to believe Tolstoy responded to music in the same way as his hero.

When he was nineteen, Tolstoy wrote down in his preposterous program of self-education: (8) "Achieve the highest degree of accomplishment in music and painting."

He did, in fact, become an accomplished pianist and made up his mind at one stage to become a great musician and composer. He was carried away by the combination of sounds, and attempted to formulate his own theory of harmony, under the title *The Fundamentals of Music and Rules for its Study*. As far as composers were concerned, Beethoven seems to have inspired in him a kind of love-hate relationship; perhaps he resented Beethoven's power to carry him out of himself. There is no doubt, then, of Tolstoy's response to music, of his initial competence to find something in a piece of music which others had missed. And there is no doubt that he was well acquainted with the formal structure of music.

We must now look briefly at the formal structure which immediately concerns us. The word 'sonata' in general refers to instrumental music arranged usually in three or four movements in different rhythms at different speeds; for instance, fast, slow, fast, sometimes with a brief, slow introduction. As a rule, there is a return during the last movement to the key of the first one. Beethoven's sonatas, according to Scholes [in the *Oxford Companion to Music*], are characterised by strong dramatic feeling, intense emotion, and violent contrasts of moods and emotion. On this last point, Beethoven's appeal for Tolstoy is obvious enough. Violent contrast is the groundwork of Tolstoy's being, as it is of Pozdnyshev's. Like his creator, Pozdnyshev is tormented by the warring impulses of the flesh and the spirit; their nature is a battle-ground; the only defence against the unsubduable flesh is to crucify it, only to find that this cannot be done without injury to the spirit. This constant yearning for a resolution, it seems to me, may have been what Tolstoy heard in the dialogue of piano and violin in the sonata.

As to dramatic feeling, Pozdnyshev's long monologue is dramatic if anything in Tolstoy ever was. This is a quality which is usually denied him; his genius, we are told, lies in his analytic power. But Pozdnyshev's monologue is a whole drama in itself; he is not only there carrying on his civil war in himself, but he evokes his wife, her presence, the tones of her voice, her appearance, as vividly as if she were present in the story as an actual antagonist. Tolstoy's artistic achievement in the person of Pozdnyshev reminds us of the great mimes, or diseurs of the stage. He peoples his setting for us with the figures of the wife, of the violinist Trukhashevsky, the guests, the servants, the children, the people in the railway carriage in his own nightmare journey within a journey. The last is a tour-de-force in atmosphere compression: the device of the journey within a journey doubles for us all the suspense, the sense of impotence, of doom, of suffocating claustrophobia, that the whole marriage relationship has meant for Pozdnyshev. The figure of the passive narrator who introduces the story performs the function of intermediary, distancing us from the central figure, preventing us from identifying with him and from identifying the author with the character. To have Pozdnyshev 'confess' direct into our ears would have meant the loss of detachment which is crucial to understanding.

The value of the sonata form as a vehicle for the expression of strong personal emotion and its relationship to the novel in this respect is too obvious to mention. Its function is analogous to that of the dramatic monologue in verse and the novel is as near to that as it could be without being written in verse. To choose a normal third-person form with the conventional omniscient narrator would have been impossible.

The description of the murder is accomplished with all the uncanny kinesthetic precision of which Tolstoy is the supreme master. Before he has finished, the reader has the physical sensation of having committed the act himself.

—*Dorothy Green*

These, it is clear enough, are large general relationships between the music and the novel. But I think there are others. The story seems to me to have three clearly marked rhythmic divisions which deserve the name of movements, and in addition to that, to have three less emphatic, but still marked movements within each of the larger ones. The tempo pattern is the same as that of the sonata, i.e. fast, slow, fast, but the whole is preceded by a short, slow introduction. The first big division in the story occurs at the end of Chapter 12, or with the beginning of Chapter 13. The pause is the more clearly marked because there is an interruption in the narrative. "Two fresh passengers entered . . ." There is still a sense of the outside world. Pozdnyshev has not yet retreated into his own nightmare territory.

The subject of the first movement concerns the general notion of solicitation between the sexes and the particular instance of this in Pozdnyshev's own courtship, wedding and honeymoon. As in the sonata, there are false starts, the subject is introduced, dropped, hinted at, in the reference to the Kunavin Fair, the lady's conversation with the lawyer and so on. Chapters 1 and 2 are a kind of overture or introduction to the theme, laying down the lines of the problem: the old man is the voice of tradition, the lawyer and the lady represent the new thought. These are quickly eliminated, for neither is capable of much insight, and the real subject is then undertaken by Pozdnyshev and his interlocutor. Pozdnyshev at first is dominant, the narrator parries the questions he raises, and Pozdnyshev finally becomes the narrator.

The second movement of the novel concerns the married life of Pozdnyshev and his wife; the begetting and rearing of their children and above all the growth of Pozdnyshev's irrational jealousy, exacerbated by the freedom acquired by his wife when she ceases to bear children. The jealousy motif is the dominant one, reflected in the husband's struggle to impose his will on his wife, in his growing intolerance, his impulses of violence. Each is contending for power, or rather, each is striving to be free from the dominance of the other, like two hostile convicts chained together.

It is important to notice that there are no further interruptions in this movement from the outside world. In Chapter 17, Pozdnyshev gets up and leaves the carriage for a moment, but he returns and the sense of constriction deepens and is sustained until the end.

The movement ends in Chapter 19, with the introduction of the change in the wife's situation, the complete breach between them, the wife's renewed interest in music and the heralding of the entrance of the musician, Trukhachevski.

Before he is introduced to the wife, there is a direct example of the kind of situation prevailing between husband and wife, an episode of violence full of the menace of destruction, which sets the seal on their separation. The final movement is the physical counterpart of the psychic murder enacted here; indeed, in a sense, this psychic murder (prepared for earlier) is the "real" murder, and the physical one an irrelevance, or at least an anti-climax. The delay between the announcement of the musician theme and its full development is a masterly stroke, enabling Tolstoy to re-introduce the notion of death (in the quarrel scene), so that it is associated with the musician theme. 'I wish you were dead as a dog!' Pozdnyshev shouts in a rage. The sentence orients our minds in the necessary direction, and then our attention is distracted by the new interest.

Chapter 20 heralds the prevailing mood of the final movement. The frenzy increases, the tempo is speeded up, there are no more interruptions until just before the catastrophe. The pivot of the movement is the sonata itself. It is prepared for by the discussion on music and its connection in the speaker's mind with the subject of adultery. There is a gradual crescendo of jealousy and the catastrophe in Chapter 27 is the actual murder. In Chapters 25 and 26 occur two more strokes of genius: the effect of the conductor's entering, putting out the candle, without supplying a fresh one and leaving the two travellers in half-darkness releases the unbearable tension for a moment before Tolstoy gives a final twist to the screw. The gesture also has strong symbolic overtones relating to the deed that is coming perhaps, but also relating to the argument itself. The story has been told so far in the semi-darkness of night; what is to follow is told in the half-daylight. That is, confession has gone as far as it can go, the problem has been laid bare, but there is no real illumination, only the half-light possible to a mind that is relieved of a burden, but not renewed in hope. The sense of tension and suspense is accentuated at the beginning of Chapter 26 by the words "At the last station but one, when the conductor had been to collect the tickets . . ." This time, of course, it is Pozdnyshev's journey home that is referred to, not the one he is engaged in at the moment of speaking. The sentence produces an effect of momentary hesitation, the last chance of a change of heart before the final action, before automatism sets in and the agent is swallowed up in the action itself. The same kind of hesitation occurs at the moment of the murder, resolved by the words "Fury has its laws . . ."

Certainly the story may be regarded as Tolstoy's confession as well as Pozdnyshev's. But if we have read it right, it is a general confession. All of us who seek to use another human being without regard to his separateness are guilty of destroying him.

—Dorothy Green

The description of the murder is accomplished with all the uncanny kinesthetic precision of which Tolstoy is the supreme master. Before he has finished, the reader has the physical sensation of having committed the act himself. The scene rivals in this respect the one in *War and Peace* where a young man stands on the window-ledge of a high building drinking a bottle of brandy, a scene which produces an actual sensation of vertigo.

The last Chapter, 28, rounds off the third movement in the manner of a coda. It sustains the violence and passion of the main subject of the movement, comments on it and then returns us to the mood of the opening of the story, the silent grief, the intense isolation, the utterly hopeless loneliness which is Pozdnyshev's inescapable lot. I am not suggesting that the structure of the story corresponds exactly with the structure of Beethoven's sonata, or that the music has any literary meaning. In any case, Tolstoy, or rather Pozdnyshev, was interested only in the first movement, particularly the Presto. But I think it does correspond to the general sonata form. And I think also that the first movement taken alone can be shown to have particular significance for the theme of the story.

It is interesting to remember that the performance that fired Tolstoy's imagination was given by two young men. In the story, the violin is given to a man, the piano to a woman. It is not possible to know what the music of the first movement suggested to Tolstoy, but I do not think it is too fanciful to suppose that it suggested first of all a dialogue between a man and a woman, and I should myself suggest that the dialogue continued into the second movement in the form of an argument, or a struggle for supremacy. In the first movement, the musical dialogue is a kind of mutual solicitation, at first mere flirtation, then developing seriously. The violin opens the movement, slowly and hesitantly; the piano replies in a restrained manner; there are modulations and hesitations, a feeling of suspense is created, then the subject is opened up with sudden determination. It is interrupted, and a fresh start is made. A great deal of use is made of a rising semitone—almost an interrogative—and one is forcibly reminded of the passage in which Pozdnyshev's wife and the violinist play together for the first time. "From the first moment his eyes met my wife's I saw that the animal in each of them, regardless of all conditions of their position and of society asked 'May I?' and answered 'Oh yes, certainly!'" In both Russian and English, the language is used merely to convey the meaning of the facial expression, the interrogation of the eyes, and this meaning is the same in all languages and is a possible way of interpreting the music. The whole of the opening Adagio suggests, or could suggest, the preliminary skirmishing, the retreats, vague fears, agitations and hesitations of a passion which wishes to declare itself and may not, and this situation is the one in which Pozdnyshev's wife and the musician find themselves: the Adagio is recapitulated, that is to say, in the third movement of Tolstoy's story, when the Musician theme is getting under way.

The Presto of the sonata is devoted to a following up of the initial advantage, the violin is the dominating instrument, the inviting instrument; the piano changes key and sidesteps the issue. There is an extraordinary progressive ascending movement at the end, which strongly suggests a dragging away by force; there is a significant silence, a kind of consent, and a haunting passage which could suggest shame, and the movement ends with a burst of passion from both instruments, with the violin in control.

Though it is impossible to know precisely the nature of the feeling the sonata produced in Tolstoy or his creation Pozdnyshev, both were profoundly stirred by the music and reacted strongly to it, while Pozdnyshev, we know, associated this, the noblest of the arts, with adultery, with voluptuousness. In Chapter 23, the playing of the sonata is introduced in this way: "His face grew serious, stern and sympathetic, and listening to the sounds he produced, he touched the strings with careful fingers. The piano answered him. The music began . . ." The overtones of the last two or three phrases are obvious. Then Pozdnyshev continues:

> Ugh, ugh, it is a terrible thing that sonata. And especially that part (i.e. the Presto). And in general music is a dreadful thing. What is it? I don't understand it. What is music, what does it do? And why does it do what it does? They say music exalts the soul. Nonsense! It is not true! It has an effect, an awful effect—I am speaking of myself—but not of an exalting kind. It has neither an exalting nor a debasing effect, but it produces an agitation . . . it transports me to some other position not my own. I can do what I cannot do.

Pozdnyshev goes on to elaborate its power of sympathetic magic, its hypnotic effect. What is clear about these two passages when they are read in full is that the feeling evoked by the sonata at the beginning changes before that movement ends. What had begun by disturbing and disgusting Pozdnyshev is submerged in a new revelation. In which, the alternative version says, jealousy had no place. It is as though the sonata, while revealing to him the nature of the relationships between men and women, also began to reveal to him that other relationships were possible besides those commonly taken for granted. Debate, argument, dialogue between two instruments can perhaps be fused into one perfect harmonious statement, in which each instrument instead of aping the other, is allowed to speak for itself, just as the two warring impulses in Pozdnyshev himself, the sensual and the aspiring, the earth and the spirit, might perhaps come to a composition, instead of each striving to eliminate the other.

Nothing comes of it, of course. Pozdnyshev has prepared us for the fact. Music belongs to another dimension: 'It makes me forget my real position; it transports me to some other position not my own.' But the suggestion of other possibilities is implanted and it is these presumably that rise to the surface, when in the act of destroying his wife, Pozdnyshev first realises that she has an independent existence.

> I looked at the children and at her bruised disfigured face and for the first time I forgot myself, my pride, and for the first time saw a human being in her. And so insignificant did all that had offended me, all my jealousy appear and so important what I had done, that I wished to fall with my face to her hand, and say: 'Forgive me,' but dared not do so.

The parallels with the sonata could I think be taken further than I have taken them, but they would require a minute musical analysis, for which there is no space here. Easier to indicate is the parallel of the general effect produced by each on the listener, or reader. And the reader of this novel, should be in a very real sense a listener. We need to remind ourselves again that Tolstoy conceived his story with the living voice of an actor in his mind. That is, it was written, as the sonata was, for an instrument. The first movement of the sonata is disturbing, passionate and at times violent, and so is the story. What Tolstoy's music finally conveys to us is the sensation of torment, of pain, of a cry like St. Paul's: 'Who will deliver me from the body of this death?' The nearest thing in our own literature is the music of *Othello,* a play on much the same subject, the destructive power of a jealousy that comes from concentration on outward appearance instead of inner reality, on what can be received, rather than on what can be given.

But there is no Iago in Tolstoy's story. Pozdnyshev's Iago is an internal one, the terrible misconception in the soul that arises from a preoccupation with the ego and its wants, a misconception whose consequences are far harder to bear than those that flow from having been wrought upon.

A superficial interpretation of the story sees it perhaps as Tolstoy's ritual murder of his wife, an act of revenge committed after twenty-seven years of marriage upon a woman who had borne him thirteen children. His wife apparently saw it as such and never forgave him. But surely, if the story must be regarded as biography, is it not more than anything else an act of confession and reparation? The whole responsibility for his situation is taken by Pozdnyshev and placed upon men and upon himself as a representative man. Right through the story runs an impassioned plea for the inviolability of woman as a

human being in her own right—the same kind of plea that Ibsen was making. All the terrible consequences are shown to flow from a failure to make this recognition, and Pozdnyshev constantly lacerates himself for his failure, which, he says, is caused by obsession with his own rights and pleasures. If the hero must be identified with his creator, then a whole identification must be made. The epigraph to the story suggests the lines along which we should think: Christ's words about lust. By extension the words apply to murder. Certainly the story may be regarded as Tolstoy's confession as well as Pozdnyshev's. But if we have read it right, it is a general confession. All of us who seek to use another human being without regard to his separateness are guilty of destroying him.

Most of us escape punishment. Pozdnyshev's, like Othello's, resulted from allowing his hand to execute the imagination of his heart. Both had to face the knowledge that the deed cannot be reversed, that to put out the light is final.

> Only when I saw her dead face did I understand all that I had done. I realised that I, I, had killed her; that it was my doing that she, living, moving and warm, had now become motionless, waxen and cold, and that this could never, anywhere, or by any means, be remedied . . .

This is the haunting note the music of the story leaves with us, just as the music of *Othello* does. And wild regret and yearning, and tragic human longings occur in the sonata, though they are overlaid in the final movement by the pressures of formalism, dissipated in the conventions of the sonata form, just as the pressures of the outside world return in the story. And Pozdnyshev's punishment is that he has to go on living in the real world, possessed of the knowledge that he murdered not only his wife's body, but her essential being as well. Perhaps Othello was more fortunate.

John Bayley   (essay date 1966)

SOURCE: "The *Nouvelle* as Hypothesis," in his *Tolstoy and the Novel,* Chatto & Windus, 1966, pp. 281-93.

[*In the excerpt below, Bayley contrasts Pozdnyshev's views about marriage expressed in* The Kreutzer Sonata *with those of Tolstoy.*]

If one married, along what lines might the relation proceed? What would happen if one became murderously jealous, or obsessed with desire for another woman? Suppose one were to contract a fatal and painful disease, or gave up the world to become a monk and hermit? These hypotheses are specialised; they depend on the rest of life being left out, so that we can concentrate on one particular possibility and problem. Yet all ask the question which is implicit in all Tolstoy's fictions: how should a man live?

Only one hypothesis became a fact for Tolstoy. He got married, and in some ways his married life resembled his forecast. Yet even *Family Happiness* . . . remains an abstract analysis, on the mental plane. In all of [his stories] Tolstoy forsakes the life of the body, even though it is problems and predicaments of the body with which most of them are so acutely concerned.

In general the characters in these stories act as Tolstoy's agents, representing his interests as if in some obsessive lawsuit. He does not *imagine* them, as he imagined the characters in his great fictions, and he does not on the whole identify himself with them, as he might be said to do with the hero of *The Live Corpse* and with Hadji Murad. The narrator of *Family Happiness* is the most successful agent, because she benefits from Tolstoy's understanding of a woman's life, even though this understanding has not the marvellous physical quality that it has in the two novels. . . .

The thankless task of acting as Tolstoy's agent in the story falls with particular weight on Pozdnyshev of *The Kreutzer Sonata.* He is required to express Tolstoy's views, but with a pathological violence and peculiarity supposedly his own. It is as if we knew that Shakespeare hated sex, but not so much as Hamlet does; and was disgusted with human beings, but not in quite so sensational a fashion as Timon. Tolstoy can neither release Pozdnyshev nor conceal himself behind him. The technical flaw in the stories, more marked in *The Kreutzer Sonata* than in the others, is that they employ a mechanism that makes for simplicity and rigidity without any compensatory detachment.

When the 'I' of *The Kreutzer Sonata* objects that if Pozdnyshev's ideas were really practised life would die out, he replies: "But why live? If life has no aim, if life is given us for life's sake, there is no reason for living." And "he evidently prized this thought very highly." So in a sense did Tolstoy, but he bestows the overt absurdity of priding himself on such a conviction upon the unfortunate Pozdnyshev. This is not the "self-derision genuinely Russian" which made Pierre so engaging a character [in *War and Peace*] and his relation to his creator so successful. The gradual externalisation of Pozdnyshev, as the climax of his story mounts, and his becoming—at the end—so touching a figure, makes this Tolstoyan use of him seem particularly jarring. When Prince Andrew denounces marriage to Pierre, or Levin tries vainly to see what makes Sviyazhsky tick [in *Anna Karenina*], we are drawn into a real dialogue, an interchange, a familiar discussion—the index of familiarity being that we know Tolstoy will address us soon in his own person. But the dramatic dialogue here is stilted and artificial, and its artifice largely thrown away.

All marriages in Tolstoy, whether described before or after his own took place, are, we feel, the same marriage—not his own, but an archetypal one. He presents the *marriageness* of marriage more directly and exhaustively than any other writer. In *Family Happiness* he envisages it; in *War and Peace* and *Anna* he describes it; in *The Kreutzer Sonata* he denounces it. Everything depends on the point of view; many of the events of the two

stories might have happened in the novels—indeed have happened—but they have not been isolated and concentrated on. Andrew and the Little Princess, Pierre and Helene, Anna, Karenin, Vronsky—they have all gone through the same kinds of disillusionment, rage, disgust, acquiescence, as the characters in the stories, but they were not able to remain in these states of mind for long. Life—the novel—carried them along; dissipating these impressions, creating new ones, and returning them to the first state without their being fully conscious of the repetition. The process of the stories is not a living one in this sense but a mental one. Like so many much more ordinary stories they have a strong element both of nightmare and of daydream in them.

> I think of running away from her, hiding myself, going to America. I get as far as dreaming of how I shall get rid of her, how splendid that will be, and how I shall unite myself with another, an admirable woman—quite different. . . .

Most married men, and women, would have to admit to occasional day-dreams something like those of Pozdnyshev. That is the intended power of the tale—to compel the individual to own up, to confess that his bosom returns an echo, and that there is some force in Pozdnyshev's contention that all marriages are secretly alike. But the accusing finger fails to disconcert us as much as it intends. For one thing, such fantasies are for most people occasional rather than obsessive; and a more serious weakness is that behind Pozdynshev's day-dream is another—that of Tolstoy himself. Tolstoy is letting himself go, and there is an element of self-indulgence in the display. The realism with which he describes the killing is particularly out of place here. The resistance of the corset; the sheath of the dagger dropped behind the sofa, and the reflection "I must remember that or it will get lost"—this is the realism of the self-told day-dream and it is highly imitable. Any competent sensationalist is Tolstoy's equal in this region of the mind.

And yet we still have the old directness—Tolstoy infects us with the terror that the fantasy arouses in him, where for most people it would be a comparatively harmless way of letting off steam inside themselves. We have something of the same feeling of horror in Dickens's description of the murder of Nancy in *Oliver Twist,* and Dostoevsky's of Nastasya Philippovna in *The Idiot*; but Dickens is fascinated rather than appalled—it was his favourite scene for recitation and used to excite him to the point of frenzy—while Dostoevsky's imagination is always on equable terms with every kind of violence. In all three we are aware of the pressure of a preoccupation—not uncommon in nineteenth-century fiction—with murder as a sexual act, but only Tolstoy seems to become fully aware as he describes it of the contrast between the insulated fantasy of the murderer and the outraged *otherness* of his victim. Pozsdnyshev's wife is not, as Nancy and Nastasya are, a natural murderee who appears to acquiesce in the atmosphere which the murderer and his creator have generated. It is significant that Norman Mailer's revival of the imagined murder as a sexual act, in his novel *An American Dream,* follows the Dickens-Dostoevsky pattern, not Tolstoy's.

Involuntarily, at the climax, the real argument of *The Kreutzer Sonata* comes out, the argument overlaid by the various diatribes indulged in through Pozdnyshev. Sex is often a hostile act, even in marriage; its consummation resembling murder in its indifference to the reality of another separate and independent being. Jealousy and hatred "have their own laws" and require their climax as inexorably as sexual passion. Only after the climax does Pozdnyshev reach the dazed awareness that his wife is, after all, "another human being".

After the evacuation of Moscow in *War and Peace,* when Natasha gets up in the night to see the wounded Prince Andrew, she says: "Forgive me". "Her face, with its swollen lips, was more than plain—it was dreadful", but Prince Andrew only sees that the jealousy which has obsessed him for months has no connection with the reality of Natasha. When he sees his wife's face, as if for the first time, and bruised and swollen where he has struck her, Pozdnyshev too says: "Forgive me". But she only looks at him "with her old expression of cold animal hatred". The ultimate horror of his act is to have put her beyond the possibility of recognising him, as he now recognises her. At the end of the story the narrator goes up to Pozdnyshev in the railway carriage to say goodbye.

> Whether he was asleep or only pretended to be, at any rate he did not move. I touched him with my hand. He uncovered his face, and I could see he had not been asleep.
>
> "Goodbye," I said, holding out my hand. He gave me his and smiled slightly, but so piteously that I felt ready to weep.
>
> "Yes, forgive me—" he said, repeating the same words with which he had concluded his story.

'Forgive' is almost the same word in Russian as 'Goodbye'. Since his wife's death deprived him of recognition and forgiveness, Pozdnyshev has to ask both of strangers.

R. F. Christian   (essay date 1969)

SOURCE: "The Later Stories," in his *Tolstoy: A Critical Introduction,* Cambridge University Press, 1969, pp. 230-46.

[In the excerpt below, Christian considers the theme of sex in The Kreutzer Sonata.*]*

'One usually thinks that most conservatives are old men and most innovators young men. This is not quite so. Most conservatives are young people who want to live, but who neither think nor have the time to think how one *should* live, and so choose as their model the life they have always known.' These controversial words from **"The

Devil"** have an unmistakably autobiographical ring, for Tolstoy as an old man was not a little proud of his nonconformity. The themes of nearly all his late stories were chosen to enable him to express his iconoclastic attitude to the organisation of society, the administration of justice and the relation between the sexes. Those on the subject of sex have attracted the greatest publicity. Uncompromising, perverse and uncharitable, they share a common loathing of the sexual act, whether lawful or unlawful, committed or merely meditated. The premise of *The Kreutzer Sonata* is that carnal love is selfish and that unselfish love needs no physical consummation. Do people go to bed together, asks its 'hero' Pozdnyshev, because of their spiritual affinities or the ideals they have in common? The knowledge and recollection of his own sexual indulgence in the past dominate his thinking to the exclusion of all else. He assumes that his wife's musician friend has only one thought in mind, and as the text for *The Kreutzer Sonata* (and **"The Devil"** reminds us): 'But I say unto you that everyone who looketh on a woman to lust after her hath committed adultery with her already in his heart.' Pozdnyshev murders his wife because he is tormented by jealousy. It follows for him that all husbands must be jealous, all wives unfaithful. His thoughts are controlled by the assumption that every possibility of evil must result in evil. The potential for good is simply discounted. Music is potentially evil because, like the presto in *The Kreutzer Sonata,* it may arouse feelings which cannot be satisfied by the music itself. Sexual passion is the root of all evil. Social conventions, low-cut dresses and the medical profession are accessories before the fact. By the second chapter of the story we already know Pozdnyshev's opinion of love and marriage and we know that he has murdered his wife. The narrator's rôle, apart from occasional interruptions, is negligible; he is not important enough to form a barrier between Pozdnyshev and the reader, or between the author and his hero.

> In *The Kreutzer Sonata,* Tolstoy adopted Turgenev's method, putting a first-person narrative in the thin frame of a third-person setting. Just as, in many of Turgenev's novels, a party of gentlemen converse at dinner until one of them begins to recount an episode of his youth, which thereupon becomes the novel, so, in *The Kreutzer Sonata,* the general conversation in a railway-carriage resolves itself into a personal confession.
>
> [D. Davie, *Russian Literature and Modern English Fiction*]

Pozdnyshev completely dominates the scene with his powerful, polemical monologue, which by its very nature is unable to actualise the character of his wife and her suspected lover or to consider them from any point of view except his own. His wife has no opportunity to state her case. Her friend is treated with the same contempt which Tolstoy reserves for Napoleon, the bureaucrats and the intelligentsia: 'He had an unusually well-developed posterior like a woman's, or like a Hottentot's, so they say.' Of course Pozdnyshev is his own prosecutor, and one who shows no mercy. As he says to himself when he decides to go and see his dying wife, whom he has stabbed: 'Yes I expect she wants to repent . . . .' He is given

> the thankless task of acting as Tolstoy's agent in the story. He is required to express Tolstoy's views, but with a pathological violence and peculiarity supposedly his own. It is as if we knew that Shakespeare hated sex, but not so much as Hamlet does; and was disgusted with human beings, but not in quite so sensational a fashion as Timon. Tolstoy can neither release Pozdnyshev nor conceal himself behind him.
>
> [J. Bayley, *Tolstoy and the Novel*]

Pozdnyshev's arguments are absurdly exaggerated and inconsistent and flavoured with Tolstoy's addiction to percentage generalisations—90% do this, 99% do that; music is responsible for 'most cases of adultery in our society. The body is the ever-present villain, the animal the symbol of unbridled incontinence, for all that it compares favourably with the human species in refraining from intercourse during pregnancy and suckling.

Significantly enough, in the light of Tolstoy's own prejudices, the whole story takes place in a railway carriage. Pozdnyshev himself comments on the emotional upheaval caused by railways. He claims to be afraid of railway carriages. He acknowledges a temptation to lie down on the rails—all this with reference to another train journey he is describing on his way to catch his wife, as he hopes, *in flagrante delicto,* a train journey within a train journey, as it were, which provides a structural basis for the story. And structurally speaking, it is taut, powerful and gripping, despite its occasional inept dialogue and its motley material culled from Tolstoy's letters to Chertkov and the books and letters he received from the American Shakers. A sensitive and, on the whole, convincing attempt has recently been made to relate the structure of the story to Beethoven's sonata itself [in Dorothy Green, 'The Kreutzer Sonata: Tolstoy and Beethoven,' *Melbourne Slavonic Studies,* Vol. I, 1967]. It is an approach which is capable of further exploration. Put briefly, the argument is that Tolstoy's story appeals mainly to the ear; that the human voice is the literary equivalent of the solo instruments; that one's attention in reading (or listening) is constantly being drawn to sounds; and that the 'confessional' form of the narrative is the nearest literary approach to the music of piano and violin, 'two voices that strive through the sonata to become one.' We are reminded that Beethoven's sonatas are characterised not only by intensity of dramatic feeling, but also by violent contrasts of moods and emotion. The structure of the story can plausibly be shown to correspond to general sonata form, and the Presto of the first movement—following an opening Adagio—which is so important for Pozdnyshev, is peculiarly important for the theme of the story as a whole. The author of the article observes that 'the violin is the dominating instrument, the inviting instrument' in the Presto; 'the piano changes key and sidesteps the issue. There is an extraordinary progressive ascending movement at the end, which strongly suggests a dragging away by force; there is a significant silence, a kind of consent, and a haunting passage which could sug-

gest shame, and the movement ends with a burst of passion from both instruments, with the violin in control.' Like the sonata, Tolstoy's story falls naturally into three movements with a slow introduction. 'The subject of the first movement concerns the general notion of solicitation between the sexes and the particular instance of this in Pozdnyshev's own courtship, wedding and honeymoon. As in the sonata, there are false starts, the subject is introduced, dropped, hinted at . . . Pozdnyshev at first is dominant, the narrator parries the question he raises and Pozdnyshev finally becomes the narrator . . . The first movement of the sonata is disturbing, passionate and at times violent, and so is the story.' The second movement (Chapters 13-19) corresponds to Pozdnyshev's married life and his growing jealousy, with each of the two partners contending for power, 'or rather striving to be free from the dominance of the other'. The third movement introduces the musician, and its pivotal point is the Kreutzer Sonata itself, the final chapter (28) rounding it off like a coda, and returning us to the mood of the Adagio opening. In musical terms the analogies could be pressed further without doing violence to the thesis which, when retailed in this eclectic manner, does less than justice to an article which is stimulating and well argued. Tolstoy's well-known receptivity to music and his intuitive feeling for musical form lend point to the musical analogies already made in the context of the Sevastopol sketches and developed further with reference to the composition, tempo and progression of *The Kreutzer Sonata.*

Structural considerations apart, few other novelists could have made compelling reading out of sentiments and arguments which are irritating and manifestly unjust. Few other novelists could have given pathos and poignancy to the ending of a story whose limits appear to be laid down by the advice proffered in its opening chapter: 'Do not trust your horse in the field, or your wife in the house.'

Keith Ellis (essay date 1971)

SOURCE: "Ambiguity and Point of View in Some Novelistic Representations of Jealousy," in *Modern Language Notes,* Vol. 86, No. 5, October, 1971, pp. 891-909.

[*In the following excerpt, Ellis identifies sexual jealousy as a major theme of* The Kreutzer Sonata, *suggesting that it provides the basis for narrative ambiguity which in turn contributes to the coherence of the novella.*]

When narrative is presented from the point of view of a jealous character a likely consequence is the occurrence of ambiguity regarding certain events in the action. Such ambiguity, deriving from a perspective affected by jealousy, determines meaning in several modern novels, and failure to take it properly into account has not only frustrated the task of interpreting some of these novels, but has also thwarted the appreciation of the possibilities of an important narrative technique. I wish to examine principally two novels: Tolstoy's *The Kreutzer Sonata* (1889) and Machado de Assis' *Dom Casmurro* (1900), in which jealousy is a major theme and where narrative ambiguity plays a greater part in the meaning than has been recognized. I will then briefly consider more recent works of prose fiction that are related by theme and technique to my subject.

For some critics, the role of jealousy is obscured in *The Kreutzer Sonata* by the strong moralizing which marks the novel itself, and to which Tolstoy returns in his "Afterword" to the work. In the "Afterword" he states his social intention or purpose in writing the story in such terms as to suggest that the work be read as a kind of *exemplum,* which, by dramatizing the perils of marriage, would make the case for celibacy. The ethical criticism of society he systematically develops there echoes the frequent periods of moralizing in the novel itself, forming a bond that is potentially so influential that interpretation of the work may be detrimentally restricted by stated authorial purpose. In order to avoid this, it is necessary to examine structural elements of the work itself, emphasizing the relationships between time and narrative point of view, the development of the narrator's arguments, and the motivating forces of the protagonist's drama and of his theories.

The reported narrator's story covers a considerable period, and it told from a point in time at which the events have already been concluded. This distance in time is particularly relevant to his moralizing, since his commentary is based on conviction drawn from a certain interpretation of the sum of the events. The moralizing is presented chiefly in the first two-thirds of the novel, where, as background to the main drama, he summarizes the story of his relationships with women, from his youth up to and including the murder of his wife. In the final third of the novel, the events leading to the murder of his wife are presented in detail. The drama of these events, as will be shown, cannot be contained by the moralizing in the novel or the statement of purpose in the "Afterword." Such statements cannot fully account for the action and may even distort certain aspects of it; for the ambiguity introduced by elusive elements makes the work susceptible of interpretations other than that given from the narrator's point of view or implied in the author's statement of purpose.

At the outset the narrator's arguments seem to be cogent and well planned. He joins in and soon monopolizes a discussion on marital relationships; his exclamations, rhetorical questions, and personal testimony scarcely giving his interlocutors a chance to interrupt. This manner wins him a certain awe from them and makes him interesting to the direct narrator of the story, who soon becomes the sole audience and behaves as an attentive though unobtrusive listener. He speaks, for the most part, only when Pozdnyshev interrupts his own narrative by emitting his peculiar choked laugh, which becomes a *leitmotif* in the novel for summits of emotional tension; and limits his comments to occasional requests for clarification and to descriptions of Pozdnyshev's gestures. About the validity of Pozdnyshev's arguments, which grow

more questionable the more he develops them, he is properly uncritical, leaving to the reader the task of perceiving contradictions and ironies.

Pozdnyshev attempts to justify his situation by presenting it as the inevitable result of a dissolute amatory life, a way of life, he insists, that is normal in his society. "Before I married I lived as we all do, loosely, and like everyone else in our particular circle, I was certain I was living as one should . . . I was not a seducer; I did not have immoral taste but I gave myself up to depravity in a restrained and decorous way for my health's sake." When he comments on his discovery that marriage is miserable and conflict-ridden he reports, "I was tormented by the awful thought that I was the only one living so badly with my wife, so unlike my expectations, while in other marriages it was different. I did not yet know at that time that this was the usual thing . . . that everyone thought as I did."

The setting itself with Pozdnyshev's story growing out of a discussion, among a random group of passengers on a train, concerning the problems of marriage, lends substance to the view that matrimony, for one reason or another, is a problematic state. Yet the strenuousness with which he argues his case comes from a new perspective, a perspective that he himself declares to be unique, and which comes at a time when he is considered to be "more or less insane" by his sister-in-law and her brother. "I myself," he says, "realized nothing of all this till recently. Now I have realized. And that is why I am tormented, because no one else seems to realize it." The narrator's attitude to marriage before the murder would seem to correspond to the present ambivalent one of his fellow passengers. In the drama itself, even in the last days of his marriage, he can still look to another, better marital situation—"Finally I began dreaming of how I would be rid of her, find another woman who would be wonderful and new"—and express love for his wife—"I woke up thinking of her and my physical love of her and about Trukhachevsky and how everything between them was over now." His fellow passengers, denying not his logic but his premise that marriage essentially is evil, are reluctant to follow him in his attack on this institution.

Pozdnyshev's theory, however, is marred by contradictions. In his moralizing he speaks in extremes as he deals with isolated aspects of his problem. At times he juxtaposes apparently contradictory positions and deals with them consciously as paradoxes as when he says, "In one way it's quite right that women are brought to the lowest depths of humiliation, and in another, that women have the ascendancy." Yet when he extends the different aspects of his argument, he does so with such denunciatory force, and in such generalized terms, that he seems to exceed the boundaries of paradox and becomes merely contradictary. He sweepingly blames, first men for pursuing women, and then women for capturing husbands by systematically inciting their lust. In attacking women's subjection to men's sexual pleasure he gives a strong and sensitive defense of women's rights, but criticizing elsewhere their cunning, he declares that "the result of all this is the ascendancy of women, from which the whole world is suffering." Consistent with his view of sexual relations, even between husband and wife, as being sinful, he can calmly advocate abstinence even with the realization that this would lead to extinction of the human race. Nevertheless, in condemning the selfishness of men who force sexual relations on their pregnant or nursing wives, he characterizes the functions of childbearing in the traditional terms of "important," "holy," and "sublime." Where he does not negate the importance of human existence altogether, his passion leads him to such extremes that his system becomes untenable for any individual human experience. His arguments which would seem to be valid when taken in isolation lose their weight in the mass of antitheses which crowd his total case.

A recognition of the two time levels operative within the work is essential in determining the nature of Pozdnyshev's self-contradictions; and in this light it is fruitful to examine the role of the murder in the novel. The narrator characterizes the murder as a routine occurrence when he discusses it in the context of his moralizing. Refuting the opinion of the jury that acquitted him, that jealousy was the motive, he declares: "The point on which I insist, is that all husbands who lead the sort of life I led," a life he has declared previously to be normal, "are bound to come to infidelity, divorce, suicide, or the murder of their wives, as I came. If anybody has avoided that, then he is a rare exception." When the murder is presented as drama, however, it stands out as an indelible event which leaves a strong residue of horror. "It was only when I saw her dead face that I realized everything I had done. I understood that I, I killed her—because of me, she who had been alive, moving, warm, was now motionless, waxen, cold. And nothing could put this right, ever. No one who has not had that experience can understand it." At this time what he has done seems to him to be beyond comprehension.

"Comprehension" comes later. "And sitting there in prison for eleven months, awaiting trial, I examined myself and my past life and came to understand it." The untidy generalization resulting from this "understanding," which puts murder and suicide on the same plane as infidelity and divorce, may well be interpreted as a desperate attempt at rationalizing his act. The "eleven months" is the link in time between the actions of the drama and the viewpoint from which he subsequently judges these actions. The murder is the last in a series of episodes that form the drama, and represents the final deterioration in the narrator's relationship with his wife. It also fixes the narrator's focus, in his search for moral justification and consolation, at its most pessimistic level as he contemplates his own amatory history and sexual relations in general. The passion and contradiction that were displayed earlier in the frame of jealousy remain strong characteristics of the narrator, but they are now channelled into arguments for self-justification. When the time relationships are understood in this way, what may otherwise seem to be obtrusive moral diatribes have their motivation within the novel and play their part in a unified work.

The murder, then, being crucial in the novel, its circumstances are worth special examination. It is clear that Pozdnyshev's immediate motive for killing his wife is jealousy. This is the emotion which, once it is objectified in the threat to the narrator represented by Trukhachevsky, puts the characters on a course of deadly conflict. There are hints in the novel of the hold jealousy has on the narrator: Pozdnyshev's attack on doctors stems most personally from the fact that their orders to his wife put her, as he says, on the path to infideltiy. "These precious doctors decided that she must not nurse her first child and so, to begin with, she was deprived of the sole antidote to flirtation . . . And as a counterpart to this I experienced the tortures of jealousy with greater acuteness . . . I was tortured by jealousy throughout my married life."

With the introduction of the theme of jealousy the pace of the novel quickens as diminishing emphasis is put on moralizing, and the drama itself comes to seize the reader's attention. The narrator's insecurity had increased sharply when his wife, for reasons of health, was supplied with a device to prevent further pregnancies. Even before the advent of Trukhachevsky, Pozdnyshev was certain that time would provide a rival. "She was a woman at the summit of her power . . . well nourished and dissatisfied . . . And I felt afraid." And "She began to dream . . . or so at least I thought." Convinced as he is that his wife will betray him, Pozdnyshev, with fatal deliberateness, encourages Trukhachevsky's attentions to her. He does this, as he says time and again, "to show that I was not afraid of him." But the preponderance of fear is revealed immediately in his wild, exaggerated suspicions. "Obviously the sound of the piano was purposely used to drown the sound of their voices—their kisses perhaps. I imagined the very worst." His jealousy is also revealed by various contradictions in his attitude toward his wife. Fearful and lustful he describes her as beautiful, "at the summit of her power"; fearful and scornful, he describes her, a short time later, as an aging mistress to whom her lover was condescending. Contradiction and conflict are presented too as oxymoron, as when he speaks of "her hated, attractive face." And finally, there is contrast in terms of emotional distance. On his way to confront his wife and Trukhachevsky he is in a violent rage, but is calmly deliberate in the actual confrontation. He has a lucid awareness of every gesture when he commits the murder which finally releases him from his jealousy; he achieves almost comic distance in the same scene when he says of Trukhachevsky, "I wanted to chase him, but realized that it was comic to rush after my wife's lover in my stocking feet, and I wanted to be terrifying and not funny."

The vehemence of the narrator's attack both by the act of murder and, subsequently, by his theorizing against sex and marriage, would seem to be revealing of weakness, of his inability to cope with a marital relationship, and above all, with jealousy. He tells us that the murder itself would not have taken place when he surprised her and Trukhachevsky by returning home early had not "her face also expressed—or so it struck me in that first moment— annoyance and displeasure that she had been interrupted in her love making and happiness with him." While recognizing that the circumstances surrounding the murder were provocative indeed for the narrator, a phrase like "or so it struck me in that first moment," given his tendency to "imagine the very worst," undermines the murder's confidence in the truth of the observation, and directs attention once more to his jealousy. Late in his story he declares that his wife "was as much a mystery now as she had always been." His jealousy is an elemental reaction to this mystery.

On listening to his wife and Trukhachevsky play Beethoven's "The Kreutzer Sonata," he comments on the inexplicability of his response to music. All the circumstances of the playing had been painful to him. He had earlier called music "the subtlest form of sensual intercourse" in speaking of it as a growing bond between his wife and Trukhachevsky. His intense delight in the music, contrasted with the pain caused him by the relationship he suspects to exist between the players makes his role of audience a highly complex and contradictory experience, which is thus related to the complexities and contradictions within the novel as a whole.

Jealousy, then, by being beyond the first-person narrator's rational control, becomes a source of complexity within the novel. It provides the basis for unreliability and ambiguity; for once its distorting presence is noticed we cannot wholly trust the narrator's judgments. The narrator's account may well be an honest one from his point of view, but his emotional state makes the presentation untrustworthy as far as any balanced view, especially of the real feelings of the other characters in his story, is concerned. Unreliability, in turn, creates a subtle irony in the work: a disparity between the narrator's and the reader's interpretation of the drama. The moralizing being inadequately served by the drama, the novel comes to hold meaning for its readers that does not result from direct acceptance of the narrator's view of events. As a result the narrator's profound and desperate loneliness is underlined. His whole narration has been a strenuous attempt to overcome this isolation; and he himself in his plea for forgiveness at the very end of his story seems to be pathetically aware of his failure. It must be emphasized, however, that the failure is the narrator's, not the author's for the novel itself, in a complex and subtle way, represents a powerful human dilemma.

To those for whom the author's purpose is the central fact to be determined in a literary work, an interpretation which is at variance with one offered by the author is *ispo facto* invalid; and it is clear that a reading of *The Kreutzer Sonata* that emphasizes jealousy and irony differs from that put forward in the "Afterword" where Tolstoy suggests that the novel supports his thesis that sexual relations constitute a depraved act, and are the source of all evil. The "Afterword" makes contact with the moralizing content of his story, while remaining somewhat removed from the specifics of the drama. In the drama told by the narrator there are points that are unaccounted for, or even distorted by the generalizations of the "Afterword." On the other hand, by regarding jeal-

ousy as the motivating force in *The Kreutzer Sonata* and antithesis as the dominant stylistic trait an interpretation is offered that would seem to reveal the novel's unity and coherence. . . .

> **The narrator's account may well be an honest one from his point of view, but his emotional state makes the presentation untrustworthy as far as any balanced view, especially of the real feelings of the other characters in his story, is concerned.**
>
> —*Keith Ellis*

To suggest an interpretation of the novel based on ambiguity is not simply to opt for a middle way. Such an interpretation seems to be indicated by certain structural features of the novel and yields important meaning especially with regard to the role of jealousy. However more subtly, however more tactfully than the narrator of *The Kreutzer Sonata,* the narrator in *Dom Casmurro* is also making a case. The motivation for self-justification discovered in *The Kreutzer Sonata* is also strong in this novel. The upheaval of the drama that took place before the time of writing is of comparable intensity in both works. But, whereas the narrator in *The Kreutzer Sonata* witnesses and reacts immediately to what he regards as the act of betrayal, the narrator of *Dom Casmurro* decides that betrayal took place some time before he discovered it and his initial torment gives way to a long period of detachment and coldness. The tone of their narrative is in keeping with the temper of the narrators. The narrator in *Dom Casmurro* persistently reveals a high degree of narrative self-consciousness: he is aware of his control over the pattern of his story and indicates this awareness to the reader in numerous asides. There is no early disclosure of the climax as there is in *The Kreutzer Sonata*; urgency and insistence give way to sophisticated resignation in *Dom Casmurro*. . . .

Tolstoy's Pozdnyshev, having been moved to decisive action, makes a strident but untenable case against marriage and sex. Machado's Dom Casmurro, in similar circumstances is unsuccessful in his case against his wife. They both admit finding their wives mysterious, and in telling their stories are not fully cognizant of the role of jealousy which comes to seem a complexly destructive and mysterious force: a force which confounds their narrative intention without their being aware of it. Their pitiful isolation at the end of their stories—for the cold Dom Casmurro who, at the end of the novel waits in vain for his lady friends to return to visit him, is quite as pitiful as Pozdnyshev—is a consequence of this irony. Machado de Assis remained aloof from discussion of his work, unlike Tolstoy, not venturing any interpretation of the novel. One cannot be sure whether his silence should be taken to indicate awareness of greater complexity than a verdict of guilt or innocence. In any case, it is fruitful for the critic to examine the literary work without being limited by authorial expressions of purpose: for in novels such as these, of Tolstoy and Machado de Assis, the workings of first-person narration with confined perspective reveal the subtlest ambiguities and contradictions in the motivations of the reporter-protagonists.

Such an understanding of the function of narration limited to the point of view of the jealous character in *Dom Casmurro* and *The Kreutzer Sontata* may illuminate the reading of more recent fiction in which this technique is structurally basic. Alain Robbe-Grillet's *Jealousy* (1957), narrated by the jealous protagonist and Eduardo Mallea's "Human Reason" (1959), a third-person story with a perspective limited for the most part to the central figure, may be considered representative.

In Mallea's story the attempt of Montuvio, the jealous husband, to know through reason whether his wife is being unfaithful ends in anguished uncertainty, because opposing facets of the emotion, such as fear of loss on the one hand and hurt pride on the other, can lead the victim to irreconcilably contradictory certainties. Thus, as in *The Kreutzer Sonata,* the inadequacy of reason in the face of jealousy is revealed. The presence in Mallea's story of a narrator who not only records everything the protagonist observes or reflects on but who, on his own initiative, also makes judgments, would seem to afford the opportunity for an objective verification. There being no verification, the limited perspective seems to be somewhat arbitrary. Yet this form of narrative gives an impression of continuous immediacy. There being no gap between the occurrence and the account of the events, the intensity of the anguish of doubt experienced by the character is well conveyed to the reader.

Greater interiorization of the functions of jealousy is to be found in Robbe-Grillet's novel *Jealousy* where the narrator, unlike those of *The Kreutzer Sonata* and *Dom Casmurro,* soliloquizes impressionistically rather than speaks to an audience. There is no laying out of a case for the reader. Absence of an ordered time also contributes to starkness in the manifestations of jealousy and to poignant anxieties and blurry contradictions revealed by a mind raw with the wounds of the emotion.

In "Human Reason" and *Jealousy* ambiguity derives from a tormented protagonist's confounded and unresolved view of events. Ambiguity in *The Kreutzer Sonata* and *Dom Casmurro* results from the narrators' representation of events in a reconstructed, personal tale intended to remove (in the case of Dom Casmurro) or at least to mitigate (in the case of Pozdnyshev) blame that might otherwise be directed against them. In these two novels ambiguity exists and functions less apparently than it does in the more recent stories. It is discovered through scrutiny of the structural features of the works themselves—a scrutiny that looks beyond expressed authorial purpose or supposed literary influences.

Ruth Crego Benson   (essay date 1973)

SOURCE: "Epilogue: Sexuality's Wasteland," in her *Women in Tolstoy: The Ideal and the Erotic,* University of Illinois Press, 1973, pp. 111-38.

[*In the following excerpt, Benson details Tolstoy's views on the nature of sex, women, and men represented in* The Kreutzer Sonata *and his other late fiction.*]

Conceived within a single year, homogenous in thought and style, three stories, *The Kreutzer Sonata,* "The Devil," and *Father Sergius,* present Tolstoy's final fictional statement on the relations between men and women. *The Kreutzer Sonata* appeared first in 1889, followed a few months later by "The Devil." Although *Father Sergius* was not finished until 1897, it is clearly kin to the other two. It is important to think of these stories not only as individual works but, taken together, as an epilogue on sexuality, love, and marriage to Tolstoy's life-work.

Though Tolstoy had renounced all his belles lettres written before 1880, including *The Cossacks, Family Happiness, War and Peace,* and *Anna Karenina,* these three stories nevertheless took fictional form. It is understandable that the desire to renounce and suppress his artistic success would accompany the broader renunciation of his former style and philosophy of life and his adoption of a self-styled Christian pacifism. For tension and contradiction supply the texture of great fiction, and Tolstoy had not so much resolved his ambivalent views of woman, love, and sexuality, as allowed them to dissipate in his abandonment of the search for an ideal way of life which would include them. Yet Tolstoy could not extinguish the force of the artist within, and quite against his will and his new convictions *The Kreutzer Sonata,* "The Devil," and *Father Sergius* all took fictional form. The content and intent of these three stories, however, are in keeping with the didactic and polemical nature of Tolstoy's other prose of the period.

To *The Kreutzer Sonata,* Tolstoy prefixed a stringent epigraph:

> But I say unto you, that whosoever looketh on a woman to lust after her hath committed adultery with her already in his heart. (Matt. 5.28)

The same epigraph precedes **"The Devil"**—with the addition of the two even more severe following verses, one of which recommends that

> if thy right hand offend thee, cut it off, and cast it from thee: for it is profitable for thee that one of thy members should perish, and not that thy whole body should be cast into hell. (Matt. 5.30)

In contrast to his earlier work, the two distinctive motifs of *The Kreutzer Sonata,* and equally of **"The Devil"** and *Father Sergius,* are Tolstoy's explicit and exacerbated preoccupation with sex as central to the relations between men and women, and the barely concealed hysteria which provides the tone of the stories. They are the fulfillment of and the self-indulgent absorption in the dark content of *Family Happiness, War and Peace,* and, of course, *Anna Karenina.* Of the three pieces, *The Kreutzer Sonata* is the most developed and the most powerful. If one were not aware that the other two were written subsequently, one might consider them preliminary sketches for the first, so similar are the concerns and details. They are, however, more appropriately described as abortive attempts to remake the statements so compellingly rendered in *The Kreutzer Sonata.*

It is important to remember that Tolstoy wrote these stories when he himself was living a personal drama almost as complicated and debilitating as those of the stories themselves. He and his wife, at the respective ages of sixty-one and forty-five, quarreled bitterly about their manner of life, the education of their children, where they should live, indeed about the total moral structure of their life. He stubbornly professed that it must change, but never changed it, and his wife tried not only to carry on their former life but to convince her husband that it was necessary.

Ironically, Sofiya Andreyevna acted out in the mid-1890s her own pale version of *The Kreutzer Sonata* in her pathetic infatuation with Sergey Ivanovich Taneyev, concert pianist and family acquaintance. Though there was no sexual infidelity involved, the indiscretion of her desperate flirtation embarrassed and exasperated her family and friends, and disgusted her husband. The fact that he could be deeply upset about this "affair," however, indicates how closely they were still emotionally entangled with each other. The memoirs of their daughter, Tanya, present an unusually fair description of their life during this period:

> It is really destructive to live among people who hate one another while you wish well to both. They have reached such a stage of exacerbation that they have to weigh every word carefully before they speak, for fear of involuntarily hurting one another's feelings.

And a year later:

> I am all the more sorry for Mamma since, first, she does not believe in anything at all, either her own or Papa's ideas; second, she is the more lonely, because since she says and does so many things which are unreasonable, of course all the children are on Papa's side, and she feels her isolation terribly. And then she loves Papa more than he loves her, and is as delighted as a child if he addresses the least kind word to her.

But this perhaps too-familiar story is noted here simply to invoke the chaotic context in which Tolstoy wrote these disturbed and disturbing tales.

The Kreutzer Sonata opens on a train, and for Tolstoy this generally means that normal modes of perception and reflection are distorted. Later in the story, its anti-hero, Pozdnyshev himself, describes the change in his mood upon boarding a train eight hours before murdering his wife:

> But that tranquil mood, that ability to suppress my feelings ended with my drive. As soon as I entered the train, something entirely different began. That eight-hour journey in a railway carriage was something dreadful, which I shall never forget all my life. Whether it was that having taken my seat in the carriage, I vividly imagined myself as having already arrived, or that railway traveling has such an exhilarating effect on people, at any rate from the moment I sat down I could no longer control my imagination.

In precisely this frame of mind, Pozdnyshev narrates his story against a background of confusion and semi-darkness. The train stops and starts, passengers come and go, candles sputter and die, conversations continue in darkness.

Aside from this murky setting, Pozdnyshev's personal appearance and habits contribute to the story's underground atmosphere. He is not actually introduced in the first scenes, but sits apart from his traveling companions, with his eyes glittering and strange sounds erupting from his throat, all the while smoking or drinking tea. He gives the impression of a chronic isolate, not belonging to this or any world. His clothes cross the limits of period and class: an old overcoat, "evidently from an expensive tailor," and underneath, a simple embroidered Russian shirt. There is nothing about him that marks his identity or suggests that he is a man of integrated character.

Carefully paced, like the piece that furnished its title, *The Kreutzer Sonata* unfolds its themes in precisely elaborated movements. Just as Pozdnyshev's identity is not fully revealed at the beginning neither is his story. Both are preceded and enhanced by a long overture. The tension of that overture is created by the motifs struck in the conversation among the passengers. The talk is concerned, in general, with men and women and their relations with each other. A lady and her companion, a lawyer, defend a "liberal" point of view, which is bitterly opposed by an old merchant whose attitude is more conventional. The discussion starts with the lawyer's remark that "then she plainly informed her husband that she was not able, and did not wish, to live with him." He goes on to say that "public opinion in Europe" was preoccupied with the question of divorce, and that cases of "that kind" were occurring more and more often in Russia.

The old merchant takes a stern and disapproving view of this. To the lawyer who asks him if these things happened in the old days, he replies: "They used to happen even then, sir, but less often. The way things are now they can't help happening. People have got too educated." What follows is, in the form of argument, a distillation of the thinking and writing that Tolstoy had done about marital relations up to that point. The lady, in essence, defends a flexible approach to marriage. No woman, she contends, should be forced to marry someone she does not love; if she finds herself married to someone she does not love, or no longer loves, she should have the right to divorce, as should the husband in similar circumstances. The old merchant replies with stern platitudes: "Human beings have a law given them"; "the first thing that should be required of a woman is fear!" (of her husband, of course); the "female sex must be curbed in time or else all is lost!" When the narrator of the story reminds the old man that he was just boasting about his own sexual exploits at a fair, the old man indignantly replies that that is "a special case."

Certainly one feels at this moment in the story that the lady and her friend are on firmer ground in the argument than the old man, even though they have not won by any means. In this argument, Tolstoy merely sets the scene and introduces the issues. But Pozdnyshev, sitting apart from the others and now greatly agitated by the discussion, will argue for him throughout the rest of the story. The second section opens with his halting question: "What kind of love . . . love . . . is it that sanctifies marriage?" This question opens his long narration about his childhood and debauched young manhood, his hypocrisy and deceit in his sexual affairs, and his irresponsible relations with women in general. He continues in great detail about the falsity of his marriage, his jealousy of his wife, and finally, his murder of her and his exile from society. It is significant that *The Kreutzer Sonata* is, to a greater degree than the other two stories, not only a personal confession but an indictment of the culture as well. . . .

In each of these three sister works, the main male characters are or were personally and socially brilliant aristocrats, whose lives and careers are ruined by events that center around a woman. Pozdnyshev murders his wife because of his rage at her response to another man. Stepan Kasatsky (Father Sergius) has three painful and destructive crises with women: the disclosure of his fiancée's love affair with the Tsar, his temptation by the divorcée, and his seduction by a suppliant girl. Evgeny Irtenev [in **"The Devil"**] has an uncontrollable passion for his serf, Stepanida, which drives him to suicide.

And it is not merely that these women act as the incidental catalysts of disaster; they are endowed with demonic powers. A decade after *The Kreutzer Sonata,* Tolstoy claimed in his *Journal* that "woman . . . is the tool of the devil. She is usually stupid, but the devil lends her his brain when she works for him. Thanks to this, she has accomplished miracles of intellect, perspective, and constancy—in order to do something vile. . . . But when there is no need for something vile, she cannot understand the simplest thing . . . and has no self-control. . . ." In *The Kreutzer Sonata* Pozdnyshev asserts that "a woman is happy and attains all she can desire when she has bewitched a man. Therefore the chief aim of a woman is to bewitch him." Father Sergius exclaims to his seductress, "You are a devil." Before, when the beautiful divorcée, Makovkina, came to his hermit cell to seduce him, he had asked, "Can it be true then as I read in the lives of the saints that the devil takes the form of a woman?" Of course, the title of **"The Devil"** speaks for

itself, but Evgeny's accusation of Stepanida makes the association clear: "She is a devil anyway. Just that, a devil. Hasn't she subjugated me against my will?"

> **In addition to reducing the act of falling in love to pure sexual attraction, Tolstoy is led from this hypothesis to suggest that all aspects of love—warmth of communication, friendship, joy in intimacy—are mere reflections or distortions of sexuality.**
>
> **—Ruth Crego Benson**

Of the three stories, however, *The Kreutzer Sonata* most clearly reveals in Pozdnyshev's image of his wife the source of this identification: the temptation of woman's sexuality. It is important to note that Pozdnyshev does not refer to his wife by name. She is neither personalized nor distinguished from any other woman. Anonymously and archetypally, she is Sexual Woman. Underneath the trappings of dress, manner, and feminine charm, there lies, in her husband's view, a malicious plan to keep him, and all men, from worthwhile and dignifying pursuits. In the full bloom of her maturity, with her children no longer an effective curb to her energies, and with the fear of further pregnancies removed, she is described by her husband as a "fresh, well fed harness horse, whose bridle has been removed." (Pozdnyshev's image calls to mind the elaborate parallel between Anna and Vronsky's mare.) *The Kreutzer Sonata*'s most serious indictment of rampant sexuality is that it alone, as the strongest and most violent of the passions, has kept humanity from reaching its goal of "goodness, righteousness, and love."

Especially in *The Kreutzer Sonata,* Tolstoy once again dismisses the reality of romantic love, or poetic love, or falling in love. In *Family Happiness,* Sergey Mikhailych and Masha fell in love, and their initial feeling for each other corresponded to the traditional view of "poetic" or romantic love. For both the lovers, however, the illusion that attended this phase in their lives, the illusion that each partner was precisely what the other wanted and would never change, was cruelly betrayed. In *The Kreutzer Sonata* there is no longer any such illusion; at least, Pozdnyshev in retrospect analyzes the illusion as something far different from romantic love. When courting his future wife, it had seemed to him on occasion that "she understood all that I felt and thought, and that what I felt and thought was very lofty. In reality it was only that her dress and her curls were particularly becoming to her and that after a day spent near her I wanted to be still closer." And further along: "The most exalted poetic love, as we call it, depends not on moral qualities but on physical nearness and on the coiffure, and the color and cut of the dress."

In addition to reducing the act of falling in love to pure sexual attraction, Tolstoy is led from this hypothesis to suggest that all aspects of love—warmth of communication, friendship, joy in intimacy—are mere reflections or distortions of sexuality. Pozdnyshev, for example, found it impossible for himself and his wife to engage in simple conversation as an expression of the "spiritual communion" that should accompany romantic love: "Well, if love is spiritual, spiritual communion, then that spiritual communion should find expression in words, in conversations, in discourse. There was nothing of the kind. It used to be dreadfully difficult to talk when we were left alone. . . . There was nothing to talk about."

Tolstoy moreover denied the possibility of communication on a deeper level, that is, the commitment and exchange that follows the recognition of a partner whose ideals meet and enhance one's own. To the woman on the train who defended this possibility, Pozdnyshev angrily, and straight to the point, retorted: "Spiritual affinity! Identity of ideals! . . . But in that case why go to bed together? (Excuse my vulgarity!)"

It may seem contradictory that even in these late stories, Tolstoy could still envision love as *agape* (if not *eros*); that is, that he could still occasionally entertain the possibility of married love built on spiritual communication and on deep reverential friendship. Such is, perhaps, the meaning of the relation of Evgeny Irtenev's wife, Liza, to her husband: emotionally warm but sexually cool. The portrait of Liza herself is almost unbelievably angelic. She is close to Tolstoy's ideal woman (along with her predecessors, Princess Marya of *War and Peace* and Pashenka of **Father Sergius**). Physically, she is presentable but not sexually attractive. Her eyes, like Princess Marya's, are her best feature: they are bright, tender, trustful, in contrast to the "black, sparkling" eyes of her rival, the serf Stepanida. Liza's eyes appeal and confide, while Stepanida's provoke and invite. Emotionally, Liza is sentimental, without passion; her infatuations with men before her marriage to Evgeny develop into tender, loving concern and pride when directed exclusively toward her husband. Her emotional make-up is primarily devoted and maternal, and her goal in her relations with her husband, indeed, of her life, is to make for him the best of all possible lives: "Liza had decided that of all the people in the world there was only her Evgeny Irtenev, a higher type, wiser, purer, nobler than all the others; and it therefore was the responsibility of everyone to serve him and to make life pleasant for him." Liza is endowed with that "spiritual communion" which Pozdnyshev found lacking between himself and his wife. In her relations with Evgeny, "she sensed every one of his moods, every shade of feeling, often, he thought, more clearly than he did himself. . . . Moreover, she understood his thoughts as well as his feelings." One might assume from this that Liza's and Evgeny's marriage should proceed tranquilly and tenderly, for Evgeny truly loves his wife as a warm and loyal friend. And that is precisely the problem; their close communication is warped by Evgeny's displaced sexual passion for Stepanida. This reveals Tolstoy's belief that these two forms of love and expression can never flow toward the same person. It is this tragic and unbearable division that dooms Evgeny.

Behind Tolstoy's idea of this apparently inevitable division, one may discern his view of sexuality and the sexual act itself. The sexual biography of each of the three men in these stories, particularly that of Pozdnyshev and Evgeny, reflects Tolstoy's view in some detail. The following passages are both typical and crucial: Evgeny, for instance,

> had spent his youth as do all young healthy bachelors; that is, he had had relationships with various kinds of women. He was not a debauchee, but neither was he . . . a monk! He indulged in this . . . only as far as it was necessary for his physical health and peace of mind. This began when he was sixteen, and had continued successfully, in the sense that he had not drowned himself in orgies, had never fallen in love, and had never caught any disease. As a result this phase of his life had been securely settled and had given him no trouble.

And Pozdnyshev says about his young manhood:

> I was not a seducer, had no unnatural tastes, did not make that the main purpose of my life as many of my associates did, but I practiced debauchery in a steady, decent way for my health's sake. I avoided women who might tie my hands by having a child or by attachment for me. There may have been children and attachments, however, but I acted as if there were not. And this I considered not only moral, I was even proud of it.

The description of Kasatsky's youth adds a new dimension: the double standard in its classic form, which introduces, in addition to premarital sexual partners, the woman who was *not* a part of the "debauched" life, the woman one could marry:

> Kasatsky belonged to those people of the forties who no longer exist, who, while consciously indulging in and inwardly not condemning unchaste sexual relations, demanded an ideal, heavenly chastity in a wife, recognized this heavenly chastity in every young girl of their own circles, and treated them accordingly. There was much that was false in this attitude, and it was harmful in the profligacy which it permitted men; but in respect to women, this viewpoint, which differs so sharply from that of today's youth, who see their potential mate in every young girl . . . did serve a purpose. Aware of this attitude, young girls tried more or less to be goddesses.

Pozdnyshev, too, says that he wallowed in a mire of debauchery and at the same time was looking for a girl chaste enough "to be worthy of [him]."

The nineteenth-century version of the double standard has always plagued men and women; but Tolstoy articulated its most painful consequences. Pozdnyshev (speaking for Tolstoy) confesses that, for himself, "dissoluteness does not lie in anything physical—no kind of physical misconduct is debauchery; real debauchery lies precisely in freeing oneself from moral relations with a woman with whom you have physical intimacy." In Tolstoy's view, *this* constituted the real double standard, and the only significant one. It was not only a double standard applied in relation to other persons, but was the mark of an interior division between act, feeling, and moral responsibility. . . .

Why such a tragic sexual schizophrenia? The later Tolstoy, as we know, regarded sexual intercourse, even between married partners, as disgusting and absurd, a shameful, "animal" act that separated the partners spiritually and emotionally. But that did not eliminate the basic problem of sexuality, the recognition of oneself and others as sexual creatures, fully available to each other. This might be called the "no barriers" theme in Tolstoy's thought, for he uses the phrase again and again to denote such recognition. This phrase indicates the mutual sudden awareness of attraction between many couples in Tolstoy's works: Pierre and Ellen, Natasha and Anatole, Anna and Vronsky, and so on. In short, throughout Tolstoy's literary work, he defines sexual attraction with a phrase connoting the consciousness of a naked confrontation between the two persons and of an uncontrolled force drawing them together.

After his wife's concert with his imagined rival, for example, Pozdnyshev feels that it was "evident already then, that there was . . . no barrier between them." In *Father Sergius,* the event is described without the specific phrase; Makovkina triumphantly realizes that when she knocked at Father Sergius's door "he put his face to the window and saw me and understood and recognized me, it was glowing and imprinted in his eyes. He loved and desired me. Yes, desired."

Of course this naked confrontation is not always matched by a frank admission of the basically erotic content of sex. The men of these stories invent verbal subterfuges, like the "safety valve" metaphor that occurs so often in Tolstoy, or better yet, they repeat the maxim that sex is necessary for the sake of one's health. In the notion that sex is necessary to the health, the mechanical idea of sex as a "safety valve" is simply rendered more explicit and concrete. Expressing these attitudes, Tolstoy was not merely reflecting his society: he was stating previous or present personal convictions. In *The Second Supplement to The Kreutzer Sonata,* he wrote: "The sexual instinct seems to me like the pressure of steam, which would cause a locomotive to explode if the pressure did not open the safety valve. The valve opens only under great pressure; otherwise it is always kept closed, and carefully closed, and it must be our conscious aim to keep it tightly closed and held down moreover by a weighted layer . . . so that it cannot open."

Both theories depersonalize man, woman, and act: first, although at this late stage Tolstoy emphasized keeping the valve closed as much as possible, in the "safety valve" theory the use of the mechanical metaphor reduces the sexual act to an annoying but necessary device which keeps the machine running smoothly. Sex "for the health" implies both that the body is, in some sense, sick, and that

the therapy is simply a matter of taking the appropriate treatment. Tolstoy's imagery evokes the dangers of a high-pressure steam boiler and suggests the regular maintenance of delicate plumbing. To ward off these perils, to service the machinery—this is woman's sexual function. Both of these dehumanizing attitudes have at their core the idea of selfish use: a woman is used by a man to keep him functioning properly.

Finally, however, the sexual bond is human, not mechanical. Yet in their rationalizations Tolstoy's characters are reluctant to admit that they feel such humanity. When Evgeny, for example, as pointed out before, seeks a woman for his "health," Danila suggests a clean healthy woman, and goes on to describe her sexual appeal. But Evgeny cuts him off because it reminds him of the purely erotic motives, the real nature of his request: "'No, no . . . that's not all what I need. On the contrary.' (What could be the contrary?)" But beyond eroticism loomed the possibility of an involvement, an emotional commitment which would inevitably fail.

In his earlier fiction, the familiar Tolstoyan solution to this dilemma was marriage, chiefly for two reasons: marriage could organize and focus the sex drive, and it could provide further justification for sex and compensation for the failure of romantic love in the creation of a family. If one takes *The Kreutzer Sonata* at face value, however, marriage as a solution to man's sexual problems is no longer possible. In the first place, love itself, and the desire to be together with one's beloved for a lifetime, are explained away as the result of an explosive pressure without a safety valve: "Try and close the safety valve . . ." Pozdnyshev warns, "and at once a stimulus arises which, passing through the prism of our artificial life, expresses itself in utter infatuation, sometimes even platonic." And he continues, further on, "Had the safety valve been open . . . I should not have fallen in love."

On this foundation, marriage would have little chance for mere survival. Pozdnyshev grudgingly admits that there are a few "true" marriages, providing a good Tolstoyan definition of an ideal marriage: "something mysterious, a sacrament binding [the partners] in the sight of God." This kind of marriage, though, is very rare; according to Pozdnyshev "ninety-nine percent of married people live in a similar hell" to the one that he experienced in his own marriage. That is, marriage is deception, a thin veil of convention, screening its real object, copulation. Such a marriage knows neither friendship nor fidelity, only an ever-increasing hatred, relieved by periods of sexual activity which, in turn, breeds further hatred. Far from softening its brutal outlines, the children of such a marriage are "not a joy but a torment." In the midst of the tensions between husband and wife, they become the object of discord and simultaneously the weapons of strife. In short, where there is sex, there can be neither love, nor marital happiness, nor the joy of family.

In *The Kreutzer Sonata* Tolstoy refers to the *Domostroy,* a sixteenth-century marriage and domestic manual. Its straightforward, no-nonsense manner of dealing with marriage is apparently prompted by a romantic notion of the past. The old man on the train, for example, who defends his old-fashioned views of marriage (women should fear their husbands, matchmaking is a sensible way to get a hard job done) is referred to by his female opponent as a "living Domostroy." Pozdnyshev refers to the *Domostroy* in another context: "You must remember that if one married according to the injunctions of the *Domostroy,* as that old fellow was saying, then the feather-beds, the trousseau, and the bedstead are all merely details appropriate to the sacrament." For his contemporaries, however, these objects are the medium of exchange in the sale of an innocent girl to a profligate. One should think of Tolstoy's nostalgic view of the *Domostroy* in this case as another example of his general wish during this period to return to a past of Arcadian simplicity and virtue, to get back to the roots, to re-create the beginnings of things. He no longer, however, actually believes in the real possibility of such a way of life. These abandoned hopes float like dream-fragments around his much more persuasive portrait of marriage as disillusion and deception.

Indeed, so powerful was the terror of sexuality and its derivative bonds in marriage that during his later period Tolstoy could readily conceive only of extreme or violent means of breaking the stalemate which they produced. Of Pozdnyshev, Irtenev, or Father Sergius, one could say as Tolstoy did of Hans Christian Andersen that "he was a confirmed rake and wanderer . . . but that only strengthens my conviction that he was a lonely man." For each of these characters is driven to isolate himself from those he loves and even from the rest of mankind: driven to the isolation of exile following the murder of his wife, driven to the ultimate isolation of death by suicide, or driven to the isolation of an ascetic religious commitment. In his youth and manhood, Tolstoy himself considered suicide; this impulse was closely linked to a sense of meaninglessness in his life, to which the problem of sexuality had contributed. And he contemplated religious asceticism as a possible escape from the torment of marriage. On one occasion (to be sure, eighteen years after writing **The Kreutzer Sonata**) he said to his friend and biographer N. N. Gusev: "I ought to have gone into a monastery. And I would have, if I hadn't had a wife". . . .

Secular celibacy is an equally possible solution for the male, as Pozdnyshev implies at the end of **The Kreutzer Sonata.** The reader is surprised to learn that immediately after stabbing his wife Pozdnyshev suddenly becomes aware of her as a human being and of the atrocity of his act. But from this belated insight, he concludes not that he should have refrained from murder, but that he should never have married! That is, only celibacy, not an agreement worked out within the marriage, could have prevented murder.

While **Father Sergius** is a curiously undigested piece, its theme of isolation receives a more significant and careful treatment in **The Kreutzer Sonata.** As previously described, Pozdnyshev appears as a loner, his albatross his only companion, the train his only home, even his natural habitat. The fact that we do not know its destination, that its few stopping places are, of course, only temporary, and that its atmosphere makes civilized communication practically impossible, are all appropriate to his previous and present life. Indeed, on a deeper level, the train is an engine of meaningless transit, from which, so long as it is in motion, one cannot escape; it is the allegory of a life over which one has no conscious control.

Dostoevsky's preoccupation with two forms of absolute violence, murder and suicide, is well known. On the other hand, because these themes are not prominent in Tolstoy's novels, he is usually assumed to have been free of the preoccupation with personal and metaphysical violence. Yet clearly in these three late stories, murder and suicide are thematically central. Pozdnyshev's final isolation, resulting from the murder of his wife, fulfills the story which he feels compelled to tell. It would, however, be a mistake to conclude that Tolstoy presents this isolation as, in any simple sense, the punishment for Pozdnyshev's crime. In fact, like the heroes of the other two stories, Pozdnyshev himself has manipulated the events leading to his isolation. On the simplest level within all three stories, the idea or act of violence has essentially the same meaning, for all three men—Pozdnyshev, Sergius, Irtenev—have manipulated their lives to a point where violence is a natural and immediate possibility. They all contemplate both murder and suicide, and two of them commit, in addition, the symbolic suicide of self-mutilation. As each contemplates or commits the murder, the actual or proposed victim is a woman whose femininity and sexuality have provoked the man to the conclusion that life is unbearable.

But suicide and murder are not, in these stories, the apocalyptic objective of events. Rather, the act of killing is instrumental. Indeed, murder and suicide share indistinguishably the same purpose. Tolstoy presents both acts, killing onself or killing another, as the means of solving an otherwise inescapable problem, to which an agony of paralysis is the only alternative. Here, violence is the means of breaking past a stalemate, or a way of bringing an intolerable series of events, an intolerable situation, to a close. Thus, like the sex in these stories, violence is finally impersonal, without real reference to the individuality of its object. In short, murder or suicide is a mode of manipulating the self, others, and events, so that in each case, the outcome leaves the agent free of self, others, and events: totally isolated.

Pozdnyshev clearly recognizes his own active agency in creating the events that simultaneously cause his downfall and justify it. He recalls, for instance, that

> a strange and fatal force led me not to repulse him [Trukhachevsky], not to keep him away, but on the contrary to invite him to the house . . . as if almost compulsively, I began talking about his playing.

> I invited him to come some evening and bring his violin to play with my wife. She glanced at me with surprise,

flushed, and as if frightened began to decline, saying that she did not play well enough. This refusal irritated me further and I insisted even more on his coming.

More conclusive, and more final, is the following confession:

> If he had not appeared, there would have been someone else. If the occasion had not been jealousy, it would have been something else. I maintain that all husbands who live as I did must either live dissolutely, separately, or kill themselves or their wives as I have done.

Pozdnyshev's admission completely separates the act of murder from the events that preceded and provoked it, since the murder has no cause apart from his own need to escape his wife's temptation and to release him from an impossible commitment. Hence, the murder cannot be entirely and exclusively identified with the sexual act, but it is analogous to it as another product of the gulf between act, feeling, and responsibility.

In Tolstoy's fiction from *Family Happiness* to *Anna Karenina,* women are primarily, and in more concrete ways than men, responsible for the failures of love and marriage. In this respect, the three late stories mark a striking departure. For in them Tolstoy indicts both woman and man; the man, in love or marriage, is no longer merely passive or unaware, essentially a victim, but personally responsible and even manipulative. Though these three characters are, properly speaking, anti-heroes, each experiences a moment of transformative self-awareness. Only for Father Sergius, however, does this self-recognition lead to a final redemption. All three men achieve self-awareness through discovery of the tragic discrepancy between what they are and what they thought or wanted themselves to be. This, in turn, leads each to an awakening, a conversion to a different way of life, thought, and action, and, in the case of Irtenev, to the end of life itself. The exiled Sergius is a partial exception, for by radically limiting both his hopes and his field of action, he overcomes the discrepancy between actuality and aspiration.

To have admitted and expressed man's share in the failure of love and marriage was a great change for Tolstoy. Ironically, he writes like a radical feminist when, in *The Second Supplement to The Kreutzer Sonata,* he argues that

> the man who has hitherto led a debauched life passes on moral corruption to the woman, infects her with his own sensuality, and taxes her with the unbearable burden of being at one and the same time mistress, mother, and human being; and she develops, too, into an excellent mistress, a tortured mother, and a suffering, nervous, and hysterical human being. And the man loves her as his mistress, ignores her as a mother, and hates her for her nervousness and hysteria which he himself has caused. It seems to me that this is the source of all the sufferings that arise in every family.

This recognition does not, however, soften Tolstoy's views of women. That is, he finds himself and all men guilty in their premarital and family relations, and for the first time he describes this guilt. Nonetheless, within this new view, he sees women as willing accomplices, as accessories before, during, and after the fact. Though men are *more* responsible for failure than in his earlier writings, women are no less responsible, and only the men are given the opportunity and the sensitivity to change or grow.

Pozdnyshev's admission completely separates the act of murder from the events that preceded and provoked it, since the murder has no cause apart from his own need to escape his wife's temptation and to release him from an impossible commitment.

—*Ruth Crego Benson*

Taken together, these three stories constituted Tolstoy's final negation of the most fundamental human institutions, commitments, and values. Implicitly and explicitly in these tales, he denied either the practical possibility or the value of chastity, love, marriage, intimacy, sexuality, and fidelity. Understandably, the public reacted strongly to the black pessimism of *The Kreutzer Sonata,* and Tolstoy was asked to explain and interpret the tale. Though he had ignored or refused requests to comment formally on earlier works, his response to this furor was an explanatory "Epilogue," which he wrote in 1890.

Tolstoy designed the Epilogue to contain "the essence of what [he] had intended to convey." In the first place, he writes, he wanted to oppose the notion that sex is necessary to health, and correspondingly to deny that social arrangements based on this premise are justified. Second, he argues that marital infidelity occurs because people mistakenly believe that sexual love is romantic and elevating, whereas it is in fact brutish and degrading. He goes so far as to say that "the violation of a promise of fidelity, given in marriage, should be punished by public opinion certainly in no lesser degree than are punished the violations of debts and business frauds." This harsh mandate for human judgment is far from the cooler tone of *Romans* 12.19, which appeared as the epigraph to *Anna Karenina.* Earlier, as we have seen, he had been content to leave judgment of such sins to God; or, more accurately, to the logic and finality of the events themselves.

As his third point, Tolstoy warns against the bad effects of birth control. His admonitions draw on his contempt for medical practice; he asserts that sexual relations make pregnant or nursing women hysterical; and he regards contraception as equivalent to murder. The fourth and fifth points are not really distinct either from each other or from the second: he says that children are educated, by clothes, sweets, excesses of food and drink, music, novels, poems, and so forth, to a life of sensuality; and that "the best part of young people's lives is passed, by men, in discovering love-affairs or marriage, and by women and girls, in alluring and drawing men into love-affairs or marriage." He repeats his belief that sexual love is not a worthy activity of human beings (men) but, quite to the contrary, keeps them from their only proper pursuit: to serve humanity, country, science, art, or God.

Needless to say, *The Kreutzer Sonata,* considered together with the other two stories, carries a much larger meaning than the strident and erratically argued Epilogue. In fact, the three stories, viewed together, may be regarded as offering a spectrum of final statements on the problem posed by women, sexuality, and moral schizophrenia. It is, however, both striking and characteristic that by the late 1880s Tolstoy could present his solutions only as utterly impracticable or productive of misery.

Basic to the shared content of the three stories is Tolstoy's assurance that women, and the sexuality that women represent, project, and provoke, are the source of man's downfall. Because of them, careers are destroyed, character is corrupted, sexual desire flares out of control. In *War and Peace* and *Anna Karenina* Tolstoy was still willing to represent marriage as an effective and acceptable way to organize sex for the purpose of bearing children. In two of these three stories, however, though the marriages could have taken such a form, Tolstoy's characters dismiss this possibility without serious consideration. In each of the three stories, when the main character faces a dilemma that is mainly sexual in nature, he feels a profound fear, distrust, or contempt of sexuality, or of intimacy of any kind. And in all three, as a direct consequence of, and indeed in direct response to, the sexual dilemma of the male tempted by the female, alienation and violence follow relentlessly.

Natasha and Pierre and Kitty and Levin had escaped this fate; Anna and Vronsky had succumbed to it. Yet there was adequate warning of this nihilism even as early as *Family Happiness,* where the possibility of happiness is concrete at the beginning, but where the deterioration of romantic illusion and the isolation of mates is inexorable. In *The Kreutzer Sonata* and its satellites, the possibility of alternatives or adjustment to this process appears as delusion or hallucination. But *The Kreutzer Sonata* penetrates beyond a tragic view of experience: like Tolstoy's own *Confession,* its orgiastic tone and its insistent self-contempt invite us to celebrate, with the penitents, their capacity for evil and their pride of guilt. In these three stories, the consistent single message is the inevitable failure of human relationships and the inescapable recognition of human alienation. In this world, like Pashenka and Father Sergius, who come together only for aid and comfort, men and women no longer live and act in concert, but in isolation.

Other great writers have substituted one vision of life for another, or have dedicated themselves to an ideal which the force of ambivalence may have destroyed. But few have equaled that relentless testing of moral sensibility

and human capacity, that indefatigable urge to break beyond limitations that characterized Tolstoy's life and fiction. In his own typically distilled yet sweeping formulation, "life is the expansion of limits." Even late in Tolstoy's life when that expansion absorbed limits and became grotesque, one feels with Gorky that "the disagreeable or hostile feelings which he aroused would assume forms that were not oppressive but seemed to explode within one's soul, expanding it, giving it greater capacity." Yet his power was tragically flawed by his consistently limited and distorted view of the nature of sex, of women, and, therefore, of the men who were his chief concern. So that, by the end of his life, the dream of the young Tolstoy—of a warm family life in the country, of a productive and benevolent estate, of friendships, of literary success, of the pursuit of culture—had vanished entirely. For this ideal, the spent but still aspiring old man finally substituted his heterodox-Christian vision of an emotionally and erotically anaesthetic world.

E. B. Greenwood   (essay date 1975)

SOURCE: "Tolstoy the Ascetic? *The Kreutzer Sonata, Father Sergius* and *Resurrection,*" in his *Tolstoy: The Comprehensive Vision,* J. M. Dent & Sons Ltd., 1975, pp. 137-46.

[*In the excerpt below, Greenwood situates the ascetic tone of* The Kreutzer Sonata *in the context of Tolstoy's life and art.*]

Aylmer Maude points out that the views approving marriage which satisfied Tolstoy in 1884 when he wrote *What I Believe* no longer satisfied him in 1889 when he wrote *The Kreutzer Sonata.* This can be brought out by considering Tolstoy's remarks on Jesus's teaching on sexual conduct in the Sermon on the Mount and his translation in *The Gospel in Brief* (1883) of Jesus's teaching on celibacy in the later passage in Matthew (19: 10-12). Let us first take Jesus's teaching on sexual conduct in Matthew 5: 27-32, part of the Sermon on the Mount:

> You have heard that it was said, 'You shall not commit adultery'. But I say to you that every one who looks at a woman lustfully has already committed adultery with her in his heart. If your right eye causes you to sin, pluck it out and throw it away; it is better that you lose one of your members than that your whole body be thrown into hell. And if your right hand causes you to sin, cut it off and throw it away; it is better that you lose one of your members than that your whole body go into hell.

> It was also said, 'Whoever divorces his wife, let him give her a certificate of divorce.' But I say to you that every one who divorces his wife, except on the ground of unchastity, makes her an adulteress: and whoever marries a divorced woman commits adultery.

In *What I Believe* (1884) Tolstoy takes this passage as implying that 'Men and women, knowing indulgence in sexual relations to lead to strife, should avoid all that evokes desire.' He shrewdly questions the *caveat* that Jesus allowed divorce on the grounds of adultery. I say shrewdly, because it appears that this caveat was not spoken by Jesus, but added by the Church.

> The central subject of *The Kreutzer Sonata* is not so much an attack on the physical side of sex . . . as the burning wish to be free of being tied to any woman, the wish which I have suggested Tolstoy could not acknowledge to himself in the case of his own wife Sonya save in the devious disguise of an ascetic moralism.
>
> —*E. B. Greenwood*

In the passage in Matthew on celibacy, the disciples had evidently been worried by the teaching forbidding a man to divorce his wife, particularly after some Pharisees had pointed out to Jesus that Moses had allowed such divorce. The disciples themselves said to Jesus, 'If such is the case of a man with his wife, it is not expedient to marry.' To this Jesus replied:

Not all men can receive this precept [presumably the precept that it is not expedient to marry], but only those to whom it is given. For there are eunuchs who have been so from birth, and there are eunuchs who have been made eunuchs by men, and there are eunuchs who have made themselves eunuchs for the sake of the kingdom of heaven. He who is able to receive this, let him receive it.

Tolstoy's version in *The Gospel in Brief* (1883) runs:

And his pupils said to Jesus: It is too hard to be always bound to one wife. If that must be, it would be better not to marry at all.

He said to them: You may refrain from marriage but you must understand what that means. If a man wishes to live without a wife, let him be quite pure and not approach women: but let him who loves women unite with one wife and not cast her off or look at other women.

It is clear that Jesus is primarily concerned to establish the spiritual superiority of celibacy to marriage for those who are 'called' to it and that Tolstoy's 1883 version interestingly shifts the emphasis to the marriage side of the issue. There is no hint in it that Tolstoy himself wishes to emphasize the importance of celibacy. But in 1889 when he wrote *The Kreutzer Sonata* he had come to see celibacy as the ideal and implicitly advocates it in that

story. In 'An Afterword to *The Kreutzer Sonata*' in the following year, though he does not rule out marriage, he certainly sees it as a kind of fall compared with the ideal of perfect chastity. Aylmer Maude is surely right in explaining this change of view on Tolstoy's part as the result of the intensification of the conflict between him and his wife Sonya over his wish to renounce his property and over his other principles. The beginnings of that conflict, it is true, go back to 1881, and in May of that year Tolstoy recorded, 'To abandon one's family is the second temptation.' At the same time he added, 'Serve not the family, but the one God.' On 26 August 1882 Tolstoy suddenly exclaimed that his most passionate wish was to go away. This deeply upset Sonya, who made her first, but not her last, attempt at suicide. Again in June 1884 after a bitter quarrel over his principles with Sonya in the final stages of pregnancy Tolstoy stalked out even as she was starting to go into labour, but turned back as feelings of guilt overcame him. This was the incident of which Shaw was so critical in his review of Maude's biography. About the change of view between 1883 and 1889 there is *no* doubt. In 1883 he could still write in *What I Believe* that the union of marriage was 'holy and obligatory.' By 1890 in the 'Afterword to *The Kreutzer Sonata*' he is calling 'sexual love, marriage . . . from a Christian point of view, a fall, a sin.'

Tolstoy's moral dilemma was to know how much, in this sudden wish to break free from marriage (the stages of which we have traced above), he was following a selfish wish for freedom (such as in many others ends in the very divorce he condemned) under the cloak of an avowed wish to serve God before his family.

What, then, are we to make of **The Kreutzer Sonata** (1889) and of 'An Afterword to *The Kreutzer Sonata*' (1890)? The first thing to be said is that Tolstoy's wife, family and first readers identified Pozdnyshev's views in the story with those of Tolstoy himself. The fact that Pozdnyshev says 'I am a sort of lunatic' could hardly deter them, for they sometimes regarded Tolstoy as a sort of lunatic. It is no wonder, then, that Sonya recorded in December 1890 her terrible fear of becoming pregnant, 'for everybody will hear of the disgrace and jubilantly repeat the recent Moscow joke: "Voilà le véritable postscriptum de la Sonate de Kreutzer".' On 6 March 1891 Sonya recorded in her diary one of the bitterest and most telling comments on the work: 'At tea we talked about . . . the vegetarianism which Lyova advocates. He said he saw a vegetarian menu in a German paper which was composed of bread and almonds. I expect the person who wrote the menu practises vegetarianism as much as the author of **The Kreutzer Sonata** practises chastity. . . .' And, after all, were not Sonya and the work's first readers right in identifying Pozdnyshev's views with Tolstoy's? A recent student of the question, G. W. Spence, writes in his book *Tolstoy the Ascetic*:

Pozdnyshev's theory is not just Pozdnyshev's: it is not contradicted by Tolstoy in anything that was written after **The Kreutzer Sonata,** and not only is the statement of the ideal of complete celibacy or perfect chastity repeated in the *Afterword* to *The Kreutzer Sonata* and in *The Kingdom of God is Within You,* IV, but also the doctrine of general suicide by means of chastity is the logical outcome of the despairing last pages of the *Confession.*

I agree with everything here except the last remark. There is no *logical* connection between *A Confession* and Tolstoy's later extreme asceticism, but at most a psychological one. Moreover, that claim obscures the fact that whatever the stresses and strains (and, as some have postulated, illness) behind *A Confession* the overt purpose of the work is to show that the view that life is 'senseless and evil' (which had also been Anna's view before her suicide) is *mistaken.* In *A Confession* Tolstoy is not putting forward the view (as some criticisms are apt to leave the impression he is) that life is meaningless, but repudiating that view. Thus if a sense of the meaninglessness of life and even of life-hatred is present in *The Kreutzer Sonata* then that work does not endorse Tolstoy's thesis in *A Confession* but undermines it, or at least leaves us merely with the psychological mood of negation and bafflement *A Confession* was designed to leave behind.

The central subject of *The Kreutzer Sonata* is not so much an attack on the physical side of sex (though that is the aspect of *The Kreutzer Sonata* which everyone remembers) as the burning wish to be free of being tied to any woman, the wish which I have suggested Tolstoy could not acknowledge to himself in the case of his own wife Sonya save in the devious disguise of an ascetic moralism. Pozdnyshev delivers tirades against tight-fitting jerseys, bustles and copulation ('our *swinish* connection') not primarily in themselves, but because they are the agents of bondage to a woman. Pozdnyshev is hopelessly confused. One moment he speaks of pregnancy as 'this sacred work' and the next he speaks of virginity as the 'highest state.' But it is very difficult to decide how much this contradictoriness was intended by Tolstoy, as artist, to be dramatically expressive of the highly-wrought state of the mind of his protagonist and how much it arises from Tolstoy's own utter bewilderment. It must be admitted that the remark which Maude quotes as having been made by Tolstoy apropos *The Kreutzer Sonata* ('The indispensable thing is to go beyond what others have done, to pick off something fresh, however small . . .') is the remark of a man who seems to have thought he was in artistic control. Be that as it may, Pozdnyshev's jealousy of the musician Trukhachevski's playing of the Kreutzer Sonata with his wife (the whole thing seems almost to become a metaphor for intercourse) is not so much jealousy as normally understood as a deliberate inflammation of the sexual bondage to her which he feels, an inflammation which at the same time affords the excuse of breaking that bondage by murder.

Pozdnyshev's twisted attack on sexuality parallels Tolstoy's own tormented attempts to convince himself that he was following the teaching of Jesus in putting God before his family, when all the time he inwardly suspected that what he was trying to do was merely to escape from them for all the world like any *roué*. What better way than to stigmatize marriage (as he does in the 'Afterword to *The Kreutzer Sonata*') as the 'service of self' when what he feared was that it might really be selfishness which underlay his own passionate desire for freedom?

Robert Louis Jackson   (essay date 1978)

SOURCE: "Tolstoj's *Kreutzer Sonata* and Dostoevskij's *Notes from the Underground,*" in *American Contributions to the Eighth International Congress of Slavists,* Slavica Publishers, Inc., 1978, pp. 280-91.

[*Below, Jackson identifies the affinities of* The Kreutzer Sonata *and Dostoevsky's* Notes from the Underground, *focusing on structure, narrative form, and use of the "irrational hero" to express each author's views of social problems.*]

1

At the end of the third chapter of *The Kreutzer Sonata* (1891) the nervous, exasperated and shrill Pozdnyšev—"landowner, university graduate and Marshal of the Nobility"—begins his account of a "critical episode" in his life, namely, the murder of his wife, with a definition of depravity. Addressing the elusive narrator, Pozdnyšev remarks:

> "Depravity really doesn't lie in anything physical, indeed, no physical outrage can be called depravity. Depravity, real depravity, consists precisely in freeing oneself from moral relations with a woman with whom you enter into physical relations. And precisely this kind of liberation I set down for myself as meritorious. I remember how I was once terribly upset when I did not manage to pay a woman who, after apparently falling in love with me, had given herself to me; and I regained my peace of mind only after I had sent her money, showing in this way that I did not consider myself bound to her in any way . . . Now don't shake your head as though you agreed with me," he suddenly shouted at me. "I really know what I'm talking about. All of us, and you too, at your best, unless you are a rare exception, share the same views that I did. Well, it makes no difference, forgive me," he continued "but the fact is that this is terrible, terrible, terrible!" "What is terrible?" I asked. "The whole abyss of error in which we live concerning women and our relations to them. Yes, I cannot speak calmly about it, and not because of this 'episode' [of the murder] as [the lawyer] just put it, but because ever since that episode occurred my eyes have been opened and I have come to see everything in quite a different light. Exactly the opposite, exactly the opposite!" He lit up a cigarette and leaning his elbows on his knees, went on talking. I could not see his face in the darkness . . .

Pozdnyšev's reminiscence of how he literally settled accounts with his mistress recalls, of course, the climax of the Underground Man's second meeting with the prostitute Liza in his flat. After a moment of catharsis—a moment in which he sobs hysterically in the arms of Liza—the Underground Man is overtaken by a feeling of "domination and possession," of alternating feelings of attraction and hatred. "One feeling intensified the other. This was almost like vengeance!" The moment of sex that follows is an utterly loveless act. His "outburst of passion," as he describes it "was precisely revenge, a further humiliation of her," a confession not only that he was "incapable of loving her," but that for him "love meant to tyrannize and be morally superior. . . . Even in my underground dreams I could not imagine love except as a struggle, and I also embarked on it with hatred." After the moment of loveless sex, the Underground Man is furious with impatience for Liza to leave. "Suddenly I ran up to her, seized her hand, opened it, put something in it, and then closed it again." This cruel gesture, the Underground Man admits, was "so insincere, so deliberately invented, so bookish" that even he could barely stand it at the time. But the gesture nonetheless signals his "depravity"—in Pozdnyšev's sense of the word—his freedom (for him an anguished freedom) from moral relations with Liza.

> Tolstoj's *Kreutzer Sonata*, originally conceived as a personal drama of a man betrayed by his wife, gradually evolved into a work in which polemical issues of broad social content involving marriage, family, and sex occupy equal space with personal history.
>
> —*Robert Louis Jackson*

More than a gesture draws the attention of the reader of *The Kreutzer Sonata* to *Notes from the Underground*. *The Kreutzer Sonata* is perhaps the most "Dostoevskian" work of Tolstoj precisely in the manner he designs his polemical work and in the way he develops his central hero, or anti-hero, Pozdnyšev. Before singling out some of the affinities of these two works one may note a certain similarity between Pozdnyšev's apocalyptic approach to marriage and sexuality and Dostoevskij's own view of this matter.

2

Pozdnyšev tells his story in a railway compartment illuminated by a single candle. The time of the narration is between twilight and dawn. The end of his narration merges with the end of his story of the journey within the journey: his return home from a trip, his discovery of his wife and suspected lover, his murder of his wife. Pozdnyšev's dawn—and that is what his monologue is about—is apocalyptic: the discovery of a tragic truth about sexuality, family, and marital relations—indeed, all human relations. "Yes, only after having fearfully suffered, only

thanks to that have I understood where the root of it all lies, understood what must be, and therefore perceived the horror of all that is." The "new light" in which he sees the world is symbolized by the Rembrandtian illumination of the candle which from time to time lights up a twitching, agitated face with "angry eyes." Pozdnyšev's indictment of upper class society—and that is the social and cultural matrix of the tragic "episode" in his life—is full of angry mutterings about an impending upheaval, chaos, an "end" to the disorder of human relations. His appeal for an ethic of sexual abstention is part of a broader, cleansing Christian fundamentalism and humanism. To the question, how the human race would be perpetuated with such an ethic, Pozdnyšev replies with irony:

> And wouldn't it be a terrible thing if the human race perished! . . . Why should it be continued—this human race? . . . If there is no goal, if life is given to us for life, there is no reason to live . . . But if there is a goal of life, then it is clear that life must come to an end when the goal is achieved . . . If the goal of mankind is well-being, goodness, love, if you wish; if the goal of mankind is what is said in the prophecies, that all men will be united in the universal love . . . then what stands in the way of attaining this goal? Human passions. Of all the passions, the most powerful and vicious and stubborn is sexual, carnal love. And therefore if the passions are annihilated and with them the most powerful—carnal love—then the prophecy will be fulfilled, men will be united, the goal of mankind will have been achieved, and there will no longer be any reason for existence.

All this, Pozdnyšev recognizes, is only an "ideal." There will be generations before the prophecy is fulfilled. In the meanwhile, he believes, some people will continue to strive for the moral ideal.

The problems raised by Tolstoj through the medium of the emotionally distraught and disturbed Pozdnyšev were by no means alien to Dostoevskij or to the inhabitants of his novelistic universe. Unlike Tolstoj, Dostoevskij never wrote explicitly on the subject of sexuality, yet the problem of sexuality in the life of the individual and society, its relation to the whole human being and social organism, concerned him deeply.

"Swinish sensuality with all its consequences, passing into cruelty, crime, the Marquis de Sade"—Dostoevskij wrote in his notebook for *The Brothers Karamazov*. Dostoevskij's "ridiculous man" has witnessed the beauty of man's primeval paradise, as well as the circumstances of his "fall," and he insists that "sensuality is the root of all evil." Though Dostoevskij clearly adheres to that view in the deepest religious sense; though he tends to identify the highest consciousness of moral beatitude with personalities in whom the sexual instinct is sublimated, undeveloped, or crippled, he refuses to idealize the asexual state. In *The Brothers Karamazov* he attempts to incorporate sexuality into a positive world view. While indicting Fedor Karamazov's "swinish sensuality," he at the same time discovers in the "earthly Karamazovian" force a deep vitality, a "thirst for life," a guarantee of spiritual rebirth.

The ideals of Zosima will presumably triumph in the journey of Aleša, but not at the expense of his humanity in the literal sense of that word.

In the final analysis, duality defines Dostoevskij's attitude towards sexuality. This is apparent in his treatment of the theme in his notebook in 1863. Here he speaks of marriage and sexuality as a manifestation of egoism and as alien to the highest spiritual ideal. "'[For in the resurrection] they neither marry nor seek to possess, but live as divine angels,'" [*Ne zenjatsja i ne posjagajut, a zivut, kak angely bozii*] (Math. 22: 30). "A profoundly noteworthy characteristic," observes Dostoevskij. And he puts down the following reflections on this theme:

> 1) They do not *get married* and do not *seek to possess*—because there is no reason to; to develop, achieve one's goal by means of changing generations is no longer necessary, and, 2) marriage and seeking to possess women is as it were the greatest deviation from humanism, the complete isolation of the pair from *everyone* (little remains for everyone). The family that is, the law of nature, but still abnormal, an egotistical state in the full sense, is a condition coming from mankind. The family is the most sacred thing of man on earth, for by means of this law of nature man achieves the goal through development (that is, through the change of generations). But at the same time, also according to the law of nature, in the name of the final ideal of his goal, man must continuously deny it.

> (Duality)

Dostoevskij's views, of course, remarkably coincide with Tolstoj's views in *The Kreutzer Sonata,* views which take on a more frenetic expression, of course, in the monologue of Pozdnyšev. Like Tolstoj, Dostoevskij believes that the whole history of humanity is a striving for a state of universality in which the "I" will merge with "everybody," that is, the "paradise of Christ." In this view, man on earth is only a "transitional, developing" creature; he is striving towards ultimate paradise. "We have no understanding of what kind of creatures we will be." One trait of this future has been "foretold and foreshadowed in Christ—the great and final ideal of the development of all humanity"; this trait is: "They *do not get married* and *do not seek to possess,* but love as divine angels."

3

In the areas of form, authorial intention and narrative timbre *The Kreutzer Sonata* and *Notes from the Underground* have something in common. Both works are narrated in the form of a confession (Tolstoj uses the device of two narrators, but it is the second narrator, Pozdnyšev, who dominates). In both works polemics—a hard core of ideological, social and philosophical discussion—are interwoven with personal narrative. *Notes from the Underground* divides into polemics (Part I) and personal reminiscences (Part II), though the division between polemics and reminiscences is by no means absolute. Tolstoj's *Kreutzer Sonata,* originally conceived as a personal drama of a man betrayed by his wife, gradually evolved into a work in which polemical issues of broad social content involving marriage, family, and sex occupy equal space with personal history. The division between polemics and personal narration is less defined in *The Kreutzer Sonata* than in *Notes from the Underground.* A consistent thread of story, or personal drama, runs from the beginning to the end of the work. Nonetheless, as in *Notes from the Underground,* the first part of the confession (chapters 1-17) tends to concentrate on polemical issues, while the last part (chapters 18-28) is by and large devoted to the tragic denouement of Pozdnyšev's relations with his wife. In both works, of course, the polemical issues lie at the core of the tragic personal drama.

The psychological motivation for the reminiscences of both the Underground Man and Pozdnyšev is a crime that weighs heavily on their consciences: Pozdnyšev's actual physical murder of his wife, and the Underground Man's spiritual murder of Liza. The Underground Man looks back on the Liza episode after sixteen years of remorse, of suffering with a "crime" on his conscience. The concept of murder as the essence of the Underground Man's crime is underscored by Dostoevskij in the final encounter of the Underground Man with Liza. "I could almost have killed her," he remarks at one point. And after his cruel tirade in which he tramples upon the feelings of trust that he had awakened in her and savagely exposes the motives of his behavior towards her, he remarks: "She turned white as a sheet, wanted to say something, her lips painfully twisted; but she collapsed in a chair as though she had been cut down by an ax."

Murder in *The Kreutzer Sonata* and *Notes from the Underground* involves a woman. In both works the theme of a depersonalized sexuality is symptomatic of social and psychological disorder. The confessions of Pozdnyšev and of the Underground Man are outpourings of men who are both conscience-stricken and bent on self-justification. But self-justification leads finally to self-indictment and involves a broad critique of society. "I am a sick man," the Underground Man declares in the opening words of his "notes"; he concludes his confession with the thought that he has "merely carried to an extreme in my life what you have not dared to carry through even half way." "All the features for the antihero have been gathered here deliberately, and, chiefly, all this creates a most unpleasant impression because we are all divorced from life, all crippled, each of us more or less." Pozdnyšev describes himself as a "kind of insane man." "I am a wreck, a cripple. But one thing I have: I know. Yes, it is clear that I know what the rest of the world does not yet know." Like Eugene Irtenev in Tolstoj's *The Devil,* Pozdnyšev finds the same indications of insanity in the so-called normal bourgeois man and women of his social class. Putting it another way, he notes that the French psychologist Charcot would probably have pronounced his wife a victim of hysteria and would have said that he, Pozdnyšev, was abnormal, "and he probably would have tried to cure us. *But there was no disease to cure.*" (My italics—RLJ). The essence of Pozdnyšev's rationalizations for his crime is that his murder of his wife simply represented an extreme manifestation of a moral and social calamity involving his whole class.

Both the Underground Man and Pozdnyšev at the moment of confession live at the periphery of the society. Both present themselves to their interlocutors as people who have gained a special knowledge of the world that is contrary to what the majority think or want to know. In their suffering and accumulated spite, both are intent on revealing the "bare" disgusting truth about themselves and their contemporaries. Theirs is the anguish and spite of disillusioned romantics, victims in their view of romantic illusions and spurious ideals. The Underground Man sarcastically expatiates on his onetime exaltation with the "beautiful and the sublime." Banality, egotism, vice lie beneath the brilliant exterior. Pozdnyšev tirelessly heaps scorn upon the notions of ideal good, Platonic love, or beauty. "It is a remarkable thing how full of illusion is the notion that beauty is good." He points to the contiguity of beauty and vice. Man—at least upper class man—finds room for Sodom in his idealism. A woman knows that "our kind lies when he talks about lofty feelings—what he wants is only the body." The romantic is deluded. "I was soiled with lewdness, and yet, at the same time, I was looking for a girl whose purity would meet my standards." Love masks vice. "Every man feels for every pretty woman what you call love." Disillusioned in their idealism, both the Underground Man and Pozdnyšev turn on the world with a terrible vengeance.

The confessions of both antiheroes are carried on in "darkness" (the darkness of the "underground" and of the night train). The light they bring to themselves, their partners and to the world is apocalyptic. They destabilize the fundamental ideals and social codes of their society. Their message about man and human relations (in Pozdnyšev's case this message is more class oriented) is one of tragic discord, a contradiction between illusion and reality, ideal and nature. Man as they present him is irrational.

Both men give evidence of the triumph of biological, instinctual man over rational, social man. This disaster is evident first of all in the over-excited, angry, disturbed manner in which the Underground Man and Pozdnyšev discuss their lives and ideas. But it is in their reminiscences of the past that both emerge as incarnations of the uncontrolled irrational. The Underground Man's terrible, tyrannical debauch of emotion in his final encounter with Liza is well known. "And what the hell do I care if you don't understand what I'm talking about? And what the hell do I care what happens to you?" He dissolves in the fury of his tormenting anguish, his self-destructive spite. "I, I can't be good." But like the man with toothache, who delights in his groans and pain, the Underground Man reaches the pitch of delight, despair, and madness in his encounters with Apollon and Liza at the climax of his stay.

The excited, shrill voice of Pozdnyšev, his odd physical behavior, his abrupt, sometimes almost hysterical utterances, recall the Underground Man. His behavior in the final hours and days preceding his crime seems wholly out of the "underground." Deliberately spiteful, full of mingled self-pity and hatred, he encourages the meeting between his wife and Truxacevskij. (There are echoes here from Dostoevskij's *Eternal Husband.*) "But, strange as it may seem, some strange, fateful force induced me not to repel him, to keep him at a distance, but, on the contrary, to bring him closer." "I smiled pleasantly [at my wife] pretending that I was very pleased." After the concert, Pozdnyšev is filled with an unnatural "genuine pleasure." In spite of his suffering and wild jealousy, some "strange feeling" compelled him to be "all the more affectionate, the more his presence was tormenting [to me]." But behind all the courteousness is a burning hatred and malice. "And the chief feeling, as always in all spite, was self-pity." "I must do something to make her suffer," Pozdnyšev recalls himself as thinking, "so that she may appreciate that I have suffered."

As his rage bursts out into the open, Pozdnyšev rouses himself to ever greater frenzy:

> For the first time I wanted to express this rage physically. I leaped up and moved towards her, but at that instant I became conscious of my anger, and asked myself, 'Is it a good thing to give way to this feeling?' and immediately answered, that it was a good thing, that it would frighten her, and immediately, instead of withholding my rage, I began to fan it in myself and to rejoice because it grew more and more intense. "Get the hell out, or I will kill you!" I shouted, approaching her and seizing her by the hand. I consciously intensified the tones of malice in my voice as I spoke these words. And, probably, I must have been terrifying . . . "Go!" I roared even more loudly. "Only you can drive me to madness. I won't be responsible for what I may do!" Having thus given rein to my madness, I delighted in it, and I wanted to do something unusual, to show the full extent of my madness. I terribly wanted to beat and kill her, but I knew that it was out of the question.

On arriving home the evening of the murder Pozdnyšev is overcome by "the same need to beat, destroy, that I felt at that time." The expressions on the face of his wife and Truxacevskij arouses in him a sense of "agonizing joy." In this final encounter, Pozdnyšev "felt this need for destruction, violence and the ecstasy of madness, and yielded to it." "I felt that I was completely mad and must be terrible, and rejoiced in this." "Madness also has its own laws," remarks Pozdnyšev as he recalls the fatal momentum of his emotions. Thus, too, the Underground Man in his profound egoism of suffering vents his rage upon Liza. And this rage and madness ends, as in the case of Pozdnyšev, with a form of murder.

4

The state of being *free from moral relations with women with whom one enters into physical relations* defines, at root, not only Pozdnyšev's relations with his causal female acquaintances in his pre-marital days, but also, in his view, his sexual relations with his wife—a woman whom he claimed to know "only as an animal." The ultimate freedom from moral relations is murder;

murder, in the case of Pozdnyšev, is the direct outcome of a relationship based on "swinishness," that is, "crime." The "mutual hatred" that Pozdnyšev and his wife had for one another was that of "accomplices in a crime."

Music, "the most subtle lust of the senses," is the precipitant in a drama that will end with adultery and murder; it breaks down the moral and aesthetic barriers to the adulterous embrace and the murderous dagger thrust—two actions which in Tolstoj's presentation are, psychologically, related.

—Robert Louis Jackson

Pozdnyšev's murder of his wife was a crime of passion in more than one sense of the word. The murder is not simply the result of jealousy; it is the displaced fulfillment of the frustrated sexual impulse. "In court I was asked: why, how did I kill my wife? Fools! They think that I killed her with a dagger on the 5th of October. I didn't kill her then, but much earlier. In exactly the same way that men are all killing their wives now, all all." "But how? (*da cem ze?*)" asks the narrator. Pozdnyšev answers by pointing to the crime of his sexual relations with his wife during her pregnancies. But the allusion to the phallic organ as a kind of murder weapon is unmistakable; it underscores the central notion of Pozdnyšev that sexual intercourse, by the very nature of the animal instincts it arouses, is incompatible with authentic moral relations or spiritual communion.

The concept of the sexual act as a form of murder, or, the other way around, of the dagger thrust as a surrogate sexual act, lies at the core of the crime of Pozdnyšev. The playing of the first presto movement of Beethoven's "Kreutzer Sonata," or, more specifically, the playing of some unnamed "passionate" and "obscenely sensual" piece of music, serves first of all, in Pozdnyšev's view, to break down the moral "barrier" between his wife and her musical partner, Truxacevskij. But what is less apparent, but equally important, is that the same music which broke down this barrier and opened the way (at least in Pozdnyšev's conjecture) for a "swinish" adulterous embrace ("was it not clear that everything was accomplished that evening?") also had a "fearful impact" on Pozdnyšev. This music aroused in him "quite new feelings, so it seemed to me, new possibilities of which I had been hitherto unaware," a strange sense of "joy" in which he saw everything "in quite a different light." Now the motif of "joy" in *The Kreutzer Sonata* is apocalyptic in its content; the word itself is linked persistently with Pozdnyšev's feelings of underground spite, his exultation in his "mad" and murderous feelings, his uncontrolled outbursts of "animal" rage and violence against his wife; and these feel-

ings have their source in his animal jealousy, his frustrated sexual impulses, his "swinishness."

Music, "the most subtle lust of the senses," is the precipitant in a drama that will end with adultery and murder; it breaks down the moral and aesthetic barriers to the adulterous embrace and the murderous dagger thrust—two actions which in Tolstoj's presentation are, psychologically, related.

The Underground Man's madness, as we have noted, in fact ends with an act of psychological and spiritual violence—symbolic murder: he fells Liza, as though with an ax, by his cynical confession. The sequel to this blow—if we disregard the ideologically important but emotionally transient moment of spiritual communication with Liza—is the loveless act of sex. The handing of money—the formal cash nexus defining relations between buyer and seller—is but the Underground Man's final signature to a relationship that for him was almost totally lacking in moral-spiritual foundations. In the case of Pozdnyšev the order of murder and sex is reversed. Animal sex—identified by Pozdnyšev with market relations and with the master-slave relationship—always in his view characterized his relationship with his wife. The real physical murder which brings to a close his tragic bedroom history is a surrogate for the frustrated sexual act—an act which Pozdnyšev perceives, in retrospect at least, as depravity, crime, murder.

5

"Both the author of the notes and the 'Notes' themselves, are, of course, fictitious," Dostoevskij wrote in his preface to *Notes from the Underground*. "Nevertheless, such persons as the author of these memoirs not only may, but even must exist in our society if we take into consideration the circumstances that led in general to the formation of our society. I wanted to bring before our public, more prominently than is usually the case, one of the characters of our recent past. This is the representative of a generation that is still with us." Tolstoj might have prefaced his *Kreutzer Sonata* with the same words. His "Afterword," however, essentially makes the same point. In the character of Pozdnyšev, in many respects as extreme in his outlook and behavior as the Underground Man, Tolstoj sought to present a number of complex and interrelated social, psychological, and cultural phenomena of his class. The polemical focus of *The Kreutzer Sonata*,—sex, marriage, the family—to be sure is removed from the main polemical focus of *Notes from the Underground*—the problems of suffering, freedom, and reason themselves. Yet *The Kreutzer Sonata* recalls *Notes from the Underground* in its structure, its special use of the confessional form and its use of the irrational hero simultaneously to expose and exemplify what in the author's view is a social calamity. Though the problem content of Pozdnyšev has deep roots in Tolstoj's life and art, the frenzied psychology and behavior of this character (though not unprecedented in Tolstoj) seems to owe something to the "underground" of *Notes from the Underground, The Eternal Husband,* as well as *The Meek One.*

Bettina L. Knapp (essay date 1988)

SOURCE: "Tolstoy's *Kreutzer Sonata*: Archetypal Music as a Demonic Force," in her *Music, Archetype, and the Writer: A Jungian View,* Pennsylvania State University Press, 1988, pp. 58-74.

[*In the following essay, Knapp details the archetypal influence of Beethoven's* Kreutzer Sonata *on Tolstoy's novella, especially as it manifests in the narrative's structure and themes and correlates with both Tolstoy's psychological condition and that of his fictional protagonist.*]

Leo Tolstoy drew the title of his short novel ***The Kreutzer Sonata*** (1891) from Beethoven's violin sonata (opus 47), an archetypal musical composition that was instrumental, according to the Russian novelist, in bringing out the animal in man. It affected Tolstoy's protagonist subliminally, *exciting* him to such an extent that he became victimized by a series of inner upheavals of volcanic force, which annihilated in him any semblance of rational behavior, balance, or logic. As Tolstoy's protagonist states:

> Music instantaneously transports me into that mental condition in which he who composed it found himself. I blend my soul with his, and together with him am transported from one mood to another; but why this is so I cannot tell. For instance, he who composed the Kreutzer sonata—Beethoven—he knew why he was in that mood. That mood impelled him to do certain things, and therefore that mood meant something for him, but it means nothing for me. And that is why music excites and does not bring to any conclusion.

Archetypal music in Tolstoy's narrative creates havoc; it unleashes repressed instincts and opens the floodgates to the irrational. Music, therefore, is *demonic.*

To understand more fully Tolstoy's strange approach to music in ***The Kreutzer Sonata*** requires some background information concerning the writer's activities and psychological condition. After putting the final touches to *Anna Karenina* (1877), Tolstoy underwent a traumatic moral and spiritual experience which almost brought him to suicide. Although he seemingly led a happy, healthy, and successful life—he was adulated by his readers for *War and Peace* (1869) and admired for his autobiographical trilogy, ***Childhood*** (1852), ***Boyhood*** (1854), and ***Youth*** (1857), and for ***The Cossacks*** (1863) and many short stories—something was gnawing at him. His marriage in 1862 to Sophia Andreyevna Bers, a well-educated woman half his age who bore him thirteen children, was marred by his infidelities, his views on wifely obligations, and his own paradoxical obsessions with chastity.

Tolstoy rejected carnal love, basing his ideas on Saint Matthew's dicta, which he quoted in ***The Kreutzer Sonata***: "But I say unto you, That whosoever looketh on a woman to lust after her hath committed adultery with her already in his heart" (5:8). In this view, the goal of marriage is to procreate, not to enjoy the fruits of sensual pleasures.

Marriage is a sacred bond. The highest earthly state for a human being is chastity.

> His disciples say unto him, if the case of the man be so with his wife, it is not good to marry.

> But he said unto them, All men cannot receive this saying, save they to whom it is given. (19:10-11)

Existence for Tolstoy at this critical stage of his life seemed devoid of interest, goalless and senseless. What was his life in terms of the infinite? God? Eternity? Tolstoy eventually concluded that religion was the only answer to his search—but not organized religion, as practiced in the Russian Orthodox Church, which he considered dogmatic and hypocritical and not in keeping with the teachings of Christ, and from which he was excommunicated in 1901. Tolstoy contended that human beings were endowed with higher and lower natures and that it is the mind which enables one to choose between good and evil. To follow Christ's message, one must practice good and live out the dictates of the Gospels (especially the Sermon on the Mount). Only by a pragmatic application of Christ's counsel would our earthly condition be improved and joy experienced. Asceticism and the banishing of sensual pleasures were Tolstoy's *way.*

Psychologically, one may say that Tolstoy was puritanical. It has been suggested that he suffered deep guilt feelings—the aftermath of a sexually active youth which continued after his marriage and included relationships with household servants and even fathering a child to one of them. These "excesses" preyed on his mind. He sought to be "clean" and "pure." His puritanical ideals were evidently at odds with his physical nature. In his writings—*Confession* (1879), *A Short Exposition of the Gospels* (1881), *What I Believe In* (1882), *What Then Must We Do* (1886), *The Law of Love and the Law of Violence* (1908), and ***The Kreutzer Sonata***—he attempted to probe his inner world through some of his protagonists. His intention was to discover and examine the motivations of certain acts and relationships. Questioning the power of evil, Tolstoy concluded that one must not resist it. One must obey Christ's commandments: not to grow angry, not to lust, not to bind oneself to oaths or to rebuff a person who is evil ("Resist not him that is evil"), Tolstoy rejected all government and religious institutions based on violence and force. Like Jean-Jacques Rousseau, whose works he had read, he admired the simple peasant, the tiller of the land, the woodcutter—those who understood the real meaning of life. Their exploitation by others caused the poor excoriating suffering; private property encouraged economic disparity. Such evils had to be eradicated. Tolstoy's decision to give his wealth to the needy aroused a bitter marital feud and a permanent break in relations with his wife. His children, save Alexandra, sided with their mother. She and her father, eighty-three years of age at the time, left home. While waiting at the railroad stationmaster's house, he caught a chill and died.

Tolstoy had always been deeply moved by music and seemed to enjoy it as much as he did his early hunting, gymnastics, and women. Throughout his student years at the University of Kazan, in the army when stationed in the Caucasus, during the Crimean War, at the siege of Sevastopol, and throughout his later years, music was one of his deep loves. In **"Sevastopol in May,"** a reportage in which he conveys his antimilitarism, Tolstoy structures various incidents, events, and scenes in sonata form with specific themes, variations, repetitions, restatements, and a coda at the finale.

In 1857, while in Europe, he composed a short story, **"Albert."** Although didactic and moralistic, it focused on something dear to Tolstoy: the fate of a violinist. His protagonist, a sensitive and talented violinist, was given to drink and desperately needed help from others. No one offered it to him because no one understood him. Society was uninterested in the fate of the artist. The feelings and ideals Tolstoy expressed in **"Albert"** were unquestionably noble, but his characters lacked depth and, worse still, he neglected to underscore the violinist's greatness. He did not encourage his readers to *experience* the instrumentalist's music, thereby precluding their taking his virtuosity seriously.

In Tolstoy's tale **"Lucerne"** (1857), we are introduced to another musician—a Tyrolean singer—whose story is based on a real incident. Tolstoy, who happened to be at a Swiss tourist center, noted the following in his diary (July 7, 1857):

> Walked to *privathaus*. On the way back at night—cloudy, with the moon breaking through—heard several marvellous voices. Two bell towers on a wide street. Little man with guitar singing Tyrolean songs—superb. Gave him something and invited him to sing opposite the Schweizerhof. He got nothing and walked away ashamed, the crowd laughing as he went. . . . Caught him up and invited him to the Schweizerhof for a drink. They put us in a separate room. Singer vulgar but pathetic. We drank. The waiter laughed and the doorkeeper sat down. This infuriated me—swore at them and got terribly worked up.

Another moral situation provoked Tolstoy to take pen in hand, but again he neglected to explore the effects of song upon him. Interested more in the tale's story line, he conveyed his annoyance with the wealthy English guests at a Swiss mountain resort who listened to and enjoyed the songs of a most charming Tyrolean singer. They admired his talent and spontaneity, but when, at the finale of the concert, he held out his cap for remuneration, not one gave a farthing. As the singer leaves the hotel, the narrator invites him to return and sip champagne with him. During the course of their conversation, the narrator points out the economic and social injustices to the singer but fails to arouse his anger; instead, he discovers the essential goodness of this country person who accepts life as it is, maintaining his jolly, buoyant, and wholesome outlook.

The Kreutzer Sonata

Tolstoy, who had based his plot on what an actor friend, Andreev-Burlak, had told him about the infidelities of a friend's wife, entitled it at first "Sexual Love." The following year, 1888, when Tolstoy saw Andreev-Burlak and the painter I. E. Repin at a party where Beethoven's *Kreutzer Sonata* was performed, the latter suggested that he write about the effects music had upon him and include these in his tale. The Russian novelist agreed, on the condition that Andreev-Burlak would read it in public and that Repin would paint a canvas based on the story. Tolstoy alone completed his part of the agreement.

Beethoven's opus 47, written for piano and violin (in 1802; published in 1805), and the best-known of his ten sonatas, was dedicated to Rodolphe Kreutzer (1766-1831), a French composer and violinist and professor at the Paris Conservatory. His forty études for violin, unequalled in their genre, must have impressed Beethoven, who wrote in a letter dated October 4, 1804, that he had heard the French violinist perform some of his works.

Tolstoy sought to convey Beethoven's infinite variety of moods, ranging from deep sorrow to rapturous exaltation, in *The Kreutzer Sonata*. It may be suggested that he used the composer's archetypal music to articulate his own emotions, dividing his tale into three parts as Beethoven had divided his violin sonata into three movements: *Adagio sostenuto Presto, Adante con variazoni, Finale (Presto)*.

Adagio sostenuto Presto

Tolstoy's *Kreutzer Sonata* is told by a narrator in the first person, but his function is minimal. He is there only as a sounding board, so that the protagonist, Pozdnyshev, can air his feelings and relate the events that preoccupy him.

The action takes place on a train. Its constant rolling and the physical closeness of those seated in a compartment encourage communication between them. A lawyer, a married woman, and an older man discuss their ideas concerning marriage and love. In addition, another person makes his presence known every now and then by a tic: "strange noises like a cough or like a laugh begun and broken off." This involuntary spasmodic reaction, usually of neurotic origin, interests the reader because it so often hides inner conflicts. While the conversation of the others in the compartment is light and lively, the narrator focuses on the man with the tic, who looks "oppressed by his loneliness." There is something arresting about him and his "extraordinarily brilliant eyes which kept roving from object to object." At times they grow flamelike, as if he were attempting in some way to restrain himself.

Only with the beginning of chapter 3 does the *adagio sostenuto* take on rapidity, leading up to the *presto*—the highly emotional and suspenseful content of the interlude. As the travelers leave the compartment or go to sleep, Pozdnyshev, the man with the tic, comforted by the constant rolling of the train and the closed and protective universe in which he finds himself, begins to withdraw into a past—his inner world. Barriers are shed; Pozdnyshev's psychic energy is mobilized and increases in activity until it reaches *presto* force.

Pozdnyshev tells the narrator that until he got married he lived like a member of the landed aristocracy. A university graduate who enjoyed his dissipated and immoral life, he decided never to get really entangled. The sight of "woman in her nakedness" at the age of sixteen tormented him for days and weeks thereafter. He felt as if he had been *corrupted* and polluted; he also realized that until now he had never known the difference between right and wrong; he had never had to choose, nor had he ever been emotionally troubled. To pursue a life of debauchery could, so the "Priests of Science" had declared, bring on illness. More significant was that he felt like weeping for the loss of his *innocence*; like a drug addict or alcoholic, he knew that the *purity* he had once known would never return, and he was "overwhelmed with horror." Although "soiled with the rottenness of lewdness," he was very fortunate to find a *pure* girl, Lily, to whom he became engaged. When he showed her his diary so that she could learn more about him, her reaction was one of despair and disillusionment. They nevertheless married. He realized that this beautiful fantasy figure would have to change if she were to fulfill her function as wife and future mother. Marriage, he had to admit, is not based exclusively on poetry, love, or morality, but on "proximity," the body—that is, low-cut gowns, hair styles, perfumes, and a woman's wiles. The *anima* in Pozdnyshev was aroused at the sight of Lily's beautiful body.

Pozdnyshev sees the world and himself in terms of extremes: chastity is equated with good; sensuality, with evil. What he does not seem to take into consideration is that good and evil are opposite poles of a moral judgment. To attempt an *imitatio Christi* and try to become all good (all light, all spirit) is to reject the notion of evil and those factors of the human condition which are identified with it.

A split results and tyrannizes Pozdnyshev: the concretization of absolute good and light at odds with Satan or the Antichrist, standing for evil, dark, material, and carnal forces. He was neither alone in his torment nor was it merely symptomatic of a contemporary malaise. The di vestiture of the Godhead's dark side in Christianity paved the way for a similar split in humankind's unconscious, since it projected onto Divinity. A dualistic formula is expressed in 2 Thessalonians: God's earthly or eschatological manifestation in Christ, and Satan's in the Antichrist. The conflict between these two opposing forces became inevitable. In Romans we read: "And the God of peace shall bruise Satan under your feet shortly" (16:20). To resist the Devil is proof of the strength of one's Christian faith (1 Peter 5:9), and of one's intelligence and understanding of Satan's ways: "Lest Satan should get an advantage of us: for we are not ignorant of his devices" (2 Corinthians 2:11). Saint Paul, a firm believer in ascetic practices, was convinced of the positive effects of discipline; it would help an individual evolve and, accordingly, rid him of his demonization: "To open their eyes, and to turn them from darkness to light, and from the power of Satan unto God, that they may receive forgiveness of sins, and inheritance among them which are sanctified by faith that is in me" (Acts 26:18).

To long to be like Christ, however—which is Pozdnyshev's goal—is not only to experience only half of one's nature and to relegate one's earthbound condition to infernal regions; it is also a paradigm of hubris. For the Greeks, hubris was one of the most serious of crimes, if not punishable by death, then by some form of chastisement. The imbalance in Pozdnyshev's attitude has created a dangerous split within his psyche.

Flesh is satanic; it is the "adversary" (the Hebrew meaning of *Satan*); it spreads chaos, doubt, and confusion. Satan's intrusion into Pozdnyshev's world has threatened his well-being—the rational order of things.

To label the *animal* in man as satanic or evil indicates psychologically, a *fear* of the irrational or instinctual domain—that whole unpredictable area within humankind and the universe. To attempt to cut away a person's sexuality is to eliminate his passionate nature, which is basic to him, and simply repress and imprison these instinctual forces in the unconscious. The natural response to imprisonment is rage. Blocked within the psyche, these negative powers become stronger and stronger. Every now and then they break out, uncontrollably and viciously.

Pozdnyshev suffers, he tells the narrator, because he feels women dominate the world in general, and his in particular. It is the woman who decides whether she wants her man or whether he must be kept at a distance. This is due, Pozdnyshev reasons, to the fact that women do not enjoy equal rights with men, and so they seek revenge; and they succeed because they know how to work on what is most vulnerable within man: his passions. They ensnare him in their nets. When a man falls under the influence of a woman's "deviltry," he "grows foolish." Here Pozdnyshev reminisces about his ancestor Adam and blames Eve for his weakness. Pozdnyshev, like countless others, was unable to assume responsibility for his acts. Rather than attempt to view Adam's acquiescence objectively, as an example of his own blindness and misguided ideas, Pozdnyshev looks for a scapegoat upon whom he can pile everything he finds objectionable. Nor does Pozdnyshev ever look upon woman as an individual, evolving being; rather he sees her in a self-serving manner—as an object to be repulsed because of her carnality and as a spreader of venality.

As Pozdnyshev describes the days and months following his marriage, his hostility toward his situation and his wife grows more and more overt. It accelerates, taking on *presto* force, as if he were overwhelmed by an unconscious rage. He regrets having married. His honeymoon was a disaster. Lily was totally unprepared for it all, and, he complains, when he put his arms around her, she burst into tears. Certainly, he must have forgotten the fact that a few days earlier he had given her his diary to read, shocking her to her very foundations. After soothing her, he realized that a "wall of cold venomous hostility" existed within, which was assuaged only when they made love. Thereafter their married life consisted, as do the introductory movements in Beethoven's sonata, in statements and restatements, in quarrels and reconciliations, which came about only after each had experienced complete sexual satisfaction. Nevertheless, beneath this veneer of passionate love, there was hatred between them. It was an "abomination."

Andante con variazoni

Chapters 13 to 19 restate similar situations in *andante* or *moderato* movement—a pace that flows along easily, steadily, with variations on the same theme.

Pozdnyshev gives examples from their conjugal life which rouse his repugnance for what people call love. "Love is something swinish," "shameful and disgusting," he remarks. Nevertheless, he fathered five children, after which the doctors told his wife that another pregnancy would endanger her life. The worst of sins was committed at this point: these men of science taught her how to avoid conception. Women, then, and specifically his wife, would no longer be fulfilling their function. Pozdnyshev grew angry as well as jealous. For her not to be pregnant meant that she would have more time to herself and, worse, that she could devote her time to making herself more beautiful. The more his diatribes took on passion, the more irrational was his reasoning. "You see I am a kind of insane man."

Pozdnyshev's jealousy of his wife grew out of proportion. That she would be able to enjoy the sexual act without being burdened with pregnancies and have time to herself without the constant presence of the children "poisoned" their life together. They were transformed, he added, into "two convicts, fastened to one chain and hating each other, each poisoning the life of the other and striving not to recognize the fact." Only then did he realize, he says, that 99 percent of couples live as if in a vise.

Why had Pozdnyshev's psychosis so increased in dimension? His constant rejection and condemnation of his earthly side made him long for its opposite: an ethereal, spiritual relationship rather than a sexual attraction between himself and his wife. Ideals, however, are incompatible with life and are virtually made to crumble, bringing into play the opposite extreme, which plunges the idealist into the most turbid of mires. Since Pozdnyshev had cut himself off so drastically from his own nature and from life in general, every time he performed the sexual act he was revulsed by his own carnality and by the pleasure which he forever equated with evil.

If, psychologically speaking, instincts are properly understood and accepted as part of the life process, they may act in concert with other factors within a personality and become positive forces. When unattended—or rejected—they crave for what is rightly theirs and thereby may become virulent and destructive. That Pozdnyshev associates his wife with evil—as he does women in general—is an age-old attitude. Woman has from time immemorial been marked with infernal, dark, chthonic, devouring, hostile, and terrifying characteristics. Such beings and supernatural forces as Medea, Gorgon, Hecate,

Cybele, and Eve, as *vagina dentata* types, are described throughout history and in religions as destroyers of man, castrators, "deadly mothers," impure creatures, and instigators of orgies. Symbolically, they have been associated with nature and the material world. Imagistically, their bodies are identified with earth, vessel, and cave, putting them in opposition to the spiritual values inherent in the male. Accordingly, they are considered inferior and damned, representatives of flesh and instinct. Eve is blamed for having seduced Adam and for the Fall. Is it any wonder that Pozdnyshev should share the universal contempt for women?

To vary the tempi and beats of their *andante* life together, with all of its variations on but a single theme—that of sexuality—Pozdnyshev decided that it might be best to move to the city. His wife's health would improve, he reasoned, and indeed it did. She not only grew more and more beautiful but also became increasingly conscious of her attractiveness. She took time out to care for herself, to see that she wore the right clothes and her hair in the right style. Her beauty became "fascinating and disturbing to men," Pozdnyshev remarked. At parties, he was convinced that all the men looked at her with longing. "She was like a well-fed and bridled horse which had not been driven for some time and from which the bridle was taken off. There was no longer any restraint. . . ." A melodic and rhythmic interchange seemed to take place between the two: as his frenzy increased, so she seemed to *awaken* to the world outside of her home and outside of her role as childbearer and mother. She started to live "for the sake of love." Pozdnyshev's speech grew to tempi and diapason as his fantasy world became more and more dynamic, acting, as it were, of its own accord, creating image upon image, freely and actively replicating his own inner phobias.

Pozdnyshev was convinced at this point that his wife was bored with him because she wanted to improve herself. Before her marriage, she had been a fine pianist, and she was now determined to pursue this art form. "That was the beginning of the end," he stated categorically. Just as sexuality undermined his spiritual longings, and so represented a threat to him, so music would also be experienced as a negative entity and as an evil force to be extirpated. Woman is a kind of *Hexe* who arouses him sexually; music is likewise demonic, penetrating as it does both his conscious and unconscious spheres. Like a seductress, it is tantalizing and therefore dangerous.

The more Pozdnyshev focuses on his wife's beauty, the more aroused he becomes. His hysterical symptoms, which are representations of unconscious events, cannot be discharged or expressed, because the contents of his fantasies are incompatible with his conscious outlook. Interiorized energy, diverted into the wrong channels, activates Pozdnyshev's fantasies, which then accrete in potency. Jung writes in this regard: "the patient constructs in his imagination little stories that are very coherent and very logical, but when he has to deal with reality, he is no longer capable of attention or comprehension." Pozdnyshev's fantasies, ideas, notions, and sensations revolve around sexuality for the most part; he relates *everything* in the outer world to the fulfillment of an inner obsession or compulsion. There is no enlightenment or evolution in his monologue. It follows the same theme and variations: those of a man who projects his *shadow*. As defined by Jung, the shadow is an unconscious aspect of the psyche which contains what the ego may consider to be inferior or negative characteristics and which it will not recognize as its own. The consequences of Pozdnyshev's inability to come to terms with his shadow, and the hysteria which results, may be dangerous.

Soon Pozdnyshev mentions a musician friend of his wife—a violinist. Interestingly enough, he cannot recall this man's first name right away, blocking out the very memory of an *evil* force. In time we learn that the violinist, a society man of sorts, was a professional or semi-professional musician. Pozdnyshev's intense jealousy of the man he believes to have been his wife's lover peppers each of his statements. "He had almond-shaped humid eyes, handsome, smiling lips, little waxed mustaches, the latest and most fashionable method of dressing his hair, an insipidly handsome face, such as women call 'not bad,' a slender build, though not ill-shaped, and with a largely developed behind such as they say characterize Hottentot women. This it is said is musical." Although underscoring the violinist's fine points, he makes certain he belittles this rival as well, lumping together both the man and his art as a destructive and evil factor in society.

"Well, this man with his music was the cause of all the trouble," Pozdnyshev said, making him the scapegoat and heaping upon him all the evils of sex and marriage. The violinist was to blame for Pozdnyshev's increasing misunderstandings with his wife. Psychologically speaking, Pozdnyshev was projecting his shadow—thereby casting out of himself onto others all those "despicable" characteristics which, in reality, existed within him. Everything Pozdnyshev associated with evil—the violinist and his art—was lumped together and condemned. Let us recall that in the olden days the collective shadow (the evils of the community) was heaped onto a goat by a priest; the animal was then sent out into the wilderness, and the clan, considered purged of its sins, did not have to face the pain of truth and the effort of resolving tensions and problems. By merely rejecting an unpleasant situation or person, one escapes a conflict that could have salutary effects.

By being projected, Pozdnyshev's shadow remains unconscious, so that he experiences it affectively and with virtually no discernment. Since the tension of opposites is nonexistent, he is now engulfed or *possessed* by his shadow. Having lost whatever capacity he had to differentiate, he can no longer be responsible for his actions. He lives in the darkened realm of his own manufacture, dominated by an ego alienated from reality.

The days, weeks, months pursue their course—as do the variations on the themes of sexuality, hostility, and jealousy. Every time he sees his wife at the piano accompanying the violinist, all blackens before him. He resents

the pleasure she takes in her musical renditions and is convinced that the man with whom she makes this music is a lecher. Something is certainly going on between them, he muses, for when they play together it is "like an electrical shock, calling forth something like a uniformity in the expression of their eyes and their smiles."

When Pozdnyshev narrates what he believes to be the evolution of the relationship between the violinist and his wife, he does so in musical terms, viewing archetypal music as a go-between or bridge that encourages an illicit affair between the two.

> In the evening he came with his fiddle, and they played together. But for a long time the music did not go very well; we had not the pieces that he wanted, and those he had my wife could not play without preparation. I was very fond of music and sympathized with their playing, arranging the music-stand for him and turning over the leaves. They managed to play something—a few songs without words and a sonata by Mozart. He played excellently, and he had to the highest degree what is called "temperament"—moreover, a delicate, noble art, entirely out of keeping with his character.

Pozdnyshev tried to remain calm that evening, pretending to be interested in music, and even encouraging his wife to play on. Inside, however, he was "tortured by jealousy." His fantasies see only "the wild beast existing in them both."

The violinist and his wife continued their musicales, their talents for art linking them powerfully together. On one occasion, after an evening of music, a strange feeling took hold of Pozdnyshev: an urge to kill the violinist on the spot. Exercising control, he makes certain he has successfully buried his urge by inviting him to stay for dinner and treating him to the finest of wines.

Instruments, tones, melodies, and rhythms are all enemies for Pozdnyshev. The performers of music (Pozdnyshev's wife and the violinist) are involved in rites and liturgies which arouse the wrath of a husband dominated by an obsession.

> Two people occupy themselves with the noblest of arts—music; in order to accomplish this a certain proximity is required, and this proximity has nothing reprehensible in it, and only a stupid, jealous husband could find anything undesirable in it. But meantime, all know that precisely by means of these very occupations, especially by music, the largest part of the adultery committed in the ranks of our society is committed.

They were days when their "proximity" caused Pozdnyshev such torment that he could barely converse with his wife. One time, virtually beside himself, he threatened to kill her and began hurling objects at her. She left the room, fully aware that he was no longer "responsible for his madness." Later that evening the usual "sexual" reconciliation took place, and again Pozdnyshev concealed his anger.

Presto

No longer working with developing themes and the difficulties involved in probing, combining, and knitting them together, Tolstoy launches into the *crisis,* which now takes on *presto* force. Emotions break loose, relationships change, human nature emerges in all of its rawness. Beethovian dynamism is released in this Tolstoyan drama—leading to its fulminating conclusion.

Pozdnyshev agrees that a musicale be given at their home. Although he feels ill at ease throughout the dinner, he watches every movement of his wife and the violinist, "their motions and glances," in an attempt to ferret out the least sign that will corroborate his obsessive jealousy. Pozdnyshev recalls every detail of the evening: how the violinist "brought his fiddle, opened the box, took off the covering which had been embroidered for him by some lady, took out the instrument and began to tune it." As for his wife, she acts relaxed and indifferent as she sits down at the grand piano and strikes the "usual *a* which was followed by the pizzicato of the fiddle and the getting into tune." After looking at each other and glancing at the audience, they start to play: "His face grew grave, stern, and sympathetic, and as he bent his head to listen to the sounds he produced, he placed his fingers cautiously on the strings. The piano replied."

An entente certainly exists between them, Pozdnyshev thinks, as he looks at them both with hatred. The violinist, in his eyes, is the living incarnation of the Devil and the instrument of perdition. He works in opposition to God and to Light, Pozdnyshev maintains. He is the Great Tempter, the Adversary, the one who prepares humankind for the Fall. He may also be regarded as a projection of Pozdnyshev's disintegrating mental condition.

It is on this particular night that Pozdnyshev's wife and the violinist play Beethoven's *Kreutzer Sonata.* "Do you know the first *presto*—You know it?" he asks the narrator.

> U!U!U! . . . That sonata is a terrible thing. And especially that movement. And music in general is a terrible thing. I cannot comprehend it. What is music? What docs it do? And why does it have the effect it has? They say music has the effect of elevating the soul—rubbish! falsehood! It has its effect, it has a terrible effect,—I am speaking about its effect on me,—but not at all by elevating the soul. Its effect is neither to elevate nor to degrade, but to excite.

The archetypal music he hears unleashes Pozdnyshev's emotions, working on his nerves, grating and grinding them so that the pain he feels becomes unbearable. The inner tensions arouse the nuclear dynamism of his psyche. For a psychopath such as Pozdnyshev, Beethoven's *Kreutzer Sonata* triggers an explosion of the ego complex, thus putting an end to relatively smooth-running conscious personality. His acts, henceforth, will be predictable. As he is carried away by the flow of libido implicit in Beethoven's music, it is as if he is being pulled by the undertow of an inner ocean.

> Music makes me forget myself, my actual position; it transports me into another state not my natural one; under the influence of music it seems to me that I feel what I don't really really feel, that I understand what I do not really understand, that I can do what I can't do. I explain this by the fact that music acts like gaping or laughing; I am not sleepy but I gape, looking at anyone else who is gaping; I have nothing to laugh at but I laugh when I hear others laugh.

Music holds the power of a drug for Pozdnyshev; it is a spirit, as is alcohol. Let us recall that when Noah began taking care of the vine he became a "man of the ground" and was no longer the "pious one." His elixir caused a disorientation of the senses: "And he drank of the wine, and was drunken; and he was uncovered within his tent" (Gen. 9:21). So, too, was Pozdnyshev uncovered by music; the melody, pitch, timbre, and rhythms encouraged him to disclose his fantasies, which emerged into life, taking on power in the empirical world. But just as wine is identified with drunkenness and ecstasy, and with the orgies and instincts of Dionysian rituals, so is it part of the Christian ceremony with its sacramental offerings (John 15:1-5).

The archetypal music emanating from the violin and piano transport Pozdnyshev into another domain, where, shedding all restraint and losing his identity, he claims that Beethoven had experienced a similar emotional condition when composing his *Kreutzer Sonata.* Pozdnyshev, then, is neither earthbound nor celestially oriented. He is in limbo. Confused and faceless, he is a pawn for any musical power that may entice him.

> Now they play a military march; the soldiers move forward under its strains, and the music accomplishes something; they play dance music and I dance, and the music accomplishes something; they perform a mass, I take the sacrament, again the music accomplishes its purpose. But in other cases there is only excitement, and it is impossible to tell what to do in this state of mind. And that is why music is so terrible, why it sometimes has such an awful effect.

Music "hypnotizes," he concedes. Like Mesmer's "animal fluid" that influences celestial bodies as well as earth beings, archetypal music is a force capable of communicating impressions and energizing the psyche. So powerful a force was Beethoven's *Kreutzer Sonata* that it took precedence over all else, and in the process it obliterated *logos.* Identifying archetypal music with the Devil, Pozdnyshev sees it as a metaphor for lovemaking, with its ultimate culmination in the orgasm.

How could anyone play the *Kreutzer Sonata*—this first *presto*—he questions, in a drawing room before ladies dressed in *décolltés*?

> To play that *presto* and then to applaud it, and then to eat ices and talk over the last bit of scandal? These things should be played only in certain grave, significant conditions, and only then when certain deeds corresponding to such music are to be accomplished:

first play the music and perform that which this music was composed for. But to call forth an energy which is not consonant with the place or the time, and an impulse which does not manifest itself in anything, cannot fail to have a baneful effect. On me, at least, it had a horrible effect. It seemed to me that entirely new impulses, new possibilities, were revealed to me in myself, such as I had never dreamed of before.

Pozdnyshev was terrified by what he felt: something so unusual, so traumatic, that it seemed to "be whispered into my soul." He did not know what was happening to him. "This new state of mind" did feel delightful. Everything seemed to be altered now that music had penetrated his being. "After the *allegro* they played the beautiful but rather commonplace and far from original *andante,* with the cheap variations and the weak *finale.*" A strange happiness flooded Pozdnyshev that evening—a feeling he attributed to the altered state of consciousness he had experienced listening to Beethoven's work.

Two days later, when Pozdnyshev had to go away on business, he was assured by his wife that she would not see the violinist during his absence. When she wrote to him and told him that the violinist had come to return some music, the "fatal step" had been taken. Pozdnyshev's fantasies about her love affair with the violinist gained full sway over his rationality. He returned to Moscow. During his long train ride home, visions of his wife kissing her lover and his own suffering were so intense that there were times when he wanted to throw himself on the tracks. "The one thing that prevented me from doing so was my self-pity which was the immediate source of my hatred for her." When Pozdnyshev arrived home in the morning, his anxiety had reached unparalleled proportions. The children were still asleep when he entered his house. He heard noises in the dining room, and when he pushed the door open, his wife and the violinist wore an expression of "despairing horror," which then turned into one of "annoyance," as if he were interrupting their pleasure. Just as love has its sensual side, so rage has its inner pulsion toward violence.

> I threw myself on her, still concealing the dagger in order that he might prevent me from striking her in the side under the breast. I had chosen the spot at the very beginning. The instant I threw myself on her he saw my design, and with an action which I never expected from him, he seized me by the arm.

To touch her even in this manner was repulsive to Pozdnyshev; it "still further inflamed" his anger, and he "exulted in it." Withdrawing his arm, he strikes his wife in the face with his elbow as hard as he can. At the height of this paroxysmal moment, she confesses her innocence. Pozdnyshev, in his madness, concludes just the opposite, convinced more than ever that his worst fears has been realized. The *crescendo* has reached its climax. "Madness also has its laws," Pozdnyshev remarks.

Rage overwhelms him. He seizes his wife by the throat and strangles her. The violinist turns white, and without uttering a word, "slipped under the piano and darted out the door." As Pozdnyshev's wife attempts to tear herself free, he "struck her with the dagger into the side under the ribs." That he recalled every detail of his act is not unusual for a psychotic.

Before his wife dies, Pozdnyshev begs her to forgive him. But she is by this time delirious, and her hatred seems to cascade forth. Pozdnyshev is taken to prison, where he spends eleven months awaiting trial. Only when he sees his wife's coffin does he realize the extent of his crime: "the terrible consciousness that I was killing and had killed a woman—a defenseless woman—my wife." He even remembers that right after plunging the dagger into her "I immediately withdrew it, with the desire to remedy what I had done and to put a stop to it."

That his protagonist reflected many of Tolstoy's thoughts and ideals is clearly evident in the "Afterword" of *The Kreutzer Sonata,* written a year later (1890). In it, he castigates doctors for spreading false rumors: that sexual relations are good for the health, that conjugal infidelity is common because relations between men and women are regarded as pleasurable ("something poetic and elevated, and a blessing to life"), that birth control allows women to enjoy sexual union without giving birth. Such aims are unworthy of mankind, although considered by some to be life's supreme goal. Chastity is the ideal: it was Christ's ideal. Tolstoy wrote: "the establishment of the kingdom of God on earth; an ideal already foretold by the prophets who spoke of a time when all men shall be taught of God, and shall beat their plowshares and their spears into pruning-hooks; when the lions shall lie down with the lambs, and all beings shall be united by love."

Morality for Tolstoy and his protagonist was looked upon as an end unto itself. As such it was a codification of life, an ossification of the human personality, and therefore it was easily turned into an evil, as in Pozdnyshev's case— perhaps even in Tolstoy's. The great Russian writer became the butt of ridicule. Concerning *The Kreutzer Sonata,* his wife noted in her diary (March 6, 1891):

> At tea we talked about . . . the vegetarianism which Lyova advocates. He said he saw a vegetarian menu in a German paper which was composed of bread and almonds. I expect the person who wrote the menu practises vegetarianism as much as the author of *The Kreutzer Sonata* practices chastity.

In December 1890 she wrote in her diary of her fear of becoming pregnant, "for everybody will hear of the disgrace and jubilantly repeat the recent Moscow joke: 'Voilà le véritable postscriptum de la Sonate de Kreutzer.'"

That Tolstoy was tyrannized or possessed by an idea or ideal indicates that he and his hero were under the spell of a powerful complex—"a splinter psyche"—or a split-off. When the shadow remains unconscious and is not integrated into the total psyche, some of its unacceptable qualities may become autonomous and go their own way. Such was Pozdnyshev's situation and, to a lesser degree,

Tolstoy's. The latter's once relatively harmonious psyche had become fragmented and split into various complexes. Each miniature complex developed a strange fantasy life of its own, assuming abnormal proportions. In Pozdnyshev's and Tolstoy's cases, fantasies may be regarded as *toxins,* because not only do they not fit into their conscious patternings but they resist all attempts on the part of the will to cope with them.

Tolstoy and Pozdnyshev were so deeply entrenched in their ideals and their ideologies that they lost contact with the world of reality and instead lived in the abyss of their own minds. There they abandoned themselves to torrents of thoughts, energized still further by Beethoven's archetypal *Kreutzer Sonata.* It was a one-way trajectory for both Tolstoy and his hero; like geologists, they burrowed deeply within their psyche, coming face to face with the raw matter that lay buried in their own rich substance. Neither was redeemed!

John M. Kopper (essay date 1989)

SOURCE: "Tolstoy and the Narrative of Sex: A Reading of 'Father Sergius,' 'The Devil,' and 'The Kreutzer Sonata,'" in *In the Shade of the Giant: Essays on Tolstoy,* edited by Hugh McLean, University of California Press, 1989, pp. 158-86.

[*In the excerpt below, Kopper concentrates on various aspects of sexuality in Tolstoy's late short fiction, emphasizing the consequences of the writer's narrative strategies for the historical development of narrative literature.*]

Like their confrères in France twenty years before, the generation of Russian writers who began their careers around midcentury—Turgenev, Goncharov, Tolstoy, and Pisemsky—found a stubborn problem of narrative lying across their path. The enterprise that they collectively pursued demanded the bodying forth of a fluid social world, filled with the motions of decay and resurgence, mobility and disruption. Railroads made travel easier and extended the possibilities of economic and social commerce both within the country and abroad. Capitalism was focusing the economic life of nations more and more in urban areas, and writers had to record not only the new importance of cities but the functions of new classes dwelling in those cities. Though change in nineteenth-century Russia moved at a slower pace than in Western Europe, her writers did begin to describe this new geographical and social mobility, the evolution of the class hierarchy, and the gradual redistribution of power. In the preceding decades Gogol in "The Overcoat" and Dostoevsky in *Poor Folk,* delving as low into the class structure as their European contemporaries Eugène Sue and Charles Dickens had done, defined the aspirations to bourgeois respectability of Russia's clerical proletariat. In *A Hunter's Notes,* Turgenev crowned the bottom man on the social ladder, the serf, as worthy and ready to bear the weight of serious fictional discourse.

These literary achievements were followed by two events which would quickly put Russia on a par with Europe in terms of political instability and social malaise. First, the Crimean War of 1853-1856 began a moral erosion of the autocracy that no ruler till Stalin absolutely succeeded in reversing. Shortly afterward followed the emancipation of the serfs, which threatened the wealthier classes, for the first time since Pugachev, with the existence of a majority of poor, who if not capable of a jacquerie could at least bankrupt the landowning class. Thus Russia experienced its French Revolution and its Revolution of 1848, though in considerably watered-down versions.

But in recording recent social changes, writers confronted a narrative paradox: an event can only be seen as an intelligible change in the given scene, and change can only be registered if it takes place against a (relatively) stable background. The Renaissance code of kingship in force at Elsinore helps make the dynastic and familial struggles that occur there distinguishable actions. Laurence Sterne's traveler can make an eventful "sentimental journey" across a landscape of social immutability. In the nineteenth century, writers, describing a world that was defined by change, were compelled to find a new reference point against which the motion of both hero and society could be measured.

One solution, available in an age when social transformation was still felt to be a novelty, was to make an event out of the conflict between a semantic field consisting of the old and inflexible and an impinging semantic field of the new and fluid. In Regency England, Jane Austen discovered this solution and applied it in many of her novels. Mary and Henry Crawford in *Mansfield Park* are infected and infecting foreign substances who invade the sanctity and torpor of English country living like germs attacking a host. Their entry into and expulsion from the aristocratic universe of the Bertrams can be seen as events. Forty years later, Russian writers would hit upon the same formula. Turgenev, Goncharov, and Pisemsky seem consciously to dramatize in their works the search for forces of flux and instability: there is a Rudin for every Pigasov, an Andrei Stolz for every Ilya Oblomov, a Kalinovich for every Flegont Godnev. In each case the agent for change transgresses a field of inertia. His very restlessness in a stagnant culture constitutes an event.

Writers found a second solution in the stratification of rates of change within the plot. As Yury Lotman has pointed out, in *War and Peace* Nikolai Rostov does not undergo the same extensive metamorphosis of person as do Prince Andrei and Pierre Bezukhov. Despite his geographic mobility, his participation in great historical events, and his evolving of a sense of family responsibility, Nikolai appears to be the unchanging member of the novel's trio of male heroes. Against him the development of the other two characters appears in bold relief. Making Nikolai a background figure entails selecting paradigms of progress (spiritual, political) according to which Nikolai will appear fixed and opposing them to others (geographical, social) that grant him mobility. The result, in Tolstoy, is a character who transverses many semantic fields but who, relative to some characters, appears fixed. Hence the usual conviction of a reader of *War and Peace* that Nikolai changes, but—crudely put—Pierre and Prince Andrei change "more."

A third solution depended very much on the reading conventions we associate with realist writing. First, plots tended to proliferate within the text. One has only to compare *Anna Karenina* with *Dead Souls* to see how dense the weave of the fictional universe had become. At the same time, narrative passed increasingly under the influence of a voice marked by its stability, articulateness, erudition, intelligence, and profound seriousness. The novels of Tolstoy record this change, as will any novel of Turgenev's, weighed against *A Hero of Our Time* and *Evgeny Onegin*; Balzac against Stendhal; or Eliot, and Dickens after 1850, with the Dickens of the late 1830s and early 1840s. The multiplication of plots led to a pretense of fictional universality, to a saturation of the narrative medium and the seeming exhaustion of its resources in every conceivable way. Narrative fiction presented a world in which every action, however cryptic and apparently unmotivated on emergence, could be recovered, traced, and described and thus be perceived as determined. Furthermore, the narrative voice became the voice of legitimacy and reconciliation in a world of indeterminate values and shifting claims to authority. By encompassing an overwhelming heterogeneity of material, the narrative came to represent a homogeneous vessel, the solid jar within which the stormy dramas of alteration and experiences of alterity could be contained. Thus nineteenth-century narrative on the one hand came to illuminate its own projected world with the light of textual determinism, and on the other hand itself became the symbol for the authoritative reconciliation of diversity. It thereby organized two new static fields against which its action could take place. The universality of its determinism and the uniformity of its narrative voice both helped to create the stability needed to describe a world in constant erosion.

This constellation of newly found narrative strategies accounts for a brief but significant moment in the history of nineteenth-century European fiction. It can be found operating in most of Dickens's and Eliot's novels and with surprisingly little qualification fits Thackeray as well. In France, it describes Balzac; and in Russia, Turgenev, Goncharov, Pisemsky, and Tolstoy up to the time of his religious crisis. For them, a narrative that can embrace everything cannot be surprised. Moreover, since it accounts for everything it narrates, its goal is to remove surprise. Finally, its reassuringly stable narrative point of view cannot *give* surprise.

Dissatisfaction and impatience with the conventions of this moment—the moment that has worn the protean label "realist" with least challenge from the critics—permeates the work of the American writers of the period and causes the curious cleavage through the middle of Flaubert's oeuvre. In Dostoevsky's novels it is reflected preeminently in the lapse of a consistently maintained narrative focus; the "gratuitous," random action; the re-

placement of action with dialogue, which is not necessarily eventful or event-producing; and the retreat of the narrative into micro-societies: the family, the political group, the individual. Dostoevsky gives such prominence to these in the organization of value hierarchies that the stable ground of larger social units fades from sight.

Tolstoy, though he reacted just as strongly as Dostoevsky to the inherited canons of writing, took his fiction down another road. In three works of the 1880s and 1890s, *The Kreutzer Sonata* (published in 1889), **"The Devil"** (written in 1889 and published posthumously), and *Father Sergius* (completed in 1898 and published posthumously), Tolstoy tries to redefine the idea of "event." These stories are often gathered up in one critical net. Grouped together for their merciless indictment of relations between women and men, they are taken to be the collective outcome of a meditation on chastity that Tolstoy began in the mid-1880s. In fact the three stories should be judged as much for their typically Tolstoyan— and equally merciless—scrutiny of narrative.

To produce the absorbent wall which would first set off, then finally blunt, the dissonances of storytelling, the author relies neither on the stability of a sententious narrator nor on the intricate density of plot connections. In fact he compounds his initial difficulty. All prose writers of the time faced the problem of establishing a notion of event in a milieu in which not only the hero but the society itself was mobile, but Tolstoy sets himself the task of describing an event in a society so permissive that it has few norms to be violated.

His conception of the permissive society has its roots in earlier works. In *War and Peace* Tolstoy appears, if not to embrace the social order, at least to identify healthy elements within it. The society of Tolstoy's construction is itself under too great a threat during the war episodes of the novel for it ever to acquire sinister force in peacetime. In *Anna Karenina*, however—the novel that only escapes to war near its conclusion, with Vronsky's departure for the Turkish war—the question of whether to belong to social groups becomes paramount. Nor does it appear that Tolstoy finds much of his culture worth participating in. Town life is rejected, and country life, unlike its manifestation in *War and Peace*, becomes in large measure the appendix of municipal cultures. Zemstvos form a rural bureaucracy that apes the St. Petersburg ministries. A city dandy like Veslovsky intrudes into the country. On Vronsky's estate, Anna and Vronsky, with their Anglophile fads, are a terrifying tableau of unsuccessful flight. It would seem that here the rural idyll of Tolstoy—perhaps in spite of the author's wish to make it otherwise—is itself a fiction; Levin must resist the fact that country estates have become moral suburbs of city life.

It is from the isolation of Anna and Vronsky that Tolstoy begins in his late stories. He has paradoxically found culture so corrupt as to be of little interest, so incapable of respect that it cannot resist, refract, or mirror the hero's ethical positions in any meaningful way. Each of the three stories is built upon a society's collective failure to understand that anything of significance is happening. Thus Tolstoy applies to fiction-making the complications inherent in a Karamazovian universe, where "all is permitted." Tolstoy's three heroes must first define what event is, and each is constrained to find a private solution, since his culture does not provide a distinct moral field within which to operate. By describing permissive societies Tolstoy infinitely stretches the elastic domain of value networks in his stories and jeopardizes the very idea of event. When the hero seems to move toward a frontier, the moral horizon retreats, leaving him still helpless to define his event. Of the three stories, only *Father Sergius* records any violation of the social code before the denouement. At the very beginning of the story, Kasatsky astonishes St. Petersburg's beau monde by taking holy orders. But the narrator quickly moves to redefine this surprise and shifts the story's focus to Kasatsky's "inner motives." By the end of its first section, the story successfully resolves the enigma of Kasatsky's renunciation, as if Tolstoy were deliberately writing "through" a conventional plot to see what lay beyond.

More remarkable is the fact that the societies of the stories so quickly forgive the heroes' most violent behavior. In both of the endings that Tolstoy wrote for **"The Devil,"** Irtenev's suicide and his murder of Stepanida are alike ascribed to his being "mentally ill." In *The Kreutzer Sonata,* Pozdnyshev kills his wife and is acquitted as a "deceived husband" for defending "his besmirched honor." In *Father Sergius,* Kasatsky cuts off his finger to save himself from a sexual fall, but the notoriety of his action only moves him more rapidly along the road to elder-hood. His action is ironic for being a cliché of hagiography. Thus even his holy exploit becomes a conventional step. Like Irtenev and Pozdnyshev, Kasatsky finds himself in a world in which he has immense difficulty violating the norms of behavior.

In these three stories, as in many of his late works, including *The Death of Ivan Ilyich* and *Hadji Murad,* Tolstoy uses a conventional notion of event as a narrative threshold. Part of Tolstoy's solution to the problem of defining event, therefore, is to transgress the reigning codes of narrative and make violation of the notion of event itself eventful. . . .

Pozdnyshev, the protagonist of *Kreutzer Sonata,* finds that every aspect of his married life revolts him. Repugnance suggests standards, and their violation would produce events. But in fact Pozdnyshev repeatedly emphasizes the absolute ordinariness of his particular marital experience. By marrying, he has located himself within a certain code of behavior that permits what he only later will conclude to be impermissible: jealousy, sex, and deceit. Thus Tolstoy has his characters choose certain isolated micro-cultures: the monastery (Kasatsky), marriage (Irtenev and Pozdnyshev), and rural life (Irtenev), but then traces the heroes' gradual recognition that these subworlds, like Leibniz's monads, in fact reduplicate the codes of a larger universe, a society of wide-ranging

permissiveness. The characters in search of an ethical landfall remain on open seas.

Tolstoy's formulation of the ethical dilemma is romantic in conception and antiromantic in conclusion. The Tolstoy subject is in fundamental conflict with a social totality and employs various strategies for removing himself from the diseased context. But precisely what the subject demands for his world is a code of discipline. In his fancied isolation, he seeks to create the law which his culture has failed to furnish. In all three stories, the protagonist ends by replacing a potential act of at most venial gravity—in "The Devil," sex with Stepanida; in *Father Sergius,* sex with Makovkina; and in *The Kreutzer Sonata,* flirting with Trukhachevsky—with murder, suicide, and dismemberment. Of the original sexual impetus only its violent component survives. Tolstoy's stories have traversed a great distance from Karamzin's "The Island of Bornholm," where the isolation of the island's microculture does *not* prove illusory and the sexual act, in opposition to its place in Tolstoy's stories, is perceived as criminal by both the social commonality and the outcast group.

The discussion has not yet acknowledged the specific forces that Tolstoy attached to his chosen topic, sex. To understand the centrality of sex to his sense of self and to his attitude toward art, one can look to the various media through which Tolstoy expressed himself, such as published conversations and his polemical works. And above all one can trace the arc plotted by his fiction over a fifty-year period. Sex and writing were closely linked for Tolstoy, because sex is preeminently a form of passion, and Tolstoy, with increasing Platonic fervor, came to believe that art aroused the passions. The remainder of this essay, however, will concentrate on sexuality not as a moral, philosophical, or biographical problem but as a semantic field possessing specific laws. In *Father Sergius, The Kreutzer Sonata,* and **"The Devil,"** the lead character puts himself in a position in which sex becomes a significant issue and therefore can be eventful. In order to move his characters onto a potentially charged narrative ground, Tolstoy finds a literary correlative for their moral impasse, a narrative where the issue is not the predicaments of plot but the difficulty of *generating* plot predicaments. His solution lies with male sexuality.

As *Anna Karenina* begins by destroying the happy families left at the end of *War and Peace,* so in the 1880s and 1890s Tolstoy seems to begin with the end of *Anna Karenina.* Sexual passion, a potential source of criminality hitherto assigned to female heroines—Natasha Rostova and Anna Karenina—now spreads to the male world. In **"The Devil,"** *The Kreutzer Sonata,* and *Father Sergius,* Tolstoy inspects the sexual component of male identity as if it were something new. Vronsky's sexual values hardly matter; he is faithful to Anna, and his earlier affairs are overlooked by his society and by the narrator who relates them. Levin's premarital liaisons, to his astonishment, shock and anger Kitty, but the problem remains Kitty's, and it is Kitty who must change, not Levin. In both *War and Peace* and *Anna Karenina,* male characters who violate the sexual codes of the society as a whole are not heroes (Dolokhov, for example). Male heroes at most run against the private standards of their loved ones.

In the eyes of the culture within which Tolstoy's male characters must function, there is little they can do that is absolutely wrong. It is extremely difficult for the hero to change position with respect to his moral environment. Levin, for example, faces a conflict between the religious standard of sexual behavior, established by the church and embraced by Kitty, and the highest practical ideal of his society, which endorses matrimonial fidelity but permits men to have premarital affairs with lower-class women. The religious ideal he must reach is *beyond* reach because he must restore his virginity to obtain it. However much Levin defers to his wife's prescripts for behavior, there is nothing he can do to alter his fallen condition and therefore no change or struggle toward change to narrate. The only taboo that his class at large would recognize is the stricture against his having affairs with women of noble birth who have never married. This line seems so fixed to Tolstoy that he rarely brings a character to cross it. Even the debauched Anatole Kuragin in *War and Peace* contemplates polygamy rather than think of running off with Natasha Rostova without marrying her.

What he perceives to be an asymmetrical relation between the sexes provides Tolstoy, from *Anna Karenina* onward, with an important field in which to explore these narrative issues. That which remains a subsidiary matter in *Anna Karenina* (the disparate receptions given Vronsky and Anna by Petersburg society while they are having their affair) becomes a central concern in some of the stories of the 1880s and 1890s: the sexuality of a man has little inherent plot interest. Because his chastity is not valued, it is more difficult for a man to create a sexual field with a distinct "here" (approved conduct) and "there" (reprehensible conduct). A woman's threatened chastity, on the other hand, will always provide the stuff of narration. . . .

In *The Kreutzer Sonata* we see Tolstoy's most radical experiment with narrative. Pozdnyshev plays a frustrated author, as it were, trying to bring his heroine to fall. Tolstoy thus correctly identifies the potential narrative interest of the threatened yet faithful woman, but also manifests his interest in evading this traditional plot. By firmly, irrationally insisting that his wife has transgressed, that she is "there" when we know her to be "here," Pozdnyshev creates the narrative. Instead of the story being about something that has happened, it is about the effort to make something from nothing, that is, about fiction-making. The irony of the story is that Pozdnyshev's wife resists participating, and Pozdnyshev must replace her inertness with his own activity. Pozdnyshev substitutes a traditional plot, the exposure of a woman's body (realized in his typically Tolstoyan obsession with low-cut gowns and with male doctors examining a nude female patient) with his own discourse, the self-exposure of confession.

This is not to say that Tolstoy's characters intend such replacements but, rather, that they perform them. Indeed, once they have created a context of potential eventfulness, his characters struggle with all their might to forestall situations in which they would have to act. The construction of barriers and their subsequent avoidance are both actions that acquire eventful force and help to constitute the story.

From here a discussion of Tolstoy's stories forks. One can look in greater detail at the replacements that the characters effect, not in their unwilled pursuit of a narrative, but in their conscious choice to avoid transgression, that is, to contain or circumvent the diffuse energies of sex. Or one can inspect the characters' actions as performance, with a view to discovering the ways their behavior dramatizes the undramatic material in the stories. We will follow both paths a little distance, knowing that farther away they will inevitably meet. What especially intrigued Tolstoy the writer about sex was that it was in two senses public. First, it was a form of commerce, a transaction that involved the potentially promiscuous possession and rejection of an ever-replaceable object of desire. And because it could be performed with a succession of people, it led, in his world of writing, to a thematic of circulation. Second, sex was public because it was performed not only with someone but before someone.

To turn first to the operations of substitution and exchange: in all three stories the protagonists alter the venue of their activities in order to defuse a sexual crisis. Irtenev journeys to the Crimea with his wife. Kasatsky enters a monastery, then changes monasteries, isolates himself in a hut, and finally takes to the road. Pozdnyshev and his wife busy themselves with the transit from city to country and back again. . . .

Pozdnyshev differs from the other two heroes, in good measure because of the autobiographical form of **The Kreutzer Sonata.** There is a schism between Pozdnyshev's narrating and narrated selves. The married, jealous Pozdnyshev reflects little; it is Pozdnyshev the narrator who is responsible for the long philippics against women, sex, marriage, and children. Thus Pozdnyshev comes to use language to replace his miserable experience. As unstoppable commentary, the narration flows over and surrounds the unhappy event of his marriage, reducing it, managing it, substituting for it a didactic and generalizing discourse. But just as Kasatsky fixed and institutionalized the experience of chastity through his choice of profession, so Pozdnyshev does not dissipate, but prolongs, his passion by describing it. The emotions of his marriage appear redivivi for recirculation in his discourse. The acts of containment that the protagonists of these stories prefer—economy, career choice, and language—simply provide alternate routes for the migration of sexuality.

Confession is also used to displace sex, and just as unsuccessfully. Irtenev speaks to his uncle, Kasatsky to a novice and then to Praskovya Mikhailovna, his cousin. Pozdnyshev addresses the train audience. (Pozdnyshev's face is never distinctly visible to his interlocutors, since he delivers his tirade at night. This darkness is also suggestive of the confessional.) . . .

The idea of confession provides a transition to the second object of Tolstoy's interest in sex: its performative aspect. Sex is not only a form of commerce but a kind of theater. Similarly, while the confession substitutes for sex, it is also like it in being an exposure of self to another. Tolstoy suggests that in the moment of revelation the self divides, becoming simultaneously a perceiving and a perceived self. In all three stories involving sex/confession, one would expect to find this schism within the "actor" self. . . .

Pozdnyshev's schizophrenia lies in the autobiographical split discussed above. Tolstoy makes explicit reference to the theater of schizophrenia by having the protagonist echo his most famous ancestor in the line of jealous spouses, Othello. . . .

> I am that Pozdnyshev, who was involved in that critical episode.

Or, as Shakespeare has it, "That's he that was Othello. Here I am" (*Othello,* Act 5, scene 2, line 284).

All three stories thus chronicle the avoidance of event through a series of displacements. They also describe a fissure of the self induced by sex, a split which cannot be escaped through the strategies of displacement but is in fact reconstituted through them. The very titles of the three stories reflect displacements: desire is caused by music, the careerist is a holy father, woman is the devil.

In harmony with his emphasis on the theatricality of sex, Tolstoy assigns a certain dramatic rhetoric to each of his stories. These lend artistic unity to the works and deserve detailed treatment, but here can only be mentioned briefly. *The Kreutzer Sonata* is obviously built on the spoken word. **"The Devil"** borrows from another aspect of the theater: its visuality. The story is permeated with references to the glance, to gazes, to darkness and day, to what can and cannot be hidden from view, to Irtenev's shortsightedness and propensity for losing his glasses (that is, his vision), especially during his encounters with Stepanida. *Father Sergius* reenacts the fluctuations of dramatic time: intense, pivotal scenes of short duration are narrated in elaborate detail, so that the time of storytelling approximates, as it does on the stage, the duration of the action. These moments are punctuated by frequent summaries that span enormous lapses of time.

The rhythms of sight, speech, and time unify the stories, but also remind one of the ever-present sexual theme, since each serves to answer a question for the hero: how can the sexual crisis be done away with? Irtenev avoids the gaze of others; Pozdnyshev incorporates his crisis into language; Kasatsky hopes that with the passage of time his sexual humiliation will be forgotten, for others will not survive to remember. . . .

If there is an aspect of sex that unites the two features that drew Tolstoy's attention—commerce and performance, exchange and theatricality—it would be repetition. Tolstoy's stories emphasize the fact that desire has the rhythm of repetition; it comes, goes, and returns, and the condition of its departure is always the same sexual act. Sexual desire is like the repetition, night after night, of a stage performance, and simultaneously like the repetitive uses to which money or words are put. The substitutions initiated by characters, and by the narrative, are all essays in repetition, and the stories are founded on this principle. Kasatsky repeats his military career as a monk. He has merely substituted the clerical hierarchy for a lay one and progresses through the churchly *tabula rangov* as quickly as he would have moved up a worldly ladder. He also duplicates a woman's body with his own. He seeks in the repetitiousness of ritual an escape from sex. Finally, his moment of temptation with Makovkina repeats in his episode with Marya, and he repeats his search for an axe. Pozdnyshev repeats his sexual misfortunes through storytelling; even the milieu is repeated. Pozdnyshev recounts to fellow train travelers the anguish he felt on his own train trip back to surprise his wife. His sense of isolation and lack of a sympathetic audience are repeated in the train ride of the story's outer frame. Pozdnyshev's audience is soon reduced to the narrator, who offers little comment on the tale he hears. Irtenev three times is on the verge of renewing his affair with Stepanida, and it is his failure each time to do so that allows the possibility of the incident repeating. Furthermore, each story underscores the repetitiveness of human life and the succession of generations. Kasatsky looks on the tsar as his father and tries to emulate him. Irtenev wants to manage the estate as his grandfather did, be as careful with his sexual activities as were both his grandfather and his father, and reproduce himself in a family (in fact his family repeats; he has two children by two women). Of all Tolstoy's characters, Pozdnyshev is concerned most with the reproductive side of sex; his speeches on bearing and raising children take up nearly half his discourse. Pozdnyshev's chief aversion to childbearing is that the repetition of a human being reminds him that the sexual act will be repeated by new generations. Tolstoy's three stories await a reading as essays on patriarchy and repetition.

To conclude, in *Father Sergius, The Kreutzer Sonata,* and **"The Devil"** Tolstoy takes a narrative situation that presents a rather infertile semiological field. What can be said about a man's sexuality when the man can do what he wants? The author makes each story into an experimental answer to his narrative dilemma. In each, first, the central characters struggle to erect moral barriers that they can then knock down. That is, they attempt to create the condition for narrative. Second, the heroes try to *avoid* knocking down the barriers of their own making, through an elaborate strategy of replacements and containments. And, third, the story itself comes to include and reduplicate many of the aspects of the sexual act which so disgusts the protagonists. It produces rituals of self-exposure and makes repetition a founding principle of the narrative.

These three "actions" become Tolstoy's subject in *Father Sergius, The Kreutzer Sonata,* and **"The Devil."** In a sense he has made narrative out of (1) the effort to make narrative, (2) the actions carried out in an effort to avoid action, and (3) the narrative's mimesis of the taboo subject. The consequences of these moves are radical enough to shake the foundations of storytelling. Tolstoy left **"The Devil"** unfinished; like a Nabokovian plot, it has a dual ending. *The Kreutzer Sonata* borrows from the literature of confession, but the protagonist is indistinctly seen, and his audience leaves; revelation has become isolation and mystery. *Father Sergius* models itself on many of the conventions of the *zhitie,* but at the moment Kasatsky has sex the genre is abandoned, and the holy father's bodily disappearance from the monastery becomes a travesty of the Resurrection and the Assumption. All three stories refuse a traditional closure and define a narrative space as fresh and interesting as the sexual politics that permits it is morbidly narrow.

FURTHER READING

Biography

Nazaroff, Alexander I. "Two Crusades." In *Tolstoy, The Inconstant Genius: A Biography,* pp. 262-83. London: George G. Harrap & Company, Ltd., 1930.

> Reads *The Kreutzer Sonata* in the context of Tolstoy's life.

Simmons, Ernest J. "'Leave Thy Wife and Follow Me.'" In *Leo Tolstoy,* pp. 427-46. Boston: Little, Brown and Company, 1946.

> Relates the genesis and themes of *The Kreutzer Sonata* to events in Tolstoy's life and thought.

Wilson, A. N. "*The Kreutzer Sonata.*" In *Tolstoy,* pp. 371-92. London: Hamish Hamilton, 1988.

> Situates *The Kreutzer Sonata* in autobiographical and cultural contexts, exposing contradictions and paradoxes in Tolstoy's life and his story.

Criticism

Baehr, Stephen. "Art and *The Kreutzer Sonata*: A Tolstoian Approach." *Canadian-American Slavic Studies* 10, No. 1 (Spring 1976): 39-46.

> Explores the "many parallels" between the novella and Tolstoy's essay *What Is Art?*

Cain, T. G. S. "The Fruits of Conversion," In *Tolstoy,* pp. 137-64. New York: Barnes and Noble Books, 1977.

> Relates the monologue form of *The Kreutzer Sonata* to its sexual and musical themes, and to the narrative's "lack of artistic balance."

Coetzee, J. M. "Confession and Double Thoughts: Tolstoy, Rousseau, Dostoevsky." *Comparative Literature* 37, No. 3 (Summer 1985): 193-232.

> Examines *The Kreutzer Sonata* in terms of the conventions of confessional fiction, showing how Tolstoy confronts the question of "truth about the self" and how the story closes as "the secular equivalent of absolution."

Gustafson, Richard F. "States of Intoxication." In *Leo Tolstoy: Resident and Stranger: A Study in Fiction and Theology,* pp. 340-54. Princeton: Princeton University Press, 1986.

> Includes an analysis of Pozdnyshev's "state of chronic intoxication" in the context of *The Kreutzer Sonata*'s plot.

Jones, M. V. "An Aspect of Tolstoy's Impact on Modern English Fiction: *The Kreutzer Sonata* and Joyce Cary's *The Moonlight.*" *The Slavonic and East European Review* 56, No. 1 (January 1978): 97-105.

> Suggests that Cary's "violent reaction" to Tolstoy's story inspired his novel.

Lynch, Hannah. "'Fécondité' versus the 'Kreutzer Sonata' or, Zola versus Tolstoi." *Fortnightly Review* 73 (January 1, 1900): 69-78.

> Compares the themes and morals of Zola's novel and Tolstoy's novella.

Redpath, Theodore. "The Pages of Fiction." In *Tolstoy,* pp. 46-88. London: Bowes & Bowes, 1960.

> Comments on the sexual theme of *The Kreutzer Sonata* in a discussion of the evolution of Tolstoy's fiction.

Slonim, Marc. "Leo Tolstoy." In *The Epic of Russian Literature: From Its Origins through Tolstoy,* pp. 309-46. New York: Oxford University Press, 1950. Reprint, 1964.

> Mentions the influence of *The Kreutzer Sonata* on Russian culture.

Wasiolek, Edward. "*Anna Karenina.*" In *Tolstoy's Major Fiction,* pp. 129-64. Chicago: University of Chicago Press, 1978.

> Concludes with brief comments about *The Kreutzer Sonata* and its themes of sex and death.

Additional coverage of Tolstoy's life and career is contained in the following sources published by Gale Research: *Contemporary Authors,* Vols. 104, 123; *DISCovering Authors; DISCovering Authors: British; DISCovering Authors: Canadian; DISCovering Authors: Most-Studied Authors Module; DISCovering Authors: Novelists Module; Short Story Criticism,* Vol. 9; *Something about the Author,* Vol. 26; *Twentieth-Century Literary Criticism,* Vols. 4, 11, 17, 28, 44; and *World Literature Criticism.*

Appendix:

Select Bibliography of General Sources on Short Fiction

BOOKS OF CRITICISM

Allen, Walter. *The Short Story in English*. New York: Oxford University Press, 1981, 413 p.

Aycock, Wendell M., ed. *The Teller and the Tale: Aspects of the Short Story* (Proceedings of the Comparative Literature Symposium, Texas Tech University, Volume XIII). Lubbock: Texas Tech Press, 1982, 156 p.

Averill, Deborah. *The Irish Short Story from George Moore to Frank O'Connor*. Washington, D.C.: University Press of America, 1982, 329 p.

Bates, H. E. *The Modern Short Story: A Critical Survey*. Boston: Writer, 1941, 231 p.

Bayley, John. *The Short Story: Henry James to Elizabeth Bowen*. Great Britain: The Harvester Press Limited, 1988, 197 p.

Bennett, E. K. *A History of the German Novelle: From Goethe to Thomas Mann*. Cambridge: At the University Press, 1934, 296 p.

Bone, Robert. *Down Home: A History of Afro-American Short Fiction from Its Beginning to the End of the Harlem Renaissance*. Rev. ed. New York: Columbia University Press, 1988, 350 p.

Bruck, Peter. *The Black American Short Story in the Twentieth Century: A Collection of Critical Essays*. Amsterdam: B. R. Grüner Publishing Co., 1977, 209 p.

Burnett, Whit, and Burnett, Hallie. *The Modern Short Story in the Making*. New York: Hawthorn Books, 1964, 405 p.

Canby, Henry Seidel. *The Short Story in English*. New York: Henry Holt and Co., 1909, 386 p.

Current-García, Eugene. *The American Short Story before 1850: A Critical History*. Twayne's Critical History of the Short Story, edited by William Peden. Boston: Twayne Publishers, 1985, 168 p.

Flora, Joseph M., ed. *The English Short Story, 1880-1945: A Critical History*. Twayne's Critical History of the Short Story, edited by William Peden. Boston: Twayne Publishers, 1985, 215 p.

Foster, David William. *Studies in the Contemporary Spanish-American Short Story*. Columbia, Mo.: University of Missouri Press, 1979, 126 p.

George, Albert J. *Short Fiction in France, 1800-1850*. Syracuse, N.Y.: Syracuse University Press, 1964, 245 p.

Gerlach, John. *Toward an End: Closure and Structure in the American Short Story*. University, Ala.: The University of Alabama Press, 1985, 193 p.

Hankin, Cherry, ed. *Critical Essays on the New Zealand Short Story*. Auckland: Heinemann Publishers, 1982, 186 p.

Hanson, Clare, ed. *Re-Reading the Short Story*. London: MacMillan Press, 1989, 137 p.

Harris, Wendell V. *British Short Fiction in the Nineteenth Century*. Detroit: Wayne State University Press, 1979, 209 p.

Huntington, John. *Rationalizing Genius: Ideological Strategies in the Classic American Science Fiction Short Story*. New Brunswick: Rutgers University Press, 1989, 216 p.

Kilroy, James F., ed. *The Irish Short Story: A Critical History*. Twayne's Critical History of the Short Story, edited by William Peden. Boston: Twayne Publishers, 1984, 251 p.

Lee, A. Robert. *The Nineteenth-Century American Short Story*. Totowa, N. J.: Vision / Barnes & Noble, 1986, 196 p.

Leibowitz, Judith. *Narrative Purpose in the Novella*. The Hague: Mouton, 1974, 137 p.

Lohafer, Susan. *Coming to Terms with the Short Story*. Baton Rouge: Louisiana State University Press, 1983, 171 p.

Lohafer, Susan, and Clarey, Jo Ellyn. *Short Story Theory at a Crossroads*. Baton Rouge: Louisiana State University Press, 1989, 352 p.

Mann, Susan Garland. *The Short Story Cycle: A Genre Companion and Reference Guide*. New York: Greenwood Press, 1989, 228 p.

Matthews, Brander. *The Philosophy of the Short Story*. New York, N.Y.: Longmans, Green and Co., 1901, 83 p.

May, Charles E., ed. *Short Story Theories*. Athens, Oh.: Ohio University Press, 1976, 251 p.

McClave, Heather, ed. *Women Writers of the Short Story: A Collection of Critical Essays*. Englewood Cliffs, N. J.: Prentice-Hall, 1980, 171 p.

Moser, Charles, ed. *The Russian Short Story: A Critical History*. Twayne's Critical History of the Short Story, edited by William Peden. Boston: Twayne Publishers, 1986, 232 p.

New, W. H. *Dreams of Speech and Violence: The Art of the Short Story in Canada and New Zealand*. Toronto: The University of Toronto Press, 1987, 302 p.

Newman, Frances. *The Short Story's Mutations: From Petronius to Paul Morand*. New York: B. W. Huebsch, 1925, 332 p.

O'Connor, Frank. *The Lonely Voice: A Study of the Short Story*. Cleveland: World Publishing Co., 1963, 220 p.

O'Faolain, Sean. *The Short Story*. New York: Devin-Adair Co., 1951, 370 p.

Orel, Harold. *The Victorian Short Story: Development and Triumph of a Literary Genre*. Cambridge: Cambridge University Press, 1986, 213 p.

O'Toole, L. Michael. *Structure, Style and Interpretation in the Russian Short Story*. New Haven: Yale University Press, 1982, 272 p.

Pattee, Fred Lewis. *The Development of the American Short Story: An Historical Survey*. New York: Harper and Brothers Publishers, 1923, 388 p.

Peden, Margaret Sayers, ed. *The Latin American Short Story: A Critical History*. Twayne's Critical History of the Short Story, edited by William Peden. Boston: Twayne Publishers, 1983, 160 p.

Peden, William. *The American Short Story: Continuity and Change, 1940-1975*. Rev. ed. Boston: Houghton Mifflin Co., 1975, 215 p.

Reid, Ian. *The Short Story*. The Critical Idiom, edited by John D. Jump. London: Methuen and Co., 1977, 76 p.

Rhode, Robert D. *Setting in the American Short Story of Local Color, 1865-1900*. The Hague: Mouton, 1975, 189 p.

Rohrberger, Mary. *Hawthorne and the Modern Short Story: A Study in Genre*. The Hague: Mouton and Co., 1966, 148 p.

Shaw, Valerie. *The Short Story: A Critical Introduction*. London: Longman, 1983, 294 p.

Stephens, Michael. *The Dramaturgy of Style: Voice in Short Fiction*. Carbondale, Ill.: Southern Illinois University Press, 1986, 281 p.

Stevick, Philip, ed. *The American Short Story, 1900-1945: A Critical History*. Twayne's Critical History of the Short Story, edited by William Peden. Boston: Twayne Publishers, 1984, 209 p.

Summers, Hollis, ed. *Discussion of the Short Story*. Boston: D. C. Heath and Co., 1963, 118 p.

Vannatta, Dennis, ed. *The English Short Story, 1945-1980: A Critical History*. Twayne's Critical History of the Short Story, edited by William Peden. Boston: Twayne Publishers, 1985, 206 p.

Voss, Arthur. *The American Short Story: A Critical Survey*. Norman, Okla.: University of Oklahoma Press, 1973, 399 p.

Walker, Warren S. *Twentieth-Century Short Story Explication: New Series, Vol. 1: 1989-1990*. Hamden, Conn.: Shoe String, 1993, 366 p.

Ward, Alfred C. *Aspects of the Modern Short Story: English and American*. London: University of London Press, 1924, 307 p.

Weaver, Gordon, ed. *The American Short Story, 1945-1980: A Critical History*. Twayne's Critical History of the Short Story, edited by William Peden. Boston: Twayne Publishers, 1983, 150 p.

West, Ray B., Jr. *The Short Story in America, 1900-1950*. Chicago: Henry Regnery Co., 1952, 147 p.

Williams, Blanche Colton. *Our Short Story Writers*. New York: Moffat, Yard and Co., 1920, 357 p.

Wright, Austin McGiffert. *The American Short Story in the Twenties*. Chicago: University of Chicago Press, 1961, 425 p.

CRITICAL ANTHOLOGIES

Atkinson, W. Patterson, ed. *The Short-Story*. Boston: Allyn and Bacon, 1923, 317 p.

Baldwin, Charles Sears, ed. *American Short Stories*. New York, N.Y.: Longmans, Green and Co., 1904, 333 p.

Charters, Ann, ed. *The Story and Its Writer: An Introduction to Short Fiction*. New York: St. Martin's Press, 1983, 1239 p.

Current-García, Eugene, and Patrick, Walton R., eds. *American Short Stories: 1820 to the Present*. Key Editions, edited by John C. Gerber. Chicago: Scott, Foresman and Co., 1952, 633 p.

Fagin, N. Bryllion, ed. *America through the Short Story*. Boston: Little, Brown, and Co., 1936, 508 p.

Frakes, James R., and Traschen, Isadore, eds. *Short Fiction: A Critical Collection*. Prentice-Hall English Literature Series, edited by Maynard Mack. Englewood Cliffs, N.J.: Prentice-Hall, 1959, 459 p.

Gifford, Douglas, ed. *Scottish Short Stories, 1800-1900*. The Scottish Library, edited by Alexander Scott. London: Calder and Boyars, 1971, 350 p.

Gordon, Caroline, and Tate, Allen, eds. *The House of Fiction: An Anthology of the Short Story withCommentary*. Rev. ed. New York: Charles Scribner's Sons, 1960, 469 p.

Greet, T. Y., et. al. *The Worlds of Fiction: Stories in Context*. Boston, Mass.: Houghton Mifflin Co., 1964, 429 p.

Gullason, Thomas A., and Caspar, Leonard, eds. *The World of Short Fiction: An International Collection.* New York: Harper and Row, 1962, 548 p.

Havighurst, Walter, ed. *Masters of the Modern Short Story.* New York: Harcourt, Brace and Co., 1945, 538 p.

Litz, A. Walton, ed. *Major American Short Stories.* New York: Oxford University Press, 1975, 823 p.

Matthews, Brander, ed. *The Short-Story: Specimens Illustrating Its Development.* New York: American Book Co., 1907, 399 p.

Menton, Seymour, ed. *The Spanish American Short Story: A Critical Anthology.* Berkeley and Los Angeles: University of California Press, 1980, 496 p.

Mzamane, Mbulelo Vizikhungo, ed. *Hungry Flames, and Other Black South African Short Stories.* Longman African Classics. Essex: Longman, 1986, 162 p.

Schorer, Mark, ed. *The Short Story: A Critical Anthology.* Rev. ed. Prentice-Hall English Literature Series, edited by Maynard Mack. Englewood Cliffs, N. J.: Prentice-Hall, 1967, 459 p.

Simpson, Claude M., ed. *The Local Colorists: American Short Stories, 1857-1900.* New York: Harper and Brothers Publishers, 1960, 340 p.

Stanton, Robert, ed. *The Short Story and the Reader.* New York: Henry Holt and Co., 1960, 557 p.

West, Ray B., Jr., ed. *American Short Stories.* New York: Thomas Y. Crowell Co., 1959, 267 p.

Short Story Criticism Indexes

Literary Criticism Series
Cumulative Author Index

SSC Cumulative Nationality Index
SSC Cumulative Title Index

How to Use This Index

The main references

> Calvino, Italo
> 1923–1985 .... **CLC 5, 8, 11, 22, 33, 39,**
> **73; SSC 3**

list all author entries in the following Gale Literary Criticism series:

BLC = *Black Literature Criticism*
CLC = *Contemporary Literary Criticism*
CLR = *Children's Literature Review*
CMLC = *Classical and Medieval Literature Criticism*
DA = *DISCovering Authors*
DAB = *DISCovering Authors: British*
DAC = *DISCovering Authors: Canadian*
DAM = *DISCovering Authors: Modules*
    DRAM: *Dramatists Module*; *MST*: *Most-Studied Authors Module*;
    MULT: *Multicultural Authors Module*; *NOV*: *Novelists Module*;
    POET: *Poets Module*; *POP*: *Popular Fiction and Genre Authors Module*
DC = *Drama Criticism*
HLC = *Hispanic Literature Criticism*
LC = *Literature Criticism from 1400 to 1800*
NCLC = *Nineteenth-Century Literature Criticism*
PC = *Poetry Criticism*
SSC = *Short Story Criticism*
TCLC = *Twentieth-Century Literary Criticism*
WLC = *World Literature Criticism, 1500 to the Present*

The cross-references

> See also CANR 23; CA 85-88;
>   obituary CA116

list all author entries in the following Gale biographical and literary sources:

AAYA = *Authors & Artists for Young Adults*
AITN = *Authors in the News*
BEST = *Bestsellers*
BW = *Black Writers*
CA = *Contemporary Authors*
CAAS = *Contemporary Authors Autobiography Series*
CABS = *Contemporary Authors Bibliographical Series*
CANR = *Contemporary Authors New Revision Series*
CAP = *Contemporary Authors Permanent Series*
CDALB = *Concise Dictionary of American Literary Biography*
CDBLB = *Concise Dictionary of British Literary Biography*
DLB = *Dictionary of Literary Biography*
DLBD = *Dictionary of Literary Biography Documentary Series*
DLBY = *Dictionary of Literary Biography Yearbook*
HW = *Hispanic Writers*
JRDA = *Junior DISCovering Authors*
MAICYA = *Major Authors and Illustrators for Children and Young Adults*
MTCW = *Major 20th-Century Writers*
NNAL = *Native North American Literature*
SAAS = *Something about the Author Autobiography Series*
SATA = *Something about the Author*
YABC = *Yesterday's Authors of Books for Children*

Literary Criticism Series
Cumulative Author Index

Akhmadulina, Bella Akhatovna 1937-   **CLC 53; DAM POET**
See also CA 65-68

Akhmatova, Anna 1888-1966   **CLC 11, 25, 64; DAM POET; PC 2**
See also CA 19-20; 25-28R; CANR 35; CAP 1; MTCW

Aksakov, Sergei Timofeyvich 1791-1859   **NCLC 2**

Aksenov, Vassily
See Aksyonov, Vassily (Pavlovich)

Akst, Daniel 1956- .... **CLC 109**
See also CA 161

Aksyonov, Vassily (Pavlovich) 1932- **CLC 22, 37, 101**
See also CA 53-56; CANR 12, 48

Akutagawa, Ryunosuke 1892-1927 . **TCLC 16**
See also CA 117; 154

Alain 1868-1951 .... **TCLC 41**
See also CA 163

Alain-Fournier .... **TCLC 6**
See also Fournier, Henri Alban
See also DLB 65

Alarcon, Pedro Antonio de   1833-1891   **NCLC 1**

Alas (y Urena), Leopoldo (Enrique Garcia) 1852-1901 **TCLC 29**
See also CA 113; 131; HW

Albee, Edward (Franklin III) 1928-   **CLC 1, 2, 3, 5, 9, 11, 13, 25, 53, 86; DA; DAB; DAC; DAM DRAM, MST; WLC**
See also AITN 1; CA 5-8R; CABS 3; CANR 8, 54; CDALB 1941-1968; DLB 7; INT CANR-8; MTCW

Alberti, Rafael 1902- .... **CLC 7**
See also CA 85-88; DLB 108

Albert the Great 1200(?)-1280 .... **CMLC 16**
See also DLB 115

Alcala-Galiano, Juan Valera y
See Valera y Alcala-Galiano, Juan

Alcott, Amos Bronson 1799-1888 ..... **NCLC 1**
See also DLB 1

Alcott, Louisa May 1832-1888 ...**NCLC 6, 58; DA; DAB; DAC; DAM MST, NOV; SSC 27; WLC**
See also AAYA 20; CDALB 1865-1917; CLR 1, 38; DLB 1, 42, 79; DLBD 14; JRDA; MAICYA; YABC 1

Aldanov, M. A.
See Aldanov, Mark (Alexandrovich)

Aldanov, Mark (Alexandrovich) 1886(?)-1957   **TCLC 23**
See also CA 118

Aldington, Richard 1892-1962 .... **CLC 49**
See also CA 85-88; CANR 45; DLB 20, 36, 100, 149

Aldiss, Brian W(ilson) 1925- ... **CLC 5, 14, 40; DAM NOV**
See also CA 5-8R; CAAS 2; CANR 5, 28, 64; DLB 14; MTCW; SATA 34

Alegria, Claribel 1924- ....

CLC 75; DAM MULT
See also CA 131; CAAS 15; CANR 66; DLB 145; HW

Alegria, Fernando 1918- .... **CLC 57**
See also CA 9-12R; CANR 5, 32; HW

Aleichem, Sholom .... **TCLC 1, 35**
See also Rabinovitch, Sholem

Aleixandre, Vicente 1898-1984 ..... **CLC 9, 36; DAM POET; PC 15**
See also CA 85-88; 114; CANR 26; DLB 108; HW; MTCW

Alepoudelis, Odysseus
See Elytis, Odysseus

Aleshkovsky, Joseph 1929-
See Aleshkovsky, Yuz
See also CA 121; 128

Aleshkovsky, Yuz .... **CLC 44**
See also Aleshkovsky, Joseph

Alexander, Lloyd (Chudley) 1924- ..... **CLC 35**
See also AAYA 1; CA 1-4R; CANR 1, 24, 38, 55; CLR 1, 5, 48; DLB 52; JRDA; MAICYA; MTCW; SAAS 19; SATA 3, 49, 81

Alexander, Samuel 1859-1938 .... **TCLC 77**

Alexie, Sherman (Joseph, Jr.) 1966- **CLC 96; DAM MULT**
See also CA 138; CANR 65; DLB 175; NNAL

Alfau, Felipe 1902- .... **CLC 66**
See also CA 137

Alger, Horatio, Jr. 1832-1899 .... **NCLC 8**
See also DLB 42; SATA 16

Algren, Nelson 1909-1981 .... **CLC 4, 10, 33**
See also CA 13-16R; 103; CANR 20, 61; CDALB 1941-1968; DLB 9; DLBY 81, 82; MTCW

Ali, Ahmed 1910- .... **CLC 69**
See also CA 25-28R; CANR 15, 34

Alighieri, Dante
See Dante

Allan, John B.
See Westlake, Donald E(dwin)

Allan, Sidney
See Hartmann, Sadakichi

Allan, Sydney
See Hartmann, Sadakichi

Allen, Edward 1948- .... **CLC 59**

Allen, Paula Gunn 1939- .... **CLC 84; DAM MULT**
See also CA 112; 143; CANR 63; DLB 175; NNAL

Allen, Roland
See Ayckbourn, Alan

Allen, Sarah A.
See Hopkins, Pauline Elizabeth

Allen, Sidney H.
See Hartmann, Sadakichi

Allen, Woody 1935- ..**CLC 16, 52; DAM POP**
See also AAYA 10; CA 33-36R; CANR 27, 38, 63; DLB 44; MTCW

Allende, Isabel 1942- ... **CLC 39, 57, 97; DAM MULT, NOV; HLC; WLCS**
See also AAYA 18; CA 125; 130; CANR 51; DLB 145; HW; INT 130; MTCW

Alleyn, Ellen
See Rossetti, Christina (Georgina)

Allingham, Margery (Louise) 1904-1966   **CLC 19**
See also CA 5-8R; 25-28R; CANR 4, 58; DLB 77; MTCW

Allingham, William 1824-1889 .... **NCLC 25**
See also DLB 35

Allison, Dorothy E. 1949- .... **CLC 78**
See also CA 140; CANR 66

Allston, Washington 1779-1843 .... **NCLC 2**
See also DLB 1

Almedingen, E. M. .... **CLC 12**
See also Almedingen, Martha Edith von
See also SATA 3

Almedingen, Martha Edith von 1898-1971
See Almedingen, E. M.
See also CA 1-4R; CANR 1

Almqvist, Carl Jonas Love 1793-1866 ...**NCLC 42**

Alonso, Damaso 1898-1990 .... **CLC 14**
See also CA 110; 131; 130; DLB 108; HW

Alov
See Gogol, Nikolai (Vasilyevich)

Alta 1942- .... **CLC 19**
See also CA 57-60

Alter, Robert B(ernard) 1935- .... **CLC 34**
See also CA 49-52; CANR 1, 47

Alther, Lisa 1944- .... **CLC 7, 41**
See also CA 65-68; CANR 12, 30, 51; MTCW

Althusser, L.
See Althusser, Louis

Althusser, Louis 1918-1990 .... **CLC 106**
See also CA 131; 132

Altman, Robert 1925- .... **CLC 16**
   See also CA 73-76; CANR 43

Alvarez, A(lfred) 1929- .... **CLC 5, 13**
   See also CA 1-4R; CANR 3, 33, 63; DLB 14, 40

Alvarez, Alejandro Rodriguez 1903-1965
   See Casona, Alejandro
   See also CA 131; 93-96; HW

Alvarez, Julia 1950- .... **CLC 93**
   See also AAYA 25; CA 147

Alvaro, Corrado 1896-1956 .... **TCLC 60**
   See also CA 163

Amado, Jorge 1912-   **CLC 13, 40, 106; DAM
   MULT, NOV; HLC**
   See also CA 77-80; CANR 35; DLB 113;
   MTCW

Ambler, Eric 1909- .... **CLC 4, 6, 9**
   See also CA 9-12R; CANR 7, 38; DLB 77;
   MTCW

Amichai, Yehuda 1924- .... **CLC 9, 22, 57**
   See also CA 85-88; CANR 46, 60; MTCW

Amichai, Yehudah
   See Amichai, Yehuda

Amiel, Henri Frederic 1821-1881 ..... **NCLC 4**

Amis, Kingsley (William) 1922-1995   **CLC 1,
   2, 3, 5, 8, 13, 40, 44; DA; DAB; DAC; DAM
   MST, NOV**
   See also AITN 2; CA 9-12R; 150; CANR 8, 28,
   54; CDBLB 1945-1960; DLB 15, 27, 100,
   139; DLBY 96; INT CANR-8; MTCW

Amis, Martin (Louis) 1949- . **CLC 4, 9, 38, 62,
   101**
   See also BEST 90:3; CA 65-68; CANR 8, 27,
   54; DLB 14, 194; INT CANR-27

Ammons, A(rchie) R(andolph) 1926-   **CLC 2,
   3, 5, 8, 9, 25, 57, 108; DAM POET; PC 16**
   See also AITN 1; CA 9-12R; CANR 6, 36, 51;
   DLB 5, 165; MTCW

Amo, Tauraatua i
   See Adams, Henry (Brooks)

Anand, Mulk Raj 1905- .. **CLC 23, 93; DAM
   NOV**
   See also CA 65-68; CANR 32, 64; MTCW

Anatol
   See Schnitzler, Arthur

Anaximander c. 610B.C.-c. 546B.C.   **CMLC 22**

Anaya, Rudolfo A(lfonso) 1937- ...... **CLC 23;
   DAM MULT, NOV; HLC**
   See also AAYA 20; CA 45-48; CAAS 4; CANR
   1, 32, 51; DLB 82; HW 1; MTCW

Andersen, Hans Christian 1805-1875   **NCLC
   7; DA; DAB; DAC; DAM MST, POP; SSC
   6; WLC**
   See also CLR 6; MAICYA; YABC 1

Anderson, C. Farley
   See Mencken, H(enry) L(ouis); Nathan, George
   Jean

Anderson, Jessica (Margaret) Queale 1916-
   CLC 37
   See also CA 9-12R; CANR 4, 62

Anderson, Jon (Victor) 1940- ... **CLC 9; DAM
   POET**
   See also CA 25-28R; CANR 20

Anderson, Lindsay (Gordon) 1923-1994   **CLC
   20**
   See also CA 125; 128; 146

Anderson, Maxwell 1888-1959 ..... **TCLC 2;
   DAM DRAM**
   See also CA 105; 152; DLB 7

Anderson, Poul (William) 1926- .... **CLC 15**
   See also AAYA 5; CA 1-4R; CAAS 2; CANR 2,
   15, 34, 64; DLB 8; INT CANR-15; MTCW;
   SATA 90; SATA-Brief 39

Anderson, Robert (Woodruff) 1917-   **CLC 23;
   DAM DRAM**
   See also AITN 1; CA 21-24R; CANR 32; DLB 7

Anderson, Sherwood 1876-1941   **TCLC 1,
   10, 24; DA; DAB; DAC; DAM MST, NOV;
   SSC 1; WLC**
   See also CA 104; 121; CANR 61; CDALB 1917-
   1929; DLB 4, 9, 86; DLBD 1; MTCW

Andier, Pierre
   See Desnos, Robert

Andouard
   See Giraudoux, (Hippolyte) Jean

Andrade, Carlos Drummond de .... **CLC 18**
   See also Drummond de Andrade, Carlos

Andrade, Mario de 1893-1945 .... **TCLC 43**

Andreae, Johann V(alentin) 1586-1654   **LC 32**
   See also DLB 164

Andreas-Salome, Lou 1861-1937 .... **TCLC 56**
   See also DLB 66

Andress, Lesley
   See Sanders, Lawrence

Andrewes, Lancelot 1555-1626 .... **LC 5**
   See also DLB 151, 172

Andrews, Cicily Fairfield
   See West, Rebecca

Andrews, Elton V.
   See Pohl, Frederik

Andreyev, Leonid (Nikolaevich) 1871-1919
   TCLC 3
   See also CA 104

Andric, Ivo 1892-1975 .... **CLC 8**
   See also CA 81-84; 57-60; CANR 43, 60; DLB
   147; MTCW

Androvar
   See Prado (Calvo), Pedro

Angelique, Pierre
   See Bataille, Georges

Angell, Roger 1920- .... **CLC 26**
   See also CA 57-60; CANR 13, 44; DLB 171,
   185

Angelou, Maya 1928-   **CLC 12, 35, 64, 77;
   BLC; DA; DAB; DAC; DAM MST, MULT,
   POET, POP; WLCS**
   See also AAYA 7, 20; BW 2; CA 65-68; CANR
   19, 42, 65; DLB 38; MTCW; SATA 49

Anna Comnena 1083-1153 .... **CMLC 25**

Annensky, Innokenty (Fyodorovich) 1856-1909
   TCLC 14
   See also CA 110; 155

Annunzio, Gabriele d'
   See D'Annunzio, Gabriele

Anodos
   See Coleridge, Mary E(lizabeth)

Anon, Charles Robert
   See Pessoa, Fernando (Antonio Nogueira)

Anouilh, Jean (Marie Lucien Pierre) 1910-1987
   **CLC 1, 3, 8, 13, 40, 50; DAM DRAM; DC
   8**
   See also CA 17-20R; 123; CANR 32; MTCW

Anthony, Florence
   See Ai

Anthony, John
   See Ciardi, John (Anthony)

Anthony, Peter
   See Shaffer, Anthony (Joshua); Shaffer, Peter
   (Levin)

Anthony, Piers 1934- ...... **CLC 35; DAM POP**
   See also AAYA 11; CA 21-24R; CANR 28, 56;
   DLB 8; MTCW; SAAS 22; SATA 84

Antoine, Marc
   See Proust, (Valentin-Louis-George-Eugene-)
   Marcel

Antoninus, Brother
   See Everson, William (Oliver)

Antonioni, Michelangelo 1912- .... **CLC 20**
   See also CA 73-76; CANR 45

Antschel, Paul 1920-1970
   See Celan, Paul
   See also CA 85-88; CANR 33, 61; MTCW

Anwar, Chairil 1922-1949 .... **TCLC 22**
   See also CA 121

Apollinaire, Guillaume 1880-1918   **TCLC 3, 8,
   51; DAM POET; PC 7**
   See also Kostrowitzki, Wilhelm Apollinaris de
   See also CA 152

Atwood, Margaret (Eleanor) 1939- **CLC 2, 3, 4, 8, 13, 15, 25, 44, 84; DA; DAB; DAC; DAM MST, NOV, POET; PC 8; SSC 2; WLC**
See also AAYA 12; BEST 89:2; CA 49-52; CANR 3, 24, 33, 59; DLB 53; INT CANR-24; MTCW; SATA 50

Aubigny, Pierre d'
See Mencken, H(enry) L(ouis)

Aubin, Penelope 1685-1731(?)................. **LC 9**
See also DLB 39

Auchincloss, Louis (Stanton) 1917- **CLC 4, 6, 9, 18, 45; DAM NOV; SSC 22**
See also CA 1-4R; CANR 6, 29, 55; DLB 2; DLBY 80; INT CANR-29; MTCW

Auden, W(ystan) H(ugh) 1907-1973 **CLC 1, 2, 3, 4, 6, 9, 11, 14, 43; DA; DAB; DAC; DAM DRAM, MST, POET; PC 1; WLC**
See also AAYA 18; CA 9-12R; 45-48; CANR 5, 61; CDBLB 1914-1945; DLB 10, 20; MTCW

Audiberti, Jacques 1900-1965 **CLC 38; DAM DRAM**
See also CA 25-28R

Audubon, John James 1785-1851 ... **NCLC 47**

Auel, Jean M(arie) 1936- **CLC 31, 107; DAM POP**
See also AAYA 7; BEST 90:4; CA 103; CANR 21, 64; INT CANR-21; SATA 91

Auerbach, Erich 1892-1957 .... **TCLC 43**
See also CA 118; 155

Augier, Emile 1820-1889 .... **NCLC 31**
See also DLB 192

August, John
See De Voto, Bernard (Augustine)

Augustine, St. 354-430 .... **CMLC 6; DAB**

Aurelius
See Bourne, Randolph S(illiman)

Aurobindo, Sri
See Aurobindo Ghose

Aurobindo Ghose 1872-1950 .... **TCLC 63**
See also CA 163

Austen, Jane 1775-1817 **NCLC 1, 13, 19, 33, 51; DA; DAB; DAC; DAM MST, NOV; WLC**
See also AAYA 19; CDBLB 1789-1832; DLB 116

Auster, Paul 1947-................................ **CLC 47**
See also CA 69-72; CANR 23, 52

Austin, Frank
See Faust, Frederick (Schiller)

Austin, Mary (Hunter) 1868-1934 .. **TCLC 25**
See also CA 109; DLB 9, 78

Autran Dourado, Waldomiro
See Dourado, (Waldomiro Freitas) Autran

Averroes 1126-1198 .... **CMLC 7**
See also DLB 115

Avicenna 980-1037 .... **CMLC 16**
See also DLB 115

Avison, Margaret 1918- . **CLC 2, 4, 97; DAC; DAM POET**
See also CA 17-20R; DLB 53; MTCW

Axton, David
See Koontz, Dean R(ay)

Ayckbourn, Alan 1939-................................**CLC 5, 8, 18, 33, 74; DAB; DAM DRAM**
See also CA 21-24R; CANR 31, 59; DLB 13; MTCW

Aydy, Catherine
See Tennant, Emma (Christina)

Ayme, Marcel (Andre) 1902-1967 ...... **CLC 11**
See also CA 89-92; CANR 67; CLR 25; DLB 72; SATA 91

Ayrton, Michael 1921-1975 .... **CLC 7**
See also CA 5-8R; 61-64; CANR 9, 21

Azorin ....**CLC 11**
See also Martinez Ruiz, Jose

Azuela, Mariano 1873-1952 .. **TCLC 3; DAM MULT; HLC**
See also CA 104; 131; HW; MTCW

Baastad, Babbis Friis
See Friis-Baastad, Babbis Ellinor

Bab
See Gilbert, W(illiam) S(chwenck)

Babbis, Eleanor
See Friis-Baastad, Babbis Ellinor

Babel, Isaac
See Babel, Isaak (Emmanuilovich)

Babel, Isaak (Emmanuilovich) 1894-1941(?) **TCLC 2, 13; SSC 16**
See also CA 104; 155

Babits, Mihaly 1883-1941 .... **TCLC 14**
See also CA 114

Babur 1483-1530 .... **LC 18**

Bacchelli, Riccardo 1891-1985 .... **CLC 19**
See also CA 29-32R; 117

Bach, Richard (David) 1936- .. **CLC 14; DAM NOV, POP**
See also AITN 1; BEST 89:2; CA 9-12R; CANR 18; MTCW; SATA 13

Bachman, Richard
See King, Stephen (Edwin)

Bachmann, Ingeborg 1926-1973 .... **CLC 69**
See also CA 93-96; 45-48; DLB 85

Bacon, Francis 1561-1626 .... **LC 18, 32**
See also CDBLB Before 1660; DLB 151

Bacon, Roger 1214(?)-1292 .... **CMLC 14**
See also DLB 115

Bacovia, George .... **TCLC 24**
See also Vasiliu, Gheorghe

Badanes, Jerome 1937- .... **CLC 59**

Bagehot, Walter 1826-1877 .... **NCLC 10**
See also DLB 55

Bagnold, Enid 1889-1981 .... **CLC 25; DAM DRAM**
See also CA 5-8R; 103; CANR 5, 40; DLB 13, 160, 191; MAICYA; SATA 1, 25

Bagritsky, Eduard 1895-1934 .... **TCLC 60**

Bagrjana, Elisaveta
See Belcheva, Elisaveta

Bagryana, Elisaveta .... **CLC 10**
See also Belcheva, Elisaveta
See also DLB 147

Bailey, Paul 1937- .... **CLC 45**
See also CA 21-24R; CANR 16, 62; DLB 14

Baillie, Joanna 1762-1851 .... **NCLC 2**
See also DLB 93

Bainbridge, Beryl (Margaret) 1933- **CLC 4, 5, 8, 10, 14, 18, 22, 62; DAM NOV**
See also CA 21-24R; CANR 24, 55; DLB 14; MTCW

Baker, Elliott 1922-............................... **CLC 8**
See also CA 45-48; CANR 2, 63

Baker, Jean H. .... **TCLC 3, 10**
See also Russell, George William

Baker, Nicholson 1957- .... **CLC 61; DAM POP**
See also CA 135; CANR 63

Baker, Ray Stannard 1870-1946 ..... **TCLC 47**
See also CA 118

Baker, Russell (Wayne) 1925- .... **CLC 31**
See also BEST 89:4; CA 57-60; CANR 11, 41, 59; MTCW

Bakhtin, M.
See Bakhtin, Mikhail Mikhailovich

Bakhtin, M. M.
See Bakhtin, Mikhail Mikhailovich

Bakhtin, Mikhail
See Bakhtin, Mikhail Mikhailovich

Bakhtin, Mikhail Mikhailovich 1895-1975 **CLC 83**
See also CA 128; 113

Bakshi, Ralph 1938(?)- .... **CLC 26**
See also CA 112; 138

Bakunin, Mikhail (Alexandrovich) 1814-1876 **NCLC 25, 58**

Baldwin, James (Arthur) 1924-1987   **CLC 1, 2, 3, 4, 5, 8, 13, 15, 17, 42, 50, 67, 90; BLC; DA; DAB; DAC; DAM MST, MULT, NOV, POP; DC 1; SSC 10; WLC**
See also AAYA 4; BW 1; CA 1-4R; 124; CABS 1; CANR 3, 24; CDALB 1941-1968; DLB 2, 7, 33; DLBY 87; MTCW; SATA 9; SATA-Obit 54

Ballard, J(ames) G(raham) 1930-   **CLC 3, 6, 14, 36; DAM NOV, POP; SSC 1**
See also AAYA 3; CA 5-8R; CANR 15, 39, 65; DLB 14; MTCW; SATA 93

Balmont, Konstantin (Dmitriyevich) 1867-1943 **TCLC 11**
See also CA 109; 155

Balzac, Honore de 1799-1850.   **NCLC 5, 35, 53; DA; DAB; DAC; DAM MST, NOV; SSC 5; WLC**
See also DLB 119

Bambara, Toni Cade 1939-1995 ... **CLC 19, 88; BLC; DA; DAC; DAM MST, MULT; WLCS**
See also AAYA 5; BW 2; CA 29-32R; 150; CANR 24, 49; DLB 38; MTCW

Bamdad, A.
See Shamlu, Ahmad

Banat, D. R.
See Bradbury, Ray (Douglas)

Bancroft, Laura
See Baum, L(yman) Frank

Banim, John 1798-1842 .... **NCLC 13**
See also DLB 116, 158, 159

Banim, Michael 1796-1874 .... **NCLC 13**
See also DLB 158, 159

Banjo, The
See Paterson, A(ndrew) B(arton)

Banks, Iain
See Banks, Iain M(enzies)

Banks, Iain M(enzies) 1954- .... **CLC 34**
See also CA 123; 128; CANR 61; DLB 194; INT 128

Banks, Lynne Reid .... **CLC 23**
See also Reid Banks, Lynne
See also AAYA 6

Banks, Russell 1940- .... **CLC 37, 72**
See also CA 65-68; CAAS 15; CANR 19, 52; DLB 130

Banville, John 1945- .... **CLC 46**
See also CA 117; 128; DLB 14; INT 128

Banville, Theodore (Faullain) de 1832-1891 **NCLC 9**

Baraka, Amiri 1934-   **CLC 1, 2, 3, 5, 10, 14, 33; BLC; DA; DAC; DAM MST, MULT, POET, POP; DC 6; PC 4; WLCS**
See also Jones, LeRoi
See also BW 2; CA 21-24R; CABS 3; CANR 27, 38, 61; CDALB 1941-1968; DLB 5, 7, 16, 38; DLBD 8; MTCW

Barbauld, Anna Laetitia 1743-1825 **NCLC 50**
See also DLB 107, 109, 142, 158

Barbellion, W. N. P. .... **TCLC 24**
See also Cummings, Bruce F(rederick)

Barbera, Jack (Vincent) 1945- .... **CLC 44**
See also CA 110; CANR 45

Barbey d'Aurevilly, Jules Amedee 1808-1889 **NCLC 1; SSC 17**
See also DLB 119

Barbusse, Henri 1873-1935 .... **TCLC 5**
See also CA 105; 154; DLB 65

Barclay, Bill
See Moorcock, Michael (John)

Barclay, William Ewert
See Moorcock, Michael (John)

Barea, Arturo 1897-1957 .... **TCLC 14**
See also CA 111

Barfoot, Joan 1946- .... **CLC 18**
See also CA 105

Baring, Maurice 1874-1945 .... **TCLC 8**
See also CA 105; DLB 34

Barker, Clive 1952-   **CLC 52; DAM POP**
See also AAYA 10; BEST 90:3; CA 121; 129; INT 129; MTCW

Barker, George Granville 1913-1991 . **CLC 8, 48; DAM POET**
See also CA 9-12R; 135; CANR 7, 38; DLB 20; MTCW

Barker, Harley Granville
See Granville-Barker, Harley
See also DLB 10

Barker, Howard 1946- .... **CLC 37**
See also CA 102; DLB 13

Barker, Pat(ricia) 1943- .... **CLC 32, 94**
See also CA 117; 122; CANR 50; INT 122

Barlow, Joel 1754-1812 .... **NCLC 23**
See also DLB 37

Barnard, Mary (Ethel) 1909- .... **CLC 48**
See also CA 21-22; CAP 2

Barnes, Djuna 1892-1982   **CLC 3, 4, 8, 11, 29; SSC 3**
See also CA 9-12R; 107; CANR 16, 55; DLB 4, 9, 45; MTCW

Barnes, Julian (Patrick) 1946- **CLC 42; DAB**
See also CA 102; CANR 19, 54; DLB 194; DLBY 93

Barnes, Peter 1931- .... **CLC 5, 56**
See also CA 65-68; CAAS 12; CANR 33, 34, 64; DLB 13; MTCW

Baroja (y Nessi), Pio 1872-1956 ....   **TCLC 8; HLC**
See also CA 104

Baron, David
See Pinter, Harold

Baron Corvo
See Rolfe, Frederick (William Serafino Austin Lewis Mary)

Barondess, Sue K(aufman) 1926-1977   **CLC 8**
See also Kaufman, Sue
See also CA 1-4R; 69-72; CANR 1

Baron de Teive
See Pessoa, Fernando (Antonio Nogueira)

Barres, (Auguste-) Maurice 1862-1923 **TCLC 47**
See also CA 164; DLB 123

Barreto, Afonso Henrique de Lima
See Lima Barreto, Afonso Henrique de

Barrett, (Roger) Syd 1946- .... **CLC 35**

Barrett, William (Christopher) 1913-1992 **CLC 27**
See also CA 13-16R; 139; CANR 11, 67; INT CANR-11

Barrie, J(ames) M(atthew) 1860-1937   **TCLC 2; DAB; DAM DRAM**
See also CA 104; 136; CDBLB 1890-1914; CLR 16; DLB 10, 141, 156; MAICYA; YABC 1

Barrington, Michael
See Moorcock, Michael (John)

Barrol, Grady
See Bograd, Larry

Barry, Mike
See Malzberg, Barry N(athaniel)

Barry, Philip 1896-1949 .... **TCLC 11**
See also CA 109; DLB 7

Bart, Andre Schwarz
See Schwarz-Bart, Andre

Barth, John (Simmons) 1930-   **CLC 1, 2, 3, 5, 7, 9, 10, 14, 27, 51, 89; DAM NOV; SSC 10**
See also AITN 1, 2; CA 1-4R; CABS 1; CANR 5, 23, 49, 64; DLB 2; MTCW

Barthelme, Donald 1931-1989   **CLC 1, 2, 3, 5, 6, 8, 13, 23, 46, 59; DAM NOV; SSC 2**
See also CA 21-24R; 129; CANR 20, 58; DLB 2; DLBY 80, 89; MTCW; SATA 7; SATA-Obit 62

Barthelme, Frederick 1943- .... **CLC 36**
See also CA 114; 122; DLBY 85; INT 122

Barthes, Roland (Gerard) 1915-1980.   **CLC 24, 83**
See also CA 130; 97-100; CANR 66; MTCW

Barzun, Jacques (Martin) 1907- .... **CLC 51**
See also CA 61-64; CANR 22

Bashevis, Isaac
See Singer, Isaac Bashevis

Bashkirtseff, Marie 1859-1884 .... **NCLC 27**

Basho
See Matsuo Basho

Bass, Kingsley B., Jr.
See Bullins, Ed

Bass, Rick 1958- .... **CLC 79**
See also CA 126; CANR 53

Bassani, Giorgio 1916- .... **CLC 9**
See also CA 65-68; CANR 33; DLB 128, 177; MTCW

Bastos, Augusto (Antonio) Roa
See Roa Bastos, Augusto (Antonio)

Bataille, Georges 1897-1962 .... **CLC 29**
See also CA 101; 89-92

Bates, H(erbert) E(rnest) 1905-1974 .. **CLC 46; DAB; DAM POP; SSC 10**
See also CA 93-96; 45-48; CANR 34; DLB 162, 191; MTCW

Bauchart
See Camus, Albert

Baudelaire, Charles 1821-1867   **NCLC 6, 29, 55; DA; DAB; DAC; DAM MST, POET; PC 1; SSC 18; WLC**

Baudrillard, Jean 1929- .... **CLC 60**

Baum, L(yman) Frank 1856-1919 ..... **TCLC 7**
See also CA 108; 133; CLR 15; DLB 22; JRDA; MAICYA; MTCW; SATA 18

Baum, Louis F.
See Baum, L(yman) Frank

Baumbach, Jonathan 1933- .... **CLC 6, 23**
See also CA 13-16R; CAAS 5; CANR 12, 66; DLBY 80; INT CANR-12; MTCW

Bausch, Richard (Carl) 1945- .... **CLC 51**
See also CA 101; CAAS 14; CANR 43, 61; DLB 130

Baxter, Charles (Morley) 1947- . **CLC 45, 78; DAM POP**
See also CA 57-60; CANR 40, 64; DLB 130

Baxter, George Owen
See Faust, Frederick (Schiller)

Baxter, James K(eir) 1926-1972 .... **CLC 14**
See also CA 77-80

Baxter, John
See Hunt, E(verette) Howard, (Jr.)

Bayer, Sylvia
See Glassco, John

Baynton, Barbara 1857-1929 .... **TCLC 57**

Beagle, Peter S(oyer) 1939- .... **CLC 7, 104**
See also CA 9-12R; CANR 4, 51; DLBY 80; INT CANR-4; SATA 60

Bean, Normal
See Burroughs, Edgar Rice

Beard, Charles A(ustin) 1874-1948 **TCLC 15**
See also CA 115; DLB 17; SATA 18

Beardsley, Aubrey 1872-1898 .... **NCLC 6**

Beattie, Ann 1947- .. **CLC 8, 13, 18, 40, 63; DAM NOV, POP; SSC 11**
See also BEST 90:2; CA 81-84; CANR 53; DLBY 82; MTCW

Beattie, James 1735-1803 .... **NCLC 25**
See also DLB 109

Beauchamp, Kathleen Mansfield 1888-1923
See Mansfield, Katherine
See also CA 104; 134; DA; DAC; DAM MST

Beaumarchais, Pierre-Augustin Caron de 1732-1799 .... **DC 4**
See also DAM DRAM

Beaumont, Francis 1584(?)-1616 **LC 33; DC 6**
See also CDBLB Before 1660; DLB 58, 121

Beauvoir, Simone (Lucie Ernestine Marie Bertrand) de 1908-1986   **CLC 1, 2, 4, 8, 14, 31, 44, 50, 71; DA; DAB; DAC; DAM MST, NOV; WLC**
See also CA 9-12R; 118; CANR 28, 61; DLB 72; DLBY 86; MTCW

Becker, Carl (Lotus) 1873-1945 ...... **TCLC 63**
See also CA 157; DLB 17

Becker, Jurek 1937-1997 .... **CLC 7, 19**
See also CA 85-88; 157; CANR 60; DLB 75

Becker, Walter 1950- .... **CLC 26**

Beckett, Samuel (Barclay) 1906-1989   **CLC 1, 2, 3, 4, 6, 9, 10, 11, 14, 18, 29, 57, 59, 83; DA; DAB; DAC; DAM DRAM, MST, NOV; SSC 16; WLC**
See also CA 5-8R; 130; CANR 33, 61; CDBLB 1945-1960; DLB 13, 15; DLBY 90; MTCW

Beckford, William 1760-1844 .... **NCLC 16**
See also DLB 39

Beckman, Gunnel 1910- .... **CLC 26**
See also CA 33-36R; CANR 15; CLR 25; MAICYA; SAAS 9; SATA 6

Becque, Henri 1837-1899 .... **NCLC 3**
See also DLB 192

Beddoes, Thomas Lovell 1803-1849 ...... **NCLC 3**
See also DLB 96

Bede c. 673-735 .... **CMLC 20**
See also DLB 146

Bedford, Donald F.
See Fearing, Kenneth (Flexner)

Beecher, Catharine Esther 1800-1878   **NCLC 30**
See also DLB 1

Beecher, John 1904-1980 .... **CLC 6**
See also AITN 1; CA 5-8R; 105; CANR 8

Beer, Johann 1655-1700 .... **LC 5**
See also DLB 168

Beer, Patricia 1924- .... **CLC 58**
See also CA 61-64; CANR 13, 46; DLB 40

Beerbohm, Max
See Beerbohm, (Henry) Max(imilian)

Beerbohm, (Henry) Max(imilian) 1872-1956   **TCLC 1, 24**
See also CA 104; 154; DLB 34, 100

Beer-Hofmann, Richard 1866-1945 **TCLC 60**
See also CA 160; DLB 81

Begiebing, Robert J(ohn) 1946- .... **CLC 70**
See also CA 122; CANR 40

Behan, Brendan 1923-1964   **CLC 1, 8, 11, 15, 79; DAM DRAM**
See also CA 73-76; CANR 33; CDBLB 1945-1960; DLB 13; MTCW

Behn, Aphra 1640(?)-1689   **LC 1, 30; DA; DAB; DAC; DAM DRAM, MST, NOV, POET; DC 4; PC 13; WLC**
See also DLB 39, 80, 131

Behrman, S(amuel) N(athaniel) 1893-1973   **CLC 40**
See also CA 13-16; 45-48; CAP 1; DLB 7, 44

Belasco, David 1853-1931 .... **TCLC 3**
See also CA 104, DLB 7

Belcheva, Elisaveta 1893- .... **CLC 10**
See also Bagryana, Elisaveta

Beldone, Phil "Cheech"
See Ellison, Harlan (Jay)

Beleno
See Azuela, Mariano

Belinski, Vissarion Grigoryevich 1811-1848   **NCLC 5**

Belitt, Ben 1911- .... **CLC 22**
See also CA 13-16R; CAAS 4; CANR 7; DLB 5

Bell, Gertrude 1868-1926 .... **TCLC 67**
See also DLB 174

Bell, James Madison 1826-1902 ..... **TCLC 43; BLC; DAM MULT**
See also BW 1; CA 122; 124; DLB 50

Bell, Madison Smartt 1957- .... **CLC 41, 102**
See also CA 111; CANR 28, 54

Bell, Marvin (Hartley) 1937- **CLC 8, 31; DAM POET**
See also CA 21-24R; CAAS 14; CANR 59; DLB 5; MTCW

Bell, W. L. D.
See Mencken, H(enry) L(ouis)

Bellamy, Atwood C.
See Mencken, H(enry) L(ouis)

Bellamy, Edward 1850-1898 .... **NCLC 4**
See also DLB 12

Bellin, Edward J.
See Kuttner, Henry

Belloc, (Joseph) Hilaire (Pierre Sebastien Rene Swanton) 1870-1953 ..... **TCLC 7, 18; DAM POET**
See also CA 106; 152; DLB 19, 100, 141, 174; YABC 1

Belloc, Joseph Peter Rene Hilaire
See Belloc, (Joseph) Hilaire (Pierre Sebastien Rene Swanton)

Belloc, Joseph Pierre Hilaire
See Belloc, (Joseph) Hilaire (Pierre Sebastien Rene Swanton)

Belloc, M. A.
See Lowndes, Marie Adelaide (Belloc)

Bellow, Saul 1915- .... **CLC 1, 2, 3, 6, 8, 10, 13, 15, 25, 33, 34, 63, 79; DA; DAB; DAC; DAM MST, NOV, POP; SSC 14; WLC**
See also AITN 2; BEST 89:3; CA 5-8R; CABS 1; CANR 29, 53; CDALB 1941-1968; DLB 2, 28; DLBD 3; DLBY 82; MTCW

Belser, Reimond Karel Maria de 1929-
See Ruyslinck, Ward
See also CA 152

Bely, Andrey .... **TCLC 7; PC 11**
See also Bugayev, Boris Nikolayevich

Belyi, Andrei
See Bugayev, Boris Nikolayevich

Benary, Margot
See Benary-Isbert, Margot

Benary-Isbert, Margot 1889-1979 ..... **CLC 12**
See also CA 5-8R; 89-92; CANR 4; CLR 12; MAICYA; SATA 2; SATA-Obit 21

Benavente (y Martinez), Jacinto 1866-1954 **TCLC 3; DAM DRAM, MULT**
See also CA 106; 131; HW; MTCW

Benchley, Peter (Bradford) 1940- ... **CLC 4, 8; DAM NOV, POP**
See also AAYA 14; AITN 2; CA 17-20R; CANR 12, 35, 66; MTCW; SATA 3, 89

Benchley, Robert (Charles) 1889-1945 **TCLC 1, 55**
See also CA 105; 153; DLB 11

Benda, Julien 1867-1956 .... **TCLC 60**
See also CA 120; 154

Benedict, Ruth (Fulton) 1887-1948 **TCLC 60**
See also CA 158

Benedikt, Michael 1935- .... **CLC 4, 14**
See also CA 13-16R; CANR 7; DLB 5

Benet, Juan 1927- .... **CLC 28**
See also CA 143

Benet, Stephen Vincent 1898-1943 .. **TCLC 7; DAM POET; SSC 10**
See also CA 104; 152; DLB 4, 48, 102; DLBY 97; YABC 1

Benet, William Rose 1886-1950 ..... **TCLC 28; DAM POET**
See also CA 118; 152; DLB 45

Benford, Gregory (Albert) 1941- .... **CLC 52**
See also CA 69-72; CAAS 27; CANR 12, 24, 49; DLBY 82

Bengtsson, Frans (Gunnar) 1894-1954 **TCLC 48**

Benjamin, David
See Slavitt, David R(ytman)

Benjamin, Lois
See Gould, Lois

Benjamin, Walter 1892-1940 .... **TCLC 39**
See also CA 164

Benn, Gottfried 1886-1956 .... **TCLC 3**
See also CA 106; 153; DLB 56

Bennett, Alan 1934- ..... **CLC 45, 77; DAB; DAM MST**
See also CA 103; CANR 35, 55; MTCW

Bennett, (Enoch) Arnold 1867-1931 **TCLC 5, 20**
See also CA 106; 155; CDBLB 1890-1914; DLB 10, 34, 98, 135

Bennett, Elizabeth
See Mitchell, Margaret (Munnerlyn)

Bennett, George Harold 1930-
See Bennett, Hal
See also BW 1; CA 97-100

Bennett, Hal .... **CLC 5**
See also Bennett, George Harold
See also DLB 33

Bennett, Jay 1912- .... **CLC 35**
See also AAYA 10; CA 69-72; CANR 11, 42; JRDA; SAAS 4; SATA 41, 87; SATA-Brief 27

Bennett, Louise (Simone) 1919- ...... **CLC 28; BLC; DAM MULT**
See also BW 2; CA 151; DLB 117

Benson, E(dward) F(rederic) 1867-1940 **TCLC 27**
See also CA 114; 157; DLB 135, 153

Benson, Jackson J. 1930- .... **CLC 34**
See also CA 25-28R; DLB 111

Benson, Sally 1900-1972 .... **CLC 17**
See also CA 19-20; 37-40R; CAP 1; SATA 1, 35; SATA-Obit 27

Benson, Stella 1892-1933 .... **TCLC 17**
See also CA 117; 155; DLB 36, 162

Bentham, Jeremy 1748-1832 .... **NCLC 38**
See also DLB 107, 158

Bentley, E(dmund) C(lerihew) 1875-1956 **TCLC 12**
See also CA 108; DLB 70

Bentley, Eric (Russell) 1916- .... **CLC 24**
See also CA 5-8R; CANR 6, 67; INT CANR-6

Beranger, Pierre Jean de 1780-1857 ..... **NCLC 34**

Berdyaev, Nicolas
See Berdyaev, Nikolai (Aleksandrovich)

Berdyaev, Nikolai (Aleksandrovich) 1874-1948 **TCLC 67**
See also CA 120; 157

Berdyayev, Nikolai (Aleksandrovich)
See Berdyaev, Nikolai (Aleksandrovich)

Berendt, John (Lawrence) 1939- .... **CLC 86**
See also CA 146

Berger, Colonel
See Malraux, (Georges-)Andre

Berger, John (Peter) 1926- .... **CLC 2, 19**
See also CA 81-84; CANR 51; DLB 14

Berger, Melvin H. 1927- .... **CLC 12**
See also CA 5-8R; CANR 4; CLR 32; SAAS 2; SATA 5, 88

Berger, Thomas (Louis) 1924- **CLC 3, 5, 8, 11, 18, 38; DAM NOV**
See also CA 1-4R; CANR 5, 28, 51; DLB 2; DLBY 80; INT CANR-28; MTCW

Bergman, (Ernst) Ingmar 1918- .. **CLC 16, 72**
See also CA 81-84; CANR 33

Bergson, Henri 1859-1941 .... **TCLC 32**
See also CA 164

Bergstein, Eleanor 1938- .... **CLC 4**
See also CA 53-56; CANR 5

Berkoff, Steven 1937- .... **CLC 56**
See also CA 104

Bermant, Chaim (Icyk) 1929- .... **CLC 40**
See also CA 57-60; CANR 6, 31, 57

Bern, Victoria
See Fisher, M(ary) F(rances) K(ennedy)

Bernanos, (Paul Louis) Georges 1888-1948 **TCLC 3**
See also CA 104; 130; DLB 72

Bernard, April 1956- .... **CLC 59**
See also CA 131

Berne, Victoria
See Fisher, M(ary) F(rances) K(ennedy)

Bernhard, Thomas 1931-1989 .. **CLC 3, 32, 61**
See also CA 85-88; 127; CANR 32, 57; DLB 85, 124; MTCW

Bova, Ben(jamin William) 1932- .... **CLC 45**
See also AAYA 16; CA 5-8R; CAAS 18; CANR 11, 56; CLR 3; DLBY 81; INT CANR-11; MAICYA; MTCW; SATA 6, 68

Bowen, Elizabeth (Dorothea Cole) 1899-1973 **CLC 1, 3, 6, 11, 15, 22; DAM NOV; SSC 3, 28**
See also CA 17-18; 41-44R; CANR 35; CAP 2; CDBLB 1945-1960; DLB 15, 162; MTCW

Bowering, George 1935- .... **CLC 15, 47**
See also CA 21-24R; CAAS 16; CANR 10; DLB 53

Bowering, Marilyn R(uthe) 1949- ...... **CLC 32**
See also CA 101; CANR 49

Bowers, Edgar 1924- .... **CLC 9**
See also CA 5-8R; CANR 24; DLB 5

Bowie, David .... **CLC 17**
See also Jones, David Robert

Bowles, Jane (Sydney) 1917-1973 .. **CLC 3, 68**
See also CA 19-20; 41-44R; CAP 2

Bowles, Paul (Frederick) 1910-1986 .... **CLC 1, 2, 19, 53; SSC 3**
See also CA 1-4R; CAAS 1; CANR 1, 19, 50; DLB 5, 6; MTCW

Box, Edgar
See Vidal, Gore

Boyd, Nancy
See Millay, Edna St. Vincent

Boyd, William 1952- .... **CLC 28, 53, 70**
See also CA 114; 120; CANR 51

Boyle, Kay 1902-1992 .... **CLC 1, 5, 19, 58; SSC 5**
See also CA 13-16R; 140; CAAS 1; CANR 29, 61; DLB 4, 9, 48, 86; DLBY 93; MTCW

Boyle, Mark
See Kienzle, William X(avier)

Boyle, Patrick 1905-1982 .... **CLC 19**
See also CA 127

Boyle, T. C. 1948-
See Boyle, T(homas) Coraghessan

Boyle, T(homas) Coraghessan 1948- ....**CLC 36, 55, 90; DAM POP; SSC 16**
See also BEST 90:4; CA 120; CANR 44; DLBY 86

Boz
See Dickens, Charles (John Huffam)

Brackenridge, Hugh Henry 1748-1816 .... **NCLC 7**
See also DLB 11, 37

Bradbury, Edward P.
See Moorcock, Michael (John)

Bradbury, Malcolm (Stanley) 1932- . **CLC 32, 61; DAM NOV**
See also CA 1-4R; CANR 1, 33; DLB 14; MTCW

Bradbury, Ray (Douglas) 1920- .... **CLC 1, 3, 10, 15, 42, 98; DA; DAB; DAC; DAM MST, NOV, POP; SSC 29; WLC**
See also AAYA 15; AITN 1, 2; CA 1-4R; CANR 2, 30; CDALB 1968-1988; DLB 2, 8; MTCW; SATA 11, 64

Bradford, Gamaliel 1863-1932 .... **TCLC 36**
See also CA 160; DLB 17

Bradley, David (Henry, Jr.) 1950- .... **CLC 23; BLC; DAM MULT**
See also BW 1; CA 104; CANR 26; DLB 33

Bradley, John Ed(mund, Jr.) 1958- .... **CLC 55**
See also CA 139

Bradley, Marion Zimmer 1930- . ..... **CLC 30; DAM POP**
See also AAYA 9; CA 57-60; CAAS 10; CANR 7, 31, 51; DLB 8; MTCW; SATA 90

Bradstreet, Anne 1612(?)-1672 ...... **LC 4, 30; DA; DAC; DAM MST, POET; PC 10**
See also CDALB 1640-1865; DLB 24

Brady, Joan 1939- .... **CLC 86**
See also CA 141

Bragg, Melvyn 1939- .... **CLC 10**
See also BEST 89:3; CA 57-60; CANR 10, 48; DLB 14

Braine, John (Gerard) 1922-1986 ...... **CLC 1, 3, 41**
See also CA 1-4R; 120; CANR 1, 33; CDBLB 1945-1960; DLB 15; DLBY 86; MTCW

Bramah, Ernest 1868-1942 .... **TCLC 72**
See also CA 156; DLB 70

Brammer, William 1930(?)-1978 .... **CLC 31**
See also CA 77-80

Brancati, Vitaliano 1907-1954 .... **TCLC 12**
See also CA 109

Brancato, Robin F(idler) 1936- .... **CLC 35**
See also AAYA 9; CA 69-72; CANR 11, 45; CLR 32; JRDA; SAAS 9; SATA 97

Brand, Max
See Faust, Frederick (Schiller)

Brand, Millen 1906-1980 .... **CLC 7**
See also CA 21-24R; 97-100

Branden, Barbara .... **CLC 44**
See also CA 148

Brandes, Georg (Morris Cohen) 1842-1927 **TCLC 10**
See also CA 105

Brandys, Kazimierz 1916- .... **CLC 62**

Branley, Franklyn M(ansfield) 1915- **CLC 21**
See also CA 33-36R; CANR 14, 39; CLR 13; MAICYA; SAAS 16; SATA 4, 68

Brathwaite, Edward Kamau 1930- ...**CLC 11; DAM POET**
See also BW 2; CA 25-28R; CANR 11, 26, 47; DLB 125

Brautigan, Richard (Gary) 1935-1984 .... **CLC 1, 3, 5, 9, 12, 34, 42; DAM NOV**
See also CA 53-56; 113; CANR 34; DLB 2, 5; DLBY 80, 84; MTCW; SATA 56

Brave Bird, Mary 1953-
See Crow Dog, Mary (Ellen)
See also NNAL

Braverman, Kate 1950- .... **CLC 67**
See also CA 89-92

Brecht, (Eugen) Bertolt (Friedrich) 1898-1956 **TCLC 1, 6, 13, 35; DA; DAB; DAC; DAM DRAM, MST; DC 3; WLC**
See also CA 104; 133; CANR 62; DLB 56, 124; MTCW

Brecht, Eugen Berthold Friedrich
See Brecht, (Eugen) Bertolt (Friedrich)

Bremer, Fredrika 1801-1865 .... **NCLC 11**

Brennan, Christopher John 1870-1932 ....
TCLC 17
See also CA 117

Brennan, Maeve 1917- .... **CLC 5**
See also CA 81-84

Brent, Linda
See Jacobs, Harriet

Brentano, Clemens (Maria) 1778-1842 **NCLC 1**
See also DLB 90

Brent of Bin Bin
See Franklin, (Stella Maria Sarah) Miles

Brenton, Howard 1942- .... **CLC 31**
See also CA 69-72; CANR 33, 67; DLB 13; MTCW

Breslin, James 1930-1996
See Breslin, Jimmy
See also CA 73-76; CANR 31; DAM NOV; MTCW

Breslin, Jimmy .... **CLC 4, 43**
See also Breslin, James
See also AITN 1; DLB 185

Bresson, Robert 1901- .... **CLC 16**
See also CA 110; CANR 49

Breton, Andre 1896-1966 .... **CLC 2, 9, 15, 54; PC 15**
See also CA 19-20; 25-28R; CANR 40, 60; CAP 2; DLB 65; MTCW

Breytenbach, Breyten 1939(?)- .. **CLC 23, 37; DAM POET**
See also CA 113; 129; CANR 61

Bridgers, Sue Ellen 1942- .... **CLC 26**
See also AAYA 8; CA 65-68; CANR 11, 36; CLR 18; DLB 52; JRDA; MAICYA; SAAS 1; SATA 22, 90

Bridges, Robert (Seymour) 1844-1930 **TCLC 1; DAM POET**
See also CA 104; 152; CDBLB 1890-1914; DLB 19, 98

Bruce, Lenny .... **CLC 21**
See also Schneider, Leonard Alfred

Bruin, John
See Brutus, Dennis

Brulard, Henri
See Stendhal

Brulls, Christian
See Simenon, Georges (Jacques Christian)

Brunner, John (Kilian Houston) 1934-1995
CLC 8, 10; DAM POP
See also CA 1-4R; 149; CAAS 8; CANR 2, 37;
MTCW

Bruno, Giordano 1548-1600 .... **LC 27**

Brutus, Dennis 1924- .... **CLC 43; BLC; DAM**
MULT, POET
See also BW 2; CA 49-52; CAAS 14; CANR 2,
27, 42; DLB 117

Bryan, C(ourtlandt) D(ixon) B(arnes) 1936-
CLC 29
See also CA 73-76; CANR 13, 68; DLB 185; INT
CANR-13

Bryan, Michael
See Moore, Brian

Bryant, William Cullen 1794-1878   **NCLC 6,**
46; DA; DAB; DAC; DAM MST, POET; PC 20
See also CDALB 1640-1865; DLB 3, 43, 59, 189

Bryusov, Valery Yakovlevich 1873-1924 ....
TCLC 10
See also CA 107; 155

Buchan, John 1875-1940 ..... **TCLC 41; DAB;**
DAM POP
See also CA 108; 145; DLB 34, 70, 156; YABC 2

Buchanan, George 1506-1582 .... **LC 4**

Buchheim, Lothar-Guenther 1918- ..... **CLC 6**
See also CA 85-88

Buchner, (Karl) Georg 1813-1837 .. **NCLC 26**

Buchwald, Art(hur) 1925- .... **CLC 33**
See also AITN 1; CA 5-8R; CANR 21, 67;
MTCW; SATA 10

Buck, Pearl S(ydenstricker) 1892-1973   **CLC**
7, 11, 18; DA; DAB; DAC; DAM MST, NOV
See also AITN 1; CA 1-4R; 41-44R; CANR 1,
34; DLB 9, 102; MTCW; SATA 1, 25

Buckler, Ernest 1908-1984 ..... **CLC 13; DAC;**
DAM MST
See also CA 11-12; 114; CAP 1; DLB 68; SATA 47

Buckley, Vincent (Thomas) 1925-1988 **CLC 57**
See also CA 101

Buckley, William F(rank), Jr. 1925- .   **CLC 7,**
18, 37; DAM POP
See also AITN 1; CA 1-4R; CANR 1, 24, 53;
DLB 137; DLBY 80; INT CANR-24;
MTCW

Buechner, (Carl) Frederick 1926- **CLC 2, 4, 6,**
9; DAM NOV
See also CA 13-16R; CANR 11, 39, 64; DLBY
80; INT CANR-11; MTCW

Buell, John (Edward) 1927- .... **CLC 10**
See also CA 1-4R; DLB 53

Buero Vallejo, Antonio 1916- .... **CLC 15, 46**
See also CA 106; CANR 24, 49; HW; MTCW

Bufalino, Gesualdo 1920(?)- .... **CLC 74**
See also DLB 196

Bugayev, Boris Nikolayevich 1880-1934
TCLC 7; PC 11
See also Bely, Andrey
See also CA 104; 165

Bukowski, Charles 1920-1994   **CLC 2, 5, 9, 41,**
82, 108; DAM NOV, POET; PC 18
See also CA 17-20R; 144; CANR 40, 62; DLB
5, 130, 169; MTCW

Bulgakov, Mikhail (Afanas'evich) 1891-1940
TCLC 2, 16; DAM DRAM, NOV; SSC 18
See also CA 105; 152

Bulgya, Alexander Alexandrovich 1901-1956
TCLC 53
See also Fadeyev, Alexander
See also CA 117

Bullins, Ed 1935- ..... **CLC 1, 5, 7; BLC; DAM**
DRAM, MULT; DC 6
See also BW 2; CA 49-52; CAAS 16; CANR 24,
46; DLB 7, 38; MTCW

Bulwer-Lytton, Edward (George Earle Lytton)
1803-1873 .... **NCLC 1, 45**
See also DLB 21

Bunin, Ivan Alexeyevich 1870-1953 ... **TCLC 6; SSC 5**
See also CA 104

Bunting, Basil 1900-1985 ....   **CLC 10, 39, 47;**
DAM POET
See also CA 53-56; 115; CANR 7; DLB 20

Bunuel, Luis 1900-1983 .... **CLC 16, 80; DAM**
MULT; HLC
See also CA 101; 110; CANR 32; HW

Bunyan, John 1628-1688 .....**LC 4; DA; DAB;**
DAC; DAM MST; WLC
See also CDBLB 1660-1789; DLB 39

Burckhardt, Jacob (Christoph) 1818-1897
NCLC 49

Burford, Eleanor
See Hibbert, Eleanor Alice Burford

Burgess, Anthony .... **CLC 1, 2, 4, 5,**
8, 10, 13, 15, 22, 40, 62, 81, 94; DAB
See also Wilson, John (Anthony) Burgess
See also AAYA 25; AITN 1; CDBLB 1960 to
Present; DLB 14, 194

Burke, Edmund 1729(?)-1797   **LC 7, 36; DA;**
DAB; DAC; DAM MST; WLC
See also DLB 104

Burke, Kenneth (Duva) 1897-1993 ..... **CLC 2,**
24
See also CA 5-8R; 143; CANR 39; DLB 45, 63;
MTCW

Burke, Leda
See Garnett, David

Burke, Ralph
See Silverberg, Robert

Burke, Thomas 1886-1945 .... **TCLC 63**
See also CA 113; 155

Burney, Fanny 1752-1840 .... **NCLC 12, 54**
See also DLB 39

Burns, Robert 1759-1796 .... **PC 6**
See also CDBLB 1789-1832; DA; DAB; DAC;
DAM MST, POET; DLB 109; WLC

Burns, Tex
See L'Amour, Louis (Dearborn)

Burnshaw, Stanley 1906- .... **CLC 3, 13, 44**
See also CA 9-12R; DLB 48; DLBY 97

Burr, Anne 1937- .... **CLC 6**
See also CA 25-28R

Burroughs, Edgar Rice 1875-1950   **TCLC 2,**
32; DAM NOV
See also AAYA 11; CA 104; 132; DLB 8;
MTCW; SATA 41

Burroughs, William S(eward) 1914-1997 **CLC**
1, 2, 5, 15, 22, 42, 75, 109; DA; DAB; DAC;
DAM MST, NOV, POP; WLC
See also AITN 2; CA 9-12R; 160; CANR 20,
52; DLB 2, 8, 16, 152; DLBY 81, 97; MTCW

Burton, Richard F. 1821-1890 .... **NCLC 42**
See also DLB 55, 184

Busch, Frederick 1941- ...... **CLC 7, 10, 18, 47**
See also CA 33-36R; CAAS 1; CANR 45; DLB 6

Bush, Ronald 1946- .... **CLC 34**
See also CA 136

Bustos, F(rancisco)
See Borges, Jorge Luis

Bustos Domecq, H(onorio)
See Bioy Casares, Adolfo; Borges, Jorge Luis

Butler, Octavia E(stelle) 1947- ......   **CLC 38;**
DAM MULT, POP
See also AAYA 18; BW 2; CA 73-76; CANR 12,
24, 38; DLB 33; MTCW; SATA 84

Butler, Robert Olen (Jr.) 1945- ......   **CLC 81;**
DAM POP
See also CA 112; CANR 66; DLB 173; INT 112

Butler, Samuel 1612-1680 .... **LC 16**
See also DLB 101, 126

Butler, Samuel 1835-1902 ... **TCLC 1, 33; DA;**
DAB; DAC; DAM MST, NOV; WLC
See also CA 143; CDBLB 1890-1914; DLB 18,
57, 174

Capra, Frank 1897-1991 .... **CLC 16**
See also CA 61-64; 135

Caputo, Philip 1941- .... **CLC 32**
See also CA 73-76; CANR 40

Caragiale, Ion Luca 1852-1912 .... **TCLC 76**
See also CA 157

Card, Orson Scott 1951- .... **CLC 44, 47, 50;
DAM POP**
See also AAYA 11; CA 102; CANR 27, 47; INT
CANR-27; MTCW; SATA 83

Cardenal, Ernesto 1925- .... **CLC 31; DAM
MULT, POET; HLC; PC 22**
See also CA 49-52; CANR 2, 32, 66; HW;
MTCW

Cardozo, Benjamin N(athan) 1870-1938
TCLC 65
See also CA 117; 164

Carducci, Giosue (Alessandro Giuseppe) 1835-
1907 ....

TCLC 32
See also CA 163

Carew, Thomas 1595(?)-1640 .... **LC 13**
See also DLB 126

Carey, Ernestine Gilbreth 1908- .... **CLC 17**
See also CA 5-8R; SATA 2

Carey, Peter 1943- .... **CLC 40, 55, 96**
See also CA 123; 127; CANR 53; INT 127;
MTCW; SATA 94

Carleton, William 1794-1869 .... **NCLC 3**
See also DLB 159

Carlisle, Henry (Coffin) 1926- .... **CLC 33**
See also CA 13-16R; CANR 15

Carlsen, Chris
See Holdstock, Robert P.

Carlson, Ron(ald F.) 1947- .... **CLC 54**
See also CA 105; CANR 27

Carlyle, Thomas 1795-1881 .... **NCLC 22; DA;
DAB; DAC; DAM MST**
See also CDBLB 1789-1832; DLB 55; 144

Carman, (William) Bliss 1861-1929 **TCLC 7;
DAC**
See also CA 104; 152; DLB 92

Carnegie, Dale 1888-1955 .... **TCLC 53**

Carossa, Hans 1878-1956 .... **TCLC 48**
See also DLB 66

Carpenter, Don(ald Richard) 1931-1995 **CLC
41**
See also CA 45-48; 149; CANR 1

Carpentier (y Valmont), Alejo 1904-1980
CLC 8, 11, 38; DAM MULT; HLC
See also CA 65-68; 97-100; CANR 11; DLB 113;
HW

Carr, Caleb 1955(?)- .... **CLC 86**
See also CA 147

Carr, Emily 1871-1945 .... **TCLC 32**
See also CA 159; DLB 68

Carr, John Dickson 1906-1977 .... **CLC 3**
See also Fairbairn, Roger
See also CA 49-52; 69-72; CANR 3, 33, 60;
MTCW

Carr, Philippa
See Hibbert, Eleanor Alice Burford

Carr, Virginia Spencer 1929- .... **CLC 34**
See also CA 61-64; DLB 111

Carrere, Emmanuel 1957- .... **CLC 89**

Carrier, Roch 1937- **CLC 13, 78; DAC; DAM
MST**
See also CA 130; CANR 61; DLB 53

Carroll, James P. 1943(?)- .... **CLC 38**
See also CA 81-84

Carroll, Jim 1951- .... **CLC 35**
See also AAYA 17; CA 45-48; CANR 42

Carroll, Lewis .... **NCLC 2, 53; PC 18; WLC**
See also Dodgson, Charles Lutwidge
See also CDBLB 1832-1890; CLR 2, 18; DLB
18, 163, 178; JRDA

Carroll, Paul Vincent 1900-1968 .... **CLC 10**
See also CA 9-12R; 25-28R; DLB 10

Carruth, Hayden 1921- **CLC 4, 7, 10, 18, 84;
PC 10**
See also CA 9-12R; CANR 4, 38, 59; DLB 5,
165; INT CANR-4; MTCW; SATA 47

Carson, Rachel Louise 1907-1964 ... **CLC 71;
DAM POP**
See also CA 77-80; CANR 35; MTCW; SATA
23

Carter, Angela (Olive) 1940-1992 **CLC 5, 41,
76; SSC 13**
See also CA 53-56; 136; CANR 12, 36, 61; DLB
14; MTCW; SATA 66; SATA-Obit 70

Carter, Nick
See Smith, Martin Cruz

Carver, Raymond 1938-1988 .... **CLC 22, 36,
53, 55; DAM NOV; SSC 8**
See also CA 33-36R; 126; CANR 17, 34, 61;
DLB 130; DLBY 84, 88; MTCW

Cary, Elizabeth, Lady Falkland 1585-1639 ... **LC 30**

Cary, (Arthur) Joyce (Lunel) 1888-1957
TCLC 1, 29
See also CA 104; 164; CDBLB 1914-1945; DLB
15, 100

Casanova de Seingalt, Giovanni Jacopo 1725-
1798 .... **LC 13**

Casares, Adolfo Bioy
See Bioy Casares, Adolfo

Casely-Hayford, J(oseph) E(phraim) 1866-1930
TCLC 24; BLC; DAM MULT
See also BW 2; CA 123; 152

Casey, John (Dudley) 1939- .... **CLC 59**
See also BEST 90:2; CA 69-72; CANR 23

Casey, Michael 1947- .... **CLC 2**
See also CA 65-68; DLB 5

Casey, Patrick
See Thurman, Wallace (Henry)

Casey, Warren (Peter) 1935-1988 ...... **CLC 12**
See also CA 101; 127; INT 101

Casona, Alejandro .... **CLC 49**
See also Alvarez, Alejandro Rodriguez

Cassavetes, John 1929-1989 .... **CLC 20**
See also CA 85-88; 127

Cassian, Nina 1924- .... **PC 17**

Cassill, R(onald) V(erlin) 1919- ..... **CLC 4, 23**
See also CA 9-12R; CAAS 1; CANR 7, 45; DLB 6

Cassirer, Ernst 1874-1945 .... **TCLC 61**
See also CA 157

Cassity, (Allen) Turner 1929- .... **CLC 6, 42**
See also CA 17-20R; CAAS 8; CANR 11; DLB
105

Castaneda, Carlos 1931(?)- .... **CLC 12**
See also CA 25-28R; CANR 32, 66; HW; MTCW

Castedo, Elena 1937- .... **CLC 65**
See also CA 132

Castedo-Ellerman, Elena
See Castedo, Elena

Castellanos, Rosario 1925-1974 ...... **CLC 66;
DAM MULT; HLC**
See also CA 131; 53-56; CANR 58; DLB 113; HW

Castelvetro, Lodovico 1505-1571 .... **LC 12**

Castiglione, Baldassare 1478-1529 .... **LC 12**

Castle, Robert
See Hamilton, Edmond

Castro, Guillen de 1569-1631 .... **LC 19**

Castro, Rosalia de 1837-1885 ... **NCLC 3; DAM
MULT**

Cather, Willa
See Cather, Willa Sibert

Cather, Willa Sibert 1873-1947 **TCLC 1, 11,
31; DA; DAB; DAC; DAM MST, NOV; SSC
2; WLC**
See also AAYA 24; CA 104; 128; CDALB 1865-1917;
DLB 9, 54, 78; DLBD 1; MTCW; SATA 30

Catherine, Saint 1347-1380 .... **CMLC 27**

Cato, Marcus Porcius 234B.C.-149B.C. **CMLC
21**

Catton, (Charles) Bruce 1899-1978 ... **CLC 35**
See also AITN 1; CA 5-8R; 81-84; CANR 7;
DLB 17; SATA 2; SATA-Obit 24

Catullus c. 84B.C.-c. 54B.C. .... **CMLC 18**

Cauldwell, Frank
See King, Francis (Henry)

Caunitz, William J. 1933-1996 .... **CLC 34**
See also BEST 89:3; CA 125; 130; 152; INT 130

Causley, Charles (Stanley) 1917- .... **CLC 7**
See also CA 9-12R; CANR 5, 35; CLR 30; DLB
27; MTCW; SATA 3, 66

Caute, (John) David 1936- .... **CLC 29; DAM
NOV**
See also CA 1-4R; CAAS 4; CANR 1, 33, 64;
DLB 14

Cavafy, C(onstantine) P(eter) 1863-1933
TCLC 2, 7; DAM POET
See also Kavafis, Konstantinos Petrou
See also CA 148

Cavallo, Evelyn
See Spark, Muriel (Sarah)

Cavanna, Betty ....**CLC 12**
See also Harrison, Elizabeth Cavanna
See also JRDA; MAICYA; SAAS 4; SATA 1, 30

Cavendish, Margaret Lucas 1623-1673 ...**LC 30**
See also DLB 131

Caxton, William 1421(?)-1491(?) .... **LC 17**
See also DLB 170

Cayer, D. M.
See Duffy, Maureen

Cayrol, Jean 1911- .... **CLC 11**
See also CA 89-92; DLB 83

Cela, Camilo Jose 1916- **CLC 4, 13, 59; DAM
MULT; HLC**
See also BEST 90:2; CA 21-24R; CAAS 10;
CANR 21, 32; DLBY 89; HW; MTCW

Celan, Paul ....**CLC 10, 19, 53, 82;
PC 10**
See also Antschel, Paul
See also DLB 69

Celine, Louis-Ferdinand .... **CLC 1, 3, 4, 7,
9, 15, 47**
See also Destouches, Louis-Ferdinand
See also DLB 72

Cellini, Benvenuto 1500-1571 .... **LC 7**

Cendrars, Blaise 1887-1961 .... **CLC 18, 106**
See also Sauser-Hall, Frederic

Cernuda (y Bidon), Luis 1902-1963 ... **CLC 54;
DAM POET**
See also CA 131; 89-92; DLB 134; HW

Cervantes (Saavedra), Miguel de 1547-1616
**LC 6, 23; DA; DAB; DAC; DAM MST,
NOV; SSC 12; WLC**

Cesaire, Aime (Fernand) 1913- .. **CLC 19, 32;
BLC; DAM MULT, POET**
See also BW 2; CA 65-68; CANR 24, 43; MTCW

Chabon, Michael 1963- .... **CLC 55**
See also CA 139; CANR 57

Chabrol, Claude 1930- .... **CLC 16**
See also CA 110

Challans, Mary 1905-1983
See Renault, Mary
See also CA 81-84; 111; SATA 23; SATA-Obit 36

Challis, George
See Faust, Frederick (Schiller)

Chambers, Aidan 1934- .... **CLC 35**
See also CA 25-28R; CANR 12, 31, 58; JRDA;
MAICYA; SAAS 12; SATA 1, 69

Chambers, James 1948-
See Cliff, Jimmy
See also CA 124

Chambers, Jessie
See Lawrence, D(avid) H(erbert Richards)

Chambers, Robert W. 1865-1933 .... **TCLC 41**
See also CA 165

Chandler, Raymond (Thornton) 1888-1959
TCLC 1, 7; SSC 23
See also AAYA 25; CA 104; 129; CANR 60;
CDALB 1929-1941; DLBD 6; MTCW

Chang, Eileen 1921- .... **SSC 28**

Chang, Jung 1952- .... **CLC 71**
See also CA 142

Channing, William Ellery 1780-1842 **NCLC 17**
See also DLB 1, 59

Chaplin, Charles Spencer 1889-1977   **CLC 16**
See also Chaplin, Charlie
See also CA 81-84; 73-76

Chaplin, Charlie
See Chaplin, Charles Spencer
See also DLB 44

Chapman, George 1559(?)-1634 **LC 22; DAM
DRAM**
See also DLB 62, 121

Chapman, Graham 1941-1989 .... **CLC 21**
See also Monty Python
See also CA 116; 129; CANR 35

Chapman, John Jay 1862-1933 .... **TCLC 7**
See also CA 104

Chapman, Lee
See Bradley, Marion Zimmer

Chapman, Walker
See Silverberg, Robert

Chappell, Fred (Davis) 1936- .... **CLC 40, 78**
See also CA 5-8R; CAAS 4; CANR 8, 33, 67;
DLB 6, 105

Char, Rene(-Emile) 1907-1988   **CLC 9, 11, 14,
55; DAM POET**
See also CA 13-16R; 124; CANR 32; MTCW

Charby, Jay
See Ellison, Harlan (Jay)

Chardin, Pierre Teilhard de
See Teilhard de Chardin, (Marie Joseph) Pierre

Charles I 1600-1649 .... **LC 13**

Charriere, Isabelle de 1740-1805 .... **NCLC 66**

Charyn, Jerome 1937- .... **CLC 5, 8, 18**
See also CA 5-8R; CAAS 1; CANR 7, 61; DLBY
83; MTCW

Chase, Mary (Coyle) 1907-1981 .... **DC 1**
See also CA 77-80; 105; SATA 17; SATA-Obit 29

Chase, Mary Ellen 1887-1973 .... **CLC 2**
See also CA 13-16; 41-44R; CAP 1; SATA 10

Chase, Nicholas
See Hyde, Anthony

Chateaubriand, Francois Rene de 1768-1848
NCLC 3
See also DLB 119

Chatterje, Sarat Chandra 1876-1936(?)
See Chatterji, Saratchandra
See also CA 109

Chatterji, Bankim Chandra 1838-1894 ...**NCLC 19**

Chatterji, Saratchandra .... **TCLC 13**
See also Chatterje, Sarat Chandra

Chatterton, Thomas 1752-1770 .. **LC 3; DAM
POET**
See also DLB 109

Chatwin, (Charles) Bruce 1940-1989 **CLC 28,
57, 59; DAM POP**
See also AAYA 4; BEST 90:1; CA 85-88; 127;
DLB 194

Chaucer, Daniel
See Ford, Ford Madox

Chaucer, Geoffrey 1340(?)-1400   **LC 17; DA;
DAB; DAC; DAM MST, POET; PC 19;
WLCS**
See also CDBLB Before 1660; DLB 146

Chaviaras, Strates 1935-
See Haviaras, Stratis
See also CA 105

Chayefsky, Paddy .... **CLC 23**
See also Chayefsky, Sidney
See also DLB 7, 44; DLBY 81

Chayefsky, Sidney 1923-1981
See Chayefsky, Paddy
See also CA 9-12R; 104; CANR 18; DAM
DRAM

Chedid, Andree 1920- .... **CLC 47**
See also CA 145

Clarke, Austin C(hesterfield) 1934- .   **CLC 8, 53; BLC; DAC; DAM MULT**
See also BW 1; CA 25-28R; CAAS 16; CANR 14, 32, 68; DLB 53, 125

Clarke, Gillian 1937- .... **CLC 61**
See also CA 106; DLB 40

Clarke, Marcus (Andrew Hislop) 1846-1881 **NCLC 19**

Clarke, Shirley 1925- .... **CLC 16**

Clash, The
See Headon, (Nicky) Topper; Jones, Mick; Simonon, Paul; Strummer, Joe

Claudel, Paul (Louis Charles Marie) 1868-1955 **TCLC 2, 10**
See also CA 104; 165; DLB 192

Clavell, James (duMaresq) 1925-1994 **CLC 6, 25, 87; DAM NOV, POP**
See also CA 25-28R; 146; CANR 26, 48; MTCW

Cleaver, (Leroy) Eldridge 1935- .....   **CLC 30; BLC; DAM MULT**
See also BW 1; CA 21-24R; CANR 16

Cleese, John (Marwood) 1939- .... **CLC 21**
See also Monty Python
See also CA 112; 116; CANR 35; MTCW

Cleishbotham, Jebediah
See Scott, Walter

Cleland, John 1710-1789 .... **LC 2**
See also DLB 39

Clemens, Samuel Langhorne 1835-1910
See Twain, Mark
See also CA 104; 135; CDALB 1865-1917; DA; DAB; DAC; DAM MST, NOV; DLB 11, 12, 23, 64, 74, 186, 189; JRDA; MAICYA; YABC 2

Cleophil
See Congreve, William

Clerihew, E.
See Bentley, E(dmund) C(lerihew)

Clerk, N. W.
See Lewis, C(live) S(taples)

Cliff, Jimmy .... **CLC 21**
See also Chambers, James

Clifton, (Thelma) Lucille 1936-..   **CLC 19, 66; BLC; DAM MULT, POET; PC 17**
See also BW 2; CA 49-52; CANR 2, 24, 42; CLR 5; DLB 5, 41; MAICYA; MTCW; SATA 20, 69

Clinton, Dirk
See Silverberg, Robert

Clough, Arthur Hugh 1819-1861 .... **NCLC 27**
See also DLB 32

Clutha, Janet Paterson Frame 1924-
See Frame, Janet
See also CA 1-4R; CANR 2, 36; MTCW

Clyne, Terence
See Blatty, William Peter

Cobalt, Martin
See Mayne, William (James Carter)

Cobb, Irvin S. 1876-1944 .... **TCLC 77**
See also DLB 11, 25, 86

Cobbett, William 1763-1835 .... **NCLC 49**
See also DLB 43, 107, 158

Coburn, D(onald) L(ee) 1938- .... **CLC 10**
See also CA 89-92

Cocteau, Jean (Maurice Eugene Clement) 1889-1963 .... **CLC 1, 8, 15, 16, 43; DA; DAB; DAC; DAM DRAM, MST, NOV; WLC**
See also CA 25-28; CANR 40; CAP 2; DLB 65; MTCW

Codrescu, Andrei 1946-**CLC 46; DAM POET**
See also CA 33-36R; CAAS 19; CANR 13, 34, 53

Coe, Max
See Bourne, Randolph S(illiman)

Coe, Tucker
See Westlake, Donald E(dwin)

Coen, Ethan 1958- .... **CLC 108**
See also CA 126

Coen, Joel 1955- .... **CLC 108**
See also CA 126

The Coen Brothers
See Coen, Ethan; Coen, Joel

Coetzee, J(ohn) M(ichael) 1940-   **CLC 23, 33, 66; DAM NOV**
See also CA 77-80; CANR 41, 54; MTCW

Coffey, Brian
See Koontz, Dean R(ay)

Cohan, George M(ichael) 1878-1942   **TCLC 60**
See also CA 157

Cohen, Arthur A(llen) 1928-1986 .. **CLC 7, 31**
See also CA 1-4R; 120; CANR 1, 17, 42; DLB 28

Cohen, Leonard (Norman) 1934-   **CLC 3, 38; DAC; DAM MST**
See also CA 21-24R; CANR 14; DLB 53; MTCW

Cohen, Matt 1942- .... **CLC 19; DAC**
See also CA 61-64; CAAS 18; CANR 40; DLB 53

Cohen-Solal, Annie 19(?)- .... **CLC 50**

Colegate, Isabel 1931- .... **CLC 36**
See also CA 17-20R; CANR 8, 22; DLB 14; INT CANR-22; MTCW

Coleman, Emmett
See Reed, Ishmael

Coleridge, M. E.
See Coleridge, Mary E(lizabeth)

Coleridge, Mary E(lizabeth) 1861-1907 **TCLC 73**
See also CA 116; DLB 19, 98

Coleridge, Samuel Taylor 1772-1834   **NCLC 9, 54; DA; DAB; DAC; DAM MST, POET; PC 11; WLC**
See also CDBLB 1789-1832; DLB 93, 107

Coleridge, Sara 1802-1852 .... **NCLC 31**

Coles, Don 1928- .... **CLC 46**
See also CA 115; CANR 38

Coles, Robert (Martin) 1929- .... **CLC 108**
See also CA 45-48; CANR 3, 32, 66; INT CANR-32; SATA 23

Colette, (Sidonie-Gabrielle) 1873-1954 **TCLC 1, 5, 16; DAM NOV; SSC 10**
See also CA 104; 131; DLB 65; MTCW

Collett, (Jacobine) Camilla (Wergeland) 1813-1895 ....

NCLC 22

Collier, Christopher 1930- .... **CLC 30**
See also AAYA 13; CA 33-36R; CANR 13, 33; JRDA; MAICYA; SATA 16, 70

Collier, James L(incoln) 1928-   **CLC 30; DAM POP**
See also AAYA 13; CA 9-12R; CANR 4, 33, 60; CLR 3; JRDA; MAICYA; SAAS 21; SATA 8, 70

Collier, Jeremy 1650-1726 .... **LC 6**

Collier, John 1901-1980 .... **SSC 19**
See also CA 65-68; 97-100; CANR 10; DLB 77

Collingwood, R(obin) G(eorge) 1889(?)-1943 **TCLC 67**
See also CA 117; 155

Collins, Hunt
See Hunter, Evan

Collins, Linda 1931- .... **CLC 44**
See also CA 125

Collins, (William) Wilkie 1824-1889 **NCLC 1, 18**
See also CDBLB 1832-1890; DLB 18, 70, 159

Collins, William 1721-1759 ... **LC 4, 40; DAM POET**
See also DLB 109

Collodi, Carlo 1826-1890 .... **NCLC 54**
See also Lorenzini, Carlo
See also CLR 5

Colman, George 1732-1794
See Glassco, John

Colt, Winchester Remington
See Hubbard, L(afayette) Ron(ald)

Colter, Cyrus 1910- .... **CLC 58**
See also BW 1; CA 65-68; CANR 10, 66; DLB 33

Colton, James
See Hansen, Joseph

Colum, Padraic 1881-1972 .... **CLC 28**
See also CA 73-76; 33-36R; CANR 35; CLR 36; MAICYA; MTCW; SATA 15

Colvin, James
See Moorcock, Michael (John)

Colwin, Laurie (E.) 1944-1992 ... **CLC 5, 13, 23, 84**
See also CA 89-92; 139; CANR 20, 46; DLBY 80; MTCW

Comfort, Alex(ander) 1920- ..... **CLC 7; DAM POP**
See also CA 1-4R; CANR 1, 45

Comfort, Montgomery
See Campbell, (John) Ramsey

Compton-Burnett, I(vy) 1884(?)-1969 **CLC 1, 3, 10, 15, 34; DAM NOV**
See also CA 1-4R; 25-28R; CANR 4; DLB 36; MTCW

Comstock, Anthony 1844-1915 .... **TCLC 13**
See also CA 110

Comte, Auguste 1798-1857 .... **NCLC 54**

Conan Doyle, Arthur
See Doyle, Arthur Conan

Conde, Maryse 1937- ..... **CLC 52, 92; DAM MULT**
See also Boucolon, Maryse
See also BW 2

Condillac, Etienne Bonnot de 1714-1780 . **LC 26**

Condon, Richard (Thomas) 1915-1996 **CLC 4, 6, 8, 10, 45, 100; DAM NOV**
See also BEST 90:3; CA 1-4R; 151; CAAS 1; CANR 2, 23; INT CANR-23; MTCW

Confucius 551B.C.-479B.C. ... **CMLC 19; DA; DAB; DAC; DAM MST; WLCS**

Congreve, William 1670-1729 . **LC 5, 21; DA; DAB; DAC; DAM DRAM, MST, POET; DC 2; WLC**
See also CDBLB 1660-1789; DLB 39, 84

Connell, Evan S(helby), Jr. 1924- **CLC 4, 6, 45; DAM NOV**
See also AAYA 7; CA 1-4R; CAAS 2; CANR 2, 39; DLB 2; DLBY 81; MTCW

Connelly, Marc(us Cook) 1890-1980 ... **CLC 7**
See also CA 85-88; 102; CANR 30; DLB 7; DLBY 80; SATA-Obit 25

Connor, Ralph .... **TCLC 31**
See also Gordon, Charles William
See also DLB 92

Conrad, Joseph 1857-1924 ...... **TCLC 1, 6, 13, 25, 43, 57; DA; DAB; DAC; DAM MST, NOV; SSC 9; WLC**
See also CA 104; 131; CANR 60; CDBLB 1890-1914; DLB 10, 34, 98, 156; MTCW; SATA 27

Conrad, Robert Arnold
See Hart, Moss

Conroy, Donald Pat(rick) 1945- . **CLC 30, 74; DAM NOV, POP**
See also AAYA 8; AITN 1; CA 85-88; CANR 24, 53; DLB 6; MTCW

Constant (de Rebecque), (Henri) Benjamin 1767-1830 .... **NCLC 6**
See also DLB 119

Conybeare, Charles Augustus
See Eliot, T(homas) S(tearns)

Cook, Michael 1933- .... **CLC 58**
See also CA 93-96; CANR 68; DLB 53

Cook, Robin 1940- .... **CLC 14; DAM POP**
See also BEST 90:2; CA 108; 111; CANR 41; INT 111

Cook, Roy
See Silverberg, Robert

Cooke, Elizabeth 1948- .... **CLC 55**
See also CA 129

Cooke, John Esten 1830-1886 .... **NCLC 5**
See also DLB 3

Cooke, John Estes
See Baum, L(yman) Frank

Cooke, M. E.
See Creasey, John

Cooke, Margaret
See Creasey, John

Cook-Lynn, Elizabeth 1930- ... **CLC 93; DAM MULT**
See also CA 133; DLB 175; NNAL

Cooney, Ray .... **CLC 62**

Cooper, Douglas 1960- .... **CLC 86**

Cooper, Henry St. John
See Creasey, John

Cooper, J(oan) California ..... **CLC 56; DAM MULT**
See also AAYA 12; BW 1; CA 125; CANR 55

Cooper, James Fenimore 1789-1851 ..... **NCLC 1, 27, 54**
See also AAYA 22; CDALB 1640-1865; DLB 3; SATA 19

Coover, Robert (Lowell) 1932- .... **CLC 3, 7, 15, 32, 46, 87; DAM NOV; SSC 15**
See also CA 45-48; CANR 3, 37, 58; DLB 2; DLBY 81; MTCW

Copeland, Stewart (Armstrong) 1952- **CLC 26**

Coppard, A(lfred) E(dgar) 1878-1957 **TCLC 5; SSC 21**
See also CA 114; DLB 162; YABC 1

Coppee, Francois 1842-1908 .... **TCLC 25**

Coppola, Francis Ford 1939- .... **CLC 16**
See also CA 77-80; CANR 40; DLB 44

Corbiere, Tristan 1845-1875 .... **NCLC 43**

Corcoran, Barbara 1911- .... **CLC 17**
See also AAYA 14; CA 21-24R; CAAS 2; CANR 11, 28, 48; DLB 52; JRDA; SAAS 20; SATA 3, 77

Cordelier, Maurice
See Giraudoux, (Hippolyte) Jean

Corelli, Marie 1855-1924 .... **TCLC 51**
See also Mackay, Mary
See also DLB 34, 156

Corman, Cid 1924- .... **CLC 9**
See also Corman, Sidney
See also CAAS 2; DLB 5, 193

Corman, Sidney 1924-
See Corman, Cid
See also CA 85-88; CANR 44; DAM POET

Cormier, Robert (Edmund) 1925- . **CLC 12, 30; DA; DAB; DAC; DAM MST, NOV**
See also AAYA 3, 19; CA 1-4R; CANR 5, 23; CDALB 1968-1988; CLR 12; DLB 52; INT CANR-23; JRDA; MAICYA; MTCW; SATA 10, 45, 83

Corn, Alfred (DeWitt III) 1943- .... **CLC 33**
See also CA 104; CAAS 25; CANR 44; DLB 120; DLBY 80

Corneille, Pierre 1606-1684 ..... **LC 28; DAB; DAM MST**

Cornwell, David (John Moore) 1931- **CLC 9, 15; DAM POP**
See also le Carre, John
See also CA 5-8R; CANR 13, 33, 59; MTCW

Corso, (Nunzio) Gregory 1930- ..... **CLC 1, 11**
See also CA 5-8R; CANR 41; DLB 5, 16; MTCW

Cortazar, Julio 1914-1984 **CLC 2, 3, 5, 10, 13, 15, 33, 34, 92; DAM MULT, NOV; HLC; SSC 7**
See also CA 21-24R; CANR 12, 32; DLB 113; HW; MTCW

CORTES, HERNAN 1484-1547 .... **LC 31**

Corwin, Cecil
See Kornbluth, C(yril) M.

Cosic, Dobrica 1921- .... **CLC 14**
See also CA 122; 138; DLB 181

Costain, Thomas B(ertram) 1885-1965 ... **CLC 30**
See also CA 5-8R; 25-28R; DLB 9

Costantini, Humberto 1924(?)-1987 .. **CLC 49**
See also CA 131; 122; HW

Crunk
See Crumb, R(obert)

Crustt
See Crumb, R(obert)

Cryer, Gretchen (Kiger) 1935- .... **CLC 21**
See also CA 114; 123

Csath, Geza 1887-1919 .... **TCLC 13**
See also CA 111

Cudlip, David 1933- .... **CLC 34**

Cullen, Countee 1903-1946 **TCLC 4, 37; BLC;
DA; DAC; DAM MST, MULT, POET; PC
20; WLCS**
See also BW 1; CA 108; 124; CDALB 1917-
1929; DLB 4, 48, 51; MTCW; SATA 18

Cum, R.
See Crumb, R(obert)

Cummings, Bruce F(rederick) 1889-1919
See Barbellion, W. N. P.
See also CA 123

Cummings, E(dward) E(stlin) 1894-1962 **CLC
1, 3, 8, 12, 15, 68; DA; DAB; DAC; DAM
MST, POET; PC 5; WLC 2**
See also CA 73-76; CANR 31; CDALB 1929-
1941; DLB 4, 48; MTCW

Cunha, Euclides (Rodrigues Pimenta) da 1866-
1909 .... **TCLC 24**
See also CA 123

Cunningham, E. V.
See Fast, Howard (Melvin)

Cunningham, J(ames) V(incent) 1911-1985
CLC 3, 31
See also CA 1-4R; 115; CANR 1; DLB 5

Cunningham, Julia (Woolfolk) 1916- **CLC 12**
See also CA 9-12R; CANR 4, 19, 36; JRDA;
MAICYA; SAAS 2; SATA 1, 26

Cunningham, Michael 1952- .... **CLC 34**
See also CA 136

Cunninghame Graham, R(obert) B(ontine)
1852-1936 .... **TCLC 19**
See also Graham, R(obert) B(ontine)
Cunninghame
See also CA 119; DLB 98

Currie, Ellen 19(?)- .... **CLC 44**

Curtin, Philip
See Lowndes, Marie Adelaide (Belloc)

Curtis, Price
See Ellison, Harlan (Jay)

Cutrate, Joe
See Spiegelman, Art

Cynewulf c. 770-c. 840 .... **CMLC 23**

Czaczkes, Shmuel Yosef
See Agnon, S(hmuel) Y(osef Halevi)

Dabrowska, Maria (Szumska) 1889-1965 ... **CLC
15**
See also CA 106

Dabydeen, David 1955- .... **CLC 34**
See also BW 1; CA 125; CANR 56

Dacey, Philip 1939- .... **CLC 51**
See also CA 37-40R; CAAS 17; CANR 14, 32,
64; DLB 105

Dagerman, Stig (Halvard) 1923-1954 **TCLC 17**
See also CA 117; 155

Dahl, Roald 1916-1990 **CLC 1, 6, 18, 79; DAB;
DAC; DAM MST, NOV, POP**
See also AAYA 15; CA 1-4R; 133; CANR 6, 32,
37, 62; CLR 1, 7, 41; DLB 139; JRDA;
MAICYA; MTCW; SATA 1, 26, 73; SATA-
Obit 65

Dahlberg, Edward 1900-1977 .... **CLC 1, 7, 14**
See also CA 9-12R; 69-72; CANR 31, 62; DLB
48; MTCW

Daitch, Susan 1954- .... **CLC 103**
See also CA 161

Dale, Colin .... **TCLC 18**
See also Lawrence, T(homas) E(dward)

Dale, George E.
See Asimov, Isaac

Daly, Elizabeth 1878-1967 .... **CLC 52**
See also CA 23-24; 25-28R; CANR 60; CAP 2

Daly, Maureen 1921- .... **CLC 17**
See also AAYA 5; CANR 37; JRDA; MAICYA;
SAAS 1; SATA 2

Damas, Leon-Gontran 1912-1978 ...... **CLC 84**
See also BW 1; CA 125; 73-76

Dana, Richard Henry Sr. 1787-1879 **NCLC 53**

Daniel, Samuel 1562(?)-1619 .... **LC 24**
See also DLB 62

Daniels, Brett
See Adler, Renata

Dannay, Frederic 1905-1982 .. **CLC 11; DAM
POP**
See also Queen, Ellery
See also CA 1-4R; 107; CANR 1, 39; DLB 137;
MTCW

D'Annunzio, Gabriele 1863-1938 **TCLC 6, 40**
See also CA 104; 155

Danois, N. le
See Gourmont, Remy (-Marie-Charles) de

Dante 1265-1321 ..... **CMLC 3, 18; DA; DAB;
DAC; DAM MST, POET; PC 21; WLCS**

d'Antibes, Germain
See Simenon, Georges (Jacques Christian)

Danticat, Edwidge 1969- .... **CLC 94**
See also CA 152

Danvers, Dennis 1947- .... **CLC 70**

Danziger, Paula 1944- .... **CLC 21**
See also AAYA 4; CA 112; 115; CANR 37; CLR
20; JRDA; MAICYA; SATA 36, 63; SATA-
Brief 30

Da Ponte, Lorenzo 1749-1838 .... **NCLC 50**

Dario, Ruben 1867-1916 .... **TCLC 4; DAM
MULT; HLC; PC 15**
See also CA 131; HW; MTCW

Darley, George 1795-1846 .... **NCLC 2**
See also DLB 96

Darwin, Charles 1809-1882 .... **NCLC 57**
See also DLB 57, 166

Daryush, Elizabeth 1887-1977 .... **CLC 6, 19**
See also CA 49-52; CANR 3; DLB 20

Dashwood, Edmee Elizabeth Monica de la Pasture
1890-1943
See Delafield, E. M.
See also CA 119; 154

Daudet, (Louis Marie) Alphonse 1840-1897
NCLC 1
See also DLB 123

Daumal, Rene 1908-1944 .... **TCLC
14**
See also CA 114

Davenport, Guy (Mattison, Jr.) 1927- ... **CLC 6,
14, 38; SSC 16**
See also CA 33-36R; CANR 23; DLB 130

Davidson, Avram 1923-
See Queen, Ellery
See also CA 101; CANR 26; DLB 8

Davidson, Donald (Grady) 1893-1968 ... **CLC 2,
13, 19**
See also CA 5-8R; 25-28R; CANR 4; DLB 45

Davidson, Hugh
See Hamilton, Edmond

Davidson, John 1857-1909 .... **TCLC 24**
See also CA 118; DLB 19

Davidson, Sara 1943- .... **CLC 9**
See also CA 81-84; CANR 44, 68; DLB 185

Davie, Donald (Alfred) 1922-1995 ... **CLC 5, 8,
10, 31**
See also CA 1-4R; 149; CAAS 3; CANR 1, 44;
DLB 27; MTCW

Davies, Ray(mond Douglas) 1944- ..... **CLC 21**
See also CA 116; 146

Davies, Rhys 1901-1978 .... **CLC 23**
See also CA 9-12R; 81-84; CANR 4; DLB 139, 191

Davies, (William) Robertson 1913-1995 ... **CLC
2, 7, 13, 25, 42, 75, 91; DA; DAB; DAC;
DAM MST, NOV, POP; WLC**
See also BEST 89:2; CA 33-36R; 150; CANR
17, 42; DLB 68; INT CANR-17; MTCW

Davies, W(illiam) H(enry) 1871-1940 .... **TCLC 5**
See also CA 104; DLB 19, 174

Davies, Walter C.
See Kornbluth, C(yril) M.

Davis, Angela (Yvonne) 1944- .... **CLC 77; DAM MULT**
See also BW 2; CA 57-60; CANR 10

Davis, B. Lynch
See Bioy Casares, Adolfo; Borges, Jorge Luis

Davis, Gordon
See Hunt, E(verette) Howard, (Jr.)

Davis, Harold Lenoir 1896-1960 .... **CLC 49**
See also CA 89-92; DLB 9

Davis, Rebecca (Blaine) Harding 1831-1910 **TCLC 6**
See also CA 104; DLB 74

Davis, Richard Harding 1864-1916 ... **TCLC 24**
See also CA 114; DLB 12, 23. 78, 79, 189; DLBD 13

Davison, Frank Dalby 1893-1970 .... **CLC 15**
See also CA 116

Davison, Lawrence H.
See Lawrence, D(avid) H(erbert Richards)

Davison, Peter (Hubert) 1928- .... **CLC 28**
See also CA 9-12R; CAAS 4; CANR 3, 43; DLB 5

Davys, Mary 1674-1732 .... **LC 1**
See also DLB 39

Dawson, Fielding 1930- .... **CLC 6**
See also CA 85-88; DLB 130

Dawson, Peter
See Faust, Frederick (Schiller)

Day, Clarence (Shepard, Jr.) 1874-1935 **TCLC 25**
See also CA 108; DLB 11

Day, Thomas 1748-1789 .... **LC 1**
See also DLB 39; YABC 1

Day Lewis, C(ecil) 1904-1972 ... **CLC 1, 6, 10; DAM POET; PC 11**
See also Blake, Nicholas
See also CA 13-16; 33-36R; CANR 34; CAP 1; DLB 15, 20; MTCW

Dazai, Osamu 1909-1948 .... **TCLC 11**
See also Tsushima, Shuji
See also CA 164; DLB 182

de Andrade, Carlos Drummond
See Drummond de Andrade, Carlos

Deane, Norman
See Creasey, John

de Beauvoir, Simone (Lucie Ernestine Marie Bertrand)
See Beauvoir, Simone (Lucie Ernestine Marie Bertrand) de

de Beer, P.
See Bosman, Herman Charles

de Brissac, Malcolm
See Dickinson, Peter (Malcolm)

de Chardin, Pierre Teilhard
See Teilhard de Chardin, (Marie Joseph) Pierre

Dee, John 1527-1608 .... **LC 20**

Deer, Sandra 1940- .... **CLC 45**

De Ferrari, Gabriella 1941- .... **CLC 65**
See also CA 146

Defoe, Daniel 1660(?)-1731 . **LC 1; DA; DAB; DAC; DAM MST, NOV; WLC**
See also CDBLB 1660-1789; DLB 39, 95, 101; JRDA; MAICYA; SATA 22

de Gourmont, Remy(-Marie-Charles)
See Gourmont, Remy (-Marie-Charles) de

de Hartog, Jan 1914- .... **CLC 19**
See also CA 1-4R; CANR 1

de Hostos, E. M.
See Hostos (y Bonilla), Eugenio Maria de

de Hostos, Eugenio M.
See Hostos (y Bonilla), Eugenio Maria de

Deighton, Len .... **CLC 4, 7, 22, 46**
See also Deighton, Leonard Cyril
See also AAYA 6; BEST 89:2; CDBLB 1960 to Present; DLB 87

Deighton, Leonard Cyril 1929-
See Deighton, Len
See also CA 9-12R; CANR 19, 33, 68; DAM NOV, POP; MTCW

Dekker, Thomas 1572(?)-1632 ... **LC 22; DAM DRAM**
See also CDBLB Before 1660; DLB 62, 172

Delafield, E. M. 1890-1943 .... **TCLC 61**
See also Dashwood, Edmee Elizabeth Monica de la Pasture
See also DLB 34

de la Mare, Walter (John) 1873-1956 **TCLC 4, 53; DAB; DAC; DAM MST, POET; SSC 14; WLC**
See also CA 163; CDBLB 1914-1945; CLR 23; DLB 162; SATA 16

Delaney, Franey
See O'Hara, John (Henry)

Delaney, Shelagh 1939- **CLC 29; DAM DRAM**
See also CA 17-20R; CANR 30, 67; CDBLB 1960 to Present; DLB 13; MTCW

Delany, Mary (Granville Pendarves) 1700-1788 **LC 12**

Delany, Samuel R(ay, Jr.) 1942- . **CLC 8, 14, 38; BLC; DAM MULT**
See also AAYA 24; BW 2; CA 81-84; CANR 27, 43; DLB 8, 33; MTCW

De La Ramee, (Marie) Louise 1839-1908
See Ouida
See also SATA 20

de la Roche, Mazo 1879-1961 .... **CLC 14**
See also CA 85-88; CANR 30; DLB 68; SATA 64

De La Salle, Innocent
See Hartmann, Sadakichi

Delbanco, Nicholas (Franklin) 1942- ... **CLC 6, 13**
See also CA 17-20R; CAAS 2; CANR 29, 55; DLB 6

del Castillo, Michel 1933- .... **CLC 38**
See also CA 109

Deledda, Grazia (Cosima) 1875(?)-1936 ... **TCLC 23**
See also CA 123

Delibes, Miguel .... **CLC 8, 18**
See also Delibes Setien, Miguel

Delibes Setien, Miguel 1920-
See Delibes, Miguel
See also CA 45-48; CANR 1, 32; HW; MTCW

DeLillo, Don 1936- **CLC 8, 10, 13, 27, 39, 54, 76; DAM NOV, POP**
See also BEST 89:1; CA 81-84; CANR 21; DLB 6, 173; MTCW

de Lisser, H. G.
See De Lisser, H(erbert) G(eorge)
See also DLB 117

De Lisser, H(erbert) G(eorge) 1878-1944 **TCLC 12**
See also de Lisser, H. G.
See also BW 2; CA 109; 152

Deloney, Thomas 1560-1600 .... **LC 41**

Deloria, Vine (Victor), Jr. 1933- ...... **CLC 21; DAM MULT**
See also CA 53-56; CANR 5, 20, 48; DLB 175; MTCW; NNAL; SATA 21

Del Vecchio, John M(ichael) 1947- .... **CLC 29**
See also CA 110; DLBD 9

de Man, Paul (Adolph Michel) 1919-1983 **CLC 55**
See also CA 128; 111; CANR 61; DLB 67; MTCW

De Marinis, Rick 1934- .... **CLC 54**
See also CA 57-60; CAAS 24; CANR 9, 25, 50

Dembry, R. Emmet
See Murfree, Mary Noailles

Demby, William 1922- .. **CLC 53; BLC; DAM MULT**
See also BW 1; CA 81-84; DLB 33

de Menton, Francisco
See Chin, Frank (Chew, Jr.)

Demijohn, Thom
See Disch, Thomas M(ichael)

de Montherlant, Henry (Milon)
See Montherlant, Henry (Milon) de

Demosthenes 384B.C.-322B.C. .... **CMLC 13**
See also DLB 176

de Natale, Francine
See Malzberg, Barry N(athaniel)

Denby, Edwin (Orr) 1903-1983 .... **CLC 48**
See also CA 138; 110

Denis, Julio
See Cortazar, Julio

Denmark, Harrison
See Zelazny, Roger (Joseph)

Dennis, John 1658-1734 .... **LC 11**
See also DLB 101

Dennis, Nigel (Forbes) 1912-1989........ **CLC 8**
See also CA 25-28R; 129; DLB 13, 15; MTCW

Dent, Lester 1904(?)-1959 .... **TCLC 72**
See also CA 112; 161

De Palma, Brian (Russell) 1940- .... **CLC 20**
See also CA 109

De Quincey, Thomas 1785-1859 .... **NCLC 4**
See also CDBLB 1789-1832; DLB 110; 144

Deren, Eleanora 1908(?)-1961
See Deren, Maya
See also CA 111

Deren, Maya 1917-1961 .... **CLC 16, 102**
See also Deren, Eleanora

Derleth, August (William) 1909-1971 **CLC 31**
See also CA 1-4R; 29-32R; CANR 4; DLB 9;
SATA 5

Der Nister 1884-1950 .... **TCLC 56**

de Routisie, Albert
See Aragon, Louis

Derrida, Jacques 1930- .... **CLC 24, 87**
See also CA 124; 127

Derry Down Derry
See Lear, Edward

Dersonnes, Jacques
See Simenon, Georges (Jacques Christian)

Desai, Anita 1937- .... **CLC 19, 37, 97; DAB;**
DAM NOV
See also CA 81-84; CANR 33, 53; MTCW; SATA 63

de Saint-Luc, Jean
See Glassco, John

de Saint Roman, Arnaud
See Aragon, Louis

Descartes, Rene 1596-1650.............. **LC 20, 35**

De Sica, Vittorio 1901(?)-1974 .... **CLC 20**
See also CA 117

Desnos, Robert 1900-1945 .... **TCLC 22**
See also CA 121; 151

Destouches, Louis-Ferdinand 1894-1961 **CLC**
9, 15
See also Celine, Louis-Ferdinand
See also CA 85-88; CANR 28; MTCW

de Tolignac, Gaston
See Griffith, D(avid Lewelyn) W(ark)

Deutsch, Babette 1895-1982 .... **CLC 18**
See also CA 1-4R; 108; CANR 4; DLB 45; SATA
1; SATA-Obit 33

Devenant, William 1606-1649 .... **LC 13**

Devkota, Laxmiprasad 1909-1959 .. **TCLC 23**
See also CA 123

De Voto, Bernard (Augustine) 1897-1955
TCLC 29
See also CA 113; 160; DLB 9

De Vries, Peter 1910-1993   **CLC 1, 2, 3, 7,**
10, 28, 46; DAM NOV
See also CA 17-20R; 142; CANR 41; DLB 6;
DLBY 82; MTCW

Dexter, John
See Bradley, Marion Zimmer

Dexter, Martin
See Faust, Frederick (Schiller)

Dexter, Pete 1943-   **CLC 34, 55; DAM POP**
See also BEST 89:2; CA 127; 131; INT 131;
MTCW

Diamano, Silmang
See Senghor, Leopold Sedar

Diamond, Neil 1941- .... **CLC 30**
See also CA 108

Diaz del Castillo, Bernal 1496-1584 ..... **LC 31**

di Bassetto, Corno
See Shaw, George Bernard

Dick, Philip K(indred) 1928-1982 **CLC 10, 30,**
72; DAM NOV, POP
See also AAYA 24; CA 49-52; 106; CANR 2,
16; DLB 8; MTCW

Dickens, Charles (John Huffam) 1812-1870
NCLC 3, 8, 18, 26, 37, 50; DA; DAB; DAC;
DAM MST, NOV; SSC 17; WLC
See also AAYA 23; CDBLB 1832-1890; DLB
21, 55, 70, 159, 166; JRDA; MAICYA; SATA
15

Dickey, James (Lafayette) 1923-1997 **CLC 1,**
2, 4, 7, 10, 15, 47, 109; DAM NOV, POET,
POP
See also AITN 1, 2; CA 9-12R; 156; CABS 2;
CANR 10, 48, 61; CDALB 1968-1988; DLB
5, 193; DLBD 7; DLBY 82, 93, 96, 97; INT
CANR-10; MTCW

Dickey, William 1928-1994 .... **CLC 3, 28**
See also CA 9-12R; 145; CANR 24; DLB 5

Dickinson, Charles 1951- .... **CLC 49**
See also CA 128

Dickinson, Emily (Elizabeth) 1830-1886
NCLC 21; DA; DAB; DAC; DAM MST,
POET; PC 1; WLC
See also AAYA 22; CDALB 1865-1917; DLB 1;
SATA 29

Dickinson, Peter (Malcolm) 1927- **CLC 12, 35**
See also AAYA 9; CA 41-44R; CANR 31, 58;
CLR 29; DLB 87, 161; JRDA; MAICYA;
SATA 5, 62, 95

Dickson, Carr
See Carr, John Dickson

Dickson, Carter
See Carr, John Dickson

Diderot, Denis 1713-1784 .... **LC 26**

Didion, Joan 1934- **CLC 1, 3, 8, 14, 32; DAM**
NOV
See also AITN 1; CA 5-8R; CANR 14, 52;
CDALB 1968-1988; DLB 2, 173, 185; DLBY
81, 86; MTCW

Dietrich, Robert
See Hunt, E(verette) Howard, (Jr.)

Dillard, Annie 1945-   **CLC 9, 60; DAM NOV**
See also AAYA 6; CA 49-52; CANR 3, 43, 62;
DLBY 80; MTCW; SATA 10

Dillard, R(ichard) H(enry) W(ilde) 1937-
CLC 5
See also CA 21-24R; CAAS 7; CANR 10; DLB 5

Dillon, Eilis 1920-1994 .... **CLC 17**
See also CA 9-12R; 147; CAAS 3; CANR 4, 38;
CLR 26; MAICYA; SATA 2, 74; SATA-Obit
83

Dimont, Penelope
See Mortimer, Penelope (Ruth)

Dinesen, Isak .... **CLC 10, 29, 95; SSC 7**
See also Blixen, Karen (Christentze Dinesen)

Ding Ling .... **CLC 68**
See also Chiang Pin-chin

Disch, Thomas M(ichael) 1940- ..... **CLC 7, 36**
See also AAYA 17; CA 21-24R; CAAS 4; CANR
17, 36, 54; CLR 18; DLB 8; MAICYA;
MTCW; SAAS 15; SATA 92

Disch, Tom
See Disch, Thomas M(ichael)

d'Isly, Georges
See Simenon, Georges (Jacques Christian)

Disraeli, Benjamin 1804-1881 ..... **NCLC 2, 39**
See also DLB 21, 55

Ditcum, Steve
See Crumb, R(obert)

Dixon, Paige
See Corcoran, Barbara

Drayham, James
See Mencken, H(enry) L(ouis)

Drayton, Michael 1563-1631 .... **LC 8**

Dreadstone, Carl
See Campbell, (John) Ramsey

Dreiser, Theodore (Herman Albert) 1871-1945
**TCLC 10, 18, 35; DA; DAC; DAM MST,
NOV; SSC 30; WLC**
See also CA 106; 132; CDALB 1865-1917; DLB
9, 12, 102, 137; DLBD 1; MTCW

Drexler, Rosalyn 1926- .... **CLC 2, 6**
See also CA 81-84; CANR 68

Dreyer, Carl Theodor 1889-1968 .... **CLC 16**
See also CA 116

Drieu la Rochelle, Pierre(-Eugene) 1893-1945
TCLC 21
See also CA 117; DLB 72

Drinkwater, John 1882-1937 .... **TCLC 57**
See also CA 109; 149; DLB 10, 19, 149

Drop Shot
See Cable, George Washington

Droste-Hulshoff, Annette Freiin von 1797-1848
NCLC 3
See also DLB 133

Drummond, Walter
See Silverberg, Robert

Drummond, William Henry 1854-1907...**TCLC 25**
See also CA 160; DLB 92

Drummond de Andrade, Carlos 1902-1987
CLC 18
See also Andrade, Carlos Drummond de
See also CA 132; 123

Drury, Allen (Stuart) 1918- .... **CLC 37**
See also CA 57-60; CANR 18, 52; INT CANR-
18

Dryden, John 1631-1700 **LC 3, 21; DA; DAB;
DAC; DAM DRAM, MST, POET; DC 3;
WLC**
See also CDBLB 1660-1789; DLB 80, 101, 131

Duberman, Martin (Bauml) 1930- .... **CLC 8**
See also CA 1-4R; CANR 2, 63

Dubie, Norman (Evans) 1945- .... **CLC 36**
See also CA 69-72; CANR 12; DLB 120

Du Bois, W(illiam) E(dward) B(urghardt) 1868-
1963 .... **CLC 1, 2, 13, 64, 96; BLC;
DA; DAC; DAM MST, MULT, NOV; WLC**
See also BW 1; CA 85-88; CANR 34; CDALB
1865-1917; DLB 47, 50, 91; MTCW; SATA 42

Dubus, Andre 1936- **CLC 13, 36, 97; SSC 15**
See also CA 21-24R; CANR 17; DLB 130; INT
CANR-17

Duca Minimo
See D'Annunzio, Gabriele

Ducharme, Rejean 1941- .... **CLC 74**
See also CA 165; DLB 60

Duclos, Charles Pinot 1704-1772 .... **LC 1**

Dudek, Louis 1918- .... **CLC 11, 19**
See also CA 45-48; CAAS 14; CANR 1; DLB 88

Duerrenmatt, Friedrich 1921-1990 **CLC 1, 4,
8, 11, 15, 43, 102; DAM DRAM**
See also CA 17-20R; CANR 33; DLB 69, 124;
MTCW

Duffy, Bruce (?)- .... **CLC 50**

Duffy, Maureen 1933- .... **CLC 37**
See also CA 25-28R; CANR 33, 68; DLB 14; MTCW

Dugan, Alan 1923- .... **CLC 2, 6**
See also CA 81-84; DLB 5

du Gard, Roger Martin
See Martin du Gard, Roger

Duhamel, Georges 1884-1966 .... **CLC 8**
See also CA 81-84; 25-28R; CANR 35; DLB 65; MTCW

Dujardin, Edouard (Emile Louis) 1861-1949
TCLC 13
See also CA 109; DLB 123

Dulles, John Foster 1888-1959 .... **TCLC 72**
See also CA 115; 149

Dumas, Alexandre (Davy de la Pailleterie) 1802-
1870 ....**NCLC 11; DA; DAB; DAC;
DAM MST, NOV; WLC**
See also DLB 119, 192; SATA 18

Dumas, Alexandre 1824-1895 **NCLC 9; DC 1**
See also AAYA 22; DLB 192

Dumas, Claudine
See Malzberg, Barry N(athaniel)

Dumas, Henry L. 1934-1968 .... **CLC 6, 62**
See also BW 1; CA 85-88; DLB 41

du Maurier, Daphne 1907-1989 **CLC 6, 11, 59;
DAB; DAC; DAM MST, POP; SSC 18**
See also CA 5-8R; 128; CANR 6, 55; DLB 191;
MTCW; SATA 27; SATA-Obit 60

Dunbar, Paul Laurence 1872-1906 **TCLC 2,
12; BLC; DA; DAC; DAM MST, MULT,
POET; PC 5; SSC 8; WLC**
See also BW 1; CA 104; 124; CDALB 1865-
1917; DLB 50, 54, 78; SATA 34

Dunbar, William 1460(?)-1530(?) .... **LC 20**
See also DLB 132, 146

Duncan, Dora Angela
See Duncan, Isadora

Duncan, Isadora 1877(?)-1927 .... **TCLC 68**
See also CA 118; 149

Duncan, Lois 1934- .... **CLC 26**
See also AAYA 4; CA 1-4R; CANR 2, 23, 36;
CLR 29; JRDA; MAICYA; SAAS 2; SATA 1,
36, 75

Duncan, Robert (Edward) 1919-1988 **CLC 1,
2, 4, 7, 15, 41, 55; DAM POET; PC 2**
See also CA 9-12R; 124; CANR 28, 62; DLB 5,
16, 193; MTCW

Duncan, Sara Jeannette 1861-1922 **TCLC 60**
See also CA 157; DLB 92

Dunlap, William 1766-1839 .... **NCLC 2**
See also DLB 30, 37, 59

Dunn, Douglas (Eaglesham) 1942- **CLC 6, 40**
See also CA 45-48; CANR 2, 33; DLB 40; MTCW

Dunn, Katherine (Karen) 1945- .... **CLC 71**
See also CA 33-36R

Dunn, Stephen 1939- .... **CLC 36**
See also CA 33-36R; CANR 12, 48, 53; DLB 105

Dunne, Finley Peter 1867-1936 .... **TCLC 28**
See also CA 108; DLB 11, 23

Dunne, John Gregory 1932- .... **CLC 28**
See also CA 25-28R; CANR 14, 50; DLBY 80

Dunsany, Edward John Moreton Drax Plunkett
1878-1957
See Dunsany, Lord
See also CA 104; 148; DLB 10

Dunsany, Lord ....**TCLC 2, 59**
See also Dunsany, Edward John Moreton Drax
Plunkett
See also DLB 77, 153, 156

du Perry, Jean
See Simenon, Georges (Jacques Christian)

Durang, Christopher (Ferdinand) 1949- **CLC
27, 38**
See also CA 105; CANR 50

Duras, Marguerite 1914-1996 **CLC 3, 6, 11, 20,
34, 40, 68, 100**
See also CA 25-28R; 151; CANR 50; DLB 83;
MTCW

Durban, (Rosa) Pam 1947- .... **CLC 39**
See also CA 123

Durcan, Paul 1944- **CLC 43, 70; DAM POET**
See also CA 134

Durkheim, Emile 1858-1917 .... **TCLC 55**

Durrell, Lawrence (George) 1912-1990 **CLC
1, 4, 6, 8, 13, 27, 41; DAM NOV**
See also CA 9-12R; 132; CANR 40; CDBLB
1945-1960; DLB 15, 27; DLBY 90; MTCW

Durrenmatt, Friedrich
See Duerrenmatt, Friedrich

Dutt, Toru 1856-1877 .... **NCLC 29**

Dwight, Timothy 1752-1817 .... **NCLC 13**
See also DLB 37

Dworkin, Andrea 1946- .... **CLC 43**
See also CA 77-80; CAAS 21; CANR 16, 39;
INT CANR-16; MTCW

Estleman, Loren D. 1952- **CLC 48; DAM NOV, POP**
See also CA 85-88; CANR 27; INT CANR-27; MTCW

Euclid 306B.C.-283B.C. .... **CMLC 25**

Eugenides, Jeffrey 1960(?)- .... **CLC 81**
See also CA 144

Euripides c. 485B.C.-406B.C. ... **CMLC 23; DA; DAB; DAC; DAM DRAM, MST; DC 4; WLCS**
See also DLB 176

Evan, Evin
See Faust, Frederick (Schiller)

Evans, Evan
See Faust, Frederick (Schiller)

Evans, Marian
See Eliot, George

Evans, Mary Ann
See Eliot, George

Evarts, Esther
See Benson, Sally

Everett, Percival L. 1956- .... **CLC 57**
See also BW 2; CA 129

Everson, R(onald) G(ilmour) 1903- ... **CLC 27**
See also CA 17-20R; DLB 88

Everson, William (Oliver) 1912-1994 **CLC 1, 5, 14**
See also CA 9-12R; 145; CANR 20; DLB 5, 16; MTCW

Evtushenko, Evgenii Aleksandrovich
See Yevtushenko, Yevgeny (Alexandrovich)

Ewart, Gavin (Buchanan) 1916-1995 . **CLC 13, 46**
See also CA 89-92; 150; CANR 17, 46; DLB 40; MTCW

Ewers, Hanns Heinz 1871-1943 ...... **TCLC 12**
See also CA 109; 149

Ewing, Frederick R.
See Sturgeon, Theodore (Hamilton)

Exley, Frederick (Earl) 1929-1992 **CLC 6, 11**
See also AITN 2; CA 81-84; 138; DLB 143; DLBY 81

Eynhardt, Guillermo
See Quiroga, Horacio (Sylvestre)

Ezekiel, Nissim 1924- .... **CLC 61**
See also CA 61-64

Ezekiel, Tish O'Dowd 1943- .... **CLC 34**
See also CA 129

Fadeyev, A.
See Bulgya, Alexander Alexandrovich

Fadeyev, Alexander .... **TCLC 53**
See also Bulgya, Alexander Alexandrovich

Fagen, Donald 1948- .... **CLC 26**

Fainzilberg, Ilya Arnoldovich 1897-1937
See Ilf, Ilya
See also CA 120; 165

Fair, Ronald L. 1932- .... **CLC 18**
See also BW 1; CA 69-72; CANR 25; DLB 33

Fairbairn, Roger
See Carr, John Dickson

Fairbairns, Zoe (Ann) 1948- .... **CLC 32**
See also CA 103; CANR 21

Falco, Gian
See Papini, Giovanni

Falconer, James
See Kirkup, James

Falconer, Kenneth
See Kornbluth, C(yril) M.

Falkland, Samuel
See Heijermans, Herman

Fallaci, Oriana 1930- .... **CLC 11**
See also CA 77-80; CANR 15, 58; MTCW

Faludy, George 1913- .... **CLC 42**
See also CA 21-24R

Faludy, Gyoergy
See Faludy, George

Fanon, Frantz 1925-1961 ... **CLC 74; BLC; DAM MULT**
See also BW 1; CA 116; 89-92

Fanshawe, Ann 1625-1680 :.................... **LC 11**

Fante, John (Thomas) 1911-1983 ...... **CLC 60**
See also CA 69-72; 109; CANR 23; DLB 130; DLBY 83

Farah, Nuruddin 1945- ... **CLC 53; BLC; DAM MULT**
See also BW 2; CA 106; DLB 125

Fargue, Leon-Paul 1876(?)-1947 .... **TCLC 11**
See also CA 109

Farigoule, Louis
See Romains, Jules

Farina, Richard 1936(?)-1966 .... **CLC 9**
See also CA 81-84; 25-28R

Farley, Walter (Lorimer) 1915-1989 ... **CLC 17**
See also CA 17-20R; CANR 8, 29; DLB 22; JRDA; MAICYA; SATA 2, 43

Farmer, Philip Jose 1918- .... **CLC 1, 19**
See also CA 1-4R; CANR 4, 35; DLB 8; MTCW; SATA 93

Farquhar, George 1677-1707 .... **LC 21; DAM DRAM**
See also DLB 84

Farrell, J(ames) G(ordon) 1935-1979 . **CLC 6**
See also CA 73-76; 89-92; CANR 36; DLB 14; MTCW

Farrell, James T(homas) 1904-1979 **CLC 1, 4, 8, 11, 66; SSC 28**
See also CA 5-8R; 89-92; CANR 9, 61; DLB 4, 9, 86; DLBD 2; MTCW

Farren, Richard J.
See Betjeman, John

Farren, Richard M.
See Betjeman, John

Fassbinder, Rainer Werner 1946-1982 **CLC 20**
See also CA 93-96; 106; CANR 31

Fast, Howard (Melvin) 1914- . **CLC 23; DAM NOV**
See also AAYA 16; CA 1-4R; CAAS 18; CANR 1, 33, 54; DLB 9; INT CANR-33; SATA 7

Faulcon, Robert
See Holdstock, Robert P.

Faulkner, William (Cuthbert) 1897-1962 **CLC 1, 3, 6, 8, 9, 11, 14, 18, 28, 52, 68; DA; DAB; DAC; DAM MST, NOV; SSC 1; WLC**
See also AAYA 7; CA 81-84; CANR 33; CDALB 1929-1941; DLB 9, 11, 44, 102; DLBD 2; DLBY 86, 97; MTCW

Fauset, Jessie Redmon 1884(?)-1961 **CLC 19, 54; BLC; DAM MULT**
See also BW 1; CA 109; DLB 51

Faust, Frederick (Schiller) 1892-1944(?) **TCLC 49; DAM POP**
See also CA 108; 152

Faust, Irvin 1924- .... **CLC 8**
See also CA 33-36R; CANR 28, 67; DLB 2, 28; DLBY 80

Fawkes, Guy
See Benchley, Robert (Charles)

Fearing, Kenneth (Flexner) 1902-1961 ... **CLC 51**
See also CA 93-96; CANR 59; DLB 9

Fecamps, Elise
See Creasey, John

Federman, Raymond 1928- .... **CLC 6, 47**
See also CA 17-20R; CAAS 8; CANR 10, 43; DLBY 80

Federspiel, J(uerg) F. 1931- .... **CLC 42**
See also CA 146

Feiffer, Jules (Ralph) 1929- .... **CLC 2, 8, 64; DAM DRAM**
See also AAYA 3; CA 17-20R; CANR 30, 59; DLB 7, 44; INT CANR-30; MTCW; SATA 8, 61

Feige, Hermann Albert Otto Maximilian
See Traven, B.

Feinberg, David B. 1956-1994 .... **CLC 59**
See also CA 135; 147

Feinstein, Elaine 1930- .... **CLC 36**
See also CA 69-72; CAAS 1; CANR 31, 68; DLB 14, 40; MTCW

Feldman, Irving (Mordecai) 1928- ...... **CLC 7**
 See also CA 1-4R; CANR 1; DLB 169

Felix-Tchicaya, Gerald
 See Tchicaya, Gerald Felix

Fellini, Federico 1920-1993 .... **CLC 16, 85**
 See also CA 65-68; 143; CANR 33

Felsen, Henry Gregor 1916- .... **CLC 17**
 See also CA 1-4R; CANR 1; SAAS 2; SATA 1

Fenno, Jack
 See Calisher, Hortense

Fenton, James Martin 1949- .... **CLC 32**
 See also CA 102; DLB 40

Ferber, Edna 1887-1968 .... **CLC 18, 93**
 See also AITN 1; CA 5-8R; 25-28R; CANR 68;
 DLB 9, 28, 86; MTCW; SATA 7

Ferguson, Helen
 See Kavan, Anna

Ferguson, Samuel 1810-1886 .... **NCLC 33**
 See also DLB 32

Fergusson, Robert 1750-1774 .... **LC 29**
 See also DLB 109

Ferling, Lawrence
 See Ferlinghetti, Lawrence (Monsanto)

Ferlinghetti, Lawrence (Monsanto) 1919(?)-
 CLC 2, 6, 10, 27; DAM POET; PC 1
 See also CA 5-8R; CANR 3, 41; CDALB 1941-
 1968; DLB 5, 16; MTCW

Fernandez, Vicente Garcia Huidobro
 See Huidobro Fernandez, Vicente Garcia

Ferrer, Gabriel (Francisco Victor) Miro
 See Miro (Ferrer), Gabriel (Francisco Victor)

Ferrier, Susan (Edmonstone) 1782-1854
 NCLC 8
 See also DLB 116

Ferrigno, Robert 1948(?)- .... **CLC 65**
 See also CA 140

Ferron, Jacques 1921-1985 ..... **CLC 94; DAC**
 See also CA 117; 129; DLB 60

Feuchtwanger, Lion 1884-1958 .... **TCLC 3**
 See also CA 104; DLB 66

Feuillet, Octave 1821-1890 .... **NCLC 45**
 See also DLB 192

Feydeau, Georges (Leon Jules Marie) 1862-1921
 TCLC 22; DAM DRAM
 See also CA 113; 152; DLB 192

Fichte, Johann Gottlieb 1762-1814 ....**NCLC 62**
 See also DLB 90

Ficino, Marsilio 1433-1499 .... **LC 12**

Fiedeler, Hans
 See Doeblin, Alfred

Fiedler, Leslie A(aron) 1917- .... **CLC 4, 13, 24**
 See also CA 9-12R; CANR 7, 63; DLB 28, 67;
 MTCW

Field, Andrew 1938- .... **CLC 44**
 See also CA 97-100; CANR 25

Field, Eugene 1850-1895 .... **NCLC 3**
 See also DLB 23, 42, 140; DLBD 13; MAICYA;
 SATA 16

Field, Gans T.
 See Wellman, Manly Wade

Field, Michael ....**TCLC 43**

Field, Peter
 See Hobson, Laura Z(ametkin)

Fielding, Henry 1707-1754 .... **LC 1; DA;**
 DAB; DAC; DAM DRAM, MST, NOV;
 WLC
 See also CDBLB 1660-1789; DLB 39, 84, 101

Fielding, Sarah 1710-1768 .... **LC 1**
 See also DLB 39

Fields, W. C. 1880-1946 .... **TCLC 80**
 See also DLB 44

Fierstein, Harvey (Forbes) 1954- ..... **CLC 33;**
 DAM DRAM, POP
 See also CA 123; 129

Figes, Eva 1932- .... **CLC 31**
 See also CA 53-56; CANR 4, 44; DLB 14

Finch, Anne 1661-1720 .... **LC 3; PC 21**
 See also DLB 95

Finch, Robert (Duer Claydon) 1900-. **CLC 18**
 See also CA 57-60; CANR 9, 24, 49; DLB 88

Findley, Timothy 1930- .. **CLC 27, 102; DAC;**
 DAM MST
 See also CA 25-28R; CANR 12, 42; DLB 53

Fink, William
 See Mencken, H(enry) L(ouis)

Firbank, Louis 1942-
 See Reed, Lou
 See also CA 117

Firbank, (Arthur Annesley) Ronald 1886-1926
 TCLC 1
 See also CA 104; DLB 36

Fisher, M(ary) F(rances) K(ennedy) 1908-1992
 CLC 76, 87
 See also CA 77-80; 138; CANR 44

Fisher, Roy 1930- .... **CLC 25**
 See also CA 81-84; CAAS 10; CANR 16; DLB
 40

Fisher, Rudolph 1897-1934 .. **TCLC 11; BLC;**
 DAM MULT; SSC 25
 See also BW 1; CA 107; 124; DLB 51, 102

Fisher, Vardis (Alvero) 1895-1968 .... **CLC 7**
 See also CA 5-8R; 25-28R; CANR 68; DLB 9

Fiske, Tarleton
 See Bloch, Robert (Albert)

Fitch, Clarke
 See Sinclair, Upton (Beall)

Fitch, John IV
 See Cormier, Robert (Edmund)

Fitzgerald, Captain Hugh
 See Baum, L(yman) Frank

FitzGerald, Edward 1809-1883 .... **NCLC 9**
 See also DLB 32

Fitzgerald, F(rancis) Scott (Key) 1896-1940
 TCLC 1, 6, 14, 28, 55; DA; DAB; DAC;
 DAM MST, NOV; SSC 6; WLC
 See also AAYA 24; AITN 1; CA 110; 123;
 CDALB 1917-1929; DLB 4, 9, 86; DLBD 1,
 15, 16; DLBY 81, 96; MTCW

Fitzgerald, Penelope 1916- ..... **CLC 19, 51, 61**
 See also CA 85-88; CAAS 10; CANR 56; DLB
 14, 194

Fitzgerald, Robert (Stuart) 1910-1985 **CLC 39**
 See also CA 1-4R; 114; CANR 1; DLBY 80

FitzGerald, Robert D(avid) 1902-1987 **CLC 19**
 See also CA 17-20R

Fitzgerald, Zelda (Sayre) 1900-1948 **TCLC 52**
 See also CA 117; 126; DLBY 84

Flanagan, Thomas (James Bonner) 1923-
 CLC 25, 52
 See also CA 108; CANR 55; DLBY 80; INT 108;
 MTCW

Flaubert, Gustave 1821-1880 **NCLC 2, 10,**
 19, 62, 66; DA; DAB; DAC; DAM MST,
 NOV; SSC 11; WLC
 See also DLB 119

Flecker, Herman Elroy
 See Flecker, (Herman) James Elroy

Flecker, (Herman) James Elroy 1884-1915
 TCLC 43
 See also CA 109; 150; DLB 10, 19

Fleming, Ian (Lancaster) 1908-1964 **CLC 3,**
 30; DAM POP
 See also CA 5-8R; CANR 59; CDBLB 1945-
 1960; DLB 87; MTCW; SATA 9

Fleming, Thomas (James) 1927- .... **CLC 37**
 See also CA 5-8R; CANR 10; INT CANR-10;
 SATA 8

Fletcher, John 1579-1625 ....**LC 33; DC 6**
 See also CDBLB Before 1660; DLB 58

Fletcher, John Gould 1886-1950 ..... **TCLC 35**
 See also CA 107; DLB 4, 45

Fleur, Paul
 See Pohl, Frederik

Flooglebuckle, Al
 See Spiegelman, Art

Frazier, Ian 1951- .... **CLC 46**
See also CA 130; CANR 54

Frederic, Harold 1856-1898 .... **NCLC 10**
See also DLB 12, 23; DLBD 13

Frederick, John
See Faust, Frederick (Schiller)

Frederick the Great 1712-1786 .... **LC 14**

Fredro, Aleksander 1793-1876 .... **NCLC 8**

Freeling, Nicolas 1927- .... **CLC 38**
See also CA 49-52; CAAS 12; CANR 1, 17, 50;
DLB 87

Freeman, Douglas Southall 1886-1953 ... **TCLC 11**
See also CA 109; DLB 17

Freeman, Judith 1946- .... **CLC 55**
See also CA 148

Freeman, Mary Eleanor Wilkins 1852-1930
TCLC 9; SSC 1
See also CA 106; DLB 12, 78

Freeman, R(ichard) Austin 1862-1943 ... **TCLC 21**
See also CA 113; DLB 70

French, Albert 1943- .... **CLC 86**

French, Marilyn 1929- **CLC 10, 18, 60; DAM DRAM, NOV, POP**
See also CA 69-72; CANR 3, 31; INT CANR-31; MTCW

French, Paul
See Asimov, Isaac

Freneau, Philip Morin 1752-1832 ..... **NCLC 1**
See also DLB 37, 43

Freud, Sigmund 1856-1939 .... **TCLC 52**
See also CA 115; 133; MTCW

Friedan, Betty (Naomi) 1921- .... **CLC 74**
See also CA 65-68; CANR 18, 45; MTCW

Friedlander, Saul 1932- .... **CLC 90**
See also CA 117; 130

Friedman, B(ernard) H(arper) 1926- ... **CLC 7**
See also CA 1-4R; CANR 3, 48

Friedman, Bruce Jay 1930- .... **CLC 3, 5, 56**
See also CA 9-12R; CANR 25, 52; DLB 2, 28;
INT CANR-25

Friel, Brian 1929- .... **CLC 5, 42, 59; DC 8**
See also CA 21-24R; CANR 33; DLB 13;
MTCW

Friis-Baastad, Babbis Ellinor 1921-1970 ... **CLC 12**
See also CA 17-20R; 134; SATA 7

Frisch, Max (Rudolf) 1911-1991 . **CLC 3, 9, 14, 18, 32, 44; DAM DRAM, NOV**
See also CA 85-88; 134; CANR 32; DLB 69,
124; MTCW

Fromentin, Eugene (Samuel Auguste) 1820-1876
NCLC 10
See also DLB 123

Frost, Frederick
See Faust, Frederick (Schiller)

Frost, Robert (Lee) 1874-1963 **CLC 1, 3, 4, 9, 10, 13, 15, 26, 34, 44; DA; DAB; DAC; DAM MST, POET; PC 1; WLC**
See also AAYA 21; CA 89-92; CANR 33;
CDALB 1917-1929; DLB 54; DLBD 7;
MTCW; SATA 14

Froude, James Anthony 1818-1894 **NCLC 43**
See also DLB 18, 57, 144

Froy, Herald
See Waterhouse, Keith (Spencer)

Fry, Christopher 1907- **CLC 2, 10, 14; DAM DRAM**
See also CA 17-20R; CAAS 23; CANR 9, 30;
DLB 13; MTCW; SATA 66

Frye, (Herman) Northrop 1912-1991 **CLC 24, 70**
See also CA 5-8R; 133; CANR 8, 37; DLB 67,
68; MTCW

Fuchs, Daniel 1909-1993 .... **CLC 8, 22**
See also CA 81-84; 142; CAAS 5; CANR 40;
DLB 9, 26, 28; DLBY 93

Fuchs, Daniel 1934- .... **CLC 34**
See also CA 37-40R; CANR 14, 48

Fuentes, Carlos 1928- **CLC 3, 8, 10, 13, 22, 41, 60; DA; DAB; DAC; DAM MST, MULT, NOV; HLC; SSC 24; WLC**
See also AAYA 4; AITN 2; CA 69-72; CANR
10, 32, 68; DLB 113; HW; MTCW

Fuentes, Gregorio Lopez y
See Lopez y Fuentes, Gregorio

Fugard, (Harold) Athol 1932- **CLC 5, 9, 14, 25, 40, 80; DAM DRAM; DC 3**
See also AAYA 17; CA 85-88; CANR 32, 54;
MTCW

Fugard, Sheila 1932- .... **CLC 48**
See also CA 125

Fuller, Charles (H., Jr.) 1939- **CLC 25; BLC; DAM DRAM, MULT; DC 1**
See also BW 2; CA 108; 112; DLB 38; INT 112;
MTCW

Fuller, John (Leopold) 1937- .... **CLC 62**
See also CA 21-24R; CANR 9, 44; DLB 40

Fuller, Margaret .... **NCLC 5, 50**
See also Ossoli, Sarah Margaret (Fuller marchesa
d')

Fuller, Roy (Broadbent) 1912-1991 **CLC 4, 28**
See also CA 5-8R; 135; CAAS 10; CANR 53;
DLB 15, 20; SATA 87

Fulton, Alice 1952- .... **CLC 52**
See also CA 116; CANR 57; DLB 193

Furphy, Joseph 1843-1912 .... **TCLC 25**
See also CA 163

Fussell, Paul 1924- .... **CLC 74**
See also BEST 90:1; CA 17-20R; CANR 8, 21,
35; INT CANR-21; MTCW

Futabatei, Shimei 1864-1909 .... **TCLC 44**
See also CA 162; DLB 180

Futrelle, Jacques 1875-1912 .... **TCLC 19**
See also CA 113; 155

Gaboriau, Emile 1835-1873 .... **NCLC 14**

Gadda, Carlo Emilio 1893-1973 .... **CLC 11**
See also CA 89-92; DLB 177

Gaddis, William 1922- ... **CLC 1, 3, 6, 8, 10, 19, 43, 86**
See also CA 17-20R; CANR 21, 48; DLB 2;
MTCW

Gage, Walter
See Inge, William (Motter)

Gaines, Ernest J(ames) 1933- ... **CLC 3, 11, 18, 86; BLC; DAM MULT**
See also AAYA 18; AITN 1; BW 2; CA 9-12R;
CANR 6, 24, 42; CDALB 1968-1988; DLB
2, 33, 152; DLBY 80; MTCW; SATA 86

Gaitskill, Mary 1954- .... **CLC 69**
See also CA 128; CANR 61

Galdos, Benito Perez
See Perez Galdos, Benito

Gale, Zona 1874-1938 .... **TCLC 7; DAM DRAM**
See also CA 105; 153; DLB 9, 78

Galeano, Eduardo (Hughes) 1940- .... **CLC 72**
See also CA 29-32R; CANR 13, 32; HW

Galiano, Juan Valera y Alcala
See Valera y Alcala-Galiano, Juan

Gallagher, Tess 1943- .... **CLC 18, 63; DAM POET; PC 9**
See also CA 106; DLB 120

Gallant, Mavis 1922- ... **CLC 7, 18, 38; DAC; DAM MST; SSC 5**
See also CA 69-72; CANR 29; DLB 53; MTCW

Gallant, Roy A(rthur) 1924- .... **CLC 17**
See also CA 5-8R; CANR 4, 29, 54; CLR 30;
MAICYA; SATA 4, 68

Gallico, Paul (William) 1897-1976 .... **CLC 2**
See also AITN 1; CA 5-8R; 69-72; CANR 23;
DLB 9, 171; MAICYA; SATA 13

Gallo, Max Louis 1932- .... **CLC 95**
See also CA 85-88

Gallois, Lucien
See Desnos, Robert

Gallup, Ralph
See Whitemore, Hugh (John)

Galsworthy, John 1867-1933 .. **TCLC 1, 45; DA; DAB; DAC; DAM DRAM, MST, NOV; SSC 22; WLC 2**
See also CA 104; 141; CDBLB 1890-1914; DLB 10, 34, 98, 162; DLBD 16

Galt, John 1779-1839 .... **NCLC 1**
See also DLB 99, 116, 159

Galvin, James 1951- .... **CLC 38**
See also CA 108; CANR 26

Gamboa, Federico 1864-1939 .... **TCLC 36**

Gandhi, M. K.
See Gandhi, Mohandas Karamchand

Gandhi, Mahatma
See Gandhi, Mohandas Karamchand

Gandhi, Mohandas Karamchand 1869-1948 **TCLC 59; DAM MULT**
See also CA 121; 132; MTCW

Gann, Ernest Kellogg 1910-1991 .... **CLC 23**
See also AITN 1; CA 1-4R; 136; CANR 1

Garcia, Cristina 1958- .... **CLC 76**
See also CA 141

Garcia Lorca, Federico 1898-1936 **TCLC 1, 7, 49; DA; DAB; DAC; DAM DRAM, MST, MULT, POET; DC 2; HLC; PC 3; WLC**
See also CA 104; 131; DLB 108; HW; MTCW

Garcia Marquez, Gabriel (Jose) 1928- **CLC 2, 3, 8, 10, 15, 27, 47, 55, 68; DA; DAB; DAC; DAM MST, MULT, NOV, POP; HLC; SSC 8; WLC**
See also AAYA 3; BEST 89:1, 90:4; CA 33-36R; CANR 10, 28, 50; DLB 113; HW; MTCW

Gard, Janice
See Latham, Jean Lee

Gard, Roger Martin du
See Martin du Gard, Roger

Gardam, Jane 1928- .... **CLC 43**
See also CA 49-52; CANR 2, 18, 33, 54; CLR 12; DLB 14, 161; MAICYA; MTCW; SAAS 9; SATA 39, 76; SATA-Brief 28

Gardner, Herb(ert) 1934- .... **CLC 44**
See also CA 149

Gardner, John (Champlin), Jr. 1933-1982 **CLC 2, 3, 5, 7, 8, 10, 18, 28, 34; DAM NOV, POP; SSC 7**
See also AITN 1; CA 65-68; 107; CANR 33; DLB 2; DLBY 82; MTCW; SATA 40; SATA-Obit 31

Gardner, John (Edmund) 1926- ...... **CLC 30; DAM POP**
See also CA 103; CANR 15; MTCW

Gardner, Miriam
See Bradley, Marion Zimmer

Gardner, Noel
See Kuttner, Henry

Gardons, S. S.
See Snodgrass, W(illiam) D(e Witt)

Garfield, Leon 1921-1996 .... **CLC 12**
See also AAYA 8; CA 17-20R; 152; CANR 38, 41; CLR 21; DLB 161; JRDA; MAICYA; SATA 1, 32, 76; SATA-Obit 90

Garland, (Hannibal) Hamlin 1860-1940 **TCLC 3; SSC 18**
See also CA 104; DLB 12, 71, 78, 186

Garneau, (Hector de) Saint-Denys 1912-1943 **TCLC 13**
See also CA 111; DLB 88

Garner, Alan 1934- .... **CLC 17; DAB; DAM POP**
See also AAYA 18; CA 73-76; CANR 15, 64; CLR 20; DLB 161; MAICYA; MTCW; SATA 18, 69

Garner, Hugh 1913-1979 .... **CLC 13**
See also CA 69-72; CANR 31; DLB 68

Garnett, David 1892-1981 .... **CLC 3**
See also CA 5-8R; 103; CANR 17; DLB 34

Garos, Stephanie
See Katz, Steve

Garrett, George (Palmer) 1929- ... **CLC 3, 11, 51; SSC 30**
See also CA 1-4R; CAAS 5; CANR 1, 42, 67; DLB 2, 5, 130, 152; DLBY 83

Garrick, David 1717-1779 .... **LC 15; DAM DRAM**
See also DLB 84

Garrigue, Jean 1914-1972 .... **CLC 2, 8**
See also CA 5-8R; 37-40R; CANR 20

Garrison, Frederick
See Sinclair, Upton (Beall)

Garth, Will
See Hamilton, Edmond; Kuttner, Henry

Garvey, Marcus (Moziah, Jr.) 1887-1940 **TCLC 41; BLC; DAM MULT**
See also BW 1; CA 120; 124

Gary, Romain .... **CLC 25**
See also Kacew, Romain
See also DLB 83

Gascar, Pierre .... **CLC 11**
See also Fournier, Pierre

Gascoyne, David (Emery) 1916- .... **CLC 45**
See also CA 65-68; CANR 10, 28, 54; DLB 20; MTCW

Gaskell, Elizabeth Cleghorn 1810-1865 **NCLC 5; DAB; DAM MST; SSC 25**
See also CDBLB 1832-1890; DLB 21, 144, 159

Gass, William H(oward) 1924- ... **CLC 1, 2, 8, 11, 15, 39; SSC 12**
See also CA 17-20R; CANR 30; DLB 2; MTCW

Gasset, Jose Ortega y
See Ortega y Gasset, Jose

Gates, Henry Louis, Jr. 1950- ..... **CLC 65; DAM MULT**
See also BW 2; CA 109; CANR 25, 53; DLB 67

Gautier, Theophile 1811-1872 **NCLC 1, 59; DAM POET; PC 18; SSC 20**
See also DLB 119

Gawsworth, John
See Bates, H(erbert) E(rnest)

Gay, Oliver
See Gogarty, Oliver St. John

Gaye, Marvin (Penze) 1939-1984 ...... **CLC 26**
See also CA 112

Gebler, Carlo (Ernest) 1954- .... **CLC 39**
See also CA 119; 133

Gee, Maggie (Mary) 1948- .... **CLC 57**
See also CA 130

Gee, Maurice (Gough) 1931- .... **CLC 29**
See also CA 97-100; CANR 67; SATA 46

Gelbart, Larry (Simon) 1923- ...... **CLC 21, 61**
See also CA 73-76; CANR 45

Gelber, Jack 1932- .... **CLC 1, 6, 14, 79**
See also CA 1-4R; CANR 2; DLB 7

Gellhorn, Martha (Ellis) 1908-1998 ... **CLC 14, 60**
See also CA 77-80; 164; CANR 44; DLBY 82

Genet, Jean 1910-1986 **CLC 1, 2, 5, 10, 14, 44, 46; DAM DRAM**
See also CA 13-16R; CANR 18; DLB 72; DLBY 86; MTCW

Gent, Peter 1942- .... **CLC 29**
See also AITN 1; CA 89-92; DLBY 82

Gentlewoman in New England, A
See Bradstreet, Anne

Gentlewoman in Those Parts, A
See Bradstreet, Anne

George, Jean Craighead 1919- .... **CLC 35**
See also AAYA 8; CA 5-8R; CANR 25; CLR 1; DLB 52; JRDA; MAICYA; SATA 2, 68

George, Stefan (Anton) 1868-1933 ... **TCLC 2, 14**
See also CA 104

Georges, Georges Martin
See Simenon, Georges (Jacques Christian)

Gerhardi, William Alexander
See Gerhardie, William Alexander

Gerhardie, William Alexander 1895-1977 **CLC 5**
See also CA 25-28R; 73-76; CANR 18; DLB 36

Gerstler, Amy 1956- .... **CLC 70**
See also CA 146

Gertler, T. .... **CLC 34**
See also CA 116; 121; INT 121

Ghalib .... **NCLC 39**
See also Ghalib, Hsadullah Khan

Ghalib, Hsadullah Khan 1797-1869
See Ghalib
See also DAM POET

Ghelderode, Michel de 1898-1962 .   **CLC 6,**
11; DAM DRAM
See also CA 85-88; CANR 40

Ghiselin, Brewster 1903- .... **CLC 23**
See also CA 13-16R; CAAS 10; CANR 13

Ghose, Zulfikar 1935- .... **CLC 42**
See also CA 65-68; CANR 67

Ghosh, Amitav 1956- .... **CLC 44**
See also CA 147

Giacosa, Giuseppe 1847-1906 .... **TCLC 7**
See also CA 104

Gibb, Lee
See Waterhouse, Keith (Spencer)

Gibbon, Lewis Grassic .... **TCLC 4**
See also Mitchell, James Leslie

Gibbons, Kaye 1960-   **CLC 50, 88; DAM POP**
See also CA 151

Gibran, Kahlil 1883-1931 .. **TCLC 1, 9; DAM**
POET, POP; PC 9
See also CA 104; 150

Gibran, Khalil
See Gibran, Kahlil

Gibson, William 1914- ..... **CLC 23; DA; DAB;**
DAC; DAM DRAM, MST
See also CA 9-12R; CANR 9, 42; DLB 7; SATA 66

Gibson, William (Ford) 1948- .... **CLC 39, 63;**
DAM POP
See also AAYA 12; CA 126; 133; CANR 52

Gide, Andre (Paul Guillaume) 1869-1951
TCLC 5, 12, 36; DA; DAB; DAC; DAM
MST, NOV; SSC 13; WLC
See also CA 104; 124; DLB 65; MTCW

Gifford, Barry (Colby) 1946- .... **CLC 34**
See also CA 65-68; CANR 9, 30, 40

Gilbert, Frank
See De Voto, Bernard (Augustine)

Gilbert, W(illiam) S(chwenck) 1836-1911
TCLC 3; DAM DRAM, POET
See also CA 104; SATA 36

Gilbreth, Frank B., Jr. 1911- .... **CLC 17**
See also CA 9-12R; SATA 2

Gilchrist, Ellen 1935- ....   **CLC 34, 48; DAM**
POP; SSC 14
See also CA 113; 116; CANR 41, 61; DLB 130;
MTCW

Giles, Molly 1942- .... **CLC 39**
See also CA 126

Gill, Patrick
See Creasey, John

Gilliam, Terry (Vance) 1940- .... **CLC 21**
See also Monty Python
See also AAYA 19; CA 108; 113; CANR 35; INT 113

Gillian, Jerry
See Gilliam, Terry (Vance)

Gilliatt, Penelope (Ann Douglass) 1932-1993
CLC 2, 10, 13, 53
See also AITN 2; CA 13-16R; 141; CANR 49;
DLB 14

Gilman, Charlotte (Anna) Perkins (Stetson)
1860-1935 .... **TCLC 9, 37; SSC 13**
See also CA 106; 150

Gilmour, David 1949- .... **CLC 35**
See also CA 138, 147

Gilpin, William 1724-1804 .... **NCLC 30**

Gilray, J. D.
See Mencken, H(enry) L(ouis)

Gilroy, Frank D(aniel) 1925- .... **CLC 2**
See also CA 81-84; CANR 32, 64; DLB 7

Gilstrap, John 1957(?)- .... **CLC 99**
See also CA 160

Ginsberg, Allen 1926-1997 **CLC 1, 2, 3, 4, 6, 13,**
36, 69, 109; DA; DAB; DAC; DAM MST,
POET; PC 4; WLC 3
See also AITN 1; CA 1-4R; 157; CANR 2, 41,
63; CDALB 1941-1968; DLB 5, 16, 169;
MTCW

Ginzburg, Natalia 1916-1991 .... **CLC 5, 11,**
54, 70
See also CA 85-88; 135; CANR 33; DLB 177;
MTCW

Giono, Jean 1895-1970 .... **CLC 4, 11**
See also CA 45-48; 29-32R; CANR 2, 35; DLB
72; MTCW

Giovanni, Nikki 1943-........... **CLC 2, 4, 19, 64;**
BLC; DA; DAB; DAC; DAM MST, MULT,
POET; PC 19; WLCS
See also AAYA 22; AITN 1; BW 2; CA 29-32R;
CAAS 6; CANR 18, 41, 60; CLR 6; DLB 5, 41;
INT CANR-18; MAICYA; MTCW; SATA 24

Giovene, Andrea 1904- .... **CLC 7**
See also CA 85-88

Gippius, Zinaida (Nikolayevna) 1869-1945
See Hippius, Zinaida
See also CA 106

Giraudoux, (Hippolyte) Jean 1882-1944
TCLC 2, 7; DAM DRAM
See also CA 104; DLB 65

Gironella, Jose Maria 1917- .... **CLC 11**
See also CA 101

Gissing, George (Robert) 1857-1903..... **TCLC**
3, 24, 47
See also CA 105; DLB 18, 135, 184

Giurlani, Aldo
See Palazzeschi, Aldo

Gladkov, Fyodor (Vasilyevich) 1883-1958
TCLC 27

Glanville, Brian (Lester) 1931- .... **CLC 6**
See also CA 5-8R; CAAS 9; CANR 3; DLB 15,
139; SATA 42

Glasgow, Ellen (Anderson Gholson) 1873-1945
TCLC 2, 7
See also CA 104; 164; DLB 9, 12

Glaspell, Susan 1882(?)-1948 .... **TCLC 55**
See also CA 110; 154; DLB 7, 9, 78; YABC 2

Glassco, John 1909-1981 .... **CLC 9**
See also CA 13-16R; 102; CANR 15; DLB 68

Glasscock, Amnesia
See Steinbeck, John (Ernst)

Glasser, Ronald J. 1940(?)- .... **CLC 37**

Glassman, Joyce
See Johnson, Joyce

Glendinning, Victoria 1937- .... **CLC 50**
See also CA 120; 127; CANR 59; DLB 155

Glissant, Edouard 1928- ... **CLC 10, 68; DAM**
MULT
See also CA 153

Gloag, Julian 1930-.............................. **CLC 40**
See also AITN 1; CA 65-68; CANR 10

Glowacki, Aleksander
See Prus, Boleslaw

Gluck, Louise (Elisabeth) 1943- .... **CLC 7,**
22, 44, 81; DAM POET; PC 16
See also CA 33-36R, CANR 40, DLB 5

Glyn, Elinor 1864-1943 .... **TCLC 72**
See also DLB 153

Gobineau, Joseph Arthur (Comte) de 1816-1882
NCLC 17
See also DLB 123

Godard, Jean-Luc 1930- .... **CLC 20**
See also CA 93-96

Godden, (Margaret) Rumer 1907- .... **CLC 53**
See also AAYA 6; CA 5-8R; CANR 4, 27, 36,
55; CLR 20; DLB 161; MAICYA; SAAS 12;
SATA 3, 36

Godoy Alcayaga, Lucila 1889-1957
See Mistral, Gabriela
See also BW 2; CA 104; 131; DAM MULT; HW; MTCW

Godwin, Gail (Kathleen) 1937- .... **CLC 5, 8,**
22, 31, 69; DAM POP
See also CA 29-32R; CANR 15, 43; DLB 6; INT
CANR-15; MTCW

Godwin, William 1756-1836 .... **NCLC 14**
See also CDBLB 1789-1832; DLB 39, 104, 142, 158, 163

Goebbels, Josef
See Goebbels, (Paul) Joseph

Goebbels, (Paul) Joseph 1897-1945 ... **TCLC 68**
See also CA 115; 148

Goebbels, Joseph Paul
See Goebbels, (Paul) Joseph

Goethe, Johann Wolfgang von 1749-1832
NCLC 4, 22, 34; DA; DAB; DAC; DAM DRAM, MST, POET; PC 5; WLC 3
See also DLB 94

Gogarty, Oliver St. John 1878-1957 **TCLC 15**
See also CA 109; 150; DLB 15, 19

Gogol, Nikolai (Vasilyevich) 1809-1852
NCLC 5, 15, 31; DA; DAB; DAC; DAM DRAM, MST; DC 1; SSC 4, 29; WLC

Goines, Donald 1937(?)-1974 . **CLC 80; BLC; DAM MULT, POP**
See also AITN 1; BW 1; CA 124; 114; DLB 33

Gold, Herbert 1924- .... **CLC 4, 7, 14, 42**
See also CA 9-12R; CANR 17, 45; DLB 2; DLBY 81

Goldbarth, Albert 1948- .... **CLC 5, 38**
See also CA 53-56; CANR 6, 40; DLB 120

Goldberg, Anatol 1910-1982 .... **CLC 34**
See also CA 131; 117

Goldemberg, Isaac 1945- .... **CLC 52**
See also CA 69-72; CAAS 12; CANR 11, 32; HW

Golding, William (Gerald) 1911-1993 .... **CLC 1, 2, 3, 8, 10, 17, 27, 58, 81; DA; DAB; DAC; DAM MST, NOV; WLC**
See also AAYA 5; CA 5-8R; 141; CANR 13, 33, 54; CDBLB 1945-1960; DLB 15, 100; MTCW

Goldman, Emma 1869-1940 .... **TCLC 13**
See also CA 110; 150

Goldman, Francisco 1954- .... **CLC 76**
See also CA 162

Goldman, William (W.) 1931- .... **CLC 1, 48**
See also CA 9-12R; CANR 29; DLB 44

Goldmann, Lucien 1913-1970 .... **CLC 24**
See also CA 25-28; CAP 2

Goldoni, Carlo 1707-1793 .... **LC 4; DAM DRAM**

Goldsberry, Steven 1949- .... **CLC 34**
See also CA 131

Goldsmith, Oliver 1728-1774 .... **LC 2; DA; DAB; DAC; DAM DRAM, MST, NOV, POET; DC 8; WLC**
See also CDBLB 1660-1789; DLB 39, 89, 104, 109, 142; SATA 26

Goldsmith, Peter
See Priestley, J(ohn) B(oynton)

Gombrowicz, Witold 1904-1969 . **CLC 4, 7, 11, 49; DAM DRAM**
See also CA 19-20; 25-28R; CAP 2

Gomez de la Serna, Ramon 1888-1963 **CLC 9**
See also CA 153; 116; HW

Goncharov, Ivan Alexandrovich 1812-1891
NCLC 1, 63

Goncourt, Edmond (Louis Antoine Huot) de 1822-1896 .... **NCLC 7**
See also DLB 123

Goncourt, Jules (Alfred Huot) de 1830-1870
NCLC 7
See also DLB 123

Gontier, Fernande 19(?)- .... **CLC 50**

Gonzalez Martinez, Enrique 1871-1952
TCLC 72
See also HW

Goodman, Paul 1911-1972 .... **CLC 1, 2, 4, 7**
See also CA 19-20; 37-40R; CANR 34; CAP 2; DLB 130; MTCW

Gordimer, Nadine 1923- **CLC 3, 5, 7, 10, 18, 33, 51, 70; DA; DAB; DAC; DAM MST, NOV; SSC 17; WLCS**
See also CA 5-8R; CANR 3, 28, 56; INT CANR-28; MTCW

Gordon, Adam Lindsay 1833-1870 **NCLC 21**

Gordon, Caroline 1895-1981 **CLC 6, 13, 29, 83; SSC 15**
See also CA 11-12; 103; CANR 36; CAP 1; DLB 4, 9, 102; DLBY 81; MTCW

Gordon, Charles William 1860-1937
See Connor, Ralph
See also CA 109

Gordon, Mary (Catherine) 1949- **CLC 13, 22**
See also CA 102; CANR 44; DLB 6; DLBY 81; INT 102; MTCW

Gordon, N. J.
See Bosman, Herman Charles

Gordon, Sol 1923- .... **CLC 26**
See also CA 53-56; CANR 4; SATA 11

Gordone, Charles 1925-1995 ..... **CLC 1, 4; DAM DRAM; DC 8**
See also BW 1; CA 93-96; 150; CANR 55; DLB 7; INT 93-96; MTCW

Gore, Catherine 1800-1861 .... **NCLC 65**
See also DLB 116

Gorenko, Anna Andreevna
See Akhmatova, Anna

Gorky, Maxim 1868-1936 **TCLC 8; DAB; SSC 28; WLC**
See also Peshkov, Alexei Maximovich

Goryan, Sirak
See Saroyan, William

Gosse, Edmund (William) 1849-1928 ... **TCLC 28**
See also CA 117; DLB 57, 144, 184

Gotlieb, Phyllis Fay (Bloom) 1926- .... **CLC 18**
See also CA 13-16R; CANR 7; DLB 88

Gottesman, S. D.
See Kornbluth, C(yril) M.; Pohl, Frederik

Gottfried von Strassburg fl. c. 1210- ... **CMLC 10**
See also DLB 138

Gould, Lois .... **CLC 4, 10**
See also CA 77-80; CANR 29; MTCW

Gourmont, Remy (-Marie-Charles) de 1858-1915 .... **TCLC 17**
See also CA 109; 150

Govier, Katherine 1948- .... **CLC 51**
See also CA 101; CANR 18, 40

Goyen, (Charles) William 1915-1983 ... **CLC 5, 8, 14, 40**
See also AITN 2; CA 5-8R; 110; CANR 6; DLB 2; DLBY 83; INT CANR-6

Goytisolo, Juan 1931- .... **CLC 5, 10, 23; DAM MULT; HLC**
See also CA 85-88; CANR 32, 61; HW; MTCW

Gozzano, Guido 1883-1916 .... **PC 10**
See also CA 154; DLB 114

Gozzi, (Conte) Carlo 1720-1806 ..... **NCLC 23**

Grabbe, Christian Dietrich 1801-1836 ... **NCLC 2**
See also DLB 133

Grace, Patricia 1937- .... **CLC 56**

Gracian y Morales, Baltasar 1601-1658 **LC 15**

Gracq, Julien .... **CLC 11, 48**
See also Poirier, Louis
See also DLB 83

Grade, Chaim 1910-1982 .... **CLC 10**
See also CA 93-96; 107

Graduate of Oxford, A
See Ruskin, John

Grafton, Garth
See Duncan, Sara Jeannette

Graham, John
See Phillips, David Graham

Graham, Jorie 1951- .... **CLC 48**
See also CA 111; CANR 63; DLB 120

Graham, R(obert) B(ontine) Cunninghame
See Cunninghame Graham, R(obert) B(ontine)
See also DLB 98, 135, 174

Graham, Robert
See Haldeman, Joe (William)

Grillparzer, Franz 1791-1872 .... **NCLC 1**
See also DLB 133

Grimble, Reverend Charles James
See Eliot, T(homas) S(tearns)

Grimke, Charlotte L(ottie) Forten 1837(?)-1914
See Forten, Charlotte L.
See also BW 1; CA 117; 124; DAM MULT, POET

Grimm, Jacob Ludwig Karl 1785-1863 ... **NCLC 3**
See also DLB 90; MAICYA; SATA 22

Grimm, Wilhelm Karl 1786-1859 ..... **NCLC 3**
See also DLB 90; MAICYA; SATA 22

Grimmelshausen, Johann Jakob Christoffel von
1621-1676 .... **LC 6**
See also DLB 168

Grindel, Eugene 1895-1952
See Eluard, Paul
See also CA 104

Grisham, John 1955- ...... **CLC 84; DAM POP**
See also AAYA 14; CA 138; CANR 47

Grossman, David 1954- .... **CLC 67**
See also CA 138

Grossman, Vasily (Semenovich) 1905-1964 ... **CLC 41**
See also CA 124; 130; MTCW

Grove, Frederick Philip .... **TCLC 4**
See also Greve, Felix Paul (Berthold Friedrich)
See also DLB 92

Grubb
See Crumb, R(obert)

Grumbach, Doris (Isaac) 1918- ... **CLC 13, 22, 64**
See also CA 5-8R; CAAS 2; CANR 9, 42; INT CANR-9

Grundtvig, Nicolai Frederik Severin 1783-1872
NCLC 1

Grunge
See Crumb, R(obert)

Grunwald, Lisa 1959- .... **CLC 44**
See also CA 120

Guare, John 1938- ... **CLC 8, 14, 29, 67; DAM DRAM**
See also CA 73-76; CANR 21; DLB 7; MTCW

Gudjonsson, Halldor Kiljan 1902-1998
See Laxness, Halldor
See also CA 103; 164

Guenter, Erich
See Eich, Guenter

Guest, Barbara 1920- .... **CLC 34**
See also CA 25-28R; CANR 11, 44; DLB 5, 193

Guest, Judith (Ann) 1936- .. **CLC 8, 30; DAM NOV, POP**
See also AAYA 7; CA 77-80; CANR 15; INT CANR-15; MTCW

Guevara, Che .... **CLC 87; HLC**
See also Guevara (Serna), Ernesto

Guevara (Serna), Ernesto 1928-1967
See Guevara, Che
See also CA 127; 111; CANR 56; DAM MULT; HW

Guild, Nicholas M. 1944- .... **CLC 33**
See also CA 93-96

Guillemin, Jacques
See Sartre, Jean-Paul

Guillen, Jorge 1893-1984 .... **CLC 11; DAM MULT, POET**
See also CA 89-92; 112; DLB 108; HW

Guillen, Nicolas (Cristobal) 1902-1989 ... **CLC 48, 79; BLC; DAM MST, MULT, POET; HLC**
See also BW 2; CA 116; 125; 129; HW

Guillevic, (Eugene) 1907- .... **CLC 33**
See also CA 93-96

Guillois
See Desnos, Robert

Guillois, Valentin
See Desnos, Robert

Guiney, Louise Imogen 1861-1920 . **TCLC 41**
See also CA 160; DLB 54

Guiraldes, Ricardo (Guillermo) 1886-1927
TCLC 39
See also CA 131; HW; MTCW

Gumilev, Nikolai (Stepanovich) 1886-1921
TCLC 60
See also CA 165

Gunesekera, Romesh 1954- .... **CLC 91**
See also CA 159

Gunn, Bill .... **CLC 5**
See also Gunn, William Harrison
See also DLB 38

Gunn, Thom(son William) 1929- .... **CLC 3, 6, 18, 32, 81; DAM POET**
See also CA 17-20R; CANR 9, 33; CDBLB 1960 to Present; DLB 27; INT CANR-33; MTCW

Gunn, William Harrison 1934(?)-1989
See Gunn, Bill
See also AITN 1; BW 1; CA 13-16R; 128; CANR 12, 25

Gunnars, Kristjana 1948- .... **CLC 69**
See also CA 113; DLB 60

Gurdjieff, G(eorgei) I(vanovich) 1877(?)-1949
TCLC 71
See also CA 157

Gurganus, Allan 1947- ... **CLC 70; DAM POP**
See also BEST 90:1; CA 135

Gurney, A(lbert) R(amsdell), Jr. 1930- .... **CLC 32, 50, 54; DAM DRAM**
See also CA 77-80; CANR 32, 64

Gurney, Ivor (Bertie) 1890-1937 .... **TCLC 33**

Gurney, Peter
See Gurney, A(lbert) R(amsdell), Jr.

Guro, Elena 1877-1913 .... **TCLC 56**

Gustafson, James M(oody) 1925- .... **CLC 100**
See also CA 25-28R; CANR 37

Gustafson, Ralph (Barker) 1909- .... **CLC 36**
See also CA 21-24R; CANR 8, 45; DLB 88

Gut, Gom
See Simenon, Georges (Jacques Christian)

Guterson, David 1956- .... **CLC 91**
See also CA 132

Guthrie, A(lfred) B(ertram), Jr. 1901-1991 ... **CLC 23**
See also CA 57-60; 134; CANR 24; DLB 6; SATA 62; SATA-Obit 67

Guthrie, Isobel
See Grieve, C(hristopher) M(urray)

Guthrie, Woodrow Wilson 1912-1967
See Guthrie, Woody
See also CA 113; 93-96

Guthrie, Woody .... **CLC 35**
See also Guthrie, Woodrow Wilson

Guy, Rosa (Cuthbert) 1928- .... **CLC 26**
See also AAYA 4; BW 2; CA 17-20R; CANR 14, 34; CLR 13; DLB 33; JRDA; MAICYA; SATA 14, 62

Gwendolyn
See Bennett, (Enoch) Arnold

H. D. .... **CLC 3, 8, 14, 31, 34, 73; PC 5**
See also Doolittle, Hilda

H. de V.
See Buchan, John

Haavikko, Paavo Juhani 1931- ..... **CLC 18, 34**
See also CA 106

Habbema, Koos
See Heijermans, Herman

Habermas, Juergen 1929- .... **CLC 104**
See also CA 109

Habermas, Jurgen
See Habermas, Juergen

Hacker, Marilyn 1942- .. **CLC 5, 9, 23, 72, 91; DAM POET**
See also CA 77-80; CANR 68; DLB 120

Haeckel, Ernst Heinrich (Philipp August) 1834-1919 .... **TCLC 80**
See also CA 157

Haggard, H(enry) Rider 1856-1925 ...... **TCLC 11**
See also CA 108; 148; DLB 70, 156, 174, 178; SATA 16

Hagiosy, L.
See Larbaud, Valery (Nicolas)

Hagiwara Sakutaro 1886-1942 ... **TCLC 60; PC 18**

Haig, Fenil
See Ford, Ford Madox

Haig-Brown, Roderick (Langmere) 1908-1976
CLC 21
See also CA 5-8R; 69-72; CANR 4, 38; CLR 31;
DLB 88; MAICYA; SATA 12

Hailey, Arthur 1920- **CLC 5; DAM NOV, POP**
See also AITN 2; BEST 90:3; CA 1-4R; CANR
2, 36; DLB 88; DLBY 82; MTCW

Hailey, Elizabeth Forsythe 1938- .... **CLC 40**
See also CA 93-96; CAAS 1; CANR 15, 48; INT
CANR-15

Haines, John (Meade) 1924- .... **CLC 58**
See also CA 17-20R; CANR 13, 34; DLB 5

Hakluyt, Richard 1552-1616 .... **LC 31**

Haldeman, Joe (William) 1943- .... **CLC 61**
See also CA 53-56; CAAS 25; CANR 6; DLB 8;
INT CANR-6

Haley, Alex(ander Murray Palmer) 1921-1992
**CLC 8, 12, 76; BLC; DA; DAB; DAC;
DAM MST, MULT, POP**
See also BW 2; CA 77-80; 136; CANR 61; DLB
38; MTCW

Haliburton, Thomas Chandler 1796-1865 ...**NCLC 15**
See also DLB 11, 99

Hall, Donald (Andrew, Jr.) 1928-   **CLC 1, 13,
37, 59; DAM POET**
See also CA 5-8R; CAAS 7; CANR 2, 44, 64;
DLB 5; SATA 23, 97

Hall, Frederic Sauser
See Sauser-Hall, Frederic

Hall, James
See Kuttner, Henry

Hall, James Norman 1887-1951 ...... **TCLC 23**
See also CA 123; SATA 21

Hall, (Marguerite) Radclyffe 1886-1943
TCLC 12
See also CA 110; 150

Hall, Rodney 1935- .... **CLC 51**
See also CA 109

Halleck, Fitz-Greene 1790-1867 ..... **NCLC 47**
See also DLB 3

Halliday, Michael
See Creasey, John

Halpern, Daniel 1945- .... **CLC 14**
See also CA 33-36R

Hamburger, Michael (Peter Leopold) 1924-
CLC 5, 14
See also CA 5-8R; CAAS 4; CANR 2, 47; DLB 27

Hamill, Pete 1935- .... **CLC 10**
See also CA 25-28R; CANR 18

Hamilton, Alexander 1755(?)-1804   .... **NCLC
49**
See also DLB 37

Hamilton, Clive
See Lewis, C(live) S(taples)

Hamilton, Edmond 1904-1977 .... **CLC 1**
See also CA 1-4R; CANR 3; DLB 8

Hamilton, Eugene (Jacob) Lee
See Lee-Hamilton, Eugene (Jacob)

Hamilton, Franklin
See Silverberg, Robert

Hamilton, Gail
See Corcoran, Barbara

Hamilton, Mollie
See Kaye, M(ary) M(argaret)

Hamilton, (Anthony Walter) Patrick 1904-1962
CLC 51
See also CA 113; DLB 10

Hamilton, Virginia 1936- .... **CLC 26; DAM
MULT**
See also AAYA 2, 21; BW 2; CA 25-28R; CANR
20, 37; CLR 1, 11, 40; DLB 33, 52; INT
CANR-20; JRDA; MAICYA; MTCW; SATA
4, 56, 79

Hammett, (Samuel) Dashiell 1894-1961 ... **CLC
3, 5, 10, 19, 47; SSC 17**
See also AITN 1; CA 81-84; CANR 42; CDALB
1929-1941; DLBD 6; DLBY 96; MTCW

Hammon, Jupiter 1711(?)-1800(?)...**NCLC 5;
BLC; DAM MULT, POET; PC 16**
See also DLB 31, 50

Hammond, Keith
See Kuttner, Henry

Hamner, Earl (Henry), Jr. 1923- .... **CLC 12**
See also AITN 2; CA 73-76; DLB 6

Hampton, Christopher (James) 1946- ...... **CLC
4**
See also CA 25-28R; DLB 13; MTCW

Hamsun, Knut .... **TCLC 2, 14, 49**
See also Pedersen, Knut

Handke, Peter 1942- .... **CLC 5, 8, 10, 15, 38;
DAM DRAM, NOV**
See also CA 77-80; CANR 33; DLB 85, 124; MTCW

Hanley, James 1901-1985 .... **CLC 3, 5, 8, 13**
See also CA 73-76; 117; CANR 36; DLB 191;
MTCW

Hannah, Barry 1942-............... **CLC 23, 38, 90**
See also CA 108; 110; CANR 43, 68; DLB 6;
INT 110; MTCW

Hannon, Ezra
See Hunter, Evan

Hansberry, Lorraine (Vivian) 1930-1965
**CLC 17, 62; BLC; DA; DAB; DAC; DAM
DRAM, MST, MULT; DC 2**
See also AAYA 25; BW 1; CA 109; 25-28R;
CABS 3; CANR 58; CDALB 1941-1968;
DLB 7, 38; MTCW

Hansen, Joseph 1923-.......................... **CLC 38**
See also CA 29-32R; CAAS 17; CANR 16, 44,
66; INT CANR-16

Hansen, Martin A. 1909-1955 .... **TCLC 32**

Hanson, Kenneth O(stlin) 1922- .... **CLC 13**
See also CA 53-56; CANR 7

Hardwick, Elizabeth 1916- .... **CLC 13; DAM
NOV**
See also CA 5-8R; CANR 3, 32; DLB 6; MTCW

Hardy, Thomas 1840-1928   **TCLC 4, 10,
18, 32, 48, 53, 72; DA; DAB; DAC; DAM
MST, NOV, POET; PC 8; SSC 2; WLC**
See also CA 104; 123; CDBLB 1890-1914; DLB
18, 19, 135; MTCW

Hare, David 1947- .... **CLC 29, 58**
See also CA 97-100; CANR 39; DLB 13;
MTCW

Harewood, John
See Van Druten, John (William)

Harford, Henry
See Hudson, W(illiam) H(enry)

Hargrave, Leonie
See Disch, Thomas M(ichael)

Harjo, Joy 1951- .... **CLC 83; DAM MULT**
See also CA 114; CANR 35, 67; DLB 120, 175;
NNAL

Harlan, Louis R(udolph) 1922- .... **CLC 34**
See also CA 21-24R; CANR 25, 55

Harling, Robert 1951(?)- .... **CLC 53**
See also CA 147

Harmon, William (Ruth) 1938- .... **CLC 38**
See also CA 33-36R; CANR 14, 32, 35; SATA
65

Harper, F. E. W.
See Harper, Frances Ellen Watkins

Harper, Frances E. W.
See Harper, Frances Ellen Watkins

Harper, Frances E. Watkins
See Harper, Frances Ellen Watkins

Harper, Frances Ellen
See Harper, Frances Ellen Watkins

Harper, Frances Ellen Watkins 1825-1911
**TCLC 14; BLC; DAM MULT, POET; PC
21**
See also BW 1; CA 111; 125; DLB 50

Harper, Michael S(teven) 1938- ..... **CLC 7, 22**
See also BW 1; CA 33-36R; CANR 24; DLB 41

Harper, Mrs. F. E. W.
See Harper, Frances Ellen Watkins

Harris, Christie (Lucy) Irwin 1907- .. **CLC 12**
See also CA 5-8R; CANR 6; CLR 47; DLB 88;
JRDA; MAICYA; SAAS 10; SATA 6, 74

Harris, Frank 1856-1931 .... **TCLC 24**
See also CA 109; 150; DLB 156

Harris, George Washington 1814-1869
NCLC 23
See also DLB 3, 11

Harris, Joel Chandler 1848-1908 ... **TCLC 2;**
SSC 19
See also CA 104; 137; CLR 49; DLB 11, 23, 42,
78, 91; MAICYA; YABC 1

Harris, John (Wyndham Parkes Lucas) Beynon
1903-1969
See Wyndham, John
See also CA 102; 89-92

Harris, MacDonald .... **CLC 9**
See also Heiney, Donald (William)

Harris, Mark 1922- .... **CLC 19**
See also CA 5-8R; CAAS 3; CANR 2, 55; DLB
2; DLBY 80

Harris, (Theodore) Wilson 1921- .... **CLC 25**
See also BW 2; CA 65-68; CAAS 16; CANR 11,
27; DLB 117; MTCW

Harrison, Elizabeth Cavanna 1909-
See Cavanna, Betty
See also CA 9-12R; CANR 6, 27

Harrison, Harry (Max) 1925- .... **CLC 42**
See also CA 1-4R; CANR 5, 21; DLB 8; SATA 4

Harrison, James (Thomas) 1937- ... **CLC 6, 14,**
33, 66; SSC 19
See also CA 13-16R; CANR 8, 51; DLBY 82;
INT CANR-8

Harrison, Jim
See Harrison, James (Thomas)

Harrison, Kathryn 1961- .... **CLC 70**
See also CA 144; CANR 68

Harrison, Tony 1937- .... **CLC 43**
See also CA 65-68; CANR 44; DLB 40; MTCW

Harriss, Will(ard Irvin) 1922- .... **CLC 34**
See also CA 111

Harson, Sley
See Ellison, Harlan (Jay)

Hart, Ellis
See Ellison, Harlan (Jay)

Hart, Josephine 1942(?)- .... **CLC 70; DAM**
POP
See also CA 138

Hart, Moss 1904-1961 .... **CLC 66; DAM**
DRAM
See also CA 109; 89-92; DLB 7

Harte, (Francis) Bret(t) 1836(?)-1902 ... **TCLC**
1, 25; DA; DAC; DAM MST; SSC 8; WLC
See also CA 104; 140; CDALB 1865-1917; DLB
12, 64, 74, 79, 186; SATA 26

Hartley, L(eslie) P(oles) 1895-1972 ..... **CLC 2,**
22
See also CA 45-48; 37-40R; CANR 33; DLB 15,
139; MTCW

Hartman, Geoffrey H. 1929- .... **CLC 27**
See also CA 117; 125; DLB 67

Hartmann, Sadakichi 1867-1944..... **TCLC 73**
See also CA 157; DLB 54

Hartmann von Aue c. 1160-c. 1205 **CMLC 15**
See also DLB 138

Hartmann von Aue 1170-1210 .... **CMLC 15**

Haruf, Kent 1943- .... **CLC 34**
See also CA 149

Harwood, Ronald 1934- .... **CLC 32; DAM**
DRAM, MST
See also CA 1-4R; CANR 4, 55; DLB 13

Hasegawa Tatsunosuke
See Futabatei, Shimei

Hasek, Jaroslav (Matej Frantisek) 1883-1923
TCLC 4
See also CA 104; 129; MTCW

Hass, Robert 1941- **CLC 18, 39, 99; PC 16**
See also CA 111; CANR 30, 50; DLB 105; SATA 94

Hastings, Hudson
See Kuttner, Henry

Hastings, Selina .... **CLC 44**

Hathorne, John 1641-1717 .... **LC 38**

Hatteras, Amelia
See Mencken, H(enry) L(ouis)

Hatteras, Owen .... **TCLC 18**
See also Mencken, H(enry) L(ouis); Nathan,
George Jean

Hauptmann, Gerhart (Johann Robert) 1862-
1946 .... **TCLC 4; DAM DRAM**
See also CA 104; 153; DLB 66, 118

Havel, Vaclav 1936- ..... **CLC 25, 58, 65; DAM**
DRAM; DC 6
See also CA 104; CANR 36, 63; MTCW

Haviaras, Stratis .... **CLC 33**
See also Chaviaras, Strates

Hawes, Stephen 1475(?)-1523(?) .... **LC 17**

Hawkes, John (Clendennin Burne, Jr.) 1925-
CLC 1, 2, 3, 4, 7, 9, 14, 15, 27, 49
See also CA 1-4R; CANR 2, 47, 64; DLB 2, 7;
DLBY 80; MTCW

Hawking, S. W.
See Hawking, Stephen W(illiam)

Hawking, Stephen W(illiam) 1942- ... **CLC 63, 105**
See also AAYA 13; BEST 89:1; CA 126; 129;
CANR 48

Hawthorne, Julian 1846-1934 .... **TCLC 25**
See also CA 165

Hawthorne, Nathaniel 1804-1864 ... **NCLC 39; DA;**
DAB; DAC; DAM MST, NOV; SSC 3, 29; WLC
See also AAYA 18; CDALB 1640-1865; DLB 1,
74; YABC 2

Haxton, Josephine Ayres 1921-
See Douglas, Ellen
See also CA 115; CANR 41

Hayaseca y Eizaguirre, Jorge
See Echegaray (y Eizaguirre), Jose (Maria Waldo)

Hayashi Fumiko 1904-1951 .... **TCLC 27**
See also CA 161; DLB 180

Haycraft, Anna
See Ellis, Alice Thomas
See also CA 122

Hayden, Robert E(arl) 1913-1980 ... **CLC 5, 9,**
14, 37; BLC; DA; DAC; DAM MST, MULT,
POET; PC 6
See also BW 1; CA 69-72; 97-100; CABS 2;
CANR 24; CDALB 1941-1968; DLB 5, 76;
MTCW; SATA 19; SATA-Obit 26

Hayford, J(oseph) E(phraim) Casely
See Casely-Hayford, J(oseph) E(phraim)

Hayman, Ronald 1932- .... **CLC 44**
See also CA 25-28R; CANR 18, 50; DLB 155

Haywood, Eliza (Fowler) 1693(?)-1756 .. **LC 1**

Hazlitt, William 1778-1830 .... **NCLC 29**
See also DLB 110, 158

Hazzard, Shirley 1931- .... **CLC 18**
See also CA 9-12R; CANR 4; DLBY 82; MTCW

Head, Bessie 1937-1986 .... **CLC 25, 67; BLC;**
DAM MULT
See also BW 2; CA 29-32R; 119; CANR 25; DLB
117; MTCW

Headon, (Nicky) Topper 1956(?)- ...... **CLC 30**

Heaney, Seamus (Justin) 1939- ... **CLC 5, 7, 14, 25,**
37, 74, 91; DAB; DAM POET; PC 18; WLCS
See also CA 85-88; CANR 25, 48; CDBLB 1960
to Present; DLB 40; DLBY 95; MTCW

Hearn, (Patricio) Lafcadio (Tessima Carlos)
1850-1904 .... **TCLC 9**
See also CA 105; DLB 12, 78

Hearne, Vicki 1946- .... **CLC 56**
See also CA 139

Hearon, Shelby 1931- .... **CLC 63**
See also AITN 2; CA 25-28R; CANR 18, 48

Heat-Moon, William Least .... **CLC 29**
See also Trogdon, William (Lewis)
See also AAYA 9

Hebbel, Friedrich 1813-1863 ....   **NCLC 43;**
DAM DRAM
See also DLB 129

Hebert, Anne 1916- ...   **CLC 4, 13, 29; DAC;**
DAM MST, POET
See also CA 85-88; DLB 68; MTCW

Hecht, Anthony (Evan) 1923- .   **CLC 8, 13,**
19; DAM POET
See also CA 9-12R; CANR 6; DLB 5, 169

Hecht, Ben 1894-1964 .... **CLC 8**
See also CA 85-88; DLB 7, 9, 25, 26, 28, 86

Hedayat, Sadeq 1903-1951 .... **TCLC 21**
See also CA 120

Hegel, Georg Wilhelm Friedrich 1770-1831
NCLC 46
See also DLB 90

Heidegger, Martin 1889-1976 .... **CLC 24**
See also CA 81-84; 65-68; CANR 34; MTCW

Heidenstam, (Carl Gustaf) Verner von 1859-
1940 .... **TCLC 5**
See also CA 104

Heifner, Jack 1946- .... **CLC 11**
See also CA 105; CANR 47

Heijermans, Herman 1864-1924 ..... **TCLC 24**
See also CA 123

Heilbrun, Carolyn G(old) 1926- .... **CLC 25**
See also CA 45-48; CANR 1, 28, 58

Heine, Heinrich 1797-1856 .... **NCLC 4, 54**
See also DLB 90

Heinemann, Larry (Curtiss) 1944- .... **CLC 50**
See also CA 110; CAAS 21; CANR 31; DLBD
9; INT CANR-31

Heiney, Donald (William) 1921-1993
See Harris, MacDonald
See also CA 1-4R; 142; CANR 3, 58

Heinlein, Robert A(nson) 1907-1988   **CLC 1,**
3, 8, 14, 26, 55; DAM POP
See also AAYA 17; CA 1-4R; 125; CANR 1, 20,
53; DLB 8; JRDA; MAICYA; MTCW; SATA
9, 69; SATA-Obit 56

Helforth, John
See Doolittle, Hilda

Hellenhofferu, Vojtech Kapristian z
See Hasek, Jaroslav (Matej Frantisek)

Heller, Joseph 1923-   **CLC 1, 3, 5, 8, 11, 36,**
63; DA; DAB; DAC; DAM MST, NOV,
POP; WLC
See also AAYA 24; AITN 1; CA 5-8R; CABS 1;
CANR 8, 42, 66; DLB 2, 28; DLBY 80; INT
CANR-8; MTCW

Hellman, Lillian (Florence) 1906-1984 ... **CLC 2,**
4, 8, 14, 18, 34, 44, 52; DAM DRAM; DC 1
See also AITN 1, 2; CA 13-16R; 112; CANR 33;
DLB 7; DLBY 84; MTCW

Helprin, Mark 1947- ...   **CLC 7, 10, 22, 32;**
DAM NOV, POP
See also CA 81-84; CANR 47, 64; DLBY 85;
MTCW

Helvetius, Claude-Adrien 1715-1771 ... **LC 26**

Helyar, Jane Penelope Josephine 1933-
See Poole, Josephine
See also CA 21-24R; CANR 10, 26; SATA 82

Hemans, Felicia 1793-1835 .... **NCLC 29**
See also DLB 96

Hemingway, Ernest (Miller) 1899-1961

CLC 1, 3, 6, 8, 10, 13, 19, 30, 34, 39, 41, 44,
50, 61, 80; DA; DAB; DAC; DAM MST,
NOV; SSC 25; WLC
See also AAYA 19; CA 77-80; CANR 34;
CDALB 1917-1929; DLB 4, 9, 102; DLBD
1, 15, 16; DLBY 81, 87, 96; MTCW

Hempel, Amy 1951- .... **CLC 39**
See also CA 118; 137

Henderson, F. C.
See Mencken, H(enry) L(ouis)

Henderson, Sylvia
See Ashton-Warner, Sylvia (Constance)

Henderson, Zenna (Chlarson) 1917-1983
SSC 29
See also CA 1-4R; 133; CANR 1; DLB 8; SATA 5

Henley, Beth .... **CLC 23; DC 6**
See also Henley, Elizabeth Becker
See also CABS 3; DLBY 86

Henley, Elizabeth Becker 1952-
See Henley, Beth
See also CA 107; CANR 32; DAM DRAM, MST;
MTCW

Henley, William Ernest 1849-1903 ... **TCLC 8**
See also CA 105; DLB 19

Hennissart, Martha
See Lathen, Emma
See also CA 85-88; CANR 64

Henry, O. .... **TCLC 1, 19; SSC 5; WLC**
See also Porter, William Sydney

Henry, Patrick 1736-1799 .... **LC 25**

Henryson, Robert 1430(?)-1506(?) .... **LC 20**
See also DLB 146

Henry VIII 1491-1547 .... **LC 10**

Henschke, Alfred
See Klabund

Hentoff, Nat(han Irving) 1925- .... **CLC 26**
See also AAYA 4; CA 1-4R; CAAS 6; CANR 5,
25; CLR 1; INT CANR-25; JRDA; MAICYA;
SATA 42, 69; SATA-Brief 27

Heppenstall, (John) Rayner 1911-1981 **CLC 10**
See also CA 1-4R; 103; CANR 29

Heraclitus c. 540B.C.-c. 450B.C. .... **CMLC 22**
See also DLB 176

Herbert, Frank (Patrick) 1920-1986 **CLC 12,**
23, 35, 44, 85; DAM POP
See also AAYA 21; CA 53-56; 118; CANR 5,
43; DLB 8; INT CANR-5; MTCW; SATA 9,
37; SATA-Obit 47

Herbert, George 1593-1633 ..... **LC 24; DAB;**
DAM POET; PC 4
See also CDBLB Before 1660; DLB 126

Herbert, Zbigniew 1924- .... **CLC 9, 43; DAM**
POET
See also CA 89-92; CANR 36; MTCW

Herbst, Josephine (Frey) 1897-1969 .... **CLC 34**
See also CA 5-8R; 25-28R; DLB 9

Hergesheimer, Joseph 1880-1954 ... **TCLC 11**
See also CA 109; DLB 102, 9

Herlihy, James Leo 1927-1993 .... **CLC 6**
See also CA 1-4R; 143; CANR 2

Hermogenes fl. c. 175- .... **CMLC 6**

Hernandez, Jose 1834-1886 .... **NCLC 17**

Herodotus c. 484B.C.-429B.C. .... **CMLC 17**
See also DLB 176

Herrick, Robert 1591-1674 .... **LC 13; DA;**
DAB; DAC; DAM MST, POP; PC 9
See also DLB 126

Herring, Guilles
See Somerville, Edith

Herriot, James 1916-1995 ...   **CLC 12; DAM**
POP
See also Wight, James Alfred
See also AAYA 1; CA 148; CANR 40; SATA 86

Herrmann, Dorothy 1941- .... **CLC 44**
See also CA 107

Herrmann, Taffy
See Herrmann, Dorothy

Hersey, John (Richard) 1914-1993   **CLC 1, 2,**
7, 9, 40, 81, 97; DAM POP
See also CA 17-20R; 140; CANR 33; DLB 6,
185; MTCW; SATA 25; SATA-Obit 76

Herzen, Aleksandr Ivanovich 1812-1870
NCLC 10, 61

Herzl, Theodor 1860-1904 .... **TCLC 36**

Herzog, Werner 1942- .... **CLC 16**
See also CA 89-92

Hesiod c. 8th cent. B.C.- .... **CMLC 5**
See also DLB 176

Hesse, Hermann 1877-1962   **CLC 1, 2, 3, 6,**
11, 17, 25, 69; DA; DAB; DAC; DAM MST,
NOV; SSC 9; WLC
See also CA 17-18; CAP 2; DLB 66; MTCW;
SATA 50

Hewes, Cady
See De Voto, Bernard (Augustine)

Heyen, William 1940- .... **CLC 13, 18**
See also CA 33-36R; CAAS 9; DLB 5

Heyerdahl, Thor 1914- .... **CLC 26**
See also CA 5-8R; CANR 5, 22, 66; MTCW;
SATA 2, 52

Heym, Georg (Theodor Franz Arthur) 1887-
1912 .... **TCLC 9**
See also CA 106

Heym, Stefan 1913- .... **CLC 41**
See also CA 9-12R; CANR 4; DLB 69

Heyse, Paul (Johann Ludwig von) 1830-1914
TCLC 8
See also CA 104; DLB 129

Heyward, (Edwin) DuBose 1885-1940   **TCLC
59**
See also CA 108; 157; DLB 7, 9, 45; SATA 21

Hibbert, Eleanor Alice Burford 1906-1993
CLC 7; DAM POP
See also BEST 90:4; CA 17-20R; 140; CANR 9,
28, 59; SATA 2; SATA-Obit 74

Hichens, Robert (Smythe) 1864-1950 ... **TCLC 64**
See also CA 162; DLB 153

Higgins, George V(incent) 1939-   **CLC 4, 7,
10, 18**
See also CA 77-80; CAAS 5; CANR 17, 51; DLB
2; DLBY 81; INT CANR-17; MTCW

Higginson, Thomas Wentworth 1823-1911
TCLC 36
See also CA 162; DLB 1, 64

Highet, Helen
See MacInnes, Helen (Clark)

Highsmith, (Mary) Patricia 1921-1995   **CLC
2, 4, 14, 42, 102; DAM NOV, POP**
See also CA 1-4R; 147; CANR 1, 20, 48, 62;
MTCW

Highwater, Jamake (Mamake) 1942(?)-   **CLC
12**
See also AAYA 7; CA 65-68; CAAS 7; CANR
10, 34; CLR 17; DLB 52; DLBY 85; JRDA;
MAICYA; SATA 32, 69; SATA-Brief 30

Highway, Tomson 1951- .....   **CLC 92; DAC;
DAM MULT**
See also CA 151; NNAL

Higuchi, Ichiyo 1872-1896 .... **NCLC 49**

Hijuelos, Oscar 1951-   **CLC 65; DAM MULT,
POP; HLC**
See also AAYA 25; BEST 90:1; CA 123; CANR
50; DLB 145; HW

Hikmet, Nazim 1902(?)-1963 .... **CLC 40**
See also CA 141; 93-96

Hildegard von Bingen 1098-1179 .. **CMLC 20**
See also DLB 148

Hildesheimer, Wolfgang 1916-1991 ... **CLC 49**
See also CA 101; 135; DLB 69, 124

Hill, Geoffrey (William) 1932-   **CLC 5, 8,
18, 45; DAM POET**
See also CA 81-84; CANR 21; CDBLB 1960 to
Present; DLB 40; MTCW

Hill, George Roy 1921- .... **CLC 26**
See also CA 110; 122

Hill, John
See Koontz, Dean R(ay)

Hill, Susan (Elizabeth) 1942-.... **CLC 4; DAB;
DAM MST, NOV**
See also CA 33-36R; CANR 29; DLB 14, 139;
MTCW

Hillerman, Tony 1925-.... **CLC 62; DAM POP**
See also AAYA 6; BEST 89:1; CA 29-32R;
CANR 21, 42, 65; SATA 6

Hillesum, Etty 1914-1943 .... **TCLC 49**
See also CA 137

Hilliard, Noel (Harvey) 1929- .... **CLC 15**
See also CA 9-12R; CANR 7

Hillis, Rick 1956- .... **CLC 66**
See also CA 134

Hilton, James 1900-1954 .... **TCLC 21**
See also CA 108; DLB 34, 77; SATA 34

Himes, Chester (Bomar) 1909-1984   **CLC 2,
4, 7, 18, 58, 108; BLC; DAM MULT**
See also BW 2; CA 25-28R; 114; CANR 22; DLB
2, 76, 143; MTCW

Hinde, Thomas .... **CLC 6, 11**
See also Chitty, Thomas Willes

Hindin, Nathan
See Bloch, Robert (Albert)

Hine, (William) Daryl 1936- .... **CLC 15**
See also CA 1-4R; CAAS 15; CANR 1, 20; DLB
60

Hinkson, Katharine Tynan
See Tynan, Katharine

Hinton, S(usan) E(loise) 1950-   **CLC 30; DA;
DAB; DAC; DAM MST, NOV**
See also AAYA 2; CA 81-84; CANR 32, 62; CLR
3, 23; JRDA; MAICYA; MTCW; SATA 19, 58

Hippius, Zinaida .... **TCLC 9**
See also Gippius, Zinaida (Nikolayevna)

Hiraoka, Kimitake 1925-1970
See Mishima, Yukio
See also CA 97-100; 29-32R; DAM DRAM;
MTCW

Hirsch, E(ric) D(onald), Jr. 1928- ...... **CLC 79**
See also CA 25-28R; CANR 27, 51; DLB 67;
INT CANR-27; MTCW

Hirsch, Edward 1950- .... **CLC 31, 50**
See also CA 104; CANR 20, 42; DLB 120

Hitchcock, Alfred (Joseph) 1899-1980 **CLC 16**
See also AAYA 22; CA 159; 97-100; SATA 27;
SATA-Obit 24

Hitler, Adolf 1889-1945 .... **TCLC 53**
See also CA 117; 147

Hoagland, Edward 1932- .... **CLC 28**
See also CA 1-4R; CANR 2, 31, 57; DLB 6;
SATA 51

Hoban, Russell (Conwell) 1925- ... **CLC 7, 25;
DAM NOV**
See also CA 5-8R; CANR 23, 37, 66; CLR 3;
DLB 52; MAICYA; MTCW; SATA 1, 40, 78

Hobbes, Thomas 1588-1679 .... **LC 36**
See also DLB 151

Hobbs, Perry
See Blackmur, R(ichard) P(almer)

Hobson, Laura Z(ametkin) 1900-1986   **CLC
7, 25**
See also CA 17-20R; 118; CANR 55; DLB 28;
SATA 52

Hochhuth, Rolf 1931-.... **CLC 4, 11, 18; DAM
DRAM**
See also CA 5-8R; CANR 33; DLB 124; MTCW

Hochman, Sandra 1936- .... **CLC 3, 8**
See also CA 5-8R; DLB 5

Hochwaelder, Fritz 1911-1986 .....   **CLC 36;
DAM DRAM**
See also CA 29-32R; 120; CANR 42; MTCW

Hochwalder, Fritz
See Hochwaelder, Fritz

Hocking, Mary (Eunice) 1921- .... **CLC 13**
See also CA 101; CANR 18, 40

Hodgins, Jack 1938- .... **CLC 23**
See also CA 93-96; DLB 60

Hodgson, William Hope 1877(?)-1918 ... **TCLC 13**
See also CA 111; 164; DLB 70, 153, 156, 178

Hoeg, Peter 1957- .... **CLC 95**
See also CA 151

Hoffman, Alice 1952- .... **CLC 51; DAM NOV**
See also CA 77-80; CANR 34, 66; MTCW

Hoffman, Daniel (Gerard) 1923-   **CLC 6,
13, 23**
See also CA 1-4R; CANR 4; DLB 5

Hoffman, Stanley 1944- .... **CLC 5**
See also CA 77-80

Hoffman, William M(oses) 1939- .... **CLC 40**
See also CA 57-60; CANR 11

Hoffmann, E(rnst) T(heodor) A(madeus) 1776-
1822 .... **NCLC 2; SSC 13**
See also DLB 90; SATA 27

Hofmann, Gert 1931- .... **CLC 54**
See also CA 128

Hofmannsthal, Hugo von 1874-1929   **TCLC 11; DAM DRAM; DC 4**
See also CA 106; 153; DLB 81, 118

Hogan, Linda 1947- ....   **CLC 73; DAM MULT**
See also CA 120; CANR 45; DLB 175; NNAL

Hogarth, Charles
See Creasey, John

Hogarth, Emmett
See Polonsky, Abraham (Lincoln)

Hogg, James 1770-1835 .... **NCLC 4**
See also DLB 93, 116, 159

Holbach, Paul Henri Thiry Baron 1723-1789
LC 14

Holberg, Ludvig 1684-1754 .... **LC 6**

Holden, Ursula 1921- .... **CLC 18**
See also CA 101; CAAS 8; CANR 22

Holderlin, (Johann Christian) Friedrich 1770-
1843 .... **NCLC 16; PC 4**

Holdstock, Robert
See Holdstock, Robert P.

Holdstock, Robert P. 1948- .... **CLC 39**
See also CA 131

Holland, Isabelle 1920- .... **CLC 21**
See also AAYA 11; CA 21-24R; CANR 10, 25, 47; JRDA; MAICYA; SATA 8, 70

Holland, Marcus
See Caldwell, (Janet Miriam) Taylor (Holland)

Hollander, John 1929- .... **CLC 2, 5, 8, 14**
See also CA 1-4R; CANR 1, 52; DLB 5; SATA 13

Hollander, Paul
See Silverberg, Robert

Holleran, Andrew 1943(?)- .... **CLC 38**
See also CA 144

Hollinghurst, Alan 1954- .... **CLC 55, 91**
See also CA 114

Hollis, Jim
See Summers, Hollis (Spurgeon, Jr.)

Holly, Buddy 1936-1959 .... **TCLC 65**

Holmes, Gordon
See Shiel, M(atthew) P(hipps)

Holmes, John
See Souster, (Holmes) Raymond

Holmes, John Clellon 1926-1988 .... **CLC 56**
See also CA 9-12R; 125; CANR 4; DLB 16

Holmes, Oliver Wendell, Jr. 1841-1935
TCLC 77
See also CA 114

Holmes, Oliver Wendell 1809-1894   **NCLC 14**
See also CDALB 1640-1865; DLB 1, 189; SATA 34

Holmes, Raymond
See Souster, (Holmes) Raymond

Holt, Victoria
See Hibbert, Eleanor Alice Burford

Holub, Miroslav 1923- .... **CLC 4**
See also CA 21-24R; CANR 10

Homer c. 8th cent. B.C.- ....   **CMLC 1, 16; DA; DAB; DAC; DAM MST, POET; WLCS**
See also DLB 176

Honig, Edwin 1919- .... **CLC 33**
See also CA 5-8R; CAAS 8; CANR 4, 45; DLB 5

Hood, Hugh (John Blagdon) 1928- ...   **CLC 15, 28**
See also CA 49-52; CAAS 17; CANR 1, 33; DLB 53

Hood, Thomas 1799-1845 .... **NCLC 16**
See also DLB 96

Hooker, (Peter) Jeremy 1941- .... **CLC 43**
See also CA 77-80; CANR 22; DLB 40

hooks, bell .... **CLC 94**
See also Watkins, Gloria

Hope, A(lec) D(erwent) 1907- .... **CLC 3, 51**
See also CA 21-24R; CANR 33; MTCW

Hope, Brian
See Creasey, John

Hope, Christopher (David Tully) 1944- ... **CLC 52**
See also CA 106; CANR 47; SATA 62

Hopkins, Gerard Manley 1844-1889 ... **NCLC 17; DA; DAB; DAC; DAM MST, POET; PC 15; WLC**
See also CDBLB 1890-1914; DLB 35, 57

Hopkins, John (Richard) 1931- .... **CLC 4**
See also CA 85-88

Hopkins, Pauline Elizabeth 1859-1930
TCLC 28; BLC; DAM MULT
See also BW 2; CA 141; DLB 50

Hopkinson, Francis 1737-1791 .... **LC 25**
See also DLB 31

Hopley-Woolrich, Cornell George 1903-1968
See Woolrich, Cornell
See also CA 13-14; CANR 58; CAP 1

Horatio
See Proust, (Valentin-Louis-George-Eugene-) Marcel

Horgan, Paul (George Vincent O'Shaughnessy) 1903-1995 .... **CLC 9, 53; DAM NOV**
See also CA 13-16R; 147; CANR 9, 35; DLB 102; DLBY 85; INT CANR-9; MTCW; SATA 13; SATA-Obit 84

Horn, Peter
See Kuttner, Henry

Hornem, Horace Esq.
See Byron, George Gordon (Noel)

Horney, Karen (Clementine Theodore Danielsen) 1885-1952 .... **TCLC 71**
See also CA 114; 165

Hornung, E(rnest) W(illiam) 1866-1921
TCLC 59
See also CA 108; 160; DLB 70

Horovitz, Israel (Arthur) 1939- ... **CLC 56; DAM DRAM**
See also CA 33-36R; CANR 46, 59; DLB 7

Horvath, Odon von
See Horvath, Oedoen von
See also DLB 85, 124

Horvath, Oedoen von 1901-1938 .... **TCLC 45**
See also Horvath, Odon von
See also CA 118

Horwitz, Julius 1920-1986 .... **CLC 14**
See also CA 9-12R; 119; CANR 12

Hospital, Janette Turner 1942- .... **CLC 42**
See also CA 108; CANR 48

Hostos, E. M. de
See Hostos (y Bonilla), Eugenio Maria de

Hostos, Eugenio M. de
See Hostos (y Bonilla), Eugenio Maria de

Hostos, Eugenio Maria
See Hostos (y Bonilla), Eugenio Maria de

Hostos (y Bonilla), Eugenio Maria de 1839-1903
TCLC 24
See also CA 123; 131; HW

Houdini
See Lovecraft, H(oward) P(hillips)

Hougan, Carolyn 1943- .... **CLC 34**
See also CA 139

Household, Geoffrey (Edward West) 1900-1988
CLC 11
See also CA 77-80; 126; CANR 58; DLB 87; SATA 14; SATA-Obit 59

Housman, A(lfred) E(dward) 1859-1936
TCLC 1, 10; DA; DAB; DAC; DAM MST, POET; PC 2; WLCS
See also CA 104; 125; DLB 19; MTCW

Housman, Laurence 1865-1959 .... **TCLC 7**
See also CA 106; 155; DLB 10; SATA 25

Howard, Elizabeth Jane 1923- .... **CLC 7, 29**
See also CA 5-8R; CANR 8, 62

Howard, Maureen 1930- .... **CLC 5, 14, 46**
See also CA 53-56; CANR 31; DLBY 83; INT CANR-31; MTCW

Howard, Richard 1929- .... **CLC 7, 10, 47**
See also AITN 1; CA 85-88; CANR 25; DLB 5; INT CANR-25

Howard, Robert E(rvin) 1906-1936 .... **TCLC 8**
See also CA 105; 157

Howard, Warren F.
See Pohl, Frederik

Howe, Fanny 1940- .... **CLC 47**
See also CA 117; CAAS 27; SATA-Brief 52

Howe, Irving 1920-1993 .... **CLC 85**
See also CA 9-12R; 141; CANR 21, 50; DLB 67; MTCW

Howe, Julia Ward 1819-1910 .... **TCLC 21**
See also CA 117; DLB 1, 189

Howe, Susan 1937- .... **CLC 72**
See also CA 160; DLB 120

Howe, Tina 1937- .... **CLC 48**
See also CA 109

Howell, James 1594(?)-1666 .... **LC 13**
See also DLB 151

Howells, W. D.
See Howells, William Dean

Howells, William D.
See Howells, William Dean

Howells, William Dean 1837-1920 ... **TCLC 7, 17, 41**
See also CA 104; 134; CDALB 1865-1917; DLB 12, 64, 74, 79, 189

Howes, Barbara 1914-1996 .... **CLC 15**
See also CA 9-12R; 151; CAAS 3; CANR 53; SATA 5

Hrabal, Bohumil 1914-1997 .... **CLC 13, 67**
See also CA 106; 156; CAAS 12; CANR 57

Hsun, Lu
See Lu Hsun

Hubbard, L(afayette) Ron(ald) 1911-1986 **CLC 43; DAM POP**
See also CA 77-80; 118; CANR 52

Huch, Ricarda (Octavia) 1864-1947 ... **TCLC 13**
See also CA 111; DLB 66

Huddle, David 1942- .... **CLC 49**
See also CA 57-60; CAAS 20; DLB 130

Hudson, Jeffrey
See Crichton, (John) Michael

Hudson, W(illiam) H(enry) 1841-1922 ... **TCLC 29**
See also CA 115; DLB 98, 153, 174; SATA 35

Hueffer, Ford Madox
See Ford, Ford Madox

Hughart, Barry 1934- .... **CLC 39**
See also CA 137

Hughes, Colin
See Creasey, John

Hughes, David (John) 1930- .... **CLC 48**
See also CA 116; 129; DLB 14

Hughes, Edward James
See Hughes, Ted
See also DAM MST, POET

Hughes, (James) Langston 1902-1967 ... **CLC 1, 5, 10, 15, 35, 44, 108; BLC; DA; DAB; DAC; DAM DRAM, MST, MULT, POET; DC 3; PC 1; SSC 6; WLC**
See also AAYA 12; BW 1; CA 1-4R; 25-28R; CANR 1, 34; CDALB 1929-1941; CLR 17; DLB 4, 7, 48, 51, 86; JRDA; MAICYA; MTCW; SATA 4, 33

Hughes, Richard (Arthur Warren) 1900-1976 **CLC 1, 11; DAM NOV**
See also CA 5-8R; 65-68; CANR 4; DLB 15, 161; MTCW; SATA 8; SATA-Obit 25

Hughes, Ted 1930- ... **CLC 2, 4, 9, 14, 37; DAB; DAC; PC 7**
See also Hughes, Edward James
See also CA 1-4R; CANR 1, 33, 66; CLR 3; DLB 40, 161; MAICYA; MTCW; SATA 49; SATA-Brief 27

Hugo, Richard F(ranklin) 1923-1982 ... **CLC 6, 18, 32; DAM POET**
See also CA 49-52; 108; CANR 3; DLB 5

Hugo, Victor (Marie) 1802-1885 ... **NCLC 3, 10, 21; DA; DAB; DAC; DAM DRAM, MST, NOV, POET; PC 17; WLC**
See also DLB 119, 192; SATA 47

Huidobro, Vicente
See Huidobro Fernandez, Vicente Garcia

Huidobro Fernandez, Vicente Garcia 1893-1948 **TCLC 31**
See also CA 131; HW

Hulme, Keri 1947- .... **CLC 39**
See also CA 125; INT 125

Hulme, T(homas) E(rnest) 1883-1917 **TCLC 21**
See also CA 117; DLB 19

Hume, David 1711-1776 .... **LC 7**
See also DLB 104

Humphrey, William 1924-1997 .... **CLC 45**
See also CA 77-80; 160; CANR 68; DLB 6

Humphreys, Emyr Owen 1919- .... **CLC 47**
See also CA 5-8R; CANR 3, 24; DLB 15

Humphreys, Josephine 1945- .... **CLC 34, 57**
See also CA 121; 127; INT 127

Huneker, James Gibbons 1857-1921 ... **TCLC 65**
See also DLB 71

Hungerford, Pixie
See Brinsmead, H(esba) F(ay)

Hunt, E(verette) Howard, (Jr.) 1918- .. **CLC 3**
See also AITN 1; CA 45-48; CANR 2, 47

Hunt, Kyle
See Creasey, John

Hunt, (James Henry) Leigh 1784-1859 **NCLC 1; DAM POET**

Hunt, Marsha 1946- .... **CLC 70**
See also BW 2; CA 143

Hunt, Violet 1866-1942 .... **TCLC 53**
See also DLB 162

Hunter, E. Waldo
See Sturgeon, Theodore (Hamilton)

Hunter, Evan 1926- .... **CLC 11, 31; DAM POP**
See also CA 5-8R; CANR 5, 38, 62; DLBY 82; INT CANR-5; MTCW; SATA 25

Hunter, Kristin (Eggleston) 1931- ..... **CLC 35**
See also AITN 1; BW 1; CA 13-16R; CANR 13; CLR 3; DLB 33; INT CANR-13; MAICYA; SAAS 10; SATA 12

Hunter, Mollie 1922- .... **CLC 21**
See also McIlwraith, Maureen Mollie Hunter
See also AAYA 13; CANR 37; CLR 25; DLB 161; JRDA; MAICYA; SAAS 7; SATA 54

Hunter, Robert (?)-1734 .... **LC 7**

Hurston, Zora Neale 1903-1960 **CLC 7, 30, 61; BLC; DA; DAC; DAM MST, MULT, NOV; SSC 4; WLCS**
See also AAYA 15; BW 1; CA 85-88; CANR 61; DLB 51, 86; MTCW

Huston, John (Marcellus) 1906-1987 **CLC 20**
See also CA 73-76; 123; CANR 34; DLB 26

Hustvedt, Siri 1955- .... **CLC 76**
See also CA 137

Hutten, Ulrich von 1488-1523 .... **LC 16**
See also DLB 179

Huxley, Aldous (Leonard) 1894-1963 **CLC 1, 3, 4, 5, 8, 11, 18, 35, 79; DA; DAB; DAC; DAM MST, NOV; WLC**
See also AAYA 11; CA 85-88; CANR 44; CDBLB 1914-1945; DLB 36, 100, 162, 195; MTCW; SATA 63

Huxley, T. H. 1825-1895 .... **NCLC 67**
See also DLB 57

Huysmans, Joris-Karl 1848-1907 **TCLC 7, 69**
See also CA 104; 165; DLB 123

Hwang, David Henry 1957- .... **CLC 55; DAM DRAM; DC 4**
See also CA 127; 132; INT 132

Hyde, Anthony 1946- .... **CLC 42**
See also CA 136

Hyde, Margaret O(ldroyd) 1917- ...... **CLC 21**
See also CA 1-4R; CANR 1, 36; CLR 23; JRDA; MAICYA; SAAS 8; SATA 1, 42, 76

Hynes, James 1956(?)- .... **CLC 65**
See also CA 164

Ian, Janis 1951- .... **CLC 21**
See also CA 105

Ibanez, Vicente Blasco
See Blasco Ibanez, Vicente

Ibarguengoitia, Jorge 1928-1983 .... **CLC 37**
See also CA 124; 113; HW

Ibsen, Henrik (Johan) 1828-1906 ... **TCLC 2, 8, 16, 37, 52; DA; DAB; DAC; DAM DRAM, MST; DC 2; WLC**
See also CA 104; 141

Ibuse Masuji 1898-1993 .... **CLC 22**
See also CA 127; 141; DLB 180

Ichikawa, Kon 1915- .... **CLC 20**
See also CA 121

Idle, Eric 1943- .... **CLC 21**
See also Monty Python
See also CA 116; CANR 35

Ignatow, David 1914-1997 .... **CLC 4, 7, 14, 40**
See also CA 9-12R; 162; CAAS 3; CANR 31, 57; DLB 5

Ihimaera, Witi 1944- .... **CLC 46**
See also CA 77-80

Ilf, Ilya .... **TCLC 21**
See also Fainzilberg, Ilya Arnoldovich

Illyes, Gyula 1902-1983 .... **PC 16**
See also CA 114; 109

Immermann, Karl (Lebrecht) 1796-1840
NCLC 4, 49
See also DLB 133

Inchbald, Elizabeth 1753-1821 .... **NCLC 62**
See also DLB 39, 89

Inclan, Ramon (Maria) del Valle
See Valle-Inclan, Ramon (Maria) del

Infante, G(uillermo) Cabrera
See Cabrera Infante, G(uillermo)

Ingalls, Rachel (Holmes) 1940- .... **CLC 42**
See also CA 123; 127

Ingamells, Rex 1913-1955 .... **TCLC 35**

Inge, William (Motter) 1913-1973 ... **CLC 1, 8, 19; DAM DRAM**
See also CA 9-12R; CDALB 1941-1968; DLB 7; MTCW

Ingelow, Jean 1820-1897 .... **NCLC 39**
See also DLB 35, 163; SATA 33

Ingram, Willis J.
See Harris, Mark

Innaurato, Albert (F.) 1948(?)- ..... **CLC 21, 60**
See also CA 115; 122; INT 122

Innes, Michael
See Stewart, J(ohn) I(nnes) M(ackintosh)

Innis, Harold Adams 1894-1952 ..... **TCLC 77**
See also DLB 88

Ionesco, Eugene 1909-1994 ... **CLC 1, 4, 6, 9, 11, 15, 41, 86; DA; DAB; DAC; DAM DRAM, MST; WLC**
See also CA 9-12R; 144; CANR 55; MTCW; SATA 7; SATA-Obit 79

Iqbal, Muhammad 1873-1938 .... **TCLC 28**

Ireland, Patrick
See O'Doherty, Brian

Iron, Ralph
See Schreiner, Olive (Emilie Albertina)

Irving, John (Winslow) 1942- ... **CLC 13, 23, 38; DAM NOV, POP**
See also AAYA 8; BEST 89:3; CA 25-28R; CANR 28; DLB 6; DLBY 82; MTCW

Irving, Washington 1783-1859 ...**NCLC 2, 19; DA; DAB; DAM MST; SSC 2; WLC**
See also CDALB 1640-1865; DLB 3, 11, 30, 59, 73, 74, 186; YABC 2

Irwin, P. K.
See Page, P(atricia) K(athleen)

Isaacs, Susan 1943- .... **CLC 32; DAM POP**
See also BEST 89:1; CA 89-92; CANR 20, 41, 65; INT CANR-20; MTCW

Isherwood, Christopher (William Bradshaw) 1904-1986 .... **CLC 1, 9, 11, 14, 44; DAM DRAM, NOV**
See also CA 13-16R; 117; CANR 35; DLB 15, 195; DLBY 86; MTCW

Ishiguro, Kazuo 1954- .... **CLC 27, 56, 59; DAM NOV**
See also BEST 90:2; CA 120; CANR 49; DLB 194; MTCW

Ishikawa, Hakuhin
See Ishikawa, Takuboku

Ishikawa, Takuboku 1886(?)-1912 . **TCLC 15; DAM POET; PC 10**
See also CA 113; 153

Iskander, Fazil 1929- .... **CLC 47**
See also CA 102

Isler, Alan (David) 1934- .... **CLC 91**
See also CA 156

Ivan IV 1530-1584 .... **LC 17**

Ivanov, Vyacheslav Ivanovich 1866-1949
TCLC 33
See also CA 122

Ivask, Ivar Vidrik 1927-1992 .... **CLC 14**
See also CA 37-40R; 139; CANR 24

Ives, Morgan
See Bradley, Marion Zimmer

J. R. S.
See Gogarty, Oliver St. John

Jabran, Kahlil
See Gibran, Kahlil

Jabran, Khalil
See Gibran, Kahlil

Jackson, Daniel
See Wingrove, David (John)

Jackson, Jesse 1908-1983 .... **CLC 12**
See also BW 1; CA 25-28R; 109; CANR 27; CLR 28; MAICYA; SATA 2, 29; SATA-Obit 48

Jackson, Laura (Riding) 1901-1991
See Riding, Laura
See also CA 65-68; 135; CANR 28; DLB 48

Jackson, Sam
See Trumbo, Dalton

Jackson, Sara
See Wingrove, David (John)

Jackson, Shirley 1919-1965 **CLC 11, 60, 87; DA; DAC; DAM MST; SSC 9; WLC**
See also AAYA 9; CA 1-4R; 25-28R; CANR 4, 52; CDALB 1941-1968; DLB 6; SATA 2

Jacob, (Cyprien-)Max 1876-1944 ..... **TCLC 6**
See also CA 104

Jacobs, Harriet 1813(?)-1897 .... **NCLC 67**

Jacobs, Jim 1942- .... **CLC 12**
See also CA 97-100; INT 97-100

Jacobs, W(illiam) W(ymark) 1863-1943
TCLC 22
See also CA 121; DLB 135

Jacobsen, Jens Peter 1847-1885 ..... **NCLC 34**

Jacobsen, Josephine 1908- .... **CLC 48, 102**
See also CA 33-36R; CAAS 18; CANR 23, 48

Jacobson, Dan 1929- .... **CLC 4, 14**
See also CA 1-4R; CANR 2, 25, 66; DLB 14; MTCW

Jacqueline
See Carpentier (y Valmont), Alejo

Jagger, Mick 1944- .... **CLC 17**

Jahiz, Al- c. 776-869 .... **CMLC 25**

Jahiz, al- c. 780-c. 869 .... **CMLC 25**

Jakes, John (William) 1932- ... **CLC 29; DAM NOV, POP**
See also BEST 89:4; CA 57-60; CANR 10, 43, 66; DLBY 83; INT CANR-10; MTCW; SATA 62

James, Andrew
See Kirkup, James

James, C(yril) L(ionel) R(obert) 1901-1989
CLC 33
See also BW 2; CA 117; 125; 128; CANR 62; DLB 125; MTCW

James, Daniel (Lewis) 1911-1988
See Santiago, Danny
See also CA 125

James, Dynely
See Mayne, William (James Carter)

James, Henry Sr. 1811-1882 .... NCLC 53

James, Henry 1843-1916 .... TCLC 2, 11, 24, 40, 47, 64; DA; DAB; DAC; DAM MST, NOV; SSC 8; WLC
See also CA 104; 132; CDALB 1865-1917; DLB 12, 71, 74, 189; DLBD 13; MTCW

James, M. R.
See James, Montague (Rhodes)
See also DLB 156

James, Montague (Rhodes) 1862-1936 ... TCLC 6; SSC 16
See also CA 104

James, P. D. .... CLC 18, 46
See also White, Phyllis Dorothy James
See also BEST 90:2; CDBLB 1960 to Present; DLB 87

James, Philip
See Moorcock, Michael (John)

James, William 1842-1910 .... TCLC 15, 32
See also CA 109

James I 1394-1437 .... LC 20

Jameson, Anna 1794-1860 .... NCLC 43
See also DLB 99, 166

Jami, Nur al-Din 'Abd al-Rahman 1414-1492 LC 9

Jammes, Francis 1868-1938 .... TCLC 75

Jandl, Ernst 1925- .... CLC 34

Janowitz, Tama 1957- .... CLC 43; DAM POP
See also CA 106; CANR 52

Japrisot, Sebastien 1931- .... CLC 90

Jarrell, Randall 1914-1965 ... CLC 1, 2, 6, 9, 13, 49; DAM POET
See also CA 5-8R; 25-28R; CABS 2; CANR 6, 34; CDALB 1941-1968; CLR 6; DLB 48, 52; MAICYA; MTCW; SATA 7

Jarry, Alfred 1873-1907 ... TCLC 2, 14; DAM DRAM; SSC 20
See also CA 104; 153; DLB 192

Jarvis, E. K.
See Bloch, Robert (Albert); Ellison, Harlan (Jay); Silverberg, Robert

Jeake, Samuel, Jr.
See Aiken, Conrad (Potter)

Jean Paul 1763-1825 .... NCLC 7

Jefferies, (John) Richard 1848-1887 NCLC 47
See also DLB 98, 141; SATA 16

Jeffers, (John) Robinson 1887-1962 ... CLC 2, 3, 11, 15, 54; DA; DAC; DAM MST, POET; PC 17; WLC
See also CA 85-88; CANR 35; CDALB 1917-1929; DLB 45; MTCW

Jefferson, Janet
See Mencken, H(enry) L(ouis)

Jefferson, Thomas 1743-1826 .... NCLC 11
See also CDALB 1640-1865; DLB 31

Jeffrey, Francis 1773-1850 .... NCLC 33
See also DLB 107

Jelakowitch, Ivan
See Heijermans, Herman

Jellicoe, (Patricia) Ann 1927- .... CLC 27
See also CA 85-88; DLB 13

Jen, Gish .... CLC 70
See also Jen, Lillian

Jen, Lillian 1956(?)-
See Jen, Gish
See also CA 135

Jenkins, (John) Robin 1912- .... CLC 52
See also CA 1-4R; CANR 1; DLB 14

Jennings, Elizabeth (Joan) 1926- .... CLC 5, 14
See also CA 61-64; CAAS 5; CANR 8, 39, 66; DLB 27; MTCW; SATA 66

Jennings, Waylon 1937- .... CLC 21

Jensen, Johannes V. 1873-1950 .... TCLC 41

Jensen, Laura (Linnea) 1948- .... CLC 37
See also CA 103

Jerome, Jerome K(lapka) 1859-1927 ... TCLC 23
See also CA 119; DLB 10, 34, 135

Jerrold, Douglas William 1803-1857 ...... NCLC 2
See also DLB 158, 159

Jewett, (Theodora) Sarah Orne 1849-1909 TCLC 1, 22; SSC 6
See also CA 108; 127; DLB 12, 74; SATA 15

Jewsbury, Geraldine (Endsor) 1812-1880 NCLC 22
See also DLB 21

Jhabvala, Ruth Prawer 1927- .... CLC 4, 8, 29, 94; DAB; DAM NOV
See also CA 1-4R; CANR 2, 29, 51; DLB 139, 194; INT CANR-29; MTCW

Jibran, Kahlil
See Gibran, Kahlil

Jibran, Khalil
See Gibran, Kahlil

Jiles, Paulette 1943- .... CLC 13, 58
See also CA 101

Jimenez (Mantecon), Juan Ramon 1881-1958 TCLC 4; DAM MULT, POET; HLC; PC 7
See also CA 104; 131; DLB 134; HW; MTCW

Jimenez, Ramon
See Jimenez (Mantecon), Juan Ramon

Jimenez Mantecon, Juan
See Jimenez (Mantecon), Juan Ramon

Jin, Ha 1956- .... CLC 109
See also CA 152

Joel, Billy .... CLC 26
See also Joel, William Martin

Joel, William Martin 1949-
See Joel, Billy
See also CA 108

John, Saint 7th cent. - .... CMLC 27

John of the Cross, St. 1542-1591 .... LC 18

Johnson, B(ryan) S(tanley William) 1933-1973 CLC 6, 9
See also CA 9-12R; 53-56; CANR 9; DLB 14, 40

Johnson, Benj. F. of Boo
See Riley, James Whitcomb

Johnson, Benjamin F. of Boo
See Riley, James Whitcomb

Johnson, Charles (Richard) 1948- ...... CLC 7, 51, 65; BLC; DAM MULT
See also BW 2; CA 116; CAAS 18; CANR 42, 66; DLB 33

Johnson, Denis 1949- .... CLC 52
See also CA 117; 121; DLB 120

Johnson, Diane 1934- .... CLC 5, 13, 48
See also CA 41-44R; CANR 17, 40, 62; DLBY 80; INT CANR-17; MTCW

Johnson, Eyvind (Olof Verner) 1900-1976 CLC 14
See also CA 73-76; 69-72; CANR 34

Johnson, J. R.
See James, C(yril) L(ionel) R(obert)

Johnson, James Weldon 1871-1938 . TCLC 3, 19; BLC; DAM MULT, POET
See also BW 1; CA 104; 125; CDALB 1917-1929; CLR 32; DLB 51; MTCW; SATA 31

Johnson, Joyce 1935- .... CLC 58
See also CA 125; 129

Johnson, Lionel (Pigot) 1867-1902   TCLC 19
See also CA 117; DLB 19

Johnson, Mel
See Malzberg, Barry N(athaniel)

Johnson, Pamela Hansford 1912-1981 ... CLC 1, 7, 27
See also CA 1-4R; 104; CANR 2, 28; DLB 15; MTCW

Kane, Paul
See Simon, Paul (Frederick)

Kane, Wilson
See Bloch, Robert (Albert)

Kanin, Garson 1912- .... **CLC 22**
See also AITN 1; CA 5-8R; CANR 7; DLB 7

Kaniuk, Yoram 1930- .... **CLC 19**
See also CA 134

Kant, Immanuel 1724-1804 .... **NCLC 27, 67**
See also DLB 94

Kantor, MacKinlay 1904-1977 .... **CLC 7**
See also CA 61-64; 73-76; CANR 60, 63; DLB 9, 102

Kaplan, David Michael 1946- .... **CLC 50**

Kaplan, James 1951- .... **CLC 59**
See also CA 135

Karageorge, Michael
See Anderson, Poul (William)

Karamzin, Nikolai Mikhailovich 1766-1826
NCLC 3
See also DLB 150

Karapanou, Margarita 1946- .... **CLC 13**
See also CA 101

Karinthy, Frigyes 1887-1938 .... **TCLC 47**

Karl, Frederick R(obert) 1927- .... **CLC 34**
See also CA 5-8R; CANR 3, 44

Kastel, Warren
See Silverberg, Robert

Kataev, Evgeny Petrovich 1903-1942
See Petrov, Evgeny
See also CA 120

Kataphusin
See Ruskin, John

Katz, Steve 1935- .... **CLC 47**
See also CA 25-28R; CAAS 14, 64; CANR 12; DLBY 83

Kauffman, Janet 1945- .... **CLC 42**
See also CA 117; CANR 43; DLBY 86

Kaufman, Bob (Garnell) 1925-1986 .. **CLC 49**
See also BW 1; CA 41-44R; 118; CANR 22; DLB 16, 41

Kaufman, George S. 1889-1961**CLC 38; DAM DRAM**
See also CA 108; 93-96; DLB 7; INT 108

Kaufman, Sue .... **CLC 3, 8**
See also Barondess, Sue K(aufman)

Kavafis, Konstantinos Petrou 1863-1933
See Cavafy, C(onstantine) P(eter)
See also CA 104

Kavan, Anna 1901-1968 .... **CLC 5, 13, 82**
See also CA 5-8R; CANR 6, 57; MTCW

Kavanagh, Dan
See Barnes, Julian (Patrick)

Kavanagh, Patrick (Joseph) 1904-1967 **CLC 22**
See also CA 123; 25-28R; DLB 15, 20; MTCW

Kawabata, Yasunari 1899-1972 **CLC 2, 5, 9, 18, 107; DAM MULT; SSC 17**
See also CA 93-96; 33-36R; DLB 180

Kaye, M(ary) M(argaret) 1909- .... **CLC 28**
See also CA 89-92; CANR 24, 60; MTCW; SATA 62

Kaye, Mollie
See Kaye, M(ary) M(argaret)

Kaye-Smith, Sheila 1887-1956 .... **TCLC 20**
See also CA 118; DLB 36

Kaymor, Patrice Maguilene
See Senghor, Leopold Sedar

Kazan, Elia 1909- .... **CLC 6, 16, 63**
See also CA 21-24R; CANR 32

Kazantzakis, Nikos 1883(?)-1957 ..... **TCLC 2, 5, 33**
See also CA 105; 132; MTCW

Kazin, Alfred 1915- .... **CLC 34, 38**
See also CA 1-4R; CAAS 7; CANR 1, 45; DLB 67

Keane, Mary Nesta (Skrine) 1904-1996
See Keane, Molly
See also CA 108; 114; 151

Keane, Molly .... **CLC 31**
See also Keane, Mary Nesta (Skrine)
See also INT 114

Keates, Jonathan 1946(?)- .... **CLC 34**
See also CA 163

Keaton, Buster 1895-1966 .... **CLC 20**

Keats, John 1795-1821 .... **NCLC 8; DA; DAB; DAC; DAM MST, POET; PC 1; WLC**
See also CDBLB 1789-1832; DLB 96, 110

Keene, Donald 1922- .... **CLC 34**
See also CA 1-4R; CANR 5

Keillor, Garrison .... **CLC 40**
See also Keillor, Gary (Edward)
See also AAYA 2; BEST 89:3; DLBY 87; SATA 58

Keillor, Gary (Edward) 1942-
See Keillor, Garrison
See also CA 111; 117; CANR 36, 59; DAM POP; MTCW

Keith, Michael
See Hubbard, L(afayette) Ron(ald)

Keller, Gottfried 1819-1890 **NCLC 2; SSC 26**
See also DLB 129

Keller, Nora Okja .... **CLC 109**

Kellerman, Jonathan 1949- ... **CLC 44; DAM POP**
See also BEST 90:1; CA 106; CANR 29, 51; INT CANR-29

Kelley, William Melvin 1937- .... **CLC 22**
See also BW 1; CA 77-80; CANR 27; DLB 33

Kellogg, Marjorie 1922- .... **CLC 2**
See also CA 81-84

Kellow, Kathleen
See Hibbert, Eleanor Alice Burford

Kelly, M(ilton) T(erry) 1947- .... **CLC 55**
See also CA 97-100; CAAS 22; CANR 19, 43

Kelman, James 1946- .... **CLC 58, 86**
See also CA 148; DLB 194

Kemal, Yashar 1923- .... **CLC 14, 29**
See also CA 89-92; CANR 44

Kemble, Fanny 1809-1893 .... **NCLC 18**
See also DLB 32

Kemelman, Harry 1908-1996 .... **CLC 2**
See also AITN 1; CA 9-12R; 155; CANR 6; DLB 28

Kempe, Margery 1373(?)-1440(?) .... **LC 6**
See also DLB 146

Kempis, Thomas a 1380-1471 .... **LC 11**

Kendall, Henry 1839-1882 .... **NCLC 12**

Keneally, Thomas (Michael) 1935- **CLC 5, 8, 10, 14, 19, 27, 43; DAM NOV**
See also CA 85-88; CANR 10, 50; MTCW

Kennedy, Adrienne (Lita) 1931- ..... **CLC 66; BLC; DAM MULT; DC 5**
See also BW 2; CA 103; CAAS 20; CABS 3; CANR 26, 53; DLB 38

Kennedy, John Pendleton 1795-1870 **NCLC 2**
See also DLB 3

Kennedy, Joseph Charles 1929-
See Kennedy, X. J.
See also CA 1-4R; CANR 4, 30, 40; SATA 14, 86

Kennedy, William 1928- .... **CLC 6, 28, 34, 53; DAM NOV**
See also AAYA 1; CA 85-88; CANR 14, 31; DLB 143; DLBY 85; INT CANR-31; MTCW; SATA 57

Kennedy, X. J. .... **CLC 8, 42**
See also Kennedy, Joseph Charles
See also CAAS 9; CLR 27; DLB 5; SAAS 22

Kenny, Maurice (Francis) 1929- ...... **CLC 87; DAM MULT**
See also CA 144; CAAS 22; DLB 175; NNAL

Kent, Kelvin
See Kuttner, Henry

Kenton, Maxwell
See Southern, Terry

Kenyon, Robert O.
See Kuttner, Henry

Kerouac, Jack .... **CLC 1, 2, 3, 5, 14, 29, 61**
See also Kerouac, Jean-Louis Lebris de
See also AAYA 25; CDALB 1941-1968; DLB 2, 16; DLBD 3; DLBY 95

Kerouac, Jean-Louis Lebris de 1922-1969
See Kerouac, Jack
See also AITN 1; CA 5-8R; 25-28R; CANR 26, 54; DA; DAB; DAC; DAM MST, NOV, POET, POP; MTCW; WLC

Kerr, Jean 1923- .... **CLC 22**
See also CA 5-8R; CANR 7; INT CANR-7

Kerr, M. E. .... **CLC 12, 35**
See also Meaker, Marijane (Agnes)
See also AAYA 2, 23; CLR 29; SAAS 1

Kerr, Robert .... **CLC 55**

Kerrigan, (Thomas) Anthony 1918- **CLC 4, 6**
See also CA 49-52; CAAS 11; CANR 4

Kerry, Lois
See Duncan, Lois

Kesey, Ken (Elton) 1935-　　**CLC 1, 3, 6, 11, 46, 64; DA; DAB; DAC; DAM MST, NOV, POP; WLC**
See also AAYA 25; CA 1-4R; CANR 22, 38, 66; CDALB 1968-1988; DLB 2, 16; MTCW; SATA 66

Kesselring, Joseph (Otto) 1902-1967 **CLC 45; DAM DRAM, MST**
See also CA 150

Kessler, Jascha (Frederick) 1929- .... **CLC 4**
See also CA 17-20R; CANR 8, 48

Kettelkamp, Larry (Dale) 1933- .... **CLC 12**
See also CA 29-32R; CANR 16; SAAS 3; SATA 2

Key, Ellen 1849-1926 .... **TCLC 65**

Keyber, Conny
See Fielding, Henry

Keyes, Daniel 1927- .....　　**CLC 80; DA; DAC; DAM MST, NOV**
See also AAYA 23; CA 17-20R; CANR 10, 26, 54; SATA 37

Keynes, John Maynard 1883-1946 **TCLC 64**
See also CA 114; 162, 163; DLBD 10

Khanshendel, Chiron
See Rose, Wendy

Khayyam, Omar 1048-1131 ...... **CMLC 11; DAM POET; PC 8**

Kherdian, David 1931- .... **CLC 6, 9**
See also CA 21-24R; CAAS 2; CANR 39; CLR 24; JRDA; MAICYA; SATA 16, 74

Khlebnikov, Velimir .... **TCLC 20**
See also Khlebnikov, Viktor Vladimirovich

Khlebnikov, Viktor Vladimirovich 1885-1922
See Khlebnikov, Velimir
See also CA 117

Khodasevich, Vladislav (Felitsianovich) 1886-1939 .... **TCLC 15**
See also CA 115

Kielland, Alexander Lange 1849-1906 **TCLC 5**
See also CA 104

Kiely, Benedict 1919- .... **CLC 23, 43**
See also CA 1-4R; CANR 2; DLB 15

Kienzle, William X(avier) 1928- ..... **CLC 25; DAM POP**
See also CA 93-96; CAAS 1; CANR 9, 31, 59; INT CANR-31; MTCW

Kierkegaard, Soren 1813-1855 .... **NCLC 34**

Killens, John Oliver 1916-1987 .... **CLC 10**
See also BW 2; CA 77-80; 123; CAAS 2; CANR 26; DLB 33

Killigrew, Anne 1660-1685 .... **LC 4**
See also DLB 131

Kim
See Simenon, Georges (Jacques Christian)

Kincaid, Jamaica 1949- ..... **CLC 43, 68; BLC; DAM MULT, NOV**
See also AAYA 13; BW 2; CA 125; CANR 47, 59; DLB 157

King, Francis (Henry) 1923- .... **CLC 8, 53; DAM NOV**
See also CA 1-4R; CANR 1, 33; DLB 15, 139; MTCW

King, Kennedy
See Brown, George Douglas

King, Martin Luther, Jr. 1929-1968　**CLC 83; BLC; DA; DAB; DAC; DAM MST, MULT; WLCS**
See also BW 2; CA 25-28; CANR 27, 44; CAP 2; MTCW; SATA 14

King, Stephen (Edwin) 1947-　　**CLC 12, 26, 37, 61; DAM NOV, POP; SSC 17**
See also AAYA 1, 17; BEST 90:1; CA 61-64; CANR 1, 30, 52; DLB 143; DLBY 80; JRDA; MTCW; SATA 9, 55

King, Steve
See King, Stephen (Edwin)

King, Thomas 1943- ..... **CLC 89; DAC; DAM MULT**
See also CA 144; DLB 175; NNAL; SATA 96

Kingman, Lee .... **CLC 17**
See also Natti, (Mary) Lee
See also SAAS 3; SATA 1, 67

Kingsley, Charles 1819-1875 .... **NCLC 35**
See also DLB 21, 32, 163, 190; YABC 2

Kingsley, Sidney 1906-1995 .... **CLC 44**
See also CA 85-88; 147; DLB 7

Kingsolver, Barbara 1955- ....　　**CLC 55, 81; DAM POP**
See also AAYA 15; CA 129; 134; CANR 60; INT 134

Kingston, Maxine (Ting Ting) Hong 1940-　**CLC 12, 19, 58; DAM MULT, NOV; WLCS**
See also AAYA 8; CA 69-72; CANR 13, 38; DLB 173; DLBY 80; INT CANR-13; MTCW; SATA 53

Kinnell, Galway 1927- .. **CLC 1, 2, 3, 5, 13, 29**
See also CA 9-12R; CANR 10, 34, 66; DLB 5; DLBY 87; INT CANR-34; MTCW

Kinsella, Thomas 1928- .... **CLC 4, 19**
See also CA 17-20R; CANR 15; DLB 27; MTCW

Kinsella, W(illiam) P(atrick) 1935- ... **CLC 27, 43; DAC; DAM NOV, POP**
See also AAYA 7; CA 97-100; CAAS 7; CANR 21, 35, 66; INT CANR-21; MTCW

Kipling, (Joseph) Rudyard 1865-1936 **TCLC 8, 17; DA; DAB; DAC; DAM MST, POET; PC 3; SSC 5; WLC**
See also CA 105; 120; CANR 33; CDBLB 1890-1914; CLR 39; DLB 19, 34, 141, 156; MAICYA; MTCW; YABC 2

Kirkup, James 1918- .... **CLC 1**
See also CA 1-4R; CAAS 4; CANR 2; DLB 27; SATA 12

Kirkwood, James 1930(?)-1989 .... **CLC 9**
See also AITN 2; CA 1-4R; 128; CANR 6, 40

Kirshner, Sidney
See Kingsley, Sidney

Kis, Danilo 1935-1989 .... **CLC 57**
See also CA 109; 118; 129; CANR 61; DLB 181; MTCW

Kivi, Aleksis 1834-1872 .... **NCLC 30**

Kizer, Carolyn (Ashley) 1925- **CLC 15, 39, 80; DAM POET**
See also CA 65-68; CAAS 5; CANR 24; DLB 5, 169

Klabund 1890-1928 .... **TCLC 44**
See also CA 162; DLB 66

Klappert, Peter 1942- .... **CLC 57**
See also CA 33-36R; DLB 5

Klein, A(braham) M(oses) 1909-1972 . **CLC 19; DAB; DAC; DAM MST**
See also CA 101; 37-40R; DLB 68

Klein, Norma 1938-1989 .... **CLC 30**
See also AAYA 2; CA 41-44R; 128; CANR 15, 37; CLR 2, 19; INT CANR-15; JRDA; MAICYA; SAAS 1; SATA 7, 57

Klein, T(heodore) E(ibon) D(onald) 1947- **CLC 34**
See also CA 119; CANR 44

Kleist, Heinrich von 1777-1811 **NCLC 2, 37; DAM DRAM; SSC 22**
See also DLB 90

Klima, Ivan 1931- .... **CLC 56; DAM NOV**
See also CA 25-28R; CANR 17, 50

Klimentov, Andrei Platonovich 1899-1951
See Platonov, Andrei
See also CA 108

Klinger, Friedrich Maximilian von 1752-1831
NCLC 1
See also DLB 94

Klingsor the Magician
See Hartmann, Sadakichi

Klopstock, Friedrich Gottlieb 1724-1803
NCLC 11
See also DLB 97

Knapp, Caroline 1959- .... **CLC 99**
See also CA 154

Knebel, Fletcher 1911-1993 .... **CLC 14**
See also AITN 1; CA 1-4R; 140; CAAS 3; CANR
1, 36; SATA 36; SATA-Obit 75

Knickerbocker, Diedrich
See Irving, Washington

Knight, Etheridge 1931-1991 ...... **CLC 40;**
BLC; DAM POET; PC 14
See also BW 1; CA 21-24R; 133; CANR 23; DLB
41

Knight, Sarah Kemble 1666-1727 .... **LC 7**
See also DLB 24

Knister, Raymond 1899-1932 .... **TCLC 56**
See also DLB 68

Knowles, John 1926- ... **CLC 1, 4, 10, 26; DA;**
DAC; DAM MST, NOV
See also AAYA 10; CA 17-20R; CANR 40;
CDALB 1968-1988; DLB 6; MTCW; SATA
8, 89

Knox, Calvin M.
See Silverberg, Robert

Knox, John c. 1505-1572 .... **LC 37**
See also DLB 132

Knye, Cassandra
See Disch, Thomas M(ichael)

Koch, C(hristopher) J(ohn) 1932- ..... **CLC 42**
See also CA 127

Koch, Christopher
See Koch, C(hristopher) J(ohn)

Koch, Kenneth 1925- ..... **CLC 5, 8, 44; DAM**
POET
See also CA 1-4R; CANR 6, 36, 57; DLB 5; INT
CANR-36; SATA 65

Kochanowski, Jan 1530-1584 .... **LC 10**

Kock, Charles Paul de 1794-1871 ... **NCLC 16**

Koda Shigeyuki 1867-1947
See Rohan, Koda
See also CA 121

Koestler, Arthur 1905-1983 ... **CLC 1, 3, 6, 8, 15, 33**
See also CA 1-4R; 109; CANR 1, 33; CDBLB
1945-1960; DLBY 83; MTCW

Kogawa, Joy Nozomi 1935- .... **CLC 78; DAC;**
DAM MST, MULT
See also CA 101; CANR 19, 62

Kohout, Pavel 1928- .... **CLC 13**
See also CA 45-48; CANR 3

Koizumi, Yakumo
See Hearn, (Patricio) Lafcadio (Tessima Carlos)

Kolmar, Gertrud 1894-1943 .... **TCLC 40**

Komunyakaa, Yusef 1947- .... **CLC 86, 94**
See also CA 147; DLB 120

Konrad, George
See Konrad, Gyoergy

Konrad, Gyoergy 1933- .... **CLC 4, 10, 73**
See also CA 85-88

Konwicki, Tadeusz 1926- .... **CLC 8, 28, 54**
See also CA 101; CAAS 9; CANR 39, 59; MTCW

Koontz, Dean R(ay) 1945- .... **CLC 78; DAM**
NOV, POP
See also AAYA 9; BEST 89:3, 90:2; CA 108;
CANR 19, 36, 52; MTCW; SATA 92

Kopit, Arthur (Lee) 1937- .... **CLC 1, 18, 33;**
DAM DRAM
See also AITN 1; CA 81-84; CABS 3; DLB 7;
MTCW

Kops, Bernard 1926- .... **CLC 4**
See also CA 5-8R; DLB 13

Kornbluth, C(yril) M. 1923-1958 ..... **TCLC 8**
See also CA 105; 160; DLB 8

Korolenko, V. G.
See Korolenko, Vladimir Galaktionovich

Korolenko, Vladimir
See Korolenko, Vladimir Galaktionovich

Korolenko, Vladimir G.
See Korolenko, Vladimir Galaktionovich

Korolenko, Vladimir Galaktionovich 1853-1921
TCLC 22
See also CA 121

Korzybski, Alfred (Habdank Skarbek) 1879-
1950 .... **TCLC 61**
See also CA 123; 160

Kosinski, Jerzy (Nikodem) 1933-1991 ... **CLC 1,**
2, 3, 6, 10, 15, 53, 70; DAM NOV
See also CA 17-20R; 134; CANR 9, 46; DLB 2;
DLBY 82; MTCW

Kostelanetz, Richard (Cory) 1940- .... **CLC 28**
See also CA 13-16R; CAAS 8; CANR 38

Kostrowitzki, Wilhelm Apollinaris de 1880-1918
See Apollinaire, Guillaume
See also CA 104

Kotlowitz, Robert 1924- .... **CLC 4**
See also CA 33-36R; CANR 36

Kotzebue, August (Friedrich Ferdinand) von
1761-1819 .... **NCLC 25**
See also DLB 94

Kotzwinkle, William 1938- .... **CLC 5, 14, 35**
See also CA 45-48; CANR 3, 44; CLR 6; DLB
173; MAICYA; SATA 24, 70

Kowna, Stancy
See Szymborska, Wislawa

Kozol, Jonathan 1936- .... **CLC 17**
See also CA 61-64; CANR 16, 45

Kozoll, Michael 1940(?)- .... **CLC 35**

Kramer, Kathryn 19(?)- .... **CLC 34**

Kramer, Larry 1935- **CLC 42; DAM POP; DC 8**
See also CA 124; 126; CANR 60

Krasicki, Ignacy 1735-1801 .... **NCLC 8**

Krasinski, Zygmunt 1812-1859 .... **NCLC 4**

Kraus, Karl 1874-1936 .... **TCLC 5**
See also CA 104; DLB 118

Kreve (Mickevicius), Vincas 1882-1954
TCLC 27

Kristeva, Julia 1941- .... **CLC 77**
See also CA 154

Kristofferson, Kris 1936- .... **CLC 26**
See also CA 104

Krizanc, John 1956- .... **CLC 57**

Krleza, Miroslav 1893-1981 .... **CLC 8**
See also CA 97-100; 105; CANR 50; DLB 147

Kroetsch, Robert 1927- .... **CLC 5, 23, 57;**
DAC; DAM POET
See also CA 17-20R; CANR 8, 38; DLB 53;
MTCW

Kroetz, Franz
See Kroetz, Franz Xaver

Kroetz, Franz Xaver 1946- .... **CLC 41**
See also CA 130

Kroker, Arthur (W.) 1945- .... **CLC 77**
See also CA 161

Kropotkin, Peter (Aleksieevich) 1842-1921
TCLC 36
See also CA 119

Krotkov, Yuri 1917- .... **CLC 19**
See also CA 102

Krumb
See Crumb, R(obert)

Krumgold, Joseph (Quincy) 1908-1980 ... **CLC 12**
See also CA 9-12R; 101; CANR 7; MAICYA;
SATA 1, 48; SATA-Obit 23

Krumwitz
See Crumb, R(obert)

Krutch, Joseph Wood 1893-1970 .... **CLC 24**
See also CA 1-4R; 25-28R; CANR 4; DLB 63

Krutzch, Gus
See Eliot, T(homas) S(tearns)

Krylov, Ivan Andreevich 1768(?)-1844 ... **NCLC 1**
See also DLB 150

Kubin, Alfred (Leopold Isidor) 1877-1959
TCLC 23
See also CA 112; 149; DLB 81

Kubrick, Stanley 1928- .... **CLC 16**
See also CA 81-84; CANR 33; DLB 26

Kumin, Maxine (Winokur) 1925-   **CLC 5, 13, 28; DAM POET; PC 15**
See also AITN 2; CA 1-4R; CAAS 8; CANR 1, 21; DLB 5; MTCW; SATA 12

Kundera, Milan 1929- ... **CLC 4, 9, 19, 32, 68; DAM NOV; SSC 24**
See also AAYA 2; CA 85-88; CANR 19, 52; MTCW

Kunene, Mazisi (Raymond) 1930- ..... **CLC 85**
See also BW 1; CA 125; DLB 117

Kunitz, Stanley (Jasspon) 1905-   **CLC 6, 11, 14; PC 19**
See also CA 41-44R; CANR 26, 57; DLB 48; INT CANR-26; MTCW

Kunze, Reiner 1933- .... **CLC 10**
See also CA 93-96; DLB 75

Kuprin, Aleksandr Ivanovich 1870-1938
TCLC 5
See also CA 104

Kureishi, Hanif 1954(?)- .... **CLC 64**
See also CA 139; DLB 194

Kurosawa, Akira 1910- **CLC 16; DAM MULT**
See also AAYA 11; CA 101; CANR 46

Kushner, Tony 1957(?)- ....   **CLC 81; DAM DRAM**
See also CA 144

Kuttner, Henry 1915-1958 .... **TCLC 10**
See also Vance, Jack
See also CA 107; 157; DLB 8

Kuzma, Greg 1944- .... **CLC 7**
See also CA 33-36R

Kuzmin, Mikhail 1872(?)-1936 .... **TCLC 40**

Kyd, Thomas 1558-1594 .... **LC 22; DAM DRAM; DC 3**
See also DLB 62

Kyprianos, Iossif
See Samarakis, Antonis

La Bruyere, Jean de 1645-1696 .... **LC 17**

Lacan, Jacques (Marie Emile) 1901-1981
CLC 75
See also CA 121; 104

Laclos, Pierre Ambroise Francois Choderlos de 1741-1803 .... **NCLC 4**

La Colere, Francois
See Aragon, Louis

Lacolere, Francois
See Aragon, Louis

La Deshabilleuse
See Simenon, Georges (Jacques Christian)

Lady Gregory
See Gregory, Isabella Augusta (Persse)

Lady of Quality, A
See Bagnold, Enid

La Fayette, Marie (Madelaine Pioche de la Vergne Comtes 1634-1693 .... **LC 2**

Lafayette, Rene
See Hubbard, L(afayette) Ron(ald)

Laforgue, Jules 1860-1887   **NCLC 5, 53; PC 14; SSC 20**

Lagerkvist, Paer (Fabian) 1891-1974   **CLC 7, 10, 13, 54; DAM DRAM, NOV**
See also Lagerkvist, Par
See also CA 85-88; 49-52; MTCW

Lagerkvist, Par ....**SSC 12**
See also Lagerkvist, Paer (Fabian)

Lagerloef, Selma (Ottiliana Lovisa) 1858-1940
TCLC 4, 36
See also Lagerlof, Selma (Ottiliana Lovisa)
See also CA 108; SATA 15

Lagerlof, Selma (Ottiliana Lovisa)
See Lagerloef, Selma (Ottiliana Lovisa)
See also CLR 7; SATA 15

La Guma, (Justin) Alex(ander) 1925-1985
CLC 19; DAM NOV
See also BW 1; CA 49-52; 118; CANR 25; DLB 117; MTCW

Laidlaw, A. K.
See Grieve, C(hristopher) M(urray)

Lainez, Manuel Mujica
See Mujica Lainez, Manuel
See also HW

Laing, R(onald) D(avid) 1927-1989 ... **CLC 95**
See also CA 107; 129; CANR 34; MTCW

Lamartine, Alphonse (Marie Louis Prat) de 1790-1869 ....

NCLC 11; DAM POET; PC 16

Lamb, Charles 1775-1834 **NCLC 10; DA; DAB; DAC; DAM MST; WLC**
See also CDBLB 1789-1832; DLB 93, 107, 163; SATA 17

Lamb, Lady Caroline 1785-1828 .... **NCLC 38**
See also DLB 116

Lamming, George (William) 1927- . **CLC 2, 4, 66; BLC; DAM MULT**
See also BW 2; CA 85-88; CANR 26; DLB 125; MTCW

L'Amour, Louis (Dearborn) 1908-1988 . **C L C 25, 55; DAM NOV, POP**
See also AAYA 16; AITN 2; BEST 89:2; CA 1-4R; 125; CANR 3, 25, 40; DLBY 80; MTCW

Lampedusa, Giuseppe (Tomasi) di 1896-1957
TCLC 13
See also Tomasi di Lampedusa, Giuseppe
See also CA 164; DLB 177

Lampman, Archibald 1861-1899 .... **NCLC 25**
See also DLB 92

Lancaster, Bruce 1896-1963 .... **CLC 36**
See also CA 9-10; CAP 1; SATA 9

Lanchester, John .... **CLC 99**

Landau, Mark Alexandrovich
See Aldanov, Mark (Alexandrovich)

Landau-Aldanov, Mark Alexandrovich
See Aldanov, Mark (Alexandrovich)

Landis, Jerry
See Simon, Paul (Frederick)

Landis, John 1950- .... **CLC 26**
See also CA 112; 122

Landolfi, Tommaso 1908-1979 ..... **CLC 11, 49**
See also CA 127; 117; DLB 177

Landon, Letitia Elizabeth 1802-1838   **NCLC 15**
See also DLB 96

Landor, Walter Savage 1775-1864   **NCLC 14**
See also DLB 93, 107

Landwirth, Heinz 1927-
See Lind, Jakov
See also CA 9-12R; CANR 7

Lane, Patrick 1939- ..... **CLC 25; DAM POET**
See also CA 97-100; CANR 54; DLB 53; INT 97-100

Lang, Andrew 1844-1912 .... **TCLC 16**
See also CA 114; 137; DLB 98, 141, 184; MAICYA; SATA 16

Lang, Fritz 1890-1976 .... **CLC 20, 103**
See also CA 77-80; 69-72; CANR 30

Lange, John
See Crichton, (John) Michael

Langer, Elinor 1939- .... **CLC 34**
See also CA 121

Langland, William 1330(?)-1400(?)   **LC 19; DA; DAB; DAC; DAM MST, POET**
See also DLB 146

Lee, Andrea 1953- .... **CLC 36; BLC; DAM MULT**
See also BW 1; CA 125

Lee, Andrew
See Auchincloss, Louis (Stanton)

Lee, Chang-rae 1965- .... **CLC 91**
See also CA 148

Lee, Don L. .... **CLC 2**
See also Madhubuti, Haki R.

Lee, George W(ashington) 1894-1976   **CLC 52; BLC; DAM MULT**
See also BW 1; CA 125; DLB 51

Lee, (Nelle) Harper 1926- .... **CLC 12, 60; DA; DAB; DAC; DAM MST, NOV; WLC**
See also AAYA 13; CA 13-16R; CANR 51; CDALB 1941-1968; DLB 6; MTCW; SATA 11

Lee, Helen Elaine 1959(?)- .... **CLC 86**
See also CA 148

Lee, Julian
See Latham, Jean Lee

Lee, Larry
See Lee, Lawrence

Lee, Laurie 1914-1997 ..... **CLC 90; DAB; DAM POP**
See also CA 77-80; 158; CANR 33; DLB 27; MTCW

Lee, Lawrence 1941-1990 .... **CLC 34**
See also CA 131; CANR 43

Lee, Manfred B(ennington) 1905-1971 .... **CLC 11**
See also Queen, Ellery
See also CA 1-4R; 29-32R; CANR 2; DLB 137

Lee, Shelton Jackson 1957(?)- ..... **CLC 105; DAM MULT**
See also Lee, Spike
See also BW 2; CA 125; CANR 42

Lee, Spike
See Lee, Shelton Jackson
See also AAYA 4

Lee, Stan 1922- .... **CLC 17**
See also AAYA 5; CA 108; 111; INT 111

Lee, Tanith 1947- .... **CLC 46**
See also AAYA 15; CA 37-40R; CANR 53; SATA 8, 88

Lee, Vernon .... **TCLC 5**
See also Paget, Violet
See also DLB 57, 153, 156, 174, 178

Lee, William
See Burroughs, William S(eward)

Lee, Willy
See Burroughs, William S(eward)

Lee-Hamilton, Eugene (Jacob) 1845-1907 **TCLC 22**
See also CA 117

Leet, Judith 1935- .... **CLC 11**

Le Fanu, Joseph Sheridan 1814-1873 ... **NCLC 9, 58; DAM POP; SSC 14**
See also DLB 21, 70, 159, 178

Leffland, Ella 1931- .... **CLC 19**
See also CA 29-32R; CANR 35; DLBY 84; INT CANR-35; SATA 65

Leger, Alexis
See Leger, (Marie-Rene Auguste) Alexis Saint-Leger

Leger, (Marie-Rene Auguste) Alexis Saint-Leger 1887-1975 .... **CLC 11; DAM POET**
See also Perse, St.-John
See also CA 13-16R; 61-64; CANR 43; MTCW

Leger, Saintleger
See Leger, (Marie-Rene Auguste) Alexis Saint-Leger

Le Guin, Ursula K(roeber) 1929- ..... **CLC 8, 13, 22, 45, 71; DAB; DAC; DAM MST, POP; SSC 12**
See also AAYA 9; AITN 1; CA 21-24R; CANR 9, 32, 52; CDALB 1968-1988; CLR 3, 28; DLB 8, 52; INT CANR-32; JRDA; MAICYA; MTCW; SATA 4, 52

Lehmann, Rosamond (Nina) 1901-1990 ... **CLC 5**
See also CA 77-80; 131; CANR 8; DLB 15

Leiber, Fritz (Reuter, Jr.) 1910-1992 ... **CLC 25**
See also CA 45-48; 139; CANR 2, 40; DLB 8; MTCW; SATA 45; SATA-Obit 73

Leibniz, Gottfried Wilhelm von 1646-1716 **LC 35**
See also DLB 168

Leimbach, Martha 1963-
See Leimbach, Marti
See also CA 130

Leimbach, Marti .... **CLC 65**
See also Leimbach, Martha

Leino, Eino .... **TCLC 24**
See also Loennbohm, Armas Eino Leopold

Leiris, Michel (Julien) 1901-1990 ...... **CLC 61**
See also CA 119; 128; 132

Leithauser, Brad 1953- .... **CLC 27**
See also CA 107; CANR 27; DLB 120

Lelchuk, Alan 1938- .... **CLC 5**
See also CA 45-48; CAAS 20; CANR 1

Lem, Stanislaw 1921- .... **CLC 8, 15, 40**
See also CA 105; CAAS 1; CANR 32; MTCW

Lemann, Nancy 1956- .... **CLC 39**
See also CA 118; 136

Lemonnier, (Antoine Louis) Camille 1844-1913 **TCLC 22**
See also CA 121

Lenau, Nikolaus 1802-1850 .... **NCLC 16**

L'Engle, Madeleine (Camp Franklin) 1918- **CLC 12; DAM POP**
See also AAYA 1; AITN 2; CA 1-4R; CANR 3, 21, 39, 66; CLR 1, 14; DLB 52; JRDA; MAICYA; MTCW; SAAS 15; SATA 1, 27, 75

Lengyel, Jozsef 1896-1975 .... **CLC 7**
See also CA 85-88; 57-60

Lenin 1870-1924
See Lenin, V. I.
See also CA 121

Lenin, V. I. .... **TCLC 67**
See also Lenin

Lennon, John (Ono) 1940-1980 ... **CLC 12, 35**
See also CA 102

Lennox, Charlotte Ramsay 1729(?)-1804 **NCLC 23**
See also DLB 39

Lentricchia, Frank (Jr.) 1940- .... **CLC 34**
See also CA 25-28R; CANR 19

Lenz, Siegfried 1926- .... **CLC 27**
See also CA 89-92; DLB 75

Leonard, Elmore (John, Jr.) 1925-   **CLC 28, 34, 71; DAM POP**
See also AAYA 22; AITN 1; BEST 89:1, 90:4; CA 81-84; CANR 12, 28, 53; DLB 173; INT CANR-28; MTCW

Leonard, Hugh .... **CLC 19**
See also Byrne, John Keyes
See also DLB 13

Leonov, Leonid (Maximovich) 1899-1994 **CLC 92; DAM NOV**
See also CA 129; MTCW

Leopardi, (Conte) Giacomo 1798-1837 **NCLC 22**

Le Reveler
See Artaud, Antonin (Marie Joseph)

Lerman, Eleanor 1952- .... **CLC 9**
See also CA 85-88

Lerman, Rhoda 1936- .... **CLC 56**
See also CA 49-52

Lermontov, Mikhail Yuryevich 1814-1841 **NCLC 47; PC 18**

Leroux, Gaston 1868-1927 .... **TCLC 25**
See also CA 108; 136; SATA 65

Lesage, Alain-Rene 1668-1747 .... **LC 28**

Leskov, Nikolai (Semyonovich) 1831-1895 **NCLC 25**

Little, Malcolm 1925-1965
See Malcolm X
See also BW 1; CA 125; 111; DA; DAB; DAC; DAM MST, MULT; MTCW

Littlewit, Humphrey Gent.
See Lovecraft, H(oward) P(hillips)

Litwos
See Sienkiewicz, Henryk (Adam Alexander Pius)

Liu E 1857-1909 .... **TCLC 15**
See also CA 115

Lively, Penelope (Margaret) 1933- ... **CLC 32, 50; DAM NOV**
See also CA 41-44R; CANR 29, 67; CLR 7; DLB 14, 161; JRDA; MAICYA; MTCW; SATA 7, 60

Livesay, Dorothy (Kathleen) 1909- ... **CLC 4, 15, 79; DAC; DAM MST, POET**
See also AITN 2; CA 25-28R; CAAS 8; CANR 36, 67; DLB 68; MTCW

Livy c. 59B.C.-c. 17 .... **CMLC 11**

Lizardi, Jose Joaquin Fernandez de 1776-1827 **NCLC 30**

Llewellyn, Richard
See Llewellyn Lloyd, Richard Dafydd Vivian
See also DLB 15

Llewellyn Lloyd, Richard Dafydd Vivian 1906-1983 .... **CLC 7, 80**
See also Llewellyn, Richard
See also CA 53-56; 111; CANR 7; SATA 11; SATA-Obit 37

Llosa, (Jorge) Mario (Pedro) Vargas
See Vargas Llosa, (Jorge) Mario (Pedro)

Lloyd, Manda
See Mander, (Mary) Jane

Lloyd Webber, Andrew 1948-
See Webber, Andrew Lloyd
See also AAYA 1; CA 116; 149; DAM DRAM; SATA 56

Llull, Ramon c. 1235-c. 1316 .... **CMLC 12**

Locke, Alain (Le Roy) 1886-1954 ... **TCLC 43**
See also BW 1; CA 106; 124; DLB 51

Locke, John 1632-1704 .... **LC 7, 35**
See also DLB 101

Locke-Elliott, Sumner
See Elliott, Sumner Locke

Lockhart, John Gibson 1794-1854 ... **NCLC 6**
See also DLB 110, 116, 144

Lodge, David (John) 1935- .... **CLC 36; DAM POP**
See also BEST 90:1; CA 17-20R; CANR 19, 53; DLB 14, 194; INT CANR-19; MTCW

Lodge, Thomas 1558-1625 .... **LC 41**
See also DLB 172

Lodge, Thomas 1558-1625 .... **LC 41**

Loennbohm, Armas Eino Leopold 1878-1926
See Leino, Eino
See also CA 123

Loewinsohn, Ron(ald William) 1937- **CLC 52**
See also CA 25-28R

Logan, Jake
See Smith, Martin Cruz

Logan, John (Burton) 1923-1987 .... **CLC 5**
See also CA 77-80; 124; CANR 45; DLB 5

Lo Kuan-chung 1330(?)-1400(?) .... **LC 12**

Lombard, Nap
See Johnson, Pamela Hansford

London, Jack .... **TCLC 9, 15, 39; SSC 4; WLC**
See also London, John Griffith
See also AAYA 13; AITN 2; CDALB 1865-1917; DLB 8, 12, 78; SATA 18

London, John Griffith 1876-1916
See London, Jack
See also CA 110; 119; DA; DAB; DAC; DAM MST, NOV; JRDA; MAICYA; MTCW

Long, Emmett
See Leonard, Elmore (John, Jr.)

Longbaugh, Harry
See Goldman, William (W.)

Longfellow, Henry Wadsworth 1807-1882 **NCLC 2, 45; DA; DAB; DAC; DAM MST, POET; WLCS**
See also CDALB 1640-1865; DLB 1, 59; SATA 19

Longinus c. 1st cent. - .... **CMLC 27**
See also DLB 176

Longley, Michael 1939- .... **CLC 29**
See also CA 102; DLB 40

Longus fl. c. 2nd cent. - .... **CMLC 7**

Longway, A. Hugh
See Lang, Andrew

Lonnrot, Elias 1802-1884 .... **NCLC 53**

Lopate, Phillip 1943- .... **CLC 29**
See also CA 97-100; DLBY 80; INT 97-100

Lopez Portillo (y Pacheco), Jose 1920- **CLC 46**
See also CA 129; HW

Lopez y Fuentes, Gregorio 1897(?)-1966 **CLC 32**
See also CA 131; HW

Lorca, Federico Garcia
See Garcia Lorca, Federico

Lord, Bette Bao 1938- .... **CLC 23**
See also BEST 90:3; CA 107; CANR 41; INT 107; SATA 58

Lord Auch
See Bataille, Georges

Lord Byron
See Byron, George Gordon (Noel)

Lorde, Audre (Geraldine) 1934-1992 ... **CLC 18, 71; BLC; DAM MULT, POET; PC 12**
See also BW 1; CA 25-28R; 142; CANR 16, 26, 46; DLB 41; MTCW

Lord Houghton
See Milnes, Richard Monckton

Lord Jeffrey
See Jeffrey, Francis

Lorenzini, Carlo 1826-1890
See Collodi, Carlo
See also MAICYA; SATA 29

Lorenzo, Heberto Padilla
See Padilla (Lorenzo), Heberto

Loris
See Hofmannsthal, Hugo von

Loti, Pierre .... **TCLC 11**
See also Viaud, (Louis Marie) Julien
See also DLB 123

Louie, David Wong 1954- .... **CLC 70**
See also CA 139

Louis, Father M.
See Merton, Thomas

Lovecraft, H(oward) P(hillips) 1890-1937 **TCLC 4, 22; DAM POP; SSC 3**
See also AAYA 14; CA 104; 133; MTCW

Lovelace, Earl 1935- .... **CLC 51**
See also BW 2; CA 77-80; CANR 41; DLB 125; MTCW

Lovelace, Richard 1618-1657 .... **LC 24**
See also DLB 131

Lowell, Amy 1874-1925 ...... **TCLC 1, 8; DAM POET; PC 13**
See also CA 104; 151; DLB 54, 140

Lowell, James Russell 1819-1891 ..... **NCLC 2**
See also CDALB 1640-1865; DLB 1, 11, 64, 79, 189

Lowell, Robert (Traill Spence, Jr.) 1917-1977 **CLC 1, 2, 3, 4, 5, 8, 9, 11, 15, 37; DA; DAB; DAC; DAM MST, NOV; PC 3; WLC**
See also CA 9-12R; 73-76; CABS 2; CANR 26, 60; DLB 5, 169; MTCW

Lowndes, Marie Adelaide (Belloc) 1868-1947 **TCLC 12**
See also CA 107; DLB 70

Lowry, (Clarence) Malcolm 1909-1957 **TCLC 6, 40**
See also CA 105; 131; CANR 62; CDBLB 1945-1960; DLB 15; MTCW

Lowry, Mina Gertrude 1882-1966
See Loy, Mina
See also CA 113

Loxsmith, John
See Brunner, John (Kilian Houston)

Maclean, Norman (Fitzroy) 1902-1990 ... **CLC 78; DAM POP; SSC 13**
See also CA 102; 132; CANR 49

MacLeish, Archibald 1892-1982 ... **CLC 3, 8, 14, 68; DAM POET**
See also CA 9-12R; 106; CANR 33, 63; DLB 4, 7, 45; DLBY 82; MTCW

MacLennan, (John) Hugh 1907-1990 ... **CLC 2, 14, 92; DAC; DAM MST**
See also CA 5-8R; 142; CANR 33; DLB 68; MTCW

MacLeod, Alistair 1936- ... **CLC 56; DAC; DAM MST**
See also CA 123; DLB 60

Macleod, Fiona
See Sharp, William

MacNeice, (Frederick) Louis 1907-1963 ... **CLC 1, 4, 10, 53; DAB; DAM POET**
See also CA 85-88; CANR 61; DLB 10, 20; MTCW

MacNeill, Dand
See Fraser, George MacDonald

Macpherson, James 1736-1796 .... **LC 29**
See also DLB 109

Macpherson, (Jean) Jay 1931- .... **CLC 14**
See also CA 5-8R; DLB 53

MacShane, Frank 1927- .... **CLC 39**
See also CA 9-12R; CANR 3, 33; DLB 111

Macumber, Mari
See Sandoz, Mari(e Susette)

Madach, Imre 1823-1864 .... **NCLC 19**

Madden, (Jerry) David 1933- .... **CLC 5, 15**
See also CA 1-4R; CAAS 3; CANR 4, 45; DLB 6; MTCW

Maddern, Al(an)
See Ellison, Harlan (Jay)

Madhubuti, Haki R. 1942- .... **CLC 6, 73; BLC; DAM MULT, POET; PC 5**
See also Lee, Don L.
See also BW 2; CA 73-76; CANR 24, 51; DLB 5, 41; DLBD 8

Maepenn, Hugh
See Kuttner, Henry

Maepenn, K. H.
See Kuttner, Henry

Maeterlinck, Maurice 1862-1949 .... **TCLC 3; DAM DRAM**
See also CA 104; 136; DLB 192; SATA 66

Maginn, William 1794-1842 .... **NCLC 8**
See also DLB 110, 159

Mahapatra, Jayanta 1928- ...... **CLC 33; DAM MULT**
See also CA 73-76; CAAS 9; CANR 15, 33, 66

Mahfouz, Naguib (Abdel Aziz Al-Sabilgi) 1911(?)-
See Mahfuz, Najib
See also BEST 89:2; CA 128; CANR 55; DAM NOV; MTCW

Mahfuz, Najib .... **CLC 52, 55**
See also Mahfouz, Naguib (Abdel Aziz Al-Sabilgi)
See also DLBY 88

Mahon, Derek 1941- .... **CLC 27**
See also CA 113; 128; DLB 40

Mailer, Norman 1923- ... **CLC 1, 2, 3, 4, 5, 8, 11, 14, 28, 39, 74; DA; DAB; DAC; DAM MST, NOV, POP**
See also AITN 2; CA 9-12R; CABS 1; CANR 28; CDALB 1968-1988; DLB 2, 16, 28, 185; DLBD 3; DLBY 80, 83; MTCW

Maillet, Antonine 1929- .... **CLC 54; DAC**
See also CA 115; 120; CANR 46; DLB 60; INT 120

Mais, Roger 1905-1955 .... **TCLC 8**
See also BW 1; CA 105; 124; DLB 125; MTCW

Maistre, Joseph de 1753-1821 .... **NCLC 37**

Maitland, Frederic 1850-1906 .... **TCLC 65**

Maitland, Sara (Louise) 1950- .... **CLC 49**
See also CA 69-72; CANR 13, 59

Major, Clarence 1936- ... **CLC 3, 19, 48; BLC; DAM MULT**
See also BW 2; CA 21-24R; CAAS 6; CANR 13, 25, 53; DLB 33

Major, Kevin (Gerald) 1949- ... **CLC 26; DAC**
See also AAYA 16; CA 97-100; CANR 21, 38; CLR 11; DLB 60; INT CANR-21; JRDA; MAICYA; SATA 32, 82

Maki, James
See Ozu, Yasujiro

Malabaila, Damiano
See Levi, Primo

Malamud, Bernard 1914-1986 ... **CLC 1, 2, 3, 5, 8, 9, 11, 18, 27, 44, 78, 85; DA; DAB; DAC; DAM MST, NOV, POP; SSC 15; WLC**
See also AAYA 16; CA 5-8R; 118; CABS 1; CANR 28, 62; CDALB 1941-1968; DLB 2, 28, 152; DLBY 80, 86; MTCW

Malan, Herman
See Bosman, Herman Charles; Bosman, Herman Charles

Malaparte, Curzio 1898-1957 .... **TCLC 52**

Malcolm, Dan
See Silverberg, Robert

Malcolm X .... **CLC 82; BLC; WLCS**
See also Little, Malcolm

Malherbe, Francois de 1555-1628 .... **LC 5**

Mallarme, Stephane 1842-1898 **NCLC 4, 41; DAM POET; PC 4**

Mallet-Joris, Francoise 1930- .... **CLC 11**
See also CA 65-68; CANR 17; DLB 83

Malley, Ern
See McAuley, James Phillip

Mallowan, Agatha Christie
See Christie, Agatha (Mary Clarissa)

Maloff, Saul 1922- .... **CLC 5**
See also CA 33-36R

Malone, Louis
See MacNeice, (Frederick) Louis

Malone, Michael (Christopher) 1942- .... **CLC 43**
See also CA 77-80; CANR 14, 32, 57

Malory, (Sir) Thomas 1410(?)-1471(?) ... **LC 11; DA; DAB; DAC; DAM MST; WLCS**
See also CDBLB Before 1660; DLB 146; SATA 59; SATA-Brief 33

Malouf, (George Joseph) David 1934- . **CLC 28, 86**
See also CA 124; CANR 50

Malraux, (Georges-)Andre 1901-1976 ... **CLC 1, 4, 9, 13, 15, 57; DAM NOV**
See also CA 21-22; 69-72; CANR 34, 58; CAP 2; DLB 72; MTCW

Malzberg, Barry N(athaniel) 1939- ..... **CLC 7**
See also CA 61-64; CAAS 4; CANR 16; DLB 8

Mamet, David (Alan) 1947- ... **CLC 9, 15, 34, 46, 91; DAM DRAM; DC 4**
See also AAYA 3; CA 81-84; CABS 3; CANR 15, 41, 67; DLB 7; MTCW

Mamoulian, Rouben (Zachary) 1897-1987 **CLC 16**
See also CA 25-28R; 124

Mandelstam, Osip (Emilievich) 1891(?)-1938(?) **TCLC 2, 6; PC 14**
See also CA 104; 150

Mander, (Mary) Jane 1877-1949 .... **TCLC 31**
See also CA 162

Mandeville, John fl. 1350- .... **CMLC 19**
See also DLB 146

Mandiargues, Andre Pieyre de .... **CLC 41**
See also Pieyre de Mandiargues, Andre
See also DLB 83

Mandrake, Ethel Belle
See Thurman, Wallace (Henry)

Mangan, James Clarence 1803-1849 ..... **NCLC 27**

Maniere, J.-E.
See Giraudoux, (Hippolyte) Jean

Manley, (Mary) Delariviere 1672(?)-1724 ..... **LC 1**
See also DLB 39, 80

Mann, Abel
See Creasey, John

Mann, Emily 1952- .... DC 7
See also CA 130; CANR 55

Mann, (Luiz) Heinrich 1871-1950 .... **TCLC 9**
See also CA 106; 164; DLB 66

Mann, (Paul) Thomas 1875-1955   **TCLC 2,**
8, 14, 21, 35, 44, 60; DA; DAB; DAC; DAM
MST, NOV; SSC 5; WLC
See also CA 104; 128; DLB 66; MTCW

Mannheim, Karl 1893-1947 .... **TCLC 65**

Manning, David
See Faust, Frederick (Schiller)

Manning, Frederic 1887(?)-1935 .... **TCLC 25**
See also CA 124

Manning, Olivia 1915-1980 .... **CLC 5, 19**
See also CA 5-8R; 101; CANR 29; MTCW

Mano, D. Keith 1942- .... **CLC 2, 10**
See also CA 25-28R; CAAS 6; CANR 26, 57; DLB 6

Mansfield, Katherine .... **TCLC 2, 8, 39;**
DAB; SSC 9, 23; WLC
See also Beauchamp, Kathleen Mansfield
See also DLB 162

Manso, Peter 1940- .... **CLC 39**
See also CA 29-32R; CANR 44

Mantecon, Juan Jimenez
See Jimenez (Mantecon), Juan Ramon

Manton, Peter
See Creasey, John

Man Without a Spleen, A
See Chekhov, Anton (Pavlovich)

Manzoni, Alessandro 1785-1873 ..... **NCLC 29**

Mapu, Abraham (ben Jekutiel) 1808-1867
NCLC 18

Mara, Sally
See Queneau, Raymond

Marat, Jean Paul 1743-1793 .... **LC 10**

Marcel, Gabriel Honore 1889-1973 .. **CLC 15**
See also CA 102; 45-48; MTCW

Marchbanks, Samuel
See Davies, (William) Robertson

Marchi, Giacomo
See Bassani, Giorgio

Margulies, Donald .... **CLC 76**

Marie de France c. 12th cent. - .... **CMLC 8**

Marie de l'Incarnation 1599-1672 .... **LC 10**

Marier, Captain Victor
See Griffith, D(avid Lewelyn) W(ark)

Mariner, Scott
See Pohl, Frederik

Marinetti, Filippo Tommaso 1876-1944 ....

TCLC 10
See also CA 107; DLB 114

Marivaux, Pierre Carlet de Chamblain de 1688-
1763 .... **LC 4; DC 7**

Markandaya, Kamala .... **CLC 8, 38**
See also Taylor, Kamala (Purnaiya)

Markfield, Wallace 1926- .... **CLC 8**
See also CA 69-72; CAAS 3; DLB 2, 28

Markham, Edwin 1852-1940 .... **TCLC 47**
See also CA 160; DLB 54, 186

Markham, Robert
See Amis, Kingsley (William)

Marks, J
See Highwater, Jamake (Mamake)

Marks-Highwater, J
See Highwater, Jamake (Mamake)

Markson, David M(errill) 1927- .... **CLC 67**
See also CA 49-52; CANR 1

Marley, Bob .... **CLC 17**
See also Marley, Robert Nesta

Marley, Robert Nesta 1945-1981
See Marley, Bob
See also CA 107; 103

Marlowe, Christopher 1564-1593 ...   **LC 22;**
DA; DAB; DAC; DAM DRAM, MST; DC
1; WLC
See also CDBLB Before 1660; DLB 62

Marlowe, Stephen 1928-
See Queen, Ellery
See also CA 13-16R; CANR 6, 55

Marmontel, Jean-Francois 1723-1799 ... **LC 2**

Marquand, John P(hillips) 1893-1960 ... **CLC 2, 10**
See also CA 85-88; DLB 9, 102

Marques, Rene 1919-1979 ...... **CLC 96; DAM**
MULT; HLC
See also CA 97-100; 85-88; DLB 113; HW

Marquez, Gabriel (Jose) Garcia
See Garcia Marquez, Gabriel (Jose)

Marquis, Don(ald Robert Perry) 1878-1937
TCLC 7
See also CA 104; DLB 11, 25

Marric, J. J.
See Creasey, John

Marryat, Frederick 1792-1848 .... **NCLC 3**
See also DLB 21, 163

Marsden, James
See Creasey, John

Marsh, (Edith) Ngaio 1899-1982 . **CLC 7, 53;**
DAM POP
See also CA 9-12R; CANR 6, 58; DLB 77;
MTCW

Marshall, Garry 1934- .... **CLC 17**
See also AAYA 3; CA 111; SATA 60

Marshall, Paule 1929- ....   **CLC 27, 72; BLC;**
DAM MULT; SSC 3
See also BW 2; CA 77-80; CANR 25; DLB 157;
MTCW

Marsten, Richard
See Hunter, Evan

Marston, John 1576-1634 ....   **LC 33; DAM**
DRAM
See also DLB 58, 172

Martha, Henry
See Harris, Mark

Marti, Jose 1853-1895 ....   **NCLC 63; DAM**
MULT; HLC

Martial c. 40-c. 104 .... **PC 10**

Martin, Ken
See Hubbard, L(afayette) Ron(ald)

Martin, Richard
See Creasey, John

Martin, Steve 1945- .... **CLC 30**
See also CA 97-100; CANR 30; MTCW

Martin, Valerie 1948- .... **CLC 89**
See also BEST 90:2; CA 85-88; CANR 49

Martin, Violet Florence 1862-1915 .... **TCLC**
51

Martin, Webber
See Silverberg, Robert

Martindale, Patrick Victor
See White, Patrick (Victor Martindale)

Martin du Gard, Roger 1881-1958 .... **TCLC**
24
See also CA 118; DLB 65

Martineau, Harriet 1802-1876 .... **NCLC 26**
See also DLB 21, 55, 159, 163, 166, 190; YABC 2

Martines, Julia
See O'Faolain, Julia

Martinez, Enrique Gonzalez
See Gonzalez Martinez, Enrique

Martinez, Jacinto Benavente y
See Benavente (y Martinez), Jacinto

Martinez Ruiz, Jose 1873-1967
See Azorin; Ruiz, Jose Martinez
See also CA 93-96; HW

Martinez Sierra, Gregorio 1881-1947 ... **TCLC**
6
See also CA 115

Martinez Sierra, Maria (de la O'LeJarraga) 1874-1974 .... **TCLC 6**
See also CA 115

Martinsen, Martin
See Follett, Ken(neth Martin)

Martinson, Harry (Edmund) 1904-1978 ... **CLC 14**
See also CA 77-80; CANR 34

Marut, Ret
See Traven, B.

Marut, Robert
See Traven, B.

Marvell, Andrew 1621-1678　**LC 4; DA; DAB; DAC; DAM MST, POET; PC 10; WLC**
See also CDBLB 1660-1789; DLB 131

Marx, Karl (Heinrich) 1818-1883 .. **NCLC 17**
See also DLB 129

Masaoka Shiki .... **TCLC 18**
See also Masaoka Tsunenori

Masaoka Tsunenori 1867-1902
See Masaoka Shiki
See also CA 117

Masefield, John (Edward) 1878-1967　**CLC 11, 47; DAM POET**
See also CA 19-20; 25-28R; CANR 33; CAP 2; CDBLB 1890-1914; DLB 10, 19, 153, 160; MTCW; SATA 19

Maso, Carole 19(?)- .... **CLC 44**

Mason, Bobbie Ann 1940-　**CLC 28, 43, 82; SSC 4**
See also AAYA 5; CA 53-56; CANR 11, 31, 58; DLB 173; DLBY 87; INT CANR-31; MTCW

Mason, Ernst
See Pohl, Frederik

Mason, Lee W.
See Malzberg, Barry N(athaniel)

Mason, Nick 1945- .... **CLC 35**

Mason, Tally
See Derleth, August (William)

Mass, William
See Gibson, William

Masters, Edgar Lee 1868-1950　**TCLC 2, 25; DA; DAC; DAM MST, POET; PC 1; WLCS**
See also CA 104; 133; CDALB 1865-1917; DLB 54; MTCW

Masters, Hilary 1928- .... **CLC 48**
See also CA 25-28R; CANR 13, 47

Mastrosimone, William 19(?)- .... **CLC 36**

Mathe, Albert
See Camus, Albert

Mather, Cotton 1663-1728 .... **LC 38**
See also CDALB 1640-1865; DLB 24, 30, 140

Mather, Increase 1639-1723 .... **LC 38**
See also DLB 24

Matheson, Richard Burton 1926- ...... **CLC 37**
See also CA 97-100; DLB 8, 44; INT 97-100

Mathews, Harry 1930- .... **CLC 6, 52**
See also CA 21-24R; CAAS 6; CANR 18, 40

Mathews, John Joseph 1894-1979 ... **CLC 84; DAM MULT**
See also CA 19-20; 142; CANR 45; CAP 2; DLB 175; NNAL

Mathias, Roland (Glyn) 1915- .... **CLC 45**
See also CA 97-100; CANR 19, 41; DLB 27

Matsuo Basho 1644-1694 .... **PC 3**
See also DAM POET

Mattheson, Rodney
See Creasey, John

Matthews, Greg 1949- .... **CLC 45**
See also CA 135

Matthews, William (Procter, III) 1942-1997
CLC 40
See also CA 29-32R; 162; CAAS 18; CANR 12, 57; DLB 5

Matthias, John (Edward) 1941- .... **CLC 9**
See also CA 33-36R; CANR 56

Matthiessen, Peter 1927-　**CLC 5, 7, 11, 32, 64; DAM NOV**
See also AAYA 6; BEST 90:4; CA 9-12R; CANR 21, 50; DLB 6, 173; MTCW; SATA 27

Maturin, Charles Robert 1780(?)-1824
NCLC 6
See also DLB 178

Matute (Ausejo), Ana Maria 1925-.... **CLC 11**
See also CA 89-92; MTCW

Maugham, W. S.
See Maugham, W(illiam) Somerset

Maugham, W(illiam) Somerset 1874-1965
CLC 1, 11, 15, 67, 93; DA; DAB; DAC; DAM DRAM, MST, NOV; SSC 8; WLC
See also CA 5-8R; 25-28R; CANR 40; CDBLB 1914-1945; DLB 10, 36, 77, 100, 162, 195; MTCW; SATA 54

Maugham, William Somerset
See Maugham, W(illiam) Somerset

Maupassant, (Henri Rene Albert) Guy de 1850-1893 .... **NCLC 1, 42; DA; DAB; DAC; DAM MST; SSC 1; WLC**
See also DLB 123

Maupin, Armistead 1944- ... **CLC 95; DAM POP**
See also CA 125; 130; CANR 58; INT 130

Maurhut, Richard
See Traven, B.

Mauriac, Claude 1914-1996 .... **CLC 9**
See also CA 89-92; 152; DLB 83

Mauriac, Francois (Charles) 1885-1970 ... **CLC 4, 9, 56; SSC 24**
See also CA 25-28; CAP 2; DLB 65; MTCW

Mavor, Osborne Henry 1888-1951
See Bridie, James
See also CA 104

Maxwell, William (Keepers, Jr.) 1908- **CLC 19**
See also CA 93-96; CANR 54; DLBY 80; INT 93-96

May, Elaine 1932- .... **CLC 16**
See also CA 124; 142; DLB 44

Mayakovski, Vladimir (Vladimirovich) 1893-1930 .... **TCLC 4, 18**
See also CA 104; 158

Mayhew, Henry 1812-1887 .... **NCLC 31**
See also DLB 18, 55, 190

Mayle, Peter 1939(?)- .... **CLC 89**
See also CA 139; CANR 64

Maynard, Joyce 1953- .... **CLC 23**
See also CA 111; 129; CANR 64

Mayne, William (James Carter) 1928- ... **CLC 12**
See also AAYA 20; CA 9-12R; CANR 37; CLR 25; JRDA; MAICYA; SAAS 11; SATA 6, 68

Mayo, Jim
See L'Amour, Louis (Dearborn)

Maysles, Albert 1926- .... **CLC 16**
See also CA 29-32R

Maysles, David 1932- .... **CLC 16**

Mazer, Norma Fox 1931- .... **CLC 26**
See also AAYA 5; CA 69-72; CANR 12, 32, 66; CLR 23; JRDA; MAICYA; SAAS 1; SATA 24, 67

Mazzini, Guiseppe 1805-1872 .... **NCLC 34**

McAuley, James Phillip 1917-1976 .... **CLC 45**
See also CA 97-100

McBain, Ed
See Hunter, Evan

McBrien, William Augustine 1930- ... **CLC 44**
See also CA 107

McCaffrey, Anne (Inez) 1926- **CLC 17; DAM NOV, POP**
See also AAYA 6; AITN 2; BEST 89:2; CA 25-28R; CANR 15, 35, 55; CLR 49; DLB 8; JRDA; MAICYA; MTCW; SAAS 11; SATA 8, 70

McCall, Nathan 1955(?)-..................... **CLC 86**
See also CA 146

McCann, Arthur
See Campbell, John W(ood, Jr.)

McCann, Edson
See Pohl, Frederik

Melmoth, Sebastian
See Wilde, Oscar (Fingal O'Flahertie Wills)

Meltzer, Milton 1915- .... **CLC 26**
See also AAYA 8; CA 13-16R; CANR 38; CLR 13; DLB 61; JRDA; MAICYA; SAAS 1; SATA 1, 50, 80

Melville, Herman 1819-1891   **NCLC 3, 12, 29, 45, 49; DA; DAB; DAC; DAM MST, NOV; SSC 1, 17; WLC**
See also AAYA 25; CDALB 1640-1865; DLB 3, 74; SATA 59

Menander c. 342B.C.-c. 292B.C. ..... **CMLC 9; DAM DRAM; DC 3**
See also DLB 176

Mencken, H(enry) L(ouis) 1880-1956 **TCLC 13**
See also CA 105; 125; CDALB 1917-1929; DLB 11, 29, 63, 137; MTCW

Mendelsohn, Jane 1965(?)- .... **CLC 99**
See also CA 154

Mercer, David 1928-1980 .... **CLC 5; DAM DRAM**
See also CA 9-12R; 102; CANR 23; DLB 13; MTCW

Merchant, Paul
See Ellison, Harlan (Jay)

Meredith, George 1828-1909 ...**TCLC 17, 43; DAM POET**
See also CA 117; 153; CDBLB 1832-1890; DLB 18, 35, 57, 159

Meredith, William (Morris) 1919- **CLC 4, 13, 22, 55; DAM POET**
See also CA 9-12R; CAAS 14; CANR 6, 40; DLB 5

Merezhkovsky, Dmitry Sergeyevich 1865-1941 **TCLC 29**

Merimee, Prosper 1803-1870 ... **NCLC 6, 65; SSC 7**
See also DLB 119, 192

Merkin, Daphne 1954- .... **CLC 44**
See also CA 123

Merlin, Arthur
See Blish, James (Benjamin)

Merrill, James (Ingram) 1926-1995 **CLC 2, 3, 6, 8, 13, 18, 34, 91; DAM POET**
See also CA 13-16R; 147; CANR 10, 49, 63; DLB 5, 165; DLBY 85; INT CANR-10; MTCW

Merriman, Alex
See Silverberg, Robert

Merritt, E. B.
See Waddington, Miriam

Merton, Thomas 1915-1968   **CLC 1, 3, 11, 34, 83; PC 10**
See also CA 5-8R; 25-28R; CANR 22, 53; DLB 48; DLBY 81; MTCW

Merwin, W(illiam) S(tanley) 1927- ... **CLC 1, 2, 3, 5, 8, 13, 18, 45, 88; DAM POET**
See also CA 13-16R; CANR 15, 51; DLB 5, 169; INT CANR-15; MTCW

Metcalf, John 1938- .... **CLC 37**
See also CA 113; DLB 60

Metcalf, Suzanne
See Baum, L(yman) Frank

Mew, Charlotte (Mary) 1870-1928 ... **TCLC 8**
See also CA 105; DLB 19, 135

Mewshaw, Michael 1943- .... **CLC 9**
See also CA 53-56; CANR 7, 47; DLBY 80

Meyer, June
See Jordan, June

Meyer, Lynn
See Slavitt, David R(ytman)

Meyer-Meyrink, Gustav 1868-1932
See Meyrink, Gustav
See also CA 117

Meyers, Jeffrey 1939- .... **CLC 39**
See also CA 73-76; CANR 54; DLB 111

Meynell, Alice (Christina Gertrude Thompson) 1847-1922 .... **TCLC 6**
See also CA 104; DLB 19, 98

Meyrink, Gustav .... **TCLC 21**
See also Meyer-Meyrink, Gustav
See also DLB 81

Michaels, Leonard 1933 ... **CLC 6, 25; SSC 16**
See also CA 61-64; CANR 21, 62; DLB 130; MTCW

Michaux, Henri 1899-1984 .... **CLC 8, 19**
See also CA 85-88; 114

Micheaux, Oscar 1884-1951 .... **TCLC 76**
See also DLB 50

Michelangelo 1475-1564 .... **LC 12**

Michelet, Jules 1798-1874 .... **NCLC 31**

Michener, James A(lbert) 1907(?)-1997 ... **CLC 1, 5, 11, 29, 60, 109; DAM NOV, POP**
See also AITN 1; BEST 90:1; CA 5-8R; 161; CANR 21, 45, 68; DLB 6; MTCW

Mickiewicz, Adam 1798-1855 .... **NCLC 3**

Middleton, Christopher 1926- .... **CLC 13**
See also CA 13-16R; CANR 29, 54; DLB 40

Middleton, Richard (Barham) 1882-1911 **TCLC 56**
See also DLB 156

Middleton, Stanley 1919- .... **CLC 7, 38**
See also CA 25-28R; CAAS 23; CANR 21, 46; DLB 14

Middleton, Thomas 1580-1627 ... **LC 33; DAM DRAM, MST; DC 5**
See also DLB 58

Migueis, Jose Rodrigues 1901- .... **CLC 10**

Mikszath, Kalman 1847-1910.......... **TCLC 31**

Miles, Jack ....**CLC 100**

Miles, Josephine (Louise) 1911-1985 ... **CLC 1, 2, 14, 34, 39; DAM POET**
See also CA 1-4R; 116; CANR 2, 55; DLB 48

Militant
See Sandburg, Carl (August)

Mill, John Stuart 1806-1873 ....**NCLC 11, 58**
See also CDBLB 1832-1890; DLB 55, 190

Millar, Kenneth 1915-1983 .... **CLC 14; DAM POP**
See also Macdonald, Ross
See also CA 9-12R; 110; CANR 16, 63; DLB 2; DLBD 6; DLBY 83; MTCW

Millay, E. Vincent
See Millay, Edna St. Vincent

Millay, Edna St. Vincent 1892-1950 ... **TCLC 4, 49; DA; DAB; DAC; DAM MST, POET; PC 6; WLCS**
See also CA 104; 130; CDALB 1917-1929; DLB 45; MTCW

Miller, Arthur 1915- .... **CLC 1, 2, 6, 10, 15, 26, 47, 78; DA; DAB; DAC; DAM DRAM, MST; DC 1; WLC**
See also AAYA 15; AITN 1; CA 1-4R; CABS 3; CANR 2, 30, 54; CDALB 1941-1968; DLB 7; MTCW

Miller, Henry (Valentine) 1891-1980   **CLC 1, 2, 4, 9, 14, 43, 84; DA; DAB; DAC; DAM MST, NOV; WLC**
See also CA 9-12R; 97-100; CANR 33, 64; CDALB 1929-1941; DLB 4, 9; DLBY 80; MTCW

Miller, Jason 1939(?)- .... **CLC 2**
See also AITN 1; CA 73-76, DLB 7

Miller, Sue 1943- .... **CLC 44; DAM POP**
See also BEST 90:3; CA 139; CANR 59; DLB 143

Miller, Walter M(ichael, Jr.) 1923- **CLC 4, 30**
See also CA 85-88; DLB 8

Millett, Kate 1934- .... **CLC 67**
See also AITN 1; CA 73-76; CANR 32, 53; MTCW

Millhauser, Steven (Lewis) 1943- ... **CLC 21, 54, 109**
See also CA 110; 111; CANR 63; DLB 2; INT 111

Millin, Sarah Gertrude 1889-1968 .... **CLC 49**
See also CA 102; 93-96

Milne, A(lan) A(lexander) 1882-1956 ...**T C L C 6; DAB; DAC; DAM MST**
See also CA 104; 133; CLR 1, 26; DLB 10, 77, 100, 160; MAICYA; MTCW; YABC 1

Milner, Ron(ald) 1938- ... **CLC 56; BLC; DAM MULT**
See also AITN 1; BW 1; CA 73-76; CANR 24; DLB 38; MTCW

Milnes, Richard Monckton 1809-1885 ... **NCLC 61**
See also DLB 32, 184

Milosz, Czeslaw 1911- .... **CLC 5, 11, 22, 31, 56, 82; DAM MST, POET; PC 8; WLCS**
See also CA 81-84; CANR 23, 51; MTCW

Milton, John 1608-1674 ..... **LC 9; DA; DAB; DAC; DAM MST, POET; PC 19; WLC**
See also CDBLB 1660-1789; DLB 131, 151

Min, Anchee 1957- .... **CLC 86**
See also CA 146

Minehaha, Cornelius
See Wedekind, (Benjamin) Frank(lin)

Miner, Valerie 1947- .... **CLC 40**
See also CA 97-100; CANR 59

Minimo, Duca
See D'Annunzio, Gabriele

Minot, Susan 1956- .... **CLC 44**
See also CA 134

Minus, Ed 1938- .... **CLC 39**

Miranda, Javier
See Bioy Casares, Adolfo

Mirbeau, Octave 1848-1917 .... **TCLC 55**
See also DLB 123, 192

Miro (Ferrer), Gabriel (Francisco Victor) 1879-1930 .... **TCLC 5**
See also CA 104

Mishima, Yukio 1925-1970 ... **CLC 2, 4, 6, 9, 27; DC 1; SSC 4**
See also Hiraoka, Kimitake
See also DLB 182

Mistral, Frederic 1830-1914 .... **TCLC 51**
See also CA 122

Mistral, Gabriela .... **TCLC 2; HLC**
See also Godoy Alcayaga, Lucila

Mistry, Rohinton 1952- .... **CLC 71; DAC**
See also CA 141

Mitchell, Clyde
See Ellison, Harlan (Jay); Silverberg, Robert

Mitchell, James Leslie 1901-1935
See Gibbon, Lewis Grassic
See also CA 104; DLB 15

Mitchell, Joni 1943- .... **CLC 12**
See also CA 112

Mitchell, Joseph (Quincy) 1908-1996 ...... **CLC 98**
See also CA 77-80; 152; DLB 185; DLBY 96

Mitchell, Margaret (Munnerlyn) 1900-1949 **TCLC 11; DAM NOV, POP**
See also AAYA 23; CA 109; 125; CANR 55; DLB 9; MTCW

Mitchell, Peggy
See Mitchell, Margaret (Munnerlyn)

Mitchell, S(ilas) Weir 1829-1914 ..... **TCLC 36**
See also CA 165

Mitchell, W(illiam) O(rmond) 1914-1998 **CLC 25; DAC; DAM MST**
See also CA 77-80; 165; CANR 15, 43; DLB 88

Mitford, Mary Russell 1787-1855 .... **NCLC 4**
See also DLB 110, 116

Mitford, Nancy 1904-1973 .... **CLC 44**
See also CA 9-12R; DLB 191

Miyamoto, Yuriko 1899-1951 .... **TCLC 37**
See also DLB 180

Miyazawa, Kenji 1896-1933 .... **TCLC 76**
See also CA 157

Mizoguchi, Kenji 1898-1956 .... **TCLC 72**

Mo, Timothy (Peter) 1950(?)- .... **CLC 46**
See also CA 117; DLB 194; MTCW

Modarressi, Taghi (M.) 1931- .... **CLC 44**
See also CA 121; 134; INT 134

Modiano, Patrick (Jean) 1945- .... **CLC 18**
See also CA 85-88; CANR 17, 40; DLB 83

Moerck, Paal
See Roelvaag, O(le) E(dvart)

Mofolo, Thomas (Mokopu) 1875(?)-1948 **TCLC 22; BLC; DAM MULT**
See also CA 121; 153

Mohr, Nicholasa 1938- ... **CLC 12; DAM MULT; HLC**
See also AAYA 8; CA 49-52; CANR 1, 32, 64; CLR 22; DLB 145; HW; JRDA; SAAS 8; SATA 8, 97

Mojtabai, A(nn) G(race) 1938- **CLC 5, 9, 15, 29**
See also CA 85-88

Moliere 1622-1673 .. **LC 28; DA; DAB; DAC; DAM DRAM, MST; WLC**

Molin, Charles
See Mayne, William (James Carter)

Molnar, Ferenc 1878-1952 ... **TCLC 20; DAM DRAM**
See also CA 109; 153

Momaday, N(avarre) Scott 1934- ... **CLC 2, 19, 85, 95; DA; DAB; DAC; DAM MST, MULT, NOV, POP; WLCS**
See also AAYA 11; CA 25-28R; CANR 14, 34, 68; DLB 143, 175; INT CANR-14; MTCW; NNAL; SATA 48; SATA-Brief 30

Monette, Paul 1945-1995 .... **CLC 82**
See also CA 139; 147

Monroe, Harriet 1860-1936 .... **TCLC 12**
See also CA 109; DLB 54, 91

Monroe, Lyle
See Heinlein, Robert A(nson)

Montagu, Elizabeth 1917- .... **NCLC 7**
See also CA 9-12R

Montagu, Mary (Pierrepont) Wortley 1689-1762 **LC 9; PC 16**
See also DLB 95, 101

Montagu, W. H.
See Coleridge, Samuel Taylor

Montague, John (Patrick) 1929- ... **CLC 13, 46**
See also CA 9-12R; CANR 9; DLB 40; MTCW

Montaigne, Michel (Eyquem) de 1533-1592 **LC 8; DA; DAB; DAC; DAM MST; WLC**

Montale, Eugenio 1896-1981 ... **CLC 7, 9, 18; PC 13**
See also CA 17-20R; 104; CANR 30; DLB 114; MTCW

Montesquieu, Charles-Louis de Secondat 1689-1755 .... **LC 7**

Montgomery, (Robert) Bruce 1921-1978
See Crispin, Edmund
See also CA 104

Montgomery, L(ucy) M(aud) 1874-1942 **TCLC 51; DAC; DAM MST**
See also AAYA 12; CA 108; 137; CLR 8; DLB 92; DLBD 14; JRDA; MAICYA; YABC 1

Montgomery, Marion H., Jr. 1925- ..... **CLC 7**
See also AITN 1; CA 1-4R; CANR 3, 48; DLB 6

Montgomery, Max
See Davenport, Guy (Mattison, Jr.)

Montherlant, Henry (Milon) de 1896-1972 **CLC 8, 19; DAM DRAM**
See also CA 85-88; 37-40R; DLB 72; MTCW

Monty Python
See Chapman, Graham; Cleese, John (Marwood); Gilliam, Terry (Vance); Idle, Eric; Jones, Terence Graham Parry; Palin, Michael (Edward)
See also AAYA 7

Moodie, Susanna (Strickland) 1803-1885 **NCLC 14**
See also DLB 99

Mooney, Edward 1951-
See Mooney, Ted
See also CA 130

Mooney, Ted .... **CLC 25**
See also Mooney, Edward

Moorcock, Michael (John) 1939- ... **CLC 5, 27, 58**
See also CA 45-48; CAAS 5; CANR 2, 17, 38, 64; DLB 14; MTCW; SATA 93

Moore, Brian 1921- **CLC 1, 3, 5, 7, 8, 19, 32, 90; DAB; DAC; DAM MST**
See also CA 1-4R; CANR 1, 25, 42, 63; MTCW

Moore, Edward
See Muir, Edwin

Moore, George Augustus 1852-1933 ... **TCLC 7; SSC 19**
See also CA 104; DLB 10, 18, 57, 135

Moore, Lorrie .... **CLC 39, 45, 68**
See also Moore, Marie Lorena

Moore, Marianne (Craig) 1887-1972 ... **CLC 1, 2, 4, 8, 10, 13, 19, 47; DA; DAB; DAC; DAM MST, POET; PC 4; WLCS**
See also CA 1-4R; 33-36R; CANR 3, 61; CDALB 1929-1941; DLB 45; DLBD 7; MTCW; SATA 20

Moore, Marie Lorena 1957-
See Moore, Lorrie
See also CA 116; CANR 39

Moore, Thomas 1779-1852 .... **NCLC 6**
See also DLB 96, 144

Morand, Paul 1888-1976 .... **CLC 41; SSC 22**
See also CA 69-72; DLB 65

Morante, Elsa 1918-1985 .... **CLC 8, 47**
See also CA 85-88; 117; CANR 35; DLB 177; MTCW

Moravia, Alberto 1907-1990 ... **CLC 2, 7, 11, 27, 46; SSC 26**
See also Pincherle, Alberto
See also DLB 177

More, Hannah 1745-1833 .... **NCLC 27**
See also DLB 107, 109, 116, 158

More, Henry 1614-1687 .... **LC 9**
See also DLB 126

More, Sir Thomas 1478-1535 .... **LC 10, 32**

Moreas, Jean .... **TCLC 18**
See also Papadiamantopoulos, Johannes

Morgan, Berry 1919- .... **CLC 6**
See also CA 49-52; DLB 6

Morgan, Claire
See Highsmith, (Mary) Patricia

Morgan, Edwin (George) 1920- .... **CLC 31**
See also CA 5-8R; CANR 3, 43; DLB 27

Morgan, (George) Frederick 1922- .... **CLC 23**
See also CA 17-20R; CANR 21

Morgan, Harriet
See Mencken, H(enry) L(ouis)

Morgan, Jane
See Cooper, James Fenimore

Morgan, Janet 1945- .... **CLC 39**
See also CA 65-68

Morgan, Lady 1776(?)-1859 .... **NCLC 29**
See also DLB 116, 158

Morgan, Robin (Evonne) 1941- .... **CLC 2**
See also CA 69-72; CANR 29, 68; MTCW; SATA 80

Morgan, Scott
See Kuttner, Henry

Morgan, Seth 1949(?)-1990 .... **CLC 65**
See also CA 132

Morgenstern, Christian 1871-1914 .. **TCLC 8**
See also CA 105

Morgenstern, S.
See Goldman, William (W.)

Moricz, Zsigmond 1879-1942 .... **TCLC 33**
See also CA 165

Morike, Eduard (Friedrich) 1804-1875 **NCLC 10**
See also DLB 133

Moritz, Karl Philipp 1756-1793 .... **LC 2**
See also DLB 94

Morland, Peter Henry
See Faust, Frederick (Schiller)

Morren, Theophil
See Hofmannsthal, Hugo von

Morris, Bill 1952- .... **CLC 76**

Morris, Julian
See West, Morris L(anglo)

Morris, Steveland Judkins 1950(?)-
See Wonder, Stevie
See also CA 111

Morris, William 1834-1896 .... **NCLC 4**
See also CDBLB 1832-1890; DLB 18, 35, 57, 156, 178, 184

Morris, Wright 1910- .... **CLC 1, 3, 7, 18, 37**
See also CA 9-12R; CANR 21; DLB 2; DLBY 81; MTCW

Morrison, Arthur 1863-1945 .... **TCLC 72**
See also CA 120; 157; DLB 70, 135

Morrison, Chloe Anthony Wofford
See Morrison, Toni

Morrison, James Douglas 1943-1971
See Morrison, Jim
See also CA 73-76; CANR 40

Morrison, Jim .... **CLC 17**
See also Morrison, James Douglas

Morrison, Toni 1931- .... **CLC 4, 10, 22, 55, 81, 87; BLC; DA; DAB; DAC; DAM MST, MULT, NOV, POP**
See also AAYA 1, 22; BW 2; CA 29-32R; CANR 27, 42, 67; CDALB 1968-1988; DLB 6, 33, 143; DLBY 81; MTCW; SATA 57

Morrison, Van 1945- .... **CLC 21**
See also CA 116

Morrissy, Mary 1958- .... **CLC 99**

Mortimer, John (Clifford) 1923- ... **CLC 28, 43; DAM DRAM, POP**
See also CA 13-16R; CANR 21; CDBLB 1960 to Present; DLB 13; INT CANR-21; MTCW

Mortimer, Penelope (Ruth) 1918- .... **CLC 5**
See also CA 57-60; CANR 45

Morton, Anthony
See Creasey, John

Mosca, Gaetano 1858-1941 .... **TCLC 75**

Mosher, Howard Frank 1943- .... **CLC 62**
See also CA 139; CANR 65

Mosley, Nicholas 1923- .... **CLC 43, 70**
See also CA 69-72; CANR 41, 60; DLB 14

Mosley, Walter 1952- ... **CLC 97; DAM MULT, POP**
See also AAYA 17; BW 2; CA 142; CANR 57

Moss, Howard 1922-1987 . **CLC 7, 14, 45, 50; DAM POET**
See also CA 1-4R; 123; CANR 1, 44; DLB 5

Mossgiel, Rab
See Burns, Robert

Motion, Andrew (Peter) 1952- .... **CLC 47**
See also CA 146; DLB 40

Motley, Willard (Francis) 1909-1965 **CLC 18**
See also BW 1; CA 117; 106; DLB 76, 143

Motoori, Norinaga 1730-1801 .... **NCLC 45**

Mott, Michael (Charles Alston) 1930- ... **CLC 15, 34**
See also CA 5-8R; CAAS 7; CANR 7, 29

Mountain Wolf Woman 1884-1960 .... **CLC 92**
See also CA 144; NNAL

Moure, Erin 1955- .... **CLC 88**
See also CA 113; DLB 60

Mowat, Farley (McGill) 1921- ... **CLC 26; DAC; DAM MST**
See also AAYA 1; CA 1-4R; CANR 4, 24, 42, 68; CLR 20; DLB 68; INT CANAR-24; JRDA; MAICYA; MTCW; SATA 3, 55

Moyers, Bill 1934- .... **CLC 74**
See also AITN 2; CA 61-64; CANR 31, 52

Mphahlele, Es'kia
See Mphahlele, Ezekiel
See also DLB 125

Mphahlele, Ezekiel 1919-1983 ... **CLC 25; BLC; DAM MULT**
See also Mphahlele, Es'kia
See also BW 2; CA 81-84; CANR 26

Mqhayi, S(amuel) E(dward) K(rune Loliwe) 1875-1945 .... **TCLC 25; BLC; DAM MULT**
See also CA 153

Nemerov, Howard (Stanley) 1920-1991　　**CLC 2, 6, 9, 36; DAM POET**
　　See also CA 1-4R; 134; CABS 2; CANR 1, 27, 53; DLB 5, 6; DLBY 83; INT CANR-27; MTCW

Neruda, Pablo 1904-1973　　　**CLC 1, 2, 5, 7, 9, 28, 62; DA; DAB; DAC; DAM MST, MULT, POET; HLC; PC 4; WLC**
　　See also CA 19-20; 45-48; CAP 2; HW; MTCW

Nerval, Gerard de 1808-1855　　**NCLC 1, 67; PC 13; SSC 18**

Nervo, (Jose) Amado (Ruiz de) 1870-1919　　**TCLC 11**
　　See also CA 109; 131; HW

Nessi, Pio Baroja y
　　See Baroja (y Nessi), Pio

Nestroy, Johann 1801-1862 .... **NCLC 42**
　　See also DLB 133

Netterville, Luke
　　See O'Grady, Standish (James)

Neufeld, John (Arthur) 1938- .... **CLC 17**
　　See also AAYA 11; CA 25-28R; CANR 11, 37, 56; MAICYA; SAAS 3; SATA 6, 81

Neville, Emily Cheney 1919- .... **CLC 12**
　　See also CA 5-8R; CANR 3, 37; JRDA; MAICYA; SAAS 2; SATA 1

Newbound, Bernard Slade 1930-
　　See Slade, Bernard
　　See also CA 81-84; CANR 49; DAM DRAM

Newby, P(ercy) H(oward) 1918-1997 .. **CLC 2, 13; DAM NOV**
　　See also CA 5-8R; 161; CANR 32, 67; DLB 15; MTCW

Newlove, Donald 1928- .... **CLC 6**
　　See also CA 29-32R; CANR 25

Newlove, John (Herbert) 1938- .... **CLC 14**
　　See also CA 21-24R; CANR 9, 25

Newman, Charles 1938- .... **CLC 2, 8**
　　See also CA 21-24R

Newman, Edwin (Harold) 1919- .... **CLC 14**
　　See also AITN 1; CA 69-72; CANR 5

Newman, John Henry 1801-1890 .... **NCLC 38**
　　See also DLB 18, 32, 55

Newton, Suzanne 1936- .... **CLC 35**
　　See also CA 41-44R; CANR 14; JRDA; SATA 5, 77

Nexo, Martin Andersen 1869-1954　　**TCLC 43**

Nezval, Vitezslav 1900-1958 .... **TCLC 44**
　　See also CA 123

Ng, Fae Myenne 1957(?)- .... **CLC 81**
　　See also CA 146

Ngema, Mbongeni 1955- .... **CLC 57**
　　See also BW 2; CA 143

Ngugi, James T(hiong'o) .... **CLC 3, 7, 13**
　　See also Ngugi wa Thiong'o

Ngugi wa Thiong'o 1938- ... **CLC 36; BLC; DAM MULT, NOV**
　　See also Ngugi, James T(hiong'o)
　　See also BW 2; CA 81-84; CANR 27, 58; DLB 125; MTCW

Nichol, B(arrie) P(hillip) 1944-1988 .. **CLC 18**
　　See also CA 53-56; DLB 53; SATA 66

Nichols, John (Treadwell) 1940- .... **CLC 38**
　　See also CA 9-12R; CAAS 2; CANR 6; DLBY 82

Nichols, Leigh
　　See Koontz, Dean R(ay)

Nichols, Peter (Richard) 1927-　　**CLC 5, 36, 65**
　　See also CA 104; CANR 33; DLB 13; MTCW

Nicolas, F. R. E.
　　See Freeling, Nicolas

Niedecker, Lorine 1903-1970 .... **CLC 10, 42; DAM POET**
　　See also CA 25-28; CAP 2; DLB 48

Nietzsche, Friedrich (Wilhelm) 1844-1900　　**TCLC 10, 18, 55**
　　See also CA 107; 121; DLB 129

Nievo, Ippolito 1831-1861 .... **NCLC 22**

Nightingale, Anne Redmon 1943-
　　See Redmon, Anne
　　See also CA 103

Nik. T. O.
　　See Annensky, Innokenty (Fyodorovich)

Nin, Anais 1903-1977 .... **CLC 1, 4, 8, 11, 14, 60; DAM NOV, POP; SSC 10**
　　See also AITN 2; CA 13-16R; 69-72; CANR 22, 53; DLB 2, 4, 152; MTCW

Nishiwaki, Junzaburo 1894-1982 .... **PC 15**
　　See also CA 107

Nissenson, Hugh 1933- .... **CLC 4, 9**
　　See also CA 17-20R; CANR 27; DLB 28

Niven, Larry .... **CLC 8**
　　See also Niven, Laurence Van Cott
　　See also DLB 8

Niven, Laurence Van Cott 1938-
　　See Niven, Larry
　　See also CA 21-24R; CAAS 12; CANR 14, 44, 66; DAM POP; MTCW; SATA 95

Nixon, Agnes Eckhardt 1927- .... **CLC 21**
　　See also CA 110

Nizan, Paul 1905-1940 .... **TCLC 40**
　　See also CA 161; DLB 72

Nkosi, Lewis 1936- ...... **CLC 45; BLC; DAM MULT**
　　See also BW 1; CA 65-68; CANR 27; DLB 157

Nodier, (Jean) Charles (Emmanuel) 1780-1844　　**NCLC 19**
　　See also DLB 119

Noguchi, Yone 1875-1947 .... **TCLC 80**

Nolan, Christopher 1965- .... **CLC 58**
　　See also CA 111

Noon, Jeff 1957- .... **CLC 91**
　　See also CA 148

Norden, Charles
　　See Durrell, Lawrence (George)

Nordhoff, Charles (Bernard) 1887-1947　　**TCLC 23**
　　See also CA 108; DLB 9; SATA 23

Norfolk, Lawrence 1963- .... **CLC 76**
　　See also CA 144

Norman, Marsha 1947- .... **CLC 28; DAM DRAM; DC 8**
　　See also CA 105; CABS 3; CANR 41; DLBY 84

Norris, Frank 1870-1902 .... **SSC 28**
　　See also Norris, (Benjamin) Frank(lin, Jr.)
　　See also CDALB 1865-1917; DLB 12, 71, 186

Norris, (Benjamin) Frank(lin, Jr.) 1870-1902　　**TCLC 24**
　　See also Norris, Frank
　　See also CA 110; 160

Norris, Leslie 1921- .... **CLC 14**
　　See also CA 11-12; CANR 14; CAP 1; DLB 27

North, Andrew
　　See Norton, Andre

North, Anthony
　　See Koontz, Dean R(ay)

North, Captain George
　　See Stevenson, Robert Louis (Balfour)

North, Milou
　　See Erdrich, Louise

Northrup, B. A.
　　See Hubbard, L(afayette) Ron(ald)

North Staffs
　　See Hulme, T(homas) E(rnest)

Norton, Alice Mary
　　See Norton, Andre
　　See also MAICYA; SATA 1, 43

Norton, Andre 1912- .... **CLC 12**
　　See also Norton, Alice Mary
　　See also AAYA 14; CA 1-4R; CANR 68; DLB 8, 52; JRDA; MTCW; SATA 91

Norton, Caroline 1808-1877 .... **NCLC 47**
　　See also DLB 21, 159

Norway, Nevil Shute 1899-1960
　　See Shute, Nevil
　　See also CA 102; 93-96

Ondaatje, (Philip) Michael 1943- .... **CLC 14, 29, 51, 76; DAB; DAC; DAM MST**
See also CA 77-80; CANR 42; DLB 60

Oneal, Elizabeth 1934-
See Oneal, Zibby
See also CA 106; CANR 28; MAICYA; SATA 30, 82

Oneal, Zibby .... **CLC 30**
See also Oneal, Elizabeth
See also AAYA 5; CLR 13; JRDA

O'Neill, Eugene (Gladstone) 1888-1953 **TCLC 1, 6, 27, 49; DA; DAB; DAC; DAM DRAM, MST; WLC**
See also AITN 1; CA 110; 132; CDALB 1929-1941; DLB 7; MTCW

Onetti, Juan Carlos 1909-1994 .... **CLC 7, 10; DAM MULT, NOV; SSC 23**
See also CA 85-88; 145; CANR 32, 63; DLB 113; HW; MTCW

O Nuallain, Brian 1911-1966
See O'Brien, Flann
See also CA 21-22; 25-28R; CAP 2

Ophuls, Max 1902-1957 .... **TCLC 79**
See also CA 113

Opie, Amelia 1769-1853 .... **NCLC 65**
See also DLB 116, 159

Oppen, George 1908-1984 .... **CLC 7, 13, 34**
See also CA 13-16R; 113; CANR 8; DLB 5, 165

Oppenheim, E(dward) Phillips 1866-1946 **TCLC 45**
See also CA 111; DLB 70

Opuls, Max
See Ophuls, Max

Origen c. 185-c. 254 .... **CMLC 19**

Orlovitz, Gil 1918-1973 .... **CLC 22**
See also CA 77-80; 45-48; DLB 2, 5

Orris
See Ingelow, Jean

Ortega y Gasset, Jose 1883-1955 ..... **TCLC 9; DAM MULT; HLC**
See also CA 106; 130; HW; MTCW

Ortese, Anna Maria 1914- .... **CLC 89**
See also DLB 177

Ortiz, Simon J(oseph) 1941- ... **CLC 45; DAM MULT, POET; PC 17**
See also CA 134; DLB 120, 175; NNAL

Orton, Joe .... **CLC 4, 13, 43; DC 3**
See also Orton, John Kingsley
See also CDBLB 1960 to Present; DLB 13

Orton, John Kingsley 1933-1967
See Orton, Joe
See also CA 85-88; CANR 35, 66; DAM DRAM; MTCW

Orwell, George .... **TCLC 2, 6, 15, 31, 51; DAB; WLC**
See also Blair, Eric (Arthur)
See also CDBLB 1945-1960; DLB 15, 98, 195

Osborne, David
See Silverberg, Robert

Osborne, George
See Silverberg, Robert

Osborne, John (James) 1929-1994 **CLC 1, 2, 5, 11, 45; DA; DAB; DAC; DAM DRAM, MST; WLC**
See also CA 13-16R; 147; CANR 21, 56; CDBLB 1945-1960; DLB 13; MTCW

Osborne, Lawrence 1958- .... **CLC 50**

Oshima, Nagisa 1932- .... **CLC 20**
See also CA 116; 121

Oskison, John Milton 1874-1947 ... **TCLC 35; DAM MULT**
See also CA 144; DLB 175; NNAL

Ossoli, Sarah Margaret (Fuller marchesa d') 1810-1850
See Fuller, Margaret
See also SATA 25

Ostrovsky, Alexander 1823-1886 ... **NCLC 30, 57**

Otero, Blas de 1916-1979 .... **CLC 11**
See also CA 89-92; DLB 134

Otto, Whitney 1955- .... **CLC 70**
See also CA 140

Ouida .... **TCLC 43**
See also De La Ramee, (Marie) Louise
See also DLB 18, 156

Ousmane, Sembene 1923- .... **CLC 66; BLC**
See also BW 1; CA 117; 125; MTCW

Ovid 43B.C.-18(?) **CMLC 7; DAM POET; PC 2**

Owen, Hugh
See Faust, Frederick (Schiller)

Owen, Wilfred (Edward Salter) 1893-1918 **TCLC 5, 27; DA; DAB; DAC; DAM MST, POET; PC 19; WLC**
See also CA 104; 141; CDBLB 1914-1945; DLB 20

Owens, Rochelle 1936- .... **CLC 8**
See also CA 17-20R; CAAS 2; CANR 39

Oz, Amos 1939- ... **CLC 5, 8, 11, 27, 33, 54; DAM NOV**
See also CA 53-56; CANR 27, 47, 65; MTCW

Ozick, Cynthia 1928- **CLC 3, 7, 28, 62; DAM NOV, POP; SSC 15**
See also BEST 90:1; CA 17-20R; CANR 23, 58; DLB 28, 152; DLBY 82; INT CANR-23; MTCW

Ozu, Yasujiro 1903-1963 .... **CLC 16**
See also CA 112

Pacheco, C.
See Pessoa, Fernando (Antonio Nogueira)

Pa Chin .... **CLC 18**
See also Li Fei-kan

Pack, Robert 1929- .... **CLC 13**
See also CA 1-4R; CANR 3, 44; DLB 5

Padgett, Lewis
See Kuttner, Henry

Padilla (Lorenzo), Heberto 1932- ...... **CLC 38**
See also AITN 1; CA 123; 131; HW

Page, Jimmy 1944- .... **CLC 12**

Page, Louise 1955- .... **CLC 40**
See also CA 140

Page, P(atricia) K(athleen) 1916- ... **CLC 7, 18; DAC; DAM MST; PC 12**
See also CA 53-56; CANR 4, 22, 65; DLB 68; MTCW

Page, Thomas Nelson 1853-1922 .... **SSC 23**
See also CA 118; DLB 12, 78; DLBD 13

Pagels, Elaine Hiesey 1943- .... **CLC 104**
See also CA 45-48; CANR 2, 24, 51

Paget, Violet 1856-1935
See Lee, Vernon
See also CA 104

Paget-Lowe, Henry
See Lovecraft, H(oward) P(hillips)

Paglia, Camille (Anna) 1947- .... **CLC 68**
See also CA 140

Paige, Richard
See Koontz, Dean R(ay)

Paine, Thomas 1737-1809 .... **NCLC 62**
See also CDALB 1640-1865; DLB 31, 43, 73, 158

Pakenham, Antonia
See Fraser, (Lady) Antonia (Pakenham)

Palamas, Kostes 1859-1943 .... **TCLC 5**
See also CA 105

Palazzeschi, Aldo 1885-1974 .... **CLC 11**
See also CA 89-92; 53-56; DLB 114

Paley, Grace 1922- ... **CLC 4, 6, 37; DAM POP; SSC 8**
See also CA 25-28R; CANR 13, 46; DLB 28; INT CANR-13; MTCW

Palin, Michael (Edward) 1943- .... **CLC 21**
See also Monty Python
See also CA 107; CANR 35; SATA 67

Palliser, Charles 1947- .... **CLC 65**
See also CA 136

Palma, Ricardo 1833-1919 .... **TCLC 29**

Pancake, Breece Dexter 1952-1979
See Pancake, Breece D'J
See also CA 123; 109

Peckinpah, (David) Sam(uel) 1925-1984 ... **CLC 20**
See also CA 109; 114

Pedersen, Knut 1859-1952
See Hamsun, Knut
See also CA 104; 119; CANR 63; MTCW

Peeslake, Gaffer
See Durrell, Lawrence (George)

Peguy, Charles Pierre 1873-1914 .... **TCLC 10**
See also CA 107

Pena, Ramon del Valle y
See Valle-Inclan, Ramon (Maria) del

Pendennis, Arthur Esquir
See Thackeray, William Makepeace

Penn, William 1644-1718 .... **LC 25**
See also DLB 24

PEPECE
See Prado (Calvo), Pedro

Pepys, Samuel 1633-1703 ... **LC 11; DA; DAB; DAC; DAM MST; WLC**
See also CDBLB 1660-1789; DLB 101

Percy, Walker 1916-1990 ... **CLC 2, 3, 6, 8, 14, 18, 47, 65; DAM NOV, POP**
See also CA 1-4R; 131; CANR 1, 23, 64; DLB 2; DLBY 80, 90; MTCW

Perec, Georges 1936-1982 .... **CLC 56**
See also CA 141; DLB 83

Percda (y Sanchez de Porrua), Jose Maria de 1833-1906 .... **TCLC 16**
See also CA 117

Pereda y Porrua, Jose Maria de
See Pereda (y Sanchez de Porrua), Jose Maria de

Peregoy, George Weems
See Mencken, H(enry) L(ouis)

Perelman, S(idney) J(oseph) 1904-1979 ... **CLC 3, 5, 9, 15, 23, 44, 49; DAM DRAM**
See also AITN 1, 2; CA 73-76; 89-92; CANR 18; DLB 11, 44; MTCW

Peret, Benjamin 1899-1959 .... **TCLC 20**
See also CA 117

Peretz, Isaac Loeb 1851(?)-1915 ... **TCLC 16; SSC 26**
See also CA 109

Peretz, Yitzkhok Leibush
See Peretz, Isaac Loeb

Perez Galdos, Benito 1843-1920 .... **TCLC 27**
See also CA 125; 153; HW

Perrault, Charles 1628-1703 .... **LC 2**
See also MAICYA; SATA 25

Perry, Brighton
See Sherwood, Robert E(mmet)

Perse, St.-John .... **CLC 4, 11, 46**
See also Leger, (Marie-Rene Auguste) Alexis Saint-Leger

Perutz, Leo 1882-1957 .... **TCLC 60**
See also DLB 81

Peseenz, Tulio F.
See Lopez y Fuentes, Gregorio

Pesetsky, Bette 1932- .... **CLC 28**
See also CA 133; DLB 130

Peshkov, Alexei Maximovich 1868-1936
See Gorky, Maxim
See also CA 105; 141; DA; DAC; DAM DRAM, MST, NOV

Pessoa, Fernando (Antonio Nogueira) 1898-1935
TCLC 27; HLC; PC 20
See also CA 125

Peterkin, Julia Mood 1880-1961 .... **CLC 31**
See also CA 102; DLB 9

Peters, Joan K(aren) 1945- .... **CLC 39**
See also CA 158

Peters, Robert L(ouis) 1924- .... **CLC 7**
See also CA 13-16R; CAAS 8; DLB 105

Petofi, Sandor 1823-1849 .... **NCLC 21**

Petrakis, Harry Mark 1923- .... **CLC 3**
See also CA 9-12R; CANR 4, 30

Petrarch 1304-1374 ... **CMLC 20; DAM POET; PC 8**

Petrov, Evgeny .... **TCLC 21**
See also Kataev, Evgeny Petrovich

Petry, Ann (Lane) 1908-1997 ..... **CLC 1, 7, 18**
See also BW 1; CA 5-8R; 157; CAAS 6; CANR 4, 46; CLR 12; DLB 76; JRDA; MAICYA; MTCW; SATA 5; SATA-Obit 94

Petursson, Halligrimur 1614-1674 .... **LC 8**

Phaedrus 18(?)B.C.-55(?) .... **CMLC 25**

Philips, Katherine 1632-1664 .... **LC 30**
See also DLB 131

Philipson, Morris H. 1926- .... **CLC 53**
See also CA 1-4R; CANR 4

Phillips, Caryl 1958- ... **CLC 96; DAM MULT**
See also BW 2; CA 141; CANR 63; DLB 157

Phillips, David Graham 1867-1911 **TCLC 44**
See also CA 108; DLB 9, 12

Phillips, Jack
See Sandburg, Carl (August)

Phillips, Jayne Anne 1952- .. **CLC 15, 33; SSC 16**
See also CA 101; CANR 24, 50; DLBY 80; INT CANR-24; MTCW

Phillips, Richard
See Dick, Philip K(indred)

Phillips, Robert (Schaeffer) 1938- ..... **CLC 28**
See also CA 17-20R; CAAS 13; CANR 8; DLB 105

Phillips, Ward
See Lovecraft, H(oward) P(hillips)

Piccolo, Lucio 1901-1969 .... **CLC 13**
See also CA 97-100; DLB 114

Pickthall, Marjorie L(owry) C(hristie) 1883-1922 .... **TCLC 21**
See also CA 107; DLB 92

Pico della Mirandola, Giovanni 1463-1494
LC 15

Piercy, Marge 1936- .... **CLC 3, 6, 14, 18, 27, 62**
See also CA 21-24R; CAAS 1; CANR 13, 43, 66; DLB 120; MTCW

Piers, Robert
See Anthony, Piers

Pieyre de Mandiargues, Andre 1909-1991
See Mandiargues, Andre Pieyre de
See also CA 103; 136; CANR 22

Pilnyak, Boris .... **TCLC 23**
See also Vogau, Boris Andreyevich

Pincherle, Alberto 1907-1990 ..... **CLC 11, 18; DAM NOV**
See also Moravia, Alberto
See also CA 25-28R; 132; CANR 33, 63; MTCW

Pinckney, Darryl 1953- .... **CLC 76**
See also BW 2; CA 143

Pindar 518B.C.-446B.C. ..... **CMLC 12; PC 19**
See also DLB 176

Pineda, Cecile 1942- .... **CLC 39**
See also CA 118

Pinero, Arthur Wing 1855-1934 .... **TCLC 32; DAM DRAM**
See also CA 110; 153; DLB 10

Pinero, Miguel (Antonio Gomez) 1946-1988
CLC 4, 55
See also CA 61-64; 125; CANR 29; HW

Pinget, Robert 1919-1997 .... **CLC 7, 13, 37**
See also CA 85-88; 160; DLB 83

Pink Floyd
See Barrett, (Roger) Syd; Gilmour, David; Mason, Nick; Waters, Roger; Wright, Rick

Pinkney, Edward 1802-1828 .... **NCLC 31**

Pinkwater, Daniel Manus 1941- .... **CLC 35**
See also Pinkwater, Manus
See also AAYA 1; CA 29-32R; CANR 12, 38; CLR 4; JRDA; MAICYA; SAAS 3; SATA 46, 76

Pinkwater, Manus
See Pinkwater, Daniel Manus
See also SATA 8

Pinsky, Robert 1940- .... CLC **9, 19, 38, 94;**
DAM POET
See also CA 29-32R; CAAS 4; CANR 58; DLBY
82

Pinta, Harold
See Pinter, Harold

Pinter, Harold 1930- CLC **1, 3, 6, 9, 11, 15,**
27, 58, 73; DA; DAB; DAC; DAM DRAM,
MST; WLC
See also CA 5-8R; CANR 33, 65; CDBLB 1960
to Present; DLB 13; MTCW

Piozzi, Hester Lynch (Thrale) 1741-1821
NCLC 57
See also DLB 104, 142

Pirandello, Luigi 1867-1936 .. TCLC **4, 29;**
DA; DAB; DAC; DAM DRAM, MST; DC
5; SSC 22; WLC
See also CA 104; 153

Pirsig, Robert M(aynard) 1928- CLC **4, 6,**
73; DAM POP
See also CA 53-56; CANR 42; MTCW; SATA
39

Pisarev, Dmitry Ivanovich 1840-1868 **NCLC**
25

Pix, Mary (Griffith) 1666-1709 .... LC **8**
See also DLB 80

Pixerecourt, (Rene Charles) Guilbert de 1773-
1844 ....NCLC **39**
See also DLB 192

Plaatje, Sol(omon) T(shekisho) 1876-1932
TCLC 73
See also BW 2; CA 141

Plaidy, Jean
See Hibbert, Eleanor Alice Burford

Planche, James Robinson 1796-1880 **NCLC**
42

Plant, Robert 1948- .... CLC **12**

Plante, David (Robert) 1940- . CLC **7, 23, 38;**
DAM NOV
See also CA 37-40R; CANR 12, 36, 58; DLBY
83; INT CANR-12; MTCW

Plath, Sylvia 1932-1963 ... CLC **1, 2, 3, 5, 9, 11,**
14, 17, 50, 51, 62; DA; DAB; DAC; DAM
MST, POET; PC 1; WLC
See also AAYA 13; CA 19-20; CANR 34; CAP
2; CDALB 1941-1968; DLB 5, 6, 152;
MTCW; SATA 96

Plato 428(?)B.C.-348(?)B.C. .... CMLC **8; DA;**
DAB; DAC; DAM MST; WLCS
See also DLB 176

Platonov, Andrei ....TCLC **14**
See also Klimentov, Andrei Platonovich

Platt, Kin 1911- .... CLC **26**
See also AAYA 11; CA 17-20R; CANR 11;
JRDA; SAAS 17; SATA 21, 86

Plautus c. 251B.C.-184B.C. .. CMLC **24; DC 6**

Plick et Plock
See Simenon, Georges (Jacques Christian)

Plimpton, George (Ames) 1927- .... CLC **36**
See also AITN 1; CA 21-24R; CANR 32; DLB
185; MTCW; SATA 10

Pliny the Elder c. 23-79 .... CMLC **23**

Plomer, William Charles Franklin 1903-1973
CLC **4, 8**
See also CA 21-22; CANR 34; CAP 2; DLB 20,
162, 191; MTCW; SATA 24

Plowman, Piers
See Kavanagh, Patrick (Joseph)

Plum, J.
See Wodehouse, P(elham) G(renville)

Plumly, Stanley (Ross) 1939- .... CLC **33**
See also CA 108; 110; DLB 5, 193; INT 110

Plumpe, Friedrich Wilhelm 1888-1931 ... TCLC
53
See also CA 112

Po Chu-i 772-846 .... CMLC **24**

Poe, Edgar Allan 1809-1849 NCLC **1, 16,**
55; DA; DAB; DAC; DAM MST, POET; PC
1; SSC 1, 22; WLC
See also AAYA 14; CDALB 1640-1865; DLB 3,
59, 73, 74; SATA 23

Poet of Titchfield Street, The
See Pound, Ezra (Weston Loomis)

Pohl, Frederik 1919- .... CLC **18; SSC 25**
See also AAYA 24; CA 61-64; CAAS 1; CANR
11, 37; DLB 8; INT CANR-11; MTCW; SATA 24

Poirier, Louis 1910-
See Gracq, Julien
See also CA 122; 126

Poitier, Sidney 1927- .... CLC **26**
See also BW 1; CA 117

Polanski, Roman 1933- .... CLC **16**
See also CA 77-80

Poliakoff, Stephen 1952- .... CLC **38**
See also CA 106; DLB 13

Police, The
See Copeland, Stewart (Armstrong); Summers,
Andrew James; Sumner, Gordon Matthew

Polidori, John William 1795-1821 .. NCLC **51**
See also DLB 116

Pollitt, Katha 1949- .... CLC **28**
See also CA 120; 122; CANR 66; MTCW

Pollock, (Mary) Sharon 1936- CLC **50; DAC;**
DAM DRAM, MST
See also CA 141; DLB 60

Polo, Marco 1254-1324 .... CMLC **15**

Polonsky, Abraham (Lincoln) 1910- CLC
92
See also CA 104; DLB 26; INT 104

Polybius c. 200B.C.-c. 118B.C. .... CMLC **17**
See also DLB 176

Pomerance, Bernard 1940- ..... CLC **13; DAM**
DRAM
See also CA 101; CANR 49

Ponge, Francis (Jean Gaston Alfred) 1899-1988
CLC **6, 18; DAM POET**
See also CA 85-88; 126; CANR 40

Pontoppidan, Henrik 1857-1943 ..... TCLC **29**

Poole, Josephine .... CLC **17**
See also Helyar, Jane Penelope Josephine
See also SAAS 2; SATA 5

Popa, Vasko 1922-1991 .... CLC **19**
See also CA 112; 148; DLB 181

Pope, Alexander 1688-1744 ....LC **3;**
DA; DAB; DAC; DAM MST, POET;
WLC
See also CDBLB 1660-1789; DLB 95, 101

Porter, Connie (Rose) 1959(?)- .... CLC **70**
See also BW 2; CA 142; SATA 81

Porter, Gene(va Grace) Stratton 1863(?)-1924
TCLC **21**
See also CA 112

Porter, Katherine Anne 1890-1980 ... CLC **1, 3,**
7, 10, 13, 15, 27, 101; DA; DAB; DAC;
DAM MST, NOV; SSC 4
See also AITN 2; CA 1-4R; 101; CANR 1, 65;
DLB 4, 9, 102; DLBD 12; DLBY 80; MTCW;
SATA 39; SATA-Obit 23

Porter, Peter (Neville Frederick) 1929- CLC
5, 13, 33
See also CA 85-88; DLB 40

Porter, William Sydney 1862-1910
See Henry, O.
See also CA 104; 131; CDALB 1865-1917; DA;
DAB; DAC; DAM MST; DLB 12, 78, 79;
MTCW; YABC 2

Portillo (y Pacheco), Jose Lopez
See Lopez Portillo (y Pacheco), Jose

Post, Melville Davisson 1869-1930 .... TCLC **39**
See also CA 110

Potok, Chaim 1929- ... CLC **2, 7, 14, 26; DAM**
NOV
See also AAYA 15; AITN 1, 2; CA 17-20R;
CANR 19, 35, 64; DLB 28, 152; INT CANR-
19; MTCW; SATA 33

Potter, (Helen) Beatrix 1866-1943
See Webb, (Martha) Beatrice (Potter)
See also MAICYA

Potter, Dennis (Christopher George) 1935-1994
CLC **58, 86**
See also CA 107; 145; CANR 33, 61; MTCW

Pound, Ezra (Weston Loomis) 1885-1972
CLC 1, 2, 3, 4, 5, 7, 10, 13, 18, 34, 48, 50;
DA; DAB; DAC; DAM MST, POET; PC 4;
WLC
See also CA 5-8R; 37-40R; CANR 40; CDALB
1917-1929; DLB 4, 45, 63; DLBD 15;
MTCW

Povod, Reinaldo 1959-1994 .... **CLC 44**
See also CA 136; 146

Powell, Adam Clayton, Jr. 1908-1972 . **CLC 89; BLC; DAM MULT**
See also BW 1; CA 102; 33-36R

Powell, Anthony (Dymoke) 1905- **CLC 1, 3, 7, 9, 10, 31**
See also CA 1-4R; CANR 1, 32, 62; CDBLB
1945-1960; DLB 15; MTCW

Powell, Dawn 1897-1965 .... **CLC 66**
See also CA 5-8R; DLBY 97

Powell, Padgett 1952- .... **CLC 34**
See also CA 126; CANR 63

Power, Susan 1961- .... **CLC 91**

Powers, J(ames) F(arl) 1917- **CLC 1, 4, 8, 57; SSC 4**
See also CA 1-4R; CANR 2, 61; DLB 130;
MTCW

Powers, John J(ames) 1945-
See Powers, John R.
See also CA 69-72

Powers, John R. .... **CLC 66**
See also Powers, John J(ames)

Powers, Richard (S.) 1957- .... **CLC 93**
See also CA 148

Pownall, David 1938- .... **CLC 10**
See also CA 89-92; CAAS 18; CANR 49; DLB 14

Powys, John Cowper 1872-1963 **CLC 7, 9, 15, 46**
See also CA 85-88; DLB 15; MTCW

Powys, T(heodore) F(rancis) 1875-1953
TCLC 9
See also CA 106; DLB 36, 162

Prado (Calvo), Pedro 1886-1952 .... **TCLC 75**
See also CA 131; HW

Prager, Emily 1952- .... **CLC 56**

Pratt, E(dwin) J(ohn) 1883(?)-1964 . **CLC 19; DAC; DAM POET**
See also CA 141; 93-96; DLB 92

Premchand .... **TCLC 21**
See also Srivastava, Dhanpat Rai

Preussler, Otfried 1923- .... **CLC 17**
See also CA 77-80; SATA 24

Prevert, Jacques (Henri Marie) 1900-1977
CLC 15
See also CA 77-80; 69-72; CANR 29, 61;
MTCW; SATA-Obit 30

Prevost, Abbe (Antoine Francois) 1697-1763
LC 1

Price, (Edward) Reynolds 1933- **CLC 3, 6, 13, 43, 50, 63; DAM NOV; SSC 22**
See also CA 1-4R; CANR 1, 37, 57; DLB 2; INT
CANR-37

Price, Richard 1949- .... **CLC 6, 12**
See also CA 49-52; CANR 3; DLBY 81

Prichard, Katharine Susannah 1883-1969
CLC 46
See also CA 11-12; CANR 33; CAP 1; MTCW;
SATA 66

Priestley, J(ohn) B(oynton) 1894-1984 ... **CLC 2, 5, 9, 34; DAM DRAM, NOV**
See also CA 9-12R; 113; CANR 33; CDBLB 1914-
1945; DLB 10, 34, 77, 100, 139; DLBY 84;
MTCW

Prince 1958(?)- .... **CLC 35**

Prince, F(rank) T(empleton) 1912- .... **CLC 22**
See also CA 101; CANR 43; DLB 20

Prince Kropotkin
See Kropotkin, Peter (Alekseievich)

Prior, Matthew 1664-1721 .... **LC 4**
See also DLB 95

Prishvin, Mikhail 1873-1954 .... **TCLC 75**

Pritchard, William H(arrison) 1932- ... **CLC 34**
See also CA 65-68; CANR 23; DLB 111

Pritchett, V(ictor) S(awdon) 1900-1997 ... **CLC 5, 13, 15, 41; DAM NOV; SSC 14**
See also CA 61-64; 157; CANR 31, 63; DLB 15,
139; MTCW

Private 19022
See Manning, Frederic

Probst, Mark 1925- .... **CLC 59**
See also CA 130

Prokosch, Frederic 1908-1989 .... **CLC 4, 48**
See also CA 73-76; 128; DLB 48

Prophet, The
See Dreiser, Theodore (Herman Albert)

Prose, Francine 1947- .... **CLC 45**
See also CA 109; 112; CANR 46

Proudhon
See Cunha, Euclides (Rodrigues Pimenta) da

Proulx, Annie
See Proulx, E(dna) Annie

Proulx, E(dna) Annie 1935- ... **CLC 81; DAM POP**
See also CA 145; CANR 65

Proust, (Valentin-Louis-George-Eugene-) Marcel
1871-1922 .... **TCLC 7, 13, 33;
DA; DAB; DAC; DAM MST, NOV; WLC**
See also CA 104; 120; DLB 65; MTCW

Prowler, Harley
See Masters, Edgar Lee

Prus, Boleslaw 1845-1912 .... **TCLC 48**

Pryor, Richard (Franklin Lenox Thomas) 1940-
CLC 26
See also CA 122

Przybyszewski, Stanislaw 1868-1927 ..... **TCLC 36**
See also CA 160; DLB 66

Pteleon
See Grieve, C(hristopher) M(urray)
See also DAM POET

Puckett, Lute
See Masters, Edgar Lee

Puig, Manuel 1932-1990 .... **CLC 3, 5, 10, 28, 65; DAM MULT; HLC**
See also CA 45-48; CANR 2, 32, 63; DLB 113;
HW; MTCW

Pulitzer, Joseph 1847-1911 .... **TCLC 76**
See also CA 114; DLB 23

Purdy, Al(fred Wellington) 1918- ... **CLC 3, 6, 14, 50; DAC; DAM MST, POET**
See also CA 81-84; CAAS 17; CANR 42, 66;
DLB 88

Purdy, James (Amos) 1923- ... **CLC 2, 4, 10, 28, 52**
See also CA 33-36R; CAAS 1; CANR 19, 51;
DLB 2; INT CANR-19; MTCW

Pure, Simon
See Swinnerton, Frank Arthur

Pushkin, Alexander (Sergeyevich) 1799-1837
**NCLC 3, 27; DA; DAB; DAC; DAM
DRAM, MST, POET; PC 10; SSC 27; WLC**
See also SATA 61

P'u Sung-ling 1640-1715 .... **LC 3**

Putnam, Arthur Lee
See Alger, Horatio, Jr.

Puzo, Mario 1920- ... **CLC 1, 2, 6, 36, 107; DAM
NOV, POP**
See also CA 65-68; CANR 4, 42, 65; DLB 6;
MTCW

Pygge, Edward
See Barnes, Julian (Patrick)

Pyle, Ernest Taylor 1900-1945
See Pyle, Ernie
See also CA 115; 160

Pyle, Ernie 1900-1945 .... **TCLC 75**
See also Pyle, Ernest Taylor
See also DLB 29

Pym, Barbara (Mary Crampton) 1913-1980
CLC 13, 19, 37
See also CA 13-14; 97-100; CANR 13, 34; CAP
1; DLB 14; DLBY 87; MTCW

Pynchon, Thomas (Ruggles, Jr.) 1937- **CLC 2, 3, 6, 9, 11, 18, 33, 62, 72; DA; DAB; DAC; DAM MST, NOV, POP; SSC 14; WLC**
See also BEST 90:2; CA 17-20R; CANR 22, 46; DLB 2, 173; MTCW

Pythagoras c. 570B.C.-c. 500B.C. ... **CMLC 22**
See also DLB 176

Qian Zhongshu
See Ch'ien Chung-shu

Qroll
See Dagerman, Stig (Halvard)

Quarrington, Paul (Lewis) 1953- .... **CLC 65**
See also CA 129; CANR 62

Quasimodo, Salvatore 1901-1968 ...... **CLC 10**
See also CA 13-16; 25-28R; CAP 1; DLB 114; MTCW

Quay, Stephen 1947- .... **CLC 95**

Quay, Timothy 1947- .... **CLC 95**

Queen, Ellery ....**CLC 3, 11**
See also Dannay, Frederic; Davidson, Avram; Lee, Manfred B(ennington); Marlowe, Stephen; Sturgeon, Theodore (Hamilton); Vance, John Holbrook

Queen, Ellery, Jr.
See Dannay, Frederic; Lee, Manfred B(ennington)

Queneau, Raymond 1903-1976   **CLC 2, 5, 10, 42**
See also CA 77-80; 69-72; CANR 32; DLB 72; MTCW

Quevedo, Francisco de 1580-1645 .... **LC 23**

Quiller-Couch, SirArthur Thomas 1863-1944 **TCLC 53**
See also CA 118; DLB 135, 153, 190

Quin, Ann (Marie) 1936-1973 .... **CLC 6**
See also CA 9-12R; 45-48; DLB 14

Quinn, Martin
See Smith, Martin Cruz

Quinn, Peter 1947- .... **CLC 91**

Quinn, Simon
See Smith, Martin Cruz

Quiroga, Horacio (Sylvestre) 1878-1937 **TCLC 20; DAM MULT; HLC**
See also CA 117; 131; HW; MTCW

Quoirez, Francoise 1935- .... **CLC 9**
See also Sagan, Francoise
See also CA 49-52; CANR 6, 39; MTCW

Raabe, Wilhelm 1831-1910 .... **TCLC 45**
See also DLB 129

Rabe, David (William) 1940- .... **CLC 4, 8, 33; DAM DRAM**
See also CA 85-88; CABS 3; CANR 59; DLB 7

Rabelais, Francois 1483-1553 ...   **LC 5; DA; DAB; DAC; DAM MST; WLC**

Rabinovitch, Sholem 1859-1916
See Aleichem, Sholom
See also CA 104

Rachilde 1860-1953 .... **TCLC 67**
See also DLB 123, 192

Racine, Jean 1639-1699 .. **LC 28; DAB; DAM MST**

Radcliffe, Ann (Ward) 1764-1823   **NCLC 6, 55**
See also DLB 39, 178

Radiguet, Raymond 1903-1923 .... **TCLC 29**
See also CA 162; DLB 65

Radnoti, Miklos 1909-1944 .... **TCLC 16**
See also CA 118

Rado, James 1939-.............................. **CLC 17**
See also CA 105

Radvanyi, Netty 1900-1983
See Seghers, Anna
See also CA 85-88; 110

Rae, Ben
See Griffiths, Trevor

Raeburn, John (Hay) 1941- .... **CLC 34**
See also CA 57-60

Ragni, Gerome 1942-1991 .... **CLC 17**
See also CA 105; 134

Rahv, Philip 1908-1973 .... **CLC 24**
See also Greenberg, Ivan
See also DLB 137

Raimund, Ferdinand Jakob 1790-1836 **NCLC 69**
See also DLB 90

Raine, Craig 1944- ....**CLC 32, 103**
See also CA 108; CANR 29, 51; DLB 40

Raine, Kathleen (Jessie) 1908- .... **CLC 7, 45**
See also CA 85-88; CANR 46; DLB 20; MTCW

Rainis, Janis 1865-1929 .... **TCLC 29**

Rakosi, Carl 1903- .... **CLC 47**
See also Rawley, Callman
See also CAAS 5; DLB 193

Raleigh, Richard
See Lovecraft, H(oward) P(hillips)

Raleigh, Sir Walter 1554(?)-1618 ... **LC 31, 39**
See also CDBLB Before 1660; DLB 172

Rallentando, H. P.
See Sayers, Dorothy L(eigh)

Ramal, Walter
See de la Mare, Walter (John)

Ramon, Juan
See Jimenez (Mantecon), Juan Ramon

Ramos, Graciliano 1892-1953 .... **TCLC 32**

Rampersad, Arnold 1941- .... **CLC 44**
See also BW 2; CA 127; 133; DLB 111; INT 133

Rampling, Anne
See Rice, Anne

Ramsay, Allan 1684(?)-1758 .... **LC 29**
See also DLB 95

Ramuz, Charles-Ferdinand 1878-1947 ...**TCLC 33**
See also CA 165

Rand, Ayn 1905-1982 .... **CLC 3, 30, 44, 79; DA; DAC; DAM MST, NOV, POP; WLC**
See also AAYA 10; CA 13-16R; 105; CANR 27; MTCW

Randall, Dudley (Felker) 1914- ... **CLC 1; BLC; DAM MULT**
See also BW 1; CA 25-28R; CANR 23; DLB 41

Randall, Robert
See Silverberg, Robert

Ranger, Ken
See Creasey, John

Ransom, John Crowe 1888-1974 ... **CLC 2, 4, 5, 11, 24; DAM POET**
See also CA 5-8R; 49-52; CANR 6, 34; DLB 45, 63; MTCW

Rao, Raja 1909- .... **CLC 25, 56; DAM NOV**
See also CA 73-76; CANR 51; MTCW

Raphael, Frederic (Michael) 1931- ...... **CLC 2, 14**
See also CA 1-4R; CANR 1; DLB 14

Ratcliffe, James P.
See Mencken, H(enry) L(ouis)

Rathbone, Julian 1935- .... **CLC 41**
See also CA 101; CANR 34

Rattigan, Terence (Mervyn) 1911-1977 ... **CLC 7; DAM DRAM**
See also CA 85-88; 73-76; CDBLB 1945-1960; DLB 13; MTCW

Ratushinskaya, Irina 1954- .... **CLC 54**
See also CA 129; CANR 68

Raven, Simon (Arthur Noel) 1927- .... **CLC 14**
See also CA 81-84

Ravenna, Michael
See Welty, Eudora

Rawley, Callman 1903-
See Rakosi, Carl
See also CA 21-24R; CANR 12, 32

Rawlings, Marjorie Kinnan 1896-1953 ... **TCLC 4**
See also AAYA 20; CA 104; 137; DLB 9, 22, 102; JRDA; MAICYA; YABC 1

Ray, Satyajit 1921-1992 .... **CLC 16, 76; DAM MULT**
See also CA 114; 137

Read, Herbert Edward 1893-1968 .... **CLC 4**
See also CA 85-88; 25-28R; DLB 20, 149

Read, Piers Paul 1941- .... **CLC 4, 10, 25**
See also CA 21-24R; CANR 38; DLB 14; SATA 21

Reade, Charles 1814-1884 .... **NCLC 2**
See also DLB 21

Reade, Hamish
See Gray, Simon (James Holliday)

Reading, Peter 1946- .... **CLC 47**
See also CA 103; CANR 46; DLB 40

Reaney, James 1926- **CLC 13; DAC; DAM MST**
See also CA 41-44R; CAAS 15; CANR 42; DLB 68; SATA 43

Rebreanu, Liviu 1885-1944 .... **TCLC 28**
See also CA 165

Rechy, John (Francisco) 1934- **CLC 1, 7, 14, 18, 107; DAM MULT; HLC**
See also CA 5-8R; CAAS 4; CANR 6, 32, 64; DLB 122; DLBY 82; HW; INT CANR-6

Redcam, Tom 1870-1933 .... **TCLC 25**

Reddin, Keith .... **CLC 67**

Redgrove, Peter (William) 1932- ... **CLC 6, 41**
See also CA 1-4R; CANR 3, 39; DLB 40

Redmon, Anne .... **CLC 22**
See also Nightingale, Anne Redmon
See also DLBY 86

Reed, Eliot
See Ambler, Eric

Reed, Ishmael 1938- **CLC 2, 3, 5, 6, 13, 32, 60; BLC; DAM MULT**
See also BW 2; CA 21-24R; CANR 25, 48; DLB 2, 5, 33, 169; DLBD 8; MTCW

Reed, John (Silas) 1887-1920 .... **TCLC 9**
See also CA 106

Reed, Lou .... **CLC 21**
See also Firbank, Louis

Reeve, Clara 1729-1807 .... **NCLC 19**
See also DLB 39

Reich, Wilhelm 1897-1957 .... **TCLC 57**

Reid, Christopher (John) 1949- .... **CLC 33**
See also CA 140; DLB 40

Reid, Desmond
See Moorcock, Michael (John)

Reid Banks, Lynne 1929-
See Banks, Lynne Reid
See also CA 1-4R; CANR 6, 22, 38; CLR 24; JRDA; MAICYA; SATA 22, 75

Reilly, William K.
See Creasey, John

Reiner, Max
See Caldwell, (Janet Miriam) Taylor (Holland)

Reis, Ricardo
See Pessoa, Fernando (Antonio Nogueira)

Remarque, Erich Maria 1898-1970. **CLC 21; DA; DAB; DAC; DAM MST, NOV**
See also CA 77-80; 29-32R; DLB 56; MTCW

Remizov, A.
See Remizov, Aleksei (Mikhailovich)

Remizov, A. M.
See Remizov, Aleksei (Mikhailovich)

Remizov, Aleksei (Mikhailovich) 1877-1957...**TCLC 27**
See also CA 125; 133

Renan, Joseph Ernest 1823-1892 .... **NCLC 26**

Renard, Jules 1864-1910 .... **TCLC 17**
See also CA 117

Renault, Mary .... **CLC 3, 11, 17**
See also Challans, Mary
See also DLBY 83

Rendell, Ruth (Barbara) 1930- .. **CLC 28, 48; DAM POP**
See also Vine, Barbara
See also CA 109; CANR 32, 52; DLB 87; INT CANR-32; MTCW

Renoir, Jean 1894-1979 .... **CLC 20**
See also CA 129; 85-88

Resnais, Alain 1922- .... **CLC 16**

Reverdy, Pierre 1889-1960 .... **CLC 53**
See also CA 97-100; 89-92

Rexroth, Kenneth 1905-1982 ... **CLC 1, 2, 6, 11, 22, 49; DAM POET; PC 20**
See also CA 5-8R; 107; CANR 14, 34, 63; CDALB 1941-1968; DLB 16, 48, 165; DLBY 82; INT CANR-14; MTCW

Reyes, Alfonso 1889-1959 .... **TCLC 33**
See also CA 131; HW

Reyes y Basoalto, Ricardo Eliecer Neftali
See Neruda, Pablo

Reymont, Wladyslaw (Stanislaw) 1868(?)-1925 **TCLC 5**
See also CA 104

Reynolds, Jonathan 1942- .... **CLC 6, 38**
See also CA 65-68; CANR 28

Reynolds, Joshua 1723-1792 .... **LC 15**
See also DLB 104

Reynolds, Michael Shane 1937- .... **CLC 44**
See also CA 65-68; CANR 9

Reznikoff, Charles 1894-1976 .... **CLC 9**
See also CA 33-36; 61-64; CAP 2; DLB 28, 45

Rezzori (d'Arezzo), Gregor von 1914- **CLC 25**
See also CA 122; 136

Rhine, Richard
See Silverstein, Alvin

Rhodes, Eugene Manlove 1869-1934 ... **TCLC 53**

R'hoone
See Balzac, Honore de

Rhys, Jean 1890(?)-1979 ... **CLC 2, 4, 6, 14, 19, 51; DAM NOV; SSC 21**
See also CA 25-28R; 85-88; CANR 35, 62; CDBLB 1945-1960; DLB 36, 117, 162; MTCW

Ribeiro, Darcy 1922-1997 .... **CLC 34**
See also CA 33-36R; 156

Ribeiro, Joao Ubaldo (Osorio Pimentel) 1941- **CLC 10, 67**
See also CA 81-84

Ribman, Ronald (Burt) 1932- .... **CLC 7**
See also CA 21-24R; CANR 46

Ricci, Nino 1959- .... **CLC 70**
See also CA 137

Rice, Anne 1941- .... **CLC 41; DAM POP**
See also AAYA 9; BEST 89:2; CA 65-68; CANR 12, 36, 53

Rice, Elmer (Leopold) 1892-1967 **CLC 7, 49; DAM DRAM**
See also CA 21-22; 25-28R; CAP 2; DLB 4, 7; MTCW

Rice, Tim(othy Miles Bindon) 1944- . **CLC 21**
See also CA 103; CANR 46

Rich, Adrienne (Cecile) 1929- **CLC 3, 6, 7, 11, 18, 36, 73, 76; DAM POET; PC 5**
See also CA 9-12R; CANR 20, 53; DLB 5, 67; MTCW

Rich, Barbara
See Graves, Robert (von Ranke)

Rich, Robert
See Trumbo, Dalton

Richard, Keith .... **CLC 17**
See also Richards, Keith

Richards, David Adams 1950- **CLC 59; DAC**
See also CA 93-96; CANR 60; DLB 53

Richards, I(vor) A(rmstrong) 1893-1979 **CLC 14, 24**
See also CA 41-44R; 89-92; CANR 34; DLB 27

Richards, Keith 1943-
See Richard, Keith
See also CA 107

Richardson, Anne
See Roiphe, Anne (Richardson)

Richardson, Dorothy Miller 1873-1957 **TCLC 3**
See also CA 104; DLB 36

Richardson, Ethel Florence (Lindesay) 1870-
1946
See Richardson, Henry Handel
See also CA 105

Richardson, Henry Handel .... **TCLC 4**
See also Richardson, Ethel Florence (Lindesay)

Richardson, John 1796-1852   **NCLC 55; DAC**
See also DLB 99

Richardson, Samuel 1689-1761 ..... **LC 1; DA;**
DAB; DAC; DAM MST, NOV; WLC
See also CDBLB 1660-1789; DLB 39

Richler, Mordecai 1931-   **CLC 3, 5, 9, 13,**
18, 46, 70; DAC; DAM MST, NOV
See also AITN 1; CA 65-68; CANR 31, 62; CLR
17; DLB 53; MAICYA; MTCW; SATA 44, 98;
SATA-Brief 27

Richter, Conrad (Michael) 1890-1968 **CLC 30**
See also AAYA 21; CA 5-8R; 25-28R; CANR
23; DLB 9; MTCW; SATA 3

Ricostranza, Tom
See Ellis, Trey

Riddell, Charlotte 1832-1906 .... **TCLC 40**
See also CA 165; DLB 156

Riding, Laura .... **CLC 3, 7**
See also Jackson, Laura (Riding)

Riefenstahl, Berta Helene Amalia 1902-
See Riefenstahl, Leni
See also CA 108

Riefenstahl, Leni .... **CLC 16**
See also Riefenstahl, Berta Helene Amalia

Riffe, Ernest
See Bergman, (Ernst) Ingmar

Riggs, (Rolla) Lynn 1899-1954 ...... **TCLC 56;**
DAM MULT
See also CA 144; DLB 175; NNAL

Riis, Jacob A(ugust) 1849-1914 ...... **TCLC 80**
See also CA 113; DLB 23

Riley, James Whitcomb 1849-1916   **TCLC**
51; DAM POET
See also CA 118; 137; MAICYA; SATA 17

Riley, Tex
See Creasey, John

Rilke, Rainer Maria 1875-1926   **TCLC 1, 6,**
19; DAM POET; PC 2
See also CA 104; 132; CANR 62; DLB 81;
MTCW

Rimbaud, (Jean Nicolas) Arthur 1854-1891
NCLC 4, 35; DA; DAB; DAC; DAM MST,
POET; PC 3; WLC

Rinehart, Mary Roberts 1876-1958 **TCLC 52**
See also CA 108

Ringmaster, The
See Mencken, H(enry) L(ouis)

Ringwood, Gwen(dolyn Margaret) Pharis 1910-
1984 .... **CLC 48**
See also CA 148; 112; DLB 88

Rio, Michel 19(?)- .... **CLC 43**

Ritsos, Giannes
See Ritsos, Yannis

Ritsos, Yannis 1909-1990 .... **CLC 6, 13, 31**
See also CA 77-80; 133; CANR 39, 61; MTCW

Ritter, Erika 1948(?)- .... **CLC 52**

Rivera, Jose Eustasio 1889-1928 .... **TCLC 35**
See also CA 162; HW

Rivers, Conrad Kent 1933-1968 .... **CLC 1**
See also BW 1; CA 85-88; DLB 41

Rivers, Elfrida
See Bradley, Marion Zimmer

Riverside, John
See Heinlein, Robert A(nson)

Rizal, Jose 1861-1896 .... **NCLC 27**

Roa Bastos, Augusto (Antonio) 1917- .... **C L C**
45; DAM MULT; HLC
See also CA 131; DLB 113; HW

Robbe-Grillet, Alain 1922- ... **CLC 1, 2, 4, 6, 8,**
10, 14, 43
See also CA 9-12R; CANR 33, 65; DLB 83;
MTCW

Robbins, Harold 1916-1997 .... **CLC 5; DAM**
NOV
See also CA 73-76; 162; CANR 26, 54; MTCW

Robbins, Thomas Eugene 1936-
See Robbins, Tom
See also CA 81-84; CANR 29, 59; DAM NOV,
POP; MTCW

Robbins, Tom .... **CLC 9, 32, 64**
See also Robbins, Thomas Eugene
See also BEST 90:3; DLBY 80

Robbins, Trina 1938- .... **CLC 21**
See also CA 128

Roberts, Charles G(eorge) D(ouglas) 1860-1943
TCLC 8
See also CA 105; CLR 33; DLB 92; SATA 88;
SATA-Brief 29

Roberts, Elizabeth Madox 1886-1941 ... **TCLC**
68
See also CA 111; DLB 9, 54, 102; SATA 33;
SATA-Brief 27

Roberts, Kate 1891-1985 .... **CLC 15**
See also CA 107; 116

Roberts, Keith (John Kingston) 1935- ... **CLC**
14
See also CA 25-28R; CANR 46

Roberts, Kenneth (Lewis) 1885-1957 **TCLC 23**
See also CA 109; DLB 9

Roberts, Michele (B.) 1949- .... **CLC 48**
See also CA 115; CANR 58

Robertson, Ellis
See Ellison, Harlan (Jay); Silverberg, Robert

Robertson, Thomas William 1829-1871
NCLC 35; DAM DRAM

Robeson, Kenneth
See Dent, Lester

Robinson, Edwin Arlington 1869-1935
TCLC 5; DA; DAC; DAM MST, POET; PC
1
See also CA 104; 133; CDALB 1865-1917; DLB
54; MTCW

Robinson, Henry Crabb 1775-1867   **NCLC 15**
See also DLB 107

Robinson, Jill 1936- .... **CLC 10**
See also CA 102; INT 102

Robinson, Kim Stanley 1952- .... **CLC 34**
See also CA 126

Robinson, Lloyd
See Silverberg, Robert

Robinson, Marilynne 1944- .... **CLC 25**
See also CA 116

Robinson, Smokey .... **CLC 21**
See also Robinson, William, Jr.

Robinson, William, Jr. 1940-
See Robinson, Smokey
See also CA 116

Robison, Mary 1949- .... **CLC 42, 98**
See also CA 113; 116; DLB 130; INT 116

Rod, Edouard 1857-1910 .... **TCLC 52**

Roddenberry, Eugene Wesley 1921-1991
See Roddenberry, Gene
See also CA 110; 135; CANR 37; SATA 45;
SATA-Obit 69

Roddenberry, Gene .... **CLC 17**
See also Roddenberry, Eugene Wesley
See also AAYA 5; SATA-Obit 69

Rodgers, Mary 1931- .... **CLC 12**
See also CA 49-52; CANR 8, 55; CLR 20; INT
CANR-8; JRDA; MAICYA; SATA 8

Rodgers, W(illiam) R(obert) 1909-1969 ... **CLC 7**
See also CA 85-88; DLB 20

Rodman, Eric
See Silverberg, Robert

Rodman, Howard 1920(?)-1985 .... **CLC 65**
See also CA 118

Rodman, Maia
See Wojciechowska, Maia (Teresa)

Rodriguez, Claudio 1934- .... **CLC 10**
See also DLB 134

Roelvaag, O(le) E(dvart) 1876-1931 **TCLC 17**
See also CA 117; DLB 9

Roethke, Theodore (Huebner) 1908-1963
**CLC 1, 3, 8, 11, 19, 46, 101; DAM POET;
PC 15**
See also CA 81-84; CABS 2; CDALB 1941-
1968; DLB 5; MTCW

Rogers, Samuel 1763-1855 .... **NCLC 69**
See also DLB 93

Rogers, Thomas Hunton 1927- .... **CLC 57**
See also CA 89-92; INT 89-92

Rogers, Will(iam Penn Adair) 1879-1935
TCLC 8, 71; DAM MULT
See also CA 105; 144; DLB 11; NNAL

Rogin, Gilbert 1929- .... **CLC 18**
See also CA 65-68; CANR 15

Rohan, Koda .... **TCLC 22**
See also Koda Shigeyuki

Rohlfs, Anna Katharine Green
See Green, Anna Katharine

Rohmer, Eric .... **CLC 16**
See also Scherer, Jean-Marie Maurice

Rohmer, Sax .... **TCLC 28**
See also Ward, Arthur Henry Sarsfield
See also DLB 70

Roiphe, Anne (Richardson) 1935- ... **CLC 3, 9**
See also CA 89-92; CANR 45; DLBY 80; INT
89-92

Rojas, Fernando de 1465-1541 .... **LC 23**

**Rolfe, Frederick (William Serafino Austin Lewis
Mary)** 1860-1913 .... **TCLC 12**
See also CA 107; DLB 34, 156

Rolland, Romain 1866-1944 .... **TCLC 23**
See also CA 118; DLB 65

Rolle, Richard c. 1300-c. 1349 .... **CMLC 21**
See also DLB 146

Rolvaag, O(le) E(dvart)
See Roelvaag, O(le) E(dvart)

Romain Arnaud, Saint
See Aragon, Louis

Romains, Jules 1885-1972 .... **CLC 7**
See also CA 85-88; CANR 34; DLB 65; MTCW

Romero, Jose Ruben 1890-1952 ..... **TCLC 14**
See also CA 114; 131; HW

Ronsard, Pierre de 1524-1585 ... **LC 6; PC 11**

Rooke, Leon 1934- .... **CLC 25, 34; DAM POP**
See also CA 25-28R; CANR 23, 53

Roosevelt, Theodore 1858-1919 ...... **TCLC 69**
See also CA 115; DLB 47, 186

Roper, William 1498-1578 .... **LC 10**

Roquelaure, A. N.
See Rice, Anne

Rosa, Joao Guimaraes 1908-1967 ...... **CLC 23**
See also CA 89-92; DLB 113

Rose, Wendy 1948- ... **CLC 85; DAM MULT;
PC 13**
See also CA 53-56; CANR 5, 51; DLB 175;
NNAL; SATA 12

Rosen, R. D.
See Rosen, Richard (Dean)

Rosen, Richard (Dean) 1949- .... **CLC 39**
See also CA 77-80; CANR 62; INT CANR-30

Rosenberg, Isaac 1890-1918 .... **TCLC 12**
See also CA 107; DLB 20

Rosenblatt, Joe .... **CLC 15**
See also Rosenblatt, Joseph

Rosenblatt, Joseph 1933-
See Rosenblatt, Joe
See also CA 89-92; INT 89-92

Rosenfeld, Samuel
See Tzara, Tristan

Rosenstock, Sami
See Tzara, Tristan

Rosenstock, Samuel
See Tzara, Tristan

Rosenthal, M(acha) L(ouis) 1917-1996 .... **CLC
28**
See also CA 1-4R; 152; CAAS 6; CANR 4, 51;
DLB 5; SATA 59

Ross, Barnaby
See Dannay, Frederic

Ross, Bernard L.
See Follett, Ken(neth Martin)

Ross, J. H.
See Lawrence, T(homas) E(dward)

Ross, Martin
See Martin, Violet Florence
See also DLB 135

Ross, (James) Sinclair 1908- ..**CLC 13; DAC;
DAM MST; SSC 24**
See also CA 73-76; DLB 88

Rossetti, Christina (Georgina) 1830-1894
**NCLC 2, 50, 66; DA; DAB; DAC; DAM
MST, POET; PC 7; WLC**
See also DLB 35, 163; MAICYA; SATA 20

Rossetti, Dante Gabriel 1828-1882 .... **NCLC
4; DA; DAB; DAC; DAM MST, POET;
WLC**
See also CDBLB 1832-1890; DLB 35

Rossner, Judith (Perelman) 1935-   **CLC 6, 9, 29**
See also AITN 2; BEST 90:3; CA 17-20R;
CANR 18, 51; DLB 6; INT CANR-18;
MTCW

Rostand, Edmond (Eugene Alexis) 1868-1918
**TCLC 6, 37; DA; DAB; DAC; DAM
DRAM, MST**
See also CA 104; 126; DLB 192; MTCW

Roth, Henry 1906-1995 .... **CLC 2, 6, 11, 104**
See also CA 11-12; 149; CANR 38, 63; CAP 1;
DLB 28; MTCW

Roth, Philip (Milton) 1933- ... **CLC 1, 2, 3, 4, 6,
9, 15, 22, 31, 47, 66, 86; DA; DAB; DAC;
DAM MST, NOV, POP; SSC 26; WLC**
See also BEST 90:3; CA 1-4R; CANR 1, 22, 36,
55; CDALB 1968-1988; DLB 2, 28, 173;
DLBY 82; MTCW

Rothenberg, Jerome 1931- .... **CLC 6, 57**
See also CA 45-48; CANR 1; DLB 5, 193

Roumain, Jacques (Jean Baptiste) 1907-1944
TCLC 19; BLC; DAM MULT
See also BW 1; CA 117; 125

Rourke, Constance (Mayfield) 1885-1941
TCLC 12
See also CA 107; YABC 1

Rousseau, Jean-Baptiste 1671-1741 .... **LC 9**

Rousseau, Jean-Jacques 1712-1778 ..   **LC 14,
36; DA; DAB; DAC; DAM MST; WLC**

Roussel, Raymond 1877-1933 .... **TCLC 20**
See also CA 117

Rovit, Earl (Herbert) 1927- .... **CLC 7**
See also CA 5-8R; CANR 12

Rowe, Nicholas 1674-1718 .... **LC 8**
See also DLB 84

Rowley, Ames Dorrance
See Lovecraft, H(oward) P(hillips)

Rowson, Susanna Haswell 1762(?)-1824
NCLC 5, 69
See also DLB 37

Roy, Arundhati 1960(?)- .... **CLC 109**
See also CA 163; DLBY 97

Roy, Gabrielle 1909-1983 ... **CLC 10, 14; DAB;
DAC; DAM MST**
See also CA 53-56; 110; CANR 5, 61; DLB 68;
MTCW

Royko, Mike 1932-1997 .... **CLC 109**
See also CA 89-92; 157; CANR 26

Rozewicz, Tadeusz 1921- ..... **CLC 9, 23; DAM
POET**
See also CA 108; CANR 36, 66; MTCW

Ruark, Gibbons 1941- .... **CLC 3**
See also CA 33-36R; CAAS 23; CANR 14, 31,
57; DLB 120

Rubens, Bernice (Ruth) 1923- ...... **CLC 19, 31**
See also CA 25-28R; CANR 33, 65; DLB 14; MTCW

Rubin, Harold
See Robbins, Harold

Rudkin, (James) David 1936- .... **CLC 14**
See also CA 89-92; DLB 13

Rudnik, Raphael 1933- .... **CLC 7**
See also CA 29-32R

Ruffian, M.
See Hasek, Jaroslav (Matej Frantisek)

Ruiz, Jose Martinez .... **CLC 11**
See also Martinez Ruiz, Jose

Rukeyser, Muriel 1913-1980   **CLC 6, 10, 15,
27; DAM POET; PC 12**
See also CA 5-8R; 93-96; CANR 26, 60; DLB
48; MTCW; SATA-Obit 22

Rule, Jane (Vance) 1931- .... **CLC 27**
See also CA 25-28R; CAAS 18; CANR 12; DLB
60

Rulfo, Juan 1918-1986 .... **CLC 8, 80; DAM
MULT; HLC; SSC 25**
See also CA 85-88; 118; CANR 26; DLB 113;
HW; MTCW

Rumi, Jalal al-Din 1297-1373 .... **CMLC 20**

Runeberg, Johan 1804-1877 .... **NCLC 41**

Runyon, (Alfred) Damon 1884(?)-1946 **TCLC
10**
See also CA 107; 165; DLB 11, 86, 171

Rush, Norman 1933- .... **CLC 44**
See also CA 121; 126; INT 126

Rushdie, (Ahmed) Salman 1947- **CLC 23, 31,
55, 100; DAB; DAC; DAM MST, NOV,
POP; WLCS**
See also BEST 89:3; CA 108; 111; CANR 33,
56; DLB 194; INT 111; MTCW

Rushforth, Peter (Scott) 1945- .... **CLC 19**
See also CA 101

Ruskin, John 1819-1900 .... **TCLC 63**
See also CA 114; 129; CDBLB 1832-1890; DLB
55, 163, 190; SATA 24

Russ, Joanna 1937- .... **CLC 15**
See also CA 25-28R; CANR 11, 31, 65; DLB 8;
MTCW

Russell, George William 1867-1935
See Baker, Jean H.
See also CA 104; 153; CDBLB 1890-1914;
DAM POET

Russell, (Henry) Ken(neth Alfred) 1927- **CLC
16**
See also CA 105

Russell, William Martin 1947- .... **CLC 60**
See also CA 164

Rutherford, Mark .... **TCLC 25**
See also White, William Hale
See also DLB 18

Ruyslinck, Ward 1929- .... **CLC 14**
See also Belser, Reimond Karel Maria de

Ryan, Cornelius (John) 1920-1974 ...... **CLC 7**
See also CA 69-72; 53-56; CANR 38

Ryan, Michael 1946- .... **CLC 65**
See also CA 49-52; DLBY 82

Ryan, Tim
See Dent, Lester

Rybakov, Anatoli (Naumovich) 1911- ... **CLC 23,
53**
See also CA 126; 135; SATA 79

Ryder, Jonathan
See Ludlum, Robert

Ryga, George 1932-1987 ... **CLC 14; DAC; DAM
MST**
See also CA 101; 124; CANR 43; DLB 60

S. H.
See Hartmann, Sadakichi

S. S.
See Sassoon, Siegfried (Lorraine)

Saba, Umberto 1883-1957 .... **TCLC 33**
See also CA 144; DLB 114

Sabatini, Rafael 1875-1950 .... **TCLC 47**
See also CA 162

Sabato, Ernesto (R.) 1911- ... **CLC 10, 23; DAM
MULT; HLC**
See also CA 97-100; CANR 32, 65; DLB 145;
HW; MTCW

Sacastru, Martin
See Bioy Casares, Adolfo

Sacher-Masoch, Leopold von 1836(?)-1895
NCLC 31

Sachs, Marilyn (Stickle) 1927- .... **CLC 35**
See also AAYA 2; CA 17-20R; CANR 13, 47;
CLR 2; JRDA; MAICYA; SAAS 2; SATA 3,
68

Sachs, Nelly 1891-1970 .... **CLC 14, 98**
See also CA 17-18; 25-28R; CAP 2

Sackler, Howard (Oliver) 1929-1982   **CLC 14**
See also CA 61-64; 108; CANR 30; DLB 7

Sacks, Oliver (Wolf) 1933- .... **CLC 67**
See also CA 53-56; CANR 28, 50; INT CANR-
28; MTCW

Sadakichi
See Hartmann, Sadakichi

Sade, Donatien Alphonse Francois Comte 1740-
1814 .... **NCLC 47**

Sadoff, Ira 1945- .... **CLC 9**
See also CA 53-56; CANR 5, 21; DLB 120

Saetone
See Camus, Albert

Safire, William 1929- .... **CLC 10**
See also CA 17-20R; CANR 31, 54

Sagan, Carl (Edward) 1934-1996 .... **CLC 30**
See also AAYA 2; CA 25-28R; 155; CANR 11,
36; MTCW; SATA 58; SATA-Obit 94

Sagan, Francoise .... **CLC 3, 6, 9, 17, 36**
See also Quoirez, Francoise
See also DLB 83

Sahgal, Nayantara (Pandit) 1927- ...... **CLC 41**
See also CA 9-12R; CANR 11

Saint, H(arry) F. 1941- .... **CLC 50**
See also CA 127

St. Aubin de Teran, Lisa 1953-
See Teran, Lisa St. Aubin de
See also CA 118; 126; INT 126

Saint Birgitta of Sweden c. 1303-1373 ... **CMLC 24**

Sainte-Beuve, Charles Augustin 1804-1869
NCLC 5

**Saint-Exupery, Antoine (Jean Baptiste Marie
Roger) de** 1900-1944 ... **TCLC 2, 56; DAM
NOV; WLC**
See also CA 108; 132; CLR 10; DLB 72;
MAICYA; MTCW; SATA 20

St. John, David
See Hunt, E(verette) Howard, (Jr.)

Saint-John Perse
See Leger, (Marie-Rene Auguste) Alexis Saint-
Leger

Saintsbury, George (Edward Bateman) 1845-
1933 .... **TCLC 31**
See also CA 160; DLB 57, 149

Sait Faik .... **TCLC 23**
See also Abasiyanik, Sait Faik

Saki .... **TCLC 3; SSC 12**
See also Munro, H(ector) H(ugh)

Sala, George Augustus .... **NCLC 46**

Salama, Hannu 1936- .... **CLC 18**

Salamanca, J(ack) R(ichard) 1922- ... **CLC 4, 15**
See also CA 25-28R

Sale, J. Kirkpatrick
See Sale, Kirkpatrick

Sale, Kirkpatrick 1937- .... **CLC 68**
See also CA 13-16R; CANR 10

Salinas, Luis Omar 1937- .... **CLC 90; DAM
MULT; HLC**
See also CA 131; DLB 82; HW

Salinas (y Serrano), Pedro 1891(?)-1951 ... **TCLC 17**
See also CA 117; DLB 134

Salinger, J(erome) D(avid) 1919- ... **CLC 1, 3, 8,
12, 55, 56; DA; DAB; DAC; DAM MST,
NOV, POP; SSC 2, 28; WLC**
See also AAYA 2; CA 5-8R; CANR 39; CDALB
1941-1968; CLR 18; DLB 2, 102, 173;
MAICYA; MTCW; SATA 67

Salisbury, John
See Caute, (John) David

Salter, James 1925- .... **CLC 7, 52, 59**
See also CA 73-76; DLB 130

Saltus, Edgar (Everton) 1855-1921 .. **TCLC 8**
See also CA 105

Saltykov, Mikhail Evgrafovich 1826-1889
NCLC 16

Samarakis, Antonis 1919- .... **CLC 5**
See also CA 25-28R; CAAS 16; CANR 36

Sanchez, Florencio 1875-1910 .... **TCLC 37**
See also CA 153; HW

Sanchez, Luis Rafael 1936- .... **CLC 23**
See also CA 128; DLB 145; HW

Sanchez, Sonia 1934- ...... **CLC 5; BLC; DAM
MULT; PC 9**
See also BW 2; CA 33-36R; CANR 24, 49; CLR
18; DLB 41; DLBD 8; MAICYA; MTCW;
SATA 22

Sand, George 1804-1876 ... **NCLC 2, 42, 57; DA;
DAB; DAC; DAM MST, NOV; WLC**
See also DLB 119, 192

Sandburg, Carl (August) 1878-1967 ... **CLC 1,
4, 10, 15, 35; DA; DAB; DAC; DAM MST,
POET; PC 2; WLC**
See also AAYA 24; CA 5-8R; 25-28R; CANR
35; CDALB 1865-1917; DLB 17, 54;
MAICYA; MTCW; SATA 8

Sandburg, Charles
See Sandburg, Carl (August)

Sandburg, Charles A.
See Sandburg, Carl (August)

Sanders, (James) Ed(ward) 1939- ...... **CLC 53**
See also CA 13-16R; CAAS 21; CANR 13, 44;
DLB 16

Sanders, Lawrence 1920-1998 ... **CLC 41; DAM
POP**
See also BEST 89:4; CA 81-84; 165; CANR 33,
62; MTCW

Sanders, Noah
See Blount, Roy (Alton), Jr.

Sanders, Winston P.
See Anderson, Poul (William)

Sandoz, Mari(e Susette) 1896-1966 ... **CLC 28**
See also CA 1-4R; 25-28R; CANR 17, 64; DLB
9; MTCW; SATA 5

Saner, Reg(inald Anthony) 1931- .... **CLC 9**
See also CA 65-68

Sannazaro, Jacopo 1456(?)-1530 .... **LC 8**

Sansom, William 1912-1976 . **CLC 2, 6; DAM
NOV; SSC 21**
See also CA 5-8R; 65-68; CANR 42; DLB 139;
MTCW

Santayana, George 1863-1952 .... **TCLC 40**
See also CA 115; DLB 54, 71; DLBD 13

Santiago, Danny .... **CLC 33**
See also James, Daniel (Lewis)
See also DLB 122

Santmyer, Helen Hoover 1895-1986 ... **CLC 33**
See also CA 1-4R; 118; CANR 15, 33; DLBY
84; MTCW

Santoka, Taneda 1882-1940 .... **TCLC 72**

Santos, Bienvenido N(uqui) 1911-1996 ... **CLC
22; DAM MULT**
See also CA 101; 151; CANR 19, 46

Sapper ....**TCLC 44**
See also McNeile, Herman Cyril

Sapphire 1950- .... **CLC 99**

Sappho fl. 6th cent. B.C.- .... **CMLC 3; DAM
POET; PC 5**
See also DLB 176

Sarduy, Severo 1937-1993 .... **CLC 6, 97**
See also CA 89-92; 142; CANR 58; DLB 113;
HW

Sargeson, Frank 1903-1982 .... **CLC 31**
See also CA 25-28R; 106; CANR 38

Sarmiento, Felix Ruben Garcia
See Dario, Ruben

Saroyan, William 1908-1981 ... **CLC 1, 8, 10, 29,
34, 56; DA; DAB; DAC; DAM DRAM,
MST, NOV; SSC 21; WLC**
See also CA 5-8R; 103; CANR 30; DLB 7, 9, 86;
DLBY 81; MTCW; SATA 23; SATA-Obit 24

Sarraute, Nathalie 1900- ... **CLC 1, 2, 4, 8, 10,
31, 80**
See also CA 9-12R; CANR 23, 66; DLB 83;
MTCW

Sarton, (Eleanor) May 1912-1995 ... **CLC 4, 14,
49, 91; DAM POET**
See also CA 1-4R; 149; CANR 1, 34, 55; DLB
48; DLBY 81; INT CANR-34; MTCW; SATA
36; SATA-Obit 86

Sartre, Jean-Paul 1905-1980 ... **CLC 1, 4, 7, 9,
13, 18, 24, 44, 50, 52; DA; DAB; DAC; DAM
DRAM, MST, NOV; DC 3; WLC**
See also CA 9-12R; 97-100; CANR 21; DLB 72;
MTCW

Sassoon, Siegfried (Lorraine) 1886-1967
**CLC 36; DAB; DAM MST, NOV, POET;
PC 12**
See also CA 104; 25-28R; CANR 36; DLB 20,
191; MTCW

Satterfield, Charles
See Pohl, Frederik

Saul, John (W. III) 1942- ... **CLC 46; DAM NOV,
POP**
See also AAYA 10; BEST 90:4; CA 81-84;
CANR 16, 40; SATA 98

Saunders, Caleb
See Heinlein, Robert A(nson)

Saura (Atares), Carlos 1932- .... **CLC 20**
See also CA 114; 131; HW

Sauser-Hall, Frederic 1887-1961 .... **CLC 18**
See also Cendrars, Blaise
See also CA 102; 93-96; CANR 36, 62;
MTCW

Saussure, Ferdinand de 1857-1913 ... **TCLC 49**

Savage, Catharine
See Brosman, Catharine Savage

Savage, Thomas 1915- .... **CLC 40**
See also CA 126; 132; CAAS 15; INT 132

Savan, Glenn 19(?)- .... **CLC 50**

Sayers, Dorothy L(eigh) 1893-1957 . **TCLC 2,
15; DAM POP**
See also CA 104; 119; CANR 60; CDBLB 1914-
1945; DLB 10, 36, 77, 100; MTCW

Sayers, Valerie 1952- .... **CLC 50**
See also CA 134; CANR 61

Sayles, John (Thomas) 1950- .... **CLC 7, 10, 14**
See also CA 57-60; CANR 41; DLB 44

Scammell, Michael 1935- .... **CLC 34**
See also CA 156

Scannell, Vernon 1922- .... **CLC 49**
See also CA 5-8R; CANR 8, 24, 57; DLB 27;
SATA 59

Scarlett, Susan
See Streatfeild, (Mary) Noel

Schaeffer, Susan Fromberg 1941- .... **CLC 6,
11, 22**
See also CA 49-52; CANR 18, 65; DLB 28; MTCW;
SATA 22

Schary, Jill
See Robinson, Jill

Schell, Jonathan 1943- .... **CLC 35**
See also CA 73-76; CANR 12

Schelling, Friedrich Wilhelm Joseph von 1775-
1854 .... **NCLC 30**
See also DLB 90

Schendel, Arthur van 1874-1946 .... **TCLC 56**

Scherer, Jean-Marie Maurice 1920-
See Rohmer, Eric
See also CA 110

Schevill, James (Erwin) 1920- .... **CLC 7**
See also CA 5-8R; CAAS 12

Schiller, Friedrich 1759-1805 .. **NCLC 39, 69;
DAM DRAM**
See also DLB 94

Schisgal, Murray (Joseph) 1926- .... **CLC 6**
See also CA 21-24R; CANR 48

Selzer, Richard 1928- .... **CLC 74**
See also CA 65-68; CANR 14

Sembene, Ousmane
See Ousmane, Sembene

Senancour, Etienne Pivert de 1770-1846
NCLC 16
See also DLB 119

Sender, Ramon (Jose) 1902-1982 ... **CLC 8;**
DAM MULT; HLC
See also CA 5-8R; 105; CANR 8; HW; MTCW

Seneca, Lucius Annaeus 4B.C.-65 ... **CMLC 6;**
DAM DRAM; DC 5

Senghor, Leopold Sedar 1906- ...**CLC 54; BLC;**
DAM MULT, POET
See also BW 2; CA 116; 125; CANR 47; MTCW

Serling, (Edward) Rod(man) 1924-1975 ...**CLC 30**
See also AAYA 14; AITN 1; CA 162; 57-60; DLB 26

Serna, Ramon Gomez de la
See Gomez de la Serna, Ramon

Serpieres
See Guillevic, (Eugene)

Service, Robert
See Service, Robert W(illiam)
See also DAB; DLB 92

Service, Robert W(illiam) 1874(?)-1958
TCLC 15; DA; DAC; DAM MST, POET; WLC
See also Service, Robert
See also CA 115; 140; SATA 20

Seth, Vikram 1952- ... **CLC 43, 90; DAM MULT**
See also CA 121; 127; CANR 50; DLB 120; INT 127

Seton, Cynthia Propper 1926-1982 ... **CLC 27**
See also CA 5-8R; 108; CANR 7

Seton, Ernest (Evan) Thompson 1860-1946
TCLC 31
See also CA 109; DLB 92; DLBD 13; JRDA;
SATA 18

Seton-Thompson, Ernest
See Seton, Ernest (Evan) Thompson

Settle, Mary Lee 1918- .... **CLC 19, 61**
See also CA 89-92; CAAS 1; CANR 44; DLB 6;
INT 89-92

Seuphor, Michel
See Arp, Jean

**Sevigne, Marie (de Rabutin-Chantal) Marquise
de** 1626-1696 .... **LC 11**

Sewall, Samuel 1652-1730 .... **LC 38**
See also DLB 24

Sexton, Anne (Harvey) 1928-1974 ... **CLC 2, 4,**
6, 8, 10, 15, 53; DA; DAB; DAC; DAM
MST, POET; PC 2; WLC
See also CA 1-4R; 53-56; CABS 2; CANR 3, 36;
CDALB 1941-1968; DLB 5, 169; MTCW;
SATA 10

Shaara, Michael (Joseph, Jr.) 1929-1988
CLC 15; DAM POP
See also AITN 1; CA 102; 125; CANR 52;
DLBY 83

Shackleton, C. C.
See Aldiss, Brian W(ilson)

Shacochis, Bob .... **CLC 39**
See also Shacochis, Robert G.

Shacochis, Robert G. 1951-
See Shacochis, Bob
See also CA 119; 124; INT 124

Shaffer, Anthony (Joshua) 1926- ...... **CLC 19;**
DAM DRAM
See also CA 110; 116; DLB 13

Shaffer, Peter (Levin) 1926- .... **CLC 5,**
14, 18, 37, 60; DAB; DAM DRAM, MST;
DC 7
See also CA 25-28R; CANR 25, 47; CDBLB
1960 to Present; DLB 13; MTCW

Shakey, Bernard
See Young, Neil

Shalamov, Varlam (Tikhonovich) 1907(?)-1982
CLC 18
See also CA 129; 105

Shamlu, Ahmad 1925- .... **CLC 10**

Shammas, Anton 1951- .... **CLC 55**

Shange, Ntozake 1948- .... **CLC 8,**
25, 38, 74; BLC; DAM DRAM, MULT; DC
3
See also AAYA 9; BW 2; CA 85-88; CABS 3;
CANR 27, 48; DLB 38; MTCW

Shanley, John Patrick 1950- .... **CLC 75**
See also CA 128; 133

Shapcott, Thomas W(illiam) 1935- .... **CLC 38**
See also CA 69-72; CANR 49

Shapiro, Jane ....**CLC 76**

Shapiro, Karl (Jay) 1913- .... **CLC 4, 8,**
15, 53
See also CA 1-4R; CAAS 6; CANR 1, 36, 66;
DLB 48; MTCW

Sharp, William 1855-1905 .... **TCLC 39**
See also CA 160; DLB 156

Sharpe, Thomas Ridley 1928-
See Sharpe, Tom
See also CA 114; 122; INT 122

Sharpe, Tom ....**CLC 36**
See also Sharpe, Thomas Ridley
See also DLB 14

Shaw, Bernard ....**TCLC 45**
See also Shaw, George Bernard
See also BW 1

Shaw, G. Bernard
See Shaw, George Bernard

Shaw, George Bernard 1856-1950 ... **TCLC 3, 9, 21;**
DA; DAB; DAC; DAM DRAM, MST; WLC
See also Shaw, Bernard
See also CA 104; 128; CDBLB 1914-1945; DLB
10, 57, 190; MTCW

Shaw, Henry Wheeler 1818-1885 .... **NCLC 15**
See also DLB 11

Shaw, Irwin 1913-1984 ... **CLC 7, 23, 34; DAM**
DRAM, POP
See also AITN 1; CA 13-16R; 112; CANR 21;
CDALB 1941-1968; DLB 6, 102; DLBY 84;
MTCW

Shaw, Robert 1927-1978 .... **CLC 5**
See also AITN 1; CA 1-4R; 81-84; CANR 4;
DLB 13, 14

Shaw, T. E.
See Lawrence, T(homas) E(dward)

Shawn, Wallace 1943- .... **CLC 41**
See also CA 112

Shea, Lisa 1953- .... **CLC 86**
See also CA 147

Sheed, Wilfrid (John Joseph) 1930- ... **CLC 2, 4,**
10, 53
See also CA 65-68; CANR 30, 66; DLB 6;
MTCW

Sheldon, Alice Hastings Bradley 1915(?)-1987
See Tiptree, James, Jr.
See also CA 108; 122; CANR 34; INT 108;
MTCW

Sheldon, John
See Bloch, Robert (Albert)

Shelley, Mary Wollstonecraft (Godwin) 1797-
1851 ...... **NCLC 14, 59; DA; DAB; DAC;**
DAM MST, NOV; WLC
See also AAYA 20; CDBLB 1789-1832; DLB
110, 116, 159, 178; SATA 29

Shelley, Percy Bysshe 1792-1822 ...**NCLC 18;**
DA; DAB; DAC; DAM MST, POET; PC 14;
WLC
See also CDBLB 1789-1832; DLB 96, 110, 158

Shepard, Jim 1956-............................. **CLC 36**
See also CA 137; CANR 59; SATA 90

Shepard, Lucius 1947- .... **CLC 34**
See also CA 128; 141

Shepard, Sam 1943- ... **CLC 4, 6, 17, 34, 41, 44;**
DAM DRAM; DC 5
See also AAYA 1; CA 69-72; CABS 3; CANR
22; DLB 7; MTCW

Shepherd, Michael
See Ludlum, Robert

Sherburne, Zoa (Morin) 1912- .... **CLC 30**
See also AAYA 13; CA 1-4R; CANR 3, 37;
MAICYA; SAAS 18; SATA 3

Sheridan, Frances 1724-1766 .... **LC 7**
See also DLB 39, 84

Sheridan, Richard Brinsley 1751-1816 ... **NCLC 5; DA; DAB; DAC; DAM DRAM, MST; DC 1; WLC**
See also CDBLB 1660-1789; DLB 89

Sherman, Jonathan Marc .... **CLC 55**

Sherman, Martin 1941(?)- .... **CLC 19**
See also CA 116; 123

Sherwin, Judith Johnson 1936- ...... **CLC 7, 15**
See also CA 25-28R; CANR 34

Sherwood, Frances 1940- .... **CLC 81**
See also CA 146

Sherwood, Robert E(mmet) 1896-1955
TCLC 3; DAM DRAM
See also CA 104; 153; DLB 7, 26

Shestov, Lev 1866-1938 .... **TCLC 56**

Shevchenko, Taras 1814-1861 .... **NCLC 54**

Shiel, M(atthew) P(hipps) 1865-1947 ... **T C L C 8**
See also Holmes, Gordon
See also CA 106; 160; DLB 153

Shields, Carol 1935- .... **CLC 91; DAC**
See also CA 81-84; CANR 51

Shields, David 1956- .... **CLC 97**
See also CA 124; CANR 48

Shiga, Naoya 1883-1971 .... **CLC 33; SSC 23**
See also CA 101; 33-36R; DLB 180

Shilts, Randy 1951-1994 .... **CLC 85**
See also AAYA 19; CA 115; 127; 144; CANR 45; INT 127

Shimazaki, Haruki 1872-1943
See Shimazaki Toson
See also CA 105; 134

Shimazaki Toson 1872-1943 .... **TCLC 5**
See also Shimazaki, Haruki
See also DLB 180

Sholokhov, Mikhail (Aleksandrovich) 1905-1984
CLC 7, 15
See also CA 101; 112; MTCW; SATA-Obit 36

Shone, Patric
See Hanley, James

Shreve, Susan Richards 1939- .... **CLC 23**
See also CA 49-52; CAAS 5; CANR 5, 38; MAICYA; SATA 46, 95; SATA-Brief 41

Shue, Larry 1946-1985 ... . **CLC 52; DAM DRAM**
See also CA 145; 117

Shu-Jen, Chou 1881-1936
See Lu Hsun
See also CA 104

Shulman, Alix Kates 1932- .... **CLC 2, 10**
See also CA 29-32R; CANR 43; SATA 7

Shuster, Joe 1914- .... **CLC 21**

Shute, Nevil .... **CLC 30**
See also Norway, Nevil Shute

Shuttle, Penelope (Diane) 1947- .... **CLC 7**
See also CA 93-96; CANR 39; DLB 14, 40

Sidney, Mary 1561-1621 .... **LC 19, 39**

Sidney, Sir Philip 1554-1586 ... **LC 19, 39; DA; DAB; DAC; DAM MST, POET**
See also CDBLB Before 1660; DLB 167

Siegel, Jerome 1914-1996 .... **CLC 21**
See also CA 116; 151

Siegel, Jerry
See Siegel, Jerome

Sienkiewicz, Henryk (Adam Alexander Pius) 1846-1916 .... **TCLC 3**
See also CA 104; 134

Sierra, Gregorio Martinez
See Martinez Sierra, Gregorio

Sierra, Maria (de la O'LeJarraga) Martinez
See Martinez Sierra, Maria (de la O'LeJarraga)

Sigal, Clancy 1926- .... **CLC 7**
See also CA 1-4R

Sigourney, Lydia Howard (Huntley) 1791-1865
NCLC 21
See also DLB 1, 42, 73

Siguenza y Gongora, Carlos de 1645-1700
LC 8

Sigurjonsson, Johann 1880-1919 .... **TCLC 27**

Sikelianos, Angelos 1884-1951 .... **TCLC 39**

Silkin, Jon 1930- .... **CLC 2, 6, 43**
See also CA 5-8R; CAAS 5; DLB 27

Silko, Leslie (Marmon) 1948- ..... **CLC 23, 74; DA; DAC; DAM MST, MULT, POP; WLCS**
See also AAYA 14; CA 115; 122; CANR 45, 65; DLB 143, 175; NNAL

Sillanpaa, Frans Eemil 1888-1964 ..... **CLC 19**
See also CA 129; 93-96; MTCW

Sillitoe, Alan 1928- .... **CLC 1, 3, 6, 10, 19, 57**
See also AITN 1; CA 9-12R; CAAS 2; CANR 8, 26, 55; CDBLB 1960 to Present; DLB 14, 139; MTCW; SATA 61

Silone, Ignazio 1900-1978 .... **CLC 4**
See also CA 25-28; 81-84; CANR 34; CAP 2; MTCW

Silver, Joan Micklin 1935- .... **CLC 20**
See also CA 114; 121; INT 121

Silver, Nicholas
See Faust, Frederick (Schiller)

Silverberg, Robert 1935- ... **CLC 7; DAM POP**
See also AAYA 24; CA 1-4R; CAAS 3; CANR 1, 20, 36; DLB 8; INT CANR-20; MAICYA; MTCW; SATA 13, 91

Silverstein, Alvin 1933- .... **CLC 17**
See also CA 49-52; CANR 2; CLR 25; JRDA; MAICYA; SATA 8, 69

Silverstein, Virginia B(arbara Opshelor) 1937-
CLC 17
See also CA 49-52; CANR 2; CLR 25; JRDA; MAICYA; SATA 8, 69

Sim, Georges
See Simenon, Georges (Jacques Christian)

Simak, Clifford D(onald) 1904-1988 ...**CLC 1, 55**
See also CA 1-4R; 125; CANR 1, 35; DLB 8; MTCW; SATA-Obit 56

Simenon, Georges (Jacques Christian) 1903-1989 ... **CLC 1, 2, 3, 8, 18, 47; DAM POP**
See also CA 85-88; 129; CANR 35; DLB 72; DLBY 89; MTCW

Simic, Charles 1938- ..... **CLC 6, 9, 22, 49, 68; DAM POET**
See also CA 29-32R; CAAS 4; CANR 12, 33, 52, 61; DLB 105

Simmel, Georg 1858-1918 .... **TCLC 64**
See also CA 157

Simmons, Charles (Paul) 1924- .... **CLC 57**
See also CA 89-92; INT 89-92

Simmons, Dan 1948- .... **CLC 44; DAM POP**
See also AAYA 16; CA 138; CANR 53

Simmons, James (Stewart Alexander) 1933-
CLC 43
See also CA 105; CAAS 21; DLB 40

Simms, William Gilmore 1806-1870 ... **NCLC 3**
See also DLB 3, 30, 59, 73

Simon, Carly 1945- .... **CLC 26**
See also CA 105

Simon, Claude 1913-1984 ... **CLC 4, 9, 15, 39; DAM NOV**
See also CA 89-92; CANR 33; DLB 83; MTCW

Simon, (Marvin) Neil 1927- ... **CLC 6, 11, 31, 39, 70; DAM DRAM**
See also AITN 1; CA 21-24R; CANR 26, 54; DLB 7; MTCW

Simon, Paul (Frederick) 1941(?)- .... **CLC 17**
See also CA 116; 153

Simonon, Paul 1956(?)- .... **CLC 30**

Simpson, Harriette
See Arnow, Harriette (Louisa) Simpson

Simpson, Louis (Aston Marantz) 1923- ... **CLC 4, 7, 9, 32; DAM POET**
See also CA 1-4R; CAAS 4; CANR 1, 61; DLB 5; MTCW

Simpson, Mona (Elizabeth) 1957- ...... **CLC 44**
See also CA 122; 135; CANR 68

Simpson, N(orman) F(rederick) 1919- ... **CLC 29**
See also CA 13-16R; DLB 13

Sinclair, Andrew (Annandale) 1935- ... **CLC 2, 14**
See also CA 9-12R; CAAS 5; CANR 14, 38; DLB 14; MTCW

Sinclair, Emil
See Hesse, Hermann

Sinclair, Iain 1943- .... **CLC 76**
See also CA 132

Sinclair, Iain MacGregor
See Sinclair, Iain

Sinclair, Irene
See Griffith, D(avid Lewelyn) W(ark)

Sinclair, Mary Amelia St. Clair 1865(?)-1946
See Sinclair, May
See also CA 104

Sinclair, May .... **TCLC 3, 11**
See also Sinclair, Mary Amelia St. Clair
See also DLB 36, 135

Sinclair, Roy
See Griffith, D(avid Lewelyn) W(ark)

Sinclair, Upton (Beall) 1878-1968 ... **CLC 1, 11, 15, 63; DA; DAB; DAC; DAM MST, NOV; WLC**
See also CA 5-8R; 25-28R; CANR 7; CDALB 1929-1941; DLB 9; INT CANR-7; MTCW; SATA 9

Singer, Isaac
See Singer, Isaac Bashevis

Singer, Isaac Bashevis 1904-1991 ...**CLC 1, 3, 6, 9, 11, 15, 23, 38, 69; DA; DAB; DAC; DAM MST, NOV; SSC 3; WLC**
See also AITN 1, 2; CA 1-4R; 134; CANR 1, 39; CDALB 1941-1968; CLR 1; DLB 6, 28, 52; DLBY 91; JRDA; MAICYA; MTCW; SATA 3, 27; SATA-Obit 68

Singer, Israel Joshua 1893-1944 ..... **TCLC 33**

Singh, Khushwant 1915- .... **CLC 11**
See also CA 9-12R; CAAS 9; CANR 6

Singleton, Ann
See Benedict, Ruth (Fulton)

Sinjohn, John
See Galsworthy, John

Sinyavsky, Andrei (Donatevich) 1925-1997
CLC 8
See also CA 85-88; 159

Sirin, V.
See Nabokov, Vladimir (Vladimirovich)

Sissman, L(ouis) E(dward) 1928-1976 ... **CLC 9, 18**
See also CA 21-24R; 65-68; CANR 13; DLB 5

Sisson, C(harles) H(ubert) 1914- .... **CLC 8**
See also CA 1-4R; CAAS 3; CANR 3, 48; DLB 27

Sitwell, Dame Edith 1887-1964 ... **CLC 2, 9, 67; DAM POET; PC 3**
See also CA 9-12R; CANR 35; CDBLB 1945-1960; DLB 20; MTCW

Siwaarmill, H. P.
See Sharp, William

Sjoewall, Maj 1935- .... **CLC 7**
See also CA 65-68

Sjowall, Maj
See Sjoewall, Maj

Skelton, Robin 1925-1997 .... **CLC 13**
See also AITN 2; CA 5-8R; 160; CAAS 5; CANR 28; DLB 27, 53

Skolimowski, Jerzy 1938- .... **CLC 20**
See also CA 128

Skram, Amalie (Bertha) 1847-1905 ... **TCLC 25**
See also CA 165

Skvorecky, Josef (Vaclav) 1924- ... **CLC 15, 39, 69; DAC; DAM NOV**
See also CA 61-64; CAAS 1; CANR 10, 34, 63; MTCW

Slade, Bernard .... **CLC 11, 46**
See also Newbound, Bernard Slade
See also CAAS 9; DLB 53

Slaughter, Carolyn 1946- .... **CLC 56**
See also CA 85-88

Slaughter, Frank G(ill) 1908- .... **CLC 29**
See also AITN 2; CA 5-8R; CANR 5; INT CANR-5

Slavitt, David R(ytman) 1935- .... **CLC 5, 14**
See also CA 21-24R; CAAS 3; CANR 41; DLB 5, 6

Slesinger, Tess 1905-1945 .... **TCLC 10**
See also CA 107; DLB 102

Slessor, Kenneth 1901-1971 .... **CLC 14**
See also CA 102; 89-92

Slowacki, Juliusz 1809-1849 .... **NCLC 15**

Smart, Christopher 1722-1771 ... **LC 3; DAM POET; PC 13**
See also DLB 109

Smart, Elizabeth 1913-1986 .... **CLC 54**
See also CA 81-84; 118; DLB 88

Smiley, Jane (Graves) 1949- .... **CLC 53, 76; DAM POP**
See also CA 104; CANR 30, 50; INT CANR-30

Smith, A(rthur) J(ames) M(arshall) 1902-1980
CLC 15; DAC
See also CA 1-4R; 102; CANR 4; DLB 88

Smith, Adam 1723-1790 .... **LC 36**
See also DLB 104

Smith, Alexander 1829-1867 .... **NCLC 59**
See also DLB 32, 55

Smith, Anna Deavere 1950- .... **CLC 86**
See also CA 133

Smith, Betty (Wehner) 1896-1972 ..... **CLC 19**
See also CA 5-8R; 33-36R; DLBY 82; SATA 6

Smith, Charlotte (Turner) 1749-1806 ... **NCLC 23**
See also DLB 39, 109

Smith, Clark Ashton 1893-1961 .... **CLC 43**
See also CA 143

Smith, Dave .... **CLC 22, 42**
See also Smith, David (Jeddie)
See also CAAS 7; DLB 5

Smith, David (Jeddie) 1942-
See Smith, Dave
See also CA 49-52; CANR 1, 59; DAM POET

Smith, Florence Margaret 1902-1971
See Smith, Stevie
See also CA 17-18; 29-32R; CANR 35; CAP 2; DAM POET; MTCW

Smith, Iain Crichton 1928- .... **CLC 64**
See also CA 21-24R; DLB 40, 139

Smith, John 1580(?)-1631 .... **LC 9**

Smith, Johnston
See Crane, Stephen (Townley)

Smith, Joseph, Jr. 1805-1844 .... **NCLC 53**

Smith, Lee 1944- .... **CLC 25, 73**
See also CA 114; 119; CANR 46; DLB 143; DLBY 83; INT 119

Smith, Martin
See Smith, Martin Cruz

Smith, Martin Cruz 1942- ...... **CLC 25; DAM MULT, POP**
See also BEST 89:4; CA 85-88; CANR 6, 23, 43, 65; INT CANR-23; NNAL

Smith, Mary-Ann Tirone 1944- .... **CLC 39**
See also CA 118; 136

Smith, Patti 1946- .... **CLC 12**
See also CA 93-96; CANR 63

Smith, Pauline (Urmson) 1882-1959 ... **TCLC 25**

Smith, Rosamond
See Oates, Joyce Carol

Smith, Sheila Kaye
See Kaye-Smith, Sheila

Smith, Stevie .... **CLC 3, 8, 25, 44; PC 12**
See also Smith, Florence Margaret
See also DLB 20

Smith, Wilbur (Addison) 1933- .... **CLC 33**
See also CA 13-16R; CANR 7, 46, 66; MTCW

Smith, William Jay 1918- .... **CLC 6**
See also CA 5-8R; CANR 44; DLB 5; MAICYA;
SAAS 22; SATA 2, 68

Smith, Woodrow Wilson
See Kuttner, Henry

Smolenskin, Peretz 1842-1885 .... **NCLC 30**

Smollett, Tobias (George) 1721-1771 ..... **LC 2**
See also CDBLB 1660-1789; DLB 39, 104

Snodgrass, W(illiam) D(e Witt) 1926-**CLC 2, 6, 10, 18, 68; DAM POET**
See also CA 1-4R; CANR 6, 36, 65; DLB 5;
MTCW

Snow, C(harles) P(ercy) 1905-1980 ... **CLC 1, 4, 6, 9, 13, 19; DAM NOV**
See also CA 5-8R; 101; CANR 28; CDBLB
1945-1960; DLB 15, 77; MTCW

Snow, Frances Compton
See Adams, Henry (Brooks)

Snyder, Gary (Sherman) 1930- ... **CLC 1, 2, 5, 9, 32; DAM POET; PC 21**
See also CA 17-20R; CANR 30, 60; DLB 5, 16,
165

Snyder, Zilpha Keatley 1927- .... **CLC 17**
See also AAYA 15; CA 9-12R; CANR 38; CLR
31; JRDA; MAICYA; SAAS 2; SATA 1, 28,
75

Soares, Bernardo
See Pessoa, Fernando (Antonio Nogueira)

Sobh, A.
See Shamlu, Ahmad

Sobol, Joshua ....**CLC 60**

Socrates 469B.C.-399B.C. .... **CMLC 27**

Soderberg, Hjalmar 1869-1941 ...... **TCLC 39**

Sodergran, Edith (Irene)
See Soedergran, Edith (Irene)

Soedergran, Edith (Irene) 1892-1923 ...**TCLC 31**

Softly, Edgar
See Lovecraft, H(oward) P(hillips)

Softly, Edward
See Lovecraft, H(oward) P(hillips)

Sokolov, Raymond 1941- .... **CLC 7**
See also CA 85-88

Solo, Jay
See Ellison, Harlan (Jay)

Sologub, Fyodor ....**TCLC 9**
See also Teternikov, Fyodor Kuzmich

Solomons, Ikey Esquir
See Thackeray, William Makepeace

Solomos, Dionysios 1798-1857 .... **NCLC 15**

Solwoska, Mara
See French, Marilyn

Solzhenitsyn, Aleksandr I(sayevich) 1918-
CLC 1, 2, 4, 7, 9, 10, 18, 26, 34, 78; DA; DAB; DAC; DAM MST, NOV; WLC
See also AITN 1; CA 69-72; CANR 40, 65;
MTCW

Somers, Jane
See Lessing, Doris (May)

Somerville, Edith 1858-1949 .... **TCLC 51**
See also DLB 135

Somerville & Ross
See Martin, Violet Florence; Somerville, Edith

Sommer, Scott 1951- .... **CLC 25**
See also CA 106

Sondheim, Stephen (Joshua) 1930- ... **CLC 30, 39; DAM DRAM**
See also AAYA 11; CA 103; CANR 47, 68

Song, Cathy 1955-................................... **PC 21**
See also CA 154; DLB 169

Sontag, Susan 1933- ... **CLC 1, 2, 10, 13, 31, 105; DAM POP**
See also CA 17-20R; CANR 25, 51; DLB 2, 67;
MTCW

Sophocles 496(?)B.C.-406(?)B.C. ... **CMLC 2; DA; DAB; DAC; DAM DRAM, MST; DC 1; WLCS**
See also DLB 176

Sordello 1189-1269 .... **CMLC 15**

Sorel, Julia
See Drexler, Rosalyn

Sorrentino, Gilbert 1929- ... **CLC 3, 7, 14, 22, 40**
See also CA 77-80; CANR 14, 33; DLB 5, 173;
DLBY 80; INT CANR-14

Soto, Gary 1952- .. **CLC 32, 80; DAM MULT; HLC**
See also AAYA 10; CA 119; 125; CANR 50; CLR
38; DLB 82; HW; INT 125; JRDA; SATA 80

Soupault, Philippe 1897-1990 .... **CLC 68**
See also CA 116; 147; 131

Souster, (Holmes) Raymond 1921- ... **CLC 5, 14; DAC; DAM POET**
See also CA 13-16R; CAAS 14; CANR 13, 29,
53; DLB 88; SATA 63

Southern, Terry 1924(?)-1995 .... **CLC 7**
See also CA 1-4R; 150; CANR 1, 55; DLB 2

Southey, Robert 1774-1843 .... **NCLC 8**
See also DLB 93, 107, 142; SATA 54

Southworth, Emma Dorothy Eliza Nevitte 1819-
1899 ....**NCLC 26**

Souza, Ernest
See Scott, Evelyn

Soyinka, Wole 1934- ... **CLC 3, 5, 14, 36, 44; BLC; DA; DAB; DAC; DAM DRAM, MST, MULT; DC 2; WLC**
See also BW 2; CA 13-16R; CANR 27, 39; DLB
125; MTCW

Spackman, W(illiam) M(ode) 1905-1990 ... **CLC 46**
See also CA 81-84; 132

Spacks, Barry (Bernard) 1931- .... **CLC 14**
See also CA 154; CANR 33; DLB 105

Spanidou, Irini 1946-........................... **CLC 44**

Spark, Muriel (Sarah) 1918- ... **CLC 2, 3, 5, 8, 13, 18, 40, 94; DAB; DAC; DAM MST, NOV; SSC 10**
See also CA 5-8R; CANR 12, 36; CDBLB 1945-
1960; DLB 15, 139; INT CANR-12; MTCW

Spaulding, Douglas
See Bradbury, Ray (Douglas)

Spaulding, Leonard
See Bradbury, Ray (Douglas)

Spence, J. A. D.
See Eliot, T(homas) S(tearns)

Spencer, Elizabeth 1921- .... **CLC 22**
See also CA 13-16R; CANR 32, 65; DLB 6;
MTCW; SATA 14

Spencer, Leonard G.
See Silverberg, Robert

Spencer, Scott 1945- .... **CLC 30**
See also CA 113; CANR 51; DLBY 86

Spender, Stephen (Harold) 1909-1995 ... **CLC 1, 2, 5, 10, 41, 91; DAM POET**
See also CA 9-12R; 149; CANR 31, 54; CDBLB
1945-1960; DLB 20; MTCW

Spengler, Oswald (Arnold Gottfried) 1880-1936
TCLC 25
See also CA 118

Spenser, Edmund 1552(?)-1599 ... **LC 5, 39; DA; DAB; DAC; DAM MST, POET; PC 8; WLC**
See also CDBLB Before 1660; DLB 167

Spicer, Jack 1925-1965 .. **CLC 8, 18, 72; DAM POET**
See also CA 85-88; DLB 5, 16, 193

Spiegelman, Art 1948- .... **CLC 76**
See also AAYA 10; CA 125; CANR 41, 55

Spielberg, Peter 1929- .... **CLC 6**
See also CA 5-8R; CANR 4, 48; DLBY 81

Spielberg, Steven 1947- .... **CLC 20**
See also AAYA 8, 24; CA 77-80; CANR 32;
SATA 32

Spillane, Frank Morrison 1918-
See Spillane, Mickey
See also CA 25-28R; CANR 28, 63; MTCW;
SATA 66

Spillane, Mickey .... **CLC 3, 13**
See also Spillane, Frank Morrison

Spinoza, Benedictus de 1632-1677 .... **LC 9**

Spinrad, Norman (Richard) 1940- ..... **CLC 46**
See also CA 37-40R; CAAS 19; CANR 20; DLB
8; INT CANR-20

Spitteler, Carl (Friedrich Georg) 1845-1924
TCLC 12
See also CA 109; DLB 129

Spivack, Kathleen (Romola Drucker) 1938- ... **CLC 6**
See also CA 49-52

Spoto, Donald 1941- .... **CLC 39**
See also CA 65-68; CANR 11, 57

Springsteen, Bruce (F.) 1949- .... **CLC 17**
See also CA 111

Spurling, Hilary 1940- .... **CLC 34**
See also CA 104; CANR 25, 52

Spyker, John Howland
See Elman, Richard (Martin)

Squires, (James) Radcliffe 1917-1993 ... **CLC 51**
See also CA 1-4R; 140; CANR 6, 21

Srivastava, Dhanpat Rai 1880(?)-1936
See Premchand
See also CA 118

Stacy, Donald
See Pohl, Frederik

Stael, Germaine de 1766-1817
See Stael-Holstein, Anne Louise Germaine
Necker Baronn
See also DLB 119

Stael-Holstein, Anne Louise Germaine Necker
Baronn 1766-1817 .... **NCLC 3**
See also Stael, Germaine de
See also DLB 192

Stafford, Jean 1915-1979 ... **CLC 4, 7, 19, 68;
SSC 26**
See also CA 1-4R; 85-88; CANR 3, 65; DLB 2,
173; MTCW; SATA-Obit 22

Stafford, William (Edgar) 1914-1993 ... **CLC 4,
7, 29; DAM POET**
See also CA 5-8R; 142; CAAS 3; CANR 5, 22;
DLB 5; INT CANR-22

Stagnelius, Eric Johan 1793-1823 .. **NCLC 61**

Staines, Trevor
See Brunner, John (Kilian Houston)

Stairs, Gordon
See Austin, Mary (Hunter)

Stannard, Martin 1947- .... **CLC 44**
See also CA 142; DLB 155

Stanton, Elizabeth Cady 1815-1902 ... **TCLC 73**
See also DLB 79

Stanton, Maura 1946- .... **CLC 9**
See also CA 89-92; CANR 15; DLB 120

Stanton, Schuyler
See Baum, L(yman) Frank

Stapledon, (William) Olaf 1886-1950 ... **TCLC
22**
See also CA 111; 162; DLB 15

Starbuck, George (Edwin) 1931-1996 ... **CLC 53;
DAM POET**
See also CA 21-24R; 153; CANR 23

Stark, Richard
See Westlake, Donald E(dwin)

Staunton, Schuyler
See Baum, L(yman) Frank

Stead, Christina (Ellen) 1902-1983 ... **CLC 2, 5,
8, 32, 80**
See also CA 13-16R; 109; CANR 33, 40; MTCW

Stead, William Thomas 1849-1912 . **TCLC 48**

Steele, Richard 1672-1729 .... **LC 18**
See also CDBLB 1660-1789; DLB 84, 101

Steele, Timothy (Reid) 1948- .... **CLC 45**
See also CA 93-96; CANR 16, 50; DLB 120

Steffens, (Joseph) Lincoln 1866-1936 ... **TCLC
20**
See also CA 117

Stegner, Wallace (Earle) 1909-1993 ... **CLC 9,
49, 81; DAM NOV; SSC 27**
See also AITN 1; BEST 90:3; CA 1-4R; 141;
CAAS 9; CANR 1, 21, 46; DLB 9; DLBY 93;
MTCW

Stein, Gertrude 1874-1946 ... **TCLC 1, 6, 28, 48;
DA; DAB; DAC; DAM MST, NOV, POET;
PC 18; WLC**
See also CA 104; 132; CDALB 1917-1929; DLB
4, 54, 86; DLBD 15; MTCW

Steinbeck, John (Ernst) 1902-1968 ... **CLC 1, 5,
9, 13, 21, 34, 45, 75; DA; DAB; DAC; DAM
DRAM, MST, NOV; SSC 11; WLC**
See also AAYA 12; CA 1-4R; 25-28R; CANR 1,
35; CDALB 1929-1941; DLB 7, 9; DLBD 2;
MTCW; SATA 9

Steinem, Gloria 1934- .... **CLC 63**
See also CA 53-56; CANR 28, 51; MTCW

Steiner, George 1929- .... **CLC 24; DAM NOV**
See also CA 73-76; CANR 31, 67; DLB 67;
MTCW; SATA 62

Steiner, K. Leslie
See Delany, Samuel R(ay, Jr.)

Steiner, Rudolf 1861-1925 .... **TCLC 13**
See also CA 107

Stendhal 1783-1842 ... **NCLC 23, 46; DA; DAB;
DAC; DAM MST, NOV; SSC 27; WLC**
See also DLB 119

Stephen, Adeline Virginia
See Woolf, (Adeline) Virginia

Stephen, SirLeslie 1832-1904 .... **TCLC 23**
See also CA 123; DLB 57, 144, 190

Stephen, Sir Leslie
See Stephen, SirLeslie

Stephen, Virginia
See Woolf, (Adeline) Virginia

Stephens, James 1882(?)-1950 .... **TCLC 4**
See also CA 104; DLB 19, 153, 162

Stephens, Reed
See Donaldson, Stephen R.

Steptoe, Lydia
See Barnes, Djuna

Sterchi, Beat 1949- .... **CLC 65**

Sterling, Brett
See Bradbury, Ray (Douglas); Hamilton,
Edmond

Sterling, Bruce 1954- .... **CLC 72**
See also CA 119; CANR 44

Sterling, George 1869-1926 .... **TCLC 20**
See also CA 117; 165; DLB 54

Stern, Gerald 1925- .... **CLC 40, 100**
See also CA 81-84; CANR 28; DLB 105

Stern, Richard (Gustave) 1928- ..... **CLC 4, 39**
See also CA 1-4R; CANR 1, 25, 52; DLBY 87;
INT CANR 25

Sternberg, Josef von 1894-1969 .... **CLC 20**
See also CA 81-84

Sterne, Laurence 1713-1768 ... **LC 2; DA; DAB;
DAC; DAM MST, NOV; WLC**
See also CDBLB 1660-1789; DLB 39

Sternheim, (William Adolf) Carl 1878-1942
TCLC 8
See also CA 105; DLB 56, 118

Stevens, Mark 1951- .... **CLC 34**
See also CA 122

Stevens, Wallace 1879-1955 ... **TCLC 3, 12, 45;
DA; DAB; DAC; DAM MST, POET; PC 6;
WLC**
See also CA 104; 124; CDALB 1929-1941; DLB
54; MTCW

Stevenson, Anne (Katharine) 1933- ... **CLC 7,
33**
See also CA 17-20R; CAAS 9; CANR 9, 33; DLB
40; MTCW

Stevenson, Robert Louis (Balfour) 1850-1894
**NCLC 5, 14, 63; DA; DAB; DAC; DAM
MST, NOV; SSC 11; WLC**
See also AAYA 24; CDBLB 1890-1914; CLR 10,
11; DLB 18, 57, 141, 156, 174; DLBD 13;
JRDA; MAICYA; YABC 2

Summerforest, Ivy B.
See Kirkup, James

Summers, Andrew James 1942- .... **CLC 26**

Summers, Andy
See Summers, Andrew James

Summers, Hollis (Spurgeon, Jr.) 1916- ... **CLC 10**
See also CA 5-8R; CANR 3; DLB 6

Summers, (Alphonsus Joseph-Mary Augustus) Montague 1880-1948 .... **TCLC 16**
See also CA 118; 163

Sumner, Gordon Matthew 1951- .... **CLC 26**

Surtees, Robert Smith 1803-1864 ... **NCLC 14**
See also DLB 21

Susann, Jacqueline 1921-1974 .... **CLC 3**
See also AITN 1; CA 65-68; 53-56; MTCW

Su Shih 1036-1101 .... **CMLC 15**

Suskind, Patrick
See Sueskind, Patrick
See also CA 145

Sutcliff, Rosemary 1920-1992 ... **CLC 26; DAB; DAC; DAM MST, POP**
See also AAYA 10; CA 5-8R; 139; CANR 37; CLR 1, 37; JRDA; MAICYA; SATA 6, 44, 78; SATA-Obit 73

Sutro, Alfred 1863-1933 .... **TCLC 6**
See also CA 105; DLB 10

Sutton, Henry
See Slavitt, David R(ytman)

Svevo, Italo 1861-1928 .... **TCLC 2, 35; SSC 25**
See also Schmitz, Aron Hector

Swados, Elizabeth (A.) 1951- .... **CLC 12**
See also CA 97-100; CANR 49; INT 97-100

Swados, Harvey 1920-1972 .... **CLC 5**
See also CA 5-8R; 37-40R; CANR 6; DLB 2

Swan, Gladys 1934- .... **CLC 69**
See also CA 101; CANR 17, 39

Swarthout, Glendon (Fred) 1918-1992 ... **CLC 35**
See also CA 1-4R; 139; CANR 1, 47; SATA 26

Sweet, Sarah C.
See Jewett, (Theodora) Sarah Orne

Swenson, May 1919-1989 ... **CLC 4, 14, 61, 106; DA; DAB; DAC; DAM MST, POET; PC 14**
See also CA 5-8R; 130; CANR 36, 61; DLB 5; MTCW; SATA 15

Swift, Augustus
See Lovecraft, H(oward) P(hillips)

Swift, Graham (Colin) 1949- .... **CLC 41, 88**
See also CA 117; 122; CANR 46; DLB 194

Swift, Jonathan 1667-1745 .... **LC 1; DA; DAB; DAC; DAM MST, NOV, POET; PC 9; WLC**
See also CDBLB 1660-1789; DLB 39, 95, 101; SATA 19

Swinburne, Algernon Charles 1837-1909 **TCLC 8, 36; DA; DAB; DAC; DAM MST, POET; WLC**
See also CA 105; 140; CDBLB 1832-1890; DLB 35, 57

Swinfen, Ann .... **CLC 34**

Swinnerton, Frank Arthur 1884-1982 ... **CLC 31**
See also CA 108; DLB 34

Swithen, John
See King, Stephen (Edwin)

Sylvia
See Ashton-Warner, Sylvia (Constance)

Symmes, Robert Edward
See Duncan, Robert (Edward)

Symonds, John Addington 1840-1893 ... **NCLC 34**
See also DLB 57, 144

Symons, Arthur 1865-1945 .... **TCLC 11**
See also CA 107; DLB 19, 57, 149

Symons, Julian (Gustave) 1912-1994 ... **CLC 2, 14, 32**
See also CA 49-52; 147; CAAS 3; CANR 3, 33, 59; DLB 87, 155; DLBY 92; MTCW

Synge, (Edmund) J(ohn) M(illington) 1871-1909 **TCLC 6, 37; DAM DRAM; DC 2**
See also CA 104; 141; CDBLB 1890-1914; DLB 10, 19

Syruc, J.
See Milosz, Czeslaw

Szirtes, George 1948- .... **CLC 46**
See also CA 109; CANR 27, 61

Szymborska, Wislawa 1923- .... **CLC 99**
See also CA 154; DLBY 96

T. O., Nik
See Annensky, Innokenty (Fyodorovich)

Tabori, George 1914- .... **CLC 19**
See also CA 49-52; CANR 4

Tagore, Rabindranath 1861-1941 ... **TCLC 3, 53; DAM DRAM, POET; PC 8**
See also CA 104; 120; MTCW

Taine, Hippolyte Adolphe 1828-1893 ... **NCLC 15**

Talese, Gay 1932- .... **CLC 37**
See also AITN 1; CA 1-4R; CANR 9, 58; DLB 185; INT CANR-9; MTCW

Tallent, Elizabeth (Ann) 1954- .... **CLC 45**
See also CA 117; DLB 130

Tally, Ted 1952- .... **CLC 42**
See also CA 120; 124; INT 124

Tamayo y Baus, Manuel 1829-1898 ... **NCLC 1**

Tammsaare, A(nton) H(ansen) 1878-1940 **TCLC 27**
See also CA 164

Tam'si, Tchicaya U
See Tchicaya, Gerald Felix

Tan, Amy (Ruth) 1952- .... **CLC 59; DAM MULT, NOV, POP**
See also AAYA 9; BEST 89:3; CA 136; CANR 54; DLB 173; SATA 75

Tandem, Felix
See Spitteler, Carl (Friedrich Georg)

Tanizaki, Jun'ichiro 1886-1965 ... **CLC 8, 14, 28; SSC 21**
See also CA 93-96; 25-28R; DLB 180

Tanner, William
See Amis, Kingsley (William)

Tao Lao
See Storni, Alfonsina

Tarassoff, Lev
See Troyat, Henri

Tarbell, Ida M(inerva) 1857-1944 .. **TCLC 40**
See also CA 122; DLB 47

Tarkington, (Newton) Booth 1869-1946 **TCLC 9**
See also CA 110; 143; DLB 9, 102; SATA 17

Tarkovsky, Andrei (Arsenyevich) 1932-1986 **CLC 75**
See also CA 127

Tartt, Donna 1964(?)- .... **CLC 76**
See also CA 142

Tasso, Torquato 1544-1595 .... **LC 5**

Tate, (John Orley) Allen 1899-1979 ... **CLC 2, 4, 6, 9, 11, 14, 24**
See also CA 5-8R; 85-88; CANR 32; DLB 4, 45, 63; MTCW

Tate, Ellalice
See Hibbert, Eleanor Alice Burford

Tate, James (Vincent) 1943- .... **CLC 2, 6, 25**
See also CA 21-24R; CANR 29, 57; DLB 5, 169

Tavel, Ronald 1940- .... **CLC 6**
See also CA 21-24R; CANR 33

Taylor, C(ecil) P(hilip) 1929-1981 ...... **CLC 27**
See also CA 25-28R; 105; CANR 47

Taylor, Edward 1642(?)-1729 ... **LC 11; DA; DAB; DAC; DAM MST, POET**
See also DLB 24

Taylor, Eleanor Ross 1920- .... **CLC 5**
See also CA 81-84

Taylor, Elizabeth 1912-1975 .... **CLC 2, 4, 29**
See also CA 13-16R; CANR 9; DLB 139;
MTCW; SATA 13

Taylor, Frederick Winslow 1856-1915 ... **TCLC 76**

Taylor, Henry (Splawn) 1942- .... **CLC 44**
See also CA 33-36R; CAAS 7; CANR 31; DLB 5

Taylor, Kamala (Purnaiya) 1924-
See Markandaya, Kamala
See also CA 77-80

Taylor, Mildred D. .... **CLC 21**
See also AAYA 10; BW 1; CA 85-88; CANR 25;
CLR 9; DLB 52; JRDA; MAICYA; SAAS 5;
SATA 15, 70

Taylor, Peter (Hillsman) 1917-1994 **CLC 1, 4, 18, 37, 44, 50, 71; SSC 10**
See also CA 13-16R; 147; CANR 9, 50; DLBY 81, 94; INT CANR-9; MTCW

Taylor, Robert Lewis 1912- .... **CLC 14**
See also CA 1-4R; CANR 3, 64; SATA 10

Tchekhov, Anton
See Chekhov, Anton (Pavlovich)

Tchicaya, Gerald Felix 1931-1988 ... **CLC 101**
See also CA 129; 125

Tchicaya U Tam'si
See Tchicaya, Gerald Felix

Teasdale, Sara 1884-1933 .... **TCLC 4**
See also CA 104; 163; DLB 45; SATA 32

Tegner, Esaias 1782-1846 .... **NCLC 2**

Teilhard de Chardin, (Marie Joseph) Pierre
1881-1955 .... **TCLC 9**
See also CA 105

Temple, Ann
See Mortimer, Penelope (Ruth)

Tennant, Emma (Christina) 1937- ... **CLC 13, 52**
See also CA 65-68; CAAS 9; CANR 10, 38, 59;
DLB 14

Tenneshaw, S. M.
See Silverberg, Robert

Tennyson, Alfred 1809-1892 .... **NCLC 30, 65; DA; DAB; DAC; DAM MST, POET; PC 6; WLC**
See also CDBLB 1832-1890; DLB 32

Teran, Lisa St. Aubin de .... **CLC 36**
See also St. Aubin de Teran, Lisa

Terence 195(?)B.C.-159B.C. .... **CMLC 14; DC 7**

Teresa de Jesus, St. 1515-1582 .... **LC 18**

Terkel, Louis 1912-
See Terkel, Studs
See also CA 57-60; CANR 18, 45, 67; MTCW

Terkel, Studs .... **CLC 38**
See also Terkel, Louis
See also AITN 1

Terry, C. V.
See Slaughter, Frank G(ill)

Terry, Megan 1932- .... **CLC 19**
See also CA 77-80; CABS 3; CANR 43; DLB 7

Tertz, Abram
See Sinyavsky, Andrei (Donatevich)

Tesich, Steve 1943(?)-1996 .... **CLC 40, 69**
See also CA 105; 152; DLBY 83

Teternikov, Fyodor Kuzmich 1863-1927
See Sologub, Fyodor
See also CA 104

Tevis, Walter 1928-1984 .... **CLC 42**
See also CA 113

Tey, Josephine .... **TCLC 14**
See also Mackintosh, Elizabeth
See also DLB 77

Thackeray, William Makepeace 1811-1863
NCLC 5, 14, 22, 43; DA; DAB; DAC; DAM MST, NOV; WLC
See also CDBLB 1832-1890; DLB 21, 55, 159, 163; SATA 23

Thakura, Ravindranatha
See Tagore, Rabindranath

Tharoor, Shashi 1956- .... **CLC 70**
See also CA 141

Thelwell, Michael Miles 1939- .... **CLC 22**
See also BW 2; CA 101

Theobald, Lewis, Jr.
See Lovecraft, H(oward) P(hillips)

Theodorescu, Ion N. 1880-1967
See Arghezi, Tudor
See also CA 116

Theriault, Yves 1915-1983 ..... .**CLC 79; DAC; DAM MST**
See also CA 102; DLB 88

Theroux, Alexander (Louis) 1939- ... **CLC 2, 25**
See also CA 85-88; CANR 20, 63

Theroux, Paul (Edward) 1941- ... **CLC 5, 8, 11, 15, 28, 46; DAM POP**
See also BEST 89:4; CA 33-36R; CANR 20, 45;
DLB 2; MTCW; SATA 44

Thesen, Sharon 1946- .... **CLC 56**
See also CA 163

Thevenin, Denis
See Duhamel, Georges

Thibault, Jacques Anatole Francois 1844-1924
See France, Anatole
See also CA 106; 127; DAM NOV; MTCW

Thiele, Colin (Milton) 1920- .... **CLC 17**
See also CA 29-32R; CANR 12, 28, 53; CLR 27; MAICYA; SAAS 2; SATA 14, 72

Thomas, Audrey (Callahan) 1935- ... **CLC 7, 13, 37, 107; SSC 20**
See also AITN 2; CA 21-24R; CAAS 19; CANR 36, 58; DLB 60; MTCW

Thomas, D(onald) M(ichael) 1935- ... **CLC 13, 22, 31**
See also CA 61-64; CAAS 11; CANR 17, 45; CDBLB 1960 to Present; DLB 40; INT CANR-17; MTCW

Thomas, Dylan (Marlais) 1914-1953 ... **TCLC 1, 8, 45; DA; DAB; DAC; DAM DRAM, MST, POET; PC 2; SSC 3; WLC**
See also CA 104; 120; CANR 65; CDBLB 1945-1960; DLB 13, 20, 139; MTCW; SATA 60

Thomas, (Philip) Edward 1878-1917 ... **TCLC 10; DAM POET**
See also CA 106; 153; DLB 19

Thomas, Joyce Carol 1938- .... **CLC 35**
See also AAYA 12; BW 2; CA 113; 116; CANR 48; CLR 19; DLB 33; INT 116; JRDA; MAICYA; MTCW; SAAS 7; SATA 40, 78

Thomas, Lewis 1913-1993 .... **CLC 35**
See also CA 85-88; 143; CANR 38, 60; MTCW

Thomas, Paul
See Mann, (Paul) Thomas

Thomas, Piri 1928- .... **CLC 17**
See also CA 73-76; HW

Thomas, R(onald) S(tuart) 1913- ... **CLC 6, 13, 48; DAB; DAM POET**
See also CA 89-92; CAAS 4; CANR 30; CDBLB 1960 to Present; DLB 27; MTCW

Thomas, Ross (Elmore) 1926-1995 .... **CLC 39**
See also CA 33-36R; 150; CANR 22, 63

Thompson, Francis Clegg
See Mencken, H(enry) L(ouis)

Thompson, Francis Joseph 1859-1907 ... **TCLC 4**
See also CA 104; CDBLB 1890-1914; DLB 19

Thompson, Hunter S(tockton) 1939- ... **CLC 9, 17, 40, 104; DAM POP**
See also BEST 89:1; CA 17-20R; CANR 23, 46; DLB 185; MTCW

Thompson, James Myers
See Thompson, Jim (Myers)

Thompson, Jim (Myers) 1906-1977(?) ... **CLC 69**
See also CA 140

Thompson, Judith .... **CLC 39**

Thomson, James 1700-1748 .... **LC 16, 29, 40; DAM POET**
See also DLB 95

Thomson, James 1834-1882 ...**NCLC 18; DAM POET**
See also DLB 35

Thoreau, Henry David 1817-1862 .... **NCLC 7, 21, 61; DA; DAB; DAC; DAM MST; WLC**
See also CDALB 1640-1865; DLB 1

Thornton, Hall
See Silverberg, Robert

Thucydides c. 455B.C.-399B.C. ...... **CMLC 17**
See also DLB 176

Thurber, James (Grover) 1894-1961 ... **CLC 5, 11, 25; DA; DAB; DAC; DAM DRAM, MST, NOV; SSC 1**
See also CA 73-76; CANR 17, 39; CDALB 1929-1941; DLB 4, 11, 22, 102; MAICYA; MTCW; SATA 13

Thurman, Wallace (Henry) 1902-1934 ... **TCLC 6; BLC; DAM MULT**
See also BW 1; CA 104; 124; DLB 51

Ticheburn, Cheviot
See Ainsworth, William Harrison

Tieck, (Johann) Ludwig 1773-1853 ... **NCLC 5, 46**
See also DLB 90

Tiger, Derry
See Ellison, Harlan (Jay)

Tilghman, Christopher 1948(?)- .... **CLC 65**
See also CA 159

Tillinghast, Richard (Williford) 1940- ... **CLC 29**
See also CA 29-32R; CAAS 23; CANR 26, 51

Timrod, Henry 1828-1867 .... **NCLC 25**
See also DLB 3

Tindall, Gillian (Elizabeth) 1938- .... **CLC 7**
See also CA 21-24R; CANR 11, 65

Tiptree, James, Jr. .... **CLC 48, 50**
See also Sheldon, Alice Hastings Bradley
See also DLB 8

Titmarsh, Michael Angelo
See Thackeray, William Makepeace

Tocqueville, Alexis (Charles Henri Maurice Clerel Comte) 1805-1859 .... **NCLC 7, 63**

Tolkien, J(ohn) R(onald) R(euel) 1892-1973 **CLC 1, 2, 3, 8, 12, 38; DA; DAB; DAC; DAM MST, NOV, POP; WLC**
See also AAYA 10; AITN 1; CA 17-18; 45-48; CANR 36; CAP 2; CDBLB 1914-1945; DLB 15, 160; JRDA; MAICYA; MTCW; SATA 2, 32; SATA-Obit 24

Toller, Ernst 1893-1939 .... **TCLC 10**
See also CA 107; DLB 124

Tolson, M. B.
See Tolson, Melvin B(eaunorus)

Tolson, Melvin B(eaunorus) 1898(?)-1966 ... **CLC 36, 105; BLC; DAM MULT, POET**
See also BW 1; CA 124; 89-92; DLB 48, 76

Tolstoi, Aleksei Nikolaevich
See Tolstoy, Alexey Nikolaevich

Tolstoy, Alexey Nikolaevich 1882-1945 ... **TCLC 18**
See also CA 107; 158

Tolstoy, Count Leo
See Tolstoy, Leo (Nikolaevich)

Tolstoy, Leo (Nikolaevich) 1828-1910 ... **TCLC 4, 11, 17, 28, 44, 79; DA; DAB; DAC; DAM MST, NOV; SSC 9, 30; WLC**
See also CA 104; 123; SATA 26

Tomasi di Lampedusa, Giuseppe 1896-1957
See Lampedusa, Giuseppe (Tomasi) di
See also CA 111

Tomlin, Lily .... **CLC 17**
See also Tomlin, Mary Jean

Tomlin, Mary Jean 1939(?)-
See Tomlin, Lily
See also CA 117

Tomlinson, (Alfred) Charles 1927- ... **CLC 2, 4, 6, 13, 45; DAM POET; PC 17**
See also CA 5-8R; CANR 33; DLB 40

Tomlinson, H(enry) M(ajor) 1873-1958 **TCLC 71**
See also CA 118; 161; DLB 36, 100, 195

Tonson, Jacob
See Bennett, (Enoch) Arnold

Toole, John Kennedy 1937-1969 .... **CLC 19, 64**
See also CA 104; DLBY 81

Toomer, Jean 1894-1967 ..... **CLC 1, 4, 13, 22; BLC; DAM MULT; PC 7; SSC 1; WLCS**
See also BW 1; CA 85-88; CDALB 1917-1929; DLB 45, 51; MTCW

Torley, Luke
See Blish, James (Benjamin)

Tornimparte, Alessandra
See Ginzburg, Natalia

Torre, Raoul della
See Mencken, H(enry) L(ouis)

Torrey, E(dwin) Fuller 1937- .... **CLC 34**
See also CA 119

Torsvan, Ben Traven
See Traven, B.

Torsvan, Benno Traven
See Traven, B.

Torsvan, Berick Traven
See Traven, B.

Torsvan, Berwick Traven
See Traven, B.

Torsvan, Bruno Traven
See Traven, B.

Torsvan, Traven
See Traven, B.

Tournier, Michel (Edouard) 1924- ... **CLC 6, 23, 36, 95**
See also CA 49-52; CANR 3, 36; DLB 83; MTCW; SATA 23

Tournimparte, Alessandra
See Ginzburg, Natalia

Towers, Ivar
See Kornbluth, C(yril) M.

Towne, Robert (Burton) 1936(?)- ...... **CLC 87**
See also CA 108; DLB 44

Townsend, Sue .... **CLC 61**
See also Townsend, Susan Elaine
See also SATA 55, 93; SATA-Brief 48

Townsend, Susan Elaine 1946-
See Townsend, Sue
See also CA 119; 127; CANR 65; DAB; DAC; DAM MST

Townshend, Peter (Dennis Blandford) 1945- **CLC 17, 42**
See also CA 107

Tozzi, Federigo 1883-1920 .... **TCLC 31**
See also CA 160

Traill, Catharine Parr 1802-1899 ... **NCLC 31**
See also DLB 99

Trakl, Georg 1887-1914 .... **TCLC 5; PC 20**
See also CA 104; 165

Transtroemer, Tomas (Goesta) 1931- ... **CLC 52, 65; DAM POET**
See also CA 117; 129; CAAS 17

Transtromer, Tomas Gosta
See Transtroemer, Tomas (Goesta)

Traven, B. (?)-1969 .... **CLC 8, 11**
See also CA 19-20; 25-28R; CAP 2; DLB 9, 56; MTCW

Treitel, Jonathan 1959- .... **CLC 70**

Tremain, Rose 1943- .... **CLC 42**
See also CA 97-100; CANR 44; DLB 14

Tremblay, Michel 1942- . **CLC 29, 102; DAC; DAM MST**
See also CA 116; 128; DLB 60; MTCW

Trevanian .... **CLC 29**
See also Whitaker, Rod(ney)

Trevor, Glen
See Hilton, James

Trevor, William 1928- ... **CLC 7, 9, 14, 25, 71; SSC 21**
See also Cox, William Trevor
See also DLB 14, 139

Trifonov, Yuri (Valentinovich) 1925-1981 ... **CLC 45**
See also CA 126; 103; MTCW

Walker, Joseph A. 1935- ... **CLC 19; DAM DRAM, MST**
See also BW 1; CA 89-92; CANR 26; DLB 38

Walker, Margaret (Abigail) 1915-...**CLC 1, 6; BLC; DAM MULT; PC 20**
See also BW 2; CA 73-76; CANR 26, 54; DLB 76, 152; MTCW

Walker, Ted ....**CLC 13**
See also Walker, Edward Joseph
See also DLB 40

Wallace, David Foster 1962- ....**CLC 50**
See also CA 132; CANR 59

Wallace, Dexter
See Masters, Edgar Lee

Wallace, (Richard Horatio) Edgar 1875-1932
TCLC 57
See also CA 115; DLB 70

Wallace, Irving 1916-1990 ... **CLC 7, 13; DAM NOV, POP**
See also AITN 1; CA 1-4R; 132; CAAS 1; CANR 1, 27; INT CANR-27; MTCW

Wallant, Edward Lewis 1926-1962 ...**CLC 5, 10**
See also CA 1-4R; CANR 22; DLB 2, 28, 143; MTCW

Walley, Byron
See Card, Orson Scott

Walpole, Horace 1717-1797 ....**LC 2**
See also DLB 39, 104

Walpole, Hugh (Seymour) 1884-1941 ... **TCLC 5**
See also CA 104; 165; DLB 34

Walser, Martin 1927- ....**CLC 27**
See also CA 57-60; CANR 8, 46; DLB 75, 124

Walser, Robert 1878-1956 .... **TCLC 18; SSC 20**
See also CA 118; 165; DLB 66

Walsh, Jill Paton ....**CLC 35**
See also Paton Walsh, Gillian
See also AAYA 11; CLR 2; DLB 161; SAAS 3

Walter, Villiam Christian
See Andersen, Hans Christian

Wambaugh, Joseph (Aloysius, Jr.) 1937- ... **CLC 3, 18; DAM NOV, POP**
See also AITN 1; BEST 89:3; CA 33-36R; CANR 42, 65; DLB 6; DLBY 83; MTCW

Wang Wei 699(?)-761(?) ....**PC 18**

Ward, Arthur Henry Sarsfield 1883-1959
See Rohmer, Sax
See also CA 108

Ward, Douglas Turner 1930- ....**CLC 19**
See also BW 1; CA 81-84; CANR 27; DLB 7, 38

Ward, Mary Augusta
See Ward, Mrs. Humphry

Ward, Mrs. Humphry 1851-1920 .... **TCLC 55**
See also DLB 18

Ward, Peter
See Faust, Frederick (Schiller)

Warhol, Andy 1928(?)-1987 .... **CLC 20**
See also AAYA 12; BEST 89:4; CA 89-92; 121; CANR 34

Warner, Francis (Robert le Plastrier) 1937-
CLC 14
See also CA 53-56; CANR 11

Warner, Marina 1946- ....**CLC 59**
See also CA 65-68; CANR 21, 55; DLB 194

Warner, Rex (Ernest) 1905-1986 .... **CLC 45**
See also CA 89-92; 119; DLB 15

Warner, Susan (Bogert) 1819-1885 ... **NCLC 31**
See also DLB 3, 42

Warner, Sylvia (Constance) Ashton
See Ashton-Warner, Sylvia (Constance)

Warner, Sylvia Townsend 1893-1978 ... **CLC 7, 19; SSC 23**
See also CA 61-64; 77-80; CANR 16, 60; DLB 34, 139; MTCW

Warren, Mercy Otis 1728-1814 ...... **NCLC 13**
See also DLB 31

Warren, Robert Penn 1905-1989 .... **CLC 1, 4, 6, 8, 10, 13, 18, 39, 53, 59; DA; DAB; DAC; DAM MST, NOV, POET; SSC 4; WLC**
See also AITN 1; CA 13-16R; 129; CANR 10, 47; CDALB 1968-1988; DLB 2, 48, 152; DLBY 80, 89; INT CANR-10; MTCW; SATA 46; SATA-Obit 63

Warshofsky, Isaac
See Singer, Isaac Bashevis

Warton, Thomas 1728-1790 ...... **LC 15; DAM POET**
See also DLB 104, 109

Waruk, Kona
See Harris, (Theodore) Wilson

Warung, Price 1855-1911 .... **TCLC 45**

Warwick, Jarvis
See Garner, Hugh

Washington, Alex
See Harris, Mark

Washington, Booker T(aliaferro) 1856-1915
TCLC 10; BLC; DAM MULT
See also BW 1; CA 114; 125; SATA 28

Washington, George 1732-1799 .... **LC 25**
See also DLB 31

Wassermann, (Karl) Jakob 1873-1934 ... **TCLC 6**
See also CA 104; DLB 66

Wasserstein, Wendy 1950- .... **CLC 32, 59, 90; DAM DRAM; DC 4**
See also CA 121; 129; CABS 3; CANR 53; INT 129; SATA 94

Waterhouse, Keith (Spencer) 1929- ... **CLC 47**
See also CA 5-8R; CANR 38, 67; DLB 13, 15; MTCW

Waters, Frank (Joseph) 1902-1995 .... **CLC 88**
See also CA 5-8R; 149; CAAS 13; CANR 3, 18, 63; DLBY 86

Waters, Roger 1944- ....**CLC 35**

Watkins, Frances Ellen
See Harper, Frances Ellen Watkins

Watkins, Gerrold
See Malzberg, Barry N(athaniel)

Watkins, Gloria 1955(?)-
See hooks, bell
See also BW 2; CA 143

Watkins, Paul 1964- ....**CLC 55**
See also CA 132; CANR 62

Watkins, Vernon Phillips 1906-1967 ... **CLC 43**
See also CA 9-10; 25-28R; CAP 1; DLB 20

Watson, Irving S.
See Mencken, H(enry) L(ouis)

Watson, John H.
See Farmer, Philip Jose

Watson, Richard F.
See Silverberg, Robert

Waugh, Auberon (Alexander) 1939- .... **CLC 7**
See also CA 45-48; CANR 6, 22; DLB 14, 194

Waugh, Evelyn (Arthur St. John) 1903-1966
CLC 1, 3, 8, 13, 19, 27, 44, 107; DA; DAB; DAC; DAM MST, NOV, POP; WLC
See also CA 85-88; 25-28R; CANR 22; CDBLB 1914-1945; DLB 15, 162, 195; MTCW

Waugh, Harriet 1944- ....**CLC 6**
See also CA 85-88; CANR 22

Ways, C. R.
See Blount, Roy (Alton), Jr.

Waystaff, Simon
See Swift, Jonathan

Webb, (Martha) Beatrice (Potter) 1858-1943
TCLC 22
See also Potter, (Helen) Beatrix
See also CA 117

Webb, Charles (Richard) 1939- .... **CLC 7**
See also CA 25-28R

Webb, James H(enry), Jr. 1946- .... **CLC 22**
See also CA 81-84

Webb, Mary (Gladys Meredith) 1881-1927
TCLC 24
See also CA 123; DLB 34

Wheelock, John Hall 1886-1978 .... **CLC 14**
See also CA 13-16R; 77-80; CANR 14; DLB 45

White, E(lwyn) B(rooks) 1899-1985 ... **CLC 10, 34, 39; DAM POP**
See also AITN 2; CA 13-16R; 116; CANR 16, 37; CLR 1, 21; DLB 11, 22; MAICYA; MTCW; SATA 2, 29; SATA-Obit 44

White, Edmund (Valentine III) 1940- .... **CLC 27; DAM POP**
See also AAYA 7; CA 45-48; CANR 3, 19, 36, 62; MTCW

White, Patrick (Victor Martindale) 1912-1990 **CLC 3, 4, 5, 7, 9, 18, 65, 69**
See also CA 81-84; 132; CANR 43; MTCW

White, Phyllis Dorothy James 1920-
See James, P. D.
See also CA 21-24R; CANR 17, 43, 65; DAM POP; MTCW

White, T(erence) H(anbury) 1906-1964 ... **CLC 30**
See also AAYA 22; CA 73-76; CANR 37; DLB 160; JRDA; MAICYA; SATA 12

White, Terence de Vere 1912-1994 .... **CLC 49**
See also CA 49-52; 145; CANR 3

White, Walter F(rancis) 1893-1955 **TCLC 15**
See also White, Walter
See also BW 1; CA 115; 124; DLB 51

White, William Hale 1831-1913
See Rutherford, Mark
See also CA 121

Whitehead, E(dward) A(nthony) 1933- **CLC 5**
See also CA 65-68; CANR 58

Whitemore, Hugh (John) 1936- .... **CLC 37**
See also CA 132; INT 132

Whitman, Sarah Helen (Power) 1803-1878 **NCLC 19**
See also DLB 1

Whitman, Walt(er) 1819-1892 ... **NCLC 4, 31; DA; DAB; DAC; DAM MST, POET; PC 3; WLC**
See also CDALB 1640-1865; DLB 3, 64; SATA 20

Whitney, Phyllis A(yame) 1903- ... **CLC 42; DAM POP**
See also AITN 2; BEST 90:3; CA 1-4R; CANR 3, 25, 38, 60; JRDA; MAICYA; SATA 1, 30

Whittemore, (Edward) Reed (Jr.) 1919- ... **CLC 4**
See also CA 9-12R; CAAS 8; CANR 4; DLB 5

Whittier, John Greenleaf 1807-1892 ... **NCLC 8, 59**
See also DLB 1

Whittlebot, Hernia
See Coward, Noel (Peirce)

Wicker, Thomas Grey 1926-
See Wicker, Tom
See also CA 65-68; CANR 21, 46

Wicker, Tom .... **CLC 7**
See also Wicker, Thomas Grey

Wideman, John Edgar 1941- ... **CLC 5, 34, 36, 67; BLC; DAM MULT**
See also BW 2; CA 85-88; CANR 14, 42, 67; DLB 33, 143

Wiebe, Rudy (Henry) 1934- .... **CLC 6, 11, 14; DAC; DAM MST**
See also CA 37-40R; CANR 42, 67; DLB 60

Wieland, Christoph Martin 1733-1813 ... **NCLC 17**
See also DLB 97

Wiene, Robert 1881-1938 .... **TCLC 56**

Wieners, John 1934- .... **CLC 7**
See also CA 13-16R; DLB 16

Wiesel, Elie(zer) 1928- ... **CLC 3, 5, 11, 37; DA; DAB; DAC; DAM MST, NOV; WLCS 2**
See also AAYA 7; AITN 1; CA 5-8R; CAAS 4; CANR 8, 40, 65; DLB 83; DLBY 87; INT CANR-8; MTCW; SATA 56

Wiggins, Marianne 1947- .... **CLC 57**
See also BEST 89:3; CA 130; CANR 60

Wight, James Alfred 1916-
See Herriot, James
See also CA 77-80; SATA 55; SATA-Brief 44

Wilbur, Richard (Purdy) 1921- ... **CLC 3, 6, 9, 14, 53; DA; DAB; DAC; DAM MST, POET**
See also CA 1-4R; CABS 2; CANR 2, 29; DLB 5, 169; INT CANR-29; MTCW; SATA 9

Wild, Peter 1940- .... **CLC 14**
See also CA 37-40R; DLB 5

Wilde, Oscar (Fingal O'Flahertie Wills) 1854(?)-1900 ... **TCLC 1, 8, 23, 41; DA; DAB; DAC; DAM DRAM, MST, NOV; SSC 11; WLC**
See also CA 104; 119; CDBLB 1890-1914; DLB 10, 19, 34, 57, 141, 156, 190; SATA 24

Wilder, Billy .... **CLC 20**
See also Wilder, Samuel
See also DLB 26

Wilder, Samuel 1906-
See Wilder, Billy
See also CA 89-92

Wilder, Thornton (Niven) 1897-1975 ... **CLC 1, 5, 6, 10, 15, 35, 82; DA; DAB; DAC; DAM DRAM, MST, NOV; DC 1; WLC**
See also AITN 2; CA 13-16R; 61-64; CANR 40; DLB 4, 7, 9; DLBY 97; MTCW

Wilding, Michael 1942- .... **CLC 73**
See also CA 104; CANR 24, 49

Wiley, Richard 1944- .... **CLC 44**
See also CA 121; 129

Wilhelm, Kate .... **CLC 7**
See also Wilhelm, Katie Gertrude
See also AAYA 20; CAAS 5; DLB 8; INT CANR-17

Wilhelm, Katie Gertrude 1928-
See Wilhelm, Kate
See also CA 37-40R; CANR 17, 36, 60; MTCW

Wilkins, Mary
See Freeman, Mary Eleanor Wilkins

Willard, Nancy 1936- .... **CLC 7, 37**
See also CA 89-92; CANR 10, 39, 68; CLR 5; DLB 5, 52; MAICYA; MTCW; SATA 37, 71; SATA-Brief 30

Williams, C(harles) K(enneth) 1936- ... **CLC 33, 56; DAM POET**
See also CA 37-40R; CAAS 26; CANR 57; DLB 5

Williams, Charles
See Collier, James L(incoln)

Williams, Charles (Walter Stansby) 1886-1945 **TCLC 1, 11**
See also CA 104; 163; DLB 100, 153

Williams, (George) Emlyn 1905-1987 .... **C L C 15; DAM DRAM**
See also CA 104; 123; CANR 36; DLB 10, 77; MTCW

Williams, Hugo 1942- .... **CLC 42**
See also CA 17-20R; CANR 45; DLB 40

Williams, J. Walker
See Wodehouse, P(elham) G(renville)

Williams, John A(lfred) 1925- ... **CLC 5, 13; BLC; DAM MULT**
See also BW 2; CA 53-56; CAAS 3; CANR 6, 26, 51; DLB 2, 33; INT CANR-6

Williams, Jonathan (Chamberlain) 1929- ... **CLC 13**
See also CA 9-12R; CAAS 12; CANR 8; DLB 5

Williams, Joy 1944- .... **CLC 31**
See also CA 41-44R; CANR 22, 48

Williams, Norman 1952- .... **CLC 39**
See also CA 118

Williams, Sherley Anne 1944- ... **CLC 89; BLC; DAM MULT, POET**
See also BW 2; CA 73-76; CANR 25; DLB 41; INT CANR-25; SATA 78

Williams, Shirley
See Williams, Sherley Anne

Williams, Tennessee 1911-1983 ... **CLC 1, 2, 5, 7, 8, 11, 15, 19, 30, 39, 45, 71; DA; DAB; DAC; DAM DRAM, MST; DC 4; WLC**
See also AITN 1, 2; CA 5-8R; 108; CABS 3; CANR 31; CDALB 1941-1968; DLB 7; DLBD 4; DLBY 83; MTCW

Williams, Thomas (Alonzo) 1926-1990 ... **CLC 14**
See also CA 1-4R; 132; CANR 2

Williams, William C.
See Williams, William Carlos

Wonder, Stevie .... **CLC 12**
See also Morris, Steveland Judkins

Wong, Jade Snow 1922- .... **CLC 17**
See also CA 109

Woodberry, George Edward 1855-1930 ... **TCLC 73**
See also CA 165; DLB 71, 103

Woodcott, Keith
See Brunner, John (Kilian Houston)

Woodruff, Robert W.
See Mencken, H(enry) L(ouis)

Woolf, (Adeline) Virginia 1882-1941 ... **TCLC 1, 5, 20, 43, 56; DA; DAB; DAC; DAM MST, NOV; SSC 7; WLC**
See also CA 104; 130; CANR 64; CDBLB 1914-1945; DLB 36, 100, 162; DLBD 10; MTCW

Woolf, Virginia Adeline
See Woolf, (Adeline) Virginia

Woollcott, Alexander (Humphreys) 1887-1943
TCLC 5
See also CA 105; 161; DLB 29

Woolrich, Cornell 1903-1968 .... **CLC 77**
See also Hopley-Woolrich, Cornell George

Wordsworth, Dorothy 1771-1855 ... **NCLC 25**
See also DLB 107

Wordsworth, William 1770-1850 ... **NCLC 12, 38; DA; DAB; DAC; DAM MST, POET; PC 4; WLC**
See also CDBLB 1789-1832; DLB 93, 107

Wouk, Herman 1915- ...... **CLC 1, 9, 38; DAM NOV, POP**
See also CA 5-8R; CANR 6, 33, 67; DLBY 82; INT CANR-6; MTCW

Wright, Charles (Penzel, Jr.) 1935- ... **CLC 6, 13, 28**
See also CA 29-32R; CAAS 7; CANR 23, 36, 62; DLB 165; DLBY 82; MTCW

Wright, Charles Stevenson 1932- ... **CLC 49; BLC 3; DAM MULT, POET**
See also BW 1; CA 9-12R; CANR 26; DLB 33

Wright, Jack R.
See Harris, Mark

Wright, James (Arlington) 1927-1980 ... **CLC 3, 5, 10, 28; DAM POET**
See also AITN 2; CA 49-52; 97-100; CANR 4, 34, 64; DLB 5, 169; MTCW

Wright, Judith (Arandell) 1915- ... **CLC 11, 53; PC 14**
See also CA 13-16R; CANR 31; MTCW; SATA 14

Wright, L(aurali) R. 1939- .... **CLC 44**
See also CA 138

Wright, Richard (Nathaniel) 1908-1960 ... **CLC 1, 3, 4, 9, 14, 21, 48, 74; BLC; DA; DAB;**

DAC; DAM MST, MULT, NOV; SSC 2; WLC
See also AAYA 5; BW 1; CA 108; CANR 64; CDALB 1929-1941; DLB 76, 102; DLBD 2; MTCW

Wright, Richard B(ruce) 1937- .... **CLC 6**
See also CA 85-88; DLB 53

Wright, Rick 1945- .... **CLC 35**

Wright, Rowland
See Wells, Carolyn

Wright, Stephen 1946- .... **CLC 33**

Wright, Willard Huntington 1888-1939
See Van Dine, S. S.
See also CA 115; DLBD 16

Wright, William 1930- .... **CLC 44**
See also CA 53-56; CANR 7, 23

Wroth, LadyMary 1587-1653(?) .... **LC 30**
See also DLB 121

Wu Ch'eng-en 1500(?)-1582(?) .... **LC 7**

Wu Ching-tzu 1701-1754 .... **LC 2**

Wurlitzer, Rudolph 1938(?)- .... **CLC 2, 4, 15**
See also CA 85-88; DLB 173

Wycherley, William 1641-1715 ... **LC 8, 21; DAM DRAM**
See also CDBLB 1660-1789; DLB 80

Wylie, Elinor (Morton Hoyt) 1885-1928 ... **TCLC 8**
See also CA 105; 162; DLB 9, 45

Wylie, Philip (Gordon) 1902-1971 ..... **CLC 43**
See also CA 21-22; 33-36R; CAP 2; DLB 9

Wyndham, John .... **CLC 19**
See also Harris, John (Wyndham Parkes Lucas) Beynon

Wyss, Johann David Von 1743-1818 ... **N C L C 10**
See also JRDA; MAICYA; SATA 29; SATA-Brief 27

Xenophon c. 430B.C.-c. 354B.C. .... **CMLC 17**
See also DLB 176

Yakumo Koizumi
See Hearn, (Patricio) Lafcadio (Tessima Carlos)

Yanez, Jose Donoso
See Donoso (Yanez), Jose

Yanovsky, Basile S.
See Yanovsky, V(assily) S(emenovich)

Yanovsky, V(assily) S(emenovich) 1906-1989
CLC 2, 18
See also CA 97-100; 129

Yates, Richard 1926-1992 .... **CLC 7, 8, 23**
See also CA 5-8R; 139; CANR 10, 43; DLB 2; DLBY 81, 92; INT CANR-10

Yeats, W. B.
See Yeats, William Butler

Yeats, William Butler 1865-1939 ... **TCLC 1, 11, 18, 31; DA; DAB; DAC; DAM DRAM, MST, POET; PC 20; WLC**
See also CA 104; 127; CANR 45; CDBLB 1890-1914; DLB 10, 19, 98, 156; MTCW

Yehoshua, A(braham) B. 1936- .... **CLC 13, 31**
See also CA 33-36R; CANR 43

Yep, Laurence Michael 1948- .... **CLC 35**
See also AAYA 5; CA 49-52; CANR 1, 46; CLR 3, 17; DLB 52; JRDA; MAICYA; SATA 7, 69

Yerby, Frank G(arvin) 1916-1991 ... **CLC 1, 7, 22; BLC; DAM MULT**
See also BW 1; CA 9-12R; 136; CANR 16, 52; DLB 76; INT CANR-16; MTCW

Yesenin, Sergei Alexandrovich
See Esenin, Sergei (Alexandrovich)

Yevtushenko, Yevgeny (Alexandrovich) 1933-
CLC 1, 3, 13, 26, 51; DAM POET
See also CA 81-84; CANR 33, 54; MTCW

Yezierska, Anzia 1885(?)-1970 .... **CLC 46**
See also CA 126; 89-92; DLB 28; MTCW

Yglesias, Helen 1915- .... **CLC 7, 22**
See also CA 37-40R; CAAS 20; CANR 15, 65; INT CANR-15; MTCW

Yokomitsu Riichi 1898-1947 .... **TCLC 47**

Yonge, Charlotte (Mary) 1823-1901 ... **TCLC 48**
See also CA 109; 163; DLB 18, 163; SATA 17

York, Jeremy
See Creasey, John

York, Simon
See Heinlein, Robert A(nson)

Yorke, Henry Vincent 1905-1974 .... **CLC 13**
See also Green, Henry
See also CA 85-88; 49-52

Yosano Akiko 1878-1942 ...... **TCLC 59; PC 11**
See also CA 161

Yoshimoto, Banana .... **CLC 84**
See also Yoshimoto, Mahoko

Yoshimoto, Mahoko 1964-
See Yoshimoto, Banana
See also CA 144

Young, Al(bert James) 1939- ... **CLC 19; BLC; DAM MULT**
See also BW 2; CA 29-32R; CANR 26, 65; DLB 33

Young, Andrew (John) 1885-1971 .... **CLC 5**
See also CA 5-8R; CANR 7, 29

Young, Collier
See Bloch, Robert (Albert)

Short Story Criticism
Cumulative Nationality Index

SSC Cumulative Title Index

Title Index

Title Index

Title Index

Title Index

Title Index